Mercer County, West Virginia

Marriages

1854–1901

Sallie Hays

Heritage Books
2024

HERITAGE BOOKS

AN IMPRINT OF HERITAGE BOOKS, INC.

Books, CDs, and more—Worldwide

For our listing of thousands of titles see our website
at
www.HeritageBooks.com

A Facsimile Reprint
Published 2024 by
HERITAGE BOOKS, INC.
Publishing Division
5810 Ruatan Street
Berwyn Heights, MD 20740

Originally published 1995

International Standard Book Number
Paperbound: 978-0-7884-7729-4

INTRODUCTION

Mercer County, West Virginia was established in 1837 from parts of Giles and Tazewell Counties in Virginia, but in 1841 a portion of Mercer County was transferred back to Giles County. The county's name was given in honor of General Hugh Mercer, of Revolutionary War fame.

Mercer County is known for its coal production through the years. After the Civil War, the West Virginia coal mines brought a large influx of different races and nationalities. After 1865, native miners included thousands of negroes, mostly from the south, with Mercer County employing approximately twenty-three percent of the new miners.

This publication concerns the marriages of Mercer County, ranging from January 1864 through December 1901. There are over 5300 entries listed with 33,600 names indexed. Since southeastern West Virginia was considered one of the finest coal fields in the world, it created a uniquely mixed breed of people because of the blend of different nationalities attracted to this place of new found labor.

Care has been taken to copy the records exactly as originally written. Some of the names are spelled differently from one page to the next, therefore, they have been copied as such. On some entries, county and state have been omitted from the original, there again, this is the way it has been copied for this book.

It is hoped you will be able to find that one twig that has been missing from your family tree.

* = an error in the typing - check the Errata on page 142

Page 1

1. 28 Jan 1854 MATHEW S. WOODALL 22 to NANCY HALDSON 30 both of Mercer Co O: farmer; by William C. Martin.

2. 1 Jan 1854 JAMES J. MASSEY single b. Patrick Co VA s/o John & Nancy Massey to PATSEY SWIMMEY single b. Mercer Co VA d/o Martin & Nancey Swimmey; by John C. Hubbard.

3. 17 Jan 1854 LAMPKIN M.K. THOMAS to ELLEN P. TILLER; by Absalom Garretson.

4. 19 Jan 1854 ADDISON C. BAILEY to OCTAVIA A.M. DAY; by James Calfee.

5. 20 Jan 1854 HENDERSON F. GORE 20 single s/o Isaac Gore to SEREPHA CAPERTON 19 single d/o Augustus W.J. Caperton O: farmer; by Leroy Keaton.

6. 11 Jan 1854 JOEL W. CHAMBERS to MARY E. COMPTON d/o Margat Compton O: farmer; by James Calfee.

7. 19 Jan 1854 SAMUEL HALDSON to SUSANA WOODALL; by William C. Martin.

8. 2 Feb 1854 THOMAS B. MASSEY s/o John Massey to LOUSA WHITE d/o William White O: farmer; by James Calfee.

9. 2 Feb 1854 HUGH M. JUSTICE single b. Mercer Co VA now of Wyoming Co s/o Henderson & Catharine Justice to MARY I. LUSTER single b. Floyd Co VA now of Mercer Co VA d/o Bird & Malinda Luster O: farmer; by John C. Hubbard.

10. 9 Feb 1854 JOHN W. CREWS single b. Pulaski Co VA s/o David & Louisiana Crews to SUSANA HEADOR single b. Mercer Co VA s/o Josiah & Judith Meador O: farmer; by John C. Hubbard.

11. 21 Feb 1854 AIDON THOMPSON wid. b. Raleigh Co VA now of Wyoming Co VA s/o Henry Gore & Jane Thompson to DASHA MEADOR single b. Mercer Co VA d/o John & Ann Meador; by John C. Hubbard.

12. 25 Feb 1854 MICHICAL PITMAN 24 single b. Fayette Co VA s/o John & Nancy Pitman to REBECA KINZER 17 single b. Montgomery Co VA d/o John & Catharine Kinzer O: farmer; by Wm C. Martin.

13. 28 Feb 1854 JAMES F. LUSK 29 wid. b. Mercer Co VA s/o Absalom & Deliah Lusk to CYNTHIA A. DUNBAR 26 yrs 6 mos single b. Mercer Co VA d/o William Dunbar O: farmer; by L.A. Smith.

14. 2 March 1854 HARRISON W. STRALEY 25 single b. Giles Co VA s/o John & Elizabeth Straley to DELILAH S. BYRONSIDE 20 single b. Mercer Co VA d/o Isaac & Mary Byronside O: merchant; by John P. Coran.

15. 27 April 1854 NICHOLAS F. HOLSTINE single b. Mercer Co VA s/o Hugh & Sarah Holstine to SUSAN DUNBAR single b. Mercer Co VA d/o William & Cintha Dunbar O: farmer; by John C. Hubbard.

16. 30 May 1854 WILLIAM S. HILL 25 single s/o John & Polly Hill to LIMMONA FRENCH 22 d/o Hugh C. French O: farmer; by Chester Bullard.

17. 20 June 1854 DAVID COBURN 45 wid. b. North Carolina s/o David Coburn to CATHARINE WIMMER 29 single b. Floyd Co VA d/o Samuel Wimmer O: farmer; by James Calfee.

18. 4 July 1854 MARCUS M. MILLER 19 single b. Appomattox Co VA s/o Grief & Nancy Miller to ELIZABETH B. HERNDON 20 single b. Campbell Co VA d/o Archer & Eliza Herndon O: farmer; by H.B. Rose.

19. 20 July 1854 WILLIAM L. BRIDGES 22 single b. Rockingham Co VA s/o William & Mary Bridges to REBECA JANE THOMPSON 24 single b. Monroe Co VA d/o Andrew & Sally Thompson O: School teacher; by James Calfee.

20. 25 July 1854 ROBERT C. LILLY wid. b. Mercer Co VA s/o Robert & Mary Lilly to VIRGINIA GORE single b. Mercer Co VA d/o Isaac & Ida Gore O: merchant; by John C. Hubbard.

21. 8 Aug 1854 HIRAM I. GARRETSON 20 yrs 6 mos 16 dys single b. Mercer Co VA s/o William & Ann Garretson to MARY A. SARVER 20 yrs 8 mos 18 dys single b. Mercer Co VA d/o James & Elizabeth Sarver O: farmer; by Abraham Garretson.

22. 10 Aug 1854 LELAND WILLS 21 single b. Monroe Co VA s/o Meredith & Lydia Wills to NANCY PACK 22 single b. Giles Co VA d/o Robert & Rhoda Pack O: farmer; John Bragg.

23. 10 Aug 1854 robert W. Saunders 22 single b. Lynchburg VA s/o David & Ann M. Saunders to ELIZABETH J. PACK 18 single b. Monroe Co VA d/o Anderson & Rebecca Pack O: merchant; by H.B. Rose.

24. 18 Aug 1854 ISAAC HARE 26 single b. Giles Co VA s/o William & Sarah Hare to LOUISA J. ROWLAND 23 single b. Giles Co VA d/o James & Elizabeth Rowland O: farmer; by James Calfee.

25. 24 Aug 1854 RILEY PENNINGTON 28 yrs 8 mos 16 dys wid. b. Monroe Co VA s/o Wm & Sarah Pennington to ELIZABETH SHREWSBURY 22 yrs 3 mos 4 dys single b. Mercer Co VA d/o Philip & Charlotte Shrewsbury O: farmer; by Samuel Scott.

26. 26 Sug 1854 JAMES COX 20 single b. Franklin Co VA s/o Joseph & Nancy Cox to DOSHA LILLY 15 single b. Mercer Co VA d/o John & Nancy Lilly O: farmer; by John Bragg.

27. 27 Aug 1854 REVOANVY CLENDONEN 23 single b. Giles Co VA s/o A.S. & Shady Clendonen to ARTEMISIA ALVIS 20 wid. b. Giles Co VA d/o Laham & Nelly Brinkley O: farmer; by Abraham Garretson.

28. 7 Sept 1854 THOMAS MOORE 28 yrs 9 mos 5 dys single b. Rockbridge Co VA s/o Samuel & Anna Moore to SARAH A. McLANE 26 yrs 6 mos 14 dys single b. Rockbridge Co VA d/o Gilliam & Hannah McLane O: farmer; by Samuel Scott.

29. 12 Sept 1854 REESE T. LUSK 28 yrs 3 mos 1 dy wid. b. Mercer Co VA s/o Cloe Lusk to REBECCA McCOMAS 21 yrs 5 mos 9 dys single b. Mercer Co VA d/o James & Rebecca McComas O: farmer; by Joseph Wright.

30. 4 Oct 1854 JEREMIAH HYLTON 31 wid. b. Floyd Co VA s/o Henry & Sarah hylton to MARY LANN REED 24 single b. Monroe Co VA d/o Joseph & Malinda Reed O: farmer; by James Calfee.

31. 19 Oct 1854 ABSOLOM LUSK, JR. 20 single b. Tazewell Co VA s/o Chico Lusk to JANE UNDERWOOD 24 single b. Floyd Co VA s/o Wm. & Rachel Underwood O: farmer by James Calfee.

32. 26 Oct 1854 ELBERT A. BELCHER 20 yrs 3 mos b. Tazewell Co VA s/o Elizabeth Belcher to MATILDA B. PAYNE 18 yrs 7 mos single b. Tazewell Co VA d/o William & Judy Payne O: farmer; by James Calfee.

33. 26 Oct 1854 NELSON FARLEY 19 single b. Mercer Co VA s/o Gideon & Dinah Farley to SARAH RUNNELS 20 single b. Montgomery Co VA d/o John & Anna Runnels O: farmer; by Leroy Keaton.

34. 2 Nov 1854 JACOB A. PECK 23 single b. Monroe Co VA s/o Benjamin & Polly Peck to LARRISSA M. GEORGE 22 single b. Tazewell Co VA d/o Thos J. & Eleanor George O: farmer; by James Calfee.

35. 8 Nov 1854 JOHN BELCHER 21 single b. Monroe Co VA s/o Minajah & Matilda Belcher to GERMNAH CASLEY 24 single b. Monroe Co VA d/o Berry & Roda Casley O: farmer; by Leroy Keaton.

36. 16 Nov 1854 ALLEN H. MEADOR 24 yrs 1 mo 21 dys single b. Giles Co VA s/o Wm M. & Celia Meador to ELIZA WHITTEN 24 yrs 4 mos 5 dys single b. Alleghany Co VA d/o Lewis & Charlotte Whitten O: farmer; by John Bragg.

37. 29 Nov 1854 GREEN DAVIS 29 single b. Giles Co VA s/o Joshua & Sally Davis to SARAH THOMAS 19 single b. Mercer Co VA d/o Jemima Thomas & David Lusk O: farmer; by Landon Duncan at Cedar Point in Giles Co VA.

38. 1 Dec 1854 ISAAC BENNET 32 yrs 6 mos 1 dy single b. Greenbrier Co VA s/o Robert & Catharine Bennet to MARY ROLLYSON 27 yrs 5 mos 21 dys single b. Giles Co VA d/o Joseph & Elizabeth Rollyson O: farmer; by John Bragg.

39. 6 Dec 1854 JOHN S. HARRIS 23 single b. Patrick Co VA s/o Robert & Elizabeth Harris to MATILDA HELMANDOLLAR 20 single b. Tazewell Co VA d/o Wm & Linda Helmandollar O: farmer; by James Calfee.

40. 26 Dec 1854 PHILIP KINZER 35 single b. Montgomery Co VA s/o John & Catharine Kinzer to SARAH MARTIN 35 single b. Giles Co VA d/o John & Susan Martin O: farmer; by Wm C. Martin.

41. 3 Jan 1855 WILLIAM H. WHITE 23 single b. Mercer Co VA s/o Wm & Edatha White to MARGARET T. SHANNON 19 single b. Campbell Co VA d/o Jno & Margaret Shannon O: farmer; by L.W. Crouch.

42. 9 Jan 1855 WILLIAM PETRY 20 single b. Mercer Co VA s/o Wm & Polly Petry to JANE FARLEY 25 single b. Mercer Co VA d/o Gideon & Dinah Farley O: farmer; by Wm C. Martin.

43. 10 Jan 1855 GORDON PENNINGTON 22 single b. Monroe Co VA s/o James Pennington & Drury Walter to JULIA BELCHER 21 single b. Mercer Co VA d/o Lewis & Rebecca Belcher O: farmer; by Wm C. Martin.

44. 10 Jan 1855 John Lane 22 yrs 5 mos 1 dy b. Monroe Co VA s/o Moses & Cintha Lane to JUDITH F. HEADOR 17 yrs 4 dys d/o Green W. & Emila Heador O: farmer; by John Bragg.

45. 11 Jan 1855 WILLIAM ELLISON 27 single b. Mercer Co VA s/o Ann & Mary Ellison to ESTER CHRISTIAN 19 single b. Giles Co VA d/o John & Nelly Christian O: farmer; by Leroy Keaton.

46. 18 Jan 1855 THOMAS D. MOTLEY 24 single b. Pittsylvania Co VA s/o Wm & Sarah Motley to HARRIET DAVIS 21 single b. Giles Co VA d/o Joshua & Sally Davis O: farmer; by Elisha G. Duncan.

47. 17 Jan 1855 CLAY BAILEY 49 yrs 10 mos 17 dys wid. b. Giles Co VA s/o Micajah & Onie Bailey to MARY A. HESS 32 yrs 2 mos 10 dys single b. Montgomery Co VA d/o Catharine Hess O: farmer; by William C. Martin.

48. 25 Jan 1855 WILLIAM G. THOMAS 22 yrs 5 mos 17 dys single b. Mercer Co VA s/o Hanley & Margaret Thomas to ANN THOMAS 19 yrs 7 mos 1 dy single b. Mercer Co VA d/o Jesse & Rachel Thomas O: farmer; by Abraham Garretson.

Page 2

1. 25 Jan 1855 WILLIAM M. BAILEY 21 yrs 10 mos 7 dys wid. b. Mercer Co VA s/o Micajah & Mahala Bailey to MATILDA SHUFFLEBARGER 25 yrs 5 mos 1 dy single b. Pulaski Co VA d/o John & Maria Shufflebarger O: farmer; by Joseph Wright.

2. 30 Jan 1855 WILSON R. JONES 34 yrs 3 mos 3 dys wid. b. Monroe Co VA s/o Wilson & Sarah Jones to FRANCES J. BLANKENSHIP 17 yrs 8 mos 25 dys single b. Mercer Co VA d/o S.M. & Catharine Blankenship O: farmer; by Abraham Garretson.

3. 6 Feb. 1855 WILLIAM J. HAGAN 20 single b. North Carolina s/o John & Elizth Hagan to MARGARET COOPER 21 single b. Giles Co VA d/o William & ---- O: farmer; by James Calfee.

4. 8 Feb 1855 GEORGE FOSTER 21 yrs 9 mos 14 dys single b. Giles Co VA s/o James & Mary Foster to MARGARET WILLIAMS 19 yrs 10 mos 5 dys b. Monroe Co VA d/o John & Anna Williams O: farmer; by Leroy Keaton.

5. 15 Feb 1855 JACKSON VEAL b. Pulaski Co VA s/o Chas & Elizth Veal to NANCY LILLY b. Mercer Co VA d/o Robt & Elizth Lilly O: farmer; by John C. Hubbard.

6. 15 Feb 1855 ANDREW WHITE 37 yrs 1 mo 11 dys wid. b. Giles Co VA s/o Wm & Edatha White to ELIZABETH E. FOLEY 17 yrs 3 mos 27 dys single b. Pulaski Co VA d/o James & Juda Foley O: farmer; by William C. Martin.

7. 27 Feb 1855 CHARLES W. BAILEY 27 single b. Mercer Co VA s/o Saml & Mary Bailey to MARY CARBAUGH 21 single b. Pulaski Co VA d/o Geo & Elizth Carbaugh O: farmer; by L.W. Crouch.

8. 6 March 1855 THOMAS MEADOWS 22 yrs 0 mos 7 dys single b. Fayett Co VA s/o Abraham & Ruth Meadows to ELIZABETH UPTON 22 yrs 11 mos 20 dys b. Monroe Co VA d/o Meredith & Sarah Upton O: farmer; by John Bragg.

9. 7 March 1855 BURLEY ELISON single b. Monroe Co VA s/o Andrew & Milly Ellison to ANNA BRAMMER single b. Patrick Co VA d/o Jno & Anna Brammer O: farmer; by John C. Hubbard.

10. 8 March 1855 GRANVILLE S. HALSTEAD single b. Monroe Co VA s/o Adam & Sarah Halstead to DIONY CLARK single b. Patrick Co VA d/o Henry & Ruth Clark O: farmer; by John C. Hubbard.

11. 8 March 1855 ALEXANDER BAILEY 26 yrs 9 mos 10 dys single b. Mercer Co VA s/o Archd & Elizth Bailey to FRANCES THOMPSON 18 yrs 3 mos 0 dys single b. Mercer Co VA d/o Lyons & Nancy Thompson O: farmer; by James Calfee.

12. 13 March 1855 WILLIAM A. TILLER 22 yrs 0 mos 4 dys single b. Mercer Co VA s/o Andr & Priscilla Tiller to NANCY J. FANNING 17 yrs 2 mos 13 dys single b. Mercer Co VA d/o Garlin & Milly Fanning O: farmer; by Abraham Garretson.

13. 15 March 1855 ERSKIN R. COX single b. Patrick Co VA s/o Francis & Boninn Cox to LOUISA SOLSBERY single b. Mercer Co VA d/o John Lilly & Phebe Solsbery O: farmer; by John C. Hubbard.

14. 21 March 1855 JAMES D. JOHNSTON 28 single b. Giles Co VA s/o Hugh & Sarah ---- to MARY CALAWAY 23 single b. Monroe Co VA d/o Granville & Susan---- O: carpenter; by Geo. Stewart.

15. 22 March 1855 BENTON WHITE 19 yrs 11 mos 18 dys single b. Mercer Co VA s/o Thos & Polly White to MARTHA M. SCOTT 17 yrs 11 mos 28 dys single b. Giles Co VA d/o Saml & Nancy Scott O: farmer; by Samuel Scott.

16. 29 March 1855 JOHN McH. THOMPSON 29 yrs 3 mos single b. Mercer Co Va s/o Lyons & Nancy Thompson to HARRIETT A. STRALEY 18 yrs 8 mos 13 dys single b. Mercer Co VA d/o John & Elizth Straley O: farmer; by James Calfee.

17. 10 Sept 1855 JACOB M. HAMMON 29 yrs 8 mos 29 dys single b. Montgomery Co VA s/o Jno & Catharine Hammon to REBECCA M. HARNDON 17 yrs 5 mos 4 dys b. Campbell Co VA d/o Archer & Sarah E.B. Herndon (both spellings are used here) O: farmer; by L.W. Crouch.

18. 12 Sept 1855 WILLIAM B. SCOTT 20 single b. Giles Co VA s/o Francis & Elizth Scott to SUSAN S. FANNING 21 single b. Giles Co VA d/o Benjn & Nancy Fanning O: farmer; by William Holroyd.

19. 14 Sept 1855 PETTER S. STUART 21 yrs 10 mos 3 dys single b. Franklin Co VA now living in Monroe Co VA s/o --- to MARY J. MEADOWS 18 yrs 2 mos 17 dys b. Monroe Co VA d/o Jefferson & Margaret Meadows O: bricklayer; by John Bragg.

20. 17 Sept 1855 GEORGE W. TONEY 24 yrs 5 mos 3 dys single b. Giles Co VA s/o Jonathan & Elizth Toney to CATHARINE MOTLEY 14 yrs 4 mos 27 dys single b. Botetourt Co VA d/o Wm & Elizth Motley O: farmer; by Abraham Garretson.

21. 17 Sept 1855 ISAAC GUNOE 26 yrs 6 mos 6 dys single b. Monroe Co VA s/o Jno & Mary Gunoe to MARY ALVIS 36 yrs 7 mos 7 dys wid. b. Giles Co VA d/o John & Phebe Thomas O: farmer; by Wm C. Martin.

22. 19 Sept 1855 HOWARD W. DAVIDSON 27 yrs 11 mos 18 dys single b. Mercer Co VA s/o Sm G & Eliza J. Davidson to RHODA G. DILLION 20 yrs 5 mos 5 dys single b. Mercer Co VA d/o Saml & Polly Dillion O: farmer; by Joseph Wright.

23. 19 Sept 1855 ANDREW J. FANING 21 yrs 1 mo 20 dys single b. Mercer Co VA s/o Benjn & Nancy Faning to NANCY F.* MARTIN 15 yrs 6 mos 5 dys single b. Mercer Co BA d/o David & Hester A. Martin O: farmer; by Wm C. Martin. (*J. appears in 1850 Mercer Co VA Census)

24. 25 Sept 1855 JUBAL CARNER* 26 yrs 1 mo 10 dys single b. Bedford Co VA s/o David & Elizabeth --- to ELIZABETH J. VASS 20 single b. Mercer Co VA d/o Robt & Mary Vass O: farmer; by Leroy Keaton. (* spelled Camer also)

25. 26 Sept 1855 HENRY BROWN 25 yrs 8 mos single b. Tazewell Co VA s/o Thos & Margaret Brown to PHEBA J. McPHERSON 23 yrs 0 mos 19 dys b. Giles Co VA d/o Polly McPherson O: farmer; by Samuel Scott.

26. 10 May 1855 JAMES L. DAY 23 yrs 8 mos 18 dys single b. Tazewell Co VA s/o Lewis & Patience Day to LOUISA C. BAILEY 19 yrs 11 mos 23 dys single b. Mercer Co VA d/o Saml & Polly Bailey O: farmer; by Joseph Wright.

27. 31 May 1855 JOSEPH MEADOWS wid. b. Mercer Co VA s/o Josiah & Judith Meadows to NANCY C. LILLY single b. Mercer Co VA d/o Turner* A. Lilly O: farmer by John C. Hubbard. (*Side Note corrected by Court Order 8/26/85)

28. 7 June 1855 WILLIAM HUDHSON* 22 yrs 10 mos single b. Franklin Co VA s/o Vincent & Rosa Hudson* to NANCY M. SONGER 14 yrs 4 mos single b. Pulaski Co VA d/o of Jno & Martha Songer O: farmer; by H.B. Rose. (*both spellings given)

29. 14 June 1855 DANL H. AGEE 37 yrs 3 mos 9 dys single b. Franklin Co VA s/o Levi & Sarah Agee to MARTHA LANE 21 yrs 1 mo 9 dys single b. Gale Co OH d/o Moses & Cyntha Lane O: farmer; by John C. Hubbard.

30. 10 July 1855 WILLIAM WADDLE 21 yrs 8 mos 28 dys single b. Giles Co VA s/o Alexr & Mary Waddle to SARAH E. FANNING* 17 yrs 8 mos 5 dys single b. Mercer Co VA d/o Benjn & Nancy Faning* O: farmer; by William C. Martin. (*both spellings given)

32. 9 Aug 1855 JOHN OLIVER 21 single b. Montgomery Co VA s/o Freeman & Cathe Oliver to ANN E. GRAYBILL 18 single b. Pulaski Co VA d/o Jno & Susan Graybill O: brickmason; by H.B. Rose.

33. 21 Augt 1855 LANDON DAVIS single b. Giles Co VA s/o Joshua & Sarah Davis to MARY MEADOWS single b. Mercer Co VA d/o Adam & Sarah Meadows O: farmer; by Abm Garretson.

34. 23 Augt 1855 ELI CLARK 21 yrs 1 mo 15 dys single b. Patrick Co VA s/o Jno & Mary Clark to ROSA M.J. MOONEY 20 yrs 4 mos 17 dys b. Mercer Co VA d/o Jno L. & Susana Mooney O: farmer; by Joseph Wright.

35. 23 Augt 1855 GREEN MEADOR 23 yrs 8 mos 17 dys single b. Mercer Co VA s/o Jno & Anna Meador to ELIZABETH HATCHER 17 yrs 5 mos 6 dys single b. Mercer Co VA d/o Edmond & Nancy Hatcher O: farmer; by John C. Hubbard.

36. 6 Sept 1855 ROBT C. SCOTT 23 yrs 6 mos 15 dys single b. Floyd Co VA s/o Jno & China Scott to SARAH A. CARR 22 yrs 2 mos 7 dys single b. Giles d/o Jno & Sarah Carr O: mechanic; by L.W. Crouch.

37. 19 Sept 1855 Wm H. SHUMATE 21 yrs 4 mos single b. Giles Co VA s/o Parkinson & R. Shumate to FIDELLA PETERS 26 yrs single b. Mercer Co VA d/o Chris & Mary Peters O: farmer; by H.B. Rose.

38. 3 Octr 1855 JNO W.O. SNAPP 24 yrs 5 mos single b. Shenandoah Co VA s/o Jno & Catharine Snapp to MATILDA J. BAILEY 16 yrs 6 mos 13 dys single b. Mercer Co VA d/o Macijah & M. Bailey O: farmer; by Joseph Wright.

39. 25 Octr 1855 SAML SHREWSBURY 25 yrs 4 mos 10 dys single b. Mercer Co VA s/o Jno & Elizth Shrewsbury to ELIZth BAILEY 20 yrs 7 mos 17 dys single b. Mercer Co VA d/o Geo & Frances Bailey O: farmer; by Joseph Wright.

40. 25 Octr 1855 MARTIN W. SWEENEY 20 yrs 8 mos 7 dys single b. Mercer Co VA s/o Martin & Nancy Sweeney to K.E. WOOD 20 yrs 11 mos 25 yrs single b. Patrick Co VA d/o Alexr & H.B. Wood O: farmer; by John C. Hubbard.

41. 1 Novr 1855 Wm K. FOSTER 27 yrs 3 mos 16 dys single b. Scott Co VA s/o Burgress & Mary B. Foster to MARGARET C. CARR 25 yrs 6 mos 16 dys single b. Giles Co VA d/o Robt & Sarah Carr O: Minister of the Gospel; by L.W. Crouch.

42. 24 Novr 1855 JNO B. ABSHER 26 yrs 8 mos wid. b. Giles Co VA s/o Sarah Absher to SARAH A. DODD 25 single b. Craig Co VA d/o Jno & Sarah Dosa O: farmer; by H.B. Rose.

43. 11 Decr 1855 JOHN TUGGLE 35 single b. Giles Co VA s/o Larkin & Malinda Tuggle now in Mercer Co VA to LUCINDA BAILEY 35 single b. Tazewell Co VA d/o Jonth & Elizth Bailey O: farmer; by M. Ellison.

44. 12 Decr 1855 Wm A. MAHOOD 20 yrs 1 mo single b. Giles Co VA s/o Alexr & Martha Mahood to ELIZth O. MARTIN 17 yrs 0 mos 17 dys single b. Campbell Co VA d/o Wm L & Elizth Martin O: merchants; by Evan H. Brown.

45. 20 Decr 1855 ARCHd JOHNSTON 23 single b. Monroe Co VA s/o Reuben & Rutha Johnston to ELIZA LUSK 22 yrs 8 mos single b. Mercer Co VA d/o Absolam & Delila Lusk O: carpenter; by H.B. Rose.

46. 27 Decr 1855 JAS A. BRAMMER 20 yrs 5 mos 22 dys single b. Patrick Co VA s/o Jas & Anna Brammer to ELIZA S. BALL 14 yrs 2 mos 13 dys single b. Monroe Co VA d/o Augustus & R. Ball O: farmer; by John C. Hubbard.

Page 3

1. 1 Jany 1856 ANDREW J. BANKS 41 yrs 1 mo 15 dys single b. Mercer Co VA s/o Saml & Anna Banks to ELIZABETH BAILEY 21 yrs 11 mos 27 dys single b. Tazewell Co VA d/o Clay & Rebecca Bailey O: farmer; by Joseph Wright.

2. 13 Feby 1856 GEORGE W. PEGRAM 22 yrs 4 mos 12 dys single b. Gilford Co NC now of Raleigh Co VA s/o George & Mary Pegram to MARGARET MANN 18 yrs 10 mos 22 dys single b. Mercer Co VA d/o Hezekiah & Elizth Mann O: carpenter; by John C. Hubbard.

3. 5 March 1856 JAME H. McKENZIE 26 single b. Giles Co VA s/o Alexr & Malinda McKenzie to SARAH E. CARPER 17 b. Botetourt Co VA d/o H.F. & E.C. Carper O: farmer; by Abraham Garretson.

4. 9 March 1856 THOMAS BRATTON 39 yrs 7 mos 10 dys wid. b. Pulaski Co VA s/o Thos & Mary Bratton to MARY E. DARE 23 yrs 6 mos 28 dys wid. b. Giles Co VA d/o Parkinson & Rhoda Shumate O: farmer; by Evans H. Brown.

5. 19 March 1856 FRANKLIN WHITTAKER 37 yrs 4 mos 15 dys wid. b. Montgomery Co VA now of Giles Co VA s/o Jas & Cath Whittaker to ELLEN WHITE 30 yrs 9 mos 19 dys single b. Mercer Co VA d/o Jas & Michae White O: farmer; by Evans H. Brown.

6. 20 March 1856 WOODSON B. MEADOR 22 yrs 2 mos 24 dys single b. Mercer Co VA s/o Jno & Anna Meador to AMANDA M. MEADOR 10 yrs* 2 mos 24 dys single b. Mercer Co VA d/o Josiah & Judity Meador O: farmer; by John C. Hubbard. (*Amanda M. is 10 yrs old in 1850 Census - household #645)

7. 20 March 1856 ASA CREWS 36 yrs 9 mos 16 dys wid. b. Patrick Co VA s/o David & Sarah Crews to NANCY MEADOR 26 yrs 2 mos 20 dys single b. Mercer Co VA d/o John & Anna Meador O: farmer; by John C. Hubbard.

8. 27 March 1856 NOAH C. BLANKENSHIP 23 single b. Giles Co VA now living in Giles Co VA s/o N. & N. Blankenship to ELIZTH E. ARMENTROUT 15 single b. Alleghany Co VA d/o Jno & B. Armentrout O: farmer; by Abram Garretson.

9. 11 April 1856 THOMPSON BLANKENSHIP 23 yrs 1 mo single b. Giles Co BA s/o S. & E. Blankenship to NARCISSA PRINCE 17 single b. Mercer Co VA d/o Jas A. & Judith Prince O: farmer; by H.B. Rose.

10. 28 May 1856 ISAAC N. GRALEY 24 yrs 4 mos single b. Franklin Co VA s/o Jas & Sarah Graley to DELILA JONES 19 yrs 3 mos single b. Floyd Co VA d/o Wm & Anna Jones O: farmer; by James Calfee.

11. 28 May 1856 JESSE JONES 22 yrs single b. Patrick Co VA s/o Wiley & Jane Jones to CATHARINE JONES 22 yrs 4 mos b. Floyd Co VA d/o Wm & Anna Jones O: farmer; by James Calfee.

12. 29 May 1856 SAMUEL MARTIN 29 yrs 6 mos single b. Montgomery Co VA now living in Montgomery Co s/o C. & C. Martin to MARY F. KERR 22 yrs 4 mos single b. Powhatan Co VA d/o Abner & Sarah Kerr O: carpenter; by James Calfee.

13. 5 June 1856 WILLIAM BASSHAM 27 yrs 10 dys wid. b. Mercer Co VA s/o Rhoda Bassham to JULINA LILLY 20 yrs 11 mos 8 dys single b. Mercer Co VA d/o Jos & Polly Lilly O: farmer; by John C. Hubbard.

14. 19 June 1856 OSCAR J. EMMONS 24 yrs 3 mos single b. Giles Co VA s/o Horton & B.Emmons to MARY E.C. ALLEN 21 yrs 7 mos single b. Monroe Co VA s/o R.M. & Ann M. Allen O: merchant; by H.B. Rose.

15. 26 June 1856 RUFUS B. LILLY 19 yrs 3 mos 6 dys single b. Mercer Co VA s/o J.& M. Lilly to MARY LILLY 18 yrs 3 mos 2dys single b. Mercer Co d/o W. & Polly Lilly O: farmer; by John C. Hubbard.

16. 26 June 1856 DAVID FERRELL 20 yrs 8 mos 26 dys single b. Monroe Co VA s/o J. & E. Ferrell now living in Monroe Co to CELIA A. MEADOR 14 yrs 8 mos 10 dys single b. Mercer Co VA d/o Wm M. & C. Meador O: farmer; by John Bragg.

17. 3 July 1856 JOHN A. HAMBRICK 22 yrs 4 mos 3 dys single b. Montgomery Co VA s/o R. & M. Hambrick to MARY J. BROYLES 16 yrs 6 mos 9 dys single b. Monroe Co VA d/o Washg & M.A. Broyles O: blacksmith; by Joseph Wright.

18. 6 Augt 1856 ALBERT WILEY 20 (26) yrs 5 mos 10 dys single b. Mercer Co VA s/o G. & T. Wiley to SARAH LANES 18 yrs 9 mos 6 dys single b. Mercer Co Va d/o Moses & C. Lane O: farmer; by William C. Martin.

19. 13 Augt 1856 JOHN J. WRIGHT 25 single b. Campbell Co VA s/o J.J. & C. Wright to ELIZABETH S. MARTIN 18 single b. Mercer Co VA d/o David & E.A. Martin O: blacksmith; by William Holroyd.

20. 21 Augt 1856 JAMES C. DAVIDSON 59 yrs 5 mos 7 dys wid. b. Wythe Co VA s/o Jos & M. Davidson to CATHARINE BAILEY 39 yrs 1 mo 6 dys single b. Tazewell d/o J. & Elizth Bailey O: farmer; by James Calfee.

21. 27 Augt 1856 GEORGE W. STUMP 19 yrs 4 mos 21 dys single b. Tazewell Co VA s/o Wm & Polly Stump to POLLY A. DILLION 19 yrs 9 mos 13 dys single b. Mercer Co VA d/o Saml & Polly Dillion O: blacksmith; by Joseph Wright.

22. 28 Augt 1856 SIMEON D. HOPKINS 22 yrs 19 dys b. Franklin Co VA s/o J. & J. Hopkins to MARY BELCHER 21 yrs 6 mos 2 dys b. Mercer Co VA d/o M. & M. Belcher O: farmer; by William C. Mercer.

23. 3 Sept 1856 MADISON F. BELCHER 22 yrs 4 mos 8 dys single b. Mercer Co VA s/o Asa & Clara Belcher to MARY J. HOUCHINS 19 yrs 1 mo 23 dys single b. Mercer Co VA d/o Jas & S. Houchins O: farmer; by William C. Mercer.

24. 9 Sept 1856 BLEDSO AUSTIN 48 yrs 7 mos 22 dys wid. b. Grayson Co VA now living in Grayson Co s/o Isaial & Lucy Austin to MATILDA P. GEORGE 30 yrs 9 mos 19 dys single b. Tazewell Co VA d/o Thos & E.H. George O: farmer; by Evan H. Brown.

25. 18 Sept 1856 JAMES M. McCUE 24 yrs 4 mos 0 dys single b. Augusta Co BA s/o John & Hannah McCue to ELIZA J. GOOCH 15 yrs 10 mos single b. Albemarle Co VA d/o Alonzo & E.J. Gooch O: farmer; by Henry B. Rose.

26. 18 Sept 1856 JAMES A. SMITH single b. Rockbridge Co VA s/o T.T. & Sarah Smith to SARAH A. TRACY single b. Giles Co. VA d/o Wm & Dicey Tracy O: farmer; by Abraham Garretson.

27. 25 Sept 1856 WILEY B.W. BLANKENSHIP single b. Mercer Co VA s/o L. & M. Blankenship to MARY E. JONES single b. Mercer Co VA s/o Israel & M. Jones O: farmer; by Abraham Garretson.

28. 21 Octr 1856 JOHN J. MEADOR 19 yrs 7 mos 25 dys single b. Mercer Co VA s/o Wm M. & Celia Meador to SARAH L. NOELL 19 yrs 28 dys single b. Bedford Co VA d/o Caleb & M. Noell O: farmer; by John Bragg.

29. 23 Octr 1856 JOHN W. WHITE 21 yrs 3 mos 6 dys single b. Mercer Co VA s/o Cornelius & M. White to NANCY BELCHER 22 yrs 1 mo 23 dys b. Mercer Co d/o Isham & R. Belcher O: farmer; by Evan H. Brown.

30. 30 Octr 1856 OVERTON C. WHITE 18 yrs 5 mos 27 dys single b. Mercer Co VA s/o Corbelius & M. White to MARY E. HOLSTINE 17 yrs 9 mos 13 dys single b. Mercer Co VA d/o Jas W. & M. Holstine O: farmer; by Evan H. Brown.

31. 12 Novr 1856 LEWIS UPTON 22 single b. Monroe Co VA s/o Sylvester & L. Upton to CHARLOTTE WHITTEN 17 yrs 5 mos 9 dys single b. Alleghany Co VA d/o Lewis & C. Whitten O: farmer; by John Bragg.

32. 13 Novr 1856 DAVID H. LILLY 20 yrs 11 mos 5 dys single b. Giles Co VA s/o Jno & Margaret Lilly to MARY UPTON 19 yrs 2 mos 27 dys b. Monroe Co VA d/o Sylvester & L. Upton O: farmer; by John Bragg.

33. 13 Novr 1856 LYENSGUS MEADOR 23 yrs 8 mos 10 dys single b. Mercer Co VA s/o Josiah & J. Meador to SARAH C. FERGUSON 19 yrs 2 mos 14 dys b. Mercer Co VA d/o Jeremiah & N. Ferguson O: farmer; by John C. Hubbard.

34. 14 Novr 1856 JOHN H. REYNOLDS 42 divorced b. Patrick Co VA s/o Richd & M. Reynolds to MALINDA WEST 19 yrs 3 mos 19 dys b. Floyd Co VA d/o Jas & Malinda West O: farmer; by John Bragg.

35. 11 Decr 1856 THOMAS B. KINZER 26 yrs 6 mos single b. Ranoke(sic) Co VA s/o Michael & Ann Kinzer now living in Tazewell Co VA to LUCRETIA COMPTON 20 yrs 3 mos 1 dy single b. Tazewell Co VA d/o Car & R.J. Compton O: farmer; by James Calfee.

36. 17 Decr 1856 ALLEN BROWN 33 single b. Monroe Co VA s/o Wm & Lucinda Brown to MARY E. ROWLAND 23 single b. Giles Co VA d/o James & E. Rowland O: farmer; by John Doyerle.

37. 18 Decr 1856 ROBERT SWADER 22 yrs 8 mos 12 dys single b. Mercer Co VA s/o Milley Swader to CYNTHIA J. HOLSTINE 15 yrs 3 mos 10 dys single b. Mercer Co VA d/o Henry & M. Holstine O: farmer; by Joseph Wright.

38. 18 Decr 1856 JESSE SIAS 44 divorced b. Monroe Co VA s/o Jas & Frances Sias to MAGDALINE BOONE 22 divorced b. Monroe Co VA d/o Jas & Sarah Scales O: farmer; by John C. Hubbard.

39. 18 Decr 1856 WILLIAM A. BOLING 29 yrs 1 mo 14 dys single b. Mercer Co VA s/o John & Sally Bowling to DEMERIUS WHITE 31 yrs 22 dys single b. Mercer Co VA d/o Cornelius & P. White O: farmer; by Joseph Wright.

40. 18 Decr 1856 ANDREW J. MARTIN 22 yrs 2 mos 10 dys single b. Monroe Co VA s/o Booker & R. Martin to SARAH A. LILLY 20 yrs 10 mos 8 dys single b. Mercer Co VA d/o Jas & Ellen Lilly O: farmer; by John Bragg.

41. 24 Decr 1856 HUGH J. MEADOR 20 yrs 9 mos 24 dys single b. Mercer Co VA s/o Jno & Anna Meador to ELIZTH M. DEEDS 16 yrs 1 mo 24 dys single b. Monroe Co VA d/o Jos & Hannah Deeds O: farmer; by John Bragg.

42. 25 Decr 1856 JAMES SNEAD 22 yrs 9 mos 15 dys single b. Patrick Co VA s/o Saml & E. Snead to MARY V. MEADOR 18 yrs 1 mo 15 dys single b. Mercer Co VA d/o Jno & Anna Meador O: farmer; by John C. Hubbard.

43. 22 Decr 1857(sic)(1856) WILLIAM M. THORNTON 20 yrs 8 mos 22 dys single b. Pulaski Co VA s/o Meredity ' Louisa Thornton to ELIZ J. HATCHER 19 yrs 8

mos 20 dys single b. Patrick Co VA d/o Simmon & Tempa Hatcher O: farmer; by James Calfee.

44. 24 Decr 1857(sic)(1856) WILLIAM HAYWOOD 23 yrs 6 mos 26 dys single b. Mercer Co VA s/o Saml & Patsy Haywood to SARAH THOMAS 26 yrs 10 mos single b. Mercer Co VA d/o Jesse & Rachel Thomas O: farmer; by Abraham Garretson.

45. 24 Decr 1857(sic)(1856) LEWIS TRAIL 24 yrs single b. Floyd Co VA s/o Elijah & Jane Trail to MARY E. CUESADAY 19 yrs 7 mos single b. Giles Co VA d/o Hiram & Martha Cuesaday O: wagoner; by. H.R.Rose.

Page 4

1. 13 Jany 1857 AUSTIN B. HARVEY 20 single b. Monroe Co VA s/o Michael & W. Harvey to MARY ANN ELLISON 14 single b. Monroe Co VA d/o Isaac & Nancy T. Ellison O: farmer; by William Holroyd.

2. 13 Jany 1867 WILLIAM JONES 21 yrs 4 mos 24 dys single b. Franklin Co VA s/o Wm & Ann Jones to ELLEN HAYWOOD 24 yrs 20 mos 2 dys single b. Mercer Co VA d/o Saml & Patsy Haywood O: farmer; by James Calfee.

3. 14 Jany 1857 ROBERT P. CASSADAY 23 yrs 11 mos single b. Wythe Co VA s/o Hiram & Martha Cassaday to LOUISA DAVIS 16 yrs 6 mos b. Patrick Co VA d/o John W. & Temperance Davis O: farmer; by H.B. Rose.

4. 14 Jany 1857 JOHN R. ELLISON 18 yrs b. Monroe Co VA s/o Isaac & Nancy T. Ellison to EMALINE HARVEY 17 single b. Monroe co VA d/o Michael & W. Harvey.

5. 25 Feby 1857 ISAAC MEADOR 28 yrs 4 mos 25 dys divorced b. Mercer Co VA s/o Thomas & Lyda Meador to MARY JANE LILLY 24 yrs 2 mos 12 dys single b. Mercer Co VA d/o James & Arminta Lilly O: farmer; by John C. Hubbard.

6. 5 March 1857 WILLIAM PENNINGTON 21 single b. Mercer Co VA s/o Wm & Sarah Pennington to NANCY SHREWSBURY 18

single b. Giles Co VA d/o Phillip & Charlotte Shrewsbury O: farmer; by William Holroyd.

7. 12 March 1857 --- LAVENDER 19 single b. Wythe Co VA s/o John & Jane Lavender to ---- CAULEY 17 single b. Mercer Co VA d/o Benjn & Phoeba Cauley O: farmer; by William Holroyd.

8. 12 March 1857 THOMAS E. LILLY 22 yrs 4 mos 10 dys single b. Raleigh Co VA where he now resides s/o Elijah & Sallie Lilley to MARY AKERS 22 yrs 6 mos 17 dys single b. Franklin Co VA d/o Hudson & nancy Akers O: farmer by John C Hubbard.

9. 26 March 1857 LORENZO D. BUCKLAND 22 yrs 7 mos 17 dys single b. Monroe Co VA s/o John & Mary Buckland to CLARA MEADOWS 20 yrs 10 mos 15 dys single b. Mercer Co VA d/o Jere. & Jane Meadows O: farmer; by Samuel Scott.

10. 8 April 1857 JESSE UNDERWOOD 22 yrs 1 mo 9 dys single b. Floyd Co VA s/o Jesse & Eleanor Underwood to MISHEL UNDERWOOD 22 yrs 1 mo 8 dys single b. Floyd Co VA d/o Adam & Elizth Underwood O: farmer; by James Calfee.

11. 23 April 1857 SAMUEL L. WILLIAMS 21 yrs 4 mos 20 dys single b. Mercer Co VA s/o Larkin & Rhoda Williams to MARY A. PETRY 18 single b. Mercer Co VA d/o Wm & Polly Petry O: farmer; by William C. Martin.

12. 5 May 1857 HENDERSON F. THOMAS 20 yrs 6 mos single b. Mercer Co VA s/o Samuel & Juliet Thomas to MARGARET H. CRAWFORD 24 yrs 17 dys single b. Mercer Co VA d/o Zachariah & Jane Crawford O: farmer; by James Calfee.

13. 14 May 1857 HENDERSON PETRY 23 yrs 3 mos single b. Mercer Co VA s/o Thomsy(sic) Petry to ALBERTINA CAPERTON 21 yrs 3 mos single b. Mercer Co VA d/o Augs & Rachel Caperton O: farmer; by Leroy Keaton.

14. 19 May 1857 Evan H. Brown 31 yrs 11 mos 20 dys single b. Mercer Co VA s/o Wm & Lucinda Brown to MARTHA E. McCLAGHERTY 17 yrs 1 mo 28 dys single

b. Giles Co VA d/o John & Phoebe McClagherty O: physician & preacher; by J.P. Gibson.

15. 21 May 1857 REECE T. LUSK 22 yrs 3 mos single b. Mercer Co VA s/o Absolom & Dilly Lusk to MARY J. GODFREY 18 yrs 3 mos b. Mercer Co VA d/o Jas B. & Nancy Godfrey O: farmer; by H.B. Rose.

16. 22 May 1857 JOHN B. CRAWFORD 37 yrs single b. Giles Co VA s/o Zachirah & Jane Crawford to MARTHA A. THOMAS 27 single b. Giles Co VA d/o Samuel & Juliet Thomas O: farmer; by Abraham Garretson.

17. 26 May 1857 JOHN E. LILLY 18 yrs 7 mos 1 dy single b. Mercer Co VA s/o Jonathan & Margaret Lilly to JULINA LILLY 17 yrs 3 mos 16 dys single b. Mercer Co VA d/o Washington & Mary Lilly O: farmer; by John C. Hubbard.

18. 27 May 1857 HUGH J. FANNING 23 single b. Giles Co VA s/o Garland B. & Millie Faning to MARINDA J. WHITE 17 single b. Giles Co VA d/o Reuben & Mary White O: farmer; by Abraham Garretson.

19. 16 June 1857 OSBORN T. DILLION 21 yrs 12 dys single b. Kanawha Co VA now living in Tazewell Co VA s/o H.J. & Elizabeth Dillion to ELISA J. BELCHER 22 yrs 2 mos 21 dys b. Mercer Co VA d/o H.D. & Anna Belcher O: farmer; by Joseph Wright.

20. 18 June 1857 GEORGE W. MEADOR 20 single b. Mercer Co VA s/o Josiah & Juda Meador to RHODA LILLY 18 single b. Mercer Co VA d/o John & Nancy Lilly O: farmer; by Rufus Pack.

21. 18 June 1857 DANIEL SHREWSBURY 19 single b. Mercer Co VA s/o --- Shrewsbury to CELIA A. LILLY 22 single b. Mercer Co VA d/o Turner & Arty Lilly O: farmer; by Rufus Pack.

22. 25 June 1857 JAMES M. LILLY 20 yrs 6 mos 25 dys single b. Mercer Co VA s/o Robt & Elizth Lilly to ELIZA J. LILLY 14 yrs 1 mo 25 dys single b. Mercer Co VA d/o Joseph & Jane Lilly O: farmer; by John C. Hubbard.

23. 30 June 1857 CHARLES A. BOLING 20 yrs 6 mos 25 dys single b. Mercer Co VA s/o John & Sarah Boling to LUCY M. BRAMMER 19 yrs 4 mos 20 dys single b. Patrick Co VA d/o Jas & Anna Brammer O: farmer; by John C. Hubbard.

24. 7 July 1857 DAVID STRONG 37 yrs 7 mos 1 dy single b. Marion Co OH s/o Horan & Abby C. Strong to MARY E. BAILEY 16 yrs 10 mos 6 dys b. Mercer Co VA d/o Amos W. & Rhoda Bailey O: farmer; by Joseph Wright.

25. 10 July 1857 JONATHAN H. BELCHER 19 yrs 3 mos 15 dys single b. Mercer Co VA s/o Asa & Clara Belcher to SARAH ANN COOK 22 yrs 19 dys sinble b. Mercer Co VA d/o Cornelius & Anna Cook O: farmer; by Leroy Keaton.

26. 16 July 1857 THOMAS NEWBURY 21 wid. b. Franklin Co VA s/o Thomas & Sarah Newbury to FRANCES J. CADLE 18 single b. Mercer Co VA d/o James & Sarah Cadle O: farmer; by Rufus Pack.

27. 22 July 1857 JOHN BASHAM 26 yrs 6 mos divorced b. Mercer Co VA s/o Meador & Patty Basham to ISABELLA PACK 26 yrs 2 mos single b. Mercer Co VA d/o Robert & Rhoda Pack O: farmer; by John C. Hubbard.

28. 11 Augt 1857 ANDREW B. BROWN 24 yrs 2 mos single b. Giles Co VA where he now lives s/o Geo W. & Hiram Brown to MARY W. SMITH 28 yrs 8 mos single b. Mercer Co VA d/o Saml P. & Agnes Smith O: farmer; by H.B. Rose.

29. 11 Augt 1857 OSCAR T. PRINCE 22 yrs 10 mos 4 dys single b. Mercer Co VA s/o Wm & Lucy Prince to MARGELINA MAXEY ---* single b. Mercer Co VA d/o Josiah & Sallie Maxey O: farmer; by Evan H. Brown. (*Note: she was 14 in the 1850 Census so about 21 here.)

30. 12 Aug 1857 ---* LILLY 27 single b. Mercer Co VA s/o John & Margaret Lilly to ---* HARVEY 18 single b. Mercer Co VA d/o Michael & Nancy Harvey O: farmer; by Rufus Pack. (*Note: This is probably William H. Lilly and Matilda Harvey as per 1850 Census #217 & #213 and 1860 Mercer Co VA Census #1005/941.)

31. 13 Aug 1857 MARTIN V. WADE 21 single b. Patrick Co VA s/o Jacob & Susan Wade to MARTHA M. BENTLEY 19 single b. Nottoway Co VA d/o Saml & Jane W. Bentley O: farmer; by Rufus Pack.

32. 26 Aug 1857 URIAH A. BOLING 22 yrs 4 mos 10 dys single b. Mercer Co VA s/o Wm & Elizth Boling to REBECCA J. REED 18 yrs 5 mos 16 dys b. Mercer Co VA d/o Joseph & Malinda Reed O: farmer; by William C. Martin.

33. 27 Aug 1857 JAMES N. WOOD 25 yrs 3 mos single b. Patrick Co VA now living in Wyoming Co VA s/o Peter & Nancy Wood to NANCY E. SWEENEY 17 yrs 4 mos 3 dys b. Mercer Co VA d/o Martin & Nancy Sweeney O: farmer; by John C. Hubbard.

34. 9 Sept 1857 WILLIAM GARRETSON 38 yrs 10 mos single b. Giles Co VA now living in Mercer Co VA s/o Abraham & Nancy Garretson to COLUMBIA BROWN 17 yrs 3 mos single b. Alleghany Co VA d/o John & Elizth Brown O: farmer; by Abraham Garretson.

35. 10 Sept 1857 JAMES T. McCORKLE 22 single b. Rockbridge Co VA now living in Mercer Co s/o John & Sarah McCorkle to MARY J. THOMPSON 18 single b. Mercer Co VA d/o Jas & Lucy Thompson O: school teacher; by William Holroyd.

36. 10 Sept 1857 JEREMIAH MEADOWS 23 single b. Fayette Co VA now living in Raleigh Co VA s/o Abraham & Rugh Meadows to LOUISA MANN 16 single b. Mercer Co VA d/o Ezekiah & Elizth Mann O: farmer; by Van Sanford.

37. 30 Sept 1857 THOMAS H. THORNILY 38 wid. b. England s/o James & Mary Thornily to EMALINE V. SCOTT 24 single b. Giles Co VA d/o Saml & Nancy Scott O: farmer; by William Holroyd.

38. 7 Octr 1857 JOHN W. NELSON 20 single b. Monroe Co VA s/o James & Lydia Nelson to ANGELINE VASS 21 single b. Mercer Co VA d/o Benjn & Julia Vass O: farmer; by Willis Tinsley.

39. 13 Oct 1857 MARCUS L. SHREWSBURY 22 yrs 10 mos 3 dys single b. Mercer Co VA now living in Wyoming Co VA s/o Jere & Elizth Shrewsbury to ELIZABETH CUNNINGHAM 28 yrs 1 mo 10 dys wid. b. Franklin Co VA s/o Henry & Ruth Clark O: farmer; by John C. Hubbard.

40. 15 Octr 1857 ROBERT SAUNDERS 21 yrs 7 mos single b. Pulaski Co VA now living in Mercer Co s/o Julius & Lydia Saunders to REBECCA J. BROWN 21 yrs 6 mos single b. Mercer Co VA d/o Geo P. & Sallie P. Brown O: farmer; by H.B. Rose.

41. 15 Octr 1857 HENRY P. WAUGH 30 single b. Monroe co VA* now a part of Holstine Conference s/o John & Ruth Waugh to BARBARA J. EVATT 26 yrs 9 mos 1 dy single b. Sullivan Co TN d/o Joseph & Phoebe Evatt O: Minister of the Gospel; by Evan H. Brown. (*Note: Henry P. Waugh was born in Monroe Co TN and was admitted to the Holston Converence of the Methodist Episcopal Church in 1855. Barbara died in 1861 and he later married again to Mrs. Mary A. Proctor. He served church in Holston and Alabama Conference and was a chaplin in the Confederate Army for two years. cf L.P. Martin's History of Holston Methodism)

42. 28 Octr 1857 ALEXANDER BAILEY 24 yrs 3 mos 10 dys wid. b. Mercer Co VA s/o Arch & Elizth Bailey to HANNAH L. LAMBERT 19 yrs 11 mos 10 dys single b. Tazewell Co VA d/o Jere. & Eleanor Lambert O: farmer; by James Calfee.

43. 3 Novr 1857 JOHN L. WALKER 25 yrs 3 mos 9 dys single b. Botetourt Co VA s/o Henry & Mary B. Walker to JANE K. CARR 24 yrs 9 dys single b. Giles Co VA d/o Robt & Sallie Carr O: farmer; by Evan H. Brown.

44. 24 Novr 1857 GEORGE D. BAILEY 27 yrs 10 mos 19 dys single b. Mercer Co VA s/o Geo & Francis Bailey to CHRISTIANA JEWELL 17 yrs 4 mos 13 dys single b. Montgomery Co VA where she now lives d/o John & Christiana Jewell O: farmer; by Evan H. Brown.

4. 20 Jany 1858 WILLIAM H. THOMPSON 22 yrs 9 mos 10 dys single b. Mercer Co VA s/o Syms & Nancy Thompson to SARAH LAMBERT 22 yrs 9 mos 2 dys single b. Tazewell Co VA d/o Jeremiah & Eleanor Lambert O: farmer; by James Calfee.

5. 20 Jany 1858 BERRY MIZE 22 yrs 3 mos single b. Patrick Co VA s/o Samson & Elizabeth Mize to FRANCES LILLY 18 yrs 1 mo 4 dys single b. Mercer Co VA d/o Robert & Elizabeth Lilly O: farmer; by Leroy Keaton.

6. 2 Feby 1858 JAMES S. ARCHER 26 yrs 16 dys single b. Wythe Co VA s/o Samson & Sarah Archer to JULINA SARVER 22 yrs 9 mos 4 dys single b. Mercer Co VA d/o James & Elizabeth Sarver O: farmer; by Abraham Garretson.

7. 4 Feby 1858 REUBEN CRAWFORD 26 yrs 1 mo 8 dys single b. Mercer Co VA s/o Zachariah & Jane Crawford to MARGARET B. BROWN 20 yrs 2 mos 18 dys single b. Tazewell Co VA d/o Thomas & Margaret Brown O: blacksmith; by W.W. Neal.

8. 4 Feby 1858 JORDAN FAULKNER 20 yrs 7 mos 4 dys single b. Montgomery Co VA s/o Hugh M. & Susannah Faulkner to ANN E. PAYNE 19 yrs 4 mos 26 dys single b. Montgomery Co VA d/o Mahala Payne O: farmer; by Joseph Wright.

9. 9 Feby 1858 JOHN T. WALKER 23 yrs 3 mos 11 dys single b. Mercer Co VA now living in Wyoming Co VA s/o Chrispianos & Eleanor Walker to RUTH S. MOONEY 18 yrs 8 mos 7 dys single b. Mercer Co VA d/o John & Susannah Mooney O: farmer; by Joseph Wright.

10. 9 Feby 1858 JOHN S. HUDSON 30 yrs 5 mos 15 dys single b. Franklin Co VA s/o James & Harriet Hudson to MARY ANN PETERS 23 yrs 9 mos single b. Mercer Co VA d/o Christian & Mary Peters O: farmer; by Leroy Keaton.

11. 11 Feby 1858 JOHN L. HARTWELL 18 yrs 10 mos single b. Mercer Co VA s/o Andrew D. & Jane Hartwell to CYNTHIA E DILLION 19 yrs 7 mos single b. Mercer Co VA d/o James P. & Julia Dillion O: farmer; by Henry B. Rose.

45. 27 Novr 1857 HIRAM A. REED 22 yrs 2 mos single b. Mercer Co VA s/o Joseph & Malinda Reed to SUSAN WORRELL 18 single b. Carroll Co VA d/o Jas B. & Rhoda Worrell O: farmer; by William C. Martin.

(Page torn here - % denotes what is missing but assumed to be correct.)

46. Decr % 1857 JOSEPH P. HUDSON 23 yrs 1 mo 20 dys single. b. Franklin Co VA s/o Vncent & Rosana Hudson to EVA A. SONGER 17 yrs 7 mos 22 dys single b. Pulaski Co VA d/o Christian & mary Ann Songer O: farmer; by James Calfee.

47. ------% 1857 WILLIAM D. STROUD 37 yrs 2 mos 16 dys single b. Dinwiddle Co VA s/o Thos & Nancy M. Stroud to LOUISA FOLEY 16 yrs 2 mos 16 dys single b. Patrick Co VA d/o James & Juda Foley O: physician; by William C. Martin.

48. --- % 1857 WILLIAM E. CARPER 20 yrs 3 mos single b. Botetourt Co VA s/o Michael & Elizth Carper to REBECCA C. TILLER 21 yrs 11 mos single b. Mercer Co VA d/o Anderson & Priscilla Tiller O: farmer; by Abraham Garretson.

Page 5

1. 1 Jany 1858 MATTHEW E. LUSK 22 yrs 7 mos 2 dys single b. Wyoming Co VA now residing same s/o Eli & Elizabeth Lusk to NANCY P. McCOMAS 18 yrs 7 mos 5 dys single b. Mercer Co VA d/o James & Rebecca McComas O: farmer; by Joseph Wright.

2. 14 Jany 1858 JOHN J. FORD 25 yrs 2 mos single b. Monroe Co VA s/o Benjamin & Peggy Ford to SARAH E. WOOD 25 yrs 5 mos single b. Augusta Co VA d/o Robert & Frances Wood O: farmer; by Leroy Keaton.

3. 15 Jany 1858 WILLIAM LAWRENCE 23 yrs 3 mos single b. Monroe Co VA residing same s/o John & Sarah Lawrence to MARY ANN BALLARD 19 yrs 2 mos 15 dys single b. Monroe Co VA d/o Wilson & Sarah Ballard O: farmer; by Leroy Keaton.

12. 25 Feby 1858 ERASTUS B MEADOR 25 yrs single b. Giles Co VA s/o William M. & Celia Meador to CLARA B. PACK 17 yrs single b. Monroe Co VA d/o Anderson & Rebecca Pack O: merchant; by Rufus Pack.

13. 11 March 1858 CHARLES ABBOT 25 yrs 9 mos 11 dys wid. b. Monroe Co VA to IDA FARLEY 24 yrs 28 dys single b. Mercer Co VA d/o Anderson & Anna Farley O: farmer; by Leroy Keaton.

14. 16 March 1858 LEWIS A. LUSK 22 yrs single b. Monroe Co VA where he now lives s/o Isaac Lusk to ---* MARTIN 16 yrs single b. Monroe Co VA d/o Booker & Rebecca Martin O: farmer; by Rufus Pack. (*Note: Probably Polly who was 8 yrs in 1850 Mercer Co Census #579.)

15. 15 April 1858 ANDREW J. HULL 26 yrs single b. Monroe Co VA now living in Raleigh Co VA s/o Henry & Emaly Hull to REBECA C. DYALE* 23 yrs single b. Montgomery Co VA d/o Crocheto* & Mary Dyale O: farmer; by Elias Kendall. (*Note: unable to read writing on these names.)

16. 15 April 1858 JOHN MARTIN 24 yrs 11 dys single b. Mercer Co VA s/o David & Nancy Martin to DIANA NOBLE 29 yrs 6 mos 10 dys single b. Mercer Co VA d/o William & Mahala Noble O: farmer; by William C. Martin.

17. 24 April 1858 CHARLES HALDREN 32 yrs 8 mos 20 dys single b. Mercer Co VA s/o Sarah Haldren to SARAH A. PENNINGTON 26 yrs 9 mos 17 dys single b. Mercer Co VA d/o James & Martha Pennington O: farmer; by William C Martin.

18. 27 April 1858 MILLON H. FRENCH 24 yrs 2 mos 10 dys single b. Giles Co VA s/o Charles C. & Rebecca French to BELINDA SCOTT 24 yrs 1 mo 26 dys single b. Floyd Co VA d/o John & China Scott O: farmer; by Evan H. Brown.

19. 7 May 1858 JOSEPH WADDLE 22 yrs single b. Giles Co VA s/o Alexander & Mary Waddle to PRISCILLA MILLS 21 yrs single b. Mercer Co VA d/o Samuel & Leenah Mills O: farmer; by Elijah Conner.

20. 25 May 1858 JOHN W. BROWN 24 yrs 8 mos 17 dys single b. Alleghany Co VA s/o John & Elizabeth Brown to RHODA M. TILLER 17 yrs 2 mos 17 dys single b. Mercer Co VA d/o Anderson & Priscilla Brown O: potter; by Abraham Garretson.

21. 7 June 1858 JOHN W. BROOKS 25 yrs single b. Sumner Co TN now living in Franklin Co VA s/o John & Nancy Brooks to LUCY W. BOWERS 22 yrs single b. Mercer Co VA d/o James & Elizabeth Bowers O: farmer; by Elias Kendall.

22. 21 June 1858 JOHN D. LYON 22 yrs single b. Patrick Co VA s/o Daniel & Lucy Lyons to MARY A MEADOR 25 yrs single b. Mercer Co VA d/o Josiah & Judith Meador O: farmer; by Rufus Pack.

23. 21 June 1858 CHARLES S. TURNER 23 yrs 6 mos 21 dys single b. Montgomery Co VA s/o Wilson & Sarah C. Turner to VICTORIA McKINZIE 13yrs 10 mos 5 dys single b. Mercer Co VA d/o John O. & Priscilla McKinzie O: farmer; by Evan H. Brown.

24. 10 Aug 1858 SYLVESTER BRAGG 30 yrs single b. Cabell Co VA now living in Greenbrier Co VA s/o Michael & Elizabeth Bragg to CAROLINE UPTON 21 yrs single b. Monroe Co VA d/o Meredith Upton O: farmer; by Paul Vanderwood.

25. 7 Sept 1858 JOHN C. PETERS 10 yrs single b. Monroe Co VA now living same s/o George W. & Margaret B. Peters to SARAH J. POINDEXTER 17 yrs single b. Henry Co VA d/o John D. & Louisa Poindexter O: farmer; by Rufus Pack.

26. 9 Sept 1858 JOHN O. SNIDER 28 yrs single b. Franklin Co VA s/o John & Susan Snider to CATHERINE SHOAS* 16 yrs single b. Giles Co VA d/o Not known O: farmer; by Leroy Keaton. (*Note: unable to read handwriting.)

27. 14 Sept 1858 JOHN R. SHANNON 23 yrs single b. Campbell Co VA s/o John & Margaret Shannon to EDITHA THOMPSON 16 yrs single b. Mercer Co VA d/o John & Elizabeth Thompson O: farmer; by William Holroyd.

28. 15 Sept 1858 JOSEPHUS ROBINSON 23 yrs 8 mos 1 dy single b. Monroe Co VA s/o Harrison & Harriett Robinson to HARRIET J. HOLSTINE 23 yrs 20 dys single b. Mercer Co VA d/o Joseph C. & Elizabeth Holstine O: farmer; by James Calfee.

29. 30 Sept 1858 BALLARD P. DILLION 21 yrs 9 mos 18 dys single b. Mercer Co VA s/o Jesse & Cynthia Dillion to ELIZA L. BELCHER 17 yrs 7 mos 17 dys single b. Mercer Co VA d/o Christian & Polly Belcher O: farmer; by Joseph Wright.

30. 6 Octr 1858 WILLIAM H. THOMPSON 23 yrs 9 mos 1 dy single b. Mercer Co VA s/o Andrew J. & Elizabeth Thompson to REBECCA J. PETERS 22 yrs 8 mos 11 dys b. Mercer Co VA d/o Christian S. & Mary Peters O: farmer; by Abraham Garretson.

31. 7 Octr 1858 JOHN W. BAILEY 17 yrs single b. Mercer Co VA s/o Samuel & Mary Bailey to SARAH E. CECIL 14 yrs single b. Mercer Co VA d/o Shelby & Mary J. Cecil O: farmer; by Elijah Conner.

32. 12 Octr 1858 WILLIAM H. LITTLE 21 yrs single b. Mercer Co VA s/o Thomas & Eleanor Little to MARY D. FANNING 18 yrs 4 mos 27 dys single b. Mercer Co VA d/o Garland B. & Martha Fanning O: farmer; by Abraham Garretson.

33. 12 Octr 1858 JOHN M. McCLAUGHERTY 26 yrs single b. Giles Co VA s/o John & Phebe McClaugherty to SUSAN A. MONROE 20 yrs single b. Campbell Co VA d/o James R. & Rhoda Monroe O: farmer; by William Holroyd.

34. 14 Octr 1858 STYNAIS L. MOONEY 23 yrs single b. Grayson Co VA s/o Martin D. & Amelia Mooney to SUSANNAH BAKER 19 yrs single b. Logan Co VA d/o John & Polly Baker O: farmer; by Joseph Wright.

35. 19 Octr 1858 PATERO A. HUBBARD 20 yrs single b. Patrick Co VA s/o Samuel & Elizabeth Hubbard to LUCY A. WORRELL 17 yrs single b. Carroll Co VA d/o James B. & Olive Worrell O: farmer; by No Name Given.

36. 26 Octr 1858 JOSEPH P. FUGATE 24 yrs 9 mos 26 dys single b. Russell Co VA now living in same s/o Zachariah & Phermba Fugate to CATHERINE DAVIS 36 yrs 9 mos 10 dys wid. b. Mercer Co VA d/o David & Rhoda Swader O: farmer; by Joseph Wright.

37. 28 Octr 1858 JOHN L. SHANNON 23 yrs 2 mos 23 dys single b. Tazewell Co VA now living in same s/o John & Rebecca Shannon to ELIZABETH DANGERFIELD 18 yrs 6 mos 23 dys single b. Mercer Co VA d/o Leonard H. & Nancy Dangerfield O: farmer; by Evan H. Brown.

38. 2 Novr 1858 WILLIAM W. BRUCE 18 yrs single b. Mercer Co VA s/o John & Catherine Bruce to MARY A.E. JOHNSTON 15 yrs single b. Giles Co VA d/o Alexander & Nancy Johnston O: farmer; by William Holroyd.

39. 3 Novr 1858 ANDERSON A. BELCHER 37 yrs wid. b. Mercer Co VA s/o Henry & Milla Belcher to CLARINDA B SCOTT 37 yrs 7 mo single b. Floyd Co VA d/o John & China Scott O: farmer; by James Calfee.

40. 9 Novr 1858 WILLIAM J. LILLY 25 yrs single b. Mercer Co VA s/o James & Nelly Lilly to MARGARET L. WHITTEN 28 yrs single b. Alleghany Co VA d/o Lewis & Charlotte Whitten O: farmer; by No Name Given.

41. 16 Novr 1858 JAMES FARLEY 34 yrs wid. b. Mercer Co VA s/o Andrew & Anna Farley to ELLEN W. ABBOTT 33 yrs single b. Monroe Co VA d/o St. Clair & Sallie Abbott O: farmer; by Leroy Keaton.

42. 23 Novr 1858 GRANVILLE WORRELL 21 yrs 9 mos 6 dys single b. Carroll Co s/o James B. & Olive Worrell to LOUISA A. HUBBARD 14 yrs 5 mos 11 dys single b. Patrick Co VA d/o Samuel & Elizabeth Hubbard O: farmer; by John C. Hubbard.

43. 25 Novr 1858 DAVID K. LUSK 30 yrs single b. Mercer Co VA s/o Absolom & Dilla Lusk to ANN S. BASHALDER 37 yrs wid. b. Montgomery Co VA d/o Robert Craig & Mary Lee O: farmer; by Joseph Wright.

44. 25 Novr 1858 HARVEY G. WHITE 18 yrs 5 mos 18 dys single b. Mercer Co VA s/o Cornelius & Polly White to SARAH E. RUHLE 17 yrs 1 mos 10 dys single b. Rockbridge Co VA d/o Samuel & Catherine Ruhle O: farmer; by Joseph Wright.

45. 25 Novr 1858 SAMUEL M. SNAPP 23 yrs single b. Augusta Co VA s/o John & Catherine Snapp to ELIZA W. HAYMAKER 19 yrs single b. Montgomery Co VA d/o Michael & Mary Haymaker O: farmer; by Paul Vanderwood.

46. 2 Decr 1858 JOHN P. TILLER 19 yrs 8 mos 27 dys single b. Mercer Co VA s/o Anderson & Priscilla Tiller to LEVINA BROWN 19 yrs 4 mos 5 dys single b. Tazewell Co VA d/o Thomas & Margaret Brown O: mechanic; by Abraham Garretson.

47. 13 Decr 1858 JOSEPH W. JOHNSON 22 yrs single b. Mechlenburg Co VA s/o Patrick & Elizabeth Johnson to PENELOPE WHITTAKER 23 yrs single b. Giles Co VA d/o Aaron & Margaret Whittabke O: waggoner; by Samuel Scott.

48. 14 Decr 1858 WILLIAM F. STEEL 19 yrs single b. Mercer Co VA s/o Sarah Steel to RHODA MEADOWS 16 yrs single b. Mercer Co VA d/o Jordan & Susann Meadows O: farmer; by Samuel Scott.

Page 6

1. 14 Decr 1858 JOHN TAYLOR 22 yrs single b. Carroll Co VA s/o John & Mary Taylor to MARY F. HARTWELL 21 yrs single b. Mercer Co VA d/o Andrew & Jane Hartwell O: farmer; by James Calfee.

2. 22 Decr 1858 CASPER L. HARLESS 28 yrs single b. Giles Co VA now residing in same s/o Alexander & Elizabeth Harless to MARY A. CALDWELL 27 yrs single b. Giles Co VA d/o John & Eliza Caldwell O: farmer; by John Dyerle.

3. 23 Decr 1858 CARY A. PITZER 21 yrs single b. Craig Co VA s/o John H. & Barbara Pitzer to AMANDA G. HARVEY 19 yrs single b. Monroe Co VA d/o James G. & Nancy Harvey O: farmer; by Paul Vanderwood.

4. 28 Decr 1858 MATTHEW W. BOLTON 31 yrs single b. Botetourt Co VA now living in Giles Co VA s/o Jacob & Elizabeth Bolton to MARY F. SMITH 25 yrs single b. Logan Co VA d/o Benjamin & Elizabeth Smith O: mill wright; by John B. Lee.

5. 6 Jany 1859 JOHN B. ST. CLAIR 27 yrs 7 mos 5 dys single b. Bedford Co VA s/o Isaac & Jane St. Clair to SARAH HALDREN 18 yrs 2 mos 3 dys single b. Mercer Co VA d/o Henry & Mahala Haldren O: farmer; by William C. Martin.

6. 9 Jany 1859 JOSEPH GOSER 79 yrs wid. b. Monroe Co VA now living in same s/o Henry & Catherine Goser to LOUISA SPRADLIN 46 yrs wid. b. Franklin Co VA d/o David & Mary Meador O: farmer; by Leroy Keaton.

7. 13 Jany 1859 JOHN A. McKINZIE 36 yrs wid. b. Mercer Co VA s/o Alex. & Malinda McKinzie to LUCINDA E. BOLING 20 yrs single b. Patrick Co VA d/o James & Ruth Boling O: farmer; by William Holroyd.

8. 18 Jany 1859 DANIEL H. EATON 24 yrs single b. Monroe Co VA now living in Wise Co VA s/o John & Elizabeth Eaton to MARY A.E. JOHNSTON 23 yrs single b. Giles Co VA d/o Adam & Susanah Johnston O: farmer; by Josiah Lorbett.

9. 26 Jany 1859 SAMUEL T.C. PERDUE 36 yrs single b. Giles Co VA now living same s/o Zach & Mary Perdue to MARY A. WAGGONER 26 yrs wid. b. Henry Co VA d/o John & Elizth Perdue O: farmer; by Abraham Garretson.

10. 27 Jany 1859 JOHN B. SMITH 29 yrs single b. Logain Co VA s/o Benj. & Eliz. S. Smith to SARAH G. NEAL 23 yrs single b. Monroe Co VA d/o Daniel & Hannah Neal O: farmer; by Elisha G. Duncan.

11. 31 Jany 1859 RUTLEDGE CALFEE 30 yrs 3 mos 3 dys single b. Pulaski Co VA s/o Saml. & Rebecca Calfee to ESTHER A. CALFEE 21 yrs 2 mos 17 dys single b. Wythe Co VA d/o Saml. T. & Jane C. Calfee O: farmer; by James Calfee.

12. 23 Feby 1859 ALEXANDER GAND 21 yrs single b. Carroll Co VA s/o Wm & Sarah Gand to LOUISA WOOD 17 yrs single b. Patrick Co VA d/o Alexr & Rathena Wood O: farmer; by Paul Vanderwood.

13. 15 March 1859 ALEXR H. MOONEY 21 yrs 11 mos 25 dys single b. Mercer Co VA s/o John L. & Susanna Mooney to MARY P. CLARK 20 yrs 11 mos 15 dys single b. Franklin Co VA d/o John & Miraine Clark O: farmer; by Russell G. French.

14. 17 March 1859 HIRAM DAVIS 20 yrs single b. Giles Co VA now living same s/o Lindsay & Jennie Davis to JULIA A. DAVIS 21 yrs single b. Giles Co VA d/o Joshua & Sarah Davis O: farmer; by Landon Duncan.

15. 8 April 1859 JAMES PETRY 70 yrs wid. b. Rockingham Co VA s/o Martin & Ann Petry to LYDIA MOSS 44 yrs wid. b. Greenbrier Co VA d/o Mary Carter O: carpenter; by William C. Martin.

16. 10 April 1859 JOHN D. MARTIN 22 yrs 5 mos 12 dys single b. Mercer Co VA s/o Wm C. & Ann Martin to LENESOR* G. GIBSON 24 yrs 8 mos 26 dys single b. Gaun* Co VA d/o Saml & Elizth Gibson O: farmer; by William C. Martin. (*Note: unable to read handwriting clearly.)

17. 28 April 1859 THOMAS H. SHREWSBURY 22 yrs 5 mos 17 dys single b. Mercer Co VA s/o John & Elizth Shrewsbury to MARYELINE M. BAILEY 22 yrs 3 mos 21 dys single b. Mercer Co VA d/o Jameson & Elizth Bailey O: farmer; by Joseph Wright.

18. 28 April 1859 JAMES J. BOLING 30 yrs 7 mos single b. Mercer Co VA s/o Wm & Elizth Boling to ISABELLA GRAYBILL 19 yrs 5 mos 12 dys single b. Montgomery Co VA d/o John & Susan Graybill O: farmer; by William C. Martin.

19. 3 May 1859 GEORGE W/ SORTER 33 yrs wid. b. Charlotte Co VA s/o John & Nancy Shorter to SARAH J. PHILLIPS 16 yrs single b. Mercer Co VA d/o Jas. & Clara Phillips O: farmer; by Garland A. Austin.

20. 26 May 1859 HIRAM G. GARRETSON 22 yrs 4 mos 13 dys single b. Mercer Co VA s/o John & Ida Garretson to NAOMA J. COMPTON 18 yrs 4 mos single b. Franklin Co VA d/o Micajah & Naoma Compton O: surveyor; by Samuel Scott.

21. 26 May 1859 ALLEN D. BELCHER 23 yrs 1 mo 16 dys b. Mercer Co VA s/o Asa & Clara Belcher to CALLEAR(?) COMPTON 21 yrs 3 mos single b. Franklin Co VA d/o Micajah & Naoma Compton O: farmer; by Samuel Scott.

22. 2 June 1859 GEORGE O. HAMBRICK 22 yrs 3 mos single b. Montgomery Co VA s/o Righly & Margaret Hambrick to EMMA FAULKNER 17 yrs 5 dys single b. Montgomery Co VA d/o Hugh M. & Susannah Faulkner O: farmer; by Joseph Wright.

23. 2 June 1859 JAMES H. THOMAS 20 yrs 11 mos 4 dys single b. Giles Co VA s/o Henley & Margaret Thomas to CAROLINE THOMAS 21 yrs 6 mos 4 dys single b. Mercer Co VA d/o Samuel & Julett Thomas O: farmer; by Abraham Garretson.

24. 8 June 1859 ALLEN THOMPSON 25 yrs single b. Mercer Co VA s/o James & Lucy A. Thompson to MANIRVA A. GORE 19 yrs single b. Mercer Co VA d/o Isaac & Ida Gore O: farmer; by William Holroyd.

25. 29 June 1859 SIMEON D. HOPKINS 24 yrs 10 mos 7 dys single b. Franklin Co VA s/o Jonathan & Jemima Hopkins to SARAH E. NEWLEE 22 yrs 11 dys single b. Lee Co VA d/o John G. & Elizth Newlee O: farmer; by Leroy Keaton.

26. 7 July 1859 DANIEL N. NEAL 20 yrs 2 mos 17 dys single b. Monroe Co VA s/o Daniel & Hannah Neal to SARAH A. ARCHER 18 yrs 4 mos 19 dys single b. Wythe Co VA d/o Samson & Sarah Archer O: farmer; by Abraham Garretson.

27. 16 July 1859 EDWARD THOMAS 50 yrs 6 mos wid. b. Giles Co VA s/o John & Phebe Thomas to MARTHA A. PERKINS 22 yrs 3 mos single b. Montgomery Co VA d/o Isom & Polly Perkins O: farmer; by Samuel Scott.

28. 20 July 1859 JOSEPH M. LESTER 22 yrs 3 mos single b. Floyd Co VA now living in Raleigh Co VA s/o Burd & Matilda Lester to ELEANOR P. MILLS 17 yrs single b. Mercer Co VA d/o Samuel Zeruah Mills O: farmer; by Russell G. French.

29. 22 July 1859 GEORGE P. MILLER 18 yrs 11 mos single b. Mercer Co VA s/o Wm & Mary Miller to SUSAN COOK 22 yrs 10 mos 22 dys single b. Mercer Co VA d/o David & Nancy Cook O: farmer; by William C. Martin.

30. 28 July 1859 IRVAN H. BAILEY 25 yrs single b. Mercer Co VA s/o Jameson & Elizth Bailey to CATHERINE T. BAILEY 18 yrs 2 mos 13 dys single b. Mercer Co VA d/o George & Frances Bailey O: farmer; by Joseph Wright.

31. 31 July 1859 MANELIUS A. CHRISTIAN 21 yrs single b. Monroe Co VA s/o Thomas H. & Cath. Christian to CINDERILLA RIFFE 22 yrs single b. Monroe Co VA d/o Joel & Susan Riffe O: farmer; by Josiah Lorbett.

32. 23 Aug 1859 JOHN W. HOGE 25 yrs 5 mos single b. Rockingham SC (NC was written above SC) now living in Giles Co VA s/o Elijah & Mary Hoge to JULIAN A. ELLISON 15 yrs single b. Monroe Co VA d/o Isaac J. & Elizth Ellison O: farmer; by Russell G. French.

33. 6 Sept 1859 JAMES LUCAS 21 yrs 5 mos single b. Giles Co VA now residing same s/o Wm & Sarah Lucas to MARY SNIDOW 21 yrs 8 mos single b. Franklin Co VA d/o John & Susan Snidow O: farmer ; by Leroy Keaton.

34. 6 Sept 1859 MILTON RATLIFF 22 yrs 2 mos single b. Floyd Co VA s/o John & Agnes Ratliff to MAHALA SNIDOW 22 yrs 9 mos single b. Franklin Co VA d/o John & Susan Snidow O: farmer; by Leroy Keaton.

35. 10 Sept 1859 MARTIN V. SHREWSBURY 23 yrs single b. Mercer Co VA now living in Wyoming Co VA s/o Jere & Elizth Shrewsbury to MAHALA A. HUBBARD 17 yrs 7 mos single b. Patrick Co VA d/o

Saml & Elizth Hubbard O: farmer; by Russell G. French.

36. 27 Sept 1859 JESSE McBRIDE 21 yrs 1 mo 21 dys single b. Bedford Co VA s/o Chas. & Sarah McBride to REBECCA CLARK 25 yrs 6 mos single b. Patrick Co VA d/o Henry & Ruth Clark O: farmer; by Russell G. French.

37. 29 Sept 1859 JAMES C. PETERS 19 yrs 8 mos 4 dys single b. Mercer Co VA s/o Chris & Mary E. Peters to POLLY A. THOMPSON 20 yrs 10 mos 13 dys single b. Mercer Co VA d/o Andrew J. & Elizth Thompson O: farmer by Abraham Garretson.

38. 30 Sept 1859 BALLARD F. BAILEY 17 yrs 15 dys single b. Mercer Co VA s/o John H. & Anna Bailey to SARAH E. CASPER 18 yrs 9 mos 19 dys single b. Botetourt Co VA d/o Isaac & Rebecca Casper O: farmer; by James Calfee.

39. 4 Octr 1859 Princeton VA JOSIAH TORBETT 30 yrs single b. Sullivan Co TN now living same s/o John & Catherine Torbett to SARAH E. HALL 20 yrs single b. Giles Co VA d/o David & Mary E. Hall O: Preacher of the Gospel; by W.W. Neal.

40. 6 Octr 1859 JAMES M. HALL 24 yrs 10 mos 7 yrs wid. b. Giles Co VA s/o James & Mary Hall to LOUISA MOWLES 24 yrs 7 mos 2 dys single b. Botetourt Co VA d/o Thos. & Elizth Mowles O: farmer; by Evan H. Brown.

41. 6 Octr 1859 SILAS B. JONES 20 yrs 6 mos 18 dys single b. Mercer Co VA s/o John & Rebecca Jones to ELIZABETH FANNING 23 yrs 9 mos 9 dys single b. Mercer Co VA d/o Garland B. & Milla Fanning O: farmer; by Abraham Garretson.

42. 13 Octr 1859 JONATHAN A. HUBBARD 25 yrs single b. Patrick Co VA s/o Saml & Elizth Hubbard to VIRGINIA E. HURST 18 yrs single b. PULASKI CO VA D/O WM & PHEBE HURST O: farmer; by Russell G. French.

43. 19 Octr 1859 WILLIAM J. KEATON 21 yrs 2 mos single b. Mercer Co VA s/o Hannon & Jane Keaton to MARTHA J. COOK 19 yrs 11 mos single b. Mercer Co VA d/o Cornelius & Anna Cook O: farmer; by Leroy Keaton.

44. 20 Octr 1859 WARD MEADOWS 26 yrs single b. Mercer Co VA s/o Anthony & Mary Meadows to HULDAH A.H. GUNOE 18 yrs single b. Mercer Co VA d/o Wm & Disa Gunoe O: farmer; by Rufus Pack.

45. 27 Octr 1859 VANDALIN B. HARVEY 25 yrs single b. Monroe Co VA s/o James G. & Nancy Harvey to NANCY PACK 16 yrs single b. Mercer Co VA d/o John & Elizth B. Pack O: tobacconist; by Rufus Pack.

46. 17 Novr 1859 RUFUS A. SHUMATE 21 yrs single b. Giles Co VA now living same s/o Parkeson & Rhoda Shumate to SARAH E. SHUMATE 22 yrs single b. Giles Co VA d/o Anderson & Sarah Shumate O: farmer; by George Stewart.

47. 27 Novr 1859 JOHN BASSHAM 29 yrs 4 dys wid. b. Monroe Co VA s/o Meador & Mary Bassham to MARTHA MEADORS 27 yrs 6 mos wid. b. Monroe Co VA d/o Jos. & Elizth Goodall O: farmer; by Leory Keaton.

48. 1 Decr 1859 THOMAS P. THORNTON 21 yrs 2 mos 7 dys single b. Pulaski Co VA s/o Meredith & Louisa Thornton to NANCY V. WHITTAKER 16 yrs 6 mos 3 dys single b. Giles Co VA d/o Franklin & Julia Whittaker O: farmer by James Calfee.

Page 7

1. 19 Decr 1859 JOEL F. MOTLEY 59 yrs 8 mos 13 dys wid. b. Pittsylvannia Co VA s/o John & Elizth Motley to ELEANOR LAMBERT 49 yrs 1 mo 6 dys wid. b. Tazewell Co VA d/o Adam & Hannah Waggoner O: grocerer; by James Calfee.

2. 22 Decr 1859 JAMES CLARK 19 yrs 14 dys single b. Franklin Co VA s/o Henry & Ruth Clark to JUDITH E. SNEAD 17 yrs 11 mos 22 dys single b. Patrick Co VA d/o

John T. & Sarah Snead O: farmer; by Russell G. French.

3. 27 Decr 1859 LEFTWICH BAILEY 21 yrs 4 mos 6 dys single b. Mercer Co VA s/o James L. & Martha Bailey to SARAH M. FARMER 21 yrs 9 mos 12 dys single b. Pulaski Co VA d/o Elijah & Mary Farmer O: farmer; by James Calfee.

4. 27 Decr 1859 JOSEPH F. WOOD 23 yrs single b. Mercer Co VA s/o Robt & Frances Wood to DERINDA CLARK 20 yrs single b. Monroe Co VA d/o Rufus & Polly Clark O: farmer; by Leroy Keaton.

5. 28 Decr 1859 HENRY CALFEE 27 yrs 11 mos 5 dys single b. Pulaski Co VA s/o Saml & Rebecca Calfee to SARAH A. BAILEY 23 yrs 9 mos 4 dys single b. Mercer Co VA d/o Jas. & Martha Bailey O: farmer; by James Calfee.

6. 29 Decr 1859 ISAAC H. MANN 23 yrs single b. Mercer Co VA s/o Elizabeth Mann to RACHEL PACK 18 yrs single b. Mercer Co VA d/o John & Elizth Pack O: farmer; by John Bragg.

7. 29 Decr 1859 JAMES A. JONES 27 yrs 9 mos 19 dys single b. Mercer Co VA s/o Judah Jones to MARY E. SMITH 21 yrs 4 mos 26 dys single b. Mercer Co VA d/o John W. & Rebecca Smith O: farmer; by Abraham Garretson.

8. 29 Decr 1859 ALEXANDER BASSHAM 24 yrs single b. Monroe Co VA s/o Meador & Mary Bassham to MARY J. PACK 25 yrs single b. Mercer Co VA d/o John & Elizth Pack O: farmer; by John Bragg.

9. 5 Jany 1860 ISAAC E. WILSON 21 yrs 10 mos 19 dys single b. Giles Co VA now living same s/o Edward & Rebecca Wilson to NANCY J. BAILEY 19 yrs 19 dys single b. Mercer Co VA d/o Arch & Elizth Bailey O: farmer; by James Calfee.

10. 5 Jany 1860 ESTILL BAILEY 24 yrs single b. Mercer Co VA now living in Tazewell Co VA s/o John C. & Polly Bailey to AGNES C. CALFEE 20 yrs 25 dys single b. Wythe Co VA d/o Saml T. & Jane Calfee O: farmer; by James Calfee.

11. 15 Jany 1860 HENDERSON F. FARLEY 24 yrs 8 mos single b. Mercer Co VA s/o Arch & Jemima Farley to ARAMINTA D. HUGHES 18 yrs 1 mo single b. Giles Co VA d/o Wm & Louisa Hughes O: plasterer; by Leroy Keaton.

12. 26 Jany 1860 PATTON R. BROWN 26 yrs 10 mos single b. Tazewell Co VA s/o Thos. & Margt Brown to SARAH W. SMITH 31 yrs 6 mos single b. Monroe Co VA d/o Jno. W. & Rebecca Smith O: farmer; by George Stewart.

13. 28 Jany 1860 JOHN T. ANDERSON 23 yrs single b. Monroe Co VA s/o C. Payne & Susan Anderson to MARTHA W. AUSTIN 27 yrs single b. Henry Co VA d/o Geo. & Elizth J. Austin O: farmer; by William C. Martin.

14. 1 Feby 1860 JOHN R. PACK 20 yrs 11 mos 16 dys single b. Mercer Co VA s/o John & Elizth B. Pack to ELIZA BASSHAM 14 yrs 5 mos 25 dys single b. Mercer Co VA d/o Meador & Mary Bassham O: farmer; by John Bragg.

15. 2 Feby 1860 PHILLIP SHREWSBURY 25 yrs 7 mos 20 dys single b. Mercer Co VA s/o John & Elizth Shrewsbury to MARY A. GODFREY 18 yrs 6 mos 2 dys single b. Mercer Co VA d/o James B. & nancy Godfrey O: farmer; by Joseph Wright.

16. 4 Feby 1860 DAVID RUSSELL 43 yrs 10 mos 1 dy wid. b. Franklin Co VA now living Morgan Co KY s/o Robt & Mary Russell to PRISCILLA MILLS 25 yrs 7 mos 5 dys single b. Mercer Co VA d/o Saml & Nancy Mills O: farmer; by Abraham Garretson.

17. 14 Feby 1860 ELI B. WORRELL 24 yrs 11 mos single b. Carroll Co VA s/o James & Olivia Worrell to ELLJA J. BAKER 18 yrs 21 dys single b. Logan Co VA d/o Polly Baker O: farmer; by James Calfee.

18. 14 Feby 1860 WILLIAM CARR 35 yrs wid. b. Scott Co VA s/o Mary Carr to ELIZABETH KINZER 42 yrs single b. Montgomery Co VA d/o John & Cath. Kinzer O: farmer; by William Holroyd.

19. 23 Feby 1860 BARRY BLANKENSHIP 63 yrs wid. b. Giles Co VA now living same s/o Shad & Edith Blankenship to SALLIE CRAWFORD 48 yrs single b. Giles Co VA s/o Zach & Jane Crawford O: farmer; by Elisha G. Duncan.

20. 1 March 1860 JOHN H. WOOD 19 yrs 9 mos single b. Monroe Co VA s/o Robt & Frances Wood to MATILDA J. LANE 18 yrs 10 mos single b. Monroe Co VA d/o Moses & Cynthia Lane O: farmer; by Leroy Keaton.

21. 15 March 1860 JAMES H. PERDUE 22 yrs single b. Franklin Co VA s/o Wm & Christinia Perdue to SARAH E. PERDUE 17 yrs single b. Franklin Co VA d/o Silas & Nancy J. Perdue O: farmer; by William C. Booth.

22. 15 March 1860 MICHAEL QUINN 28 yrs 6 mos wid. b. Ireland s/o Patrick & Winnie M. Quinn to MANERVA J. ANDERSON 25 yrs 6 mos single b. Franklin Co VA d/o Jabez & Julia Anderson O: blacksmith; by Leroy Keaton.

23. 5 April 1860 OSCAR J. SHREWSBURY 23 yrs single b. Mercer Co VA s/o Phillip & Charlotte Shrewsbury to REBECCA H. RISK 20 yrs single b. Rockbridge Co VA d/o Joseph & Sicily Risk O: farmer; by Garland A. Austin.

24. 11 April 1860 WILLIAM R. BOAG 23 yrs 5 mos 1 dy single b. Campbell Co VA s/o James & Tabha S. Bong to ARDELIA ROBINSON 14 yrs 8 mos 19 dys single b. Monroe Co VA d/o Har. & Hart. Robinson O: mill wright; by James Calfee.

25. 12 April 1860 JOHN H. JUSTICE 35 yrs wid. b. Tazewell Co VA s/o Hen. & Catharine Justice to SUSAN NEELY 48 yrs single b. Monroe Co VA d/o John & Delila Neely O: farmer; by Leroy Keaton.

26. 8 May 1860 JAMES T. FOLEY 27 yrs single b. Patrick Co VA s/o James & Judity Foley to SUSANNAH WHITE 20 yrs single b. Mercer Co VA d/o Thomas & Polly White O: farmer; by Samuel Scott.

27. 22 May 1860 RICHARD A. MILLER 21 yrs single b. Monroe Co VA s/o James & Sarah Miller to REBECCA J. TILLER 18 yrs single b. Mercer Co VA d/o Kinzie & Juda Tiller O: farmer; by Abraham Garretson.

28. 2 June 1860 JOHN H. CHRISTIAN 45 yrs 11 mos 25 dys wid. b. Monroe Co VA s/o Elizabeth Christian to MARTHA FARLEY 32 yrs 11 mos 7 dys wid. b. Logan Co VA d/o Priscilla Shields O: farmer; by William C. Martin.

29. 7 June 1860 ANDREW J. BAILEY 21 yrs 11 mos 7 dys single b. Mercer Co VA s/o Eli & Charlotte Bailey to SALLIE BELCHER 23 yrs 5 mos 2 dys single b. Mercer Co VA d/o Isaac & Rebecca Belcher O: farmer; by Joseph Wright.

30. 12 June 1860 WILLIAM R. NEAL 34 yrs single b. Monroe Co VA s/o David & Sarah Neal to MARTHA J. SMITH 28 yrs single b. Logan Co VA d/o Benj & Elizth Smith O: farmer; by William Holroyd.

31. 14 June 1860 JOHN A DOUGLASS 27 yrs single b. Augusta Co VA s/o John A. & Eleanor Douglass to MARY E. FRENCH 19 yrs single b. Mercer Co VA d/o N.B. & Jane French O: lawyer; by George Stewart.

32. 26 July 1860 WILLIAM K. MARTIN 24 yrs single b. Mercer Co VA s/o John & Elizth Martin to CYNTHIA J. MARTIN 17 yrs single b. Giles Co VA d/o Lorenzo D. & Sarah Martin O: farmer; by William C. Martin.

33. 7 Aug 1860 EASOM SNIDER 23 yrs single b. Franklin Co VA s/o John & Susan Snider to RHODA A. WILEY 17 yrs single b. Mercer Co VA d/o Vincent & Cynthia Wiley O: farmer; by Garland A. Austin.

34. 9 Aug 1860 ANDERSON BRAMMER 23 yrs 3 dys single b. Patrick Co VA s/o Jonathan & Maria Brammer to MARY MASSEY 20 yrs 9 mos single b. Patrick Co VA d/o Insel & Elizth Massey O: farmer; by Leroy Keaton.

35. 16 Aug 1860 ELI HUNT 20 yrs 8 mos 16 dys single b. Mercer Co VA s/o Cynthia Hunt to ARBELIA OYLER 14 yrs 8 mos 16 dys single b. Franklin Co VA d/o Martha Oyler O: farmer; by William C. Martin.

36. 21 Aug 1860 WILLIAM HEARN 23 yrs 29 dys single b. Mercer Co VA s/o Levi G. & Arora Hearn to IDA J. SMITH 25 yrs 7 mos 13 dys single b. Mercer Co VA d/o John W. & Rebecca Smith O: farmer; by W.W. Neal.

37. 6 Sept 1860 JOSEPH GAUTIER 24 yrs wid. b. Buford Co NC s/o Joseph & Mary Gautier to LUCY A. SHREWSBURY 26 yrs single b. Mercer Co VA d/o Phil & Char Shrewsbury O: farmer; by Garland A. Austin.

38. 13 Sept 1860 NATHANIEL R. MILLS 26 yrs single b. Mercer Co VA s/o Saml & Zernah Mills to JULIA A. KARNES 19 yrs single b. Mercer Co VA d/o Had. & Nancy Karnes O: merchant; by George Stewart.

39. 25 Sept 1860 GEORGE W. HALDRON 25 yrs single b. Mercer Co VA s/o Henry & Mahala Haldron to LOUISA C. WILEY 27 yrs single b. Mercer Co VA d/o Edward Wiley O: farmer; by No Name Given.

40. 2 Octr 1860 JAMES A. BELCHER 21 yrs single b. Tazewell Co VA s/o Lewis & Rebecca Belcher to MARGARET J. ALVIS 16 yrs single b. Mercer Co VA d/o David & Mary Alvis O: farmer; by William Holroyd.

41. 2 Octr 1860 JOHN D. FARMER 19 yrs 5 mos 5 dys single b. Pulaski Co VA s/o Elijah & Mary E. Farmer to RHODA G. BAILEY 18 yrs 10 mos 7 dys single b. Mercer Co VA d/o James L. & Martha Bailey O: farmer; by James Calfee.

42. 11 Octr 1860 THOMAS C. GOOCH 21 yrs single b. Albemarle Co VA s/o Alonzo & Jane F. Gooch to NANCY J. JOHNSTON 21 yrs single b. Giles Co VA d/o Adam & Susannah Johnston O: farmer; by John Deyerle.

24. 25 Sept 1855 JUBAL CARNER* 26 yrs 1 mo 10 dys single b. Bedford Co VA s/o David & Elizabeth --- to ELIZABETH J. VASS 20 single b. Mercer Co VA d/o Robt & Mary Vass O: farmer; by Leroy Keaton. (* spelled Camer also)

25. 26 Sept 1855 HENRY BROWN 25 yrs 8 mos single b. Tazewell Co VA s/o Thos & Margaret Brown to PHEBA J. McPHERSON 23 yrs 0 mos 19 dys single b. Giles Co VA d/o Polly McPherson O: farmer; by Samuel Scott.

26. 10 May 1855 JAMES L. DAY 23 yrs 8 mos 18 dys single b. Tazewell Co VA s/o Lewis & Patience Day to LOUISA C. BAILEY 19 yrs 11 mos 23 dys single b. Mercer Co VA d/o Saml & Polly Bailey O: farmer; by Joseph Wright.

27. 31 May 1855 JOSEPH MEADOWS wid. b. Mercer Co VA s/o Josiah & Judith Meadows to NANCY A. LILLY single b. Mercer Co VA d/o Turner* A. Lilly O: farmer by John C. Hubbard. (*Side Note: corrected by Court Order 8/26/85)

28. 7 June 1855 WILLIAM HUDSON* 22 yrs 10 mos single b. Franklin Co VA s/o Vincent & Rosa Hudson* to NANCY M. SONGER 14 yrs 4 mos single b. Pulaski Co VA d/o of Jno & Martha Songer O: farmer; by H.B. Rose. (*both spellings given)

29. 14 June 1855 DANL H. AGEE 37 yrs 3 mos 9 dys single b. Franklin Co VA s/o Levi & Sarah Agee to MARTHA LANE 21 yrs 1 mo 9 dys single b. Gale Co OH d/o Moses & Cyntha Lane O: farmer; by John C. Hubbard.

30. 10 July 1855 WILLIAM WADDLE 21 yrs 8 mos 28 dys single b. Giles Co VA s/o Alexr & Mary Waddle to SARAH E. FANNING* 17 yrs 8 mos 5 dys single b. Mercer Co VA d/o Benjn & Nancy Faning* O: farmer; by William C. Martin. (*both spellings given)

32. 9 Aug 1855 JOHN OLIVER 21 single b. Montgomery Co VA s/o Freeman & Cathe Oliver to ANN E. GRAYBILL 18 single b. Pulaski Co VA d/o Jno & Susan Graybill O: brickmason; by H.B. Rose.

33. 21 Aug 1855 LANDON DAVIS single b. Giles Co VA s/o Joshua & Sarah Davis to MARY MEADOWS single b. Mercer Co VA d/o Adam & Sarah Meadows O: farmer; by Abm Garretson.

34. 23 Aug 1855 ELI CLARK 21 yrs 1 mo 15 dys single b. Patrick Co VA s/o Jno & Mary Clark to ROSA M.J. MOONEY 20 yrs 4 mos 17 dys b. Mercer Co VA d/o Jno L. & Susana Mooney O: farmer; by Joseph Wright.

35. 23 Aug 1855 GREEN MEADOR 23 yrs 8 mos 17 dys single b. Mercer Co VA s/o Jno & Anna Meador to ELIZABETH HATCHER 17 yrs 5 mos 6 dys single b. Mercer Co VA d/o Edmond & Nancy Hatcher O: farmer; by John C. Hubbard.

36. 6 Sept 1855 ROBT C. SCOTT 23 yrs 6 mos 15 dys single b. Floyd Co VA s/o Jno & China Scott to SARAH A. CARR 22 yrs 2 mos 7 dys single b. Giles d/o Jno & Sarah Carr O: mechanic; by L.W. Crouch.

37. 19 Sept 1855 Wm H. SHUMATE 21 yrs 4 mos single b. Giles Co VA s/o Parkinson & R. Shumate to FIDELLA PETERS 26 yrs single b. Mercer Co VA d/o Chris & Mary Peters O: farmer; by H.B. Rose.

38. 3 Octr 1855 JNO W.O. SNAPP 24 yrs 5 mos single b. Shenandoah Co VA s/o Jno & Catharine Snapp to MATILDA J. BAILEY 16 yrs 6 mos 13 dys single b. Mercer Co VA d/o Macijah & M. Bailey O: farmer; by Joseph Wright.

39. 25 Octr 1855 SAML SHREWSBURY 25 yrs 4 mos 10 dys single b. Mercer Co VA s/o Jno & Elizth Shrewsbury to ELIZTH BAILEY 20 yrs 7 mos 17 dys single b. Mercer Co VA d/o Geo & Frances Bailey O: farmer; by Joseph Wright.

40. 25 Octr 1855 MARTIN W. SWEENEY 20 yrs 8 mos 7 dys single b. Mercer Co VA s/o Martin & Nancy Sweeney to K.E. WOOD 20 yrs 11 mos 25 dys single b. Patrick Co VA d/o Alexr & H.B. Wood O: farmer; by John C. Hubbard.

41. 1 Novr 1855 Wm K. FOSTER 27 yrs 3 mos 16 dys single b. Scott Co VA s/o Burgress & Mary B. Foster to MARGARET C. CARR 25 yrs 6 mos 16 dys single b. Giles Co VA d/o Robt & Sarah Carr O: Minister of the Gospel; by L.W. Crouch.

42. 24 Novr 1855 JNo B. ABSHER 26 yrs 8 mos wid. b. Giles Co VA s/o Sarah Absher to SARAH A. DODD 25 single b. Craig Co VA d/o Jno & Sarah Dodd O: farmer; by H.B. Rose.

43. 11 Decr 1855 JOHN TUGGLE 35 single b. Giles Co VA s/o Larkin & Malinda Tuggle now in Mercer Co VA to LUCINDA BAILEY 35 single b. Tazewell Co VA d/o Jonth & Elizth Bailey O: farmer; by M. Ellison.

44. 12 Decr 1855 Wm A. MAHOOD 20 yrs 1 mo single b. Giles Co VA s/o Alexr & Martha Mahood to ELIZTH O. MARTIN 17 yrs 0 mos 17 dys single b. Campbell Co VA d/o Wm L & Elizth Martin O: merchants; by Evan H. Brown.

45. 20 Decr 1855 ARCHd JOHNSTON 23 single b. Monroe Co VA s/o Reuben & Rutha Johnston to ELIZA LUSK 22 yrs 8 mos single b. Mercer Co VA d/o Absolam & Delila Lusk O: carpenter; by H.B. Rose.

46. 27 Decr 1855 JAS A. BRAMMER 20 yrs 5 mos 22 dys single b. Patrick Co VA s/o Jas & Anna Brammer to ELIZA S. BALL 14 yrs 2 mos 13 dys single b. Monroe Co VA d/o Augustus & R. Ball O: farmer; by John C. Hubbard.

Page 3

1. 1 Jany 1856 ANDREW J. BANKS 41 yrs 1 mo 15 dys single b. Mercer Co VA s/o Saml & Anna Banks to ELIZABETH BAILEY 21 yrs 11 mos 27 dys single b. Tazewell Co VA d/o Clay & Rebecca Bailey O: farmer; by Joseph Wright.

2. 13 Feby 1856 GEORGE W. PEGRAM 22 yrs 4 mos 12 dys single b. Gilford Co NC now of Raleigh Co VA s/o George & Mary Pegram to MARGARET MANN 18 yrs 10 mos 22 dys single b. Mercer Co VA d/o Hezekiah & Elizth Mann O: carpenter; by John C. Hubbard.

3. 5 March 1856 JAMH H. McKENZIE 26 single b. Giles Co VA s/o Alexr & Malinda McKenzie to SARAH E. CARPER 17 b. Botetourt Co VA d/o H.F. & E.C. Carper O: farmer; by Abraham Garretson.

4. 9 March 1856 THOMAS BRATTON 39 yrs 7 mos 10 dys wid. b. Pulaski Co VA s/o Thos & Mary Bratton to MARY E. DARE 23 yrs 6 mos 28 dys wid. b. Giles Co VA d/o Parkinson & Rhoda Shumate O: farmer; by Evans H. Brown.

5. 19 March 1856 FRANKLIN WHITTAKER 37 yrs 4 mos 15 dys wid. b. Montgomery Co VA now of Giles Co VA s/o Jas & Cath Whittaker to ELLEN WHITE 30 yrs 9 mos 19 dys single b. Mercer Co VA d/o Jas & Michae White O: farmer; by Evans H. Brown.

6. 20 March 1856 WOODSON B. MEADOR 22 yrs 2 mos 24 dys single b. Mercer Co VA s/o Jno & Anna Meador to AMANDA M. MEADOR 10 yrs* 2 mos 24 dys single b. Mercer Co VA d/o Josiah & Judity Meador O: farmer; by John C. Hubbard. (*Amanda M. is 10 yrs old in 1850 Census - household #645).

7. 20 March 1856 ASA CREWS 36 yrs 9 mos 16 dys wid. b. Patrick Co VA s/o David & Sarah Crews to NANCY MEADOR 26 yrs 2 mos 20 dys single b. Mercer Co VA d/o John & Anna Meador O: farmer; by John C. Hubbard.

8. 27 March 1856 NOAH C. BLANKENSHIP 23 single b. Giles Co VA now living in Giles Co VA s/o N. & N. Blankenship to ELIZTH E. ARMENTROUT 15 single b. Alleghany Co VA d/o Jno & B. Armentrout O: farmer; by Abram Garretson.

9. 11 April 1856 THOMPSON BLANKENSHIP 23 yrs 1 mo single b. Giles Co BA s/o S. & E. Blankenship to NARCISSA PRINCE 17 single b. Mercer Co VA d/o Jas A. & Judith Prince O: farmer; by H.B. Rose.

10. 28 May 1856 ISAAC N. GRALEY 24 yrs 4 mos single b. Franklin Co VA s/o Jas & Sarah Graley to DELILA JONES 19 yrs 3 mos single b. Floyd Co VA d/o Wm & Anna Jones O: farmer; by James Calfee.

11. 28 May 1856 JESSE JONES 22 yrs single b. Patrick Co VA s/o Wiley & Jane Jones to CATHARINE JONES 22 yrs 4 mos b. Floyd Co VA d/o Wm & Anna Jones O: farmer; by James Calfee.

12. 29 May 1856 SAMUEL MARTIN 29 yrs 6 mos single b. Montgomery Co VA now living in Montgomery Co s/o C. & C. Martin to MARY F. KERR 22 yrs 4 mos single b. Powhatan Co VA d/o Abner & Sarah Kerr O: carpenter; by James Calfee.

13. 5 June 1856 WILLIAM BASSHAM 27 yrs 10 dys wid. b. Mercer Co VA s/o Rhoda Bassham to JULINA LILLY 20 yrs 11 mos 8 dys single b. Mercer Co VA d/o Jos & Polly Lilly O: farmer; by John C. Hubbard.

14. 19 June 1856 OSCAR J. EMMONS 24 yrs 3 mos single b. Giles Co VA s/o Horton & B.Emmons to MARY E.C. ALLEN 21 yrs 7 mos single b. Monroe Co VA d/o R.M. & Ann M. Allen O: merchant; by H.B. Rose.

15. 26 June 1856 RUFUS B. LILLY 19 yrs 3 mos 6 dys single b. Mercer Co VA s/o J.& M. Lilly to MARY LILLY 18 yrs 3 mos 2 dys single b. Mercer Co d/o W. & Polly Lilly O: farmer; by John C. Hubbard.

16. 26 June 1856 DAVID FERRELL 20 yrs 8 mos 26 dys single b. Monroe Co VA s/o J. & E. Ferrell now living in Monroe Co to CELIA A. MEADOR 14 yrs 8 mos 10 dys single b. Mercer Co VA d/o Wm M. & C. Meador O: farmer; by John Bragg.

17. 3 July 1856 JOHN A. HAMBRICK 22 yrs 4 mos 3 dys single b. Montgomery Co VA s/o R. & M. Hambrick to MARY J. BROYLES 16 yrs 6 mos 9 dys single b. Monroe Co VA s/o Washg & M.A. Broyles O: blacksmith; by Joseph Wright.

18. 6 Augt 1856 ALBERT WILEY 20 (26) yrs 5 mos 10 dys single b. Mercer Co VA s/o G. & T. Wiley to SARAH LANES 18 yrs 9 mos 6 dys single b. Mercer Co Va d/o Moses & C. Lane O: farmer; by William C. Martin.

19. 13 Augt 1856 JOHN J. WRIGHT 25 single b. Campbell Co VA s/o J.J. & C. Wright to ELIZABETH S. MARTIN 18 single b. Mercer Co VA d/o David & E.A. Martin O: blacksmith; by William Holroyd.

20. 21 Augt 1856 JAMES C. DAVIDSON 59 yrs 5 mos 7 dys wid. b. Wythe Co VA s/o Jos & M. Davidson to CATHARINE BAILEY 39 yrs 1 mo 6 dys single b. Tazewell d/o J. & Elizth Bailey O: farmer; by James Calfee.

21. 27 Augt 1856 GEORGE W. STUMP 19 yrs 4 mos 21 dys single b. Tazewell Co VA s/o Wm & Polly Stump to POLLY A. DILLION 19 yrs 9 mos 13 dys single b. Mercer Co VA d/o Saml & Polly Dillion O: blacksmith; by Joseph Wright.

22. 28 Augt 1856 SIMEON D. HOPKINS 22 yrs 19 dys b. Franklin Co VA s/o J. & J. Hopkins to MARY BELCHER 21 yrs 6 mos 2 dys b. Mercer Co VA d/o M. & M. Belcher O: farmer; by William C. Mercer.

23. 3 Sept 1856 MADISON F. BELCHER 22 yrs 4 mos 8 dys single b. Mercer Co VA s/o Asa & Clara Belcher to MARY J. HOUCHINS 19 yrs 1 mo 23 dys single b. Mercer Co VA d/o Jas & S. Houchins O: farmer; by William C. Mercer.

24. 9 Sept 1856 BLEDSO AUSTIN 48 yrs 7 mos 22 dys wid. b. Grayson Co VA now living in Grayson Co s/o Isaial & Lucy Austin to MATILDA P. GEORGE 30 yrs 9 mos 19 dys single b. Tazewell Co VA d/o Thos & E.H. George O: farmer; by Evan H. Brown.

25. 18 Sept 1856 JAMES M. McCUE 24 yrs 4 mos 0 dys single b. Augusta Co BA s/o John & Hannah McCue to ELIZA J. GOOCH 15 yrs 10 mos single b. Albemarle Co VA d/o Alonzo & E.J. Gooch O: farmer; by Henry B. Rose.

26. 18 Sept 1856 JAMES A. SMITH single b. Rockbridge Co VA s/o T.T. & Sarah Smith to SARAH A. TRACY single b. Giles Co. VA d/o Wm & Dicey Tracy O: farmer; by Abraham Garretson.

27. 25 Sept 1856 WILEY B.W. BLANKENSHIP single b. Mercer Co VA s/o L. & M. Blankenship to MARY E. JONES single b. Mercer Co VA d/o Israel & M. Jones O: farmer; by Abraham Garretson.

28. 21 Octr 1856 JOHN J. MEADOR 19 yrs 7 mos 25 dys single b. Mercer Co VA s/o Wm H. & Celia Meador to SARAH L. NOELL 19 yrs 28 dys single b. Bedford Co VA d/o Caleb & M. Noell O: farmer; by John Bragg.

29. 23 Octr 1856 JOHN W. WHITE 21 yrs 3 mos 6 dys single b. Mercer Co VA s/o Cornelius & M. White to NANCY BELCHER 22 yrs 1 mo 23 dys b. Mercer Co d/o Isham & R. Belcher O: farmer; by Evan H. Brown.

30. 30 Octr 1856 OVERTON C. WHITE 18 yrs 5 mos 27 dys single b. Mercer Co VA s/o Corbelius & M. White to MARY E. HOLSTINE 17 yrs 9 mos 13 dys single b. Mercer Co VA d/o Jas W. & M. Holstine O: farmer; by Evan H. Brown.

31. 12 Novr 1856 LEWIS UPTON 22 single b. Monroe Co VA s/o Sylvester & L. Upton CHARLOTTE WHITTEN 17 yrs 5 mos 9 dys single b. Alleghany Co VA d/o Lewis & C. Whitten O: farmer; by John Bragg.

32. 13 Novr 1856 DAVID H. LILLY 20 yrs 11 mos 5 dys single b. Giles Co VA s/o Jno & Margaret Lilly to MARY UPTON 19 yrs 2 mos 27 dys b. Monroe Co VA d/o Sylvester & L. Upton O: farmer; by John Bragg.

33. 13 Novr 1856 LYENSGUS MEADOR 23 yrs 8 mos 10 dys single b. Mercer Co VA s/o Josiah & J. Meador to SARAH C. FERGUSON 19 yrs 2 mos 14 dys b. Mercer Co VA s/o Jeremiah & N. Ferguson O: farmer; by John C. Hubbard.

34. 14 Novr 1856 JOHN H. REYNOLDS 42 divorced b. Patrick Co VA s/o Richd & M. Reynolds to MALINDA WEST 19 yrs 3 mos 19 dys b. Floyd Co VA d/o Jas & Malinda West O: farmer; by John Bragg.

35. 11 Decr 1856 THOMAS B. KINZER 26 yrs 6 mos single b. Rannke(sic) Co VA s/o Michael & Ann Kinzer now living in Tazewell Co VA to LUCRETIA COMPTON 20 yrs 3 mos 1 dy single b. Tazewell Co VA d/o Car & R.J. Compton O: farmer; by James Calfee.

36. 17 Decr 1856 ALLEN BROWN 33 single b. Monroe Co VA s/o Wm & Lucinda Brown to MARY E. ROWLAND 23 single b. Giles Co VA d/o James & E. Rowland O: farmer; by John Doyerle.

37. 18 Decr 1856 ROBERT SWADER 22 yrs 8 mos 12 dys single b. Mercer Co VA s/o Milley Swader to CYNTHIA J. HOLSTINE 15 yrs 3 mos 10 dys single b. Mercer Co VA d/o Henry & M. Holstine O: farmer; by Joseph Wright.

38. 18 Decr 1856 JESSE SIAS 44 divorced b. Monroe Co VA s/o Jas & Frances Sias to MAGDALINE BOONE 22 divorced b. Monroe Co VA d/o Jas & Sarah Scales O: farmer; by John C. Hubbard.

39. 18 Decr 1856 WILLIAM A. BOLING 29 yrs 1 mo 14 dys single b. Mercer Co VA s/o John & Sally Bowling to DEMERIUS WHITE 31 yrs 22 dys single b. Mercer Co VA d/o Cornelius & P. White O: farmer; by Joseph Wright.

40. 18 Decr 1856 ANDREW J. MARTIN 22 yrs 2 mos 10 dys single b. Monroe Co VA s/o Booker & R. Martin to SARAH A. LILLY 20 yrs 10 mos 8 dys single b. Mercer co VA d/o Jas & Ellen Lilly O: farmer; by John Bragg.

41. 24 Decr 1856 HUGH J. MEADOR 20 yrs 9 mos 24 dys single b. Mercer Co VA s/o Jno & Anna Meador to ELIZTH H. DEEDS 16 yrs 1 mo 24 dys single b. Monroe Co VA d/o Jos & Hannah Deeds O: farmer; by John Bragg.

42. 25 Decr 1856 JAMES SNEAD 22 yrs 9 mos 15 dys single b. Patrick Co VA s/o Saml & E. Snead to MARY V. MEADOR 18 yrs 1 mo 15 dys single b. Mercer Co VA d/o Jno & Anna Meador O: farmer; by John C. Hubbard.

43. 22 Decr 1857(sic)(1856) WILLIAM M. THORNTON 20 yrs 8 mos 22 dys single b. Pulaski Co VA s/o Heredity ' Louisa Thornton to ELIZ J. HATCHER 19 yrs 8

43. 18 Octr 1860 JOHN A. BAILEY 24 yrs single b. Foryette Co VA s/o Zach & Rachel Bailey to SARAH BRUNTY 19 yrs single b. Wythe Co VA d/o James & Tabitha Brunty O: wheel wright; by William C. Booth.

44. 8 Novr 1860 JOHN W. BROWN 28 yrs single b. Mercer Co VA s/o Wm & Lucinda Brown to MARTHA J. BELCHER 20 yrs single b. Mercer Co VA d/o Asa & Clarinda Belcher O: farmer; by Garland A. Austin.

45. 8 Novr 1860 FRANCIS FARLEY 20 yrs 9 mos single b. Mercer Co VA s/o Gideon & Dinah Farley to MARIETTA LANE 24 yrs 11 mos single b. Mason Co VA d/o Moses & Cynthia Lane O: farmer; by Leroy Keaton.

46. 13 Novr 1860 HUBERT B. BARBER 33 yrs single b. Manchester Eng s/o Alex & Elizth Barber to FANNIE E.C.GRIGSBY 19 yrs single b. Rockbridge Co VA d/o Jas. S. & Judith E. Grigsby O: farmer; by John Deyerle.

47. 15 Novr 1860 JAMES M. SHANNON 19 yrs 6 mos 19 dys single b. Botetourt Co VA now living in Tazewell Co VA s/o Chris & Susan Shannon to ELIZA J. KERR 38 yrs 9 dys single b. Powhatan Co VA d/o Abner & Sarah Kerr O: farmer; by James Calfee.

48. 21 Novr 1860 DRURY T. MURRELL 23 yrs 7 mos 9 dys single b. Bedford Co VA s/o James & Mary Murrell to ELLEN GRIM 34 yrs 11 mos 6 dys single b. Botetourt Co VA d/o Wm & Rebecca Grim O: carpenter; by James Calfee.

Page 8

1. 22 Novr 1860 FREDERICK HARVEY 20 yrs 11 mos 19 dys single b. Monroe Co VA s/o Jacob W. & Cath Harvey to ALLEY CLARK 21 yrs 2 mos single b. Franklin Co VA d/o Henry & Ruth Clark O: farmer; by Russell G. French.

2. 29 Novr 1860 JOHN Q. SPANGLER 31 yrs 5 mos 19 dys single b. Monroe Co VA now living same s/o John & Jane Spangler to VALERA J. STRALEY 18 yrs 11 mos 1 dy single b. Franklin Co VA d/o John & Elizth Straley O: farmer; by James Calfee.

3. 12 Decr 1860 WOODSON A. SHORTER 42 yrs wid. b. Charlotte Co VA s/o John & Nancy Shorter to ELIZABETH PHILLIPS 21 yrs single b. Mercer Co VA d/o James & Clara Phillips O: farmer; by Garland A. Austin.

4. 12 Decr 1860 JAMES H. DILLION 29 yrs 9 mos 18 dys single b. Mercer Co VA s/o Jesse & Cynthia Dillion to MATILDA J. BRUNTY 21 yrs single b. Wythe Co VA d/o James & Tabitha Brunty O: farmer; by William C. Booth.

5. 20 Decr 1860 SAMUEL W. JACKSON 27 yrs 9 mos 2 dys single b. Alleghany Co VA now living same s/o Abel & Elizth Jackson to LYNN OLIVER 27 yrs 7 mos 2 dys single b. Bath Co VA d/o Jas. & Mary Oliver O: farmer; by William Holroyd.

6. 20 Decr 1860 RICHARD BUNYON 27 yrs 3 mos 19 dys wid. b. Pulaski Co VA s/o Stephan & Nancy Runyon to ELIZABETH F. PRIVOTT 18 yrs single b. Carroll Co VA d/o Sarah Bowden O: farmer; by James Calfee.

7. 27 Decr 1860 JOHN CAULEY 40 yrs wid. b. Bedford Co VA s/o Berry & Rhoda Cauley to LOUISA FARLEY 31 yrs 9 mos single b. Mercer Co VA d/o Arch & Jemima Farley O: farmer; by Leroy Keaton.

8. 19* Decr 1860 REUBEN C. FARMER 20 yrs 11 mos 26 dys single b. Carroll Co VA s/o John L. & Nancy Farmer to MARY M. SHREWSBURY 16 yrs 10 mos 25 dys single b. Mercer Co VA d/o Henry & Jane Shrewsbury O: farmer; by Joseph Wright. (*Note: 19 written probably should read 29)

9. 8 Jany 1861 GEORGE O. TABOR 17 yrs single b. Mercer Co VA s/o Jesse & Eliza Tabor to OLIVIA WORRELL 16 yrs single b. Carroll Co VA d/o James & Olivia Worrell O: farmer; by Russell G. French.

10. 20 Jany 1861 FRANCIS A.J. KING 26 yrs 4 mos single b. Jackson Co VA now living in Raleigh Co VA s/o Samuel & Mary King to RUFINA C. WILSON 21 yrs single b. Alleghany Co VA d/o Andrew & Nancy M. Wilson O: farmer; by Andrew Workmon.

11. 12 Feby 1861 JAMES S. WILEY 23 yrs single b. Giles Co VA s/o Absolom & Elizabeth Wiley to AMERICAS S. RATLIFF 23 yrs single b. Monroe Co VA d/o John & Agnes Ratliff O: farmer; by Wm Holroyd.

12. 19 Feby 1861 JAMES HEARN 29 yrs 8 mos 9 dys single b. Mercer Co VA s/o Levi G. & Anna Hearn to ESTHER DEWEESE 16 yrs single b. Floyd Co VA d/o Andrew & Rosine Deweese O: farmer; by Wm. Holroyd.

13. 20 Feby 1861 JOHN GOLLIER 34 yrs 6 mos 15 dys single b. Shropshire Engld s/o John & Elizabeth Gollier to POLLY D. DILLION 21 yrs 7 mos 9 dys single b. Mercer Co VA d/o James P. & Juliet Dillion O: farmer; by John Dierle (Deyirle).

14. 21 Feby 1861 ISAAC A. SMITH 23 yrs single b. Logan Co VA s/o Benjamin & Elizabeth Smith to SARAH J. CHATTING 13 yrs single b. Botetourt Co VA d/o William & Mary Chatting O: farmer; by Elisha G. Dunson.

15. 25 Feby 1861 ELI W. CHRISTIAN 24 yrs 1 mos 10 dys single b. Mercer Co VA s/o John H. & Permilia Christian to ELIZA F. COOK 24 yrs 10 mos 6 dys single b. Mercer Co VA d/o Cornelius & Anna Cook O: farmer; by Leroy Keaton.

16. 6 March 1861 CHARLES E. WHITLOCK 24 yrs 5 mos single b. Patrick Co VA s/o Joseph R. & Anna Whitlock to ELIZABETH LILLY 16 yrs single b. Mercer Co VA d/o Robert & Elizabeth Lilly O: farmer; by Leroy Keaton.

17. 6 March 1861 WILLIAM ADKINSON* 22 yrs 3 mos 16 dys single b. Fayette Co VA s/o John H. & Mary Adkins* to NANCY C. REASE 16 yrs 10 mos 19 dys single b. Mercer Co VA s/o Jesse & Rosanna Rease O: farmer; by Leroy Keaton.(*Note: names spelled both ways.)

18. 8 March 1861 WILLIAM G. DWIGGINS 26 yrs 7 mos 5 dys single b. North Carolina s/o Thomas C. Dwiggins to ANNA FARLEY 20 yrs 7 mos 9 dys single b. Mercer Co VA d/o Andrew & Anna Farley O: farmer; by Leroy Keaton.

19. 8 March 1861 JAMES M. SNEAD 20 yrs 4 mos 16 dys single b. Patrick Co VA s/o John B. & Sarah B. Snead to ELIZABETH C. COOPER 17 yrs 28 dys b. Mercer Co VA d/o Nancy Cooper O: farmer; by Russell G. French.

20. 14 March 1861 WILLIAM A. SHOWVEN* 23 yrs single b. Craig Co VA now living in Tazewell Co VA s/o Alex Showven* & Malinda Sarver to NANCY B. FARMER 23 yrs single b. Pulaski Co VA d/o Elijah & Mary Farmer O: farmer; by James Calfee.

21. 21 March 1861 JOHN J. COTTLE 22 yrs 8 mos 15 dys single b. Monroe Co VA now living same s/o George & Maria Cottle to CATHERINE E. WOOD 21 yrs 3 mos 21 dys single b. Monroe Co VA d/o Robert & Frances Wood O: farmer; by P.B. Bober.

22. 23 March 1861 BALLARD R. HALDRON 22 yrs 8 mos 21 dys single b. Mercer Co VA s/o Henry & Mahala Haldron to SUDOMY C. PAULEY 20 yrs 5 mos 5 dys single b. Giles Co VA d/o Harvey & Barbara Pauley O: farmer; by Wm. Holroyd.

23. 28 March 1861 JOSEPH H. MARTIN 22 yrs 1 mos 10 dys single b. Pittsylvania Co VA now living in Monroe Co VA s/o Donsil W. & Sallie Martin to SARAH V. CALDWELL 18 yrs single b. Craig Co VA d/o William & Sophia Caldwell O: farmer; by Wm. Holroyd.

24. 28 March 1861 HENRY S. CALFEE 26 yrs 4 mos 3 dys single b. Wythe Co VA s/o Samuel T. & Jane Calfee to LOUISA J. BAILEY 18 yrs 6 mos 19 dys single b. Mercer Co VA d/o Phillip P. & Louisa Bailey O: farmer; by James Calfee.

25. 4 April 1861 JAMES A. THOMAS 22 yrs 4 mos 14 dys single b. Mercer Co VA s/o Jemima Thomas to RUTH J. DAVIS 17 yrs 4 mos 14 dys single b. Giles Co VA d/o Maria Davis O: farmer; by Benj. W. Bishop.

26. 4 April 1861 THOMAS S. BRAG* 19 yrs single b. Raleigh Co VA now living name s/o Abraham & Rachel Bragg* to MARY UPTON 21 yrs single b. Monroe Co VA d/o Meredith & Sallie Upton O: farmer; by T.H. Jennie King. (*Note: name spelled both ways.)

27. 11 April 1861 SAMUEL HOPKINS 24 yrs 3 mos single b. Franklin Co VA s/o Jonathan & Jemimah Hopkins to RACHEL FARLEY 24 yrs 19 dys single b. Mercer Co VA d/o Gideon & Dinah Farley O: farmer; by Leroy Keaton.

28. 16 April 1861 ROBERT H. BROTHERTON 30 yrs 1 mos wid. b. Jefferson Co VA now living in Giles Co VA s/o Thomas & Elizabeth Brotherton to PRISCILLA J. WILBURN 26 yrs 10 mos 6 dys single b. Giles Co VA d/o Stephen & Nancy Wilburn O: farmer; by Benj. W.S. Bishop.

29. 18 April 1861 CHRISTIAN B. PETERS 25 yrs 2 mos single b. Mercer Co VA s/o Christian & Mary T. Peters to JULINA WILEY 20 yrs 8 mos single b. Mercer Co VA d/o James & Nancy Wiley O: farmer; by Russel G. French.

30. 18 April 1861 WILLIAM H. WILLIAMS 18 yrs 4 mos 7 dys single b. Mercer Co VA s/o Andrew & Ann Williams to LUCINDA M. CADLE 16 yrs single b. Mercer Co VA d/o John H. & Julia Cadle O: farmer; No Return Made.

31. 7 May 1861 SAMUEL A. EAST 30 yrs 1 mos 17 dys single b. Pittsylvania Co VA s/o Thomas & Elizabeth East to FANNIE D. CUSTARD 27 yrs 4 mos 12 dys single b. Mercer Co VA d/o John D. & Catherine Custard O: farmer; by James Calfee.

32. 16 May 1861 JOHN RUNYON 33 yrs 5 mos 6 dys wid. b. Pulaski Co VA s/o Stephen & Nancy Runyon to MARY PRIVETT 20 yrs single b. Smith Co VA d/o William & Sarah Privett O: farmer; by James Calfee.

33. 23 May 1861 NICHOLAS B. BAILEY 22 yrs 11 mos 21 dys single b. Mercer Co VA s/o John & Mary Bailey to ELLEN M. ALLEN 18 yrs 9 mos 16 dys single b. Monroe Co VA d/o Richard M. & Ann M. Allen O: farmer; by Benj. W.S. Bishop.

34. 6 June 1861 ANDREW McPHERSON 40 yrs 2 mos single b. Franklin Co VA s/o Polly McPherson to SUSAN McCAHN 33 yrs 7 mos single b. Botetourt Co VA d/o Stephen & Milla McCahn O: farmer; by Samuel Scott.

35. 7 June 1861 WILLIAM H. ROBINSON 22 yrs 11 mos single b. Ronoake Co VA now living in Giles Co VA s/o John & Ellen Robinson to MARGARET T. CALLOWAY 21 yrs 10 mos 15 dys single b. Monroe Co VA d/o Granville & Susan Calloway O: farmer; by Benj W.S. Bishop.

36. 18 June 1861 HARVEY D. MEADORS 23 yrs 6 mos 9 dys single b. Mercer Co VA s/o Jeremiah & Jane Meadors to VICTORIA WILKS* 16 yrs 11 mos single b. Bedford Co VA d/o John & Tempa J. Welks* O: farmer; by Samuel Scott. (*Note: name spelled both ways.)

37. 18* July 1861 SAMUEL J. SNEED 21 yrs 9 mos 8 dys single b. Patrick Co VA s/o John T. & Sarah Sneed to EMOZELLA WALKER 25 yrs single b. Mercer Co VA d/o Council & Nancy Walker O: farmer; by Wm Holroyd. (*Note: probably should read 8 instead of 18.)

38. 10 July 1861 HENRY DAVIDSON 21 yrs 11 mos single b. Mercer Co VA s/o William G. & Betsy Davidson to LUCINDA DANGERFIELD single b. Mercer Co VA d/o Samuel H. & Nancy Dangerfield O: farmer; No Return Made.

39. 11 July 1861 JAMES D. ANDERSON 24 yrs 1 mos 16 dys single b. Monroe Co VA s/o John & Judy Anderson to LOUISE M. ANDERSON 25 yrs 2 mos 16 dys single b. Pittsylvania Co VA d/o G.A. & Elizabeth J. Abteshin* O: farmer; by Leroy Keaton.(*Note: unable to read handwriting.)

40. 25 July 1861 JOHN SNIDER 65 yrs wid. b. Pensylvania(sic) s/o John & Sarah Snider to NANCY ADKINSON 18 yrs single b. Franklin Co VA d/o Shedrick & Polly Adkinson O: farmer; by Leroy Keaton.

41. 15 Augt 1861 ANDREW COLE 28 yrs 8 mos single b. Mercer Co VA s/o Augustus D. & Hanah Cole to MARY M. DEWESE 17 yrs 3 mos 16 dys single b. Montgomery Co VA d/o Andrew & Rosena Dewese O: farmer; No Return Made.

42. 21 Augt 1861 FLOYD MILLER 42 yrs 7 mos 1 dy wid. b. Mercer Co VA s/o William & Polly Miller to CYNTHIA COPERTON 44 yrs wid. b. Mercer Co VA d/o Charles & Sallie Deov(sic) O: farmer; No Return Made.

43. 27 AUGT 1861 LEWIS SHUFFLEBURGER 30 yrs single b.Montgomery Co VA to A.* PETERS 22 yrs single b. Mercer Co VA d/o Christian & Polly Peters O: farmer; No Return Made.(*Note: 1850 Mercer Co Census an Amcille was 12 yrs old.)

44. * Sept 1861 WILLIAM TILLER 70 yrs wid. b. Giles Co VA s/o Samuel Tiller to * JONES 22 yrs single b. Mercer Co VA d/o John & Rebecca Jones O: farmer; No Return Made.(*Note: left blank)

45. 31 Octr 1861 FIELDING STACK 30 yrs single b. Washington Co VA now living Prestonsburg KY s/o Wm & Elizabeth Stack to ELIZABETH BOWLING 21 yrs single b. Mercer Co VA d/o Wm & Elizabeth Bowling O: taylor; by Wm Holroyd.

46. 25 Novr 1861 JOHN H. FLOWERS 21 yrs single b. Franklin Co VA s/o James & Sarah Flowers to CATHERINE F. WALDSON 21 yrs single b. Franklin Co VA d/o James & Margaret Waldson O: farmer; by Leroy Keaton.

47. 29 Novr 1861 TAZEWELL WORLEY 20 yrs single b. Franklin Co VA s/o George & Polly Worley to MARTHA LILLY 18 yrs single b. Mercer Co VA d/o John & Nancy Lilly O: farmer; by Leroy Keaton.

48. 12 Decr 1861 BALLARD F. SARVER 26 yrs 8 mos 26 dys s/o John & Francis Sarver to LYDIA J. ARCHER 17 yrs 10 mos 23 dys single b. Wythe Co VA d/o Sampson & Sarah Archer O: farmer; No Return Made.

49. 24 Decr 1861 WILLIAM H. BELCHER 21 yrs 1 mos 17 dys single b. Mercer Co VA s/o James & Mahala Belcher to ELEANOR P. FRENCH 23 yrs 8 mos 20 dys single b. Mercer Co VA d/o Charles & Rebecca French O: farmer; No Return Made.

50. 26 Decr 1861 Wm. T. ELLISON 33 yrs wid. b. Mercer Co VA s/o Asa & Mary Ellison to MARY E. VEST 21 yrs single b. Mercer Co VA d/o L. Vest O: farmer; by Leroy Keaton.

Page 9

1. 24 Aug 1865 WILLIAM J. FARLY 21 yrs 11 mos single b. Mercer Co W VA s/o Gideon Farly to MARY A. MILLER 25 yrs 7 mos single b. Mercer Co W VA d/o Dinah Farly(sic) O: farmer; by William C. Martin; REMARKS: A mistake in the names of wife's parents.

(NOTE: A line was drawn through entire entry.)
2. 24 Aug 1865 JNO. G. CAPERTON 19 yrs 11 mos single b. Mercer Co W VA s/o Adam Caperton to ALBERTINA WILLY 19 yrs 8 mos single b. Mercer Co W VA d/o Nancy Pauley O: farmer; by William C. Martin; REMARKS: parents never married.

3. 7 Sep 1865 JNO. W. WOOD 26 yrs single b. Patrick Co VA s/o Alex. & Bethany Wood to CELIA LILLY 23 yrs single b. Mercer Co W VA d/o Wash & Mary Lilly O: farmer; by Benj. T. Bird.

4. 12 Oct 1865 GEO. W. BIRCH 27 yrs single b. Putnam Co W VA s/o Martha Birch to S.J. FANNING 22 yrs single b. Mercer Co W VA d/o Benj. F. Fanning O: farmer; by Wm C. Martin.

12. 25 Feby 1858 ERASTUS B MEADOR 25 yrs single b. Giles Co VA s/o William M. & Celia Meador to CLARA B. PACK 17 yrs single b. Monroe Co VA d/o Anderson & Rebecca Pack O: merchant; by Rufus Pack.

13. 11 March 1858 CHARLES ABBOT 25 yrs 9 mos 11 dys wid. b. Monroe Co VA to IDA FARLEY 24 yrs 28 dys single b. Mercer Co VA d/o Anderson & Anna Farley O: farmer; by Leroy Keaton.

14. 16 March 1858 LEWIS A. LUSK 22 yrs single b. Monroe Co VA where he now lives s/o Isaac Lusk to ---* MARTIN 16 yrs single b. Monroe Co VA d/o Booker & Rebecca Martin O: farmer; by Rufus Pack. (*Note: Probably Polly who was 8 yrs in 1850 Mercer Co Census #579.)

15. 15 April 1858 ANDREW J. HULL 26 yrs single b. Monroe Co VA now living in Raleigh Co VA s/o Henry & Emaly Hull to REBECA C. DYALE* 23 yrs single b. Montgomery Co VA d/o Crocheto* & Mary Dyale O: farmer; by Elias Kendall. (*Note: unable to read writing on these names.)

16. 15 April 1858 JOHN MARTIN 24 yrs 11 dys single b. Mercer Co VA s/o David & Nancy Martin to DIANA NOBLE 29 yrs 6 mos 10 dys single b. Mercer Co VA d/o William & Mahala Noble O: farmer; by William C. Martin.

17. 24 April 1858 CHARLES HALDREN 32 yrs 8 mos 20 dys single b. Mercer Co VA s/o Sarah Haldren to SARAH A. PENNINGTON 26 yrs 9 mos 17 dys single b. Mercer Co VA d/o James & Martha Pennington O: farmer; by William C Martin.

18. 27 April 1858 MILLON H. FRENCH 24 yrs 2 mos 18 dys single b. Giles Co VA s/o Charles C. & Rebecca French to BELINDA SCOTT 24 yrs 1 mo 26 dys single b. Floyd Co VA d/o John & China Scott O: farmer; by Evan H. Brown.

19. 7 May 1858 JOSEPH WADDLE 22 yrs single b. Giles Co VA s/o Alexander & Mary Waddle to PRISCILLA MILLS 21 yrs single b. Mercer Co VA d/o Samuel & Lernah Mills O: farmer; by Elijah Conner.

20. 25 May 1858 JOHN W. BROWN 24 yrs 8 mos 17 dys sinble b. Alleghany Co VA s/o John & Elizabeth Brown to RHODA M. TILLER 17 yrs 2 mos 17 dys single b. Mercer Co VA d/o Anderson & Priscilla Brown O: potter; by Abraham Garretson.

21. 7 June 1858 JOHN W. BROOKS 25 yrs single b. Sumner Co TN now living in Franklin Co VA s/o John & Nancy Brooks to LUCY W. BOWERS 22 yrs single b. Mercer Co VA d/o James & Elizabeth Bowers O: farmer; by Elias Kendall.

22. 21 June 1858 JOHN D. LYON 22 yrs single b. Mercer Co VA s/o Daniel & Lucy Lyons to MARY A MEADOR 25 yrs single b. Mercer Co VA d/o Josiah & Judith Meador O: farmer; by Rufus Pack.

23. 21 June 1858 CHARLES S. TURNER 23 yrs 6 mos 21 dys single b. Montgomery Co VA s/o Wilson & Sarah C. Turner to VICTORIA McKINZIE 13 yrs 10 mos 5 dys single b. Mercer Co VA d/o John O. & Priscilla McKinzie O: farmer; by Evan H. Brown.

24. 10 Aug 1858 SYLVESTER BRAGG 30 yrs single b. Cabell Co VA now living in Greenbrier Co VA s/o Michael & Elizabeth Bragg to CAROLINE UPTON 21 yrs single b. Monroe Co VA d/o Meredith Upton O: farmer; by Paul Vanderwood.

25. 7 Sept 1858 JOHN C. PETERS 10 yrs single b. Monroe Co VA now living same s/o George W. & Margaret B. Peters to SARAH J. POINDEXTER 17 yrs single b. Henry Co VA d/o John D. & Louisa Poindexter O: farmer; by Rufus Pack.

26. 9 Sept 1858 JOHN O. SNIDER 28 yrs single b. Franklin Co VA s/o John & Susan Snider to CATHERINE SUOAS* 16 yrs single b. Giles Co VA d/o Not known O: farmer; by Leroy Keaton. (*Note: unable to read handwriting.)

27. 14 Sept 1858 JOHN R. SHANNON 23 yrs single b. Campbell Co VA s/o John & Margaret Shannon to EDITHA THOMPSON 16 yrs single b. Mercer Co VA d/o John & Elizabeth Thompson O: farmer; by William Holroyd.

28. 15 Sept 1858 JOSEPHUS ROBINSON 23 yrs 8 mos 1 dy single b. Monroe Co VA s/o Harrison & Harriett Robinson to HARRIET J. HOLSTINE 23 yrs 20 dys single b. Mercer Co VA d/o Joseph C. & Elizabeth Holstine O: farmer; by James Calfee.

29. 30 Sept 1858 BALLARD P. DILLION 21 yrs 9 mos 18 dys single b. Mercer Co VA s/o Jesse & Cynthia Dillion to ELIZA L. BELCHER 17 yrs 7 mos 17 dys single b. Mercer Co VA d/o Christian & Polly Belcher O: farmer; by Joseph Wright.

30. 6 Octr 1858 WILLIAM H. THOMPSON 23 yrs 9 mos 1 dy single b. Mercer Co VA s/o Andrew J. & Elizabeth Thompson to REBECCA J. PETERS 22 yrs 8 mos 11 dys b. Mercer Co VA d/o Christian S. & Mary Peters O: farmer; by Abraham Garretson.

31. 7 Octr 1858 JOHN W. BAILEY 17 yrs single b. Mercer Co VA s/o Samuel & Mary Bailey to SARAH E. CECIL 14 yrs single b. Mercer Co VA d/o Shelby & Mary J. Cecil O: farmer; by Elijah Conner.

32. 12 Octr 1858 WILLIAM H. LITTLE 21 yrs single b. Mercer Co VA s/o Thomas & Eleanor Little to MARY D. FANNING 18 yrs 4 mos 27 dys single b. Mercer Co VA d/o Garland B. & Martha Fanning O: farmer; by Abraham Garretson.

33. 12 Octr 1858 JOHN M. McCLAUGHERTY 26 yrs single b. Giles Co VA s/o John & Phebe McClaugherty to SUSAN A. MONROE 20 yrs single b. Campbell Co VA d/o James R. & Rhoda Monroe O: farmer; by William Holroyd.

34. 14 Octr 1858 STYNAIS L. MOONEY 23 yrs single b. Grayson Co VA s/o Martin D. & Amelia Mooney to SUSANNAH BAKER 19 yrs single b. Logan Co VA d/o John & Polly Baker O: farmer; by Joseph Wright.

35. 19 Octr 1858 PATERO A. HUBBARD 20 yrs single b. Patrick Co VA s/o Samuel & Elizabeth Hubbard to LUCY A. WORRELL 17 yrs single b. Carroll Co VA d/o James B. & Olive Worrell O: farmer; by No Name Given.

36. 26 Octr 1858 JOSEPH P. FUGATE 24 yrs 9 mos 26 dys single b. Russell Co VA now living in same s/o Zachariah & Phermba Fugate to CATHERINE DAVIS 36 yrs 9 mos 10 dys wid. b. Mercer Co VA d/o David & Rhoda Swader O: farmer; by Joseph Wright.

37. 28 Octr 1858 JOHN L. SHANNON 23 yrs 2 mos 23 dys single b. Tazewell Co VA now living in same s/o John & Rebecca Shannon to ELIZABETH DANGERFIELD 18 yrs 6 mos 23 dys single b. Mercer Co VA d/o Leonard H. & Nancy Dangerfield O: farmer; by Evan H. Brown.

38. 2 Novr 1858 WILLIAM W. BRUCE 18 yrs single b. Mercer Co VA s/o John & Catherine Bruce to MARY A.E. JOHNSTON 15 yrs single b. Giles Co VA d/o Alexander & Nancy Johnston O: farmer; by William Holroyd.

39. 3 Novr 1858 ANDERSON A. BELCHER 37 yrs wid. b. Mercer Co VA s/o Henry & Milla Belcher to CLARINDA B SCOTT 37 yrs 7 mo single b. Floyd Co VA d/o John & China Scott O: farmer; by James Calfee.

40. 9 Novr 1858 WILLIAM J. LILLY 25 yrs single b. Mercer Co VA s/o James & Nelly Lilly to MARGARET L. WHITTEN 28 yrs single b. Alleghany Co VA d/o Lewis & Charlotte Whitten O: farmer; by No Name Given.

41. 16 Novr 1858 JAMES FARLEY 34 yrs wid. b. Mercer Co VA s/o Andrew & Anna Farley to ELLEN W. ABBOTT 33 yrs single b. Monroe Co VA d/o St. Clair & Sallie Abbott O: farmer; by Leroy Keaton.

42. 23 Novr 1858 GRANVILLE WORRELL 21 yrs 9 mos 6 dys single b. Carroll Co s/o James B. & Olive Worrell to LOUISA A. HUBBARD 14 yrs 5 mos 11 dys single b. Patrick Co VA d/o Samuel & Elizabeth Hubbard O: farmer; by John C. Hubbard.

43. 25 Novr 1858 DAVID K. LUSK 30 yrs single b. Mercer Co VA s/o Absolom & Dilla Lusk to ANN S. BASHALDER 37 yrs wid. b. Montgomery Co VA d/o Robert Craig & Mary Lee O: farmer; by Joseph Wright.

44. 25 Novr 1858 HARVEY C. WHITE 18 yrs 5 mos 18 dys single b. Mercer Co VA s/o Cornelius & Polly White to SARAH E. RUHLE 17 yrs 1 mos 10 dys single b. Rockbridge Co VA d/o Samuel & Catherine Ruhle O: farmer; by Joseph Wright.

45. 25 Novr 1858 SAMUEL M. SNAPP 23 yrs single b. Augusta Co VA s/o John & Catherine Snapp to ELIZA W. HAYMAKER 19 yrs single b. Montgomery Co VA d/o Michael & Mary Haymaker O: farmer; by Paul Vanderwood.

46. 2 Decr 1858 JOHN P. TILLER 19 yrs 8 mos 27 dys single b. Mercer Co VA s/o Anderson & Priscilla Tiller to LEVINA BROWN 19 yrs 4 mos 5 dys single b. Tazewell Co VA d/o Thomas & Margaret Brown O: mechanic; by Abraham Garretson.

47. 13 Decr 1858 JOSEPH W. JOHNSON 22 yrs single b. Mechlenburg Co VA s/o Patrick & Elizabeth Johnson to PENELOPE WHITTAKER 23 yrs single b. Giles Co VA d/o Aaron & Margaret Whittabke O: waggoner; by Samuel Scott.

48. 14 Decr 1858 WILLIAM F. STEEL 19 yrs single b. Mercer Co VA s/o Sarah Steel to RHODA MEADOWS 16 yrs single b. Mercer Co VA d/o Jordan & Susann Meadows O: farmer; by Samuel Scott.

Page 6

1. 14 Decr 1858 JOHN TAYLOR 22 yrs single b. Carroll Co VA s/o John & Mary Taylor to MARY F. HARTWELL 21 yrs single b. Mercer Co VA d/o Andrew & Jane Hartwell O: farmer; by James Calfee.

2. 22 Decr 1858 CASPER L. HARLESS 28 yrs single b. Giles Co VA now residing in same s/o Alexander & Elizabeth Harless to MARY A. CALDWELL 27 yrs single b. Giles Co VA d/o John & Eliza Caldwell O: farmer; by John Dyerle.

3. 23 Decr 1858 CARY A. PITZER 21 yrs single b. Craig Co VA s/o John H. & Barbara Pitzer to AMANDA G. HARVEY 19 yrs single b. Monroe Co VA d/o James G. & Nancy Harvey O: farmer; by Paul Vanderwood.

4. 28 Decr 1858 MATTHEW W. BOLTON 31 yrs single b. Botetourt Co VA now living in Giles Co VA s/o Jacob & Elizabeth Bolton to MARY F. SMITH 25 yrs single b. Logan Co VA d/o Benjamin & Elizabeth Smith O: mill wright; by John B. Lee.

5. 6 Jany 1859 JOHN B. ST. CLAIR 27 yrs 7 mos 5 dys single b. Bedford Co VA s/o Isaac & Jane St. Clair to SARAH HALDREN 18 yrs 2 mos 3 dys single b. Mercer Co VA d/o Henry & Mahala Haldren O: farmer; by William C. Martin.

6. 9 Jany 1859 JOSEPH GOSER 79 yrs wid. b. Monroe Co VA now living in same s/o Henry & Catherine Goser to LOUISA SPRADLIN 46 yrs wid. b. Franklin Co VA d/o David & Mary Meador O: farmer; by Leroy Keaton.

7. 13 Jany 1859 JOHN A. McKINZIE 36 yrs wid. b. Mercer Co VA s/o Alex. & Malinda McKinzie to LUCINDA E. BOLING 20 yrs single b. Patrick Co VA d/o James & Ruth Boling O: farmer; by William Holroyd.

8. 18 Jany 1859 DANIEL H. EATON 24 yrs single b. Monroe Co VA now living in Wise Co VA s/o John & Elizabeth Eaton to MARY A.E. JOHNSTON 23 yrs single b. Giles Co VA d/o Adam & Susannah Johnston O: farmer; by Josiah Lorbett.

9. 26 Jany 1859 SAMUEL T.C. PERDUE 36 yrs single b. Giles Co VA now living same s/o Zach & Mary Perdue to MARY A. WAGGONER 26 yrs wid. b. Henry Co VA d/o John & Elizth Perdue O: farmer; by Abraham Garretson.

10. 27 Jany 1859 JOHN B. SMITH 29 yrs single b. Lognin Co VA s/o Benj. & Eliz. S. Smith to SARAH G. NEAL 23 yrs single b. Monroe Co VA d/o Daniel & Hannah Neal O: farmer; by Elisha G. Duncan.

11. 31 Jany 1859 RUTLEDGE CALFEE 30 yrs 3 mos 3 dys single b. Pulaski Co VA s/o Saml. & Rebecca Calfee to ESTHER A. CALFEE 21 yrs 2 mos 17 dys single b. Wythe Co VA d/o Saml. T. & Jane C. Calfee O: farmer; by James Calfee.

12. 23 Feby 1859 ALEXANDER GAND 21 yrs single b. Carroll Co VA s/o Wm & Sarah Gand to LOUISA WOOD 17 yrs single b. Patrick Co VA d/o Alexr & Bathena Wood O: farmer; by Paul Vanderwood.

13. 15 March 1859 ALEXR H. MOONEY 21 yrs 11 mos 25 dys single b. Mercer Co VA s/o John L. & Susanna Mooney to MARY P. CLARK 20 yrs 11 mos 15 dys single b. Franklin Co VA d/o John & Miraine Clark O: farmer; by Russell G. French.

14. 17 March 1859 HIRAM DAVIS 20 yrs single b. Giles Co VA now living same s/o Lindsay & Jennie Davis to JULIA A. DAVIS 21 yrs single b. Giles Co VA d/o Joshua & Sarah Davis O: farmer; by Landon Duncan.

15. 8 April 1859 JAMES PETRY 70 yrs wid. b. Rockingham Co VA s/o Martin & Ann Petry to LYDIA MOSS 44 yrs wid. b. Greenbrier Co VA d/o Mary Carter O: carpenter; by William C. Martin.

16. 10 April 1859 JOHN D. MARTIN 22 yrs 5 mos 12 dys single b. Mercer Co VA s/o Wm C. & Ann Martin to LENESOR* G. GIBSON 24 yrs 8 mos 26 dys single b. Grun* Co VA d/o Saml & Elizth Gibson O: farmer; by William C. Martin. (*Note: unable to read handwriting clearly.)

17. 28 April 1859 THOMAS H. SHREWSBURY 22 yrs 5 mos 17 dys single b. Mercer Co VA s/o John & Elizth Shrewsbury to MARYELINE H. BAILEY 22 yrs 3 mos 21 dys single b. Mercer Co VA d/o Jameson & Elizth Bailey O: farmer; by Joseph Wright.

18. 28 April 1859 JAMES J. BOLING 30 yrs 7 mos single b. Mercer Co VA s/o Wm & Elizth Boling to ISABELLA GRAYBILL 19 yrs 5 mos 12 dys single b. Montgomery Co VA d/o John & Susan Graybill O: farmer; by William C. Martin.

19. 3 May 1859 GEORGE W/ SORTER 33 yrs wid. b. Charlotte Co VA s/o John & Nancy Shorter to SARAH J. PHILLIPS 16 yrs single b. Mercer Co VA d/o Jas. & Clara Phillips O: farmer; by Garland A. Austin.

20. 26 May 1859 HIRAM C. GARRETSON 22 yrs 4 mos 13 dys single b. Mercer Co VA s/o John & Ida Garretson to NAOMA J. COMPTON 18 yrs 4 mos single b. Franklin Co VA d/o Micajah & Naoma Compton O: surveyor; by Samuel Scott.

21. 26 May 1859 ALLEN D. BELCHER 23 yrs 1 mo 16 dys b. Mercer Co VA s/o Asa & Clara Belcher to CALLEAR(?) COMPTON 21 yrs 3 mos single b. Franklin Co VA d/o Micajah & Naoma Compton O: farmer; by Samuel Scott.

22. 2 June 1859 GEORGE O. HAMBRICK 22 yrs 3 mos single b. Montgomery Co VA s/o Righly & Margaret Hambrick to EMMA FAULKNER 17 yrs 5 dys single b. Montgomery Co VA d/o Hugh H. & Susannah Faulkner O: farmer; by Joseph Wright.

23. 2 June 1859 JAMES H. THOMAS 20 yrs 11 mos 4 dys single b. Giles Co VA s/o Henley & Margaret Thomas to CAROLINE THOMAS 21 yrs 6 mos 4 dys single b. Mercer Co VA d/o Samuel & Julett Thomas O: farmer; by Abraham Garretson.

24. 8 June 1859 ALLEN THOMPSON 25 yrs single b. Mercer Co VA s/o James & Lucy A. Thompson to MANIRVA A. GORE 19 yrs single b. Mercer Co VA d/o Isaac & Ida Gore O: farmer; by William Holroyd.

25. 29 June 1859 SIMEON D. HOPKINS 24 yrs 10 mos 7 dys single b. Franklin Co VA s/o Jonathan & Jemima Hopkins to SARAH E. NEWLEE 22 yrs 11 dys single b. Lee Co VA d/o John G. & Elizth Newlee O: farmer; by Leroy Keaton.

26. 7 July 1859 DANIEL N. NEAL 20 yrs 2 mos 17 dys single b. Monroe Co VA s/o Daniel & Hannah Neal to SARAH A. ARCHER 18 yrs 4 mos 19 dys single b. Wythe Co VA d/o Samson & Sarah Archer O: farmer; by Abraham Garretson.

27. 16 July 1859 EDWARD THOMAS 50 yrs 6 mos wid. b. Giles Co VA s/o John & Phebe Thomas to MARTHA A. PERKINS 22 yrs 3 mos single b. Montgomery Co VA d/o Isom & Polly Perkins O: farmer; by Samuel Scott.

5. 21 Sep 1865 JOHN W. LILLY 35 yrs single b. Mercer Co W VA s/o John & Ellen Lilly to MARTHA WHITTEN 22 yrs single b. Alleghany Co W VA d/o L. & Charlotte Whitten by Jno. C Hubbard; REMARKS: No occupation given.

6. 20 Sep 1865 CALVIN E. STEPHENSON 23 yrs single b. Monroe Co W VA s/o J. Hintin & N. Stephenson to MARY DEEDS 38 yrs wid. b. Bedford Co VA d/o Lewis & Charlotte Whitten O: farmer; by Jno. C. Hubbard. REMARKS: name of wife's father not given.

7. 29 Novr 1865 SAMP. G. MEADOR 28 yrs wid. b. Mercer Co W VA s/o Jordan & Susan Meador to CAROLINE THOMAS 24 yrs single b. Mercer Co W VA d/o Jemima Thomas O: farmer; by Saml Scott.

8. 25 Oct 1865 GEO. S. BOWLING 20 yrs 9 mos 5 dys single b. Mercer Co W VA s/o Jesse & Jane Bowling to ELIZ. HUTCHINSON 18 yrs single b. Craig Co VA d/o H. & Ann Hutchinson O: farmer; by Saml. Scott.

9. 5 Oct 1865 MATH. F. BENNETT 19 yrs single b. Greenbrier Co W VA now living same s/o Robt. & Elcinda Bennett to MARTHA J. BENNETT 20 yrs single b. Raleigh W VA d/o Jeff. & Nancy Bennett O: farmer; by Rufus Pack.

10. 6 Sep 1865 JAS. W LILLY 20 yrs single b. Mercer Co W VA s/o Wash. & Mary Lilly to RACHEL MEADOR 17 yrs single b. Mercer Co W VA d/o John & Anna Meador O: farmer; by B.T. Bird.

11. 24 Aug 1865 THOS. J. BOWLING 24 yrs single b. Mercer Co W VA s/o Jno. & Sarah Bowling to VIRGINIA KEARNS 18 yrs single b. Mercer Co W VA d/o Madison & N. Kearns O: farmer; by Charles Walker.

12. 29 Aug 1865 THOS. McBRIDE 25 yrs single b. Bedford Co VA s/o Chas & Sarah McBride to SUE F. FERGUSON 24 yrs single b. Mercer Co W VA d/o E.W. & Amelia Ferguson O: farmer; by B.T. Bird.

13. 31 Aug 1865 W.M. MEADOR 20 yrs 14 dys single b. Mercer Co W VA s/o Jos. & Julia Meador to SUSAN LILLY 17 yrs 7 mos 23 dys single b. Mercer Co W VA d/o Jno. & Nancy Lilly O: farmer; by Chas. Walker.

14. 29 Aug 1865 WM. LILLY 61 yrs 8 mos wid. b. Giles Co VA s/o Thos. & Profoana(?) Lilly to NANCY COOPER 49 yrs 4 mos wid. b. Giles Co VA d/o James M. Couchins O: farmer; by Chas. Walker.

15. 30 Aug 1865 WM. MEADOR 28 yrs single b. Mercer Co W VA s/o Wm & Margaret Lilly(sic) to MARG. M. LILLY 23 yrs single b. Mercer Co W VA d/o Green W. & Emily Meador(sic) O: farmer; by B.T. Bird.

16. 24 Aug 1865 WILSON L. BAILY 26 yrs 17 dys single b. Mercer Co W VA s/o Russel B. & N. Baily to ELIZTH McCOMAS 24 yrs 5 mos 6 dys single b. Mercer Co W VA d/o Jos. & Rebecca McComas O: farmer; by B.T. Bird.

17. 14 Sep 1865 ARCH MARTIN 22 yrs single b. Mercer Co W VA s/o David & Mahala Martin to LOUISA J. HOUCHINS 20 yrs single b. Mercer Co W VA d/o Chas. & Catharine Houchins O: farmer; by B.T. Bird

18. 30 Aug 1865 JAMES LILLY 23 yrs single b. Mercer Co W VA s/o Jas. & Nelly Lilly to MARY E. BARKER 21 yrs single b. Mercer Co W VA d/o M.C. & Julia A. Barker O: farmer; by B.T. Bird.

19. 13 Sept 1865 W.P. LILLY 23 yrs single b. Mercer Co W VA s/o Wilson & Tabatha A. Lilly to MANERVA UPTON 17 yrs single b. Mercer Co W VA d/o Sylvester & Letha Upton O: farmer; by B.T. Bird.

20. 31 Sept 1865 GREENVILLE C. BAILY 23 yrs 6 mos single b. Mercer Co W VA s/o Eli & Charlotte Baily to JANE BOWLING 23 yrs 10 mos single b. Mercer Co W VA d/o John & Sarah Baily(sic) O: farmer; by Joseph Wright.

21. 29 Aug 1865 JOHN MILLS 20 yrs 10 mos single b. Mercer Co W VA now living in Wyoming Co VA s/o David & Nancy Mills to JANE SIZEMORE 18 yrs 15 dys single b. Logan Co W VA d/o Jno. & Jane Sizemore O: farmer; by Chas. Walker.

22. 29 Aug 1865 JNO. G. CAPERTON 19 yrs single b. Mercer Co W VA s/o Adam Caperton & Nancy Pauly to ALBTa. WILEY 19 yrs 8 mos single b. Mercer Co W VA d/o Vincent & Cynthia Wiley O: farmer; by W.C. Martin. REMARKS: Regstd. by mistake see 2nd line. (Note: 2nd entry page 9.)

23. 29 Aug 1865 W.T. FARLEY* 21 yrs 11 mos single b. Mercer Co W VA s/o Gideon Farly* to MARY A. MILLER 25 yrs 7 mos single b. Mercer Co W VA d/o Dinah Farly(sic) O: farmer; by Wm. C. Martin; REMARKS: Mistake in names of wife's parents. (*Note: name spelled both ways.)

24. 12 Sep 1865 JONATHAN K. LILLY 24 yrs single b. Mercer Co W VA s/o Jos. & Elizabeth Lilly to ALABAMA GORE 16 yrs single b. Mercer Co W VA d/o Isaac & Ida Gore O: farmer; by B.T. Bird.

25. 29 Aug 1865 JOHN B. McBRIDE 46 yrs wid. b. Bedford Co VA s/o Thos. & Catharine McBride to SARAH E. BAKER 21 yrs single b. Logan Co W VA d/o Jno. & Mary Baker O: farmer; by B.T. Bird.

26. 24 Oct 1865 WM. FARMER 23 yrs single b. Carroll Co VA s/o Jno. & Nancy Farmer to SARAH E. ROACH 26 yrs single b. Logan Co W VA d/o Reuben & M. Roach O: farmer; by Joseph Wright.

27. 26 Oct 1865 WM. R. HOUCHINS 23 yrs single b. Mercer Co W VA s/o James & S. Houchins to N.E. SPRADLIN 20 yrs single b. Bedford Co VA d/o Jno. & Louisa Spradlin O: farmer; by Garland A. Austin.

28. 2 Nov 1865 THOS. LILLY 25 yrs single b. Mercer Co W VA s/o Robt & Mary Lilly to ELIZTH CALLAWAY 26 yrs single b. Mercer Co W VA d/o Granville & --- Callaway O: farmer; by B.T. Bird.

29. 5 Oct 1865 SAMP. TAYLOR 48 yrs wid. b. Carroll Co VA s/o MOTHER Wealthy Taylor to MARTHA TAYLOR 22 yrs 7 mos single b. Carroll Co VA d/o Jno. & Mary Taylor O: farmer; by Joseph Wright; REMARKS: Wife's mother's name not given.

30. 5 Oct 1865 MICAJAH B. SAUNDERS 25 yrs single b. Pulaski Co W VA s/o Julias & Lydia Saunders to DRUCILLA P. GRIMM 19 yrs single b. Roanoke Co VA d/o Wm & Cath. Grimm O: farmer; by Joseph Wright and Evan H. Brown.

31. 30 Nov 1865 JAMES PHILLIPS 57 yrs wid. b. Franklin Co VA s/o James & Sarah Phillips to LUCY KENT 47 yrs wid. b. Franklin Co VA d/o Squire & S. Dillion O: farmer; by G.A. Austin.

32. 25 Oct 1865 HARVY M. HEDRICK 22 yrs single b. Wythe Co VA now living in Tazewell Co VA s/o Jas. & Diannah Hedrick to NANCY BAILY 20 single b. Tazewell Co VA d/o Jas. L. & M. Baily O: farmer; by Evan H. Brown.

33. 23 Sep 1865 PETER ROLLISON 41 yrs single b. Monroe Co W VA s/o Jos. & Elizth Rollison to MARY A. WILLIAMS 21 yrs single b. Mercer Co W VA d/o Fielding & N. Williams O: farmer; by B.T. Bird.

34. 11 Oct 1865 W.H. ROACH 20 yrs single b. Logan Co W VA s/o Reub. & Margarett Roach to CHRISTIAN F. BAILY 20 yrs wid. b. Montgomery Co VA d/o John & Christian Jewell O: farmer; by Joseph Wright.

35. 15 Oct 1865 WM. R. MARTIN 23 yrs single b. Monroe Co W VA s/o Hudson to E. Martin to MARINDA ELLISON 21 yrs single b. Mercer Co W VA d/o Jos. & Mary Ellison O: farmer; by B.T. Bird.

36. 28 Sep 1865 ANDW. J. DAVIS 35 yrs single b. Patrick Co VA s/o Jno. W. & Temperance Davis to MARTHA D. STANLY 32 yrs single b. Mercer Co W VA d/o Jno. & Elizabeth Stanly O: farmer; by B.T. Bird.

37. 29 Sep 1865 CHAS. WINFRY 20 yrs 11 mos single b. Franklin Co VA s/o Burrell & Orina Winfry to JULIANN PETERS 25 yrs 2 mos wid. b. Raleigh Co W VA d/o Jas & Cynthia Wiley O: farmer; by Chas. Walker.

38. 19 Oct 1865 CRAWFORD H. WOOD 22 yrs single b. Patrick Co VA s/o Alexr. & Bethina Wood to VINICE S. HOWELL 20 yrs single b. Patrick Co VA d/o Jno & Setha Howell O: farmer; by Chas. Walker.

39. 12 Oct 1865 JAS. R.P. BAILY 28 yrs single b. Mercer Co W VA s/o Arch. & Elizth Baily to ELEANOR P. LAMBERT 19 yrs single b. Tazewell Co VA d/o Jeremiah & E. Lambert O: farmer; by Jas. Calfee.

40. 19 Oct 1865 ABR. R. BIRCHFIELD 21 yrs single b. Rupell Co VA s/o Thos. & A. Birchfield to MARY J. WOOD 18 yrs single b. Patrick Co VA d/o Alex & Bethena Wood O: farmer; by Chas. Walker.

41. 17 Oct 1865 JACOB L. WILLIAMS 22 yrs single b. Mercer Co W VA s/o Andrew & Ora Williams to MARTHA M. FEAZEL 26 yrs single b. Franklin Co VA d/o Marshall & M. Feazel O: farmer; by Wm C. Martin.

42. 12 Oct 1865 M.D.L. GORE 30 yrs single b. Mercer Co W VA s/o Isaac & Ida Gore to MARY E. HUGHS 17 yrs single b. Giles Co VA d/o Wm & Louisa Hughs O: farmer; by Benj. T. Bird.

43. 21 Sept 1865 A.N. THOMPSON 26 yrs single b. Giles Co VA s/o Joshua B. Thompson to JULIANA H. BIRD 21 yrs single b. Franklin Co VA d/o Benj. T. & Vina Bird O: mechanic; by A.A. Ashworth.

44. 30 Aug 1865 GI---* AL----* 43 yrs wid. b. Mercer Co W VA s/o Robt. & Mary Lilly(sic) to EMILY MEADOR 29 yrs single b. Mercer Co W VA d/o Green W. & E. Meador O: miller; by B.T. Bird. (*Note: unable to read handwriting.)

45. 29 Novr 1865 SAML. G. LILLY 22 yrs single b. Mercer Co W VA s/o Jonathan & M. Lilly to MARY COCHRAN 26 yrs single b. Mercer Co W VA d/o Brick & W. Cochran O: farmer; by B.T. Bird.

46. 5 Dec. 1865 JNO. D. THOMPSON 34 yrs single b. Mercer Co W VA s/o A.J. & Elizth. Thompson to EMILY N. DEWEY 17 yrs single b. Floyd Co VA d/o A.G. & Rosa Dewey O: farmer; by A.G. Thompson.

47. 29 Jan 1862 WM. SOLESBURY 42 yrs wid. b. Mercer Co W VA s/o Phil. & Elizth Solesbury to SARAH A.J. BAILY 16 yrs single b. Mercer Co W VA d/o Floyd & Zelpha Baily O: farmer; by Russell G. French; REMARKS: returned by Clk of C.C

48. 9 Jan 1862 WM. HOLDRON 24 yrs single b. Mercer Co W VA s/o Sally Holdron to MARY F. HARLESS 28 yrs single b. Montgomery Co VA d/o Phil & Susan Harless O: farmer; by Saml. Scott; REMARKS: returned by Clk of C.C.

Page 10

1. 11 March 1862 JOHN A. BROWN 27 yrs single b. Giles Co VA s/o Geo. P. & Sarah P. Brown to MARGARET THOMPSON 19 yrs single b. Wythe Co VA d/o David & Ang. Thompson O: farmer; by Joseph Wright; REMARKS: county co(urt) ... released with ...* (*Note: edge of page missing.)

2. 6 March 1862 ISAAC FLETCHER 40 yrs wid. b. Giles Co VA s/o Jas & Elizth Fletcher to SARAH E. SHREWSBURY 22 yrs single b. Mercer Co VA d/o Jas. & Elizth Shrewsbury O: farmer; by James Calfee; REMARKS: same (as above).

3. ? Oct 1865 WM. FARMER 23 yrs single b. Carroll Co VA s/o John & Mary Farmer to SARAH E. ROACH 26 yrs single b. Logan Co VA d/o Ruben & M. Roach O: farmer; by Joseph Wright. (?= day not given)

4. 25 Dec 1865 ADISON JOHNSTON 24 yrs single b. Charlotte Co VA s/o Pat & Eliz. Johnston to FRANCIS GIVENS 22 yrs single b. Monroe Co W VA d/o Jas. H. & Mary Givens O: farmer; by Saml. Scott.

5. 21 Dec 1865 BALLARD BLANKENSHIP 27 yrs single b. Giles Co VA now living in same s/o Steph & E. Blankenship to MARTHA NEELY 19 yrs single b. Mercer Co W VA d/o Wm. & Delila Neely O: farmer; by E.G. Duncan.

6. 28 Novr 1861 JOHN C. BOLEN 57 yrs wid. b. Nelson Co VA s/o Marvel & Sarah Bolen to HELEN JONES 39 yrs single b. Giles Co VA d/o Jeremiah Jones O: farmer; by Samuel Scott.

7. 8 Jany 1865 ISOM BELCHER 22 yrs 15 dys single b. Mercer Co W VA now living in Boone Co W VA s/o Micajah & Malinda Belcher to NANCY WINFREY 18 yrs 11 mos 22 dys single b. Mercer Co W VA d/o Birrel & Reney Winfrey O: farmer; REMARKS: License not r(eturned)* (*Note: the edge of page was missing, probably should read "License not returned".)

8. 13 Jany 1865 GEORGE UPTON 21 yrs single b. Monroe Co W VA now living in Mercer Co W VA d/o Sylvester & Letha Upton to LOUISA J. LILLY 19 yrs single b. Mercer Co W VA d/o Wilson & Tabitha Lilly O: farmer; by Rufus Pack.

9. 17 Jany 1865 GEORGE HUGHES 18 yrs single b. Giles Co VA s/o John & Delila Hughes to SARAH V. MARTIN 22 yrs wid. b. Botetourt Co VA d/o Wm & Sophia Caldwell O: farmer; by Samuel Scott.

10. 31 Jany 1865 ROBERT G. CLENDERSON 45 yrs wid. b. Mercer Co W VA s/o John & Mary Clenderson to MARY E. TRAIL 26 yrs wid. b. Giles Co VA d/o H. & M. Cassaday O: farmer; by William Holroyd.

11. 6 Feby 1865 JAMES TAYLOR 37 yrs 9 mos 28 dys single b. West Meath Ireland now living in Wood Co W VA s/o George & Eleanor Taylor to MARY H. DEYERLE 39 yrs 10 mos wid. b. Darby Co Ireland d/o R. & Mary Henderson O: soldier; by Joseph Wright.

12. 7 Feby 1865 WILLIAM SHANNON 23 yrs single b. Campbell Co VA s/o Wm & Mary Shannon to MARTHA ALVIS 30 yrs wid. b. Giles Co VA d/o Thos. & Agnus Neale O: farmer; by Samuel Scott.

13. 8 Feby 1865 ALBERT P. BRIANS 28 yrs single b. Mercer Co W VA s/o J.M. & Chloe Brians to SUSAN ROWLAND 28 yrs wid. b. Giles Co VA d/o Wm & Sarah Heare O: farmer; REMARKS: License not r(eturned).

14. 9 Feby 1865 GEORGE W. SURFACE 50 yrs 10 mos 18 dys wid. b. Montgomery Co VA s/o A. & Mary A. Surface to EMARILLA DILLION 22 yrs 2 mos 25 dys single b. Mercer Co W VA d/o Jas. P. & Juliet Dillion O: farmer; by Joseph Wright.

15. 16 Feby 1865 ANDREW THORNTON 23 yrs 3 mos 28 dys single b. Pulaski Co VA s/o H & L Thornton to MATILDA J. DEWEESE 18 yrs 3 mos 28 dys single b. Roanoke Co VA d/o A & R Deweese O: farmer; REMARKS: license not (returned).

16. 2 March 1865 JAMES A. PERDUE 26 yrs single b. Giles Co VA s/o Jas. & C. Perdue to LURESY MEADOWS 18 yrs single b. Mercer Co W VA d/o Jordan & Su Meadows O: farmer; by John West.

17. 15 March 1865 DAVID B. PENDLETON 46 yrs single b. Buckingham Co VA s/o H & Susan Pendleton to NANCY V. THORNTON 21 yrs wid. b. Giles Co VA d/o F. & Julia Whittaker O: farmer; by Milton L. Clendenon.

18. 28 March 1865 JACOB WOODALL 62 yrs 6 mos wid. b. Prince Edward Co VA s/o J & R Woodall to SARAH KINZER 50 yrs wid b. Giles Co VA d/o John & S. Martin O: farmer; by William C. Martin.

19. 6 April 1865 JEFFREY THOMAS 22 yrs single b. Giles Co VA s/o Ed & May Thomas to ELLEN MEADOWS 32 yrs single b. Mercer Co W VA d/o J & S Meadows O: farmer; by John West.

20. 25 April 1865 CALEB ANGLE 18 yrs 11 mos single b. Franklin Co VA s/o David & E Angle to MARY E CRUM 24 yrs 7 mos single b. Franklin Co VA d/o A & J.A. Crum O: farmer; by William C. Booth.

21. 4 May 1865 WILLIAM S. MOORE 24 yrs 11 mos 11 dys single b. Tazewell Co VA now living same s/o Wm. S. & M.H. Moore to ELIZA L. DILLION 24 yrs 2 mos 17 dys wid. b. Mercer Co W VA d/o Chris & Mary Belcher O: saddler; by Joseph Wright.

22. 11 May 1865 JAMES O. CASSADAY 29 yrs 3 mos 11 dys single b. Wythe Co VA s/o H & M Cassaday to MARTHA C. CASPER 24 yrs 4 mos 18 dys single b. Giles Co VA d/o H & E. Casper O: farmer; by Milton L. Clendenon.

23. 18 May 1865 STEPHEN ARTHUR 23 yrs single b. Tazewell Co VA now living Fayette Co W VA s/o A & T. Arthur to RACHEL ROLLYSON 18 yrs 5 dys single b. Mercer Co W VA d/o J & E Rollyson O: farmer; by Rufus Pack.

24. 1 June 1865 WM H.H. HERNDON 22 yrs 11 mos 22 dys single b. Campbell Co VA s/o A & S.E.B. Herndon to MARY E. BELCHER 20 yrs 8 mos 4 dys single b. Mercer Co W VA d/o C. & Mary Belcher O: farmer; by Joseph Wright.

25. 22 June 1865 ISOM D. BELCHER 24 yrs 6 mos 16 dys single b. Mercer Co W VA s/o H.D. & Anna Belcher to MARTHA J. BROWN 25 yrs 5 mos 12 dys wid. b. Mercer Co W VA d/o Asa & Clara Belcher O: farmer; by Benjamin T. Bird.

26. 4 July 1865 WILLIAM M. BLANKENSHIP 25 yrs 5 mos 28 dys wid. b. Mercer Co W VA s/o A.H. & C. Blankenship to GRIGGELLE P. MOTLEY 25 yrs single Pike Co MO d/o Wm & E. Motley O: farmer; by Milton L. Clendenon.

27. 7 July 1865 JOHN D. SMITH 25 yrs 5 mos 8 dys single b. Desmoins Iowa now living in Guadaloupe TX s/o Vearis & Darcas Smith to NANCY H. THOMPSON 16 yrs 8 mos 19 dys single b. Mercer Co W VA d/o S & N Thompson O: farmer; by Milton L. Clendenon.

28. 10 July 1865 SAMUEL H. NEWBURY 35 yrs 21 dys single b. Wythe Co VA now living in Bland Co VA s/o A.J. & E. Newbury to MARY A. REPASS 16 yrs 1 mo 5 dys single b. Wythe Co VA d/o J.L & E.J. Repass O: farmer; by G.W. Penley.

29. 18 July 1865 HIRAM D. TILLER 19 yrs 1 mo 5 dys single b. Mercer Co W VA s/o A. & D. Tiller to ELIZABETH C. WHITTAKER 18 yrs single b. Giles Co VA d/o F. & (Ellen *) Whittaker O: farmer; by G.W. Penly. (*Note: 1860 Mercer Co VA Census, Ellen was the wife.)

30. 19 July 1865 MANDEVILLE COOK 22 yrs 8 mos 15 dys single b. Mercer Co W VA s/o E. & Jennie Cook to MARY FARLEY 26 yrs 3 mos 6 dys single b. Mercer Co W VA d/o Anna Farley O: farmer; by John C. Hubbard.

31. 25 July 1865 ALBERT G. PAULEY 23 yrs 2 mos single b. Giles Co VA s/o H. & B. Pauley to JULIA F. BIRD 23 yrs 5 mos 5 dys single b. Franklin Co VA d/o John & A. Bird O: farmer; by Benjamin T. Bird.

32. 27 July 1865 JOHN W. ARMONTROUT 20 yrs single b. Alleghany Co VA s/o J. & B. Armontrout to BERTHA A. THOMAS 24 yrs single b. Mercer Co W VA d/o H. & M. Thomas O: farmer; by Elisha G. Duncan.

33. 8 Aug 1865 JAMES R. MILLS 22 yrs 9 mos 28 dys single b. Mercer Co W VA s/o D. & Nancy Mills to NANCY A. COOPER 16 yrs 23 dys single b. Mercer Co W VA d/o J. & Nancy Cooper O: farmer; by Charles Walker.

34. 8 Novr 1865 ANDREW J. WILLIAMS 27 yrs 6 mos single b. Mercer Co W VA s/o J.L. & A. Williams to LUCINDA WOOD 21 yrs single b. Monroe Co W VA d/o G.W. & S.F. Wood O: farmer; by John C. Hubbard.

35. 16 Novr 1865 ANDREW L. LILLY 24 yrs 11 mos 20 dys single b. Mercer Co W VA s/o W. & L. Lilly to ELIZABETH E. HOLSTINE 21 yrs single b. Mercer Co W VA d/o J. & E. Holstine O: farmer; by George W. Martin.

36. 30 Novr 1865 WILLIAM J. WELCH 27 yrs single b. Louisville KY s/o Wm & Ellen Welch to ELIZABETH DAVIS 30 yrs wid. b. Franklin Co VA d/o Wm & Julia Palmer O: shoemaker; by James Calfee.

37. 12 Decr 1865 WILLIAM HANCOCK 25 yrs single b. Alleghany Co VA s/o M. & N. Hancock to PERMELIA A. SHORTER 19 yrs single b. Franklin Co VA d/o Geo. W. & P. Shorter O: farmer; by Garland A. Austin

38. 14 Decr 1865 BALLARD SHUMATE 23 yrs single b. Giles Co VA now living same s/o A. & S. Shumate to JUDITH E. MEADOR 22 yrs single b. Mercer Co W VA d/o Wm. & C. Meador O: farmer; by Benjamin T. Bird.

39. 22 Decr 1865 JAMES H. WILSON 31 yrs single b. Giles Co VA now living Bland Co VA s/o E. & R. Wilson to MARINDA BAILEY 27 yrs single b. Mercer Co W VA d/o J. & E. Bailey O: farmer; by James Calfee.

40. 26 Decr 1865 JOHN A. WILLIAMS 27 yrs single b. Monroe Co W VA s/o J.S. & A. Williams to MARTHA A. BUTLER 21 yrs single b. Monroe Co W VA d/o P. & D. Butler O: farmer; by Garland A. Austin.

41. 26 Decr 1865 JAMES H. BUTLER 23 yrs single b. Monroe Co W VA s/o P. & D. Butler to MARGARET LADD 20 yrs single b. Bedford Co VA d/o Thos. & E. Ladd O: farmer; by Garland A. Austin.

42. 27 March 1862 RICHARD TUTOR 18 yrs single b. N. Car. s/o Henry & Susan Tutor to MIRAM REED 17 yrs single b. Floyd Co VA d/o Elijah & Disa Reed O: farmer; by Russell G. French.

43. 23 Octr 1862 WM B. SMITH 22 yrs 10 mos single b. Washington Co VA now living Smith Co VA s/o Wm & Elizth Smith to MALINDA JAMEY 14 yrs 11 mos 26 dys single b. Pulaski Co VA d/o John W. & Elizth Jamey O: carpenter; by Joseph Wright.

44. 25 Decr 1862 REED M. FOLEY single b. Patrick Co VA s/o James & Judith Foley to Mary J. Cooper single b. Pulaski Co VA d/o ? & Nancy Cooper O: farmer; by Charles Walker.(*Note: father's name not given.)

45. 12 March 1863 JOHN A.J. WOODALL 20 yrs single b. Mecklenburg Co VA s/o Jacob & Martha B. Woodall to REBECCA J. PAULEY 18 yrs single b. Mercer Co VA d/o Nancy Pauley O: farmer; by William C. Martin.

46. 12 March 1863 JAMES A. HOBBS 21 yrs single b. Madison Co AL now living same s/o Calvin & Alabama Hobbs to ADELINE THOMPSON 18 yrs single b. Monroe Co VA d/o Arch & Elizth Thompson O: farmer; by Alexander S. Hutchinson.

47. 26 March 1863 GEORGE W. JARRELL 49 yrs 9 mos 29 dys wid. b. Madison Co VA s/o Jere. & Sarah Jarrell to ELIZABETH T. HARMAN 16 yrs 10 mos 7 dys single b. Tazewell Co VA d/o James P. & Rinda Harman; O: farmer; by James Calfee.

48. 27 March 1863 JOHN G. SNEAD 48 yrs wid. b. Patrick Co VA s/o Samuel & Esther Snead to MARY J. FERGUSON 20 yrs single b. Mercer Co VA d/o (Jere.) & Nancy Ferguson O: farmer; by Russell G. French.

1. 21 April 1863 LEWIS EVANS 20 yrs 10 dys single b. Botetourt Co VA now living same s/o Ab. & Sarah A. Evans to LEE A.S. SURFACE 24 yrs 25 dys single b. Montgomery Co VA d/o Geo. W. & Sarah Surface O: farmer; by Joseph Wright.

2. 3 May 1863 WILLIAM TAYLOR 22 yrs 10 mos single b. Carroll Co VA s/o Sampson & Mary Taylor to MARY A. TAYLOR 22 yrs 3 mos single b. Carroll Co VA d/o John & Mary Taylor O: farmer; by Joseph Wright.

3. 27 May 1863 MANELIUS CALDWELL 27 yrs single b. Giles Co VA s/o John & Eliza Caldwell to CAROLINE HOUELIUS(?) 23 yrs single b. Mercer Co VA d/o Wm. & Wilmouth Houelius O:farmer; REMARKS: No License retu(rned)*. (*Note: edge of page missing.)

4. 31 may 1863 GEORGE W. HEYLTON 21 yrs single b. Patrick Co VA s/o A. & Martha Heylton to RACHEL WILLIAMS 23 yrs single b. Monroe Co VA s/o James & Eliza Williams O: farmer; by Charles Walker

NOTE: Place of marriage is listed as Mercer Co, W VA-Instead of Mercer Co VA

5. 28 July 1863 THOMAS PRITCHARD 36 yrs single b. England s/o Thos. & Mary Pritchard to SARAH J. CALLOWAY 20 yrs single b. Monroe Co W VA d/o Jas. & Margt. Calloway O: carpenter; by William C. Martin.

6. 4 August 1863 JAMES WHITE 20 yrs single b. Logan Co W VA now living same s/o Elijah & Mahala White to CAROLINA WHITE 17 yrs single b. Floyd & Rhoda White O: farmer; by Samuel Scott.

7. 13 August 1863 BENJAMIN RUSSELL 55 yrs wid. b. Franklin Co VA s/o Robert & Mary Russell to SARAH J. VEST 37 yrs wid. b. Franklin Co VA d/o Chloe Boyd O: farmer; by Martin Bibb.

8. 13 August 1863 EDWARD THOMAS 54 yrs wid. b. Giles Co VA s/o John & Phebe Thomas to TERROPY WILKES 46 yrs single b. Franklin Co VA d/o Archibald & ? Wilkes O: farmer; by Samuel Scott.

9. 27 August 1863 ELISHA BOWLING 21 yrs 2 mos single b. Floyd co VA s/o Joshua & Nancy Bowling to ELIZA PACK 17 yrs 20 dys wid. b. Mercer Co W VA d/o Meador & Mary Balpham O: farmer; by M.E. Robinson.

10. 27 August 1863 SAMUEL G. HENDERSON 25 yrs single b. VA now living Nicholas Co W VA to SARAH E. MILLS 21 yrs single b. Mercer Co W VA d/o Benj. & Mary M. Mills O: farmer; by Jacob Brillhart.

11. 3 Sept 1863 EDMOND BLANKENSHIP wid. b. Giles Co VA s/o Stephen & -- Blankenship to RUTH HUBBARD wid. b. Mercer Co W VA O: farmer; by William Sturgis.

12. 16 Sept 1863 WILLIAM H. ELLIS (No other info given) to PRISCILLA RUSSELL b. Mercer Co W VA d/o Samuel & Nancy Mills O: farmer; by Jacob Brillhart.

13. 15 Octr 1863 MOSES D. TILLER 24 yrs single b. Logan Co W VA now living same to MICHEY THOMAS single b. Mercer Co W VA d/o Samuel Thomas O: farmer; by Jacob Brillhart.

14. 26 Octr 1863 ELI H. BLANKENSHIP 23 yrs single b. Logan Co W VA now living same s/o Jesse & H. Blankenship to ELIZABETH BAILEY 29 yrs single b. Mercer Co W VA d/o Micajah & M. Bailey O: farmer; by Jacob Brillhart.

15. 27 Octr 1863 CHRISTIAN L. WAUGHT 26 yrs single b.Giles Co VA now living same s/o William & Peggy Vaught to CLARESSA C. ABSHIRE single b. Mercer Co W VA d/o Christian & J. Abshire O: farmer; by Jacob Brillhart.

16. 29 Octr 1863 JOEL ASHWORTH 24 yrs single b. Cabell Co W VA now living same s/o John & Nancy Ashworth to ANN S. HOLSTINE 23 yrs single b. Mercer Co W VA d/o Jas. C & Elizth Holstine O: farmer; by Jacob Brillhart.

17. 3 Novr 1863 CROCKETT McDONALD 24 yrs single b. Wyoming Co W VA now living in MO s/o Stephen & S. McDonald to ELLEN V. NEALL 21 yrs single b.Mercer Co W VA d/o David & Mary E. Hall O: farmer; by Burwell Spurlock.

18. 1 Decr 1863 JOHN S. WISEMOUR 20 yrs 1 mos 4 dys single b. Monroe Co W VA now living same to MARGARET BAILEY 18 yrs 7 mos single b.Mercer Co W VA d/o Amos & ? Bailey O: farmer; by James Calfee.

19. 10 Decr 1863 JOHN A. PARKINS 21 yrs 11 mos 4 dys single b. Meggs Co OH now living in Putnam Co W VA s/o Saml & Elizth Parkins to HESTER A. MARTIN 20 yrs 7 mos single b. Mercer Co W VA d/o Wm. C. & Anna Martin O: farmer; by Benjamin T. Bird.

20. 18 Decr 1863 JOSEPH C. BURDITT 46 yrs wid. b. Monroe Co W VA s/o Joseph & Dicy Burditt to ARENA W. THOMAS 19 yrs single b. Mercer Co W VA d/o Henley & Margt Thomas O: farmer; by Elisha G. Duncan.

21. 24 Decr 1863 FLOYD G. MEADOR 40 yrs wid. b. Monroe Co W VA now living Tazewell Co VA to ADELINE H. HOLSTINE 24 yrs single b. Mercer Co W VA d/o Joseph C. & Elizth Holstine O: carpenter; by James Calfee.

22. 28 Oct 1863 LORENZA BALLENGER 36 yrs single b. Greenbrier Co W VA now living same s/o Polly Ballenger to SUSAN ROLYSON* 28 yrs single b. Mercer Co W VA d/o Joseph & Elizth Rollyson* O: farmer; by Rufus Pack. (*Note: name spelled both ways.)

23. 7 Jany 1864 WILLIAM S. HOBBS 24 yrs single b. Giles Co VA now living same s/o Thos. & Julina Hobbs to DEMARIUS K. CHRISTIE 21 yrs single b. Monroe Co W VA d/o James H. & C. Christie O: farmer; by Elisha G. Duncan.

24. 19 Jany 1864 KPHATJAH C/ JARVEH 22 yrs single b. Mercer co W VA s/o Isaac G. & ? Harvey to MARY E. HARVEY 22 yrs single g. Mercer Co W VA d/o Jacob H. & ? Harvey O: farmer; by Charles Walker.

25. 22 Jany 1864 JOHN PACK 56 yrs wid. b. Giles Co VA s/o Matthew & Frances Pack to ELIZABETH ROLLYSON 36 yrs single b. Mercer Co W VA d/o Joseph & E. Rollyson O: farmer; by Charles Walker.

26. 27 Jany 1864 JOHN REYNOLDS 56 yrs wid. b. Patrick Co VA now living in Monroe Co W VA s/o Richd. & Milla Reynolds to DELILA WHITE 45 yrs wid. b. Bedford Co VA d/o James & Elizth Cauley O: farmer; by Leroy Keaton.

27. 2 Feby 1864 JOHN LAMBERT 60 yrs wid. b. Wythe Co VA now living in Bland Co VA s/o Thomas & Anna Lambert to EMILY SARVER 30 yrs single b. Mercer Co W VA d/o James & Elizth Sarver O: farmer; by John West.

28. 22 Feby 1864 MILTON M. BELCHER 27 yrs single b. Mercer Co W VA s/o Lewis & R. Belcher to MARGARET C. BELCHER 29 yrs single b. Mercer Co W VA d/o Asa & Clara Belcher O: farmer; by William Holroyd.

29. 5 April 1864 MATTHEW B. ATKINS 21 yrs single b. Raleigh Co W VA s/o Matthew & Elizth Adkins to CELIA A. HARVEY 18 yrs single b. Mercer Co W VA d/o Michael W. & N. Harvey O: farmer; REMARKS: License not ret(urned).

30. 13 April 1864 THOMAS C. PULLIAM 22 yrs single b. Hanover Co VA now living in Greenbrier Co W VA s/o John C. & M.B. Pulliam to SALLIE B. SMITH 17 yrs single b. Campbell Co VA d/o Saml B. & Agnes Smith O: farmer; Milton L. Clendenon.

31. 14 April 1864 JOHN S. LILLY 20 yrs single b. Mercer Co W VA s/o A.L. & Sarah Lilly to SARAH C. HARVEY 21 yrs single b.(unable to read) d/o John W. & Sarah Harvey O: farmer; by Rufus Pack.

32. 22 April 1864 EDMUND H. HATCHER 22 yrs single b. Mercer Co W VA s/o Elijah & Jennie Hatcher to NANCY McBRIDE 19 yrs single b. Bedford Co VA d/o Charles & Sarah McBride O: farmer; by Leroy Keaton.

33. 5 May 1864 JESSE THOMAS 62 yrs wid. b. Giles Co VA s/o John & Phebe Thomas to LUCY M. WRIGHT 51 yrs single b. Campbell Co VA d/o George & Agnes Wright O: farmer; by John West.

34. 9 June 1864 ELIHS REED 28 yrs 29 dys single b. Mercer Co W VA now living in Wyoming Co W VA s/o Elijah & Dica Reed to SARAH G. WADDLE 21 yrs 10 dys single b. Mercer Co W VA d/o James & Susan Waddle O: farmer; by Charles Walker.

35. 9 July 1864 ROBERT PATRICK 24 yrs wid. b. Tazewell Co VA now living same s/o Wilson & Ruth Patrick to ARAMINTA DAVIDSON 20 yrs single b. Giles Co VA d/o David & A. Davidson O: farmer; by Elisha G. Duncan.

36. 13 July 1864 JOSEPH W. VANVAETER 29 yrs single b. Loudon Co VA s/o Sol. & Charity Vanvaeter to RUFINA MOTLEY 18 yrs single b. Botetourt Co VA d/o Wm & Elizth Motley O: farmer; by Milton L. Clendenon.

37. 18 July 1864 ALLEN P. SHREWSBURY 25 yrs single b. Mercer Co W VA now living Wyoming Co W VA s/o Jere. & Elizth Shrewsbury to ELIZABETH BLANKENSHIP 20 yrs single b. Mercer Co W VA d/o A.M. & Cath. Blankenship O: farmer; by Milton L. Clendenon.

38. 21 July 1864 JOHN H. CLINE 23 yrs 6 mos 6 dys single b. Wyoming Co W VA s/o James & Elizth Cline to RACHEL REED 22 yrs 10 mos single b. Floyd Co VA s/o Elijah & Dicy Reed O: farmer; by Charles Walker.

39. 11 Aug 1864 WILSON HARVEY 23 yrs 7 mos single b. Deleware Co (? unable to read) s/o John W. & Sarah Harvey to MARY J. BASSHAM 29 yrs 7 mos 15 dys wid. b. Mercer Co W VA s/o John & Elizth B. Park O: farmer; by Charles Walker.

40. 17 Aug 1864 SAMUEL CARPENTER 51 yrs wid. b. Mecklenburg Co VA s/o Samuel & Nancy Carpenter to NANCY J. BIRD 27 yrs single b. Franklin Co VA d/o John & Agineth Bird O: farmer; by Benjamin T. Bird.

41. 20 Sept 1864 BERRY CAULEY wid. b. Bedford Co VA s/o David & ? Cauley to ELIZABETH PETERS wid. b. Franklin Co VA d/o David Farmer O: farmer; by Benjamin T. Bird.

42. 24 Sept 1864 ANDREW WILLIAMS 45 yrs wid. b. Giles Co VA s/o Landon & R. Williams to MARY A. LAW 25 yrs single b. Patrick Co VA d/o Wm & Jane Law O: farmer; by Benjamin T. Bird.

43. 28 Sept 1864 JAMES CLARK 23 yrs wid. b. Franklin Co VA s/o Henry & Ruth Clark to CELIA E. MEADOR 21 yrs single b. Mercer Co W VA d/o John & Ann Meador O: farmer; by Charles Walker.

44. 28 Sept 1864 WILLIAM H. BOYD 24 yrs wid. b. Wythe Co VA now living same s/o thos. & Manerva Boyd to MARINDA F. JONES 22 yrs single b. Mercer Co W VA d/o Isaac & Martha Jones O: farmer; by Samuel Scott.

45. 4 Octr 1864 ELIJAH MOYE 64 yrs wid. b. N. Car. now living Giles Co VA s/o Mar. & Mary Moye to ELIZA TABOR 33 yrs wid. b. Botetourt Co VA d/o Hugh & Sarah Holstine O: farmer; by Benjamin T. Bird.

46. 6 Octr 1864 HARVEY S. TRACY 23 yrs single b. Giles Co VA s/o Wm & ? Tracy to MANERVA H. TILLER 20 yrs single b. Mercer Co W VA d/o Kinzer & Judith Tiller O: farmer; by Samuel Scott.

47. 19 Octr 1864 JOHN L. HUFFMAN 24 yrs single b. Monroe Co W VA now living same s/o Jno & Margt. Huffman to SARAH A. COX 23 yrs single b. Franklin Co VA d/o Moses & Cynthia Cox O: farmer; by Charles Walker.

48. 26 Octr 1864 ROBERT LILLY 33 yrs wid. b. Mercer Co W VA s/o Thomas & Delila Lilly to HAHALA FARLEY 34 yrs single b. Mercer Co W VA d/o Arch & Jemima Farley O: farmer; by Garland A. Austin.

Page 12

1. 27 Octr 1864 JAMES N. BRANHAM 25 yrs single b. Greenbrier Co W VA now living same s/o Beverly & Rachel Branham to MARY A. NEELY 18 yrs single b. Mercer Co W VA d/o Wm & Delila Neely O: farmer; by Samuel Scott.

2. 27 Oct 1864 JOHN F. DEEDS 22 yrs single b. Monroe Co W VA s/o Joseph & Hannah Deeds to AMANDA E. HOGAN 19 yrs single b. Monroe Co W VA d/o Peter & Nancy Hogan O: farmer; by Rufus Pack.

3. 9 Novr 1864 GRANVILLE H. HOGAN 22 yrs single b. Monroe Co W VA s/o Peter & Nancy Hogan to EMILY LILLY 24 yrs single d/o James & Nelly Lilly O: farmer; by Rufus Pack.

4. 22 Novr 1864 JACKSON BOWLING 17 yrs single b. Floyd Co VA s/o Joshua & Nancy Bowling to ELIZABETH E. LILLY 19 yrs single b. Mercer Co W VA d/o John & Nancy Lilly O: farmer; by Charles Walker.

5. 24 Novr 1864 HARDIN H. CASPER 23 yrs 8 mos single b. Monroe Co W VA now living in Raleigh Co W VA s/o Joseph & Jane Casper to MALINDA SWINNEY 15 yrs 11 mos 12 dys single b. Monroe Co W VA d/o Arch & Lucinda Swinney O: farmer; by Claibourne Curtis; REMARKS: License nor return(ed).

6. 16 Decr 1864 VINCENT P. HUDSON 56 yrs wid. b. Franklin Co VA s/o Wm. & Elizth Hudson to HESTER H. RUSSELL 17 yrs single b. Giles Co VA d/o Benj & Sarah Russell O: miller; by Samuel Scott.

7. 22 Decr 1864 ANDREW C. PRINCE 19 yrs single b. Mercer Co W VA s/o James & Juliet Prince to ADELINE Y. JANNEY 18 yrs single b. Pulaski Co VA d/o John & Elizth Janney O: farmer; by Charles Walker

8. 25 Decr 1864 ROBERT WORKMAN 22 yrs 10 mos 5 dys single b. Mercer Co W VA s/o Robert & Dolly Workman to LEUDERNA J. SURFACE 17 yrs 7 mos 5 dys single b. Mercer Co W VA d/o Geo. W. & Sarah Surface O: farmer; by Joseph Wright.

9. 27 Decr 1864 GREENVILLE SWADER 21 yrs 5 mos 27 dys single b. Mercer Co W VA s/o John & Nancy Swader to REBECCA WOLFE 21 yrs single b. Mercer Co VA d/o Lucinda Wolfe O: farmer; by Joseph Wright.

10. 28 Decr 1864 ALEXANDER SWADER 21 yrs 10 mos single b. Mercer Co W VA s/o Wm & Julia Swader to CATHERINE A. SURFACE 24 yrs 1 mo 3 dys single b. Montgomery Co VA d/o Geo. W. & Sarah Surface O: farmer; by Joseph Wright.

11. 26 Feby 1865 ANDREW THORNTON 23 yrs 3 mos 26 dys single b. Pulaski Co VA s/o M. & Louise Thornton to MATILDA J. DEWESE 18 yrs 9 mos 13 dys single b. Floyd Co VA d/o A. & Rosena Dewese O: farmer; by James Calfee.

12. 10 May 1865 ROBERT R. HUDSON 28 yrs 9 mos 12 dys single b. Franklin Co VA s/o Vincent & R. Hudson to MARTHA E. PARMER 21 yrs 6 dys single b. Patrick Co VA d/o Wm & Julia Parmer O: farmer; by James Calfee.

13. 21 July 1865 JAMES M. STOWERS 24 yrs 6 mos 9 dys single b. Tazewell Co VA now living Bland Co W VA s/o Hick. & Sarah Stowers to MOLLIE STOWERS wid. b. Wythe Co VA d/o Jno & Elizth Lambert O: farmer; by J.A. Cowgill.

14. 1 Jany 1866 ABRAM MEADOR 27 yrs single b. Monroe Co W VA now living Raleigh Co W VA s/o Abe & Ruth Meador to MARY A. HOGAN 27 yrs single b. Raleigh Co W VA d/o Peter & Nancy Hogan O: farmer; by Rufus Pack.

15. 2 Jany 1866 HENDERSON F. ELLISON 31 yrs single b. Mercer Co W VA s/o Jas. & Mary Ellison to SUSAN C. NEELY 24 yrs single b. Mercer Co W VA d/o Nelson H. & Clara Neely O: farmer; by Benjamin T Bird

16. 4 Jany 1866 OSCAR F. BLANKENSHIP 31 yrs single b. Giles Co VA now living same s/o S. & E. Blankenship to SARAH A. MEADOR 30 yrs wid. b. NC d/o H. & Fannie Skeens O: farmer; by John West.

17. 4 Jany 1866 HUGH H. BELCHER 23 yrs single b. Mercer Co W VA s/o C. & M.Mn Belcher to LIONA R. HAMBRICK 22 yrs single b. Montgomery Co VA d/o R. & M. Hambrick O: farmer; by Joseph Wright.

18. 9 Jany 1866 JAMES T. HOPKINS 29 yrs single b. Bedford Co VA s/o J.T. & M. Hopkins to MARY E. BROWN 29 yrs wid. b. Mercer Co W VA d/o Jas. & Elizth Rowland O: farmer; by William Holroyd.

19. 10 Jany 1866 THOMAS C. MEEKS 29 yrs single b. Henry Co VA s/o C. & Susan Meeks to CAROLINE MOYE 22 yrs single b. Guilford Co NC d/o Elijah Moye O: farmer; by G.T. Gray.

20. 24 Jany 1866 JOSEPH H. HAMBRICK 23 yrs single b. Montgomery Co VA s/o R. & M. Hambrick to ELLEN P. FAULKNER 17 yrs single b. Montgomery Co VA d/o H.M. & S. Faulkner O: farmer; by Joseph Wright.

21. 23 Jany 1866 JAMES BRAMMER 68 yrs wid. b. Patrick Co VA s/o John & Sarah Brammer to NANCY MASSIE 45 yrs single b. Patrick Co VA d/o John & Nancy Massie O: farmer; by Charles Walker.

22. 25 Jany 1866 ELIAS JOHNSTON 23 yrs single b. Ohio s/o Wm Johnston to THARISA GARRETSON 18 yrs single b. Mercer Co W VA d/o A. & B. Garretson O: farmer; by Andrew J. Thompson.

23. 1 Feby 1866 WILLIAM J. BURDITT 20 yrs single b. Giles Co VA s/o J.C. & A. Burditt to SARAH ARMONTROUT 16 yrs single b. Mercer Co W VA d/o J. & B. Armontrout O: farmer; by Andrew J. Thompson.

24. 1 Feby 1866 JAMES M. HOLDREN 24 yrs single b. Mercer Co W VA s/o Polly Holdren to FRANCES E. BLANKENSHIP 23 yrs single b. Mercer Co W VA d/o L. & M. Blankenship O: farmer; by Andrew J. Thompson.

25. 1 Feby 1866 ANDREW J. WHITTAKER 26 yrs single b. Giles Co VA s/o A. & M. Whittaker to CYLISTINA F. HOLSTINE 19 yrs single b. Mercer Co W VA d/o J.C. & E. Holstine O: farmer; by Samuel Scott.

26. 7 Feby 1866 GEORGE C. MILLER 40 yrs single b. Pittsylvanie Co VA s/o J. & E. Miller to ELIZABETH A. RIGHT 39 yrs wid. b. Pittsylvania Co VA d/o Wm & S. Goin O: farmer; by William C. Martin.

27. 15 Feby 1866 ISAAC F. McKINNEY 25 yrs single b. Mercer Co W VA s/o P. & S. McKinney to MARY A. CAPERTON 20 yrs single b. Mercer Co W VA d/o T.H. Caperton O: farmer; by William Holroyd.

28. 18 Feby 1866 ARCHIBALD B. LESTER 27 yrs single b. Logan Co W VA now living in Wyoming Co W VA s/o J.L. & Dicie Lester to MARTHA L. MORGAN 20 yrs single b. Logan Co W VA d/o A. & Chloe Morgan O: farmer; by Evan H. Brown

29. 22 Feby 1866 WILLIAM J. SWEENEY 28 yrs wid. b. Mercer Co W VA s/o Wm & N. Sweeney to ISABELLE F. PETERS 17 yrs single b. Mercer Co W VA d/o Chris & Mary Peters O: farmer; by Charles Walker.

30. 23 Feby 1866 JOHN ROLES 30 yrs single Monroe Co W VA s/o M. & Susan Roles to ELIZABETH LILLY 18 yrs single b. Mercer Co W VA s/o J.L. & E Lilly O: farmer; by John C. Hubbard.

31. 23 Feby 1866 BALLARD HOUCHINS 23 yrs single b. Mercer Co W VA s/o Wm & W. Houchins to NANCY J. MEADOR 17 yrs single b. Mercer Co W VA d/o J. & E. Meador O: farmer; by John C. Hubbard.

32. 1 March 1866 EDGAR MAXEY 28 yrs single b. Giles Co VA s/o J. & Sarah Maxey to ANN LILLY 24 yrs single b. Mercer Co W VA d/o J.L. & E. Lilly O: farmer; by John C. Hubbard.

33. 25 Feby 1866 LORAINE STINSON 19 yrs single b. Giles Co VA s/o C. & E. Stinson to RHODA J. SMITH 18 yrs single b. Roanoke Co VA s/o Abs. & A. Smith O: farmer; by William Holroyd.

34. 1 March 1866 WILLIAM M.H. BELCHER 23 yrs single b. Mercer Co W VA s/o Lewis & R. Belcher to JULIA A. BLANKENSHIP 16 yrs single b. Mercer Co W VA d/o Leantha Blankenship O: farmer; by William Holroyd.

35. 3 March 1866 WINTON B. TRACY 30 yrs single b. Tazewell Co VA now living in Bland Co VA s/o John & E. Tracy to SARAH M. MINCY 22 yrs single b. Giles Co VA now living in Bland Co VA d/o D. & P.P. Mincy O: farmer; by Andrew J. Thompson.

36. 3 March 1866 JOHN VEST 21 yrs single b. Franklin Co VA s/o M. & Sarah Vest to VIRGINIA P. HOUCHINS 18 yrs single b. Mercer Co W VA d/o C. & C. Houchins O: farmer; by John C. Hubbard.

37. 7 March 1866 ALLEN T. CLARK 24 yrs single b. Monroe Co W VA s/o R. & Mary Clark to ISABELL H. BROWN 21 yrs single b. Mercer Co W VA d/o Wm & L. Brown O: farmer; by George T. Gray.

38. 9 March 1866 CHARLES J. VEST 26 yrs single b. Franklin Co VA s/o A. & Rhoda Vest to MARY J. HARVEY 18 yrs single b. Mercer Co W VA d/o M.W. & N.N. Harvey O: farmer; by Charles Walker.

39. 10 March 1866 CHRISTOPHER SUTPHIN 70 yrs wid. b. Bedford Co VA s/o Wm Sutphin to REBECCA J. KINZER 18 yrs single b. Mercer Co W VA d/o Elizabeth Kinzer O: farmer; by Garland A. Austin.

40. 22 March 1866 FLEMING PACK 18 yrs single b. Monroe Co W VA s/o S. & Mary Spense to ROSANA MYERS 25 yrs wid. b. Giles Co VA d/o J. & Docie Carr O: farmer; by Evan H. Brown; REMARKS: colored.

41. 24 March 1866 ISAAC H. MEADOWS 26 yrs wid. b. Mercer Co W VA s/o J. & N. Meadows to ELIZA PACK 20 yrs wid. b. Mercer Co W VA d/o M. & M. Bassham O: farmer; by John C. Hubbard.

42. 25 March 1866 THOMPSON PETERS 60 yrs wid. b. Giles Co VA now living same s/o John & Sarah Peters to MAHILDA LESTER 46 yrs wid. b. Mercer Co W VA d/o C.A. & F. Walker O: farmer; Charles Walker.

43. 29 March 1866 SAMUEL HUNT 23 yrs single b. Stokes Co TN s/o Saml. & S.P. Hunt to MARTHA BELCHER 20 yrs single b. Mercer Co W VA d/o James & M. Belcher O: farmer; by Samuel Scott.

44. 3 April 1866 JOHN T. WHITTAKER 26 yrs single b. Pulaski Co VA s/o N. & E. Whittaker to MARIA A. THOMPSON 24 yrs single b. Tazewell Co VA d/o D. & A. Thompson O: farmer; by George W. Martin.

45. 4 April 1866 JOSHUA DAY 20 yrs 5 mos 14 dys single b. Giles Co VA s/o Lewis & E. Day to SARAH E. KEGLEY 16 yrs single b. Wythe Co VA d/o Daniel & M. Kegley O: merchant; by William Holroyd.

46. 5 April 1866 WILLIAM R. KINZER 21 yrs 10 mos 3 dys single b. Montgomery Co VA s/o Mary Kinzer to MARGARET E. FARMER 20 yrs 1 mo 20 dys single b. Carroll Co VA d/o J.L. & N. Farmer O: farmer; by Joseph Wright.

47. 10 April 1866 WILLIAM H. FLETCHER 23 yrs 6 mos 1 dy single b. Mercer Co W VA s/o I. & E. Fletcher to MARTHA J. EASTER 16 yrs 7 mos 26 dys single b. Campbell Co VA d/o Wm. W. & Susan Easter O: farmer; by Andrew J. Thompson.

48. 12 April 1866 JOSEPH H. McCLAUGHERTY 31 yrs single b. Giles Co VA s/o J. McClaugherty to EMALINE E. WRIGHT 20 yrs single b. Mercer Co W VA d/o Jas. & E. Wright O: merchant; by Joseph Wright.

Page 13

1. 23 May 1866 HARDIN K. MARTIN 24 yrs 10 mos 5 dys single b.Mercer Co W VA s/o D. & Esther Martin to ANGELINE C. KIRTNER 18 yrs single b.Pulaski Co VA d/o E. & Ellen E. Kirtner O: farmer; by William C. Martin.

2. 31 May 1866 JESSE I. BOWLING single b.Mercer Co W VA s/o John & S. Bowling to JANE KARNES 18 yrs single b. Monroe Co W VA d/o Henry & R. Karnes O: farmer; by Benjamin T. Bird.

3. 1 June 1866 SAMUEL HARRUP 23 yrs 11 mos 29 dys single b. Alleghany Co VA s/o Jas. & Mary Harrup to VIRGINIA C. SHANNEN 22 yrs single b. Campbell Co VA d/o John & M. Shannen O: moulder; by Andrew J. Thompson.

4. 5 June 1866 GEORGE HARMAN 34 yrs single b. Carroll Co VA s/o Pete & Polly Harman to WEALTHY TAYLOR 28 yrs single b. Wythe Co VA d/o John & Mary Taylor O: farmer; by Joseph Wright.

5. 6 June 1866 SAMUEL M. TRAIL 21 yrs 1 mo 5 dys single b. Franklin Co VA s/o Jacob & Locka Trail to SARAH M. McKINNEY 21 yrs 8 mos 21 dys single b.Mercer Co W VA d/o P&S McKinney O: farmer; by Samuel Scott.

6. 13 June 1866 GEORGE W. WHITE 20 yrs 11 mos 10 dys single b. Mercer Co W VA s/o Reuben & Mary White to REBECCA S. JONES 15 yrs single b. Wyoming Co W VA d/o John & Rebecca Jones O: farmer; by Andrew J. Thompson.

7. 13 June 1866 HENDERSON F. MARTIN 25 yrs 14 mos single b. Mercer Co W VA s/o Wm C. & Ann Martin to NANCY E. FANNING 20 yrs 9 mos 22 dys d/o Benj. & Nancy Fanning O: farmer; by William C. Martin.

8. 24 June 1866 DAVIDSON C. ROSS 31 yrs 11 mos single b. Alleghany Co VA s/o G. & Harriet E. Ross to EMALINE V. THOMILY 24 yrs 11 mos wid. b. Giles Co VA d/o Samuel & N. Scott O: farmer; by George W. Martin.

9. 24 June 1866 POWHATAN B. McKINNEY 52 yrs 2 mos 28 dys wid. b. Mercer Co W VA s/o Polly McKinney to ELIZABETH M. SCOTT single b. Mercer Co W VA d/o Saml. & Nancy Scott O: farmer; by George W. Martin.

10. 27 June 1866 AUGUSTUS C. GODFREY 19 yrs 4 mos 26 dys single b. Wyoming Co W VA now living same s/o Thos. & Margt. Godfrey to CHLOE BAILEY 17 yrs 6 dys single b. Mercer Co W VA d/o Jas. M. & Sarah Bailey O: farmer; by George T. Gray

11. 11 July 1866 DAVID COLLINS 33 yrs 1 mos 5 dys wid. b. Giles Co VA s/o Sol, & Jeme Collins to LEVINA PAULEY 21 yrs 8 mos 9 dys single b. Cabell Co VA now living in Bland Co VA d/o Jos & Sue Pauley O: farmer; by Evan H. Brown.

12. 19 July 1866 JOHN H. COLE 21 yrs 2 mos 23 dys single b. Mercer Co W VA s/o Aug. & Margt Cole to MARTHA J. COMER 20 yrs 3 mos single b. Mercer Co W VA d/o John & Jane Comer O: farmer; by Andrew J. Thompson.

13. 21 July 1866 JAMES A. CRUSENBURY 45 yrs wid. b. Bedford Co VA s/o Elizabeth Anderson to NANCY PETRY 43 yrs single b. Mercer Co W VA d/o James & Pollie Petry O: farmer; by Leroy Kenton

14. 9 Aug 1866 JOHN A. LILLY 28 yrs single b. Mercer Co W VA s/o Robt. & Mary Lilly to SARAH A. LILLY 16 yrs single b. Mercer Co W VA d/o A.L. & Sarah Lilly O: physician; by Rufus Pack.

15. 19 Aug 1866 WILLIAM A. HOON 24 yrs single b. Franklin Co VA s/o John & Celia Hoon to MARY BASSHAM 22 yrs single b. Mercer Co W VA d/o Dave & R. Bassham O: farmer; by Willis Tinsley.

16. 23 Aug 1866 JOHN W.N. TILLER 18 yrs single b. Mercer Co W VA s/o Hiram & Polly Tiller to SUSAN E. THORNTON 20 yrs single b. Pulaski Co VA d/o Mer. Thornton O: farmer; by Andrew J Thompson

17. 30 Aug 1866 JOHN WHITTEN 28 yrs single b. Mercer Co W VA s/o Lewis Whitten to AGNES UPTON 17 yrs single b. Mercer Co W VA d/o M. & Martha Upton O: farmer; by Rufus Pack.

18. 4 Sept 1866 JAMES H. HURST 23 yrs 10 mos 5 dys single b. Pulaski Co VA s/o Wm & Phebe Hurst to SARAH F. BAILEY 22 yrs 8 mos 1 dy single b. Mercer Co W VA d/o B.B. & Nancy Bailey O: farmer; by Joseph Wright.

19. 13 Sept 1866 BLUFORD W. BIRD 25 yrs 4 mos 15 dys single b. Franklin Co VA s/o Benj. T. & Irena Bird to LETHA A. HATCHER 23 yrs 1 mos 23 dys single b. Patrick Co VA d/o Ammon T. Hatcher O: farmer; by John C. Hubbard.

20. 19 Sept 1866 JOHN W. STOWERS 27 yrs 3 mos 29 dys single b. Tazewell Co VA now living same s/o A. & Elizth Stowers to ELIZABETH F. MURRELL 22 yrs 1 mo 20 dys d/o James & S. Murrell O: clerk; by J.T. Frazier.

21. 20 Sept 1866 JOHN COOPER 22 yrs single b. Mercer Co W VA s/o Austin & Jane Cooper to LOUISA F. KEGLEY 16 yrs single b. Wythe Co VA d/o Daniel & M. Kegley O: merchant; by George W. Martin.

22. 24 Sept 1866 GREEN C. BRAMMER 19 yrs 18 dys single b. Mercer Co W VA s/o J.H. & Mary Brammer to ROSABELLA FOLEY 16 yrs single b. Patrick Co VA d/o R.B. & P. Foley O: farmer; by John C. Hubbard.

23. 27 Sept 1866 ARMSTED A. HURST 19 yrs 7 mos 22 dys single b. Carroll Co VA s/o Wm. & Susan Hurst to SARAH C. HONAKER 19 yrs 11 mos 18 dys single b. Giles Co VA d/o J. & M. Honaker O: farmer; by Joseph Wright.

24. 2 Octr 1866 HUGH J. HUGHES 21 yrs 11 mos 10 dys single b. Giles Co VA s/o Wm Hughes to ALBERTINE PETRY 30 yrs 6 mos 23 dys wid. b. Mercer Co W VA d/o A.W.J. & R. Caperton O: merchant; by William C. Martin.

25. 4 Octr 1866 JOHN W. BELCHER 27 yrs 8 mos 29 dys single b. Mercer Co W VA now living Tazewell Co VA s/o Henry D. & Anna Belcher to REBECCA PAYNE 22 yrs 1 mo 25 dys single b. Mercer Co W VA d/o Wm. & Julia A. Payne O: farmer; by Evan H. Brown.

26. 4 Octr 1866 PLEASANT H. LILLY 24 yrs 4 mos 19 dys single b. Mercer Co W VA s/o Robt. & E. Lilly to MARY A. LILLY 23 yrs single b. Mercer Co W VA d/o W. & T.A. Lilly O: farmer; by Rufus Pack.

27. 19 Octr 1866 JOSIAH MEADOR 63 yrs wid. b. Mercer Co W VA s/o J. & Judith Meador to MARGARET LILLY 55 yrs wid. b. Mercer Co W VA d/o John & Nancy Walker O: farmer; by Russel G. French.

28. 23 Octr 1866 DAVID T. LILLY 19 yrs single b. Mercer Co W VA s/o W. & M. Lilly to ELIZABETH J. ELLISON 18 yrs single b. Mercer Co W VA d/o S.J. & E. Ellison O: farmer; by Benjamin T. Bird.

29. 24 Octr 1866 HENRY AKERS 23 yrs single b. Franklin Co VA s/o Hudson & Nancy Akers to ELIZABETH LILLY 17 yrs single b. Mercer Co W VA d/o Wash. & Mary Lilly O: farmer; by Benjamin T. Bird.

30. 24 Octr 1866 JOHN W. ARCHER 29 yrs 8 mos 27 dys single b. TN now living in Tazewell Co VA s/o S. & Sarah Archer to MARY A. CARR 17 yrs single b. Giles Co VA d/o Thos & Rachel Carr O: farmer; by Benjamin T. Bird.

31. 25 Octr 1866 ROBERT S. SHANNON wid. b. Campbell Co VA s/o John & M. Shannon to RHODA LITTLE single b. Mercer Co W VA d/o Thomas & Ellen Little O: farmer; by Andrew J. Thompson.

32. 5 Novr 1866 ASA H. JEWELL 30 yrs single b. Montgomery Co VA s/o John & C. Jewell to LOUISA PAYNE 20 yrs single b. Mercer Co W VA d/o Wm. & Julia A. Payne O: farmer; by Joseph Wright.

33. 15 Novr 1866 JAMES M. HODGE 31 yrs 4 mos 20 dys single b. Wythe Co VA now living in Tazewell Co VA s/o Anderson & E. Hodge to NANCY PAYNE 28 yrs single b. Mercer Co W VA d/o Wm & Julia A. Payne O: farmer; by Joseph Wright.

34. 27 Novr 1866 THOMPSON P. BAILEY 40 yrs wid. b. Mercer Co W VA s/o Geo C. & F. Bailey to ELIZABETH MINOR 36 yrs 8 mos 20 dys wid. b. Mercer Co W VA d/o Saml. & Polly Bailey O: farmer; by Joseph Wright.

35. 27 Novr 1866 SAMUEL HOLDREN 37 yrs wid. b. Mercer Co W VA s/o Sarah Holdren to DARCUS BLANKENSHIP 33 yrs b. Mercer Co W VA d/o L & M Blankenship O: farmer; by Andrew J. Thompson.

36. 6 Decr 1866 JOEL A. BUTLER 27 yrs 9 mos 20 dys single b. Monroe Co W VA s/o P & Louisa Butler to SARAH E. CLARK 28 yrs 9 mos 14 dys single b. Monroe Co W VA d/o Rufus & Mary Clark O: farmer; by William C. Martin.

37. 12 Decr 1866 STEPHEN T. VERMILLION 22 yrs 6 mos 23 dys single b. Pulaski Co VA s/o J A & E Vermillion to RHODA A. BIRD single b. 18 yrs 8 mos 14 dys d/o b t & Vina Bird O: farmer; by John C. Hubbard.

38. 13 Decr 1866 JOHN S.H. BIRD 23 yrs 8 mos 29 dys single b. Franklin Co VA s/o B T & Nena Bird to ELIZABETH S. VERMILLION 17 yrs 5 mos 1 dy single b. Mercer Co W VA d/o J R & E Vermillion O: farmer; by John C. Hubbard.

39. 18 Decr 1866 ISAAC COOK 34 yrs 10 mos 2 dys single b. Henry Co Ind s/o David & Nancy Cook to EMILY HOUCHINS 28 yrs 2 mos 1 dy single b. Mercer Co W VA d/o Jas. & Sarah Houchins O: farmer; by John C. Hubbard.

40. 19 Decr 1866 ELIJAH CLARK 21 yrs 3 mos 20 dys single b. Franklin Co W VA s/o Henry & Ruth Clark to ELIZA. E. HARVEY 23 yrs 7 mos single b. Mercer Co W VA d/o Isaac N & E Harvey O: farmer; by Benjamin T. Bird.

41. 20 Decr 1866 BIRREL W. WALKER 21 yrs 5 mos 5 dys single b. Mercer Co W VA s/o C & Nancy D. Walker to VICTORIA McCOMAS 19 yrs 3 mos 9 dys single b. Mercer Co W VA d/o Eli & J.A. McComas O: farmer; by Joseph Wright.

42. 31 Decr 1866 JAMES R. WHITE 23 yrs single b. Mercer Co W VA s/o Reuben & Mary White to SARAH J. OWENSBY 20 yrs single b. Tazewell Co VA now living same d/o M & C Owensby O: farmer; by Andrew J. Thompson.

43. 31 Decr 1866 MATTHEW MEADOR 25 yrs 3 mos 2 dys single b. Mercer Co W VA s/o T & Malinda Meador to RHODA A. WEST 28 yrs 2 mos single b. Mercer Co W VA O: farmer; by George W. Martin.

44. 23 Novr 1866 Tazewell Co VA LEWIS FORDE* 22 yrs single b. Raleigh Co W VA now living same s/o Lutitia Forde* to MARY HILL 21 yrs single b. Tazewell Co VA d/o Alexr. & Rosena Hill O: farmer; by Evan H. Brown; REMARKS: Colored.(*Note: name spelled both ways.)

45. 7 Decr 1866 ALLEN LINDSAY 27 yrs 9 mos 7 dys single b. Hanover Co VA s/o Joshua & Nancy Lindsay to MARGARET A. GAINES 17 yrs 5 mos 14 dys single b. Pulaski Co VA d/o Charlotte Gaines O: farmer; by James Calfee; REMARKS: colored.

46. 28 Decr 1866 BALLARD P. PETRY 21 yrs 3 mos 16 dys wid. b. Mercer Co W VA s/o Wm & Polly Petry to ARDELIA PETRY 23 yrs 3 mos 14 dys single b. Mercer Co W VA d/o Nancy Anderson O: farmer; by Leroy Kenton.

47. 10 Jany 1867 JOHN FARLEY 27 yrs single b. Mercer Co W VA s/o Gideon & Dinah Farley to RACHEL FARLEY 24 yrs single b. Mercer Co W VA d/o Isaac & Elizth Farley O: farmer; by John C. Hubbard.

48. 10 Jany 1867 JAMES R. LILLY 23 yrs 4 mos 23 dys single b. Mercer Co W VA s/o Jonth & Margt Lilly to MARTHA TURPIN 21 yrs 8 mos single b. Mercer Co W VA d/o Henry & Rebecca Turpin; by Benjamin T. Bird.

Page 14

1. 15 Jany 1867 JAMES G. CLARK 23 yrs 9 mos 6 dys single b. Monroe Co W VA s/o Rufus & Mary Clark to MARINDA BUTLER 18 yrs 2 mos 18 dys single b. Monroe Co W VA d/o Powell & Veroca Butler O: farmer; by William C. Martin.

2. 22 Jany 1867 SAMUEL SHANNON 22 yrs single b. Campbell Co VA s/o Wm & Sarah Shannon to MARY A ARMONTROUT 24 yrs wid. b. Giles Co VA d/o Noah & Nancy Blankenship O: farmer; by John West.

3. 24 Jany 1867 JOSEPH T. HETHERINGTON 23 yrs 4 mos 5 dys single b. Giles Co VA s/o Jos J & Rhoda Hetherington to JULIETTE H. CARR 20 yrs 20 dys single b. Giles Co VA s/o John & Sarah Carr O: farmer; by Evan H. Brown.

4. 6 Feby 1867 WILLIAM M. ARMONTROUT 23 yrs single b. Alleghany Co VA s/o Jas & Bar. Armontrout to MARY F. SHANNON 22 yrs single b. Campbell Co VA d/o Wm & Sarah Shannon O: farmer; by John West.

5. 6 Feby 1867 HENRY HONAKER 46 yrs 10 mos 22 dys wid. b. Montgomery Co VA now living Bland Co W VA s/o Abram & Sarah Honaker to SARAH HAGER 35 yrs 6 mos 8 dys wid. b. Tazewell Co VA d/o Wm & Mary Stump O: blacksmith; by Evan H. Brown.

6. 7 Feby 1867 JACOB T. SINGLETON 22 yrs 7 mos 29 dys single b. Lafayette Miss. s/o Adam & Winnie Singleton to ELIZABETH F. MARTIN 21 yrs 17 dys single b. Mercer Co W VA d/o Adam & Rebecca Martin O: shoe & boot maker; by William C. Martin.

7. 9 Feby 1867 ISAAC E. FRENCH 28 yrs single b. Mercer Co W VA s/o Austin & Lee French to CHRISTERINA S. ROBINETT 21 yrs single b. Tazewell Co VA d/o Hiram & Dica Robinett O: farmer; by Samuel Scott.

8. 12 Feby 1867 PURRIS L. DAVIS 20 yrs 11 mos 26 dys single b. Mercer Co W VA s/o John W. & Tempa Davis to KEZIAH C. BOWLING 26 yrs 3 mos 16 dys single b. Patrick Co VA d/o Jas. & Ruth M. Bowling O: farmer; by Benjamin T. Bird.

9. 14 Feby 1867 MARSHALL M. FEAZEL 17 yrs 7 mos 20 dys single b. Henry Co VA s/o Jno M & Mary E. Feazel to RHODA A. BAKER 19 yrs 6 mos 21 dys single b. Mercer Co W VA d/o John & Polly Baker O: farmer by Harrison Robinson

10. 14 Feby 1867 JOHN R HATCHER 18 yrs 8 mos single b. Mercer Co W VA now living in Wyoming Co VA s/o Silas & Anadia Hatcher to NANCY E. FERGUSON 15 yrs 4 mos 21 dys single b. Mercer Co W VA d/o Elijah & Aurelia Ferguson O: farmer; by Benjamin T. Bird.

11. 14 Feby 1867 WILLIAM HARGO 22 yrs 9 mos 16 dys single b. Mercer Co W VA s/o Rebecca Hargo to MARY GORE 25 yrs 6 mos 20 dys single b. Mercer Co W VA d/o Matilda Gore O: farmer; by J.W. Bennett; REMARKS: colored.

12. 24 Feby 1867 WILLIAM F. MILLS 19 yrs single b. Mercer Co W VA s/o Wm & Emmarilla Mills to SARAH F. SHREWSBURY 19 yrs single b. Mercer Co W VA d/o Wm & Vashti Shrewsbury O: farmer; by Russell G. French.

13. 26 Feby 1867 SAMUEL T. CRUM 19 yrs 1 mo 24 dys single b. Franklin Co VA s/o Abr & Julia Crum to ARAMINTA TAYLOR 17 yrs 13 dys single b. Mercer Co W VA d/o Sam & Mary Taylor O: farmer; by Joseph Wright.

14. 27 Feby 1867 WILLIAM J. RUSSBURG 25 yrs 5 mos 24 dys single b. Monroe Co W VA s/o S. Woolford & M E Pennington to NANCY J. ROUR 21 yrs 9 mos 20 dys single b.Patrick Co VA d/o Isom H & Jane Rour O: farmer; by William C. Martin.

15. 28 Feby 1867 DOCTOR DAVIS 27 yrs single b. Bushingham W VA s/o Wm & Jane Davis to ARAMINTA DAVIDSON 23 yrs wid. b. Giles Co VA d/o Docia Thompson O: blacksmith; by George W. Martin; REMARKS: colored.

16. 28 Feby 1867 WILSON FARLEY 45 yrs 11 mos 14 dys wid. b. Mercer Co W VA s/o Andrew & Anna Farley to NANCY ROLES 27 yrs 9 mos 22 dys single b. Monroe Co W VA d/o Mordica & Susan Roles O: farmer; by John C. Hubbard.

17. 6 March 1867 JAMES H. NEAL single b. Monroe Co W VA s/o H.M. & Sarah A. Neal to CYNTHA BAILEY single b. Mercer Co W VA d/o Eli & Charlotte Bailey O: farmer; by Joseph Wright.(**NOTE** This entry was illegible-name & birthplace of hus. & wife was based on 1860 Mercer Co TN Census.)

18. 12 March 1867 SILAS J. BIRD single b. Franklin Co VA s/o Thos. A. & emily J. Bird to MARY J. CARPENTER single b. Mercer Co W VA d/o Saml & M. Carpenter O: farmer; by Andrew J. Thompson.

19. 14 March 1867 WINFIELD S. HAWLEY 23 yrs 8 mos 27 dys single b. Montgomery Co VA s/o John & Charlotte Hawley to MARY J. HAMBRICK 27 yrs 2 mos 11 dys wid. b. Monroe Co VA d/o Wash & Mary A. Broyles O: farmer; by Evan H. Brown.

20. 18 March 1867 DAVID P. BAILEY 18 yrs 4 mos 2 dys single b. Mercer Co W VA s/o Jameson & Polly Bailey to MARY J. THOMPSON 15 yrs 2 mos 25 dys single b. Mercer Co W VA d/o Gordon & Louisa Thompson O: farmer; by John W. Bailey.

21. 21 March 1867 SAMUEL G. LILLY 22 yrs wid. b.Mercer Co W VA s/o Jon & Margt Lilly to JUDITH TURPIN 17 yrs single b. Mercer Co W VA d/o Henry & Nancy Turpin; by Joseph Lilly.

22. 21 March 1867 AUGUSTUS McDOWELL 22 yrs 11 mos 26 dys single b. Tazewell Co VA s/o Terry Steel to AGNES SULLENDER 16 yrs 8 mos 19 dys single b. Mercer Co W VA d/o Christenia Sullender O: farmer; by James Calfee; REMARKS: colored.

23. 28 March 1867 HARVEY G. TILLER 17 yrs 3 mos 11 dys single b. Monroe Co W VA s/o A & Priscilla Tiller to PRISCILLA B. McKINNEY 18 yrs 8 mos single b. Mercer Co W VA d/o D.A. & Rhoda McKinney O: farmer; by James O Cassaday.

24. 29 March 1867 ROWLAND F. STOWERS 21 yrs 1 mos 8 dys single b. Mercer Co W VA now living same s/o Jno L & Dina Stowers to MARY E. YOUNG 21 yrs 2 mos 14 dys single b. Mercer Co W VA d/o Isaac S. & Sarah Young O: farmer; by William Holroyd.

25. 28 March 1867 CHARLES A. HAMBRICK 21 yrs 1 dy single b. Tazewell Co VA s/o R & Margt Hambrick to SARAH L. HOUCHER 17 yrs 6 mos 1 dy single b. Bland Co VA d/o Wm C. & S.A. Houcher O: farmer; by Joseph Wright.

26. 28 March 1867 LEWIS GARNER 42 yrs 10 mos 8 dys single b. Wythe Co VA s/o Joanah Ross to CHRISTENIA SULLENDER 43 yrs 1 mo 8 dys single b. Botetourt Co VA s/o (No first name) Sullender O: farmer; by James Calfee; REMARKS: colored.

27. 4 Apr 1867 NAPOLEON F. HARLESS 27 yrs 8 mos 8 dys single b. Montgomery Co VA s/o John & Elizth Harless to EMMAZELLA SNEAD 31 yrs 21 dys wid. b. Mercer Co W VA d/o C & Nancy D. Walker O: farmer; by John W. Bailey.

28. 4 Apr 1867 EDWARD M. ONEY 30 yrs 8 mos 11 dys single b. Giles Co VA s/o Wm & Nancy Oney to VIRGINIA F. BROWN 22 yrs 1 mo 24 dys single b. Mercer Co W VA d/o Geo P & Sarah Brown O: farmer; by James O. Cassaday.

29. 16 Apr 1867 HENDERSON F. DILLION 21 yrs 26 dys single b. Mercer Co W VA s/o Jesse & Cynthia Dillion to MEREAHA F. WALKER 29 yrs 6 mos 23 dys single b. Mercer Co W VA d/o C & Nancy D. Walker O: farmer; by John W. Bailey.

30. 17 Apr 1867 GORDON L. WILBURN 25 yrs 5 mon 21 dys single b. Giles Co VA now living same s/o Lewis & M.B. Wilburn to JULIA HOUCHINS 20 yrs 5 mon 9 dys single b. Mercer Co W VA d/o Jas. & Sarah Houchins O: farmer; by Tyre T. Salyer.

31. 25 Apr 1867 ANDREW J. FRENCH 20 yrs single b. Mercer Co W VA s/o Wm M & Rhoda French to NANCY M MILLER 20 yrs single b. Mercer Co W VA d/o F. & Elphicy Miller O: farmer; by Andrew J. Thompson.

32. 25 Apr 1867 GASTON C. BAILEY 24 yrs 8 mon 16 dys single b. Mercer Co W VA s/o Jas M. & Julia T. Bailey to MOLLIE M. JARRELL 20 yrs single b. Mercer Co W VA d/o Geo. W. & Reb. Jarrell O: farmer; by James Calfee.

33. 28 Apr 1867 ALBERT B. NASH 35 yrs 5 mon 23 dys single b. Campbell Co VA s/o Abner & Rebecca Nash to FRANCES J. WOODALL 41 yrs 1 mo 11 dys single b. Campbell Co VA d/o S & Sarah Woodall O: farmer; by William Holroyd.

34. 7 May 1867 ADAM HALSTEAD 66 yrs 11 mon 20 dys wid. b. Monroe Co W VA s/o John & Elizth Halstead to MARY M. SHACK 36 yrs wid. b. Greenbrier Co W VA d/o Leo & Elizth Osborne O: farmer; by Joseph R. Lilly.

35. 7 May 1867 ARTHUR HERNDON 19 yrs 9 mos single b. Campbell Co VA s/o A & S.E.B. Herndon to LOUISA KARNES 22 yrs 1 mo 7 dys single b. Mercer Co W VA d/o M. & Nancy Karnes O: farmer; by John W. Bailey.

36. 9 May 1867 JAMES N. WILEY 24 yrs 1 mo 18 dys single b. Giles Co VA now living Monroe Co W VA s/o Squire & Ellen Wiley to LOUISA J. DARE 16 yrs 6 mos 10 dys single b. Mercer Co W VA d/o Chas. & Elizth Dare O: farmer; by James O. Cassaday.

37. 30 May 1867 JAMES GRIM 29 yrs 11 mos 8 dys single b. Botetourt Co VA s/o Wm & Cath Grim to JANE A. WILSON 26 yrs 9 mon 21 dys single b. Pulaski Co VA d/o Erastus & S. Wilson O: carpenter; by Evan H. Brown.

38. 22 May 1867 NELSON H. McCLAUGHERTY 24 yrs 9 mon 28 dys single b. Mercer Co W VA s/o Jno. & P. McClaugherty to MOLLIE C. COSE 21 yrs single b. Sullivan Co TN d/o Seimul & Sarah Cose O: clerk; by George W. Martin.

39. 30 May 1867 RUSSEL S. HICKS 28 yrs 5 mon 26 dys single b. Tazewell Co VA now living in Bland Co VA s/o J.T. & Rebecca Hicks to MATILDA F. WHITTAKER 21 yrs 5 mon 10 dys single b. Mercer Co W VA d/o S.J. & Elizth Whittaker O: farmer; by William Holroyd.

40. 5 June 1867 LEWIS C. HOLSTINE 18 yrs 6 mon 14 dys single b. Mercer Co W VA s/o Jos. C. & Elizth Holstine to SARAH L. CALDWELL single b. Craig Co VA d/o Hugh & F. Caldwell O: farmer; by William Holroyd.

41. 9 Jany 1867 JOHN A. CALFEE 31 yrs 1 mo 4 dys wid. b. Pulaski Co VA s/o Wm & Evaline Calfee to JULIA A. DAVIDSON 20 yrs 8 mon 16 dys single b. Mercer Co W VA d/o Jos. & Jane Davidson O: farmer; by James Calfee.

42. 13 June 1867 HENRY C. THORNTON 23 yrs single b. Pulaski Co VA s/o M. & Louisa Thornton to AMANDA M. PRIVETT 17 yrs 11 mon 23 dys single b. Wythe Co VA d/o Isaac & Sarah Privett O: farmer; by James Calfee.

43. 13 June 1867 MIDDLETON H. BELCHER 29 yrs 4 mon 14 dys single b. Mercer Co W VA s/o Jas. C. & Mahala Belcher to HESTER M. UNDERWOOD 33 yrs 3 mos 23 dys single b. Franklin Co VA d/o Wm. & Elizth Underwood O: farmer; by James Calfee.

44. 27 June 1867 SAMUEL WIMMER 21 yrs 29 dys single b. Mercer Co W VA now living in Bland Co VA s/o Saml. & Massie Wimmer to RHODA J. MILLS 23 yrs 8 mos single b. Mercer Co W VA d/o Wm. & Emmarilla Mills O: farmer; by Russel G. French.

45. 11 July 1867 JAMES R. FARLEY 20 yrs 8 mon 28 dys single b. Mercer Co W VA s/o Jas. & Martha Farley to MARY J. MARTIN 21 yrs single b. Mercer Co W VA d/o H. & Eliza Martin O: farmer; by John C. Hubbard.

46. 16 July 1867 ANDREW J. HOLDREN 21 yrs 11 mon 8 dys single b. Mercer Co W VA s/o Henry & M. Holdren to LOUISA CASSADAY wid. b. Patrick Co VA d/o J.W. & Laupee Davis O: farmer; by Andrew J. Thompson.

47. 18 July 1867 ALLEN H. BOWLING 20 yrs 8 mos 13 dys single b. Mercer Co W VA s/o Wm. & Elizth Bowling to ELIZABETH S. MARTIN 19 yrs 3 mon 11 dys single b. Mercer Co W VA d/o A. & Eliza Martin O: farmer; by William Holroyd.

48. 18 July 1867 WILLIAM C. BAILEY 27 yrs 3 mon 16 dys single b. Mercer Co W VA s/o Henry & Polly Bailey to MARY E.M.B. SHUTT 16 yrs 9 mon single b. Mercer Co W VA d/o David & Elizth Shutt O: farmer; by John W. Bailey.

Page 15

1. 25 July 1867 ANDREW P. FARLEY 21 yrs 2 mos 4 dys single b. Mercer Co W VA s/o Arch & J. Farley to EMALINE HUBBARD 16 yrs 3 mon 16 dys single b. Patrick Co VA d/o J.C. & Anna Hubbard O: farmer; by Benjamin T. Bird.

2. 31 July 1867 FRANCIS M. CAMPBELL 24 yrs 11 mon 20 dys single b. Mercer Co W VA now living Monroe Co W VA s/o Caroline Campbell to RACHEL J. FARLEY 18 yrs 2 mon 12 dys single b. Mercer Co W VA d/o James & M. Farley O: farmer; by John C. Hubbard.

3. 6 Augt 1867 JAMES A. UNDERWOOD 25 yrs 8 mon 26 dys single b. Franklin Co VA s/o Wm. & Elizth Underwood to MARY A. HARRY 19 yrs 4 mon 29 dys single b. Mercer Co W VA d/o R. & Ruth Harry O: farmer; by James O. Cassaday.

4. 14 Augt 1867 ELIAS HALE 65 yrs 1 mo 26 dys wid. b. Giles Co VA s/o Ed & Martha Hale to ELIZA F. PARKER 38 yrs single b. Franklin Co VA d/o A. & Mary Parker O: farmer; by James Calfee.

5. 27 Augt 1867 JOHN PERDUE 65 single b. Giles Co VA now living same s/o Rias & Polly Perdue to CLARISSA MEADOR 30 yrs single b. Mercer Co W VA d/o Jere & J. Meador O: farmer; by Andrew J. Thompson.

6. 21 Augt 1867 GEORGE W. PAULEY 26 yrs 1 mon 17 dys single b. Mercer Co W VA s/o Nancy Pauley to SARAY A. PENNINGTON 22 yrs 2 mon 4 dys single b. Monroe Co W VA d/o Nancy Pennington O: farmer; by William Holroyd.

7. 22 Augt 1867 JOHN WILEY 26 yrs single b. Monroe Co W VA s/o Abs. & Elizth Wiley to MAHALA Y. COOK 27 yrs single b. Mercer Co W VA d/o Cor. & Anna Cook O: farmer; by Benjamin T. Bird.

8. 20 Augt 1867 WILLIAM A. SHELTON 21 yrs 8 mon 20 dys single b. Patrick Co VA s/o Fred & Esther Shelton to MARY J. WELLS 23 yrs 19 dys single b. Stokes Co NC d/o Danl. & Elizth Wells O: farmer; by James O. Cassaday.

9. 27 Augt 1867 DAVID P. ST. CLAIR single b. Bedford Co VA s/o Isaac & Jane St. Clair to ALICE J. JONES single b. Mercer Co W VA d/o Julia A. Jones O: farmer; by Andrew J. Thompson.

10. 29 Augt 1867 CORNELIUS HARRIS 26 yrs 5 mon 21 dys single b. Patrick Co VA s/o Jas & Nancy Harris to SARAH M. WAUHOP 21 yrs 8 mon 25 dys single b. Floyd Co VA d/o John K. & E. Wauhop O: farmer; by Benjamin T. Bird.

11. 18 Sept 1867 HEUDLEY C. FARLEY 23 yrs 1 dy single b. Mercer Co W VA s/o Arch & Jem. Farley to MARTHA J. JUSTICE 16 yrs single b. Mercer Co W VA d/o J.H. & Margt. Justice O: farmer; by John C. Hubbard.

12. 28 Sept 1867 BAZEWELL SUTPHIN 38 yrs single b. Carroll Co VA s/o Chris & M. Sutphin to ANN HELM 35 yrs single b. Carroll Co VA d/o Adam & Rachel Helm O: farmer; by William C. Martin.

13. 3 Octr 1867 JOHN GRIFFITH 25 yrs 1 mo 21 dys single b. Franklin Co VA now living Raleigh Co W VA s/o John T. & Juda Griffith to EMALINE BRAMMER 23 yrs 5 mon single b. Patrick Co VA d/o Jon & Maria Brammer O: farmer; by Matthew Ellison.

14. 3 Octr 1867 ANDREW W. MANN 20 yrs 7 mos 19 dys single b. Mercer Co W VA s/o Hez & Elizth Mann to NANCY C.

LILLY 23 yrs 9 mos 10 dys single b. Mercer Co W VA d/o Jos. & Elizth Lilly O: farmer; by Rufus Pack.

15. 7 Octr 1867 RICHARD FOLEY 20 yrs 6 mos 11 dys single b. Patrick Co VA s/o Alf. & Nancy A. Foley to MARY D. WILKES 19 yrs 8 mos 4 dys single b. Franklin Co VA d/o Tempy Thomas O: farmer; by William Holroyd.

16. 10 Octr 1867 OBEDIAH BELCHER 21 yrs 5 mos 18 dys single b. Mercer Co W VA s/o Chris & Mary M. Belcher to MARGARET A. DILLION 17 yrs 1 mo single b. Mercer Co W VA d/o Jesse & Cynth. Dillion O: farmer; by Joseph Wright.

17. 17 Octr 1867 JOHN W. LILLY 24 yrs 1 mo single b. Mercer Co W VA s/o Turner & Rutha Lilly to JOSEPHINE KIDWELL 16 yrs 7 mos single b. Mercer Co W VA d/o Mich & Litta. Kidwell O: farmer; by William C. Martin.

18. 22 Octr 1867 GEORGE W. WEST 17 yrs single b. Floyd Co VA s/o John & Marinda West to MARTHA PETRY 13 yrs 3 mos single b. Mercer Co W VA d/o John & Sarina Petry O: farmer; by John C. Hubbard.

19. 30 Octr 1867 ANDERSON PACK 20 yrs single b. Mercer Co W VA s/o James A. & Mary Pack to AMA PARK 26 yrs single b. Mercer Co W VA d/o Rob & Rhoda Park O: farmer; by William C. Martin.

20. 31 Octr 1867 ROMULUS SWADER 20 yrs 5 mos 16 dys single b. Mercer Co W VA s/o Wm & Julia Swader to RHODA SWADER 17 yrs 11 mos 29 dys single b. Mercer Co W VA d/o David & Chloe Swader O: farmer; by Joseph Wright.

21. 31 Octr 1867 PRICE K.M. BIRD 26 yrs single b. Franklin Co VA now living in Bland Co VA s/o Wm M. & Cath. Bird to SARAH F. NOBLE 27 yrs single b. Monroe Co VA d/o Wm & Nancy Noble O: farmer; by Benjamin T. Bird.

22. 16 Novr 1867 HIRAM G. DAVIS 31 yrs 11 mos 4 dys wid. b. Mercer Co W VA s/o Jesse & Margt Davis to CLEMANTINE C. BAILEY 22 yrs 1 mo 4 dys single b. Mercer Co W VA d/o Eli, & Char, Bailey O: shoe & boot maker; by Benjamin T. Bird.

23. 25 Novr 1867 SAMUEL MILLS 52 yrs wid. b. Mercer Co W VA now living Vermillion Co IL s/o Saml & Rachel Mills to MARTHA J. BROWN 31 yrs wid. b. Monroe Co W VA d/o Mad. & Nancy Karnes O: farmer; by Russel G. French.

24. 21 Novr 1867 DANIEL W. BELCHER 20 yrs 8 mos 21 dys single b. Mercer Co W VA s/o A.A. & Letta A. Belcher to REBECCA J. BELCHER 20 yrs 6 mos 1 dy single b. Mercer Co W VA d/o Isom & Rebecca Belcher O: farmer; by James Calfee.

25. 21 Novr 1867 JAMES CARR 17 yrs 3 mos 9 dys single b. Bland Co VA s/o Wm & Sallie Carr to SARAH J. BOWLING 24 yrs 5 mos 9 dys single b. Patrick Co VA d/o John & Sallie Bowling O: farmer; by William C. Martin.

26. 24 Novr 1867 JAMES H. JONES 21 yrs single b. Mercer Co W VA s/o Helen Jones to MARTHA M. BLANKENSHIP 22 yrs single b. Mercer Co W VA d/o Leantha Blankenship O: farmer; by Andrew J. Thompson.

27. 27 Novr 1867 HENRY CLARK 24 yrs 8 mos 4 dys single b. Patrick C. VA s/o Henry & Ruth Clark to VIRGINIA MEADOR 19 yrs 5 mos 26 dys single b. Mercer Co W VA d/o John & Ann Meador O: farmer; by Russel G. French.

28. 28 Novr 1867 GEORGE W. HEDRICK 24 yrs single b. Greenbrier Co W VA now living Wyoming Co W VA s/o Phil, & Nan, Hedrick to ELIZABETH A. MEADOR 20 yrs single b. Mercer Co W VA d/o G.W. & Emily Meador O: farmer; by Rufus Pack.

29. 28 Novr 1867 TURPIN M. FINK 21 yrs 11 mos 24 dys single b. Wyoming Co W VA now living same s/o Wm A. & Rachel Fink to EMILY C. MEADOR 21 yrs 11 mos 22 dys single b. Mercer Co W VA d/o G.W. & Emily Meador O: farmer; by Rufus Pack.

30. 1 Decr 1867 ALBERT WILEY 31 yrs 9 mos 5 dys wid. b. Mercer Co W VA s/o Gor. & Tomsy Wiley to LOUISA PETRY 20 yrs 11 mos 5 dys single b. Mercer Co W VA d/o J & Elizth Petry O: farmer; by William C. Martin.

31. 3 Decr 1867 DAVID H. COOK 22 yrs 11 mos 2 dys single b. Mercer Co W VA s/o Jas & Nancy Cook to MARY S. ELLISON 17 yrs single b. Mercer co W VA d/o Jas & Mary Ellison O: farmer; by Benjamin T. Bird.

32. 7 Decr 1867 WILLIAM MEDLIN 24 yrs single b. Mercer Co W VA s/o Araminta Medlin to NANCY SHANKLIN 24 yrs single b. Monroe Co W VA d/o Polly Shanklin O: farmer; by William C. Martin: REMARKS: colored.

33. 7 Decr 1867 ISAAC N. FITZWATER 21 yrs single b. Nicholas Co W VA s/o Jno & Sarah Fitzwater to RHODA THOMAS 23 yrs single b. Mercer Co W VA d/o Jesse & Rachel Thomas O: farmer; by Andrew J. Thompson.

34. 19 Decr 1867 ERSKINE COX 18 yrs 6 mos 28 dys single b. Raleigh Co W VA s/o Danl R. & S.A. Cox to HARRIET COOK 33 yrs wid. b. Raleigh Co W VA d/o Ben, & N. Couchins O: farmer; by John C. Hubbard.

35. 19 Decr 1867 LEVI V. STOVALL 21 yrs single b. Mercer Co W VA s/o A.G. & N.K. Stovall to ANGELINE KARNES 21 yrs single b. Monroe Co W VA d/o Henry & R. Karnes O: farmer; by Benjamin T. Bird.

36. 24 Decr 1867 JAMES P. WILLIAMS 20 yrs 10 mos 20 dys single b. Mercer Co W VA s/o Anl & Mary A. Williams to NANCY A. ROLLYSON 22 yrs 10 dys single b. Mercer Co W VA d/o Jos & Elizth Rollyson O: farmer; by George W. Crook.

37. 19 Decr 1867 MADISON W. JOHNSTON 23 yrs 11 mos 20 dys single b. Giles Co VA s/o Adam & S. Johnston to MARY C. HETHERINGTON 21 yrs 1 mo 20 dys single b. Giles Co VA d/o John & R. Hetherington O: farmer; by J.W. Bennett.

38. 12 Decr 1867 ROBERT HARMAN 21 yrs single b. Tazewell Co VA s/o Sallie Harman to MATILDA N. CALLENDER 18 yrs single b. Mercer Co W VA d/o Susan Callender O: farmer; by Evan H. Brown; REMARKS: colored.

39. 1 Jan 1868 URIAH A. BAILEY 21 yrs 9 mos 23 dys single b. Mercer Co VA s/o Johnathan S. & H. Bailey to SARAH B. FRENCH 23 yrs 11 mos 7 dys single b. Giles Co VA d/o And & R. French O: farmer; by J.W. Bennett.

40. 2 Jan 1868 ERASMUS BROYLES 22 yrs 5 mos 2 dys single b. Mercer Co VA s/o Washington & M. Broyles to JOSEPINE BAILEY 20 yrs 5 mos 12 dys single b. Mercer Co W VA d/o James L. & M. Bailey O: farmer; by James Calfee.

41. 7 Jan 1868 ROBERT L. SHELTON 23 yrs single b. Patrick Co VA s/o ? & H. Shelton to NANCY J. FRENCH 19 yrs single b. Mercer Co W VA d/o C.C. & R. French O: farmer; by J.O. Cassaday.

42. 16 Jan 1868 DAVID W. FRENCH 21 yrs 1 mos 9 dys single b. Giles Co VA s/o Andrew & K. French to POLLY W. BAILEY 16 yrs 3 mos 11 dys single b. Mercer Co W VA d/o Jameson & Polly Bailey O: farmer; by J.W. Bennett.

43. 23 Jan 1868 THOMAS G. TABOR 23 yrs 11 mos 23 dys single b. Tazewell Co VA now living same s/o J.H. & Nell Tabor to ANN E. PARKER 19 yrs 4 mos 19 dys single b. Patrick Co VA d/o Anderson & M. Parker O: farmer; by Evan H. Brown.

44. 23 Jan 1868 JOHN E. SNODGRASS 21 yrs 10 mos single b. Montgr Co VA s/o E.N. & S.A. Snodgrass to ARAMINTA CALDWELL 16 yrs 1 mo single b. Craig Co VA d/o Lucinda E. Duncan O: farmer; by William C. Martin.

45. 11 Feby 1868 DAVID McCLANAHAN 65 yrs wid. b. Botetourt Co VA s/o Wm & A. McClanahan to MARGARET J. WAGNER 23 yrs single b. Henry Co VA d/o D. & M. Wagner O: blacksmith; by Samuel Scott.

46. 13 Feby 1868 RUFUS MELVIN 24 yrs 5 mos 28 dys single b. Mercer Co W VA s/o Hez. & E. Melvin to NANCY CARR 19 yrs single b. Giles Co VA d/o Wm & S. Carr O: farmer; by John West MS.

47. 18 Feby 1868 JAMES A. THOMAS 29 yrs 2 mos 28 dys wid. b. Mercer Co W VA s/o Jemison Thomas to MARY J. CARR 19 yrs 11 mos single b. Giles Co VA d/o Wm & S. Carr O: farmer; by John West MS.

48. 12 March 1868 GEO W. LILLY 25 yrs 1 mo 1 dy single b. Mercer Co W VA s/o Levi Lilly & Reb Shrewbury to MARTHA J. WHORLEY 18 yrs single b. Franklin Co VA d/o G.W. & P. Whorley O: farmer; by J.C. Hubbard.

Page 16

1. 19 March 1868 ANDREW L. COOPER 24 yrs single b. Reighley(sic) Co W VA now living in Wyoming Co W VA s/o John & Nancy Cooper to NANCY C. SCOTT 18 yrs 2 mos b. Mercer Co W VA d/o Samuel & Nancy Scott O: farmer; by John Hoverton, Priest.

2. 3 April 1868 JOHN A. PHILLIPS 21 yrs 1 mos 23 dys single b. Mercer Co W VA s/o James & Clare Phillips to SEREPTA P. CHRISTIAN 19 yrs 10 mos 27 dys single b. Mercer Co W VA d/o John H. & Priscilla Christian O: farmer; by William C. Martin.

3. 5 April 1868 BARNEY MERRICK 24 yrs 6 mos 19 dys single b. Giles Co VA s/o Dodson & Mary Merrick to MARY C. BOLING 24 yrs 6 mos 19 dys wid. b. Lee Co VA O: blacksmith; by J.W. Bennett.

4. 14 April 1868 JACKSON ANDREWS 30 yrs wid. b. Bland Co VA s/o Russell & Julia Andrews to NANCY FISHER 30 yrs wid. b. Mercer Co W VA d/o Micajah & M. Belcher O: farmer; by James O. Casnaday.

5. 23 April 1868 PLEASANT C. LILLY 17 yrs 4 mos 22 dys single b. Mercer Co W VA s/o Hiram & P.R. Lilly to SARAH F. MEADOR 15 yrs 6 mos 7 dys single b. Mercer Co W VA d/o Joseph & Nancy C. Meador O: farmer; by R.G. French.

6. 3 May 1868 J. WEAVER MELVIN 29 yrs 1 mo 10 dys single b. Mercer Co W VA s/o Hez & Eliz. Melvin to REBECCA GATTON 35 yrs wid. b. Giles Co VA d/o Jeremiah Thomas O: farmer; by John West MS.

7. 19 May 1868 HENRY A. HARVEY 18 yrs 11 mos 16 dys single b. Monroe Co VA now living same s/o James L. & Eliza Harvey to LEAH M. HARVEY 21 yrs single b. Mercer Co W VA d/o Isaac N. & Elizabeth Harvey O: farmer by J.C Hubbard

8. 26 May 1868 MEDDLETON HUNT 21 yrs single b. Mercer Co W VA s/o James & M.A. Hunt to NANCY JANE HORNESBY 14 yrs single b. Mercer Co W VA d/o Johnathan & C. Hornesby O: farmer; by William C. Martin.

9. 27 May 1868 JAS. B. HONAKER 18 yrs single b. Bland Co VA now living same s/o Petter & M.A. Honaker to SARAH J. BAILEY 18 yrs single b. Mercer Co W VA d/o Jas M. & J.J. Bailey O: farmer; by J.W. Bennett.

10. 5 July 1868 ROBERT C. HOYE 19 yrs single b. Mercer Co W VA s/o Wm & M.J. Hoye to MARY M. WAUHOP 18 yrs single b. Grayson Co VA d/o John Wauhop O: farmer; by Harrison Robinson.

11. 13 July 1868 WILLIAM R. WHITE 21 yrs 8 dys single b. Mercer Co W VA s/o Andrew & Mary White to POLLY J. MARTIN 21 yrs 8 mos 22 dys single b. Mercer Co W VA d/o Geo W. & Nancy Martin O: farmer; by William Holrhoyd.

12. 17 July 1868 LEE DAVIS 20 yrs 6 mos single b. Mercer Co W VA s/o Joshua & P. Davis to MARY E. BURDETT 16 yrs 8 mos single b. Giles Co VA d/o Joseph Burdett O: farmer; by John West MS.

13. 2 Aug 1868 ISAAC GRIFFITH 21 yrs 11 mos single b. Franklin Co VA s/o John & J. Griffith to LUCINDA A. LILLY 16 yrs 2 mos single b. Mercer Co W VA d/o Joseph & E. Lilly O: farmer; by B.T. Bird.

14. 6 Aug 1868 ISAAC R. JOHNSTON 23 yrs 6 mos single b. Giles Co VA s/o A & N Johnston to SARAH ANN KARR 25 yrs single b. Giles Co VA d/o Robert & S Karr O: farmer; by Evan H. Brown.

15. 14 Aug 1868 CORNELIUS W. COOK 19 yrs single b. Mercer Co W VA s/o Corns & Ann Cook to RHODA A. WILEY 21 yrs single b. Mercer Co W VA d/o Absalom & E Wiley O: farmer; by William A. Martin.

16. 18 Aug 1868 JOHN F. MARTIN 27 yrs single b. Mercer Co W VA s/o Adam & R. Martin to SARAH J. CALOWAY* 25 yrs single b. Mercer Co W VA d/o G. & S. Calloway* O: farmer; by William Holrhoyd. (*Note: name spelled both ways.)

17. 20 Aug 1868 RUSSELL F. KARNES 25 yrs single b. Monroe Co W VA s/o Henry & Elizabeth Karnes to JULIA E THOMPSON 25 yrs single b. Tazewell Co VA d/o D & A Thompson O: farmer; by R.G. French.

18. 2 Sept 1868 LEVI L. HEARN 20 yrs single b. Mercer Co W VA s/o L.G. & A. Hearn to RHODA L. TILLER 21 yrs single b. Mercer Co W VA d/o K & J Tiller O: farmer; by John West MS.

19. 3 July 1868 ANDREW MEADOR 40 yrs single b. Mercer Co W VA s/o E. & E. Meador to ELIZABETH FRENCH 34 yrs single b. Mercer Co W VA d/o Adam & Sarah Meador O: farmer; by John West MS.

20. 10 Sept 1868 CYRUS B. FANNING 20 yrs 10 mos 5 dys single b. Wyoming Co W VA s/o G.B. & Nancy Fanning to NANCY H. BURDETT 17 yrs single b. Mercer Co W VA d/o Sy. & Ca. Burdett O: farmer; by John West MS.

21. 16 Sept 1868 JAMES C. HARMAN 20 yrs single b. Tazewell Co VA s/o Jas. P. & M. Harman to MARY J. BAILEY 21 yrs single b. Mercer Co W VA d/o E & S Bailey O: farmer; by James Calfee.

22. 16 Sept 1868 JAMES H. HARVY 19 yrs 7 mos single b. Mercer Co W VA s/o J.N. & E. Harvy to ADALINE HARVY 25 yrs single b. Mercer Co W VA d/o Jacob W. & C. Harvy O: farmer; by W.C. Martin.

23. 5 Oct 1868 JOHN W. BIRD 20 yrs 2 mos 24 dys single b. Franklin Co VA s/o Thos A & E.J. Bird to LAURESY PERDUE 19 yrs 11 mos 4 dys wid. b. Mercer co W VA d/o Jordan & S. Meador O: farmer; by B.T. Bird.

24. 7 Oct 1868 GEORGE P. BROWN 56 yrs wid. b. Giles Co VA s/o J. & R. Brown to MARY A. McPHERSON 27 yrs single b. Giles Co VA d/o G. & E. McPherson O: farmer; by Wm Holrhoyd.

25. 9 Oct 1868 THOMAS WHITE 65 yrs single b. Giles Co VA s/o John & Susan White to REBECCA S. BLANKENSHIP 30 yrs single b. Giles Co VA d/o L. & P. Blankenship O: farmer; by William Holrhoyd.

26. 15 Oct 1868 RUFUS MEADOWS 21 yrs single b. Mercer Co W VA now living Wyoming Co W VA s/o J. & N. Meadows to SARAH JANE CARMACK 17 yrs single b. Mercer Co W VA d/o R. & N. Carmack O: farmer; by Rufus Pack.

27. 15 Oct 1868 JOHN J. VEST 24 yrs single b. Franklin Co W VA s/o John M. & A Vest to NICY A. VEST 21 yrs single b. Mercer Co W VA d/o Fleming & Jane Vest O: farmer; by B.T. Bird.

28. 18 Oct 1868 ALEXANDER WOOD 64 yrs wid. b. Franklin Co VA s/o R. & R. Wood to SARAH VEST 54 yrs wid. b. Franklin Co VA d/o Isom & S. Cochran O: farmer; by M. Elison.

29. 19 Oct 1868 JAMES M. WALKER 26 yrs single b. Mercer Co W VA now living Wyoming Co W VA s/o Charles & R Walker to MADALINE BRAMHER 27 yrs single b. Mercer Co W VA d/o J & M Brammer O: farmer; by B.T. Bird.

30. 20 Oct 1868 JAMES H. HITE 33 yrs single b. Campbell Co W VA s/o Samuel & Mary Hite to REBECCA J. BUTLER 27 yrs single b. Monroe Co W VA d/o Powell & Nancy J. Butler O: carpenter; by W.C. Martin.

31. 28 Oct 1868 THOMAS M. COOK 52 yrs wid. b. Logan Co W VA now living in Wyoming Co W VA s/o Wm & Catherine Cook to NANCY P. LUSK 31 yrs wid. b. Mercer Co W VA s/o Jas. McComas O: farmer; by John S. Mullins.

32. 5 Nov 1868 JAS P. LILLEY 24 yrs 7 mos single b. Mercer C W VA s/o David & Mary V. Lilley to VALLERIA LILLEY 22 yrs single b. Mercer Co W VA d/o Andrew & Marinda Lilley O: farmer.

33. 11 Nov 1868 GEORGE W. PERDUE 20 yrs 5 mos single b. Franklin Co VA s/o Silas & Nancy Jane Perdue to FRANCES POWEL 22 yrs 10 mos single b. Franklin Co VA d/o Wm A & Julia Powel O: farmer; by Andrew Workman.

34. 11 Nov 1868 SAMUEL D. LILLEY 21 yrs 7 mos single b. Mercer Co W VA s/o Robert & Mary Lilley to EMILY COMMACK

16 yrs single b. Monroe Co W VA d/o Robert & Nancy Commack O: farmer; by Benj. T. Bird.

35. 19 Nov 1868 MARCUS P. ANDERSON 28 yrs single b. Monroe Co W VA s/o Jabez & J.A. Anderson to ELIZABETH F. HOGAN 21 yrs single b. Mercer Co W VA d/o Peter & Nancy Hogan O: farmer; by Rufus Pack.

36. 1 Decr 1868 NAPOLION COLEMAN 22 yrs single b. Henry Co VA s/o Jaba & Serena Taylor to AGNESS AYMES 25 yrs wid. b. Madison Co AL d/o [no name given] O: farmer; by R.G. French.

37. 1 Decr 1868 JACKSON CALFEE 38 yrs single b. Wyatt Co VA s/o James & Hannah Calfee to MARGARET J. BROWN 27 yrs wid. b. Tazewell Co VA d/o David & Angeline Thompson O: farmer; by Wm Holroyd.

38. 1 Decr 1868 ISSAC D. MARTIN 26 yrs single b. Campbell Co VA s/o Samuel W. & Sally Martin to MARY C. DRIGGINS 18 yrs single b. NC d/o Thomas & Nancy Driggins O: farmer; by John Brag.

39. 3 Decr 1868 CARDWELL M.D. SPRADLIN 28 yrs single b. Franklin Co VA s/o John & L. Spradlin to SAREPTA HOUCHINS 19 yrs single b. Mercer Co W VA d/o James & S. Houchins O: farmer; by J.C. Hubbard.

40. 8 Decr 1868 BENJAMIN M. TINSLEY 25 yrs single b. Rochbridge Co VA s/o Willis & Eliz. Tinsley to DORIAS C. STRALEY 31 yrs single b. Giles Co VA d/o John & Eliz. Straley O: farmer; by H.C. Tinsley.

41. 17 Decr 1868 JOHN HAZELWOOD 23 yrs single b. Patrick Co VA s/o Joshua & Charity Hazlewood to MARY J. ST. CLAIR 22 yrs single b. Mercer Co W VA d/o William & Eliz. St. Clair O: farmer; by A.J. Thompson.

42. 24 Decr 1868 WILBER F. BECKETT 23 yrs single b. Monroe Co W VA now living same s/o Wm C. & Margt. Beckett to VIRGINIA P. DEWEES* 17 yrs single b. Floyd Co W VA d/o Andrew & B. Deewees* O: farmer; by A.J. Thompson. (*Note: name spelled both ways.)

43. 24 Decr 1868 JOHN S. SHREWBURY 22 yrs single b. Mercer Co W VA s/o H & J Shrewsbury to VICTORIA GODFREY 22 yrs single b. Mercer Co W VA d/o James & N. Godfrey O: farmer; by Andrew L. French.

44. 24 Decr 1868 ABNER C. CALAHAN 48 yrs wid. b. Campbell Co VA s/o Stephen E. & P. Calahan to NANCY P. PERKINS 15 yrs single b. Franklin Co W VA d/o James & E Perkins O: mill wright; by H. Robinson.

45. 24 Decr 1868 JAMES HOLDREN 25 yrs single b. Mercer Co W VA s/o Henry & Mahala Holdren to MARY B. PAULY 24 yrs single b. Giles Co VA d/o Harry & B A Pauley O: farmer; by A.J.F. Thompson.

46. 29 Decr 1868 ROBERT M. BLANKENSHIP 23 yrs single b. Mercer Co W VA s/o L & M Blankenship to SYNTHA J. WHITE 19 yrs single b. Mercer Co W VA d/o Louisa Massey O: farmer; by A.J.Thompson.

47. 30 Decr 1868 DAVID H. AKERS 21 yrs single b. Patrick Co VA s/o N.B. & S.J. Akers to JOSEPHINE ELLISON* 17 yrs single b. Mercer Co W VA d/o F.T. & H. Elison* O: farmer; by B.T. Bird. (*Note: name spelled both ways.)

48. 31 Decr 1868 JOHN T. LILLEY 19 yrs single b. Mercer Co W VA s/o John & Nancy Lilley to ELIZA J. FARLEY 19 yrs single b. Mercer Co W VA d/o John & Lucy Farley O: farmer; by B.T. Bird.

Page 17

1. 31 Decr 1868 JOSIAH LILLEY 22 yrs single b. Mercer Co W VA s/o Josiah & Jane Lilley to EMILIA A. WORLEY 22 yrs single b. Franklin Co VA d/o George & Mary Worley O: farmer; by B.T. Bird.

2. 6 Jan 1869 EVAN NEELY 21 yrs single b. Mercer co W VA s/o Nelson & Clara Neely to SARAH ELLISON 30 yrs single b. Mercer Co W VA d/o James & Mary Ellison O: farmer; by J.C. Hubbard.

3. 13 Jan 1869 JOHN ANGLE 19 yrs single b. Franklin Co VA s/o Danl. & Elizabeth Angle to ELIZABETH DILLION 21 yrs single b. Smyth Co VA d/o Mastin & Margaret W. Dillion O: farmer; by Andrew L. French, Minst.

4. 13 Jan 1869 LEROY THOMPSON 19 yrs single b. Monroe Co W VA s/o Arch & Elizabeth Thompson to REBECCA J. DILLION 23 yrs single b. Smyth Co VA d/o Mastin & Margaret W. Dillion O: farmer; by Andrew L. French, Minst.

5. 20 Jan 1869 TIMOTHY N. HESLIP 37 yrs wid. b. Botetourt Co VA s/o Joseph & Rebecca Heslip to LOUISA CATH DWIGGINS 24 yrs single b. NC d/o Thomas & Mary Dwiggins O: farmer; by John Bragg.

6. 20 Jan 1869 LEVI N. MARTIN 21 yrs single b. Mercer Co W VA s/o David & Hester Martin to LOUISE F. KIRTNER 16 yrs single b. Pulaski Co VA d/o Crockett & Ellen F. Kirtner O: farmer; by William C. Martin.

7. 20 Jan 1869 JAMES W. BALL 19 yrs single b. Mercer Co W VA s/o Johnathan & Temperance Hopkins to NANCY B. PETRY 21 yrs single b. Mercer Co W VA d/o Wm & Polly Petry O: farmer; by William C. Martin.

8. 24 Jan 1869 ROBERT LILLEY 22 yrs single b. Mercer Co W VA s/o William & Francis Lilley to AMANDA L. ACRES 19 yrs single b. Patrick Co VA d/o Nathaniel & Sarah Acres O: farmer; by B.T. Bird.

9. 26 Jan 1869 JACOB McPHERSON 23 yrs single b. Craig Co VA s/o George & Elizabeth McPherson to ELIZABETH E. SHREWSBURY 21 yrs single b. Mercer Co W VA d/o Henry & Jane Shrewsbury O: farmer; by William C. Martin.

10. 4 Feby 1869 ALEXANDER M. WOOD 21 yrs single b. Patrick Co VA s/o German & Nancy Wood to ELIZABETH MASSEY 14 yrs single b. Mercer Co W VA d/o Thomas J. & Mary J. Massey O: farmer; by B.T. Bird.

11. 10 Feby 1869 HARVY R. BAILEY 32 yrs single b. Mercer Co W VA s/o Hy & Mary Bailey to LOUISA C. DAY 23 yrs wid. b. Mercer Co W VA s/o Saml. & Mary Bailey O: farmer; by Andrew L. French.

12. 15 Feby 1869 FRANCIS M. CARR 38 yrs wid. b. Kanawha Co VA s/o Thomas & Dinah Carr to PATSY OILER 42 yrs wid. b. Patrick Co VA d/o William & Eliz. Miller O: farmer; by William C. Martin.

13. 15 Feby 1869 SYLVESTER STEWART 21 yrs single b. Mercer Co W VA s/o Wm & Catherine Stewart to MARINDA A. HALE 22 yrs single b. Henry Co VA d/o Julia Hale O: farmer; by J.O. Casaday.

14. 5 Mar 1869 S.N. FRENCH 22 yrs single b. Giles Co VA now living in Bland Co VA s/o M. Blair & Maria French to SUSAN S. SCOTT 32 yrs wid. b. Mercer Co W VA d/o Benj & Nancy Fanning O: teacher; by William Holroyd.

15. 11 Mar 1869 ROBERT FLETCHER 21 yrs single b. Mercer Co W VA s/o Hiram A. & Rhoda Fletcher to MARY FLETCHER 18 yrs single b. Mercer Co W VA d/o James H & Jane Fletcher O: farmer; by A.J. Thompson.

16. 15 Mar 1869 WARD C. KEATON 23 yrs single b. Mercer Co W VA s/o Harmon & Jane Keaton to MARTHA J. COOK 16 yrs 9 mos 10 days single b. Mercer Co W VA d/o James & Nancy Cook O: farmer; by Benjamin T. Bird.

17. 13 Mar 1869 WILSON A. LILLEY 21 yrs single b. Mercer Co W VA s/o Wilson & Tabitha Lilley to ELLEN FARLEY 21 yrs single b. Mercer Co W VA d/o Hiram & Mary A Farley O:farmer; by Rufus Pack.

18. 16 May 1869 FRENCH BAILEY 21 yrs single b. Mercer Co W VA s/o Reuben & Jane Bailey to GRIZELLE W. CHATTING 16 yrs single b. Botetourt Co VA d/o Wm & Mary Chatting O:farmer by Theodore Smith.

19. 24 Mar 1869 CHARLES R. YOUNG 25 yrs single b. Craig Co VA s/o John & Mary Young to LOUISA UPTON 23 yrs wid. b. Jackson Co W VA d/o Clifford* O: farmer; by N.C. Beckley. (*Note: only name given.)

20. 1 Feb 1869 ROBERT M. THOMAS 21 yrs single b. Mercer Co W VA s/o Jessee & Rachael Thomas to MARTHA FITSWATER 19 yrs single b. Nicholas Co W VA d/o John & Sarah Fitswater O: farmer; by John Garretson.

21. 11 March 1869 HENRY HASKIN 22 yrs single b. Pulaski Co VA s/o Elen Haskin to PHEBE DICKINSON 20 yrs single b. Giles Co VA d/o Ansel & Lucinda Dickinson O: farmer; by J.O. Cassady(sic) (REMARKS: colored).

22. 22 March 1869 CHARLES W. BAILEY 41 yrs wid. b. Mercer Co W VA s/o Samuel & Poly Bailey to SARAH FURGUSON 38 yrs wid. b. Mercer Co W VA d/o Nancy Karnes O: farmer; by Andrew L. French.

23. 1 April 1869 JOHN LILLEY 22 yrs single b. Mercer Co W VA s/o Wilson & T. Lilley to MARY E. NELLY 17 yrs single b. Mercer Co W VA d/o Levi & Rebeca Nelly O: farmer; by Rufus Pack.

24. 1 April 1869 JOHN M. DEEDS 26 yrs single b. Alegany(sic) Co VA s/o John & Patsey Deeds to AGNES D. DONAHOE 22 yrs single b. Craig Co VA d/o Thos. H. & Jane Donahoe O: farmer; by G.W. Crook.

25. 7 April 1869 ARON ANGLE 21 yrs single b. Franklin Co VA s/o Don & Eliz Angle to SARAH LAMBERT 21 yrs single b. McDowell Co W VA d/o Kenly & Shar. Lambert O: farmer; by Andrew L. French.

26. 9 April 1869 WM. A. SHORTER 25 yrs single b. Franklin Co VA s/o W.A. & M.C. Shorter to NANCY J. KIDWELL 21 yrs single b. Mercer Co W VA d/o Green & Sarah Kidwell O: farmer; by Wm C. Martin.

27. 9 April 1869 PRESTON PACK 22 yrs single b. Mercer Co W VA s/o John & E.B. Pack to AMANDA J. COOPER 21 yrs single b. Wythe Co VA d/o Alexander Cooper O:farmer; by Rufus Pack.

28. 9 April 1869 JAMES A. MARTIN 25 yrs single b. Mercer Co W VA s/o Hudson & Eliza Martin to MARTHA J. KEATON 29 yrs wid. b. Mercer Co W VA d/o C & Annie Cook O: farmer; by Wm C. Martin.

29. 15 April 1869 JAMES H. JOHNSTON 48 yrs single b. Halifax Co VA s/o Elvira Johnston to AMANDA PACK 38 yrs single b. Monroe Co W VA d/o Thomas & Celia Pack O: farmer; by Rufus Pack.

30. 18 April 1869 JOSEPH HUBBARD 20 yrs 4 mos 7 dys single b. Patrick Co VA s/o J.C. & Anna Hubbard to CELIA HOUCHINS 21 yrs single b. Mercer Co W VA d/o Wm & Wilmon Houchins O: farmer; by Granville Houchins.

31. 18 April 1869 WAIN THOMAS 25 yrs single b. Mercer Co W VA s/o Jessee & R. Thomas to SARAH ANN JOHNSTON 24 yr single b. Mercer Co W VA d/o William Johnston O: farmer; by John Garretson.

32. 22 April 1869 AUGUSTUS A. YOUNG 18 yrs single b. Craig Co VA s/o John & M.A. Young to AMANDA E. EVERLY 18 yrs single b. Raleigh Co VA d/o Ira & Martha Everly O: farmer; by F.H.K. King.

33. 22 April 1869 WILLIAM R. FARLEY 22 yrs single b. Mercer Co W VA s/o Isaac F. Farley to MARY JANE VEST 15 yrs single b. Franklin Co VA d/o John & Delphia Vest O: farmer; by George W. Crook.

34. 26 April 1869 WILLIAM FRENCH 18 yrs single b. Giles Co VA s/o A. & R. French to LOUISA V. WHITE 16 yrs single b. Mercer Co W VA d/o Albert J. & S. White O: farmer; by Andrew L. French.

35. 29 April 1869 LEWIS DUNAGAN 25 yrs single b. Surry Co NC s/o L. & N. Dunagan to NANCY J. MOSLEY 30 yrs wid. b. Campbell Co VA d/o W. & E. Wright O: farmer; by W. Tinsley.

36. 29 April 1869 VALEIUS* W COOPER 21 yrs 17 mos(sic) subgke b. Wyoming Co VA s/o F. & N. Cooper to LOUISA M. WORLEY 17 yrs single b. Franklin Co VA d/o G. & M. Worley O:farmer; by B.T. Bird. (*Note: handwriting difficult to read)

37. 6 May 1869 BALLARD SNYDER 21 yrs single b. Mercer Co W VA s/o J. & S. Snyder to LOUISA WILLIAMS 22 yrs single b. Giles Co VA d/o Job & J. Williams O: farmer; by George W. Crook.

38. 11 May 1869 SAMUEL G. HUBBARD 22 yrs single b. Patrick Co VA s/o S. & E. Hubbard to M.J. SHREWSBURY 25 yrs single b. Mercer Co W VA d/o L.E. Shrewsbury O: farmer; by Harrison Robinson

39. * * 1869 JOHN H. HONAKER 21 yrs single b. Bland Co VA s/o Wm C. & S. Honaker to SARAH A. BELCHER 21 yrs single b. Mercer Co W VA d/o Ch. & M. Belcher O: farmer; by Andrew L. French. (*Note:* unable to read, too dark)

40. 19 May 1869 JOHN W. MEADOR 29 yrs single b. Mercer Co W VA s/o A. & Sarah Meador to ARDELIA DAVIS 19 yrs single b. Giles Co VA d/o Linsey & J. Davis O: farmer; by Theodore Smith.

41. 27 May 1869 GEORGE WHITE 19 yrs single b. Mercer Co W VA s/o Benjk & Eliz White to ALICE L. BAILEY 15 yrs single b. Mercer Co W VA d/o J.M. & M. Bailey O: farmer; by T.W. Bennett.

42.*2 June 1869 JOHN F. LILLEY 19 yrs single b. Mercer Co W VA s/o A & M.A. Lilley to VIRGINIA V. PACK 19 yrs single b. Mercer Co W VA d/o J.A. & M. Bailey O: farmer; by Rufus Pack. (*Note:* hard to read, copy very dark)

43.*3 June 1869 PETER MINOR 22 yrs single b. Mercer Co W VA s/o Thompson & E Minor to NANCY OSBORN 15 yrs single b. Mercer Co W VA d/o John & Sarah Osborn O: farmer; by John H. Honaker.

44. 17 June 1869 JOHN CARBOUGH 31 yrs single b. Pulaski Co VA s/o Geo & Elizabeth Carbough to ALMEDA KARNES 17 yrs single b. Mercer Co W VA d/o Madison & Nancy Karnes O: farmer; by G.W.K. Green.

45. 22 June 1869 GASTON BLANKENSHIP 21 yrs single b. Mercer Co W VA to H.S. LITTLE 20 yrs single b. Mercer Co W VA d/o L.D. & Rue Little O: farmer; by John Garretson.

46. 14 July 1869 WILLIAM A. PACK 25 yrs single b. Monroe Co W VA s/o Samuel & Eliz. Pack to SARAH E. LILLEY 18 yrs single b. Mercer Co W VA d/o David & Mary Lilley O: farmer; by Rufus Pack.

47. 9 July 1869 JESSEE THOMAS, JR. 22 yrs single b. Mercer Co W VA s/o Jessee & Rachel Thomas to ELIZABETH BLANKENSHIP 26 yrs single b. Mercer Co W VA d/o Leantha Blankenship O: farmer; by John Garretson.

48. 11 July 1869 RUFUS B. McCOMAS 19 yrs single b. Monroe Co W VA s/o Arch & L.F. McComas to O.A. HONAKER 20 yrs single b. Giles Co VA d/o Jas. & Manerva Honaker O: farmer; by John H. Honaker.

49. 9 Aug 1869 KAIBURN BUCKLAND 57 yrs wid. b. Monroe Co W VA s/o Stephen & Malinda Buckland to NANCY GANOE 32 yrs single b. Raleigh Co W VA d/o Wm & Dicia Ganoe O: farmer; by Rufus Pack.

50. 20 Aug 1869 SYLVESTER PETRY 21 yrs single b. Mercer Co W VA s/o Nancy Petry to MARY E. WILLIAMS 24 yrs single b. Mercer Co W VA d/o Jno L. & Ann Williams O: farmer; by William C. Martin.

51. 17 Aug 1869 JAMES L. REYNOLDS 51 yrs wid. b. Craig Co VA now living Tazewell Co VA s/o Wm E. & Elizabeth Reynolds to ADALINE M. MEADOR 28 wid. b. Mercer Co W VA s/o Jos. & Eliz Holstine O: farmer; by J.O. Cassady.

52. 26 Aug 1869 TURNER T. LILLEY 19 yrs single b. Mercer Co W VA s/o Turner & Urto(sic) Lilley to VIRGINIA SHREWSBURY 30 yrs single b. Mercer Co W VA d/o John & Susan Shrewsbury O: farmer; by R.G. French.

53. 14 Sept 1869 SAMUEL PACK 23 yrs single b. Mercer Co W VA s/o John & Elizabeth B. Pack to RHODA A.E. COOPER 19 yrs single b. Wythe Co VA d/o Ax & Ann Cooper O: farmer; by N.C. Beckley.

54. 14 Sept 1869 MATHEW CALOWAY 23 yrs single b. Mercer Co W VA s/o Granville & Susan Caloway to CHORA ALICE CALLOWAY* 19 yrs single d/o J.W. Callahan O: farmer; by Wm Holroyd. (*Note: this may be an error in comparison to parent's name)

55. 9 Sept 1869 BARTLEY PANE 21 yrs single b. Tazewell Co VA s/o Wm & Juliet Pane to LUCINDA C BELCHER 26 yrs single b. Mercer Co W VA d/o Asa & Clare Belcher O:farmer; by John H Honaker

56. 15 Sept 1869 JAMES H. DANIEL 30 yrs single b. Roanoke Co VA now living Raleigh Co W VA s/o Jane Daniel to MATILDA A. PACK 21 yrs single b. Mercer Co W VA d/o Tandy & Vga* Pack O: farmer; by Rufus Pack; REMARKS: colored. (*Note: handwriting difficult to read.)

57. 16 Sept 1869 GEORGE W.N. WALKER 23 yrs single b. Mercer Co W VA s/o Charles & Rachel Walker to MINERVA A. FARLEY 16 yrs single b. Raleigh Co W VA d/o Adam & Marg Farley O: farmer; by William C. Dobins.

58. 16 Sept 1869 JOSEPH A. LILLEY 20 yrs single b. Raleigh Co W VA now living same s/o Elijah & Sarah Lilley to JULIA A. LILLEY 16 yrs single b. Mercer Co W VA d/o Wash. & Mary Lilley O: farmer; by William C. Dobins.

59. 13 Sept 1869 WILLIAM R. HICKS 21 yrs single b. Wythe Co VA s/o Lorenzo D. & Lucinda Hicks to HANNAH L. FAULKNER 16 yrs single b. Montgomery Co VA d/o Hugh M. & Susannah Faulkner O: farmer; by Andrew L. French.

60. 22 Sept 1869 JOHN A. LILLEY 25 yrs wid. b. Mercer Co W VA s/o A.L. & Sarah A Lilley to VIRGINIA A. HOGAN 17 yrs single b. Mercer Co W VA d/o Peter & Nancy Hogan O: farmer; by N.C. Beckley.

61. 30 Sept 1869 RUFUS R. BELCHER 30 yrs single b. Mercer Co W VA s/o Isom & Rebecca Belcher to MELVINA BELCHER 21 yrs single b. Mercer Co W VA d/o Asa & Clara Belcher O: farmer; by John H. Honaker.

62. 3 Octr 1869 ST. CLAIR ABBOTT 64 yrs wid. b. Mercer Co W VA s/o Joseph & Minerva Abbott to FRANCIS P. GARRETSON 53 yrs wid. b. Mercer Co W VA d/o John & Mary Ann Garretson O: farmer; by William C. Martin.

63. 13 Octr 1869 GEORGE WITTEN 27 yrs single b. Tazewell Co VA now living same s/o Edmond & Patience Witten to EMALINE WITTEN 22 yrs single b. Tazewell Co W VA d/o Jacob & Nina Witten O: farmer; by John H. Honaker; REMARKS: colored.

64. 5 Octr 1869 ELEANA FERGUSON 22 yrs single b. Mercer Co W VA s/o Daniel W. & Lironia Ferguson to ELIZABETH McBRIDE 28 yrs single Bedford Co VA d/o Charles & Sarah McBride O: farmer; by William C. Dobins.

65. 21 Octr 1869 HENRY JONES 26 yrs single b. Greenbrier Co W VA s/o Thomas & Rachel Jones to ANNY OLIVER 15 yrs single Giles Co VA d/o Lizzie Oliver O: farmer; by William J. Oliver; REMARKS: colored.

66. 13 Octr 1869 MILLARD F. ELLISON 19 yrs single b. Monroe Co VA s/o Isaac J & Eliza Ellison to MARTHA J. FRENCH 18 yrs single b. Giles Co VA d/o Russel G. & Martha A. French O: farmer; by Harrison Robinson.

67. 21 Octr 1869 ALBERT G.P. FARLEY 28 yrs single b. Mercer Co W VA s/o Arch'd & Jemima Farley to MARY B. DONAHOO 24 yrs single b. Craig Co VA d/o Thos H. & June Donahoo O: farmer; by F.H.J. King.

68. 19 Novr 1869 ALLEN L. NEELY 24 yrs single b. Mercer Co W VA s/o Nelson H. & Clara Neely to LUVERNA FARLEY 21 yrs single b. Mercer Co W VA d/o Andrew & Judah Farley O: farmer; by J.C. Hubbard.

69. 18 Novr 1869 SAML. G.W. CALDWELL 29 yrs single b. Giles Co W VA s/o Hugh & Francis Caldwell to SARAH A. GRIM 26 yrs single b. Roanoke Co VA d/o Wm & Cahine(sic) Grim O: farmer; by Evan H Brown.

70. 23 June 1869 WM A. HARRIS 40 yrs single b. Patrick Co VA s/o Robt & Elizabeth Harris to MARY MARGT. CALFEE 20 yrs single b. Pulaski Co VA d/o John & Virginia Calfee O: farmer; by James Calfee.

71. 28 Octr 1869 WM C. FARLEY 20 yrs single b. Mercer Co W VA s/o Hiram & Mary Farley to ANN E. COOPER 17 yrs single b. Mercer Co W VA d/o Jonah & Narcissus Cooper O: farmer; by Charles Walker.

72. 24 Nov 1869 GILBERT MORGAN 20 yrs single b. Greenbrier Co VA now living same s/o Baswell & Urwean Morgan to SARAH FARLEY 22 yrs single b. Raleigh Co W VA d/o Isaac & Elizabeth Farley O: farmer; by N.C. Beckley.

73. 24 Nov 1869 JOHN MORGAN 30 yrs single b. Greenbrier Co VA now living same s/o Baswell & Urwean Morgan to SUSAN FARLEY 25 yrs single b. Raleigh Co W VA d/o Isaac & Elizabeth Farley O: farmer; by N.C. Beckley.

74. 18 Nov 1869 SAMUEL R. CROTTY 25 yrs single b. Bedford Co VA s/o Michael & Mary Ann Crotty to MARY E. ROBINSON 23 yrs single b. Monroe Co W VA d/o Harrison & Harriet (Robinson) O: carpenter; by B.F. Bird.

75. 10 Dec 1869 JAMES WM PETRIE 19 yrs single b. Mercer Co W VA s/o Jacob & Elizabeth Petrie to JULIA MILLER 18 yrs single b. Mercer Co W VA d/o Floyd & Rucy Miller O: carpenter; by W.C. Martin.

76. 23 Dec 1869 JAMES C. WALL 24 yrs single b. Mercer Co W VA s/o Wm & Elizabeth Wall to MARTHA F. HERNDON 18 yrs 11 mos 16 dys single b. Campbell Co VA d/o Authur & S.E.B. Herndon O: farmer; by E.H. Brown.

77. 2 Dec 1869 JOSEPH J. BUCKLAND 21 yrs single b. Monroe Co VA now living same s/o John & Nancy Buckland to MARY J. COX 21 yrs single b. Mercer Co W VA d/o Joseph & Sidney Cox O: farmer; by N.C. Beckley.

78. 5 Dec 1869 WM A. MEADOWS 21 yrs single b. Mercer Co W VA s/o Sylvester & Mary Meadows to ALABAMA MEADOWS 17 yrs single b. Mercer Co W VA d/o Joab & Lida Meadows O: farmer; by John Bragg.

79. 16 Dec 1869 ELIJAH BAILEY 59 yrs wid. b. Mercer Co W VA s/o Henry & Elizth Bailey to ARAMINTA STRABY 40 yrs single b. Mercer Co W VA d/o John & Elizth, Straby O: farmer; by W. Tinsley.

80. 23 Dec 1869 CALVIN WHITLOCK 21 yrs single b. Kanawha Co W VA s/o Joseph R. & Annie Whitlock to MARY J. LILLY 17 yrs single b. Mercer Co W VA d/o Thomas & Rebecca Lilly O: farmer; by J.C. Hubbard.

81. 30 Dec 1869 CHAS. A. WILLIAMS 19 yrs single b. Mercer Co W VA s/o Andw. & Ore. Lucy Williams to GABELLA ROLLYSON 27 yrs single b. Mercer Co W VA d/o Jos. & Bettie Rollyson O: farmer; by N.C. Beckley.

(**NOTE: #'s 82 - 85 are either 1869 or 1870**)

82. 6 Jany 1869 CALVIN COOK 20 yrs single b. Wyoming Co VA now living same s/o Thos. & Rebecca Cook to REBECCA BAILEY 22 yrs single b. Mercer Co W VA d/o Jamison Jr. & Polly Bailey O: farmer; by Andrew L. French.

83. 9 Nov 1869 DANIEL CADLE 22 yrs single b. Mercer Co W VA s/o Martin & Elizabeth Cadle to NANCY PETRIE 23 yrs single b. Mercer Co W VA d/o Jacob Petrie O: farmer; by Rufus Pack.

84. 5 Jany 1870 THOS J. HAMLIN 20 yrs single b. Montgomery Co VA s/o S.W. & Lucinda Hamlin to JANE SCOTT 15 yrs single b. Mercer Co W VA d/o Eliz. Scott O: blacksmith; by Benj. F. Bird.

85. 16 Jany 1869 STAUNTON GRIFFITH 22 yrs single b. Raleigh Co VA now living same s/o John & Juda Griffith to AD. R.* BRAMMER 20 yrs single b. Mercer Co W VA d/o Jesse & Sarah Brammer O: farmer; by J.W. Lilly. (*Note: 1860 Mercer Co TN Census listed Adaline R. 11 yrs #825.)

86. 20 Jany 1870 LEONARD T. HAMBRIC 24 yrs single b. Mercer Co W VA s/o Riley & Marg Hambric to REBECCA J. BAILEY single b. Mercer Co W VA d/o Jas. L. & Martha Bailey O: farmer; by Andrew L. French.

87. 10 Feby 1870 FOUNTAIN S. MEADOR 18 yrs single b. Mercer Co W VA s/o Wm M & Selia Meador to MARY L.F. LILLY 16 yrs single b. Mercer Co W VA d/o David & Mary V. Lilly O: farmer; by Rufus Pack.

MERCER COUNTY, WEST VIRGINIA
Marriages 1854 - 1901

56. 15 Sept 1869 JAMES H. DANIEL 30 yrs single b. Roanoka Co VA now living Raleigh Co W VA s/o Jane Daniel to MATILDA A. PACK 21 yrs single b. Mercer Co W VA d/o Tandy & Vga* Pack O: farmer; by Rufus Pack; REMARKS: colored. (*Note: handwriting difficult to read.)

57. 16 Sept 1869 GEORGE W.N. WALKER 23 yrs single b. Mercer Co W VA s/o Charles & Rachel Walker to MINERVA A. FARLEY 16 yrs single b. Raleigh Co W VA d/o adam & Marg Farley O: farmer; by William C. Dobins.

58. 16 Sept 1869 JOSEPH A. LILLEY 20 yrs single b. Raleigh Co W VA now living same s/o Elijah & Sarah Lilley to JULIA A. LILLEY 16 yrs single b. Mercer Co W VA d/o Wash. & Mary Lilley O: farmer; by William C. Dobins.

59. 13 Sept 1869 WILLIAM R. HICKS 21 yrs single b. Wythe Co VA s/o Lorenzo D & Lucinda Hicks to HANNAH L. FAULKNER 16 yrs single b. Montgomery Co VA d/o Hugh H. & Susannah Faulkner O: farmer; by Andrew L. French.

60. 22 Sept 1869 JOHN A. LILLEY 25 yrs wid. b. Mercer Co W VA s/o A.L. & Sarah A Lilley to VIRGINIA A. HOGAN 17 yrs single b. Mercer Co W VA d/o Peter & Nancy Hogan O: farmer; by N.C. Beckley.

61. 30 Sept 1869 RUFUS R. BELCHER 30 yrs single b. Mercer Co W VA s/o Isom & Rebecca Belcher to MELVINA BELCHER 21 yrs single b. Mercer Co W VA d/o Asa & Clara Belcher O: farmer; by John H. Honaker.

62. 3 Octr 1869 ST. CLAIR ABBOTT 64 yrs wid. b. Mercer Co W VA s/o Joseph & Minerva Abbott to FRANCIS P. GARRETSON 53 yrs wid. b. Mercer Co W VA d/o John & Mary Ann Garretson O: farmer; by William C. Martin.

63. 13 Octr 1869 GEORGE WITTEN 27 yrs single b. Tazewell Co VA now living same s/o Edmond & Patience Witten to EMALINE WITTEN 22 yrs single b. Tazewell Co W VA d/o Jacob & Nina Witten O: farmer; by John H. Honaker; REMARKS: colored.

64. 6 Octr 1869 ELEANA FERGUSON 22 yrs single b. Mercer Co W VA s/o Daniel W. & Lironia Ferguson to ELIZABETH McBRIDE 28 yrs single Bedford Co VA d/o Charles & Sarah McBride O: farmer; by William C. Dobins.

65. 21 Octr 1869 HENRY JONES 26 yrs single b. Greenbrier Co W VA s/o Thomas & Rachel Jones to ANNY OLIVER 15 yrs single Giles Co VA d/o Lizzie Oliver O: farmer; by William J. Oliver; REMARKS: colored.

66. 13 Octr 1869 MILLARD F. ELLISON 19 yrs single b. Monroe Co VA s/o Isaac J & Eliza Ellison to MARTHA J. FRENCH 18 yrs single b. Giles Co VA d/o Rusnel G. & Martha A. French O: farmer; by Harrison Robinson.

67. 21 Octr 1869 ALBERT G.P. FARLEY 28 yrs single b. Mercer Co W VA s/o Arch'd & Jemima Farley to MARY B. DONAHOO 24 yrs single b. Craig Co VA d/o Thos H & June Donahoo O: farmer; by F.H.J. King.

68. 19 Novr 1869 ALLEN L. NEELY 24 yrs single b. Mercer Co W VA s/o Nelson H & Clara Neely to LUVERNA FARLEY 21 yrs single b. Mercer Co W VA d/o Andrew & Judah Farley O: farmer; by J.C. Hubbard.

69. 18 Novr 1869 SAML. G.W. CALDWELL 29 yrs single b. Giles Co VA s/o Hugh & Francis Caldwell to SARAH A. GRIM 26 yrs single b. Roanoke Co VA d/o Wm & Cahine(sic) Grim O: farmer; by Evan H Brown.

70. 23 June 1869 WM A. HARRIS 40 yrs single b. Patrick Co VA s/o Robt & Elizabeth Harris to MARY MARGT. CALFEE 20 yrs single b. Pulaski Co VA d/o John & Virginia Calfee O: farmer; by James Calfee.

71. 28 Octr 1869 WM C. FARLEY 20 yrs single b. Mercer Co W VA s/o Hiram & Mary Farley to ANN E. COOPER 17 yrs single b. Mercer Co W VA d/o Jonah & Narcissus Cooper O: farmer; by Charles Walker.

72. 24 Nov 1869 GILBERT MORGAN 20 yrs single b. Greenbrier Co VA now living same s/o Baswell & Urvean Morgan to SARAH FARLEY 22 yrs single b. Raleigh Co W VA d/o Isaac & Elizabeth Farley O: farmer; by N.C. Beckley.

73. 24 Nov 1869 JOHN MORGAN 30 yrs single b. Greenbrier Co VA now living same s/o Baswell & Urvean Morgan to SUSAN FARLEY 25 yrs single b. Raleigh Co W VA d/o Isaac & Elizabeth Farley O: farmer; by N.C. Beckley.

74. 18 Nov 1869 SAMUEL R. CROTTY 25 yrs single b. Bedford Co VA s/o Michael & Mary Ann Crotty to MARY E. ROBINSON 23 yrs single b. Monroe Co W VA d/o Harrison & Harriet (Robinson) O: carpenter; by B.F. Bird.

75. 10 Dec 1869 JAMES WM PETRIE 19 yrs single b. Mercer Co W VA s/o Jacob & Elizabeth Petrie to JULIA MILLER 18 yrs single b. Mercer Co W VA d/o Floyd & Rucy Miller O: carpenter; by W.C. Martin.

76. 23 Dec 1869 JAMES C. WALL 24 yrs single b. Mercer Co W VA s/o Wm & Elizabeth Wall to MARTHA F. HERNDON 18 yrs 11 mos 16 dys single b. Campbell Co VA d/o Authur & S.E.B. Herndon O: farmer; by E.H. Brown.

77. 2 Dec 1869 JOSEPH J. BUCKLAND 21 yrs single b. Monroe Co VA now living same s/o John & Nancy Buckland to MARY J. COX 21 yrs single b. Mercer Co W VA d/o Joseph & Sidney Cox O: farmer; by N.C. Beckley.

78. 5 Dec 1869 WM A. MEADOWS 21 yrs single b. Mercer Co W VA s/o Sylvester & Mary Meadows to ALABAMA MEADOWS 17 yrs single b. Mercer Co W VA d/o Joab & Lida Meadows O: farmer; by John Bragg.

79. 16 Dec 1869 ELLIAH BAILEY 59 yrs wid. b. Mercer Co W VA s/o Henry & Elizth Bailey to ARAMINTA STRABY 40 yrs single b. Mercer Co W VA d/o John & Elizth Straby O: farmer; by W. Tinsley.

80. 23 Dec 1869 CALVIN WHITLOCK 21 yrs single b. Kanawha Co W VA s/o Joseph R. & Annie Whitlock to MARY J. LILLY 17 yrs single b. Mercer Co W VA d/o Thomas & Rebeca Lilly O: farmer; by J.C. Hubbard.

81. 30 Dec 1869 CHAS. A. WILLIAMS 19 yrs single b. Mercer Co W VA s/o Andw. & Ore. Lucy Williams to GABELLA ROLLYSON 27 yrs single b. Mercer Co W VA d/o Jos. & Battie Rollyson O: farmer; by N.C. Beckley.

(**NOTE: #'s 82 - 85 are either 1869 or 1870**)

82. 6 Jany 1869 CALVIN COOK 20 yrs single b. Wyoming Co VA now living same s/o Thos. & Rebecca Cook to REBECCA BAILEY 22 yrs single b. Mercer Co W VA d/o Jamison Jr. & Polly Bailey O: farmer; by Andrew L. French.

83. 9 Nov 1869 DANIEL CADLE 22 yrs single b. Mercer Co W VA s/o Martin & Elizabeth Cadle to NANCY PETRIE 23 yrs single b. Mercer Co W VA d/o Jacob Petrie O: farmer; by Rufus Pack.

84. 5 Jany 1870 THOS J. HAMLIN 20 yrs single b. Montgomery Co VA s/o S.W. & Lucinda Hamlin to JANE SCOTT 15 yrs single b. Mercer Co W VA d/o Eliz. Scott O: blacksmith; by Benj. F. Bird.

85. 16 Jany 1869 STAUNTON GRIFFITH 22 yrs single b. Raleigh Co VA now living same s/o John & Juda Griffith to AD. R.* BRAMMER 20 yrs single b. Mercer Co VA d/o Jesse & Sarah Brammer O: farmer; by J.W. Lilly. (*Note: 1860 Mercer Co TN Census listed Adaline R. 11 yrs #825.)

86. 20 Jany 1870 LEONARD T. HAMBRIC 24 yrs single b. Mercer Co W VA s/o Riley & Marg Hambric to REBECCA J. BAILEY single b. Mercer Co W VA d/o Jas. L. & Martha Bailey O: farmer; by Andrew L. French.

87. 10 Feby 1870 FOUNTAIN S. MEADOR 18 yrs single b. Mercer Co W VA s/o Wm H & Selia Meador to MARY L.F. LILLY 16 yrs single b. Mercer Co W VA d/o David & Mary V. Lilly O: farmer; by Rufus Pack.

88. 20 Jany 1870 DAVID SLOAN 19 yrs single b. NC s/o Jack & Deborah Sloan to MARTHA M. MILLER 20 yrs single b. Mercer Co W VA O: farmer; by Wm C. Martin.

89. 20 Feby 1870 ELIJAH P. MEADOWS 22 yrs single b. Mercer Co W VA now living in Wyoming Co VA s/o Jerry & Nancy Meadows to DISA J. REED 20 yrs single b. Mercer Co W VA d/o Elijah & Disa Reed O: farmer.

90. 23 Feby 1870 HANELIUS C. CALDWELL 35 yrs wid. b. Giles Co VA s/o John & Eliza Caldwell to ALICE M. FARLEY 18 yrs single b. Mercer Co W VA d/o Andrew & Judith Farley O:farmer; by Wm C.Dobbins.

91. 24 Feby 1870 DAVID R. PAYNE 21 yrs single b. Mercer Co W VA s/o James & Mary Payne to VIRGINIA S. FAULKNER 21 yrs single b. Giles Co VA d/o Hardy & Mary Faulkner O: farmer; by A.J. Thompson

92. 8 Mar 1870 JOHN H. BAILEY 20 yrs single b. Mercer Co W VA s/o Reubin R. & Jane Bailey to SARAH F. DAVIS 20 yrs single b. Mercer Co W VA d/o John & Elizabeth Davis O: farmer; by Theodore Smith.

93. 9 Mar 1870 ANDREW L. CALLOWAY 21 yrs single b. Mercer Co W VA s/o Granville & Susan G. Calloway to JULIA A. FRY 21 yrs single b. Alleghany Co VA d/o Rebecca J. Fry O: farmer; by James O. Casaday.

94. 25 Feby 1870 FERDIMAN DOVE 21 yrs single b. Henry Co VA s/o Sherwood & Sally Dove to ISABELLA FANNING 20 yrs single b. Mercer Co W VA d/o Benj. & Nancy Fanning O: farmer; by William C. Martin.

95. 15 Mar 1870 JOSEPH ENOCHS 29 yrs wid. b. Ross Co OH s/o Henry & Rhoda Enochs to LOLLIE ENOCHS(SIC) single b. Tazewell Co VA d/o John & Sarah Osburn O: trader; by A.L. French.

96. 28 Mar 1870 WILLIAM MIRICK 21 yrs single s/o John & Lucinda Mirick to L.B. PETRY single b. Mercer Co W VA d/o William & Polly Petry O: farmer; by W.C. Martin.

Page 19

1. * * 1870 CORNELIUS W. BAILEY 22 yrs single b. Mercer Co W VA s/o Eli & Charlotte Bailey to SUSAN A. NEAL 15 yrs single b. Monroe Co W VA d/o Henry M. & Sarah A. Neal O:farmer; by Jno D Honaker. (*Note: No day or month given.)

2. 19 April 1870 HENRY MEADOR 20 yrs single b. Mercer Co W VA s/o Woodson B. Meador to SARAH COX 23 yrs single b. Patrick Co VA d/o Joseph & Nancy Cox O: farmer; by Rufus Pack.

3. 19 April 1870 THOS J BELCHER 18 yrs single b. Mercer Co W VA s/o Christian & May Belcher to ALMEDA BAILEY 17 yrs single b. Mercer Co W VA d/o Eli Bailey O: farmer; by Jno D Honaker.

4. 5 May 1870 JACK TYRUS 23 yrs single b. Hallifax VA s/o Peyton Tyrus & Geanna Green to JULIA CALLANDER 19 yrs single b. Mercer Co W VA d/o Susan Callander O: farmer; by Evan H. Brown; REMARKS: colored.

5. 9 March 1870 JNO H. CAMPBELL 21 yrs single b. Mercer Co W VA s/o Thos K. Campbell to SARAH E.A. STOVALL 24 yrs single b. Mercer Co W VA d/o Albert & S.M.K. Stovall O: farmer; by Jas W. Lilly.

6. 4 May 1870 WM S. COSNER 30 yrs single b. Mercer Co W VA s/o John & Jane Cosner to MARTHA BLANKENSHIP 23 yrs wid b. Mercer Co W VA d/o Delilah Blankenship O: farmer; by Theodore Smith.

7. 6 June 1870 JAMES GANTIER 18 yrs single b. Tazewell Co VA s/o Jos & Mary F. Gantier to PALINA V. WHITTAKER 18 yrs single b. Giles Co VA d/o Jas. & Hulda Whittaker O: farmer; by Andrew J. Thompson.

8. 21 July 1870 ANDREW HEARN 28 yrs single b. Mercer Co W VA s/o Levi Hearn to MARTHA C. BRUCE 15 yrs single b. Mercer Co W VA d/o Amy Hearn(sic)* O:farmer; by Andrew Workman. (*Note: 1870 Mercer Co TN Census parents are Josiah G & Mary Bruce #324. Martha is 5 yrs.)

9. 8 Aug 1870 JOEL DAVIS 23 yrs single b. Campbell Co VA now living in Giles Co VA s/o Elijah & Mary Davis to MAHALA EASTER 19 yrs single b. Giles Co VA d/o Wm & Susan Easter O: farmer; by A.J. Thompson

10. 4 Aug 1870 AUGUSTUS COMER 28 yrs single b. Mercer Co W VA s/o John & Jane Comas to MARTHA J. CLEMONS 21 yrs single b. Mercer Co W VA d/o John R. & Mary Clemons O: farmer; by A.J. Thompson.

11. 11 Aug 1870 JAMES M. CREWS 24 yrs single b. Franklin Co VA s/o Asa V. Crews to RHODA ANN REED 23 yrs single b. Mercer Co W VA d/o Joseph & Malinda Reed O: farmer; by Benj. T. Bird.

12. 23 Aug 1870 ALLEN McNUTT 20 yrs single b. Bland Co VA s/o --- & Charlotte Praus to EMILY ANN KING 20 yrs single b. Pulaski Co VA d/o Floyd Hurst & Sally King O: blacksmith; by Wm J. Oleser; REMARKS: colored.

13. 11 Aug 1870 WM F. NEELY 18 yrs single b. Mercer Co W VA s/o Wm G. & Delilah Neely to VICTORIA CYNTHIA RUSSELL 15 yrs single b. Mercer Co W VA d/o Benj. & Sarah A. Russell O: farmer; by Theodore Smith.

14. 25 Aug 1870 ANDREW GOTT 58 yrs wid. b. Ireland s/o Andrew & Alice Gott to EMILY C. ELKINS 40 yrs wid. b. Pulaski Co VA d/o Elizabeth Bowden O: farmer; by Theodore Smith.

15. 2 Sept 1870 BALLARD F. PHILIPS 20 yrs single b. Mercer Co W VA s/o Jas. & Clary Philips to CLEOPATRIA SHORTER 18 yrs single b. Franklin Co VA d/o Woodson A & Martha A Shorter O: farmer; by G.A. Austin.

16. 8 Aug 1870 GREEN F. MEADOR 25 yrs single b. Mercer Co W VA s/o Wm M & Celia Meador to WILSONIA JOSEPHINE DEEDS 16 yrs single b. Allaghany Co VA d/o C.B. & S.C. Deeds O: farmer; by Rufus Pack.

17. * Sep 1870 ANDREW HARMAN 20 yrs single b. Patrick Co VA s/o Geo & Bettie Harman to LYDIA DAY 19 yrs single b. Mercer Co W VA d/o Elijah & Dicy J. Reed(sic) O: farmer; by Jno. W. Honaker. (*Note: no day given.)

18. * Sep 1870 THEO TAYLOR 20 yrs single b. Mercer Co W VA s/o Sampson & Mary Taylor to NANCY E. REED 17 yrs single b. Mercer Co W VA d/o Elijah & Dicy J. Reed O: farmer; by J.W. Honaker. (*Note: no day given.)

19. * Sep 1870 ELIAS BAILEY 21 yrs single b. Mercer Co W VA s/o Burrell & Nancy Bailey to LUCINDA ELIZTH McCOMAS 19 yrs single b. Mercer Co W VA d/o Eli & Julia Ann McComas O: farmer; by A.G. French. (*Note: no day given.)

20. 14 Sep 1870 BALLARD A. MANN 21 yrs single b. Mercer Co W VA s/o Jacob & Sarah E. Mann to LUCY A. VEST 21 yrs single b. Mercer Co W VA d/o Aud. & Rhoda Vest O: farmer; by James W. Lilly.

21. 22 Sep 1870 BENJN. H. OXLY 23 yrs single b. Giles Co VA s/o Sanford & Delilah Oxly to NANCY M. VERMILLION 17 yrs single b. Mercer Co W VA d/o Jas A. & Elizabeth Vermillion O: farmer; by Wm C. Dobins.

22. 22 Sep 1870 JNO S. YOUNG 21 yrs single Craig Co VA s/o John and Mary Ann Young to SAREFITA WILEY 20 yrs single b. Mercer Co W VA d/o Gordon & Tomsey Wiley O: farmer; by Jno W. Crook.

23. 20 Oct 1870 JAMES BROWN 22 yrs single b. Montgomery Co VA s/o Ned & Nelly Brown to VIRGINIA LYBROOK 18 yrs single b. Giles Co VA d/o Harry & Maima Lybrook O: farmer; by Theodore Smith; REMARKS: colored.

24. 31 Oct 1870 HUGH SWADER 18 yrs single b. Mercer Co W VA s/o Jno & Nancy Swader to MARY JANE FERGUSON 17 yrs single b. Franklin Co VA d/o Jos. & Elizth Ferguson O: farmer; by A.L. French.

25. 3 Oct 1870 JOSIAH YOUNG 21 yrs single b. Monroe Co W VA s/o Lewis and Mary Young to AMANDA J. SIMMONS 22 yrs single b. Mercer Co W VA d/o Ephraim & Sarah J. Simmons O: farmer; by Rufus Pack.

26. 7 Oct 1870 GEO WILLIAMS 21 yrs single b. Mercer Co W VA s/o Andrew Williams to REBECCA CADLE 19 yrs single b. Mercer Co W VA d/o Martin & Elizabeth Cadle O: farmer; by Rufus Pack.

27. 17 Nov 1870 JAS ANDERSON WHITE 17 yrs single b. Mercer Co W VA s/o Jas R & Juliet White to DERENZIE H.McKINZIE 17 yrs single b. Mercer Co W VA d/o Jno & Martha McKinzie O:farmer; by W. Linsley

28. 13 Oct 1870 JAS. W. BENNETT 44 yrs wid. b. Hampton VA now living Monroe Co W VA s/o Thos. & Ann W. Bennett to CLARA A. FRENCH 29 yrs single b. Mercer Co W VA d/o Wm M. & Mahala French O: Minister of the Gospel; by J.J. Crickenburgen.

29. 24 Nov 1870 LEWIS LILLY 28 yrs single b. Mercer Co W VA s/o Milly Lilly to NANCY UPTON 30 yrs single b. Mercer Co W VA d/o Sylvester & Martha Upton O: farmer; by G.W. Crook.

30. 3 Nov 1870 JOSEPH LILLY 18 yrs single b. Raleigh Co W VA now living same s/o Wm & Francis Lilly to MARY D. AKERS 17 yrs single b. Mercer Co W VA d/o Nathaniel & Sarah Akers O: farmer; by James W. Lilly.

31. 1 Dec 1870 THOMAS H. WITT 20 yrs single b. Giles Co VA now living Monroe Co W VA s/o Jesse & Sephrous T. Witt to NANCY E. WEATHERFORD 23 yrs single b. Pitsylvania VA d/o Jno. M. & Adeline M. Weatherford O: farmer; by John Bragg.

32. 8 Dec 1870 JOSEPH E. FRENCH 24 yrs single b. Giles Co VA s/o A.L. & R.D. French to EMILINE V. BATCHELOR 18 yrs single b. Montgomery Co VA d/o Reuben & Arine Batchelor O: farmer; by John H Honaker.

33. 24 Nov 1870 RUFUS A McCOMAS 21 yrs single b. Mercer Co W VA s/o Eli & Julie McComas to AMANDA J. WALKER 19 yrs single b. Mercer Co W VA d/o Council & Nancy Walker O: farmer; by A.L. French

34. 24 Nov 1870 CLIAS W. BAILEY 20 yrs single b. Wyoming Co W VA s/o Jamison & Poly Bailey to FRANKIE J.C. WALKER 16 yrs single b. Mercer Co W VA d/o * & Adaline Walker O: farmer; by A.L. French. (*Note: handwriting difficult to read.)

35. 24 Nov 1870 FERDINAND MITCHELL 22 yrs single b. Pitsylvania Co VA s/o Joel & C. Mitchell to S.J. HIGGINBOTHAM 17 yrs single b. Mercer Co W VA d/o -- & Sarah E. Higginbothan O: farmer; by A.J. Thompson.

36. 28 Dec 1870 DAVID H. SAUDERS 25 yrs single b. Pulaski Co W VA s/o Julius & Lydia Sauders to NANCY JANE WILSON 28 yrs wid. b. Mercer Co W VA d/o Arch & Eliz Bailey O: farmer; by John H. Honaker.

37. 15 Nov 1870 ALLEN LAW 39 yrs single b. Franklin co VA s/o Allen & -- Law to HARRIET NEWLON* * 19 yrs single b. Mercer Co W VA d/o Reuben & Nancy Hairtz O: blacksmith; by David Noll; REMARKS: colored. (*Note: handrwriting difficult to read.)

38. 25 Oct 1870 HARRY L. RICHMAN 21 yrs single b. Frankclin Co VA now living in Raleigh Co W VA s/o James & Lucinda Richman to LYDIA A. WOOD 21 yrs single b. Mercer Co W VA d/o Rbt. & Frankie Wood O: farmer; by John C. Hubbard.

39. 8 Dec 1870 WM HINTON 26 yrs single b. Monroe Co W VA now living same s/o Jno & Ann. Hinton to JULIA DONEHOE 16 yrs single b. Alleghany Co VA d/o Thos & Jane Donehoe O: farmer; by Geo W. Crook.

40. 29 Nov 1870 LORENZO MEADOR 21 single b. Mercer Co W VA s/o Joseph & Julia Meador to RHODA E. SOLESBURY 18 yrs single b. Mercer Co W VA d/o Pleasant Lilly & Nancy Solesbury O: farmer; by James W. Lilly.

41. 22 Dec 1870 BALLARD P. WHITE 19 yrs single b. Mercer Co W VA s/o R & Julia White to MARY JANE WOOLWINE 17 yrs single b. Greenbriar Co W VA d/o Jus. L & Nancy Woolwine O: farmer; by W. Holroyd.

42. 29 Dec 1870 ROBT. M. GODFREY 20 yrs single b. Mercer Co W VA s/o James & Nancy M. Godfrey to URSULA M. SHREWSBURY 18 yrs single b. Mercer Co W VA d/o Henry & Jane Shrewsbury O: farmer; by Andrew L. French.

43. 30 Dec 1870 JESSE G.L. FERGUSON 20 yrs single b. Mercer Co W VA s/o Susanah Ferguson to REBECCA PACK 22 yrs single b. Mercer Co W VA d/o Robt & Rhoda Pack O: farmer; by Jas. W. Wiley.

44. 25 Oct 1870 HENRY TUGGLE 22 yrs single b. Mercer Co W VA s/o John & Emily Tuggle to ESTHER JANE CALFEE 21 yrs single b. Mercer Co W VA d/o James & Elizabeth Calfee O: farmer; by E.H. Brown.

(*NOTE: #45 is believed to be the beginning of 1871 marriages, even though it states 1870 on #44 and no year is given on #'s 45 - 48.*)

45. 25 Jany * WM A. POWELL 21 yrs single b. Franklin Co VA s/o Wm A. & Julia Powell to JULIA E. PERDUE 19 yrs single b. Franklin Co VA d/o Silas & Nancy J. Perdue O: farmer; by John H Honaker.

46. 20 Jany * ELLET. H. CANTERBURY 21 yrs single b. Wyoming Co W VA now living same s/o D.D. & Lucinda Canterbury to MARY A.E. LUSK 22 yrs single b. Mercer Co W VA d/o R.T. & Lucinda Lusk O: farmer; by Andrew L. French.

47. 19 Jany * WM B. LUSK 19 yrs single b. Mercer Co W VA s/o R.T. & Lucinda Lusk to MARY J. HURST 17 yrs single b. Mercer Co W VA d/o Wm & - Hurst O: farmer; by Andrew L. French.

48. 19 Jany * MANELIUS C. CALDWELL 20 yrs single to OLIVA A. CALDWELL 17 yrs single. (All other information was missing.)

Page 20

1. 22 Jany 1871 JOHNATHAN L. PENDRY 21 yrs single b. Grayson Co VA s/o Morgan Pendry to ELIZABETH BARTON 22 yrs single b. Grayson Co VA d/o - & Poly Barton O: cooper; by W. Holroyd.

2. 24 Dec 1870 ROBT M. GODFREY 20 yrs single b. Mercer Co W VA s/o James & Nancy M. Godfrey to URSULA M. SHREWSBURY 18 yrs single b. Mercer Co W VA d/o Henry & Jane Shrewsbury O: farmer; by Andrew L. French; REMARKS: Entered preceeding page.)

3. 26 Jany 1871 JOHN W. BARKER 21 yrs single b. Mercer Co W VA s/o M.C. & Julia A. Barker to MARY M. MEADOR 17 yrs single b. Mercer Co W VA d/o W.H. & Rebecca Meador O: farmer; by Wm C. Dobbins.

4. 30 Jany 1871 JOHN R. NEWKIRK 28 yrs single b. Montgomery Co VA s/o Stephen & Mary A. Newkirk to MARY C. NEWLEE 17 yrs single b. Mercer Co W VA d/o Geo. B. & Amanda Newlee O:farmer;by G.A. Austin.

5. 31 Jany 1871 ALLEN G. COLE 29 yrs single b. Mercer Co W VA s/o Alb. & M. Cole to JEMSHA H. MASSEY 16 yrs single b. Mercer Co W VA d/o Thos. & Louisa Hassey O: farmer; by B.T. Bird.

6. 2 Feby 1871 WM J. SAUNDERS 28 yrs single b. Pulaski Co VA s/o Julius & Lidia Saunders to CLARY C. BELCHER 28 yrs single b. Mercer Co W VA d/o Isham & Sallie Belcher O:farmer; by John H Honaker

7. 28 Nov 1870 WM P. ROGERS 39 yrs wid. b. Stokes Co NC s/o Lot & Pheba Rogers to MARY SHREWSBURY 26 yrs single b. Mercer Co W VA d/o Phil & Sarah Shrewsbury O: farmer; by Wm C. Dobbins.

8. 4 Dec 1870 WILLIAM F. MARTIN 20 yrs single b. Mercer Co W VA s/o David & Esther Martin to MARY E. OXLEY 19 yrs single b. Bland Co VA d/o Sanford & Delilah A. Oxley O: farmer; by Wm C. Dobbins.

9. 8 Dec 1870 ALEXANDER BELCHER 33 yrs single b. Mercer Co W VA s/o Henry & Ann Belcher to JANE WALL 37 yrs wid. b. Mercer Co W VA d/o Henry & Polly Bailey O: farmer; by John H. Honaker.

10. 9 Feby 1871 SIMON B. LILLY 18 yrs single b. Mercer Co W VA s/o Wm & - Lilly to SARAH E. DAVIS 20 yrs single b. Mercer Co W VA d/o Lindsey & Mary N. Davis O: farmer; by B.T. Bird.

11. 15 Feby 1871 ANDREW J. HOLSTINE 27 yrs single b. Mercer Co W VA Jos. C. & Elizabeth Holstine to VIRGINIA WHITE 20 yrs single b. Mercer Co W VA d/o Cornelius & Polly White O: frmer; by J.O. Cassaday.

12. 23 Feby 1871 GEORGE BAXLER 39 yrs single b. Giles Co VA s/o Geo & Sarah Baxler to ANN McGEO 21 yrs single b. Pulaski Co VA d/o Chas. & Ailsey McGeo O: laborer; by J.O. Cassaday; REMARKS: colored.

13. 23 Feby 1871 WARD C. KEATON 25 yrs single b. Mercer Co W VA s/o Hannon & Jane Keaton to SARAH J. FARLEY 17 yrs single b. Mercer Co W VA d/o John & Salina Farley O: farmer; by J.C. Hubbard.

14. 5 Mar 1871 ALEXANDER FARLEY 21 yrs single b. Mercer Co W VA s/o Drury & Sarah E. Farley to SARAH P. DWIGGINS 21 yrs single b. Gilford Co NC d/o Thomas C. Dwiggins O: farmer; by John Bragg.

15. 2 Mar 1871 ALBERT B. SMITH 22 yrs single b. Mercer Co W VA s/o Theodore & Elizth J. Smith to LORIA E. DEWESE 17 yrs single b. Montgomery Co VA d/o Andr. & - Dewese O: farmer; by A.J. Thompson.

16. 12 Jany 1871 GEORGE D. MILLER 20 yrs single b. Monroe Co VA s/o Moses & Susan Miller to MARTHA L. BURDITT 18 yrs single b. Mercer Co W VA d/o J.C. & L. Burditt O: farmer; by A.J. Cumins.

17. 10 Mar 1871 BALLARD P. LILLY 23 yrs single b. Mercer Co W VA s/o Johnathan & Margaret Lilly to LALUDA MEADOR 22 yrs single b. Mercer Co W VA O: farmer; by Rufus Pack.

18. 16 April 1871 JOHN S. LILLY 19 yrs single b. Mercer co W VA s/o Washington & Mary Lilly to ELIZABETH C. MEADOR 19 yrs single b. Mercer Co W VA d/o Josiah & Elizabeth Meador O: farmer; by R G French.

19. 8 Mar 1871 HENRY W. DAVIS 21 yrs single b Mercer Co W VA s/o Ira W. & Temperance Davis to MARY E. BALLARD 21 yrs single b. Monroe Co W VA d/o Harrison Ballard & wife O: farmer.

20. 7 Mar 1871 ANDREW BENNETT 22 yrs single b. Raleigh Co VA s/o Jefferson & Mary Bennett to MARIAH L. WILLS 28 yrs single b. Giles Co VA d/o E.G. Wills O: farmer; by Geo W. Crook.

21. 18 Jany 1871 JARVIS NELSON 21 yrs single b. Patrick Co VA s/o Elisha & Chardy Nelson to ELIZABETH HOLDREN 17 yrs single d/o Geo & - Holdren O: farmer; by A.J. Thompson.

22. 16 Mar 1871 JAMES H. WHITTAKER 24 yrs single b. Giles Co VA s/o Wm & Rutha Whittaker to CLARA A. WRIGHT 18 yrs single b. Campbell Co VA s/o Camden G. & Eliz. Wright O: farmer; by J.O. Cassaday

23. 14 Mar 1871 JOHN E MARTIN 22 yrs single b. Franklin Co VA s/o Judson & Eliza Martin to SARAH E CALDWELL 22 yrs single b. Mercer Co W VA d/o Jno & Eliza Caldwell O:farmer; by H.C. Thompson

24. 15 Mar 1871 THOMAS K. LAMBERT 20 yrs single b. McDowell Co W VA now living same s/o Thos K & Charlotte Lambert to CYNTHIA M. BAILEY 17 yrs single b. Mercer Co W VA d/o Jno S. & Ursula Bailey O:farmer; by Thos K Lambert

25. 28 Mar 1871 FRANCIS M. GEORGE 35 yrs single b. Pitsylvania Co VA to ANNIE CRAWFORD 30 yrs single d/o Isaac & - Crawford O: farmer; by G.W. Bennett.

26. 6 April 1871 HARMON LILLY 21 yrs single b. Mercer Co W VA now living Summers Co W VA s/o James & Nelly Lilly to SARAH ANN MEADOR 15 yrs single b. Mercer Co W VA d/o John W. & Clinantina Meador O: farmer; by R.G. French.

27. 11 April 1871 THOMAS B. LILLY 20 yrs single b. Mercer Co W VA s/o Josiah & Leah Lilly to DOSHA H. COOPER 16 yrs single b. Mercer Co W VA d/o Josiah & Norium Cooper O:farmer; by R G French.

28. 11 April 1871 ROBERT B. TURNER 28 yrs single b. Montgomery Co VA s/o Wilson & Sarah Turner to MARY H. THORNTON 16 yrs single b. Mercer Co W VA d/o Merideth & Louisa Thornton O: farmer; by Benjamin T. Bird.

29. 21 April 1871 SIDNEY A. THORNTON 19 yrs single b. Mercer Co W VA s/o Merideth & Louisa Thornton to CYNTHIA J. BURDETT 21 yrs single b. Giles Co VA d/o Joseph & Adelade Burdett O: farmer; by Samuel Scott.

30. 26 April 1871 HENRY MEADOWS 22 yrs single b. Mercer Co W VA s/o Jeremiah Meadows to LONEMA DAVIS 21 yrs single b. Giles Co VA d/o Lindsey & Jane Davis O: farmer; by John West.

31. 16 March 1871 WILSON McKINNEY 21 yrs single b. Wyoming Co VA s/o Eliah & Matilda McKinney to MARY THOMPSON 18 yrs single b. Tazewell Co VA d/o Archibald & Elizth Thompson O: farmer; by John H. Honaker.

32. 18 May 1871 JAMES C. TAYLOR 22 yrs single b. Grayson Co VA s/o Joseph A. & Mary B. Taylor to MARGRET A. JUSTICE 17 yrs single b. Mercer Co W VA d/o Henry & Polly A. Justice O: farmer; by J.O. Cassaday.

33. 18 May 1871 22 yrs single b. Mercer Co W VA s/o Jas. & Mary Payne to MARY E. SADLER 18 yrs single b. Pulaski Co VA d/o Henry & Araminta Sadler O: farmer; by John H. Honaker.

34. 25 May 1871 JAMES E. JOHNSTON 38 yrs single b. Giles Co VA s/o Adam & Susanah Johnston to ELLA C.E. WALL 21 yrs single b. Mercer Co W VA d/o Wm & Elizth Wall O: farmer; by N. Tinsley.

35. 16 March 1871 ADAM HARVEY 22 yrs single b. Monroe Co W VA s/o Jacob W. & Catherine Harvey to ELECTRA A. GADD 19 yrs single b. Mercer Co W VA d/o Andrew & Delila Gadd O: farmer; by James W. Lilly.

36. 1 June 1871 HENDERSON F. PRINCE 24 yrs single b. Mercer Co W VA s/o Jos. & Susan Prince to MARY E. HUBBARD 22 yrs single b. Patrick Co VA d/o Samuel & Elizth Hubbard O: farmer; by R.G. French.

37. 8 June 1871 JOHN H. FARMER 22 yrs single b. Mercer Co W VA s/o John L. & Nancy Farmer to MILLEY SHREWSBURY 21 yrs single b. Mercer Co W VA d/o Henry & Jane Shrewsbury O: farmer; by John H. Honaker.

38. 18 June 1871 GUMARD WOOD 55 yrs wid. b. Franklin Co VA s/o Richard & Rachel Wood to NANCY BRAMMER 52 yrs wid. b. Patrick Co VA d/o John & Nancy Massey O: farmer; by James W. Lilly.

39. 28 June 1871 JACOB A. WALKER 19 yrs single b. Wyoming Co W VA now living same s/o Christian & Mahala Walker to NANCY A. WOOD 24 yrs single b. Mercer co W VA d/o German & Nancy Wood O: farmer; by James W. Lilly.

40. 10 June 1871 JACOB MEADOR 25 yrs single b. Mercer Co W VA s/o Adam & Sarah Meador to JULIA A. FLETCHER 21 yrs single b. Mercer co W VA d/o Jas. H. & Jane Fletcher O: farmer; by A.J. Thompson.

41. 22 June 1871 SAMUEL G. TABOR 20 yrs single b. Tazewell Co VA now living same s/o James & Nancy Tabor to VIRGINIA W. JOHNSTON 20 yrs single b. Mercer Co W VA d/o Jno W. & Marg. Johnston O: farmer; by Evan H. Brown.

42. 29 June 1871 WM M. FOSTER 23 yrs single b. Mercer Co W VA s/o Richard & Zalpha Foster to MARY C. ROSER 19 yrs single O: farmer; by W.C. Martin.

43. 23 Aug 1871 JOHNATHAN LILLY 20 yrs single b. Mercer Co W VA now living in Summers Co VA s/o Johnathan & Margaret Lilly to LUCINDA MEADOR 18 yrs single b. Mercer Co W VA d/o Josiah & Elizabeth Meador O: farmer; by James H. Lilly.

44. 7 August 1871 ISAH BELCHER 64 yrs wid. b. Tazwell Co VA s/o Isam & Nancy Belcher to ANN S. LUSK 51 yrs wid. b. Montgomery Co VA d/o Robert & Mary Lusk 0: farmer; by John H. Honaker.

45. 21 Aug 1871 JAS. F. TILLER 19 yrs single b. Mercer Co W VA s/o W.D. & R. Tiller to ANN C. LYNCH 14 yrs single b. Monroe Co VA d/o Emaline Lynch 0: farmer; by A.L. French.

46. 29 Aug 1871 BALLARD F. COOPER 24 yrs single b. Craig Co VA s/o Isaac & Rebecca Cooper to MARTHA WIMER 18 yrs singler b. Mercer Co W VA d/o Jas & Elizth Wimer 0: farmer; by J.O. Cassaday.

47. 20 Sept 1871 JOHNATHAN P. MEADOWS 19 yrs single b. Mercer Co W VA s/o Jeremiah & Jane C. Meadows to CATHERING DAVIS 16 yrs single b. Giles Co VA d/o John & Sarah Davis 0: farmer; by John West.

48. 21 Sept 1871 HARRISON PERDUE 27 yrs single b. Giles Co VA s/o Fergus & Nancy Perdue to MARGARET J. SKEONG* b. Giles Co VA d/o Thos. & Francis Skeong* 0: farmer; by Theodore Smith. (*Note: handwriting difficult to read.)

Page 21

1. 26 Sept 1871 DANIEL C. BURGESS 23 yrs single b. Mercer Co W VA s/o Hiram & Nancy Burgess to AMANDA J. ROSS 23 yrs single b. Alleghany Co VA 0: Griffith & Harriet Ross 0: farmer; by B.T. Bird.

2. 3 Oct 1871 JAMES F. BAILEY 18 yrs single b. Mercer Co W VA s/o Jamison & Polly Bailey to MARTHA M. SHREWSBURY 15 yrs single b. Mercer Co W VA d/o Jno. & Martha M. Shrewsbury 0: farmer; by Andrew L. French.

3. 11 Oct 1871 WILLIAM A. MARTIN 20 yrs single b. Mercer Co W VA s/o William C. & Ann Martin to VIRGINIA WILEY 20 yrs single b. Mercer Co W VA d/o Vincent & Cynthia Wiley 0: farmer; by William C Martin.

4. 18 Oct 1871 JOHNATHAN S. BAILEY 20 yrs single b. Mercer Co W VA s/o Burrel & Nancy Bailey to TIMEANDRE M. GODFREY 19 yrs single b. Mercer Co W VA d/o Jno. D. & Martha Godfrey 0: farmer; by John H. Honaker.

5. 26 Sept 1871 LEWIS A. WILEY 22 yrs single b. Giles Co VA now living same s/o John & Mary Wiley to JULIA A. CLEMENTS 18 yrs single b. Henry Co VA d/o John & Mary Clements 0: farmer; by John West.

6. 1 Novr 1871 JOSEPHUS BELCHER 20 yrs single b. Mercer Co W VA s/o Asa & Clarinda Belcher to MARY E. BUICE 18 yrs single b. Bland Co VA d/o Charles & Sarah Buice 0: farmer; by W. Holroyd.

7. 7 Novr 1871 ARMINUS L. NEAL 19 yrs single b. Monroe Co VA s/o Henry M. & Sarah Neal to MARY A.P. BAILEY 26 yrs single b. Mercer Co W VA d/o Eli & Ellotta Bailey 0: farmer; by Andrew L. French.

8. 15 Novr 1871 RUFUS A. HALE 41 yrs single b. Giles Co VA s/o Elias & Nancy Hale to MARY E. BAILEY single b. Mercer Co W VA d/o Johnathan & Elizabeth Bailey 0: farmer; by James Calfee.

9. 2 Decr 1871 JAMES O. PERDUE 22 yrs single b. Franklin co VA s/o Silas & Nancy Perdue to LUMHA L. BRUNTY 19 yrs single b. Tazewall Co VA 0: farmer; by James Calfee.

10. 5 Decr 1871 JOHN H. ROBINSON 32 yrs single b. Monroe Co W VA s/o Harrison & Harret Robinson to VIRGINIA L. CALFEE 18 yrs single b. Mercer Co W VA d/o Chas. W. & Nancy D. Calfee 0: dental surgeon; by James Calfee.

11. 13 Decr 1871 Princeton LEROY BROYLES 21 yrs single b. Monroe Co W VA s/o Washington & - Broyles to SARAH E. CARR 20 yrs single b. Giles Co VA d/o Harry & - Carr 0: farmer; by Andrew L. French.

12. 21 Decr 1871 JOHN B. MILLS 20 yrs single b. Wyoming Co W VA now living same s/o Robert & Liddy Mills to MANERVA FALEY 16 yrs single b. Mercer Co W VA d/o A.B. & P. Faley 0: farmer; by Charles Walker.

13. 21 Decr 1871 HARMON W. BIRD 22 yrs single b. Bland Co VA s/o Stephen W & Malinda Bird to HESTER F. VERMILLION 16 yrs 6 mos 14 dys single b. Mercer Co W VA d/o Jas. R. & Elizth Vermillion 0: farmer; by Benjamin T. Bird.

14. 14 Sept 1871 ELI SHREWSBURY 19 yrs single b. Mercer Co W VA s/o Jno & Martha Shrewsbury to TILICE BAILEY 15 yrs single b. Mercer Co W VA d/o Thompson P & Mary J Bailey 0: farmer; by J.H. Honaker.

15. 19 Dec 1871 Princeton JOHN W. McCREERY 26 yrs wid. b. Monroe Co W VA now living Raleigh Co VA s/o Wm & Daurarius McCreery to MARY C. LACY 17 yrs single b. Ritchie Co VA d/o Henry & Mary Lacy 0: lawyer; by James H. Humphreys.

This was noted in the REMARKS between entry #15 & #16.
REMARKS: listed to here for auditon & mail.

16. 4 Jany 1872 WILLIAM H. EVANS 27 yrs single b. Luzarn Co TN s/o George & - Evans to MARY J. TUGGLE single b. Monroe Co VA d/o John & - Tuggle 0: farmer; by James Calfee.

17. 16 Jany 1872 LARKIN L. STINSON 26 yrs single b. Giles Co VA s/o Charles & Elizabeth Stinson to ELIZABETH L. DAVIS 28 yrs single b. Patrick Co VA d/o Jno W. & Temperance Davis 0: farmer; by J.O. Cassaday.

18. 16 Jany 1872 JAMES W. SCOTT 18 yrs single b. Mercer Co W VA s/o Saml. & Margaret A. Scott to NANCY E. McKINNEY 21 yrs single b. Wyoming Co W VA d/o Powhatton B. & Susan E. McKinney 0: farmer; by J.O. Cassaday.

19. 21 Decr 1871 JAMES M. CALDWELL 28 yrs single b. Mercer Co W VA now living Tazewell Co VA s/o Ed & Margaret Caldwell to SARAH E. ROSS 21 yrs single b. Montgomery Co VA d/o Griffith & Harriet Ross 0: farmer; by B.T. Lacy; REMARKS: this one listed to auditor.)

20. 17 Jany 1872 JOHN M. SMITH 17 yrs single b. Montgomery Co VA s/o Jno N. & Sarah C. Smith to ALWILDAY DAVIS 16 yrs single b. Mercer Co W VA d/o Green & Sarah Davis 0: farmer; by A.J. Thompson.

21. 18 Jany 1872 SOLOMON D. BROYLES 21 yrs single b. Monroe Co W VA s/o Thompson & Lucinda Broyles to MARTHA J. PENNINGTON 22 yrs single b. Mercer Co W VA d/o John A. & Ellen Pennington 0: farmer; by A.J. Thompson.

22. 18 Jany 1872 WILLIAM H. MEADOWS 27 yrs single b. Mercer Co W VA s/o Jeremiah & Jane Meadows to ELIZABETH S. PATTERSON 27 yrs single b. Bedford Co VA d/o Jas. & Gilen Patterson 0: farmer; by A.J. Thompson.

23. 11 Jany 1872 JAS. H. CUNNINGHAM 19 yrs single b. Wyoming Co VA now living same s/o James & Elizabeth Cunningham to SARAH J. WEIMER 22 yrs single b. Tazewell Co VA d/o Sam. & Massey Weimer 0: farmer; by James W. Lilly.

24. 7 Feb 1872 JAMES W. VINES 27 yrs single b. Monroe Co VA s/o Silas & Eliza Vines to SARAH F. CALFEE 20 yrs single b. Mercer Co W VA d/o Saml T. & Matilda D. Calfee 0: farmer; by J.O. Cassaday.

25. 15 Feb 1872 JOHN T. SKEENS 19 yrs 5 mos 3 dys single b. Giles co VA s/o Joseph & Nancy A. Skeens to AMANDA SHANNON 21 yrs 9 mos 5 dys single b. Campbell Co VA d/o Wm & Sarah Shannon 0: farmer; by Theodore Smith.

26. 15 Feb 1872 HARVEY PETERS 27 yrs single b. Giles Co VA s/o Thompson & Nancy Peters to MARTHA McCOMAS 35 yrs single b. Mercer Co W VA s/o James & Rebecca McComas 0: farmer; by Andrew L. French.

27. 14 Feb 1872 JOHN W. JOHNSTON 24 yrs single b. Mercer Co W VA s/o Alex & Nancy D. Johnston to MARY E. RICE 19 yrs single b. Green Co TN d/o David & Nancy A. Rice O: farmer; by Geo. Stewart.

28. 20 Feb 1872 ANDREW MELVIN 24 yrs single b. Mercer Co W VA s/o Hezekiah & Elizth Melvin to SUSAN E. DURHAM 19 yrs single b. Surry Co NC d/o Wm H. & Phoebe Durham O:farmer; by J.O. Cassaday.

29. 22 Feb 1872 PEMBROOK F. REED 18 yrs single b. Mercer Co W VA s/o John C. & Sarah J. Reed to MARY J. KARNES 15 yrs single b. Mercer Co W VA d/o Henry & Elizabeth Karnes O: farmer; by H. Robinson.

30. 18 Jany 1872 SAMUEL P. GEORGE 40 yrs single b. Tazewell Co VA s/o - & Henrietta George to ELMIRA HIGGINBOTHAM 25 yrs single b. Giles co VA d/o - & Susan Higginbotham O: farmer; by Evan H. Brown.

31. 13 Mar 1872 CHAS. J. TILLER 18 yrs single b. Mercer Co W VA s/o Wm D. & Rhoda Tiller to ELIZTH H. BELCHER 18 yrs single b. Mercer Co W VA d/o A.A. & ? Belcher O: farmer; by John H. Honaker.

32. 14 Mar 1872 JNO W. THOMAS 18 yrs single b. Mercer Co W VA s/o (Unknown) & Malvina Thomas to HARRIET N. HALE 22 yrs single b. Mercer Co W VA d/o Jno C. & - Hale O: farmer; by Theodore Smith.

33. 1 Feb 1872 JOHN R. JOHNSTON 17 yrs single b. Campbell Co VA s/o Saml & Mary J Johnston to JULIA A. MAFEY 17 yrs single b. Patrick Co VA d/o James B. & Ellen A. Mafey O:farmer; by A.J. Thompson.

34. 26 Mar 1872 PETER H. GRAVELLY 24 yrs single b. Henry Co VA now living in Carroll Co VA s/o John & Winney Gravelly to LOUISA GIBBS 24 yrs wid. b. Pittsylvania Co VA d/o Joseph & Martha James O: farmer; by H. Robinson.

35. 18 April 1872 LEWIS C. SHREWSBURY 24 yrs single b. Mercer Co W VA s/o Jas & Elizth Shrewsbury to NANCY ROSE 19 yrs single b. Grayson Co VA d/o Bryant & Ranzy Rose O: farmer; by Charles Walker.

36. 24 April 1872 JAMES A. MURRAY 17 yrs 11 mos single b. Bland Co VA s/o Skidmon & Julia A. Murray to AGORA N. CLENDENON 22 yrs single b. Mercer Co W VA d/o Robert C. & Almeda Clendenon O: farmer; by James O. Cassady.

37. 28 April 1872 GREEN W. FERGUSON 20 yrs single b. Mercer Co W VA s/o John & Swauna S. Ferguson to OCTAVIA WOOD 21 yrs single b. Mercer Co W VA d/o German & Nancy Wood O: farmer; by J.C. Hubbard.

38. 7 May 1872 JOHN CLEAVER 22 yrs single b. Tazewell Co VA s/o David & Polly Cleaver to NANCY E. ABSHER 16 yrs single b. Tazewell Co VA d/o Jas & Nancy Absher O: farmer; by James Calfee.

39. 16 May 1872 GEORGE B. WADDLE 25 yrs single b. Giles Co VA now living Raleigh Co VA s/o John A. & Polly Waddle to MINERVA A. BOLING 27 yrs single b. Mercer Co W VA d/o Wm & Elizth Boling O: farmer; by Samuel Scott.

40. 23 May 1872 MASTIN DILLION 65 yrs wid. to REBECCA LUSK 39 yrs wid. b. Mercer Co W VA d/o Jas. & Rebecca McComas O: farmer; by John H Honaker.

41. 21 May 1872 SAMUEL MINOR 21 yrs single b. Mercer Co W VA s/o Thos & E. Minor to LUCINDA BURGE 22 yrs single b. Tazewell Co VA d/o Jno & N. Burge O: farmer; by John H Honaker.

42. 1 June 1872 RIGHT. E. DANGERFIELD 25 yrs single b. Mercer Co W VA s/o Leonard H. & Nancy Dangerfield to SUSAN E. CARR 28 yrs single b. Giles Co VA d/o John & Sarah Carr O: Tanner & *?; by Wm E. Neal. (*Note: handwriting difficult to read.)

43. 8 June 1872 JOHN COX 50 yrs single b. Ash Co NC to RHODA MILLER 38 yrs single b. Ash Co NC O: farmer; by Chas. Walker.

44. 3 July 1872 P.T. SHREWSBURY 20 yrs single b. Mercer Co W VA s/o Phillip & Charlotte Shrewsbury to IOWA MAXEY 18 yrs single b. Mercer Co W VA d/o Preston & Celia A. Maxey O: farmer; by Wm C. Martin.

45. 1 July 1872 JOHN W. McKINNEY 21 yrs single b. Wyoming Co W VA s/o Han McKinney to EMILY F. RINEHART 21 yrs single b. Wyoming Co W VA d/o Jno & Juliet Rinehart O: farmer.

46. 6 July 1872 LEE C. MORAN 24 yrs wid. b. Ash Co NC s/o Jas M & Sarah Moran to FANNY E. SADDLER 21 yrs single b. VA d/o Henry Saddler O: farmer; by John H Honaker.

47. 19 July 1872 GREEN PENNINGTON 21 yrs single b. Mercer Co W VA s/o Jno & Ellen Pennington to MARTHA WHITTAKER 20 yrs single b.Giles Co VA d/o Wm & Ruth Whittaker O: farmer; by A.J. Thompson.

48. 23 July 1872 R.B. SOLESBURY 20 yrs single b. Mercer Co W VA s/o Jno & Elizth Solesbury to MARY CLENDENON 18 yrs single b. Wyoming Co W VA d/o Arglen & M. Clendenon O:farmer; by Chas. Walker.

Page 22

1. 1 Aug 1872 THOS. BELCHER 20 yrs single b. Mercer Co W VA s/o Obadiah Belcher to RACHEL DILLION 18 yrs single b. Mercer Co W VA d/o Mastin & R. Dillion O: farmer; by R.V. Godfrey.

2. 3 Aug 1872 R.A. CRAWFORD 19 yrs single b. Mercer Co W VA s/o Thos & Elizth Crawford to S.E. THORNTON 17 yrs single b. Pulaski Co VA d/o Wm R. & S.E. Thornton O: farmer; by R.A. Miller.

3. 3 Aug 1872 B.P. HARMAN 23 yrs single b. Mercer Co W VA s/o Sallie Harman to M.C. CALENDER 15 yrs single b. Mercer Co W VA d/o Susan Calender O: farmer; by Evan H. Brown.

4. 27 Aug 1872 H. HIGGINBOTHAM 30 yrs single b. Mercer Co W VA s/o Mary Higginbotham to MARY S. AUSTIN 28 yrs single b. Pittsylvania Co VA d/o G.A. & E.J. Austin O: farmer; by E.A. Austin.

5. 29 Aug 1872 WM F. KEATON 22 yrs single b. Mercer Co W VA now living in Summers Co W VA s/o Leroy & Eliza J. Keaton to S.R. FARLEY 16 yrs single b. Mercer Co W VA d/o N.H. & S.E. Farley O: farmer; by John Bragg.

6. 2 Sep 1872 SAML. HUBBARD 58 yrs wid. b. Floyd Co VA to E. BLANKENSHIP 22 yrs single b. Giles Co VA d/o Ed. & Sus. Blankenship O: farmer; by J.O. Cassaday.

7. 3 Sep 1872 STEP G.J. BIRD 17 yrs single b. Franklin Co VA s/o F.A. & H.A.E. Bird to SUSAN J. PERDUE 24 yrs single b. Giles Co VA d/o Fierg. & Nancy Perdue O: farmer; by Theodore Smith.

8. 4 Sep 1872 W.E. MARTIN 20 yrs single b. Mercer Co W VA s/o Acles & E. Martin to JUDA V. WHITE 16 yrs single b. Mercer Co W VA d/o And & Elizth White O: farmer; by William Holroyd.

9. 4 Sep 1872 CH. W. MILLS 24 yrs single b. Mercer Co W VA s/o Benj & Mary O. Mills to ESTHER A. WEINER 18 yrs single b. Mercer Co W VA d/o Jas. & Elizth Weiner O: farmer; by J.O. Cassaday.

10. 7 Sep 1872 GEO. W. BELL 20 yrs single b. Mercer Co W VA s/o Jas. & J.A. Bell to S.E. TOTTON 18 yrs single b. McDowell Co VA d/o Wm & Elizth Totton O: farmer; by John H Honaker.

11. 20 Sep 1872 GEO N. HALL 29 yrs single b. Tazewell Co VA s/o Geo. & Earsley Irskins to MALINDA HENDERSON 19 yrs single b. Pulaski Co VA d/o Perry & Christianna Henderson O: shoemaker; by J.O. Cassaday; REMARKS: cold.

12. 7 Oct 1872 THOMAS LILLY wid. s/o Robt & Mary Lilly to NANCY BOWLING single d/o John & Sallie Bowling O: farmer; by R.G. French. (Note: no other information given.)

13. 10 Oct 1872 JAMES B. RECK 29 yrs single b. Giles Co VA now living same s/o George H. & Sarah Reck to MARY G. McNUTT 22 yrs single b. Mercer Co W VA d/o Robt B. & Ellen McNutt O: lawyer; by Geo. Stuart.

14. 9 Sept 1872 GEORGE SMITH 22 yrs single b. Montgomery Co VA s/o George & Jane Smith to VICTORIA TURNER 26 yrs wid. b. Mercer Co W VA d/o Jno A. & - McKinzie O: farmer; by Richard A. Miller.

15. 4 Nov 1872 R.W. GADD 19 yrs single b. Mercer Co W VA s/o A.P & Delila Gadd to E.M. MARTIN 19 yrs single b. Mercer Co W VA d/o Adam Martin O: farmer; by William Holroyd.

16. 11 Nov 1872 GREEN A. JOHNSTON 20 yrs single b. Mercer Co W VA s/o John L. & M.N. Johnston to LOUISA WELLS* 20 yrs single b. Mercer Co W VA d/o Danl. & Elizabeth Well* O: farmer; by Richard A. Miller. (*Note: name spelled both ways.)

17. 4 Dec 1872 WM. MILLER 79 yrs wid. b. Mercer Co W VA to SUSANAH HYLE* 56 yrs wid. O: farmer; by B.T. Bird. (*Note: black smear on name, difficult to read.)

18. 10 Dec 1872 PETER MILLER 36 yrs single b. Monroe Co VA s/o Peter & Mary Miller to CLARA OLIVER 17 yrs single d/o * & Eliza * O: farmer; by J.O. Cassaday. (*Note: no other name given.)

19. 10 Dec 1872 WM CLARK 21 yrs single b. Mercer Co W VA s/o Wm Clark & E. Oliver to SOPHONIA COWLING 18 yrs single b. Campbell Co VA O: farmer; by J.O. Cassaday.

20. 14 Dec 1872 JOHN R. GOTT 23 yrs single b. Giles co VA s/o Andrew & Francis Gott to M.A.J. CARR 20 yrs single b. Mercer Co W VA d/o John & Sallie Carr O: carpenter; by W.J. Philips.

21. 24 Dec 1872 ISAIAH W. DUNN 24 yrs single b. Pitsylvania Co VA s/o M.W. & Millie J. Dunn to ANNIE SNODGRASS 22 yrs single b. Giles Co VA s/o Sarah Snodgrass O: farmer; by J.O. Cassaday.

22. 31 Dec 1872 M.B. SMITH 24 yrs single b. Rockbridge Co VA s/o Thos. & Sallie Smith to V.B. CALFEE 20 yrs single b. Mercer Co W VA d/o S.T. & Matilda Calfee O: farmer; by J.O. Cassaday.

23. 24 Dec 1872 T.T. DILLION 24 yrs single b. Mercer Co W VA s/o Jesse & Cynthia Dillion to SALLIE A. HERNDON 17 yrs single b. Mercer Co W VA d/o Arthur & S.E.B. Herndon O: farmer; by J.H. Honaker.

24. 28 Dec 1872 SAMUEL W. BELCHER 23 yrs single b. Mercer Co W VA s/o Chris & Mary Belcher to NANCY C. HARRY single b. Mercer Co W VA d/o Calvin & Mary Harry O: farmer; by J.H. Honaker.

25. 8 Jany 1873 LEWIS WOOLWINE 27 yrs single b. Montgomery Co VA s/o Jno L. & Nancy Woolwine to ELMIRA H. ROBERTSON 27 yrs single b. Buckingham Co VA d/o Jno L. & Amanda Robertson O: farmer; by William Holroyd.

26. 30 Jany 1873 JOHN D. MOYE 21 yrs single b. Wyoming Co VA s/o Wm & Martha J. Moye to MARTHA F. MAXEY 21 yrs single b. Mercer Co W VA d/o Josiah & Mary Maxey O: farmer; by Benj T. Bird.

27. 6 Feby 1873 JACOB H. WHITE 21 yrs single b. Mercer Co W VA s/o Patton & Rhoda White to RHODA H. BLANKENSHIP 22 yrs single b. Mercer Co W VA d/o Lewis & Mary Blankenship O: farmer; by Andrew J. Thompson.

28. 6 Feby 1873 JAMES K. WHITE 18 yrs single b. Mercer Co W VA s/o Patton & Rhoda White to JULIA ANN HALDREN 17 yrs single b. Mercer Co W VA d/o Saml. & Lonsan Haldren O:farmer; by Andrew J. Thompson.

29. 13 Feby 1873 AUGUSTUS J. BAILEY 23 yrs single b. Mercer Co W VA s/o Floyd & Zelpha Bailey to ANNA COOK 16 yrs single b. Wyoming Co VA d/o Thomas & Nancy Cook O:farmer; by Andrew J French.

30. 19 Feby 1873 WM E. SHUFFLEBARGER 19 yrs single b. Pulaski Co VA now living Tazewell Co VA s/o David & Elizabeth Shufflebarger to MARY M. JOHNSTON 18 yrs single b. Mercer Co W VA d/o Jno W. & Margaret Johnston O: carpenter; by Evan H. Brown.

31. 13 Feby 1873 JNO SNEED 20 yrs single b. Mercer Co W VA s/o Jno T. & Sally Sneed to ANN E. SWIMNEY 21 yrs single b. Mercer Co W VA d/o James J. & Martha Massey O: farmer; by Elias Reed.

32. 20 Jan 1873 REUBEN G. HUGHS 24 yrs single b. Giles Co VA now living same s/o Geo W. & Susan Hughs to SARAH J. MARTIN 21 yrs single b. Mercer Co W VA d/o Wm C. & Ann Martin O: farmer; by Benjamin T. Bird.

33. 13 Jan 1873 GEO P. WILLIAMS 22 yrs single b. Giles Co VA now living same s/o Jno M. & Catharine Williams to ALICE J. GIBSON 18 yrs single b. Pitsylvanic Co VA d/o Jas M. & L.M. Gibson O: farmer; by G.A. Austin.

34. 29 Dec 1872 JOSHUA HAZELWOOD 19 yrs single b. Patrick Co VA s/o Joshua & Charity Hazelwood to NANCY J. HUGHS 16 yrs single b. Giles Co VA d/o Geo W. & Susan Hughs O: farmer; by B.T. Bird.

35. 20 Feby 1873 JESSE THOMAS 70 yrs wid. b. Giles Co VA s/o John & Pheba Thomas to MARY C. HUFFMAN 32 yrs wid. b. Craig Co VA d/o Wm & Sofa Caldwell O: farmer; by J.O. Cassaday.

36. 20 Feby 1873 HENRY G. MILLS 23 yrs single b. Mercer Co W VA s/o Robert & Tepla Mills to CLARA C. SHREWSBURY 27 yrs single b. Mercer Co W VA d/o James & Elizth Shrewsbury O: farmer; by Elias Reed.

37. 20 Feby 1873 WM E. REYNOLDS 40 yrs single b. Craig Co VA s/o Wm E. & Eliza. Reynolds to MINERVA J. STINSTON 30 yrs single b. Giles Co VA d/o Chas & Elizabeth Stinston O: farmer; by J.O. Cassaday; REMARKS: Listed to here auditor & mail.

38. 6 Marcy 1873 JOHN COOPER 21 yrs single b. Raleigh Co W VA now living same s/o Lewis & Polly A. Cooper to SARAH M. GADD 14 yrs single b. Mercer Co W VA d/o And., P. & Delila E. Gadd O: farmer; by James W. Lilly.

39. 4 March 1873 JOSEPH H. BIRD 22 yrs single b. Franklin co VA s/o John & Sarah Bird to ELIZABETH WILEY 19 yrs single b. Wyoming co W VA d/o James & Nancy Wiley O: farmer; by Wm C Dobbins.

40. 6 March 1873 DAVID SIER 22 yrs single b. Roanoke Co VA s/o Soloman & Sarah Sier to ZILPHIA A. BAILEY 28 yrs single b. Mercer Co W VA d/o Henry & Polly Bailey O: farmer; by John H Honaker.

41. 11 March 1873 JOHNSTON HALL 54 yrs wid. b. Mercer Co W VA s/o John & Rhoda Hall to IDA ABBOTT 35 yrs wid. b. Mercer Co W VA d/o And & Anna Farley O: shoemaker; by Benj T. Bird.

42. * March 1873 HIRAM THOMPSON 55 yrs wid. b. Montgomery Co VA s/o Clabum & Omey Thompson to JANE H. HALL 20 yrs single b. Franklin Co VA d/o Preston B. & Mary Hall O: farmer. (*Note: no date given.)

43. 20 March 1873 JOHN M. PAINE 21 yrs single b. Mercer Co W VA now living Tazewell Co VA s/o Wm & July Paine to CYNTHIA TAYLOR 21 yrs single b. Mercer Co W VA d/o Sampson & Martha Taylor O: farmer; by Evan H. Brown.

44. 31 March 1873 ECL. FLICK 17 yrs single b. Mercer Co W VA s/o Jn. M.N. & Ann M. Flick to ANN HALE 18 yrs single b. Giles Co VA d/o Jno D. & Jane Hale O: farmer; by William Holroyd.

45. 3 Apl 1873 GEO. W. DEVOR 23 yrs single b. Bland Co VA now living same s/o John & Conbull Decor to T.T. FANNING 19 yrs single b. Mercer Co W VA d/o Benjamin & Nancy Fanning O: carpenter; by B.T. Bird.

46. 3 Apl 1873 GEO W. BELCHER 39 yrs single b. Mercer Co W VA s/o Obediah & Martha Belcher to MARY E. BAILEY 23 yrs single b. Mercer Co W VA d/o Philip P. & Francis Bailey O: farmer; by James Calfee.

47. 9 Apl 1873 WM G. MEMX 29 yrs single. b. Pitsylvania Co VA now living in Giles Co VA s/o Dotsey & Maur Memx to MARGARET A. ADAMS 28 wid. d/o * & * Jordan O: farmer; by B.T. Bird. (*Note: no name given.)

Page 23

1. 13 Apl 1873 WILLIAM HURST 53 yrs wid. b. Wythe Co VA s/o Thos. & Jemima Hurst to MARY E. BAILEY 40 yrs single b. Giles Co VA d/o Jamison & Elz. Bailey O: farmer; by John H. Honaker.

2. 13 Apl 1873 AMOS D. THOMPSON 24 yrs single b. Tazewell Co VA s/o David & Angeline Thompson to DONNIE HERNDON 19 yrs single b. Mercer co W VA d/o Arthur & S.E.B. Herndon O: farmer; by John H. Honaker.

3. 1 May 1873 JOEL E. HOPKINS 37 yrs single b. Bedford Co VA s/o James F. & Marn P. Hopkins to LOUISA J. BROWN 16 yrs single b. Mercer Co W VA d/o Allen & Mary Brown O:farmer; by William C Martin.

4. 15 May 1873 RALPH SHRADER 20 yrs single b. Mercer Co W VA s/o David & Cloe Shrader to JULIANA V. BELCHER 15 yrs single b. Mercer Co W VA d/o Bartley & Sallie Belcher O: farmer; by John H. Honaker.

5. 22 May 1873 WILLIAM W. HAGER 24 yrs single b. Mercer Co W VA s/o - & Beckey Smith* to BECKY A. SMITH 24 yrs single b. Mercer Co W VA d/o Russel & Sarah Hager* O: farmer. (*Note: the parents' names should be reversed.)

6. 29 May 1873 TILLUSON CHRISTY 21 yrs single b. Monroe Co VA s/o Thos & Cath. Christy to SARAH G. DEWESE 16 yrs single b. Montgomery Co VA d/o Andrew J. & Rosanah Dewese O: farmer.

7. 14 June 1873 JOSEPH H. BANE 32 yrs single b. Tazewell Co VA s/o Wm R. & Nancy Bane to RACHEL C. WITTEN 21 yrs single b. Mercer Co W VA d/o Wm H. & Mary Witten O: farmer; by Evan H. Brown.

8. This entire line is blank.

9. 17 July 1873 BASTON ROSE 19 yrs single b. Grayson Co VA to REBECCA J. McCOMAS 16 yrs single b. Mercer Co W VA; by A.L. French.

10. 29 July 1873 DANIEL T. LILLY 26 yrs wid. b. Mercer Co W VA s/o Washington & Mary Lilly to ALMIRA F. FARLEY 18 yrs single b. Mercer Co W VA d/o Andrew & Sarah Farler O: farmer; by James W. Lilly.

NOTE: #11 - #48 DO NOT contain the parents' names or the occupation for either the husband or the bride. When able have obtained parents' names from 1860 Mercer Co VA-WV Census.

11. 30 July 1873 WILLIAM J. HIX 26 yrs single b. Roanoke co VA; by J.O Cassaday.

12. 13 Aug 1873 RICHD W. ROBERTSON 24 yrs single b. Buckingham Co VA to MARIA L.V. SHEPHARD 22 yrs single b. Buckingham Co VA; by W.J. Phillips.

13. 7 Aug 1873 SYNCH P. SHELTIN 27 yrs b. Pitsylvania Co VA to ETHAL ELIZTH MASSEY 18 yrs b. Carroll Co VA; by R.G. French.

14. 7 Aug 1873 CONRAD SHRADER 18 yrs b. Mercer Co W VA (s/o John & Nancy, #39) to VIRGINIA A. RATLIFF 18 yrs b. Mercer Co W VA; by A.L. French.

15. 14 Aug 1873 OBEDIAH TABOR 20 yrs b. Tazewell Co VA now living same to LUMHA J. HONAKER 18 yrs b. Mercer Co W VA; by A.L. French.

16. 28 Aug 1873 WILLIAM H. GADD 18 yrs b. Mercer Co W VA (s/o Andrew P. & Delila E, #779) to LUCINDA E. WOOD 16 yrs b. Raleigh Co VA; by James W. Lilly.

17. 4 Sep 1873 RAISON A. BIRD 28 yrs b. Bland Co VA now living same to MINTERY R. BONSLANG 21 yrs b. Patrick Co VA; by A.A. Ashworth.

18. 18 Sep 1873 DANL H. BUICE 27 yrs b. Bland Co VA to MARTHA M. CARR 22 yrs b. Mercer Co W VA (d/o Robert & Sarah Carr, #234); by W.O Phillips.

19. 2 Oct 1873 WILLIAM R. SHREWSBURY 19 yrs b. Wyoming Co VA to CYNTHIA WEIMER 20 yrs b. Mercer Co W VA; R.G. French.

20. 21 Oct 1873 JOHN H. HOLSTIN 19 yrs b. Mercer Co W VA to SUSAN E. SNIDOW 18 yrs b. Mercer Co W VA; by B.T. Bird.

21. 30 Oct 1873 LEVI PENNINGTON 26 yrs b. Mercer Co W VA (s/o John A. & Ellen, #452) to SALLIE A BROYLES 16 yrs b. Monroe Co VA; by A.J. Thompson.

22. 22 Nov 1873 THOMAS D. SINK 20 yrs b. Franklin Co VA to HARRIET L. FAULKNER 17 yrs b. Mercer Co W VA (d/o Hugh M. & Susannah, #54); by Jno H. Honaker.

23. 20 Nov 1873 WM McH TILLER 26 yrs b. Mercer Co W VA to MINERVA A. WHITE 17 yrs b. Mercer Co W VA; by Richard A. Miller.

24. 23 Nov 1873 23 NOV 1873 WM WHITTAKER 50 yrs b. Pulaski Co VA to MARY JANE HEARN 30 yrs b. Mercer Co W VA (d/o Levi & Paulina Hearn, #576).

25. 4 Decr 1873 MONDACAI NELSON 21 yrs b. Patrick Co VA to MARY BELCHER 21 yrs b. Mercer Co W VA; by Wm Holroyd.

26. 13 Decr 1873 BALLARD P. PENNINGTON 20 yrs single b. Mercer Co W VA to RUSH H. LINIS* 18 yrs single b. Mercer Co W VA; by Richard A. Miller. (*Note: handwriting difficult to read.)

27. 20 Decr 1873 JOHN W. PEFRAM 26 yrs single b. NC to ALMEDA H. BURGESS 24 yrs single b. Raleigh Co W VA; by R.G. French.

28. 30 Decr 1873 ROBERT G. WILLIAMS 20 yrs b. Mercer Co W VA to RHODA JANE SCOTT 17 yrs b. Mercer Co W VA (d/o Samuel & Margaret A. Scott, #188); by Wm Holroyd.

This is the beginning of the entries for 1874, though not stated on this page.

29. 1 Jany 1874 MIFFLIN W. WINFREY 22 yrs single b. Mercer Co W VA now living Summers Co W VA (s/o Burrell & Orina Winfrey, #164) to MARY V.H. BROWN 18 yrs single b. Mercer Co W VA; by J.O. Cassaday.

30. 15 Jany (1874) PASCAL BUTLER 23 yrs b. Monroe Co W VA to ELIZABETH A. DUNN 23 yrs b. Pitsylvania Co VA; by J.O. Cassaday.

31. 14 Jany (1874) JOHN W. DUNN 20 yrs b. Mercer Co W VA to MARY C. DAVIS 22 yrs b. Mercer Co W VA; by Richd. A. Miller.

32. 13 Jany (1874) JOHN H. SHELTON 25 yrs single b. Patrick Vo VA to ELIZA E. BOWLLING 21 yrs single b. Patrick Co VA; by J.O. Cassaday.

33. 16 Jany (1874) A.C. BAILEY 35 yrs b. Mercer Co W VA to CYNTHIA J. DILLION 18 yrs; by John H. Honaker.

34. 17 Jany (1874) J.W. HAWLEY 27 yrs single b. Montgomery Co VA now living Tazewell Co VA to E.J. PRUNTY 27 yrs single b. Wythe Co VA; by Evan H. Brown.

35. 17 Jany (1874) G.F. BAILEY 38 yrs single b. Mercer Co W VA to E.A. GODFRY 34 yrs wid. b. Wythe Co VA; by James Calfee.

36. 27 Jany (1874) RUSSELL SWADER 20 yrs single b. Mercer Co W VA to SARAH HICKSON 20 yrs single b. Mercer Co W VA; by L. Goodwin.

37. 2 Feby (1874) AECE. WILKMAN 24 yrs b. Wyoming Co VA now living in Wayne Co W VA to MARGARET J. WORKMAN 18 yrs b. Wyoming co W VA; by John H. Honaker.

38. 2 Feby (1874) SAMUEL SHITT 20 yrs single b. Mercer Co W VA to MAY S. WRIGHT 19 yrs single b. Mercer Co W VA; by John H. Honaker.

39. 9 Feby (1874) AUGUSTUS B. GODFREY 24 yrs single b. Mercer Co W VA (s/o John D. & Martha Godfrey, #56) to SARAH M. TILLER 14 yrs single b. Mercer Co W VA (d/o William D. & Rhoda Tiller, #136); by A.L. French.

40. 10 Feby (1874) M.M. WALKER 19 yrs single b. Raleigh Co VA to MILLE HURST 19 yrs single b. Mercer Co W VA; by John H. Honaker.

41. 12 Feby (1874) THOMAS PUCKETT 22 yrs single b. Franklin Co VA now living in Tazewell Co VA to CYNTHIA M. FLORANCE 17 yrs single b. Tazewell Co VA; by Evan H. Brown.

42. 25 Feby (1874) WINFIDA T. SHORTER 25 yrs single b. Franklin Co VA to MARY WILEY 19 yrs single b. Mercer Co W VA; by G.A. Austin.

43. 2 March (1874) WILLIAM J. ***LEWOOD 22 yrs single b. Patrick Co VA to AMANDA VIDWELL 28 yrs single b. Raleigh Co W VA;by J.W. Bennett. (***Note: unable to read handwriting.)

44. 8 March (1874) WM L. HARVEY 22 yrs single b. Summers Co W VA now living same to ADALINE FARLEY 18 yrs single b. Mercer Co W VA (d/o William & Lucy A. Farley, #815); by James W. Lilley.

45. 8 March (1874) JASPER M. HARVEY 29 yrs b. Monroe Co W VA to ANNETTA J. FERGUSON 21 yrs b. Mercer Co W VA; by James W. Lilley.

46. 12 March (1874) AHAM GARRETSON 20 yrs b. Wyoming co W VA to CHARLOTTE J. OWNBY 15 yrs b. Tazewell Co VA; by R.A. Miller.

47. 19 March (1874) ANDERSON BELCHER 17 yrs b. Mercer Co W VA to MATILDA HURST 16 yrs b. Mercer Co W VA; by A.P.L. French.

48. 5 April (1874) IVIN H. SHREWSBURY 18 yrs b. Mercer Co W VA to JULIET Y. CLENDENEN 17 yrs b. Wyoming co W VA; by Russell G. French.

Page 24

1. 13 July 1873 JONATHAN RAINS 52 yrs b. Wythe Co VA to CAUSBY HARMAN 25 yrs b. Tazewell Co VA; by A.L. French; REMARKS: colored.

2. 22 Sept 1873 CHARLES HERNDEN 26 yrs b. Campbell Co VA to HANA NICKISON 17 yrs; by Harrison Robinson; REMARKS: colored.

3.(NOTE: this entry has been marked through.) 15 April (?) DAVID P. COOK 19 yrs single b. Mercer Co W VA to MAHALA WILEY 17 yrs single b. Mercer co W VA; REMARKS: colored. (? Unsure of year.)

4. 25 Nov 1874 JORDAN WALKER 21 yrs single b. Monroe Co W VA now living in Summers Co W VA s/o Hannah Walker to CAROLINE GORE 24 yrs single b. Mercer Co W VA d/o Matilda Gore O: farmer; by J.W. Bennett; REMARKS: colored.

5. 3 Mar 1875 JOHN CLARK 41 yrs wid. b. Madison Co AL s/o Nizy Clark to ELZA OLIVER 44 yrs wid. b. Monroe Co W VA O: farmer; by Harrison Robinson; REMARKS: colored.

6. 29 Sept 1875 PHILIP WASHINGTON 30 yrs single b. Rockbridge Co VA s/o Geo & Harriet Washington to MILLE NICHSON 36 yrs single b. Pulaski Co VA d/o Thomas & Nicy Clark O: farmer; by Harrison Robinson; REMARKS: colored.

Page 25

(The following two names were written at top of page without a number.)

5 Nov 1875 MAS. W. BAILEY 56 yrs wid. b. Mercer Co W VA to ELIZA SMITH 40 yrs single b. Logan Co W Va; by Wm M. Crawford.

2 July 1874 JOHN BAILEY 25 yrs single b. Mercer Co W VA to SARAH KENZER 26 yrs single b. Tazewell Co VA; by A.P.L. French.

1. 9 Apl 1874 AUGUSTUS C. MAXEY 28 yrs b. Mercer Co W Va (s/o Josiah & Mary Maxey, #717) to ELZ. F. ROWLAND 20 yrs b. Mercer Co W VA (d/o Jackson & Sarah, #615); by Russell G. French.

2. 15 Apl 1874 WILLIAM L. DUDLEY 25 yrs b. Bland Co VA to BECKY ANN HALL 18 yrs b. Franklin Co VA;by J.O. Cassaday

3. 14 Apl 1874 JOHN T. SHUMATE 33 yrs b. Giles Co VA now living same to LOUISA F. THOMPSON 20 yrs b. Mercer Co W VA (d/o Phillip & Mary J. Thompson, #538); by A.J. Thompson.

4. 16 Apl 1874 DANIEL P. COOK 19 yrs b. Mercer Co W VA (s/o Cornelius & Ann Cook, #707) to MAHALA WILEY 17 yrs b. Mercer Co W VA (d/o Vincent & Cyntha Wiley, #652).

5. 18 May 1874 JOHN H. CARTER 21 yrs b. Tazewell Co VA now living same to EMILINA HARLEY 22 yrs b. Bland Co VA now living Tazewell Co VA; by James Calfee.

6. * * 1874 JAMES B. SHREWSBURY 27 yrs b. Mercer Co W VA to MARY A. MASSEY 18 yrs b. Carroll Co VA.

7. 9 June 1874 WILLIAM A. PENDLETON 21 yrs b. Campbell Co W VA (s/o Wyatt W. & Rachel A. Pendleton, #467) to MARY JANE TANNER 22 yrs b. Botetourt Co VA; by Geo A. Miller.

8. 16 June 1874 J.H. HIGGINBOTHAM 25 yrs b. Mercer Co W VA to SAVELETT D. KAHLE 16 yrs b. Mercer Co W VA; by E.H. Brown.

9. 23 June 1874 THOS P. MORGAN 25 yrs b. Wyoming Co VA to MARTHA HEDLIN 16 yrs b. Bedford Co VA; by Jas. Calfee.

10. 16 July 1874 ISHAM D. BELCHER 33 yrs b. Mercer Co W VA (s/o Henry D. & Ann, #862) to MARTHA HURST 22 yrs b. Mercer Co W VA; by A.L. French.

11. 15 July 1874 GEORGE B. MARTIN 24 yrs b. Mercer Co W VA to MARY KEATLEY 22 yrs b. Mercer Co W VA; by B.T. Bird.

12. 11 Aug 1874 JAMES F.M. LILLEY 26 yrs b. Mercer Co W VA to MARY V. LILLEY 21 yrs b. Mercer Co W VA.

13. 23 July 1874 ANDERSON M. BAILEY 21 yrs b. Mercer Co W VA to MATILDA J. GODFREY 17 yrs b. Mercer Co W VA; by A.R.L. French.

14. 30 July 1874 WILEY W. BAILEY 22 yrs b. Mercer Co W VA (s/o Jonathan S. & Julia Bailey, #5) to ELECTRA V. DAY 17 yrs b. Mercer Co W VA; by A.R.L. French.

15. 30 July 1874 PURVIS A. BOWLING 23 yrs b. Mercer Co W VA to CYNTHIA J. BIRD 22 yrs b. Mercer Co W VA; by A.A. Ashworth.

16. 13 Aug 1874 HENRY BELL 18 yrs b. Mercer Co W VA (s/o James & Julia A. Bell, #274) to JULIA ANN BELCHER 22 yrs b. Mercer Co W VA; by A.R.L. French.

17. 13 Aug 1874 JAS. W. LAMBERT 22 yrs b. Bland Co VA to CATHARINE F. CALFEE 22 yrs b. Mercer Co W VA; by James Calfee.

18. 13 Aug 1874 RUFUS G. MEADOR 23 yrs b. Mercer Co W VA (s/o Elizabeth Meador, #881) to ELZ. R. OXLEY 17 yrs b. Bland Co VA; by B.T. Bird.

19. 20 Aug 1874 GIDEON BURCHETT 21 yrs b. NC to MARY J. TAYLOR 15 yrs b. Mercer Co W VA; by A.R.L. French.

20. 20 Aug 1874 ROBERT O. CARPER 23 yrs b. Craig Co VA to ARDELIA C. McKINZIE 16 yrs b. Mercer Co W VA; by Jas O. Cassaday.

21. 22 Oct 1874 HARMAN WHITE 18 yrs b. Mercer Co W VA to SARAH J. PENNINGTON 21 yrs b. Mercer Co W VA (d/o Riley & Elizabeth Pennington, #558); by R.J. Thompson.

22. 21 Oct 1874 JAMES A. FARLEY 20 yrs b. Mercer Co W VA now living in Summers Co VA (s/o Henley & Sarah Farley, #953) to RACHEL A. MEADOR 17 yrs b. Mercer Co W VA; by John A. Meador.

23. 21 Oct 1874 ACLES MARTIN 53 yrs b. Giles Co VA to ELIZABETH MEADOR 45 yrs b. Monroe Co VA; by Wm C. Martin.

24. 21 Oct 1874 WM R. CARR 34 yrs b. Giles Co VA to MELISSA V. BRATTEN 18 yrs b. Mercer Co W VA; by Jas O. Cassaday.

25. 19 Nov 1874 ISAAC J. LILLEY 23 yrs b. Mercer Co W VA (s/o Johnathan & Ruhama Lilly, #762) to SUSAM B. STOVALL 16 yrs b. Mercer Co W VA (d/o Albert G. & Nancy Stovall, #182); by Jas. W. Lilley.

26. 20 Nov 1874 DAVID H. SMITH 19 yrs b. Montgomery Co VA to ALLICE J. WHITTAKER 16 yrs b. Mercer Co W VA; by R.A. Miller.

27. 16 Dec 1874 GASTON M. WILEY 25 yrs b. Giles Co VA to EMMA F. CLEMONS 19 yrs b. Henry Co VA; by A.J. Thompson.

28. 5 Dec 1874 AMOS L. PETRY 20 yrs b. Mercer Co W VA to PERMELIA PETRY 21 yrs b. Mercer Co W VA; by Wm C. Martin.

29. 8 Dec 1874 JOHN A. HOLDREN 22 yrs b. Mercer Co W Va to MOLLIE S. CLEMMONS 22 yrs; by A.J. Thompson.

30. 12 Dec 1874 JAMES A. BURNETT 20 yrs b. Mercer Co W VA to MARY W. DAY 18 yrs b. Giles Co VA; by A.P.L. French.

31. 15 Dec 1874 JOHN S. BAILEY 18 yrs b. Mercer Co W VA to LINA N. GODFREY 19 yrs b. Mercer Co W VA; by A.P.L. French.

32. 16 Dec 1874 WILLIAM L. DAVIS 19 yrs b. Giles Co VA now living same to ELIZABETH CHATTING 16 yrs b. Mercer Co W VA; by R.A. Miller.

33. 16 Dec 1874 CHARLES A. DEATIN 35 yrs b. Roanoke Co VA to SARAH F. McCLAUGHERTY 36 yrs b. Giles Co VA; by Evan H. Brown.

34. 23 Dec 1874 RICHD. H. KINZER 21 yrs b. Tazewell Co VA now living same to ALICE A. GODFREY 18 yrs b. Pulaski Co VA; by James Calfee.

35. 31 Dec 1874 FIELDING COMPTON 21 yrs b. Tazewell Co VA to BATHILDA LARRUE 23 yrs b. Grayson Co VA; by Evan H. Brown.

36. 28 Dec 1874 JOHN W.C. WALKER 19 yrs b. Wyoming Co VA now living in Raleigh Co W VA to NANCY BAILEY 19 yrs b. Mercer Co W VA; by Chas. Walker.

37. 29 Dec 1874 GEORGE T. HETHERINGTON 25 yrs b. Monroe Co VA to C.T.J. JOHNSTON 18 yrs b. Giles Co VA; by ? Kimkaid; REMARKS: Sisteo & Hd to auditor. (?= unable to read handwriting.)

38. 6 Jany 1875 W.R. WALTERS 19 yrs single b. Mercer Co W VA s/o Moses & S. Walters to MARGARET J. WINFREY 21 yrs single b. Mercer Co W VA d/o Burrell & Orina Winfrey O: farmer; by J.O. Cassaday.

39. 7 Jany 1875 JOHNSTON B. ROSS 28 yrs single b. Bath Co VA to JANE HAMLIN 19 yrs single b. Mercer Co W VA O: farmer; by R.B. McKinney.

40. 14 Jany 1875 MITCHELL HAWKS 19 yrs single b. Wythe Co VA s/o A. & Bulia Hawks to SUSAN HARMAN 17 yrs single b. Carroll Co VA d/o Geo & Elzth Harman O: farmer; by A.P.L. French.

41. 26 Jany 1875 GEORGE W. FANNING 38 yrs wid. g. Giles Co VA now living in Bland Co VA s/o Joseph & Jane Fanning to HANNAH M. DAVIDSON 26 yrs single b. Mercer Co W VA d/o Joseph & Jane Davidson O: farmer; by Evan H. Brown.

42. 16 Jany 1875 GEORGE W. SHREWSBURY 21 yrs b. Mercer Co W VA to ELZ A. McCOMAS 22 yrs b. Mercer Co W VA O: farmer; by Chas. Walker.

43. 14 Jany 1875 ROBT ROBINSON 22 yrs b. Buckingham Co VA to VIRGINIA E. WHITE 17 yrs b. Mercer Co W VA O: farmer; by R.A. Miller.

44. 14 Jany 1875 JOHN HAZLEWOOD 21 yrs single b. NC s/o Joshua Hazlewood to OLIVE M. WHITTAKER 19 yrs single b. Giles Co VA d/o Jas. & Hulda Whittaker O: farmer; by A.J. Thompson.

45. 21 Jany 1875 ROBT S. EASTER 20 yrs single b. Montgomery Co VA s/o W.W. Easter & Susan to MARTHA H.J. DAVIS 16 yrs single b. Mercer Co W VA d/o Landon & Mary Davis O: farmer; by R.A. Miller.

46. 28 Jany 1875 CLARKSTON C. REED 36 yrs single b. Mercer Co W VA to ELIZA J. WORRELL 33 yrs single O: farmer; by R.G. French.

47. 3 Feby 1875 JAS P. PITZER 20 yrs single b. Monroe Co VA now living in Summers Co VA s/o Geo W. & Martha Pitzer to ELZ. E.J. WILLIAMS 24 yrs single b. Mercer Co W VA d/o Jno L. & Annie Williams O: farmer; by Jas M. Lucas.

48. 4 Feby 1875 WM W. CHATTING 50 yrs wid. b. Pittsylvania Co VA s/o Jos & Mary Chatting to JULIA ANN DEWESE 33 yrs single b. Montgomery Co VA d/o Andrew & T. Dewese O: farmer; by A.J. Thompson.

49. 25 Jany 1875 BURRELL B. BAILEY 56 yrs wid. b. Mercer Co W VA s/o Geo & Frances Bailey to NANCY TAYLOR 39 yrs single b. Mercer Co W VA d/o S & Mary Taylor O: farmer; by A.P.L. French.

Page 26

1. 6 Feby 1875 JAMES M. BLANKENSHIP 21 yrs single b. Giles Co VA s/o E.G. & Sarah Blankenship to RACHEL W. SHANNON 23 yrs single b. Campbell Co VA d/o Wm & Sarah Shannon O: farmer; by R.A. Miller.

2. 9 Feby 1875 SAML. P. LAMBERT 19 yrs single b. McDowell Co W VA now living same s/o T.K. & C. Lambert to MARTHA J. McCOMAS 20 yrs single b. Mercer Co W VA d/o E & J. McComas O: farmer; by T.K. Lambert.

3. 10 Feby 1875 JOSEPH HAZELWOOD 21 yrs single b. Stokes Co NC s/o Joshua & Charity Hazelwood to NANCY HALDREN 22 yrs single b. Mercer Co W VA d/o Henry & Mahala Haldren O: farmer; by A.J. Thompson.

4. 10 Feby 1875 JACOB L. PETRY 22 yrs single b. Mercer Co W VA s/o Jacob & Elz. Petry to ELZ. ISABELLA MARTIN 26 yrs single b. Mercer Co W VA d/o L.D. & Susan Martin O: farmer; by Wm C. Martin.

5. 15 Feby 1875 A.W. GORE 20 yrs single b. Mercer Co W VA s/o A.W. Gore & Serepta to SARAH L.N. MARTIN 20 yrs single b. Mercer Co W VA d/o Acles & Alcy Martin O: farmer; by Wm C. Martin.

6. 16 Feby 1875 HENRY BAILEY 38 yrs wid. b. Mercer Co W VA s/o Jonathan & Elz. Bailey to SUDOHA JANE LAMBERT 25 yrs single b. McDowell Co VA d/o Kenly & Charlotte Lambert O: farmer; by T.K. Lambert.

7. 22 Feby 1875 JAMES C. WALKER 22 yrs single b. Logan Co VA s/o Anderson & Louisa to RHODA J. FERGUSON 18 yrs single b. Mercer Co W VA d/o Jno & Susana Ferguson O:farmer; by Chas. Walker.

8. 4 Mar 1875 ISAAC R. McKINNEY 34 yrs wid. b. Giles Co VA s/o Pauhanan & Susan to MARGARET A. CAPERTON 23 yrs single b. Giles Co VA d/o John S & Manerva Caperton O: carpenter; by A.J. Thompson.

9. 5 Mar 1875 CYRUS TABOR 21 yrs single b. Mercer Co W VA s/o Abraham & Nancy Tabor to VICTORIA SADDLER 25 yrs single b. Giles Co VA d/o Henry Saddler O: farmer; by Wm. M. Crawford.

10. 11 Mar 1875 JOHN HARRISON BAILEY 18 yrs single b. Mercer Co W VA s/o Jas M. & Sally Bailey to JULIA ANN BURTON 18 yrs single b. Mercer Co W VA d/o Elias & Sally Burton O: farmer; by Wm. M. Crawford.

11. 22 Feb 1875 GEO P. SCOTT 15 yrs single b. Giles Co VA s/o W.R. & Mary E. Scott to AMANDA MINOR 14 yrs single b. Mercer Co W VA d/o Thompson & Eliz. Minor O: farmer; by A.P.L. French.

12. 23 Mar 1875 JNO W. MEADOR 28 wid. b. Mercer Co W VA s/o Josiah & Judah Meador to AGNES PERMELIA HATCHER 27 yrs single b. Mercer Co W VA d/o Elijah & Nancy Hatcher O: farmer; by James W. Lilley.

13. 3 Apl 1875 GRANVILLE M. FIELDER 19 yrs single b. Grayson Co VA s/o Dennis & Polly Fielder to VICTORIA W. FRENCH 19 yrs single b. Tazewell Co VA d/o A.P.L. & Rebecca French O: farmer; by P.B. McKinney.

14. 8 Apl 1875 JOHN FERGUSON 55 yrs single b. Mercer Co W VA s/o Josiah & Milla Ferguson to ELIZTH MARY MAXEY 33 yrs single b. Mercer Co W VA d/o Josiah & Sarah Maxey O: farmer; by P.B. McKinney.

15. 10 Apl 1875 JAMES ABHER 19 yrs single b. Wythe Co VA now living in Tazewell Co VA s/o John & Nancy Ann Abher to SARAH J. COFER 19 yrs single b. OH d/o & Sarah Ann Cofer O: farmer.

16. 10 Apl 1875 SAMUEL M. CRAWFORD 25 yrs single b.Floyd Co VA now living in Summers Co W VA s/o Isaac & Nancy Crawford to EMILY F. PINE 23 yrs single b. Mercer Co W VA d/o Alexd & Rebecca Pine O: farmer; by J.W. Bennett.

17. 26 Apl 1875 JOHN TAYLOR 85 yrs wid. b. Grayson Co VA s/o Jesse & Aley Taylor to CAROLINE WOOD 45 yrs single b. Wilkes Co NC d/o John & Nancy Wood O: farmer; by Wm M. Crawford.

18. 29 Apl 1875 ANDREW B. PETRY 21 yrs single b. Mercer Co W VA s/o Jacob & Elzth Petry to ELIZA MARTIN 21 yrs single b. Mercer Co W VA d/o Wm C. & Ann Martin O: farmer; by Wm C. Martin.

19. 30 Apl 1875 JOSEPH PETERS 25 yrs single b. Raleigh Co VA s/o Stephen & Elizabeth Peters to MARY A. ELLISON 18 yrs single b. Mercer Co W VA d/o Isaac & Elizabeth Ellison O: school teacher; by B.T. Bird.

20. 3 May 1875 ISAAC GORE 72 yrs wid. b. Giles Co VA s/o Robert Gore to MARY GREELY 25 yrs wid. b. VA O: farmer; by R.G. French.

21. 20 May 1875 WINFIELD THOMPSON 27 yrs single b. Mason Co W VA s/o Philip & Margt Thompson to EMMA C. FLETCHER 21 yrs single b. Mercer Co W VA d/o Calvin & Rhoda Fletcher O: farmer; by A.J. Thompson.

22. 5 June 1875 DAVID SLOANE 26 yrs wid. b. NC s/o Joel Sloane to EMILY L. COOK 27 yrs single b. Cornelius & Annie Cook O: farmer; by Wm C. Martin.

23. 8 June 1875 BENJAMIN HALDREN 21 yrs single b. Mercer Co W VA s/o Saml Harans Haldren to EASTHA S. DAVIS 22 yrs single b. Mercer Co W VA d/o Lee & Christina Davis O: farmer; by R.A. Miller.

24. 14 June 1875 JAMES H. DARE 22 yrs single b. Mercer Co W VA s/o Chas & Elizabeth Dare to SARAH V. BELCHER 15 yrs single b. Mercer Co W VA d/o Anderson & Clarissa Belcher O: farmer; by J.O. Cassaday.

25. 14 June 1875 ALEXANDER H. LILLY 21 yrs single b. Mercer Co W VA s/o Huff J. & Mahala J. Lilly O: farmer; by R.G. French.

26. 15 June 1875 WM H. McCRURY 28 yrs single b. Monroe Co VA now living in Ralaigh Co W VA s/o Wm & Demarus McCrury to IDA M. COWLING 20 yrs single b. Lynchburg Co VA d/o Willis J. & Mary Cowling O: farmer; by George Stuart.

27. 17 June 1875 WILLIAM ADAIR, JR. 32 yrs single b. Monroe Co VA now living same s/o Wm & Sarah Adair to HARRIET A. FRENCH 28 yrs single b. Mercer Co W VA d/o N.B. & Jane French O: D. Shffmon; by George Stuart.

28. 22 June 1875 JAMES M. LUCUS 23 yrs single b. Giles Co VA now living same to MARIA ELZTH HIGGINBOTHAM 20 yrs single b.Mercer Co W VA by J.O. Cassaday

29. 5 July 1875 LEONIDAS M. PENDLETON 21 yrs single b. Campbell Co VA s/o Samuel & Elzth Pendleton to MANERVA E. TANNER 21 yrs single b. Putnam Co VA d/o Frederick & Zula Tanner O: school teacher; by R.A. Miller.

30. 7 July 1875 ERASTUS W. PENNINGTON 21 yrs single b. Mercer Co W VA s/o Riley & Elzth Pennington to LUCINDA A. STOVALL 21 yrs single b. Patrick Co VA d/o Archad F & Mary Stovall O: farmer; by Wm C. Martin.

31. 21 July 1875 LYNCH GRAHAM 18 yrs single b. Wyoming Co VA now living same s/o James & Sarah Graham to NANCY M. HOWELL 16 yrs single d/o John D. & Setha Howell O: farmer; by Elias Reed.

32. 29 July 1875 CHARLES L. DEATON 22 yrs single b. Alleghany Co VA s/o John Deaton to ELECTRA SHRADER 26 single b. Mercer Co W VA d/o David & Chloe Shrader O:carpenter; by A.P.L. French.

33. 1 Aug 1875 JAMES J. MEADOWS 22 yrs single b. Monroe Co W VA s/o St. Clair & Eliza Meadows to ELIZABETH A. LYNCH 17 yrs single b. Mercer Co W VA d/o John C. & Emilia Lynch O: farmer; by R.A. Miller.

34. 17 July 1875 MADISON P. MAXEY 24 yrs single b. Franklin Co VA s/o James B & Ala Maxey to LELIA S. HERNDON 17 yrs single b. Mercer Co W VA d/o Arthur & Eliza Herndon O: farmer; by W.M. Crawford.

35. 30 July 1875 GEORGE W. TAYLOR 20 yrs single b. Mercer Co W VA s/o Sampson & Mary Taylor to SARAH M. LUSK 18 yrs single b. Mercer Co W VA d/o Reese & Rebecca Lusk O: farmer; by T.K. Lambert.

36. 25 Aug 1875 WILLIAM P. MINOR 21 yrs single b. Mercer Co W VA s/o Thompson & Elizbth Minor to MARTHA E. HARLESS 31 yrs single b. Montgomery Co VA d/o Philip & Elizabeth Harless O: farmer; by A.R.L. French.

37. 10 Sept 1875 DANIEL LILLY 19 yrs single b. Mercer Co W VA d/o Daniel & Lavina Lilly to NANCY M.J. WOOD 16 yrs single b. Montgomery Co VA d/o Gabriel & Luetta Wood O: farmer; by James W. Lilley

38. 18 Sept 1875 FOUNTAIN J. HOGGE 22 yrs single b. Franklin Co VA s/o Dale & Dellah Hogge to MARTHA JANE PERDUE 21 yrs single b. Franklin Co VA d/o wm & Tinah Perdue O:farmer; by Wm M. Crawford

39. 22 Sept 1875 FREDERICK H. SHELTON 23 yrs single b. Patrick Co VA s/o Frederick & Esther Shelton to SARAH V. SNODGRASS 23 yrs single b. Craig Co VA d/o Estill & - Snodgrass O: shoemaker; by B.T. Bird.

40. 22 Sept 1875 PUNNARD C. WINFREY 21 yrs single b. Mercer Co W VA s/o Burrell & Oina Winfrey to LYDIA A. SAUNDERS 21 yrs single b. Pulaski Co VA d/o Julius & Lillie Saunders O: farmer; by J.O. Cassaday.

41. 25 Sept 1875 JOHN GRIM 20 yrs single b. Mercer Co W VA s/o Wm & Catherine Grim to REBECCA J. SHRADER 17 yrs single b. Mercer Co W VA d/o John & Nancy Shrader O: farmer; by A.P.L. French

42. 7 Oct 1875 SAMUEL C. HARVEY 21 yrs single b. Mercer Co W VA s/o Isaac N. & Elizth Harvey to LUCINDA JANE BROYLES 15 yrs single b. Monroe Co VA d/o Thompson & Lucinda Broyles O: farmer; by John West.

43. 10 Oct 1875 JAS. D. JOHNSTON 50 yrs wid. b. Giles Co VA s/o Hugh & Sarah Johnston to MAHALA A. WOODALL 48 yrs single b. Campbell Co VA d/o Sampson & Sally Woodall O: miller; by J.W. Bennett.

44. 12 Oct 1875 STEPHEN SAUNDERS 24 yrs single b. Pulaski Co VA s/o Julius & Lillie Saunders to EURY ELLAN WINFREY 23 yrs single b. Mercer Co W VA d/o Burrell & Onina Winfrey O: farmer; by Wm Wriston.

45. 21 Oct 1875 CLONNEY S. HEDRICK 26 yrs single b. Greenbriar Co W VA now living in Raleigh Co VA s/o Peter Hedrick to SARAH E. THOMPSON 22 yrs single b. Mercer Co W VA d/o David & Angeline Thompson O: farmer; by J.O. Cassaday.

46. 2 Sept 1875 DOUGLASS MORGAN 21 yrs single b. Monroe Co W VA to ELIZA WHITE 17 yrs single b. Mercer Co W VA O: farmer; by R.A. Miller.

47. 16 Oct 1875 ALBERT S. DAWSON 28 yrs single b. Pulaski Co VA s/o Hiram A. & Sarah Dawson to REBECCA J. HURRELL 23 yrs single b. Mercer Co W VA d/o Jas A. & Saray Hurrell O: blacksmith; by James Calfee.

48. 15 Oct 1875 ELI WHITE 17 yrs single b. Mercer Co W VA now living in Wyomming Co W VA s/o Patton & Rhoda White to REBECCA J. BAILEY 16 yrs single b. Mercer Co W VA d/o Madison & Sally Bailey O: farmer; by Thomas K. Lambert.

MERCER COUNTY, WEST VIRGINIA
Marriages 1854 - 1901

Page 27

1. 15 Oct 1875 JNO W. HATCHER 22 yrs single b. Mercer Co W VA now living in Raleigh Co W VA s/o Silas & Permelia Hatcher to NANCY R. WOLF 22 yrs single b. Mercer Co W VA d/o Richard A. & Lucinda W. Wolf O: farmer; by J.W. Lilley.

2. 20 Nov 1875 JAS H. BRINKLEY 22 yrs single b. Mercer Co W VA s/o Green & Nancy Brinkley to RACHAEL JONES 19 yrs single b. Mercer Co W VA d/o Elisha & Sarah Jones O: farmer; by R.A. Miller.

3. 22 Nov 1875 GRANVILLE H. HEDRICK 42 yrs wid. b. Wythe Co VA s/o Joseph & Dianna Hedrick to REBECCA O'DANIEL 27 yrs single b. Mercer Co W VA d/o Isaac & Rebecca O'Daniel O: carpenter; by A.P.L. French.

4. 24 Nov 1875 GEORGE L. KARNES 26 yrs single b. Mercer Co W VA s/o Madison & Nancy Karnes to ESTHER F. CALFEE 22 yrs single b. Mercer Co W VA d/o Wilson D. & Jane Calfee O: farmer; by James Calfee.

5. 25 Nov 1875 DOCK HASKINS 22 yrs single b. Pulaski Co VA s/o David & Louisa Haskins to REBECCA HENDERSON 19 yrs single b. Pulaski Co VA d/o Pier & Christina Henderson O: farmer; by J.O. Cassaday; REMARKS: colored.

6. 27 Nov 1875 WILLIAM C. ROLES 21 yrs single b. Raleigh Co W VA now living same s/o Alex. & Elzth Roles to ELIZA R. THOMPSON 17 yrs single b. Mercer Co W VA d/o Winton & R.J. Thompson O: farmer; by Charles Walker.

7. 30 Nov 1875 THOMAS J. GARRETSON 21 yrs single b. Mercer Co W VA s/o Ruah Garretson to MARY JANE FLETCHER 24 yrs wid. b. Mercer Co W VA d/o Jas H. & Columbia J. Fletcher O: farmer; by John West.

8. 6 Dec 1875 THOMAS K. MASSEY 23 yrs single b. Mercer Co W VA s/o Richard S. & Mary Massey to NANNIE P. PHIPPS 19 yrs single b. Grayson Co VA d/o Aaron & Charlotte Phipps O: farmer; by A.J. Thompson.

9. 21 Dec 1875 CHARLES W. BUTLER 23 yrs single b. Monroe Co W VA now living Summers Co VA s/o Powell & Davien Butler to MARY E. GAUTIER 16 yrs single b. Mercer Co W VA d/o Joseph & Jane Gautier O: farmer; by J.W. Bennett.

10. 5 Jany 1876 WILLIAM A. BAILEY 23 yrs single b. Mercer Co W VA s/o Floyd & Zilphia Bailey to VIRGINIA E. FOLEY 17 yrs single b. Mercer Co W VA d/o Richd & P. Foley O: farmer; by Elias Read.

11. 8 Jany 1876 LEWIS M. COOPER 24 yrs single b. Franklin Co VA s/o Alex & Mary Cooper to MARGARET A. ROBERTSON 23 yrs single b. Pulaski Co VA d/o Henry & - Robertson O: farmer; by R.A. Miller.

12. 10 Jany 1876 ROBERT HEDRICK 18 yrs single b. Tazewell Co VA s/o Granville H. & M. Hedrick to BIDDY LAREW 17 yrs single b. Grayson Co VA d/o John & Mary Larew O: farmer; by A.L.P. French.

13. 10 Jany 1875 JOHN A. WORRELL 21 yrs single b. Carroll Co VA s/o Luke & Milla Worrell to ELIZABETH WOOD 22 yrs single b. Patrick Co VA O: farmer; by James W. Lilley.

14. 15 Jany 1876 JAMES A. WOOD 20 yrs single b. Mercer Co W VA s/o Richard A. & Luanda Wood to SARAH A.E. DODD 17 yrs single b. Mercer Co W VA d/o Anderson & Elzth Dodd O: farmer; by James W. Lilley.

15. 19 Jany 1876 GEORGE W. CADE 22 yrs single b. Wood Co VA s/o - & Elizabeth Cade to MARY W. AUSTIN 18 yrs single b. Bland Co VA d/o Isaac E. & Malinda Austin O: farmer; by B.T. Bird.

16. 20 Jany 1876 REUBEN G. BLANKENSHIP 28 yrs single b. Mercer Co W VA s/o Lewis & Mary Blankenship to ESTHER A. MARTIN 23 yrs single b. Mercer Co W VA d/o Danl & Esther A. Martin O: farmer; by William Holroyd.

17. 7 Feby 1876 JAMES P. FRANKLIN 22 yrs single b. Tazewell Co VA now living same s/o Thomas & Abbia Franklin to AMERICA L. BELCHER 20 yrs single b. Tazewell Co VA d/o Bartley & Sarah Belcher O:farmer; by A.P.L. French.

18. 16 Feby 1876 WM R. BROYLES 20 yrs single b. Monroe Co W VA s/o Thompson & Lucinda Broyles to MARY J. COMER 19 yrs single b. Mercer Co W VA d/o W.I. & Sarah Comer O: farmer; by A.J. Thompson.

19. 24 Feby 1876 REESE B. SHREWSBURY 24 yrs wid. b. Mercer Co W VA s/o John & Elizabeth Shrewsbury to ALMEDA L. THOMPSON 21 yrs single b. Mercer Co W VA d/o Gordon & L. Thompson O: farmer; by R.G. French.

20. 24 Feby 1876 JOHN W. BURTON 21 yrs single b. Bland Co VA s/o Elias & Sarah Burton to MARTHA J. BELCHER 29 yrs single b. Mercer Co W VA d/o John N. & Nancy Belcher O: farmer; by A.P.L. French

21. 9 March 1876 ERASTUS N. JOHNSTON 21 yrs single b. Mercer Co W VA s/o Wm & Sarah Johnston to ELLA A. FLETCHER 18 yrs single b. Mercer Co W VA d/o Isaac & Ellen Fletcher O: farmer; by J.O. Cassaday.

22. 23 Feby 1876 AARAS HILL 23 yrs single b. Alleghany Co NC s/o - & Ala Hill to CAUSHY BELL 16 yrs single b. Mercer Co W VA d/o James Bell O: farmer; by Evan H. Brown.

23. 14 March 1876 BENJAMIN L. MEADOR 18 yrs single b. Mercer Co W VA s/o Solon & Malinda Meador to CELIA CLARK 30 yrs wid. b. Mercer Co W VA d/o John & Ann Meador O: farmer; by R.G. French.

24. 20 March 1876 JOHN W. PENNINGTON 19 yrs single b. Mercer Co W VA s/o John A. & Ellen Pennington to MALINDA E. PENNINGTON 19 yrs single b. Mercer Co W VA d/o Levi & Eliz. Pennington O: farmer; by A.J. Thompson.

25. 18 March 1876 MAZARINO BELCHER 18 yrs single b. Mercer Co W VA s/o Christian & Mary M. Belcher to ELECTRA P. BAILEY 18 yrs single b. Mercer Co W VA d/o Eli & Charlotte Bailey O: farmer; by Henry M. Neal.

26. 19 Apl 1876 CARROLL BLARK 55 yrs wid. b. Morgan Co s/o Samuel & Ankar Clark to ELIZABETH FERGUSON 56 yrs wid. b. Mercer Co W VA d/o Henry & Elizth Bailey O: Minister of Gospel; by R.J. Thompson.

27. 19 Apl 1876 JAMES COBURN 21 yrs single b. Mercer Co W VA s/o David & Ursula Coburn to SARAH A. SHANNON 23 yrs single b. Campbell Co VA d/o Wm & Sarah E. Shannon O: farmer; by R.A. Miller

28. 25 Apl 1876 ANDREW THORNTON 22 yrs wid. b. Pulaski Co VA s/o Robt & Charlotte Thornton to ELIZTH S. COMER 15 yrs single b. Mercer Co W VA d/o Jacob & Elzth Comer O: farmer; by Richd. A. Miller.

29. 15 Apl 1876 STEPHEN FARMER 23 yrs single b. Grayson Co W VA s/o David & Rhoda Farmer to REBECCA TAYLOR 18 yrs single b. Mercer Co W VA d/o Sampson & Tracy Taylor O: farmer; by Henry M. Neal.

30. 13 May 1876 FRANKLIN WHITED 34 yrs wid. b. Smyth Co VA s/o - & Rhoda Whited to EMMA J. MAULY 21 yrs single b. Augustus Co VA O: farmer; by R.A. Miller.

31. 18 May 1876 HENRY SADDLER 52 yrs wid. b. Botetourt Co VA s/o Jacob & Mary Saddler to SARAH A. JEFFRES 18 yrs single b. Tazewell Co VA d/o John J. & - Jeffres O: farmer; by Henry M. Neal.

32. 10 June 1876 JAMES SIMPSON 21 yrs single b. Sullivan Co TN s/o - Simpson to ELIZA T. CAMPBELL 18 yrs single b. Mercer Co W VA d/o thos K. & Mary Campbell O: farmer; by R.G. French.

33. 10 June 1876 THOMAS J. MULLINS 25 yrs wid. b. Franklin Co VA s/o Abe & Polly Mullins to JANE BELCHER 30 yrs wid. b. Mercer Co W VA d/o Wm & ? Alvis O: farmer; by William Holroyd.

34. 10 June 1876 WM H. CALES 25 yrs single b. Greenbriar Co W VA now living in Giles Co VA s/o James & Sarah Cales to MARY E. WAGONER 18 yrs single b. Henry Co VA d/o Mary A. Wagoner O: farmer; by R.A. Miller.

35. 16 Sept 1876 JOHN C. FITZWATER 23 yrs single b. Nicholas Co VA s/o Jno & Sarah Fitzwater to MARIA E. GARRETSON 17 yrs single b. Mercer Co W VA d/o Wm & Columbia A. Garretson O: farmer; by C. Crawford.

36. 23 Sept 1876 JOSEPH S. WHITE 20 yrs single b. Mercer Co W VA s/o Harman & C.M. White to JOSEPHINE S. MUNSEY 19 yrs single b. Bland Co VA d/o Skidmore & Julia Munsey O: farmer; by Harrison Robinson.

37. 27 Sept 1876 P.A. CASON 36 yrs single b. Essex Co VA now living in Cabell Co VA s/o Jas B. & Elzth D. Cason to SALLIE M. PACK 21 yrs single b. Mercer Co w VA d/o Jno A. & Mary R. Pack O: Conductor R.R.; by L.H. Renfro.

38. 9 Oct 1876 ISAAC E. ROGERS 20 yrs single b. Giles Co VA now living same s/o John & Sarah Rogers to SARAH O. FRAZIER 16 yrs single b. Giles Co VA d/o William & Louisa Frazier O: farmer; by James H. Johnston.

39. 12 Oct 1876 JOHN NEELEY 26 yrs single b. Mercer Co W VA s/o Wm G. & Delilah Neeley to RACHEL WILEY 21 yrs single b. Mercer Co W VA d/o James & Elizth Wiley O: farmer; by A.J. Thompson.

40. 12 Oct 1876 GEO. SHREWSBURY 22 yrs single b. Mercer Co W VA s/o Wm Basty Shrewsbury to ELEANDER WORRELL 18 yrs single b. Carroll Co VA d/o Luke & Mille Worrell O: farmer; by R.G. French.

41. 19 Oct 1876 ELLIOTT V. BLANKENSHIP 19 yrs single b. Mercer Co W VA s/o Thompson & Silvester Blankenship to MARY E. SHELTON 21 yrs single b. Patrick Co VA d/o Frederick & Esther Shelton O: farmer; by J.O. Cassaday.

42. 24 Oct 1876 WILLIAM R. KEGLEY 22 yrs single b. Wythe Co VA s/o Danl & Margaret Kegley to RHODA C. ROBINSON 19 yrs single b. Mercer Co w VA d/o Harrison & Harriet Robinson O: farmer; by J.O. Cassaday.

43. 30 Oct 1876 ALEXANDER HAGER 21 yrs single b. Mercer Co W VA s/o Russell & Sarah Hager to CYNTHIA COBURN 30 yrs single b. Mercer Co W VA d/o David & Ursula Coburn O: farmer; by James Calfee.

44. 6 Nov 1876 JAS E.P. ST. CLAIR 30 yrs single b. Bedford Co VA s/o Wm & Batsey St. Clair to MARY ANN KIDWELL 27 yrs single b. Raleigh Co VA d/o Michael B. & A. Kidwell O: farmer; by J.W. Bennett.

45. 2 nov 1876 JOHN D. SCOTT 20 yrs single b. Giles co VA s/o Wm & - Scott to ANN E. NEAL 28 yrs single b. Monroe Co VA d/o Henry M. & Sallie Neal O: farmer; by A.P.L. French.

46. 8 Nov 1876 JAS. W. STINSON 22 yrs single b. Mercer Co W VA s/o Chas & Elzth Stinson to NANCY HALE 17 yrs single b. Giles Co VA d/o Danl P. & Martha Hale O: farmer; by J.O. Cassaday.

47. 9 Nov 1876 DANIEL BEASLEY 52 yrs wid. b. Giles Co VA s/o Thos & Amy Beasley to MARGARET A. LINDSAY 30 yrs wid. O: farmer; by J.O. Cassaday; REMARKS: colored.

48. 11 Nov 1876 WM OR. ELLISON 26 yrs single b. Summers Co W VA now living same s/o Jas. & Polly Ellison to ELIZABETH LILLY 23 yrs single b. Mercer Co W VA d/o Lewis Lilly O: farmer; by James W. Lilley.

Page 28

1. 16 Nov 1876 JOHN A. JOHNSTON 25 yrs single b. Mercer Co W VA s/o Adam & Susan Johnston to ADDIE S. RICE 21 yrs single b. TN d/o David & Nancy Rice O: farmer; by J.O. Cassaday.

2. 21 nov 1876 HENRY C. BLANKENSHIP 24 yrs single b. Wyoming Co VA now living same s/o Jesse & Hannah Blankenship to JANA P. BAILEY 15 yrs single b. Mercer Co W VA d/o J.M. & Sarah Bailey O: farmer; by J.K. Lambert.

3. 29 Nov 1876 DANIEL L. OXLEY 22 yrs single b. Bland Co VA s/o Buford H & Rhoda J. Oxley to RUTHA M. BOWLING 22 yrs single b. Mercer Co W VA d/o Jesse & Jane Bowling O: farmer; by B.T. Bird.

4. 6 Dec 1876 JACOB P. ROBINSON 26 yrs single b. Pulaski Co VA s/o Thos & Louisa Robinson to JULIA ANN RIDDLE 23 yrs single b. Logan Co VA d/o Tobia & Sophia Riddle O: farmer; by Richard A. Miller.

5. 13 Dec 1876 MORRIS H. KENT 22 yrs single b. Pulaski Co VA s/o Henry & Lucy Kent to EMMA A. MASSEY 18 yrs single b. Floyd Co VA d/o Matilda C. Prince O: farmer; by R.G. French.

6. 21 Dec 1876 WILLIAM CALFEE 22 yrs single b. Mercer Co W VA s/o James & Elzth Calfee to LANDONIA P. JOHNSTON 17 yrs single b. Mercer Co W VA d/o John W. Johnston O: farmer; by James Calfee.

7. 25 Dec 1876 EDWARD P. WILLIAMS 21 yrs single b. Raleigh Co VA now living same s/o John L. & M.A. Williams to MALINDA E. HONCHINS 21 yrs single b. Raleigh Co VA d/o Shom & Edme J. Houchins O: farmer; by James W. Lilley.

8. 27 Dec 1876 GEORGE WILLIAM SELLERS 23 yrs single b. Rockingham Co VA now living Sevier Co TN s/o Wm & Eliza J. Sellers to SARAH E. STAFFORD 18 yrs single b. Mercer Co W VA d/o Wm H. & Louisa A. Stafford O: farmer; by William Holroyd; REMARKS: listed to auditor.

9. 1 Jan 1877 JAMES W. YOUNG 22 yrs single b. Summers Co W VA s/o Lewis & Nancy Young to VICTORIA A. THOMPSON 16 yrs single b. Mercer Co W VA d/o Eli & Sarah Thompson O: farmer; by J.W. Bennett.

10. 16 Jan 1877 HENRY MEADOWS 26 yrs single b. Mercer Co W VA s/o Causby Young to SARAH E. MEADOWS 20 yrs single b. Giles Co VA d/o S.G. & Mary Meadows O: farmer; by Richard A. Miller.

11. 17 Jan 1877 WILLIAM H. RUSSELL 27 yrs single b. Summers NC & England(sic) s/o Henry & Susan Russell to NANCY K. HARVEY 25 yrs single b. Monroe Co W VA d/o Jacob & Martha K. Harvey O: ditcher & pruner; by Elias Reed.

12. 20 Jan 1877 WILLIAM L. WILLIAMS 19 yrs single b. Monroe Co W VA s/o Saml L. & Mary A. Williams to SARAH E. CHRISTIAN 18 yrs single b. Mercer Co W VA d/o Jno H. & Martha Christian O: farmer; by J.W. Bennett.

13. 23 Jan 1877 WILSON THOMAS 23 yrs single b. Mercer Co W VA s/o James H. & Sallie Thomas to HANNIE A. DAVIS 25 yrs single b. Mercer Co W VA d/o John & Tempe Davis O: farmer; by C. Crawford.

14. 24 Jan 1877 FERDINAND BACHELOR 24 yrs single b. Montgomery Co VA s/o Reuben & Ann Bachelor to SARAH J. HEDRICK 16 yrs single b. Tazewell Co VA d/o Granville & Ann Hedrick O: farmer; by A.P.L. French.

15. 30 Jan 1877 BERNARD F. FOLEY 20 yrs single b. Mercer co w VA s/o Richard B & P. Foley to MARY J. DODD 16 yrs single b. Summers Co W VA d/o Anderson A. & Elzth Dodd O: farmer; by Elias Reed.

16. 5 Feby 1877 JOHN A. PENNINGTON 54 yrs wid. b. Monroe Co VA s/o William & Sarah Pennington to MARGARET S. SIMPKINS 28 yrs single b. Giles co VA d/o Elias & Elizabeth Simpkins O: farmer; by A.J. Thompson.

17. 5 Feby 1877 POWHATTAN DOVE 24 yrs single b. Halifax Co VA now living in Summers co W VA s/o S.B. & Sallie Dove to BEATRICE A. SHORTER 17 yrs single b. Mercer Co W VA d/o Geo & Sarah J. Shorter O: farmer; by William Holroyd.

18. 5 Feby 1877 HENRY A.W. PENNINGTON 20 yrs single b. Mercer Co W VA s/o P.F. & M.E. Pennington to CLARA A. PHILLIPS 20 yrs single b. Mercer Co W VA d/o James Phillips O:farmer; by William Holroyd.

19. 13 Feby 1877 WILSON COLEMAN 18 yrs single b. Pulaski Co VA s/o Kelson Coleman to CLARA MILLER 18 yrs wid. b. Mercer Co W VA d/o Eliza Oliver O: farmer; by Harrison Robinson; REMARKS: colored.

20. 21 Feby 1877 JAMES J. BECKET 21 yrs single b. OH s/o Solomon & Sarah Becket to JOSEPHINE LILLEY 25 yrs wid. b. Mercer Co W VA d/o Jonathan Lilley O: farmer; by Harrison Robinson.

21. 26 Feby 1877 WILLIAM C. COOPER 20 yrs single b. Grayson Co VA s/o Wm A. & Melvina Cooper to MINERVA E. BIRD 21 yrs single b. Bland co VA d/o Benj F. & Irene Bird O: farmer; by J.O. Cassaday.

22. 5 March 1877 JOHN F. PENNINGTON 25 yrs single b. Mercer Co W VA s/o Parkison F. & Susan Pennington to SUSAN C. MILLER 19 yrs single b. Mercer Co W VA d/o James & Rachel Miller O: farmer; by Wm C. Martin.

23. 8 March 1877 WILLIAM F. MILLS 25 yrs single b. Raleigh Co VA now living same s/o Robt & Lydia Mills to ELECTRA JANE CLENDENON 18 yrs single b. Mercer Co W VA d/o Anglen & Margery Clendenon O: farmer; by Elias Reed.

24. 19 March 1877 ELI H. WALTERS 18 yrs single b. Mercer Co W VA s/o Moses & Serenia Walters to OLENA M. FARMER 15 yrs single b. Mercer Co W VA d/o Reuben & Mary M. Farmer O: farmer; by J.O. Cassaday.

25. *19 March 1877 WILLIAM H. HAGER 36 yrs single b. Bland Co VA s/o Squire & Elizth Hager to MARTHA UNDERWOOD 37 yrs single b. Franklin Co VA d/o William & Elizth Underwood O: farmer; by James Calfee.

26. 19 March 1877 RUFUS F. JONES 19 yrs single b. Mercer Co W VA s/o John & Rebecca Jones to SARAH M. JONES 15 yrs single b. Mercer Co W VA d/o Elisha R. & Rnah Jones O: farmer; by L. Goodwin.

27. 21 March 1877 ALEXANDER JOHNSTON 58 wid. b. Giles Co VA s/o John & Elizth Johnston to ARAMINTA F. BRYANS 45 yrs single b. Mercer Co W VA d/o Jno & Chloe Bryans O: farmer; by William Holroyd.

28. 28 March 1877 ISHAM UNDERWOOD 28 yrs single b. Mercer Co VA s/o Wm & Elizth Underwood to MARY JANE WALTERS 27 yrs single b. Mercer Co W VA d/o Moses & Serenia Walters O: farmer; by J.O. Cassaday.

29. 30 March 1877 ANDREW P.L. FRENCH 60 yrs wid. b. Giles Co VA s/o James & Susan French to ELIZABETH HOPKINS 47 yrs single b. Botetourt Co VA d/o Jas. T. & Mary F. Hopkins O: farmer; by P.B. McKinney.

30. 31 March 1877 JOSEPH MAXEY 19 yrs single b. Mercer Co W VA s/o Preston & Celia Maxey to VIRGINIA HOUCHINS 17 yrs single b. Raleigh Co W VA d/o Irvin Houchins O: farmer; by Benjamin T. Bird.

31. 31 March 1877 JOHN L. BRAMMER 25 yrs single b. Mercer co W VA now living in Summers Co VA s/o Jonathan & Maria Brammer to SARAH E. MAXEY 16 yrs single b. Mercer Co W VA d/o Preston & Celia Maxey O: farmer; by Benj. T. Bird.

32. 4 Apl 1877 JOSHUA LILLEY* 55 yrs wid. b. Giles Co VA s/o Thomas & Rosana Lilly* to ELENDER PRINCE 40 yrs single b. Giles Co VA d/o Jas & Ellen Prince O: rail splitter; by R.G. French. (*Note: name spelled both ways.)

33. 4 Apl 1877 SAMUEL WASHINGTON 24 yrs single b. Washington Co VA s/o Geo & Harriet Washington to ALICE BROWN 17 yrs single b. Pulaski Co VA d/o Smal & Brown O: farmer; by Wm Holroyd; REMARKS: colored.

34. 7 Apl 1877 CLINTON G. LAUVE 25 yrs single b. Grayson Co VA s/o John & Mary Lauve to MARY ANN SHRADER 25 yrs single b. Mercer Co W VA d/o David & Chloe Shrader O: farmer; by A.P.L. French.

35. 10 Apl 1877 CHRISTOPHER A. FRAZIER 22 yrs single b. Mercer Co W VA s/o Robt Frazier to CLARA F. WILEY 19 yrs single b. Mercer Co W VA d/o Sophia A. Wiley O: farmer; by J.W. Bennett.

36. 13 Apl 1877 JOHN W. MILKE 23 yrs single b. Monroe Co VA s/o Henry S. & Mary J. Mikle to KATHARINE SNODGRASS 23 yrs single b. Mercer Co W VA d/o Estill & Sarah Snodgrass O: farmer; by P.B. McKinney.

37. 10 Apl 1877 CASVILLE C. BELCHER 21 yrs single b. Mercer Co W VA s/o Christian Belcher to NANCY B. MAXEY 18 yrs single b. Franklin Co VA d/o Burrell & Ala Maxey O: farmer; by T.K. Lambert.

38. 24 Apl 1877 GEORGE BILLIPS 21 yrs single b. Tazewell Co VA s/o Wesley & Nancy Billips to BIRDIE EMSWELLER 16 yrs single d/o Ira Emsweller O: farmer; by J.O. Cassaday.

39. 28 Apl 1877 GEO. C. TABOR 22 yrs single b. Tazewell Co VA now living same s/o Jas. H. & Nancy Tabor to FANNIE JOHNSTON 20 yrs single b. Mercer Co w VA d/o Jno W. & Margaret Johnston O: farmer; by James Calfee.

40. 10 May 1877 RUSH GARDNER 25 yrs single b. Wythe Co VA s/o Hardin & Rosanah Gardner to LOUISIA HERNDON 21 yrs single b. Mercer Co w VA d/o Jno W. & Martha O: farmer; by Phil S. Sutton; REMARKS: colored.

41. 15 May 1877 JOHN W. ANDREWS 17 yrs single b. Bland Co VA s/o A.J. & Nancy M. to ALICE A. BILLIPS 17 yrs single b. Tazewell Co VA d/o John & Francis O: farmer; by Phil S. Sutton.

42. 15 May 1877 JOHN H. DANIELLEY 26 yrs single b. Giles Co VA s/o Nehemiah & Jerusha to MARY JANE PHIPPS 20 yrs single b. Allaghany Co NC d/o A.B. & Margaret A. O: farmer; by Wm Holroyd.

43. 16 May 1877 BENJAMIN F. KIDWELL 23 yrs single b. Mercer Co W VA s/o Michael B. & Latishia to MARTHA E. PERDUE 21 yrs single b. Giles Co VA d/o Fergus & Nancy O:farmer; by J.W. Bennett.

44. 22 May 1877 WILLIAM ABSHER 24 yrs single b. Wythe Co VA now living in Tazewell Co VA s/o Nancy Absher to MARTHA WELLS 22 yrs single b. Mercer Co W VA d/o David & Elizabeth; by P.S. Sutton.

45. 26 May 1877 BENJAMIN PARKER 21 yrs single b. Mercer Co W VA s/o Jas. & Mary to SARAH F. SHREWSBURY 16 yrs single b. Mercer Co W VA d/o F.K.J. Shrewsbury O: farmer; by T.K. Lambert.

46. 9 June 1877 BAITLEY D. FARLEY 22 yrs single b. Wyoming Co W VA now living in Raleigh Co W VA s/o John & Lucy Farley to MARY A. FARLEY 22 yrs single b. Mercer Co W VA d/o Wm & Lucy A. Farley O: farmer; by James W. Lilly.

47. 11 June 1877 SAMUEL H. HAGER 18 yrs single b. Mercer Co W VA s/o A.G. & Nancy Hager to REBECCA WINFREY 17 yrs single b. Mercer Co W VA d/o Burrell & Orina O: farmer; by Phil S. Sutton.

48. 21 June 1877 GEO W. KEATLEY* 23 yrs single b. Mercer Co W VA s/o John & Susan Keatly* to MARY J. MARTIN 19 yrs single b. Mercer Co W VA d/o David & Esther Martin O: farmer; by Wm Holroyd.

Page 29

1. 16 July 1877 GEORGE M. BAILEY 20 yrs single b. Mercer Co W VA s/o Jonathan S. & Ursula to MARY L. HEDRICK 17 yrs single b. Tazewell Co VA d/o Granville H. & Mary O: farmer; by James Calfee.

2. 18 July 1877 ALBERT SCOTT 23 yrs single b. Tazewell Co VA now living same s/o William & Sarah to ROSA LEWIS 26 yrs single b. Tazewell Co VA d/o ? & Mary O: farmer; by Phil S. Sutton; REMARKS: colored.

3. 25 July 1877 SAMUEL A. BAILEY 22 yrs single b. Mercer Co W VA s/o Jamison & Polly to JULIA A. SHREWSBURY 18 yrs single b. Mercer Co W VA d/o John W. & Martha M. O: farmer; by J.O. Cassaday.

4. 28 July 1877 JOSEPH L. ESKEY 23 yrs single b. Roanoke Co VA s/o William & Avis to MINERVA B. MASSEY 18 yrs single b. Mercer Co W VA d/o Thomas B. & Louisa O: farmer; by J.W. Bennett.

5. 10 July 1877 JESSEE G. HATCHER 22 yrs single b. Mercer Co W VA s/o Elijah & Jemima to NANCY ELIZABETH NEELEY 15 yrs single b. Mercer Co W VA d/o Nathaniel M. & Katherine O: farmer; by Elias Reed.

6. 31 July 1877 ABSOLOM WILEY 66 yrs wid. b. Giles Co VA s/o James Wiley to MARY ANN KEATON 56 yrs wid. b. Green Co VA d/o ? Gibson O: farmer; by J.W. Bennett.

7. 6 Aug 1877 WILLIAM M. DOYLES 22 yrs single b. Montgomery Co VA s/o James A. & Martha A. to SARAH E. WINFREY 18 yrs single b. Mercer Co VA d/o Burrell & Orina; by J.O. Cassaday.

8. 10 Aug 1877 DANIEL WELLS 55 yrs wid. b. Dinviddie Co VA s/o ? & Nancy Wells to DORCAS E. WINFREY 25 yrs single b. Mercer Co W VA d/o Burrell & Orina J. Winfrey O: farmer; by J.O. Cassaday.

9. 22 Aug 1877 SAMUEL S. CORDER 19 yrs single b. Bland Co VA s/o Benj. & Julia Corder to HENRIETTA WILLIAMS 15 yrs single b. Giles Co VA d/o Preston & Francis Williams O: farmer; by James Calfee.

10. 16 Aug 1877 JOHN T. ROBINSON 19 yrs single b. Giles Co VA s/o Thomas & Louisa Robinson to VICTORIA THOMAS 17 yrs single b. Mercer Co W VA d/o W.G. & Annie Thomas O: farmer; by (Unable to read.)

11. 11 Aug 1877 WILEY G. HILL 27 yrs single b. Alleghany Co NC s/o Hardin H. & Jane Hill to NANCY B. PERDUE 22 yrs single b. Franklin Co VA d/o Silas & Nancy Perdue O: farmer; by Evan H. Brown.

12. 20 Aug 1877 ROBERT F. REED 21 yrs single b. Campbell Co VA s/o Thomas & Suffronia to RHODA HAYWOOD 18 yrs single b. Mercer Co W VA d/o Wm & Sarah O: farmer; by J.O. Cassaday.

13. 3 Sept 1877 WILLIAM A. NORE 21 yrs single b. Franklin Co VA now living in Bland Co VA s/o Thomas & Nancy to PAHALATHA E. HOLT 22 yrs single b. Mercer Co W VA d/o Richard & Elender O: farmer; by James Calfee.

14. 5 Sept 1877 JOHN H. CARBOUGH 35 yrs wid. b. Pulaski Co VA s/o George & Elizabeth to NANCY BAILEY 17 yrs single b. Mercer Co W VA d/o Leftwich & Sarah O: farmer; by J.O. Cassaday.

15. 5 Sept 1877 ABRAM L. CARTER 21 yrs single b. Tazewell Co VA now living same s/o Gordan & Kate to MARGARET M. WADE 17 yrs single b. Bland Co VA now living Tazewell Co VA d/o Joshua & Margaret O: farmer; by James Calfee.

16. 7 Sept 1877 JONATHAN A. ROLLINS 28 yrs single b. Randolph Co NC now living in Tazewell Co VA s/o Jonathan & Nancy to SARAH F. DEATON 30 yrs single b. Roanoke Co VA d/o Nathan & O: farmer; by T.K. Lambert.

17. 10 Sept 1877 JACOB A. HARVEY 19 yrs single b. Mercer Co w VA s/o Jacob W. & Katharine to NANCY M. MEADOR 17 yrs single b. Mercer Co W VA d/o Lycungus & Nancy O:farmer; by Elias Reed.

18. 10 Sept 1877 SQUIRE T. LYON 24 yrs single b. Mercer Co W VA s/o ? & Mary to MARY ANN MASSEY 21 yrs single b. Floyd Co VA d/o Theodore & Matilda O: farmer; by Jas. W. Lilley.

19. 10 Sept 1877 HENRY SHRADER 19 yrs single b. Mercer Co W VA s/o robt & Cynthia Jane to CATHARINE HILL 21 yrs single b. Tazewell Co VA d/o ? & Ala Hill O: farmer; by Evan H. Brown.

20. 18 Sept 1877 JAMES A. LUSK 20 yrs single b. Mercer Co W VA s/o Alfred E. & Henrietta to LUEMMA A. TURNER 17 yrs single b. Mercer co W VA d/o Charles G. & Victoria O: farmer; by Louidas Goodwyn.

21. 29 Aug 1877 PARIS W. WAGONER 21 yrs single b. Tazewell Co VA now living same s/o Adam C. & Julina E to PATRIA A. PERDUE 21 yrs single b. Franklin Co VA d/o Silas & Nancy Perdue O: farmer; by Evan H. Brown.

22. 25 Sept 1877 STAUNTON GRIFFITH 28 yrs wid. now living Raleigh Co W VA s/o John & Juda to LOUISA LILLEY 15 yrs single b. Mercer Co W VA d/o Joseph & Elizabeth O: farmer; by James W. Lilley.

23. 29 Sept 1877 WILLIAM H. JOHNSTON 22 yrs single b. Mercer Co W VA s/o John W. & Margaret D. to MATILDA E. CALFEE 21 yrs single b. Mercer Co W VA d/o James & Jane O: farmer; by James Calfee.

24. 1 Oct 1877 JNO L. BOGGESS 20 yrs single b. Monroe Co VA s/o Kinrod & Margaret A. to SARAH F. CALFEE 21 yrs single b. Mercer Co W VA d/o Chas W. & Nancy D. O: farmer; by James Calfee.

25. 4 Oct 1877 JAS. M. WRIGHT 20 yrs single b. Mercer Co W VA s/o Thos & Sarah Jane to NANCY MILLER 21 yrs single b. Fayette Co VA d/o Willoughby & ? O: farmer; by Phil S. Sutton.

26. 24 Sept 1877 GEORGE W. TABOR 22 yrs single b. Tazewell Co VA now living same s/o Jefferson & Sarah to MARTHA A. PERDUE 20 yrs single b. Mercer Co W VA d/o Silas & Nancy O: farmer; by Evan H. Brown.

27. 9 Oct 1877 ELI C. LUSK 17 yrs single b. Mercer Co W VA s/o Reese T. & Rebecca to LOUICIE E. WALKER 18 yrs single b. Mercer Co W VA d/o Underwood & Louisa O: farmer; by T.K. Lambert.

28. 20 Oct 1877 MATHEW E. BAILEY 18 yrs single b. Mercer Co W VA s/o Jamison & Polly to MARY M.S.E.E. SHREWSBURY 17 yrs single b. Mercer Co W VA d/o Thomas & Margy O: farmer; by A.A. Ashworth.

29. 25 Oct 1877 THOMAS B. COOK 19 yrs single b. Wyoming Co W VA s/o Thomas H. & Rebecca to LOUISA E. THOMPSON 16 yrs single b. Mercer Co W VA d/o Gordan & Louisa O: farmer; by T.K. Lambert.

30. 29 Oct 1877 JOHN A. GORE 22 yrs single b. Mercer Co W VA s/o Henderson F. & S.R. to LOUISA MARTIN 21 yrs single b. Mercer Co W VA d/o David & Esther O: farmer; by Wm Holroyd.

31. 30 Oct 1877 WILLIAM MEDLEY 32 yrs wid. b. Mercer Co W VA now living Summers Co W VA s/o Fielding & Araminta to MARGARET SHUMATE 27 yrs single b. Mercer Co W VA O: farmer; by J.W. Bennett; REMARKS: colored.

32. 6 Nov 1877 JOSEPH N. PENNINGTON 19 yrs single b. Mercer Co W VA s/o John A. & Ellen to FANNIE G. NEELEY 20 yrs single b. Mercer Co W VA s/o William G. & Delilah O: farmer; by A.J. Thompson.

33. 7 Nov 1877 JAMES B. DAVIS 24 yrs single b. Mercer Co W VA now living in Wyoming Co VA s/o Jesse & Margaret to ELIZA JANE DAVIS 17 yrs single b. Mercer Co W VA d/o Lee & Christine O: farmer; by Lonidas Goodwyn.

34. 20 Nov 1877 HASTIN BAILEY 19 yrs single b. Wyoming Co W VA s/o John P & Nancy to ESTER A. BAILEY 18 yrs single b. Mercer Co W VA d/o Wm M. & Matilda O: farmer; by T.K. Lambert.

35. 29 Nov 1877 OSCAR J. FARLEY 20 yrs single b. Mercer Co W VA now living in Summers Co W VA s/o Andrew & Judith to NANCY G. CAPERTON 21 yrs single b. Mercer Co w VA d/o Thompson N. & - O: farmer; by J.J. Meador.

36. 3 Dec 1877 DANIEL C. TICKLE 23 yrs single b. Giles Co VA now living in Tazewell Co VA s/o S & F.C. Tickle to LAURA E. JOHNSTON 16 yrs single b. Mercer Co W VA d/o Jno W. & Margaret O: farmer.

37. 3 Dec 1877 WILLIS GORE 24 yrs single b. Mercer Co W VA now living in Boone Co W VA s/o Mary Gore to CATHARINE GORE 21 yrs single b. Mercer Co W VA d/o - & Sarah Gore O: farmer; by J.W. Bennett; REMARKS: colored.

38. 17 Dec 1877 BENJAMIN B. PENDLETON 22 yrs single b. Mercer Co w VA s/o Wyatt W. & Rachael to CHARLOTTE A. TANNER 17 yrs single b. Botetourt Co VA d/o Frederick & Miuonsi(sic) O: farmer; by Leonidas Goodwin.

39. 19 Dec 1877 LAFAYETTE CHAMP 19 yrs single b. Tazewell Co VA s/o Elkahah & Nancy to CENA DUDLEY 19 yrs single b. Bland Co VA d/o John & Lucy O: farmer; by J.O. Cassaday.

40. 21 Dec 1877 ALLEN T. GORE 25 yrs single b. Mercer Co W VA now living in Summers Co W VA s/o Robert & Elizabeth to EMMA PHIPPS 18 yrs single b. Alleghany Co NC d/o Aaron B. & ? O: farmer; by Wm Holroyd.

41. 24 Dec 1877 JOHN L. MILLER 20 yrs single b. Mercer Co W VA s/o Floyd & Lucretia to JOANNA ARMONTROUT 18 yrs single b. Mercer Co W VA d/o George & Mary Ann O: farmer; by A.J. Thompson.

42. 24 Dec 1877 EDWARD K. FRENCH 30 yrs single b. Mercer Co W VA s/o Napoleon B. & Jane B. to EUPHERNIA BARBERIES 22 yrs single b. Sussex England d/o John & Maria Ann O: surveyor; by Wm H. Barnes.

43. 26 Dec 1877 JOSEPH W. WOOLWINE 32 yrs single b. Montgomery Co VA s/o John L. & Nancy to SALLIE A. BROWN 22 yrs single b. Giles Co VA d/o James L. & ? O: farming; by Wm H. Barnes; REMARKS: listed to auditor.

44. 3 Jany 1878 JOSEPH A. STAFFORD 22 yrs single b. Mercer Co W VA s/o Wm M. & Louisa H. to MIRIAM E. HALE 16 yrs single b. Giles Co VA d/o Danl P. & Martha A. O: farming; by William Holroyd.

45. 22 Jany 1878 W.R. CRADDOCK 22 yrs single now living in Giles Co VA s/o Ezekiah & Lucy R. to SERVILLA J. CLEMONS 19 yrs single b. Pitsylvania Co VA d/o John R. & Mary S. O: school teaching; by Jas H. Johnston.

46. 17 Jany 1878 EDMOND REDMAN 48 yrs wid. b. Wythe Co VA s/o Joseph & Sarah to KATHARINE WILSON 37 yrs wid. b. Mercer Co W VA d/o W.H. Barnes O: farming; by William H. Barnes; REMARKS: colored.

47. 27 Dec. 1877 JOHN C. HOLBROOK 27 yrs single b. Tazewell Co VA now living same s/o Randall & Mary B. to MARY WITTEN 22 yrs single b. Mercer Co W VA d/o Wm H. & Mary O: farming; by Wm E. Neal.

48. 4 Feby 1878 WM A. GORE 33 yrs single b. Monroe Co W VA s/o & Sarah Gore to CAROLINE JONES 24 yrs single b. Mercer co W VA d/o Poval & Lucy Jones O: farming; by J.W. Bennett.

Page 30

1. 5 Feby 1878 ISAAC G. FLETCHER 22 yrs single b. Mercer Co W VA s/o Isaac & Ellen Fletcher to ELVIRA V. CALDWELL 18 yrs single b. Craig Co VA d/o Madison A. & Ann Caldwell O: farming; by William Holroyd.

2. 7 Feby 1878 FILLMORE M. THORNTON 21 yrs single b. Mercer Co W VA s/o Meredith & Louisa W. Thornton to ALICE JANE WHITE 18 yrs single b. Mercer Co W VA d/o John & Melvina White O: farming; by L. Goodwyn.

3. 7 Feby 1878 HIRAM LITTLE 25 yrs single b. Mercer Co W VA now living in Wyoming Co VA to MARTHA A. HEARN 23 yrs single b. Mercer Co W VA d/o Levi G. & Ora Hearn O: farming; by C.F. Johnston.

4. 7 Feby 1878 DANIEL C. PETRY 22 yrs single b. Mercer Co W VA s/o ? & Terry Petry to MARY JANE MILLER 17 yrs single b. Mercer Co W VA d/o James & Rachel Miller O: farming; by William C. Martin.

5. 20 Feby 1878 THOMAS J. MEADOWS 21 yrs single b. Mercer Co W VA s/o B.P & S.A Meadows to ALEC J. CRAWFORD 21 yrs single b. Mercer Co W VA d/o Thos & Elizabeth Crawford O: farming; by Leonidas Goodwin.

6. 26 Feby 1878 REUBEN PETTIFORD 50 yrs wid. b. NC to RHODA THOMAS 40 yrs wid. b. Pulaski Co VA O: farming; by J.W. Bennett; REMARKS: colored.

7. 2 March 1878 LEVI GORE 21 yrs wid. b. Mercer Co VA s/o ? & Sarah Gore to HARRIET VORGE 19 yrs single b. Mercer Co W VA d/o ? & Harriet Vorge O: farming; by J.W. Bennett; REMARKS: colored.

8. 7 March 1878 MARSHAL W. WALKUP 27 yrs single b. Greenbriar Co VA now living in Giles Co VA s/o Joseph & Susan J. to LIZZIE F. CANNADY 16 yrs single b. Mercer Co W VA d/o Flemming & Clara O: lumber dealing; by Jas. H. Johnston.

9. 11 April 1878 HARRISON A. RICHMOND 25 yrs single b. Raleigh Co VA now living same s/o Moses & Elizabeth to JULIA E. MASSIE 21 yrs single b. Mercer Co W VA d/o Jas J. & Patsey O: farming; by Jas. W. Lilly.

10. 12 March 1878 DAVID A. BARGER 27 yrs single b. Tazewell Co VA s/o Jacob & Dianna to DELIA W. TRAILE 22 yrs single b. Mercer Co W VA d/o Jacob & Lockey O: carpenter; by J.O. Cassaday.

11. 19 March 1878 SAMUEL L. PALMER 23 yrs single b. Campbell Co VA s/o Robt T. & Elizabeth A. to LUCINDA T. DAVIS 21 yrs single b. Mercer Co W VA d/o George R. & Elizabeth O: carpenter; by L. Goodwin.

12. 25 March 1878 FABIAS N. SHORTER 24 yrs single b. Franklin Co VA s/o Woodson A. & Martha C. to ELIZTH G. CAPERTON 26 yrs single b. Mercer Co W VA d/o Thompson & Laura O: farmer; by Caroll Clark.

13. 28 March 1878 WILLIAM S. BROWN 19 yrs single b. Alleghany Co VA s/o Marchall B. & Elizth to HARRIET A. PENNINGTON 19 yrs single b. Mercer Co W VA d/o Gordan E & Julia A. O: farming; by William Holroyd.

14. 24 April 1878 BALLARD P. DELP 19 yrs single b. Carroll Co VA s/o Elphraim & Lucy A. to SARAH E. DILLION 18 yrs single b. Mercer Co W VA d/o Wm & Martha O: farming; by Evan H. Brown.

15. 8 May 1878 GEORGE B. NADDLE 29 yrs wid. b. Giles Co VA s/o Jno A. & Polly Naddle to MARY E. SHORTER 16 yrs single b. Mercer Co W VA d/o W.A. & Eliz. Shorter O: farming; by Carroll Clark.

16. 14 May 1878 DAVID SHRADER 55 yrs wid. b. Mercer Co W VA s/o David & Rhoda Shrader to ELIZABETH COLEMAN 43 yrs single b. Mercer Co W VA d/o Jno. & Eliza Coleman O: farming; by Lewis G. Day.

17. 23 May 1878 JESSE G. NEELEY 17 yrs single b. Mercer Co W VA s/o N.M. & Catharine to V.E. FERGUSON 23 yrs single b. Mercer Co W VA d/o D.M. & Livonia O: farming; by Charles Walker.

18. 5 June 1878 EVERMONT W. HOYE 17 yrs single b. Mercer Co W VA now living in Summers Co VA s/o John W. & Julia Ann to SARAH E. LILLY 22 yrs single b. Raleigh Co VA d/o Wm H. & Jane O: farming; by James W. Lilly.

19. 26 June 1878 JOHN D. JOHNSTON 21 yrs single b. Giles Co VA s/o Jno L. & Minerva A. to ELIZTH F. SPADE 15 yrs angle b. Mercer Co W VA d/o Saml A. & Rhoda O: farming; by J.O. Cassaday.

20. 27 June 1878 NICHOLAS PENNINGTON 21 yrs single b. KY s/o Green & Avena to ARAMINTA K. PENNINGTON 17 yrs angle b. Mercer Co W VA d/o Levi & Elizabeth O: farming; by Wm C. Martin.

21. 1 Aug 1878 L.P.G. STAFFORD 24 yrs single b. Mercer Co W VA now living in Giles co Va s/o Edward & Lucilla to REBECCA A. WOOLWINE 22 yrs single b. Montgomery Co VA d/o Jno L. & Nancy O: carpenter; by J.O. Cassaday.

22. 18 July 1878 JNO A. PENNINGTON 22 yrs single b. Mercer Co W VA s/o Gordan E. & Juliet to MARGARET A. DILLION 19 yrs single b. Mercer Co W VA d/o Mastin & Peggy O: farmer; by E.F. Kahle.

23. 17 July 1878 MASTIN C. McCORKLE 24 yrs single b. Monroe Co W VA now living same s/o samuel & Julia to RHODA J. CANNADAY 19 yrs single b. Mercer Co W VA d/o flemming & Clara O: lumber dealer; by Leonidas Goodwyn.

24. 23 July 1878 WM H. CHAMPE 22 yrs single b. Tazewell Co VA s/o Elkanah & Nancy to ELIZ A. DUDLEY 23 yrs single b. Bland Co VA d/o Jno S. & Lucy O: farming; by J.O. Cassaday.

25. 25 July 1878 JAMES NONE 24 yrs single b. Franklin Co VA s/o Thomas & Nancy to NANCY FLETCHER 20 yrs single b. Mercer Co W VA d/o Hiram H. & Rhoda O: farming; by James Calfee.

26. 8 Aug 1878 JAMES A. McCOMAS 19 yrs single b. Mercer Co W VA s/o Archibald & Savilla to MARY A. MANGUS 19 yrs single b. Wyoming Co VA d/o Joseph & Julina O:farming; by A. McComas.

27. 8 Aug 1878 FLOYD A. BOLIN 33 yrs single b. Mercer Co W VA s/o William & Elizabeth to MARY A HUNT 24 yrs single b. Bland Co VA d/o H.W. & Hannah C. O: merchant; by William Holroyd.

28. 15 Aug 1878 CHARLES D. ROBINSON 22 yrs single b. Giles Co VA s/o Chas. & Katharine to MARY E. BYRD single b. Bland Co VA d/o Wm & Cynthia; by B.T. Bird.

29. 23 Aug 1878 L.S. PETRY 19 yrs single b. Mercer Co W VA s/o Jacob & Elizabeth to N.A. WHITE 14 yrs single b. Wyoming Co W VA d/o Geo P. & Rhoda O: farmer; by Wm C. Martin.

30. 9 Sept 1878 F.M. CALDWELL 28 yrs single b. Craig Co VA s/o Hugh & Frances M. to MAY KARNES 16 yrs single b. Mercer Co W VA d/o Isaac & Lucinda O: farmer; by J.O. Cassaday.

31. 26 Sept 1878 WM C. GORE 26 yrs wid. b. Mercer Co W VA s/o ? & Matilda to MARY SHUMATE 30 yrs wid. b. Mercer Co W VA O: farmer; by Leonidas Goodwyn; REMARKS: colored.

32. 26 Sept 1878 WILSON W. SMITH 25 yrs single b. Montgomery Co VA s/o John H. & Sarah to ELIZA J. COMER 24 yrs single b. Mercer Co W VA d/o Jacob & Elizabeth O: farmer; by Leonidas Goodwyn.

33. 10 Oct 1878 WM A. NOBLE 20 yrs single b. Mercer Co W VA now living Summers Co W VA s/o L.B. W. & Permelia to ELIZA T.T. BOLIN 17 yrs single b. Mercer Co W VA d/o Wm & Elizabeth O: farmer; by B.T. Bird.

34. 28 Nov 1878 W.E. MASTON 46 yrs wid. b. Wilkes Co NC s/o John & Elisabeth to LOUISA HERNDON 34 yrs wid. b. Mercer Co W VA d/o Madison & Nancey O: farmer; by Archibald McComas.

35. 24 Oct 1878 NOAH CHARLTON 21 yrs single b. Tazewell Co VA s/o Noah & Kisy J. to SARAH CALLANDER 25 yrs single b. Mercer Co W VA d/o ? & Susan O: farmer; by Evan H. Brown.

36. 24 Oct 1878 LEWIS G. HICKS 22 yrs single b. Giles Co VA to NANCY SWADER 18 yrs single b. Mercer Co W VA O: farmer; by Lewis G. Day.

37. 29 Oct 1878 JAMES ADAMS 32 yrs single b. Smythe Co VA s/o A.A. & S.A. to VICTORIA E. McKINNEY 22 yrs single b. Mercer Co W VA d/o Powhattan & Susan O: carpenter; by J.O. Cassaday.

38. 29 Oct 1878 JAMES E. AUSTIN 23 yrs single b. Giles Co VA s/o Isaac E. & Malinda L. to JULIA A. McKINNEY 17 yrs single b. Mercer Co W VA O: carpenter; by J.O. Cassaday.

39. 3 Nov 1878 LAZARUS HAZELWOOD 22 yrs single b. Stokes Co NC s/o Asa & Rachel to ELIZA NELSON 22 yrs single b. Stokes Co NC O:farmer; by A.J. Thompson.

40. 14 Nov 1878 ROBERT D. MEADOWS 23 yrs single b. Giles Co VA s/o Richard & Mary to NANCY A FRENCH 23 yrs single b. Mercer Co W VA d/o R.G. & Martha A. O: farmer; by Benjamin T. Bird.

41. 21 Nov 1878 JOSHUA L. JOHNSTON 20 yrs single b. Giles Co VA s/o Jno L. & Minerva A. to SARAH E. THOMPSON 17 yrs single b. Mercer Co W VA d/o Wm R. & Jane O: farmer; by A.J. Thompson.

42. 20 Nov 1878 REESE A. HARMAN 31 yrs single b. Tazewell Co VA s/o Danl C. & Margaret to ELIZABETH R. THOMPSON 23 yrs single b. Tazewell Co VA s/o Wm & Marinda O: farmer; by Romulus Harry.

43. 30 Nov 1878 REESE MOORE 31 yrs wid. b. Tazewell Co VA s/o Richard & Ellen to NANCY MOORE 17 yrs single b. NC d/o Lewis & Frances O: farmer; by John Trigg; REMARKS: colored.

44. 26 Nov 1878 ARCHIBALD B. MORGAN 25 yrs single b. Wyoming Co W VA s/o Anthony & Chloe to RIERDELL SHREWSBURY 18 yrs single b. Mercer Co W VA d/o Philip & Margery O: farmer; by J.O. Cassaday.

45. 5 Dec 1878 JAS M. LUSK 19 yrs single b. Mercer Co W VA s/o Reese & Rebecca to ABBIE C. STRONG 18 yrs single b. Mercer Co W VA d/o Daniel & Elizth O: farmer; by thomas K. Lambert.

46. 7 Dec 1878 ROBERT C. WHITE 24 yrs single b. Mercer Co W VA s/o Reuben & Martha to MARTHA ISABELL COX 21 yrs single b. Mercer Co W VA d/o J.C. & C.H. Cox O: farmer; by Wm Holroyd.

47. 15 Dec 1878 GEO W. HOPKINS 20 yrs single b. Mercer Co W VA now living Summers Co W VA s/o Reuben & Nancy to LILLY F. BELCHER 17 yrs single b. Mercer Co W VA d/o Russell & Sarah O: farmer; by John J. Meador.

48. 26 Dec 1878 GEO P. BAILEY 18 yrs single b. Mercer Co W VA s/o Zilphia & Floyd to VASTY SHREWSBURY 17 yrs single b. Mercer Co W VA d/o Wm & Vasty O: farmer; by Archibald McComas.

Page 31

1. 25 Dec 1878 THOMPSON W. DICKINSON 30 yrs single b. Giles Co VA now living same s/o Henry & Nancy to ELIZABETH PINE 30 yrs single b. Mercer Co W VA d/o Alexander & Rebecca O: farming; by J.W. Bennett.

2. 24 Dec 1878 WILLIAM WILLIAMS 50 yrs single b. Kanawha Co W VA to MARY E. CARTER 40 yrs wid. b. Wythe Co VA O: farming; by G.W.K. Green.

3. 31 Dec 1878 JAMES T. WEATHERFORD 21 yrs single b. Monroe Co W VA now living in Summers Co VA s/o John M. & Adeline M. to VICTORIA E. SHORTER 21 yrs single b. Pitsylvania Co VA d/o Jno & Sarah A. O: farming; by G.A. Austin.

4. 1 Jany 1879 JNO W. MELVIN 35 yrs wid. b. Mercer Co W VA s/o Hezekiah & Elizabeth to NANCY F. PERDUE 31 yrs wid. b. Giles Co VA d/o Thomas & Frances O: farming; by Leonidas Goodwyn.

5. 4 Jany 1879 ERASTUS B. LILLY 21 yrs single b. Mercer Co W VA s/o Jonathan & Rebecca to LUCINDA CREWS 19 yrs single b. Mercer Co W VA d/o Asa & Nancy O: farming; by Joseph Lilly.

6. 4 Jany 1879 JOHN D. FLETCHER 23 yrs single b. Mercer Co W VA s/o Jas H. & Columbia to ELIZ. C. DAVIS 18 yrs single b. Mercer Co w VA d/o Green & Sarah O: farming; by A.J. Thompson.

7. 4 Jany 1879 JACOB MEADOWS 33 yrs wid. b. Mercer Co W VA s/o Adam & Sarah to MARY E. BOLIN 26 yrs single b. Mercer Co W VA d/o Wm & Elizabeth O: farming; by Benj. T. Bird.

8. 4 Jany 1879 HIRAM PRINCE 23 yrs single b. Wayne Co VA now living same s/o Hiram & - to ELLEN TABOR 23 yrs single b. Mercer Co W VA d/o Abram & Nancy O: farming; by T.K. Lambert.

9. 18 Jany 1879 SILAS J. McVEY 30 yrs single b. Kanawha Co W VA s/o James & Phoebe to VICTORIA J. AUSTIN 38 yrs single b. Pitsylvania Co VA d/o Garland A. & E.J. O: farming; by G.A. Austin.

10. 22 Jany 1879 JOHN C. GORE 19 yrs single bl Boone Co W VA now living same s/o Jacob & Sarah Jane to MINERVA JANE GORE 18 yrs single b. Mercer Co W VA d/o ? & Sarah O: farming; by J.W. Bennett; REMARKS: colored.

11. 25 Jany 1879 WILLIAM CALDWELL 70 yrs wid. b. Botetourt Co VA s/o William & Priscilla to LOUISA TILLER 38 yrs wid. b. Mercer Co W VA d/o John & - O: farming; by Thomas C. Pulliam.

12. 29 Jany 1879 BENJAMIN M. HOLDRON 25 yrs wid. b. Mercer Co W VA s/o Samuel & 7 to ELIZABETH HILL 18 yrs single b. Franklin Co VA d/o James R. & Delia A. O: farming; by A.J. Thompson.

13. 10 Feb 1879 MATTHIAS J. CASEY 19 yrs single b. Russell Co VA s/o Henry D. & Sarah to SARAH J. BAILEY 18 yrs single b. Mercer Co W VA d/o George D. & Christina O: farming; by Joseph Lilly.

14. 13 Feb 1879 JAMES SARVER, JR. 23 yrs single b. Mercer Co W VA s/o Wm A. & Mary A. to ELIZABETH S. GARRETSON 15 yrs single b. Wyoming Co VA d/o Hiram J. & Mary A. O: farming; by thomas C. Pulliam.

15. 16 Feb 1879 ALLEN G. LILLY 30 yrs wid. b. Mercer Co W VA now living in Summers Co W VA s/o Thomas & Rebecca to TEXAS A. PHILLIPS 17 yrs single b. Mercer Co W VA d/o James & Clara O: farming; by John J. Meador.

16. 20 Feb 1879 ELISHA E. HAZELWOOD 17 yrs single b. Stokes Co NC s/o Asa & Rachael to NANCY E. WHITE 17 yrs single, b. Mercer Co W VA d/o Reuben & Martha O: farming; by A.J. Thompson.

17. 28 Feb 1879 HIRAM TILLER 54 yrs wid. b. Mercer Co W VA s/o William & Rebecca to PERCILLA LITTLE 23 yrs single b. Mercer Co W VA d/o Lorenzo D. & Zernah O:farming; by Thomas C. Pulliam.

18. 26 Feb 1879 ALEXANDER ALIFF 20 yrs single b. Mercer Co W VA s/o Perry & Julia A. to MARY JONES 18 yrs single b. Mercer Co W VA d/o Elisha P. & Zernah O: farming; by thomas C. Pulliam.

19. 5 March 1879 CHARLES H. ROBINSON 22 yrs single b. Pulaski Co VA s/o Henry & Pheobe to SUE E. CALDWELL 23 yrs wid. b. Pulaski Co VA d/o John & Emma O: farming; by Leonidas Goodwyn.

20. 13 March 1879 MILLARD F. THOMAS 22 yrs single b. Mercer Co W VA s/o William G. & Annie to SARAH L. PERDUE 22 yrs single b. Giles Co VA d/o Asa C. & Rhoda J. O: farming; by Thomas C. Pulliam.

21. * * * STEPHEN EVANS 30 yrs single b. PA s/o George & Caroline to ? THOMPSON 33 yrs wid. b. Tazewell Co VA d/o William & Manerva O: farming; by James Calfee. (*Note: no date given) (?=no first name given)

22. 25 March 1879 ANDREW P. WILLIAMS 24 yrs single now living Giles Co VA to VIRGINIA A. LILLY 17 yrs single d/o Jonathan & ? O: farming; by Benj T. Bird.

23. * March 1878(sic) PORTER W. BOGGESS 25 yrs single b. Monroe Co W VA now living same to MARY E. BAILEY 24 yrs single b. Mercer Co W VA d/o John M. & Sarah A. O: farming; by Jas. Sweeney. (*Note: no date given.)

24. 18 March 1879 JOHN F. McKINNEY 26 yrs single b. Wyoming Co VA s/o Powhattan B. & Susan E. to AINCETTA A. BURNETT 18 yrs single b. Carroll Co VA d/o B.C. & Adaline O: farming; by J.O. Cassaday.

25. 3 April 1879 CHARLES LEWIS HALDRON 22 yrs single b. Monroe Co W VA s/o Smithen(?) & Nancy to ADILAH A. BELL 17 yrs single b. Floyd Co VA d/o Thomas & Martha A. O: farming; by Benjamin T. Bird. (?= handwriting difficult to read.)

26. 10 April 1879 JOHN C. TABOR 21 yrs single b. Mercer Co W VA now living in Tazewell Co VA s/o Stephen B. & Lucinda O. to MARY A. BELL 22 yrs single b. Mercer co W VA d/o James & Julia Ann O: farming; by Evan B. Brown.

27. 10 April 1879 OWEN S. HURST 20 yrs single b. Mercer Co W VA s/o Wm & Susan to LUVENIA C. BAILEY 22 yrs single b. Mercer Co W VA d/o Addison & Octavia O: farming; by A. McComas.

28. 15 April 1879 WM BOLIN 50 yrs wid. b. Mercer Co W VA s/o Wm & ? to

RUTHA J. CALDWELL 33 yrs single b. Mercer Co W VA d/o Jno & Eliza O: farming; by Benjamin T. Bird.

29. 10 April 1879 EVERMONT W. TILLER 18 yrs single b. Mercer Co W VA s/o Wm & Louisa to JULIA L. THORNTON 18 yrs sngle b. Mercer Co W VA d/o Nancy V. & Thos P. O: farming; by Thos C. Pulliam.

30. 19 May 1879 CORNELIUS B. ST CLAIR 22 yrs single b. Mercer Co W VA s/o Edward & ? to SARAH C. MEANS 20 yrs single b. Mercer Co W VA d/o Charles & Elizabeth O: farming; by J.W. Bennett.

31. 22 April 1879 LEWIS M. HALE 21 yrs single b. Giles Co VA s/o Daniel P. & Martha A. to JOSEPHINE STINSON 21 yrs single b. Mercer Co W VA d/o Charles & Elizabeth O: farming; by G.W.K. Green.

32. * * * EDGAR P. KIRTNER 22 yrs single b. Pulaski Co VA s/o Crockett J. & Ellen E. to MARIETTA REATON 18 yrs single b. Monroe Co VA d/o ? & Mary A. O: farming. (*Note: no dates given.)

33. 22 May 1879 WILLIAM T. RAHLE 28 yrs single b. Amhurst Co VA d/o Samuel K. & Catherine K. to CYNTHIA J. HUTCHINSON 22 yrs single b. Mercer Co W VA d/o Alex & Lydia Ann O: farming; by G.W.K. Green.

34. 25 May 1879 JOSEPH MILLS 20 yrs single b. Mercer Co W VA s/o William & Marilia to TRIFANIE REED 16 yrs single b. Raleigh Co W VA d/o Calvin & Nancy O: farming; by Elias Read.

35. 5 June 1879 JOHN C. MORAN 26 yrs single b. Ash Co NC s/o James M. & Sarah to ELIZABETH BELL 30 yrs single b. McDowell Co VA d/o David E. & 7 O: farming; by T.K. Lambert.

36. 25 June 1879 RUSSEL F. LILLY 21 yrs single b. Mercer Co W VA s/o Joseph & Elizabeth to LUCINDA V. LILLY 21 yrs single b. Mercer Co W VA d/o Wm H. & Jane O: farming; by James W. Lilly.

37. 8 July 1879 JOHN ABSHER 31 yrs single b. Mercer Co W VA now living in Tazewell Co VA s/o Christian & 7 to RACHAEL SHREWSBURY 22 yrs single b. Mercer Co W VA d/o Henry & Sarah O: farming; by Lewis G. Day.

38. 23 July 1879 JOHN W. CANTERBURY 25 yrs single b. Monroe Co W VA now living same to ALICE V. CAPERTON 26 yrs single b. Mercer Co W VA d/o thompson & Laura O: farming; by Carroll Clark.

39. 31 July 1879 JAMES B. MULLINS 27 yrs sngle b. Mercer Co W VA s/o Wm P. & Abagie Ann to MARTHA JANE LESLIE 19 yrs single b. Pulaski Co VA d/o Jno P. & Elvina Leslie O: farming; by James Calfee.

40. 6 Aug 1879 JAMES W. LESLIE 21 yrs single b. Pulaski Co VA s/o John P. & Melvina to ELLEN HONAKER 22 yrs single b. Tazewell Co VA d/o Henry & Elizabeth O: carpenter; by Carroll Clark.

41. 10 Aug 1879 ISAAC PAINE 20 yrs single b. Mercer Co W VA s/o James & Mary to CELIA HARMAN 22 yrs single b. Grayson Co VA d/o George & 7 O: farmer; by T.K. Lambert.

42. 24 Aug 1879 ANDREW J. HUFFMAN 46 yrs wid. b. Botetourt Co VA s/o Solamon & Ellen to MINERVA J. HUBBARD 35 yrs wid. b. Mercer Co W VA d/o Jas & - Shrewsbury O: farmer; by Carroll Clark.

43. 9 Sep 1879 PLEASANT H. FARLEY 18 yrs single b. Mercer Co W VA now living in Summers Co VA s/o Hendley & Sarah to MARY E. MEADOR 16 yrs single b. Mercer Co W VA d/o ? & Susannah O: farmer; by Joseph Lilly.

44. 6 Sep 1879 LEWIS J. LESTER 21 yrs single b. Wyoming Co W VA now living same s/o Isaac & Mary to REBECCA GODFREY 21 yrs single b. Mercer Co W VA d/o John D. & Martha O: farmer; by Archibald McComas.

MERCER COUNTY, WEST VIRGINIA
Marriages 1854 - 1901

45. 11 Sep 1879 HENLEY BUICE 22 yrs single b. Bland Co VA now living same s/o James & ? to MARINDA ANN DAY 17 yrs single b. Mercer Co W VA d/o Lewis G. & Eliz. Ann O: farmer; by G.W.K. Green.

46. 11 Sep 1879 H.W. FRANKLIN 25 yrs single b. Tazewell Co VA now living same s/o William & Mary to D.A. CALDWELL 24 yrs single b. Montgomery Co VA d/o Edward & Margaret O: farmer; by J.O. Cassaday.

47. 15 Sep 1879 WM P. MALONE 22 yrs single b. Dublin Ireland s/o Jonathan & Mary to VIRGINIA SHREWSBURY 22 yrs single b. Mercer Co W VA d/o ? & Virginia O: carpenter; by Joseph Lilly.

48. 18 Sep 1879 STARLING HAZELWOOD 18 yrs single b. Patrick Co VA s/o John & Nancy to OCTABIA L. BELCHER 18 yrs single b. Mercer Co W VA d/o Anderson & Jane O: farmer; by J.O. Cassaday.

Page 32

1. 21 Sep 1879 JOSEPH S. BECKNER 22 yrs single b. Roanoke Co VA now living Summers Co W VA s/o Hoab & Sarah A. to SARAH A. ABBOTT 19 yrs single b. Summers Co W VA d/o Chas. & Ida Abbott O: farmer; by John J. Headlor.

2. 24 Sep 1879 RICHARDSON C. CHRISTIE 27 yrs single b. Monroe Co W VA s/o James M. & Cynthia P. to ELIZABETH P. WHITE 21 yrs single b. Mercer Co W VA d/o Benj & Elizabeth O: lawyer; by Phillip S. Sutton.

3. 1 Oct 1879 WILIAM MANN 40 yrs wid. b. Campbell Co VA to MARY DORHAN 35 yrs wid. b. Augustus Co VA O: laborer; by A.J. Thompson; REMARKS: colored.

4. 2 Oct 1879 GRIFFITH ELLIS 60 yrs wid. b. Monroe Co W VA to AWANDA SHUE 25 yrs single b. Monroe co W VA d/o Joseph B. & Sarah O: farmer; by J.O. Cassaday.

5. 15 Oct 1879 Z.A. MURFY* 20 yrs single b. Logan Co W VA now living same s/o Joseph & Jane to FAMIE E. BAILEY 22 yrs single b. Mercer Co W VA d/o William & Matilda O: farmer; by T.K. Lambert.

6. 16 Oct 1879 ANDREW J. LILLY 19 yrs single b. Mercer Co W VA now living in Summers Co VA s/o Wm H. & Lucinda to SARAH E. LYON 17 yrs single b. Mercer Co W VA d/o Jno D. & Mary Ann O: farmer; by Joseph Lilly.

7. 19 Oct 1879 JAMES O. SCOTT 18 yrs single b. Giles Co VA s/o Wm & Elizabeth to PHOEBE K. HARMAN 22 yrs single b. Carroll Co VA d/o Joseph & Nancy O: farmer; by James Calfee.

8. 1 Nov 1879 JOHN J. MULLINS 21 yrs single b. Pulaski co VA now living in Tazewell Co Va s/o Austin & Sarah J. to JOSEPHINE C. BAILEY 19 yrs single b. Mercer Co W VA d/o Irvin & Telia O: farmer; by Archibald McComas.

9. 30 Oct 1879 CHARLES H. FINE 20 yrs single b. Wyoming co W VA now living in Raleigh Co W VA s/o Wm A. & Rachael S. to ELIZA S. VINES 20 yrs single b. Monroe Co W VA d/o Silas & ? O: farmer; by Charles Walker.

10. 30 Oct 1879 ROBERT P. ELLISON 26 yrs single b. Mercer Co W VA s/o Isaac J. & Elizabeth to MINERVA J. LILLY 22 yrs single b. Mercer Co W VA d/o Washington & Mary O: farmer; by Joseph Lilly.

11. 30 Oct 1879 MARTIN L. CARTER 24 yrs single b. Tazewell Co Va now living same s/o Gordon & Catherine to ARLEVA B. HARMAN 21 yrs single b. Tazewell Co VA d/o James & Jane O: farmer.

12. 30 Oct 1879 IRVIN H. SHREWSBURY 24 yrs wid. b. Mercer Co W VA s/o John & Elizabeth to SARAE ANN KING 23 yrs single b. Mercer Co W VA d/o Riley & Hannah O: farmer; by Archibald McComas.

13. 12 Nov 1879 REESE WINSTON 24 yrs wid. b. Loring Co MS s/o Robert & Mary to MAY E. KIDD 20 yrs single b. Bland Co VA d/o William & May O: farmer; by Wm C. Martin.

14. 27 Nov 1879 BARNETT J. SNEAD 19 yrs single b. Mercer Co W VA s/o John & ? to ELIZABETH R. GADD 17 yrs single b. Mercer Co W VA d/o Andrew P. & Delilah E. O: farmer; by Elias Reed.

15. 18 Nov 1879 JOSEPH T. OLIVER 31 yrs single b. Mercer Co W VA s/o Wm & Nancy to JULIA V. HARRY 22 yrs single b. Mercer Co W VA d/o Calvin & Mary O: farmer; by J.O. Cassaday.

16. 19 Nov 1879 CHARLES W. WIMMER 23 yrs single b. Mercer Co W VA s/o James & Elizabeth to MARTHA J. NEAL 19 yrs single b. Mercer Co W VA s/o Daniel N. & Ann O: farmer; by James O. Cassaday.

17. 20 Nov 1879 GEORGE BAXTER 51 yrs wid. b. Giles Co VA s/o George & Sarah to PATSY CALFEE 37 yrs wid. b. Giles Co VA O: farmer; by Wm A. Claxton; REMARKS: colored.

18. 20 Nov 1879 WM J. TABOR 44 yrs wid. b. Tazewell Co Va s/o Richard & Millie to MANERVA A. REYNOLDS 36 yrs wid. b. Mercer Co W VA d/o Charles & ? O: farmer; by Lewis G. Day.

19. 28 Nov 1879 WILLIAM T. AKERS 21 yrs single b. Pulaski Co VA s/o David & Rachel to VICTORIA UNDERWOOD 20 yrs single b. Giles Co VA d/o Joshua & Litha O: farmer; by Wm H. Barnes.

20. * * * GEORGE W. TUGGLE 27 yrs single b. Mercer Co W VA s/o John & Emily to ELECTRA ANN BAILEY 23 yrs single b. Mercer Co W VA d/o Henry B. & Martha O: farmer. (*Note: no date given.)

21. 4 Dec 1879 WM J. JOHNSTON 21 yrs single b. Giles Co VA s/o J.R. & Martha E. to LYDIA SHRADER 19 yrs single b. Mercer Co W VA d/o David & Chloe O: farmer; by Evan H. Brown.

22. 9 Dec 1879 GEORGE D. SADDLER 22 yrs single b. Giles Co VA s/o Henry & Chloe to KATHARINE WOOD 18 yrs single b. Mercer Co W VA d/o ? & Caroline O: farmer; by James Calfee.

23. 10 Dec 1879 ANDREW E. FINK 24 yrs single b. Greenbriar Co W VA now living in Raleigh Co VA s/o Andrew L. & Ruth to JANE E. VINES 17 yrs single b. Monroe Co VA s/o Silas S. & Eliza P. O: farmer; by Charles Walker.

24. 2 Feb 1880 JNO W. VINES 31 yrs single b. Monroe Co VA s/o Silas & Eliza P. to MATTIE L. ELLISON 24 yrs single b. Monroe Co VA d/o Saml & Susan O: farmer; by Charles Walker.

25. 1 Jan 1880 ALBERT C. BOWLING 20 yrs single b. Greenbriar Co W VA s/o Chas. A. & Lucy M. to RACHEL LILLY 19 yrs single b. Mercer Co W VA d/o Lewis & Frances O: farmer; by William P. Lilly.

26. 11 Dec 1879 FRANCIS K. FARLEY 21 yrs single b. Mercer Co W VA s/o John W. & Elizabeth to LUCY A. GRIMM 21 yrs single b. Mercer Co W VA d/o John & ? O: farmer; by J.O. Cassaday.

27. 11 Dec 1879 ALLEN T. COLE 35 yrs wid. b. Mercer Co W VA s/o Augustus W. & Margaret to MARTHA V. PETTIT 19 yrs single b. Henry Co VA d/o Robert & Martha O: farmer; by Leonidas Goodwyn.

28. 17 Dec 1879 WM W. GEORGE 23 yrs single b. Greenbriar Co W VA s/o John & Mollie to MARTHA F. ELLIS 21 yrs single b. Monroe Co W VA d/o Obedia & Jane O: farmer; by James O. Cassaday.

29. 24 Dec 1879 JAMES M. MIDCAFF 21 yrs single b. Carroll Co VA s/o Mathew & Jane to SARAH E. KINZER 22 yrs single b. Tazewell Co VA d/o Thos B. & Lucretia O: farmer; by L.G. Day.

30. 31 Dec 1879 JOSEPH O. CROTTY 26 yrs single b. Mercer Co W VA now living in Monroe Co W VA s/o Wm & Julia to MARTHA S. DUNCAN 20 yrs single b. Monroe Co W VA d/o Josephus & Malinda J.; by J.O. Cassaday.

31. 6 Jan 1880 R.A. MILLER 39 yrs wid. b. Monroe Co W VA s/o James & Sallie to MARY J. FRENCH 31 yrs single b. Mrcer Co W VA d/o John & ? O: farmer; by J.C. Pulliam.

32. 20 Jan 1880 LEANDER H. BAILEY 20 yrs single b. Wyoming Co VA now living same s/o Jas O. & Martha J. to SARAH C. STRING 21 yrs single b. Mercer Co W VA d/o Daniel & Rhoda O: farmer; by T.K. Lambert.

33. 19 Jan 1880 THOMAS EVANS 22 yrs single b. Montgomery Co VA s/o Edwin & Mary Ann to WILLIE LEFTRIDGE 23 yrs single b. Smith Co VA O: farmer; by Wm H. Barnes.

34. 21 Jan 1880 DAVID D. WAGONER 30 yrs single b. Russel Co VA now living same s/o William & Nancy to LUCINDA FARLEY 23 yrs single b. Giles Co VA d/o John W. & Elizabeth O: farmer; by J.O. Cassaday.

35. 22 Jan 1880 C.W. GORE 24 yrs single b. Mercer Co W VA now living in Summers Co W VA s/o Robert & Elizabeth to NANNIE T. HOLROYD 22 yrs single b. Mercer Co W VA s/o William & Sarah O: farmer; by J.W. Bennett.

36. 2 Feb 1880 CEPHAS LILLY 23 yrs single b. Mercer Co W VA s/o Lewis & Francis to MARY A.V. ELLISON 27 yrs single b. Mercer Co W VA d/o Samuel & Susan O: farmer; by Charles Walker.

37. 8 Feb 1880 CROCKET C. KIRTNER 22 yrs single b. Mercer Co W VA s/o Crockett & Ellen to MARY J. CAPERTON 22 yrs single b. Mercer Co W VA s/o John & Minerva O: farmer; by Carroll Clark.

38. 12 Feb 1880 JAMES W. BOWLING 24 yrs single b. Mercer Co W VA s/o Wm & Elizabeth to CELESTIA G. SHORTER 24 yrs single b. VA d/o Woodson A. & Martha C. O:farmer; by G.A. Austin.

39. 18 Feb 1880 BARBER B. BOLING 21 yrs single b. Mercer Co W VA s/o Anderson & Dement to AMY R. KARNES 17 yrs single b. Mercer Co W VA d/o Isaac & Lucretia O: farmer; by J.O. Cassaday.

40. 11 March 1880 JOSEPH B. GADD 22 yrs single b. Mercer Co W VA s/o Andrew P. & Delilah to EMMA Z. HOWELL 18 yrs single b. Mercer Co W VA d/o John P. & Letha O: farmer; by Elias Reed.

41. 26 Feb 1880 CHAS W. SNEED 20 yrs single b. Mercer Co W VA now living in Raleigh Co VA s/o John T. & Sarah to MARY ANN GADD 20 yrs single b. Mercer Co W VA d/o Andrew P & Delilah O: farmer; by Elias Reed.

42. 4 March 1880 D.C. HARVEY 18 yrs single b. Giles Co VA s/o Jacob W. & Catharine to ELVIRA M. HALL 18 yrs single b. Giles Co VA d/o Daniel & May M. O: farmer; by Elias Reed.

43. 4 March 1880 LEROY F. BAILEY 17 yrs single b. Mercer Co W VA s/o Floyd & Zilphia to NANCY E. GARRETSON 19 yrs single b. Mercer Co W VA d/o John & Delia O: farmer; by Archibald McComas.

44. 9 March 1880 WILLIAM E. BAYWOOD 19 yrs single b. Mercer Co W VA s/o Wm & Sarah to MATILDA FANNING 16 yrs single b. Summers Co VA d/o Garland & Nancy O: farmer; by T.C. Pulliam.

45. 18 March 1880 WM A. HARMAN 20 yrs single b. Carrol Co VA s/o Joseph & Nancy to MARTHA C. SCOR 15 yrs single b. Mercer Co W VA d/o William & Elizabeth O: farmer; by T.K. Lambert.

46. 18 March 1880 GEORGE B. GALE 42 yrs wid. b. Washington Co AL now living in Giles Co VA s/o Levin & Anna to SARAH B. THOMPSON 23 yrs single b. Giles Co VA d/o James & Abbe O: farmer; by Wm H. Barnes.

47. 1 March 1880 GEORGE C. WHITTAKER 23 yrs single b. Pulaski Co VA s/o ? & Katie to MALINDA J. FISHER 21 yrs single b. Boone Co W VA d/o Henry & Nancy O: farmer; by James Calfee.

48. 8 Apr 1880 WM B. MABE 21 yrs single b. Alleghany Co NC s/o Wm & Louisa to EMILY BELL 25 yrs single b. Mercer Co W VA d/o James & Julia O: farmer; by T.K. Lambert.

Page 33

1. 8 Apr 1880 EDWARD E. WHITE 19 yrs single b. Mercer Co W VA s/o James & Juliet to NECTJIE(sic) V. McKENZIE 19 yrs single b. Mercer Co W VA d/o John & Lucinda E. O: farmer; by James H. Johnston.

2. 14 Apr 1880 JAMES W. VINES 36 yrs wid. b. Monroe Co VA s/o Silas S. & Eliza P. to JEANNETTIE N. HEDRICK 20 yrs single b. Mercer Co W VA d/o Perry & Mary Jane O: farmer; by C. Walker.

3. 14 Apr 1880 THOMAS LUDLOW 20 yrs single b. Boone Co VA s/o - & May to MALINDA SHUCK 21 yrs single b. Raleigh Co VA d/o Wm & Margaret O: farmer; by C. Walker.

4. 22 Apr 1880 ERASTUS G. RINEHART 24 yrs single b. Wyoming Co VA now living Fayette Co VA s/o John & Juliet to MARY M. GARRETSON 21 yrs single b. Mercer Co W VA d/o John & Ardelia O: farmer; by Archibald McComas.

5. 28 Apr 1880 JOHN R. GROSS 24 yrs single b. Bland Co VA now living McDowell Co W VA s/o Harvey & Mary E. to SARAH J. GREER 21 yrs single b. Grayson Co VA d/o John C. O:physician; by Evan H Brown.

6. 28 Apr 1880 EDWARD G. HICKS 21 yrs single b. Mercer Co W VA s/o Lorenzie & Lucinda to POLLY ANN FLETCHER 19 yrs single b. Mercer Co W VA d/o Hiram A. & Rhoda O: farmer; by Lewis G. Day.

7. 28 Apr 1880 W.D. HOLBROOK 31 yrs single b. Tazewell Co VA s/o Randal & Polly to HARRIET D.B. NEAL 24 yrs single b. Tazewell Co VA d/o R. Matthew & Martha A. O: farmer; by Wm H. Barnes.

8. 13 May 1880 JAMES P. AKERS 23 yrs single b. Mercer Co W VA s/o Nathaniel B. & Sarah J. to POLLY E. McCOMAS 17 yrs single b. Mercer Co W VA d/o Archibald & Sevilla F. O: farmer; by Joseph Lilly.

9. 12 May 1880 HIRAM HAZLEWOOD 21 yrs single b. Stokes Co NC now living Giles Co VA s/o Asa & Rachael to SARAH E. FLETCHER 21 yrs single b. Mercer Co W VA d/o Harrison & Jane O: blacksmith; by A.J. Thompson.

10. 26 May 1880 MILLARD C. DILLS 24 yrs single b. Tazewell Co VA now living same s/o Peter H. & Nancy J. to MARIA E. LUCAS 24 yrs wid. b. Mercer Co W VA d/o John B. & Mary O: farmer; by A.J. Frazier.

11. 20 May 1880 JAMES MITCHELL 23 yrs single b. McDowell Co W VA s/o Elijah & Matilda to HARRIET O. RUSSEL 16 yrs single b. Mercer Co W VA d/o Benj O. & Jane O: farmer; by J.O. Cassaday.

12. 26 May 1880 JOHN W. MEADOR 21 yrs single b. Mercer Co W VA s/o ? & Judy to ALLYFARE V. LILLY 15 yrs single b. Mercer Co W VA d/o Joseph & Elizabeth O: farmer; by Wm P. Lilly.

13. 5 June 1880 JAMES D. THOMAS 18 yrs single b. Mercer Co W VA s/o James H. & Caroline to SARAH C. JONES 23 yrs single b. Mercer Co W VA d/o Wilson & Francis J. O: farmer; by James H. Johnston.

14. 8 June 1880 HENDERSON B. HAGER 25 yrs single b. Mercer Co W VA s/o A. Greenville & Nancy to CLARINDA SWADER 26 yrs single b. Mercer Co W VA d/o Henry & Sarah O: farmer; by Lewis G. Day.

15. 11 June 1880 JOHN F. MASSIE 23 yrs single b. Mercer Co W VA s/o Thomas B. & Louisa to BETTIE D. NASH 17 yrs single b. Mercer Co W VA O: farmer; by A.J. Thompson.

16. 14 June 1880 EVERMONT W. WHITE 21 yrs single b. Mercer Co W VA s/o Patton & Rhoda to LOUISA FLETCHER 18 yrs single b. Mercer Co W VA d/o James H. & Jane O: farmer; by A.J. Thompson.

17. 1 July 1880 ROBERT W. FARLEY 22 yrs single b. Mercer Co W VA now living Summers Co W VA s/o Hendley & Sarah to LOUISA FLETCHER 18 yrs single b. Mercer Co W VA d/o William & Lucy Ann O: farmer; by Joseph Lilly.

18. 27 June 1880 ROBT A. SHREWSBURY 23 yrs single b. Mercer Co W VA s/o Samuel & Elizabeth R. to LOUISA MAXEY 23 yrs single b. Mercer Co W VA d/o Josiah & Mary O: farmer; by Carroll Clark.

19. 23 July 1880 ALEXANDER FARMER 21 yrs single b. Campbell Co VA s/o John H. & Augustus to MARY A.P. WHITTAKER 21 yrs single b. Mercer Co W VA d/o William & ? O: farmer; by L. Goodwyn.

20. 3 Aug 1880 JAMES A. THOMPSON 22 yrs single b. Mercer Co W VA s/o Gordon & Louisa J. to VIRGINIA BAILEY 19 yrs single b. Mercer Co W VA d/o Eli & Lottie O: farmer; by Archibald McComas.

21. 28 July 1880 MARION COLRIN 21 yrs single b. Mercer Co W VA s/o ? & Luzena A. to MARGARET D. HUGHES 26 yrs single b. Mercer Co W VA O: farmer; by James Calfee.

22. 7 Aug 1880 CHARLES HOWARD 23 yrs single b. Pulaski Co VA s/o Grandville & Betsey to ELVIRA ADDISON 20 yrs single b. Giles Co VA d/o Lewis & Dicey O: farmer; by J.O. Cassaday.

23. * * * JOHN SHREWSBURY 21 yrs single b. Mercer Co W VA s/o Wm & Vanty Ann to JULIA GARRETSON 19 yrs single b. Mercer Co W VA d/o John & Delia O: farmer; by J.O. Cassaday. (*Note: no dates given.)

24. 12 Aug 1880 J.M. ELLISON 21 yrs single b. Mercer Co W VA s/o Samuel G. & Susan to ALICE T. MILLER 17 yrs single b. AK d/o Mark M. & Edie E. O: farmer; by William P. Lilly.

25. 16 Sept 1880 WM R. McCOMAS 25 yrs single b. Mercer Co W VA s/o Archibald & Sevilla F. to MARTHA A. BAILEY 20 yrs sngle b. Mercer Co W VA d/o Thompson P. & - O: farmer; by Archibald McComas.

26. 7 Sept 1880 DANIEL M. SNAPP 22 yrs single b. Mercer Co W VA s/o Jno W. & Matilda J. to LOUELLA BAILEY 18 yrs single b. Mercer Co W VA d/o Wm M. & Matilda O: farmer; by Wm H. Barnes.

27. 16 Sept 1880 WILLIAM SNEED 20 yrs single b. Mercer Co W VA s/o James & Mary to EMELINE MEADOR 20 yrs single b. Mercer Co W VA d/o Isaac & Mary J. O: farmer; by Joseph Lilly.

28. 16 Sept 1880 JAMES G. BOWDEN 19 yrs single b. Pulaski Co VA s/o James G. & Lucinda to IDA REED 15 yrs single b. Mercer Co W VA d/o Thomas & Sephrona O: farmer; by Leonidas Goodwyn.

29. 21 Sept 1880 M.F. CALDWELL 22 yrs single b. Mercer Co W VA s/o George W. & Elizabeth A. to SARAH E. FLESHMAN 19 yrs single b. Raleigh Co VA d/o - & Jane O: farmer; by Wm Bolroyd.

30. 29 Sept 1880 ANDERSON BASHAM 18 yrs single b. Raleigh Co VA s/o John & Martha A. to SARAH A. CREWS 21 yrs single b. Mercer Co W VA d/o John W. & - O: farmer; by Joseph Lilly.

31. 29 Sept 1880 BOYD S. BELCHER 24 yrs single b. Mercer Co W VA s/o Anderson A. & Lettie to NANNIE E. THOMPSON 19 yrs single b. Mercer Co W VA d/o Wm H. & Sarah O: farmer; by J.O. Cassaday.

32. 5 Oct 1880 CHAS W.J. WALKER 21 yrs single b. Mercer Co W VA s/o Council & Nancy D. to ARDELIA TAYLOR 18 yrs single b. Mercer Co W VA d/o Sampson & ? O: farmer; by Archibald McComas.

33. 6 Oct 1880 WM H. McCOY 26 yrs single b. Monroe Co VA s/o Charles F. & Lucinda to SAVILLA J. MORGAN 21 yrs single b. Wyoming Co VA d/o Anthony & Chloe O: shoemaker; by James Sweeney.

34. 8 Oct 1880 A.J. MEADOR 21 yrs single b. Mercer Co W VA now living in Summers Co W VA s/o George W. & Rhoda to SARAH E. MEADOR 20 yrs single b. Mercer Co W VA d/o Solar & Malinda O: farmer; by Joseph Lilly.

35. 29 Oct 1880 ELIJAH C. CLARK 19 yrs single b. Mercer Co W VA s/o James & Judath to JUDATH A. LILLY 19 yrs single b. Raleigh Co VA d/o Wm H. & Jane O: farmer; by James W. Lilly.

36. 26 Oct 1880 R.J. WICH 23 yrs single b. Roanoke Co VA s/o John & Nancy to E.N. SCOTT 18 yrs single b. Mercer Co W VA d/o Brown & Susan O: carpenter; by Carroll Clark.

37. 20 Oct 1880 LEWIS MARTIN 21 yrs single b. Mercer Co W VA now living in Summers Co VA s/o ? & Rebecca to CYNTHIA J. OXLEY 22 yrs single b. Wythe Co VA d/o Sanford H. & Delila A. O: farmer; by J.O. Cassaday.

38. * * * LEWIS A. MARTIN 20 yrs single b. Mercer Co W VA s/o David & Hester to JULIA F. CAPERTON 20 yrs single b. Mercer Co W VA d/o Thompson & ? O: farmer. (*Note: no date given.)

39. * * * B.J. CAMPBELL 26 yrs single b. Mercer Co W VA s/o Thomas K. & Mary to NANNIE J. SINK 22 yrs single b. Mercer Co W VA d/o Daniel & Emily O: miller. (*Note: no date given.)

40. 1 Nov 1880 DAVID P. PERRY 31 yrs wid. b. Tazewell Co VA now living same to MARGARET M. WHITT 19 yrs single b. Tazewell Co VA; by Wm K. Barnes.

41. 11 Nov 1880 COUNCIL WALKER 67 yrs wid. b. Giles Co VA s/o Chrispianos & Frances to MARTHA J. WOOD 39 yrs single b. Mercer Co W VA German & ? O: farmer; by Joseph Lilly.

42. 17 Nov 1880 JAMES J. LYON 21 yrs single b. Mercer Co W VA s/o Mary A. & John D. to ELIZABETH J. FARLEY 30 yrs single b. Mercer Co W VA d/o Andrew & ? O: farmer; by Joseph Lilly.

43. 15 Nov 1880 GEO W.E. CALDWELL 21 yrs single b. Giles Co VA s/o James & Emenira to MARY PENNINGTON 17 yrs single b. Mercer Co W VA d/o William & Catherine O: farmer; by Leonidas Goodwyn.

44. 17 Nov 1880 E.R. McWALL 27 yrs single b. Mercer Co W VA s/o Henry D. & Jane to MARGARET E. MANNING 22 yrs single b. Mercer Co W VA d/o ? & Nancy J. O: farmer; by J.O. Cassaday.

45. 22 Nov 1880 EDGAR G. NELSON 22 yrs single b. Rockbridge Co VA now living in St George Co IN s/o John R. & Sallie to V.H. SONGER 20 yrs single b. Kanawha Co VA d/o A.I. & Charlotte O: book agent; by James Calfee.

46. 2 Decr 1880 P.H. WHITLOCK 19 yrs single b. Mercer Co W VA now living in Summers Co W VA s/o Charles E. & Elizabeth M. to MARY LILLY 22 yrs single b. Mercer Co W VA d/o Wm P. & Leerie O: farmer; by Joseph Lilly.

47. 7 Decr 1880 ROBERT D. KARNES 23 yrs single b. Mercer Co W VA s/o Madison & Nancy to ARTHELLA E. BOWLING 18 yrs single b. Mercer Co W VA d/o Uriah A. & Rebecca J. O: farmer; by Carroll Clark.

48. 9 Decr 1880 CHAS E. THOMPSON 20 yrs single b. Giles Co VA s/o Chas & Haltilda to HARRIET GRIGSBY 23 yrs single b. Mercer Co W VA O: farmer; by And. J. Thompson; REMARKS: colored.

Page 34

1. 16 Decr 1880 HENRY WHITE 21 yrs single b. Summers Co W VA now living Monroe Co W VA s/o George & Amanda to SALLIE A. BEAU 22 yrs single b. Mercer Co W VA d/o Saml Lee & Martha L. O: farmer; by J.O. Cassaday; REMARKS: colored.

2. 22 Decr 1880 SAML MULLINS 21 yrs single b. Wyoming Co VA s/o John S. & Nancy to ELLA McPHERSON 22 yrs single b. Mercer Co W VA d/o George & Cynthia O: farmer; by Wm H. Barnes.

3. 29 Decr 1880 HESEKEAH MURRELL 22 yrs single b. Mercer Co W VA s/o James A & Sarah A. to HARRIET V. HAMBRICK 21 yrs single b. Tazewell Co VA d/o John & Jane O: farmer; by Evan H. Brown.

4. 7 Jan 1881 MAC C. HOLDRON 20 yrs single b. Mercer Co W VA s/o Henry & Mahaia to ELIZ A. RATLIFFE 17 yrs single b. Monroe Co W VA d/o Milton & Mary O: farmer; by J.W. Bennett.

5. 13 Jan 1881 R.G. BLANKENSHIP 33 yrs wid. b. Mercer Co W VA s/o Lewis & Mary to MARTHA F. WILEY 17 yrs single b. Mercer Co W VA d/o Vincent & Cynthia O: farmer; by A.J. Thompson.

6. 20 Jan 1881 MURAIN* Y. HARVEY 20 yrs single b. Mercer Co W VA now living in Summers Co W VA s/o Austin B. & ? to JULIA A. MAXEY 17 yrs single b. Mercer Co W VA d/o Preston & Celia A. O: farmer; by James W. Lilly. (*NOTE: handwriting difficult to read.)

7. 1 Feb 1881 HENRY W. BASHAM 20 yrs single b. Mercer Co W VA s/o John & Martha to LOUISIANA D. CREWS 18 yrs single b. Mercer Co W VA d/o John W. & Susan O: farmer; by Joseph Lilly.

8. 2 Feb 1881 SAMUEL T. BILLINGSLY 22 yrs single b. TX s/o ? & Elizabeth to NANCY J. WANHOP 19 yrs single b. Floyd Co VA d/o John R. & Elizth O: farmer; by William P. Lilly.

9. 2 Feb 1881 JESSE H. BRAMMER 27 yrs single b. Mercer Co W VA s/o John H. & Sarah L. to ELIZABETH BASHAM 16 yrs single b. Mercer Co W VA d/o John & Martha O: farmer; by William P. Lilly.

10. 31 Jan 1881 JEFF W. THOMAS 40 yrs wid. b. Mercer Co W VA s/o Edward & Margaret to FRANCES JONES 42 yrs wid. b. Mercer Co W VA d/o Robert & - O: farmer; by John West.

11. 3 Feb 1881 EDGAR P. KIRTNER 23 yrs single b. Mercer Co W VA s/o Crockett J. & Ellen E. to ELVIRA E.A. KIDD 18 yrs single b. Bland Co VA d/o William & Mary J. O: farmer; by Wm Holroyd.

12. 10 Feb 1881 WILBURN WORRELL 21 yrs single b. Carroll Co VA s/o Luke & Millie to JULITIA HALL 13 yrs single b. Giles Co VA d/o Daniel & Mary O: farmer; by William P. Lilly.

13. 16 Feb 1881 JEREMIAH S. THOMPSON 22 yrs single b. Mercer Co W VA s/o Wm H. & Sarah to ELLY C. WHITE 19 yrs single b. Mercer Co W VA d/o Harvey G. & Sarah E. O: farmer; by J.O. Cassaday.

14. 1 March 1881 JAMES SWADER 21 yrs single b. Mercer Co W VA s/o Robert & Cynthia J. to CYNTHIA SWADER 23 yrs single b. Mercer Co W VA d/o Wm & Juliet O: farmer; by Evan H. Brown.

15. 9 March 1881 R.W. JOHNSTON 24 yrs single b. Giles Co VA s/o Jas D. & Nancy to SUSAN A. BUTRY 17 yrs single b. Russell Co VA d/o Nathaniel & Mary O: miller; by J.W. Bennett.

16. 22 March 1881 WM E. ARGABRIGHT 24 yrs single b. Franklin Co VA s/o Wm & Birtie A. to JENNIE A. WHITE 19 yrs single b. Mercer Co W VA d/o Albert J. & Sarah A. O: farmer; by A.T. Brooks.

17. 23 March 1881 GORDAN C. MADISON 24 yrs single b. Giles Co VA s/o Gordan C. & Eliza to AMERICA J. HOLLY 23 yrs single b. Tazewell Co VA d/o Charles & Maurinda O: farmer; by James Calfee; REMARKS: colored.

18. 31 March 1881 HENRY GORE 22 yrs single b. Mercer Co W VA s/o Green & Sarah to CHRISTINA DAVIDSON 24 yrs wid. b. Mercer Co W VA d/o Hiram & Nancy O: farmer; by J.W. Bennett; REMARKS: colored.

19. 12 Apl 1881 WM T. BAKER 29 yrs single b. Mercer Co W VA s/o John & Polly to MARTHA S. KESLER 24 yrs single b. Carroll Co VA d/o John M. & Elizabeth O: farmer; by Joseph Lilly.

20. 12 Apl 1881 S.G.C. BOWLING 26 yrs single b. Patrick Co VA s/o James & Ruth M. to MARY A. WIMMER 23 yrs single b. Mercer Co W VA d/o James & Elizabeth O: farmer; by J.O. Cassaday.

21. 13 Apl 1881 THOS. H. THORNTON 19 yrs single b. Mercer Co W VA s/o Thomas P. & Nancy to JOSEPHINE J. HOLT 19 yrs single b. Mercer Co W VA d/o ? & Gracey O: farmer; by J.O. Cassaday.

22. 29 Apl 1881 JAMES A. ROWLAND 21 yrs single b. Mercer Co W VA s/o Jackson & Sarah to SARAH M. SNODGRASS 22 yrs single b. Giles Co VA d/o Estill & ? O: farmer; by Wm Holroyd.

23. 11 May 1881 WM B. BONAKER 23 yrs single b. Bland Co VA now living same s/o Peter C. & Mary A. to LAURA V. TRACEY 20 yrs sngle b. Mercer Co W VA d/o rowland J. & Frankie O: farmer; by Robt M. Ashworth.

24. 4 May 1881 ELBERT C. WRIGHT 25 yrs single b. Giles Co VA s/o thomas & Sarah J. to MARY S. ELLIS 21 yrs single b. Monroe Co W VA d/o Overton & Jane O: farmer; by J.O. Cassaday.

25. 13 May 1881 PHILIP J. BAILEY 21 yrs single b. Mercer Co W VA s/o Enos & Elizabeth to FANNIE L. BOLTON 17 yrs single b. Mercer Co W VA d/o Mathew & Mary O: farmer; by A.T. Brooks.

26. 9 June 1881 GEO W. HOPKINS 22 yrs wid. b. Mercer Co W VA s/o Reuben & Nancy to AMANDA P. PHILIPS 22 yrs single b. Mercer Co W VA d/o James & Clara O: farmer; by Wm Holroyd.

27. 7 July 1881 CHAS. W. BAILEY 53 yrs wid. b. Mercer Co W VA s/o Saml & Polly to MATILDA WEAVER 35 yrs single b. NC O: farmer; by James Calfee.

28. 14 July 1881 GEO W. TERRY 27 yrs wid. b. Tazewell Co VA s/o Joseph & Mary Ann to JULIET M. HARTWELL 21 yrs single b. Mercer Co W VA d/o John & Synthia E. O: farmer; by Phil S. Sutton.

29. 19 July 1881 JAMES SWEENEY 55 yrs wid. b. Monroe Co W VA now living same to P.C. PEARIS 46 yrs wid. b. Giles Co VA d/o John & Agnes O: Minister of the Gospel; by M. Ellison.

30. 21 July 1881 LARKIN ELLISON 26 yrs single b. Mercer Co W VA now living in Summers Co W VA s/o William & Easter to MARGARET MANNING 21 yrs single b. Giles Co VA d/o James & Hester Ann O: farmer; by Phil S. Sutton.

31. 6 Aug 1881 WM E. DUDLEY 23 yrs single b. Tazewell Co VA now living same s/o Hugh D. & Jane to MAGGIE L. GILLESPIE 18 yrs single b. Tazewell Co VA d/o Robt & Kate E. O: farmer; by Jas. Calfee.

32. 21 Aug 1881 L.F. THOMAS 35 yrs single b. Carter Co TN s/o Joseph & ? to OLLIE PARKER 22 yrs single b. Mercer Co W VA d/o James & Mary O: farmer; by Archd. McComas.

33. 19 Aug 1881 JAS S. BAXTER 23 yrs single b. Carroll Co VA s/o William & Martha to LAURA C.C. WHITTAKER 21 yrs wid. b. Giles Co VA d/o Harvey & Sarah O: farmer; by Isaac S. Hanuau.

34. 6 Sept 1881 WM E. BUTT 33 yrs single b. Botetourt Co VA now living in Tazewell Co VA s/o Harrison & Lucretia to VIRGINIA SHUTT 18 yrs single b. Mercer Co W VA d/o David & Betsy O: carpenter; by J.O. Cassaday.

35. 7 Sept 1881 PATRICK BLANKENSHIP 22 yrs single b. Wyoming Co W VA now living in Raleigh Co W VA s/o ? & Rebecca to JULIA A. GARRETSON 18 yrs single b. Mercer Co W VA d/o John & Ardelia O: farmer; by E. Howerton.

36. 8 Sept 1881 GILFORD BURCHETT 23 yrs single b. Wilkes Co NC s/o Lawson & Elizabeth to LAVENIA BELCHER 25 yrs sinble b. Mercer Co W VA d/o Henry & Annie O: farmer; by T.K. Lambert.

37. 20 Sept 1881 JAS B. WORRELL 25 yrs single b. Carroll Co VA s/o Luke & ? to MARY L. KESTER 19 yrs single b. Carroll Co VA d/o John & Elizabeth O: farmer; by Archd. McComas.

38. 22 Sept 1881 CHAS L. TABOR 20 yrs single b. Tazewell Co VA now living same s/o Andrew J. & Julina to MARY A. DOYLE 16 yrs single b. Mercer Co W VA d/o Jas A. & Martha A. O: farmer; by P.S. Sutton.

39. 28 Sept 1881 HENRY B. KITTS 20 yrs single b. Bland Co VA s/o Peter & Mary A. to ARAMINTA A. KAHLE 20 yrs single b. Mercer Co W VA d/o Saml & Katharine O: publisher; by P.S. Sutton.

40. 2 Oct 1881 GILES M. BUTT 25 yrs single b. Pulaski Co VA s/o Harrison & Lucetia to REBECCA E. GREAR 20 yrs single b. Grayson Co VA d/o John C. & - O: farmer; by Adam E. Wagoner.

41. 7 Oct 1881 JAMES F. MABE 21 yrs single b. Wilkes Co NC s/o - & Eliza to SARAH BELL 17 yrs angle b. Mercer Co W VA d/o James & Julia O: farmer; by T.K. Lambert.

42. 22 Oct 1881 GEORGE W. THORNTON 22 yrs single b. Pulaski Co VA s/o Peter & Mary to MALINDA F. UNDERWOOD 21 yrs single b. Mercer Co W VA d/o Jesse & Marshall H. O: farmer; by J.O. Cassaday.

43. 20 Oct 1881 ALONZO G. HARTWELL 19 yrs single b. Mercer Co W VA s/o Jno L. & Cynthia E. to JANE PENNINGTON 25 yrs single b. Mercer Co W VA d/o Gordan & Juliet O: farmer; by Jas Sweeney.

44. 27 Oct 1881 PHILLIP B. LAMBERT 19 yrs single b. McDowell Co W VA now living same s/o T.K. & Lottie to NANCY JANE SNEAD 19 yrs single b. Mercer Co W VA d/o Enemarella O: farmer; by T.K. Lambert.

45. 27 Oct 1881 CHAS. T. FIELDER 22 yrs single b. Grayson Co VA s/o Deweese & Mary to VIOLA T. TABOT 18 yrs single b. Tazewell Co VA d/o William J. & Sarah O: farmer; by L.G. Day.

46. 17 Nov 1881 HENRY H. SHUMATE 21 yrs single b. Giles Co VA s/o Rufus A. & Sarah E. to RHODA C. BURTON 21 yrs single b. Giles Co VA d/o Elisha & Martha O: farmer; by J.O. Cassaday.

47. 16 Nov 1881 BARKLEY TABOR 24 yrs single b. Tazewell Co VA now living same s/o Andrew & Julina to JULIA A. SINK 18 yrs single b. Tazewell Co VA d/o Daniel & Emily A. O: miller; by Evan H. Brown.

48. 20 Nov 1881 WILLOUGHBY TAYLOR 20 yrs single b. Mercer Co W VA s/o Sampson & Mary to SERRILDIA CECIL 18 yrs single d/o Jas & Jane O: farmer; by T.K. Lambert.

49. 16 Oct 1881 JOHN A. * 27 yrs single b. Randolph Co VA now living in Summers Co W VA to MARTHA C. SHORTER 21 yrs single b. Mercer Co W VA; by G.A. Austin. (*Note: small piece torn off original copy.)

Page 35

1. * Nov 1881 GEORGE W. BOLIN 21 yrs single b. Mercer Co W VA s/o William & Elizabeth to MARY E. PENNINGTON 16 yrs single b. Mercer Co W VA d/o Levi & Elizabeth O: farmer. (*Note: no day given.)

2. 17 Nov 1881 JONAS CLYBURN 22 yrs single b. Mercer Co W VA s/o James & Angeline to DEMARIES W. PERDUE 21 yrs single b. Mercer Co W VA d/o William & Sarah O: farmer; by A.J. Thompson.

3. 24 Nov 1881 CHARLES DAVIDSON 21 yrs single b. Mercer Co W VA now living in Summers W VA s/o Hairam & Nancy to ANGELINE GORE 21 yrs single b. Monroe Co W VA d/o George & Mary O: farmer; by J.W. Bennett; REMARKS: colored.

4. 23 Nov 1881 JAMES B. BAILEY 24 yrs single b. Mercer Co W VA s/o Leland & Rebecca to MALINDA C. TUGGLE 21 yrs single b. Mercer Co W VA d/o John & Lucinda O: farmer; by Jas Calfee.

5. 24 Nov 1881 JOHN MASSEY 22 yrs single b. Mercer Co W VA s/o Jackson & Patsey to MINERVA E. DODD 18 yrs single b. Monroe Co W VA d/o Anderson & Elizabeth O: farmer; by Joseph Lilly.

6. 29 Nov 1881 WILLIAM WALL 64 yrs wid. b. Montgomery Co VA s/o John & Elizabeth to MARY B. KAHLE 43 yrs single d/o Samuel & -- O: farmer; by J.O. Cassaday.

7. 1 Dec 1881 L.W.D. LILLY 23 yrs single b. Summers Co W VA now living same s/o Andrew L. & Sarah E. to SARAH E. ELLISON 21 yrs single b. Mercer Co W VA d/o Isaac J. & Elizabeth O: farmer; by Joseph Lilly.

8. 1 Dec 1881 ANDREW J. HARTWELL 20 yrs single b. Mercer Co W VA s/o John & Cynthia to REBECCA BELCHER 20 yrs single b. Mercer Co W VA d/o Anderson & Jane O: farmer; by P.S. Sutton.

9. 1 Dec 1881 M.A.W. YOUNG 35 yrs single b. Craig Co VA now living in Summers Co VA s/o John & Mary A. to HENRIETTA M. WRIGHT 22 yrs single b. Mercer Co W VA d/o Camden G. & ? O: commercial agent; by L. Goodwyn.

10. 6 Dec 1881 HENRY J. BASHAM 22 yrs single b. Mercer Co W VA s/o William & Julina to AMANDA E. PENNINGTON 17 yrs single b. Mercer Co W VA d/o Riley & Margaret O: farmer; by Jas. Sweeney.

11. 14 Dec 1881 THOMAS J. HURST 20 yrs single b. Mercer Co W VA s/o Wm & Susan to MARTHA Z. HUFFMAN 24 yrs single b. Tazewell Co VA d/o Andrew J. & ? O: farmer; by Archd. McComas.

12. 15 Dec 1881 JOHN H. MILLER 21 yrs single b. Mercer Co W VA s/o George C. & ? to ELIZABETH F. NEAL 17 yrs single b. Mercer Co W VA d/o Danl N. & Sarah A. O: farmer; by J.O. Cassaday.

13. 15 Dec 1881 DAVID G. LILLY 23 yrs single b. Mercer Co W VA s/o Robt C. & Virginia to MARGARET E. THOMPSON 25 yrs single b. Mercer Co W VA d/o Philip & Mary J. O: farmer; by J. Sweeney.

14. 15 Dec 1881 WM T. CHATTING 23 yrs single b. Mercer Co W VA s/o W.W. & Mary to OZELLA R. McKENZIE 16 yrs single b. Mercer Co W VA d/o Jno & Lucinda E. O: merchant; by L. Goodwyn.

15. 21 Dec 1881 JOHN D. CALDWELL 28 yrs single b. Mercer Co W VA s/o Geo W. & Elizabeth to VIRGINIA D. BROWN 19 yrs single b. Tazewell Co VA d/o Evan H. & Martha E. O: farmer; by K.H. Carr.

16. 22 Dec 1881 ROBERT N. WHELER 36 yrs wid. Carroll Co VA now living Bland Co VA s/o Andrew M. & Nancy to ARAMINTA FLETCHER 26 yrs single b. Mercer Co W VA d/o Hiram A. & Rhoda O: farmer; by James Calfee.

17. 29 Dec 1881 WINTON E. BAILEY 23 yrs single b. Mercer Co W VA s/o Addison & Octava to JOSEPHINE MASTON 23 yrs single b. NC d/o William E. & ? O: farmer; by L.G. Day.

18. 1 Jan 1882 JAMES SADDLER 22 yrs single b. Giles Co VA s/o Henry & ? to LEFTWICH A. SURFACE 16 yrs single b. Mercer Co W VA d/o ? & Sarah O: farmer; by A.J. Brooks.

19. 5 Jan 1882 THOMAS B. LUSK 21 yrs single b. Wyoming Co W VA s/o William & Amanda to ENERZETER E. ARGABRIGHT 18 yrs single b. Franklin Co VA d/o Geo W. & Elizabeth A. O: merchant; by A. McComas.

20. 4 Jan 1882 J.B. WHITTAKER 20 yrs single b. Mercer Co W VA s/o William & Rutha to SUSAN C. JOHNSTON 21 yrs single b. Mercer Co W VA d/o John L. & ? O: farmer; by A.J. Thompson.

21. 5 Jan 1882 SAMPSON TAYLOR 22 yrs single b. Mercer Co W VA s/o Sampson & Polly to JENNETTA H. HILL 15 yrs single b. NC d/o ? & Alie O: farmer; by T.K. Lambert.

22. 6 Jan 1882 WM B. PITZER 33 yrs single b. Alleghany Co VA to MAGGIE J. WRIGHT 22 yrs single b. Augusta Co VA O: bookkeeper; by J.Sweeney.

23. 25 Jan 1882 BALLARD P. WILSON 28 yrs single b. Bland Co VA now living same s/o Edward & Rebecca to HESTER A.C. BAILEY 22 yrs single b. Mercer Co W VA d/o Alex J. & Hannah L. O: farmer; by R.H. Ashworth.

24. 15 Feb 1882 JOHN H. WYRICK 54 yrs wid. b. Gilford Co NC now living Summers Co W VA s/o Daniel & Leanna to ARDELIA BOWLING 47 yrs single O: farmer; by J.W. Bennett.

25. * * * JOHN L. WILEY 22 yrs single b. Mercer Co W VA s/o Vincent & Cynthia to ROSELLA E. PAULEY 16 yrs single b. Bland Co VA d/o John & Ellen O: farmer.

26. 28 Feb 1882 GEO W. BARGER 28 yrs single b. Tazewell Co VA now living same s/o Jacob & ? to SARAH E. FAULKNER 20 yrs single b. Mercer Co W VA d/o Gordon & Anne O: farmer; by Evan H. Brown.

27. 21 Feb 1882 GEO W. BURGESS 25 yrs single b. Raleigh Co W VA s/o Hiram & Nancy to CORA A. ROSS 15 yrs single b. Mercer Co W VA d/o Davidson C. & Emeline O: farmer; by A. McComas.

28. 22 Feb 1882 CHAS. S. KAHLE 26 yrs single b. Mercer Co w VA s/o Samuel & Catherine T. to NANNIE WITTEN 21 yrs single b. Tazewell Co VA d/o James R. & Matilda J. O: farmer; by P.S. Sutton.

29. 22 Feb 1882 MARCUS A. SLUSS 18 yrs single b. Tazewell Co VA now living same s/o James & Clarinda to MILLE F. SHRADER 17 yrs single b. Mercer Co w VA d/o David & Chloe O: farmer; by Lewis G. Day.

30. 5 March 1882 JAS A. MEADOWS 21 yrs single b. Mercer Co w VA s/o Harvey & ? to VICTORIA A. FOLEY 17 yrs single b. Mercer Co W VA d/o Richard & Mary D. O: farmer; by Eliza Reed.

31. 22 Feb 1882 ROBERT H. FRENCH 22 yrs single b. Wise Co VA s/o James M. & Rhoda to H. VICTORIA FRENCH 21 yrs single b. Mercer Co w VA d/o Russel G. & ? O: lawyer; by James Sweeney.

32. 19 March 1882 LEE D. MASTIN 22 yrs single b. Wilkes Co NC s/o William E. & Amanda M. to AMANDA DAY 21 yrs single b. Giles Co VA d/o James S. & Louisa C. O: teacher; by L.G. Day.

33. 15 March 1882 JOSEPH CALDWELL 32 yrs single b. Montgomery Co VA s/o Harper W. & Mary to MARY E. THOMPSON 27 yrs wid. b. Mercer Co W VA d/o John & Sarah Hardy O: farmer; by J.O. Cassaday.

34. 23 March 1882 WM A. HELTON 23 yrs single b. Carroll Co VA now living in Bristol TN s/o Newman & Nancy to HARBARY E. RUNYON 18 yrs single b. Bland Co VA d/o Jas F. & Elizabeth O: farmer; by Romulus Harry.

35. 22 March 1882 JAS A. GODFREY 28 yrs single b. Mercer Co w VA s/o John D. & Martha to MARY E. MILLER 25 yrs single b. Fayette Co W VA d/o Willoughby & ? O: miller; by T.K. Lambert.

36. 4 April 1882 JNO W. BOWLING 26 yrs single b. Patrick Co VA s/o A.W. & Lucinda to SARAH E.V. HARRY 20 yrs single b. Mercer Co W VA d/o Romulus & Ruthy Jane O: farmer; by Romulus Harry.

37. 6 April 1882 HENRY FARLEY 22 yrs single b. Mercer Co W VA s/o William & Lucy Ann to EMILY MASSEY 16 yrs single b. Mercer Co W VA d/o James J. & Patsy O: farmer; by J. Lilly.

38. 20 April 1882 RICHARD BROWN 22 yrs single b. Stafford Co VA now living same s/o Alex & Catharine to JULIET JANE REED 22 yrs single b. Mercer Co W VA d/o Thomas & Saphronia O: farmer; by L. Goodwyn.

39. 20 April 1882 WM WHITTAKER 60 yrs wid. b. Pulaski Co VA s/o Aaron & Margaret to ELIZA F. SALE 48 yrs wid. b. Mercer Co W VA O: farmer; by P.S. Sutton.

40. 24 May 1882 WM N. DICKINSON 27 yrs single b. Giles Co VA now living same s/o Henry & Nancy Ann to SARAH E. PETERS 20 yrs single b. Monroe Co VA d/o James C. & ? O: farmer; by J.W. Bennett.

41. 28 May 1882 WRITON JACKSON 25 yrs wid. b. Bland Co VA s/o Andrew & Minney to HULDAH CHARLTON 21 yrs single b. Tazewell Co VA d/o Saml & Kizima O: farmer; by Wm A. Claxton; REMARKS: colored.

42. 5 June 1882 JEFFERSON D. CREWS 20 yrs single b. Mercer Co W VA s/o Asa & Nancy to ANNA L. LILLY 18 yrs single b. Mercer Co W VA d/o Wm H. & Jane O: farmer; by Jas W. Lilly.

43. 3 June 1882 GEORGE CALENDER 19 yrs single b. Wythe Co VA s/o ? & Eliza to POLLY HENDERSON 18 yrs single b. Pulaski Co VA d/o Perry & Christina O: farmer; by D.H. Carr; REMARKS: colored.

44. 21 June 1882 JOHN BOWLING 24 yrs single b. Mercer Co w VA s/o M.A. & Demaries to MARY J. MUNCEY 16 yrs single b. Giles Co VA d/o Wiley & Martha O: farmer; by A.J. Brooks.

45. * * * WM C. ROBERTSON 22 yrs single b. Pulaski Co VA s/o Chas. & Catherine to SUSAN M. RIDDLE 28 yrs single d/o Tobias & Sophia O: farmer.

46. 5 July 1882 PHILIP T. HOLDRON 26 yrs single b. Mercer Co W VA s/o Harry & Mahala to RUTH E. CLEMMONS 21 yrs single b. Mercer Co W VA d/o John R. & Mary O: farmer; by J.H. Johnston.

47. 7 July 1882 JNO W. CRAFT 21 yrs single b. Alleghany Co VA s/o Geo W. & Mary E. to SALLIE VEST 23 yrs single b. Mercer Co W VA O: farmer; by J.O. Cassaday.

48. 15 July 1882 O.E. CALDWELL 45 yrs wid. b. Montgomery Co VA s/o Edward & Margaret to MARY A. CALFEE 36 yrs single b. Mercer Co W VA d/o James & Elizabeth O: farmer; by James Calfee.

49. 22 June 1882 O.J. WOODS 26 yrs single b. Giles Co VA to DORA LEE KING 18 yrs single b. TN O: physician; by Phil S. Sutton.

Page 36

1. 30 July 1882 R.R. HARTWELL 24 yrs single b. Mercer Co w VA s/o ? & Mary to NORA CARR 20 yrs single b. Wayne Co W VA d/o William & Mary O: farmer; by Carroll Clark.

2. 9 Aug 1882 WM J.E. FLUMMER 22 yrs swid b. Tazewell Co VA s/o Jas H. & Catherine to MARTHA A. CHATTING 18 yrs single b. Mercer Co W VA d/o William & Mary O: farmer; by Jas N. Johnston.

3. 20 Aug 1882 JAMES O. BIRD 26 yrs single b. Bland Co VA s/o Stephen & Malinda to MARY JANE RUNYON 20 yrs single b. Giles Co VA d/o ? & Elizabeth F. O: farmer; by R.M. Ashworth.

4. 24 Aug 1882 LEWIS DUNAGAN 37 yrs wid. b. Surrey Co NC s/o Lewis & Nancy to ELIZA WHITTAKER 36 yrs single b. Giles Co VA d/o William & Ruth O: farmer; by L. Goodwyn.

5. 24 Aug 1882 GORDON FAULKNER 45 yrs wid. b. Montgomery Co VA s/o Hugh M & Susan to RHODA FARLEY 28 yrs single b. Giles Co VA d/o John W. & Elizabeth O: farmer; by J.O. Cassaday.

6. 23 Aug 1882 WAYNE H. PENNINGTON 23 yrs single b. Mercer Co W VA s/o William & Catherine to MARIA S. MELVIN 21 yrs single b. Mercer Co W VA d/o Weaver & Rebecca O: farmer; by L. Goodwyn.

7. 3 Sep 1882 CYRIS M. BROWN 26 yrs single b. Tazewell Co VA now living same s/o E.G. & Rebecca to MOLLIE HARRY 22 yrs single b. Mercer Co w VA d/o Calvin & Mary O: merchant; by Evan H. Brown.

8. 4 Sep 1882 JEFFERSON D. MULLINS 20 yrs single b. Mercer Co W VA s/o Wm P. & Abagail to ENRIVA J. DOYLE 20 yrs single b. Mercer co W VA d/o James A. & Martha A. O: farmer; by D.N. Saunders.

9. 7 Sep 1882 ALONZO W. PENINGTON 22 yrs single b. Bland Co VA s/o Gordon E. & Julia to MARY F. IRVINE 21 yrs single b. Mercer Co w VA d/o Isaac N. & Lucinda O: farmer; by J.O. Cassaday.

10. 7 Sep 1882 THOMAS G. LITTLE 25 yrs single b. Mercer Co W VA s/o Thomas & Ellen to MEDIA A. MILLER 22 yrs single b. Fayette Co W VA d/o Willoughby & Elizabeth O: school teacher; by David N. Saunders.

11. 12 Sep 1882 JOHN A. SHIELDS 23 yrs single b. Montgomery Co VA now living in Omaha NE s/o Hamilton & ? to MINNIE B. FRENCH 22 yrs single b. Giles Co VA d/o David & Mary O:clerk; by W.L. Richardson.

12. 14 Sep 1882 JOSEPH PITTMAN 23 yrs single b. Mercer Co W VA now living in Kanawha Co W VA s/o Michael & Rebecca M. to AMANDA HARVEY 16 yrs single b. Mercer Co W VA d/o Frederick & Alley O: miner; by Jas W. Lilly.

13. 21 Sep 1882 JOHN A. HAMBRICK 28 yrs single b. Tazewell Co VA s/o John A. & Mary Jane to NANNIE E. MERRETT 21 yrs single b. Mercer Co W VA d/o Drury T & Ellen O: farmer; by Evan H. Brown.

14. 7 Oct 1882 WILSON E. GAUTIER 21 yrs single b. Mercer Co W VA s/o Joseph & Lucy to REBECCA FIZER 15 yrs single b. Montgomery Co VA d/o Charles & Susan O: farmer; by P.S. Sutton.

15. 12 Oct 1882 AUGUSTUS B. CALFEE 35 yrs single b. Mercer Co W VA s/o Wilson D. & Jane P. to VIRGINIA STINSON 25 yrs single b. Giles Co VA d/o Charles & Elizabeth O: farmer; by Carroll Clark.

16. 19 Oct 1882 BOOKER T. PERDUE 21 yrs single b. Mercer Co W VA s/o Silas & Nancy Jane to HARRIET A. DILLION 17 yrs single b. Mercer Co W VA d/o James H. & Matilda O:farmer; by Evan H. Brown.

17. 25 Oct 1882 ALBERT HARVEY 20 yrs single b. Mercer Co W VA s/o Frederick & Allie to SARAH E. BASSHAM 16 yrs single b. Mercer Co W VA d/o John & Martha O: farmer; by Jas H. Lilley.

18. 28 Oct 1882 CORNELIUS H. FOLEY 21 yrs single b. Mercer Co W VA s/o Toliver & Susan to VILEY JANE FOLEY 16 yrs single b. Mercer Co W VA d/o Richard B. & Parshaudalha O: farmer; by Jos. Lilley.

19. 26 oct 1882 GEORGE PRESTON 35 yrs wid. b. Bland Co VA s/o Reece & Caroline to AGNES HEDDICK 34 yrs wid. b. Tazewell Co VA O: farmer; by Jas. Calfee; REMARKS: colored.

20. 2 Nov 1882 THOS. T. LILLY 33 yrs wid. b. Mercer Co W VA s/o Turner & Artie to MARTHA J. HATCHER 30 yrs single b. Mercer Co W VA d/o Elijah & Minney O: farmer; by Joseph Lilley.

21. 8 Nov 1882 JOSHUA L. JOHNSTON 23 yrs wid. b. Giles Co VA s/o John S. & Minerva A. to PERLINA MILLER single d/o Richard A & ? O: farmer; by L. Goodwyn.

22. 12 Nov 1882 THOS N. LYNCH 40 yrs single b. Monroe Co W VA s/o John C. & Ann to MARY E. TILLER 26 yrs single b. Mercer Co W VA d/o William & Rhoda O: farmer; by David N. Saunders.

23. 16 Nov 1882 JOS R.A. MEADOWS 17 yrs single b. Mercer co W VA s/o Ward & Huldah to MARY J. LILLY 14 yrs single b. Mercer Co W VA d/o Jas W. & Rachel O: farmer; by John Bragg.

24. 16 Nov 1882 BALLARD R. BAILEY 31 yrs single b. Mercer Co W VA s/o Jonathan & Jula to MARY E. DAY 19 yrs single b. Tazewell Co VA d/o Lewis G. & Elizabeth O: farmer; by Evan H. Brown.

25. 22 Nov 1882 STEWART C. MITCHELL 24 yrs single b. Carroll Co VA now living in Tazewell Co VA s/o John W. & Martha J. to JOSEPHINE V. PERDUE 19 yrs single b. Mercer Co W VA d/o Silas & Nancy J. O: farmer; by A.T. Brooks.

26. 25 Nov 1882 ROBERT M. COOPER 23 yrs single b. Mercer Co W VA s/o C.W. & Harriet to REBECCA BASHAM 23 yrs single b. Monroe Co VA d/o Joseph & Polly O: farmer; by A. McComas.

27. 28 Nov 1882 JAMES H. JONES 24 yrs single b. Hagerstown MD s/o Barvey & Titia to NANNIE PECK 17 yrs single b. Mercer Co W VA d/o Flemming & Rosa O: farmer; by P.S. Sutton.

28. 12 Dec 1882 JOHN A. SHREWSBURY 23 yrs single b. Mercer Co W VA s/o Wm & Vastie to LOUISA E McCOMAS 15 yrs single b. Mercer Co W VA d/o Archibald & Survilla O: farmer; by A. McComas.

29. 14 Dec 1882 JAMES L. HAMBRICK 22 yrs sinble b. Mercer Co W VA s/o G.O & Emma P. to MARTHA ANN HYPES 19 yrs single b. Craig Co VA d/o Geo A. & Sallie E. O: farmer; by Evan H. Brown.

30. 14 Dec 1882 LEWIS H. GOODE 24 yrs single b. Franklin Co VA s/o Geo W. & Parmelia to AMANDA A. OXLEY 23 yrs single b. Bland Co VA d/o Sanford H. & Delila A. O: farmer; by R.M. Ashworth.

31. 20 Dec 1882 JAS M. PRUETT 23 yrs single b. Bland Co VA now living same s/o Henry H. & Isabella to ELIZABETH BAILEY 23 yrs single b. Mercer Co W VA d/o Alex J. & Hannah L. O: farmer; by R.M. Ashworth.

32. 28 Dec 1882 JOHN H. HALL 21 yrs single b. Franklin Co VA s/o Andrew J. & Eliza to RHODA J. BAILEY 18 yrs single b. Mercer Co W VA d/o Chas W. & Mary O: farmer; by A.J. Young.

33. 26 Dec 1882 AND J. HEARN 21 yrs sngle b. Mercer Co W VA s/o James & Easter to SARAH L. WHITE 22 yrs single b. Mercer Co W VA d/o Benj. & Elizabeth O: farmer; by P.S. Sutton.

34. 27 Dec 1882 CHAS R. POOL 31 yrs single b. Montgomery Co VA s/o Moses & Matilda to SARAH J. PRINCE 21 yrs single b. Mercer Co W VA d/o O.F. & Margaline O: farmer; by A. McComas.

35. 27 Dec 1882 WM H. JONES 21 yrs single b. Greenbriar W VA now living in Summers Co VA s/o Thos J. & Elizabeth to MARY B. GORE 16 yrs single b. Mercer Co W VA d/o Robert & Eliz. M. O: teacher; by Wm Holroyd.

36. 28 Dec 1882 GREEN A. JOHNSTON 31 wid. b. Giles Co VA s/o John L. & Minerva A. to MARTHA JANE VEST 26 yrs single b. Montgomery Co VA d/o Wm & Jane O: farmer; by L. Goodwyn.

37. 27 Dec 1882 RICHARD WILSON 31 yrs single b. Mercer Co W VA s/o ? & Catherine to ELIZ. SERUTH* 21 yrs single b. Montgomery Co VA d/o George & Kittie O: farmer; by P.S. Sutton; REMARKS: colored. (*Note: handwriting difficult to read.)

38. 29 Dec 1882 JOS. H. GARRETSON 26 yrs single b. Wyoming Co W VA s/o H.L & Mary A. to MARY H. WELLER 17 yrs single b. PA d/o E.B. & M.B. O: R.R. Conductor; by L. Goodwyn.

39. 3 Jan 1883 WM R. HAWKS 38 yrs wid. b. Grayson Co VA s/o Abraham & Beula to ARAMINTA CRUMB* 35 yrs wid. b. Mercer Co w VA d/o Sampson & Polly O: farmer; by T.K. Lambert. (*NOTE: handwriting difficult to read.)

40. 1 Jan 1883 BEN H. BURTON 32 yrs single b. Pulaski Co VA now living in Giles Co VA s/o Saml F. & Sarah R. to M.E. REYNOLDS 23 yrs single b. Craig Co VA d/o Silas T. & Araminta O: farmer; by J.O. Cassaday; REMARKS: Parties colores, Returned Not Executed.

41. * * * OSCAR GLASCOW 21 yrs single b. Tazewell Co VA s/o Alfred & Emeline to CHARLOTTE FRANSCOW 21 yrs single b. Kanawha Co W VA O: blacksmith. (*Note: no date given.)

42. 4 Jan 1883 LEWIS A. BASSHAM 24 yrs single b. Monroe Co W VA s/o Jos A. & Polly A. to MARY F. SHUTT 16 yrs single b. Montgomery Co VA d/o Henderson F. & Ellen O: farmer; by Archd. McComas.

43. 4 Jan 1883 TAZEWELL C. RUTLEDGE 23 yrs single now living in Summers Co VA s/o Saml & Adeline to ELLA JANE BASHAM 18 yrs single b. Monroe Co W VA d/o Jos A. & Polly A. O: farmer; by A.T. Brooks.

44. 10 Jan 1883 WM H. AYRES 19 yrs single b. Carroll Co VA now living in Tazewell Co VA s/o Granville & Susan to LUCY H. PERDUE 17 yrs single b. Mercer Co W VA d/o Silas & Nancy Jane O: farmer; by A.T. Brooks.

45. 10 Jan 1883 DANIEL J. WAGNER 20 yrs single b. Tazewell Co VA s/o Adair e. & Julina E. to SUSAN M. HAMBRICK 16 yrs single b. Mercer Co W VA d/o Geo O. & Amy P. O: merchant; by D.N. Saunders.

46. 18 Jan 1883 WM J. HALL 22 yrs single b. Franklin Co VA s/o ? & Susan Hall to LOUISA F. FLETCHER 20 yrs single b. Mercer Co W VA d/o Hiram A. & Rhoda O: farmer; by John West.

47. 19 Jan 1883 WILLIS WONK 24 yrs single s/o Silas & ? to ELIZABETH AKERS 16 yrs single d/o Crockett & Martha O: farmer; by E.Howerton.

Page 37

1. 17 Jan 1883 JAMES W. BOLIN 22 yrs single b. Mercer Co W VA s/o J.J. & Isabella to ALLIE M. THOMPSON 24 yrs single b. Mercer Co W VA d/o David & Angeline O: miller; by J.W. Bennett.

2. 25 Jan 1883 HUGH J. SHREWSBURY 25 yrs single b. Mercer Co W VA s/o ? & Rebecca to RHODA SHREWSBURY 35 yrs single b. Mercer Co W VA d/o Philip & Charlotte O: farmer; by Joseph Lilly.

3. 28 Jan 1883 WM A. BROWN 19 yrs single b. Mercer Co W VA s/o John W. & Rhoda M. to OLIVIA K. BROYLES 16 yrs single b. Monroe Co W VA d/o Andrew W. & Amanda O: farmer; by John West.

4. 31 Jan 1883 ROBT KENSLEY 25 yrs single b. Madison Co VA now living in Green Co VA s/o Avaline & Aaron to BELLE BEACKENRIDGE 19 yrs single b. Giles Co VA d/o Cary & Matilda O: black-smith; by Phil S. Sutton; REMARKS: colored.

5. 7 Feb 1883 JAMESON BAILEY 17 yrs single b. Mercer Co W VA s/o Floyd & Zilpha S. to VIRGINIA E. BAILEY 16 yrs single b. Mercer Co W VA d/o Daniel P. & Mary J. O: farmer; by Archibald McComas.

6. 8 Feb 1883 CHARLES WARD 22 yrs single b. Giles Co VA s/o ? & Mary to SARAH TURNER 17 yrs single b. Mercer Co W VA d/o Charles L. & Victoria O: farmer; by L. Goodwyn.

7. 14 Feb 1883 B.G. LEOVEL* 21 yrs single b. Culpeper Co VA s/o Alexander & Mary to PRISCILLA JONES 15 yrs single b. Mercer Co v VA d/o Elisha & Rhuey O: farmer; by L. Goodwyn.(*NOTE: Handwriting difficult to read.)

8. 21 Feb 1883 JAS T. BOWER 33 yrs wid. b. Floyd Co VA now living same s/o David & Nancy to MARY E. JONES 23 yrs single b. Mercer Co W VA d/o Wilson & Frances O: farmer; by L. Goodwyn.

9. 15 Feb 1883 CHARLES R. McNUTT 28 yrs single b. Mercer Co W VA s/o R.B. & Elizabeth E. to E?? B. BARNES 25 yrs single b. Washington Co VA d/o Wm & Mary O: Clerk County Clerk; by Phil S. Sutton.(?=unable to read name.)

10. 8 March 1883 W.B. KEATON 21 yrs single b. Summers Co W VA now living same s/o Nelson & Jane to THEODOSIA E. CAPERTON 19 yrs single b. Mercer Co w VA d/o Thompson K. & Lora O: farmer; by J.W. Bennett.

11. 29 March 1883 GEO E. CARNEFIX 20 yrs single b. Monroe Co W VA s/o Benj F. & Elizabeth A. to NANNIE E. LUSK 27 yrs single b. Mercer Co W VA d/o Alfred E. Henrietta W. O: Saw Mill W.K; by L. Goodwyn.

12. 29 March 1883 WM E. MARTIN 30 yrs wid. b. Mercer Co W VA s/o Achilles & Ailsey to SARAH C. HEARN 30 yrs single b. Mercer Co W VA d/o Levi G. & Ora O: farmer; by J.W. Bennett.

13. 8 April 1883 HIRAM A. PRINCE 23 yrs single b. Mercer Co W VA s/o Oscar F. & Margaline to FRANCES SAFERTY 21 yrs single b. Wyoming Co W VA O: farmer; by Archibald McComas.

14. 12 April 1883 RUFUS CRADDOCK 27 yrs wid. b. Monroe Co W VA s/o Ezekial & Lucy R. to MARY KEYTON 23 yrs single b. Monroe Co W VA d/o ? & Mary A. O: farmer; by James H. Johnston.

15. 12 April 1883 JOHN A.L.LILLY 20 yrs single b. Mercer Co W VA s/o John E. & Julina to SARAH J. BARKER 19 yrs single b. Mercer Co W VA d/o Saml L. & Mary O: farmer; by R.H. Stuart; REMARKS: Court Order 10/30/85.

16. 12 April 1883 JOHN M.SKELTON 21 yrs single b. Tazewell Co VA s/o Milton & Elizabeth to ELIZA A. MEADOR 16 yrs single b. Mercer Co W VA d/o Folon & Malinda O: farmer; by Joseph Lilly.

17. 19 April 1883 LEONIDAS A. SHORTER 26 yrs single b. Franklin Co VA s/o Woodson A. & Martha A.C. to E?? J. Sublett 17 yrs single b. Montgomery Co VA d/o W.R. & Rebecca F. O: farmer; by J.W. Bennett.

18. 18 April 1883 JOHN W. CAPERTON 29 yrs single b. Mercer Co W VA s/o John S. & Minerva A. to ELIZABETH L. WILLIAMS 20 yrs single b. Monroe Co W VA d/o London & Julia O: farmer; by J.W. Bennett.

19. 19 April 1883 GODFREY CHARLTON 21 yrs single b. Tazewell Co VA s/o Saml & Kis. to HESTER STOCK 15 yrs single b. Mercer Co W VA d/o Flem & Sally O: farmer; by Jas. Calfee; REMARKS: colored.

20. 16 April 1883 GEO. C. MILLER 58 yrs wid. b. Pittsylvania Co VA to MARGARET BELCHER 30 yrs single b. Mercer Co w VA d/o Lewis & Rebecca O: miller; by P.S. Sutton.

21. 26 April 1883 U.S. WHITE 17 yrs single b. Mercer Co W VA s/o Abraham & Milly F. to VICTORIA E. SHREWSBURY 17 yrs single b. Mercer Co W VA d/o John & Elizabeth O: farmer; by Archd McComas.

22. 3 May 1883 GRANGER H. GORE 20 yrs single b. Mercer Co W VA s/o H.F. & Sarepta R. to LUCY W. VAUGHT 22 yrs single b. MO d/o Ransom & Minerva O: farmer; by J.W. Bennett.

23. 4 May 1883 THOS. C. ANDERSON 29 yrs single b. Mercer Co W VA s/o Berry & Sally to NANCY J. KINZER 24 yrs single b. Mercer Co W VA d/o Philip & Sally O: farmer; by J.W. Bennett.

24. 23 May 1883 JAS. ESTEL BAILEY 21 yrs single b. Giles Co W VA s/o James & Sarah J. to RUTHA J. JONES 29 yrs single b. Mercer Co W VA d/o Francis & Wilson O: farmer; by James H. Johnston.

25. 27 May 1883 DAVID HURLEY 23 yrs single b. Rockingham Co VA s/o David & Mary to LAURA TILLER 18 yrs single b. Mercer Co W VA d/o Wm & Louisa O: railroader; by J.O. Cassaday.

26. 14 June 1883 JOHN H. NEAL 21 yrs single b. Mercer Co W VA s/o D.N. & Sarah A. to REBECCA A. BAILEY 18 yrs single b. Mercer Co W VA d/o Ballard P. & Sarah O: farmer; by J.O. Cassaday.

27. 21 June 1883 CHAS A. SHREWSBURY 21 yrs single b. Mercer Co W VA s/o Thos & Margaline to SALLIE B. KINZER 16 yrs single b. Mercer Co W VA d/o Thos B. & Sucretia A. O: farmer; by A.J. Young.

28. 21 June 1883 L.J. ELLISON, JR. 21 yrs single b. Mercer Co W VA s/o Isaac J. & Elizabeth to A. CHARLOTTE BRAMMER 21 yrs single b. Raleigh Co W VA d/o James & ? O: farmer; by Wm P. Lilly.

29. 21 June 1883 JOHN J. DOYLE 23 yrs single b. Mercer Co W VA s/o James A. & Martha to HARRIET E. ELLIS 18 yrs single b. Mercer Co W VA d/o Pricsilla & Wm O: farmer; by J.O. Cassaday.

30. 20 June 1883 JOHN E. MULLIN 24 yrs single b. Green Co OH s/o Calvin & Elizabeth to LON WOODYARD 21 yrs single d/o Wm S. & Nancy J. O: saw mill buens; by James Calfea.

31. 28 June 1883 DANIEL R. BAILEY 21 yrs single b. Tazewell Co VA s/o Henderson F. & Sarah to MOLLIE PEDIGO 16 yrs single b. Giles Co VA d/o Saml E. & Susan M. O: farmer; by J.O. Cassaday.

32. 7 July 1883 BALLARD P. WILEY 22 yrs single b. Summers Co W VA s/o ? & Catherine to ALICE FLETCHER 22 yrs single b. Mercer Co W VA d/o Davison & Martha O: farmer; by A.J. Thompson.

33. 19 July 1883 AUGUSTUS B. BELCHER 20 yrs single b. Mercer Co W VA s/o William & Ellen to MARY J. VAUGHT 19 yrs single b. Tazewell Co VA d/o C.L. & Clara C. O: farmer; by J.O. Cassaday.

34. 23 July 1883 CAPHAS D. HARRY 29 yrs single b. Mercer Co W VA s/o Romulus & Rutha J. to MARY E. BAILEY 21 yrs single b. Mercer Co W VA d/o Ballard P. & Sarah E. O: farmer; by J.O. Cassaday.

35. 2 Aug 1883 WM H. SNIDER 21 yrs single b. Mercer Co W VA s/o Wm Riley & Dimortha to RHODA C. ROBERTSON 20 yrs single b. Giles Co VA d/o Chas P. Catharine O: farmer; by Wm Holroyd.

36. * * * J.H. MOYE 29 yrs single b. Mercer Co W VA s/o William W. & Martha J. to AMERICA A. WORRELL 18 yrs single b. Mercer Co W VA d/o Eli & Eliza Jane O: farmer. (*Note: no date given.)

37. 29 Aug 1883 CHAS W. WILEY 21 yrs single b. Mercer Co W VA s/o James L. & America to XANTIPPI F. HALL 17 yrs single b. Montgomery Co VA d/o John M. & Henrietta B. O: farmer; by A.J. Thompson.

38. 30 Aug 1883 JOHN B. HARTWELL 21 yrs single b. Mercer Co W VA s/o John & Cynthia to ISABELLA BELCHER 18 yrs single b. Mercer Co W VA d/o Anderson & Margaret J. O: farmer; by Phil S. Sutton.

39. 5 Sept 1883 JOHN M. HONAKER 22 yrs single b. Bland Co VA s/o Henry & Elizabeth to JENNETTA A. GRIM 18 yrs single b. Mercer Co W VA d/o Peter & Martha A. O: carpenter; by Andrew J. Young.

40. 3 Oct 1883 M.C. BAILEY 23 yrs single b. Mercer Co W VA s/o H.F. & Sarah to SARAH L. BURTON 17 yrs single b. Mercer Co W VA d/o Elias & Sarah O: merchant; by T.K. Lambert.

41. 21 Sept 1883 B.H. VEST 24 yrs single b. Mercer Co W VA s/o Alex McCann & S.J. Vest to CELIA HAGERMAN 20 yrs single b. Fayette Co W VA d/o Wm Hagerman & Roxy Nicholas O: farmer; by J.O. Cassaday; REMARKS: colored.

42. 25 Sept 1883 GORDON L. SAUNDERS 38 yrs single b. Pulaski Co VA s/o Julius & Lydia to NANCY BAILEY 40 yrs wid. b. Mercer Co W VA d/o Sampson Tayler & Polly O: school teacher; by T.K. Lambert.

43. 26 Sept 1883 ALLEN H. CARR 32 yrs wid. b. Mercer Co W VA s/o John S. & Araminta J. to SARAH F. BRATTON 19 yrs single b. Mercer Co W VA d/o Thomas & Mary E. O: physician; by D.B. Carr.

44. 3 Oct 1883 HENRY BELCHER 24 yrs single b. Mercer Co W VA s/o Henry D. & Anna to AMY SHRADER 19 yrs single b. Mercer Co W VA d/o John & Nancy O: farmer; by A.J. Young.

45. 4 Oct 1883 WM F. NEELEY 29 yrs wid. b. Mercer Co W VA s/o Wm & Delilah to SUSAN A.E. VEST 21 yrs single b. Giles Co VA d/o William & Mary J. O: farmer; by L. Goodwyn.

46. 10 Oct 1883 R.T. BANGLES 23 yrs single b. Wilkes Co NC s/o Reuben & Mary to LAURA FAULKNER 16 yrs single b. Mercer Co W VA d/o Hugh M. & Mary O: farmer; by A.J. Young.

47. 12 Oct 1883 WM BALL 22 yrs single b. Mercer Co W VA s/o Jos H. & Elizabeth to SARAH A. PETTRY 16 yrs single b. Mercer Co W VA d/o ? & Albertena O: farmer; by Wm Holroyd.

48. 15 Oct 1883 ELIAS BURTON 46 yrs wid. to MARY E. BAILEY 18 yrs single b. Mercer Co W VA d/o H.F. & Sarah O: merchant; by J.O. Cassaday.

Page 38

1. 24 Oct 1883 SILAS W. PERDUE 21 yrs single b. Mercer Co W VA s/o James H. & Sarah E. to MARY HILL 20 yrs single b. Allegheny Co NC d/o Harden & Jane O: farmer; by T.K. Lambert.

2. 23 Nov 1883 CAMPBELL PRICE 23 yrs single b. Washington Co VA s/o Charles & Mary to SUSAN SURFACE 22 yrs single b. Mercer Co W VA d/o Leftridge & Sarah O: farmer; by Evan H. Brown.

3. 23 Oct 1883 LEWIS B. BRATTON 22 yrs single b. Mercer Co W VA s/o Thos & Mary E. to NANNIE E. CARR 20 yrs single d/o D.B. & Sarah O: farmer; by Phil S. Sutton.

4. 24 Oct 1883 JOHN S. SCOTT 23 yrs single b. Mercer Co W VA s/o Crockett & Sarah to MARY V. BRATTON 20 yrs single b. Mercer Co W VA d/o Thos & Mary E. O: farmer; by D.B. Carr.

5. 25 Oct 1883 ANDREW J. WHITE 60 yrs wid. b. Rockbridge Co VA s/o Sampson & Eliza to KIZZIAH CHARLTON 44 yrs wid. b. Monroe Co W VA O: stone mason; by Wm A. Claxton; REMARKS: colored.

6. 25 Oct 1883 MOSES DAWSON 23 yrs single b. Amhurst Co VA s/o Willis & Nancy to MARTHA TAYLOR 24 yrs single b. Tazewell Co VA d/o William & Rosa O: farmer; by Wm A. Claxton; REMARKS: colored.

7. 1 Nov 1883 GEO W. MEADOWS 18 yrs single b. Mercer Co W VA now living Summers Co W VA s/o Sylvester & Mary to MARY A. SNEAD 18 yrs single b. Mercer Co W VA d/o ? & Mary O: farmer; by James W. Lilly.

8. 1 Nov 1883 ISAAC G. CARDEN 42 yrs single b. Monroe Co W VA now living in Summers Co VA s/o Isaac & Rebecca to MARTHA M. PINE 29 yrs single b. Mercer Co W VA d/o Alexdr & Rebecca O: farmer; by J.W. Bennett.

9. 7 Nov 1883 JOSEPH R. GOODE 23 yrs single b. Franklin Co VA s/o Geo. W. & Pamelia to ANNA J. HUNT 22 yrs single b. Gland Co VA d/o Harvey & Hannah C. O: farmer; by J.W. Bennett.

10. 21 Nov 1883 FIELDING E. FAULKNER 24 yrs single b. Mercer Co W VA s/o Gordon & Anna E. to OCTAVIA J. BELCHER 21 yrs single b. Mercer Co W VA d/o Allen D. & Sallie E. O: farmer; by J.O. Cassaday.

11. 21 Nov 1883 BALLARD J. HAGAR 20 yrs single b. Mercer Co W VA s/o A. Green & Nancy to SARAH A. SHRADER 17 yrs single b. Mercer Co W VA d/o Henry & Sarah O: farmer; by David N. Saunders.

12. 22 Nov 1883 THOS A. MARTIN 23 yrs single b. Mercer Co W VA s/o Achilles & Ailsey to EASTER S. STEARN 23 yrs single b. Mercer Co W VA d/o Levi G. & Aury O: farmer; by J.W. Bennett.

13. 21 Nov 1883 CHAS D. McMANAWAY 22 yrs single b. Montgomery Co VA s/o James & Sarah A. to NANCY A. WHITE 17 yrs single b. Wyoming Co VA d/o Allen & Mary O: farmer; by A.J. Thompson.

14. 24 Nov 1883 ZACH TAYLOR ROGERS 35 yrs wid. b. Clayton Co TN s/o Jefferson & Mary Ann to MARY A DILLION 20 yrs single b. Mercer Co W VA d/o Jas. Harvey & Matilda O: merchant; by Evan H. Brown.

15. 5 Dec 1883 WM H.H. MEADER 24 yrs single b. Mercer Co W VA s/o Josiah & Susanna to MARY O. KESSINGER 23 yrs single b. Giles Co VA d/o Silas & Anna Jane O: farmer; by Wm P. Lilly.

16. 20 Nov 1883 ANTHONY ANDERSON 25 yrs single b. Fayette Co W VA s/o Jack & Mary to JULIANN GALLIHER 14 yrs single b. Mercer Co W VA d/o Jack & Polly O: farmer; by Evan H. Brown.

17. 5 Dec 1883 WATSON C. BOWLING 22 yrs single b. Mercer Co W VA s/o Wm A. & Devarius to MOLLIE J. REED 21 yrs single b. Mercer Co W VA d/o Hiram & Susan O: farmer; by James W. Lilly.

18. 5 Dec 1883 JOSEPH R. ARGABRIGHT 34 yrs wid. b. Franklin Co VA s/o George W. & Elizabeth A. to CLARINDA E. MASSEY 19 yrs single b. Floyd Co VA d/o Charles & Elizabeth P. O: carpenter; by J.W. Bennett.

19. 5 Dec 1883 HENRY SNOW 30 yrs div. to MARIA HERNDON 25 yrs div. O: farmer; by J.O. Cassaday; REMARKS: colored.

20. 6 Dec 1883 GABRIEL UNDERWOOD 22 yrs single b. Floyd Co W VA s/o Martin & Elizabeth to SARAH JANE BAILEY 20 yrs single b. Mercer Co W VA d/o Andrew & Sarah O: farmer; by Evan H. Brown.

21. 6 Dec 1883 LUTHER CROTTY 18 yrs single b. Monroe Co W VA s/o Geo W. & India H. to FANNIE M. SOUTHERN 17 yrs single b. Mercer Co W VA d/o Wm & Rachel O: farmer; by A.J. Thompson.

22. * Dec 1883 BLUFORD B. BAILEY 29 yrs single b. Mercer Co W VA s/o Eli & Charlotte to CATHERINE A. GRIM 16 yrs single b. Mercer Co W VA d/o Peter & Martha A. O: farmer; by A.J. Young. (*Note: no day given.)

23. 13 Dec 1883 JAMES F. HILL 23 yrs single b. Alleghany Co NC s/o Harium & Janey to BETTIE C. NEAL 23 yrs single b. Mercer Co W VA d/o Henry M. & Sarah O: farmer; by A.T. Brooks.

24. 11 Dec 1883 HENRY P. NOBLE 28 yrs single b. Mercer Co W VA s/o L.B.W. & Parmelia Ann to NANNIE L. HUNT 25 yrs single b. Wythe Co VA d/o Harvey W. & Hannah O: farmer; by J.W. Bennett.

25. 18 Dec 1883 CHAS. W. GRAHAM 26 yrs single b. Wythe Co VA s/o David E. & Rebecca to NANNIE M. BROWN 19 yrs single b. Tazewell Co VA d/o Evan H & Martha E. O: farmer; by James Calfee.

MERCER COUNTY, WEST VIRGINIA
Marriages 1854 - 1901

26. 20 Dec 1883 NATHAN BAILEY 21 yrs single b. Tazewell Co VA now living same s/o Z.H. & Elizabeth to ALICE TAYLOR 19 yrs single b. Mercer Co W VA d/o John & Mary F. O: farmer; by A.J. Young.

27. 27 Dec 1883 NEWTON F. HOYE 20 yrs single b. Mercer Co W VA s/o John W. & Julia A. to BARBARA A. FARLEY 15 yrs single b. Mercer Co W VA d/o ? & Sarah A. O: farmer; by James W. Lilly.

28. 20 Dec 1883 JNO D. GOTT 22 yrs single b. Giles Co VA s/o Andrew & ? to MARY J. BELCHER 21 yrs single b. Mercer Co W VA d/o And. A. & Clarinda O: farmer; by J.O. Cassaday.

29. 24 Dec 1883 B.A. PENNINGTON 25 yrs single b. Monroe Co W VA now living same s/o William & Nancy to MARY E. WHITE 15 yrs single b. Mercer Co W VA d/o Reuben & Martha O: school teacher; by A.J. Thompson.

30. 25 Dec 1883 HARVEY W. DUDLEY 24 yrs single b. Giles Co VA s/o Tobias & Jane to HENRIETTA THOMAS 16 yrs single b. Mercer Co W VA d/o James A. & Mary O: farmer; by L. Goodwyn.

31. 25 Dec 1883 JAMES T. TABOR 19 yrs single b. Galliher Co OH s/o Geo. O. & Olive to DOLLY KISSINGER 17 yrs single b. Giles Co VA d/o Silas & Anna Jane O: farmer; by James W. Lilly.

32. 25 Dec 1883 GEO R. TABOR 21 yrs single b. Mercer Co W VA s/o Geo. O. & Olive to MALINDA A. BOWLING 18 yrs single b. Mercer Co W VA d/o M.A. & r.J. O: farmer; by James W. Lilly.

33. 26 Dec 1883 AUGUSTUS L. STEELE 18 yrs single b. Mercer Co W VA s/o Wm F. & Rhoda to FLORA WHITE 16 yrs single b. Mercer Co W VA d/o J.A. & Mary E. O: farmer; by A.J. Thompson.

34. 27 Dec 1883 JOSEPH RYAN 41 yrs single b. Montgomery Co VA now living in Summers Co VA s/o W.G. & N.J. Ryan to SARAH L. PINE 34 yrs single b. Mercer Co W VA d/o Alex & R. Pine O: farmer; by J.W. Bennett.

35. 2 Jan 1884 MILLARD F. FRENCH 25 yrs single b. Mercer Co W VA s/o R.G & Martha A. to MOLLIE L. KARNES 21 yrs single b. Mercer Co W VA d/o Jas. A. & Addie E. O: farmer; by J.W. Bennett.

36. 2 Jan 1884 GEORGE A. BUTT 22 yrs single b. Tazewell Co VA now living same s/o Harrison Butt to REBECCA J. BAILEY 22 yrs single b. Mercer Co W VA d/o Harry & Rosina O: farmer; by James Calfee.

. 27 Dec 1883 ESTELL R. BRUCE 22 yrs single b. Mercer Co W VA s/o Wm A. & Martha H. to MARY L. MANN 20 yrs single b. Mercer Co W VA O: farmer; by J.W. Bennett. (Note: no number given.)

37. 3 Jan 1884 THOS G. DAMERON 28 yrs single b. Smythe Co VA now living in Washington s/o Michael & Catherine to DELIA A. BELCHER 18 yrs single b. Mercer Co W VA d/o Wm A. & Ellen R. O: wagon maker; by J.O. Cassaday.

38. 12 Jan 1884 GEO W. MARTIN 21 yrs single b. Mercer Co W VA s/o David & Hester to HANNAH J. BIRD 16 yrs single b. Mercer Co W VA d/o Wm A. & Cynthia O: farmer; by Wm Holroyd.

39. 21 Jan 1884 NAPOLEON EUBANKS 30 yrs single b. Amherst Co VA now living in Tazewell Co VA s/o Dawnie & Caroline to NELLIE THORP 21 yrs single b. Bedford Co VA O: railroader(sic); by J.O. Cassaday; REMARKS: colored.

40. 29 Jan 1884 IRA W. WALKER 28 yrs single b. Mercer Co W VA s/o Council & Nancy D. to LIORIA C. KINZER 21 yrs single b. Mercer Co W VA d/o Thomas & Lucretia O: merchant; by Archibald McComas.

41. 31 Jan 1884 WM A. ELTON 27 yrs single b. Hosford Co MD now living in Tazewell Co VA s/o Henry S. & Eliza to NANNIE HEATH 23 yrs single b. Smythe Co VA d/o Jefferson & Perlinia O: hotel keeper; by W.A. Dickinson.

42. 4 Feb 1884 JAS. HERBERT BEASLEY 21 yrs single b. Nicholas Co W VA s/o Jerry & Hannah to LAURA ANN E. BECHELHYMER 17 yrs single b. Floyd Co VA d/o Abraham & Mary O: farmer; by Archibald McComas; REMARKS: colored.

43. 7 Feb 1884 LEWIS J. AKERS 18 yrs single b. Raleigh Co W VA s/o Crockett & Martha to MINERVA J. FLETCHER 20 yrs single b. Mercer Co W VA d/o Isaac & Sarah O: farmer; by Geo W. McKinney.

44. 20 Feb 1884 LEWIS D. MARTIN 25 yrs single b. Mercer Co W VA s/o L.D. & Sarah to DERENZIE RORER 20 yrs single b. Patrick Co VA d/o Wm R. & Mary O: farmer; by Wm Holroyd.

45. 20 Feb 1884 JAS B. MARTIN 23 yrs single b. Mercer Co W VA s/o L.D. & Sarah to EMMA RUMBURG 14 yrs single b. Mercer Co W VA d/o Wm J. & Nancy O: farmer; by Wm Holroyd.

46. 22 Feb 1884 CARR MUSE 20 yrs single b. Pitsylvanie Co VA now living in Tazewell Co Va s/o Abe & Mille Muse to LUCY JOHNSON 14 yrs single b. Franklin Co VA d/o Abe & Isabell O: farm hand; by Evan H. Brown; REMARKS: colored.

47. 26 Feb 1884 J.W. HENDERSON FLETCHER 28 yrs wid. b. Mercer Co W Va s/o Calvin & Rhoda to CYNTHIA E. MASSEY 25 yrs single b. Mercer Co W VA d/o Richard S. & Mary O: farmer; by J.W. Bennett.

48. 27 Feb 1884 RUFUS K.G. WALL 23 yrs single b. Mercer Co W VA s/o Henry D. & Mary J. to QUEEN V. AUSTIN 23 yrs single b. Mercer Co W VA d/o Isaac E. & Malvina O: farmer; by Jas. O. Cassaday.

Page 39

1. 29 Feb 1884 JESSE G.J. DUNFORD 21 yrs single b. Montgomery Co VA s/o Albert & Eliza to SARAH J. THOMPSON 22 yrs div. b. Montgomery Co VA d/o James & Lucy O: farmer; by James Calfee.

2. 27 Feb 1884 WM C. OLIVER 27 yrs single b. Mercer Co W VA s/o Wm & Nancy to JANE R. THORN 20 yrs single b. Giles Co VA d/o James P. & Mahala T. O: farmer; by D.H. Carr.

3. 28 Feb 1884 F.W. HALE 22 yrs single b. Giles Co Va now living same s/o Wm W. & Martha H. to CATHARINE J. BRUCE 17 yrs single b. Giles Co VA d/o Charles & Polly O: farmer; by Wm Holroyd.

4. 6 March 1884 WM H. DUNCAN 23 yrs single b. Mercer Co W VA s/o Wm & Lucinda to MARIA A. BROWN 19 yrs single b. Mercer Co W VA d/o Patten R. & Sarah W. O: farmer; by J.W. Bennett.

5. 19 March 1884 JAS. A. REED 24 yrs single b. Mercer Co W VA s/o Hiram A. & Susan to ONIE E. KESSINGER 16 yrs single b. Giles Co VA d/o Silas & Tolley O: farmer; by Jas W. Lilly.

6. 13 March 1884 JAS. GARNER 36 yrs wid. b. Mercer Co W VA s/o Lewis & Charlotte to LOLLIE ADAMS 20 yrs single b. Pulaski Co VA d/o Pleasant & Minerva O: farmer; by Phil S. Sutton; REMARKS: colored.

7. 16 March 1884 JAS. R. KARNES 28 yrs single b. Monroe Co W VA s/o Jacob & Elizabeth M. to VICTORIA HENDERSON 23 yrs single d/o ? & Hannah O: farmer; by R.H. Stuart.

8. 26 March 1884 JAS. W. WHITE 27 yrs single b. Mercer Co W VA s/o Andrew & Elizabeth to LAURA P. MORGAN 22 yrs single b. Mercer Co W VA d/o Swan H. & Francis A. O: farmer; by J.W. Bennett.

9. 27 March 1884 LEWIS H. PENNINGTON 25 yrs single b. Mercer Co W VA s/o Levi & Elizabeth to MARY J. JOHNSTON 17 yrs single b. Mercer Co W VA d/o John L. & ? O: farmer; by A.J. Thompson.

10. 7 April 1884 HENRY W. ROLES 24 yrs single b. Mercer Co W VA s/o Andrew & Elizabeth to ALA. B. LILLY 16 yrs single b. Mercer Co W VA d/o Wm H. & Jane O: farmer; by Wm P. Lilly.

11. 2 April 1884 H.F. SHRADER 22 yrs single b. Mercer Co W VA s/o Robert & Cynthia J. to MARY J. TAYLOR 19 yrs single b. Mercer Co W VA d/o Wm & Mary O: farmer; by T.K. Lambert.

12. 6 April 1884 THOS M. CAMPBELL 19 yrs single b. Tazewell Co VA s/o Thos K. & ? to SUSANAH B. CAMPBELL 19 yrs single b. Mercer Co W VA d/o Wm E. & Lucinda O: farmer; by Phil S. Sutton.

13. 8 April 1884 JOHN R. PHIPPS 21 yrs single b. Alleghany Co NC s/o Aaron B. & Margaret A. to JANE B. WADDLE 18 yrs single b. Raleigh Co VA d/o William & Sarah O: farmer; by J.W. Bennett.

14. 10 April 1884 JNO. H. SHREWSBURY 22 yrs single b. Mercer Co W VA s/o Riley & Jane to MATILDA MEDOW 26 yrs single b. Mercer Co W VA d/o Isaac & Jane O: farmer; by James W. Lilly.

15. 10 April 1884 THOMAS W. HIBBS 27 yrs single b. Loudon Co VA s/o William & Mary E. to SARAH M.P. MARTIN 29 yrs single b. Mercer Co W VA d/o Geo W. & Nancy O: blacksmith; by J.W. Bennett.

16. 9 April 1884 AUGUSTUS NEAL 37 yrs wid. b. Tazewell Co VA s/o ? & Terry to SELENIA BRECKENRIDGE 23 yrs single b. Giles Co VA d/o Cary & Matilda O: farmer; by Isaac S. Harmon.

17. 28 April 1884 CHAS A. DEATON 43 yrs wid. b. Tazewell Co VA now living same s/o Nathan & Sarah to ANN MARTIN 29 yrs single b. Pulaski Co VA d/o Sanford & Margaret O: merchant; by D.H. Carr.

18. 26 April 1884 THOS C. FARLEY 21 yrs single b. Raleigh Co W VA s/o Nelson & Malinda to VICTORIA L. MOYE 14 yrs single b. Mercer Co W VA d/o Robt E. & Lucinda O: merchant; by Jas W. Lilly.

19. 30 April 1884 J.A. CLEGHON 28 yrs single b. Smythe Co VA s/o J.B. & Mary to VIRGINIA B. HEDRICK 17 yrs single b. Tazewell Co VA d/o G.H. & ? O: farmer; by L. Goodwyn.

20. 19 May 1884 NOAH R. RUSSEL 18 yrs single b. Mercer Co W VA s/o B.O. & Jane to ARAMINIA UNDERWOOD 21 yrs single b. Mercer Co W VA d/o ? & Ester O: farmer; by J.O. Cassaday.

21. 21 May 1884 ALEX W. BAILEY 20 yrs single b. Mercer Co W VA s/o Leland & Rebecca to LAURA F. CALFEE 23 yrs single b. Mercer Co W VA d/o James & Elizabeth O: farmer; by James Calfee.

22. 22 May 1884 JACOB BELSEL 21 yrs single b. Benford Co PA s/o Joseph & Barbara to SUSAN J. CHAUEP(?) 18 yrs single b. Wythe Co VA d/o James H. & Causby O: farmer; by J.O. Cassaday.

23. 5 June 1884 GEO D. CARPER 23 yrs single b. Floyd Co VA s/o ? & Mary to ELIZA J.B. MANN 19 yrs single b. Mercer Co W VA d/o Wm & Mary O: farmer; by A.J. Thompson; REMARKS: colored.

24. 5 June 1884 HUGHIE G. MILLS 44 yrs wid. b. Mercer Co W VA s/o Robt & Rebecca to CATHARINE KEELEY 45 yrs wid. b. Beaford Co VA d/o Chas & Sarah McBride O: farmer; by Charles Walker.

25. 3 June 1884 HARMAN A. WHITE 27 yrs single b. Mercer Co W VA s/o Albert J. & Sarah A. to MARY H. MASTIN 20 yrs single d/o Wm E. & ? O: farmer; by J.W. Bennett.

26. 5 June 1884 JNO. J.T. ALLEN 25 yrs wid. b. Nelson Co VA s/o George G. & Jane S. to REBECCA A. REED 28 yrs wid. b. Mercer Co W VA d/o Sampkin & Ellen Thomas O: farmer; by L. Goodwyn.

27. 11 June 1884 SAML ARMSTRONG 22 yrs single b. Smyth Co VA s/o Obadiah & Elizabeth to BELLE RATLIFF 14 yrs single b. Mercer Co W VA d/o ? & Jane O: farmer; by Evan H. Brown.

28. 17 June 1884 JAS H. HOGE 63 yrs wid. b. Pulaski Co VA now living in Giles Co VA s/o James & Ellen to ELIZ. J. HOOGE 45 yrs single b. Giles Co VA d/o Geo D. & Rebecca O: farmer; by P.S. Sutton.

29. 22 June 1884 AUSCAI PERDUE 20 yrs single b. Mercer Co W VA s/o Forgus & Nannie to ALICE B. HAZLEWOOD 17 yrs single b. Mercer Co W VA d/o John & Mary J. O: farmer; by A.J. Thompson.

30. 22 June 1884 WM J. KEATON 19 yrs single b. Mercer Co W VA s/o Judson & Martha J. to LUCINDA E. FARLEY 16 yrs single b. Mercer Co W VA d/o Auden. P. & Emaline O: farmer; by Ward C. Keaton.

31. 19 June 1884 JASPER JAMES 24 yrs single b. Mercer Co W VA s/o Anderson James & Maria Stephens to GILLIE A. HENDERSON 32 yrs wid. b. Mercer Co W VA d/o John A. & Rebecca J. Rutter O: farmer; by L. Goodwyn.

32. 3 July 1884 HUGH A. DANNELEY 30 yrs single b. Mercer Co W VA s/o Nehemiah & Gerusha to JULIA A. ROWLAND 30 yrs single b. Mercer Co W VA d/o Jonathan J. & Sarah O: farmer; by J.W. Bennett.

33. 3 July 1884 SAMUEL P. PEARIES 26 yrs single b. Mercer Co W VA s/o George W. & Phoebe C. to MARY H. BARBER 22 yrs single b. Mercer Co W VA d/o Herbert B. & Tammie C. O: Dep. Clk. Coty. Co; by P.S. Sutton.

34. 17 July 1884 JOHN A. BAILEY 48 yrs wid. b. Mercer Co W VA now living in Wyoming Co W VA s/o Mashu & Jutst to MELVINA M. BAILEY 29 yrs single b. Mercer Co W VA d/o Eli & Lottie O: farmer; by T.K. Lambert.

35. 27 July 1884 EDWIN J. KNOWELS 24 yrs subgke b. England now living in Tazewell Co VA s/o James & Elizabeth to WILLIE BUFFALOW 21 yrs single b. Floyd Co VA d/o William & Susan O: miner; by F.A. Hendr.

36. 30 July 1884 WM H. HOLROYD 24 yrs single b. Mercer Co W VA s/o William & Sarah to BETTIE B. JOHNSTON 20 yrs single b. Giles Co VA d/o H.S. & Sarah O: physician; by C.E. Higgins.

37. 30 July 1884 CHAS W. WOODSON 20 yrs single b. Tazewell Co VA now living same s/o Agnes Preston & ? to JOSEPHINE DAVIDSON 17 yrs single b. Mercer Co W VA d/o Saml & Elvira O: farmer; by Romulus Harry.

38. * * * A.D. McMANAWAY 23 yrs single b. Monroe Co W VA s/o John W. & Mary E. to ABAGAIL VIA 27 yrs single b. Franklin Co VA d/o ? & Rachel O: farmer. (*NOTE: No date given.)

39. 14 Aug 1884 JOS M. HYPES 22 yrs single b. Craig Co VA s/o Jacob L. & Francis J. to ADELINE BILLIPS 20 yrs single b. Tazewell Co VA d/o Kiah & Rhew O: farmer; by J.O. Cassaday.

40. 24 Aug 1884 A.J. MEADOWS 25 yrs single b. Mercer Co W VA s/o ? & Ellen to MARY E. BROYLES 20 yrs single b. Monroe Co W VA d/o A.W. & Amanda O: farmer; by J.L. Hubbard.

41. 25 Aug 1884 B.S. BURKET 34 yrs single b. Wythe Co VA now living same s/o George & Ann to MARY FULLER 38 yrs wid. b. Wythe Co VA d/o Daul & Betsy Wright O: farmer; by L. Goodwyn.

42. 28 Aug 1884 W.S. HAWLEY 42 yrs wid. b. Montgomery Co VA s/o John A. & Charlotte to MARGARET L. FAULKNER 21 yrs single b. Mercer Co W VA d/o Gordon & Ann B. O: farmer; by Evan H. Brown.

43. 3 Sept 1884 JNO T. KING 29 yrs single b. Baltimore MD s/o Thomas & Sarah to VIRGINIA E. COWLING 27 yrs single b. Mercer Co W VA d/o Willis J. & Mary E. O: bridge builder; by Phil S. Sutton.

44. 18 Sept 1884 JEREMIAH R. SNEED 19 yrs single b. Mercer Co W VA s/o John & Mary J. to ROMANSA C. MEADOW 16 yrs single b. Mercer Co W VA d/o Lycurgus & Mary C. O: farmer; by Charles Walker.

45. 2 Sept 1884 THOS NORTHCUTT 19 yrs single b. TN to VIRGINIA SWADER 17 yrs single b. Mercer Co W VA d/o Alexander & Catherine O: farmer; by Evan H. Brown.

46. No Entry.

47. 10 Sept 1884 NEHEMIAH WATSON 70 yrs wid. b. Harrison Co OH to PARSHANDATHA FOLEY 52 yrs wid. b. Patrick Co VA O: farmer; by Charles Walker.

48. 18 Sept 1884 JNO C. PRICE 21 yrs single b. Montgomery Co VA s/o Henry & Catherine to M.J. SHREWSBURY 19 yrs single b. Mercer Co W VA d/o Wm & Sarah O: farmer; by Archibald McComas.

Page 40

1. 15 Sept 1884 WILLIAM T. MOORE 21 yrs single b. Monroe Co W VA now living same s/o Thos & Sally Moore to ELIZA F. JOHNSTON 21 yrs div. b. Mercer Co W VA d/o Saml A. & Rhoda Shade O: farmer; by J.O. Cassaday.

2. 1 Oct 1884 JAS. W. GRAHAM 21 yrs single b. Raleigh Co W VA now living same s/o Jas & Sarah to PHILENA A WOOD 14 yrs single b. Mercer Co W VA d/o Alexander N. & Eliz. O: farmer; by George R. McKinney.

3. 25 Sept 1884 GEO E. CALDWELL 27 yrs single b. Montgomery Co VA s/o Edward & Margaret to LURISA C. BAILEY 25 yrs single b. Mercer Co W VA d/o Buron & Martha O: farmer; by Carroll Clark.

4. 2 Oct 1884 JOSEPH T. HOLT 24 yrs single b. Mercer Co W VA s/o Richard & Eleanor Holt to LUCINDA SHRADER 18 yrs single b. Mercer Co W VA d/o John & Nancy Shrader O: farmer; by David N. Saunders.

5. 2 Sept 1884 PERRY G. CAHILL 23 yrs single b. Giles Co VA now living same s/o Perry J. & Eliz. Cahill to FANNIE C. CLEGHORN 29 yrs single b. Smythe Co VA d/o J.B. Cleghorn O: farmer; by P.S. Sutton.

6. 2 Sept 1884 T.J. BENNETT 26 yrs single b. Stokes Co NC now living Carroll Co VA s/o T.J. & Delilah Bennett to MARY C. WRIGHT 23 yrs single b. Mercer Co W VA d/o C.G. & Elizabeth O: farmer; by L. Goodwyn.

7. 8 Sept 1884 ROBT L. WHITE 22 yrs single b. Monroe Co W VA s/o Robt & Martha to MARTELAH HARRISON 19 yrs single b. Tazewell Co VA d/o ? & Jane O: farmer; by P.S. Sutton; REMARKS: colored.

8. * * * LORENZO D. BURNETT 22 yrs single b. Floyd Co VA now living in Monroe Co W VA s/o Josiah & Jemima to MARINDA A. CRAWFORD 23 yrs single b. Raleigh Co W VA; O: farmer. (*Note: no date given.)

9. 8 Sept 1884 WM McINNES 45 yrs single b. Edinburgh Scotland s/o John & Catharine to CATHARINE A WRIGHT 45 yrs single b. Appomattox Co VA; by J.O. Cassaday.

10. 21 Oct 1884 FLOYD L. AKERS 22 yrs single b. Mercer Co W VA s/o N.B. & Sarah J. to LAURA MOOREY 18 yrs single b. Mercer Co W VA d/o Stynax L. & Susanah O: farmer; by Archibald McComas.

11. 19 Oct 1884 B.G. WRIGHT 25 yrs single b. Mercer Co W VA s/o Camden G. & Elizabeth to ELIZ. J. CLEGHON 21 yrs single b. Smyth Co VA d/o J.B. & Mary O: farmer; by P.S. Sutton.

12. 23 Oct 1884 SUTTON BURKS 21 yrs single b. Pulaski Co VA to SARAH J. MAY 16 yrs single b. Mercer Co W VA d/o William & Mary O: farmer; by A.J. Thompson; REMARKS: colored.

13. 25 Oct 1884 JOHN G. PROFIT 26 yrs single b. Johnston Co TX s/o Hiram & Betsy to ALICE FLETCHER 22 yrs single b. Mercer Co W VA d/o B.A. & ? O: farmer; by J.O. Cassaday.

14. 27 Oct 1884 WM G. CALFEE 24 yrs sngle b. Mercer Co W VA s/o Rutlege & Easter Ann to SALLIE MANNING 22 yrs single b. Mercer Co W VA d/o ? & Margaret J. O: farmer; by J.O. Cassaday.

15. 30 Oct 1884 WM B. CROCKETT 21 yrs single b. Tazewell Co VA s/o Jas A. & Rachel E. to NANCY E. TAYLOR 16 yrs single b. Mercer Co W VA d/o John & Mary F. O: farmer; by James Calfee.

16. 30 Oct 1884 JACOB R. SAUNDERS 21 yrs single b. Montgomery Co VA s/o George & Liona to NANCY A.A. FARMER 18 yrs single b. Mercer Co W VA d/o Reuben C. & Mary M. O: farmer; by Phil S. Sutton.

17. 6 Nov 1884 J.C.W. HEADER 24 yrs single b. Mercer Co W VA s/o Beildy & Susan to BELLE J. LILLY 17 yrs single b. Raleigh Co W VA d/o James W. & Mary M. O: farmer; by Wm P. Lilly.

18. 12 Nov 1884 CHAS D. HAWLEY 24 yrs single b. Mercer Co W VA s/o John H. & Charlotte to LELIA A. TAYLOR 16 yrs single b. Pittsylvania Co VA d/o Wm F. & Martha E. O: farmer; by J.W. Bennett.

19. 12 Nov 1884 ENON E. LILLY 18 yrs single b. Mercer Co W VA s/o Johnston K. & Allie to LAURA A. WRIGHT 16 yrs single b. Giles Co VA d/o Ranson & Sarah M. O: farmer; by Evan H. Brown.

20. 12 Nov 1884 GEO R. ROWLAND 28 yrs single b. Mercer Co W VA s/o J.J. & Sarah to OCTAVIA H. ROBINSON 29 yrs single b. Mercer Co W VA d/o Harrison & Harriet O: farmer; by J.W. Bennett.

21. 12 Nov 1884 MILTON G. PENNINGTON 22 yrs single b. Mercer Co W VA s/o Gordon E & Julia Ann to ELIZA JANE LIKENS 18 yrs single b. Floyd Co VA d/o Wm & Martha J. O: farmer; by J.O. Cassaday.

22. 13 Nov 1884 THOS H. BATEMAN 29 yrs single b. Bedford Co VA s/o Joseph & Amanda to NELIA J. HUMPHREYS 21 yrs single b. Augusta Co VA s/o John & Malinda O: stonemason; by P.S. Sutton.

23. * * * AUSTIN SMITH 26 yrs single b. Summers Co W VA now living same s/o Moses & Agness to ELIZA GORE 21 yrs single b. Mercer Co W VA d/o ? & Louisa O: boatman; REMARKS: colored.

24. 25 Nov 1884 JAMES R. FOSTER 23 yrs single b. Monroe Co W VA s/o Milton & ? to LUVENA RANSON 21 yrs single b. Raleigh Co W VA d/o James T. & Lucinda O: railroader; by P.S. Sutton.

25. 27 Nov 1884 JAMES JOHNSTON 28 yrs single b. Martinsburg Co W VA now living in Tazewell Co VA s/o William & Mary to SALLIE J. BAILEY 21 yrs single b. Tazewell Co VA d/o John & Rebecca O: miner; by P.S. Sutton.

26. 4 Dec 1884 COUNCIL WALKER 72 yrs wid. b. Giles Co VA now living in Raleigh Co W VA s/o Chrispianos & Francis to MALISSA O. McDONALD 47 yrs wid. b. John & Francis O: farmer; by Archibald McComas.

27. 10 Dec 1884 CHAS C. WALKER 26 yrs single b. Mercer Co W VA s/o John L. & Jane K. to BELLE D. WITTEN 26 yrs single b. Mercer Co W VA d/o William & Mary O: farmer; by J.T. Stovall.

28. 11 Dec 1884 W.S.G. McKENZIE 25 yrs single b. Mercer Co W VA s/o John A. & Lucinda to HARRIET J. THORNTON 21 yrs single b. Mercer Co W VA d/o James A. & Harriet L. O: farmer; by L. Goodwyn.

29. 16 Dec 1884 JOSEPH KEATEN 65 yrs wid. b. Mercer Co W VA now living in Summers Co W VA s/o Wm & Mary to DRUCILLA AKERS 45 yrs wid. b. Franklin Co VA d/o David & ? Crews O: farmer; by Ward C. Keaten.

30. 16 Dec 1884 JAS H. MARTIN 21 yrs single b. Frederick Co MD now living in Montgomery Co VA s/o John & Sarah to S. SUE LESLIE 17 yrs single b. Pulaski Co VA d/o John C. & melvina O: railroader; by J.O. Cassaday.

31. 21 Dec 1884 C.F. FIELDER 19 yrs single b. Grayson Co NC s/o Dennis & Mary to ELLA A. BAILEY 22 yrs single b. Mercer Co W VA d/o Jonathan & Ursula O: farmer; by D.N. Saunders.

32. 24 Dec 1884 JOS B. BYRD 22 yrs single b. Floyd Co VA s/o John S. & Sarah C. to DORA L. TABOR 16 yrs single b. Tazewell Co VA d/o Henry H. & Mary M. O: carpenter; by A.T. Brooks.

33. 26 Dec 1884 THOS. SAUNDERS 21 yrs single b. Floyd Co VA s/o Henry & ? to MARY H. CARPER 18 yrs single b. Floyd Co VA d/o ? & Mary O: farmer; by A.J. Thompson; REMARKS: colored.

34. 25 Dec 1884 S.B. GRIFFITH 21 yrs single b. Pulaski Co VA s/o Shadrack B. & Catherine to MARY J. GRIFFITH 20 yrs single b. Pulaski Co VA d/o ? & Louisa O: farmer; by Romulus Harry.

35. 24 Dec 1884 THOS A. DUNN 21 yrs single b. Monroe Co W VA s/o Ballard P. & Amanda to ELIZ. C. MULLINS 20 yrs single b. Mercer Co W VA d/o Wm P. & Abagail O: teamster.

36. 26 Dec 1884 WM SIPHERS 22 yrs single b. Wythe Co VA s/o Andrew & Elizabeth to M.E. DILLION 17 yrs single b. Mercer Co W VA d/o James & Matilda O: farmer; by Evan H. Brown.

37. 27 Dec 1884 CORNELIUS WOOD 20 yrs single b. Wilkes Co NC s/o Ransom & ? to SARAH DELP 23 yrs wid. b. Mercer Co W VA d/o Wm & Martha Dillion O: farmer; by Evan H. Brown.

38. 25 Dec 1884 ED J. BELCHER 18 yrs 4 mos single b. Mercer Co W VA s/o Isham & Nancy to MARGIE SHREWSBURY 16 yrs single b. Mercer Co W VA d/o Henry & F.J. O: farmer; by A. McComas.

39. 25 Dec 1884 JNO K. SMITHICANN 22 yrs single b. Amherst Co VA now living in Tazewell Co VA s/o Robert M. & Eliza. A. to M.C. LUSK 18 yrs single b. Raleigh Co W VA d/o Alfred E & ? O: railroader; by C. Clark.

40. 30 Dec 1884 CHAS McF. WALL 23 yrs single b. Mercer Co W VA s/o Wm & Elizabeth to SALLIE B. WALKER 23 yrs single b. Mercer Co W VA d/o John L. & Jane N. O: farmer; by J.O. Cassaday.

(NOTE: #'s 41 - 46 DOES NOT list parents for husband or wife.)

41. 1 Sept 1884 WM A. FEDIGO 21 yrs single b. KY now living in Tazewell Co VA to ISABELLA DENNSON 21 yrs single b. PA; by P.S. Sutton.

42. 24 March 1884 JAS H. POOL 19 yrs single b. Montgomery Co VA to M.J. BECKLEHYMER 16 yrs single b. Franklin Co VA; by A. McComas.

43. 1 May 1884 L.D. PATRICK 30 yrs wid. b. W VA now living in Tazewell Co VA to EMMA COMER 27 yrs single b. Montgomery Co VA; by P.S. Sutton.

44. 12 June 1884 EVAN EVANS 52 yrs wid. b. PA to JULIA BLANKENSHIP 22 yrs wid. b. Mercer Co W VA O: stone mason; by Romulus Harry.

45. 17 May 1884 JOSEPH K. COLE 20 yrs single b. Raleigh Co W VA now living same to TEXAS FOLEY 15 yrs single b. Mercer Co W VA O: farmer; by Charles Walker.

46. 16 Oct 1884 JOHN T. CALBIRD 23 yrs single b. Ash Co NC now living in Bland Co VA to ELIZABETH CANTRELL 21 yrs single b. Rockingham Co NC O: farmer; by Evan H. Brown.

47. 25 Dec 1884 GEO LIKENS 23 yrs single b. Floyd Co VA s/o Wm & Martha J. to ALMEDIA V.M.J. PENNINGTON 15 yrs single b. Mercer Co W VA d/o Gordon & Julia Ann O: farmer; by J.O. Cassaday.

Page 41

1. 7 Jan 1885 WM H. RANSOM 27 yrs single b. Buckingham Co VA s/o Henry T & Caroline V to ANNIE R. JOHNSON 19 yrs single b. Mercer Co W VA d/o John W. & M.D. O: lawyer; by James Calfee.

2. 14 Jan 1885 LEVI G. COMER 20 yrs single b. Mercer Co W VA s/o Jacob & Elizabeth to DICY A. PERDUE 15 yrs single b. Mercer Co W VA d/o Forgus & Nancy O: farmer; by A.J. Thompson.

3. 13 Jan 1885 GEORGE A. KIDD 31 yrs single b. Mercer Co W VA to NANCY A. KARNES 19 yrs single b. Summers Co VA d/o Wm & Catherine O: farmer; by James W. Lilly.

4. 18 Jan 1885 L.W. ROBINSON 35 yrs single b. Mercer Co W VA s/o Harrison & Harriet to MARGARET A. CALDWELL 20 yrs single b. Mercer Co W VA d/o Madison A. & Ann O: dentist; by Jas. O. Cassaday.

5. 19 Jan 1885 WM M. BAXTER 20 yrs single b. Giles Co VA now living same s/o W.D. & M.H. to MARINDA A. CRAWFORD 23 yrs single b. Raleigh Co VA d/o John & Susan O: railroader; by L. Goodwyn.

6. 4 Feb 1885 FLOYD DOSS 27 yrs wid. b. Giles Co VA to AMELIA HAUEKS(?) 22 yrs single b. Carrol Co NC d/o Wm & Polly O: farmer; by A.J. Young.

7. 11 Feb 1885 ELI JONES 24 yrs single b. Russell Co VA s/o Henry & Mary to ARMINDA R. BOWLING 18 yrs single b. Mercer Co W VA d/o A.W. & Lucinda O: farmer; by Romulus Harry.

8. 19 Feb 1885 WM A. STOVALL 24 yrs single b. Mercer Co W VA now living in Tazewell Co VA s/o A.G. & Nancy K. to HATTA A. HARRY 18 yrs single b. Mercer Co W VA d/o Calvin & Mary E. O: merchant; by D.H. Carr.

9. 25 Feb 1885 HENRY L. PETERS 22 yrs single b. Mercer Co W VA s/o Christian & Julina to ANNA E. RUNION 20 yrs sngle b. Mercer Co W VA d/o Elizabeth & ? O: farmer; by J.O. Cassaday.

10. 26 Feb 1885 WM L. JOHNSTON 23 yrs single b. Mercer Co W VA now living in Giles Co VA s/o Saml. & Mary E. to SALLIE F. SEUCE 23 yrs single b. Bedford Co VA d/o Saml H. & Sarah F. O: farmer; by Jas H. Johnston.

11. * * * JOHN T. VIA 25 yrs single b. Franklin Co VA s/o ? & Rachel to MARGARET A. HAULDRONZ 17 yrs single b. Mercer Co W VA d/o Tyressa J. HaldronZ O: farmer. (*Note: no date given) (ZNote: name spelled both ways.)

12. 4 Mar 1885 WM R. IRVIN 28 yrs single b. Bland Co VA s/o Isaac N. & Lucinda to WILLIE N. WALTHALT 26 yrs single b. Giles Co VA d/o Robt B. & Mary B. O: farmer; by Evan H. Brown.

13. 10 Mar 1885 CHARLES BOOTH 30 yrs single b. Franklin Co VA to HARRIET WILLIAMS 33 yrs wid. b. Franklin Co VA O: farmer; by A.J. Thompson; REMARKS: colored.

14. 11 Mar 1885 THOS W. LYNCH 47 yrs wid. b. Mercer Co W VA s/o John & Ann to MEDORA A. FAULKNER 33 yrs single b. Montgomery Co VA d/o ? & Susan O: farmer; by Evan H. Brown.

15. 12 Mar 1885 RUSSEL K. CALFEE 33 yrs single b. Mercer Co W VA s/o Wilson D. & Jane P. to MARY C. PINE 25 yrs single b. Mercer Co W VA d/o Alex & Rebecca O: farmer; by J.W. Bennett.

16. 19 Mar 1885 RUFUS H. BASHAM 23 yrs single s/o Joseph A. & Polly A. to MARY J. JESSIE 15 yrs single b. Monroe Co W VA d/o B.A. & Sarah O: farmer; by Andrew J. Young.

17. 30 Mar 1885 JAS H. WHITT 31 yrs div. b. Pulaski Co VA s/o Burgess & Mary to EMMA WAIMER 16 yrs single b. Tazewell Co VA d/o Isaac & Rebecca O: farmer; by J.T. Glover.

18. 8 April 1885 JOSHUA LILLY 66 yrs wid. b. Mercer Co W VA to NANCY E. LILLY 21 yrs single b. Mercer Co W VA O: farmer; by Jas W. Lilly.

19. 9 April 1885 JAS W. HARMAN 21 yrs single b. Floyd Co VA s/o Jos & Nancy to SARAH CECIL 19 yrs single b. Tazewell Co VA d/o James W. & Jane O: farmer; by T.K. Lambert.

20. 15 April 1885 JOS H. COMER 29 yrs single b. Mercer Co W VA s/o Jacob & Elizabeth to MARY E. WILEY 19 yrs single b. Mercer Co W VA d/o ? & Sina O: farmer; by A.J. Thompson.

21. 16 April 1885 GEO W. BOWLING 23 yrs single b. Mercer Co W VA s/o A.W. & Lucinda to LILLY ALICE HARRY 22 yrs single b. Mercer Co W VA d/o Romulus & Rutha J. O: farmer; by Romulus Harry.

22. 16 April 1885 RUFUS J. CARR 21 yrs single b. Giles Co VA s/o John T. & Nancy A. to ALBANY V. BAILEY 19 yrs single b. Mercer Co W VA d/o Leland & Rebecca O: farmer; by D.H. Carr.

23. 26 April 1885 JAS F. BAILEY 22 yrs single b. Mercer Co W VA s/o Henderson F. & Sarah to REBECCA J. SPADE 18 yrs single b. Mercer Co W VA d/o Saml A. & Rhoda O: farmer; by J.O. Cassaday.

24. 28 April 1885 WM HUFFMAN 22 yrs single b. Giles Co VA s/o Andrew J. & ? to NANCY E. FARMER 16 yrs single b. Mercer Co W VA d/o Wm H. & Sarah O: farmer; by Arch. McComas.

25. 4 May 1885 JAS WM. SCOTT 22 yrs single b. Monroe Co W VA s/o Joseph & Nancy to CORLIE V. WHITTAKER 22 yrs single b. Wythe Co VA d/o George O: carpenter; by Jas. Calfee.

26. * * * RO. N. KESSINGER 26 yrs single b. Giles Co VA s/o Silas M. & Annie J. to PERCILLA M. JONES 16 yrs single b. Franklin Co VA d/o Pinkney & Joanna O: carpenter; REMARKS: not used miss fit. (*Note: no date given.)

27. * * * CHAS G.C. WALKER 18 yrs single b. Raleigh Co W VA now living in Summers Co W VA s/o Numa & Martha A. to MINIAH S. STAFFMAN 17 yrs single b. Raleigh Co W VA d/o John L. & ? O: farmer. (*Note: no date given.)

28. 24 May 1885 DAVIS THORN 23 yrs single b. Giles Co VA s/o James P. & Mahavala T. to PAMELA STINSON 24 yrs single b. Mercer Co W VA d/o Chas & Elizabeth O: farmer; by J.T. Clover.

29. 28 May 1885 GEO W. HEARN 22 yrs single b. Raleigh Co W VA now living in Wyoming Co VA s/o William & Ida to VICTORIA ANGLE 15 yrs single d/o Aron & Sarah O: farmer; by T.K. Lambert.

30. 28 May 1885 ALLEN W. BROWN 25 yrs single b. Mercer Co W VA s/o John W. & Martha J. to EMMA E. BOLTON 25 yrs single b. Mercer Co W VA d/o Mathew W. & Mary F. O: farmer; by J.W. Bennett.

31. 3 June 1885 J.F. BUTTREY 22 yrs single b. Wilkes Co NC now living in Tazewell Co VA s/o J.T. & - to NANNIE BILLIPS 21 yrs single b. Tazewell Co VA d/o - & Francis O: farmer; by Evan H. Brown.

32. 11 June 1885 JONATHAN H. HOYA 27 yrs single b. Mercer Co W VA s/o Wm & Martha J. to CLARISON A. FARLEY 28 yrs single b. Mercer Co W VA d/o Jas H. & Mary O: farmer; by Jas W. Lilly.

33. 17 June 1885 JNO MILTON SNIDOW 30 yrs single b. Giles Co VA now living same s/o Wm B. & Nancy B. to MARTHA E. WALKER 22 yrs single b. Giles Co VA d/o Lewis & Jane D. O: farmer; by Phil S. Sutton.

34. 18 June 1885 JAS J. VIA 25 yrs single b. Franklin Co VA s/o Anderson & Nancy to LECTORY J. MILLS 17 yrs single b. Mercer Co W VA d/o Jas H. & Mary O: farmer; by Jas. O. Cassaday.

35. * * * R.A. LIPFORD 25 yrs single b. Tazewell Co VA now living in Pike Co KY s/o Richard A. & Fannie to CAROLINE BALL 24 yrs single b. Russell Co VA d/o Alfred & Annie O: saddle & harness maker. (*Note: no date given.)

36. 25 June 1885 ANDREW M. LAMBERT 19 yrs single b. McDowell Co W VA now living same s/o T.K. & Charlotte to ALICE G. BAILEY 21 yrs single b. Mercer Co W VA d/o Harry & Rosena O: farmer; by T.K. Lambert.

37. 27 June 1885 WM P. TAYLOR 23 yrs single b. Mercer Co W VA s/o William & Mary to WELTHY C. HODGE 20 yrs single b. Mercer Co W VA d/o George W. & Elizabeth O: farmer; by T.K. Lambert.

38. 2 July 1885 GEO W. STOWERTON 27 yrs single b. Wyoming Co W VA now living same s/o Reuben & Martha Ann to JENNIE BLANKENSHIP 17 yrs single b. Mercer Co W VA d/o Eli S. & Eliza O: farmer; by E. Howerton.

39. 30 June 1885 RUFUS W. FARLEY 26 yrs single b. Mercer Co W VA s/o Wilson & Lucinda to ALLEYFAIR V. MEADOR 21 yrs single b. Mercer Co W VA d/o Joseph & Elizabeth O: farmer; by Drewery Farley.

40. 5 July 1885 GREEN MOURIZ 24 yrs wid. b. Lincon Co W VA to VICTORIA SURFACE 26 yrs single b. Mercer Co W VA d/o Lef & Sarah O: farmer; by A.J. Young.

41. 29 July 1885 J.A. HARMAN 20 yrs single b. Grayson Co VA s/o Patrick & Sarah J. to JULIA A. SHRADER 15 yrs single b. Mercer Co W VA d/o Henry & Sarah O: farmer; by A.J. Young.

42. 29 July 1885 GEO T. RATLIFFE 21 yrs single b. Mercer Co W VA s/o James & Elizabeth to ARTHA C. HARMAN 17 yrs single b. Carroll Co VA d/o Patrick & Sarah J. O: farmer; by A.J. Young.

43. 9 Aug 1885 WM G. HELTON 26 yrs single b. Floyd Co VA s/o Elijah & Emily to MARIA J. DAVIS 21 yrs single b. Mercer Co W VA d/o Geo & Elizabeth J. O: farmer; by R.H. Hughes.

44. 25 Aug 1885 C.D. ROSS 23 yrs single b. Mercer Co W VA s/o John B. & Lee A. to SARAH E. LILLY 19 yrs single b. Mercer Co W VA d/o Rufus B. & Mary O: farmer; by Wm P. Lilly.

45. 27 Aug 1885 JOHN W. SHORTER 20 yrs single b. Mercer Co W VA s/o Woodson A. & Elizabeth to LOUENNA J. COOK 16 yrs single b. Mercer Co W VA d/o C.W. & Rhoda O: farmer; by Ward C. Keaton.

46. 17 Sept 1885 CHAS H. BURDETT 20 yrs single b. Mercer Co W VA s/o Jos C. & Anna W. to MARY F. DAVIS 18 yrs single b. Giles Co VA d/o Wm G. & Nancy O: farmer; by L. Goodwyn.

47. 15 Sept 1885 JOSEPH MURPHY 60 yrs single b. Logan Co W VA now living in Wyoming Co W VA s/o John & Jane to MARY L. MEDLEY 29 yrs single b. Mercer Co W VA O: farmer; by T.K. Lambert.

48. 3 Sept 1885 JEFFERSON D. SHUTT 23 yrs single b. Mercer Co W VA to MOLLY C. BAILEY 19 yrs single b. Mercer Co W VA O: farmer; by A.J. Young.

Page 42

1. 19 Sept 1885 F. HANAR COX 26 yrs single b. Mercer Co W VA now living in Tazewell Co VA s/o Mary & Joseph to MARY BAILEY 22 yrs single b. Mercer Co W VA d/o Leftwich & Sarah O: farmer; by D.N. Saunders.

2. 24 Sept 1885 JOHN C. MEADOWS 24 yrs single b. Mercer Co W VA to VICTORIA A. CLARK 16 yrs single b. Mercer Co W VA O: merchant; by W.C. Dobbins.

3. * * * JOHN MUNDA 25 yrs single b. VA to JULIA A. DUNFORD 25 yrs single b. Tazewell Co VA d/o J.W. & Phoebe E. O: farmer. (*Note: no date given.)

4. 27 Sept 1885 HENRY THOMPSON 27 yrs wid. b. Campbell Co VA s/o Jackson & Fansey to VICEY TAYLOR 17 yrs single b. Tazewell Co VA d/o William & Rosa O: railroader; by Romulus Harry.

5. 14 Oct 1885 WM W. HEYPES 19 yrs single b. Craig Co VA to VIRGINIA FARMER 17 yrs single b. Campbell Co VA O: farmer; by D.N. Saunders.

6. 14 Oct 1885 WALTER C. WALKER 26 yrs single b. Pittsylvanie Co VA now living in Tazewell Co VA s/o Thos H. & Lucy A. to MAURICE R. DUDLEY 15 yrs single b. Pulaski Co VA d/o Andrew J. & Elizabeth O: carpenter; by M.A. Wilson.

7. 21 Oct 1885 CHAS STINSON 63 yrs wid. b. Giles Co VA s/o Jacob & Mary S. to MARY L. DAWSON 36 yrs single b. Pulaski Co VA d/o Hiram A. & Sallie Dawson O: mason; by Phil S. Sutton.

8. 24 Oct 1885 WM F. LONGWORTH 29 yrs single b. Forsyth Co NC s/o Wm & Sarah Longworth to RUTHY NEWKIRK 22 yrs single b. Buchanan Co VA d/o Prather O: railroader; by Evan H. Brown.

9. 29 Oct 1885 JOHN MURRAY 22 yrs single b. Mayo Co Ireland now living in Tazewell Co VA s/o Thomas & Mary to ELIZABETH CROCKETT 18 yrs single b. Tazewell Co VA d/o James A. & Rachel O: miner; by James Calfee.

10. 1 Nov 1885 PHIL WASHINGTON 45 yrs wid. b. Rockbridge Co VA s/o George & Harriet to EMMA SMITH 23 yrs single b. Montgomery Co VA d/o ? & Catherine O: farmer; by P.C. Mays; REMARKS: colored.

11. 29 oct 1885 JNO D. CREWS 21 yrs single b. Mercer Co W VA s/o Aeg & Nancy to MARY J. MOYE 21 yrs single b. Mercer Co W VA d/o William & Martha O: farmer; by Jas W. Lilly.

12. 2 Nov 1885 JNO M. KESTER 25 yrs single b. Carroll Co VA s/o John & Elizabeth F. to EMMA F. ARCHER 23 yrs single b. Mercer Co W VA d/o James & Julina O: farmer; by P.C. Hays.

13. 11 Nov 1885 THOS P. CRAWFORD 36 yrs single b. Monroe Co W VA s/o Isaac & Nancy Crawford to ARTHELIA N. THOMPSON 22 yrs single b. Mercer Co W VA d/o Allen & Minerva A. O: farmer; by J.W. Bennett.

14. 2 July 1885 JOSEPH GARNER 40 yrs wid. b. Floyd Co VA now living in Tazewell Co VA to MALINDA F. VEST 25 yrs single b. Giles Co VA O: fcarpernter; by Benj. Dennis.

15. 8 Nov 1885 SAML P. SMITH 21 yrs single b. Washington Co TN s/o John H. & Mary J. to ROSA BELL LUSK 16 yrs single b. Raleigh Co W VA d/o Alfred E. & Henrietta W. O: railraoder; by L. Goodwyn.

16. 12 Nov 1885 WM R. HAMBRICK 21 yrs single b. Mercer Co W VA s/o Geo O. & Amy P. to NANCY R. BELCHER 18 yrs single b. Mercer Co W VA d/o Jas E. & Amanda Bel O: farmer; by Evan H. Brown.

17. 12 Nov 1885 PASCHAL B. BLANKENSHIP 19 yrs single b. Mercer Co W VA s/o Rebecca L. White to LILLY HAZLEWOOD 17 yrs single b. Mercer Co W VA d/o John & Nancy Hazlewood O: farmer; by A.J. Thompson.

18. 15 Nov 1885 WH FOSTER 19 yrs single b. Giles Co VA s/o ? & Lucy to MARY JANE BELCHER 21 yrs single b. Tazewell Co VA d/o Obediah & ? O: railraoder; by Evan H. Brown.

19. 17 Nov 1885 A.N. HAZLEWOOD 21 yrs single b. Stokes Co NC s/o Asa & Rachel to MARY E. KIDWELL 15 yrs single b. Giles Co VA d/o ? & Amanda E. O: farmer; by A.J. Thompson.

20. 20 Nov 1885 JOHN LILLY 28 yrs single s/o James & Elizabeth to KATE HARMAN 26 yrs single b. Orange Co OH d/o Richard & Mary O: mining; by Joseph Mullen.

21. 8 Dec 1885 R.J. STOKE 26 yrs single b. Alleghemy Co VA now living in Monroe Co W VA s/o Josiah & Margaret to L.F. GOTT 19 yrs single b. Mercer Co W VA d/o Andrew & Loucinda J. O: sewing machine agt; by Phil S. Sutton.

22. 13 Dec 1885 SAML G. SAWER 20 yrs single b. Mercer Co W VA to LARISSA E. LITTLE 18 yrs single b. Mercer Co W VA O: farmer; by P.C. Hays.

23. 24 Dec 1885 WM T. BALL 21 yrs single b. Montgomery Co VA s/o John M. & Henrietta B. to DELLIE M. COLE 18 yrs single b. Mercer Co W VA d/o Andrew J. & Mary O: farmer; by A.J. Thompson.

24. 17 Dec 1885 ED EVANS 20 yrs single b. Mechlenburg Co VA s/o Osborne & Rebecca to MARY LAMBERT 18 yrs single b. Tazewell Co VA d/o Jas H. & Amanda O: farmer; by Jas Calfee.

25. 17 Dec 1885 JAS W. TAYLER 20 yrs single b. Mercer Co W VA s/o John & Mary L. to MARY N. BAILEY 21 yrs single b. Mercer Co W VA d/o Thompson P. & Elizabeth O: farmer; by A.J. Young.

26. 26 Dec 1885 RUFUS M. DAVIDSON 22 yrs single b. Mercer Co W VA s/o James & Margaret A. to PEGGY ANN HILL 16 yrs single b. Mercer Co W VA d/o Davey & Louisa O: farmer; by T.K. Lambert.

27. 24 Dec 1885 EPHRAIM G. DEEP 22 yrs single b. Grayson Co VA s/o Ephraim & Lucy to LAURA E. MURRELL 19 yrs single b. Mercer Co W VA d/o Drury T. & Ellen O: farmer; by Jas Calfee.

28. 24 Dec 1885 B.W. BSREWSBURY 26 yrs single b. Mercer Co W VA s/o Saml & Elizabeth to JULIA F. McCOMAS 20 yrs single b. Mercer Co W VA d/o Archibald & Lewilla O: farmer; by D.K. Saunders.

29. 28 Dec 1885 F.D. ANDREWS 21 yrs single b. Mercer Co W VA s/o A.J. & Nancy Andrews to MARGARET C. CANDIFF 16 yrs single b. Bland Co VA d/o Nancy O: farmer; by C. Clark.

30. 31 Dec 1885 DENNIS HOGINS 67 yrs wid. b. Wythe Co VA s/o Patrick & Chloe to HANNAH IRVIN 50 yrs wid. b. Washington Co VA d/o Polly Craig & ? O: farmer; by C. Clark; REMARKS: colored.

31. 31 Dec 1885 FRANK IRVAN 26 yrs single b. Washington Co VA s/o Andrew & Sarah to FANNIE J.E. WALKINS 21 yrs single b. Washington Co VA d/o Wilson & Cynthia A. O: farmer; by C. Clark; REMARKS: colored.

32. 31 Dec 1885 D.L.G. LAMBERT 21 yrs single b. McDowell Co W VA now living same s/o Thos K. & Charlotte to MARY S. BAILEY 17 yrs single b. Mercer Co W VA d/o Henry & Rozenia O: farmer; by Jas. Calfee.

33. 24 Nov 1885 WM A. COOPER 44 yrs single b. Grayson Co VA to LOUCINDA N. CALFEE 32 yrs single b. Mercer Co W VA O: farmer; by Jas. Calfee.

34. 3 Dec 1885 LANDON E. DAVIS 22 yrs single b. Mercer Co W VA to NANCY ELLEN LYON 22 yrs single b. Wythe Co VA O: farmer; by A.J. Thompson.

Page 43

1. 1 Jan 1886 HENRY WOLLEN 30 yrs wid. b. Gallia Co OH now living in Tazewell Co VA s/o Alvin & Lucinda E. to ANN SADLER 23 yrs single b. Mercer Co W VA d/o Henry & Araminta O: miner; by E.F. Kahle.

2. 7 Jan 1886 NED T. BRIDGES 25 yrs single s/o Ned T. & ? to MARY E. LILLY 15 yrs single b. Mercer Co W VA d/o J.K. & Alabama O: farmer; by J.W. Bennett.

3. 13 Jan 1886 GEO A. WINFREY 19 yrs single b. Mercer Co W VA s/o Charles & Julina to LORETTA B. PETERS 19 yrs single b. Mercer Co W VA d/o Elijah C. & Tainer O: farmer; by Romulus Harry.

4. 26 Jan 1886 S.P. WHEELER 27 yrs single b. Bland Co VA s/o Henry P. & Bathsheba to MARTHA J. KINZER 26 yrs single b. Tazewell Co VA d/o Thos B. & Lucretia O: farmer; by Giles M. Johnston.

5. 4 Feb 1886 URLEY W. LITTLE 25 yrs single b. Mercer Co W VA now living in Wyoming Co W VA s/o Wm H. & Mary D. to JULIA A. ACORD 18 yrs single b. Wyoming Co W VA d/o Floyd & Elizabeth O: farmer; by T.K. Lambert.

6. 10 Feb 1886 TURNER D. WELLS 33 yrs wid. b. Mercer Co W VA s/o Alexander & Mary C. to M.B. GARRETSON 25 yrs single d/o H. Ingram & Ann O: carpenter; by M.A. Wilson.

7. 11 Feb 1886 FREDERICK JENNINGS 19 yrs single b. Carroll Co VA s/o Churchwell M. & Mary to LOURINDA HUBBARD 20 yrs single b. Mercer Co W VA d/o Jonathan & Virginia O: farmer; by James W. Lilly.

8. 24 Feb 1886 CHAS A. MORGAN 29 yrs single b. Campbell Co VA s/o Swan H. & Francis A. to JOSIE PINE 22 yrs single b. Mercer Co W VA d/o Alex & Rebeca O: farmer; by J.W. Bennett.

9. 1 Mar 1886 W. WINTON KARNES 25 yrs single b. Mercer Co W VA s/o Jas A. & Elizabeth to MARIETTA WHITE 19 yrs single b. Mercer Co W VA d/o Harman & Cynthia M. O: farmer; by J.W. Bennett.

10. 6 Mar 1886 A. JACKSON WILLIS 23 yrs single b. Floyd Co VA s/o D.R. & Stana to POLLY PETTRY 19 yrs single b. Mercer Co W VA d/o Jacob & Elizabeth O: farmer; by J.W. Bennett.

11. 3 Mar 1886 ROBERT MOORE 32 yrs single b. Durham Co Gt Britian s/o Wm & Mary Ann to ALLA RUNYON 24 yrs single b. Mercer Co W VA d/o James & Betsy O: miner; by E.F. Kahle.

12. 10 Mar 1886 LEE HUDGENS 23 yrs single b. Buckingham Co VA to LURENDA LOVINGS 18 yrs single b. Grayson Co VA d/o Thos & Adaline O: miner; by J.M. Spencer.

MERCER COUNTY, WEST VIRGINIA
Marriages 1854 - 1901

13. 8 Mar 1886 MARCUS W. HANCOCK 30 yrs single b. Bland Co VA s/o George & Julia to MAHALA HUGHES 23 yrs single b. Giles Co VA d/o George & Susan O: farmer; by L. Goodwyn; REMARKS: M.W. Hancock sworn.

14. 13 Mar 1886 JAMES CORNETT 22 yrs single b. Tazewell Co VA to LOUVENIA JAMISON 20 yrs single b. Mercer Co W VA d/o Steptor & ? O:miner; by J.H. Spencer.

15. 15 Mar 1886 ERASTUS W. COOPER 21 yrs single b. Summers Co W VA now living same s/o John S. & ? to MALISSA A. LILLY 21 yrs single b. Summers Co W VA d/o Josiah & Narcissa O: miller; by J.O. Cassaday; REMARKS: E.W.C. sworn.

16. 17 Mar 1886 WM ROBT. HUDSON 23 yrs single b. Pulaski Co VA s/o Wm & Elizth Hudson to CALLIE D. BAILEY 24 yrs single b. Mercer Co W VA d/o Jno M. & Sarah O: depot agent; by E.F. Kahle.

17. 25 Mar 1886 ADOLPHUS E. BROWN 25 yrs single b. Mercer Co W VA s/o John W. & Rhoda M. to SUSAN A. SHUMATE 15 yrs single b. Mercer Co W VA d/o Rufus & Sarah E. O: farmer; by P.C. Mays.

18. 26 Mar 1886 WM BARTRUM 21 yrs single b. Boyd Co KY s/o Wm & Malissa to ALMEDA F. SHREWSBURY 27 yrs wid. b. Mercer Co W VA d/o James & Louisa O: farmer; by A. McComas; REMARKS: Wm Bartrum sworn.

19. 28 Mar 1886 LOUIS LEVIDEER 36 yrs wid. b. Dominion of Canada s/o James W. & Phoebe E. to BELLE WILSON 17 yrs wid. b. Marshall Co W VA O: miller; by Cl Clark.

20. 20 Mar 1886 WM R. WHITEHEAD 21 yrs single b. Russell Co VA s/o Franklin C. & Mary A. to ARDELIA A. MEADOWS 19 yrs single b. Mercer Co W VA d/o Harvey D. & Victoria O: farmer; by A.J. Thompson.

21. 31 Mar 1886 CHAS L. HARVEY 29 yrs single b. Monroe Co W VA now living same to RHODA A MILLER 19 yrs single b. Mercer Co W VA d/o Richard & Rebecca J. O: farmer; by L. Goodwyn.

22. 31 Mar 1886 JAMES WIMMER 21 yrs single b. Mercer Co W VA s/o James & Elizabeth to EUGENIA A. BAILEY 19 yrs single b. Mercer Co W VA d/o Ballard P. & Sarah E. O: farmer; by Romulus Harry.

23. 1 April 1886 CEAS L HALL 21 yrs single b. Franklin Co VA s/o John R. Amanda E. to REBECCA MARTIN 24 yrs single b. Mercer Co W VA d/o Geo W. & ? O: farmer; by P.C. Mays.

24. 8 April 1886 IRVIN E. BAILEY 25 yrs single b. Mercer Co W VA s/o Jamison & Polly to ELECTRA V. SHREWSBURY 22 yrs single b. Mercer Co W VA d/o William & Sarah A.J. O: farmer; by A. McComas.

25. 9 April 1886 LEWIS HOBBS 21 yrs single b. Bland Co V s/o Thos & Julia to ELIZABETH BROWN 23 yrs single b. Mercer Co W VA d/o Ross & Eannah O: farmer; by E.F. Kahle; REMARKS: colored.

26. * * * HENRY LAWSON 31 yrs wid. b. Walabusha MS s/o Joseph & Vina to ELIZA LIN FLEMING 21 yrs single b. Giles Co VA d/o Jerry & Caroline O: shoemaker; REMARKS: colored. (*Note: no date given.)

27. 15 April 1886 NELSON PENNINGTON 22 yrs single b. Mercer Co W VA s/o Levi & Elizabeth to HATTIE SWINDLER 16 yrs single b. Mason Co W VA d/o John O: farmer; by J.G. Vicars.

28. 21 April 1886 WALTER V. PECK 25 yrs single b. Mercer Co W VA s/o Jacob A. & Larissa to SUE PECK 25 yrs single b. Monroe Co W VA d/o Erastus & Sarah O: farmer; by Giles M. Johnston.

29. 22 April 1886 JOHN F. NASH 21 yrs single b. Mercer Co W VA s/o ? & Ellen Meadors to MARIAH R.E. DAVIS 17 yrs single b. Mercer Co W VA d/o William & ? O: farmer; by John Wax.

30. 28 April 1886 MONTGOMERY LINKONS 24 yrs single b. Montgomery Co VA s/o Thos & Ellen to JANE HUBBARD 23 yrs single b. Mercer Co W VA d/o Jonathan & ? O: farmer; by Jas W. Lilly.

31. 28 April 1886 JOHN W. BLANKENSHIP 19 yrs single b. Mercer Co W VA s/o ? & Ellen to AGNES J. CALFEE 22 yrs single b. Mercer Co W VA d/o John & Jane O: farmer; by E.F. Kahle.

32. 29 April 1886 NELSON EAVES 30 yrs single b. Pulaski Co VA to LUCY DESPER 25 yrs single b. Louisa Co VA d/o John & Patience O: hotel waiter; by E.F. Kahle; REMARKS: colored.

33. 5 May 1886 JOS B. MEADOWS 25 yrs single b. Giles Co VA s/o Sampson & Mary to AMANDA M. NEELY 25 yrs single b. Mercer Co W VA d/o Wm G. & Delilah O: farmer; by L. Goodwyn.

34. 13 May 1886 ROBT L. CREWS 19 yrs single b. Mercer Co W VA s/o Acy & Nancy to LELIA C. BOWLING 18 yrs single b. Mercer Co W VA d/o M.A. & R.J. O: farmer; by Jas W. Lilly.

35. 13 May 1886 H.G. JONES 21 yrs single b. Kanawha Co W VA s/o Silas B. & Elizabeth to ROZENA LESLIE 22 yrs single b. Monroe Co W VA d/o John P. & Melvina O: farmer; by James B. Johnston.

36. 15 May 1886 CHAS W. McPEEK 30 yrs single b. Floyd Co VA s/o Clayburn & Celia A. to ELMIRA LOFFLIN 30 yrs single b. Adkin Co NC d/o Benj & Adith O: farmer; by Jas O. Cassaday.

37. 23 May 1886 WM CUNDIFF 34 yrs wid. b. Franklin Co VA s/o Eli & Rebecca to SALLIE SURFACE 20 yrs single b. Mercer Co W VA d/o G.W. & Amariliah O: carpenter; by D.N. Saunders.

38. 22 Aug 1886 CHESTINE GOINS 26 yrs single b. Pittsylvania Co VA s/o George & Eliza to NANNIE JAMISON 19 yrs single b. Wythe Co VA d/o Steptoe & Sidney O: miner; by Floyd Meadows; REMARKS: colored.

39. 2 June 1886 JOHN L. BOWDEN 19 yrs single b. Monroe Co W VA s/o J.C. & Mary Jane to ELIZABETH A. FARLEY 19 yrs single b. Mercer Co W VA d/o Wm & Elizabeth O: farmer; by James W. Lilly.

40. 16 June 1886 HENDERSON H. HALL 17 yrs single b. Montgomery Co VA s/o Jno H. & Henrietta to NAOMI HANKS 21 yrs single b. Floyd Co VA d/o Wm & Susan O: farmer; by A.J. Thompson.

41. 18 June 1886 HENRY HORTON 25 yrs single b. Carroll Co VA s/o Jacob & Sine to CALLIE R. ARGABRIGHT 15 yrs single b. Franklin Co VA d/o ? & Catherine O: farmer; by Carroll Clark.

42. 23 June 1886 CONRAD SPANGLER 25 yrs single b. Monroe Co W Va s/o Danl W. & Sarah C. to MARY A. JONES 25 yrs single b. Russell Co VA d/o Henry & Mary O: farmer; by Romulus Harry.

43. 28 June 1886 JAS A. PENNINGTON 21 yrs single b. Mercer Co W VA s/o Riley & Margaret to ETTABELL BROOKMAN 19 yrs single b. Pulaski Co VA d/o C. & Mary M. O: farmer; by J.W. Bennett.

44. 28 June 1886 C.B. SOWERS 24 yrs single b. Floyd Co VA now living in Tazewell Co VA s/o Major & Docia A.M. to CYNTHIA DAMEWOOD 19 yrs single b. Blank Co VA d/o S.M. & ? O: shoemaker; by Isaac Harman.

45. 1 July 1886 JAMES B. TERRY 29 yrs single b. Floyd Co VA s/o Saml B. & Lucinda to JULIA E. FLETCHER 16 yrs single b. Mercer Co W VA d/o ? & Mary J. O: farmer; by L. Goodwyn.

46. 6 July 1886 ALEXR. ABSHERE 25 yrs single b. Wythe Co VA s/o John & Nancy to ELIZABETH JONES 19 yrs wid. b. Bland Co VA d/o Wm & Sarah O: farmer; by Carroll Clark; REMARKS: Jas A. & Alex Abshere sworn.

47. 12 July 1886 JOS. TAYLOR 41 yrs wid. b. York England s/o Elias & Mary to SALLIE J. MINER 27 yrs single d/o T.P. & Elizth E. O: miner; by J.M. Spencer.

48. 18 July 1886 ROBT T. SHRADER 22 yrs single b. Mercer Co W VA s/o Robt & Cynthia J. to MARTHA SHRADER 18 yrs single b. Mercer Co W VA d/o David & Chloe O: farmer; by D.N. Saunders.

Page 44

1. 18 July 1886 JOHN T. SHUMATE 46 yrs wid. b. Mercer Co W VA now living in Giles Co VA s/o Anderson & Sallie to NANCY J. THOMPSON 36 yrs single b. Mercer Co W VA d/o Philip & Mary O: merchant; by J.P. Campbell.

2. 18 July 1886 JAMES P. FRENCH 22 yrs single b. Mercer Co W VA s/o John E. & malinda to ELIZA A. SMITH 20 yrs single b. Mercer Co W VA d/o John B. & Sarah G. O: farmer; by Jas. H. Johnston.

3. 23 July 1886 ALFRED PETTRY 20 yrs single b. Mercer Co W VA s/o ? & Louisa to NANNIE B. BROOKMAN 16 yrs single b. Pulaski Co VA d/o Augustus & Mary M. O: farmer; by J.W. Bennett.

4. 21 July 1886 JNO B. HEARN 36 yrs single b. Mercer Co W VA s/o Levi G. & Ora to ELIZABETH T. JARRELL 38 yrs wid. b. Tazewell Co VA d/o James & ? O: merchant; by J.O. Cassaday.

5. 28 July 1886 CHAVESS WATKINS 24 yrs single b. Halifax Co VA s/o Chavess & Sarah to SARAH JOHNSON 16 yrs single b. Pulaski Co VA d/o Abe & ? O: mining; by H.A. Wilson; REMARKS: colored.

6. 29 July 1886 CHAS G. TILLER 22 yrs single b. Tazewell Co VA s/o William & Louisa to MATILDA E. SHELTON 23 yrs single b. Patrick Co VA s/o Frederick & Easter O: shoemaker; by E.F. Kahle.

7. 5 Aug 1886 GEO T. DAVIS 20 yrs single b. Giles Co VA s/o Hiram & Julia Ann to REBECCA M.F. STEELE 17 yrs single b. Mercer Co W VA d/o Wm F. & Rhoda O: farmer; by A.J. Thompson.

8. 4 Aug 1886 JAS W. JONES 22 yrs single b. Tazewell Co VA s/o Elisha P. & Jeruha to ROSA BELLE DUNIGAN 16 yrs single b. Mercer Co W VA d/o Lewis & Nancy Jane O: farmer; by P.C. Mays.

9. 5 Aug 1886 LEANDER DISHMEL 24 yrs single b. Ardel Co NC now living in Tazewell Co VA s/o Wm & Hila Ann to SARAH KIRK 17 yrs single b. Tazewell Co VA d/o John F. & Annie O: mining; by Evan H. Brown.

10. 18 Aug 1886 JOSHUA L. CLYBURN 26 yrs single b. Giles Co VA now living in Giles Co VA s/o Wm B. & Maria to MARGARET A. JOHNSTON 23 yrs single b. Giles Co VA d/o James D. & Mary B. O: farmer; by J.W. Bennett.

11. 17 Aug 1886 GEORGE SHERWOOD 41 yrs single b. Essex England s/o George & Eliza to SARAH V. HUGHES 39 yrs wid. (No other info given) by E.F. Kahle.

12. 24 Aug 1886 THOS B. VIA 24 yrs single b. Floyd Co VA s/o George & Ann to VICTORIA J. BEARK 21 yrs single b. Mercer Co W VA d/o Jas & Esther C. O: railroader; by Jas B. Johnston.

13. 29 Aug 1886 JNO W. POWELL 24 yrs single b. Monroe Co W VA s/o John W. & Jane to MARY D. LITTLE 21 yrs single b. Mercer Co W VA d/o L.D. & Rhua O: railroader; by L. Goodwyn.

14. 2 Sept 1886 M.W. CHRISTIE 32 yrs single b. Monroe Co W VA s/o Jas M. & Cynthia P. to OZELLO R. CHATTING 22 yrs wid. b. Mercer Co W VA d/o John A. & Lucinda O: farmer; by Jas H. Johnston.

15. 2 Sept 1886 JAMES M. CANTRELL 23 yrs single b. Kanawha Co W VA to REBECCA J. RATLIFFE 19 yrs single b. Mercer Co W VA d/o James & Amanda E. O: carpenter; by D.K. Saunders.

16. 2 Sept 1886 GEORGE HOLLY 23 yrs single b. Tazewell Co VA s/o Henderson Holly & Malinda Compton to CHRISTENA ELIZ. NEAL 22 yrs single b. Bland Co VA d/o Gus Neal & Nancy J. Robinet O: farmer; by E.F. Kahle; REMARKS: colored.

17. 8 Sept 1886 AS K. KESSINGER 28 yrs single b. Giles Co VA s/o Silas M. & Annie J. to MARY E. JEWELL 17 yrs single b. Jackson Co W VA d/o Wm H. & Elizabeth O: carpenter; by Wm P. Lilly.

18. 9 Sept 1886 JNO W. TERRY 19 yrs single b. Floyd Co VA s/o A.J. & Martha J. to EDMONIA C. SMITH 17 yrs single b. Giles Co VA d/o Daniel L. & Fannie B. O: farmer; by L. Goodwyn.

19. 8 Sept 1886 EDWD. JONES 20 yrs single b. Augusta Co VA s/o James & Fanny to MARY HARRIS 19 yrs single b. Tazewell Co VA d/o Ab & Jane O: farmer; by Phil S. Sutton; REMARKS: colored.

20. 14 Sept 1886 JNO C. VERMILLION 28 yrs single b. Pulaski Co VA s/o J.B. & ? to CARRIE A. MEADOWS 19 yrs single b. Summers Co W VA d/o Uriah & Nancy O: physician; by Saml R. Wheeler.

21. 24 Sept 1886 WM G. MEADOW 26 yrs single b. Mercer Co W VA s/o Woodson & Amanda to VIRGINIA EMMA TEXAS HARVEY 13 yrs single b. Mercer Co W VA d/o Adam M. & Electra A. O: farmer; by Drewry Farley.

22. 23 Sept 1886 S.M. RICE 28 yrs single b. TN s/o David & Nancy to MINNIE T. JOHNSTON 17 yrs single b. Mercer Co W VA d/o Watson & Mary C. O: farmer; by J.S. Spencer.

23. 23 Sept 1886 THOS W. BROWN 20 yrs single b. Mercer Co W VA s/o John W. & Rhoda M. to REBECCA A. BROYLES 19 yrs single b. Monroe Co W VA d/o Andrew W. & Amanda O: farmer; by L. Goodwyn.

24. 28 Sept 1886 ISAAC CARTER 22 yrs single b. Buckingham Co VA s/o Charles & Sarah to MALINDA WEAVER 16 yrs single b. Floyd Co VA d/o James & Eliza O: railroader; by David Smith; REMARKS: colored.

25. 14 Oct 1886 RICHARD BAUHER 21 yrs single b. Forsythe Co NC s/o Dick & Chloe to MARY E. PASSEL 20 yrs single b. Franklin Co VA O: mining; by J.W. Patterson; REMARKS: colored.

26. 5 Oct 1886 WM H. STAFFORD 23 yrs single b. Montgomery Co VA s/o David & Henrietta to ANNA MAUD WILLIS 18 yrs single b. Mercer Co W VA s/o Wm H. & Louisa O: farmer; by Isaac S. Harman.

27. 7 Oct 1886 JOS B. ARGABRIGHT 20 yrs single b. Franklin Co VA s/o Jacob & Sene to JANE E. SCOTT 28 yrs single b. Mercer Co W VA d/o Crocket & Sarah A. O: farmer; by E.F. Kahle.

28. 14 Oct 1886 JAS W. DEWESE 21 yrs single b. Mercer Co W VA s/o Andrew & Rozena to MARTHA C. JOHNSTON 15 yrs single b. Mercer Co W VA d/o John L. & ? O: farmer; by A.J. Thompson.

29. 14 Oct 1886 THOS MANN 21 yrs single b. Mercer Co W VA to GEORGIE A. HEDLEY 18 yrs single b. Mercer Co W VA O: farmer; by A.J. Thompson; REMARKS: colored.

30. 14 Oct 1886 ELLIAH W. McBRIDE 20 yrs single b. Mercer Co W VA s/o Thos. & Lucetta to NANCY F. FERGUSON 17 yrs single b. Mercer Co W VA d/o J.B. & Sarah C. O: farmer; by Charles Walker.

31. 14 Oct 1886 FRANK C. FIELDER 24 yrs single b. Grayson Co VA s/o Dennis & Mary M. to MINNIE M. HONCHINS 17 yrs single b. Mercer Co W VA d/o Geo H. & Sarah A. O: clerk; by Wm P. Lilly.

32. 14 Oct 1886 JAS C. HUGHES 22 yrs single b. Mercer Co W VA s/o Cluff & Hollie to RENIE DANIELEY 26 yrs single b. Mercer Co W VA d/o Nehemiah & Derusha O: farmer; by Isaac S. Harman.

33. 28 Oct 1886 JEHIAL M. FLAMMER 23 yrs single b. Tazewell Co VA now living same m/o Jas H. & Elizabeth to LILLIE E. BROWN 19 yrs single b. Tazewell Co VA d/o Evan H & Martha E. O: miner; by Evan H. Brown.

34. 20 Oct 1886 MAXEY G. WITTEN 23 yrs single b. Tazewell Co VA now living same s/o Zachariah S. & Julia A. to SARAH H. BAILEY 19 yrs single b. Mercer Co W VA d/o Robt H. & Emma J. O: Cerus. of Revenue; by Edmund A. Tilly.

35. 21 Oct 1886 CHAS W. SHANNON 19 yrs single b. Mercer Co W VA s/o Saml. & Sarah A. to FLORILLA B. WRIGHT 19 yrs single b. Mercer Co W VA d/o ? & Lucy A. Wright O: farmer; by L. Goodwyn.

36. 21 Oct 1886 J.W.R. EVANS 22 yrs single b. Mercer Co W VA s/o Lewis & Susan to JANE GRIFFITH 24 yrs single b. Franklin Co VA d/o Beverly & Catherine O: blacksmith; by Jas H. Johnston.

MERCER COUNTY, WEST VIRGINIA
Marriages 1854 - 1901

37. 21 Oct 1886 JAS M. BAILEY 22 yrs single b. Mercer Co W VA s/o Geo P. & Elizabeth to ARAMINTA E. SHREWSBURY 19 yrs single b. Mercer Co W VA d/o Saml & Elizabeth R. O:farmer; by D.N. Saunders.

38. 28 Oct 1886 WM F. HEDRICK 30 yrs single b. Tazewell Co VA s/o Granville & Mary to COSBY SWADER 24 yrs single b. Mercer Co W VA d/o John & Nancy O: farmer; by D.N. Saunders.

39. 25 Oct 1886 ROBT BURNEY 46 yrs wid. b. Cumberland Co England now living in Tazewell Co VA s/o James & Sarah to SUSAN ADAMS 35 yrs div. b. Patrick Co VA d/o Daniel E. & Elizabeth O: mining; by L. Goodwyn.

40. 25 Oct 1886 DANL E. WRIGHT 63 yrs wid. b. Pittsylvania Co VA s/o Wm & Tetney to MARY BURNETT 21 yrs single b. Carroll Co VA d/o Benj. & ? O: miller; by L. Goodwyn.

41. 27 Oct 1886 GERMAN PENN 24 yrs single b. Roanoke Co VA to SOPHIA A. McCLINTOCK 23 yrs single b. Rome GA O: miner; by Jas H. Johnston; REMARKS: colored.

42. 3 Nov 1886 HIRAM HENDERSON 21 yrs single b. Pulaski Co VA s/o Peer & Christina to CLARISSA CHAPMAN 16 yrs single b. Mercer Co W VA d/o J. & Mary O: farmer; by D.N. Saunders; REMARKS: colored.

43. 11 Nov 1886 A.L. BICKNELL 20 yrs single s/o A.R. & M. Bicknell to M.J. LILLEY 15 yrs single b. Mercer Co W VA d/o Rufus & Mary O: farmer; by Wm P. Lilly.

44. 10 Nov 1886 MOSES DAWSON 25 yrs wid. b. Amherst Co VA s/o Willis & Nancy to ALICE MATHEWS 22 yrs single b. Pulaski Co VA d/o ? & Milley O: farmer; by Phil S. Sutton; REMARKS: colored.

45. 18 Nov 1886 WM J. LYON 18 yrs single b. Mercer Co W VA s/o John D. & Mary A. to AMANDA L. TABOR 19 yrs single b. Fayette Co W VA d/o George & Oliva O: farmer; by Jas W. Lilly.

46. 18 Nov 1886 EPHRAIM CALES 57 yrs wid. b. Greenbrier Co VA now living in Raleigh Co W VA s/o John & Mary to SARAH F. CREWS 43 yrs single b. Bedford Co VA d/o Asa & Martha O: farmer; by W.C. Dobbins.

47. * * * JAS H. CALDWELL 31 yrs single b. Mercer Co W VA s/o Geo W. & Elizabeth A. to FANNIE A. BELCHER 18 yrs single b. Mercer Co W VA d/o Wm W. & Julia A. O: farmer.(*No date given.)

48. 18 Nov 1886 WM R. MANNING 25 yrs single b. Mercer Co W VA s/o Andrew & Nancy J. to ARAMINTA C. CRAWFORD 24 yrs single b. Mercer Co W VA d/o Reuben & Margt B. O: blacksmith; by E.F. Kahle.

1. 24 Nov 1886 OLIVER J. SHEGGS 25 yrs single b. Fayette Co W VA s/o Jesse & Mary to ARAMINTA BAILEY 16 yrs single b. Mercer Co W VA d/o Thompson P. & Elizabeth O: carpenter; by J.R. Greever.

2. 24 Nov 1886 SAML SCOTT 24 yrs single b. Prince Edward Co VA s/o Robt Scott & Lettie Stills to MARY MILLER 16 yrs single b. Mercer Co W VA d/o Thomas & Elizabeth O: railroader; by Simon L. Mann; REMARKS: colored.

3. 2 Dec 1886 JESSE J. WEST 24 yrs single b. Bunkum Co NC s/o Zach & Elizabeth to ELIZABETH MARTIN 28 yrs single b. Mercer Co W VA d/o Geo W. & Nancy O: carpenter; by Jesse F. Snodgrass.

4. 20 Dec 1886 JEFFERSON SHELDON 25 yrs single b. Appomattox Co VA to BELLE JOHNSON 23 yrs single b. Russell Co VA O: miner; by A.J. Young; REMARKS: colored.

5. 14 Dec 1886 FRANK ROBINSON 25 yrs single b. Hanover Co VA to BETTIE FERGUSON 21 yrs single b. Russell Co VA O: miner; by Moses Johnson; REMARKS: colored.

6. 9 Dec 1886 WALTER D. EASTBURN 22 yrs single b. Galveston Co TX s/o David & Sarah to CATHARINE A. HARE 18 yrs single b. Mercer Co W VA d/o Isaac & Araminta O: railroader; by L. Goodwyn.

7. 16 Dec 1886 F.W. MITCHELL 36 yrs div. b. Pittsylvania Co VA to MARY J. PENDLETON 19 yrs single b. Raleigh Co W VA d/o ? & S.A. Pendleton O: farmer; by L. Goodwyn.

8. * * * THOS P. HAZLEWOOD 20 yrs 11 mos 18 dys single b. NC s/o John & Nancy to SARAH A. BELCHER 20 yrs single b. Raleigh Co W VA d/o J. Floyd & Martha O: farmer. (*Note: no date given.)

9. 29 Dec 1886 URA SPICER 21 yrs single b. Wilkes Co NC s/o Harvey & Nancy to NANCY J. HARMAN 16 yrs single b. Mercer Co W VA d/o Andrew & Lydia O: farmer; by T.K. Lambert.

10. 23 Dec 1886 JAS W. DAVIS 24 yrs single b. Mercer Co W VA s/o Len & Polly Ann to MARY F. GOODE 20 yrs single d/o George W. & ? O: carpenter; by J.W. Bennett.

11. 26 Dec 1886 ABNEW H. OVERSTREET 42 yrs single b. Bedford Co VA s/o Wm W. & Sophia to MATTIE S. ANGLE 21 yrs single b. Bedford Co VA d/o Henry Boswell & Paulina O: farmer; by L. Goodwyn.

12. 29 Dec 1886 SAML E. SEAL 25 yrs single b. Monroe Co W VA s/o James W. & Catherine to LOUISA C. SPANGLER 19 yrs single b. Giles Co VA d/o Danl W. & Sarah C. O: farmer; by Thos R. Morris.

13. 30 Dec 1886 JAS R. DUNFORD 19 yrs single b. Tazewell Co VA s/o J.W. & P.E. Dunford to ROSA B. GRIFFITH 17 yrs single b. Mercer Co W VA d/o S.B. & Catherine O:railroader; by Jas H. Johnston.

14. 29 Dec 1886 JAS McH. BAILEY 33 yrs wid. b. Mercer Co W VA s/o John M. & Sarah to ELIZTH F. ELLIS 19 yrs single b. Greenbrier Co W VA d/o O.J. & Jane Ellis O: farmer; by C. Clark.

1. 6 Jany 1887 GEO A. FORD 18 yrs single b. Mercer Co W VA s/o Lewis & Mary to LOUISA MERCHANT 24 yrs single b. Mercer Co W VA d/o Chas & ? O: farmer; by A.J. Thompson; REMARKS: colored.

2. 12 Jany 1887 JOS B. WHITT 25 yrs single b. Montgomery Co VA s/o F.T. & Mary to MARY B. THOMPSON 20 yrs single b. Mercer Co W VA d/o Wm H. & Rebecca O: farmer; by A.J. Thompson.

3. * * * JOHN R. TAYLOR 21 yrs single b. Bland Co VA s/o Jno N. & Martha J. to SARAH E. GILLS 21 yrs single b. Bland Co VA d/o Bingman & Mary M. O: farmer. (*Note: no date given.)

4. * * * WM RILEY SNYDER 22 yrs single b. Mercer Co W VA s/o Esom & Rhoda A. to MALINDA J. SNYDER 17 yrs single b. Mercer Co W VA d/o Wm R. & Dimotha O: farmer. (*Note: no date given.)

5. * * * JNO WM PURDUE 23 yrs single b. Giles Co VA s/o Council & Mary to ROSANIA PENNINGTON 27 yrs single b. Mercer Co W VA d/o Wm K. & Catherine O: farmer. (*Note: no date given.)

6. 20 Jany 1887 WM W. FORTNER 23 yrs single b. Pulaski Co VA s/o Jno & Minerva to PERMELIA A. WILLIAMS 16 yrs single b. Mercer Co W VA d/o Jno A. & ? O: farmer; by J.W. Bennett.

7. 8 Feby 1887 HENI J. WELLER 25 yrs single b. PA s/o E.B. & Margaret to CAROLINE W. CRAWFORD 23 yrs 11 mos single b. Mercer Co W VA d/o Thos B. & Elizabeth O: railroader; by L. Goodwyn.

8. * * * ELIAS JAS. HALE 33 yrs single b. Mercer Co W VA s/o Jno E. & Mary K. to MELISSA C. BAILEY 27 yrs single b. Mercer Co W VA d/o Leland & Rebecca O: farmer. (*Note: no date given.)

9. 17 Feby 1887 GEO HCALES 25 yrs single b. Patrick Co VA to NANCY M. STARKWELL 17 yrs single d/o F.T. & Mary Ann O: farmer; by J.M. Spencer; REMARKS: colored.

10. 17 Feby 1887 HENRY L. FARLEY 21 yrs single b. Summers Co W VA s/o James H. & Mary to ELIZA J. WANHOP 18 yrs single b. Mercer Co W VA d/o John K. & Elizabeth O: farmer; by Wm P. Lilly.

11. 16 Feby 1887 LOYD P. WALKER 26 yrs single b. Tazewell Co VA now living same s/o Saml & Sallie to EMMA GIVENS 25 yrs single b. Craig Co VA d/o Isaiah & Harriet O: farmer; by Jas H. Johnston.

12. 22 Feby 1887 FRED H. STREWBUCHER 22 yrs single b. Dorhmund Co Germany s/o Starmond & Henrietta to SARAH W. CALDWELL 18 yrs single b. Tazewell Co VA d/o J.H. & ? O: mining; by Edmund F. Tilly.

13. 23 Feby 1887 LEWIS A. PINE 30 yrs single b. Mercer Co W VA s/o Alexander & Rebecca to MARY C. BRIDGES 20 yrs single b. Franklin Co VA d/o Ned T. & Tupps O: farmer; by J.P. Campbell.

14. 14 Feby 1887 CYRUS M. BAILEY 23 yrs single b. Mercer Co W VA s/o Thompson & Mary to HARRIETT L. SINK 26 yrs wid. b. Mercer Co W VA d/o Morris & Susan O: farmer; by E.F. Kahle.

15. 3 Mar 1887 BENJ F. LAMBERT 23 yrs single b. Fayette Co OH s/o Edward & Mary to LAURA J. CRAWFORD 21 yrs single b. Tazewell Co VA d/o Reuben & Margaret O: mechanic; by J.O. Cassaday; REMARKS: Thos Crawford sworn.

16. 6 Mar 1887 GEO THOS FRENCH 21 yrs single b. Pulaski Co OH s/o Jno W. & Sallie to LOUVENIA J. BURNETT 21 yrs single b. Pulaski Co VA d/o J.B. & S.D. O: miner; by C.R. Brown; REMARKS: G.T. French sworn.

17. 10 Mar 1887 CHRIS C. IRVINE 19 yrs single b. Blanc Co VA s/o LN. & Lucinda to ELIZA C. SHORT 20 yrs single b. Russell Co VA d/o James & Elizabeth O: railroader; by Evan H. Brown.

18. 6 April 1887 WM C. WHITEKER 33 yrs single b. Wythe Co Va s/o Andrew & Virginia to MARGARET J. FARMER 18 yrs single b. Mercer Co W VA d/o Wm H & Sarah O: carpenter; by Archd. McComas.

19. 9 April 1887 ROBT LEWIS 24 yrs single b. Durham Co England s/o Thomas & Margaret to NELLIE CULLISS 19 yrs single b. Worsteishire Co England d/o Hezekiah & Sarah Ann O: miner; by M.A. Wilson.

20. 17 April 1887 JOHN W. FLETCHER 28 yrs single b. Mercer Co W VA s/o Isaac G. & Ardelia E. to ANN DARNELEY 36 yrs single b. Mercer Co W VA d/o Nehemiah & Derusha O: farmer; by J.W. Bennett.

21. 26 April 1887 THOS R. SHUPE 19 yrs single b. Johnson Co TN s/o John & Elizabeth to NANCY L. SPICER 15 yrs single b. Wilkes Co NC d/o William & Martha M. O: mining; by Thos R. Morris; REMARKS: R.C. Christie appt guardn. & consent given.

22. 27 April 1887 THOS F. BRAMMER 27 yrs single b. Mercer Co W VA now living in Raleigh Co W VA s/o James A. & Louisa to RACHEL E.B. LILLY 17 yrs single b. Mercer Co W VA d/o James & Estaline O: farming; by Wm P. Lilly.

23. 27 April 1887 E.K. RUMBURG 19 YRS single b. Mercer Co W VA s/o Wm J. & Nancy J. to ELIZA MOONEY 19 yrs single b. Mercer Co W VA d/o Stynax L. & Susannah O: farming; by A.J. Young.

24. 27 April 1887 ANDRW C.F. FRENCH 20 yrs single b. Tazewell Co VA now living same s/o Jas D. & Reddie E. to MARTHA E. DOYLE 19 yrs single b. Mercer Co W VA d/o Jas A. & Martha A. O: farming; by J.O. Cassaday.

25. 5 May 1887 FLOURNOY C. JEWEL 20 yrs single b. Montgomery Co VA now living same s/o Thos & Catherine to IDA B. PICKERING 22 yrs single b. TN d/o David & Sarah O: farming; by Carroll Clark.

26. 9 May 1887 BENJ P. PENNINGTON 28 yrs single b. Mercer Co W VA s/o John A. & Ellen to ELIZABETH KENTLEY 24 yrs single b. Mercer Co W VA d/o John & Susan O: farming; by A.J. Thompson.

27. 27 May 1887 JAMES BALL 27 yrs single b. Russell Co VA s/o Alfred & Anna to JANE RATLIFF 35 yrs single O: farming; by Evan H. Brown.

28. 22 May 1887 F.C. WHITEHEAD 47 yrs wid. b. Smythe Co VA s/o Jas Sprinkle & Rhoda Whitehead to ELIZTH BAILEY 25 yrs single b. Johnson Co TN d/o Robert & Elizth A. O: farming; by Jas O. Cassaday.

29. 22 May 1887 DANL F. HALE 21 yrs single b. Giles Co VA now living same s/o Danl P. & Martha to SENORA BELL KARNES 20 yrs single b. Mercer Co W VA d/o Jas A. & ? O: Asst. Depot Agt; by Thos R. Morris.

30. 25 May 1887 WM MILLER 22 yrs single b. Montgomery Co VA s/o John & Harriett to MARY COBURN 22 yrs single b. Mercer Co W VA d/o David & Catherine O: farmer; by D.N. Saunders.

31. 31 May 1887 HENRY L. CARVER 21 yrs single b. Bland Co VA s/o James & Mary to ALMEDA PENNINGTON 15 yrs single b. Mercer Co W VA d/o Wm R & Catherine O: farmer; by L. Goodwyn; REMARKS: H. Carver sworn.

32. 2 June 1887 W.B. HAVELY 29 yrs wid. b. Claiborne Co TN now living in Tazewell Co VA s/o Charles & Eliza to NANNIE P. HAMMOCK 29 yrs wid. b. Franklin Co VA d/o Amos & Mary J. Gore O: blacksmith; by Edmund Tilly.

33. 2 June 1887 W.H.B. WRIGHT 36 yrs single b. Mercer Co W VA s/o Wm J. & ? to VIOLA T. FIELDER 24 yrs wid. b. Tazewell Co VA d/o Joseph & Cynthia O: farmer; by E.F. Kahle.

34. 2 June 1887 T.D. WALDRON 26 yrs single b. Pittsylvania Co VA s/o Andrew & Martha to JULIA A. HARE 21 yrs single b. Giles Co VA d/o Joseph & Julia O: farmer; by A.J. Thompson.

35. 8 June 1887 VINCENT W. WILSON 21 yrs single b. Buchannon Co VA s/o Wm & Martha to EASTER J. HAGAR 18 yrs single b. Mercer Co W VA d/o A.G. & Nancy O: farmer; by D.N. Saunders.

36. 18 June 1887 WM F. ROSS 22 yrs single b. Mercer Co W VA s/o Burley & Nancy to ROMANZIE B. LILLY 20 yrs single b. Mercer Co W VA d/o Jno E. & Julina O: farmer; by Jas Sweeney.

37. 19 June 1887 JOHN R. BOYD 23 yrs single b. Mercer Co W VA s/o Wm S. & Marinda to A.L.J. STEARN 17 yrs single b. Mercer Co W VA d/o L.L. & Rhoda O: depot agent; by L. Goodwyn.

38. 22 June 1887 MORTON R. EMMONS 30 yrs single b. Mercer Co W VA now living in Tazewell Co VA s/o Oscar J. & Mary E.C. to VIRGINIA E. WILSON 24 yrs single b. Rockbridge Co VA d/o M.A. & Elizth J; by J.P. Campbell.

39. 27 June 1887 C.L. CROTTY 38 yrs wid. b. Monroe Co W VA now living same s/o Michael & Mary to MATILDA CAMPBELL 32 yrs single b. Monroe Co W VA d/o Cyrus & Susan O: farmer; by J.P. Campbell.

40. 20 June 1887 ROBT LEE AUSTIN 23 yrs single b. Mercer Co W VA s/o Edwd & Malinda to MARGT L. CARTER 15 yrs single b. McDowell Co W VA d/o Thos & Elizabeth O: farmer; by E.F. Kahle.

41. 30 June 1887 JAS W. WOOD 26 yrs single b. Mercer Co W VA s/o German & Nancy to MARY J. HILLON 31 yrs single b. Raleigh Co W Va d/o Davis & ?; by James W. Lilly.

42. 30 June 1887 W.A. SARVER 20 yrs single b. Giles Co VA s/o James M. & Matilda to MARY L. BAILEY 17 yrs single b. OH d/o ? & Nancy O: farmer; by Carroll Clark.

43. 30 June 1887 W.L.G. FRENCH 25 yrs single b. Mercer Co W VA now living in Tazewell Co VA s/o Wm K. & Martha to FANNIE W. BAILEY 19 yrs single b. OH d/o ? & Nancy O:farmer; by Carroll Clark.

44. 1 July 1887 J. MARSHALL HALL 21 yrs single b. Franklin Co VA s/o Preston B. & Mary J. to MARY L. GRIFFITH 17 yrs single b. Mercer Co W VA d/o S.B. & R.C. O: farmer; by J.C. Hannon; REMARKS: J. Marsh Hall sworn.

45. 4 July 1887 JACOB STOBBS 22 yrs single b. Washington Co VA s/o Madison & Nancy to EMILY E. MARTIN 23 yrs single b. Giles Co VA d/o Chas & Elizabeth O: farmer; by Jacob Hobbs.

46. 8 July 1887 FRANCIS H. RULOFF 30 yrs single b. Prusia Germany s/o Herman & Annie to MATTIE E. KIOUS 23 yrs single b. Fayette Co W VA d/o Jas H. & Isabella O: mining; by J.B. Simpson.

47. 12 July 1887 DENNIS HOLT 22 yrs single b. Floyd Co VA s/o James & Julia to MINERVA E. HIX 17 yrs single b. Mercer Co W Va d/o ? & Jane O: farmer; by D.N. Saunders.

48. 15 July 1887 JOHN LOCK 31 yrs single b. Roan Co NC s/o Joseph & Eliza to MARY FULLER 30 yrs single b. Wythe Co VA d/o John & ? O: mining; by A.J. Young; REMARKS: colored.

49. 19 May 1887 COLUMBUS ROSE 19 yrs single b. Grayson NC to ELIZA ANN WOOD 18 yrs single b. Mercer Co W VA O: farming; by James W. Lilly.

50. * NOTE:* Line is cut off at bottom - Cannot be read on original.

Page 47

1. 6 Sept 1887 THOMAS MILES 35 yrs single b. Campbell Co VA s/o Moses Miles & Milly Oley(sic) to ALICE OLEY 23 yrs single b. Bedford Co VA d/o Edward & Lucinda O: mining; by J.C. Maness; REMARKS: colored, Thos Miles sworn.

2. 24 July 1887 J.H. NORMAN 23 yrs single b. NC s/o ? & Mary Norman to LAURA E. GORDON 24 yrs single b. NC d/o Granville & Mary O: mining; by A.J. Young.

3. 24 July 1887 WILLIAM RISKY 24 yrs single b. Gauldapa Germany s/o Joseph & Anna Risky to JOSEPHINE GRIFFITH 20 yrs single b. Pulaski Co VA d/o S.B. & M.C. Griffith O: mining; by A.J. Young; REMARKS: sworn by S.B. Griffith & Wm Risky.

4. 28 July 1887 JAS H. SHREWSBURY 17 yrs single b. Raleigh Co W VA now living same s/o Geo W. & Malinda to SARAH E. CUNNINGHAM 14 yrs single b. Wyoming Co W VA d/o Jas H. & Sarah J. O: farmer; by Archd McComas.

. 11 Aug 1887 WM A. JEWELL 22 yrs single b. Montgomery Co VA s/o J.G. & H.M. to FLORENCE A.LVIPPERMON 21 yrs single b. Pulaski Co VA d/o Emanl J. & Rachel O: miner; by J.C. Maness; REMARKS: Mr. Jewell sworn.

6. 9 Aug 1887 A.B. ARGABRIGHT 22 yrs single b. Franklin Co VA s/o C.W. & Elizabeth to HARRIET P. BELCHER 22 yrs single b. Mercer Co W VA d/o H.M. & Clemintine O: farmer; by E.F. Kahle.

7. 7 Sept 1887 MAT S. WOODALL 52 yrs wid. b. Mechlenburg Co VA s/o Jacob & Martha to SARAH E. BLANKENSHIP 34 yrs single b. Mercer Co W VA d/o ? & Lucinda O: farmer; by Jas H. Johnston.

8. 13 Aug 1887 JAS E. POE 23 yrs single b. Alleghany Co NC s/o Jeremiah & Cynthia to MARTHA J. KENNEDY 23 yrs single b. Franklin Co VA d/o Jas L. & Mary O: farmer; by Romulus Harry.

9. 24 Aug 1887 CHAS H.F. HALL 19 yrs single b. Mercer Co W VA s/o Preston B. & Mary J. to MARTHA BUCKLAND 23 yrs sngle b. Tazewell Co VA d/o Hugh & ? O: farmer; by J.O. Cassaday.

10. 30 Aug 1887 FRANK W. TINCHER 20 yrs single b. Monroe Co VA now living in Summers Co W VA s/o W.C. & E.A. to PAULINE A. DAVIS 18 yrs single b. Giles Co VA d/o Wm L. & Rhoda O: farmer; by L. Goodwyn.

11. 10 Sept 1887 BENJ. HENDERSON 24 yrs single b. Pulaski Co VA s/o Peer & Christina to RHODA HAYWOOD 21 yrs single b. Mercer Co W VA O: farmer; by Phil S. Sutton; REMARKS: colored.

12. 4 Sept 1887 HENRY HARRIS 21 yrs single b. Amherst Co VA s/o Anderson & Susan to MARY RICHARDSON 22 yrs single; by J.C. Maness; REMARKS: colored.

13. 11 Sept 1887 ELLIAH D. MITCHUM 61 yrs single b. McDowell Co VA s/o Jordan & Hannah to JANE THOMPSON 38 yrs single b. Franklin Co VA d/o Preston B. & Mary O: farmer; by Jas O. Cassaday.

14. 14 Sept 1887 JNO D. KUTZNER 25 yrs single b. Northumberland Co PA now living in Luzerue Co PA s/o Wm R. & Anna M. to PHOEBE W. BOWEN 25 yrs single b. Schuylkill Co PA d/o Jonathan & ? O: pharmacist; by J.C. Maness.

15. 18 Sept 1887 H.H. CLARK 42 yrs single b. Halifax Co VA s/o Thos M. & Susan E. to ELVIRA J. HAMBRICK 36 yrs single b. Mercer Co W VA d/o Riley & Margaret O: mining; by A.J. Young; REMARKS: by Riley Hambrick.

16. 22 Sept 1887 LEANDER J. LILLY 29 yrs single b. Mercer Co W VA s/o Turner & Artie to CYNTHIA PITMAN 27 yrs single b. Raleigh Co W VA d/o John & Malinda O: farmer; by James W. Lilly.

17. 9 Oct 1887 LANDAN HALO 28 yrs single b. Franklin Co VA s/o Doc & Louisa to JULIA A. TURNER 26 yrs wid. b. Franklin Co VA d/o Mose & Louise Radford O: mining; by A.J. Young; REMARKS: by letter of A.J. Young.

18. 13 Oct 1887 W.C. DUGGER 22 yrs single b. Johnson Co TN s/o Wm & Mary to CYNTHIA C. BURNETT 18 yrs single b. Pulaski Co VA d/o J.B. & S.D. O: mining; by J.H. Spencer.

19. 12 Oct 1887 ELLIAH L. BAILEY 23 yrs single b. Mercer Co W VA s/o Leftwich & Sarah to HARRIET L. SAUNDERS 16 yrs single b. Mercer Co W VA d/o D.N. & Jane O: farming; by D.N. Saunders; REMARKS: permission of D.N. Saunders.

20. 16 Oct 1887 HIRAM A. PRINCE 27 yrs wid. b. Mercer Co W VA s/o Oscar F. & Margaline to SARAH E. GRIFFITH 27 yrs single b. Montgomery Co VA d/o Shedrach & Cathrine O: farming; by A.J. Young.

21. 8 Nov 1887 WM H. THOMAS 25 yrs single b. Wales now living in Tazewell Co VA s/o Wm H. & Margaret to ANNIE E. COOPER 20 yrs single d/o John & Maria O: clerk store; by E.A. Filly.

22. 3 Nov 1887 HENRY B. POE 18 yrs single b. Mercer Co W VA s/o Thomas F. & Nancy E. to ELIZABETH FORTUNE 17 yrs single O: farmer; by D.N. Saunders.

23. 3 Nov 1887 EDWARD HUFF 21 yrs single b. Franklin Co VA s/o Jas V. & ? to VIRGINIA F. DILLION 18 yrs single b. Mercer Co W VA d/o ? & Matilda J. O: farmer; by J.C. Maness; REMARKS: by J.H. Kincade.

24. 6 Nov 1887 JOEL NOBLE 23 yrs single b. Summers Co W VA now living same s/o L.B. & Eliza to JANE DANIELEY 24 yrs single b. Mercer Co W VA d/o Nehemiah & Jerisha O: farmer; by J.C. Maness.

25. 10 Nov 1887 RICHARD JOHNSTON 22 yrs single to LUCY JOHNSTON 19 yrs single d/o ? & Charlotte; by J.C. Maness; REMARKS: by C.H. Dahring.

26. 10 Nov 1887 JAS W. JOHNSTON 26 yrs single b. Mercer Co W VA s/o Wm & Sarah to NANNIE J. CAHILL 29 yrs single b. Giles Co VA d/o Perry J. & Elizth A. O: farmer; by J.O. Cassaday.

27. 12 Nov 1887 JOHN W. KING 22 yrs single b. Floyd Co VA s/o Jas H. & Mildrege J. to SARAH E. MAXIE 17 yrs single b. Mercer Co W VA d/o Edgar & Annie O: farmer; by James W. Lilly.

28. 27 Nov 1887 J.E.T. SEUCE 24 yrs single b. Botetourt Co VA to FANNIE J. CALFEE 18 yrs single b. Mercer Co W VA d/o Henry S. & L.J. O: Asst R.R. Agt; by J.H. Johnston; REMARKS: by T.L. Henritze.

29. 23 Nov 1887 WM J. RICE 28 yrs single b. Green Co TN s/o David & Nancy A. to EMMA T. NEAL 21 yrs single b. Mercer Co W VA d/o Henry M. & Sallie O: carpenter; by John H. Romano.

30. 24 Nov 1887 ALBERT EDWIN BAILEY 25 yrs single b. Tazewell Co VA s/o Estill & Agnes to MARY ELLEN CALFEE 25 yrs single b. Mercer Co W VA d/o Wilson D. & Jane O: jailer; by Carroll Clark.

31. 28 Nov 1887 CHAS T. GARLICK 25 yrs single b. Montgomery Co VA s/o Jas F. & Boreus to IDA J. AKERS 24 yrs single b. Franklin Co VA d/o ? & Bettie; by J.H. Kennedy.

32. 10 Dec 1887 J.H. CLARE 27 yrs single b. Wuthe Co VA s/o Thomas & Clarinda to ELLA B. HODGE 23 yrs single b. Giles Co VA d/o James & Araminta O: farmer; by J.P. Campbell.

33. 21 Dec 1887 GEO T. DAVIDSON 26 yrs single b. Mercer Co W VA s/o Joseph & Jane to MARY A. FREEMAN 22 yrs single d/o John O: farmer; by J.C. Maness.

34. 17 Dec 1887 JOHN SCALES 21 yrs single b. Patrick Co VA s/o Jno & Ann to FANNEY L. HARTWELL 17 yrs single b. Pulaski Co VA d/o Z.T. & Mary Ann O: farmer; by J.C. Maness; REMARKS: colored, by mail to Wm Booth & Co.

35. 22 Dec 1887 CHAS A. DINGER 28 yrs single b. Campbell Co KY s/o Aug & Kate to SARAH JANE PERDUE 18 yrs single b. Mercer Co W VA d/o James & Sarah E. O: miner; by Evan H. Brown.

36. 22 Dec 1887 JOHN SWADER 23 yrs single b. Mercer Co W VA s/o Henry & Sarah to GERUSHA B. DILLION 19 yrs single b. Mercer Co W VA d/o H.F. & Hercina O: miner; by J.C. Maness.

37. 26 Dec 1887 FRANK GOFF 26 yrs single b. Albemarle Co VA now living in McDowell Co W VA s/o John & Maggie to BELL GRIFFIN 27 yrs single b. Lynchburg VA d/o Elliott & Maggie; by A.J. Young; REMARKS: colored.

38. 23 Dec 1887 JNO H. KING 24 yrs single b. Floyd Co VA s/o John T. & Serelda F. to ELIZTH N.B. HARMAN 16 yrs single b. Mercer Co W VA d/o Patrick & Sarah J. O: farmer; by Phil S. Sutton.

39. 24 Dec 1887 JAMES RUDISILL 27 yrs single b. Wuthe Co VA to AMERICA RATCLIFF 16 yrs single b. Mercer Co W VA d/o James & Elizabeth O: miner; by A.J. Young; REMARKS: by Edward Hugg.

40. 24 Dec 1887 THOS J. PENNINGTON 21 yrs single b. Mercer Co W VA s/o Fordon E. & Juliet to MALINDA WORKMAN 18 yrs single b. Mercer Co W VA d/o Robt & Jane O: farmer; by J.H. Kennedy.

41. 25 Dec 1887 JAS L. CALFEE 30 yrs single b. Mercer Co W VA s/o Wilson D. & Jane to MARY JANE BAILEY 27 yrs single b. Mercer Co W VA d/o Essill & Agnes O: farmer; by Jas H. Johnston.

42. 26 Dec 1887 FRANK HAWKS 22 yrs single b. Grayson Co VA s/o Wm R. & Polly to RACHEL H. BELCHER 17 yrs single b. McDowell Co W VA d/o Robt C. & Louise L. O: farmer; by T.R. Lambert.

43. 28 Dec 1887 THOS L. CATO 24 yrs single b. Smyth Co VA s/o David & Rachel to AGNES L. SHELTON 17 yrs single b. Nelson Co VA d/o London & ? O: farmer; by J.C. Maness; REMARKS: colored.

44. 28 Dec 1887 CHAS M. BELCHER 20 yrs single b. Tazewell Co VA s/o Isom G. & Mary E. to MAGGIE M. DAY 18 yrs single b. Mercer Co W VA d/o Lewis G. & Elizth A. O: farmer; by J.O. Cassaday.

45. 29 Dec 1887 CHARLES BELL 21 yrs single b. Mercer Co W VA s/o James & Julia to BELL A. MOORE 26 yrs single b. Roanoke VA d/o Napoleon A. & Martha O: farmer; by D.N. Saunders.

46. * * * JAMES E. JONES 28 yrs single b. Giles Co VA s/o Alex & ? to EDNA E. HARE 19 yrs single b. Marion Co Iowa d/o Isaac & Araminta O: farmer; by D.N. Saunders. (*Note: no date given.)

Page 48

1. 12 Jan 1888 CURVIN L. POE 20 yrs single b. Mercer Co W VA s/o Hezekiah & Henrietta to ELIZTH C. FIELDER 19 yrs single b. Grayson Co VA d/o Dennis & Mary; by Evan H. Brown.

2. 18 Jan 1888 JAS D. SURFACE 24 yrs single b. Montgomery Co VA s/o Augustus & Jane A. to MARY E. SURFACE 27 yrs single b. Mercer Co W VA d/o Marta & Tobitha; by D.N. Saunders.

3. 18 Jan 1888 BOSTON THOMAS 42 yrs single b. Mercer Co W VA s/o Jesse & Rachel to NALE KING 21 yrs single b. Giles Co W VA O: farmer; by L. Goodwyn.

4. 19 Jan 1888 A.M. THORNTON 30 yrs single b. Mercer Co W VA s/o Jas A. & Louisa to LULA RICE 17 yrs single b. Monroe Co W VA d/o ? & Malinda; by L. Goodwyn.

5. 19 Jan 1888 ALLEN A. PARKER 26 yrs single b. Mercer Co W VA s/o Jas. & Mary J. to MARY J. UNDERWOOD 37 yrs wid. b. Mercer Co W Va s/o Moses & Serena O: farmer; by M.A. Wilson; REMARKS: A.A. Parker sworn.

6. 19 Jan 1888 HENRY P. NEAL 52 yrs wid. now living in Bland Co VA to AMANDA J. ELLIS 34 yrs wid. b. Monroe Co W VA O: farmer; by Thos R. Morris.

7. 2 Feb 1888 R.L. LESLIE (No other on husband given) to ELIZABETH J. CARTER 39 yrs div. b. Tazewell Co VA d/o ? & Polly; by M.A. Wilson.

8. 24 Jan 1888 JONATHAN K. JENNINGS 24 yrs single b. Carrol Co VA s/o Churchwell M. & Mary to LUCY A. McKINNEY 18 yrs single b. Mercer Co W VA d/o Powhatan & M. O: carpenter; by J.O. Cassaday.

9. 29 Jan 1888 CORNELIUS TURPIN 23 yrs single b. Bedford Co VA s/o ? & Emily to NANCY FANTROY 26 yrs wid. b. Bedford Co VA d/o Geo. Clark O: miner; by A.J. Young; REMARKS: colored.

10. 2 Feb 1888 WILLIS C. WHITE 27 yrs single b. Mercer Co W VA s/o Harman & Cynthia M. to AMANDA H. KARNES 16 yrs single b. Mercer Co W VA d/o Henry & Elizabeth C. O: farmer; by J.W. Bennett.

11. 2 Feb 1888 H.C. JEWELL 34 yrs single b. Pike Co KY s/o Soloman & Jane to MARY TUCKETT 23 yrs single b. NC d/o James; by Evan H. Brown.

12. 2 Feb 1888 JORDAN MANUAL 23 yrs single b. Montgomery Co VA s/o ? & Jennie to CATHERINE WADE 25 yrs wid. b. Franklin Co VA d/o Jackson & Margaret O: miner; by A.J. Young; REMARKS: colored.

13. 2 Feb 1888 CHAS C. STEVENS 20 yrs single b. Giles Co VA s/o John & Sarah A. to GEORGIANA GRIGGSBY 21 yrs single b. Mercer Co W VA d/o ? & Mary O: farmer; by A.J. Thompson; REMARKS: colored.

14. 2 Feb 1888 WILSON LEE BAILEY 50 yrs wid. b. Mercer Co W VA s/o Burrell B. & Nancy to LOUISA J. FLETCHER 39 yrs single b. Mercer Co W VA d/o Isaac & ? O: miller; by Archd McComas.

15. 9 Feb 1888 ALBERT TABOR 22 yrs single b. Tazewell Co VA s/o Albert & Matilda to MARTHA P. PERDUE 16 yrs single b. Mercer Co W VA d/o Jas H. & Sarah E. O: farmer; by Evan H. Brown.

16. 7 Feb 1888 JAS J. MARTIN 20 yrs single b. Mercer Co W VA s/o Wm K. & Cynthia J. to ARRAHAH E. ROWEN 21 yrs single b. Patrick Co VA d/o P.F. & Nancy J. O: farmer; by J.W. Bennett.

17. 9 Feb 1888 ANDW JACKN NEAL 28 yrs single b. Bland Co VA s/o Robt M. & Martha to HOLLIE CARPER 19 yrs single b. Tazewell Co VA d/o Jeremh & Rebecca O: farmer; by Thos R. Morris.

18. 14 Feb 1888 EDWIN V. BARR 35 yrs wid. b. Little Falls NJ to LILLIE S. JOHNSON 21 yrs single b. Mercer Co W VA d/o Jas D. & Mary V. O: dyer; by J.W. Bennett.

19. 15 Feb 1888 THOS J. MONROE 39 yrs single b. Campbell Co VA s/o John & Parmelia to MINNIE B. BLANKENSHIP 16 yrs single b. Mercer Co W VA d/o Robt & Cynthia O: merchant; by J.F. Campbell.

20. 19 Feb 1888 JAS P. SHREWSBURY 24 yrs single b. Mercer Co W VA s/o Philip & Margie to AMANDA B. HURST 19 yrs single b. Mercer Co W VA d/o Jas H. & Sarah O: farmer; by Archd. McComas.

21. * * * JOHN WOODS 27 yrs single b. Surry Co NC s/o ? & Ludemin to LUVERNIE V. COOK 35 yrs single b. Mercer Co W VA d/o Cornelius & Ann O: farmer. (*Note: no date given.)

59

22. 22 Feb 1888 FRANK E. MATEEN 27 yrs single b. Huntington Co PA s/o Henry & Elizabeth to DORA G. COLE 17 yrs single b. Mercer Co W VA d/o A.J. & Mary O: lumberman; by L. Goodwyn.

23. 22 Feb 1888 FOUNTAIN SNIDER 19 yrs single b. Mercer Co W VA s/o Esom & Rhoda A. to IDA A.H. BIRD 18 yrs single b. Mercer Co W VA d/o Wm A. & Cynthia J. O: farmer; by Wm Holroyd.

24. 22 Feb 1888 ALLAN CAPERTON 20 yrs single b. Mercer Co W VA s/o John G. & Alberteany to MAUD SHORTER 16 yrs single b. Mercer Co W VA d/o Woodson A. & Elizabeth O: farmer; by Wm Holroyd; REMARKS: by Jas W. Bolin.

25. 26 Feb 1888 J.K. WHITE 33 yrs div. b. Mercer Co W VA s/o Patton & R. White to LUSANE WOODALL 22 yrs single b. Mercer Co W VA d/o Rhoda Holson O: farmer; by A.J. Thompson; REMARKS: By John W. Dunn.

26. 9 March 1888 JOHN CALLOWAY 27 yrs single b. Pittsylvania Co VA to MARY ALLISON 16 yrs single b. Danville VA d/o Jas & L.E. Allison O: miner; by Jno M. Douglass; REMARKS: colored, certificate of A.J. Young, J.P.

27. 11 March 1888 RICHARD JOYCE 26 yrs single b. NC s/o Jake & Mollie to LIZZIE SANFARD 24 yrs single b. Wythe Co VA s/o George & Sallie O: miner; by John M. Douglass; REMARKS: colored, certificate of A.J. Young, J.P.

28. 6 March 1888 WM HENRY BOOK 24 yrs single b. Craig Co VA now living in Pulaski Co VA s/o Henry L. & Mary E. to KATE McKENZIE 22 yrs single b. Mercer Co W VA s/o Jno A. & Lucinda E. O: minister; by P.B. Baber.

29. 9 March 1888 ISAAC F. GRIFFITH 24 yrs single b. Roanoke Co VA s/o Shadreck B. & Catharine to SARAH C. SAUNDERS 19 yrs single b. Mercer Co W VA d/o M.B. & D.P. O: farmer; by J.C. Haness.

30. 8 March 1888 WM BARRETT 20 yrs single b. Grayson Co VA s/o Reuben & Margaret to MOLLIE JONES 17 yrs single b. Mercer Co W VA d/o Kenney & Ann O: farmer; by J.W. Bennett; REMARKS: colored, by permission of parents.

31. 11 March 1888 ALLEN T. CAPERTON 30 yrs single b. Mercer Co W VA s/o Thompson H. & Laura to RHODA A. COOK 38 yrs wid. b. Giles Co VA d/o Wm & Polly Miller O: farmer; by W.C. Keaton.

32. 15 March 1888 HARVEY E. THOMAS 27 yrs single b. Mercer Co W VA s/o James B. & Caroline to ALICE PERDUE 21 yrs single b. Giles Co VA d/o Mac & Nancy O: farmer; by L. Goodwyn.

33. 18 March 1888 ISAAC H. LILLY 19 yrs single b. Mercer Co W VA s/o Johnston K. & Alabama to JOSIE L. FLETCHER 17 yrs single b. Giles Co VA d/o Wm H. & Martha O: farmer; by J.W. Bennett.

34. 21 March 1888 JAMES C. DOWDY 27 yrs wid. b. Giles Co VA s/o Benjn & Susan to MARY L. TILLER 18 yrs single b. Mercer Co W VA d/o John M. & Susan E. O: farmer; by L. Goodwyn.

35. 25 March 1888 DANIEL LILLY 31 yrs wid. b. Mercer Co W VA s/o Daniel & Servina to MANORA A. MEADOR 33 yrs single b. Mercer Co W VA d/o Josiah & Susan O: farmer; by James W. Lilly.

36. 21 March 1888 ROBT H. HIGGINBOTHAM 27 yrs single b. Mercer Co W VA s/o ? & Sarah to NANNIE L. SKEENS 18 yrs single b. Giles Co VA d/o Joseph & Nancy O: farmer; by A.J. Thompson.

37. 29 March 1888 GEO D. GODFREY 25 yrs single b. Mercer Co W VA s/o John D. & Martha to REBECCA J. BAILEY 23 yrs single b. Mercer Co W VA d/o Irvin H. & Telia C. O: farmer; by Archd McComas.

38. 29 March 1888 HENRY M. SMITH 27 yrs single b. Richmond VA now living in Fayette Co AL s/o Hiram M. & Caroline to ALBERTA C. PECK 18 yrs single b. Mercer Co W VA d/o Jacob A. & Malissa O: railroader; by J.W. Bennett.

39. 5 April 1888 HADEN CONNOR 23 yrs single b. Floyd Co VA s/o Danl R. & Liddie to ARRISTER CLEMMONS 21 yrs single b. Mercer Co W VA d/o James H. & Betsy O: farmer; by A.J. Thompson.

40. 10 April 1888 ERASTUS L. BASHAM 18 yrs single b. Mercer Co W VA s/o John & Martha A. to AVIS A. MEADOR 14 yrs single b. Mercer Co W VA d/o Lycurgus & Catharine O: farmer; by Wm P. Lilly.

41. 9 April 1888 JAMES McCLOSKEY 38 yrs single b. Susquehann Co. PA s/o Byrnard & Catharine to MAGGIE S. WAGONER 27 yrs div. d/o Geo O. & ? O: laborer; by M.A. Wilson.

42. 12 April 1888 JAS A. LILLY 23 yrs single b. Mercer Co W VA s/o ? & Rhoda J. to MARY E. CLENDENON 17 yrs single b. Mercer Co W VA d/o A. Mc & Nancy J. O: farmer; by J.O. Cassaday.

43. 18 April 1888 L.F. PORTERFIELD 26 yrs single to VINNIE R. BRAY 17 yrs single; by J.W. Bennett.

44. 14 April 1888 EZRA TABOR 21 yrs single b. Tazewell Co VA s/o Wm J. & Sarah to ALBINA R.J. PETERS 20 yrs single b. Raleigh Co W VA d/o Elijah C. & Tamor O: farmer; by C. Clark.

45. 25 April 1888 NATHAN SCALES 26 yrs single b. Stewart VA s/o John & A.P. to DAISY COUSINS 21 yrs single b. Birmingham AL d/o Carter & Sarah H; by Moses A. Pannill; REMARKS: colored.

46. 26 April 1888 JOS DAVID WRIGHT 23 yrs single b. Mercer Co W VA s/o A.W. & Lucy A. to ELIZA ANN COMER 27 yrs single b. Mercer Co W VA d/o Wallace J. & Sarah O: farmer; by A.J. Thompson.

47. 28 April 1888 MAJOR HAWKINS 24 yrs single b. Notaway Co VA s/o Abram & Sarah B. to FANNY MUSE 21 yrs single b. Floyd Co VA d/o Abe & Millie O: miner; by Moses A. Pannill; REMARKS: colored.

48. 1 May 1888 GEO W. SCOTT 30 yrs single b. Mercer Co W VA s/o Brown & Susan to MARY WADDLE 29 yrs single b. Mercer Co W VA d/o Wm & Sarah E. O: farmer; by J.W. Bennett.

1. 6 May 1888 CHAS F. CROMER 21 yrs single b. Montgomery Co VA s/o J.C. & Mary to WILLIE H. BECKETT 15 yrs single b. Monroe Co W VA d/o Wm & Margaret O: miner; by J.C. Haness.

2. 8 May 1888 JOS N. PERMINGTON 28 yrs div. b. Mercer Co W VA s/o Jno A. & Ellen to SARAH WILEY 27 yrs single b. Mercer Co W Va O: farmer; by A.J. Thompson.

3. 10 May 1888 R.A. BLANKENSHIP 18 yrs single b. Mercer Co W VA s/o Eli H. & Elizabeth to MARY E. WHITT 17 yrs single b. Tazewell Co VA d/o Charter M. & Martha S. O: farmer; by T.K. Lambert.

4. 12 May 1888 JOHNSON HAWKINS 25 yrs single b. Pulaski VA s/o James & Eliza Jane to VICTORIA MUSE 24 yrs single b. Franklin Co VA d/o Abe & Millie O: miner; by Jno M. Douglass; REMARKS: colored.

5. 15 May 1888 GEO W. PRICE 25 yrs single b. Scott Co VA s/o Geo J. & Amy to SUSAN E. HARVEY 19 yrs single d/o Saml M. & Susan O: miner; by A.J. Young.

6. 20 May 1888 JAS A. BLANKENSHIP 23 yrs single b. Giles Co VA s/o Olie B. & Lucinda to FLORA R. SKEENS 20 yrs single b. Giles Co VA d/o Josiah & Nancy O: farming; by A.J. Thompson.

7. 21 May 1888 WM S. HARLESS 20 yrs single b. Mercer Co W VA s/o N.F. & Emma S. to MARTHA L. COOK 16 yrs single b. Mercer Co W VA d/o Thomas M. & Nancy P. O: farming; by T.K. Lambert.

8. 23 May 1888 CHAS S. THOMPSON 28 yrs single b. Mercer Co W VA s/o Wm H. & Rebecca to SUSAN E. WILEY 17 yrs single b. Mercer Co W VA d/o Gordon & Giney O: farming; by A.J. Thompson.

9. 4 June 1888 ALBERT K. WALKER 22 yrs 3 mos 9 dys single b. Wyoming Co W VA now living in Raleigh Co W VA s/o Jno M. & Mary J. to ROSA LEE HOUCHINS 16 yrs 4 mos 11 dys single b. Mercer Co W VA d/o Geo H. & Sarah O: farmer; by Wm P. Lilly.

10. 29 May 1888 JAS T. AKERS 22 yrs single b. Pulaski Co VA now living in Montgomery Co VA s/o Amos & Missouri to QUINDORA HEARN 18 yrs single b. Mercer Co W VA d/o Jas & E.C. O: fireman; by R.A. Kelly.

11. 31 May 1888 ALEXR D. CRAWFORD 24 yrs single b. Summers Co W VA now living same s/o ? & Rebecca J. to ENDORA F. FURGUSON 13 yrs single b. Mercer Co W VA d/o Jno & Elizabeth O: dentist; by Archd McComas.

12. 31 May 1888 LEWIS F. EDWARDS 20 yrs single b. Carrol Co VA s/o Newel M. & Charity to SARAH J. BAILEY 18 yrs single b. Mercer Co W VA d/o Jas R.P. & Perlina O: railroading; by D.N. Saunders.

13. 7 June 1888 GORDON J. MOORE 21 yrs single b. Roanoke VA s/o N.D. & Martha M. to ANNIE J. TILLER 15 yrs single b. Mercer Co W VA d/o J.F. & Clementine A. O: public works; by Robt Hughes.

14. 6 June 1888 JAS S. NICHOLS 27 yrs single b. Bedford Co VA s/o Wm G. & Kate to SUSAN A. FARMER 17 yrs single b. Appomatox Co VA d/o John & Augusta L. O: merchant; by H.A. Wilson.

15. 1 August 1888 RICHD JNO WHITE 28 yrs wid. b. Cornwall England s/o George & Mary A. to SARAH CALLIS 22 yrs wid. b. Raffordshire England O: miner; by J.C. Maness; REMARKS: R.J. White sworn.

16. 14 June 1888 HENRY W. DAVIS 40 yrs div. b. Patrick Co VA s/o John & Terripy to ALICE REED 21 yrs angle b. Mercer Co W VA d/o Thomas & Saphrona O: farmer; by J.O. Cassaday.

17. 16 June 1888 WH J. HAMILTON 22 yrs single b. Rockbridge Co VA now living in Tazewell Co VA s/o John & Fannie to LIZZIE M. LAREW 21 yrs single b. Rockbridge Co VA s/o Fortner & Lizzie O: miner; by H.A. Wilson; REMARKS: J.R. Templeton & Howard Hughes sworn.

18. 30 June 1888 JAS H. ANDERSON 25 yrs single b. Amherst Co VA s/o Reuben & Frances to LAURA WINBUSH 24 yrs single b. Halifax Co VA d/o Raleigh & Sarah O: miner; by J.B. Harwell; REMARKS: colored.

19. 29 June 1888 ALBERT KEATLEY 24 yrs single b. Mercer Co W VA s/o John & Susan to MINNIE S. GORE 19 yrs single b. Mercer Co W VA d/o B.F. & Sarepta R. O: farmer; by Wm Holroyd.

20. 5 July 1888 JAS MAD. ENGLAND 22 yrs single b. Jackson Co W VA s/o Aug J.S. & Mary E. to RHODA J. BALE 17 yrs single b. Mercer Co W VA d/o Elias & Eliza F. O: farmer; by J.B. Kennedy.

21. 8 July 1888 REUBEN A. CRAWFORD 36 yrs div. b. Mercer Co W VA s/o Thos & Elizabeth to NANCY C. DAVIS 21 yrs single b. Mercer Co W VA d/o Green & Sarah O: farmer; by L. Goodwyn.

22. 12 July 1888 JNO P. RICHARDS 28 yrs single b. Franklin Co VA s/o Robt E. & Sarah J. to NELLIE C. WALKER 19 yrs single b. Mercer Co W VA d/o B.H. & Victoria O: merchant; by Archd. McComas.

23. 14 July 1888 ALANZO P. SHELTON 19 yrs single b. Mercer Co W VA s/o Wm & Eunice to MALINDA LESLIE 17 yrs single d/o J.P. & Melvina O: farmer; by Thos R. Horris.

24. 17 July 1888 THEE L. FAULKNER 23 yrs single b. Mercer Co W VA s/o Gordon & Sarah E. to JENNIE J. BAILEY 28 yrs single b. Mercer Co W VA d/o ? & Zula O: farmer; by J.B. Kennedy.

25. 18 July 1888 MACK STARMAN 26 yrs single b. Carroll VA s/o Joseph & Nancy to PRISCILLA STARMAN 28 yrs single b. Carroll VA d/o Wm & Rebecca O: farmer; by A.J. Young.

26. 27 July 1888 EDGAR CANDLER 24 yrs single b. Lynchburg VA s/o John W. & Sallie to MARTHA POE 19 yrs single b. Mercer Co W VA d/o Jeremiah & Cynthia O: carpenter; by D.N. Saunders; REMARKS: James Even Poe.

27. 29 July 1888 GARLAND PINKARD 29 yrs single b. Pitsylvania Co VA s/o Terris & Ellen to MARY JEMISON 17 yrs single d/o Step & Sydney O: miner; by J.C. Maness; REMARKS: A.J. Young, J.P; (colored.)

28. 26 July 1888 JOHN CONRAD PACK 22 yrs single b. Summers Co W VA s/o Jas W. & Mary A. to EMMA H. JOHNSTON 21 yrs single d/o Manl S. & Sallie A. O: merchant; by J.P. Campbell.

29. 29 July 1888 LARKIN BLANKENSHIP 22 yrs single b. Buchanan Co VA now living same s/o Daniel & Mary to ELIZABETH S. PARKER 33 yrs single b. Mercer Co W VA d/o James & Mary O: farmer; by John M. Romans.

30. 2 Aug 1888 CHAS E. COMPTON 20 yrs single b. Tazewell Co VA now living same s/o Ballard P. & Delilah to EMMA J. POE 16 yrs single d/o James A. & ?; by Eva H. Brown.

31. 31 July 1888 BALLARD WADE 29 yrs single b. Franklin Co VA s/o Moses & Abigail to ELIZA PERKINS 22 yrs single b. Bedford Co VA d/o Henry & Mary O: miner; by B.J. Hargraves; REMARKS: colored.

32. 2 Aug 1888 JOHN H. FARMER 18 yrs single b. Mercer Co W VA s/o Reuben C. & Mary H. to ELIZA J. FARMER 20 yrs single b. Kanawha Co W VA d/o Jas T. & Sarah A. O: farmer; by Phil S. Sutton.

33. 2 Aug 1888 JOSEPH E. STARMAN 19 yrs single b. Mercer Co W VA s/o Patrick & Sarah J. to NANCY E. KINZER 21 yrs single b. Mercer Co W VA d/o Wm R. & Margaret O: farmer; by Phil S. Sutton.

34. 16 Aug 1888 JNO OTE PERDIN 21 yrs single b. Mercer Co W VA s/o J.H. & Sarah E. to MINNIE A. GARLICK 16 yrs single b. Montgomery Co VA d/o F.T. & Sarah J. O: farmer; by Evan H. Brown.

35. * * * ALLEN H. MAY 21 yrs angle b. Montgomery Co VA s/o Amanias & Emma to MOLLIE SMELCHER 23 yrs single b. Montgomery Co VA d/o ? & Mary O: miner. (*Note: no date given.)

36. 16 Aug 1888 ADAM H. CAPERTON 18 yrs single b. Mercer Co W VA s/o Jno G. & Albertina to SARAH E. BIRD 22 yrs single b. Mercer Co W VA d/o Wm A. & Cynthia J. O: farmer; by Wm Holroyd.

37. 15 Aug 1888 ANDREW J. HILL 20 yrs single b. Floyd Co VA s/o Robert & Martha A. to LUCINDA O. BROYLES 16 yrs single b. Mercer Co W VA d/o A.W. & Amanda O: farmer; by A.J. Thompson.

38. 23 Aug 1888 JOHN H. HARVEY 20 yrs single b. Monroe Co W VA s/o Floyd & Emeline to SUSAN E. HILL 17 yrs single b. Floyd Co VA d/o Robert & Martha O: farmer; by A.J. Thompson.

39. 18 Aug 1888 WM A. THOMPSON 20 yrs single b. Mercer Co W VA s/o Wm H. & Rebecca J. to PARTHELA J. WILEY 15 yrs single b. Mercer Co W VA d/o Gordon & Sina O: farmer; by A.J. Thompson.

40. 23 Aug 1888 HENRY BROWN 20 yrs single b. Tazewell Co VA s/o Wm & Jane to TINY DAVIS 23 yrs single b. TN d/o Saml & Susan O:farmer; by Evan H. Brown.

41. 27 Aug 1888 SAML JOHNSTON 54 yrs wid. b. Mechlinburg Co VA now living in Giles Co VA s/o Richard & Elizabeth to MARTHA J. JOHNSTON 38 yrs single b. Mercer Co W VA d/o Alexander & Nancy D. O: farmer; by J.O. Cassaday.

42. 27 Aug 1888 BALLARD P. WOODS single b. Franklin Co VA s/o Saml & Jane to MIMA HUFF single b. Franklin Co VA d/o Harvey & Martha O: miner; by B.J. Hargraves; REMARKS: colored.

43. 29 Aug 1888 ABRAHAM L GARRETSON 22 yrs single b. Mason Co W VA s/o Wm P. & Mary J to VIRGINIA JONES 21 yrs single b. Mercer Co W VA d/o Elisha P. & Zerhus O: farmer; by L. Goodwyn.

44. 29 Aug 1888 HENRY F. WARD 28 yrs wid. b. Raleigh Co W VA now living same s/o Henry & ? to MARY I. UPTON 24 yrs single b. Monroe Co W VA O: mining; by Wm P. Lilly.

45. 29 Aug 1888 JAS M. WIMMER 22 yrs single b. Mercer Co W VA s/o ? & Ellen to MARGARET M. SHRADER 20 yrs single b. Mercer Co W VA d/o John & Nancy O: farmer; by D.N. Saunders.

46. 30 Aug 1888 CHAS H. VEST 21 yrs single b. Giles Co VA now living same s/o Wm & ? to ALICE BLANKENSHIP 21 yrs single b. Mercer Co W VA d/o Ballard & Martha O: farmer; by R.W. Fitzgerald.

47. 2 Sept 1888 JAS W. WHIRLEY 21 yrs single b. Montgomery Co VA to MARGARET J. SHANNON 18 yrs single b. Mercer Co W VA d/o Saml & Mary Ann O: farmer; by T.C. Pulliam.

48. 7 Sept 1888 WM J. PREECE 33 yrs single b. Worcestershire England to M.M. WILLIAMS 40 yrs div. b. Tafeshire Scotland d/o Alex & Christina O: Coal inspector; by A.J. Young.

Page 50

1. 15 Sept 1888 MICHAEL J. GEARHEART 21 yrs single b. Floyd Co VA s/o Andrew & Elizabeth to ROSA L. WHITE 17 yrs single b. Mercer Co W VA d/o John A. & Mary J. O: farming; by J.P. Campbell.

2. 6 Sept 1888 WM J. FARLEY 24 yrs sngle b. Mercer Co v VA s/o Wm & Lucy Ann to CELIA R. MASSEY 18 yrs single b. Mercer Co W VA d/o Jackson & Patsy O: farming; by J.T. Swinney.

3. 5 Sept 1888 PHIL M. SHREWSBURY 21 yrs single b. Mercer Co W VA s/o Wm & Sarah A. to C.M. MASTIN 18 yrs single d/o Wm E. & Elizabeth O: farming; by Archd. McComas.

4. 6 Sept 1888 JOS H. COX 17 yrs sngle b. Summers Co W VA s/o James & Docia to MARY A. MERCER 18 yrs single b. Mercer Co W VA d/o Andrew & Nancy C. O: farming; by Drewry Farley.

5. 6 Sept 1888 H.G.C. SHREWSBURY 24 yrs single b. Mercer Co W VA s/o Saml & Elizabeth to EMMA A. BASHAM 18 yrs single b. Mercer Co W VA d/o Joseph A. & Polly O: farming; by Archd McComas.

6. 6 Sept 1888 WHITNEY E. WILLIS 27 yrs div. b. Giles Co VA now living in Bland co VA s/o Wm V. & Margt. to SARAH E. LESTER 15 yrs single b. Mercer Co W VA d/o A.B. & Martha L. O: farming; by Thos R. Morris.

7. 9 Sept 1888 JAS E. BRYANT 25 yrs single b. Rockbridge VA s/o J.M. & Sarah J. to VIRGINIA FLUMMER 20 yrs single b. Mercer Co W VA d/o Jas H. & C.E. O: railroad; by David McCrackin.

8. 13 Sept 1888 JEREMIAH COBURN 31 yrs single b. Mercer Co W VA s/o David & Catharine to MARY E.A. HAGAR 16 yrs single b. Mercer Co W VA d/o And. G. & Nancy O: farmer; by Carroll Clark.

9. 13 Sept 1888 M.T. ADDISON 27 yrs single b. Russell Co VA s/o William & Mary J. to LUCY J. DARMER 21 yrs single b. Bedford Co VA d/o John E. & Jane O: engineer R.R.; by M.A. Wilson.

10. 19 Sept 1888 JAS F. DANGERFIELD 22 yrs single b. Mercer Co W VA s/o Owen & Matilda to EMELINE NEWSOM 21 yrs single b. W VA O: engineer; by Eli B. Rose; REMARKS: Jas T. Dangerfield sworn.

11. 18 Sept 1888 JOHN P. RICHMOND 20 yrs single b. Raleigh Co W VA now living same s/o Parkison & Elizabeth to MARTHA H. PRINCE 18 yrs single b. Mercer Co W VA d/o O.T. & Margalina O: farmer; by Jas W. Lilly.

12. 19 Sept 1888 RUFUS E. SHUMATE 48 yrs wid. now living in Giles Co VA s/o Anderson & ? to JOSIE BROWN 27 yrs single b. Mercer Co W VA d/o Allen & Mary E. O: farmer; by J.W. Bennett.

13. 26 Sept 1888 WAL E. MILLS 21 yrs single b. Raleigh Co W VA now living same s/o Robert & Lydia to SERVILLA T. McCOMAS 17 yrs single b. Mercer Co W VA d/o Rufus B. & Olivia A. O: farmer; by Archd. McComas.

14. 24 Sept 1888 FLOYD PAGE 21 yrs single b. Nottoway Co VA s/o Alfred & Amanda to DORA JONES 18 yrs wid. b. Pulaski Co VA d/o Henry & Martha J. O: miner; by Moses A. Pannill; REMARKS: Henry Boyd sworn; colored.

15. 26 Sept 1888 WM MOODY LILLY 22 yrs single b. Mercer Co W VA s/o Wm H. & Virginia J. to MARTHA E. BICKNELL 25 yrs single b. SC d/o Larkin & Myrinda O: farmer; by Wm P. Lilly.

16. 27 Sept 1888 IRVIN DANL BRINDLE 30 yrs div. b. Davidson Co NC now living in Pulaski Co VA s/o Chas A. & Amanda R. to MARGT JANE COLE 21 yrs single b. Mercer Co W VA d/o Jno W. & Martha J. O: lumberman; by L. Goodwyn.

17. 28 Sept 1888 REUBEN McGEE 24 yrs single b. Fluvanna Co VA s/o John & Betsie to EMELINE JOHNSON 30 yrs single b. Roanoke Co VA d/o John & Esther O: miner; by Edmond Johnson; REMARKS: colored.

18. 1 Oct 1888 CHAS JOHNSON 26 yrs single b. Monroe Co W VA s/o Wesley & Phoebe to FANNIE WASHINGTON 23 yrs single b. Bristol TN d/o George & ? O: miner; by J.H. Harwell; REMARKS: colored.

19. 7 Oct 1888 TAYLOR O'NEAL 19 yrs single b. Kanawha Co W VA s/o Daniel & Ellen to ELIZA JANE TERRY 21 yrs single b. Floyd Co VA d/o Saml B. & Lucinda O: railroader; by L. Goodwyn.

20. 10 Oct 1888 CHAS A. WISEMAN 22 yrs single b. Mercer Co W VA now living in Monroe Co W VA s/o Jno L. & Margt A. to HENRI V. DAVIDSON 23 yrs single b. Mercer Co W VA d/o Henry P. & Lucinda O: railroader; by Phil S. Sutton.

21. 18 Oct 1888 SAML H. PRINCE 21 yrs sngle b. Raleigh Co W Va now living same s/o Hugh G. & ? to GEORGIE ANN MINK 21 yrs single b. NC d/o Silas & Elizabeth O: farmer; by Jacob Hylton.

22. 11 Oct 1888 JAS W. DEVANEY 33 yrs single b. Alleghany Co VA s/o Thomas & Martha to ROXIE HAMILTON 18 yrs single b. Bland Co VA d/o W.W. & D.H. O: miner; by John McBride.

23. 10 Oct 1888 WM G. WYANT 27 yrs single b. Summers Co W VA now living same s/o F.B. & Isabella A. to LUCY N. BUTLER 19 yrs single b. Mercer Co W VA d/o Joel A. & Sarah E. O: farmer; by G.M. Johnston.

24. 18 Oct 1888 DAVID W. THOMAS 22 yrs single b. Kanawha Co W VA s/o Lampkin & Ellen to MARY S. COMER 19 yrs single b. Mercer Co W VA d/o Jacob & Betsy O: farmer; by John West.

25. 13 Oct 1888 JAS PETRIE 27 yrs single b. Kanawha Co W VA s/o Martin & Melie to LOTTIE LITTLE 23 yrs single b. Mercer Co W VA d/o Lorenza & Rucy O: miner; by A.J. Young.

26. 17 Oct 1888 HOUSTON STREET 24 yrs single b. Lunenburg Co W VA s/o Jas P. & Mary E. to HANNIE REYNOLDS 19 yrs single b. Mercer Co W VA d/o Silas T. & ? O: lumberman; by J.H. Kennedy.

27. 16 Oct 1888 JAS LAFAYETTE ROGUS 23 yrs single b. Mercer Co W VA s/o Wm P. & ? to MALONA SLONE 18 yrs single b. Mercer Co W VA d/o David A. & Martha M. O: farmer; by Wm Holroyd.

28. 25 Oct 1888 GARLAND C. ANDERSON 22 yrs single b. Mercer Co W VA now living in Summers Co W VA s/o Jno T. & Martha W. to JOSIE E. GODFREY 26 yrs single b. Mercer Co W VA d/o Jno D. & Martha O: farmer; by Carroll Clark.

29. 24 Oct 1888 JAS N. FARLEY 20 yrs single b. Raleigh Co W VA now living same s/o ? & Margaret to MARTHA J. BAILEY 20 yrs single b. Mercer Co W VA d/o Henderson F. & Sarah O: farmer; by Jas W. Lilly.

30. 24 Oct 1888 SAML J. CONNOR 27 yrs single b. Floyd Co VA s/o Danl R. & Lydia to LOUISA M. MASSIE 20 yrs single b. Mercer Co W VA d/o F.B. & Louisa O: farmer; by J.P. Campbell.

31. 25 Oct 1888 RALEIGH M. ANDERSON 25 yrs single b. Mercer Co W VA now living in Summers Co W VA s/o Jno T. & Martha W. to VIRGINIA J. GODFREY 18 yrs single b. Mercer Co W VA d/o Jno D. & Martha O: farmer; by Carroll Clark.

32. 1 Nov 1888 WM WHITTAKER 68 yrs div. b. Pulaski Co VA s/o Aaron & Margaret to MARGARET A. CROTTY 33 yrs single b. Mercer Co W VA d/o Wm A. & Julia O: farmer; by L. Goodwyn.

33. 29 Oct 1888 JNO L. RICHARDS 22 yrs single b. Montgomery Co VA now living in McDowell Co W VA to SARAH E. CROTTY 22 yrs single b. Mercer Co W VA d/o Wm A. & Julia O:blacksmith; by Phil S. Sutton.

34. 21 Oct 1888 GILES M. WILLIAMS 38 yrs wid. b. Giles Co VA now living same s/o Wm & Harriet to NELLIE J. CHRISTIAN 22 yrs single b. Mercer Co W VA d/o Robt G. & Jane O: farmer; by Wm Holroyd.

35. 11 Nov 1888 THOS M. MILES 29 yrs single b. Montgomery Co VA s/o Wm & Rachael to EMMA G. SOUTHERN 19 yrs single b. Mercer Co W VA d/o Asa & Sarah O: farmer; by A.J. Thompson.

36. 7 Nov 1888 JAS W. CREWS 19 yrs single b. Mercer Co W VA s/o John W. & Susan to ARAMINTA BASHAM 16 yrs single b. Mercer Co W VA d/o John & Martha A. O: farmer; by Wm P. Lilly.

37. 8 Nov 1888 JAS E. VAUGHAN 27 yrs div. b. Montgomery Co VA s/o Thos J. & Easter J. to ARAMINTA BOOSE 16 yrs single b. Montgomery Co VA d/o Wm G. & Nancy A. O: farmer; by J.H. Kennedy.

38. 8 Nov 1888 ROBT L. MOONEY 27 yrs single b. Mercer Co W VA s/o S.L. & Susannah to CLARA C. AKERS 25 yrs single b. Mercer Co W VA d/o Nathl B. & Sarah O: miner; by Wm J. Sage.

39. 8 Nov 1888 JOHN PATTERSON 23 yrs single b. Franklin Co VA s/o Gilford & Nancy to SUSAN DICKSON 17 yrs single b. Russell Co VA d/o John & Sallie O: miner; by J.B. Simpson; REMARKS: colored.

40. 15 Nov 1888 ROBT BENJ MILLS 22 yrs single b. Mercer Co W VA s/o Hugh G. & Catherine to SARAH J. HATCHER 19 yrs single b. Mercer Co W VA d/o Edmond H. & Nancy O: farmer; by Jas W. Lilly'

41. 14 Nov 1888 JAMES A. MONK 24 yrs single b. Mercer Co W VA s/o Silas & ? to DELILA SWADER 15 yrs single b. Mercer Co W VA d/o David & Clora O: farmer; by Chas Walker; REMARKS: C.H. Jenning sworn.

42. 15 Nov 1888 ROBT J.L. HILL 23 yrs single b. Floyd Co VA to WILMOTH C. DAVIS 20 yrs 11 mos 9 dys single b. Giles Co VA d/o ? & Rhoda O: farmer; by R.W. Fitzgerald.

43. 21 Nov 1888 EDWD L. MELVIN 25 yrs single b. Mercer Co W VA s/o John W. & Beckey to ALICE PERDUE 16 yrs single b. Mercer Co WV d/o Harison & Margarett O: farmer; by L. Goodwyn.

44. 22 Nov 1888 RUSSEL F. CONLEY 24 yrs single b. Giles Co VA now living same s/o Guy P. & Almedia to MARY P. WHITE 19 yrs single b. Mercer Co W VA d/o G.W.P. & Rebecca S. O: farmer; by T.C. Pulliam.

45. 21 Nov 1888 JEREMIAH J. MILLS 21 yrs single b. Mcer Co W VA s/o Green & Catharine to ELIZA J.E. McBRIDE 21 yrs single b. Mercer Co W VA d/o Jno B. & Sarah O: farmer; by Jas W. Lilly.

46. 28 Nov 1888 THOS G. SNEED 23 yrs single b. Mercer Co W VA s/o Jas & Mary V. to ELLA M. OKES 17 yrs single b. Floyd Co VA d/o Jesse A. & Polly O: farmer; by Drewry Farley.

47. 29 Nov 1888 THOS J. HEDRICK 25 yrs single b. Tazewell Co VA s/o Granville H. & Polly to VIRGINIA J. SMITH 15 yrs single b. Mercer Co W VA d/o H.W. & Victoria O: saw mill hand; by L. Goodwyn.

48. 5 Dec 1888 FRANK W. PRICE 35 yrs wid. b. Craig Co VA s/o Jacob L. & Amanda M. to CARRIE HAMILTON 33 yrs wid. b. Alleghany Co VA d/o Wm & K.L. Evans O: farmer; by A.J. Young; REMARKS: Squire Caldwell & Price sworn.

Page 51

1. * * * WM E. BURTON 21 yrs single b. Giela Co VA now living same s/o Elias & Easter to ALICE J. DAVIS 21 yrs single b. Mercer Co W VA d/o Lee & Christine O: farmer. (*Note: no date given.)

2. 10 Dec 1888 JOHN S. RILEY 31 yrs single b. Rockbridge Co VA s/o John S. & Francis to MAKALA C. GRIFFITH 24 yrs single b. Roanoke Co VA d/o S.B. & Catharine O: farmer; by J.C. Haness.

3. 6 Dec 1888 PETER ALEXD HILL 22 yrs single b. Floyd Co VA s/o Robert & Martha to JOSIE B. BROYLES 18 yrs single b. Mercer Co W VA d/o Joshua G. & Olivia O: farmer; by A.J. Thompson.

4. 13 Dec 1888 JACOB E. HILTON 21 yrs single s/o David & Mary A. to LOUISA A. PRINCE 17 yrs single b. Mercer Co W VA d/o Oscar F. & Margeline O: farmer; by James W. Lilly.

5. * Dec 1888 HENRY BOLING 23 yrs single b. Raleigh Co W VA s/o Jackson & ? to PHOEBE A. MITCHELL 17 yrs single b. Wyoming Co W VA d/o John W. & Causby Mitchell O: mining; by A.J. Young. (*Note: no day given.)

6. 16 Dec 1888 CHAS A. WHITE 23 yrs single b. Kanawha Co VA s/o Reuben & Martha to LAURA F. STEELE 17 yrs single b. Mercer Co W VA d/o Wm F. & Rhoda O: farmer; by A.J. Thompson.

7. 19 Dec 1888 MACK H. WILEY 19 yrs single b. Summers Co W VA s/o Geordon & Suicy to TINEY E. SKEENS 15 yrs single b. Giles Co VA d/o John F. & Amanda H. O: farmer; by R.W. Fitzgerald.

8. 20 Dec 1888 ROBERT GILLS 21 yrs single b. Bland Co VA s/o Benj F. & Mary to SARAH E. SCOTT 18 yrs single b. Mercer Co W VA d/o Wm R. & Elizabeth O: farmer; by J.M. Romans.

9. 27 Dec 1888 FREDERICK JONES 32 yrs single b. Buckingham Co VA s/o Lindsey & Chancy to ANNIE SHOWARLER* 21 yrs single d/o Shelton & Jennie O: mining; by John M. Douglass; REMARKS: colored. (*Note: difficult to read handwriting – could be Showaler.)

10. 23 Dec 1888 MOSES WRIGHT 23 yrs single b. Roanoke Co VA s/o James & Fannie to JENNIE SHOWALER 30 yrs single b. Giles Co VA; by Jno M. Douglass; REMARKS: colored.

11. 25 Dec 1888 BALLARD P. WHITE 37 yrs wid. b. Mercer Co W VA s/o Jas R. & Julia to LAURA A. HURLEY 22 yrs wid. b. Mercer Co W VA d/o Wm Tiller & ? O: farmer; by J.O. Cannaday.

12. 25 Dec 1888 HORACE L. BINGHAM 28 yrs single b. Appomattox Co VA s/o Chris T. & Emaline to EDNA A. TAYLOR 17 yrs single b. Mason Co W VA d/o And J. & Victoria E. O: mining; by C.T. Kirtner.

13. 27 Dec 1888 WM J. MASSEY 26 yrs single b. Mercer Co W VA s/o Jas & Patsy to LOW CLARK 16 yrs single b. Mercer Co W VA d/o John & Emma O: farmer; by James W. Lilly.

14. 25 Dec 1888 ROBT HY WALKER 28 yrs single b. Campbell Co VA s/o Drury Lacy & Mary A. to REBECCA E. TUCKER 28 yrs single b. Montgomery Co VA d/o Littleton W. & Julia A. O: carpenter; by J.J.W. Mathis.

15. 25 Dec 1888 WM H. MARTIN 40 yrs wid. b. Mercer Co W VA s/o Adam H. & Rebecca to MOLLIE K. HOLDERN 21 yrs single b. Mercer Co W VA d/o ? & Jane O: farmer; by A.J. Thompson.

16. 26 Dec 1888 LOUIS N. TALLICHET 32 yrs single b. Switzerland s/o Francois & Charlotte to LUCY K. TAMPLIN 20 yrs single b. Kanawha Co W VA d/o Wm & Elizabeth O: clerk; by J.C. Haness.

17. 30 Dec 1888 E.J. MAURY 25 yrs b. Buckingham Co VA s/o Stirling & Cudie to OLLIE RIPPEY 22 yrs b. Pulaski Co Va d/o John & Sarah O: miner; by R.J. Buckner; REMARKS: colored.

18. 30 Dec 1888 JOHN W. TRAIL 21 yrs single b. Mercer Co W VA s/o Saml M. & Sarah M. to SUSAN E. SPANGLER single d/o G.W. & ? O:carpenter; by J.C. Haness.

19. 27 Dec 1888 CHAS G. GILLESPIE 24 yrs single b. Montgomery Co VA now living same s/o Wm E. & Jane to MATTIE L. LUCAS 24 yrs single b. Giles Co VA d/o Jno M. & Mary Ann O: fireman; by J.C. Haness.

Page 52

1. 16 Jan 1889 JAS H. HUFFMAN 23 yrs single b. Giles Co VA s/o A.J. & Ellen to LUCINDA R.R. ROBINS 20 yrs single b. Monroe Co W VA d/o Wm H. & Henrietta O: farmer; by Jas W. Lilly; REMARKS: J.H. Huffman sworn.

2. 16 Jan 1889 CHAS R. DUNCAN 29 yrs single b. Mobile AL s/o ? & Mary A. to DORA TILLER 19 yrs single b. Mercer Co W VA d/o Wm & Louisa O: railroader; by Phil S. Sutton.

3. 17 Jan 1889 JOHN CRENSHAW 21 yrs single b. Bedford Co VA s/o Fred & Flora to JENNIE BROWN 16 yrs single b. Wytheville VA d/o ? & Martha O: miner; by John M. Douglass; REMARKS: colored.

4. 23 Jan 1889 JESSE G. O'DANIEL 22 yrs single b. Mercer Co W VA s/o Wm & Lizzie to SARAH M. LOVELL 19 yrs single b. Carrol Co VA d/o Wm C. & Margt A. O: farmer; by Phil S. Sutton; REMARKS: Caldwell sworn.

5. 23 Jan 1889 ROBT R. HARRY 23 yrs single b. Mercer Co W VA s/o Romulus & Rutha to SARAH E. SMITH 18 yrs single b. Mercer Co W VA d/o Danl L. & Annie B. O: farmer; by T.C. Pulliam.

6. 23 Jan 1889 BALLARD P. SMITH 22 yrs single b. Montgomery Co VA s/o Rich & Catherine to MATILDA STEVENS 19 yrs single b. Giles Co VA d/o John & Sarah A. O: public works; by A.J. Thompson; REMARKS: colored.

7. 24 Jan 1889 WM HETTERMAN 21 yrs single b. Kanawha Co W VA s/o Patrick & Mary to HETTIE GILMORE 18 yrs single b. Boone Co W VA d/o Milton & Alice O: miner; by J.C. Haness.

8. 29 Jan 1889 DAN P. MOREHEAD 26 yrs single b. Bland Co VA now living same s/o Dan F. & Elizabeth to NANNIE V. McCLAUGHETY 20 yrs single b. Mercer Co W VA d/o Jos H. & Evaline O: farmer; by J.H. Kennedy.

9. 13 Feb 1889 JACOB C. SIMPSON 27 yrs single b. Pulaski Co Va s/o Shack & Lucy to JULIA A. GEORGE 17 yrs single b. Pulaski Co VA d/o Ellison & Elvira O: teamster; by R.J. Buckner; REMARKS: colored.

10. 7 Feb 1889 JOHN H. SURFACE 30 yrs wid. b. Montgomery Co VA s/o James H. & Julia to LOUISA L. MULLIN 27 yrs single b. Mercer Co W Va d/o James & Sally O: carpenter; by J.J.W. Mathis.

11. 8 Feb 1889 ROBT F. BLEVENS 21 yrs single b. Ash Co NC now living in Wyoming Co W VA s/o Daniel & Laura to LAURA L. BAILEY 20 yrs single b. Mercer Co W VA d/o ? & Eliza J. O: mining; by A.J. Young.

12. 8 Feb 1889 JAS B. RICHARDS 28 yrs single b. Franklin Co VA s/o Bruce W. & Sophia M. to INDICA F. BAILEY 17 yrs single b. Mercer Co W VA d/o ? & Eliza J. O: mining; by A.J. Young.

13. 8 Feb 1889 WM R. DAVIW 27 yrs single b. Mercer Co W VA s/o Lee & Christina to KORA J.E. LEFLER 20 yrs single b. Giles Co VA d/o John & M.O. Lefler O: farmer; by L. Goodwyn.

14. 14 Feb 1889 WM MARROW 22 yrs single b. Kottoway Co VA s/o Saml & Julia to MARTHA MORTIN 19 yrs single b. Franklin Co VA d/o ? & Emaline O: miner; by John M. Douglass; REMARKS: colored.

15. 15 Feb 1889 TEOS A. LYON 18 yrs single b. VA s/o Jas & Jane to MARTHA F. HIGGINBOTHAM 15 yrs single b. Mercer Co W VA d/o G.L. & Elizth O: farmer; by John West.

16. 7 March 1889 JAMES D. ALVIS 21 yrs single b. Giles Co VA s/o John & Josephine to AMERICA J. VAUGHT 16 yrs single b. Giles Co VA d/o Ransom & Sarah M. O: farmer; by J.P. Campbell; REMARKS: Jas D. Alvis sworn.

17. 6 March 1889 WM M. FOSTER 40 yrs wid. b. Mercer Co W VA s/o Richd & Zilthia to SARAH MARTIN 35 yrs single b. Mercer Co W VA d/o Adam & Rebecca O: farmer; by J.P. Campbell

18. 16 March 1889 WM REED 23 yrs single b. Botetourt Co VA s/o Abraham & Adeline to JENNIE SLAUGHTER 16 yrs single b. Wythe Co VA d/o Edward & Nancy R. O: miner; by D.C. Horne; REMARKS: Wm Reed sworn; colored.

19. 2 May 1889 SAML CLARK 30 yrs single b. Albemarle Co VA s/o Lewis & Harriet to FANNIE DARBIN 28 yrs single b. Floyd Co VA d/o ? & Mary O: miner; by John M. Douglass; REMARKS: colored.

20. 31 March 1889 JOHN T. WILKES 21 yrs single b. Franklin Co VA s/o R.F. & Sarah C. to MARY E. BLANKENSHIP 17 yrs single b. Giles Co VA d/o A.J. & Mary O: farmer; by Jas O. Cassaday; REMARKS: Wilkes sworn.

21. 3 April 1889 HENSLEY HOWLS 21 yrs single b. Mercer Co W VA s/o David C. & Nancy to LAURA A. PARKER 22 yrs single b. Mercer Co W VA d/o Isaac & Betsy O: railroader; by J.J.W. Mathis.

22. 2 April 1889 STEPHEN F. CLEGHON 22 yrs single b. Smythe Co VA s/o Jerome B. & Mary to MARY JANE BOLIN 20 yrs single b. Mercer Co W VA d/o Allen H. & Elizth O: farmer; by J.H. Kennedy.

23. 3 April 1889 PARIS M. MATHENA 22 yrs single b. Tazewell Co VA s/o Jeo W. & Harriett to IOWA M. BOWLING 19 yrs single b. Mercer Co W VA d/o A.W. & ? O: farmer; by Jas O. Cassaday; REMARKS: C.W. Mathena sworn.

24. 4 April 1889 LEE BROADNAX 29 yrs wid. b. Rockingham NC s/o Adam & Louisa to MARY CLARK 25 yrs single b. Bedford Co VA d/o Geo & Merritt O: miner; by J.C. Haness; REMARKS: colored.

25. 28 April 1889 E.V. KIRK 21 yrs single b. Giles Co VA s/o James & Sarah to PERLINA B. IMFREWILLER(?) 17 yrs single b. Tazewell Co VA d/o Saml & Nancy O: miner; by D.C. Horne.

26. 11 April 1889 WM L. McCRAY 24 yrs single b. Staunton VA s/o G.S. & Fanny to JULIA McPHERSON 18 yrs single b. Bedford Co VA d/o H.H. & M.L. O: depot agent; by J.C. Haness.

27. 9 April 1889 RUSH H. BROWN 20 yrs single b. Mercer Co W VA s/o Paris & Mary A. to JULIA McPHERSON 18 yrs single b. Mercer Co W VA d/o Jacob & Elizabeth O: farmer; by J.H. Kennedy.

28. 17 April 1889 WM A. SMITH 22 yrs single b. Montgomery Co VA s/o Richd L. & Cath J. to FANNIE ERWIN 19 yrs single b. TN d/o Andrew & Hannah O: mill hand; by A.J. Thompson; REMARKS: colored.

29. 17 April 1889 CHAS I. BROWN 27 yrs single b. Tazewell Co VA s/o Evan H. & Mary E. to MATILDA G. PECK 22 yrs single b. Mercer Co W VA d/o Jacob A. & Larissa O: farmer; by John M. Romans.

30. 24 April 1889 CHRISTIAN BELCHER 66 yrs wid. b. Tazewell Co VA s/o Obediah & Martha to FANNIE McCRAY 42 yrs wid. b. Augusta Co VA d/o John Lohr & Margt L. O: farmer; by J.M. Romans.

31. 30 April 1889 GEO CUNNINGHAM 26 yrs single b. Danville VA to KITTY MORRIS 23 yrs single b. Floyd Co VA O: railroader; by John M. Douglass; REMARKS: colored.

32. 2 May 1889 WM SHEPARD 21 yrs single b. Grayson Co VA s/o George & Caroline to ORINIE J. BELCHER 16 yrs single b. Mercer Co W VA d/o Leom & Nancy O: carpenter; by Romulus Harry; REMARKS: J.H. Dare & W. Shepard sworn.

33. 12 May 1889 JAMES McINDOR 57 yrs wid. b. Lanarkshire Scotland now living in McDowell Co VA s/o James & Cathrine to ELIZA J. BROYLES 47 yrs wid. b. VA O: Engineer; by J.J.W. Mathis.

34. 15 May 1889 LUTHER S. KESSINGER 19 yrs single b. Giles Co VA s/o Silas M. & Charlotte Ann to MARY E. LILLY 20 yrs single b. Mercer Co W VA d/o Danl T. & Elmira O: farmer; by Jas W. Lilly; REMARKS: L.S. Kessinger sworn.

35. 12 May 1889 CALVIN NICHOLS 25 yrs single b. Wythe Co VA s/o Wm & Susan to MARTHA BELL JEWELL 18 yrs single b. Jackson Co W VA d/o Hamilton & Elizth Ann O: mining; by Thos R. Morris.

36. 30 May 1889 ANDREW L. STAMBRICK 28 yrs single b. Liberty Bedford Co VA s/o A.L. & Rebecca to BELLE SUITZ 16 yrs single b. Bedford Co VA d/o S.H. & S.T. O: plastered; by M.A. Wilson.

37. 31 May 1889 WELLINGTON COX 31 yrs wid. b. Summers Co W VA now living same s/o James & Docia to CELIA E. MEADOR 24 yrs single b. Mercer Co W VA d/o Green & Elizabeth O: farming; by Drury Farley; REMARKS: colored.

38. 9 June 1889 F.A. SMITH 24 yrs single b. Floyd Co VA s/o Jeff & Clouy to LORIE BUMGARDNER 22 yrs single b. Augusta Co VA d/o George & Ann; by R.J. Buckner.

39. 9 June 1889 JAS H. COLLINS 22 yrs single b. Mercer Co W VA s/o David & Luvina to NANCY V. TACKET 21 yrs single b. Grayson Co VA d/o Wm A. & Ellen J. O: farmer; by R.A. Kelly.

40. 7 June 1889 ROBT B. SMITH 21 yrs single b. Mercer Co W VA s/o ? & Olivia J. to LUCY B. DAVIDSON 18 yrs single b. Mercer Co W VA d/o Henry P. & Lucinda A. O: miner; by Phil S. Sutton.

41. 9 June 1889 JOS PRES KUSTER 28 yrs single b. Montgomery Co VA s/o Jacob & Mary A. to NANNIE M. COOPER 19 yrs single b. Mercer Co W VA d/o Wm A. & Melvina O: plasterer; by R.A. Kelly; REMARKS: Wm C. Cooper sworn.

42. 12 June 1889 CHAS A. VAUGHT 23 yrs single b. Gallier Co OH s/o Ransom & Sarah M. to M. WILLIE BURCH 20 yrs single b. Mercer Co W VA d/o George W. & ?; by J.W. Bennett.

43. 17 June 1889 NELSON MEADOWS 19 yrs single b. Mercer Co W VA s/o John L. & Marinda to CHARLOTTE S. BAILEY 15 yrs single b. Mercer Co W VA d/o Augustus L & Ann O: farming; by E. Howerton.

44. 16 June 1889 JOHN E. GODFREY 22 yrs single b. Mercer Co W VA s/o John D. & Martha to POLLIE E. BAILEY 22 yrs single b. Mercer Co W VA d/o Irvin & Telia O: farming; by Chas Walker.

45. 3 July 1889 LARKIN J. BENNETT 21 yrs single b. Yadkin Co NC s/o Green & Mary E. to MARY L THOMPSON 16 yrs single b. Bland Co VA d/o Hiram & Jane O: farming; by R.A. Kelly; REMARKS: W.W.Tacket sworn.

46. 4 July 1889 WILBUR J. HAWKS 21 yrs single b. Grayson Co VA s/o Wm R. & Polly Ann to SARAH ODLE 17 yrs single b. Carroll Co VA d/o Abram & Martha O: mining; by T.K. Lambert; REMARKS: W.J. Hawks sworn.

47. 9 July 1889 HENRY TALO 22 yrs single b. Pittsylvania Co VA s/o Geo & Mary to LIAALE TURKER 23 yrs single b. Washington Co VA d/o Geo & Mattie O: miner; by D.C. Borne: REMARKS: colored.

48. 9 July 1889 ROBT LEE DONITHAN to MINNIE BOLLIN O: miner; by A.M. Craft. (No other information was given.)

Page 53

1. 17 July 1889 GEORGE COUSINS 27 yrs single b. Washington Co TN s/o Jas & Lou Cousins to OLLIE JOKES 18 yrs single b. Montgomery Co VA d/o ? & Alice O: barber; by R.J. Buckner; REMARKS: colored.

2. 23 July 1889 STEPHEN M. TICKLE 32 yrs single b. Giles Co VA s/o Soloman D. & Francis C. to SUE M. GOOCH 23 yrs single b. Mercer Co W VA d/o Thos C. & Nancy J. O: merchandising; by E.F. Kahle.

3. 19 July 1889 JAS M. STEWART 23 yrs single b. Smith Co VA to SARAH HOWARD 16 yrs single b. Tazewell Co VA d/o ? & Malinda O: mining; by John M. Douglass; REMARKS: colored.

4. 28 July 1889 JAKE WADE 21 yrs single b. Franklin Co VA s/o James & Winnie to MAGGIE FERGUSON 19 yrs single b. Rusel Co VA d/o ? & Mary O: mining; by M.A. Pannill; REMARKS: colored.

5. 31 July 1889 WM J. JONES 21 yrs single to GEORGIA HOLBROOK 20 yrs wid. d/o Russel & Delila West O: railroading; REMARKS: Cyrus M. Bailey.

6. 8 Aug 1889 IRVIN H. BAILEY 24 yrs single b. Mercer Co W VA s/o Jonathan S. & Ursula to MARY J. SHREWSBURY 23 yrs single b. Mercer Co W VA d/o Philip & Margie A. O: farming; by J.M. Romans.

7. 8 Aug 1889 ALLEN B. HAMBRICK 21 yrs single b. Mercer Co W VA s/o Jos H. & Ellen to SARAH PAYNE 15 yrs single b. Mercer Co W VA d/o Andrew & Eliza O: farming; by D.N. Saunders.

8. 7 Aug 1889 SAML H. GILLS 19 yrs single b. Bland Co VA s/o Benj F. & Mary to MOLLIE HICKS 18 yrs single b. Mercer Co W VA d/o Wm R. & Hannah O: farming; by D.N. Saunders.

9. 11 AUG 1889 HENRY LEE 22 yrs single b. TN to MALINDA ARMSTEAD 24 yrs wid. b. Lynchburg VA O: waiter; by G.W. Stoples; REMARKS: colored.

10. 11 Aug 1889 WALTER E. DIXON 28 yrs b. Washington Co VA s/o Chas & Ninie to JENNIE DAVENPORT 25 yrs b. Tazewell Co VA d/o Tom & Bettie; by J.W. Stoples; REMARKS: colored.

11. 11 Aug 1889 WILLIE ROBERTSON 22 yrs b. Pittsylvania Co VA s/o Reed & Patsie to CLARA CRAFT 21 yrs b. Pittsylbania Co VA d/o Armstead & Dissie; by J.C. Maness; REMARKS: colored.

12. 11 Aug 1889 ARTHUR W. RODE 30 yrs wid. b. Sullivan Co NY s/o John C. & Bridget to MARY JANE CLOWERS 17 yrs single b. Montgomery Co VA d/o John D. & Mary Jane O: railroading; by J.J.W. Mathis.

13. 15 Aug 1889 A.J. HORTON 22 yrs wid. s/o ? & Ana to MARGARET N. HONAKER 17 yrs single b. Tazewell Co VA d/o Wm C. & Mary Jane O: farmer; by R.A. Kelly; REMARKS: Wm C. Honaker.

14. 29 Aug 1889 WILLIAM LANIER 22 yrs single b. Pittsylbania Co VA s/o Alfred & Betty to EMMA THOMAS 21 yrs single b. Pittsylbanic Co VA d/o ? & Mary O: miner; by T.J. Brandon.

15. 3 Sept 1889 CLARK JACKSON 26 yrs single b. Roanoke Co VA to LOTTA JOHNSON 17 yrs single b. Albemarle Co VA O: miner; by J.C. Maness; REMARKS: By A.C. Davidson.

16. 29 Aug 1889 JAMES BURNS 48 yrs single b. Renslow Co NY s/o Michael & Norah to SALLIE P. DAVIS 25 yrs single b. Bland Co VA d/o Isaac J. & Amelia O: moulder; by John H. Kennedy.

17. 31 Aug 1889 LEWIS STEWARD 33 yrs wid. b. Wythe Co VA s/o Granville & Cynthia to MARY HARRELL 25 yrs single b. Wythe Co VA O: farmer; by R.J. Buckner; REMARKS: colored.

18. 4 Sept 1889 MICHAEL CLARK 27 yrs single b. Maids Co OH s/o Patrick & Catherine to CATHERINE G. ALLEN 23 yrs single b. Nelson Co VA d/o George & Jane S. O: mining; by John McBride.

19. 8 Sept 1889 JOHN W. SMITH 19 yrs single b. Alleghany Co NC s/o Asbury & Julia Ann to SARAH NELSON 22 yrs single b. Tazewell Co VA d/o Jordan & Temperance O: mining; by D.C. Horne.

20. 18 Sept 1889 GEO P. WILLIAMS 38 yrs div. b. Giles Co VA s/o John M. & Cathering to SARAH P. WARD 22 yrs wid. b. Mercer Co W VA d/o John & Victoria Timer; by J.H. Johnston; REMARKS: Geo P. Williams sworn.

21. 9 Sept 1889 JAMES WETHERFOOT 24 yrs single b. Pittsylvania Co VA to MINIE HOWARD 21 yrs single b. Russell Co VA d/o ? & Malinda Swader O: miner; by John M. Douglass; REMARKS: colored.

22. 8 Sept 1889 WILLIAM T. CREWS 32 yrs single b. Mercer Co W VA s/o Acy & Nancy to ANNIE L. CREWS 25 yrs single b. Mercer Co W VA d/o Wm H. & Jane Lilly O: farmer; by Jas W. Lilly.

23. 10 Sept 1889 JAMES W. DELPH 19 yrs single b. Mercer Co W VA s/o Ephraim & Lucy to LILY DILLON 14 yrs single b. Mercer Co W VA d/o Henderson F. & Mercena F. O: farmer; by D.N. Saunders.

24. 17 Sept 1889 JAMES W. HURST 22 yrs single b. Mercer Co W VA s/o Armstead & Sarah E. to IDA E. WHITE 17 yrs single b. Raleigh Co VA d/o T.H. & Zuriah D. O: farmer; by J.M. Romans.

25. 15 Sept 1889 ROBERT G. CAPERTON 23 yrs single b. Mercer Co W VA s/o T.H. & Laura to ELLA HANCOCK 21 yrs single b. Monroe Co VA d/o Wm H. & Julia O: farmer; by J.P. Campbell.

26. 23 Sept 1889 W.C. THOMSON 23 yrs single b. SC s/o ? & Mary Ann to ALICE CLAYTON 22 yrs single b. Bedford Co VA O: mining; by John M. Douglass; REMARKS: colored.

27. 23 Sept 1889 WM L. PETTITT 31 yrs single b. Kanawha Co W VA s/o George & Elizabeth to MARIA SMITH 21 yrs single b. England d/o Eli & ? O: mining; by J.C. Maness.

28. 25 Sept 1889 WM B. ELMORE 40 yrs wid. b. Craig Co VA s/o James & Ellen to SARAH M. TAYLOR 21 yrs single b. Craig Co VA d/o George A. & Almira O: farmer; by Jas O. Cassaday.

29. 28 Sept 1889 WM M. HARDY 25 yrs single b. Mercer Co W VA s/o John L. & Sarah C. to RHODA J. TILLER 20 yrs single b. Mercer Co W VA d/o Wm D. & Rhoda O: farmer; by Phil S. Sutton.

30. 2 Oct 1889 CHAS W. HALL 22 yrs single b. Montgomery Co VA s/o J.N.J. & Margaret G. to MARIA B. KIRK 18 yrs single b. Mercer Co W VA d/o J.G. & Ann O: farmer; by J.J.W. Mathis.

31. 3 Oct 1889 CHAS R. THOMPSON 21 yrs single b. Mercer Co W VA s/o Levi E. & Cathering to MARY E. WIMMER 22 yrs single b. Mercer Co W VA d/o Saml D. & Rhoda J. O: farmer; by Jas O. Cassaday.

32. 3 Oct 1889 GEO W. DEAN 22 yrs single b. Lynchburg VA s/o Lee & Fanny to EMMA J. GREEN 23 yrs single b. Lynchburg VA d/o Frank & Jane O: mining; by T.J. Brandon; REMARKS: colored.

33. 3 Oct 1889 JOHN V. BROWNING 26 yrs single b. McDowell Co VA s/o L.H. & Lucinda to BETTIE A. HARLESS 18 yrs single b. Mercer Co W VA d/o N.F. & Emily O: farmer; by D.N. Saunders.

34. 5 Oct 1889 LUTHER MEADOWS 19 yrs single b. Wyoming Co VA s/o Harvey & Victoria to SARAH A. LEFLER 21 yrs single b. Monroe Co VA d/o ? & M.C. O: farmer; by L. Goodwyn.

35. 8 Oct 1889 JAMES FARTHING 26 yrs wid. b. Pittsylvania Co VA s/o A.P & Parthenia to IDA J. TAYLER 15 yrs single b. Pittsylvania Co VA d/o W.T. & ? O: farmer; by D.N. Saunders.

36. 28 Oct 1889 THOS R. BROWN 22 yrs single b. Northampton Co NC s/o Thos & Elizabeth to MARGARET E. WEAVER 15 yrs single b. Pulaski Co W VA d/o James & Eliza O: shoemaker; by M.A. Pannill; REMARKS: colored.

37. 14 Oct 1889 JASPER DUNEVANT 31 yrs single b. Henry Co VA s/o James & Becky to IDELLA S. GOODE 31 yrs single b. Montgomery Co VA d/o G.W. & Permelia O: farmer; by David McCracken.

38. 16 Oct 1889 R.E. GREEAR 23 yrs single b. Grayson Co VA s/o J.C. & Joania to MARY E. DUDLEY 16 yrs single b. Mercer Co W VA d/o A.J. & A.E. O: merchant; by M.A. Wilson.

39. 16 Oct 1889 WM H. CALDWELL 27 yrs single b. Mercer Co W VA s/o G.W. & E.A. to LOCHIE BUTLER 18 yrs single b. Mercer Co W VA d/o Joel A. & S.E. O: farmer; by Giles M. Johnston.

40. 20 Oct 1889 SIDNEY J. BAILEY 23 yrs single b. Mercer Co W VA s/o Harry & Rosina to ELLA L. DAY 17 yrs single b. Mercer Co W VA d/o Giles & Elizabeth O: farmer; by D.N. Saunders.

41. 17 Oct 1889 CHAS R. HALE 23 yrs single b. Franklin Co VA s/o Sparrell & Eliza to CHRISTINA PERDUE 18 yrs single b. Mercer Co W VA d/o J.H. & Sarah E. O: miner; by A.M. Craft.

42. 22 Oct 1889 JOHN C. HUGHES 33 yrs wid. b. Giles Co VA s/o Cluff & Holley to LAURA P. WHITE 28 yrs wid. b. Mercer Co W VA O: physician; by D. McCracken.

43. 23 Oct 1889 JONATHAN W. LILLY 22 yrs single b. Mercer Co W VA s/o J.E. & Julina to CORA N. HOUCHINS 18 yrs single b. Mercer Co W VA d/o G.H. & ? O: farmer; by Wm P. Lilly.

44. 28 Oct 1889 ED COLES 25 yrs single b. Pittsylvania Co VA s/o ? & Jane to ELIZA BURNETT 37 yrs single b. Henry Co VA O: miner; by M.A. Pannill; REMARKS: colored.

45. 25 Oct 1889 J.H. COBURN 20 yrs single b. Mercer Co W VA s/o John & Sarah to LOU WADDLE 22 yrs single b. Mercer Co W VA d/o Wm & ? O: farmer; by J.W. Bennett.

46. 27 Oct 1889 LB. BELCHER 50 yrs wid. b. Boone Co VA s/o ? & Malinda to RHODA SHREWSBURY 36 yrs single b. Mercer Co W VA d/o Henry & Jane O: farmer; by J.B. Grewer.

47. 28 Oct 1889 JOHN MILLS 27 yrs single b. Staffordshire Engd. s/o John & Jane to ALICE J. COULEY 21 yrs single b. Mercer Co W VA d/o J.F. & Mary O: engineer; by J.J.W. Mathis.

48. 1 Nov 1889 FEILDON DUNN 22 yrs single b. NC s/o Junius & Milley to LUVINA GRIM 21 yrs single b. Mercer Co W VA d/o Peter & M.A. O: miner; by W.D. Sanford.

Page 54

1. 30 Oct 1889 C.W. LEFLER 42 yrs wid. b. Roanoke Co VA s/o Aaron & M.A. to LOUISA J. HOPKINS 32 yrs wid. b. Mercer Co W VA O: railroader; by J.W. Bennett.

2. 2 Nov 1889 J.A. HEAD 26 yrs single b. Grayson Co VA s/o Alexd & Nancy to ALICE DAVIS 21 yrs single b. Grayson Co VA d/o Albert & Betty O: railroader; by H.G. Dillion.

3. 3 Nov 1889 GUSTUS SMITH 25 yrs single b. Pittsylvania Co VA s/o Hampton & Harriet to BELLE GOFF 28 yrs wid. b. Lynchburg VA d/o Alex Griffin & Henrietta O: mining; by T.J. Brandon; REMARKS: colored.

4. 6 Nov 1889 C.W. HATCHER 20 yrs single b. Mercer Co W VA now living in Raleigh Co VA s/o John R. & Nancy E. to J.A. FERGUSON 17 yrs single b. Mercer Co W VA d/o E.R. & Elizabeth O: farming; by Chas Walker.

5. 4 Nov 1889 ROBEY DUNN 18 yrs single b. Ash Co NC s/o Junius & Milly to LUCINDA J. KING 16 yrs single b. Mercer Co W VA d/o Wm R. & Margaret O: mining; by Phil S. Sutton.

6. 5 Nov 1889 JOHN D. SCOTT 33 yrs wid. b. Giles Co VA s/o Wm R. & Mary E. to MARY E. HERNDON 44 yrs wid. b. Mercer Co W VA d/o Christian & ? Belcher O: merchant; by D.N. Saunders.

7. 6 Nov 1889 J.H. CHANNING 22 yrs single b. Monroe Co W VA now living in Giles Co VA s/o W.J. & E.A. to MINNIE D. PICKERING 22 yrs single b. Morristown TN d/o D.Y. & Sarah O: depot agent; by R.A. Kelly.

8. 14 Nov 1889 J.W. WALLER 24 yrs single b. Henry Co VA s/o Gabe & Minnie to ELIZA TURNER 21 yrs single b. Montgomery Co VA d/o Andy Turner & S.T. Denton O: miner; by John M. Douglass; REMARKS: colored.

9. * * * S.N. BLANTON 23 yrs single b. Tazewell Co VA s/o Bartley & Sarah to KATE FREEMAN 21 yrs single b. Fire Creek W VA d/o John & ? O: telegraph operator. (*Note: no date given.)

10. 13 Nov 1889 W.O. BELCHER 42 yrs wid. b. Tazewell Co VA s/o Bartley & Sarah to HADEN M. POWELL 29 yrs single b. Franklin Co VA d/o Wm & Julia O: farmer; by D.C. Horne.

11. * * * JOS R. WILSON 26 yrs single b. Monroe Co W VA s/o John A. & Emily to ALICE M. JOHNSTON 18 yrs single b. Mercer Co W VA d/o Wm W. & Margaret O: butcher; REMARKS: License returned, not used. (*Note: no date given.)

12. * * * THOS B. LUSK 29 yrs wid. b. Wyoming Co W VA s/o William & Amanda to REBECCA SHARP 17 yrs single b. Smythe Co VA d/o Stephen & Catharine O: mining. (*Note: no date given.)

13. 28 Nov 1889 R.A. PENN 28 yrs single b. Bedford Co VA s/o James & Fanny to ADDIE SHERMAN 25 yrs single b. Bedford Co VA d/o ? & Martha O: mining; by W.J. Carter.

14. 28 Nov 1889 J.R. PIGGOTT 25 yrs single b. James City Co VA s/o Person & Minerva to BLANCH GILMORE 20 yrs single b. Bedford Co VA d/o Wm & Fannie O: mining; by W.J. Carter; REMARKS: colored.

15. 28 Nov 1889 WESLEY COX 28 yrs single b. Campbell Co VA s/o Anselin & Judy to LILLY CHEATHAM 26 yrs single b. Appomatox Co VA d/o Wash & Eliza O: mining; by r.J. Buckner; REMARKS: colored, W. Cox sworn.

16. 1 Dec 1889 WM G. McBRIDE 19 yrs single b. Mrcer Co W VA s/o Thomas & S.F. to EMMA C. WOOD 15 yrs single b. Mrcer Co w VA d/o A.N. & Elizabeth O: farming; by Chas Walker.

17. 17 Dec 1889 J.S. BALDWIN 21 yrs single b. Alleghany Co NC s/o John M. & Tabitha to MARY ANN SPICER 19 yrs single b. Wilkes Co NC d/o Wm & Martha H. O: mining; by J.H. Roberts.

18. 3 Dec 1889 WM WINFREY 24 yrs single b. Mercer Co W VA s/o Burrell & Orina to SALLIE E. CARBAUGH 19 yrs single b. Mercer Co W VA d/o W.T. & Esther O: farmer; by J.H. Kennedy.

19. 5 Dec 1889 OVID BUMGARDNER 21 yrs single b. Augusta Co VA s/o George & Mary to MARTHA CONNOR 21 yrs single b. Pulaski Co VA d/o Henry & Miranda O: miner; by R.J. Buckner; REMARKS: colored, J.H. Kyle.

20. 8 Dec 1889 JOHN BAILEY 34 yrs single b. Stokes NC s/o Wm D. & P.F. to SARAH WADE 30 yrs single b. Franklin Co VA d/o Geo & Harriett O: miner; by R.J. Buckner; REMARKS: colored.

21. 8 Dec 1889 N.C. CROCKETT 25 yrs single b. Montgomery Co VA s/o J. & Caroline to ANNIE GLOVER 21 yrs single b. Campbell Co NC d/o John & Betty O: miner; by D.C. Horne; REMARKS: colored.

22. 10 Dec 1889 BALLARD L. PERDUE 19 yrs single b. Mercer Co W VA s/o Silas & Nancy to IDA HARRIS 15 yrs single b. Mercer Co W VA d/o Wm A. & Mary M. O: farming; by R.A. Kelly.

23. * * * SAML M. CHRISTIE 27 yrs single b. Gilmer Co W VA s/o James M. & Cynthia P. to EMMA C. BURDITTE 18 yrs single b. Mercer Co W VA d/o Jos C. & Arrena W. O: merchant. (*Note: no date given.)

24. 12 Dec 1889 JACOB J. HOLT 30 yrs single b. Mrcer Co W VA s/o Richard & Ellender to LOUISA SHRADER 19 yrs single b. Mercer Co W VA d/o Granville & Rebecca O: farming; by D.N. Saunders.

25. 12 Dec 1889 SAML W. SAMPLES 24 yrs single b. Kanawha Co W VA s/o Harvey & Emeline to RUTH WHITWORTH 19 yrs single b. Montgomery Co VA d/o Thos L. O: miner; by D.C. Horne.

26. 12 Dec 1889 B.P. LESLY 24 yrs single b. Pulaski Co VA s/o Pearis to FANNIE E. ROLAND 19 yrs single b. Bland Co VA d/o M.B. & M.E. O: railroading; by J.J.W. Mathis.

27. 12 Dec 1889 GEO W. SCOTT 33 yrs wid. b. Mercer Co W VA s/o Brown & Susan to MARY E. BALL 28 yrs single b. Franklin Co VA d/o John r. & Amanda E. O: farmer; by J.W. Bennett.

28. 19 Dec 1889 C.W. HARMAN 22 yrs single b. Carroll Co VA s/o Joseph & Mary to JULIA A. BAILEY 16 yrs single b. Tazewell Co VA d/o Z. & Elizabeth O: farmer; by T.K. Lambert.

29. 24 Dec 1889 JAS R. BOOTH 22 yrs single b. Northumberland Co PA s/o Thomas & Ellen to DAISY B. FITCH 17 yrs single b. Augusta Co VA d/o George B. & Hattie A. O: Asst mining boss; by D.C. Horne.

30. 22 Dec 1889 DANL D. McNEIL 28 yrs single b. Moore Co NC s/o Peter McNare & R. McNeil to JANIE SAUNDERS 18 yrs single b. Roanoke Co VA s/o W. Webb & S. Saunders O: Asst mining boss; by R.J. Buckner; REMARKS: colored.

31. 22 Dec 1889 GEO E. WILLIAMS 21 yrs single b. Giles Co VA s/o James A. & R.E. to E.V. NISWANDES 24 yrs single b. Bland Co VA d/o W.S. & Ann O: fireman; by D.C. Horne.

32. 22 Dec 1889 C.E. TABOR 23 yrs single b. Tazewell Co VA s/o Henry H. & Mary M. to HALLIE A. TILLER 27 yrs single b. Mercer Co W VA d/o Wm D. & Rhoda O: carpenter; by M.A. Wilson.

33. 24 Dec 1889 ARMSTEAD MILLER 24 yrs single b. Prince Edward Co VA s/o William & Elizabeth to JENNIE RICHARDS 23 yrs single b. Giles Co VA d/o Henry & S. O: railroading; by L. Goodwyn; REMARKS: colored.

34. 26 Dec 1889 WM B. AKERS 18 yrs single b. Raleigh Co W VA s/o Crockett & Martha to MARY J. AKERS 16 yrs single b. Raleigh Co W VA d/o Louis & Josie F. O: farming; by S.M. McKinney.

35. 24 Dec 1889 LS. ARCHER 20 yrs single b. Mercer Co W VA s/o James to M.E. LOVELL 17 yrs single b. Carroll Co VA d/o Wm & M.A. O: farming; by Thos Parris.

36. 23 Dec 1889 W.S. STEEL 22 yrs single b. Mercer Co W VA s/o Wm F. & Rhoda to CORA TAYLOR 16 yrs single b. Mercer Co W VA d/o ? & Matilda O: mining; by E.F. Kahle.

37. 24 Dec 1889 BRADY B. DUNCAN 22 yrs single b. Mercer Co W VA s/o Wm H. & Lucinda E. to EMMA L. GOODE 18 yrs single d/o Geo W. & Permelia O: carpenter; by D. McCracken.

38. 25 Dec 1889 A.G. McCUE 30 yrs single b. Mercer Co W VA s/o Jas & Josephine to BERTHA BARBORA 25 yrs single b. England d/o Jno & Julia O: lumberman; by E.F. Kahle.

39. 25 Dec 1889 JOHN GRAVES 31 yrs single b. NC s/o Geo & Mille to ISABELLA KING 17 yrs single b. VA d/o Isham & Mary; by R.J. Buckner; REMARKS: colored.

40. 26 Dec 1889 C.W. SMITH 37 yrs single b. Mercer Co W VA s/o Theodore & Eliza J. to MARY S. SUTTON 19 yrs single b. Giles Co VA d/o Philip S. & Victoria O: Atty at law; by Phil S. Sutton.

41. 28 Dec 1889 E.S. WALKER 18 yrs single b. Mercer Co W VA s/o Burrel & Victoria to ROSABEL BAILEY 19 yrs single b. Mercer Co W VA d/o Irvin H. & Telia O: farmer; by T.K. Lambert.

42. 2 Jan 1890 SAML A. TOY 28 yrs single b. England s/o Saml & Mary to CAROLINE BILBIE 28 yrs single b. Northumberland Co PA d/o Joseph & Isabella O: bookkeeper; by D.C. Horne.

43. * * * JAMES H. PERDUE 21 yrs single b. Mercer Co W VA s/o McHenry & Nancy F. to JENNELLIE A. THOMAS 21 yrs single b. Mercer Co W VA d/o Jas H. & Caroline O: railroading. (*Note: No date given.)

44. 31 Dec 1889 R.H. FLETCHER 21 yrs single b. Mercer Co W VA s/o Wm H. & Martha J. to SARAH J. CALDWELL 21 yrs single b. Mercer Co W VA d/o Had & Ann O: farmer; by J.W. Bennett.

45. 1 Jan 1890 JOS C. JOHNSON 42 yrs wid. b. Holloway Co VA s/o Richard & Catherine to MALINDA GOODE 35 yrs single b. Franklin Co VA d/o Geo W. & Parindia O: farmer; by D. McCracken.

Page 55

1. 9 Jan 1890 WM I. LUSK 23 yrs single b. Wyoming Co W VA s/o Wm & Malinda to MARY O. KENNEDY 16 yrs single b. Montgomery Co VA d/o Joseph E & Susah J. O: farmer; by D.C. Horne.

2. 14 Jan 1890 GEORGE HAIDY 23 yrs single b. Roanoke Co VA s/o Henry & Martha to NANNIE BELCHER 21 yrs single b. Roanoke Co VA d/o Daniel & Julia O: farmer; by L. Diggs.

3. 9 Jan 1890 HENRY W. BRADLEY 34 yrs single b. Roanoke Co VA now living same s/o David & Ann to JULIA A. GILLESPIE 22 yrs single b. Montgomery Co VA d/o W.E. & Jane O: R.R. man; by J.O. Cassaday.

4. 12 Jan 1890 JOHN FULLEN 30 yrs wid. b. Russell Co VA s/o ? & Bettie to ELSIE HEAD 27 yrs single b. Washington Co VA d/o Zeb & Susan O: miner; by M.A. Wilson.

5. 16 Jan 1890 C.W. MYERS 22 yrs single b. Roanoke Co VA s/o Harden & Jane to VICTORIA WEAVER 17 yrs single b. Pulaski Co VA d/o James & Lizie O: teamster; by A.J. Buckner.

6. 18 Jan 1890 J.B. SIMPSON 26 yrs single b. Jonesborough TN to NANNIE J. BAILEY 26 yrs single b. Mercer Co W VA d/o John M. & ? O: minister; by D.C. Horne.

7. 28 Jan 1890 C.E. STAUFFER 26 yrs single b. Washington Co MS s/o Chas S. & Mary E. to SD. VIOLA KINGBURY 19 yrs single b. Carrol Co VA d/o Lawrence D. & Mariam A. O: Chief clerk machine shop; by R.A. Kelly.

8. 29 Jan 1890 RUFUS F. JONES 33 yrs wid. b. Mercer Co W VA s/o John & Reba to LUCINDA BLANKENSHIP 23 yrs single b. Giles Co VA d/o Harrison & Luisa O: farmer; by R.W. Fitzgerald.

9. 30 Jan 1890 JOHN J. LAWSON 24 yrs single b. Pulaski Co VA now living in Summers Co W VA s/o ? & Joannah to LUCINDA E. MANN 21 yrs single b. Summers Co W VA d/o Andrew & Nancy C. O: farmer; by J.W. Lilly.

10. 29 Jan 1890 S.W. BAILEY 27 yrs single b. Mercer Co W VA s/o Thompson & Mary to SALLIE A. MILLS 21 yrs single b. Franklin Co VA d/o John A. & Elizabeth O: butchering; by J.R. Morris.

11. 31 Jan 1890 WM L. WHITE 18 yrs single b. Mercer Co W VA s/o Ballard P. & Mary Jane to MINNIE B. PAULEY 17 yrs single b. Mason Co W VA d/o George & Elizabeth O: farmer; by J.O. Cassaday; REMARKS: applied for by B.P. White.

12. 2 Feb 1890 H.F.P. OWNBY 35 yrs div. b. Tazewell Co VA s/o Monroe & Charlotta to VERONE P. BRAY 20 yrs single b. Summers Co W VA d/o M.H. & Fannie O: carpenter; by J.O. Cassaday.

13. 4 Feb 1890 WM B. WILLIAMS 21 yrs single b. Giles Co VA s/o B.F. & Frances E. to JENNIE B. KIRK 15 yrs single b. Mercer Co W VA d/o J.F. & Anna O: farmer; by M.A. Wilson.

14. 5 Feb 1890 M.G. PENINGTON 28 yrs div. b. Mercer Co W VA s/o Gordon E. & Julia P. to ARDELIA WORKMAN 22 yrs single b. Mercer Co W VA d/o Bobt(sic) & Jane O: lumberman; by M.A. Wilson.

15. 6 Feb 1890 E.M. GOFF 21 yrs single b. Campbell Co VA s/o Joph L. & Sarah E. to MARY E. STREET 28 yrs single b. Lunenburg Co VA d/o Jas P. & Sarah O: laborer; by D.C. Horne.

16. 11 Feb 1890 LEVI ROSE 23 yrs single b. Ash Co NC s/o Bryan F. & Rosamand to ANNA L. MOYE 18 yrs single b. Summers Co W VA d/o Jno W. & Julia A. O: farmer; by J.W. Lilly.

17. 20 Feb 1890 BERT F. DINGMAN 24 yrs single b. NY to MARTHA SMITH 19 yrs single b. England d/o Eri & Emma Smith; by J.C. Maness.

18. 9 Feb 1890 HIRAM P. BELCHER 21 yrs single b. Tazewell Co VA s/o Robert & Relia to LAURA E. PEUCE 17 yrs single b. Monroe Co W VA d/o Pendleton G. & J.K. O: farmer; by B.E. Thompson.

19. 20 Feb 1890 WILEY W. SADLER 27 yrs single b. Giles Co VA s/o Henry & Araminta to VIRGINIA B. CHANESS 16 yrs single b. Tazewell Co VA d/o Jas H. & Cosby C. O: farmer; by J.O. Cassaday.

20. 20 Feb 1890 DAVID M. RYAN 19 yrs single b. Pulaski Co VA s/o John F. & Rebecca to ELLA GALLIER 18 yrs single b. Mercer Co W VA d/o Mary A. & John O: farmer; by M.A. Wilson.

21. 23 Feb 1890 JAS J. BONAKER 22 yrs single b. Bland Co VA s/o A.J. & Lucy A. to LUTICIA V. GRIM 22 yrs single d/o James & ? O: mining; by R.A. Kelly.

22. 23 Feb 1890 JASPER CLICK 19 yrs single b. Washington Co VA s/o Henry & Mary F. to FLORENCE L. GALDIN 13 yrs single b. Campbell Co VA d/o William & Louisa O: mining; by D.C. Horne.

23. 23 Feb 1890 M.H. BRAY 48 yrs wid. b. Henry Co VA to C.A. GARRETSON 46 yrs wid. b. Allegahany Co VA; by R.W Fitzgerald.

24. 26 Feb 1890 LEWIS WARD 29 yrs single b. Campbell Co VA s/o ? & Fannie to MARY JOHNSTON 20 yrs single b. Tazewell Co VA d/o Richard & Elizabeth O: railroading; by J.R. Morris; REMARKS: colored.

25. 26 Feb 1890 J.N. THOMPSON 27 yrs single b. Mercer Co W VA s/o David & Angeline to S.E. FIELDER 21 yrs single d.o Wm S. & R.J. O: farming; by P.S. Sutton.

26. 27 Feb 1890 B.F. PETTREY 29 yrs single b. Mercer Co W VA s/o Jacob & Elizabeth to REBECCA M. MANAWAY 23 yrs single d/o James & Sarah O: farming; by J.W. Bennett.

27. 1 March 1890 J.A. FOLEY 20 yrs single b. Mercer Co W VA s/o R.F. & Mary D. to BELL HUBBARD 17 yrs single b. Mercer Co W VA d/o Jonathan & V.E. O: mining; by J. Hylton.

28. 12 March 1890 JOHN A. HAWKINS 26 yrs to DARRIE RANDOLPH 38 yrs O: mining; by Robt Davis; REMARKS: colored, Applied for by B. Moore by letter.

29. 9 March 1890 WM CARDWELL 24 yrs single b. Campbell Co VA s/o L. & Watson to MALINDA WILLIAMS 22 yrs single d/o John & Lori O: mining; by D.C. Horne; REMARKS: colored.

30. 10 March 1890 WH DAVIS 22 yrs single b. Mounta NC s/o R. & R. to VICTORIA GRAVLEY 22 yrs wid. b. Roanoke Co VA d/o Steve & Victoria O: mining; by A.J. Carter; REMARKS: colored.

31. 9 March 1890 PLEASANT ADAMS 48 yrs wid. b. Bedford Co VA s/o Humphrey & Rhoda to MILLE SIMMS 30 yrs single b. Mercer Co W VA d/o ? & Kizzie O: farmer; by P.S. Sutton; REMARKS: colored.

32. 12 March 1890 GENERAL WASHINGTON BECKLEHEIMER 26 yrs single b. Floyd Co VA s/o Abram & Mary A. to RHODA E. FARMER 16 yrs single b. Mercer Co W VA d/o Reuben & Mary M. O: farmer; by P.S. Sutton.

33. 13 march 1890 GEO G. THOMAS 24 yrs single b. Mercer Co W VA s/o Jas H. & Caroline to ISABELLA DAVIS 21 yrs single b. Mercer Co W VA d/o Lee & Christina O: farmer; by J.H. Johnston.

34. 11 March 1890 BALLARD P. JONES 22 yrs single b. Mercer Co W VA s/o Wilson & Frances to FANNIE BAILEY 16 yrs single b. Giles Co VA d/o James & Sarah J. O: farmer; by J.H. Johnston.

35. 16 March 1890 GEO E.L. NEAL 27 yrs single b. Mercer Co W VA s/o Wm R. & Martha J. to EMMA M. McCLAUGHERTY 18 yrs single b. Mercer Co W VA d/o Jos H. & Emaline O: farmer; by J.H. Kennedy.

36. 20 March 1890 W.J. GORDEN 22 yrs single b. Giles Co VA s/o Geo W. & Elizabeth to DELLIE B. DAVIS 17 yrs single b. Mercer Co W VA d/o Lee & Christina O: farmer; by J.H. Johnston.

37. 19 March 1890 JNO S. KIRK 34 yrs single b. Giles Co W VA s/o Jos & Sarah to LIZZIE J. JOHNSTON 28 yrs single b. Mercer Co W VA d/o Adam & H.E. O: butchering; by G.H. Johnston.

38. 20 March 1890 F.L.A. WILSON 28 yrs single b. Rockbridge Co VA now living in Bell Co KY s/o M.A. & E.J. to LULA A. JOHNSTON 21 yrs single b. Giles Co VA d/o David E. & Sarah E. O: physician; by Jas Sweeney.

39. 26 March 1890 JNO L. LEE 30 yrs single b. Campbell Co VA s/o J.R. & Martha J. to WILLIE E. CALFEE 18 yrs single b. Mrcer Co W VA d/o H.S. & L.J; by J.B. Greaver.

40. 26 March 1890 CHAS CRAWFORD 33 yrs single b. Mercer Co W VA s/o Thos B. & Elizabeth to MARY V. SHUMATE 23 yrs single b. Giles Co VA d/o R.A. & Elizath O: farmer; by J.H. Johnston.

41. 26 March 1890 C.W. AKERS 22 yrs single b. Mercer Co w VA s/o J.W. & Sarah J. to FLORA H. BAILEY 22 yrs single b. Montgomery Co VA d/o John M. & ?; by J.B. Simpson.

42. 27 March 1890 H. SARVER 27 yrs single b. Mercer Co W VA s/o Wm A. & Mary A. to MINNIE J. HARE 21 yrs single b. Bland Co VA d/o Jas F. & ? O: farmer; by R.W. Fitzgerald.

43. 26 March 1890 H.A. HOUCHINS 23 yrs single b. Summers Co W VA s/o W.R. & Elizabeth to JENNIE F. CRAWFORD 16 yrs single b. Mercer Co W VA d/o Reuben & Margaret B. O: Rich Land Coal Co.; by J.H. Kennedy.

44. 26 March 1890 B.P. BRATTON 31 yrs single b. Mercer Co W VA s/o Thos & Mary E. to CELESTINE STINSON 30 yrs single b. Mercer Co W VA d/o Chas & ? O: farmer; by D.N. Saunders.

45. 27 March 1890 WM R. ADKINS 25 yrs single b. Mercer Co W VA s/o Wm & Caroline to V.L. CREWS 35 yrs wid. b. Mercer Co W VA d/o Soleri & Malinda Heador O: farmer; by D. Farley.

46. 28 March 1890 WM CARR 25 yrs single b. Bland Co VA s/o James & Fannie to LIZZIE L. HAYNES 21 yrs single b. Floyd Co VA d/o Isaac N. & Ann O: farmer; by J.H. Kennedy.

47. 1 April 1890 ISSAC A. BOWLING 29 yrs single b. Mercer Co W VA s/o M.A. & Rebecca J. to NANNIE J. REED 17 yrs single b. Mercer Co W VA d/o Washington & Rhoda O: farmer; by A.J. Thompson.

48. 3 Apr 1890 R.E.L. HOLT 24 yrs single b. Mercer Co W VA s/o ? & Gracy A. to O.E. THORNTON 17 yrs single b. Mercer Co W VA d/o A.J. & ? O: merchant; by J.O. Cassaday.

Page 56

1. 9 Apr 1890 F.A. WORRELL 29 yrs single b. Mercer Co W VA s/o Eli & Eliza to MARY E. JENNINGS 21 yrs single b. Carroll Co VA d/o Riley & Rebecca O: farmer; by J.W. Lilly.

2. 9 Apr 1890 OSCAR BLANKENSHIP 53 yrs wid. b. Mercer Co W VA s/o Stephen & Ellen to NANCY THOMAS 45 yrs single b. Mercer Co W VA d/o Harly & Peggy O: farmer; by J.H. Johnston.

3. 12 Apr 1890 JOHN CAMBELL 27 yrs single b. GA to EMMA TAYLOR 34 yrs single b. Raleigh NC O: miner; by J.H. Douglass; REMARKS: colored.

4. 17 Apr 1890 CHAS E. LITCHFORD 26 yrs single b. Amherst Co VA now living in Tazewell Co VA s/o Edward L. & Catherine to ROSA E. WHITEHEAD 17 yrs single b. Nelson Co VA d/o Kade & Annie F. O: failroading; by D.C. Borne.

5. 20 Apr 1890 G.H. TANNER 27 yrs single b. Appomattox Co VA s/o John M. & A.L. to M.A. TANNER 21 yrs single b. Campbell Co VA d/o Nathan & Martha C. O: painter; by L. Goodwyn.

6. 24 Apr 1890 JAS C. HONAKER 21 yrs single b. Bland Co VA now living same s/o James D. & Bell to SALLIE B. JARRELL 21 yrs single b. Mercer Co W VA d/o Geo W. & Lizzie T. O: merchant; by R.M. Ashworth.

7. 1 May 1890 JULIAS COOK 24 yrs single b. NC s/o Jas W. & Mary M. to M.E. SURFACE 22 yrs single b. Mercer Co W VA d/o Geo W. & Amarilla O: miner; by D.N. Saunders.

8. 1 May 1890 JAS D. MEADOWS 23 yrs single b. Mercer Co W VA s/o S.G. & Caroline to SARAH J. MEADOWS 20 yrs single b. Mercer Co W VA d/o J.W. & Andelia O: carpenter; by J.H. Johnston.

9. 12 May 1890 LAYNE BURNETTE 30 yrs div. b. Floyd Co VA s/o Jeremiah & Sarah to E.E. MILLS 18 yrs single b. Franklin Co VA d/o Jno A. & Elizath O: miner; by M.A. Wilson.

10. 1 May 1890 ANDREW SHUCK 22 yrs single b. Greenbriar Co W VA s/o Wm & Mary J. to JOSEPHINE SPICER 18 yrs single b. Mercer Co W VA d/o ? & Nancy O: miner; by M.A. Wilson.

11. 5 May 1890 WM G. REEDE 39 yrs single b. Mercer Co W VA s/o Jos & Malinda to MARY E. THOMPSON 33 yrs single b. Mercer Co W VA d/o Eli & Sarah O: farmer; by A.J. Thompson.

12. 5 May 1890 J.F. CALLAWAY 34 yrs single b. Sarah Co NC now living in Pocahontas (Co W VA) s/o J.R. & Mary to OLLIE M. CYPERS 21 yrs single b. MO d/o J.S. & Mollie O: butcher; by M.A. Wilson.

13. 8 May 1890 WASH WEST 26 yrs single b. Campbell Co VA s/o Peter & Leeanna to LUCY ERBY 24 yrs single b. Mercer Co W VA d/o John & Anna O: railroading; by J.M. Douglass; REMARKS: colored, sworn, applied for by W.A. Jewell, sworn.

14. 12 May 1890 R. HACKER 22 yrs single b. Kanawha Co W VA s/o Pery & Nannie to MARTHA VIPERMAN 20 yrs single b. Patrick Co VA d/o E.J. & Rachel O: mining; by J.C. Cook.

15. 11 May 1890 WM T. WOODS 76 yrs wid. b. England s/o Thos & Jane to ARMINTA SWANGGIN 24 yrs wid. b. Mercer Co W VA d/o James & Julet O: farmer; by J.W. Lilly.

16. 11 May 1890 CHAS REYNOLDS 26 yrs single b. Tazewell Co Va s/o Wash & ? to JESSIE STRANGER 16 yrs single b. Tazewell Co VA d/o Thos & Elizabeth; by R.J. Buckner.

17. 11 May 1890 EULAS KING 21 yrs single b. Caswell Co NC s/o Isain & Mary to NANCY GRAVES 21 yrs single b. Pitsylvania Co VA d/o Geo & Millie O: miner; by r.J. Buckner; REMARKS: col'd, sworn.

18. 12 May 1890 EDWARD COX 24 yrs single b. Campbell Co VA s/o Aslum & Judia to MRS. ELLEN HALE 25 yrs wid. b. Franklin Co VA d/o Henry & Mima Taylor O: miner; by J.M. Douglass; REMARKS: col'd, applied for by C.M. Kyle.

19. 20 May 1890 JAS R. HONAKER 22 yrs single b. Bland Co VA now living same s/o Andrew & ? Honaker to ELLA M. WINFREY 17 yrs single b. Mercer Co W VA d/o Charles & Julina O: farmer; by R.M. Ashworth.

20. This line was entirely omitted.

21. 21 May 1890 G.C. GEORGE 22 yrs single b. Tazewell Co VA now living same s/o Hiram & Edith to MARY McNUTT 19 yrs single b. Mercer Co W VA d/o Allen & Emma L. O: farmer; by R.J. Buckner; REMARKS: col'd.

22. 29 May 1890 DUDLEY ANGLE 19 yrs single b. Mercer Co W VA now living in Wyoming Co W VA s/o Silas & Cloey A. to AMANDA CRIME 16 yrs single b. Mercer Co W VA d/o thos & Arminta O: farmer; by D. Strong; REMARKS: Applied for by a.J. Bailey, sworn.

23. 25 May 1890 C.W. GRIM 19 yrs single b. Mercer Co W VA s/o Peter & Martha to C.N. BAILEY 16 yrs single b. Mercer Co W VA d/o C.W. & Sue A. O: miner; by D. Strong; REMARKS: Applied for by B.b. Bailey, sworn.

24. 27 May 1890 WM B. EARLE 48 yrs wid. b. Augusta Co VA now living in Braenbrier Co W VA s/o Jacob & Jane to MARGARET A. CROTTY 35 yrs single b. Monroe Co W VA d/o Daniel L & ? O: carpenter; by R.A Kelley.

25. * * * WASH MARTIN 33 yrs to MATILDA WRIGHT 31 yrs ** (*Note: no date or any other information given.)

26. 8 June 1890 GEO CASEY 26 yrs single b. Franklin Co Va s/o John & Susan to ROSA MEADOWS 21 yrs single b. Pulaski Co VA d/o Abram & Sallie O: miner; by J.M. Douglass; REMARKS: Applied for by B. Moore.

27. 9 June 1890 ANDREW COCHRAN 27 yrs single b. Larrence Co KY s/o Danl & Nancy to MOLLIE ENSLEY 22 yrs wid. b. MO d/o John & Mary O: railroading; by P.S. Sutton.

28. 11 June 1890 WM HENDRICKS 22 yrs single b. Pulaski Co VA s/o Wm & Maria to ANNA DAVENPORT 18 yrs single b. Russel Co VA d/o Thomas & Eliza O: miner; by J.M. Douglass.

29. 18 June 1890 ALFRED E. BURTON 22 yrs single b. Giles Co VA s/o A.D. & Arbell to NANNIE B. NEAL 18 yrs single b. Bland Co VA d/o ? & Mollie O: carpenter; by J.C. Cook; REMARKS: sworn.

30. 11 June 1890 J.V. CARR 27 yrs wid. b. Floyd Co VA to MARY J. VIA 38 yrs single b. Franklin Co VA d/o S. & Mary J. O: farmer; by J.P. Campbell.

31. 12 June 1890 JOHN MITCHELL 35 yrs single b. Campbell Co VA s/o Lucinda to MOLLIE GARDNER 18 yrs single b. Mercer Co W VA d/o Rush & Viney O: farming; by M.A. Wilson.

32. 15 June 1890 G.W. THORNTON 20 yrs single b. Mercer Co W VA s/o H.C. & Amanda to LELIA M. BRAY 22 yrs single d/o M.H. & ? O:railroading; by L. Goodwyn.

33. 16 June 1890 WM P. HAWLEY 22 yrs single b. Raleigh Co W VA s/o Addison M. & Mary E. to HATTIE L. KARNES 18 yrs single b. Mercer Co W VA d/o James A. & Elizabeth O:merchandising; by Jas Sweeney.

34. 18 June 1890 JOHN L. BIGGS 21 yrs single b. Monroe Co W VA now living same s/o Augustus C. & Lydia to METTIE J. HEARN 21 yrs angle b. Mercer Co W VA d/o L.L. & Rhoda L. O: railroading; by P.S. Sutton.

35. 19 June 1890 HENRY BELL 22 yrs single b. Calh(oun) Co W VA s/o H. & Eliza to MELVINA HAWKINS 24 yrs single b. Grason Co NC d/o ? & Polly O: laborer; by D.N. Saunders.

36. 22 June 1890 FRED KNIGHT 24 yrs single b. Chatham Co NC s/o John J. & Sarah Jane to NANCY GRIFFITH 19 yrs single b. Franklin Co VA d/o Beverly & Chatherine O: mining; by J.C. Cook.

37. 23 June 1890 ELI W. SNIDER 23 yrs single b. Mercer Co W VA s/o Wm Riley & Dimotha to SALLIE E. SHUTT 31 yrs single b. Mercer Co W VA d/o David & Elizabeth O: farmer; by J.R. Morris.

38. 27 June 1890 H.C. CLAY 46 yrs single b. Augusta Co GA s/o Burg & Sarah to SALLIE FARMER 26 yrs single b. Tazewell Co VA O: carpenter; by P.S. Sutton.

39. 2 July 1890 ROBERT A. KARNES 25 yrs single b. Mercer Co W VA s/o James A. & Elizabeth A. to ENDORA MASTIN 23 yrs single b. NC d/o Wm E. & ? O: merchant; by J.R. Morris.

40. 22 July 1890 HENRY CUNINGHAM 25 yrs single b. Franklin Co VA s/o Miles & Lucy to FLORENCE HANCOCK 18 yrs single b. Franklin Co VA O: miner; by J.H. Brown; REMARKS: col'd.

41. 3 July 1890 GEORGE ADAMS 26 yrs single b. Wythe Co VA s/o Charles & Ester to KATE WHITE 21 yrs single b. Wythe Co VA d/o Fred & Kate O: miner; by J.M. Douglass; REMARKS: colored.

42. 15 July 1890 L.D. BRICKEY 22 yrs single b. Montgomery Co VA s/o E.G. & Christina to TERESSA MONSEY 21 yrs single b. Floyd Co VA d/o W.J. & Anna O: farmer; by J.C. Cook.

43. 10 July 1890 E.A. SANDRIDGE 28 yrs single b. Albermarle Co VA s/o Austn & Sarah J. to SUE GRAHAM 20 yrs single b. Montgomery Co VA d/o ? & Fannie O: mining; by M.A. Wilson.

44. 17 July 1890 D.T. MILLS 35 yrs wid. b. Franklin Co VA s/o C.M. & Sallie to AMANDA HALL 18 yrs single b. Montgomery Co VA d/o J.D. & L.S. O: mining; by J.C. Cook.

45. 20 July 1890 SAML. S. MILLER 33 yrs single b. Monroe Co W VA now living same s/o Saml & ? to JOSEPHINE V. BOWLING 26 yrs single b. Mercer Co W VA d/o Chas A. & Lucy O: farmer; by Chas Walker.

46. 28 July 1890 B.L GEARHEART 41 yrs wid. b. Floyd Co VA s/o Washington & Mary to NANNIE C. WILLIAMS 33 yrs single b. Franklin Co VA d/o ? & Mary B. O: mining; by J.L. Prater.

47. 26 July 1890 R.L. DOVE 20 yrs single b. Mercer Co W VA s/o Toot. W. & Isabella to JENNIE JOHNSTON 21 yrs single b. Grayson Co VA d/o Joseph C. & Martha J. O: farmer; by J.W. Bennett.

48. 28 July 1890 OVERTON MEAD 33 yrs single b. Louisa Co VA s/o Jos & Bettie to MARTHA PLUNTER 32 yrs single b. KY d/o ? & Harriett O: miner; by W.J. Prater.

Page 57

1. 4 Aug 1890 JAMES SMITH 29 yrs single b. Campbell Co VA s/o Thos & Annie to ELLA SMITH 18 yrs angle b. Mercer Co W Va d/o ? & Emma O: railroading; by P.S. Sutton.

2. 4 Aug 1890 JAMES S. WYRICK 60 yrs wid. b. Bland Co VA s/o Asa & Marinda to NANCY J. HAZLEWOOD 32 yrs wid. b. Giles Co VA d/o Geo W. & Susanna O: farming; by J.H. Kennedy.

3. 9 Aug 1890 HENRY P. BLANKENSHIP 34 yrs single b. Mercer Co W VA s/o Edward & ? to NANNIE B. MATHEREY 18 yrs single b. Tazewell Co VA d/o Floyd W. & Hulda J. O: farming; by J.O. Cassaday.

4. 13 Aug 1890 F.J. TABOR 33 yrs wid. b. Tazewell Co VA s/o Richard & Permilia to A.R. DAWSON 35 yrs single b. Wythe Co VA d/o Hiram & Sarah O: farming; by J.H. Kennedy.

5. 31 Aug 1890 HENRY DICKERSON 21 yrs single b. Bedford Co VA s/o Saml & Jennett to HATTIE GLOVER 21 yrs single b. Campbell Co VA d/o John & Bettie O: miner; by M.A. Pannill.

6. 26 Aug 1890 SEXTON STEELE 29 yrs single b. Carrol Co VA now living same s/o James & Mary to WILLIE M. THOMPSON 26 yrs single b. Monroe Co W VA d/o William & Marinda O: merchant; by H.C. Thompson.

7. 27 Aug 1890 CHAS W. THAXTON 33 yrs wid. b. Amhurst Co VA s/o Saml & Sallie to MARY C. MANNING 19 yrs single b. Mercer Co W VA d/o Andrew & Nancy J. O: engineer; by J.O. Cassaday.

8. 2 Sept 1890 ROBT E. BRIDGES 21 yrs single b. Franklin Co VA s/o N.T. & Sallie P. to MARY M. PHILLIPS 16 yrs single b. Mercer Co W VA d/o Ballard P. & C.P. O: farming; by Wm Holroyd.

9. 4 Sept 1890 ROBT E. PENDLETON 23 yrs single b. Mercer Co W VA s/o Wyatt & Rachael to SARAH M. BONHAM 15 yrs single b. Smythe Co VA d/o ? & Amanda O: farming; by L. Goodwyn.

10. 4 Sept 1890 MACK H. SHRADER 20 yrs single b. Mercer Co W VA s/o David & Cloria to ELIZTH M. MILLS 14 yrs single b. Mercer Co W VA d/o H.G. & Amanda E. O: farming; by Chas Walker.

11. 6 Sept 1890 MOSES TABOR 51 yrs wid. b. Tazewell Co VA s/o Albert & Hatilda to LILLIE MEADOWS 16 yrs single b. Mercer Co W VA d/o Harvey & Victoria O: laborer; by A.J. Thompson.

12. 7 Sept 1890 AUGUSTUS WALKER 23 yrs single b. Brunswick Co VA s/o Ferd & Louisa to SARAH L. SMITH 21 yrs single b. Montgomery Co VA d/o John H. & Annie O: railroading; by L. Goodwyn.

13. 9 Sept 1890 SIDNEY M. WALL 40 yrs single b. Mercer Co W VA s/o Henry & Jane to AMANDA A. SCOTT 22 yrs single b. Mercer Co W VA d/o Wm R. & Elizabeth O: farming; by D.N. Saunders.

14. 10 Sept 1890 VINT C. FAULKNER 22 yrs single b. Tazewell Co VA s/o Gordon & Annie E. to SARAH M.J. POE 16 yrs single b. Mercer Co W VA d/o Thos E. & M.E. Poe O: farming; by D.N. Saunders.

15. 10 Sept 1890 AMAJIAH L GODFREY 42 yrs single b. Tazewell Co VA s/o John D. & Martha B. to SOPHIA WITTEN 30 yrs single b. Mercer Co W VA d/o Wm H. & Mary O: Town Seargent Barnwell; by J.L. Prater.

16. 12 Sept 1890 GEO W. FARMER 20 yrs single b. Campbell Co VA s/o James & Polly to MAGGIE L. HYPES 22 yrs single b. Crayg(sic) Co VA d/o G.A. & S.E. O: carpenter; by J.H. Kennedy.

17. 15 Sept 1890 J.B. MARTIN 30 yrs div. b. Mercer Co W VA s/o L.D. & Sarah to MOLLIE M. BELCHER 19 yrs single b. Mercer Co W VA d/o W. McH. & Julia A. O: farmer; by Wm Holroyd.

18. 17 Sept 1890 C.W. MARTIN 22 yrs single b. Campbell Co VA s/o Wm & Mary J. to LENA G. FARMER 26 yrs single b. Pulaski Co VA d/o Frank M. & Victoria O: railroading; by J.R. Morris.

19. 21 Sept 1890 HENRY CECIL 21 yrs single b. Mercer Co W VA s/o James & Jane to MARTHA HILL 16 yrs single b. Mercer Co W VA d/o David & Louisa O: mining; by D. Strong.

20. 22 Sept 1890 EDWARD LEE 21 yrs single b. Caswell Co NC s/o Wm & Manerva to RACHEL LAWSON 21 yrs single b. Halifax Co VA d/o Albert & Emma O: railroading; by Jas Sweeney; REMARKS: col'd, both sworn.

21. 24 Sept 1890 ROBT JEFFERSON 22 yrs single b. Prince Edward Co VA s/o Andrew & Harriet to ANNIE SALES 21 yrs single b. Washington Co VA d/o Harry & Ann O: railroading; by J.H. Douglass; REMARKS: col'd, sworn.

22. 30 Sept 1890 J.A. FRANKLIN 29 yrs single b. Tazewell Co VA now living same s/o Wm & Mary J. to LEVICIE WITTEN 24 yrs single b. Mercer Co W VA d/o Wm H. & Mary O: farmer; by R.A. Kelly.

23. 1 Oct 1890 J.L. UNDERWOOD 25 yrs single b. Franklin Co VA s/o Murrell & Martha to SALLIE J. BREWER 30 yrs single b. Franklin Co VA d/o Hopkins & Susan A. O: farmer; by J.W. Bennett; REMARKS: applied for by J.F. Holroyd.

24. 1 Oct 1890 W.J. WINSON 25 yrs single b. Fayett Co W VA s/o Anderson & Martha to ANNA WOLF 20 yrs single b. OH d/o Peter & Mary O: miner; by M.A. Wilson; REMARKS: applied for by Z.T. Rodgers.

25. 5 Oct 1890 ARCHER WOODS 38 yrs single b. Campbell Co VA s/o Geo & Mary to ALICE GOWINGS 21 yrs single b. Grayson Co VA d/o Andrew & Hariet O: miner; by J.H. Douglass; REMARKS: col'd, sworn.

26. 30 Nov 1890 WALKER MILLS 27 yrs single b. Pulaski Co VA s/o Jacob & Mary to CATHARINE CALLOWAY 28 yrs single b. Franklin Co VA d/o ? & Louisa O: miner; by J.H. Douglass; REMARKS: col'd, sworn.

27. 2 Oct 1890 CHAS H. WHITE 22 yrs single b. Mercer Co W VA s/o J.G. & Elizzie to MARY E. HATHERINGTON 21 yrs single b. Mercer Co W VA d/o J.T. & J.H. O: railroading; by J.O. Cassaday.

28. 2 Oct 1890 J.B. WOOD 22 yrs single b. Richmond VA s/o R.B. & Susan to SUE DICKERSON 21 yrs single b. Floyd Co VA d/o John & Mary O: stone cutter; by M.A. Wilson.

29. 5 Oct 1890 S.K. GORE 20 yrs single b. Mercer Co W VA s/o J.F. & S.R. to EURAH E. KING 15 yrs single b. Floyd Co VA d/o Henry A. & J.E. O: farmer; by J.W. Bennett.

30. 7 Oct 1890 GARLAND BRUCE 24 yrs single b. Pittsylvania Co VA s/o Willis & Agnes to MARY TINLEY 21 yrs single b. Amherst Co VA d/o Dick & Jinnie O: miner; by Jas Sweeney; REMARKS: col'd, both sworn.

31. 12 Oct 1890 MOSES DANCE 34 yrs wid. b. Dinwiddie Co VA s/o Henry & Sophia to ANNA MILLS 22 yrs single b. NC d/o M. & Rhoda O: miner; by J.H. Douglass.

32. 15 Oct 1890 J.K. MEADOR 24 yrs single b. Summers Co W VA now living same s/o John J. & ? to MOLLIE L. BURCH 19 yrs single b. Mercer Co W VA d/o Geo W. & Sarepta O: merchant; by J.P. Campbell.

33. 11 Oct 1890 W.E. MORGAN 36 yrs wid. b. Northampton Co NC s/o Robt H. & Sarah E. to MINNIE N. FIZIER 15 yrs single b. Montgomery Co VA d/o Chas F. & Sue K. O: railroading; by L. Goodwyn.

34. 11 Oct 1890 S.M. BLANTON 23 yrs single b. Halifax Co MA s/o M.D. & Nannie to KATE FREEMAN 22 yrs single b. Fire Creek W VA d/o John & Bell O: telegraph operator; by M.A. Wilson.

35. 15 Oct 1890 RUSSELL MEREDITH(sic) 32 yrs wid. b. Montgomery Co VA to ANGELINE POE 16 yrs single b. Mercer Co W VA d/o Jerery & Cyntha O: farmer; by D.N. Saunders.

36. 15 Oct 1890 ROBT B. CRAWFORD 26 yrs single b. Giles Co VA s/o Wm & Mary to NANNIE ATKINS 27 yrs wid. b. Fayette Co VA d/o Harvey & Eliza J. Kincaid O: railroader; by J.H. Kennedy.

37. 21 Oct 1890 WM H. PENNINGTON 21 yrs single b. KY s/o Wheeler & Wilmouth to A.A. OYLER 16 yrs single b. Montgomery Co VA d/o Emanuel & Mollie R. O: miner; by A.H. Croft; REMARKS: W.J. Penington sworn.

38. 19 Oct 1890 J.P. GOODE 30 yrs wid. b. VA s/o Geo W. & Permelia to ALICE V. DAVIS 30 yrs single b. Mercer Co W VA d/o Len & Polly A. O: farmer; by Wm Holroyd; REMARKS: applied for by Jas C. Hughes.

39. 22 Oct 1890 P.S. BUCHANAN 24 yrs single b. Logan Co W VA s/o Henry & Riziah to MAY M. CARR 20 yrs single b. Mercer Co W VA d/o John T. & Ardelia O: engineer; by P.S. Sutton.

40. 30 Oct 1890 R.L. STOVALL 25 yrs single b. Mercer Co W VA s/o A.G. & Nancy K. to MARY A. JOHNSTON 18 yrs single b. Mercer Co W VA d/o James D. & Mary O: farmer; by J.W. Bennett.

41. 29 Oct 1890 F.D. EVANS 27 yrs single b. Greenbriar Co W VA s/o John J. & Ruth A. to MARY J. MOORE 19 yrs single b. Roanoke Co VA d/o N.D. & H.M. O: miner; by D.N. Saunders.

42. 29 Oct 1890 D.C. EVANS 24 yrs single b. Greenbriar Co W VA s/o John J. & Ruth A. to E.C. MOORE 20 yrs single b. Roanoke Co VA d/o N.D. & H.M. O: miner; by D.N. Saunders.

43. 5 Nov 1890 WM K. BLANKENSHIP 21 yrs single b. Mercer Co W VA s/o Robt H. & Cyntha J. to NORA D. FERGUSON 16 yrs single b. Floyd Co VA d/o C.L. & S.M. O: farmer; by J.W. Bennett.

44. 5 Nov 1890 H.B. SMITH 23 yrs single b. Giles Co VA s/o John J. & Rachel to MARY J. WHITE 16 yrs single b. Mercer Co W VA d/o Jas R. & Sarah J. O: machanic(sic); by L. Goodwyn.

45. 9 Nov 1890 ISAAC IRBY 24 yrs single b. Halifax Co VA s/o Peyton & Jennie to MATTIE DICKERSON 21 yrs single b. Franklin Co VA d/o Henry & Jane O: miner; by M.A. Pannill.

46. 9 Nov 1890 J.W. HALL 29 yrs single b. Smith Co VA s/o A. & Elizabeth to LIZZIE HUTCHINSON 29 yrs single b. Mercer Co W VA d/o Alex & Lydia O: railroader; by J.H.C. Buckwall.

47. 9 Nov 1890 J.L. BOWLING 27 yrs single b. Mercer Co W VA s/o J.J. & Isabella to SARAH A. MAXWELL 21 yrs single b. Mercer Co W VA d/o Wm & Melvina O: farmer; by P.S. Sutton.

48. 13 Nov 1890 JAS L. ROACH 22 yrs single b. Summers Co W VA s/o Wm & Mary to LAURA PERDUE 20 yrs single b. Giles Co VA d/o Hack & Nancy F. O: carpenter; by J.O. Cassaday.

Page 58

1. 21 Nov 1890 J.K. KIDD 21 yrs single b. Bland Co VA s/o W.H. & Mary T. to R.M.L. HAGER 16 yrs single b. Mercer Co W VA d/o W.W. & R.A. O: farmer; by Jas. Sweeney.

2. 27 Nov 1890 W.A. THOMPSON 27 yrs single b. Mercer Co W VA s/o Wm H. & Sarah to SARAH CALFEE 27 yrs single b. Mercer Co W VA d/o Jas & Elizabeth Calfee O: farmer; by J.O. Cassaday.

3. 27 Nov 1890 FOUNTAIN WILEY 20 yrs single b. Mercer Co W VA s/o Albert & Louisa to IDA MARTIN 15 yrs single b. Mercer Co W VA d/o W.J. & Martha O: farmer; by Wm Holroyd; REMARKS: F.Wiley sworn.

4. 29 Nov 1890 J.P. WOODS 21 yrs wid. b. Raleigh Co W VA now living same s/o James & Nancy E. to R.B. MEADOR 18 yrs single b. Mercer Co W VA d/o G.W. & Elizabeth N. O: farmer; by D. Farley.

5. 4 Dec 1890 JNO P. MUSE 23 yrs single b. Franklin Co VA s/o Austn & Rosazella to LAURA HARMAN 18 yrs single b. Mercer Co W VA d/o Ballard & Fannie O: railroading; by G.W. Thrasher; REMARKS: sworn.

6. 7 Dec 1890 ALBERT PRANT 27 yrs single b. Germany s/o Charles & ? to KATE WARD 28 yrs div. b. Wythe Co VA d/o David & Sarah A. O: fireman; by C.W. Kelley.

7. 22 Dec 1890 M.B. PHILLIPS 23 yrs single b. Raleigh Co W VA now living same s/o Clark & Catherine to S.B. CHRISTIAN 15 yrs single b. Mercer Co W VA d/o Eli W. & L. O: farmer; by G.H. Johnston.

8. 10 Dec 1890 NEEL FITCH 22 yrs sngle b. Franklin Co VA s/o Jordon & Caroline to MARY HALL 23 yrs wid. b. Henry Co VA d/o John & Julia O: miner; by J.H. Douglass; REMARKS: col'd.

9. Number and line entirely omitted.

10. 11 Dec 1890 JAS DILLARD 46 yrs single b. Amhurst Co VA s/o Jno & Lucy to REBECCA C. KING 50 yrs wid. b. Franklin Co VA d/o Fleming & Mary O: farmer; by D.N. Saunders.

11. 11 Dec 1890 A.B. SHOOT 31 yrs single b. NC s/o Wash. Cowan & Amanda Smoot to BETTIE STANLEY 27 yrs single b. Roanoke Co VA d/o ? & Ailsie Gary O: miner; by W.J. Carter; REMARKS: col'd.

12. 11 Dec 1890 WM S. FONTY 25 yrs single b. Franklin Co PA s/o Michieal(sic) & Rebecca to MARY E. JOHNSON 19 yrs single b. Botetourt Co VA d/o Geo S. & Nannie O: lumberman; by S.C. Dorsey.

13. 11 Dec 1890 J.E. BOND 29 yrs single b. Franklin Co VA s/o Wm P. & Bettie A. to SALLIE B. JOHNSON 20 yrs single b. Botetourt Co VA d/o Geo S. & Nannie O: merchant; by S.C. Dorsey.

14. 14 Dec 1890 C.L. BELCHER 23 yrs single b. Tazewell Co Va s/o R.H. & Reely to CELESTIA A. MAXWELL 27 yrs single b. Mercer Co w VA d/o Wm & ? O: farmer; by J.W. Bennett; REMARKS: sworn.

15. 24 Dec 1890 JAS S. CHAMBERS 22 yrs single b. Monroe Co W VA now living Summers Co W VA s/o A.F. & Mary J. to ALLIE W. WILEY 17 yrs single b. Mercer Co W VA d/o Jno A. & Mahala O: farmer; by J.W. Bennett; REMARKS: sworn.

16. 17 Dec 1890 D.L. EPLING 20 yrs single b. Giles Co VA s/o L.A. & Ellen to LONIE C. TABOR 17 yrs sngle b. Mercer Co W VA d/o Geo O. & Ollie O: farmer; by J.W. Lilly.

17. 18 Dec 1890 A.C. DAVIDSON 18 yrs single b. Mercer Co W VA s/o Henry & Cassander to ALICE L. POWELL 18 yrs single b. Mercer Co W VA d/o W.A. & Mollie O: farmer; by D.N. Saunders.

18. 18 Dec 1890 J.W. PRICE 28 yrs signle b. Bedford Co VA s/o Morris & Mary to JULIAN SPENCER 23 yrs single b. Charlotte VA d/o C.H. & Rhoda O: railroading; by G.W. Thrasher; REMARKS: sworn, col'd.

19. 18 Dec 1890 DAVID K. BAILEY 19 yrs single b. McDowell Co W VA s/o Martin & Nannie C. to MEDA B. BROWN 19 yrs single b. Mercer Co W VA d/o M & Martha O: farmer; by I.K. Lambert; REMARKS: sworn.

20. 21 Dec 1890 ESLIE SALE 28 yrs single b. Amherst Co VA now livng in Rockbridge Co Va s/o Wm H. & Sarah to EUNICE E. BAILEY 16 yrs single b. Mercer Co W VA d/o Greenville C. & Sarah E.J. O: mechanic; by S.C. Dorsey.

21. 24 Dec 1890 R.C. BRITTON 26 yrs single b. Halifax Co VA s/o Scot & Edie to SALLIE JONES 22 yrs single b. Halifax Co VA d/o Robt & Sallie O: miner; by G.F. Johnston; REMARKS: col'd.

22. 25 Dec 1890 JAMES YEATS 22 yrs single b. Pittsylvania Co VA s/o Geo W. & Nannie to JULIA BELL 16 yrs single b. Mercer Co W VA d/o Geo & Sarah O: miner; by C.W. Kelley; REMARKS: sworn.

23. 24 Dec 1890 JAS W. VAUGHT 23 yrs single b. Mercer Co W VA s/o Lewis C. & Clara C. to SARAH F. HURT 16 yrs single b. Mercer Co W VA d/o W.S. & Martha J. O: farmer; by J.O. Cassaday.

24. 24 Dec 1890 JOS M.S. KEENES 25 yrs single b. Giles Co W VA s/o Joseph & ? to NANCY J. SOUTHERN 16 yrs sngle b. Mercer Co W VA d/o Wm & Rachael O: farmer; by A.J. Thompson.

25. 25 Dec 1890 W.H. RUCKER 25 yrs single b. Campbell Co VA now living same s/o Ambros & Martha to CORA WITTEN 18 yrs single b. Mercer Co W VA d/o Wm H. & Nancie O: railroader; by J.C. Prater.

26. 25 Dec 1890 SAMUEL SCOTT 27 yrs wid. b. Prince Edward Co VA s/o Robt & Lettie to MARGARET ELDRIDGE 21 yrs single b. Giles Co VA d/o ? & Rachel O: railroader; by R. Harris; REMARKS: col'd.

27. 24 Dec 1890 SAML FIERCE 23 yrs single b. Mitchell Co NC to CALLIE L. HINES 20 yrs single b. Mitchell Co NC d/o Ben & Adeline O: mining; by J.L. Prater.

28. 24 Dec 1890 JOHN A. WOLFORD 24 yrs single b. Augusta Co VA s/o ? & C. Wolford to CLARINDA McLAUGHLIN 22 yrs single b. Russell Co VA d/o Harvey & Serilda A. O: railroading; by J.L. Prater.

29. 25 Dec 1890 JAMES T. WIMMER 21 yrs single b. Mercer Co W VA s/o Isaac & Rebecca J. to NANCY C. ROLAND 17 yrs single b. Mercer Co W VA d/o Miles B. & Mary O: farming; by R. Harry.

30. 25 Dec 1890 GEO L. PETIT 24 yrs wid. b. Henry Co VA s/o Wm W. & Matilda to SARAH E. SARVER 19 yrs single b. Giles Co VA d/o James M. & Matilda A. O: railroading; by L. Goodwyn.

31. 25 Dec 1890 ANDREW R. BONHAM 22 yrs single b. Smythe Co VA s/o John F. & amanda S. to DERINZIE B. SMITH 15 yrs single b. Mercer Co W VA d/o Wm H. & Victorie O: railroading; by L. Goodwyn.

32. 25 Dec 1890 SILAS COBBS 24 yrs single b. Bedford Co VA s/o Jacob & Caroline to ANN BIRD 28 yrs wid. b. Moore Co NC d/o James & Martha O: railroading; by A.J. Thompson; REMARKS: col'd.

33. 29 Dec 1890 JAMES P.D. JONES 21 yrs single b. Mercer Co W VA s/o ? & Caroline to NANCY R. GORE 19 yrs single b. Mercer Co W VA d/o Wm & Minerva O: farming; by J.P. Campbell.

34. 31 Dec 1890 CHAS A. MARSHALL 37 yrs single b. England now living in Knoxville TN s/o Wm & Elizabeth to IRENE H. BARBOR 22 yrs single b. Monroe Co W VA d/o H.b. & Fannie C. O: clerk; by P.S. Sutton.

35. 13 Jan 1891 L.R. BAILEY 22 yrs single b. Giles Co W VA s/o James & Jane to ZEALIE E. GORDON 18 yrs single d/o George W. & Sallie O: farmer; by H.E. Bailey.

36. * * * ALBERT LAWSON 38 yrs wid. b. Marion Co VA s/o John & Mary to MARY J. CLOWERS 32 yrs wid. b. Pulaski Co VA O: mill right. (*Note: no date given.)

37. * * * JAMES REED 23 yrs single b. Franklin Co VA s/o Flem & Sarah to ALICE C. PAYNE 20 yrs single b. Mercer Co W VA d/o Bartly & Caroline O: farming; by L. Goodwyn. (*Note: no date given.)

Page 59

1. 8 Jan 1891 J.W. BROWNING 25 yrs single to LIEUVENIA HAMBRICK 21 yrs single b. Mercer Co W VA d/o Joseph & Ellen O: miner; by D.N. Saunders.

2. 8 Jan 1891 MOSES E. BELCHER 25 yrs single b. Tazewell Co VA s/o Robt H. & Arrolie to LURA M. HURST 16 yrs single b. Mercer Co W VA d/o Jas B. & Sarah P. O: farmer; by John H. Kennedy.

3. 13 Jan 1891 G.W. WALKER 21 yrs single b. Mercer Co W VA s/o ? & Caroline Walker to OSHIE WILLIAMS 21 yrs single b. Mercer Co W VA d/o A.J. Thompson; REMARKS: col'd, G.W. Walker sworn.

4. 14 Jan 1891 J.F. WITT 21 yrs single b. Tazewell Co VA s/o J.F. & J.T. Witt to EMMA DOUTHAT 19 yrs single b. Pulaski Co VA d/o C.F. & Mary F. Douthat O: clerk master mech; by Frank Jackson; REMARKS: information by J.F. Witt and M.S. Johnson.

5. 14 Jan 1891 JOHN T. VIA 32 yrs single b. Tazewell Co VA to MAHALA COOK 33 yrs wid. b. Mercer Co W VA d/o Vincent & Cynthia Wiley O: farmer; by G.M. Johnston; REMARKS: informed by G.W. Caldwell

6. 14 Jan 1891 E.V. MAXWELL 34 yrs single b. Mercer Co W VA s/o Wm & Melvina Maxwell to SALLIE KARNES 22 yrs single b. Mercer Co W VA d/o J.A. & E.A. Karnes O: merchant; by John B. Kennedy; REMARKS: informed by J.B. Kennedy.

7. 22 Jan 1891 S.F. LYONS* 38 yrs wid. b. OH s/o Elijah & Lucy Lyon* to SINA A. UNDERWOOD 22 yrs single b. Franklin Co VA d/o Asa L. & H.J. Underwood O: farmer; by Thos Parris. (*Note: name spelled both ways.)

8. 28 Jan 1891 THOMAS ROBINSON 38 yrs single b. Giles Co VA now living same s/o Henry & Phoebe to MARY E. SKEENS 21 yrs single b. Giles Co VA d/o H.A. & M.E. Skeens O: farmer; by T.C. Pulliam.

9. 5 Feb 1891 ANDREW J. FLETCHER 23 yrs single b. Mercer Co W VA s/o Jas H. & Columbia Jane to NANCY JANE HILL 21 yrs single b. VA d/o ? & Martha Hill O: farmer; by A.J. Thompson.

10. 11 Feb 1891 OLIVER M. GLASS 26 yrs single b. Albermarle Co VA s/o Jesse M. & Martha to EDNA LITTLE 28 yrs single b. Mercer Co W VA O: railroader; by M.A. Wilson.

11. 12 Feb 1891 B.F. BEAMER 54 yrs wid. b. Monroe Co W VA now living n Montgomery Co VA s/o Michael & Jane Beamer to LIZZIE CARR 40 yrs single b. Mercer Co W VA d/o Robert & Sarah O: saw mill; by Phil S. Sutton.

12. 12 Feb 1891 J.P. ROBINETT 29 yrs single b. Bland Co VA s/o John & Mary Robinett to M.B. LEFLER 22 yrs single b. Mercer Co W VA d/o C.W. & ? O: railroader; by R.W. Kite.

13. 22 Feb 1891 GEORGE M. BAILEY 34 yrs wid. b. Mercer Co W VA s/o J.S. & Urzula to ELLA E. KING 20 yrs sngle b. Roanoke Co VA d/o Jacob O. & Rebecca C. O: farmer; by D.N. Saunders.

14. 22 Feb 1891 C.O. WRIGHT 25 yrs single b. Albermarle Co VA s/o John J. & M.R. to H. WINTERS McCUE 20 yrs single b. Mercer Co W VA d/o James & E.J; by Phil S. Sutton.

15. 25 Feb 1891 BALLARD P. McGUIRE 21 yrs div. b. Montgomery Co VA s/o Lee & Sarah E. McGuire to EASTER JANE BOOZE 21 yrs single b. Montgomery Co VA d/o Wm & Nancy Booze O: farmer; by James Sweeney.

16. 26 Feb 1891 JOHN W. SMITH 24 yrs single b. Mercer Co W Va now living in Giles Co VA s/o Isaac A. & Sarah to JOSIE M. BOLTON 24 yrs single b. Mercer Co W VA d/o Matthew & Mary O: farmer; by S.C. Dorsey.

17. 24 Feb 1891 Oakvale W VA JOHN C. WILLIAMS 24 yrs single b. Giles Co VA s/o Floyd G. & Mary to ROSIE E. CAMPBELL 18 yrs single b. Mercer Co W VA d/o John & Eliza O: railroader; by L. Goodwyn.

18. 24 Feb 1891 Bramwell W VA JOHN T. COLLINS 36 yrs wid. b. Monroe Co W VA s/o Edw & Elizabeth to JOSIE E. HUNTER 21 yrs single b. Monroe Co W VA d/o Geo W. & Eveline O: mason & bricklayer; by C.W. Kelley.

19. 24 Feb 1891 Bramwell W VA G.W.L. HONAKER 22 yrs single b. Tazewell Co VA s/o Andrew & Lucy to RACHEL E. BAILEY 21 yrs single d/o Zachariah & Elizabeth O: miner; by C.W. Kelley.

20. 25 Feb 1891 Oakvale W VA W.P. BOGGESS 28 yrs single b. Mercer Co W VA s/o Nimrod & Margaret to MARY H. BOYD 20 yrs single b. Mercer Co w VA d/o Wm B. & Marinda O: merchant; by L. Goodwyn.

21. 4 Mar 1891 J.J. KESSINGER 19 yrs single b. Giles Co VA s/o Silas M. & Charlotte A. to L.B. ELLISON 17 yrs single b. Mercer Co W VA d/o Benj Ellison & Josie Lilly O: farmer; by Jas W. Lilly; REMARKS: consent of J.H. Campbell who raised the lady.

22. 30 Mar 1891 CORNELIUS MARTIN 24 yrs single b. NC s/o Thos & Martha to VIOLIA WILLIAMS 22 yrs single b. Giles Co VA d/o Harvey & ? O: bricklayer; by A.M. Craft.

23. 14 Mar 1891 Bluefield W VA WM A. COOPER 53 yrs wid. b. Grason Co VA s/o John & Rachel S. Cooper to CHRISTIN KNOBLOUCH 22 yrs single b. Germany d/o Peter & Babett Knoblouch O: Agt for Real Estate; by Frank Jackson.

24. 6 Mar 1891 DAVID C. HEADOR 22 yrs single b. Summers Co W VA s/o Isaac & Mary Jane to VIRGINIA A. HEADOR 17 yrs single b. Summers Co W VA d/o Josephus & Catherine O: farm laborer; by Drewry Farley.

25. 8 Mar 1891 Simmons W VA WM ANTHONY 23 yrs single b. VA s/o ? & Emily to FRANCES WHEELER 24 yrs single b. Campbell Co VA d/o Jacob & Mary O: miner; by G.F. Johnson; REMARKS: col'd, applied for by B. Moore.

26. 8 Mar 1891 Simmons W VA CHAS SMITH 22 yrs single b. Appomattox Co VA s/o Wm & Ada to LIZZIE JONES 20 yrs single b. Halifax Co VA d/o Robt & Elmira; by G.F. Johnson; REMARKS: col'd, applied for by C.M. Kyle.

27. 10 Mar 1891 ABRAHAM WITT 22 yrs sngle b. Montgomery Co VA now living same s/o James & Emaline to JATHINA A. HUDSON 18 yrs single b. Mercer Co W VA d/o R.R. & Martha E. O: railroader; by Jas O. Cassaday.

28. 12 Mar 1891 PERRY G. CAHILL 29 yrs wid. b. Giles Co VA s/o Perry J. & Elizabeth A. to SARAH J. BRUCE 22 yrs single b. Mercer Co W VA d/o Wm W. & Martha O: farmer; by L. Goodwyn.

29. 18 Mar 1891 Simmons W VA JAMES JORDAN 27 yrs single b. Halifax Co VA s/o Elijah & Martha to MOLLIE CAVILL 16 yrs single b. Tazewell Co VA d/o Frank & Ellen O: miner; by M.A. Pannill; REMARKS: col'd, applied for by C.M. Kyle.

30. 18 Mar 1891 Coopers W VA T.C. MONTGOMERY 22 yrs single b. Giles Co VA to DOLLIE EDWARDS 17 yrs single b. Pittsylvania Co VA d/o W.H. & Bia R. Edwards O: miner; by C.W. Kelly.

31. 19 Mar 1891 Bluefield W VA JOHN STOCKTON 23 yrs single b. Franklin Co VA s/o Jenk Kidd & Patsy Stockton to MARY JOHNSON 22 yrs single b. Campbell Co VA d/o Creed & ? O: railroading; by G.W. Trasher; REMARKS: colored.

32. 22 Mar 1891 Hill Creek W VA HAT BETHEL 27 yrs single b. Pittsylvania Co VA s/o Joseph & Lucy to ROSE McDANIEL 23 yrs single b. Amherst Co VA d/o David & ? O: miner; by R.S. Umberger; REMARKS: colored.

33. 26 Mar 1891 Freemans W VA JEFF MITCHELL 22 yrs single b. Nelson Co VA s/o Jeff & Agnes to EVALINE NICHOLS 23 yrs single b. Giles Co VA d/o John & Rosy O: miner; by M.A. Pannill; REMARKS: colored.

34. 28 Mar 1891 Goodwill W VA WILLIAM HERON 24 yrs single b. Durham Co England s/o John & Mary to MARY TWEDDLE 22 yrs single b. Northumberland Co England d/o Robert & Isabella O: miner; by C.W. Kelley; REMARKS: W.J. Preece gave information.

35. 27 Mar 1891 Bramwell W VA HARVEY HOSTON 26 yrs single b. NC s/o Abraham & Jennette to MARY ANNIE TAYLOR 23 yrs single b. Roanoke Co VA d/o West & Laura O: miner; by C.W. Kelley; REMARKS: colored, H. Hoston sworn.

36. 27 Mar 1891 Bramwell W VA JOHN PATTERSON 26 yrs single b. Franklin Co VA s/o ? & Sally Ann to SALLY ANN FULLER 28 yrs single b. Danville VA ? & Chaney Fuller O: miner; by C.W. Kelley.

37. 2 April 1891 JEFFERSON D. LILLY 18 yrs single b. Mercer Co W VA now living in Raleigh Co W VA s/o Joseph & Betsey to ELIZABETH C. LILLY 16 yrs single b. Mercer Co W VA d/o Jas W. & Rachel O: teacher; by James Sweeney.

38. 1 April 1891 Freeman's W VA CHAS GIBSON 22 yrs single b. Czmpbell Co VA s/o Charles & Nancy to ANNIE COX 21 yrs single b. Campbell Co VA d/o Anderson & Juda O: miner; by G.F. Johnson; REMARKS: col'd.

39. 2 April 1891 Mill Creek W VA ALBERT VIERNOW 34 yrs single b. Germany s/o Henry & Alvena to NANNIE H. PARKER 28 yrs single b. Mercer Co W VA d/o A.A. & Mary O:miner; by C.W. Kelley.

40. 2 April 1891 Bluefield W VA VAIDEN GILES 29 yrs wid. b. Pittsylvania Co VA s/o Nat & Sally to WILLIE HAINES 20 yrs single b. Giles Co VA d/o John & Harriet O: railroader; by G.W. Thrasher; REMARKS: col'd.

41. 2 April 1891 Bramwell W VA BOSE JACKSON 22 yrs single b. Hecklenburg Co VA s/o Charles & Harriet to SALLIE JOHNSON 21 yrs single b. Halifax Co VA d/o ? & Chaney Barksdale O: miner; by C.W. Kelley; REMARKS: col'd.

42. 20 April 1891 Simmons W VA MADISON CAIN 32 yrs single b. Ballahack VA s/o Cha & Mariah to VIOLET SAUNDERS 38 yrs single b. Bedford Co VA d/o Leroy & Charity O: engineer; by G.F. Johnson; REMARKS: col'd, applied for by B. Moore.

43. 8 April 1891 Bluefield W VA DEXTER STOKES 24 yrs single b. Montgomery Co VA s/o Scotland & Parthena to VIOLA CARDWELL 21 yrs single b. Giles Co VA O: railroading; by G.W. Thrasher.

44. 8 April 1891 JAMES M. ROSE 20 yrs single b. Grason Co VA s/o Bryan & Rosamand to M. GIRTRUDE ELLISON 15 yrs single b. Mercer Co w VA d/o M.F. & H.J. Ellison O: farmer; by Jas W. Lilly.

45. 8 April 1891 WM R. WHITE 31 yrs single b. Carroll Co VA s/o Thomas & ? to MARY FOLEY 22 yrs single b. Mercer Co W VA O: farmer; by D.N. Saunders.

46. 8 April 1891 Bluefield W VA V.V. AUSTIN 34 yrs single b. Henry Co VA now living in Hinton W VA s/o Albert C. & Matilda B. to ALICE V. HERNDON 20 yrs single b. Mercer Co W VA d/o Arthur & N.L. O: clerk; by Frank Jackson.

47. 8 April 1891 Princeton W VA WM M. BRIDGES 22 yrs single b. Mercer Co W VA s/o Wm & Jane Alvis to HATTIE L. RYAN 18 yrs single b. Pulaski Co VA d/o John F. & Rebecca S. O: railroader; by M.A. Wilson.

48. 16 April 1891 Oakvale W VA B.P. THOMAS 21 yrs single b. Mercer Co W VA s/o J.W. & F. Jane Thomas to MARGRET ANN JONES 25 yrs single b. Mercer Co W VA d/o Wilson & Francis Jones O: farmer; by L. Goodwyn; REMARKS: applied for by J.W. Thomas.

Page 60

1. 16 April 1891 JOHN CONDEXTER 32 yrs single b. Davis Co NC to JULIA SMITH 19 yrs single b. Mercer Co W VA d/o Richard & Esther Smith O: farmer; by A.J. Thompson; REMARKS: by Richard Smith, col'd.

2. 30 April 1891 Bluefield W VA WM J. JENKS 21 yrs single b. Wake Co NC s/o Wm S. & Ianna R. to SALLIE C. BALDWIN 21 yrs single b. Tazewell Co VA d/o Don B. & Sallie W. O: train dispatcher; by W. H. Burkhardt.

3. 22 April 1891 B.E. TANNER 20 yrs single b. Mercer Co W VA s/o Jas A. White & Mary J. Tanner to SARAH A. HAXEY 21 yrs single b. Franklin Co VA O: farmer; by L. Goodwyn; REMARKS: R.E. Pendleton sworn.

4. 22 April 1891 WM MATSIN 40 yrs wid. b. Harrison Co OH s/o Nehemiah & Mary to ELLEN SHRADER 20 yrs single b. Mercer Co W VA d/o Robert & Jane O: merchant; by Phil S. Sutton.

5. 23 April 1891 AMBROSE WOODIN 27 yrs single b. Pittsylvania Co VA s/o George & Betty to IDA McDANIEL 22 yrs single b. Amherst Co VA d/o David & Paulina O: miner; by S.C. Dorsey; REMARKS: col'd.

6. 26 April 1891 TUCK S. WINGERISH 27 yrs single b. France s/o Peter & Annie Wingerish to ELLEN C. MILLER 26 yrs single b. Craig Co VA d/o George & Milvina Miller O: farmer; by J.O. Cassaday.

7. * * * JOHN HARE 21 yrs single b. Giles Co VA s/o Isaac & Araminta to LAURA A. GRIMM 20 yrs single b. Mercer Co W VA d/o James & Jane O: railroading; REMARKS: License returned without mark or certificate. (*Note: no date given.)

8. 29 April 1891 Simmons W VA R.D. BECKETT 26 yrs single b. Monroe Co W VA s/o William & Margaret to A. JULIA ROBERTSON 21 yrs single b. Franklin Co VA d/o ? & Bish O: miner; by C.W. Kelley; REMARKS: sworn, R.D. Beckett.

9. 28 April 1891 Bramwell W VA JAS A. CHAPMAN 26 yrs single b. Halifax Co NC s/o Aaron D. & Sarah J. to IDA MAY 22 yrs single b. VA d/o Dut. & Annie O: miner; by C.W. Kelley; REMARKS: sworn, J.A. Chapman.

10. 29 April 1891 JAS K. WHITE 36 yrs wid. b. Mercer Co W VA s/o Patton & Rhoda to JULIA A. HOLDRON 26 yrs wid. b. Mercer Co W VA d/o Saml & ? O: farming; by A.J. Thompson; REMARKS: applied for by J.A. White.

11. 30 April 1891 Bramwell W VA JOHN MARTIN 38 yrs wid. b. Russell Co VA now living in Pocahontas VA s/o ? & Peggy to BETTIE HALL 38 yrs single b. Bedford Co VA d/o Randall & Rissie Roberts O: miner; by C.W. Kelley; REMARKS: col'd.

12. 30 April 1891 Simmons W VA JOHN W. RUDD 28 yrs single b. Chesterfield Co VA s/o Arelius & Caroline to SYLVIA SMITH 18 yrs single b. England d/o Eu & Emma Smith O: miner; by C.W. Kelley; REMARKS: applied for by B. Moore.

13. 6 May 1891 Freemans W VA LONDON IRBY 23 yrs single b. Halifax Co VA s/o Peyton & Jennie to CARRIE FIELDS 21 yrs single b. Pittsylvania Co VA d/o Robt & Amanda O: miner; by G.F. Johnson; REMARKS: col'd, applied for by C.M. Ryle.

14. 6 May 1891 JOSHUA A. DAVIS 20 yrs single b. Mercer Co W VA s/o Wm & ? to H.JANE PENNINGTON 15 yrs single b. Mercer Co W VA d/o B.P & Rush Pennington O: laborer; by A.J. Thompson.

15. 9 May 1891 CALVIN DESWIM 22 yrs single b. NC s/o M.F. & Amanda to L. THOMPSON 19 yrs single b. Bland Co VA d/o J.H. & Margaret O: farmer; by J.O. Cassaday.

16. 10 May 1891 RADFORD DICKENSON 24 yrs single b. Bedford Co VA s/o Saml & Jennie to ELLA JONES 22 yrs single b. Botetourte Co VA d/o Harry & Mary O: miner; by G.F. Johnson; REMARKS: col'd, A.F. Godfrey.

17. 10 May 1891 JAS D. GREEN 25 yrs single b. Halifax Co VA s/o Albert & Winnie to HENRIETTA HOPSON 23 yrs single b. Bedford Co VA d/o Willis & Catharine O: miner; by G.F. Johnson; REMARKS: col'd.

18. 11 May 1891 ARTHUR S. THORN 23 yrs single b. Giles Co VA s/o James P. & Mahavala to LULA L. HALE 23 yrs single b. Giles Co VA d/o Jas W. & C.B. O: minister; by J.H. Kennedy.

19. 14 May 1891 C.W. HURST 23 yrs single b. Mercer Co W VA s/o James H. & Sarah F. to L.A. BELCHER 17 yrs single b. Mercer Co w VA d/o Danl W. & Rebecca J. O: merchant; by Phil S. Sutton.

20. 16 May 1891 JAMES H. MONTGOMERY 30 yrs wid. b. Smythe Co VA s/o John Montgomery & Mary Clayton to SARAH BELCHER 18 yrs single b. Smythe Co VA d/o LC. & ? O: blacksmith; by H.E. Bailey; REMARKS: L.D. Hunter sworn.

21. 20 May 1891 JAS W. PENNINGTON 25 yrs single b. Lawrence Co KY s/o G.W. & Wilmouth Pennington to LOUISA H. PETTREY 14 yrs single b. Mercer Co W VA d/o Amos L. & Cornelia O: carpenter; by J.W. Bennett.

22. 20 May 1891 WM T. AGEE 19 yrs single b. Rauley Co W VA now living same s/o Absom & Elvira Agee to NANCY V. FURGUSON 18 yrs single b. Mercer Co W VA d/o Grano N. & Octova F. O: farmer; by Charles Walker; REMARKS: Green N. Furguson.

23. 19 May 1891 C. MABE 22 yrs single b. Sloan Co NC s/o Joseph & Sophia to NANCY DAVIS 21 yrs single d/o Saml & Susan O: farmer; by D.N. Saunders; REMARKS: sworn.

24. 22 May 1891 WM S. HUBBARD 24 yrs single s/o Jonathan & V.E. to ALLIE R. McPHERSON 15 yrs single b. Mercer Co W VA d/o J.R. & Lizzie O: farmer; by Jas W. Lilly.

25. 25 May 1891 Simmons W VA J.D. STAMPER 23 yrs single b. Ashe Co NC s/o H.D. & Catherine to NANNIE HOLLOWAY 19 yrs single b. Carroll Co VA d/o Chas E. & Eliza A. O: teamster; by C.W. Kelley; REMARKS: applied for by Z.T. Rogers.

26. 23 May 1891 Bramwell W VA PAYTON DICKISON 21 yrs single b. Pittsylbania Co VA s/o Lewis & Lucy to REBECCA JOHNSTON 21 yrs angle b. Botetourt Co VA d/o ? & Katy Manuel O: miner; by H.A. Pannill; REMARKS: applied for by B. Moore.

27. 23 May 1891 JOHN B. PARKER 19 yrs single b. Mercer Co W VA s/o ? & Sarah Berks to PHOEBE L. McPHERSON 17 yrs single b. Mercer Co W VA d/o Jacob R. & Lizzie E. O: farmer; by S.C. Dorsey.

28. 25 May 1891 THOMAS M. CASEY 21 yrs single b. Wilkes Co NC s/o Henry & Millie to MOLLIE MEADOWS 22 yrs wid. b. Floyd Co VA d/o Chas & Lucy Wert O: miner; by C.r. Brown; REMARKS: applied for by B. Moore.

29. 27 May 1891 Simmons W VA R.H. PRICE 30 yrs single b. Franklin Co VA s/o ? & Octavia Price to MATILDA MUSE 21 yrs single b. Floyd Co VA d/o Abram & Milly O: miner; by M.A. Pannill; REMARKS: Johnston Hawkins sworn.

30. 6 June 1891 Princeton W VA CHARLES ROWLAND 21 yrs single b. Mercer Co W VA s/o Kinzie & Nancy to SARAH E. ARCHER 23 yrs single b. Mercer Co W VA d/o J.S. & Julina O: farmer; by P.S. Sutton; REMARKS: applied for by J.S. Archer.

31. 4 June 1891 HARVEY HYLTON 22 yrs single b. Floyd Co VA s/o Hiram & Sarah to JULIA A. ANDERSON 21 yrs wid. b. Mercer Co W VA d/o Jack & Polly Galliher O: laborer; by H.E. Bailey; REMARKS: applied for by G.W. Terry.

32. 6 June 1891 Bluefield W VA WILEY SMITH 24 yrs single b. Franklin Co VA s/o George & Victoria to MARY ANN NAPIER 26 yrs wid. b. Montgomery Co VA O: railroader; by G.W. Thrasher.

33. 12 July 1891 Bramwell W VA GEO W. JACKSON 31 yrs single b. Taylor Co W VA s/o ? & Mary Daniel to ELLA YOUNG 21 yrs single b. SC d/o ? & Sylvia Booker O: miner; by G.F. Johnson; REMARKS: col'd.

34. 18 June 1891 Freemans W VA JOHN PRUNTY 23 yrs single b. Pittsylvania Co VA s/o Joseph & Ella to ANNA BERTA LEE 18 yrs single b. Pittsylvania Co VA d/o Sullis & Ann O: miner; by M.A. Pannill; REMARKS: col'd, applied for by S.A. Toy.

35. 20 June 1891 WM T. GIBSON 25 yrs single b. Bland Co VA s/o Thompson Givson to ALICE E. BAILEY 19 yrs single b. Mercer Co W VA O: farmer; by Phil S. Sutton.

36. 20 June 1891 CLOYD AUSTIN CARTER 21 yrs single b. Tazewell Co VA s/o Aaron & Nancy to RHODA JONES 19 yrs angle b. Mercer Co W VA d/o E.P & Zeruah O: farmer; by J.O. Cassaday; REMARKS: R.F. Jones, C.A. Carter both sworn.

37. 1 July 1891 WEBB HUNT 27 yrs div. b. Charleston SC s/o John & Sallie to LELIA CLAYTOR 28 yrs single b. Bedford Co VA d/o ? & Jentry Claytor O: miner; by G.F. Johnson; REMARKS: colored, sworn.

38. 8 July 1891 L.A. BOWES 27 yrs angle b. Attleboro MA s/o Joseph & Mary E. to PEARLY MAY COLE 19 yrs single b. Mercer Co W VA d/o Allen T. & Jennie O: telegraph operator; by L. Goodwyn.

39. 23 June 1891 J.R. MILLER 30 yrs single b. Mercer Co W VA s/o R.A. & Rebecca J. to SUE ANIE WILLIAMS 17 yrs single b. Giles CoVA d/o G.P & ? O: silversmith; by L. Goodwyn.

40. 28 June 1891 THELBERT MEADOWS 22 yrs single b. Mercer Co W VA s/o H.D. & Victoria to ROSEBEL ALTIZER 15 yrs single b. Montgomery Co VA d/o J.E. & Miniam O: farmer; by L. Goodwyn.

41. 28 June 1891 Bluefield W VA JOHN RIPPY 22 yrs single b. Pulaski Co VA s/o Saunders & Sarah to SUE BURTON 21 yrs single b. Pulaski Co VA d/o John & ? O: railroader; by G.W. Thrasher; REMARKS: col'd, John Rippy sworn.

42. 30 June 1891 Bluefield W VA J.L DAVIS 23 yrs single b. Botetourt Co VA s/o D.J. & V.A. to ZORAH E. SURFACE 17 yrs single b. Montgomery Co VA d/o S.D. & ? O: railroader; by Frank Jackson; REMARKS: J.L Davis sworn.

43. 29 June 1891 Oakvale W VA PRESTON VANCE 21 yrs single b. Mercer Co W VA s/o Marvel & Margaret to LIZZIE BAILEY 20 yrs single b. Mercer Co W VA d/o J.H. & Sarah O: miner; by L. Goodwyn; REMARKS: information by Jeff Thomas & J.H. Bailey.

44. 3 July 1891 WINFIELD BELCHER 30 yrs single b. Summers Co W VA s/o M.F. & M.J. to MARY ELLEN FARMER 20 yrs single b. Kanawha Co VA d/o Jas t. & Sarah E. O: farmer; by D.N. Saunders.

45. 5 July 1891 GEO R. MURPHY 19 yrs single s/o Geo. & Lucinda to SALLIE CLARK 27 yrs single b. Roanoke VA d/o James & Sallie A. O: laborer; by M.A. Wilson.

46. 9 July 1891 AMOS GORE 58 yrs wid. b. Franklin Co VA s/o Wm & Elizabeth to ELIZE J. WEBB 42 yrs single b. Monroe Co W VA d/o Warner & Martha O: mner; by C.R. Brown.

47. 8 July 1891 B.J. McCULLOCH 29 yrs single b. Montgomery Co VA s/o Benj & Elizabeth to G.J. WILLIAMS 25 yrs single b. VA d/o E.T. & Leo J. O: merchant; by Frank Jackson.

48. 10 July 1891 ROBT HASKINS 23 yrs single b. Prince Ed Co VA s/o Lacy & Julia to ROSE AKERSON 21 yrs single b. Monroe Co W VA d/o Geo & Sarah O: railroader; by J. McC. Duckwall; REMARKS: col'd, sworn.

Page 61

1. 14 July 1891 WM B. JONES 21 yrs single b. Mercer Co W VA s/o E.P & Zeruah to LILLY A. COOPER 18 yrs single b. Franklin Co VA d/o Joseph & Sarah M. O: farmer; by J.O. Cassaday.

2. 16 July 1891 WM BIGGER 23 yrs single b. Franklin Co VA s/o Wm & ? to EMMA EANS 25 yrs wid. b. Pittsylvania Co VA d/o Henry & Chainie Fuller O: miner; by G.F. Johnson; REMARKS: col'd, sworn (husband).

3. 16 July 1891 WM H. McGINNIS 35 yrs single b. Raleigh Co W VA s/o James H. & Mary McGinnis to SALLIE E. HOLROYD 26 yrs single b. Mercer Co W VA d/o Wm & Sarah Holroyd O: lawyer; by D. McCrackin.

4. 23 July 1891 WM D. KNIGHT 22 yrs single b. Floyd Co VA s/o Robert & ? to SARAH COBERN 17 yrs single b. Wyoming Co W VA d/o John D. & Sarah O: farmer; by J.W. Bennett.

5. 29 July 1891 ALBERT GARRISON 26 yrs single b. Mercer Co W VA s/o William & C.A. Garrison to LISHA C. SUTER 21 yrs single b. Bland Co VA d/o Jand & Joshua O: miner; by J.O. Cassaday.

6. 28 July 1891 ROBIE PHIPPS 22 yrs single b. Ashe Co NC s/o Benj & Rebecca to GILLIE YATES 22 yrs single b. Pittsylvania Co VA d/o Geo W. & Nannie A. O: miner; by C.R. Brown.

7. 30 July 1891 WESLEY ROSE 24 yrs single b. Pittsylvania Co VA s/o Lawson & Mary to CARRIE BROWN 24 yrs wid. b. Tazewell Co VA O: railroader; by M.A. Wilson; REMARKS: col'd.

8. 29 July 1891 C.A. THOMAS 25 yrs single b. Kanawha Co W VA s/o L.H. & Ellen to MINNIE L. COLE 19 yrs single b. Mercer Co W VA d/o Andrew J. & Mary O: carpenter; by L. Goodwyn.

9. 4 Aug 1891 JOSEPH CLARK 22 yrs single b. Mercer Co W VA s/o Elijah & Eliza to EMMA L RUHBURG 21 yrs div. b. Mercer Co W VA d/o Wm J. & Nancy J. O: farmer; by Jas W. Lilly.

10. 29 July 1891 WM P. HULL 33 yrs div. b. Raleigh Co W VA now living in McDowell Co W VA s/o Lewis & Elizabeth to VIRGINIA BAILEY 26 yrs single b. Mercer Co W VA d/o William & Matilda O: carpenter; by S.C. Dorsey.

11. 2 Aug 1891 WALTER T. BAILEY 21 yrs single b. Mercer Co W VA s/o Estill & Agnes C. to NANNIE C. CALFEE 20 yrs single b. Mercer Co W VA d/o Wm D. & Mary F. O: railroader; by M.A. Wilson.

12. 4 Aug 1891 W.A. STRALEY 23 yrs single b. Giles Co VA s/o D.C. & S.A.E. to M.G. ONEY 18 yrs single b. Mercer Co W VA d/o E.M. & V.F. O: R.R. conductor; by J.O. Cassaday.

13. 5 Aug 1891 THOS C. GOOCH 52 yrs wid. b. Albermarle Co VA s/o Alonzo & Jane F. to MRS. ELLA C. JOHNSTON 42 yrs wid. b. Mercer Co W VA d/o Wm & Elizabeth Wall O:farmer; by J.O. Cassaday.

14. 6 Aug 1891 ROBT L. STUMP 24 yrs single b. Franklin Co VA s/o John & Martha J. to SARAH E. BRINKLEY 15 yrs single b. Mercer Co W VA d/o Jas H. & Rachel A. O: farmer; by J.O. Cassaday.

15. 15 Aug 1891 W.A. SHREWSBURY 18 yrs single b. Mercer Co W VA s/o Wm A. & Julin A. to MELIA C. PRICE 18 yrs single b. Montgomery Co VA d/o Henry D. & Katharine O: farmer; by Charles Walker.

16. 2 Sept 1891 JAS S. ARNOLD 27 yrs single b. Johnson Co TN s/o C.M. & Sarah to ANNA B. WOOLWINE 19 yrs single b. Montgomery Co VA d/o R.P & Jane O: carpenter; by Frank Jackson.

17. 22 Aug 1891 GEO D. GODFREY 29 yrs wid. b. Mercer Co W VA s/o John D. & Martha to HATTIE BASHAM 26 yrs single b. Monroe Co W VA d/o Joseph & ? O: farmer; by G.C. Anderson.

18. 26 Aug 1891 W.W. DODD 20 yrs single b. Mercer Co W VA s/o A.A. & E.C. Dodd to MARY E. FURGUSON 16 yrs single b. Mercer Co VA d/o J.J. & S.C. Furguson O: farmer; by Jas W. Lilly.

19. 27 Aug 1891 JAS R. FANNING 30 yrs sngle b. Mercer Co W VA s/o J.J. & Annie J. to ANNIE J. BOLIN 21 yrs single b. Mercer Co W VA d/o G.S. & Bettie O: farmer; by D. McCracken.

20. 27 Aug 1891 R.A. PICKETT 22 yrs single b. Anne Arundel Co MD now living in Fayette Co PA s/o W.W. & Susannah M. to MAGDALENA C. COLE 20 yrs single b. Mercer Co W VA d/o A.J. & M.M. Cole O: bricklayer; by L. Goodwyn.

21. 27 Aug 1891 J.E. DEER 23 yrs single b. Giles Co VA s/o Wm H. & Elizth R.L. to MARY HONAKER 17 yrs single b. Bland Co VA d/o A.J. & Lucy O: carpenter; by H.E. Bailey.

22. 30 Aug 1891 Simmons W VA SMITH WINBUSH 26 yrs single b. Campbell Co VA s/o Wilson & Catherine to FRANCES MEASE 21 yrs single b. Pittsylvania Co VA d/o Booker & Bindie O: miner; by G.W. Pinkard; REMARKS: col'd, information B. Moore.

23. 29 Aug 1891 Bluefield W VA D.V. MILLISON 28 yrs single b. Chalk Md KS to IDA B. WIBIRT 23 yrs single b. Andover OH; by M.A. Wilson. (No other information given.)

24. 29 Aug 1891 Bluefield W VA W.H. MONTGOMERY 22 yrs single b. Smythe Co VA s/o J.R. & Mary C. to BETIE COOLEY 18 yrs single b. Washington Co VA d/o Isaiah & L.C. O: railroader; by H.E. Bailey.

25. 1 Sept 1891 S.J. CLENDENEN 25 yrs single b. Mercer Co W VA s/o R.G. & Mary E. to ALICE V. ONEY 20 yrs single b. Mercer Co W VA d/o E.M. & V.F. O: telegraph operator; by J.O. Cassaday.

26. * * * JAS W. LILLY 46 yrs wid. b. Mercer Co W VA s/o Washg & Mary to JUDA A. DOVE 24 yrs single b. Mercer Co W VA d/o Wm & Elizabeth O: farmer. (*Note: no date given.)

27. 3 Sept 1891 W.G. WRIGHT 21 yrs single b. Mercer Co W VA s/o Lucy A. Wright to MAT. J. MARTIN 24 yrs single b. Mercer Co W VA d/o A.& ? Martin O: farmer; by L. Goodwyn.

28. 8 Sept 1891 W.P. DIXIE 35 yrs single b. NC s/o ? & Louisa Dixie to WILLIE B. BROWN 22 yrs single b. Christiansburgh PA d/o ? & Nana Brown O: barber; by W. Green; REMARKS: col'd, information by J.S. Young.

29. 30 Sept 1891 Flipping W VA JOHN BROWN 26 yrs single b. Buckingham Co VA s/o Randall & Lucy to JULIA TAYLOR 30 yrs wid. b. Franklin Co VA O: miner; by G.W. Pinkard; REMARKS: colored.

30. 6 Sept 1891 Princeton W Va WM HYE 27 yrs single b. Patrick Co VA s/o Henry & Silvia to ELMIRA HOWARD 31 yrs wid. b. Giles Co VA d/o Lewis & Dicey Addison O: farmer; by Phil S. Sutton; REMARKS: colored.

31. 8 Sept 1891 ALLEN C. WILEY 22 yrs single b. Mercer Co W VA s/o John A. & Mahala to LIDA TAYLOR 19 yrs single b. NC d/o James & Nannie O: farmer; by J.W. Bennett.

32. 8 Sept 1891 B.Z. BURCH 24 yrs single b. Mercer Co W VA s/o Geo W. & ? to LURA J. WILEY 20 yrs single b. Mercer Co W VA d/o John A. & Mahala O: farmer; by J.W. Bennett.

33. 9 Sept 1891 WM LEE O'BRYANT 31 yrs wid. b. Buckingham Co VA s/o Francis & Julianne to SARAH H.E. MILLER 22 yrs single b. Mercer Co W VA d/o R.A. & Rebecca O: farmer; by L. Goodwyn.

34. 8 Sept 1891 THOS AUSTIN 50 yrs wid. b. Franklin Co VA to ALICE A SPANGLER 37 yrs single b. Monroe Co W VA d/o D.W. & S.C. Spangler O: farmer; by Romulus Harry.

35. 9 Sept 1891 ROBT McNUTT HURT 74 yrs wid. b. Mercer Co W VA s/o Wm Saml & Martha J. to SALINA M. VAUGHT 22 yrs single b. Mercer Co W Va d/o C.L. & C.C. Vaught O: farmer; by J.O. Cassaday; REMARKS: G.B. Belcher informant.

36. 16 Sept 1891 FREELIN H. DILLION 20 yrs single b. Mercer Co W VA s/o Henderson & M.F. to MARY M. McCOMAS 17 yrs single b. Raleigh Co W VA d/o R.B. & Olivia A. O:farmer; by A.J. Young.

37. 16 Sept 1891 Princeton W VA J.J.D. HEDLEY 30 yrs single b. Bedford Co VA now living in Hogan Co W VA s/o Isaac & Amanda M. to MINNIE J. ELLIS 21 yrs single b. Monroe Co W VA d/o O.J. & Jane O: teacher; by M.A. Wilson.

38. 20 Sept 1891 SANDY VAIDEN 23 yrs single b. Pittsylvania Co VA s/o Alex & Susan to BETTIE STRADER 22 yrs single b. Pittsylvania Co VA d/o Sidney & Rachel O: miner; by G.F. Johnson; REMARKS: col'd, Sandy Vaiden sworn.

39. 22 Sept 1891 J.B. SETTLE 24 yrs single b. Fayette Co W VA now living same b. F.A. & M.F. to LELIA G. CAMPBELL 23 yrs single b. Monroe Co W VA d/o J.P & Fannie O: Atty at Law; by W.F. Hank; REMARKS: by S.R. Holroyd.

40. 30 Sept 1891 ARTHUR L. PETERS 25 yrs single b. Giles Co VA s/o J.D. & Hollie to EMMA V. THOMAS 22 yrs single b. Montgomery Co VA d/o Geor W. & Josie O: druggist; by J.L. Prater.

41. 29 Sept 1891 THOS OSBURN 28 yrs single b. Washington Co VA s/o Aaron & Elizabeth to MATILDA PECK 32 yrs wid. b. Pike Co KY d/o Wm & Elizabeth Lee O: farmer; by D.N. Saunders.

42. 30 Sept 1891 Flipping W VA JOHN HASKIN* 22 yrs single b. Prince Edward VA s/o Lacey & Julia to RACHEL CLAYTOR 21 yrs single b. Salem VA d/o Ned & Bettie O: miner; by G.W. Pinkard; REMARKS: John Haskins* sworn, col'd. (*Note: name spelled both ways.)

43. 2 Oct 1891 SIDNEY HURKEY 25 yrs single b. Prince Edward VA s/o Henry Throat & ? to LIZZIE WILKE 26 yrs single b. Halifax Co VA d/o ? & Susan Wilke O: miner; by J.V. Dickinson; REMARKS: information by W.J. Clark, J.P.

44. 30 Sept 1891 JAS T. GODFREY 22 yrs single b. Mercer Co W VA s/o A.C. & Clois to EMMA F. AUSTIN 23 yrs single b. Montgomery Co VA d/o A.J. & Athalinda O: railroader; by L. Goodwyn.

45. 3 Oct 1891 Bramwell W VA SIBERT ROBINSON 26 yrs single b. Carroll Co VA s/o Berry & Sily to MARTHA EVANS 22 yrs single b. Prince Edward Co VA d/o Thornton & Louisa; by G.W. Pinkard; REMARKS: applied for by Mayor Young of Br*. (*Note: copy cut off, probably Bramwell W VA.)

46. 3 Oct 1891 Roseville W VA FRED L. CROWDER 35 yrs single b. VA s/o Wm & Augusta to KATIE HAMPTON 25 yrs single b. VA d/o Lawson & Louisa; by J.V. Dickinson; REMARKS: information by Wm L. McGlocklin.

47. * * * HENRY MASON 26 yrs single b. Danville VA to L.E. ALLISON 21 yrs single b. Prince Edward Co VA d/o James & Mary O: driver in mines; by G.W. Pinkard; REMARKS: no date, applied for by Geo. Wooding. (*Note: no date given.)

48. * * * HENRY TOLIVER 25 yrs single b. Roanoke Co VA to FANNY BOYD 22 yrs single b. Radford VA; REMARKS: certificate partially filled and unsigned. (*Note: no date given.)

Page 62

1. * * * JAMES WOODING 21 yrs single b. Appomattax Co VA s/o Geo & Kitty to LAURA CLAYTOR 21 yrs single O: miner; by G.W. Pinkard; REMARKS: col'd, no date, applied for by Geo. Wooding. (*Note: no date given.)

2. 8 Oct 1891 Flipping (W VA) J.F. FOY 28 yrs single b. Union Co PA s/o Geo & Katharine to M.E. JEWELL 18 yrs single b. Jackson Co W VA d/o Wm H. & Elizth Ann O: railroader; by J.V. Dickinson

3. 7 Oct 1891 WM H. RUMBURG 20 yrs single b. Mercer Co W VA s/o Wm J. & Nancy J. to ARMANDA KESTER 21 yrs single b. Carroll Co VA d/o John & Elizabeth O: farmer; by Phil S. Sutton.

4. 30 Oct 1891 JNO H. THOMPSON 37 yrs single b. Ironton OH s/o Jno H. & Katharine to OLLIE V. COOK 26 yrs single b. Montgomery Co VA d/o Montgomery & Hattie O: miner; by C.W. Kelley.

5. 18 Oct 1891 HAYWOOD THOMPSON 21 yrs single b. Surry Co NC s/o Elihu & Francis to MINNIE LEE HOLLOWAY 15 yrs single b. Franklin Co VA d/o Chas E. & Eliza Ann; by J.V. Dickinson.

6. * Oct 1891 J.H. HOWARD 23 yrs single b. Rockingham Co NC s/o James & Mary to DELPHA HURT 25 yrs single b. Halifax Co VA d/o Epp & Delie; by G.W. Pinkard; REMARKS: no date given.

7. 22 Oct 1891 J.G.W. MEADOR 30 yrs wid. b. Mercer Co W VA s/o Josiah & Susan to EVA BRAHMER 22 yrs single b. Raleigh Co W VA d/o James & Lou O: farmer; by James W. Lilly.

8. 21 Oct 1891 Princeton W VA H.L. BURKS 33 yrs single b. Botetourt Co VA now living in Roanoke Co VA s/o R.S. & M.E. to NANNIE B. GEORGE single b. Tazewell Co VA O: railroader; by Eugene Blake.

9. 1 Nov 1891 JNO R. PHIPPS 28 yrs wid. b. Grayson Co VA s/o A.B. & Margt A. to SARAH C. MARTIN 39 yrs wid. b. Mercer Co W VA d/o David & Jane O: carpenter; by A.B. Phipps; REMARKS: A.B. Phipps applicant.

10. 28 Oct 1891 WM LEE DEWESE 20 yrs single b. Floyd Co VA s/o Wm P. & Jane to FLORA E. SPICER 15 yrs single b. Wilks Co NC d/o Wm & Martha M. O: carpenter; by C.W. Kelly; REMARKS: W.S. Dewese sworn.

11. 1 Nov 1891 EMMET R. BOURNE 23 yrs single b. Grayson Co VA s/o H.A. & Julia F. to FANNIE A. EVANS 18 yrs single b. Mercer Co W VA d/o Lewis & Susan O: flagman; by H.A. Wilson; REMARKS: permit from parents.

12. 28 Oct 1891 JAMES E. GOTT 21 yrs single b. Mercer Co W VA s/o Andrew & L.G. to L.R. BRATTON 18 yrs single b. Mercer Co W VA d/o Thos & Mary E. O: farmer; by Phil S. Sutton.

13. * * * MAC EDMUNDS 24 yrs single b. Halifax Co VA s/o Cavness & Dilsey to PRISCILLA JONES 22 yrs single b. Prince Edward Co VA d/o Joseph & Charlotte O: miner; REMARKS: colored, applied for by C.M. Kyle. (*Note: no date given.)

14. 28 Oct 1891 Princeton W VA JAS A. KITTS 20 yrs single b. Bland Co VA s/o Peter & Mary A. to CLARRIE H. SMITH 18 yrs single d/o John T. & ? O: printer; by Wm H. Burkhardt.

15. 1 Nov 1891 W.C. KELLY 24 yrs single b. Greenbrier Co W VA now living in Pocahontas VA s/o John E. & Rachel to MARTHA BAILEY 19 yrs single b. Mercer Co W VA d/o Leftwich & Sarah O: miner; by J.O. Cassaday; REMARKS: applied for by Leftwich Bailey.

16. 8 Nov 1891 JAMES WRIGHT 24 yrs single b. Campbell Co VA s/o Henry & Fanny to MARY DAVIS 21 yrs single b. Wuthe Co VA d/o Sandy & Perfina O: miner; by H.A. Pannill; REMARKS: applied for by Wm J. Clark, col'd.

17. 4 Nov 1891 LEVI TAYLOR 21 yrs single b. Mercer Co W VA s/o Sampson & Matilda to MERTIE R. BAILEY 18 yrs single b. Mercer Co W VA d/o D.P & Mary J. O: miner; by G.C. Anderson.

18. 5 Oct 1891 DOCK FUDGE 24 yrs single b. Tazewell Co VA s/o Milton & Elyn to BETIE J. BROOKS 22 yrs single b. Campbell Co VA d/o ? & Fannie Brooks O: railroad switchman; by Wm Green; REMARKS: col'd.

19. 5 Nov 1891 GEO W. HUBBARD 20 yrs single b. Mercer Co W Va s/o P.A. & L.A. to AMELIA H. HOONY 14 yrs single b. Mercer Co W VA d/o S.L & Susannah O: farmer; by Jas W. Lilly; REMARKS: applied for by T.C. Hubbard.

20. 15 Nov 1891 THEODOR THOMSON 49 yrs single b. Denmark s/o Wm & Anna K. to ARAMINTA JANE TAYLOR 43 yrs single b. W VA d/o ? & ? Hall O: time keeper; by H.E. Bailey; REMARKS: information by L.C. Tabb.

21. 10 Nov 1891 JOSEPH H. HOPKINS 18 yrs single b. Summers Co W VA now living same s/o Saml & Rachel to LUTICIA A. CHRISTIAN 16 yrs single b. Mercer Co W VA d/o Gideon & Jane Christian O: farmer; by G.H. Johnson.

22. 15 Nov 1891 Bramwell W VA C.H. ERBY 25 yrs single b. Pulaski Co VA s/o Isaac & Lucinda to MOLLIE HILL 30 yrs wid. b. Montgomery Co VA O: miner; by H.A. Pannill; REMARKS: colored, inf by Jos Young Mayor Br.

23. 11 Nov 1891 H.A. RESSINGER 26 yrs single b. Giles Co VA s/o Wm & Manerva to MINNIE J. ALVIS 18 yrs single b. Mercer Co W VA d/o John H. & Josephine M. O: farming; by J.W. Bennett; REMARKS: J.D. Alvis sworn.

24. 12 Nov 1891 JOHN COOPER 22 yrs single b. Franklin Co VA s/o Joseph & Sarah A. to CORA C. GARRETSON 16 yrs single b. Mercer Co W VA d/o Thomas & Mary O: carpenter; by L. Goodwyn; REMARKS: fathers both present.

25. 20 Nov 1891 ERI SMITH 52 yrs wid. b. England to MARTHA OGDEN 52 yrs wid. b. England O: miner; by C.W. Kelley; REMARKS: inf by A.C. Davidson.

26. 14 Nov 1891 J.W. HOOD 25 yrs single b. Johnson Co NC s/o David & Fannie Hood to ELLIE DIE 25 yrs single b. Tazewell Co VA d/o John & Sarah Die O: brickmason; by A.M. Craft; REMARKS: Inf by Wm J. Clark sworn.

27. 19 Nov 1891 JOHN W. DAVIS 29 yrs wid. b. Lynchburg VA to ROSE ARMSTEAD 30 yrs wid. b. Roanoke VA O: hotel waiter; by Chas W. Kelley; REMARKS: Inf by Wm J. Clark, sworn.

28. 16 Nov 1891 Bluefield W VA JOHN BLAKEY 24 yrs single b. Albemarle Co VA s/o Henry & Charlotte to ANNIE TRAYNHAM 23 yrs single b. Salem VA d/o ? & Sally Traynham O: railroad hand; by J. McC. Duckwall; REMARKS: John Blakey sworn.

29. 26 Nov 1891 C.W. BAILEY 29 yrs single b. Mercer Co W VA s/o C.W. & Mary to LUCY TABOR 17 yrs single b. Mercer Co w VA d/o William J. & Sarah O: farmer; by Phil S. Sutton.

30. 25 Nov 1891 W.J. WILLIAMS 28 yrs single b. Chesterfield VA s/o J.B. & Martha A. to MINNIE SNIDOW 20 yrs single b. Giles Co VA d/o Harvey & M.V. Snidow O: miner; by Jas H. Johnson; REMARKS: Inf by W.J. & C.A Williams.

31. 22 Nov 1891 FERD, H. HARDNEY 27 yrs single b. Pittsylvania Co Va s/o Moses & J. Vney to ELLA BRACKENBRIDGE 19 yrs single b. Mercer Co W VA d/o Carey & Matilda O: hosler; by Eugene Blake.

32. 22 Nov 1891 ISA H. THOMPSON 24 yrs single b. Bland co Va s/o Jos H. & Margt. F. to PRISCILLA SEVELL 24 yrs div. b. Mercer Co W VA d/o E.P & Z. Jones O: farmer; by Jas O. Cassaday; REMARKS: cert of Clk Cir Ct.

33. 25 Nov 1891 WILLIE HORTON 24 yrs wid. b. Winston NC s/o Chas & Esther to MARY REED 16 yrs sngle b. OH d/o Anderson & Harriet O: butcher; by Jno C. Cook; REMARKS: col'd.

34. 25 Nov 1891 ELBERT W. MAXWELL 31 yrs single b. Mercer Co W VA s/o Wm & Melvina P. to THEODOSIA SAUNDERS 18 yrs single b. Mercer Co W VA d/o David N. & nancy J. O: merchant; by Eugene Blake; REMARKS: consent of S.N.S & wife.

35. 25 Nov 1891 ANDREW A. BIRD 22 yrs single b. Mercer Co W VA s/o Wm A. & Cynthia to LOUISA V. SHORTER 17 yrs single b. Mercr Co W VA d/o W.T. & Mary O: farmer; by Wm Holroyd; REMARKS: consent of W.T. Shorter.

36. 25 Nov 1891 ALBERT BARLEY 24 yrs single b. Davidson Co NC s/o Peter & Mary to LAURA A. KING 21 yrs sngle b. Mercr Co W VA O: railroader; by Jno C. Cook; REMARKS: husband sworn.

37. 26 Nov 1891 ROBT L. SPANGLER 28 yrs single b. Mercr Co W VA s/o Jno L. & Valaria L. to NANNIE E. CARR 23 yrs single b. Mercer Co W VA d/o Jno T. & Nancy A. O: farmer; by Phil S. Sutton.

38. 29 Nov 1891 JAS F. HILL 31 yrs wid. b. Alhega Co NC s/o Hardon & Jane to MAGGIE CROCKETT 23 yrs single b. Tazewell Co VA d/o Jas A. & Rachel O: farmer; by A.M. Craft.

39. 28 Nov 1891 E.L. CLARK 28 yrs single b. Floyd Co Va now living in McDowell Co W VA s/o E.J. & Katharine to LAURA B. BAILEY 25 yrs single b. Mercer Co W VA d/o G.C. & Jane O: carpenter; by W.A. Nichols.

40. 2 Nov 1891 JOHN H. WHITE 28 yrs single b. Mercer Co W VA s/o Harman & Cynthia M. to LUCINDA A. HUBBARD 21 yrs single b. Mercer Co W VA d/o Green & Manervia O: farmer; by Charles Walker; REMARKS: applied by J.S. White.

41. 30 Nov 1891 LEE PENNINGTON 23 yrs div. b. Mercer Co W VA s/o Isac G. & Irene to EVA PENNINGTON 15 yrs single b. Lincoln Co W VA d/o ? & Sarah A. O: farmer; by Phil S. Sutton.

42. 2 Dec 1891 W.G. BARGER 25 yrs single b. Summers Co W VA now living same s/o W.H. & Mary J. to EMMA J. VAUGHT 20 yrs single b. Giles Co VA d/o Ransom & Sarah M. O: farmer; by J.W. Bennett.

43. 3 Dec 1891 J.L. STRALEY 29 yrs single b. Bradley Co TN now living in Giles Co VA s/o D.C. & S.A.E. to E.J ONEY 23 yrs single b. Mercer Co W VA d/o E.M. & V.F. O: railroader; by J.O. Cassaday.

44. 5 Dec 1891 JOHN L. HORTON 24 yrs single b. Russell Co VA s/o Lewis & Lucinda to LULA K. FINNEY 23 yrs single b. Russell Co VA d/o Lilburn & Melissa O: jeweler; by W.H. Burkhardt.

45. 9 Dec 1891 OSCAR REED 23 yrs single b. Cash's Corner, VA s/o ? & Ellen Reed to RHODA SAUNDERS 24 yrs wid. b. Franklin Co VA d/o ? & Emily Saunders O: miner; by thos Coleman; REMARKS: col'd, Inf by B. Moore.

46. 13 Dec 1891 JAS C. HOLLOWAY 17 yrs single b. Franklin Co VA s/o Chas E. & Eliza Ann to MARY LOUISA BOWLES 21 yrs single b. Franklin Co VA d/o Thos t. & Mary A. O: miner; by W.E. Hart; REMARKS: information by E.M. Kyle.

47. 22 Dec 1891 JAMES T. MEADOWS 23 yrs single b. Summers Co W VA s/o Ward & Huldah to MARY J. RORER 22 yrs single b. Patrick Co VA O: farmer; by Jas W. Lilly.

48. 24 Dec 1891 G.W. HARMAN 18 yrs single b. Mercer co W VA s/o Andrew & Lydia to MARGRET E. SISCLE 18 yrs single b. Mercer Co W VA d/o James & Prucilia O: farmer; by G.C. Anderson; REMARKS: information by Andy Harman.

Page 63

1. 24 Dec 1891 R.C. LILLY, JR. 19 yrs single b. Summers Co W VA now living in Raleigh Co W VA s/o Robt C. & Virginia to WILLIE E. REED 16 yrs single b. Mercer Co w VA d/o V.C. & Eliza O: farmer; by Wm L. Simmons; REMARKS: applied for by F.A. Worrell on cert of both fathers.

2. 23 Dec 1891 JAS H. DICKENSON 28 yrs single b. Giles Co VA now living same s/o Henry & Nancy to ELMIRA C. BOLIN 24 yrs single b. Mercer Co W VA d/o G.S. & E.M. O: farmer; by J.W. Bennett.

3. 23 Dec 1891 J.R. GROSS 35 yrs wid. b. Bland Co Va now living in Tazewell Co VA s/o Frank & ? to LAURA J. WITEN 26 yrs single b. Mercer Co W VA d/o Wm H. & ? O: doctor; by C.W. Kelley.

4. 23 Dec 1891 JOHN R. BRATTON 23 yrs single b. Mercer Co W VA s/o Thomas & Elizabeth to NANNIE E. CARBAUGH 21 yrs single b. Mercer Co W VA d/o John & Almada O: farmer; by J.O. Cassaday.

5. 24 Dec 1891 GEORGE S. OXLEY 26 yrs single b. Mercer Co W VA s/o Sanford H. & Delilah to LIDA W. WILLIS 20 yrs single b. Montgomery Co VA d/o D.R. & ? O: farmer; by J.P. Campbell.

6. 26 Dec 1891 WASH SMITH 22 yrs single b. Appomattax Co VA s/o Henry & Flora to ANNA SMITH 20 yrs single b. Appomattax Co VA d/o Wm & Ada O: miner; by M.A. Pannill; REMARKS: colored, applied for by C.M. Kyle.

7. 24 Dec 1891 GEO A. HARRY 23 yrs single b. Mercer Co W VA s/o Calvin & ? to LOUISA SEAL 24 yrs wid. b. Giles Co VA d/o D.W. & S.C. Spangler O:lumberman; by J.O. Cassaday.

8. 7 Jan 1892 WILEY J. TILLER 18 yrs single b. Mercer Co W VA now living in Wyoming Co W VA s/o Wm McH & Minerva A. to MARY E. SHREWSBURY 20 yrs single b. Mercer Co W VA s/o James W. & Julia A. O: farmer; by Saml M. McKinney.

9. 29 Dec 1891 C.R. BROWN 27 yrs single b. Tazewell Co VA now living in Knoxville TN to SALLIE IRENE COOPER 21 yrs single d/o John & Maria O: minister; by C.W. Kelley.

10. 28 Dec 1891 SILA WELCH 19 yrs single b. Mercer Co W VA s/o ? & Elizabeth Welch to RUTH J. SWIM 19 yrs single d/o M.F. & Mandy O: laborer; by J.O. Cassaday.

11. 2 Jan 1892 E.W. WELCH 23 yrs single s/o ? & Nannie Welch to SARAH KNAPIER 22 yrs single d/o Joshua & Nancy; by Wm Green.

12. 29 Dec 1891 A.B. HYLTON 19 yrs single b. Floyd Co VA s/o Hiram & Louisa to JULIA F. BROWN 15 yrs single b. Roanoke Co VA d/o S.B. & Fanny O: carpenter; by M.A. Wilson.

13. 30 Dec 1891 WALTER L. WHITE 22 yrs single b. Mercer Co W VA s/o Harrison & Mary to JOSEPHINE V. BAILEY 17 yrs single b. Mercer Co W VA d/o James F. & Margaret O: farmer; by J.W. Bennett.

14. 30 Dec 1891 J.B. WINFREY 23 yrs single b. Mercer Co W VA s/o Burwell & Drina to IDA K. BAILEY 18 yrs single b. Mercer Co W VA d/o Leftwich & Sarah M. O: farmer; by J.O. Cassaday.

15. 30 Dec 1891 CHAS C. BRAMMER 24 yrs single b. Mercer Co W VA s/o Jas A. & Louisa to VIRGINIA ALICE FARLEY 22 yrs single b. Raleigh Co W VA d/o Jas H. & Mary O: teacher; by Jas W. Lilly.

16. 2 Jan 1892 CHAS C. THOMPSON 21 yrs single b. Tazewell Co VA s/o Geo T. & Mary to DICIE S. HARMAN 16 yrs single b. Mercer Co W VA d/o A.J. & Lizzie O: miner; by G.C. Anderson; REMARKS: applied for by A.J. Harman.

Page 64

1. 3 Jan 1892 CHAS G. HUBBARD 26 yrs single b. OH s/o P.A. & Lucy A. to EFFIE A. STOVALL 23 yrs single b. Mercer Co W VA d/o L.V. & Ann O: teacher; by Jas W. Lilly.

2. 14 Jan 1892 G.L. STONE 31 yrs wid. b. Henry Co VA s/o G.L. & Malinda to SARAH E. BELL 16 yrs single b. Mercer Co W VA d/o Henry & Julia O: lumberman; by A.M. Craft.

3. 5 Jan 1892 R.H. BAILEY 48 yrs wid. b. Mercer Co W VA s/o Elijah & Sarah F. to CASS DAVIDSON 44 yrs wid. b. Tazewell Co VA d/o Addison & Jane Crockett O: farmer; by M.A. Wilson.

4. 5 Jan 1892 FOUNTAIN CARTERBURY single b. Wyoming Co W VA now living same s/o George & Emaline to SUSAN B. COOK 22 yrs single b. Wyoming Co W VA d/o Floyd & Mary A. O: farmer; by W.W. Workman.

5. 4 Feb 1892 G.L. SMITH 19 yrs single b. Franklin Co VA s/o John & ? to VIRGINIA BELL 15 yrs single b. Mercer Co W VA d/o Henry & Julia Ann O: miner; by A.M. Craft.

6. 11 Jan 1892 HARVEY WIMMER 60 yrs wid. b. Floyd Co VA s/o Saml & Massie to SARAH E. COBURN 41 yrs single b. Mercer Co W VA d/o David & ? O: farmer; by D.N. Saunders.

7. 27 Jan 1892 ALBERT P. BONHAM 48 yrs wid. b. Monroe Co W VA now living in Summers Co w VA s/o Nehemiah & Regina to VICTORY MELISSA GADD 22 yrs single b. Mercer Co W VA d/o A.P & Delilah; by Jas W. Lilly.

8. 12 Jan 1892 CHARLES LEWIS ZOLL 27 yrs single b. Monroe Co W VA s/o Jacob & Mary to SARAH WILLIS McEWEN 23 yrs single b. Ashe Co NC d/o Alex C. & Mary A. O: clerk; by C.W. Kelly; REMARKS: information by A.J. Clark, J.P.

9. 14 Jan 1892 CHAS H. BEARD 24 yrs single b. Augusta Co VA now living in Roanoke Co W VA s/o Geo W. & M.A. to SUSAN E. PENDLETON 19 yrs single b. Mercer Co W VA d/o D.B. & Susan O: conductor; by J.O. Cassaday; REMARKS: information by writing & sworn.

10. 20 Jan 1892 JOSEPH H. CALFEE 21 yrs single b. Mercer Co W VA s/o A.J. & Maggie to N.A.E. HURST 19 yrs single b. Mercer Co W VA d/o Jas H. & Sarah F. O: farmer; by Jas W. Lilly; REMARKS: information by Ben Belcher.

11. 27 Jan 1892 H.L. WINGFIELD 31 yrs single b. Huston Co TN s/o L.H. & S.E.V. to ELIZA B. DAWSON 23 yrs single b. Tazewell Co VA d/o R.D. & ? O: railroader; by A.B. Hunter.

12. 28 Jan 1892 D.W. FERGUSON 30 yrs single b. Mercer Co W VA s/o D.W. & Live Owney to NANNIE J. BRAY 17 yrs single b. Mercer Co W VA d/o M.H. & ? O: farmer; by J.O. Cassaday; REMARKS: information by D.W. Ferguson.

13. 30 Jan 1892 L.W. EASTER 21 yrs single b. Franklin Co VA s/o E.W. & Bettie E. to H.J. CLEAVER 21 yrs single b. Wythe Co VA d/o Wm & Ellen O: miner; by J.L. Prater; REMARKS: information by L.W. Easter & sworn.

14. 10 Feb 1892 ALLEN L. WILEY 24 yrs single b. Mercer Co W VA s/o Vincent & Cynthia to ANNIE L. SUBLETT 17 yrs single b. Montgomery Co VA d/o Dock & Rebecca O: farmer; by Wm Holroyd.

15. 10 Feb 1892 AMANUEL ROSE 38 yrs wid. b. Tazewell Co VA s/o Saml & Kizzie R. to LAURA A. JARRELL 21 yrs single b. McDowell Co VA d/o Geo & Mattie O: farmer; by J.O. Cassaday.

16. 10 Feb 1892 WM H. HAHOOD 31 yrs single b. Giles Co VA s/o Wm A. & Bettie O. to KATIE A. STRALEY single b. Mercer Co W VA d/o H.W. & D.A. O: merchant; by Jas Sweeney.

17. 18 Feb 1892 JAMES H. THORNTON 25 yrs single b. Mercer Co W VA s/o A.J. & H.J. to BELL DAVIS 19 yrs single b. Mercer Co W VA d/o C.S. & Kizziah O: farmer; by L. Goodwyn.

18. 17 Feb 1892 EDWARD HILL 32 yrs wid. b. Augusta Co VA now living in Pulaski Co VA s/o Reuben & Martha Hill to RHODA ADAMS 22 yrs single b. Pulaski Co VA d/o Peasant & Minerva O: farmer; by Phil S. Sutton.

19. 18 Feb 1892 W.A. SHANNON 20 yrs single b. Mercer Co W VA s/o Saml & Mary A. to LUNDA V. TURNER 19 yrs single b. Mercer Co W VA d/o Robt B. & Mary J. O: farmer; by L. Goodwyn.

20. 18 Feb 1892 E.E. REED 19 yrs single b. Mercer Co W VA s/o Thomas & Saphrona to JOSEPHINE LEVALLEY 15 yrs single d/o Charles & Lizzie LeValley O: railroader; by L. Goodwyn; REMARKS: applied for by H.B. Smith.

21. 23 Feb 1892 MARSHAL FOWLER 27 yrs single b. Carroll Co VA s/o John L. & Elizabeth to MARY EULA YATES 21 yrs single b. Pittsylvania Co VA d/o Wash & Nannie Yates O: miner; by A.M. Craft.

22. 25 Feb 1892 JAMES BLANKENSHIP 22 yrs single b. Giles Co VA s/o Harrison & Louisa to MARY OLA BLANKENSHIP 16 yrs single b. Giles Co VA d/o Noah & Elizabeth O: farmer; by J.O. Cassaday.

23. * * * C.H. STRUM 24 yrs single b. Granville Co NC s/o Wm & F.B. Tucker to H.B. TOLBERT 20 yrs single b. Summers Co W VA d/o G.W. & Mary H. O: railroader; REMARKS: cert not filled or signed-. (*Note: no date given.)

24. 3 Mar 1892 W.R. PARKER 21 yrs single b. Floyd Co VA s/o ? & Jane Parker to SARAH REDDIX 17 yrs single b. Smyth Co VA d/o Henry & Caroline O: farmer; by J.F. Hill; REMARKS: col'd.

25. 2 Mar 1892 D.R. DAY 22 yrs single b. Mercer Co W VA s/o Joshua & Sarah E. to EMMA L. BOWLING 17 yrs single b. Mercer Co w VA d/o Thos J. & ? O: farmer; by J.W. Bennett.

26. 3 Mar 1892 CHAS R. WISE 24 yrs single b. Buckingham Co VA s/o W.G. & Bettie G. Wise to JENNIE CALDWELL 21 yrs single b. OH d/o J.H. & Julia Caldwell O: miner; by W.E. Hurt; REMARKS: applied for by B. Moore.

27. 9 Mar 1892 T.J. McELRATH 33 yrs single b. Giles Co VA to LIZZIE C. VAUGHT 19 yrs single b. Giles Co VA d/o Rufus F. & Elizabeth H. O: dentist; by J.W. Bennett.

28. 10 Mar 1892 THOMAS McGHEE 22 yrs single b. Giles Co VA to MARY WHITENBURGER 23 yrs single b. TN O: cook; by J.H.C. Duckwall.

29. 8 Mar 1892 THOS BONDS 21 yrs single b. NC s/o Wm & Mary to ANNA B. THOMPSON 21 yrs single b. Mercer Co W VA d/o Levi & katherine O: laborer; by Phil S. Sutton; REMARKS: both parties sworn.

30. 10 Mar 1892 A.J. HOLLAND 25 yrs single b. Franklin Co VA now living in McDowell Co W VA s/o Cornelius & Griselda to HATTIE WILLIS 22 yrs single b. Amherst Co VA d/o ? & Mahala Willis O: miner; by T.J. Brandart; REMARKS: A.J. Holland & Jeff Willis sworn.

31. 10 Mar 1892 HENDERSON C. HAWKS 18 yrs single b. Mercer Co W VA s/o Wm R. & Mary Ann to RACHEL AKERS 15 yrs single b. Mercer Co W VA d/o Luke & Susan O: farmer; by G.C. Anderson.

32. 16 Mar 1892 ROBT L. ROWLAND 26 yrs single b. Mercer Co W VA s/o Kinzie & Nancy to JAVA A. MASSIE 16 yrs single b. Mercer Co W VA d/o ? & Mary A. O: farmer; by J.W. Bennett; REMARKS: applied for by Geo W. Burgess guardn J.A. Massie.

33. 16 Mar 1892 JOHN BAILEY 23 yrs single b. Giles Co VA s/o Louie & ? to MINNIE KIDWELL 16 yrs single b. Mercer Co W VA d/o Green & Sarah Kidwell O: farmer; by A.J. Thompson; REMARKS: by certification.

34. 23 Mar 1892 NELSON BOWLS 21 yrs single b. Yadkin Co NC s/o Danl & Loucinda to ALICE DAWSON 28 yrs div. b. Pulaski Co VA d/o ? & Millie Mathews O: dragman; by Eugene Blake; REMARKS:col'd.

35. 27 Mar 1892 A.N. HAZLEWOOD 28 yrs div. b. Sarah Co NC s/o Aasy(sic) & Rachel to D.E. BOGGLESS 29 yrs single b. NC d/o Reuben & Polly O: farmer; by W.W. Workman.

36. 26 Mar 1892 J.A. SAMMONS 24 yrs div. b. Carroll Co VA s/o Alfred & Zaida to ELIZABETH FERGUSON 52 yrs wid. b. Mercer Co W VA d/o Josiah & Sarah Maxey O: farmer; by Eugene Blake.

37. * * * LEE A. CHARLTON 21 yrs single b. Bland Co VA s/o Saml & Kizzie M.J. to ELIZA CARINGTON 22 yrs single b. Appomattox Co VA d/o Wm & Mary Smith O: railroader; REMARKS: no cert or signature, col'd, sworn. (*Note: no date given.)

38. 30 Mar 1892 OPIE O. WHITE 20 yrs single b. Mercer Co W VA s/o H. & Mary to ROSA E. HURST 17 yrs single b. Mercer Co v VA d/o Wm & Pollie O: farmer; by Jas W. Lilly.

39. 29 Mar 1892 J.J. O'DELL 23 yrs single b. Nicholas Co VA s/o Jacob & Manerva to LORA HARLESS 21 yrs single b. Montgomery Co VA O: blacksmith; by H.E. Bailey; REMARKS: sworn.

40. 29 Mar 1892 W.J. POWERS 33 yrs single b. Botetourt Co VA now living in McDowell Co W VA s/o C.H. & Mary to EMMA J. GARRETSON 24 yrs single b. Kanawha Co W VA d/o H.F. & Mary J. O: carpenter; by W.W. Workman.

41. 30 Mar 1892 JOHN W. WHITE 23 yrs single b. Mercer Co W VA s/o James & Sallie to ADA B.GREENS 17 yrs single b. Mercer Co W VA d/o John L. & Amanda H. O: lawyer; by L. Goodwyn.

42. 29 Mar 1892 J.J. SMITH 24 yrs single b. Giles Co VA s/o R.A. & Sarah to LOUISA W. THORNTON 24 yrs single b. Mercer Co W VA d/o James A. & Louisa O: farmer; by Jas H. Johnston.

43. 31 Mar 1892 ALBERT MILLER 29 yrs single b. Schuyrill Co PA s/o Jos & Mary to S.D. JEWELL 20 yrs single d/o W.H. & E.A. O: miner; by C.W. Kelley.

44. 2 April 1892 LEE J. SHIP 30 yrs wid. b. Smyth Co VA s/o Gaines & Margaret to FANNIE BOYD 17 yrs single b. Smyth Co VA s/o A.J. & Margaret O: railroader; by H.E. Bailey.

45. 4 April 1892 WM DICKSON 26 yrs single s/o Sam Serge & Ginnet Dickson to MARY MILLER 24 yrs single b. Danville VA d/o Ben & Nancy; by G.W. Pinkard; REMARKS:col'd, applied for by J.S. Young.

46. 6 May 1892 JAMES BURK 23 yrs single b. Monroe Co W VA s/o Wallace & Selah to ROSA MANN 19 yrs single b. Mercer Co W VA d/o Wm & Mary O: railroader; by A.J. Thompson; REMARKS: col'd, sworn.

47. 13 April 1892 WALTER TAYLOR 22 yrs single b. Pittsylvania Co VA to ELIZABETH HAWKS 17 yrs single b. Mercer Co W VA d/o Eli & Nancy O: miner; by C.W. Kelley; REMARKS: applied for by Jno Taylor.

Page 65

1. 13 April 1892 R.B. BROYLES 19 yrs single b. Mercer Co W VA s/o Leroy & S.E. to L.R. POE 20 yrs single b. Mercer Co W VA d/o Thos E. & N.E. O: farmer; by Chas W. Kelley; REMARKS: applied for by T.E. Poe.

2. * * * C.H. JENNINGS 24 yrs single b. Carroll Co VA s/o C.H. & Mary to ROSA A. CROTTY 24 yrs single b. Monroe Co W VA d/o Geo W. & India M. O: railroader; REMARKS: return not made out. (*Note: no date given.)

3. 17 April 1892 JAMES HOWEL 21 yrs single b. Tazewell Co VA s/o Thomas & Virginia to NANNIE C. CRUMBE 21 yrs single b. Mercer Co W VA d/o Thomas & Araminta O: miner; by G.C. Anderson; REMARKS: Willoughby Taylor.

4. 21 April 1892 A.J. GEARHEART 25 yrs single b. Floyd Co VA s/o Jenry & Mollie to LAURA B. LILLY 19 yrs single b. Raulie(sic) Co W VA d/o C.D. & Julia Lilly O: mine labor; by Chas W. Kelley.

5. 21 April 1892 E.B. HORRIS 29 yrs single b. Giles Co VA now living in Bland Co VA s/o Saml H. & Rachel to JULIA E. BURTON 21 yrs single b. Giles Co VA d/o H.B. & Mary A. O: carpenter; by H.E. Bailey.

6. 29 April 1892 THOMAS DAY 22 yrs single now living in Pocahontas VA s/o David & Josephine to JENNIE MORRIS 20 yrs single d/o ? & Katie Cummingham O: miner; by W.J. Carter; REMARKS: information by Jos Young.

7. 26 April 1892 JAMES POE 43 yrs wid. b. Mercer Co W VA s/o Henry & Jane Poe to MARY DILLION 19 yrs single b. Monroe Co VA d/o William & Mary O: carpenter; by Chas W. Kelley.

8. 27 April 1892 ROBT L. CHRISTIAN 23 yrs single b. Mercer Co W VA s/o Robt G. & Jane to ANGELA WHITE 16 yrs single b. Mercer Co W VA d/o Harman & Jane O: carpenter; by Giles M. Johnston; REMARKS: cert. by father.

9. 26 April 1892 THOS GRIFFITH 21 yrs single b. Mercer Co W VA to NANCY HOWELL 21 yrs single b. Floyd Co VA d/o Thos & Virginia O: miner; by Andw J. Young.

10. 27 April 1892 MOSES C. RICHMOND 29 yrs wid. s/o Aster & Malinda J. to EMMADORA S. FERGUSON 20 yrs single b. Raleigh Co W VA d/o Feo W. & Mary Ferguson; by Chas W. Kelley.

11. 5 May 1892 JNO W. CLEMONS 29 yrs single s/o Jno R. & Mary to MALINDIA VIA 25 yrs single b. Floyd Co VA d/o ? & Mary J. O: farmer; by A.J. Thompson.

12. 10 May 1892 JAMES WORKMAN 35 yrs single b. Mercer Co W VA s/o ? & Polly to RACHEL SHRADER 23 yrs single b. Mercer Co W VA d/o Jackson & Elvira O: railroader; by D.N. Saunders.

13. 11 May 1892 JAS H. BOWLING 32 yrs single b. Raleigh Co W VA s/o Wm A. & Demarris to MOLLIE L. HARMAN 20 yrs single b. Tazewell Co VA d/o Wm B & P.J. O: farmer; by Jas W. Lilly.

14. 18 May 1892 JAS R. HEATH 23 yrs single b. Russell Co VA now living in Elkhorn W VA s/o Milton & Elizabeth to MARY M. THOMPSON 21 yrs single b. Tazewell Co VA d/o Albert & Mariah J. O: miner; by M.A. Pannill; REMARKS: col'd, C.M. Kyle.

15. 23 May 1892 JNO A. THOMPSON 20 yrs single b. Mercer Co W VA d/o Levy & Catherine to SARAH WIMMER 20 yrs single b. mercer Co v VA d/o S.D. & R.J. O: farmer; by L. Goodwyn; REMARKS: Levy Thompson.

16. 26 May 1892 W.A. SAYLOR 25 yrs wid. b. Junioretta Co PA s/o John H & Katherine E. to E.F. MONTGOMERY 22 yrs single b. Henry Co MD d/o S.M. & ? O: engineer; by H.E. Bailey.

17. 29 May 1892 G.W. ROBINSON 46 yrs single b. VA s/o Henry & Millie Wysong to ARTHELIA BURKS 40 yrs wid. b. Mercer Co W VA d/o Fielden Walker & Mistie Medley O: cook; by L. Goodwyn; REMARKS: applied for by letter, col'd.

18. 25 Aug 1892 LORENZO D. HARVEY 19 yrs single b. Summers Co W VA s/o Joshua & Susan to ELIZA E. BASHAM 17 yrs single b. Mercer Co W VA d/o John & Martha Ann O: farmer; by Allen M. McKinney.

19. 5 June 1892 GEORGE WOODING 30 yrs single b. Pittsylvania Co VA s/o George & Kittie to NANIE SCALES 23 yrs wid. b. Pulaski Co VA O: miner; by M.A. Pannill.

20. 3 June 1892 JAS LEWIS 24 yrs single b. Albermarle Co VA s/o Robt & mary to ALICE WILSON 22 yrs single b. Botetourt Co VA d/o Walker & Rhoda O: railroader; by Phil S. Sutton; REMARKS: Both sworn wife & husband, col'd.

21. 7 June 1892 GEORGE E. PATRICK 20 yrs single b. Montgomery Co VA s/o Jas & Nannie Patrick to ELLA P. AUSTIN 16 yrs

single b. Montgomery Co VA d/o G.W. & Maggie Austin O: telegraph operator; by J.McC. Duckwall; REMARKS: sworn.

22. 8 June 1892 WM T. BURROUGHS 28 yrs wid. b. Bedford Co VA s/o Tazewell W. & L.R. to ALICE H. WILLIAMS 17 yrs single b. Giles Co VA d/o B.P & Frances E. O: house painter; by Gran: Houchins; REMARKS: Mr. Burroughs sworn.

23. 9 June 1892 H.F. COPING 33 yrs wid. b. Mercer Co W VA s/o ? & L.A. to JENNIE ROBERTSON 34 yrs single d/o Chas & ? O: farmer; by Wm Holroyd.

24. 19 June 1892 JAMES H. WILLIAMS 39 yrs wid. b. Montgomery Co VA s/o Jno M. & Sarah to FANNIE J. PENNINGTON 33 yrs div. b. Mercer Co W VA d/o Wm & Delilah Neely O: farmer; by L. Goodwyn.

25. 16 June 1892 LEE SURFACE 22 yrs single b. Montgomery Co VA s/o Augustus & ? to CYNTHIA D. SHRADER 18 yrs single b. Mercer Co W VA d/o Robert & Cynthia J. O: farmer; by D.N. Saunders.

26. 16 June 1892 THOMAS PINKARD 22 yrs single b. Franklin Co VA s/o John & Fannie to MATTIE CALLOWAY 21 yrs single b. Franklin Co VA d/o Jas & Chloe O: working store; by Chas W. Kelley; REMARKS: colored.

27. 22 June 1892 GEORG L. REID 24 yrs single b. VA s/o James & Jennie Reid to NORAH E. STOVALL 17 yrs single b. Mercer Co VA d/o Ann & L.V. Stovall O: merchant; by Jas W. Lilly.

28. 23 June 1892 GEORGE H. PENN 28 yrs single b. Roanoke Co VA s/o Charles Penn & Dicy Hostin to PHOEBE ELLEN DICKISON 18 yrs single b. Tazewell Co VA d/o John & Sallie O: miner; by J.H. Adams; REMARKS: colored.

29. 22 June 1892 WM PAYNE 19 yrs single b. Mercer Co W VA s/o Andrew & Elizabeth Payne to NANNIE A. WILLIS 23 yrs wid. b. Bland Co VA O: lawier(sic); by Jno H. Honaker.

30. 23 June 1892 J.W. MILLER 21 yrs single b. Mercer Co W VA s/o R.A. & Mary J. Miller to WILLIE H. CROMER 20 yrs wid. b. Monroe Co W VA d/o Kinzie & Judie Tiller O: lawier(sic); by L. Goodwyn.

31. 29 June 1892 B.S. HIGGINBOTHAM 27 yrs single s/o John B. & M.E. to FLORA L. AIKINSON 19 yrs single b. Summers Co W VA d/o L.F. & Mary P. O: real estate; by Frank Jackson.

32. 29 June 1892 MILTON HENRY 19 yrs single b. White Co TN s/o Milton & Jane to SYLVIA SMYTH 23 yrs single b. Pulaski Co VA d/o Peter & Sarah O: laborer; by Jas E. Thompson, REMARKS: col'd.

33. * * * W.F. LORD 29 yrs single b. Camden Co NJ s/o F.C. & Adella Co to ZORAH M. MIREAL 17 yrs single b. Pulaski Co VA d/o H.S. & Mary A. O: laundryman. (*Note: no date given.)

34. 30 June 1892 A.P. ELMORE 28 yrs single b. Craig Co VA s/o J.E. & Clementine to LAURA N. SHANNON 22 yrs single b. Giles Co VA d/o Saml & ? O: railroader; by L. Goodwyn; REMARKS: applied for by Sam Shannon.

35. 30 June 1892 WM BURKS 23 yrs single b. Wythe Co VA s/o Joseph & Ann to ALICE GORDON 22 yrs single c. Wythe Co VA d/o Columbus & Sophia O: miner; by Phil S. Sutton; REMARKS: both present, colored.

36. 3 July 1892 JOHN SARVER 24 yrs single b. Bland Co VA now living in McDowell Co W VA s/o Jerry & Francis to TINA BARGER 21 yrs single b. Tazewell Co VA d/o Jacob & Lucy O: farmer; by A.M. Craft.

37. 6 July 1892 JOS CALIVER 35 yrs div. b. Washington Co VA s/o Joseph & Amanda to MARTHA GHERRANT 31 yrs single b. Floyd Co VA d/o ? & Lidia O: sta. engineer; by W.J. Carter; REMARKS: both (colored).

38. 7 July 1892 A.H. MEADOWS 23 yrs single b. Monroe Co W VA s/o A.P. & Vinny to LUCY B. BILLINGS 20 yrs single b. KY d/o W.M. & M.J. O: mining; by James Sweeney.

39. 17 July 1892 SAMUEL SAUNDERS 21 yrs single b. Montgomery Co VA s/o Calvin & Jemima to RUTHA ROBERTSON 24 yrs single b. Montgomery Co VA d/o Robert & Jane O: miner; by J.H. Adams; REMARKS: col'd.

40. 14 July 1892 N.F. WHITE 18 yrs wid. now living in McDowell Co W VA s/o John H. & Francis to MARY E. HOLLINS 30 yrs single b. Floyd Co VA O: stable boss; by D.M. Cracken; REMARKS: applied for by wife's father J.M. Hollins.

41. 21 July 1892 FRANCIS MARION STEELE 20 yrs single b. Kanawha Co W VA s/o Wm F. & Rhoda to ALZODO M. WHITE 18 yrs single b. Kanawha Co W VA d/o T.H. & Dessie O: farming; by Andw J. Young.

42. 28 July 1892 JAMES O. KELLEY 22 yrs single b. Floyd Co VA s/o Moses G. & Kizziah to ALZORA J. HALL 16 yrs single b. Floyd Co VA d/o Ira D. & Mary E. Hall O: farming; by W.W. Workman.

43. 4 Aug 1892 LUKOUS H. SHREWSBURY 18 yrs single b. Mercer Co W VA now living in Wyoming Co W VA s/o James & M.J. to LUEWINA SHREWSBURY 15 yrs single b. Mercer Co W VA d/o Wm & S.R.J. O: farming; by E.W. Cooper; REMARKS: sworn.

44. 26 July 1892 COLUMBUS BOWLES 34 yrs wid. b. Yadkin Co NC s/o Daniel & Lucinda to BELL CARTER 31 yrs wid. b. Pittsylvania Co VA d/o ? & Jane Cole O: railroader; by T.H. Gardner; REMARKS: cd.

45. 27 July 1892 FRANK NESBIT 25 yrs single b. SC s/o Isaac & Nancy to P.A. MORRISON 24 yrs single b. NC O: miner; by W.J. Carter; REMARKS: col'd.

46. * * * J.R. HONAKER 23 yrs single b. Bland Co VA s/o Chas W. & Mary J. to MARY L.G. RATLIFFE 15 yrs single b. Tazewell Co VA d/o Wm D. & Missouri C. O: wagoner; REMARKS: applied for by father of wife.

47. 4 Aug 1892 HARVEY FORTNER 19 yrs single b. Tazewell Co VA s/o ? & Now(sic) Fortner to MARTHA CARVER 16 yrs single b. Tazewell Co VA d/o ? & Mary Carver O: miner; by A.M. Craft; REMARKS: Henry Carver witness.

48. 1 Aug 1892 W.R. MONTGOMERY 22 yrs wid. b. Smith Co VA s/o ? & Mary to MARTHA COLLINS 22 yrs wid. b. Smith Co VA d/o J.R. & Sallie O: miner; by A.A. Ashworth; REMARKS: W.R. Montgomery sworn.

Page 66

1. 3 Aug 1892 WILLIAM B. DILLION 22 yrs single b. Tazewell Co VA s/o W.H. & Julia to SUSAN BAILEY 17 yrs single b. Tazewell Co VA d/o Z.H. & Elizabeth O: blacksmith; by Chas W. Kelley.

2. 3 Aug 1892 ROBT A. MARTIN 20 yrs single b. Mercer Co W VA s/o Wm A. & Virginia to LUCINDA R. RORER 18 yrs single b. Patrick Co VA d/o Wm R. & Mary A. O: farmer; by J.W. Bennett; REMARKS: applied for by the father of Robt A. Martin.

3. 3 Aug 1892 JNO W. LILLY 22 yrs single b. Mercer Co W VA s/o Wm H. & Jane to MOLLIE E. EPLING 19 yrs single d/o L.A. & Ellen O: farmer; by Jas W. Lilly; REMARKS: applied for by E.W. Hoye.

4. 3 Aug 1892 JOHN W. SIMPSON 26 yrs single b. Roanoke Co VA s/o Vincent R. & Franie J. to CORA L. SMITH 19 yrs single b. Pulaski Co VA d/o Robert & Mary O: railroader; by M.A. Wilson REMARKS: Evidence of J.C. Elliott.

5. 10 Aug 1892 W.W. WRIGHT 25 yrs single b. Bland Co VA s/o David O. & H.J. to EUGENIA BAILEY 15 yrs single b. Mercer Co W VA d/o Cornelius W. & S.A. O: carpenter; by Eugene Blake.

6. 10 Aug 1892 REUBEN C. FARMER 52 yrs wid. b. Carroll Co VA s/o John N. & Nancy to HARRIET O.O. CADLWELL 40 yrs single b. Craig Co VA d/o Hugh & Frances O: carpenter; by Phil S. Sutton.

7. 11 Aug 1892 ANGELO D'AGOSTIN 28 yrs single b. Italy s/o Angelo & Marie to MARY FRANCIS MILLS 26 yrs single b. Mercer Co W VA d/o Jas H. & Mary A. O: stone cutter; by J.O. Cassaday.

8. 18 Aug 1892 WH W. BELCHER 25 yrs single b. Tazewell Co VA s/o Waddy C. & Phoebe A. to ELIZABETH KIRBY 18 yrs single b. Montgomery Co VA d/o Jas W. & E.E. Kirby O: carpenter; by Jno C. Cook.

9. 16 Aug 1892 WH H. GAINS 23 yrs single b. Wythe Co VA s/o Anderson & Harriet to ELIZA BILLINGS 25 yrs wid. b. Henry Co VA d/o Danl & Kizziah Reynolds O: barber; by Phil S. Sutton; REMARKS: both sworn, colored.

10. 18 Aug 1892 ROBT CARPER 24 yrs single b. Floyd Co VA s/o Wesley & Mary to VICTORIA SMITH 22 yrs single b. Mercer Co W VA d/o ? & Victoria O: railroader; by A.J. Thompson; REMARKS: Robt. Carper sworn, col'd.

11. 18 Aug 1892 VISSENSO SONSENIE 22 yrs single b. Italy s/o John & Rosa to ELIZABETH VAUGHT 17 yrs single b. Mercer Co W VA d/o C.L. & C.C. O: stone cutter; by J.O. Cassaday.

12. 25 Aug 1892 IRVIN S. RENN 22 yrs single b. Sunberry PA s/o J.S. & Katherine to BESSIE POWERS 15 yrs single b. Bland Co VA d/o ? & Mary S. O: miner; by Chas W. Kelley; REMARKS: applied for by J.F.Foy.

13. 25 Aug 1892 JOS KEISER 21 yrs single b. Dorken Co PA s/o Wm & ? to GERTRUDE POWERS 17 yrs single b. Bland Co VA d/o ? & Mary S. O: miner; by Chas W. Kelley; REMARKS: applied for by J.F. Foy.

14. 20 Aug 1892 A.C. PRINCE 47 yrs wid. b. Mercer Co W VA s/o Jas & Julia to MARY J. BIRD 31 yrs wid. b. Giles Co VA d/o Richard & Elizabeth O: farmer; by Phil S. Sutton; REMARKS: applied for by H.W. Blankenship.

15. 22 Aug 1892 JAS A. BURNETT 25 yrs single b. Middlesex Co MS s/o John & Olibia(sic) T. to MARY C. EDWARDS 23 yrs wid. b. Pulaski Co VA d/o John & Esther Brady O: painter; by R.A. Kelley.

16. 25 Aug 1892 JAS E. HALE 22 yrs single b. Franklin Co VA s/o Sparrel & E.A. to ARREDELLA SMITH 17 yrs single d/o H.C. & Mary E. O: miner; by Chas W. Kelley; REMARKS: applied for by J.E.T. Senty.

17. 24 Aug 1892 W.B. HURT 21 yrs single b. Mercer Co W VA s/o W.S. & Martha J. to MARTHA A. VAUGHT 20 yrs single b. Mercer Co w VA d/o C.L. & Clara C. O: farmer; by J.O. Cassaday.

18. 26 Aug 1892 DOUGLAS PITMAN 21 yrs single b. Raleigh Co W VA s/o Peter & Cynthia to ELLA ELLIS 25 yrs single b. Raleigh Co VA d/o ? & Sally O: farmer; by Eugene Blake; REMARKS: D. Pitman sworn.

19. 1 Sept 1892 ROBT A. WRIGHT 31 yrs single b. Randolph Co NC s/o John D. & Emily to CHRISTEN BELCHER 22 yrs single b. Mercer Co W VA d/o Green & Martha O: miner; by A.M. Craft.

20. 1 Sept 1892 ALEX H. BARBOR 26 yrs single b. Mercer Co W VA s/o H.B. & Fannie C. to KATIE A. SUTTON 18 yrs single b. Mercer Co W VA d/o Phil S. & Victoria O: Deputy Clerk County Court; by Phil S. Sutton.

21. 3 Sept 1892 JOSEPH STROUSE 23 yrs single s/o John & Mary to MAGGIE BAILEY 25 yrs single b. Russell Co VA; by Chas W. Kelley; REMARKS: applied for by J.S. Young.

22. 8 Sept 1892 ARCHIE BROWN 23 yrs single b. Campbell Co VA s/o Noke & Eliza Ann to LAURA KIRKPATRICK 27 yrs wid. b. Pittsylvania Co VA d/o Doctor & Lucy Graves O: miner; by M.A. Pannill; REMARKS: applied for by C.M. Kyle.

23. 5 Sept 1892 GEO WAS SNIDER 22 yrs single b. Mercer Co W VA s/o Wm R. & Dimotheus to LURINDA A. BOWLING 25 yrs single b. Mercer Co W VA d/o A.W. & Lucinda O: farmer; by R.M. Ashworth; REMARKS: applied for by G.W. Snider.

24. 18 Sept 1892 GABRIEL BRYANT 29 yrs single b. Fauquier Co VA to PARTHENIA HENDERSON 28 yrs single b. Danville VA O: miner; by W.H. Harris; REMARKS: applied for by W. Miller.

25. 7 Sept 1892 WILBERT J. LILLY 20 yrs single b. Mercer Co W VA s/o John S. & Elizbth C. to VIRA E. REID 22 yrs single b. Monroe Co W VA d/o ? & V.E. Reid O: merchant; by Jas W. Lilly; REMARKS: applied for by permits filed.

26. 18 Sept 1892 GEORGE WOMACK 26 yrs single b. Halifax Co VA s/o Samuel & Sallie to MARY JONES 23 yrs single b. Halifax Co VA d/o ? & Charlotte Jones O: miner; by W.H. Harris.

27. 7 Sept 1892 ED. JOHNSTON GOUCH 22 yrs single b. Mercer Co W VA s/o Thomas C. & Mary Jane to VIR BELLE BLAKE 24 yrs single b. Fayette Co W VA d/o W.E. & Mary V.E. O: farmer; by Eugene Blake.

28. 8 Sept 1892 VINCENT WILEY 72 yrs wid. b. Mercer Co W VA s/o Jas & Annie to RHODA J. LILLY 54 yrs single b. Mercer Co W VA d/o Joseph & Polly O: farmer; by Wm Holroyd; REMARKS: James A. Lilly.

29. 8 Sept 1892 THOS ROYESTER 23 yrs single b. Granville Co NC s/o Spotts & Mary to MARY M. ARMSTRONG 22 yrs single b. Giles Co VA d/o John & Susan O: railroader; by R.O. Johnson; REMARKS: colored, sworn.

30. 9 Sept 1892 THOS H. WHITE 23 yrs single b. Mercer Co W VA s/o George & Susan to SUSAN E. SARVER 27 yrs wid. b. Mercer Co W VA d/o Ingraham & Polly Garretson O: farmer; by J.O. Cassaday.

31. 14 Sept 1892 LAWRENCE S. GANDY 25 yrs single b. Preston Co W VA s/o Cornelius & Mary J. to FANNIE H. BURDISS 18 yrs single b. KY d/o James & Martha O: miner; by Jno McBride; REMARKS: certificate from parents.

32. 15 Sept 1892 CHAS W. KESINGER 24 yrs single b. Monroe Co W VA now living in McDowell Co W VA s/o Jas H. & Martha to ORPHA BOWLING 22 yrs single b. Mercer Co w VA d/o Jesse I & Jane O: carpenter; by Eugene Blake.

33. 17 Sept 1892 J.F. DREBERT 27 yrs single b. Kittaming PA s/o John & Mary to SALLIE SHEPHERD 21 yrs single b. Lewistown PA d/o Peter & Mary O: mine foreman; by Chas W. Kelley; REMARKS: applied for by P.W. Anderson.

34. 18 Sept 1892 WILTON W. LILLY 26 yrs single b. Summers Co W VA now living same s/o Andw L. & Elizbth E. to ALICE BEE ROSE 17 yrs single b. Mercer Co W VA d/o Barton & Rebecca J. O: farmer; by Chas Walker; REMARKS: written permission parents.

35. 21 Sept 1892 J.I. VIA 23 yrs single b. Franklin Co VA s/o Spirel & Mary J. to MARY E. SHRADER 18 yrs single b. Mercer Co W VA d/o Conrad & Virginia O: farmer; by A.J. Thompson; REMARKS: certificate from parents.

36. 22 Sept 1892 J.W. WILSON 23 yrs single b. Mercer Co W VA s/o J.H. & Marinda to JULIA F. STAFFORD 23 yrs single b. Mercer Co W VA d/o Wm M. & Louisa H. O: farmer; by C.B. LeFew.

37. 25 Sept 1892 ALLEN CHAPMAN 22 yrs single b. Tazewell Co VA s/o George & Hulda to MARY GEORGE 17 yrs single b. Mercer Co W VA d/o Sam & Elvira O: laborer; by S.M. Gaines; REMARKS: applied for by L.A. Campbell, cert filed, both col'd.

38. 27 Sept 1892 E.T. SHELDON 35 yrs div. b. Heigs Co OH s/o Thos S. & Alvira to MAGGIE MILLS 18 yrs single b. Franklin Co Va d/o J.A. & Elizabeth O: miner; by Chas W. Kelley; REMARKS: E.D. Sheldon sworn.

39. 28 Sept 1892 CHAS A. LAYNE 32 yrs single b. Pittsylvania Co VA s/o Wm & Minerva to SARAH YOUNG 25 yrs single b. Tazewell Co VA d/o Dan'l ' Mary O: railroader; by S.M. Gaines; REMARKS: col'd, sworn.

40. 29 Sept 1892 J.B. BIRD 21 yrs single b. Mercer Co W VA s/o Stephen J. & Susan J. to SARAH J. BLANKENSHIP 17 yrs single b. Mercer Co W VA d/o Jas H. & R.A. O: railroader; by L. Goodwyn; REMARKS: J.B. Bird sworn.

41. 6 Oct 1892 WILSON LEE BAILEY 54 yrs div. b. Mercer Co W VA s/o Burwell & Nancy to POLLY BAILEY 38 yrs single b. Mercer Co W VA d/o Floyd & Sylvia O: farmer; by Gar. C. Anderson.

42. 5 Oct 1892 S.B. McKINNEY 24 yrs single b. Mercer Co W VA s/o Powstan & Elizth S. to NANNIE E. THORN 17 yrs single b. Bland Co VA d/o J.D. & Nancy O: farmer; by Phil S. Sutton; REMARKS: certificate of parents.

43. 5 Oct 1892 A.D. RICE 22 yrs single b. Pulaski Co VA s/o David & Nancy A. to CORA L. HILL 21 yrs single b. Mercer Co W VA d/o F.S. & Nannie S. O: carpenter; by J.McC. Duckwall; REMARKS: certificate of parents.

44. 6 Oct 1892 JAS F. SURFACE 18 yrs single b. Mercer Co W VA s/o G.W. & Emirilla to EVY HARTWELL 14 yrs single b. Mercer Co W VA d/o Gooch & Jane O: farmer; by D.N. Saunders; REMARKS: certificate from both parents, Jas F. Surface sworn.

45. 5 Oct 1892 G.E. CROY 25 yrs single b. Giles Co VA s/o Isaac & Sarah F. to JULIA F. HILLS 21 yrs single b. Roanoke Co VA d/o J.A. & Elizabeth O: miner; by Chas W. Kelley; REMARKS: G.E. Croy sworn.

46. 24 Oct 1892 Pocahontas VA AUGUSTUS HOWARD 26 yrs single b. Charlotte NC s/o Wm & Eliza M. to ROSA DILLS 21 yrs single b. Salem VA d/o ? & Cynthia O: miner; by Ed Scarboro P.E.

47. 9 Oct 1892 EDWARD BELL 24 yrs single b. Mercer Co W VA s/o Jas & Julia Ann to LILIAN J. HALL 17 yrs single b. Pulaski Co VA d/o Saml A. & Julia F. O: miner; by A.M. Craft; REMARKS: Saml A. Hall sworn.

48. 5 Oct 1892 J. HENRY MATHENA 22 yrs single b. Tazewll Co VA s/o Floyd & Hulda to R.E. UNDERWOOD 21 yrs single b. Mercer Co W VA d/o Jas A. & Mary Ann O: farmer; by J.O. Cassaday; REMARKS: Jas A. Underwood.

19. 9 Nov 1892 H.W. EGGLERTON 29 yrs wid. b. Lynchburg VA s/o Beverly & Mary to LOUISA COLES 21 yrs single b. Pittsylvania Co VA d/o Wyatt & Jane O: railroader; by W.J. Carter; REMARKS: col'd, sworn.

20. 10 Nov 1892 JAS D. CUMFORD 21 yrs single b. Bland Co VA now living same s/o Wm H. & Margt to MELISSA E. PRUETT 21 yrs single b. Bland Co VA d/o I.F. & Lucinda F. O: farmer; by J.O. Cassaday; REMARKS: I.F. Pruett.

21. 10 Nov 1892 W.L. GARHART 40 yrs wid. b. Floyd Co VA s/o Washington & Mary to EMMILINE NELSON 30 yrs single b. Roanoke Co VA O: miner; by Isaac P. Martin; REMARKS: applied for by F.M. Hall.

22. 16 Nov 1892 G. MILTON WALL 33 yrs single b. Mercer Co W VA s/o Henry & Jane to NANCY E. PETERS 18 yrs single b. Mercer Co W VA d/o Wm H. & Martha O: farmer; by G.C. Anderson; REMARKS: cert filed of minors parents.

23. 16 Nov 1892 LAWSON E. P. STEWART 18 yrs single b. Wyoming Co VA now living in McDowell Co W VA s/o Jno H. & Martha to LAURA A. LESTER 21 yrs single b. Mercer Co W VA d/o A.B. & Martha O: miner; by A.B. Hunter; REMARKS: both sworn.

24. 17 Nov 1892 T.W.H. SIMPKINS 30 yrs wid. b. Giles Co Va now living in Summers Co W VA s/o Elias & Elizabth to JOSIE THOMAS 22 yrs single b. Mercer Co W VA d/o Jas H. & Caroline O: farmer; by L. Goodwyn; REMARKS: parties sworn.

25. 17 Nov 1892 W.R. FOSTER 21 yrs single b. Putman Co W VA s/o Wm & Mary to MARTHA BLANKENSHIP 18 yrs single b. Mercer Co W VA d/o Wm H.H. & Louisa J. O: laborer; by J.O. Cassaday; REMARKS: parents of wife present.

26. 17 Nov 1892 S.L. NEELY 76 yrs wid. b. Mercer Co W VA now living in Raleigh Co W VA s/o John & Delily to JANE CHRISTIAN 52 yrs wid. b. Raleigh Co W VA d/o Sparril & ? Bailey O: farmer; by Giles H. Johnston.

10. 30 Oct 1892 GUS HARISON 25 yrs single b. VA to ALICE SMITH 27 yrs single b. VA O: miner; by S.M. Gaines; REMARKS: applied for by S.M. Gaines, col'd.

11. 26 Oct 1892 CHAS M. WINFREY 24 yrs single b. Mercer Co W VA s/o Chas & Julia to LAURA V. BROYLES 16 yrs single b. Mercer Co W VA d/o W.A. & Amanda O: farmer; by Gran Houchins.

12. 26 Oct 1892 WM J. BRATTON 26 yrs single b. Mercer Co W VA s/o Thos & Elizth to SALLIE M. HARMAN 19 yrs single b. Mercer Co W VA d/o Chas & Mary J. O: farmer; by Phil S. Sutton.

13. 27 Oct 1892 WM A. MILLER 26 yrs single b. Craig Co VA s/o Geo C. & Nancy to EUGENIA L. STINSON 22 yrs single b. Mercer Co W VA d/o L. & Rhoda O: merchant; by J.O. Cassaday.

14. 1 Nov 1892 CHAS G. WEISER 27 yrs sngle b. Burke Co PA to CORA M. SCHWANN 21 yrs single b. Schuylrill Co PA s/o Jos & Matilda O: machanist; by A.B. Hunter.

15. 29 Oct 1892 JOS W. WHITLOW 21 yrs single b. Floyd Co Va s/o P.H. & Rebecca to LAURA A. CONNER 18 yrs single b. Floyd Co VA d/o W.N. & R.J. O: farmer; by L. Goodwyn; REMARKS: cert filed for both husband & wife.

16. 31 Oct 1892 CYRUS BUCHANAN 22 yrs single b. Tazewell Co VA s/o Andrew & Mary to ELIZA CLARK 16 yrs single b. Mercer Co W VA d/o Wm & Willie O: railroader; by Jas Sweeney; REMARKS: colored, father's permission.

17. 2 Nov 1892 SAML E. CROY 21 yrs single b. Giles Co VA s/o Isaac & Sarah F. to MARY H. LOUERN* 23 yrs single b. Montgomery Co VA d/o J.R. & Catherine; by J.McC. Duckwall.(*Note: name smudged.)

18. 6 Nov 1892 JNO B. KAHLE 46 yrs wid. b. Rockbridge Co VA s/o Saml & Katherine to LOUVENY WILEY 36 yrs wid. b. Mercer Co W VA O: farmer; by Wm Holroyd.

Page 67

1. 6 Oct 1892 WM R. DAVIDSON 62 yrs wid. b. Tazewell Co VA s/o James C. & Julia to ISABELLE A. RICE 31 yrs single b. TN d/o David & ? O: farmer; by J.McC. Duckwall.

2. 11 Oct 1892 BENJ C. HORTON 25 yrs single b. KY s/o Jno C. & Nancy J. to HATTIE H. WITTEN 22 yrs single b. Mercer Co W VA d/o William & Mary O: minister; by Chas W. Kelley.

3. 13 Oct 1892 RUFUS E. LILLY 22 yrs single b. Mercer Co W VA s/o Jas W. & Rachel to ALLIE H. FARLEY 16 yrs single b. Summers Co W VA d/o J.R. & M.J. O: clerk; by Jas W. Lilly; REMARKS: applied for by James W. Lilly.

4. 14 Oct 1892 J.W. CLEMENT 25 yrs single b. Franklin Co Va s/o Stephen & Sarah to SARAH ROSS 18 yrs single O: miner; by J.B. Adams; REMARKS: col'd, applied for by N.J. Charles.

5. 13 Oct 1892 WILLIAM L. COOPER 18 yrs single b. Raleigh Co W VA now living same s/o John & Millison to FLORIDA GRIFFITH 18 yrs single b. Raleigh Co W VA d/o John & Mary O: farmer; by Chas Walker; REMARKS: applied for by Lewis Lilly.

6. 16 Oct 1892 EDWARD COLES 29 yrs wid. b. Pitsylvania Co Va s/o Jane Coles to HARIET FRANKLIN 38 yrs wid. b. Franklin Co Va d/o Nancy Hurt O: miner; by W.H. Harris; REMARKS: colored.

7. * * * CHAS BAYS 35 yrs wid. b. Tazewell Co VA s/o Wm & Louisa to RUHAMER HUGHES 22 yrs single b. Mercer Co W VA d/o Washn & Arminta O: farmer; REMARKS: C. Bays sworn. (* Note: no date given.)

8. * * * THOS PATTERSON single to DORA PAGE wid. O: miner; REMARKS: no return, not filled out, col'd, C.D. Bray. (*Note: no date given.)

9. 25 Oct 1892 WM M. SMITH 22 yrs single b. Giles Co VA now living same s/o Isaac A. & Sarah to CLEMENTINE A. NEAL 20 yrs single b. Mercer Co W VA d/o Wm R. & Martha J. O: farmer; by Jas Sweeney.

27. 23 Nov 1892 T.J. HIGGINBOTHAM 22 yrs single b. Mercer Co W VA s/o Jno B.& M.E. to CECELIA KEISLER 18 yrs single b. Montgomery Co VA d/o H.J. & U.M. O: merchant; by Frank Jackson.

28. 23 Nov 1892 C.J. SHELTON 23 yrs single b. Mercer Co W VA s/o Fred & Rebecca to MARY E. BOWLING 18 yrs single b. Mercer Co W VA d/o A.J. & Allie O: farmer; by J.O. Cassaday; REMARKS: C.J. Shelton sworn & cert. A.J. Bowling on file.

29. 30 Nov 1892 M.C. ADAMS 30 yrs wid. b. Indian Territory s/o Wm C. & Melissa to NANNIE C. JEWELL 23 yrs single b. Montgomery Co VA d/o J.G. & Mary M. O: clerk; by J.McC. Duckwall; REMARKS: permit J.G. Jewell.

30. 1 Dec 1892 SAML J. HENRY 22 yrs single b. Roanoke Co VA s/o Thos H. & Virginia to ANNIE A. GEARHART 21 yrs single b. Montgomery Co VA d/o Henry J. O: miner; by J.V. Dickinson; REMARKS: applied for by G.G. Williams, cert of parents filed.

31. 1 Dec 1892 CHAS L. HUFFMAN 20 yrs single b. Mercer Co w VA s/o James & Mary C. to ALICE GIBSON 21 yrs single b. Mercer Co w VA d/o James & Jane Belcher O: teamster; by Phil S. Sutton; REMARKS: cert of husband & mother on file & sworn.

32. * * * W.B. SANDERS 23 yrs single b. Franklin Co VA now living in McDowell Co W VA s/o Absolum & Adeline to EMMA G. CLAYTOR 21 yrs single b. Floyd Co VA d/o Peter & Harriet O: miner; REMARKS: W.B. Sanders & Fletcher Claytor both sworn. (*Note: no date given.)

33. 13 Dec 1892 JOSEPH DRUGAN 51 yrs single b. Ireland s/o John & Jane to LUCY MAYFIELD 34 yrs wid. b. Grayson Co VA O: plasterer; by J. McC. Duckwall.

34. 5 Dec 1892 WM J. BROWN 23 yrs wid. b. Louisville KY s/o McDonald & S.P to MARY J. GLOVER 20 yrs single b. Abrigdon VA d/o C.W. & ? O: boiler maker; by M.A. Wilson.

35. 7 Dec 1892 SOLOMON GILLISPIE 38 yrs single b. Smith Co Va s/o Robt & Martha to MAGGIE TURNER 33 yrs single b. Smith Co VA d/o Aaron & Jaxeina O: laborer; by Phil S. Sutton; REMARKS: Solomon Gillispie sworn.

36. 7 Dec 1892 JOHN M. CROTTY 33 yrs single b. Mercer Co W VA now living in McDowell Co W VA s/o Wm A. & Julia to LOULA N. CALFEE 20 yrs single b. Mercer Co W VA d/o A.J. & Maggie O: stockman; by James Sweeney.

37. 7 Dec 1892 JOHN HOWELL 21 yrs single b. Floyd Co VA s/o Thos & Jennie to JULIA A. CRUM 19 yrs single b. Mercer Co W VA d/o Thos & Arminta O: miner; by Andw J. Young.

38. 19 Dec 1892 AARON BROOKS 29 yrs div. b. Wilkes Co NC s/o John & Polly to JENNIE BROOKS 33 yrs single b. Wilkes Co NC d/o James Burchett & Sally Brooks O: miner; by M.A. Wilson.

39. 31 Dec 1892 THOS E. BREAZEALE 22 yrs single b. MA s/o Chas & Sallie to SARAH A. ELLIOTT 16 yrs single b. Newcastle Eng d/o robt P. & Esther O: miner; by Jno E. Naff; REMARKS: cert of father.

40. 21 Dec 1892 CHAS M. EASTER 44 yrs wid. b. Campbell Co VA s/o Wm M. & Susan A. to MOLLIE D.C. HANKS 23 yrs single b. Montgomery Co VA d/o C.P & Oney E. O: farmer; by J.W. Bennett.

41. 21 Dec 1892 CHARLES ROYSTER 22 yrs single b. Granville Co NC s/o ? & Marinda to HULDAH WAGONER 21 yrs single b. Pulaski Co VA d/o Jno W. & Sarah O: laborer; by S.M. Gaines; REMARKS: (col'd), Jas Hearn.

42. 21 Dec 1892 JAS T. GILPEN 36 yrs single b. Smyth Co VA s/o Wm & Elizabeth to LILLIE G. THORNTON 22 yrs single b. Mercer Co W VA d/o Jas & ? O: merchant; by M.A. Wilson.

43. 22 Dec 1892 JNO W. THOMPSON 21 yrs single b. Bland Co VA s/o Johile & Margt F. to MARY J. WILLIAMS 21 yrs single d/o Jas H. & ? O: laborer; by L. Goodwyn; REMARKS: L.H. Thompson.

44. 21 Dec 1892 WM A. HUGHES 25 yrs single b. Mercer Co W VA s/o Hugh J. & ? to MOLLIE L. HOUCHINS 15 yrs single b. Mercer Co W VA d/o Geo H. & Sarah A. O: merchant; by Jas W. Lilly; REMARKS: cert of father.

45. 22 Dec 1892 JNO A. McKINZIE JR. 24 yrs single b. Mercer Co W VA s/o Jno A. & Loucinda to LILLIE M. POLLIE 22 yrs single b. Mercer Co W VA d/o Allen & ? O: farmer; by L. Goodwyn.

46. 21 Dec 1892 THOS S. SHREWSBURY 23 yrs single b. Mercer Co W VA s/o Jno S. & Victoria to MARY P. BAILEY 20 yrs single b. Mercer Co W VA d/o Addison & Octava O: farmer; by Gar C. Anderson.

47. 22 Dec 1892 G.T. BAILEY 20 yrs single b. Mercer Co W VA s/o ? & Emily Dillard to BETTY F. BAILEY 20 yrs single b. Mercer Co W VA d/o J.S. & Timandry M. O: farmer; by Gar. C. Anderson; REMARKS: G.T. Bailey sworn, cert of parents of both parties.

48. 22 Dec 1892 JOHN DILLARD 23 yrs single b. Campbell Co VA s/o ? & Emily Dillard to OLLIE GRAVES 20 yrs single b. VA O: miner; by G.W. Alexander; REMARKS: (col'd) applied for by E.W. Freeman.

Page 68

1. 28 Dec 1892 JOS L. SMITH 22 yrs single b. Henry Co VA s/o Robert & Martha to THEODOCIA E. AUSTIN 17 yrs single b. Mercer Co W VA d/o A.J. & A. O: railroader; by L. Goodwyn; REMARKS: cert of parents.

2. 24 Dec 1892 WM NELSON TAYLOR 30 yrs single b. Franklin Co VA s/o ? & Ann Taylor to BARBARA ABINGTON 25 yrs single b. Franklin Co VA d/o Peter & Lucinda O: miner; by G.W. Alexander.

3. 29 Dec 1892 JNO J. AUSTIN 23 yrs single b. Wythe Co VA s/o Umphery & Margaret to MAY G. FORD 22 yrs single b. Montgomery Co VA d/o Saml & Loucinda O: railroader; by S.M. Gaines; REMARKS: col'd.

4. 27 Dec 1892 ISAAC L. HYLTON 22 yrs single b. Floyd Co VA s/o Hiram & Louisa to LUCY J. ARGABRIGHT 17 yrs single b. Montgomery Co VA d/o J.H. & Sarah A. O: farmer; by James Sweney.

5. 28 Dec 1892 BIRD F.F. McBRIDE 21 yrs single b. Mercer Co W VA s/o Bird & Flowretta to VIRGINIA F. FERGUSON 17 yrs single b. Mercer Co W VA d/o G.N. & Octava O: farmer; by J.W. Lilly; REMARKS: cert of parents.

6. 28 Dec 1892 JAS H. HARVEY 20 yrs single b. Mercer Co W VA s/o Adam M. & Electra A. to BROOK CLARK 19 yrs single b. Mercer Co W VA d/o John & Ellen O: teacher; by Jas W. Lilly; REMARKS: cert of parents.

7. 28 Dec 1892 HENRY ARMSTEAD 24 yrs single b. Prince Edward Co Va s/o Jacob & Polly to WILLIE CODWILL 22 yrs single b. Giles Co VA d/o Robt & Sallie O: barber; by S.M. Gaines; REMARKS: colored, aff'd.

8. 28 Dec 1892 E.B. LAMBERT 19 yrs single b. Bland Co VA s/o William & Mary E. to NANNIE N. HAGEN 15 yrs single b. Bland Co VA d/o J.R. & Mary O: farmer; by R.M. Ashworth.

Page 69

1. 3 Jan 1893 S.J. BURTON 20 yrs single b. Giles Co VA s/o H.P. & M.A. to ESTELLA MONTGOMERY 17 yrs single b. MO d/o S.M. & D. O: fireman; by Alfred B. Hunter.

2. 4 Jan 1893 CHAS B. BAILEY 28 yrs single b. Tazewell Co VA now living same s/o Harvey G. & Nancy J. to SARAH LOUTHEN 23 yrs single b. Smith Co VA d/o Isaac P. & ? O: butcher; by Phil S. Sutton.

3. 5 Jan 1893 CROCKETT SCOTT 19 yrs single b. Mercer Co W VA s/o Wm R. & ? to LUCETTA BELCHER 15 yrs single b. Mercer Co W VA d/o Anderson & Matilda O: farmer; by John H. Honaker; REMARKS: cert & wife's parents.

4. 11 Jan 1893 ROBERT S. COOK 22 yrs single b. Wyoming Co W VA s/o John N. & Margaret Cook to BETTIE E. HUFFMAN 18 yrs single b. Giles Co VA d/o A.J. & Dicie E. Huffman O: farmer; by E.W. Cooper.

5. 16 Jan 1893 G.M. JACKSON 38 yrs single b. Halifax Co W VA now living Rockingham Co NC s/o Abel & Emily to LELIA H. NEAL 17 yrs single b. Rockingham Co NC d/o Phil & Rebecca V. O: barkeeper; by A.B. Hunter; REMARKS: G.M. Jackson sworn.

6. 15 Jan 1893 W.H. POWELL 26 yrs single b. Rockingham Co VA s/o M.F. & Rebecca to SARAH C. COMER 21 yrs single b. Mercer Co W VA d/o Wallace J. & Sarah A. O: lumberman; by L. Goodwyn.

7. 19 Jan 1893 ABSOLUM WILLIAMS 21 yrs single b. Carrol Co VA s/o Connaily & Eliza Jane to ELEN DANILY 16 yrs single b. NC d/o Thomas & Willmouie O: miner; by Jno E. Noff; REMARKS: Absolum Williams sworn.

8. 25 Jan 1893 E.L. BILLIPS 22 yrs single b. Tazewell Co VA now living name s/o Gidieon & Eliza to SARAH V. HYPES 22 yrs single b. Mercer Co W VA d/o J.L. & Francis J. O: farmer; by J.O. Cassaday.

9. 18 Jan 1893 LUCIEN WHITE 29 yrs single b. Roanoke Co VA s/o Saml M. & Bettie M. to MRS. J.C. JONES 37 yrs wid. b. Bland Co VA d/o Isaac J. & M. Davis O: painter; by P.S. Sutton.

10. 22 Jan 1893 WM HOLCOMB 53 yrs wid. b. Yadkin Co SC(sic) s/o Geo L. & Nancy to JANE HITCHEH 33 yrs wid. b. Franklin Co VA d/o Preston & Mary Hall O: farmer; by W.A. Pearson.

11. 21 Jan 1893 LEON R. PRICE 29 yrs single b. Knox Co Tn now living in Baltimore MD s/o Allen J. & ? to ELIZA O. BURNS 21 yrs single b. Russell Co VA d/o ? & Sarah O: salesman; by P.S. Sutton; REMARKS: applied for by J.E. Town.

12. 25 Jan 1893 C. CUMBY 26 yrs single b. Giles Co VA s/o Thos & Arminta to SALLIE MURPHY 18 yrs single b. Roanoke Co VA d/o ? & Loucinda O: lawyer; by P.S. Sutton; REMARKS: C. Cumby sworn.

13. 29 Jan 1893 SAML A. MINOR 21 yrs single b. Mercer Co W VA s/o Peter & Nancy to FANNY HANGER 18 yrs single b. Washington Co VA d/o A.H. & Sarah O: blacksmith; by D.N. Saunders; REMARKS: J.M. Wimmer & S.A. Minor sworn.

14. 6 Feb 1893 CHARLES W. LILLY 21 yrs single b. Washington Co TN s/o J.J. & Vina Lilly to ARDELIA BLANKENSHIP 18 yrs single b. Mercer Co W VA d/o A.J. Blankenship O: miner; by J.B. Dickinson.

15. 19 Feb 1893 THOS Q. WILCOX 27 yrs single b. Surry Co NC now living in McDowell Co W VA s/o J.B. & Elizabeth to ROSA E. HOWELL 19 yrs single b. VA d/o Thomas & Jennie O: mine foreman; by Jno E. Noff; REMARKS: certificate of father.

16. 7 Feb 1893 WOODSON SHORTER 25 yrs single b. Mercer Co W VA s/o Woodson & Bettie to ALMETA SNIDER 29 yrs single b. Mercer Co W VA d/o Esom & Rhoda O: farmer; by Wm Holrody; REMARKS: A.J. Caperton.

17. 8 Feb 1893 JOS M. NORRIS 22 yrs single b. Pulaski Co VA s/o H.L. & E.F. to NANCY GREEN 21 yrs single b. NC d/o ? & Louisa O: railroader; by J.V. Dickinson; REMARKS: cert. Norris sworn.

18. 16 Feb 1893 P.E. SCOTT 23 yrs single b. Boone Co W VA s/o Wm & Mary E. to L.C. HUBBARD 18 yrs single b. Mercer Co W VA d/o Saml & Ellen O: saw mill; by G.C. Anderson; REMARKS: consent of GON.

19. 15 Feb 1893 JAS H. PETTET 23 yrs single b. Henry Co VA s/o W.W. & Harriet H. to MARY A. AUSTIN 21 yrs single b. Montgomery Co VA d/o A.J. & Athalinda O: railroader; by L. Goodwyn.

20. 15 Feb 1893 W.C. BROYLES 28 yrs single b. Monroe Co W VA s/o W.H. & Katherine to NANNIE S. ANDERSON 27 yrs single b. Bedford Co VA d/o John W. & ? O: carpenter; by Phil S. Sutton.

21. 20 Feb 1893 LEVI TABOR 23 yrs single b. Tazewell Co VA s/o S.H. & Loucinda to ALICE O. COMPTON 17 yrs single b. Tazewell Co VA d/o Docn & Bathelda O: miner; by D.N. Saunders; REMARKS: L. Tabor sworn.

22. 20 Feb 1893 ROBT E. GULLION 20 yrs single b. Tazewell Co VA s/o Reuben & Elizth M. to STELLA C. COMPTON 16 yrs single b. Tazewell Co VA d/o Docn & Bathelda O: miner; by D.N. Saunders; REMARKS: R.E. Gullion sworn.

23. 27 Feb 1893 RAY R. LOWDER 26 yrs single b. Tazewell Co VA s/o Geo W. & Luranie B. to MARY SHELTON 26 yrs single b. Pittsylvania Co VA d/o P.T. & Rebecca O: conductor; by A.B. Hunter.

24. 2 March 1893 JOSHUA S. MEADOWS 20 yrs single b. Mercer Co W VA s/o J.F. & Katherine to MARY R.J. WEEKS 19 yrs single b. Floyd co VA d/o Jno W. & E.J. O: farmer; by James H. Johnson; REMARKS: cert of wife's parents filed, J.F. Meadows gave the information.

25. 27 Feb 1893 ANDREW CAMPBELL 55 yrs wid. to ROSANE PENINGTON 35 yrs single b. Mercer Co W VA d/o Wm R. & Katherine O: farmer; by L. Goodwyn; REMARKS: applied for in writing by A. Campbell.

26. 27 Feb 1893 E.M. MONTGOMERY 25 yrs single b. MO s/o Sydney M. & Del to NANNIE TABOR 17 yrs single b. Falls Mills VA d/o S.G. & Virginia O: barber; by H.E. Willson; REMARKS: cert of father.

27. 3 March 1893 J.W. SHREWSBURY 19 yrs single b. Mercer Co W VA s/o Jas W. & Julia to VIR E. McCOMAS 20 yrs single b. Raleigh Co W VA d/o R.B. & Oa'eoc O: farmer; by E.W. Cooper; REMARKS: cert of father & fathers per*. (*Note: copy cut off.)

28. 1 March 1893 JESSE D. RESSEE 31 yrs single b. Pittsylvania VA s/o John & Gallina to ALICE ROSE 21 yrs single b. Mercer Co W VA O: miner; by Jno E. Noff; REMARKS: applied for by J.D. Reesee.

29. 9 March 1893 CHARLES STEDEDCIDE* 26 yrs single b. Nashville TN s/o Jack & Lythia Stindell* to SARAH EVANS 18 yrs single b. Wythe Co Va d/o Lee & Sarah A. Evans O: enjineer(sic); by Jno E. Noff. (*Note: both times handwriting difficult to read.)

30. 15 March 1893 JOS F. BONHAM 26 yrs single b. Smythe Co VA s/o Jno F. & Amanda to NOGIE SARVER 21 yrs single b. Giles Co VA d/o ? & Mary A. O: railroader; by L. Goodwyn.

31. 15 March 1893 JOHN LAWRENCE 21 yrs single b. Floyd Co W VA s/o James & Cynthia to LULA WILLS 22 yrs single b. Monroe Co W VA d/o John & Eliza O: bricklayer; by A.B. Hunter; REMARKS: J. Lawrence sworn.

32. 22 March 1893 R.L. FARLEY 21 yrs single b. Mercer Co W VA s/o Wm & ? to MARY I. SNEED 18 yrs single b. Mercer Co W VA d/o John & E.A. O: farmer; by James W. Lilly; REMARKS: inf. by John Snead.

33. 22 March 1893 A.W. SUBLETT 63 yrs wid. b. Campbell Co VA s/o Mathew & Francis to ELLEN V. NEAL 22 yrs single b. Bland Co VA d/o Robt H. & Martha A. O: farmer; by J.O. Cassaday; REMARKS: inf. by A.W. Sublett.

34. 26 March 1893 JAS W. FINNEY 22 yrs single b. Franklin Co VA s/o ? & Rinda to HATTIE CALSAW 21 yrs angle b. Bedford Co VA d/o Eliza & Nathan O: engineer; by J.H. Adams; REMARKS: col'd, J.W. Finney sworn.

35. 28 March 1893 CHARLES WOODEY 23 yrs single b. Franklin Co VA s/o Joseph & Betty to MORA SAUNDERS 25 yrs single b. Bedford Co VA d/o Henry & Martha O: laborer; by M.A. Pannill; REMARKS: inf. by B. Moore.

36. 29 March 1893 ABERT J. MEDLY 27 yrs single b. Summers Co W VA s/o Minnie Medly to LUCY V. GORE 17 yrs single b. Mercer Co W VA d/o William & Caroline O: farmer; by A.J. Thompson.

37. 30 March 1893 ROBERT BAILEY 22 yrs single b. Mercer Co W VA to EMMA BAILEY 21 yrs single b. Mercer Co W VA d/o John & Julia Ann O: miner; by John H. Honaker; REMARKS: applied for by W.C. Patterson.

38. 30 March 1893 EZEKIEL B. BELCHER 23 yrs single b. Mercer Co W VA s/o Obediah & Margt W. to ELIZA J. NEAL 21 yrs single b. Mercer Co W VA d/o D.N. & Sarah A. O: farmer; by J.O. Cassaday.

39. 29 March 1893 CHAS THOS DOYLE 22 yrs single b. Mercer Co W VA s/o Jas A. & Martha to ZORA M. CONNER 21 yrs single b. Montgomery Co VA d/o Jas H. & L.F. O: farmer; by T.K. Lambert.

40. 30 March 1893 R.S. McCOY 25 yrs single b. VA s/o D. & ? to MAGGIE HOUCHINS 20 yrs single b. Tazewell Co VA d/o J.B. & Patria O: railroading; by Granvill Houchins; REMARKS: applied for by J.B. Houchins.

41. 3 April 1893 T.F. DILLON 23 yrs single b. Mercer Co W VA s/o Wm & ? to FANNIE POE 16 yrs single b. Lincoln Co W VA d/o James & ? O: railroader; by John H. Honaker; REMARKS: cert filed T.F. Dillon sworn.

42. 5 April 1893 L.H. PHETTHLACE 21 yrs single b. Smithsburg MD s/o Danl H. & Elizabeth to MAY BERNES 17 yrs single b. Philadelphia PA d/o Martin & Naomi O: train dispatcher; by J. McC Duckwall; REMARKS: cert filed.

43. 5 April 1893 F.D. CARPER 22 yrs single b. Mercer Co w VA s/o Fleming & Sally to KATE HUDSON 22 yrs single b. Mercer Co W VA d/o Robert & ? O: R.R. brakeman; by J.O. Cassaday.

44. 15 April 1893 GEORGE H. HILL 25 yrs single b. Schuylkill Co PA s/o Chas M. & Ellen to LOUISE C. HAWES 28 yrs single b. Farmville VA d/o Rev H.H. & Hattie A. O: civil engineer; by H.H. Hawes.

45. 12 April 1893 JOHN W. BOOTH 35 yrs single b. Northumberland PA s/o Thos & Ellen to MAGGIE HARMAN 20 yrs single b. Tazewell Co VA d/o Wm B.C. & Paulina O: bottler of soda wtr; by J.L. Prater; REMARKS: father of bride present.

46. 11 April 1893 JNO A. PERKINS 18 yrs single b. Russell Co VA s/o J.W. & Mary to MAGGIE E. COMPTON 18 yrs single b. Rusell Co VA d/o Starling & Lou O: farmer; by Phil S. Sutton.

47. 22 April 1893 W.H. YOUNG 30 yrs single b. Mercer Co W VA now living in McDowell Co W VA s/o Isaac & Sarah to ROXIE L. BAILEY 22 yrs single b. Mercer Co W VA d/o G.C. & S.E. Jane O: D.S. McD Co.; by J.T. Frazier.

page 70

1. 23 April 1893 MILTON MARSHALL 29 yrs single b. Chester Co PA s/o Geo C. & Minerva to EDNA J. HATHLEY 27 yrs single b. Bedford Co VA d/o Wm & Bettie A. O: miner; by A.H. Craft; REMARKS: M. Marshall sworn.

2. 26 April 1893 ULYSSUS S. ALLEN 24 yrs single b. Nelson Co VA now living in McDowell Co W VA s/o Geo C. & Jane S. to RHODA REED 16 yrs single b. Mercer Co W VA d/o James H. & Rebecca A. O: miner; by L. Goodwyn; REMARKS: U.S. Allen & A.E. Brown sworn.

3. 27 April 1893 BENJAMIN BARKSDALE 24 yrs single b. Halifax Co VA s/o Daniel & Sallie to PRUDENCE HUFF 20 yrs single b. Franklin Co VA d/o Watt & Melinda O: laborer; by M.A. Pannill.

4. 4 May 1893 G.J. THORNTON 30 yrs div. b. Pulaski Co VA now living in Raleigh Co W VA s/o G.J. & Margt E. to SARAH C. BURTON 19 yrs single b. Mercer Co W VA d/o Wm H. & Elvira E. O: farmer; by Saml W. McKinney; REMARKS: G.J. Thornton sworn, divorced in Raleigh Cir Ct.

5. 14 May 1893 G.E. BATTLES 22 yrs single b. Middlesex Co MA s/o E.M. & Louisa M. to PRISCILLA WAKEFIELD 22 yrs single b. Phila Co PA d/o Theodore & Isabella D. O: clerk; by W. Hullihan Burkhart.

6. 14 May 1893 ROBERT CHEATHAM 28 yrs single b. Appomattox Co Va s/o Spencer & Charity to MOLLIE DAVIS 22 yrs single b. Appomattox Co VA d/o Sol & Betty O: miner; by W.H. Harris; REMARKS: colored.

7. 20 May 1893 WALTER HALL 21 yrs single b. England s/o Jas & Melinna to SUSAN RATLIFF 17 yrs single b. Mercer Co W VA d/o Jas F. & M.E. O: miner; by A.H. Craft.

8. 14 May 1893 WESLEY H. BAILEY 25 yrs single b. McDowell Co W VA s/o Zachariah H. & Elizabeth to SARAH C. CROWDER 28 yrs wid. b. TN d/o Lawson & Sarah Hampton O: miner; by Jno E. Noff.

9. 22 May 1893 CALLIE HOUCHINS 24 yrs single b. Russell Co VA s/o Geo & Mary to ELLEN HUGHES 22 yrs single b. Smith Co VA d/o Gabe & ? O: railroader; by Granville Houchins.

10. 24 May 1893 ELIAS KING 27 yrs wid. b. Tazewell Co VA s/o Walter & Matilda to JOSIE BROWN 23 yrs single b. Tazewell Co VA d/o Chas & Rosa O: laborer; by Anderson Ward; REMARKS: col'd, E. King sworn.

11. 23 May 1893 WM BURGESS 23 yrs single to CORA JARHER 22 yrs single b. Smith Co VA d/o Jno J. & Lucy O: painter; by A.B. Hunter; REMARKS: applied for by J.F. Loyd sworn, cert. filed.

12. 25 May 1893 B.I RORRER 22 yrs single b. Patrick Co VA to VIRGIN M. NEELY 18 yrs single b. Mercer Co W VA d/o W.F. & Victoria O: agent; by James H. Johnson; REMARKS: applied for by Wm F. Neeley, cert filed.

13. 24 May 1893 THOS C. HUBBARD 23 yrs single b. Mason Co W VA s/o Payton A. & Lucy A. to NANNIE E. KARNES 17 yrs single b. Mercer Co W VA d/o Jas A. & Adaline O: farmer; by J.W. Lilly; REMARKS: consent of father.

14. 31 May 1893 A.M. SLUSHER 26 yrs single b. Floyd Co VA s/o Lafayette & Louisa to MINNIE J. ANDERSON 17 yrs single b. Bedford Co VA d/o Geo W. & Manerva O: photographer; by W.A. Pearson.

15. 31 May 1893 JOHN W. PATRICK 23 yrs single b. Montgomery Co VA s/o James & Nannie A. to LILLIE V. WHITE 17 yrs single b. Mercer Co W VA d/o Geo W.P. & Rebecca S. O: car inspector; by J.O. Cassaday; REMARKS: cert of father filed.

16. 1 June 1893 ARTHUR M. HERNDON 23 yrs single b. Mercer Co W VA s/o W.H. & Mary E. to MINERVA GEARHART 17 yrs single b. Floyd Co VA d/o W.L. & Evaline O: mining; by John H. Honaker; REMARKS: cert of father filed.

17. 1 June 1893 ROBT L. LAWLESS 23 yrs single b. Patrick Co VA s/o G.W. & R.M. to FLORENCE D. HALL 16 yrs single b. Floyd Co VA d/o J.T. & Sarah E. O: mining; by D.A. Rauney; REMARKS: cert of father filed.

18. 1 June 1893 EDWARD P. WINSTON 23 yrs single b. Tazewell Co VA s/o Robt & Mary to ALICE M. PEERY 18 yrs single b. Tazewell Co VA d/o Reese & Elizth Jane Tinner; by Granville Houchins; REMARKS: cert of father filed.

19. 5 June 1893 FRANK SHAFFER 23 yrs single b. Lackawanna Co PA s/o Sidney & Kate to LULA KELLER 17 yrs single b. Clearfield Co PA d/o John & ? O: conductor; REMARKS: cert of father filed.

20. 7 June 1893 ROBT L. SMITH 29 yrs single b. Tazewell Co VA s/o Geo P. & Martha L to NANCY ANN HEADOWS 20 yrs single b. Raleigh Co W VA d/o John L. & Marinda O: farmer; by Phil S. Sutton; REMARKS: cert of father filed.

21. 8 June 1893 A.J. ALIFF 24 yrs single b. Raleigh Co W VA s/o Thos E. & Fluvanna to EDNA E. FERFUSON 17 yrs single b. Franklin Co VA d/o Thos S. & M.W. O: miner; by A.H. Craft; REMARKS: father present and gave his consent.

22. 8 June 1893 J.H. GENT 22 yrs single b. Cline Co PA s/o Wm & Magaret(sic) to MARTHA W. FERFUSON 15 yrs single b. Franklin Co VA d/o thos S. & M.W. O: miner; by A.H. Craft; REMARKS: father present and gave his consent.

23. 10 June 1893 SAM CONWELL 36 yrs single b. Rockingham Co NC s/o James & Harriet to PARTHENIA CALAWAY 30 yrs single b. Franklin Co VA d/o Simeon & Annie; by D.A. Raney; REMARKS: colored, sworn.

24. 11 June 1893 W.H. BALLARD 20 yrs single b. Alheg Co NC s/o R.F. & A.H. to ROSA E. HAWKS 22 yrs single b. Carroll Co VA d/o Wm R. & Polley A. O: laborer; by John H. Honaker; REMARKS: H.G. Woods, guardn. of W.H. Ballard gave cons. personally.

25. 13 June 1893 S.C. NIEWANDER 21 yrs single b. Bland Co VA s/o Alex & Mary to LINDA J. DENT 17 yrs single b. NC d/o Thos & Charlotte O: miner; by Jno E. Noff; REMARKS: certs of both parents filed & parties sworn.

26. 21 June 1893 JNO C. HIGGINBOTHAM 34 yrs wid. b. Mercer Co W VA s/o Jno B. & Mary to LEEOTA D. JOHNSTON 23 yrs single b. Pulaski Co VA d/o M.S. & Sallie A. O: gentleman; by Phil S. Sutton.

27. 5 June 1893 EDWARD G. DAVIDSON 21 yrs single b. Mercer Co W VA s/o James & ? to MARTHA E. HAMBRICK 20 yrs single b. Mercer Co W VA d/o L.T. & Rebecca J. O: laborer; by John H. Honaker; REMARKS: applied for by L.T. Hambrick.

28. 20 June 1893 JAMES W. LILLY 48 yrs wid. b. Mercer Co W VA s/o Washington & Polly to MARY E. MEADOR 26 yrs div. b. Mercer Co W VA d/o Geo W. & Oney Meador O: farmer; by Drury Farley; REMARKS: divorced at Hinten.

29. 25 June 1893 CHARLES JONES 21 yrs single b. Lynchburg VA s/o James & Elize to HATTIE PATTERSON 21 yrs single b. Franklin Co VA d/o Surry & Julia O: miner; by S.H. Gaines; REMARKS: col'd.

30. 30 June 1893 WM J. ARMSTEAD 31 yrs wid. b. Lynchbury VA s/o Reuben & Anna to MARY ELLA WHITE 24 yrs single b. Washington Co VA O: hotel; by J.H. Carter; REMARKS: col'd.

31. 25 June 1893 JNO H. WARD 41 yrs wid. b. Tazewell Co VA s/o Anderson & Malinda to MARGARET HILL 49 yrs wid. b. Henry Co VA d/o Jubel & Sophia O: laborer; by J.W. Payne; REMARKS: colored.

32. 29 June 1893 J.G. HARWOOD 29 yrs single b. Bath Co VA s/o Wm & Sarah to MARY A. BALES 22 yrs single O: hostler R.R.; by A.B. Hunter.

33. 3 July 1893 EDWARD BUCHANAN 24 yrs sngle b. Wyoming Co W VA s/o Geo & Caroline to SARAH RATLIFF 26 yrs single b. Mercer Co W VA d/o Jas & Elizabeth O: miner; by Phil S. Sutton.

34. 4 July 1893 WM H. HAYS 52 yrs wid. now living in Lawrence Co O(sic) to POLLY A. TAYLOR 39 yrs single b. Craig Co VA d/o Geo A. & Elmira O: farmer; by J.O. Cassaday.

35. 7 July 1893 PHILIP MEADOWS 19 yrs single b. Mercer Co W VA s/o Sampson & Caroline to MOLLIE E. SMITH 16 yrs single b. Mercer Co W VA d/o John M. & Louisa A. O: laborer; by L. Goodwyn; REMARKS: consent of guardian & father.

36. 20 July 1893 CHAS DAY 23 yrs single b. Fayette Co W VA s/o Davis & Josephine to BETTIE BAGLEY 21 yrs single d/o Sam & Tina O: hotel waiter; by W.J. Carter.

37. 16 July 1893 JAS T. GREER 25 yrs single b. Floyd co VA s/o J.L. Greer & Elizabeth to MARTHA W. SMITH 19 yrs single b. Mercer co W VA d/o Daniel L. & Fannie B. O: farmer; by T.C. Pulum; REMARKS: consent of father.

38. 16 July 1893 WALTER S. GREER 23 yrs single b. Floyd Co VA s/o J.L. Greer & Elizabeth to LAURA E. SMITH 17 yrs single b. Mercer Co W VA d/o Daniel L. & Fannie B. O: farmer; by T.C. Pulum; REMARKS: consent of father.

39. 19 July 1893 J.S. FRENCH 21 yrs single b. Tazewell Co VA s/o J.D. & Henrietta to NANNIE NISWANDER 17 yrs single b. Bland Co VA d/o W.H.H. & Ann O: engineer; by C.E. Painter; REMARKS: consent of father.

40. 20 July 1893 WM R. BRUMFIELD 22 yrs single b. Montgomery Co VA s/o T.W. & Jane to MARY E. PUGH 17 yrs single b. Floyd Co VA d/o Flern & Adelia O: miner; by A.M. Craft; REMARKS: consent of mother.

41. 27 July 1893 JOHN HURT 25 yrs single b. Franklin Co VA d/o Mac & Mandy to SARAH CHARLTON 22 yrs single b. Tazewell Co VA d/o Sam & Kizziah O: coke drawer; by Rev Floyd Meadows; REMARKS: col'd.

42. 27 July 1893 HENRY YOUNG 30 yrs wid. b. Halifax Co VA s/o Henry & Fannie to LUCY M. NOBLE 36 yrs wid. b. Franklin Co VA d/o Jno P. & Sarah DeHaven O: railroader; by H.J. Carter; REMARKS: col'd.

43. 26 July 1893 N.A.H. BOGGESS 28 yrs single b. Mercer Co w VA s/o Nimrod & H.A. to ANNIE LAURA JOHNSTON 23 yrs single b. Mercer Co W VA d/o Wm & S.E. O: farmer; by J.L. Prater.

44. 27 July 1893 CHARLES A. PEYTON 48 yrs wid. b. Mercer Co w VA s/o John C. & Julina to FRANCES PRINCE 35 yrs div. b. Wyoming Co W VA d/o ? & Drucilla Pettry O: farmer; by Phil S. Sutton.

45. 29 July 1893 GEORGE P. HONAKER 21 yrs single b. Tazewell Co VA s/o Chas Wm & Mollie J. to ISABELL ALIFF 16 yrs single b. Franklin Co VA d/o J.T. & S.C. Aliff O: farmer; by W.A. Pearson; REMARKS: cert filed, F.P. Honaker sworn.

46. 3 July 1893 HENRY CEPHAS 27 yrs single b. Appomattox Co VA s/o Bob Cephas & Nancy Baker to MARY JANE DOWNS 22 yrs single b. Tazewell Co VA d/o Elisha & Emma Downs O: miner; by J.H. Adams.

47. 3 Aug 1893 W.S. HAZLEWOOD 21 yrs single b. Mercer Co w VA s/o W & Nancy Hazlewood to MARINDA C. BELCHER 16 yrs single b. Mercer co W VA d/o J.F. & M.J. Belcher O: laborer; by D.N. Saunders.

48. * * * ANDREW SCOTT 38 yrs single b. England s/o Jacob & Amelia to MAGGIE PARRY 24 yrs single b. OH d/o William & eliza O: bricklayer; by J.L. Prater. (*Note: date torn off of original copy.)

1. 20 April 1893 THOS J. HALL 21 yrs single b. Mercer Co W VA s/o J.R. & Amanda E. to LETITIA H. WILKINSON 21 yrs single b. Bland Co VA d/o ? & Causby Ann O: farmer; by J.W. Bennett; REMARKS: certificates.

2. 10 Aug 1893 LEONARD H. SMITH 24 yrs single b. Giles Co VA s/o G.H. & Ellen B. to CORA L. BRUCE 19 yrs single b. Mercer Co W VA d/o W.W. & Martha H. O: farmer; by J.O. Cassaday; REMARKS: certificates.

3. 9 Aug 1893 T.J.F. ASHWORTH 28 yrs single b. Wythe Co VA now living in McDowell Co W VA s/o J.S. & Eliza A. to SARAH J. BAILEY 19 yrs single b. Mercer Co W VA d/o C.A. & Eliza O: clerk in comesoy(sic); by W.A. Parson; REMARKS: certificates.

4. 10 Aug 1893 S.E. JACK* 31 yrs single b. Yadkin Co NC s/o Alex & J.C. to IDA F. HALL 16 yrs single b. Mercer Co W VA d/o P.B. & Mary J. O: farmer; by W.A. Pearson; REMARKS: certificates filed both sworn.

5. 9 Aug 1893 J. LEWIS JOHNSON 20 yrs single b. Grayson Co VA s/o Jos C. & Martha to LUCY J. GOODE 16 yrs single b. Giles Co VA d/o ? & Malinda O: farmer; by J.W. Bennett; REMARKS: certificates filed both sworn.

6. 12 Aug 1893 R.L. BLANKENSHIP 23 yrs single b. Mercer Co w VA s/o Thompson & Elizabeth to ALICE J. BLANKENSHIP 25 yrs single b. Mercer Co W VA d/o Oscar & Sarah O: laborer; by J.O. Cassaday.

7. 20 Aug 1893 WM FREEMAN 30 yrs single b. Mercer Co W VA s/o Edward & Mary to JANE CARVER 21 yrs single b. Tazewell Co VA d/o ? & Mary O: miner; by Jno E. Noff; REMARKS: Wm Freeman sworn.

8. 24 Aug 1893 T.L. WILLIAMS 23 yrs single b. Montgomery Co VA s/o Thos P. & Mollie B. Williams to RACHEL ANN WORREN 28 yrs wid. b. Mercer Co W VA d/o John Shrewsbury O: farmer; by A.B. Hunter.

18. 17 Sept 1893 BENJ B. LILLY 20 yrs single b. Raleigh Co W VA now living same s/o Thos E. & Sarah A. to CELIA J. LILLY 16 yrs single b. Mercer Co W VA d/o John E. & Julina O: farmer; REMARKS: cert filed; by Drury Farley.

19. 6 Sept 1893 HERALD FULTON BRUCE 56 yrs wid. b. Wythe Co W VA now living in Bland Co VA s/o James & Elizabeth to FANNIE C. THOMPSON 38 yrs single b. Mercer Co W VA d/o David & Adaline O: farmer; by J.L. Prater.

20. * * * H. AUSTIN 69 yrs wid. b. Wythe Co VA s/o James & Millie to GEORGE 46 yrs wid. b. Bland Co VA O: butchers asst; REMARKS: col'd. (*Note: no date given).

21. 7 Sept 1893 RICE PILLARS 22 yrs single b. McDowell Co W VA s/o Thos G. & H.C. to ELIZA A. HATCHER 22 yrs wid. b. Mercer Co W VA O: miner; by D.A. Rously; REMARKS: Rice Pillars sworn.

22. 8 Sept 1893 LAWSON G. BURCHETT 34 yrs wid. b. Surry Co NC s/o Lawson & Elizabeth to AMANDA SCOTT 33 yrs wil. b. Mercer Co W VA d/o Thompson & Eliz Minor O: miner; by John H. Honaker.

23. 10 Sept 1893 FRANKLIN McGUIRE 21 yrs single b. Ash Co NC s/o Granville & Matilda to LELA JANE SHUTT 17 yrs single b. Mercer Co W VA d/o H.F. & Ellen O: farmer; by Rufus M. Wheeler; REMARKS: cert. filed.

24. 15 Sept 1893 JOHNATHAN K. WALKER 21 yrs single b. Mercer Co W VA s/o Counsel R. & Emily to LOLA D. WALKER 15 yrs single b. Mercer Co W VA d/o G.P & Harriet O: farmer; by I.R. Lambert.

25. 12 Sept 1893 JAMES A. SISR 22 yrs single b. Wythe Co VA s/o Gideon & Eliza to MARY L. BUCHANON 19 yrs single b. Wyoming(sic) d/o George & Annie C. O: farmer; by D.A. Rously.

26. 13 Sept 1893 MILES C. HOYE 27 yrs single b. Raleigh Co W VA now living in Summers Co VA s/o Calvin C. & Mary E. to NOMMIE LEE BIRD 25 yrs single b. Mercer Co W VA d/o Jno S.H. & Elizabeth O: merchant; by J.O. Campbell.

27. 27 Sept 1893 LETCHER McPHILLIPS 23 yrs single b. Raleigh Co W VA now living same s/o R.S. & H.F. to PHILLIPS 19 yrs single b. Mercer Co W VA d/o Jno A. & Serepta J. O: farmer; by G.W. Johnson; REMARKS: permission.

28. 28 Sept 1893 BAILEY STRONG 23 yrs single b. Monroe Co W VA s/o Daniel & Mary E. to ZOLLIE M. WHEELER 14 yrs single b. Giles Co VA d/o T.B. & Mollie O: farmer; by G.C. Anderson; REMARKS: fathers permission in unity.

29. 21 Sept 1893 WALTER W. PALMER 20 yrs single b. Giles Co VA s/o ? & Agnes Palmer to MARY A. SMITH 25 yrs single b. Mercer Co W VA d/o D.L. & Fannie B. O: farmer; by J.O. Cassaday; REMARKS:

30. 27 Sept 1893 SAML O. WHITE 22 yrs single b. Mercer Co W VA s/o H.G. & Sarah E. to MARTHA SIMPSON 18 yrs single b. Washington Co VA d/o ? & ? O: railroader; by M. McC. Duckwall; REMARKS: cert filed & H.G. White.

31. 28 Sept 1893 THOS B. BROWNING 23 yrs single b. Boone Co W VA s/o L.D. & Mary J. to NORA E. WRIGHT 18 yrs single b. Bland Co VA d/o Jas D. & Sarah E. O: farmer; by John H. Honaker; REMARKS: cert filed T.B.B. sworn.

32. 23 Sept 1893 J.B. WOODY 22 yrs wid. b. Wilkes Co NC s/o Bryant & nancy to HARY TOLIVER 16 yrs single b. Mercer Co W VA d/o Creesl & Frankie O: stone mason; by C.E. Painter; REMARKS: cert filed J.B.W. sworn.

33. * * * S.T. SMITH 25 yrs single b. Floyd Co VA s/o J.W. & Sarah A. to MARY A. GRAHAM 23 yrs single b. Floyd Co VA O: carpenter. (*Note: no date given).

34. 28 Sept 1893 WILLIAM CROW 30 yrs single b. Watauga NC s/o Fayette & Kate to SARAH CECIL 31 yrs single b. by John H. Honaker.

35. 28 Sept 1893 GORDON single b. Cannole s/o Hira SUSAN BROWN 31 yrs sin W.R. & S.W. O:engineer; by

36. 28 Sept 1893 JAS A. wid. b. Monroe Co W VA n s/o Wm & Nancy to MARY yrs wid. d/o Jos & Fran farmer; by

37. 1 Oct 1893 GEO SMITH single b. Surry Co NC s/o to GLENNA LEFTWICH 24 Montgomery Co VA d/o Wm miner; by W.H. Hartin; REMA

38. 4 Oct 1893 JAMES S. single b. Tazewell Co V Martha to HANNAH M. HAI b. PA d/o F.J. & Emma O: hunter; REMARKS: father's

39. 4 Oct 1893 JOHN H. P single b. Tazewell Co W Jane to ALICE FARLEY 2 Mercer Co W VA d/o Lev farmer; by Phil S. Sutton.

40. 4 Oct 1893 JOSEPHUS single b. Surry Co NC s/o Mary P. to MOLLIE V. BI single b. Mercer Co W VA Martha O: farmer; by T.R. 1

41. 4 Oct 1893 LLOYD E. yrs single b. Marion VA s/o S. Nelson Co VA d/o Wm & O: brakeman; by W.A. Pearn

42. 7 Oct 1893 JAMES T. single b. Marion VA s/o S. to HATTIE A. BRYANT ; single b. Mercer Co W VA b. Mercer Co W VA d/o White O: railroader; by Joh

43. 7 Oct 1893 LACEY single b. Rockbridge Co Martha to ROSA GEARHAR b. Mercer Co W VA d/o REMARKS: certificate of he

44. 11 Oct 1893 W.H. single b. Augusta Co VA VAUGHT 18 yrs single b. R.F. & Co O: farmer; by

45. 12 Oct 1893 ROBERT M. SHIREY 36 yrs single b. Augusta Co VA to ALICE HARVES 30 yrs single b. Prnce Edward Co VA d/o H.H. & ?; by Herbert H. Haws.

46. 11 Oct 1893 JOHN HUSE 38 yrs wid. b. Pittsylvania Co VA s/o Jack & Lucinda to LIZZIE SAUNDERS 23 yrs single b. Floyd Co VA d/o Wm & Mary O: farmer; by John L. Walton.

47. 17 Oct 1893 W.W. BOYD 27 yrs single b. Smyth Co VA s/o A.J. & Margaret to RHODA J. SMITH 16 yrs single b. W VA d/o W.B. & Habrida O: com. laborer; by S.E. Boyd; REMARKS: cert of parents filed, W.W. Boyd sworn.

48. 18 Oct 1893 L.H. PAYNE 22 yrs single b. Carrol Co VA s/o Noah & Augusta Payne to ROSIA F. HUBBARD 18 yrs sngle b. Mercer Co W VA d/o Green & Morus Hubbard O: farmer; by James W. Lilly.

Page 72

1. 16 Oct 1893 JAMES W. COLE 21 yrs single b. Raleigh Co W VA now living same s/o Bartley D. & E.A. to VIRGINIA R. FARLEY 21 yrs single b. Raleigh Co W VA d/o Wm & Victoria O: farmer; by Rev. E.W. Cooper.

2. 18 Oct 1893 E.L. DAY 26 yrs single b. Mercer Co W VA s/o Joshua & Sarah E. to MOLLIE DARE 17 yrs single b. Mercer Co W VA d/o J.H. & Jennie O: merchant; by J.O. Cassaday; REMARKS: fathers' consent filed.

3. 25 Oct 1893 W.N. EDWARDS 21 yrs sngle b. Pittsylvania Co VA s/o W.H. & Bettie R. to MINNIE H. PERDUE 19 yrs single b. Franklin Co VA d/o J.A. & N.A. O: miner; by C.E. Painter; REMARKS: consent of bride's father filed.

4. 26 Oct 1893 A.K. DAVIS 21 yrs sngle b. OH s/o H.G. & C.C. to MARTHA E. PRIM 18 yrs single b. Mercer Co W VA d/o Peter & martha A. O: carpenter; by G.C. Anderson; REMARKS: consent of bride's father filed.

5. 22 Oct 1893 WM SCOTT 60 yrs wid. b. Giles Co VA to CYNTHIA SHILLING 46 yrs single (No other info given on bride) O: farmer; by John H. Honaker.

6. 25 Oct 1893 J.H. HIGGINBOTHAM 43 yrs wid. b. Mercer Co W VA s/o J.C. & M.C.H. to HOLLIE L. BROWN 33 yrs wid. b. Mercer Co W VA d/o Calvin & Mary Harvy O: farmer; by G.W. Summers.

7. 25 Oct 1893 JESSE WATTS 26 yrs single b. Campbell Co VA s/o Lee & Jane to NANNIE CREWS 20 yrs single b. Pittsylvania Co VA d/o James & ? O: miner; by M.A. Pannill; REMARKS: consent of father, (col'd).

8. 26 Oct 1893 LEE BROOKMAN 25 yrs single b. Pulaski Co VA s/o Augustus & Mollie to LIZZIE PETTREY 18 yrs single b. Mercer Co W VA d/o Jas W. & Julia O: clerk; by Jas A. Johnston; REMARKS: consent of father filed.

9. 28 Oct 1893 JAS C. CUNNINGHAM 19 yrs single b. Mercer Co W VA s/o Jas H. & Sarah to MINNIE F. MONK 17 yrs sngle b. Mercer Co W VA d/o Jesse A. & Frances O: farmer; by Charles Walker; REMARKS: consent of parents.

10. 25 Oct 1893 LEWIS E. CARLIN 19 yrs single b. Tazewell Co VA s/o Wm & May to HINNIE A. DUNCAN 20 yrs single b. Mercer Co W VA d/o Wm & Lucnda O: farmer; by James Sweeney.

11. 30 Oct 1893 REUBEN A. GULLION 19 yrs single b. Tazewell Co VA s/o Reuben & E.M. to CORRIE COMPTON 15 yrs single b. Mercer Co W VA d/o F.P. & Bathilda O: miner; by A.M. Craft; REMARKS: consent of parents.

12. 1 Nov 1893 H.H. SHRADER 27 yrs single b. Mercer Co W VA s/o Robt & Cynthia J. to MARCY C. BELCHER 22 yrs single b. Mercer Co W VA s/o Hands C. O: farmer; by Phil S. Sutton; REMARKS: consent of parents filed , H.H. Shrader sworn.

13. 1 Nov 1893 W.H. JOHNSON 22 yrs single b. Charlestown W VA now living in Radford VA s/o Chas G. & Jessie E. to

CORINNE ANDERSON 20 yrs single b. Fincastle VA d/o C.T. & Olivia C. O: train dispatcher; by F.T. McFaden; REMARKS: consent of C.T. Anderson in person.

14. 1 Nov 1893 EVAN DAVID 26 yrs single b. Wailes(sic) s/o Evan & Katherine to AGNES PARRY 21 yrs single b. OH d/o Wm & Eliza O: tipple boss; by John E. Noff; REMARKS: Evan David sworn.

15. 6 Nov 1893 ROBT N. ECHOLS 30 yrs wid. b. Giles Co VA now living in Pocahontas VA to VIRGINIA V. FARMER 18 yrs single b. Tazewell Co VA d/o J.r. & Martha A. O: overhauler; by J. McC. Duckwall; REMARKS: cert of mother filed.

16. 7 Nov 1893 J.R. WEBB 21 yrs single b. Washington Co VA s/o F.N. & J.O. to AUDREY KILMER 20 yrs single b. Montgomery Co VA d/o G.W. Kilmer & Mary J. O: railroader; by J. McC. Duckwall; REMARKS: cert of mother filed.

17. 7 Nov 1893 JAMES E. HALE 20 yrs sngle b. Mercer Co W VA s/o Bailey & Martha to ISADOR O. RANSOM 20 yrs single b. Buckingham VA d/o John & ? O: farmer; by D.A. Ramey; REMARKS: certification of parents filed.

18. 8 Nov 1893 D.W. WILLIAMS 35 yrs wid. b. Montgomery Co VA now living in Floyd Co VA s/o Matthew & Elizabeth to MOLLIE P. SCOTT 40 yrs wid. b. Campbell Co VA d/o Pickney & Nancy Scott O: merchant; by J.O. Cassaday.

19. 12 Nov 1893 G.W. AUSTIN 20 yrs single b. Mercer Co W VA s/o LE. & Halinda to HELVINA STWART(sic) 21 yrs single b. Montgomery Co VA d/o Sparel & Mary O: farmer; by Jas Sweeney; REMARKS: certificate of parties filed.

20. 14 Nov 1893 J.F. BELCHER 27 yrs single b. Mercer Co W VA s/o Hugh H. & Viola to LOUISA ELLISE TILLER 17 yrs single b. Mercer Co W VA d/o C.I & Elizabeth O: farmer; by D.N. Saunders; REMARKS: applied for by C.I. Tiller.

21. 15 Nov 1893 D.E. WRIGHT 27 yrs single b. Mercer Co W VA s/o John H. & Elizabeth to DELLA J. TABOR 18 yrs sngle b. Tazewell Co VA d/o Mary Tabor O: carpenter; by T.C. Sheeler; REMARKS: consent of guardian.

22. 14 Nov 1893 JAS A. BLACKBURN 22 yrs single b. Wilks Co NC s/o Jordan & Eliza to ELIZA A. DUNFORD 21 yrs single d/o Wm & Lina O: farmer; by John H. Honaker; REMARKS: consent of fathers filed, J.A.B. sworn.

23. 15 Nov 1893 GEORGE REED 25 yrs single b. Mercer Co W VA s/o Thos & Sofrana to AMANDA THORNTON 43 yrs wid. b. Wythe Co VA d/o Isaac & Sarah Privett o: farmer; by L. Goodwyn.

24. 15 Nov 1893 SAMUEL GRAY 21 yrs single b. Franklin Co VA now living in Bland Co VA s/o Henry & Octavia to ANNA STEVENS 18 yrs single b. Giles Co VA d/o John & Sarah O: railroader; by A.J. Thompson; REMARKS: consent of father of girl filed.

25. 16 Nov 1893 J.H. WILLIAMS 23 yrs single b. Buckingham VA s/o Saml & Susanna to MARY H. BENNETT 18 yrs single b. Franklin Co VA d/o Geo D. & Martha L. O: mining; by D.A. Ramey; REMARKS: father present.

26. 16 Nov 1893 DANL G. COOK 20 yrs single b. Mercer Co W VA s/o Ward & Rhoda to SARAH V. KEATON 17 yrs sngle b. Mercer Co W VA d/o Wm F. & Sarepta O: farmer; by C.H. Johnston; REMARKS: Cook's guardn. present & cert. filed.

27. 29 Nov 1893 W.P. LAYNE 29 yrs single b. Pittsylvania Co VA s/o W.C. & Elizabeth to ZONA M. BUTLER 17 yrs single b. Mercer Co W VA d/o Z.R. & ? O: Jack of all trades; by G.H. Johnston; REMARKS: consent of father personally given.

28. 16 Nov 1893 R.W. MILLS 19 yrs single b. Mercer Co W VA s/o Hy G. & C. Katharine to V.R. SHREWSBURY 17 yrs single b. Mercer Co W VA d/o Jas W. & Julia O: farmer; by J.W. Lilly; REMARKS: consent of father filed.

29. 22 Nov 1893 H.P. SNIDER 26 yrs single b. Mercer Co W VA s/o Esom & Rhoda to H.R. AUSTIN 26 yrs single b. Summers Co W VA d/o Albert & Matilda O: teacher; by J.W. Bennett; REMARKS: applied for by C.A. Vaught sworn.

30. 29 Nov 1893 D.P. TICKEL 26 yrs single b. Bland Co Va s/o ? & Mary to NANNIE P. EDWARDS 18 yrs single b. Pittsylvania Co VA d/o Wm H. & Bettie R. O: engineer; by J.H. Romans; REMARKS: applied for by W.H. Edwards.

31. 22 Nov 1893 ALBERT W. BLANKENSHIP 21 yrs single b. Mercer Co W VA s/o Harrison & Louisa to OLLIE* SNODGRASS 21 yrs single b. Mercer Co W VA d/o John & Araminta O: farmer; by J.O. Cassaday; REMARKS: wife's name suggested as Hollie instead of Ollie, J.O. Cassaday. (*Note: wife's name was underlined on original).

32. 22 Nov 1893 STARLING COMPTON 45 yrs div. b. Russell Co VA s/o Peyton & Mary to TERUPA PERKINS 35 yrs wid. b. Russell Co VA O: farmer; by J.L. Prater.

33. 20 Dec 1893 H.J.M. WILKIE 27 yrs single b. Mar London England s/o Hosea J. & L.E. to MINNIE B. WHITE 16 yrs single b. Mercer Co W VA d/o J.S. & M.S.J. O: painter; by W.A. Pearson.

34. 26 Nov 1893 M.J. SAUNDERS 35 yrs wid. b. Franklin Co VA s/o A.J. & Ann to IDA B. MILLS 18 yrs single b. Franklin Co VA d/o D.T. & Fanny O: miner; by D.A. Ramey; REMARKS: certificate of D.T. Mills filed.

35. 29 Nov 1893 UNDERWOOD PRIER 26 yrs single b. Bedford Co VA s/o Morris & Mary to FRANCIS SPENCER 20 yrs single b. Charlotte Co VA d/o C.H. & Rhody O: miner; by W.J. Carter; by cert of C.H. Spencer filed.

36. 30 Nov 1893 JAMES KEYS 26 yrs single b. Washington Co VA s/o James & Martha to SALLIE WIDNER 22 yrs single b. Washington Co VA d/o Steven & Lydia O: miner; by John H. Honaker.

37. 6 Dec 1893 HENRY P. POE 24 yrs wid. b. Mercer Co W VA s/o Thos E. & Nancy E. to MARTELIA V. BAILEY 25 yrs single b. Mrcer Co W VA d/o H.A. & Sarah O: farmer; by J.W. Rader; REMARKS: H.P. Poe sworn & writing filed.

38. 7 Dec 1893 CHAS W. HONAKER 22 yrs single b. Bland Co VA s/o A.J. & Lucy to MAGGIE E. PERRY 20 yrs single b. Tazewell Co VA d/o Jas H. & E.J. O: loco. fireman; by S.E. Boyd; REMARKS: J.E. Deak sworn & writing filed.

39. 14 Dec 1893 W.E. HARRY 38 yrs single b. Mercer Co W VA s/o Calvin & Mary E. to CAROLINE BALL 30 yrs single b. Russell Co VA d/o Alford & ? O: farmer; by J.McC. Duckwall.

40. 8 Dec 1893 GASTON K. PENNINGTON 36 yrs wid. b. Mercer Co W VA s/o Wm K. & Kate K. to MARTHA J. FRENCH 38 yrs single b. Giles Co VA d/o Jas & Lizzie O: farmer; by L. Goodwyn; REMARKS: G.K. Pennington sworn.

41. * * * HOLCOMB W. BEASLEY JR. 26 yrs single b. Lynchburg VA s/o H.W. & Jemima to BETTIE HAIRSTON 26 yrs wid. b. Christiansburg VA d/o ? & Martha O: miner; REMARKS: colored.(*Note: no date given.)

42. 9 Dec 1893 T.J.J. FRANKLIN 32 yrs single b. Lynchburg VA s/o Thos G. & Dollie M. to GILLIE E. FRAZIER 23 yrs single b. Bedford Co VA O: plasterer; by W.A Pearson; REMARKS: T.J.J. Franklin sworn.

43. 14 Dec 1893 A.C. McGUIRE 21 yrs single b. Ash Co NC s/o Jno & M.E. to MOLLIE WHITWORTH 22 yrs single b. Montgomery Co VA d/o Thos & Oney O: miner; by D.A. Ramey; REMARKS: A.C.McGuire sworn.

44. * * * JOHN S. BROYLES 19 yrs single b. Mercer Co W VA s/o Leroy & Sarah E. to PATRIA F. DILLON 19 yrs single b. Mercer Co W VA d/o Jas & Matilda J. O: farmer; REMARKS: certification filed. (*Note: no date given.)

45. 14 Dec 1893 GEO L. TILLER 33 yrs single b. Mercer Co W VA s/o Wm D. & Rhoda to JULIA A. DONALLY 20 yrs single b. Henry Co VA d/o Anderson & Sallie A. O: farmer; by J.L. Prater; REMARKS: father present & consent.

46. 14 Dec 1893 JAS L. BAILEY 70 yrs wid. b. Tazewell Co VA to NANNIE A. WITT 46 yrs wid. b. Montgomery Co VA d/o H.H. & Elizabeth Graham O: farmer; by D.N. Saunders.

47. 16 Dec 1893 ALEX WALLACE 27 yrs single to CATHERINE C. MASSEY 22 yrs single b. Mercer Co W VA d/o Jackson & Patsey O: lawyer; by J.J. Meador Jr; REMARKS: Thos Hughes.

48. 20 Dec 1893 MARION B. POSTLETHWAITE 25 yrs single b. Meigs Co OH s/o G.W. & Olive to JUANITA B. BAILEY 21 yrs single b. Mercer Co W VA d/o John M. & Sallie A. O: salesman; by J. McC. Duckwall.

Page 73

1. 20 Dec 1893 C.C. LILLY 19 yrs single b. Mercer Co W VA s/o Danl T. & Almira to ALICE S. MEADOR 20 yrs single b. Summers Co W VA d/o Isaac & P.E. O: farmer; by Drury Farley; REMARKS: applied for by J.A. Lilly who is witness to both signings.

2. 20 Dec 1893 JNO W. CARVER 19 yrs single b. Tazewell Co VA s/o Jas & Mary to SYNTHA M. TAYLOR 16 yrs single b. Mercer Co W VA d/o Wm & Mary O: farmer; by John H. Honaker; REMARKS: C.C. Taylor sworn & cert by parents filed.

3. 21 Dec 1893 THEODORE CHAPMAN 24 yrs single b. Green Co KY s/o Wm & Sarah to IDA F. TAYLOR 20 yrs single b. Montgomery Co VA d/o Jacob & Martha O: miner; by A.M. Craft; REMARKS: cert parents filed.

4. * * * WH GENT JR. 24 yrs single to FLORENCE DYE 15 yrs single b. Russell Co VA d/o Prior & Sarahan O: miner; REMARKS: applied for by G.N. Lewis. (*Note: no date given.)

5. 24 Dec 1893 WM MOSES PENCE 20 yrs single b. Monroe Co W VA s/o P.C. & Jennie K. to ELLA HOLDREN 19 yrs single b. Wayne Co IL O: laborer; by John E. Noff; REMARKS: certificates filed.

6. 25 Dec 1893 JOHN D. SWEENEY 33 yrs single b. Tyler Co W VA to MAUD REID 22 yrs single b. Summers Co W VA d/o Wm A. & Louisa O: teacher; by J.P. Campbell; REMARKS: corrected from Geo W. & Eliza to Wm A. & Louisa 10-31-1930 - authority(sic) Mrs. D.E. French.

7. 24 Dec 1893 W.W. BOEHM 21 yrs single b. Shenandoah Co VA s/o J.S. & J.T. to JESSIE PROPHET 19 yrs single b. Mercer Co W VA d/o Anderson & Rebecca O: miner; by J. McC. Duckwall; REMARKS: certificate filed.

8. 26 Dec 1893 G.W. GOODE, JR. 24 yrs single b. Franklin Co VA s/o G.W. & Permela to LULA BOLING 19 yrs single b. Mercer Co W VA d/o J.J. & Isabel O: farmer; by J.W. Bennett; REMARKS: certificate filed.

9. 29 Dec 1893 W. WIRT BOLTON 25 yrs single b. Mercer Co W VA s/o Mathew & Mary F. to FRANKIE BAILEY 25 yrs single b. McDowell Co W VA d/o Elijah & Polly O: carpenter; by T.K. Lambert.

10. 29 Dec 1893 JNO A. HYLTON 36 yrs wid. b. Mercer Co W VA s/o Absolom & Mary J. to MARY L. DOUDY 24 yrs div. b. Mercer Co W VA d/o Jno & ? O: farmer; by Phil S. Sutton.

11. 31 Dec 1893 WM R. HAGER 19 yrs single b. Mercer Co W VA s/o A.G. & Nancy to RHODA J. BRUSTER 18 yrs single b. Tazewell Co VA d/o R.B. & Sarah O: farmer; by D.N. Saunders; REMARKS: both parents file certs & ptys sworn.

12. 2 Jan 1894 JOHN ANDREWS 21 yrs single b. VA s/o Wm & Caroline to TISHY BROWN 21 yrs single b. Campbell Co VA d/o Rolen & Kate O: miner; by G.W. Alexander; REMARKS: col'd.

Page 74

1. * * * JOSEPH AUER 32 yrs div. b. Germany s/o Ignaty & Mary to NANCY L. PETERS 17 yrs single b. Raleigh Co W VA d/o Geo P. & Maria O: stone mason; REMARKS: cert. of both parents of wife filed.

2. 7 Jan 1894 MOSES TABOR 36 yrs wid. b. Mercer Co W VA to RHODA A. MARTIN 30 yrs single b. Mercer Co W VA d/o Geo W. & ? O: public works; by Wm Holroyd.

3. 3 Jan 1894 C.W. STOVALL 21 yrs single b. Mercer Co W VA s/o Levi & Ann to MARY JANE MOYE 20 yrs single b. Mercer Co W VA d/o Jno D. & Martha F. O: farmer; by J.W. Lilly; REMARKS: father of wife present.

4. 7 Jan 1894 BOOKER HALL 22 yrs single b. Franklin Co VA s/o Preston & Mary to ELLA CARTER 21 yrs single b. Tazewell Co VA d/o ? & Rachel O: farmer; by W.A. Pearson; REMARKS: father present & cert filed.

5. 9 Jan 1894 ORESTEES LIGHT 19 yrs single b. Floyd Co VA s/o Mat & Ganzettie to LAURA B. HALL 16 yrs single b. Floyd Co VA d/o C.D. & Adaline O: farmer; by L. Goodwyn; REMARKS: cert of both parents filed.

6. 10 Jan 1894 GEO B. FRENCH 21 yrs single b. Mercer Co W VA s/o H.B. & Mary to TELIA TESTER 22 yrs single b. Mercer Co W VA d/o Danl & Lina O: farmer; by J.O. Cassaday; REMARKS: cert of father filed.

7. 10 Jan 1894 WH R. HARMAN 24 yrs single b. Mercer Co W VA s/o Chas & Mary J. to AMANDA BELCHER 24 yrs single b. Summers Co W VA d/o M.F. & Mary O: farmer; by P.S. Sutton.

8. 10 Jan 1894 GEO P. DAMEWOOD 22 yrs single b. Bland Co VA s/o Saml M. & ? to MARY C. PENTURFF 19 yrs single b. Holowdaysbury PA d/o W.J. & Gertrude O: carpenter; by A.S. Thorn; REMARKS: cert of W.J.P. filed.

9. 16 Jan 1894 JOSEPH W. MAXIE 20 yrs single b. Mercer Co W VA s/o Nancy E.* to JINN V. CLARK 18 yrs single b. Mercer Co W VA d/o Edgar & Annie* O: farmer; by J.W. Lilly; REMARKS: applied for by John Clark. (*Note: parents believed to be reversed - ATTN to #11.)

10. 13 Jan 1894 J.C. MEADOR 36 yrs div. b. Mercer Co W VA to VIRGINIA B. GODFREY 23 yrs wid. b. Monroe Co W VA d/o Wallace & Nancy Robbins O: teacher; by G.C. Anderson; REMARKS: copy of divorce filed.

11. 17 Jan 1894 A.R. BOWLING 17 yrs single b. Mercer Co W VA s/o H.A. & Rebecca J. to LOUISA H. MAXEY 22 yrs single b. Mercer Co W VA d/o Edgar & Annie O: farmer; by J.W. Lilly; REMARKS: cert filed & wit. present.

12. 17 Jan 1894 JOSEPH SAUNDERS 21 yrs single b. Floyd Co VA s/o Henry & Lucy to LUCY PARRETT 22 yrs single b. Mercer Co W VA d/o Reuben & Margaret O: laborer; by J.P. Campbell.

13. 20 Jan 1894 JOHN L. HEADOR 19 yrs single b. Mercer Co W VA s/o Solon & Malinda to ROXIE B. LILLY 21 yrs single b. Mercer Co W VA d/o Jas W. & Rachal O: farmer; by J.J. Meador, Jr; REMARKS: applied for by J.W. Lilly.

14. 18 Jan 1894 J.T. JOHNSON 24 yrs single b. Fayette Co VA s/o W.C. & ? to BELL FAULKNER 19 yrs single b. Mercer Co W VA d/o H.M. & Mollie O: driver in mines; by D.A. Ramey; REMARKS: cert of H.M. Faulkner filed.

15. 24 Jan 1894 L.A. CAMPBELL 45 yrs single b. Summers Co W VA now living same s/o Isaac H. & Nancy A. to MAGGIE E. THORN 27 yrs single b. Giles Co VA d/o J.D. & Nancy O: merchant; by J. McC. Duckwall.

16. 28 Jan 1894 JOHN R. FARLEY 19 yrs single b. Summers Co VA s/o John & Mary J. to ELIZA A. GADD 17 yrs single b. Mercer Co W VA d/o Wm H. & L.E. O: farmer; by J.W. Lilly; REMARKS: certification of parents of both filed & J.R.F. sworn.

17. 11 Feb 1894 JAS ED. HAMPTON 23 yrs single b. Patrick Co VA s/o Isaac & Jane to SARAH M. HICKMAN 37 yrs single b. Franklin Co VA d/o John & Phillis O: miner; by S.M. Gaines; REMARKS: colored.

18. 9 Feb 1894 CHRIS COL ROMAN 29 yrs single b. Russell Co VA now living same s/o James & Betsy to FANNIE EDWARDS 15 yrs single d/o H.H. & Jane O: farmer; by J.V. Dickinson; REMARKS: consent of parents by cert.

19. 18 Feb 1894 WM G. HELMANDOLLAR 18 yrs single b. Tazewell Co VA s/o Thomas & Anga G. to DELLA R. NICEWANDER 18 yrs single b. Bland Co VA d/o R.F. & Julia A. O: farmer; by E.W. Tiller; REMARKS: consent of parents by cert.

20. 18 Feb 1894 ROMA V. NICEWANDER 21 yrs single b. Bland Co VA s/o R.F. & Julia A. to MARY J. HELMANDOLLAR 15 yrs single b. Tazewell Co VA d/o Thomas & Angie G. O: farmer; by J.W. Bennett; REMARKS: consent of parents by cert.

21. 21 Feb 1894 DOUGLASS MORGAN 39 yrs wid. b. Monroe Co W VA s/o Swan H. & Francis A. to SARAH E. BOLIN 39 yrs single b. Mercer Co W VA d/o Jesse & Jane O: carpenter; by J.W. Bennett.

22. 21 Feb 1894 K. THOMPSON 21 yrs single b. Mercer Co W Va s/o Robert & Mary to HARRIET E. CROTTY 21 yrs single b. Mercer Co W VA d/o S.R. & Mary O: farmer; by J.L. Prater.

23. 4 Mar 1894 GEORGE SMITH 22 yrs single b. Newbury SC s/o Frank & Dinah to BERTIE MONROE 22 yrs single b. Pulaski Co VA d/o ? & Lou O: miner; by J.H. Adams.

24. 7 Mar 1894 E.W. RHODES 27 yrs single b. Davidson Co NC s/o Isaac & Huldah to CALLIE J. RIDER 18 yrs single b. Bland Co VA d/o W.H. & Ella O: miner; by S.B. Vaught; REMARKS: father of wife present.

25. 7 Mar 1894 H.L. LOVILL 20 yrs single b. Carroll Co VA s/o Wm & M.A. to A.B. HERNDON 19 yrs single b. MO d/o ? & N.L. O: farmer; by Charles Walker; REMARKS: cert of mothers filed & wit. sworn.

26. 14 Mar 1894 MATHEW HOLDREN 22 yrs single b. Mercer Co v VA s/o Jas H. & Rhoda to HALISA A. BAILEY 16 yrs single d/o John & Sarah O: farmer; by A.J. Thompson; REMARKS: cert of parents filed & wit. sworn.

27. 12 Mar 1894 WILLIAM N. LILLY 22 yrs single b. Raleigh Co W VA now living in Summers Co W VA s/o Joseph & Drucilla to MARY A. LILLY 16 yrs 9 mos 17 dys single b. Raleigh Co W VA d/o Jas W. & Mary H. O: farmer; by Drury Farley; REMARKS: cert of parents filed.

28. 14 Mar 1894 CHAS H. BURDETT 29 yrs wid. b. Mercer Co W VA s/o Joseph & Irene to MANDA L. PERDUE 18 yrs single b. Mercer Co W VA d/o Mack & Nancy F. O: lumberman; by L. Goodwyn; REMARKS: cert of wife's parents filed.

29. 21 Mar 1894 LEE BAILEY 18 yrs single b. Mercer Co W VA s/o Leftwich & Sarah M. to NANNIE B. LINCONS 18 yrs single b. Montgomery Co VA d/o Thomas & Ellen O: farmer; by E.W. Tiller; REMARKS: cert of parents of both filed.

30. 22 Mar 1894 HENRY JONES 27 yrs single b. Giles Co VA s/o ? & Mary Thompson to BETTIE FOLKNER 17 yrs single b. PA d/o ? & Sally Trotter O: farmer; by A.J. Thompson; REMARKS: cert of mother, father dead.

31. 28 Mar 1894 WM R. VAWTER 37 yrs single b. Mercer Co W VA s/o Edward & ? to FANNIE L. MILLER 21 yrs single b. Sommerset Co PA d/o M.A. & ? O: farmer; by Jno S. Lightbourn; REMARKS: applied for by W.H. Millar & Letter of M.A. Miller filed.

32. 3 Apr 1894 FRANK NICEWANDER 24 yrs single b. Bland Co VA s/o Wm H. & Ann to R. LEE WILLIAMS 15 yrs single b. Giles Co VA d/o Jas A. & ? O: fireman; by S.B. Vaught; REMARKS: cert of wife's father filed.

33. 29 Mar 1894 C.W. SMITH 33 yrs single b. Fayette Co W VA s/o Jno J. & Margaret A. to WILLIE A. NICEWANDER 28 yrs single b. Bland Co VA d/o Wm H. & Ann O: carpenter; by S.V. Vaught.

34. 1 Apr 1894 CHAS C. HILL 30 yrs single b. Patrick Co VA s/o Philip W. & Harriet E. to LINNIE B. CLENDENIN 20 yrs single b. Summers Co VA d/o Mac & N.J. O: miner; by A.M. Craft; REMARKS: cert of mother.

35. 3 Apr 1894 C.C. FALKE 21 yrs single b. Marion, Smyth Co VA s/o H.H. Falke & Eliza to SADIE E. SHEPHERDSON 16 yrs single b. Richmond VA d/o James F. & Willie O: com. laborer; by W.A. Pearson; REMARKS: cert of father filed.

36. 3 Apr 1894 J.W. SHUTT 21 yrs single b. Mercer Co W VA s/o H.F. & Ellen to MOLLIE E. BELCHER 18 yrs single b. Mercer Co W VA O: farmer; by Jno H. Honaker; REMARKS: cert filed & consent of guardn given in person.

37. 15 Apr 1894 HENRY SADLER 25 yrs single b. Mercer Co W VA s/o Henry & Araminta to LILLIE BAILEY 22 yrs single b. Mercer Co W VA d/o J.F. & Sarah O: farmer; by E.S. Bettis.

38. 16 Apr 1894 B.B. BELCHER 22 yrs single b. Tazewell Co VA s/o Robert & ? to ELVIRA C. HAIRMAN 19 yrs single b. Tazewell Co VA d/o Wm B. & Paulina J. O: farmer; by J.L. Prater; REMARKS: father of bride.

39. 16 Apr 1894 LEE TILLEY 25 yrs single b. NC to NANCY E. COMSTOCK 24 yrs wid. b. Mrcer Co W VA d/o Wm & Mary Taylor; by Jno H. Honaker; REMARKS: sworn to by C.C. Taylor.

40. 18 Apr 1894 A.P. WILEY 22 yrs single b. Mercer Co W VA s/o Jno & Ellen to JENNIE R. BIRD 22 yrs single b. Mercer Co W VA d/o B.W. & L.A. O: farmer; by R.M. Ashworth; REMARKS: cert filed.

41. 19 Apr 1894 OWEN P. GRIFFITH 19 yrs single b. Raleigh Co W VA now living same s/o Isaac & ? to MARTHA LILLY 23 yrs single b. Mercer Co W VA d/o Wm P. & Valeria O: farmer; by M.H. Giffith; REMARKS: cert filed.

42. 20 Apr 1894 W.T. BASHAM 28 yrs single b. Monroe Co W VA s/o Jos & Polly A. to VIRGINIA E. FARMER 17 yrs single b. Mercer Co w VA d/o R.C. & Mary M. O: farmer; by G.C. Anderson; REMARKS: father of bride present.

43. 20 Apr 1894 M.G. ARCHER 20 yrs single b. Mercer Co w VA s/o Jas S. & Julina to MARTHA HUBBARD 24 yrs angle b. Mercer Co W VA d/o Jonathan & Virginia O: farmer; by J.W. Rader; REMARKS: cert of Jas S. Archer filed.

44. 26 Apr 1894 GEO W. ALVIS 24 yrs single b. Mercer Co W VA s/o Jno H. & Josephine to ELIZA A. MARTIN 17 yrs single b. Mercer Co W VA d/o Wm E. & Victoria O: farmer; by J.W. Bennett; REMARKS: applied for by A. White.

45. 29 Apr 1894 PETER GENT 25 yrs single b. PA s/o Wm & Margaret to FANNIE DYE 21 yrs single b. Russell Co VA d/o Prior & Sarah O: miner; by G.H. Alexander.

46. * * * JOHN HOLLAND 27 yrs single Franklin Co VA s/o ? & Bettie to FANNIE B. TYREE 21 yrs single b. Franklin Co VA d/o ? & Mary O: miner; REMARKS: col'd. (*Note: no date given.)

47. * * * THOMAS W. JOHNSON 29 yrs single b. Tazewell Co VA s/o Anthony & Marietta to ROSA FINLEY 19 yrs single b. Carroll Co VA d/o Rufus & Eliza O: railroader; REMARKS: col'd. (*Note: no date given.)

48. 3 May 1894 F.A. HALLANO 23 yrs single b. Floyd Co VA s/o William & Evaline to AMANDA J. SWIM 20 yrs single b. Yadkin Co NC d/o Robecca O: miner; by J.O. Cassaday.

Page 75

1. 10 May 1894 W.T. CORUM 21 yrs single b. Johnson Co TN s/o Janckney & Elizabeth to EVALANOR C. DAVIDSON 20 yrs single b. Mercer Co W VA d/o Jas & Margaret A. O: farmer; by Jno H. Honaker; REMARKS: father's consent filed.

2. 17 May 1894 WM L. SMITH 21 yrs single b. Mercer Co W VA s/o J.B. & Sarah to ELLA O. BARNETT 18 yrs single b. Tazewell Co VA d/o William & Maggie O: farmer; by Romulus Harry; REMARKS: consent of guardian given.

3. 17 May 1894 ANDREW DAVIDSON 23 yrs single b. Mercer Co W VA s/o Jas & Margaret to CANDIS BELL 16 yrs single b. Mercer Co W VA d/o Henry & Julia A.; by Jno H. Honaker.

4. * * * WM W. PILLERS 25 yrs angle b. Mercer Co W VA s/o Thomas & M.C. Pillers to STELOH NORRIS 18 yrs single b. Mercer Co W VA d/o Harvey & E.F. Norris O: miner; REMARKS: order from his mother.(*Note: no date given.)

5. 23 May 1894 W.I. GANTIER 32 yrs div. b. Mercer Co W VA s/o Joseph & Lucy to IDA B. LILLY 20 yrs single b. Mercer Co W VA d/o J.K. & Alabama O: teacher; by Jas H. Johnston; REMARKS: certificate of fther's consent filed.

6. 23 May 1894 W.J. WINESETT 29 yrs single b. Carroll Co VA s/o Noah & Darthula to ANNIE RADFORD 23 yrs single b. Floyd Co VA O: stone mason & builder; by Eugene Blake.

7. 26 May 1894 L.A. FOLEY 20 yrs single b. Mercer Co W VA s/o Chas A. & Mary J. to S.J. SNEED 17 yrs single b. Mercer Co W VA d/o John & Ann O: farmer; by Romulus Harry; REMARKS: cert of all parents filed.

8. 28 May 1894 ALBERT AMERINGTIN* 21 yrs single b. Mercer Co W VA s/o Isaac G. & Nancy to ELLA TAYLER 22 yrs wid. b. Mercer Co W VA d/o ? & Araminta Hughes O: farmer; by Phil S. Sutton.

9. 30 May 1894 LAFAYETTE TURNER 33 yrs wid. b. Smyth Co VA s/o Peyton & Susan to MARY J. MEADOWS 23 yrs single b. Raleigh Co W VA d/o Jno L. & Melina O: railroader; by J.O. Cassaday.

10. 29 May 1894 JAS M. SLAUGHTER 26 yrs single b. Belle Co KY s/o Wm & Martha to VICTORIA C. HARMAN 19 yrs single b. Mercer Co W VA d/o Patrick & Sarah J. O: miner; by Phil S. Sutton; REMARKS: cert of father.

11. 7 June 1894 SAML C. WIMMER 21 yrs single b. Tazewell Co VA s/o Isaac C. & Rebecca to SALLIE NEAL 21 yrs single b. Bland Co VA d/o Randall & Nancy O: farmer; by D.N. Saunders; REMARKS: Jas T. Wimmer.

12. 10 June 1894 F.J. ANDERSON 23 yrs single b. VA to ELLA A. WHITTAKER 24 yrs single b. Mercer Co W VA d/o William & ? O: carpenter; by Jno H. Honaker; REMARKS: T.C. Whittaker.

13. 14 June 1894 ANDREW PHILLIPS 27 yrs single b. Albermarle Co VA s/o Henry & Alice to MARY E. JOHNSON 16 yrs single b. Hinton W VA d/o G.W. & Rebecca O: railroader; by T.J. Brandon; REMARKS: cert of consent filed.

14. 20 June 1894 J.F. TOBOR 20 yrs single b. Mercer Co w VA s/o Charles & Cynthia to WILLHATH D. DAVIDSON 26 yrs single b. Mercer Co W VA d/o James & Margret O: farmer; by Jno H. Honaker; REMARKS: cert of parents filed.

15. 28 June 1894 GEORGE SIMPSON 35 yrs single b. Pittsylvania Co VA s/o Geo & Susan to RADER GRAVES 31 yrs wid. b. Pittsylvania Co VA d/o Geo Ward & Eliza O: miner; by G.W. Alexander.

16. 20 JUNE 1894 PAUL C. SMITH 22 yrs single b. Mercer Co W VA s/o Daniel & Fannie to MARY C. UNDERWOOD 21 yrs single b. Mercer Co W VA d/o J.A. & Mary Ann O: farmer; by R. Harry.

17. 26 June 1894 DANL DEARMON 33 yrs single b. Stokes Co NC s/o Anthony & Caroline to VICIE THOMPSON 28 yrs wid. b. Mercer Co W VA d/o Wm Taylor & Sarah O: miner; by T.J. Brandon; REMARKS: colored.

18. 3 July 1894 JOHN CURRY 29 yrs single b. Powhatan Co VA s/o Meshach & Maria to NANNIE HOLLAND 23 yrs wid. b. Franklin Co VA O: miner; by T.J. Brandon; REMARKS: colored, Jo. Thaxton.

19. 27 June 1894 DANL W. HALL 20 yrs single b. Mercer Co W VA s/o Jno R. & Amanda to MAGGIE WORRELL 21 yrs single b. Carroll Co VA d/o Jesse & Elizabeth O: farmer; by J.D. Strader; REMARKS: H.H. Martin & cert of father.

20. * * * MILTON GILMORE 36 yrs wid. b. Montgomery Co VA to HATTIE DICKINSON 22 yrs single b. Franklin Co VA O: mine boss. (*Note: no date given.)

21. 5 July 1894 C.W. MAHAN 25 yrs wid. b. NC s/o Adam & Francis Reynolds to ALICE WRIGHT 24 yrs single b. Bedford Co VA d/o Peter & Ad. Wright O: laborer; by S.M. Gaines; REMARKS: C.W. Mahan sworn.

22. 12 July 1894 JAS TABOR 28 yrs single b. Tazewell Co VA s/o Stephen & Lucinda to ROSA O'DONELL 21 yrs sngle b. Mercer Co W VA d/o William & Elizabeth O: miner; by A.M. Craft; REMARKS: Jas Tabor sworn.

23. 11 July 1894 EDWARD J. BELCHER 28 yrs wid. b. Mercer Co W VA s/o Isham & Nancy to SALLIE HAVENS 28 yrs single b. Bland Co VA d/o John & Lizzie O: carpenter; by Thos C. Shuler.

24. 13 July 1894 EDWARD ANAHEIM 23 yrs single b. PA s/o Adrian & Sarah to LIZZIE BAKER 22 yrs single b. England d/o Wm & Sarah J. O: driver in mines; by Jno E. Noff; REMARKS: Edwd Anaheim sworn.

25. 18 July 1894 WM ED SHARP 24 yrs single b. Alamance Co NC s/o ? & Emily Sharp to LULA BARNES 22 yrs single b. Tazewell Co VA d/o Helen Dyerly O: public work; by S.M. Gaines; REMARKS: W.E. Sharp & J.W. Fields sworn.

26. 18 July 1894 JAMES TAYLOR 21 yrs single b. Ashe Co NC s/o B. & M. Taylor to SARAH BLANKENSHIP 21 yrs single b. Tazewell Co VA d/o Jasper & Julia Ann O: farmer; by Jas Sweeney; REMARKS: Sarah Blankenship sworn.

27. 19 July 1894 POMPEY NEWBILL 30 yrs wid. b. Franklin Co VA s/o Anderson & Harriet to EMMA LAW 28 yrs wid. b. Rockingham Co NC s/o Sam & Pauline Moore O: miner; by G.W. Alexander; REMARKS: Pompey Newbill sworn, (col'd).

28. 21 July 1894 JAMES MONROE 21 yrs single b. Bristol TN s/o Calvin & Annie to ITHLA DEHART 18 yrs single b. Patrick Co VA d/o Thomas & Martha O: R.R. brakeman; by J.L. Prater; REMARKS: consent of guardian given.

29.*24 July 1894 L.E. BEE 27 yrs single b. Mercer Co W VA s/o Isaiah & Mary V. to IDA WHITE 22 yrs single b. Mercer Co W VA d/o Jas A. & ? O: physician; REMARKS: I.E. Bee sworn; Returned not executed. (*Note: date marked through.)

30. 24 July 1894 P.H. BAILEY 23 yrs single b. Mercer Co W VA s/o R.H. & Emma to LUCINDIA ABSHER 18 yrs single b. Tazewell Co VA d/o Jas A. & Sarah Jane O: farmer; by J. McC. Duckwall; REMARKS: Jas A. Absher.

31. 26 July 1894 WM TWIGGS 22 yrs single b. Carter Co TN s/o Timothy & Eliza to LIDDIE ANN STAHL 22 yrs single b. Dauphin Co PA d/o Elias & Susannah O: miner; by S.E. Buchanan; REMARKS: Alfred Stahl sworn.

32. 24 July 1894 ALFRED STAHL 25 yrs single b. Cass Co IN s/o Elias & Susannah to ZORA SHAFER 21 yrs single b. Summerc Co W VA d/o Peter & Mary O: miner; by A.S. Thorn; REMARKS: Alfred Stahl sworn.

33. 23 July 1894 J.W. ASHWORTH 23 yrs single b. Wise Co VA now living same s/o F.A. & Susan to NANNIE R. HALL 20 yrs single b. Montgomery Co VA d/o Asa R. & Lucy O: merchant; by Eugene Blake; REMARKS: father of bride present.

34. 26 July 1894 BENJAMIN BARKSDALE 25 yrs wid. b. Halifax Co VA s/o Daniel & Sallie to MOLLIE R. JONES 24 yrs single b. Smyth Co VA d/o Henry & Lucinda O: miner; by T.J. Brandon; REMARKS: col'd.

35. 26 July 1894 CHARLES HARMAN 21 yrs single b. Mercer Co W VA s/o Bal & Martha to MINNIE ROLES 19 yrs single b. Monroe Co VA O: railroader; by J.H. Gardner; REMARKS: col'd.

36. 30 July 1894 W.J. LEWIS 21 yrs single b. Washington Co VA s/o James L. & H.J. to L.A. GILLOM* 17 yrs single b. Patric(sic) Co VA d/o J.W. & H.A. Gillum* O: miner; by Jno H. Honaker; REMARKS: white. (*Note: name spelled both ways.)

37. 5 Aug 1894 A.L. FOLEY 20 yrs single b. Mercer Co W VA s/o Richard Phasin Dary to ALICE SNEAD 18 yrs single b. Raleigh Co W VA d/o Wiley & Martha O: farmer; by R. Harry; REMARKS: white.

38. 10 Aug 1894 W.R. FARMER 21 yrs single b. Mercer Co W VA s/o Jas T. & Sarah E. to ALMEDA CRUM 15 yrs single b. Mercer Co W VA d/o Hiram & Araminta O: farmer; by G.C. Anderson; REMARKS: J.T. Farmer sworn.

39. 14 Aug 1894 A.J. SHREWSBURY 21 yrs single b. Mercer Co W VA s/o P.t. & Iowa to ARTHELIA PETTRY 23 yrs single b. Mercer Co W VA d/o Jas & Julia O: farmer; by J.W. Bennett.

40. 12 Aug 1894 CHARLES H. RHOADS 25 yrs single b. Amherst Co VA s/o G.W. & Bettie to MOLLIE HOLLOWAY 15 yrs single b. Franklin Co VA d/o Chas E. & Eliza A. O: miner; by Jno E. Noff; REMARKS: father present.

41. 12 Aug 1894 SAMUEL D. CROMER 28 yrs single b. Montgomery Co VA s/o John C. & Mary to MOLLIE HARLESS 26 yrs sngle b. Montgomery Co VA d/o Phlegar & Mary O: miner; by A.M. Craft.

42. 13 Aug 1894 G.L. ROBINSON 25 yrs single b. Giles Co VA s/o W.H. & Margaret to MAGGIE A. PRITCHARD 23 yrs single b. Mercer Co W VA d/o Thos & Sallie O: machin(sic); by Phil S. Sutton; REMARKS: G.L. Robinson sworn.

43. 16 Aug 1894 THOMAS MILLER 52 yrs wid. b. Monroe Co w VA s/o Peter & Mary to LIZZIE BROOKS 29 yrs single b. Mercer Co W VA d/o Wm & Mary O: farmer; by S.M. Gaines; REMARKS: col'd.

44. 14 Aug 1894 S.S. HILL 17 yrs single b. Franklin Co VA s/o Jas R. & H.A. to MAHALA M.A. BROYLES 22 yrs single b. Mercer Co W VA d/o J.G. & M.O. O: farmer; by L. Goodwyn; REMARKS: cert of mother filed.

45. 20 Aug 1894 JOHN SINCOCK 25 yrs single b. England now living in Tazewell Co VA s/o Edwin & Mary to OSHIE FRENCH 17 yrs single b. Bland Co VA d/o Jas M. & Rhoda L. O: teacher; by J.T. French.

46. 5 SEPT 1894 LUTHER L. BUTLER 20 yrs single b. Mercer Co W VA now living in Summers Co W VA s/o Jas H. & M.E. to NANNIE HAZLEWOOD 19 yrs single b. Mercer Co W VA d/o John & Mary O: farmer; by B.P. Pennington; REMARKS: cert of father & mother filed.

47. 29 Aug 1894 D.B. COLE 21 yrs single b. Mercer Co W VA now living in McDowell Co W VA s/o A.J. & Mary to LEONAH B. CLOWER 18 yrs single b. Floyd Co VA d/o J.T. & M.F. O: miner; by L. Goodwyn; REMARKS: cert of parents filed & D.B. Cole sworn.

48. 12 Sept 1894 JAMES D. THOMPSON 23 yrs single b. Mercer Co W VA s/o John D. & Nancy E. to MINNESOTA VEST 18 yrs single b. Summers Co W VA d/o S.J. & E.A. O: farmer; by A.J. Thompson; REMARKS: cert of parents filed.

Page 76

1. 6 Sept 1894 G.D. BAILEY 27 yrs single b. Mercer Co W VA s/o Wilson L. & Elizabeth to MARY ODLE 17 yrs single b. NC d/o Abram & ? O: farmer; by G.C. Anderson; REMARKS: cert of A. Odle filed.

2. 12 Sept 1894 J.A. TAGUE 25 yrs single b. NC s/o Andrew & Hollie to OLIIA HUNSY 21 yrs single b. Floyd Co VA d/o W.J. & Hannah O: blacksmith: by Jno E. Noff; REMARKS: cert of parent filed & sworn.

3. 5 Sept 1894 CHAS C. RUMBURG 19 yrs single b. Mercer Co W VA s/o Wm J. & Nancy J. to ETTIE MAXIE 18 yrs single b. Mercer Co W VA d/o Edgar & Annie O: farmer; by R.H. Ashworth; REMARKS: cert of girl mother filed & Wm J. Rumburg present in person.

4. 5 Sept 1894 E.R. CLOWER 23 yrs single b. Floyd Co VA s/o Jas & ? to SHIRLE K. SMITH 18 yrs single b. Mercer Co W VA d/o D.H. & Alice O: farmer; by L. Goodwyn; REMARKS: father of bride present.

MERCER COUNTY, WEST VIRGINIA
Marriages 1854 - 1901

5. 7 Sept 1894 GEO E. HARRIS 22 yrs single b. Henrico Co VA s/o W.H. & Virginia to MARY L. WEAVER 18 yrs single b. Franklin Co VA; by T.A. Brandon; REMARKS: cert of consent filed.

6. 13 Sept 1894 WARD B. MEADOWS 20 yrs single b. Mercer Co W VA s/o Ward & Huldah to CENORA A. RORRER 20 yrs single b. Patrick Co VA d/o P.T. & Nancy J. O: farmer; by Jas W. Lilly; REMARKS: cert of consent filed.

7. 12 Sept 1894 FLOYD P. FERGUSON 24 yrs single b. Mercer Co W VA s/o E.R. & Elizabeth to MARTHA ALICE McBRIDE 22 yrs single b. Mercer Co W VA d/o J. Bird & Sally O: farmer; by Jas W. Lilly.

8. 19 Sept 1894 McC. MUNSEY 20 yrs single b. Mercer Co W VA s/o Jas A. & N.A. to LETTIE WELLS 17 yrs single b. Mercer Co W VA d/o Danl & D. O: farmer; by J.O. Cassaday; REMARKS: father H C Munsey present in person & cert, & wife's parents filed & wit sworn.

9. 19 Sept 1894 JOHN DAVIS 19 yrs sngle b. Mercer Co W VA s/o Lee & Mary to VALARY JONES 20 yrs single b. Mercer Co W VA d/o Elisha & Jerusha O: farmer; by J.O. Cassaday; REMARKS: cert of parents & husband sworn.

10. 25 Sept 1894 C.A. FINNEY 22 yrs single b. Franklin Co VA s/o Silas & Marinda to BELLE NESBIT 21 yrs single b. Charlotte NC d/o Isaac & Nannie O: miner; by J.H. Adams; REMARKS: C.A. Finney sworn, (col'd).

11. 27 Sept 1894 B.N. FITZWATER 37 yrs wid. b. Fayette Co W VA s/o Isaiah & Octavia to ANNIE L. DAVIS 25 yrs single b. Washington Co OH d/o H.G. & C.C. O: Minister gospel; by T.K. Lambert.

12. 26 Sept 1894 CLIFTON W. TAYLOR 20 yrs single b. Craig Co VA s/o Geo A. & Elmira to ADA E. MILLS 16 yrs single b. Mercer Co W VA d/o Jas H. & Mary A. O: farmer; by J.O. Cassaday; REMARKS: C.W. Taylor sworn, parents certs filed.

13. 26 Sept 1894 GEO G. CLENDENON 22 yrs single b. Mercer Co W VA s/o Mc & Nancy J. to ELLA M. DUNCAN 17 yrs single b. Smyth Co VA d/o Jas W. & Sarah A. O: R.R. brakeman; by Thos C. Shuler; REMARKS: W.S. Aker sworn, parents filed cert.

14. 28 Sept 1894 DAVID S. JOSEPH 22 yrs single b. Wales s/o Benj & Mary J. to LILLIE GILMORE 18 yrs single b. Boone Co W VA d/o Milton & Alice O: miner; by Jno E. Noff; REMARKS: Milton Gilmore present in person.

15. 10 Oct 1894 DANIEL F. PENNINGTON 23 yrs single b. KY s/o G.W. & Wilmoth to JULIA A. NELSON 17 yrs single b. Mercer Co W VA d/o Morgan & Mary O: farmer; by J.W. Bennett; REMARKS: G.W. Pennington sworn, cert of Morgan Nelson filed.

16. 3 Oct 1894 J.R. ALLEN 22 yrs single b. NC s/o Jas & Maria to A.A. DANIELS 22 yrs single b. VA O: miner; by T.J. Brandon; REMARKS: sworn, col'd.

17. 3 Oct 1894 JOS BURCH 53 yrs wid. b. Sweden s/o Jos & Katherine to VIRGINIA STRALEY 43 yrs wid. b. Mercer Co W VA O: farmer; by A.S. Thorn.

18. 4 Oct 1894 CHARLES L. CARPER 25 yrs single b. Mercer Co W VA s/o ? & Mary J. to ALICE COOPER 25 yrs single b. Grason(sic) Co VA d/o Jas M. & Phamy O: farmer; by J.O. Cassaday.

19. 12 Oct 1894 GAY LEWIS 22 yrs single b. Pittsylvania Co VA s/o John & Jane to LELIA E. MITCHELL 22 yrs single b. Montgomery Co VA d/o Henry & Amanda O: miner; by T.J. Brandon.

20. 6 Oct 1894 ISAAC J. KINGRY 27 yrs single b. Franklin Co VA s/o Fleming & Martha to NORA L. HARRIS 20 yrs single b. Appomattox Co VA d/o S.S. & ? O: miner; by Jno e. Noff; REMARKS: cert filed & L.J. Kingry sworn.

21. * * * SAUL GREENSPAN 24 yrs single b. Russia s/o A. & L Greenspan to MARRIE COHEN 22 yrs single b. Russia d/o H. & J. Cohen O: merchant. (*Note: no date given.)

22. 19 Oct 1894 THOS GRAY 30 yrs single b. Wythe Co VA s/o James & Mary to JULIA SHAFFER 28 yrs single b. Montgomery Co VA O: carpenter; by Geo. H. Pettis; REMARKS: col'd.

23. 9 Oct 1894 JAS E. MURPHY 29 yrs single b. Lynchburg VA s/o John & Annora to ELIZABETH A. RILEY 25 yrs single b. Nelson Co VA d/o Edward & Catharine O: cabinmaker; by J.J. McGurk (Priest).

24. 10 Oct 1894 GEO. L. OWENS 24 yrs single b. Roanoke Co VA s/o J.B. & Julia M. Owens to BILLIE L. FLOYD 21 yrs single b. Henry Co VA d/o H.D. & Namie M. Floyd O: r.roading; by Thos C. Shuler.

25. 10 Oct 1894 THOS R. HUGHES 33 yrs single b. Mercer Co W VA s/o Cluff & Hollie to MARY STAFFORD 38 yrs single b. Mercer Co W VA d/o Wm H & Louisa O: farmer; by Phil S. Sutton.

26. 11 Oct 1894 J.J. PERRYMAN 22 yrs single b. Henry Co VA now living in McDowell Co W VA s/o R.B. & S.E. to ELLA C. TAYLOR 17 yrs single b. Henry Co VA d/o W.T. & Martha O: carpenter; by D.N. Saunders.

27. 17 Oct 1894 RICHARD D. LALEY 52 yrs wid. b. Mercer Co W VA s/o Alfoid & ? to SARAH J. HONK 37 yrs single b. Russell Co VA d/o Silas & ? O: farmer; by Chas Walker.

28. 23 Oct 1894 LEWIS JONES 38 yrs single b. Amherst Co VA s/o James & Eliza to BETTIE LUMPKINS 28 yrs wid. b. Franklin Co VA d/o Henry & Maria O: miner; by T.J. Brandon.

29. 14 Oct 1894 MUNFORD CROWDER 23 yrs single b. Lulenburg(sic) Co VA s/o Amon & Lucy to LIZZIE FORD 23 yrs single b. Winston NC d/o George & Mary Ford O: r.roder(sic); by S.M. Gaines; REMARKS: col'd.

30. 18 Oct 1894 JNO R. GUNTER 22 yrs sngle b. Carroll Co VA s/o Wm & Pheby Jane to ALICE L. O'DONALD 22 yrs single b. Mercer Co W VA d/o Wm & Lizzie O: farmer; by Jas W. Lilly; REMARKS: Jno R. Gunter sworn.

31. 17 Oct 1894 PEARIS M. MATHEWS 26 yrs wid. b. Tazewell Co VA s/o G.W. & Harriet L. to L.B. BOWLING 25 yrs single b. Mercer Co W VA d/o A.W. & Lucinda O: farmer; by Granville Houchins.

32. 24 Oct 1894 G.H. WADE 28 yrs single b. Motgomery Co VA s/o H.D. & M.E. to ANNIE C. McDANIEL 19 yrs single b. VA d/o John W. & Mary L. O: druggist; by N.F. Marshall.

33. 21 Oct 1894 SAMUEL WHITE 24 yrs single b. Wythe Co VA s/o Cornelius & Ann to CHARLOTTE DUHRING 24 yrs single b. Stanton VA d/o Geo & Eliza O: miner; by T.J. Brandon; REMARKS: col'd, Saml White sworn.

34. 1 Nov 1894 U.S. BECKER 36 yrs single b. York Co PA s/o Jesse & Mary to IDA COMER 22 yrs single b. Mercer Co W VA d/o James & Martha O: R.R. conductor; by N.F. Marshall.

35. 22 Oct 1894 WALTER BAILEY 21 yrs single b. Mercer Co W VA s/o ? & Nancy to FLORENCE E. PATRICK 19 yrs single b. Montgomery Co VA d/o Jas F. & Nannie Bailey O: farmer; by E.W. Tiller; REMARKS: certificate filed.

36. 24 Oct 1894 SAM A. TABOR 18 yrs single b. Mercer Co W VA s/o Geo & Olive to M.E. CLARK 18 yrs single b. Mercer Co W VA d/o E. & E.E. Clark O: farmer; by Drewry Farley; REMARKS: certificate filed.

37. 24 Oct 1894 JOHN R. GREENAWALT 45 yrs wid. b. PA now living in McDowell s/o Philip & Dorcas to ADA A. FARLIN 27 yrs single b. Giles Co VA d/o W.C. & Octva O: merchant; by Phil S. Sutton.

38. 25 Oct 1894 WM WRIGHT 25 yrs single b. Mercer Co W VA s/o C.G. & Bettie to LEANNA ROBINSON 19 yrs single b. Mercer Co W VA d/o R.G. & Virginia O: farmer; by L. Goodwyn; REMARKS: father of wife.

39. 1 Nov 1894 HORRUS H. McALEANDER 25 yrs single b. Floyd Co VA now living in Raleigh Co W VA s/o Lester & Bire E. to HARRETT(sic) M. DODD 21 yrs single b. Mercer Co W VA d/o Anderson & E.C. O: farmer; by Wm L. Summons; REMARKS: certificate filed.

40. 15 Nov 1894 M.H. MORGAN 26 yrs single b. Hollins VA now living same s/o D.A. & L.I. to KATHERINA A. SHIREY 19 yrs single b. Augusta Co VA d/o W.H. & L.H. O: farmer.

41. 3 Nov 1894 JAMES BANNER 37 yrs b. Mount Airy NC s/o M. & A. Banner to LULA MOHOARN(sic) 28 yrs b. Montgomery Co VA d/o B. & E. Momoarn O: miner; by T.J. Brandon; REMARKS: certificate filed.

42. 31 Oct 1894 JOS WILLIAMS 54 yrs wid. b. Hanover Co VA s/o S & M Williams to NANCY MIDTIFF 34 yrs single b. Patrick Co VA d/o ? & I Midtiff O: farmer; by C.H. Payne; REMARKS: col'd, Jos Williams sworn.

43. 2 Nov 1894 ISAAC PAYNE 36 yrs wid. b. Mercer Co W VA s/o James & Mary to RABECCA MIMICK 20 yrs wid. b. PA O: farmer; by Jno H. Honaker; REMARKS: certificate, sworn.

44. 1 Nov 1894 W.H. COOK 19 yrs single b. Mercer Co W VA s/o Ward & Rhoda to LUCRECIA VAUGHT 18 yrs single b. Giles Co VA d/o Ransom & Sarah H. O: farmer; by Jas H. Johnston.

45. 1 Nov 1894 ZANCY KING 22 yrs single b. Halifax Co VA now living in McDowell Co W VA s/o Edmon & ? to MARY GARNER 21 yrs single b. Johnson City TN d/o Arche Garner O: miner; by A.M. Craft; REMARKS: certifed(sic)-certificate filed.

46. 31 Oct 1894 E.F. COOPER 27 yrs single b. Grason(sic) Co VA s/o William A. & Malvina to IREAN E. VIRMILLION 23 yrs single b. Mercer Co W VA d/o S.T. & roda O: manufactin(sic); by J.W. Bennett.

47. 1 Nov 1894 JNO MUSGROVE 22 yrs single b. Bedford Co VA s/o Marshall & Adeline to EMMA BOOKER 20 yrs single b. Prince Edward Co VA d/o Calvin & Mary O: miner; by Eugene Blake.

48. 6 Nov 1894 WH J. TABOR 62 yrs wid. b. Tazewell Co VA s/o Richard & Millie to EMMA WHEELER 39 yrs single d/o Henry O: farmer; by D.N. Saunders.

Page 77

1. 4 Nov 1894 JEFFERSON WILLIS 25 yrs single b. Amherst Co VA now living in McDowell Co W VA s/o ? & Mahala to MINNIE HOLLAND 23 yrs single b. Franklin Co VA d/o Cornelius & Gruzela O: miner; by T.J. Brandon; REMARKS: J. Willis & Hy Areis sworn (col'd).

2. 14 Nov 1894 A.L. BOWLING 23 yrs single b. Mercer Co W VA s/o T.J. & Jennie F. to WILLIE CLARK 19 yrs single b. Mercer Co W VA d/o A.F. & Martha O: merchant; by G.M. Johnston; REMARKS: certificate filed.

3. 8 Nov 1894 JAS H. WILEY 28 yrs single b. Mercer Co W VA s/o Vincent & Cynthia to RHODA A. BIRD 19 yrs single b. Mercer Co W VA d/o Wm A. & Cynthia O: farmer; by J.P. Campbell; REMARKS: certificate filed.

4. 13 Nov 1894 C.E. PAINTER 28 yrs wid. b. Tazewell Co VA now living same s/o John A. & Elvira to CORDELIA E. JOHNSON 18 yrs single b. Fayette Co VA d/o Jacob S. & Sally O: Minister; by S.B. Vaught; REMARKS: certificate filed.

5. 8 Nov 1894 G.W. WILLIAMS 24 yrs single b. Giles Co VA s/o J.M. & Katherine to BELLE CALFEE 28 yrs single b. Mercer Co W VA d/o Jas & Elizabeth O: mechanic; by J.O. Cassaday.

6. 14 Nov 1894 WH K. PETERS 22 yrs single b. Mercer Co W VA now living in Summers Co VA s/o James & Pollie to IDA D. BUTLER 18 yrs single b. Mercer Co W VA d/o Zachariah R. & Caroline O: farmer; by G.M. Johnston; REMARKS: cert of father filed.

7. 10 Nov 1894 WM TAYLOR 26 yrs single b. GA s/o John & Marinda to ALICE COFFEY 14 yrs single b. NC d/o J.G. & Lois O: miner; by A.M. Craft; REMARKS: father of bride present.

8. 14 Nov 1894 JNO S. JEWELL 27 yrs single b. Mercer Co W VA s/o J.G. & Mary M. to SARA O.S. KING 15 yrs single b. Roanoke Co VA d/o Jas H. & Mildred O: farmer; by Jas W. Lilly; REMARKS: cert of father.

9. 14 Nov 1894 GRAYSON MAXWELL 20 yrs single b. Mercer Co W VA s/o Wm & Melvina to CATHARINE PRITCHARD 17 yrs single b. Mercer Co W VA d/o Thomas & ? O: miller; by J.W. Bennett; REMARKS: applied for by J.L. Bolin & cert filed.

10. 14 Nov 1894 THOS J. CALFEE 21 yrs 7 mos single b. Mercer Co W VA s/o A.J. & Margaret to JOSIE M. HURST 16 yrs single b. Mercer Co W VA d/o Jas H. & Sarah O: farmer; by G.C. Anderson; REMARKS: cert of J.H. Hurst & sworn.

11. 14 Nov 1894 WILLIAM MANN 50 yrs wid. b. VA to SALLY TROTTER 40 yrs wid. b. VA O: farmer; by A.J. Thompson; REMARKS: colored.

12. 14 Nov 1894 JOS ALEX HUDNALL 34 yrs single b. Warren Co VA s/o Richd A. & Mary E. to CALLIE B. GOODMAN 38 yrs wid. b. Mercer Co W VA d/o Jno W. & H.A. Sherwood O: carpenter; by Phil S. Sutton; REMARKS: sworn.

13. 21 Nov 1894 E.A. COOK 22 yrs single b. Mercer Co W VA s/o Calvin J. & R.I. to ANGIE LEE DILLION* 18 yrs single b. Mercer Co W VA d/o J. Bailey & M.F. Dillon* O: butcher; by G.C. Anderson; REMARKS: certificate filed. (*Note: name spelled both ways)

14. 21 Nov 1894 E.R. WHITLOW 22 yrs single b. Franklin Co VA s/o E.H. & Sallie C. to LILLIE KING 16 yrs single b. Wythe Co VA d/o E.W. & Sarah V. O: painter; by Phil S. Sutton; REMARKS: cert filed.

15. 22 Nov 1894 WM LAMB 21 yrs single b. Bland Co Va now living in Giles Co VA s/o A. & Martha Louisa to GEORGIA GAUTIER 18 yrs single b. Giles Co VA d/o James & Paulina O: farmer; by P.L. Prater; REMARKS: cert filed.

16. 12 Nov 1894 C.B. LEE 27 yrs single b. Montgomery Co VA s/o W.P F. & Nannie S. to DORA WORKMAN 21 yrs single b. Dauphin Co PA d/o Levi & Elizabeth O: physician; by jno E. Noff.

17. 25 Nov 1894 JACOB HALE 28 yrs single b. Franklin Co VA s/o Chas & Bettie to JANE WADE 24 yrs wid. b. Franklin Co VA O: miner; by Jno Coleman; REMARKS: J. Hale sworn, colored.

18. 28 Nov 1894 W.J. PENTURFF 46 yrs div. b. Shenandoah Co VA s/o Richard C. & Catherine to MARY THORN 24 yrs single b. Giles Co VA d/o James P. & Mahavala O: blacksmith; by J.L. Prater.

19. 30 Nov 1894 G.W. HALE 34 yrs wid. b. Giles Co VA now living same s/o John & Jane to LIZZIE F. WALKUP 32 yrs div. b. Mercer Co W VA d/o ? & Clara Canaday O: farmer; by Jas H. Johnston.

20. 30 Nov 1894 JONAS CLYBURN 23 yrs wid. b. Giles Co VA s/o E.B. & Eliza to AMANDA L. COHER 16 yrs single b. Mercer Co W VA d/o Wm S. & Martha O: farmer; by Jas H. Johnston; REMARKS: certificate of parents.

21. 1 Dec 1894 H.F. KINZER 25 yrs single b. Mercer Co W VA s/o Wm R. & Margaret to RHODA C. HAWKS 19 yrs single b. Mercer Co W VA d/o Wm R. & ? O: farmer; by G.C. Anderson; REMARKS: cert filed by A.B. Calfee.

22. 6 Dec 1894 JACOB H. BROWN 34 yrs single b. Garrett Co MI now living in Logan Co W VA s/o Hanson & Elizabeth to LIZZIE MOORE 28 yrs wid. b. Mercer Co W VA d/o Saml & Rhoda Spade O: lumberman; by J.O. Cassaday; REMARKS: J.H. Brown.

23. 5 Dec 1894 WH H. CROY 26 yrs single b. Bedford Co MA s/o Wm D. & Ellen M. to JUDIA HOWLES 21 yrs single b. Mercer Co W VA d/o D.C. & nancy C. O: blacksmith; by Thos C. Shuler; REMARKS: cert filed by Wm H. Croy.

24. 12 Dec 1894 H.C. OSBORN 21 yrs single b. Tazewell Co VA s/o J.r. & Sarilda to CHRISTENA MYERS 18 yrs single b. Tazewell Co VA d/o A.J. & Sally O: mechanic; by Thos C. Shuler; REMARKS: cert filed & H.C.O. sworn.

25. 12 Dec 1894 JAS B. JOHNSTON 18 yrs single b. Mercer Co W VA s/o Green A. & Louisa to LAURA R. WINFREY 18 yrs single b. Mercer Co W VA d/o Columbus & Lydia A. O: farmer; by G. Houchins.

26. 19 Dec 1894 S. WALTER MOORE 21 yrs single b. Appomattox Co VA s/o Peter & Sue to FLORENCE WADE 23 yrs single b. Montgomery Co VA d/o Ned & Bettie O: miner; by T.J. Brandon; REMARKS: S.W. Moore sworn.

27. 18 Dec 1894 J.D. CREWS 19 yrs single b. Mercer Co W VA s/o A.G.W. & D.R. to E.P. LILLY 21 yrs single b. Summers Co W VA d/o Joseph & Mary D. O: farmer; by Jas W. Lilly; REMARKS: cert filed.

28. 19 Dec 1894 HENRY CARROLL 24 yrs single b. Mercer Co W VA s/o Elishua & Sarah C. to MARY ANN BROWN 19 yrs single b. Mercer Co W VA d/o Marshal & Elizabeth B. O: railroader; by L. Goodwyn;

29. 19 Dec 1894 FLOYD ROWDEN 22 yrs single b. Buckingham Co VA s/o Danl & Winnie to POLLY GEORGE 21 yrs single b. Tazewell Co VA d/o Hugh & Margaret O: brakeman; by S.M. Gaines; REMARKS: colored.

30. 19 Dec 1894 THOS J. SANDERS 25 yrs single b. Alleghany Co NC s/o Riley & Sarah to POLLY ANN PETERS 18 yrs single b. Mercer Co W VA d/o Harvey & Martha O: farmer; by G.C. Anderson; REMARKS: certificate of father.

31. 20 Dec 1894 GEO THOS HALL 22 yrs single b. Montgomery Co VA s/o Jas K. & Hollie S. to VICIE J.F. CARTER 21 yrs single b. Tazewell Co VA d/o Wm & Mary O: lawyer; by J.L. Prater; REMARKS: certificate of father.

32. 19 Dec 1894 JOHN H. HYPES 27 yrs single b. Mercer Co W VA s/o J.L. & Frances Jane to IDA L BAILEY 21 yrs single b. Mercer Co W VA d/o Ballard P. & Sarah O: farmer; by J.O. Cassaday.

33. 25 Dec 1894 OTIS T. CASTLE 29 yrs wid. b. Russell Co VA now living in Monroe Co W VA s/o Abram & Mary D. to SUSIE EDWARDS 18 yrs single b. Wythe Co Va d/o H.H. & Jane O: miner; by V.I Masten; REMARKS: cert filed.

34. 24 Dec 1894 L.E. THOMPSON 27 yrs single b. Bland Co VA now living same s/o A.N. & J.H. to LULA JANE COOPER 17

yrs single b. Mercer Co W VA d/o Wm A. & ? O: carpenter; by Thos C. Shuler; REMARKS: cert filed.

35. 25 Dec 1894 FLEMING E. STONE 28 yrs single b. Franklin Co VA s/o Stephen & Clementine to AMANDA A. BOWLES 22 yrs single b. Franklin Co VA d/o Wm & Mary O: miner; by thos C. Shuler.

36. 24 Dec 1894 JOHN ROBBINS 21 yrs single b. Summers Co W VA s/o Wallace & Nancy P. to MINNIE ST.CLAIR 20 yrs single b. Mercer Co W VA d/o David P. & alice O: railroader; by L. Goodwyn; REMARKS: cert filed.

37. 25 Dec 1894 ALONZO P. SHELTON 25 yrs wid. b. Mercer Co W VA now living in Logan Co W VA s/o Wm & Mary J. to ALMEDA THOMAS 21 yrs single b. Giles Co VA d/o James & Mary J. O: railroader; by Thos C. Shuler.

38. 25 Dec 1894 A.D. BELCHER 24 yrs single b. Mercer Co W VA s/o David & Rebecca J. to LOVIE HAMBRICK 17 yrs single b. Mercer Co W VA d/o Geo & Amy O: farmer; by Jno H. Honaker; REMARKS: cert filed.

39. 28 Dec 1894 L. EASLEY CUMBY 20 yrs single b. Giles Co Va s/o Aaron T. & Annie to VIRGIE E. COMPTON 19 yrs single b. Tazewell Co VA s/o Granga B. & E.G. O: stableman; by J. McC. Duckwall; REMARKS: certificate of parents.

40. 31 Dec 1894 GEORGE WILLIAMS 24 yrs single b. Tazewell Co VA s/o Chas & Sarah to VIRGINIA REDIX 24 yrs single b. Tazewell Co VA d/o Henry & Ida O: laborer; by Geo T. Wright; REMARKS: (col'd), G. Williams sworn.

41. 2 Jan 1895 A.A. HUBBARD 28 yrs single b. Mercer Co W VA s/o M.F. & Martha A. to N.V. ELLISON 17 yrs sngle b. Mrcer Co W VA d/o P.A. & Lucy Ann O: farmer; by Jas W. Lilly; REMARKS: cert of parent filed.

42. 1 Jan 1895 DOLLIVER B. MILLS 19 yrs single b. Mercer Co W VA s/o H.G. & C.C. to VIOLA JANE BAILEY 18 yrs single b. Mercer Co W VA d/o Augustus I & Ann O: farmer; by G.C. Anderson; REMARKS: cert of parent filed & D.B. Mills sworn.

43. 9 Jan 1895 LEWIS MURRY 21 yrs single b. Buchanan Co VA s/o Sterling & Curdy to FANNIE BRANCH 24 yrs wid. b. Lynchburg VA d/o Jerry & Fannie Leftridge O: miner; by A.M. Craft; REMARKS: affidavit filed.

Page 78

1. 3 Jan 1895 H.L. GORE 22 yrs single b. Mercer Co W VA s/o H.F. & S.R. to MARY A. CAPERTON 17 yrs single b. Mercer Co W VA d/o John G. & Albertena O: farmer; by J.P. Campbell; REMARKS: certificate filed.

2. 2 Jan 1895 A.M. TABOR 24 yrs single b. Tazewell Co VA s/o Henry H. & Mary M. to CELESTE V. WILSON 19 yrs single b. Floyd Co VA d/o Raleigh G. & Alean O: miner; by Jno E. Naff; REMARKS: cert filed & A.M. Tabor sworn.

3. 9 Jan 1895 ELISHA R. DONALLEY 34 yrs single b. Henry Co VA s/o Andrson & Sarah to COSBY L. SMITH 19 yrs single b. McDowell Co W VA d/o G.P & Martha L O: farmer; by J.L. Prater; REMARKS: cert filed.

4. 10 Jan 1895 SAML A. STROCK 22 yrs single b. Bland Co Va s/o Jno F. & Sarah to SARAH E. MILLER 18 yrs single b. Wythe Co Va d/o Willoughby & R.E. O: miner; by A.M. Craft; REMARKS: cert filed & S.A. Strock sworn.

5. 15 Jan 1895 B.A. POE 21 yrs single b. Mercer Co W Va s/o H. & Henrietta J. to MINNIE HICKS 18 yrs single b. Mercer Co W VA d/o Wm R. & H.L. O: farmer; by A.M. Craft; REMARKS: cert filed & H. Poe present.

6. 17 Jan 1895 WM J. CALDWELL 22 yrs single b. Hancock Co TN s/o Glen & Sarah A. to MINNIE E. MORGAN 17 yrs single b. Mercer Co W VA d/o Thos P. & Martha O: carpenter; by R. Harry; REMARKS: cert filed of parent.

7. 23 Jan 1895 FLOYD PHIPPS 30 yrs single b. NC s/o Noah & Nancy to LUCILLA S. GRAHAM 16 yrs single d/o

W.E. & ? O: merchant's clerk; by Jno E. Naff.

8. 27 Jan 1895 R.C. WHITE 38 yrs wid. b. Mercer Co W VA s/o Reuben & Martha A. to ELIZA JANE SOUTHERN 22 yrs single b. Mercer Co W VA d/o ? & Minta O: farmer; by A.J. Thompson.

9. 30 Jan 1895 LEWIS L. MATHEWS 19 yrs single b. Tazewell Co VA s/o Geo W. & H.L. to REBECCA E. CARPET 17 yrs single b. Mercer Co W VA d/o Henry & Martha A. O: farmer; by J.O. Cassaday; REMARKS: cert of both parents filed & L.L. Mathews sworn.

10. 31 Jan 1895 CROCKETT JENNINGS 26 yrs single b. Halifax Co VA s/o Lewis & Polly to JENNIE JESSUT 25 yrs single b. Pulaski Co VA d/o Alfred & Ruth O: farm hand; by S.H. Gaines; REMARKS: affidavit filed, col'd.

11. 30 Jan 1895 WH F. GRIMES 21 yrs single b. Greenbrier Co W VA s/o P.H. & A.M. to MARY J. LAWSON 16 yrs single b. Tazewell Co VA d/o Z.P. & ? O: railroader; by J.McC. Duckwall; REMARKS: cert of father.

12. 4 Feb 1895 RASTUS B. SWADER 19 yrs single b. Mercer Co W VA s/o Alexander & Catherine to MARY WORKMAN 17 yrs single b. Mercer Co W VA d/o Robert & Jane O: blacksmith; by A.M. Craft; REMARKS: cert of father.

13. 28 Feb 1895 J.E. BELCHER 19 yrs single b. Mercer Co W VA s/o A.G. & Martha A. to NANCY R. BURTON 16 yrs single b. Mercer Co W VA d/o Wm H. & elvira A. O: farmer; by Jno H. Honaker; REMARKS: cert of both parents.

14. 6 Feb 1895 A.J. PHIPPS 21 yrs single b. NC s/o Harvey & Sally to KATIE B. COOPER 21 yrs single b. Mercer Co W VA d/o Wm A. & ? O: mason & plasterer; by Thos C. Shuler; REMARKS: cert of father.

15. 26 Feb 1895 JAS H. GOFORTH 24 yrs single b. NC s/o Jas T. & Hannah to NANCY C. PERDUE 21 yrs single b. Mercer Co W VA d/o Jas H. & Sarah E. O: farmer; by A.M. Craft; REMARKS: cert of father.

16. 20 Feb 1895 WM GORDON HARVEY 26 yrs single b. Monroe Co W Va now living same s/o John & ? to LOCKEY ISABEL SKEENS 19 yrs single b. Mercer Co W VA d/o Henry A. & Mary E. O: farmer; by E.S. Bettis; REMARKS: applied for by bride's father.

17. 27 Feb 1895 HENRY FARLEY 35 yrs wid. b. Mercer Co W VA s/o Wm & Lucy Ann to MARTHA J. GRAHAM 18 yrs single b. Mercer co W VA d/o Lynch & Mary O: farmer; by Jas W. Lilly; REMARKS: certificate of parents.

18. 27 Feb 1895 THOS J. GULLION 24 yrs single b. Tazewell Co VA s/oReuben & elizabeth to EMMA J. CLENDENEN 15 yrs single b. Mercer Co W VA d/o ? & N.J. O: miner; by A.H. Craft; REMARKS: certificate of mother.

19. 27 Feb 1895 JOHN B. NEAL 29 yrs single b. Mercer Co W VA s/o Wm R. & Martha J. to IDA A. BAILEY 19 yrs single b. Mercer Co W VA d/o A.C. & c.J. O: C.E.; by Jno E. Naff; REMARKS: certificate of bride's parents.

20. 27 Feb 1895 S.H. TRETWELL 23 yrs single b. Henry Co VA s/o ? & Nanie M. to MARY L. FLOYD 17 yrs single b. Henry CoVA d/o N.S. & W.H. O: railroading; by W.A. Pearson; REMARKS: certificate of bride's parents.

21. 28 Feb 1895 A.L. BAILEY 19 yrs single b. Tazewell Co VA s/o John & Julia Ann to LUCINDA TAYLOR 21 yrs single b. Mercer Co W VA d/o Wm & Mary O: miner; by Jno H. Honaker; REMARKS: certificate of parents filed.

22. 23 Mar 1895 JAS H. HOLDRON 48 yrs wid. b. Mercer Co w VA s/o Henry & Mahala to SNOWIE J. WHITE 42 yrs single b. Mercer Co W VA d/o Reuben & Martha O: farmer; by A.J. Thompson.

23. 5 Mar 1895 ROBT S. PUGH 24 yrs single b. Franklin Co VA s/o Flem & Emiline to MARY E. CLARK 18 yrs single b. Gland Co VA d/o Rufus W. & Nannie L. O: miner; by W.A. Pearson; REMARKS: father.

24. 7 Mar 1895 PAT J. SMITH 28 yrs single b. McDowell Co W VA s/o Geo P. & Martha L. to ELHETTIE L. SPANGLER 29 yrs div. b. Carroll Co VA d/o Eli & Rhoda O: farmer; by D.N. Saunders; REMARKS: see Cir Ct Chy O.B. No 9 p 157.

25. 6 Mar 1895 E.V. NEEL 24 yrs single b. Mercer Co W VA s/o Henry M. & Sarah A. to IDA M. HERNDON 21 yrs single b. Mercer Co W VA d/o Wm H. & Mary E. O: miner; by J.T. Frazier; REMARKS: E.V. Neel sworn.

26. 7 Mar 1895 C.H. KIRBY 22 yrs single b. Montgomery Co VA s/o R.R. & Mary A. to ELLA L. JOHNSTON 20 yrs single b. Montgomery Co VA d/o John & Mary L. O: miner; by Jno H. Honaker; REMARKS: cer of parent filed.

27. 22 Mar 1895 GRIFFITH JONES 30 yrs single b. Roanoke Co VA s/o ? & Nancy to NETTIE CHAPELL 24 yrs single b. Roanoke Co VA d/o John & Susan O: miner; by Phil S. Sutton; REMARKS: both parties sworn.

28. 12 Mar 1895 JAS W. BIRD 25 yrs single b. Mercer Co W VA s/o Jno S.H. & Elizabeth to LUTIE SHEANARD 18 yrs single b. Mercer Co W VA d/o ? & Sarah O: farmer; by R.M. Ashworth; REMARKS: cert of mother.

29. 28 Mar 1895 ALBERT G. PENNINGTON 23 yrs single b. Monroe Co W VA now living same s/o William & Nancy to LIONA WILEY 17 yrs single b. G.N. & Emily O: farmer; by B.P. Pennington; REMARKS: cert of father.

30. 13 Mar 1895 WALKER CALFEE 22 yrs single b. Mercer Co W VA s/o Henry & Sarah to MAGGIE H. COY 21 yrs wid. b. Tazewell Co W VA d/o J.b. Houchins & Clara P. O: brakeman; by W.A. Pearson; REMARKS: sworn.

31. 15 Mar 1895 WM HARRISON BUTT 79 yrs wid. b. Botetourt Co VA s/o Abram & Peggy to LULA E. HOPKINS 18 yrs single b. Mercer Co W VA d/o Joel & L.E. O: farmer; by d.N. Saunders; REMARKS: cert of mother filed.

32. 20 Mar 1895 LEVI J. COOK 45 yrs div. b. Hancock Co IN s/o Mat F. & Sarah to SARAH V. SHELTON 41 yrs wid. b. Craig Co VA d/o Estill & ? Snodgrass O: harness & shoe maker; by J.W. Bennett.

33. 20 Mar 1895 T.L. REED 20 yrs single b. Mercer Co W VA s/o Jas & Rebecca A. to LILLIE M. WHITLOW 17 yrs single b. Floyd Co VA d/o P.H. & Rebecca O: farmer; by L. Goodwyn; REMARKS: certificates of parents filed.

34. 28 Mar 1895 LUTHER R. BRAGG 19 yrs single b. Summers Co W VA now living same s/o A.J. & Malinda to VIRGINIA C. CHRISTIN 17 yrs single b. Mercer Co W VA d/o Eli & Luticia O: farmer; by G.H. Johnston; REMARKS: certificates of parents filed.

35. 28 Mar 1895 JAS CHILDRESS 23 yrs single b. Nelson Co VA now living in Wise Co VA s/o Edw & Mary F. to ELLA PAYTON 23 yrs wid. b. Cabell Co W VA d/o Jas & Julia Farror O: railroader; by S.M. Gaines; REMARKS: col'd, Jas Childress sworn.

36. 26 Apr 1895 WALTER DAY 22 yrs single b. Yadkin Co NC s/o C.C. & Mary to REBECCA CROCKETT 17 yrs single b. Tazewell Co VA d/o Jas A. & Rachel O: coal miner; by G.C. Anderson; REMARKS: Walter Day sworn, cert filed.

37. * * * SIDNEY WOOD 27 yrs single b. Armenlah(sic) Co VA s/o Sidney & Martha to MARTHA SHIPMAN 25 yrs single b. Sharlotte(sic) Co VA d/o Edmond & ? O: railroader; REMARKS: S. Wood sworn, col'd. (*Note: no date given.)

38. 10 Apr 1895 O.W. HOLSTINE 27 yrs single b. Mercer Co W VA s/o Lewis C. & Sarah L. to MARY R. BELCHER 16 yrs single b. Mercer Co W VA d/o Isham & Martha O: farmer; by J.W. Rader; REMARKS: O.W.H. sworn & cert filed.

39. 11 Apr 1895 JAS W. JOHNSON 23 yrs single b. S. Orange Co VA s/o W.C. & Mary H. to CORA E. WALL 23 yrs single b. Mercer Co W VA d/o Jas C. & ? O: miner; by R.K. Sutherland; REMARKS: W.C. Johnson.

40. * * * W.H. FOSTER 30 yrs wid. b. Alimance Co NC s/o Squire & Nancy to SUSAN A. ADAMS 22 yrs wid. b. Pillesvaina(sic) Co VA d/o Oliver & Julia Stone O: miner; REMARKS: applied for by A.L. Godfrey sworn statement filed. (*Note: no date given.)

41. 16 Apr 1895 GEO B. SINCLAIR 25 yrs single b. Albermarle Co VA s/o Geo A. & E.G.F. to NITA McNUTT 26 yrs single b. Mercer Co W VA d/o Robt B. & Ellen E. O: asst. cashier; by Eugene Blake.

42. 16 Apr 1895 W.B. HELVIN 26 yrs single b. Mercer co W VA s/o John W. & Rebecca to ROSA PERDEW 18 yrs single b. Mercer Co W VA d/o Harrison & Peggy O: saw mill; by L. Goodwyn; REMARKS: cert of bride's father filed.

43. 18 Apr 1895 B.F. LILLY 23 yrs single b. Mercer Co W VA s/o S.F. & Sarah E. to ALLIE R. LILLY 22 yrs single b. Mercer Co W VA d/o Jas & Linn O: farmer; by Jas A. Matherly; REMARKS: B.F. Lilly sworn.

44. 21 Apr 1895 CHARLES CARR 22 yrs single b. Tazewell Co VA s/o ? Haywood to MARY A. SHORTER 22 yrs single b. Mercer Co W VA d/o Wm T. & Nancy O: farmer; by B.P. Pennington; REMARKS: Chas Carrsworn.

45. 21 Apr 1895 LEWIS C. REED 23 yrs single b. Mercer co W VA s/o G.W. & rhoda to LIDA H. HOLDREN 17 yrs single b. Mercer Co W VA d/o H.S. & J.A. O: farmer; by B.P. Pennington; REMARKS: cert of father & mother.

46. 24 Apr 1895 ZEPHANIAH BELCHER 21 yrs single b. Mercer Co W VA s/o A.R. & Matilda to W.E. HARMAN 18 yrs single b. Mercer Co W VA d/o A.J. & Lydia O: miner; by Jno H. Honaker; REMARKS: cert of father & mother.

47. 23 Apr 1895 HENRY FRAZIER HAWKS 18 yrs single b. Mrcer Co W VA s/o Mitchell & Susan to MARTHA J. BAILEY 16 yrs single b. Mercer Co W VA d/o Wilson L. & Elizabeth O: farmer; by G.C. Anderson; REMARKS: cert of father & mother.

48. 24 Apr 1895 G.F. AKERS 49 yrs wid. b. Montgomery Co VA s/o Jordan & Julina to MARY ANN EAST 40 yrs single b. Pulaski Co VA d/o Galen & Nancy O: farmer; by J.W. Bennett.

Page 79

1. 24 Apr 1895 J.E. CARR 36 yrs wid. b. Giles Co VA s/o Thos & Lucinda to MARY S. DAVIDSON 23 yrs single b. Mercer Co W VA d/o Henry P. & Lucinda O: merchant; by J.W. Rader.

2. 25 Apr 1895 JOHN C. LOVERN 24 yrs single b. Montgomery Co VA s/o John K. & Catherine to MARY E. PAYNE 16 yrs single b. Mercer Co W Va d/o Andrew & Eliza O: coal mining; by Jno H. Honaker; REMARKS: J.C. Lovern sworn & cert filed.

3. 28 Apr 1895 W.S. WHITLOW 24 yrs single b. Floyd Co VA s/o P.H. & Rebecca to M.S. McPHERSON 20 yrs single b. Giles Co VA d/o J.L. & S.E. O: farmer; by L. Goodwyn.

4. 2 May 1895 H.E. HUBBARD 22 yrs single b. Mercer Co W VA s/o Peyton A. & Lucy Ann to ADA MARIA MOYE 15 yrs single b. Mercer Co W VA d/o E.W. & s.E. Moye O: farmer; by Jas W. Lilly; REMARKS: father of bride.

5. 3 May 1895 CHAS H. RICE 20 yrs single b. Monroe Co W VA s/o Geo & Malinda J. to CORA TURNER 17 yrs single b. Mercer Co W VA d/o Robt D. & mary J. O: farmer; by L. Goodwyn; REMARKS: guardn present & cert filed.

6. 7 May 1895 S.M. FOWLER 52 yrs single b. NC s/o D.W. & ? to SALLIE E. BELCHER 42 yrs wid. b. W VA O: grader on R.R.; by W.A. Pearson.

7. 10 May 1895 GERMAN P. HATCHER 21 yrs single b. Mercer Co W Va now living in Raleigh Co W VA s/o Jno R. & Nancy E. to ALICE BELLE COOK 21 yrs single b. Wyoming Co W VA d/o Geo W. & Margaret A. O: farmer; by Jas A. Hatherly.

8. 14 May 1895 NATHAN A. BLEOIUS 23 yrs single b. Russell Co VA now living in Benefield W VA s/o David A. & Aley to ADIUS JOHNSON 18 yrs single b. Wise Co VA d/o Nathan & ? O: R.R. brakeman; by H.H. Hawks; REMARKS: cert father filed.

9. 23 May 1895 EDWARD THOMPSON 20 yrs single b. Tazewell Co VA s/o George & Mary A. to MARY MATILDA TACKETT 16 yrs single b. Mercer Co W VA d/o W.A. & Ellen G. O: miner; by T.C. Shuler; REMARKS: cert of parents filed.

10. 23 May 1895 VERNIE NICEWANDER 25 yrs single b. Bland Co VA s/o Rufus & Christina to REBECCA BAILEY 27 yrs single b. Mercer Co W VA d/o Geo P. & elizabeth O: railroader; by T.C. Shuler.

11. 23 May 1895 HENRY WHITTEN 29 yrs single b. Bowling Green KY s/o Wm Harris & Roberta to POCA ARMSTRONG 21 yrs single b. Bland Co VA d/o John & Susan O: railroader; by S.M. Gaines; REMARKS: colered.

12. 5 June 1895 FRANK M. SHIREY 27 yrs single b. Augusta Co VA s/o Wm H. & Lucy M. to MARY V. HAWKS 25 yrs single b. Augusta Co VA d/o Herbert H. & Hattie B. O: clerk; by H.H. Hawks.

13. 29 May 1895 H.D. VASS 26 yrs single b. Monroe Co W VA now living same s/o A.C. & H.E. to ALLIE L. PERDUE 21 yrs single b. Mercer Co W VA d/o Geo W. & Fannie O: operator(telegraph); by S.b. Vaught; REMARKS: cert. G.W. Perdue filed.

14. 29 May 1895 E.M. LEFLER 23 yrs single b. Giles Co VA s/o James & ? to SUNDY M. BROCE 16 yrs single b. Montgomery Co VA d/o B.P & Mary O: farmer; by T.C. Shuler; REMARKS: cert filed.

15. 29 May 1895 JOS S. GOLDSMITH 24 yrs single b. St Marys Co MD now living in Montgomery Co VA s/o J.H. & Mary L to MIRA L. HAMMERSLEY 23 yrs single b. Campbell Co VA d/o Jas & H.L. O: tel. operator; by N.F. Marshall.

16. 29 May 1895 CREED F. SHELTON 24 yrs single b. Wythe Co VA s/o Creed & Elizabeth to BARBARA J. LAWSON 18 yrs single b. Tazewell Co VA d/o ? & Sarah E. O: R.R. fireman; by T.C. Shuler.

17. 30 May 1895 GEO W. CALDWELL 61 yrs wid. b. Giles Co VA s/o Jno & Eliza to E.R. TRAIL 27 yrs angle b. Mercer Co W VA d/o Jacob & Lockie O: county surveyor; by J.O. Cassaday.

18. 5 June 1895 RICHARD MULLINS 24 yrs single b. Montgomery Co VA s/o P.H. & Adeline to EMMA VAUGHAN 19 yrs single b. Giles Co VA d/o Thos J. & Esther J. O: railroader; by W.A. Pearson; REMARKS: R. Mullins sworn & cert filed.

19. 9 June 1895 JAMES W. SUBLETT 28 yrs single b. Montgomery Co VA s/o W.R. & Rebecca to MANERVA CAPERTON 19 yrs single b. Mercer Co W VA d/o John G. & Albertiny O: farmer; by G.H. Johnston; REMARKS: cert of mother filed.

20. 13 June 1895 JNO C. FITZWATER 42 yrs wid. b. Nicholas Co W VA s/o Jno & Sarah to CORA L. TERRY 19 yrs single b. Montgomery Co VA d/o A.J. & Martha J. O: farmer; by E.S. Bettis; REMARKS: bride's father present.

21. 10 June 1895 ALFRED CLARK 20 yrs single b. Mercer Co W VA s/o Henry & Virginia to LILLY MAY MOYE 16 yrs single b. Summers Co W VA d/o E.W. & S.E. O: saw mill; by Jas W. Lilly; REMARKS: cert of parents' filed.

22. 12 June 1895 CHARLES DAVIDSON 34 yrs wid. b. Bland Co VA now living same s/o Hugh & Ailsa Davidson to CALLIE JONES 17 yrs angle b. Mercer Co W VA d/o Kinnen & Ann O: farmer; by O.E. Bumgardner; REMARKS: cert of father filed.

23. 13 June 1895 G.A. WINFREY 29 yrs wid. b. Mercer Co W VA s/o Charles & Julina to REBECCA JANE ADKINS 33 yrs wid. b. Monroe Co W VA d/o Alison & Eleanor Found O: farmer; by R.H. Ashworth.

24. 24 June 1895 JAMES A. CORNER 21 yrs single b. Summers Co W VA s/o William & Catherine to MARTHA RIDWELL 32 yrs wid. b. Monroe Co W VA d/o Frog & Nancy O: farmer; by A.J. Thompson; REMARKS: cert filed.

25. 24 June 1895 CHAS W. BELCHER 23 yrs single b. Kanawha Co W VA s/o Floyd & Martha to MARIA L. MATHEWS 21 yrs single b. Tazewell Co VA d/o G.W. & H.L.E. O: sawmill; by Jas W. Lilly.

26. 24 June 1895 JAS L. DALTON 24 yrs single b. Carroll Co VA s/o ? & Mahala to SARAH F. UNDERWOOD 21 yrs single b. Mercer Co W VA d/o A.L & Mary J. O: farmer; by Jas W. Lilly; REMARKS: applied for by Robt Stovall.

27. 25 June 1895 WM H. SHINALL 50 yrs wid. to LOUDERMA HAGER 30 yrs single b. Bland Co VA d/o ? & Lucinda O: farmer; by E.W. Tiller; REMARKS: applied for by N.E. Hager.

28. 25 June 1895 SHIELDS BALLARD JONES 23 yrs single b. Franklin Co VA now living in Summers Co W VA s/o Pickney & Joanna to ROSIE E. BROOKS 17 yrs single b. Franklin Co VA d/o Robt L. & Mary A. O: farmer; by Drewry Farley; REMARKS: cert of mother filed.

29. 28 June 1895 BAL W. LILLY 24 yrs single b. Mercer Co W VA s/o Rufus & Mary to MINERVA MEADOWS 17 yrs single b. Summers Co W VA d/o ? & O.E. Meador O: farmer; by Drewry Farley; REMARKS: cert of mother filed.

30. 25 June 1895 H.L. DONATHAN 40 yrs div. b. Hanifae Co KY s/o Aaron & Martha to L.E. BUTLER 26 yrs single b. Mercer Co W VA d/o Jas H. & M.E. O: laborer; by Phil S. Sutton; REMARKS: copy of divorce filed.

31. 1 July 1895 JOHN M. HARMAN 38 yrs single b. Bland Co VA s/o John W. & Ann to CORDELIA AYERS 25 yrs wid. b. Carroll Co VA O: carpenter; by J.W. Rader.

32. 14 Nov 1895* RANSOM VAUGHT 56 yrs wid. b. Giles Co VA s/o Levi H. & Lucinda to NANCY TAYLOR 48 yrs wid. b. Mercer Co W VA d/o James Thompson & Lucy O: farmer; by J.W. Bennett. (*Note: perhaps the date should be 1894 - Unsure)

33. 4 July 1895 J.S. ALIFF 21 yrs single b. Franklin Co VA s/o Josiah & Sarah C. to LUCINDA F. THOMAS 17 yrs single b. NS d/o Andrew & M.H. O: shop labor; by W.A. Pearson; REMARKS: certificate of bride's mother filed.

34. 3 July 1895 CHAS KIRBY 21 yrs single b. Montgomery Co VA s/o Jas & Calley A. to DORA BISHOP 16 yrs single b. Montgomery Co VA d/o A. & Martha O: fireman; by W.A Pearson; REMARKS: kirby sworn, bride's father present.

35. 4 July 1895 JNO D. ST.CLAIR 23 yrs single b. Mercer Co W VA s/o D.P & Alice to LELIA M. McDANIEL 15 yrs single b. Montgomery Co VA d/o E.F. & Lizzie O: public works; by L. Goodwyn; REMARKS: cert of parents.

36. 7 July 1895 R.S. HAMBRICK 24 yrs single b. Mercer Co W VA s/o L.T. & R.J. to CORRIE L. HEDRICK 21 yrs single b. Tazewell Co VA d/o H.M. & Nancy O: farmer; by W.H. Ayres.

37. 11 July 1895 SAMUEL KINZER 19 yrs single b. Mercer Co W VA s/o Wm R. & Margaret E. to ROSETTA HAWKS 16 yrs single b. Mercer Co W VA d/o Wm R. & Polly O: farmer; by G.C. Anderson; REMARKS: cert of parents.

38. 19 July 1895 H.P. NEAL 22 yrs angle b. Wyoming Co W VA s/o ? & Ellen Neal to FRANKLIN B. FRANKLIN 17 yrs single b. Bland Co VA d/o C.W. & Mary E. O: farmer; by W.A. Pearson; REMARKS: cert of parents.

39. 28 July 1895 R.K. HILL 40 yrs wid. b. Alleghany Co NC s/o ? & Ala Hill to MARY ANN SHUMATE 16 yrs single b. Wyoming Co W VA d/o Matthew Shumate O: farmer; by A.H. Craft; REMARKS: cert of parents.

40. 24 July 1895 WM H. McKEE 24 yrs single b. Alton IL s/o Wm & Lucy to MAY B. TERRY 22 yrs single b. Bland Co VA d/o Saml & Meggie O: painter; by W.A. Pearson.

41. 24 July 1895 JNO H. JOHNSTON 35 yrs single b. Mercer Co W VA s/o Wm & Sarah E. to MINNIE A. SHUMATE 23 yrs single b. Giles Co VA d/o H.N. & allie O: railroader; by Giles M. Johnston.

42. 26 July 1895 HUGHEY G. HILLS 24 yrs single b. Mercer Co W VA s/o Hugh & Margt E. to SOPHIA A.H. McBRIDE 26 yrs single b. Mercer Co w VA d/o Jno B. & Sallie O: farmer; by Jas W. Lilly; REMARKS: J.G. Nealey.

43. 28 July 1895 ROBT A. WOOD 26 yrs single b. Sarah Co NC s/o Ransom & Debie to HARRIET A. GRIM 18 yrs single b. Mercer Co W VA d/o Peter & Martha A. O: farmer; by G.C. Anderson; REMARKS: father present.

44. 31 July 1895 H.F. PRINCE 49 yrs wid. b. Mercer Co W VA s/o Joseph & Susan to LUCETTIA F. HATCHER 23 yrs single b. Mercer Co W VA d/o Edmond & Nancy O: farmer; by Jas W. Lilly.

45. 29 July 1895 MARK W. HOWELL 21 yrs single b. Floyd CoVA s/o Thos & Virginia to LUCY E. BLESSING 19 yrs single b. KY d/o ? & Caroline O: miner; by G.C. Anderson; REMARKS: cert of mother.

46. 31 July 1895 MELVIN SWIM 19 yrs single b. Yadkin Co NC s/o H.F. & Handy J. to EMMA WELLS 15 yrs single b. Mercer Co W VA d/o Daniel & Dorcas O: farmer; by J.O. Cassaday; REMARKS: cert of parents of both.

47. 4 Aug 1895 R.L. JOHNSON 25 yrs single b. Carroll Co VA s/o Jos C. & Martha L. to ROSA WORRELL 19 yrs single b. Carroll Co VA d/o ? & Elizabeth O: farmer; by J.W. Bennett; REMARKS: applied for by J.C. Johnson.

48. 7 Aug 1895 JOHN McGRAW 21 yrs single b. Franklin Co VA s/o Mitchell & Sarah to MYRTLE SPANGLER 22 yrs single b. Monroe Co W VA d/o ? & Willie O: public works; by J.McC. Duckwall; REMARKS: applied for by Jas A. McGraw.

Page 80

1. 8 Aug 1895 FLOURNOY BOWLING 20 yrs single b. Mercer Co W VA s/o A.W. & Lucinda to LULA ALBERTA HILL 16 yrs single d/o J.R. & Martha Hill O: farmer; by R.M. Ashworth; REMARKS: applied for by A.W. Bowling, cert of mother filed.

2. 8 Aug 1895 BOYD M. BROWN 21 yrs single b. Mercer Co W VA s/o Marshal & Elizabeth to MARTHA A. ALIFF 16 yrs div. b. Mercer Co W VA d/o Elisha & Mary O: farmer; by J.O. Cassaday; REMARKS: cert filed.

3. 14 Aug 1895 PED. STOVALL 32 yrs wid. b. Montgomery Co VA s/o Silas & Sarah to MARIA V. FOX 26 yrs single b. Bland Co VA d/o Mathias & Ann C. O: stone mason; by J.McC. Duckwall.

4. 14 Aug 1895 BEN. ISAAC SNIDER 20 yrs single b. Mercer Co w VA s/o Wm R. & Dimothy to NANCY J. SNIDER 18 yrs single b. Mercer Co W VA d/o Esom & Rhoda O: lawyer; by J.W. Bennett; REMARKS: certificates of parents.

5. * * * JOHN L. FRANCISCO 28 yrs single b. Washington Co VA s/o L.M. & S.E. to EMMA L. DILLON 18 yrs single b. Mercer Co W VA d/o Z.T. & Sally O: R.R. man; REMARKS: certificates of parents. (*Note: no date given.)

6. 22 Aug 1895 JAMES BARRETT 22 yrs single b. Hawkins Co TN s/o Saml & Nancy to MINNIE B. JOHNSON 20 yrs single d/o W.C. & Mary H. O: miner; by D.A. Ramey; REMARKS: Jas Barrett sworn & cert filed.

7. 27 Aug 1895 B.F. SHARP 29 yrs wid. b. Wythe Co VA s/o Jas & Sarah to ELLEN WESTMORELAND 23 yrs single b. VA O: miner; by A.M. Craft; REMARKS: applied for by Gideon Sisk & sworn.

8. 10 Sept 1895 JOHN C. TILLY 59 yrs div. b. Ash Co NC now living in Wyoming Co W VA s/o ? & Mary to JULIA ANN BAILEY 36 yrs wid. b. Mercer Co W VA d/o Elias & ? O: farmer; by Jno H. Honaker; REMARKS: copy of decree filed.

9. 28 Aug 1895 MARK HARTWELL 21 yrs single b. Mercer Co W VA s/o John & Cynthia to SINAI GODFREY 22 yrs single b. Mercer Co W VA d/o Robt & ? O: farmer; by Phil S. Sutton; REMARKS: M. Hartwell sworn.

10. 4 Sept 1895 McCLELLAN PERDUE 25 yrs single b. Mercer Co W VA s/o Geo W. & Fannie to IDA E. CRAFT 18 yrs single b. Franklin Co VA d/o A.M. & Sally O: carpenter; by W.H. Ayers; REMARKS: cert of A.M. Craft filed.

11. 31 Aug 1895 D.E. NEEL 43 yrs wid. b. Tazewell Co VA to MARY NEEL 34 yrs single b. Tazewell Co VA d/o H.P. & Lydia O: laborer; by W.A. Pearson; REMARKS: applied for by R.M. Neel.

12. 3 Sept 1895 WESLEY WOODSON 32 yrs wid. b. Tazewell Co VA s/o ? & Agnes Preston to SARAH CARTER 24 yrs div. b. Bristol TN O: public labor; by Jno L. Witten.

13. 5 Sept 1895 WILLIAM H. SHREWSBURY 19 yrs single b. Mercer Co W VA s/o Wm R. & Cynthia to ARMINTA E. SHREWSBURY 16 yrs single b. Mercer Co W VA d/o J.B. & Elizabeth O: farmer; by Irvin H. Bailey.

14. 6 Sept 1895 SAML M. NICEWANDER 23 yrs single b. Bland Co VA s/o Nannie Nicewander to JOSIE L. NICEWANDER 16 yrs b. Bland Co VA d/o Ardetia J. O: miner; by D.A. Ramsey; REMARKS: cert of bride's mother filed.

15. 12 Sept 1895 JOS M. OARS 22 yrs single b. Floyd Co VA s/o Jesse & Mary to LEORA EFFA COOK 16 yrs single b. Mercer Co W VA d/o Thos B. & Louisa O: teacher; by G.C. Anderson; REMARKS: J.M. Oaks sworn.

16. 12 Sept 1895 W.H. BUCHANAN 23 yrs single b. Wyoming Co W VA s/o Geo & ? to MARTHA J. BELL 14 yrs single b. Mercer Co W VA d/o Henry & Julia O: miner; by A.M. Craft; REMARKS: cert of bride's father filed.

17. 13 Sept 1895 LEWIS WETZEL HARVEY 18 yrs single b. Mercer Co W VA s/o A.H. & Sarah J. to MARY ANN LILLY 14 yrs single b. Mercer Co W VA d/o A.M. & Electra A. O: farmer; by James W. Lilly; REMARKS: A.H. Lilly & A.M. Harvey.

18. 16 Sept 1895 JNO H. JENNINGS 19 yrs single b. Carroll Co VA s/o Garland H. & Sarah to ELIZA J. MEADOWS 16 yrs single b. Mercer Co W VA d/o russell & Nancy A. O: farmer; by James W. Lilly; REMARKS: certs of parents.

19. 18 Sept 1895 H.G. HOLDRON 23 yrs single b. Mercer Co w VA s/o Saml & Dorcas W. to NANCY J. THOMPSON 20 yrs single b. Mercer Co W VA d/o Wm Henderson & Rebecca J. O: farmer; by A.J. Thompson; REMARKS: applied for by bride's father.

20. 17 Sept 1895 HARRY H. STEWART 29 yrs single b. Cabell Co W VA now living same s/o James & Sarah to DELLA H. RATCLIFFE 19 yrs single b. Pulaski Co VA d/o D.S. & M.V. O: farmer; by W.C. Lindsey; REMARKS: father of bride.

21. 18 Sept 1895 SAML L. CALFEE 23 yrs single b. Mercer Co W VA s/o Henry & Sarah to CLARA A. BELCHER 16 yrs single b. Mercer Co W VA d/o B.P & C. O: lumberman; by D.N. Saunders; REMARKS: certificate filed & S.L. Calfee sworn.

22. 20 Sept 1895 M.H. CHILDERS 24 yrs single b. Surrey Co NC s/o James & Ollie to MARY D. RADFORD 22 yrs single b. Franklin Co VA d/o Jacob & Chaterine O: farmer; by E.W. Tiller; REMARKS: Mr. Childers sworn.

23. 25 Sept 1895 ROBT L BOWLING 29 yrs single b. Mercer Co W VA now living in Giles Co VA s/o John & Helen to MARY E. SINCLAIR 34 yrs single b. Mercer Co W VA d/o Bluford & Betty O: farmer; by R.H. Ashworth; REMARKS: Mr. Bowling sworn.

24. 23 Sept 1895 BEN W. PECK 21 yrs single b. Summers Co W VA now living same s/o Erastus H. & C.H. to HAZIE B. TAYLOR 16 yrs single b. Mt. Airy, NC d/o ? & Nannie O: clerk; by J.W. Bennett; REMARKS: certificates.

25. 26 Sept 1895 PETER STESSEL 33 yrs single b. Germany to JULINIE HILL 22 yrs wid. bo Mercer Co W VA d/o H.C. & Nancy Jane; by R.K. Sutherland; REMARKS: certificate.

26. 25 Sept 1895 WADE H. TAYLOR 24 yrs single b. Mercer Co W VA s/o Sampson & Martha to MAGGIE A. MILLS 21 yrs single b. Mercer Co W VA d/o Thompson & E.G. O: miner; by A.M. Craft; REMARKS: certificate.

27. 27 Sept 1895 GEO W. AKERS 24 yrs single b. Mercer Co W VA s/o Henry H. & ? to RACHEL E. RAMBURG 17 yrs single b. Mercer Co W VA d/o Wm J. & Nancy J. O: farmer; by Jas W. Lilly; REMARKS: father of bride present.

28. 2 Oct 1895 EDWD S. HEARN 21 yrs single b. Mercer Co W VA s/o James & ? to POLLY TAYLOR 22 yrs single b. Mercer Co W VA d/o Sampson & Martha O: miner; by Jno H. Honaker; REMARKS: cert of parents.

29. 2 Oct 1895 CANEY DUNFORD 22 yrs single b. Giles Co VA s/o Wm & Paulina to DOSIE UNDERWOOD 23 yrs wid. b. Floyd Co VA d/o Martin & Elizabeth O: saw mill help; by Phil S. Sutton; REMARKS: C. Dunford sworn.

30. 2 Oct 1895 ROBERT HALE 22 yrs single b. Grayson Co VA s/o John & Luderna to NORA B. WILSON 19 yrs single b. Floyd Co VA d/o R.G. & A.A. O: miner; by R.K. Sutherland; REMARKS: Arch Tabor & R. Hale sworn.

31. 3 Oct 1895 ASA B. DAVIS 20 yrs single b. Mercer Co W VA s/o Lee & Christine to SALLIE M. GORDON 21 yrs single b. Giles Co VA d/o G.W. & Elizabeth O: farmer; by L. Goodwyn; REMARKS: cert of parents.

32. 25 Oct 1895 CHAPMAN HUNTER 38 yrs wid. b. Bedford Co VA to ALMEDA SIMS 38 yrs wid. b. Atlanta GA O: miner; by H.C. Smith; REMARKS: by Wm Taylor.

33. 6 Oct 1895 HENRY ROBINSON JR. 24 yrs single b. Wythe Co VA s/o Henry & Letta to LAURA JENKINS 22 yrs single b.

Wythe Co VA d/o Chas & Maria O: railroader; by Jno H. Honaker; REMARKS: sworn.

34. 9 Oct 1895 LEONIDAS JASPER NEAL 23 yrs single b. Mercer Co W VA s/o A.S. & A.P to NORA ANN BURTON 17 yrs single b. Giles Co VA d/o H.P & Mary A. O: painter; by T.C. Shorter; REMARKS: cert filed.

35. 8 Oct 1895 SAMUEL S. KARNES 22 yrs single b. Mercer Co W VA s/o Gad & Robecca to NANNIE E. McKINNEY 22 yrs single b. Mercer Co W VA d/o ? & Elizabeth O: farmer; by J.S. Rader.

36. 8 Oct 1895 JOHN A. KIMBLE 20 yrs single b. Patrick Co VA s/o Jno A. & Mahala to FRANCIS E. GUNTER 26 yrs single b. Carroll Co VA d/o William & Pheba O: farmer; by J.W. Lilly; REMARKS: certificate.

37. 15 Oct 1895 CHAS V. FERGUSON 26 yrs single b. New York City NY now living in May Beary W VA s/o Chas A. & Mary Louisa to DAISY LILLIAN BURTON 19 yrs single b. Amherst Co VA d/o Geo H. & Vestina J. O: bookkeeper; by J.B. Simpson; REMARKS: certificate.

38. 15 Oct 1895 WALTER S. HOLDREN 24 yrs single b. Mercer Co W VA s/o Saml & Dorcas W. to JENNIE THOMPSON 22 yrs single b. Mercer Co W VA d/o Danl & Minerva O: farmer; by J.W. Bennett; REMARKS: certificate.

39. 15 Oct 1895 ORAB A. HENING 25 yrs single b. OH s/o Frank & Mina to GEORGIA A.F. DUNCAN 14 yrs single b. Tazewell Co VA d/o G.W. & Sarah O: com. labor; by W.W. Smith; REMARKS: father of bride present.

40. 14 Oct 1895 CHARLES RICE 24 yrs single b. Charlotte Co VA now living in McDowell Co W VA s/o Doctor & Amanda to HATTIE DOYLE 20 yrs single b. Pittsylvania Co VA d/o ? & Sariah O: miner; by S.L. Tucker; REMARKS: certificate, col'd.

41. 16 Oct 1895 FRANK E. SKAGGS 24 yrs single b. Monroe Co W VA now living same s/o Andrew A. & Martha to MAY B. HENDERSON 21 yrs single b. Guadaloupe Co TX d/o Wm A. & Annie O: farmer; by W.A. Wynne.

42. 16 Oct 1895 C.H. WILEY 23 yrs single b. Mercer Co v VA s/o J.R. & Louisa J. to E.J. CARPER 21 yrs single b. Mercer Co W VA d/o B.P & Martha O: railroading; by J.O. Cassaday; REMARKS: C.H. Wiley sworn.

43. 17 Oct 1895 F.S. IRVINE 22 yrs single b. Giles Co VA s/o Isaac & Lucinda to LIZZIE ANDERSON 22 yrs single b. Giles Co VA d/o Geo & ? O: railroading; by J.HcC. Duckwall; REMARKS: F.S. Irvine sworn.

44. 24 Oct 1895 J. BALLARD LAMBERT 21 yrs single b. McDowell Co W VA now living same s/o Thos K. & Cynthia M. to REBECCA A. TAYLOR 20 yrs single b. Mercer Co W Va d/o G.W. & Sarah O: farmer; by T.K. Lambert; REMARKS: certificates, sworn.

45. 23 Oct 1895 JAS SANDERS DUNN 31 yrs single b. Washington Co VA s/o T.E. & C.V. Dunn to HASSIE J. KIESTER 21 yrs single b. Montgomery Co VA d/o J.H. & S.M. O: engineer; by W.C. Lindsay; REMARKS: certificates, sworn.

46. 23 Oct 1895 T.J. BURKET 23 yrs single b. Marion, Smyth Co VA now living in Marion VA s/o Abraham & Sofia H. to LAURA ALICE TURNER 18 yrs single b. Marion VA d/o Jos H. & Mary M. O: railroading; by W.A. Pearson; REMARKS: certificates, sworn.

47. 23 Oct 1895 WM E. WILLIAMS 28 yrs div. b. Rensselaer Co NY now living in Wayne Co W VA s/o Chas B. & Frances M. to CYNTHIA M. CRAWFORD 27 yrs single b. Tazewell Co VA d/o Reuben & Margaret O: fireman; by E.S. Bettis; REMARKS: certificates, sworn.

48. 24 Oct 1895 THOS J. ANTON 23 yrs single b. Maclenbury Co NC now living in Wautauka Co NC s/o John & Annie to NANCY I. HAMLIN 19 yrs single b. Montgomery Co VA d/o T.H. & Cassie O: railroading; by REMARKS: father of wife present.

Page 81

1. 30 Oct 1895 CHARLIE WARREN 25 yrs single b. TN s/o Richard & Mary J. to ROSIE SOUTHERN 19 yrs single b. Mercer Co W VA d/o ? & Betty O: miner; by G.C. Anderson; REMARKS: consent of guardian.

2. 30 Oct 1895 BENJ J. LILLY 21 yrs single b. Raleigh Co W VA now living same s/o Naaman W. & Elizabeth to LULA MAUD LILLY 16 yrs single b. Mercer Co W VA d/o J.H. & Araminta O: farmer; by J.J. Meador; REMARKS: cert filed.

3. 30 Oct 1895 JOHN R. CALLOWAY 28 yrs single b. Nelson Co VA s/o Anthony & Louisa to ADDIE DILLARD 20 yrs single b. Appomattox Co VA d/o Marsh & ? O: railroader; by R.C. Fox; REMARKS: Jno R. Calloway sworn & cert filed.

4. 30 Oct 1895 JOHN DAVIS 23 yrs single b. Lunenburg Co VA s/o Edmund & Martha to JULIA WISDOM 21 yrs single b. Tazewell Co VA d/o Humphrey & ? O: railroader; by R.C. Fox; REMARKS: Jno Davis sworn.

5. 6 Nov 1895 GEO W. PENN 33 yrs single b. Henry Co VA s/o John J. & Amanda to SALLY M. MULLIN 19 yrs single b. Mercer Co W VA d/o John & Jane O: farmer; by S.E. Houk; REMARKS: cert of mother, colored.

6. 6 Nov 1895 ADAM L. LILLY 21 yrs single b. Mercer Co W VA s/o Rufus & , Mary to J.A. CLARK 30 yrs wid. b. Mercer Co W VA d/o Wm Lilly & ? O: farmer; by Drewry Farley; REMARKS: cert of mother & sworn.

7. 7 Nov 1895 ROBERT FIELDS 23 yrs single b. Bedford Co VA s/o ? & Linia Fields to SARAH E. HARTWELL 16 yrs single b. Giles Co VA d/o ? & Mary Ann O: mine driver; by T.J. Brandon; REMARKS: applied for by Z.T. Hartwell.

8. 13 Nov 1895 JAS E.V. SWEENEY 27 yrs single b. Monroe Co W VA s/o Frank & ? to BELLE THOMPSON 22 yrs single b. Mercer Co W VA d/o W.H. & Sallie O: teacher; by T.C. Shuler.

9. 20 Nov 1895 ROBT A. ANDERSON 44 yrs wid. b. Edinburgh Scotland s/o Robt S. & Margaret Kelly to PEARL MOORE ANDERSON 26 yrs single b. Fincastle VA d/o E.T. & Olivia O: merchant; by Norman F. Marshall.

10. 13 Nov 1895 JULIUS C. HIGHT 24 yrs single b. Summers Co W VA now living same s/o J.H. & Rebecca to RAVENA E. WILEY 19 yrs single b. Mercer Co W VA d/o Jno A. & Mahala Y. O: merchant; by J.W. Bennett; REMARKS: cert of parents.

11. 13 Nov 1895 SAML A. BOWLING 24 yrs single b. Mercer Co W VA s/o Andrew & Lucinda to HAGGIE C. MATHENA 15 yrs single b. Tazewll Co VA d/o Geo W. & Harriet O: farmer; by R.M. Ashworth; REMARKS: cert of parents.

12. 14 Nov 1895 HENRY L. MARTIN 32 yrs single b. Mercer Co W Va s/o Aclas & Ails A. to JOANNA BRUCE 19 yrs single b. Mercer Co W VA d/o W.W. & Martha O: farmer; by L. Goodwyn; REMARKS: cert of parents.

13. 18 Nov 1895 BUDD ALIFF 23 yrs single b. Montgomery Co VA s/o Thomas & Nannie to RHODA FLORENCE ALIFF 23 yrs single b. Mercer Co W VA d/o Jos S. & Sarah C. O: railroading; by Norman F. Marshall; REMARKS: Budd Aliff sworn.

14. 9 Dec 1895 EDWARD B. KIRTNER 39 yrs div. b. Pulaski Co VA s/o C.I & Ellen E. to SARAH RYE 28 yrs single d/o Hiram & ? O: farmer; by J.W. Bennett.

15. 22 Nov 1895 FLEMING COMPTON 23 yrs single b. Russell Co VA s/o Starling & Temperance to ANGELINE PERKINS 23 yrs single b. Rusell Co VA d/o John & Mary O: farmer; by D.N. Saunders.

16. 20 Nov 1895 W.W. McCLAUGHERTY 25 yrs single b. Mercer Co W Va s/o Jos W. & Eveline to MARY E. POWELL 19 yrs single b. Mercer Co W VA d/o Wm A. & Catherine O: merchant; by W.A. Pearson; REMARKS: cert of W.A. Powell.

17. 21 Nov 1895 LEWIS EVANS 49 yrs wid. b. Botetourt Co VA now living in Graham VA s/o Abraham & Sarah to SARAH C. RATCLIFFE 27 yrs single b. Bland Co VA d/o Jas S. & Elizabeth D. O: blacksmith; by W.H. Ayers.

18. 20 Nov 1895 AMOS E. DILLON 22 yrs single b. Mercer Co W VA s/o Zach & Sallie to WILLIE G. PETERS 19 yrs single b. Summers Co VA d/o Joseph & Alice O: lawyer; by Jas W. Lilly; REMARKS: cert of Jos Peters.

19. 21 Nov 1895 ALBERT F. CALDWELL 32 yrs single b. Giles Co VA s/o Geo W. & E.A. to CLA A. UNDERWOOD 17 yrs single b. Montgomery Co VA d/o C.R. & Sarah F. O: farmer; by J.B. Simpson; REMARKS: cert of C.R. Underwood.

20. 27 Nov 1895 GEO H. BARGER 38 yrs single b. Montgomery Co VA s/o Daniel & Bessie to FLORENCE MAYNARD 22 yrs single b. Russell Co VA d/o ? & Cosby O: conductor; by W.A. Pearson.

21. 25 Nov 1895 JOS W. BOOTHE 29 yrs div. b. Montgomery Co Va s/o Elisha & Mary J. to ANNIE J. MUNSEY 22 yrs single b. Mercer Co W VA d/o M.P. & ? O: miner; by G.C. Anderson; REMARKS: cert of clerk Mercer Co Ct.

22. 28 Nov 1895 JAS S. GRIFFITH 20 yrs b. Pike Co KY s/o W.A. & Francis to ALVERTY RUDISILL 22 yrs b. Pulaski Co VA d/o ? & Louzena O: miner; by W.A. Wynne; REMARKS: cert filed.

23. 4 Dec 1895 GEO R. McKINEY 19 yrs single b. Wyoming Co W VA now living same s/o Jno W. & Jane to POLLY A. AKERS 20 yrs single b. Wyoming Co W VA d/o Crockett & Martha A. O: farmer; by S.M. McKinney; REMARKS: cert filed.

24. 5 Dec 1895 WM HAWKS 22 yrs single b. Mercer Co W VA s/o Eli & Nancy J. to MARY BAILEY 18 yrs single b. Tazewell Co VA d/o Z.H. & Elizabeth O: miner; by A.H. Craft; REMARKS: cert filed.

25. 4 Dec 1895 JNO T. FAULKNER 26 yrs single b. mercer Co W VA s/o Gordon P & Ann E. to SARAH L. BELCHER 26 yrs single b. Mercer Co V VA d/o J.E. & Amanda E. O: farmer; by A.H. Craft.

26. 4 Dec 1895 W.R. McGUYER 31 yrs single b. Montgomery Co VA now living in Roanoke Co VA s/o A. & M.F. to FLORA B. PECK 20 yrs single b. MO d/o J.P & Annie C. O: conductor; by W.A. Pearson; REMARKS: cert filed.

27. 11 Dec 1895 HENRY FRANK DAUGHERTY 24 yrs single b. Montgomery Co VA now living in Monroe Co W VA s/o H.T. & Landonia to ELIZABETH C. EVANS 24 yrs wid. b. Montgomery Co VA d/o N.D. & M.M. Moore O: teacher; by J.W. Bennett.

28. 8 Dec 1895 SAML P. CROTTY 35 yrs wid. b. Mercer Co W VA s/o Wm & Julia to A. SUE WHITTAKER 18 yrs single b. Mercer Co W VA d/o Wm & ? O: farmer; by L. Goodwyn; REMARKS: cert filed.

29. 11 Dec 1895 JOHN F. VANDIKE 20 yrs single b. Tazewell Co VA s/o Louisa to MARY S. HILTON 19 yrs single b. Floyd Co VA d/o Louisa O: dray majors(sic); by E.S. Battis; REMARKS: cert filed.

30. 15 Dec 1895 CHARLES H. STUAT* 22 yrs single b. Bedford Co VA s/o Kitt & Vilet* to MAMIE WILLIAMS 22 yrs single b. Rauhlie* NC d/o Haniva* O: gen house work; by T.J. Brandon; REMARKS: cert filed. (*Note: names & city copied exactly)

31. 12 Dec 1895 W.F. WINFREY 21 yrs single b. Mercer Co W Va s/o M.W. & V.M. to LILLIE CRAWFORD 25 yrs single b. Tazewell Co VA d/o Reuben & Margaret O: farmer; by E.S. Battis.

32. 17 Dec 1895 W.R. BALLARD 24 yrs wid. b. Monroe Co V VA s/o Riley & Emily to HATTIE MOWLS 19 yrs single b. Mercer Co W VA d/o D.C. & Nancy G. O: carpenter; by W.A. Pearson; REMARKS: certificate filed.

33. 19 Dec 1895 A.B. HILL 22 yrs single b. Floyd Co VA s/o Robert & Martha A. to MARY JANE BIRD 19 yrs single b. Mercer Co W VA d/o Stephen & Susan O: teamster; by L.Goodwyn L.M.; REMARKS: applied for by J.H. Harvey, cert filed.

34. 17 Dec 1895 CHAS F. BROOKS 32 yrs single b. Franklin Co Va now living in McDowell Co W VA s/o Clough M. & Emaline to MINNIE L. WILLIAMS 18 yrs single b. Monroe Co W VA d/o G.G. & Fannie O: carpenter; by A.M. Craft; REMARKS: father present.

35. 18 Dec 1895 GEO H. JENNINGS 23 yrs sngle b. Carroll Co VA s/o Garland & Sarah to L.C. REED 22 yrs single b. Mercer Co v VA d/o Hiram & Susan O: farmer; by J.W. Lilly.

36. 18 Dec 1895 ALX, H. SUTTON 26 yrs single b. Giles Co VA s/o P.S. & Victoria to MARGRET BARBRIE 29 yrs single b. England d/o John & Julia O: lawyer; by S.E. Houk.

37. 18 Dec 1895 A.H. HARMAN 22 yrs single b. Mercer Co W VA s/o Patrick & Sarah J. to ELIZABETH ROSS 18 yrs single b. Mercer Co W VA d/o J.B. & ? O: farmer; by S.E. Houk; REMARKS: cert of J.B. Ross filed.

38. 25 Dec 1895 CHAS F. HYLTON 21 yrs single b. Floyd Co VA s/o Lewis & Millie to LAURA B. FRENCH 20 yrs single d/o Wm L. & Louisa O: farmer; by G.W. Bailey; REMARKS: Wm L. French present.

39. 24 Dec 1895 W.D. GIBSON 23 yrs single b. Pittsylvania Co VA to MARY J. GODFREY 23 yrs single b. Mercer Co W VA d/o A.C. & ? O: engineer; by A.M. Craft; REMARKS: applied for by J.S. Collins.

40. 25 Dec 1895 RANSOM BUTT 22 yrs single b. Tazewell Co Va now living in McDowell Co VA s/o Chas W. & Virgnia C. to ALICE BOSTWICK 22 yrs single b. Montgomery Co VA d/o Ira H. & Pelariam O: carpenter; by W.A. Pearson; REMARKS: R. Butt sworn.

41. 26 Dec 1895 C.A. MORGAN 39 yrs wid. b. Campbell Co VA s/o Swan H. & Francis A. to M.H. CARDEN 41 yrs div. b. Mercer Co W VA d/o Alex & Rebecca Price O: farmer; by J.P. Campbell; REMARKS: copy decree filed.

42. 24 Dec 1895 W.J. PETERS 22 yrs single b. Wyoming Co VA s/o G.P. & Maria to CORA A. MAXEY 22 yrs single b. Mercer Co W VA d/o Preston & Celia O: merchant; by D.A. Ramey; REMARKS: cert filed.

43. 25 Dec 1895 J.F. BROWN 26 yrs single b. mercar Co W VA s/o Marshall & Elizabeth to MARY J. HEARN 23 yrs sngle b. Mercer Co v VA d/o Andrew & Hattie O: railroader; by J.W. Bennett; REMARKS: F.J. Brown sworn.

44. 24 Dec 1895 R.A. TACKETT 22 yrs single b. Tazewell Co VA s/o W.A. & Ellen to TERESSA C.P. GILLASPIA 14 yrs single b. Mercer Co W VA d/o Isaac & Jennie O: quaryman; by E.S. Bettis; REMARKS: certificate of mother filed.

45. 25 Dec 1895 OSCAR LEFLER 21 yrs single b. Giles Co VA s/o Jas A. & Fannie to MONTIE THOMAS 20 yrs single b. Kanawha Co W VA d/o Robt M. & Sarah M. O: laborer; by J.O. Cassaday; REMARKS: cert filed.

46. 26 Dec 1895 ROBERT KING 24 yrs single b. Bland Co VA s/o Jas & Jane to ELLIE LEFLER 19 yrs single b. Giles Co VA d/o Jas A. & Fannie O: laborer; by E.W. Tiller; REMARKS: cert filed.

47. 24 Dec 1895 WILLIAM CARR 32 yrs wid. b. Bland Co VA s/o Jas & Fannie to LIZZIE FARMER 21 yrs single b. Mercer Co W VA d/o William & Sarah E. O: farmer; by D.A Ramey; REMARKS: cert filed.

48. 25 Dec 1895 JAS PALMER 28 yrs single b. Albemarle Co VA s/o Jerry & Priscilla to ANNA LEVERAGE 18 yrs single b. Louisville KY d/o Daniel & ? O: railroader; by W.J. Carter; REMARKS: cert filed, colored.

Page 82

1. 26 Dec 1895 GEO JOHNSON 30 yrs single b. Roanoke Co Va s/o Richard & Emiline to LUCY CARTER 22 yrs single b. Danville VA d/o ? & Sallie O: section hand; by A.L. Thompson; REMARKS: colored.

2. 24 Dec 1895 HARVEY R. HALL 23 yrs single b. Montgomery Co Va s/o Ama & Lucy to FANNIE M. THOMPSON 21 yrs sngle b. Lincoln Co W VA d/o H.C. & ? O: farmer; by S.E. Houk.

3. 25 Dec 1895 JOHN MORRISON 23 yrs single b. Pittsylvania Co VA s/o Ephraim & Emaline to LIZZIE JACKSON 23 yrs single b. Bland Co VA d/o Winton & ? O: railroader; by R.C. Fox; REMARKS: colored.

4. 25 Dec 1895 CHAS H. BAXTER 23 yrs single b. Mercer Co v VA s/o George & Ann to B. ANN LEWIS 19 yrs single b. Mercer Co W VA d/o Sanders & Harriet O: hack driver; by S.E. Houk; REMARKS: colored, father present.

5. 1 Jan 1896 D.C. MEADER 27 yrs wid. b. mercer Co W VA s/o Isaac & Mary Jane to NORA ESTALINE HATCHER 14 yrs single b. Mercer Co v VA d/o J.G. & Nancy O: farmer; by Drewry Farley; REMARKS: cert of father filed.

6. 26 Dec 1895 W.W. SHREWSBURY 23 yrs single b. Mercer Co W VA s/o John S. & Victoria to ANNIE R. MUNCY 21 yrs single b. Giles Co VA d/o W.W. & Martha O: farmer; by G.W. Bailey.

7. 2 Jan 1896 ERASTUS MEADOWS 17 yrs single b. Monroe Co W VA now living same s/o Joseph & Sarah J. to ARDELIA HAZLEWOOD 18 yrs single b. Mercer Co W VA d/o John & Mary O: farmer; by J.B. Chambers; REMARKS: certs filed.

8. 31 Dec 1895 MICHAEL KIPPINGER 55 yrs wid. b. Niagara Co NY s/o Adam & Catherine to VICTORIA LUIKONS 31 yrs sngle b. Montgomery Co VA d/o Thomas & Ellen O: fireman; by E.W. Tiller.

Page 83

1. 1 Jan 1896 THOS DUNCAN 26 yrs div. b. Tazewell Co Va s/o Wm & Jane to MARTHA A. DUNCAN 20 yrs single b. Grayson Co VA d/o G.W. & Sarah O: farmer; by W.A. Pearson; REMARKS: wife's father consenting.

2. 7 Jan 1896 CHAS ELDRIDGE 26 yrs single b. Giles Co Va s/o Wm & Rachel to SUSIE BORSDICKS 21 yrs single b. Roanoke Co VA d/o Wilburn & Ann O: miner; by T.J. Brandon; REMARKS: applied for by A.I Godfrey, sworn statement filed.

3. 8 Jan 1896 WM A. PECK 32 yrs single b. Tazewell Co VA s/o J. Austin & Larissa to FLORA A. HAROLD 17 yrs single b. VA d/o H.C. & Edie O: farmer; by J.W. Bennett; REMARKS: cert of father.

4. 15 Jan 1896 J.W. GRAHAM 25 yrs single b. Knox Co TN s/o Wm A. & Louisa to LOUISE SUTTON 23 yrs single b. lenoir Co NC d/o S.I. & Mary O: tel. operator; by Thos J. Eskridge; REMARKS: applied for by J.S. Wigginton.

5. 16 Jan 1896 CHARLES A. MILLS 23 yrs single b. Mercer Co W VA now living in Raleigh Co W VA s/o Anderson & ? to NANCY E. WALLACE 27 yrs single b. VA d/o Thos & Mary O: farmer; by S.H. McKinney.

6. 22 Jan 1896 WM A. VAWTER 24 yrs sngle b. Monroe Co v VA s/o Jno Wm & Elizth D. to MABEL CLARE SHORTER 21 yrs single b. Augusta Co VA d/o J.O. & Rebecca A. O: railroader; by Wm C. Lindsay; REMARKS: cert filed & W.A. Vawter sworn.

7. 21 Jan 1896 SIMON L. TRIGG 33 yrs wid. b. Tazewell Co VA s/o Elijah & Deborah to HATTIE HARVEY 21 yrs single b. VA d/o ? & Wyett O: farmer; by G.T. Wright.

8. 29 Jan 1896 WM HICKS 27 yrs single b. Rockcastle Co KY s/o Jesse & Pulina to HELEN WALL 22 yrs single b. Mercer Co v Va d/o Harvey & ? O: merchant; by T.C. Shular.

9. 29 Jan 1896 GREELY WHITE 23 yrs single b. Mercer Co v VA s/o Allen & Mary to NANNIE BURCH 20 yrs single b. Mrcer Co W VA d/o Geo W. & S.J. O: farmer; by J.W. Bennett; REMARKS: cert filed of G.W.B.

10. 10 Feb 1896 CHARLES SAUNDERS 37 yrs sngle b. Montgomery Co VA s/o Noah & Maria to ESTELLA CALLAHAN 22 yrs single b. Montgomery Co VA d/o Ben & Martha O: miner; by J.W. Johnson; REMARKS: col'd, Chas Saunders sworn.

11. 5 Feb 1896 D.C. RORRER 25 yrs single b. Patrick Co VA s/o W.R. & mary A. to THEORA E. LILLY 23 yrs single b. mercer Co W VA d/o J.K. & Alabama O: teacher; by Granvill Houchins.

12. 5 Feb 1896 A.G. HEARN 30 yrs div. b. Mercer Co W VA s/o James & Easter C. to EMMA RAMEY 17 yrs single b. Johnston Co KY d/o Own(sic) & M.M. O: railroader; by E.W. Tilley; REMARKS: cert filed.

13. 5 Feb 1896 WM H. GILLS 23 yrs single b. Bland Co VA s/o Benjn & Mary to HATTIE F. HUBBARD 17 yrs sngle b. mercer Co W VA d/o Saml & Ellen O: railroader; by T.F. Suthers; REMARKS: consent of grdn.

14. 5 Feb 1896 HARRISON C. WALKER 19 yrs single b. Mercer Co W VA s/o John W.C. Walker & Nancy to LILLY D. ROSE 15 yrs single b. Mercer Co W VA d/o Barlin & Rebecca J. O: farmer; by L.H. Bailey; REMARKS: cert filed.

15. 12 Feb 1896 ALLEN B. McCOMAS 26 yrs wid. b. Mercer Co W VA now living in McDowell s/o Archabald & Savilla to FLORA E. WALKER 20 yrs single b. Mercer Co W VA d/o John M. & Millie O: carpenter; by L.H. Bailey; REMARKS: cert filed.

16. 12 Feb 1896 WILLIAM CLARK 43 yrs div. b. Mercer Co W VA s/o ? & Eliza to MALINDA HALL 40 yrs wid. b. Pulaski Co VA d/o Perry & Christian Henderson O: laborer; by S.E. Houk; REMARKS: colored.

17. 13 Feb 1896 LEWIS H. WILEY 21 yrs single b. Giles Co VA s/o Gordon & Sinai to RHODA E. WHITTAKER 16 yrs single b. Mercer Co W VA d/o William & Mary J. O: farmer; by L. Goodwyn; REMARKS: certificate & affidavit.

18. 17 Feb 1896 HENRY NELSON 21 yrs single b. Mercer Co W VA s/o Ward & Mary to SUSAN S. PETTREY 20 yrs single b. Mercer Co W VA d/o J.L. & Isabell O: farmer; by J.P. Campbell; REMARKS: certificate.

19. 26 Feb 1896 THOS WATTS 26 yrs single b. Rome GA s/o Elijah & Laurinda to MARIA J. RUMBURG 16 yrs sngle b. Mercer Co W VA d/o Wm J. & Nancy J. O: miner; by T.J. Eskridge; REMARKS: certificate of father.

20. 4 Mar 1896 FRANKLIN T. SHITER 25 yrs single b. Bland Co VA now living same s/o Peter & Margaret to LUCINDA A. BOWLING 16 yrs single b. mercer Co W VA d/o Andrew J. & Almanie O: farmer; by J.O. Cassaday; REMARKS: certificate.

21. 4 Mar 1896 C.L. RICHMOND 23 yrs single b. Raleigh Co W Va s/o Jno P. & Elizabeth to IDA E. COX 16 yrs sngle b. Summers Co w VA d/o Wellington A ? O: farmer; by Drewry Farley; REMARKS: certificate of father & C.L.R. sworn.

22. 4 Mar 1896 OPIE BATEMAN 28 yrs wid. b. Charlotte Co VA s/o Albert & Mary to MARIA LOWRY 32 yrs wid. b. NC d/o ? & Harriet Mills O: miner; by W.E. Mitchell; REMARKS: col'd.

23. 11 Mar 1896 J.W. MAXIE 27 yrs single b. Mercer Co W VA s/o Edgar & Annie to NANNIE R. STOVALL 25 yrs single b. Mercer Co w VA d/o Levi V. & Ann O: farmer; by Jas W. Lilly.

24. 13 Mar 1896 CHRIS FITZGERALD 32 yrs single b. Pittsylvanic Co VA s/o David & Rachel to GEORGIE HALE 22 yrs single b. Giles Co VA d/o John & Ama O: brakeman; by T.C. Shuler; REMARKS: col'd.

25. 13 Mar 1896 WM MOSS 23 yrs single b. Campbell Co VA s/o James & Tilda to DELPHIA HOWARD 30 yrs wid. b. VA d/o ? & Kitty O: railroader; by T.C. Shuler; REMARKS: col'd.

26. 17 Mar 1896 JAS R. ROLAND 24 yrs single b. tazewell Co VA s/o Miles B. & Mary E. to BETIE E. BAILEY 20 yrs single b. Mercer Co w VA d/o J.R.P. & E.P. O: farmer; by E.W. Tiller; REMARKS: cert of parents.

27. 18 Mar 1896 CLARENCE GUTRIDGE 23 yrs single b. Newark OH to BERTHA M. THOMPSON 17 yrs single b. Mercer Co W VA d/o W.S. & Emma C. O: lawyer; by T.C. Pulliam; REMARKS: father present.

28. 25 Mar 1896 LEWIS PRESTON HYLTON 29 yrs single b. Floyd Co VA s/o Wm A. & Rutha E. to CALLIE D. LOVE 17 yrs single b. Smyth Co VA d/o James & M.F. O: miner; by D.A. Daugherty; REMARKS: cert filed.

29. 26 Mar 1896 WM BARKSDALE 26 yrs single b. Halifax Co Va now living in Tazewell Co Va s/o Clem & Lillie to GIRTIE GRAVES 23 yrs single b. Pittsylvania Co VA d/o Jesse & Mary A. O: miner; by J.W. Johnson; REMARKS: applied for by Chas Pulman, sworn, col'd.

(NOTE: Entry #30 marked through.)
30. * * * L.A. SHUMATE 38 yrs single b. Wyoming Co W VA to S.A. SHREWSBURY 17 yrs single b. Mercer Co W VA d/o Geo Wm & Ellen. (*Note: no date given.)

31. 30 Mar 1896 J.E. JONES 38 yrs div. b. IA s/o Alex & Laura to R.V. PETERS 18 yrs single b. Raleigh Co W VA d/o E.C. & Tamor O: lawyer; by E.W. Tiller.

32. 2 Apr 1896 A.C. LEFFEW 25 yrs single b. Franklin Co VA s/o W.K. & Elizabeth to H.EMMA JONES 21 yrs single b. Montgomery Co VA d/o Geo W. & Martha J. O: miner; by D.A. Ramey; REMARKS: father present & gave consent.

33. 1 Apr 1896 LOUIS TURNES 21 yrs single b. Appomattox Co VA s/o Pleasant & Fannie to LULA A. LILLY 15 yrs single b. Mercer Co W VA d/o J.K. & Alabamma O: farmer; by W.I Gantier; REMARKS: cert filed.

34. 3 Apr 1896 JAMES H. WALTON 22 yrs single b. Floyd Co VA s/o Davis & Mary to MARY J. REED 17 yrs single b. Mercer Co W VA d/o Elias & Catherine O: farmer; by S.M. McKinney; REMARKS: Elias Reed.

35. 3 Apr 1896 JAS H. FLETCHER 40 yrs wid. b. Mercer Co W VA s/o Calvin & Rhoda to NANNIE J. BURTON 28 yrs single b. Bland Co VA d/o Travis & Mary H. O: farmer; by L. Goodwyn.

36. 12 Apr 1896 ISAAC THOMPSON 28 yrs single b. Mercer Co W VA s/o Allen & Minerva to LIZZIE PAYNE 23 yrs single b. Mercer Co W VA d/o Bartley O: farmer; by A.J. Thompson.

37. 9 Apr 1896 A.J. HEADOR 36 yrs div. b. Summers Co W VA now living same s/o Geo & Rhoda to B.D. RICHMOND 16 yrs single b. Raleigh Co W VA d/o Parkerson & Elizabeth O: farmer; by Drewry Farley; REMARKS: cert filed.

38. 11 Apr 1896 J. ROBT SHRADER 19 yrs single b. Mercer Co W VA s/o Alex & Katherine to CORA L. BRUSE 18 yrs sngle b. Pulaski Co VA d/o Jos N. & M.J. O: railroader; by D.N. Saunders; REMARKS: consent given for both parties by guardn & father.

39. 8 Apr 1896 W.A. SIMPSON 27 yrs single b. Bathe Co VA now living in Kanawha Co W VA s/o Geo W. & Mary A. to MARY E. THORNTON 24 yrs single b. Charlotte Co VA d/o F.B. & Mary S. O: carpenter; by W.C. Lindsey.

40. 14 Apr 1896 WM C. BARKER 24 yrs single b. Wake Co NC s/o Wm C. & M.E. to THALESTROUS VERMILLION 27 yrs single b. Mercer Co W VA d/o S.T. & Rhoda O: clerk; by J.P. Campbell

41. 15 Apr 1896 COY R. COLE 23 yrs single b. Mercer Co w VA s/o Allen & Virginia to AMERICUS WINFREY 16 yrs single b. Mercer Co W VA d/o Columbus & Lydia O: lawyer; by E.W. Tiller; REMARKS: cert of mother.

42. 25 Apr 1896 JOHN LUKAC 27 yrs single b. Austria s/o Andrew & Mary to MARY ORNEFER 19 yrs single b. Austria d/o John & Annie O: farmer; by E.Olivier.

43. 30 Apr 1896 PETER AVINGTON 21 yrs single b. Roanoke VA s/o Peter & Loucinda A. to NANNIE BUTLER 22 yrs single b. Roanoke Co VA d/o Geo & Mary O: miner; by J.W. Johnson; REMARKS: cert filed.

44. 20 Apr 1896 HORTON COWAN 33 yrs single b. Wythe Co VA s/o Saml W. & Maggie to CORA A. FOWLER 19 yrs single b. Tazewell Co VA d/o S.M. & S.E. O: loc engineer; by E.S. Bettis; REMARKS: cert filed.

45. 2 May 1896 FLOYD ODELL 22 yrs single b. Carroll Co VA s/o Abraham & Martha to PAULINA L REED 17 yrs single b. Mercer Co W VA d/o Geo W. & Marinda C. O: farmer; by G.C. Anderson; REMARKS: father of wife.

46. 27 May 1896 CHARLES A. BALL 67 yrs wid. b. Tazewell Co VA s/o James & Catherine to EMAIRILO BROOKS 43 yrs single b. Tazewell Co VA d/o William & Elizabeth O: farmer; by E.S. Bettis.

47. 5 May 1896 J. CHANCY VAUGHT 20 yrs single b. Giles Co VA s/o Rufus & E.H. to MARY E. COOK 19 yrs single b. Mercer Co W VA d/o Ward & Rhoda O: farmer; by W.I Gantier; REMARKS: cert filed & wit sworn.

48. 10 May 1896 JOS A. HEDRICK 25 yrs single b. Mercer Co W VA s/o Harvey M. & Nannie J. to ALICE B. AUSTIN 24 yrs single b. Mason Co W VA d/o I.S. & M.L O: conductor; by D.M. Austin.

Page 84

1. 12 May 1896 CHAS H. EVANS 30 yrs single b. Campbell Co VA s/o D.S. & Sarah E. to KATE H. EASLEY 23 yrs single b. Giles Co VA d/o Jno W. & M.B. O: clerk; by W.A. Pearson.

2. 21 May 1896 ELISHA D. LILLY 22 yrs single b. Raleigh Co W VA now living same s/o Robert & Amanda L. to ELIZA OAKS 17 yrs single b. Mercer Co W VA d/o Jesse N. & Polly O: farmer; by Allen H. McKinney; REMARKS: cert filed.

3. 21 May 1896 FLOYD W. DOSS 40 yrs wid. b. Giles Co VA s/o Jno R. & Elzine to LOU J. BAILEY 30 yrs div. b. Mercer Co W VA d/o ? & Martha O: farmer; by Thos B. Cook; REMARKS: decree filed.

4. 20 May 1896 FRED B. YORK 25 yrs single b. Chatum Co NC s/o R.W. & Lou F. to SALLIE SPICER 17 yrs single b. Mercer Co W VA d/o William & Martha O: miner; by T.J. Eskridge.

5. * * * GEO SPARKS 26 yrs single b. Pittsburgh PA s/o Jno & Annie to FRANCES M. WARNER 17 yrs single b. Franklin Co OH d/o Geo & Belle O: engineer; REMARKS: guardian. (*Note: no date given.)

6. 27 May 1896 STONEWALL J. NEAL 33 yrs single b. Mercer Co W VA s/o Henry H. & Sarah A. to EVALINE FRENCH 25 yrs single b. Mercer Co W VA d/o Harvey & Belinda O: farmer; by J.W. Bennett.

7. 27 May 1896 GEO S. LAWSON 19 yrs single b. Tazewell Co VA s/o Wm W. & Luie to LYDIA A. HYLTON 18 yrs single b. Floyd Co VA d/o Hiram & Louisa O: miner; by E.S. Bettis; REMARKS: both witnesses (affirmed), cert filed.

8. 28 May 1896 JOSEPH MACK 23 yrs single b. Prince Edward Co VA now living in McDowell Co W VA s/o Charles & Nancy to MARY A. MURRAY 19 yrs single b. Buckingham Co VA d/o Sterling & ? O: miner; by J.W. Johnson; REMARKS: guardian present.

9. 2 June 1896 ROBT L. COLVARD 25 yrs single b. Ash Co NC now living same s/o Wm M. & Sallie to LUCY LOWRY 25 yrs single b. Roanoke Co VA d/o S.H. & Fannie A. O: farmer; by T.C. Shuler.

10. 30 May 1896 HEROD A. PAGE 27 yrs single b. Buckingham Co VA s/o Herod & Louisa to CHARLOTTE CAMPBELL 28 yrs single b. Tazewell Co VA d/o Delawar & Ami O: miner; by J.W. Johnson.

11. 2 June 1896 JNO H. DICKERSON 33 yrs single b. Bedford Co VA s/o Sam & Jenette to LUCY SHELVY 23 yrs single b. Roanoke Co VA d/o Lewis & Martha O: miner; by J.W. Johnson; REMARKS: Jno H. Dickerson sworn, col'd.

12. 2 June 1896 JNO B. RATCLIFFE 22 yrs single b. Fayette Co VA s/o David S. & Mary V. to MOLLIE B. ROBERTSON 19 yrs single b. Pittsylvania Co VA d/o W.H. & Mary A. O: chacker; by W.A. Pearson; REMARKS: cert filed.

13. 2 June 1896 W.T. WHITE 30 yrs single b. Allamarl Co VA s/o Nelson & Ardenia to EMMA EAVES 25 yrs single b. Giles Co VA d/o Jacob & Elizabeth O: miner; by J.W. Johnson; REMARKS: W.S. White sworn, col'd.

14. 2 June 1896 STEPHEN PEARISH 29 yrs single b. Pittsylvania Co VA now living in McDowell Co W VA s/o Fountain & Martha to LOUISA HURT 31 yrs single b. Franklin Co VA d/o ? & Vanie O: coke drawer; by J.W. Johnson; REMARKS: S. Pearish sworn, col'd.

15. 2 June 1896 WM E. B. JOHNSTON 31 yrs single b. Mercer Co W VA s/o William & Sarah E. to VIRGIE R.V.S. STAFFORD 22 yrs single b. Mercer Co W VA d/o Wm H. & Louisa A. O: farmer; by S.E. Houk.

16. 3 June 1896 WILLIS L HAGER 16 yrs single b. Mercer Co W Va s/o S.H. & R.A. to EUGENIA THOMASON 17 yrs single b. Tazewell Co VA d/o T.L. & Ellen O: farmer; by E.W. Tiller; REMARKS: cert filed & wit. sworn & his father present in person.

17. 3 June 1896 LEH L. MARTIN 22 yrs single b. Mercer Co W VA s/o Wm E. & Julia V. to RHODA C. LILLY 17 yrs single b. Mercer Co W VA d/o J.K. & Alabama O: carpenter; by J.W. Bennett; REMARKS: cert filed of parents.

18. 4 May 1896 WM J. LILLY 35 yrs single b. Mercer Co W VA now living in Summers Co W VA s/o Rufus B. & Mary to BERTIE A. OAKES 19 yrs single b. Mercer Co W VA d/o Jesse s. & ? O: farmer; by Allen H. McKinney; REMARKS: cert filed of father.

19. 8 June 1896 O.T. HARRIS 33 yrs single b. Louise Co VA s/o Winston & Louisa to SARAH E. GORE 22 yrs single b. Mercer Co W VA d/o Jake & Sara J. O: minister; by C.H. Booker; REMARKS: both col'd.

20. 9 June 1896 HARVEY DUNKIN 19 yrs single b. Floyd Co VA now living in Giles Co VA s/o A.T. & Rebecca to JENNIE HELTON 24 yrs single b. Giles Co VA d/o ? & Mary Helton O: carpenter; by A.J. Thompson; REMARKS: cert filed of father.

21. 10 June 1896 W.C. LINROWE 25 yrs single b. Bland Co VA s/o ? & Martha to ELHORA WILLIAMS 20 yrs single b. Mercer Co W VA d/o A.M. & Mary J. O: farmer; by J.W. Bennett; REMARKS: bride's father present.

22. 17 June 1896 SOL D. STEPHENS 23 yrs single b. Giles Co VA s/o Wm & Nancy J. to EVELINE LAWSON 16 yrs single b. Tazewell Co VA d/o Wm W. & Lue O: stone mason; by E.S. Bettis; REMARKS: cert of father & mother.

23. * * * JOHN ANDREW SOUTHERN 19 yrs single b. Mercer Co W VA s/o Wm & Rachel to SEVILLA COHER 20 yrs single b. Mercer Co W VA d/o Augustus & Martha O: farmer; REMARKS: No Return; cert of parents filed. (*Note: no date given.)

24. 18 June 1896 JOHN E. SMITH 36 yrs wid. b. Huntingdon PA s/o Paul & Veronia to SARAH E. HILL 38 yrs div. b. NC d/o Wm & Sarah M. Chandler O: flagman; by T.C. Shuler.

25. 18 June 1896 D. ENZER SIMPSON 24 yrs single b. Washington Co VA s/o V.R. & F.T. to IDA B. BAILEY 18 yrs single b. Mercer Co W VA d/o L.K.P. & E.P O: hostler; by E.S. Bettis; REMARKS: cert of parents.

26. 22 June 1896 O.H. CAPERTON 28 yrs single b. Mercer Co W VA now living in Summers Co W VA s/o O.H. & Martha H. to ELIZA E. CRAWFORD 25 yrs single b. Mercer Co W VA d/o Saml H. & Emily O: railroader; by J.P. Campbell; REMARKS: cert of father.

27. 23 June 1896 HEN B. THOMPSON 26 yrs single b. Mercer Co W VA s/o Wm H. & Sarah to ANNIE L. ALLEN 22 yrs single b. Philadelphia PA d/o Elijah & Alice O: butcher; by W.A. Pearson.

28. 24 June 1896 ISAIAH W. BRADY 51 yrs wid. b. Preston Co W Va s/o Saml & ? to MARY W. GRAHAM 41 yrs wid. b. Montgomery Co VA d/o Andrew & Tinsey O: laborer; by T.J. Eskridge.

29. 24 June 1896 PHIL K. BLANKENSHIP 22 yrs single b. Mercer Co W VA s/o R.M.B. & Cynthia to IDA B. DUNN 21 yrs single b. Mercer Co W VA d/o Jno W. & Mary O: farmer; by A.J. Thompson.

30. 24 June 1896 AND L. HALDREN 21 yrs single b. Mercer Co W VA s/o Saml & Dorcas W. to ZORA J. DUNN 16 yrs single b. Mercer Co W VA d/o Jno W. & Mary C. O: farmer; by A.J. Thompson; REMARKS: cert of father.

31. 24 June 1896 EDMON D. JOHNSON 23 yrs single b. Goochland VA now living in Roanoke VA s/o James & Mary to SADIE F. FINCH 17 yrs single b. Montgomery Co VA d/o Thomas R. & Lizzie O: railroader; by T.T. Suthers.

32. 24 June 1896 GEO W. HANCE 25 yrs single b. Giles Co VA s/o ? & Lena to ELIZA V. DABNEY 22 yrs single b. Campbell Co VA d/o ? & Bettie O: hotel waiter; by R.C. Fox; REMARKS: col'd.

33. 25 June 1896 JESSE H. LINSEY 23 yrs single b. Randolph Co NC now living in McDowell Co W VA s/o Alford & Martha to LILLIE R. HAVIS 16 yrs single b. Leon Co NC d/o James & Campline O: miner; by J.W. Johnson; REMARKS: col'd.

34. 25 June 1896 J.E. SAUNDERS 27 yrs single b. Mercer Co W VA s/o Micajah & Drucilla to CHLOE L. LESTER 17 yrs single b. Mercer Co W VA d/o A.B. & Martha L. O: blacksmith; by E.W. Tiller; REMARKS: cert of father filed.

35. 28 June 1896 ROBT LINHONS 24 yrs single b. Montgomery Co VA s/o Thomas & Ellen to MATTIE SHEPARD 23 yrs single b. NC d/o James & Julina O: farmer; by E.W. Tiller.

36. 26 June 1896 SAMUEL BUEL 21 yrs single b. Wytheville VA s/o Douglass & Bettie to SALLIE B. WALKER 19 yrs single b. Monroe Co W VA d/o Floyd & Julia O: hotel waiter; by G.T. Wright; REMARKS: col'd, consent of guardian.

37. 2 July 1896 HENRY WOODS 23 yrs single b. Mercer Co W VA s/o ? & Loudenia to LOUISA SCOTT 16 yrs single b. Mercer Co W Va d/o John & Nancy O: farmer; by G.C. Anderson; REMARKS: applied for by L. Burchett (step-father).

38. 7 July 1896 NEHEMIAH MINOR 22 yrs single b. Kanawha Co VA s/o Peter & Nancy to NANCY BAILEY 25 yrs single b. Mercer Co W VA d/o Wilson Lee & Lizzie O: farmer; by G.C. Anderson.

39. 2 July 1896 A.H. SHELTON 27 yrs single b. Stoke Co NC s/o G.H. & Eliza to CYNTHIA A. TAYLOR 18 yrs single b. Mercer Co W VA d/o Thomas & Bettie O: miner; by John H. Honaker; REMARKS: cert of bride's father filed.

40. 2 July 1896 WM BROOKS 23 yrs single b. Franklin Co Va now living in McDowell W VA s/o ? & Paulina Brooks to SALLIE B. HARRELL 21 yrs single b. Caswell Co NC d/o Robt & Catherine O: coal miner; by J.W. Johnson; REMARKS: col'd.

41. 2 July 1896 A.B. HALL 23 yrs single b. Patrick Co VA s/o Absalom B. & Elizabeth to MARY E. HUNT 23 yrs single b. Tazewell Co VA d/o H.F. & Louisa O: railroader; by S.E. Houk; REMARKS: A.B. Hall sworn.

42. 3 July 1896 J.R. GANTIER 17 yrs single b. Mercer Co W VA s/o Rufus A. & Alice to MARY GOODSON 15 yrs single b. Montgomery Co VA d/o Floyd & Sarah O: farmer; by W.I Gantier; REMARKS: cert of parents filed.

43. 5 July 1896 W.W. HICKS 24 yrs single b. Bedford Co VA s/o Wesley & Annie to H.B. PATTERSON 28 yrs single b. Prince Edward Co Va d/o Jackson & ? O: coal mner; by R.C. Fox; REMARKS: col'd.

44. 9 July 1896 A.J. TAYLOR 26 yrs single b. Mercer Co W VA s/o John & Mary to JENNIE SAUNDERS 23 yrs single b. Mercer Co W VA d/o Gordon & Nancy O: farmer; by A.M. Craft.

45. 9 July 1896 WILLIAM HACK 23 yrs single b. Appomattox Co VA s/o Calvin Mason & Margaret Hack to EMMA BOARD 25 yrs div. b. Bedford Co VA d/o Chas & Narcissus Robinson O: coal miner; by J.W. Johnson; REMARKS: col'd.

46. 8 July 1896 ALBERT MOONEY 24 yrs single b. Mercer Co W VA s/o Stonix L. & Susannah to LILLIAN SHELTON 19 yrs angle b. Mercer Co W VA d/o F.H. & S.V. O: carpenter; by r.M. Ashworth; REMARKS: cert of mother.

47. 13 July 1896 WILLIAM G SHREWSBURY 21 yrs single b. Raleigh Co W VA s/o John B. & Elizabeth to MASSIE M. SHREWSBURY 21 yrs single b. Wyoming Co W VA d/o William A. & Allie O: farmer; by W.A. Bailey; REMARKS: affidavit filed.

48. 14 July 1896 BASCOM HALL 19 yrs single b. Bland Co VA s/o Saml H. & Mary S. to LAURA DOVE 18 yrs angle b. Mercer Co W VA d/o Foote W. & Isabella O: farmer; by R.M. Ashworth; REMARKS: Bas Hall sworn & cert filed.

Page 85

1. 14 July 1896 CALVIN REED 22 yrs single b. Montgomery Co VA s/o Wm H. & Bettie to ZENA B. BLANKENSHIP 17 yrs single b. Mercer W VA d/o J.H. & Rachel A. O: railroader; by T.J. Eskridge; REMARKS: J.H. Blankenship present.

2. 21 July 1896 CALVIN SHENALL 20 yrs single b. Smyth Co VA s/o Wm H. & Orrie Jane to ARAMINTA HONAKER 20 yrs single b. Tazewell Co VA d/o W.C. & ? O: farmer; by E.W. Tiller; REMARKS: cert of W.C. Honaker filed, Wm H. Shenall present.

3. 22 July 1896 SCOTT BURKS 22 yrs single b. Wytheville VA s/o Adams & Victoria to HATTIE HERNDON 19 yrs single b. Mercer Co W VA d/o Chas & Mariah O: farmer; by S.E. Houk; REMARKS: consent of mother of bride.

4. 6 Aug 1896 GILBERT L. WALKER 18 yrs single b. Mercer Co W VA s/o Jas B. & Rebecca C. to ELSIE A. McCOMAS 19 yrs single b. Mercer Co W VA d/o R.B. & Oliva A. O: miner; by T.K. Lambert; REMARKS: cert of parents.

5. 26 July 1896 B.V. WHITE 20 yrs single b. Mercer Co W VA s/o Allen & Mary J. to FLORA M. STEELS 17 yrs single b. Meigs Co OH d/o Wm F. & Rhoda O: farmer; by A.J. Thompson; REMARKS: cert of M.J. White & W.F. Steels present.

6. 28 July 1896 S.B. WRIGHT 30 yrs wid. b. Prince Edw Co VA s/o Watson & Jane to MAGGIE BELL 24 yrs single b. Prnce Edw Co VA d/o Havner & Mollie O: miner; by A.M. Craft.

7. 20 July 1896 ELLIS M. BOWINE 25 yrs single b. Grayson Co VA s/o Houstin & Julia to HATTIE NEAL 15 yrs single b. Tazewell Co VA d/o W.C. & Rhoda J. O: stone mason; by W.A.Pearson; REMARKS: cert of W.C. Neal filed.

8. 31 July 1896 W.F.M. BENNETT 24 yrs angle b. Chattanooga TN now living same s/o Jackson & Amanda to MINTA JANE THOMAS 15 yrs single b. Wythe Co VA d/o Giles B. & Rosa L. O: railroader; by E.S. Bettis; REMARKS: cert of G.B. Thomas filed.

9. 3 Aug 1896 HARRY LUCAS 24 yrs single b. Franklin Co OH s/o Jas & Martha to POLLY MULLINS 26 yrs single b. Wyoming Co W VA d/o Jos & Mollie O: painter; by S.E. Houk.

10. 5 Aug 1896 ISAAC GIBERSON 23 yrs single b. Northumberland Co VA s/o James & ? to LULA B. HARRIS 21 yrs single b. Giles Co Va d/o G.A. & Charlotte O: fireman; by Thos C. Shuler; REMARKS: applied for by G.A. Harris, cert filed.

11. 13 Aug 1896 WM NORRIS 24 yrs single b. Giles Co VA s/o Harvey & Emily to ROSA M. PERDUE 22 yrs single b. Mercer Co W VA d/o Isaac & Margaret O: miner; by A.M. Craft; REMARKS: Wm Norris.

12. 13 Aug 1895 ELIJAH C. PAYNE 20 yrs single b. Mercer Co W VA s/o Andrew & Elizth to ADA C. BURGERS 16 yrs single b. Raleigh Co W VA d/o Jas C. & ? O: blacksmith; by John H. Honaker; REMARKS: certificates of parents.

13. 9 Aug 1896 RODK.B. FERGUSON single b. Carter Co TN s/o Andrew & Effie to MOLLIE HOUCHINS div. b. Tazewell Co VA d/o Saml & Jennie Tabor O: plasterer; by E.S. Bettis; REMARKS: copy divorce filed.

14. * * * HACK MELVIN 21 yrs single b. Mercer Co W VA s/o ? & Sarah to S.E. PETTREY 17 yrs single b. Mercer Co W VA d/o Amos L. & Cornelia O: laborer; REMARKS: No Return, cert of parents & J.W. Pennington. (*Note: no date given.)

15. 15 Aug 1896 JAS S. HALL 19 yrs sngle b. Mercer Co W VA s/o Harvey & Lizzie to JULIA HAYWOOD 21 yrs single b. Mercer Co W VA O: laborer; by Arthur S. Thorn; REMARKS: parents present.

16. 22 Aug 1896 HERBERT MAYES 28 yrs single b. Germany s/o Peter & Francis to HATIE STAHL 17 yrs single b. Dolphan Co PA d/o Elias & Susan O: miner; by G.C. Anderson; REMARKS: cert filed.

17. 19 Aug 1896 WH S. AKERS 27 yrs single b. Mrcer Co W VA s/o H.H. & Elizabeth to ALMIRA V. LILLY 19 yrs single b. Mercer Co w VA d/o Enf. & Clarie E. O: merchant; by James W. Tilly; REMARKS: her father present.

18. 2 Sept 1896 D.H. THOMAS 29 yrs single b. Wales now living in Algoma W VA s/o W.H. & Margaret to EMMA L. COOPER 20 yrs single b. Shamorin PA d/o Jno & Maria O: physician; by Norman F. Marshall REMARKS: cert filed.

19. 23 Aug 1896 JOHN H. LESTER 20 yrs 12 mos 9 dys b. Monroe Co W VA now living in Tazewell Co Va s/o W.F. & Mary A. to CLARISY M. GINTHER 17 yrs 2 mos single b. Giles Co VA d/o J.S. & G.Z. O: farmer; by S.B. Vaught; REMARKS: cert filed.

20. 23 Aug 1896 WH J. FRANKLIN 24 yrs single b. Tazewell Co VA s/o John & Victoria to ALICE JOHNSTON 23 yrs single b. Roanoke Co VA d/o John & Alice O: breakman(sic); by R.C. Fox; REMARKS: col'd.

21. 24 Aug 1896 ISAAC B. AUSTN 29 yrs wid. b. Mercer Co W VA s/o I.E. & Malinda to NELLIE V. JOHNSTON 20 yrs single b. VA d/o D.B. & Rosa W. O: carpenter; by W.A. Pearson; REMARKS: cert filed.

22. 24 Aug 1896 JOS W. THOMPSON 20 yrs single b. Mercer Co W VA s/o John D. & Nancy E. to NANNIE E. DUNN 18 yrs single b. Mercer Co W VA d/o John W. & Mary C. O: farmer; by A.J. Thompson; REMARKS: cert of J.W. Dunn filed, applied for by J.D. Thompson.

23. 31 Aug 1896 JACOB EDWARDS 22 yrs single b. Washington Co TN s/o Thomas & Martha J. to MARY J. McINTOSH 21 yrs single b. Washington Co TN s/o Jacob & Mary O: miner; by T.F. Suthers; REMARKS: Jacob Edwards sworn.

24. 28 Aug 1896 WH NUNLEY 30 yrs single b. Pittsylvania Co VA s/o James & Mary J. to JENNIE F. WHITE 27 yrs single b. Roanoke Co VA d/o Taylor & Mary S. O: miner; by J.W. Johnson; REMARKS: col'd.

25. 2 Sept 1896 J.S. HETHERINGTON 25 yrs single b. Mercer Co W VA s/o J.T. & Juliett H. to LULA M. GOODALL 21 yrs single b. Monroe Co W VA O: fireman; by E.S. Bettis.

26. 1 Sept 1896 JNO FLICK 21 yrs single b. Giles Co VA s/o Edward & Ann to JENNIE L. CALDWELL 17 yrs single b. Mercer Co W VA d/o Wm & Louisa O: saw mill; by Arthur S. Thorn; REMARKS: cert filed & sworn.

27. 2 Sept 1896 KELLEY J. LILLY 19 yrs single b. Mercer Co W VA s/o J.K. & Allabamma to BERTHA J. REID 16 yrs single b. Mercer Co W VA d/o Wm F. & Mary E. O: farmer; by W.L. Gantier; REMARKS: cert filed & sworn.

28. 2 Sept 1896 ROBT L. WEAVER 57 yrs wid. b. Hardy Co W VA now living in McDowell Co W VA to NANNIE JANE BELCHER 36 yrs wid. b. Bland Co VA d/o Colby & S. Stowers O: coke boss; by D.A. Daugherty.

29. 2 Sept 1896 HY LEWIS MOORE 22 yrs single b. Floyd Co VA s/o H.G. & Adeline to FLORENCE L. BURGESS 22 yrs single b. Mercer Co W VA d/o Danl E. & Amanda O: bartender; by J.W. Bennett; REMARKS: sworn.

30. 2 Sept 1896 WH LEWIS 24 yrs single b. Chesterfield Co VA s/o Harry & Agnes to LOUISA MORRIS 23 yrs single b. Smythe Co VA d/o John & Ann O: miner; by R.C. Fox; REMARKS: colored.

31. 10 Sept 1896 R.G. CLAYTOR 24 yrs single b. Bedford Co VA now living in McDowell Co W VA s/o Pleasant & Elizabeth to LOCHIE A. YOUNG 21 yrs single b. Franklin Co VA d/o S.H. & Nannie O: coal mining; by A.M. Craft.

32. 9 Sept 1896 DECATUR BROOKMAN 22 yrs single b. Pulaski Co VA s/o Augustus & Rachel to NETTA L. FRENCH 18 yrs single b. Mercer Co w VA d/o W.L. & Louisa Vorg O: farmer; by G.W. Baily; REMARKS: father of wife present.

33. 28 Sept 1896 HENRY A. SOUTHERN 24 yrs single b. Giles Co VA s/o Wm & Rachel to HESTER J. COMER 18 yrs single b. Mercer Co W VA d/o Augustus & Martha O: farmer; by A.J. Thompson; REMARKS: cert of parents.

(NOTE: Entry #34 marked through.)
34. * * * W.R. DRISCOLL 25 yrs to LYDIA C. TALBERT 20 yrs. (*Note: no date given.) **LOOK AT ENTRY #37**

35. 19 Sept 1896 PETER HAGER 25 yrs single b. Bland Co VA s/o Floyd & Cyntha to LULA B. COLLINS 22 yrs single b. Wythe Co VA d/o James & Elizth O: railroader; by E.W. Tiller.

36. 23 Sept 1896 E.L. HARRIS 24 yrs single now living in McDowell Co W VA to DORA JANE BELL 17 yrs single b. Mercer Co W VA d/o Geo W. & Sarah E. O: conductor R.R.; by T.F. Suthers; REMARKS: father present.

37. 23 Sept 1896 W.R. DRISCOLL 25 yrs single b. Allejanie(sic) Co VA s/o Dennis & Virginia E. to LYDIA C. TALBERT 20 yrs single b. Summers Co W VA d/o G.W. & Mary M. O: plasterer; by E.S. Bettis; REMARKS: cert filed.

38. 23 Sept 1896 WH SMITH 30 yrs single b. Buckingham Co VA s/o Wm & Jennie to FANNIE HOLLAND 24 yrs single b. Franklin Co VA d/o Geo & Creasy O: miner; by R.H. McCoy; REMARKS: colored.

39. 27 Sept 1896 ARCHIE S. LAWSON 41 yrs wid. b. Patrick Co VA s/o Wm & Lucy to SARAH BARNES 25 yrs single b. Stokes Co NC d/o Wm & Lucy(sic) O: farmer; by S.E. Houk.

40. 25 Sept 1896 PRESTON SCOTT 18 yrs single b. Mercer Co v VA s/o Pearis & Amanda to ANNIE MILLS 22 yrs single b. England d/o Emily O: farmer; by G.C. Anderson; REMARKS: Gilford Burchett.

41. 27 Sept 1896 WH DILLION 23 yrs single b. mercer Co W VA s/o Wm & Mary to VICIE J.F. HALL 23 yrs wid. b. Tazewell Co VA d/o Wm & Mary Carter O: miner; by S.E. Houk.

42. 21 Sept 1896 JNO C. GODSEY 47 yrs wid. b. Rockingham NC now living in McDowell Co W VA s/o T.C. & Charlotte to HUSSIE SMITH 17 yrs single b. Monroe Co W VA d/o C.P. & Jennie O: carpenter; by T.C. Shuler; REMARKS: father of wife present.

43. 1 Oct 1896 JAS M. NEEL 28 yrs single b. Bland Co VA s/o Robt M. & Martha A. to ARLENIA E. WALKER 29 yrs wid. b. Tazewell Co VA d/o Thos J. Neel & Sarah E.(sic) O: carpenter; by E.W. Tiller.

44. 2 Oct 1896 CALLEY GRAD 22 yrs single b. Carrol Co VA s/o Andrew J. & Maggie to LUCY A. SMITH 19 yrs single b. CarrolCo VA d/o John & Caroline O: farmer; by James W. Tilly; REMARKS: certificate filed.

45. 6 Oct 1896 LE. AUSTIN 68 yrs wid. b. Campbell Co VA s/o Miles & Macy to N.K. BAILEY 64 yrs single b. Mercer Co W VA d/o Philip Bailey O: carpenter; by D.N. Saunders.

46. 13 Oct 1896 GABE BENNETT 28 yrs single b. Surrey Co NC now living in Tazewell Co VA s/o Jno m. & Nancy to ALICE SWADER 23 yrs single b. Mercer Co W VA d/o Alex & Cassie O: railroader; by A.M. Craft.

47. 7 Oct 1896 M.C. LANE 19 yrs single b. Nelson Co VA now living in Montgomery Co VA s/o H.N. & Georgia to LULA SNEAD 20 yrs single b. Giles Co VA d/o A.J. & Mary C. O: machinist; by J.W. Bennett.

48. 14 Oct 1896 ALONZO B. SIMPSON 19 yrs single b. Mercer Co W VA s/o James & Eliza to LUVERNIE HUBBARD 16 yrs single b. Mercer Co W VA d/o P.A. & Lucy Ann O: farmer; by James W. Tilly; REMARKS: consent of guardian.

Page 86

1. 14 Oct 1896 E. JACKSON VIPPERMAN 54 yrs wid. b. Patrick Co VA s/o Danl & ? to JANE HICKS 50 yrs single b. Mercer Co W VA d/o ? & Nancy O: farmer; by D.N. Saunders; REMARKS: applied for by Jas Tanner & sworn.

2. 14 Oct 1896 ALLEN L. BRATTON 25 yrs single b. Mercer Co W VA s/o Thos & Mary Elizth to MARY J. GOTT 21 yrs single b. Mercer Co W VA d/o Andrew & Louemona J. O: farmer; by S.E. Houk.

3. 21 Oct 1896 ERNEST M. CASH 23 yrs single b. Nelson Co VA s/o J.R. & Annie E. to VIOLA M. CLENDONEN 24 yrs single b. Mercer Co W VA d/o Robt G. & Mary O: loco engineer; by I.C. Shuler.

4. 24 Oct 1896 JOHN H. DILLION 21 yrs single b. Monroe Co WVA s/o wm & Mary to LUEMMA VICTORIA FLETCHER 26 yrs single b. Mercer Co W VA d/o Isaac & Sarah E. O: farmer & laborer; by G.W. Bailey.

(NOTE: Entry #5 marked through)
5. * * * DELAWARE PAGE 26 yrs to OLLIE ROPPY 29 yrs. (*Note: no date given.)

6. 29 Oct 1896 WM R. CHRISTIAN 24 yrs single b. Halifax Co VA now living in McDowell Co W VA s/o Arthur & Fanny to NANNIE B. ABINGDON 22 yrs single b. Roanoke Co VA d/o Peter & Lucinda O: miner; by J.W. Johnson; REMARKS: colored.

7. 30 Oct 1896 JNO A. DAULTON 29 yrs single b. Carroll CoVA s/o ? & Polly to KANSAS S. COMPTON 16 yrs single b. Mercer Co W VA d/o Feilden T. & Berthilda O: farmer; by W.H. Ayres; REMARKS: father present.

8. 28 Oct 1896 NOAH BALL 24 yrs single b. Carroll Co VA s/o ? & Cath Ball to LUCINDA B. PAULEY 28 yrs single b. Mercer Co W VA d/o Feilden T. & Berthilda O: farmer; by W.H. Ayres; REMARKS: father present.

9. 29 Nov 1896 NELSON JAMES 26 yrs single b. Campbell Co VA s/o Thomas & Sarah to RESSIE ROBERSON 17 yrs single b. Patrick Co VA d/o John H. & Julia O: miner; by J.H. Johnson; REMARKS: colored.

10. 4 Nov 1896 W.T. GEORGE 24 yrs single b. Summers Co W VA s/o F.M. & Annie to LILLY D. FLETCHER 17 yrs single b. Mercer Co W VA d/o Jas H. & Mary Ann O: farmer; by T. Goodwyn; REMARKS: father of bride present.

11. 5 Nov 1896 WM D. PENDLETON 25 yrs single b. Mercer Co W VA s/o D.B. & Nancy Va to FANNIE M. MILLS 20 yrs single b. Mercer Co W VA d/o C.W. & E.A. O: merchant; by J.O. Cassaday; REMARKS: cert of parents filed.

12. 5 Nov 1896 CHARLES W. HARRY 26 yrs single b. Mercer Co W VA s/o Calvin & Mary E. to MATTIE B. HALE 24 yrs single b. Tazewell Co VA d/o C.A. & Julide O: farmer; by W.H. Ayres.

13. 11 Nov 1896 C.R. MATHEWS 21 yrs single b. Tazewell Co VA s/o F.H. & Huldah J. to RENA O. GREER 22 yrs single b. Franklin Co VA d/o J.L. & E.A. Greer O: farmer; by J.O. Cassaday.

14. 11 Nov 1896 W.J. COMER 71 yrs wid. b. Monroe Co W VA s/o John & Jane to MARTHA HILL 54 yrs wid. b. Floyd Co VA O: farmer; by F. Goodwyn.

15. 11 Nov 1896 PHILIP MELANCHON PEERMAN 37 yrs single b. Campbell Co VA now living same s/o Wm H. & Catharine S. to ELIZABETH M. KITTS 23 yrs single b. Bland Co VA d/o Peter & Mary A. O: farmer; by S.E. Houk.

16. 18 Nov 1896 SAML J. EVANS 26 yrs single b. Schuylkill Co PA now living McDowell Co W VA s/o Jno B. & Sarah A. to ADA P. CAWLEY 21 yrs single b. Monroe Co VA d/o L.A. & Pearl O: mechanic; by J.B. Ward; REMARKS: affidavit filed.

17. 18 Nov 1896 GEO J. HEDRICK 38 yrs div. b. Tazewell Co VA s/o Asken & Cathrine to FANNIE WARD 22 yrs single b. Pittsylvania Co VA d/o Geo. & Eliza O: preacher; by J.W. Johnson; REMARKS: copy decree filed, col'd.

18. 2 Dec 1896 A.B. COBURN 39 yrs wid. b. Monroe Co W VA now living in Giles Co VA s/o Wm T. & Sarah E. to LEAH BELCHER 24 yrs single b. Mercer Co W VA d/o Hilton & Clementine O: merchant; by E.S. Bettis.

19. 19 Nov 1896 J.W. McKINNEY 28 yrs single b. Mercer Co W VA s/o P.B. & Elizabeth to NANCY ALICE PALMER 23 yrs single b. Floyd Co VA d/o Eden & Nancy O: farmer; by J.H. McClaugherty; REMARKS: certify copy filed.

20. 25 Nov 1896 H.S. BROYLES 21 yrs single b. Mercer Co W VA s/o Leroy & Elizabeth to MARY HEDRICK 19 yrs single b. Mercer Co W VA d/o Rufus & Biddy O: farmer; by W.H. Ayres.

21. 24 Nov 1896 WM E. WHITE 21 yrs single b. Mercer Co W VA s/o Jas A. & D.H. to ETTA M. TILLER 21 yrs single b. Mercer Co W VA d/o Jno & ? O: railroader; by F. Goodwyn; REMARKS: W.E. White sworn.

22. 25 Nov 1896 JAMES KENNEDY 35 yrs single b. Franklin Co VA to CAROLINE BLESSING 30 yrs wid. b. Mercer Co W VA O: coal miner; by G.W. Bailey; REMARKS: applied for by T.F. Dillon.

23. 30 Nov 1896 F.H. ATKINS 25 yrs single b. Smith Co VA s/o Jackson & Susan to CORDELIA HOWNEN 25 yrs single b. Smith Co VA d/o Chas & Eliza O: painter; by W.A. Pearson.

24. 2 Dec 1896 R.T. CHRISTIAN 25 yrs wid. b. Montgomery Co VA s/o W.W. & Carrie T. to MARGARET L. YOUNG 17 yrs single b. Tazewell Co VA d/o Robt W. & Margt A. O: engineer; by W.A. Pearson; REMARKS: cert of R.W. Young filed.

25. 2 Dec 1896 C.W. THORNTON 28 yrs single b. Mercer Co W VA s/o Wm M. & Eliza J. to IRENE M. BIRD 22 yrs single b. Mercer Co W VA d/o J.S.H. & Lizzie O: conductor; by R.H. Ashworth.

26. 10 Dec 1896 J.T. HALL 38 yrs wid. b. Floyd Co VA s/o Henry & Allie to DEANEY NORRIS 24 yrs single b. Mercer Co W VA d/o John & Emily O: coal miner; by A.M. Craft.

27. 6 Dec 1896 IRA L. WHITE 21 yrs single b. Mercer Co W VA s/o T.H. & Z.D. to MARTHA A. RICHARDS 18 yrs single b. Franklin Co VA d/o B.W. & S.M. O: machinist; by E.S. Bettis.

28. 7 Dec 1896 HENDERSON M. PENNINGTON 39 yrs div. b. Mercer Co W VA s/o Wm K. & Catherine to TNIE HELVIN 17 yrs single b. Mercer Co W VA d/o N.B. & Ann O: farmer; by F. Goodwyn; REMARKS: cert of B. Helvin filed.

29. 9 Dec 1896 W.D. PENNINGTON 21 yrs single b. Mercer Co W VA s/o Levi & S.A. to FLORA JANE MEADOWS 17 yrs single b. Mercer Co W VA d/o ? & Mary E. O: farmer; by a.J. Thompson; REMARKS: certificates of parents filed.

30. 16 Dec 1896 CHAS J. PEDIGO 26 yrs single b. Franklin Co VA s/o Saml E. & Susan to ALICE BELLE STEPHENS 20 yrs single b. Giles Co VA d/o S.B. & I.M. O: wagoner; by E.S. Bettis; REMARKS: certificates of parents filed.

31. 22 Dec 1896 EDW H. TILLER 21 yrs single b. Mercer Co W VA s/o Wm & Louisa Caldwell to LAURA M. BONHAM 17 yrs single b. Smith Co VA d/o Jno & Amanda O: farmer; by F. Goodwyn; REMARKS: cert of parents filed.

32. 23 Dec 1896 JAMES COX 26 yrs single b. Campbell Co VA s/o Absolum & Judia to PULINA F. MOORE 22 yrs single b. Appomatox Co VA d/o Peter & Sue O: miner; by G.W. Alexander; REMARKS: col'd.

33. 23 Dec 1896 ALX JENNINS 34 yrs single b. Carrol Co VA s/o Riley & Rebecca to SARAH J. WALLACE 22 yrs single b. Carrol Co VA d/o Mary O: farmer; by James W. Tilly; REMARKS: Rob Tabor.

34. 23 Dec 1896 WILLIAM ADAMS 23 yrs single b. Pulaski Co VA s/o Pleasant & Minerva to ANNIE GARDNER 21 yrs single b. Mercer Co W VA d/o Rush & Lina O: farmer; by Arthur S. Thorn; REMARKS: col'd.

35. 23 Dec 1896 GEORGE EDWARD BAXTER 21 yrs single b. Mercer Co W VA s/o George & Ann to ADA GARDNER 17 yrs single b. Mercer Co W VA d/o Rush & Lina O: teamster; by Arthur S. Thorn; REMARKS: col'd.,

36. 24 Dec 1896 GEO MOORE 47 yrs wid. b. Bedford Co VA now living in Pulaski Co VA s/o Jesse & Minty to MARY CHOCKLET 30 yrs single b. Giles CoVA d/o Wm & Cynthia O: farmer; by J.D. Leftwich; REMARKS: col'd.

37. 26 Dec 1896 CHARLES TYLER 35 yrs single b. Rockbridge Co VA now living in McDowell Co W VA s/o S.P & Sarah Tyler to ANNIE PRICE 22 yrs single b. Montgomery Co VA d/o Thos F. & Edith M. O: coal miner; by R.A. kelly; REMARKS: applied for by G.W. Hale.

38. 28 Dec 1896 THOMAS ATKINS 23 yrs single b. Franklin Co VA now living in Salem VA s/o Daniel & Patsey to MARGIE ROBERSON 21 yrs single b. Giles Co VA d/o John & Charlott O: railroader; by O.T. Harris; REMARKS: colored, certificate.

39. 1 Jan 1897 P.J. LILLY 23 yrs single b. Summers Co W Va now living same s/o John S. & Virginia to M.E. MANN 19 yrs single b. Summers Co W VA d/o Andrew & N.C. O: farmer; by J.J. Meador; REMARKS: cert of mother filed.

40. 30 Dec 1896 MARION T. ROBERTS 31 yrs single b. Nelson Co VA s/o H.H. & L.J. to LIZZIE W. ABOS 30 yrs single b. NY s/o Wm H. & S.P. O: postle(sic) clerk; by S.E. Houk.

41. 31 Dec 1896 N.L. BOLIN 23 yrs single b. Mercer Co W VA s/o J.J. & Isabell to M.J. LILLY 23 yrs single b. Mercer Co w VA d/o S.P. & Sarah E. O: farmer; by James W. Lilly.

Page 87

1. 25 Jan 1897 DELAWARE L. PAGE 26 yrs single b. Buckingham VA now living in McDowell Co W VA s/o Harold & Louisa Page to OLLIE MURRY 29 yrs div. b. Pulaski Co VA d/o Sanders & Sarah Rippey O: miner; by G.W. Alexander; REMARKS: col'd.

2. 4 Jan 1897 HENRY C. BRINKLEY 19 yrs single b. Mercer Co W VA s/o Hen & Rachel Brinkley to LOU P. THORNTON 15 yrs single b. Mercer Co W VA d/o Henry & A.M. Thornton O: farmer; by L. Goodwyn.

3. 6 Jan 1897 ADAM BRANCH 23 yrs single b. Prince Edward VA s/o Adam & Jane Branch to EDNA BROWN 19 yrs single b. Tazewell Co VA d/o Andrew & Fannie Brown O: railroading; by R.C. Fox; REMARKS: colored.

4. 14 Jan 1897 JOHN MITCHEL 25 yrs single b. Franklin Co VA s/o Jack & Elvira Mitchel to JOCKEY CUNNINGHAM 17 yrs single b. Franklin Co VA d/o Miles & Lucy Cunningham O: mining; by G.W. Alexander; REMARKS: colored.

5. 13 Jan 1897 JOHN W. AMOS 27 yrs single b. Floyd Co VA s/o James W. & Elvira F. Amos to EVIE M. WOOLWINE 17 yrs single b. Montgomery Co VA d/o Ruben P. & Sallie J. Woolwine O: railroading; by W.A. Pearson.

6. 14 Jan 1897 JOHN W. FOSTER 23 yrs single b. Mercer Co W VA s/o Hatison & Katie Foster to ROSA BELL AKERS 32 yrs wid. O: farmer; by Granville Houchins.

7. 23 Jan 1897 ERASTUS WILEY 19 yrs single b. Mercer Co W VA s/o Albert & Louisa Wiley to HESTER PEARLY WHITE abt. 16 yrs wid. b. Mercer Co W VA d/o John A. White & Mary J. O: farmer; by W.L Gautier.

8. 21 Jan 1897 JESSIE C. HATCHER 44 yrs wid. b. Mercer Co W VA s/o Elijah & Jemima Hatcher to MATILDA SHREWSBURY 39 yrs wid. b. Mercer Co W VA d/o Isaac & Mary J. Meadow O: farmer; by Drewry Farley.

9. 27 Jan 1897 THOMAS B. GODFREY 20 yrs single b. Mercer Co W VA s/o A.B. & S.M. Godfrey to JANETTE A.D. SHREWSBURY 17 yrs single b. Mercer Co W VA d/o Eli B. & M. Shrewsbury O: farmer; by L.H. Bailey.

10. 27 Jan 1897 ROBERT W. AUSTIN 23 yrs single b. Campbell Co VA s/o Anthony & Ellen Austin to JENNIE B. KESLER 22 yrs single b. Franklin Co VA d/o James & Jannie Kesler O: railroading; by R.C. Fox; REMARKS: col'd.

11. 3 Feb 1897 ROBERT W. JORDAN 22 yrs single b. Montgomery AL s/o Catlett & Dolly Jordan to MARGARET SANDERS 21 yrs single b. Christiansbury VA d/o Calvin & Jemima Sanders O: railroading; by R.C. Fox; REMARKS: col'd.

12. 27 Jan 1897 BISHOP A. AYERS 38 yrs wid. b. Bedford Co VA s/o Thomas & Jenne Ayers to EMMA V. HARE 37 yrs single b. Giles Co VA O: railroading; by S.E. Houk; REMARKS: white.

13. 2 Feb 1897 JAMES SANDERS 31 yrs wid. b. Franklin Co VA s/o Gustavus & Amy Sanders to WILLIE WHALES 21 yrs single b. Roanoke VA d/o James & Lucy Whales O: miner; by J.W. Johnson; REMARKS: col'd.

14. 10 Feb 1897 ARMINE WILEY 19 yrs single b. Mercer Co W VA s/o Josie Perdue to ROBERTIE H. KING 15 yrs single b. Floyd Co VA d/o H.A. King & L.E. King O: farmer; by W.L Gautier.

15. 11 Feb 1897 ROBERT GRIGGSBY 24 yrs single b. Bedford Co VA s/o Edmond & Margaret Griggsby to JENNIE CRIDER 16 yrs single b. Pitsylvania Co VA d/o J.W. & Catherine Crider O: miner; by G.W. Alexander; REMARKS: col'd.

16. 17 Feb 1897 ADAM H. CAPERTON 35 yrs div. b. Mercer Co W VA now living in Summers Co W VA s/o O.H. & Martha H. Caperton to LOCHIE J. WILEY 25 yrs single b. Mercer Co w VA d/o John A. & Mahala J. Wiley O: farmer; by J.W. Bennett.

17. 17 Feb 1897 GEORGE W. ALVIS 27 yrs wid. b. Mercer Co W VA s/o John H. & Margaret J. to ELIZA JANE PENNINGTON 19 yrs single b. Mercer Co W VA d/o John F. & Susan C. O: farmer; by James T. Tabor.

18. 21 Feb 1897 JAMES H. KEISTER 24 yrs single b. Floyd Co VA s/o James B. & Nannie to STELLAR S. TABOR 17 yrs angle b. Tazewell Co VA d/o S.G. & Virginia O: farmer; by E.S. Bettis.

19. 24 Feb 1897 GEORGE W. CHATTING 21 yrs single b. Mercer Co W VA s/o W.W. & Julia to MAGIE M. HOBBS 20 yrs single b. Giles Co VA d/o W.S. & D.C. O: farmer; by R.H. Ashworth.

20. 4 Mar 1897 O.H. SNIDER 22 yrs single b. Mercer Co W VA s/o L.A. to CARRIE T. GOODSON 19 yrs single b. Floyd Co VA d/o Floyd & Sallie O: farmer; by W.L Gautier.

21. 23 Feb 1897 JOSEPH W. WILLIS 24 yrs single b. Giles Co VA s/o J.T. & N.J. to MINTIE E. MEADOWS 34 yrs wid. b. Montgomery Co VA O: railroader; by W.A. Pearson.

22. 26 Feb 1897 HENRY ROBINSON 38 yrs single b. Henry Co VA s/o John & Rachel Robinson to ELLA B. PARKER 21 yrs single b. Patrick Co VA d/o Saml H. & Mary J. O: railroader; by O.T. Harris; REMARKS: col'd.

23. 24 Feb 1897 ELIJAH MACK 24 yrs single b. Prince Ed Co VA s/o John & Caroline to WILLIE BROWN22 yrs single b. Bedford Co VA d/o John & Ella O: railroading; by R.C. Fox; REMARKS: col'd.

24. 24 Feb 1897 HENRY C. GARRETT 22 yrs single b. Scott Co VA s/o Jim & Rachel to NANNIE PULLERHAN 21 yrs div. b. Pulaski Co VA d/o John & ? O: railroading; by R.C. Fox; REMARKS: col'd.

25. 26 Feb 1897 MINOR B. BARTLEY 30 yrs single b. Orange Co VA s/o Henry A. & H. to EMMA S. BYRD 27 yrs single b. Franklin Co VA d/o Arch A. & Francis O: railroading; by W.A. Pearson.

26. 3 Mar 1897 J.J. VANCE 23 yrs single b. Cook Co TN s/o Wm & Margaret to IDA M. BOWLING 16 yrs single b. Tazewell Co VA d/o G.W. & M.J. O: miner; by D.A. Ramey.

27. 1 Mar 1897 STEPHEN F. TESTERMAN 25 yrs single b. Ash Co NC s/o Stephen & Susan to LEW BOOSE 18 yrs single b. Montgomery Co VA d/o W.G. & N.A. O: railroading; by W.A. Pearson.

28. 3 Mar 1897 K.H. SMITH 23 yrs single b. Giles Co VA s/o G.H. & E.V. to ALICE V. SHIELDS 16 yrs single d/o A.M. & Mary A. O: farmer; by J.O. Cassaday.

29. 4 Mar 1897 WILLIAM SAUNDERS 34 yrs wid. b. Franklin Co VA s/o Chris & Emma to LULA MANNS 24 yrs single b. Montgomery Co VA d/o Lewis & Martha O: laborer; by S.M. Grimes; REMARKS: col'd.

30. 17 Mar 1897 E.W. BONHAM 27 yrs single b. Summers Co W VA now living in McDowell Co VA s/o A.P & A.J. to ROMA A. SMITH 23 yrs single b. Mercer Co W VA d/o H.A. & H.M. O: carpenter; by R.A. Kelly.

31. 17 Mar 1897 J.L. WYGAL 38 yrs single b. Pulaski Co VA s/o J.G.W. & M.W. to PATTIE DUNLAP 26 yrs single b. Washington Co VA O: laborer; by E.S. Bettis.

32. 16 Mar 1897 J.H. SNEED 21 yrs single b. Mercer Co W VA s/o James & Mary V. to SARAH E. LAWSON 22 yrs div. b. Summers Co W VA d/o ? & Rosa Lawson O: farmer; by James W. Lilly.

33. 19 Mar 1897 RUFUS A. LUSK 19 yrs single b. Mercer Co W VA s/o E.C. & D.M. to NORA BELL HARMAN 19 yrs single b. Mercer Co w VA d/o A.J. & L. O: miner; by John H. Honaker.

34. 19 Mar 1897 WM EDWARDS 38 yrs wid. b. Washington Co TN to AURORA JOHNSON 28 yrs single b. Grayson Co VA d/o T.J. & M.A. O: miner; by D.A. Ramey.

35. * * * NICHOLAS BIBY 84 yrs wid. b. Stokes Co NC s/o John & Nancy to MARY PENNINGTON 17 yrs single b. Giles Co VA d/o ? & Rozenia Pennington O: laborer; REMARKS: Not Returned. (*Note: no date given.)*NOTE: See entry #45.*

36. 24 Mar 1897 CLAUDE KERNS 22 yrs single b. PA s/o H.& S. to SUSAN J. BALDWIN 22 yrs single b. SC O: fireman; by S.H. Greener.

37. 24 Mar 1897 CHARLES R. COGER 24 yrs single b. Franklin Co VA s/o S.& A. to L.R. HARMAN 21 yrs single b. Tazewell Co VA O: railroading; by R.C. Fox; REMARKS: col'd.

38. 26 Mar 1897 G.W. TAYLOR 26 yrs single b. Prince Edward Co VA s/o James & Harriett to SALLIE TUCKER 27 yrs single b. Franklin Co VA O: R.R. brakeman; by J.D. Leftwich; REMARKS: col'd.

39. 26 Mar 1897 DAVID HARRIS 25 yrs single b. Tazewell Co VA s/o John & Ellen to JENNIE HOLLAND 24 yrs single b. Montgomery Co VA O: railroading; by J.D. Leftwich; REMARKS: col'd.

40. 26 Mar 1897 H.L. MEADOWS 22 yrs single s/o Hunt to LIDA BASHAM 16 yrs single d/o D.A. & Manerva J. O: farmer; by James W. Lilly.

41. 27 Mar 1897 CHAS J.W. HUFFMAN 30 yrs single b. Montgomery Co VA s/o John & Elvira Huffman to LETHA A. SNIDER 26 yrs single b. Mercer Co W VA d/o Enom & Rhoda Ann O: farmer; by James T. Tabot.

42. 1 Apr 1897 EUGENE B. SEANLAND 26 yrs single b. Montgomery Co VA s/o Nathan & Sallie to NANNIE E. BROWN 23 yrs single b. Tazewell Co VA d/o Frank & Mary O: stone mason; by W.A. Greener.

43. 30 Mar 1897 M.E. KARNES 36 yrs single b. Mercer Co w VA s/o H.A. & R. to LUCETTIE P. HATCHER 18 yrs single b. Mercer Co W VA d/o ? & N.E. O: farming; by Wm B. Cook.

44. 1 Apr 1897 LEWIS McNUTT 21 yrs single b. Mercer Co w VA s/o Allen & Emma to SUSAN CALANDER 22 yrs single b. Mercer Co W VA d/o Wm & Ann O: farming; by D.N. Saunders; REMARKS: col'd.

45. 10 Apr 1897 NICHOLAS BIBY 84 yrs wid. b. Stokes Co NC s/o John & Nancy to MARY PENNINGTON 17 yrs single b. Giles Co VA d/o ? & Rozena Pennington O: laborer; by D.A. Ramey.

46. 5 Apr 1897 W.T. BOWMAN 23 yrs single b. Patrick Co VA s/o Peter & Hattie to MARY E. GLETCHER 22 yrs single b. Mercer Co W VA d/o Isaac & Sarah E. O: farming; by John H. Honaker.

47. 7 Apr 1897 KING WIRGHT 38 yrs to LIZZIE ANDREWS 25 yrs; by G.N. Alexander.

Page 88

48. 7 Apr 1897 THOS W. BAILEY 28 yrs div. b. McDowell Co W VA s/o E.P. & Mary A. Bailey to PATRA M. JENKINS 30 yrs single b. Bedford Co VA d/o O.H. & Tabitha Jenkins O: farming; by Jno C. Reed.

49. 7 Apr 1897 LAFAYETT F. TURNER 34 yrs wid. b. Tazewell Co VA s/o P. & Susan to M.L. CARPER 24 yrs single b. Mercer Co w VA d/o B.P & Martha O: RR; by W.A. Pearson.

50. 8 Apr 1897 WILLIAM HENRY FARMER 23 yrs single b. Mercer Co W VA to MARY FRANCIS THOMAS 15 yrs single b. Mercer Co W VA d/o Wm H. & Ollie A. O: farmer; by T.H. McClaugherty.

51. 10 Apr 1897 C.W. BROWN 21 yrs single b. Ash Co NC s/o Jim & Ellen to DELLER C. GRIM 16 yrs single b. Mercer Co W VA d/o Peter & Martha a. O: farming; by G.C. Anderson.

52. 14 Apr 1897 H.D. PENNINGTON 20 yrs single b. Monroe Co W VA s/o W.M. & Nancy to ARDELIA L. WILEY 21 yrs single b. Mercer Co W VA O: farming; by W.L Gautier.

53. 12 Apr 1897 E.W. ATKINSON 21 yrs single b. Floyd Co VA s/o L.F. & ? to M.C. CROFT 22 yrs single b. PA d/o D.H. & T.C. O: stenographer; by W.A. Pearson.

54. 13 Apr 1897 J.W. LINDSAY 27 yrs single b. Pulaski Co VA s/o J.L.C. & Nancy to L.B. FISHER 33 yrs wid. b. Caroll Co VA d/o James & ? O: RR conductor; by L.M. Broyles.

55. 14 Mar 1897 W.M. MUNSEY 21 yrs single b. Mercer Co W VA s/o J.L. & Sarah to COUSBY T. BAILEY 24 yrs single b. Tazewell Co VA d/o Z.H. & E. O: farmer; by John H. Honaker.

56. 15 Apr 1897 ROBT H. WILLIAMS 26 yrs single b. Giles Co VA s/o B.P & F.E. Williams to ROSE M. SHELTON 23 yrs single b. Mercer Co w VA d/o ? & M.E. Shelton O: farmer; by E.W. Tiller.

57. 22 Apr 1897 ROBERT SULLIVAN 30 yrs single b. Washington Co VA to M. DELLA GEARHEART 25 yrs single b. Floyd co VA d/o H.L & Sarah O: laborer; by D.A. Ramey.

58. 21 Apr 1897 JAMES B. HUBBARD 21 yrs single b. Mercer Co W VA s/o Payton A. & L.A. to CORA L. AKERS 18 yrs single b. Mercer Co W VA d/o H.H. & Lizie O: farmer; by James W. Lilly.

59. 22 Apr 1897 LEANDER J. LILLY 21 yrs single b. Raleigh Co W VA s/o A.E. & Adaline to ELIZABETH S. CUX 28 yrs single b. Summers Co W VA d/o Mathew & Mary O: farmer; by James W. Lilly.

60. 28 Apr 1897 W.S. HONAKER 27 yrs single b. Mercer Co w VA s/o W.C. & S.A. to CLORIE E. STUMP 20 yrs single b. Floyd Co VA d/o J.B. & S.M. O: carpenter; by John H. Honaker.

61. 27 Apr 1897 ANDERSON FRANKLIN 24 yrs single b. Prince Edward Co VA s/o Thos & Jennie Franklin to BESSIE L. BANKS 20 yrs single b. VA d/o Geo & Adaline Banks O: railroader; by R.C. Fox.

62. 29 Apr 1897 JNO HENRY KENNEDY 37 yrs wid. Franklin Co VA s/o J.L. & Mary Kennedy to ANGELINE HEREDITH 22 yrs wid. b. Mercer Co W VA d/o Jerry & Cynthia Poe O: farmer; by D.N. Saunders.

63. 29 Apr 1897 ELISHA BURTON 62 yrs single b. giles Co VA s/o Cobe & Lucinda to ELLEN T. HYLTON 40 yrs single b. Floyd Co VA O: farmer; by Denison O. Baldwin.

64. 30 Apr 1897 C.S.W. BROWN 21 yrs single b. NC s/o J.H. & Georgia to PRISCILLA CONNER 23 yrs single b. VA d/o McCracken O: barber; by R.C. Fox.

65. 30 Apr 1897 WM E. LEWIS 23 yrs single b. NE s/o Lewis to BIRDY KILMER 20 yrs single b. VA d/o Mollie Kilmer O: blacksmith; by W.A. Pearson.

66. 2 May 1897 J.E. APSHER 52 yrs single b. Tazewell Co VA now living same s/o C. & Celina to CATHERINE LEWEY 51 yrs wid. O: farmer; by E.W. Tiller.

67. 8 May 1897 CHARLES PRESTON 28 yrs single to JULIA HOWARD 19 yrs single; by G.N. Alexander.

68. 5 May 1897 THOS W. SUITER 22 yrs single b. Bland Co VA s/o Wm & Sarah J. to LOTTIE T. CHRISTIAN 20 yrs single b. Tazewell Co VA d/o R.B. & Elizabeth O: plumber; by L.H. Broyles.

69. 8 May 1897 GEO WOLFE 23 yrs single b. Albany NJ to VIRGILLA G. FAULKNER 18 yrs single b. Mercer Co W VA d/o H.M. & M.D. Faulkner O: bookkeeper; REMARKS: No Return, returned April 1st, (18)98.

70. 5 May 1897 GORDAN J. HUGHES 25 yrs single b. Mercer Co W VA now living in Summers Co W VA s/o H.J. & A.A. Hughes to RACHEL C. GORE 19 yrs angle b. Mercer Co W VA d/o H.F. & S.R. Gore O: merchant; by J.P. Campbell.

71. 9 May 1897 JAMES HOLLAWAY 22 yrs wid. b. Franklin Co VA s/o C.E. & E.A. to ROSA A. SHREWSBURY 21 yrs single b. Mercer Co W VA d/o Phillip & Margaret O: farming; by G.H. Johnston.

72. 6 May 1897 J.L.L. HOY 28 yrs single b. Augusta Co VA now living in Stanton VA s/o LL. & S.M. to MILDRED R. SHOTH 26 yrs single b. Augusta Co VA d/o D.W. & L.B. O: miller; by L.H. Broyles.

73. 11 May 1897 A.M. STEWART 22 yrs single b. Montgomery Co VA now living same to MARTHA O. DOYLE 18 yrs single b. Mercer Co W VA d/o Wm M. & S.E. O: RR man; by A.M. Lambert.

74. 13 May 1897 EDWARD HALE 22 yrs single b. Giles Co VA now living same s/o J.A. & J.B. to NORA A. ALVIS 20 yrs single b. Mercer Co W VA d/o John H. & Josephine O: lawyer; by James T. Tabor.

75. 13 May 1897 C.A. CARTER 25 yrs div. b. Tazewell Co VA to SARAH A. WILEY 24 yrs single b. Mercer Co W VA d/o Allen & Louisa O: farmer; by R.H. Ashworth.

76. 15 May 1897 JOHN CLTER(sic) 40 yrs wid. b. Smythe Co VA s/o Wm & Jane to EADY SHULL 40 yrs wid. b. Russell Co VA O: farmer; by L.H. Broyles.

77. 15 May 1897 J.E. SHEFFEY 22 yrs single b. Abington VA s/o Thomas & Jane to NANNIE R. THOMPSON 21 yrs single b. Graham VA O: barber; by S.H. Gaines.

78. 19 May 1897 CHAS W. MARTIN 19 yrs single b. Mercer Co W VA s/o W.A. & Virginia to LILLY B.P. GAUTIER 16 yrs single b. Mercer Co W VA d/o Rufus A. & Alisa O: farmer; by W.L Gautier.

79. 19 May 1897 A.W.H. MARTIN 22 yrs single b. Mercer Co W VA s/o W.E. & Victoria to OLIVE WILEY 16 yrs single b. Mercer Co W VA d/o Allen & Louisa O: farmer; by B.H. Ashworth.

80. 14 July 1897 D.A. SNIDER 24 yrs single b. Mercer Co W VA s/o W.R. & D. to L. VICTORIA BIRD 22 yrs wid. b. Mercer Co W VA d/o Taylor & Mary O: merchant; by W.L Gautier.

81. 27 May 1897 WALTER S. DAVIS 23 yrs single b. Mercer Co W VA s/o Wm & Nancy to NINNIE H. HEADOWS 18 yrs single b. Mercer Co W VA d/o Henry & Sarah O: farmer; by L. Goodwyn.

82. 26 May 1897 A.D. READ 26 yrs single b. South Boston VA s/o Alfred & Emma to MARTHA ORR 18 yrs single b. Franklin Co VA d/o Sam & Margaret O: miner; by S.N. Patterson.

83. 3 June 1897 JAMES SAUL 28 yrs single b. Italy to LUCY A. DELP 19 yrs single b. Mercer Co W VA d/o E. & Lucy O: RR; by N.H. Ayers.

84. 2 June 1897 ED B. GARNETT 22 yrs single b. Smith Co VA s/o S.W. & Ellen T. to CARRIE D. GARRETT 22 yrs single b. Montgomery Co VA d/o ? & B.S. O: RR; by S.B. Vaught.

85. 7 June 1897 EDWARD J. SHAWVER 24 yrs single b. Tazewell Co VA s/o J.H. & Alice to ANNIE V. EVANS 22 yrs angle b. Pulaski Co VA d/o Joseph & S.A. O: RR; by L.H. Broyles.

86. 13 June 1897 EMANUEL S. WARWICK 24 yrs single b. Washington Co VA s/o Richd & Anna Warwick to NANNIE B. ROSS 22 yrs single b. Stokes Co NC d/o Wm & Anna Ross O: barber; by G.T. Wright; REMARKS: col'd.

87. 15 June 1897 THOMAS PEAKS 29 yrs wid. b. Nelson Co VA s/o Clayborne & Amanda to SARAH WASHINGTON 23 yrs single b. Wythe Co VA d/o Ed & ? Washington O: railroader; by J.D. Leftwich; REMARKS: col'd.

88. 19 June 1897 LONNIE L. LILLY 30 yrs single b. Mercer Co W VA s/o J.A. & Hit. Lilly to H. SUE CONIMACK 30 yrs wid. b. Greenbrier Co W VA d/o John & ? Yates O: physician; by J.J. Meador.

89. 24 June 1897 GARNET JACKSON 23 yrs single b. Prince Edward Co VA s/o Stephen & Bettie to SALLY A. BOWLES 23 yrs single b. Richmond VA d/o Richd & Melvina O: laborer; by G.W. Alexander; REMARKS: col'd.

90. 23 June 1897 FLETCHER J. HARPER 28 yrs single b. Harpers Ferry to VINIA HARRISON 18 yrs single b. Reidaville NC d/o ? & Caroline O: minister; by R.H. McKay; REMARKS: col'd.

91. 26 June 1897 JOHN TATURN 36 yrs single b. Rockingham Co NC s/o Coleman & Hannah to CALLIE DYLA 25 yrs single b. Wythe Co VA d/o Jeff & Ellen Dyla O: miner; by M.S. Simmons; REMARKS: col'd.

92. 19 June 1897 WM L SHORT 24 yrs single b. Roanoke Co VA s/o G.W. & Nannie Short to SALLY J. EDWARDS 25 yrs wid. b. Mercer Co W VA d/o J.K.P. & Paulina Bailey O: groceryman; by E.W. Tiller.

93. 20 June 1897 JAS B. WOOD 22 yrs single b. Patrick Co VA s/o W.T. & H.H. Wood to MARY A. TABOR 23 yrs single b. Bland Co VA; by L.H. Broyles.

94. 22 June 1897 JAS C. BURTON 20 yrs single b. Mercer Co W VA s/o John W. & Martha J. to MARTHA E. AKERS 16 yrs single b. Mercer Co W VA d/o Crockett & Martha O: farmer; by E.A. Cooper.

95. 22 June 1897 W.W. KARNES 36 yrs wid. b. Mercer Co W VA s/o J.A. & Adaline to SUSAN V. BOLING 31 yrs single b. Mercer Co W VA d/o Jackson & ? O: farmer; by J.W. Bennett.

Page 89

96. 27 June 1897 GILES F. PAYNE 21 yrs single b. Carroll Co VA s/o Noah & Augusta to MELDORA D. BAILEY 17 yrs angle b. Mercer Co W VA d/o C.W. & Susan Bailey O: farmer; by M.C. Reed.

97. 30 June 1897 C.H. BRADLEY 27 yrs single b. Bedford Co VA s/o C.F. & M.J. to L.H. COWLING 25 yrs single b. Mercer Co W VA d/o W.J. & Mary O: fireman; by L.H. Broyles.

98. 30 June 1897 E.J. GOOCH 27 yrs wid. b. Mercer Co W VA s/o t.C. & Nancy J. to VIRGINIA B. MILLER 20 yrs single b. Mercer Co W VA d/o R.A. & ? O: farmer; by D.O. Baldwin; REMARKS: Reported to Ste. B of H.

99. 4 July 1897 WM C. TATE 21 yrs single b. Giles Co VA s/o C. & Vira to EVA C. WILSON 19 yrs single b. Mercer Co W VA d/o W.T. & M.E. O:farmer; by W.L Gautier.

100. 4 July 1897 DAVID B. HAGER 18 yrs single b. Mercer co W VA s/o A.J. & Syntha F. to VICTORIA HAGER 21 yrs single b. Pike Co KY d/o A. Bailey & Phoeby O: farmer; by D.N. Saunders.

101. 4 July 1897 ALBERT W. BLANKENSHIP 23 yrs div. b. Mercer Co W VA s/o Harrison & Louisa to AMANDA M. REED 46 yrs wid. b. Mercer Co W VA O: farmer; by L. Goodwyn.

102. 7 July 1897 WM ARTHUR 23 yrs single b. Franklin Co VA s/o John & Sarah to LUCINDA BELCHER 16 yrs single b. Mercer Co W VA d/o Isom & Nancy O: farmer; by T.F. Suthers.

103. 8 July 1897 W.G. HALE 30 yrs single to MARY E. PENNINGTON 19 yrs single b. Mercer Co W VA d/o A.W. & Lucinda O: farmer; by W.L. Gantier.

104. 11 July 1897 WM CARNES 24 yrs single b. Greenbrier Co W VA s/o Wm & Catherine to VIRGIE WOOD 18 yrs single d/o John H. & Mary E. O: farmer; by James F. Campbell.

105. 8 July 1897 T.W. CHRISTIE 22 yrs single b. Mercer Co W VA s/o T.M. & Sarah G. to ANNA LAURA NEEL 21 yrs single b. Mercer Co W VA d/o R.H. & Martha O: farmer; by J.O. Cassaday.

106. 7 July 1897 G.S. BOLIN 51 yrs wid. b. Mercer Co W VA s/o Jessie & Jane to MOLLIE B. BOLIN 31 yrs single b. Mercer Co W VA d/o J.J. & Isabella O: farmer; by J.W. Bennett.

107. 10 July 1897 JOHN WYATT 39 yrs div. b. Grayson Co VA s/o Boston & Mary L. to MARY JANE WYATT 38 yrs div. b. Ash Co NC d/o J.C. & Sarah Tilley O: farmer; by Peter Grim.

108. 9 July 1897 J.W. HAZLEWOOD 22 yrs single b. Smith Co VA to CARRIE GULLION 19 yrs wid. b. Mercer Co W VA d/o Dock & Tilda O: miner; by A.M. Craft.

109. 8 July 1897 HENRY TOLER 27 yrs div. b. Pitsylvania Co VA now living in Pocahontas VA s/o George & Mary to NANNIE GAINES 16 yrs single b. Tazewell Co VA d/o ? & Julia Gaines O: miner; by G.T. Wright.

110. 19 July 1897 ROBT LEE SAYERS 28 yrs single b. Wythe Co VA s/o Jas A. & Elizabeth to ELIZABETH NORMAN 31 yrs wid. O: miner; by James T. Tabor.

111. 22 July 1897 JOEL SLOAN 73 yrs wid. b. Davie Co NC s/o K. & Anne to SARAH E. ADKINS 48 yrs wid. b. Patrick Co VA O: farmer; by M.S. Simmons.

112. * * * DOUGLAS McELRATH 27 yrs single b. Burke Co NC s/o James & Louisa to ZANIE WALKER 26 yrs single b. Franklin Co VA O: miner; REMARKS: No Return. (*Note: no date given.)

113. 28 July 1897 J.C. KESTER single b. Carrol Co VA s/o J.L. & Nancy to GENNETTIE BAILEY single b. Wyoming Co W VA d/o A.I. & Annie O: farmer; by T.B. Cook.

114. 25 July 1897 H.L. HULLER 26 yrs single b. Rochester NY s/o J.J. & ? to ELLEN MANDINE WEIMER 17 yrs single b. Shamakin PA O: carpenter; by S.M. Broyles.

115. * * * FRANK ROBERTS 47 yrs wid. b. Rockingham Co NC s/o Robt & Peggy to EVILINE GIBSON 48 yrs wid. b. Wythe Co VA O: job work; REMARKS: No Return of certificate. (*Note: no date given) (?-40 something, ink smudge on age).

116. 29 July 1897 RUFUS WORKMAN 23 yrs single b. Mercer Co W VA s/o Robt & Sallie to RACHEL McCLOUD 17 yrs single b. Rusel(sic) Co VA d/o Henry & Sarah O: farmer; by W.H. Ayres.

117. 1 Aug 1897 JOSHUA R. RIGGIN 26 yrs single b. Serna Co NC s/o Riggin to SOPHRONIA J. NEAL 18 yrs single b. Bland Co VA d/o Erastur G. & LV. Neal O: farmer; by W.A. Pearson.

118. 5 Aug 1897 T.J. BOLEN 22 yrs single b. Carrol Co VA s/o Isaac & Mary E. to BLANCH GIRST 15 yrs single b. Mercer Co W VA d/o Luke & ? O: miner; by D.A. Ramey.

119. 5 Aug 1897 BOYD FARMER 21 yrs single b. Mercer Co W VA s/o James & Sarah E. to THIRSEY HAWKS 14 yrs single b. Mercer Co W VA d/o W.R. Hawks & Armitta O: farmer; by Peter Grim.

120. 12 Aug 1897 ASH PRATT 27 yrs single b. Johnson Co TN s/o Overton & Nellie S. to JENNIE D. BOWER 18 yrs single b. Floyd Co VA d/o R.H. & S.E. O: miner; by R.A. Kelly; REMARKS: father present.

121. 11 Aug 1897 ROBERT NEEL 24 yrs single b. Mercer Co W VA s/o R.M. & M.A. to LAURA A. FITZWATER 18 yrs single b. Mercer Co W VA d/o J.C. & H.E. O: carpenter; by J.O. Cassaday; REMARKS: sworn.

122. 11 Aug 1897 J.W. CLYBURN 42 yrs single b. Giles Co VA s/o Wm B. & Mariah to MARY A. HARRIS 39 yrs wid. b. Giles Co VA d/o Flern S. & Clara Canady O: farmer; by James H. Johnston.

123. 25 Aug 1897 N.A. KEATON 22 yrs single b. Mercer Co W VA s/o W.F. & S.R. to EFFIE BRAHMER 19 yrs single b. Mercer Co W VA d/o John L. & Sarah E. O: farmer; by G.M. Johnston; REMARKS: sworn.

124. 18 Aug 1897 S.H. TABOR 21 yrs single b. Mercer Co W VA s/o H.H. & H.M. to C.C. POWELL 17 yrs single b. Franklin Co VA d/o E.L. & L.A. O: miner; by R.A. Kelly; REMARKS: sworn, father of lady present.

125. 20 Aug 1897 JOHN PERDUE 37 yrs single b. Giles Co VA s/o C. & Mary Ann to SUSAN JANE BIRD 35 yrs wid. b. Mercer Co W Va d/o F. & Nancy O: farmer; by R.A. Kelly.

126. 25 Aug 1897 W.E. DUDLEY 38 yrs wid. b. Tazewell Co VA s/o H.D. & Jane to MINNIE B. ETTER 20 yr single b. Tazewell Co VA d/o ? & Ellen J. O: RR; by W.A. Pearson.

127. 25 Aug 1897 JAMES H. WYRICK 38 yrs wid. b. Mercer Co W VA s/o Henry to AVARILLA SHORTER 27 yrs single b. Mercer Co W VA & Elizabeth O: farmer; by James T. Tabor.

128. 26 Aug 1897 JAMES O. DAVIS 26 yrs single b. Grayson Co VA s/o Elbert & ? to COSBY SIZEMORE 24 yrs single O: miner; by L. Goodwyn; REMARKS: mode swim sworn as to age.

129. 24 Aug 1897 DANIEL M. SMITH 23 yrs single b. Montgomery Co VA s/o Dan & Malinda to AMY LEE MARTIN 22 yrs single b. Montgomery Co VA O: miner; by G.W. Alexander.

130. 26 Aug 1897 J.F. KINZER 32 yrs single b. Tazewell Co VA s/o Thos B. & S.S. to NEVADA MAY GRIM 17 yrs single b. Mercer Co W VA d/o Peter & Martha A. O: carpenter; by G.C. Anderson; REMARKS: sworn.

131. 1 Sept 1897 G.E. EVANS 33 yrs single b. Scranton PA s/o Robt & Angeline to E.H. RICH 33 yrs div. b. Bainbridge PA O: engineer; by L.M. Broyles.

132. 28 Sept 1897 RALEIGH IDDINGS 55 yrs wid. b. Floyd Co VA s/o ? & Ollie to RACHEL SOUTHERN 60 yrs wid. O: farmer; by L. Goodwyn.

133. 8 Sept 1897 EDDIE B. RORRER 23 yrs single b. Patrick Co VA s/o Peter & Nancy to THEODOSIA BRINKEY 18 yrs single b. Mercer Co w VA d/o J.H. & Rachel O: farmer; by L. Goodwyn.

134. 8 Sept 1897 HENRY R. YOUNG 33 yrs wid. b. Halifax Co VA s/o Henry & Fannie to JANE B. HIGGENBOTHAM 22 yrs single b. Halifax Co VA d/o George & Fannie O: RR man; by S.H. Gaines.

135. 14 Sept 1897 C.H. BALL 36 yrs single b. Bland Co VA s/o Peter H. & Mary M. to SARAH E. BUTTERWORTH 28 yrs single b. Carter Co TN d/o Charles E. & Julie A. O: teacher; by D.A. Ramey.

136. 13 Sept 1897 R.H. WHITTAKER 44 yrs wid. b. Mercer Co W VA to R.E. MEADOWS 17 yrs single d/o John L. & Marinda O: miner; by W.A. Bailey.

137. 21 Sept 1897 J.W. LOVILL 19 yrs single b. Carroll Co VA s/o Wm C. & M.A. to DORTHA L HATCHER 17 yrs single b. Wyoming Co W VA d/o John & Nancy E. O: farmer; by Thos B. Cook; REMARKS: witness sworn.

138. 6 Oct 1897 G.W. ARNOLD 30 yrs single b. Patrick Co VA s/o Thomas & Mary to MARY DEETON 30 yrs single b.

Mt. Eva NC d/o John & Parcilla O: RR; by S.W. Patterson; REMARKS: col'd, certificate swimt to.

139. 21 Sept 1897 LEWIS TARPLER 21 yrs single b. Pitsylvania Co VA s/o Ben & Harriet to SUSAN ANN WASHINGTON 19 yrs single b. Mercer Co W VA d/o Sam & Alice O: farmer; by S.E. Houk; REMARKS: col'd.

140. 22 Sept 1897 WM H. AYERS 25 yrs single b. Henry Co VA now living in Giles Co VA s/o L.L. & Flora to WILLIE BRUCE 18 yrs single b. Mercer Co W VA d/o Wm & Martha O:saw mill man; by L. Goodwyn.

141. 22 Sept 1897 WATSON THOMPSON 19 yrs single b. Mercer Co W VA s/o Hiram & Jane to MARY MIRTIE FARMER 20 yrs single b. Mercer Co W VA d/o John R Farmer & Jane O: farmer; by John H. Honaker.

142. 25 Sept 1897 HASEY WEEKS 22 yrs single b. Raleigh Co W VA s/o Joseph & Arbela to ADDIE L. WEEKS 20 yrs sngle b. Floyd Co VA d/o J.W. & E.J. O: farmer; by R.A. Miller.

143. 28 Sept 1897 H.W. BOWMAN 26 yrs single b. Memphis TN now living in Richmond VA s/o Francis H. & Rosalie to FANNIE C. FARMER 19 yrs single b. Richmond VA d/o James H. & Roxana O: shipping clerk; by L.M. Broyles.

Page 90

144. 28 Sept 1897 SAML E. PEDIGO 56 yrs wid. b. Henry Co VA s/o Lewis & nancy Pedigo to PATRICA AMOS 51 yrs wid. b. Bedford Co VA O: farming; by E.S. Bettis.

145. 29 Sept 1897 J.H. FALEY 22 yrs single b. Mason Co OH s/o Toliver & Susan to H.A. WOOD 17 yrs wid. b. Mercer Co W VA d/o Peter & Martha O: farming; by G.C. Anderson.

146. 29 Sept 1897 JAMES ANDERSON 24 yrs single b. Tazewell Co VA s/o H.& S. to EDNA R. LYBROOK 22 yrs single b. Giles Co VA d/o John & ? O: RR; by G.T. Wright.

147. 30 Sept 1897 M.L. STEELE 22 yrs single b. Meigs Co OH s/o W.F. & Rhoda to MARY E. MOTLEY 17 yrs single b. Mercer Co W VA d/o Wm & Parthena P-farmer; by W.L Gantier.

148. 6 Oct 1897 LEWIS A. COMER 27 yrs single b. Mercer Co w Va s/o Wm & Martha to ELLA J. PENNINGTON 19 yrs single b. Mercer Co W VA d/o Levi & S.A. O: farmer; by L. Goodwyn.

149. 6 Oct 1897 J.W. BRAG 24 yrs single b. Tazewell Co VA to MARY ELIZA JOHNSON 20 yrs single b. Fayette Co VA d/o W.C. & Mary H. O: farmer; by G.C. Anderson.

150. 6 Oct 1897 DOMINEK BIRKY 47 yrs single b. Germany to JENNIE DUNFORD 32 yrs div. b. Tazewell Co VA O: miner; by Wm A. Wynn.

151. 8 Oct 1897 A.W. COLE, JR. 24 yrs single b. Mercer Co W VA s/o John & Martha to NANNIE ALVIS 26 yrs single b. Mercer Co W VA d/o John & Jocie O: farmer; by W.L Gantier.

152. 5 Oct 1897 JOHN S. HALL 19 yrs single b. Mercer Co W VA s/o J.R. & Amanda to HATTIE I. PANLEY 16 yrs single b. Mercer Co W Va d/o H.C. & S.M. O: farmer; by R.H. Ashworth; REMARKS: both parents present - given consent.

153. 8 Oct 1897 JOHN TAYLOR 62 yrs wid. b. Carrol Co VA s/o Jno & Mary to NANCY SPICER 63 yrs wid. b. NC d/o Wm & ? Evans O: farmer; by John H. Honaker.

154. 20 Oct 1897 WM GARRETT 24 yrs single b. NC s/o Wm Garett & Ellen to FLORENCE MUSSELFIELD? 21 yrs single b. Montgomery Co VA d/o Marshall & Ollie O: laborer; by S.H. Gaines. (?Note: handwriting difficult to read)

155. 7 Oct 1897 J.H. BALEY 20 yrs single b. Giles Co VA s/o J.C. Baley & Mary to JULIA A. BELCHER 15 yrs single b. Mercer Co W VA d/o W.C. & Ann O: miner; by A.M. Craft.

156. 7 Oct 1897 JOSHUA DAVIS 22 yrs single b. Mercer Co W VA s/o Lee & Mary E. to MARY E. COOPER 20 yrs single b. Mercer Co W Va d/o Lewis & M.A. O: farmer; by James H. Johnston.

157. 10 Oct 1897 S.L. BOEHM 21 yrs single b. Shenandoah Co VA s/o John S. & Catherine to RHOLLETA MAY HEARN 21 yrs single b. Raleigh Co w VA d/o Wm & J. O: farmer; by G.C. Anderson.

158. 13 Oct 1897 ELGIN C. TABOR 27 yrs single b. Tazewell Co VA s/o Wm & Sarah Tabor to MARY B. STINSON 24 yrs single b. Mercer Co W VA d/o L.L. & Elizabeth Stinson O: farmer; by G.W. Bailey.

159. 14 Oct 1897 RICE PILLARS 27 yrs wid. b. McDowell Co W VA s/o Thos G. & M.C. to NANNIE HYLTON 30 yrs single b. Floyd Co Va O: miner; by A.M. Craft.

160. 25 Oct 1897 DAVID D. DAVIS 38 yrs single b. McDowell Co W VA now living same. s/o Thomas & Elizabeth to IMOGENE WEAVER 21 yrs single b. Mercer Co W VA d/o Robt L. & Lizzie H; by J.B. Ward.

161. 19 Oct 1897 J.M. COOPER 22 yrs single b. Mercer Co W VA s/o J.M. & Jane to ALICE NICKLES 20 yrs single b. Pulaski Co VA d/o Wm & Luzena O: farmer; by S.E. Houk.

162. 25 Oct 1897 WM W. CATRAN 35 yrs div. b. Wythe Co VA s/o J.W. & Nancy to MARGARET BRINDLE 31 yrs div. b. Mercer Co W VA d/o John & Martha Cole O: farmer; by A.B. Hunter.

163. 27 Oct 1897 SIDNEY CARTER 35 yrs div. b. Pittsylvania Co VA s/o Dab & Eliza Carter to MARY A. JONES 27 yrs wid. b. Bedford Co VA d/o Payton & Maria Jones O: railroader; by W.G. Harris; REMARKS: colored.

164. 27 oct 1897 WM FLETCHER SMITH 47 yrs div. b. Foresythe(sic) Co GA to MILLIE YOUNG 33 yrs div. b. Tazewell Co VA; by S.M. Gailres.

165. 27 Oct 1897 WADE MILLER 25 yrs single b. Montgomery Co VA s/o E.J. & J.R. Miller to ANNIE E. WATKINS 19 yrs single b. Charlotte Co VA d/o W.J. & C.S. Watkins O: L. engineer; by W.A. Pearson.

166. 27 Oct 1897 BRADE ATKINSON 21 yrs single to ANNA L. GANT 17 yrs single b. Clarion Co PA s/o Thos & Elizabeth Gant O: miner; by R.A. Kelly.

167. 27 Oct 1897 WM ROY 27 yrs single b. Louisa Co VA s/o John & Martha Roy to MARIA CLARK 22 yrs single b. Tazewell Co VA d/o C.A. & a.V. Clark O: railroader; by s.W. Patterson; REMARKS: colored.

168. 27 Oct 1897 DAVID A. BURCH 24 yrs single b. Mercer Co W Va s/o Geo W. & Sorraptra Burch to EMMA S. SKEENS 16 yrs single b. Mercer Co W VA d/o Jno T. & Amanda Skeens O: cabinet maker; by R.M. Ashworth.

169. 5 Nov 1897 CHARLES SEALS 27 yrs single b. Tazewell Co VA s/o Henry & Lilly Seals to AMANDA ROGGERS 23 yrs single b. Danville VA d/o Saml & Rachel Boggess O: miner; by J.W. Johnston.

170. 28 Oct 1897 JOHN COLES 27 yrs single b. Charlotte Co VA s/o Bedford & Catherine to MARY SCOTT 25 yrs single b. Smith Co VA d/o Alfred & Ann Scott O: miner; by M.S. Simmons.

171. 28 Oct 1897 CHAS M. MULLINS 21 yrs single b. Mercer Co W VA s/o Jos & Jane Mullins to FANNY MARTIN 21 yrs single b. Wyoming Co W Va d/o Jas & Rhoda Martin O: laborer; by S.E. Houk.

172. 28 Oct 1897 H.B. WALTERS 30 yrs div. b. Montgomery Co VA s/o Henry & Rutha to MARY E. TUCKER 24 yrs single b. Montgomery Co VA d/o L.W. & Julia A. O: miner; by A.B. Hunter.

173. 30 Oct 1897 WM D. MEADOWS 20 yrs single b. Mercer Co W VA s/o J.F. & Catherine to MARY S. EASTER 17 yrs single b. Mercer Co W VA d/o R.S. & Martha J. Easter O: farming; by R.A. Miller.

174. 4 Nov 1897 W.F. ALEXANDER 26 yrs single b. Smith Co VA s/o Franklin & Mary to LAURA E. THOMAS 27 yrs single b. Montgomery Co VA d/o G.W. Thomas & Josephine O: bank clerk; by A.B. Hunter.

175. 2 Nov 1897 C.W. HALDREN 30 yrs single b. Mercer Co W VA s/o Saml & Darcus W. to CHRISTIE WHITE 22 yrs single b. Mercer Co W VA s/o John Allen & Mary J. O: doctor; by W.L Gantier.

176. 4 Nov 1897 THOMAS REED, SR. 69 yrs wid. b. Campbell Co VA s/o Keziah Reed to EDNA CALDWELL 55 yrs single b. Appomatox Co VA d/o James & Polly O: farmer; by L. Goodwyn.

177. 5 Nov 1897 CHAS C. RUMBURG 22 yrs wid. b. Mercer Co W VA s/o W.J. & Nancy J. Rumburg to SARAH E. LILLY 19 yrs single b. Mercer Co W VA d/o Ed. & Elizabeth Lilly O: farmer; by Jas W. Lilly.

178. 8 Nov 1897 LITTLETON BOLES 25 yrs single b. Cumberland Co VA s/o James & Alice to MARY KING 27 yrs single b. Monroe Co VA d/o Wm & Elizabeth O: RR; by C.D. Leftwich; REMARKS: col'd.

179. 7 Nov 1897 ALEX C. VINES 27 yrs single b. Augusta Co VA now living in Fayette Co W VA s/o W.F. & Susan Vines to MAY L HAMBRICK 26 yrs single b. Mercer Co W VA d/o J.H. & E.P. Hambrick O: laborer; by W.A. Pearson.

180. 7 Nov 1897 WILLIAM TURNER 23 yrs single s/o Meador & ? Turner to BESSIE BELCHER 18 yrs single b. Tazewell Co VA d/o Obediah & Visa Belcher O: railroader; by W.H. Ayers.

181. 7 Nov 1897 OBEDIAH D. BELCHER 22 yrs single b. Tazewell Co VA s/o Obediah & Visa Belcher to LUCY J. DUDLEY 18 yrs single b. Mercer Co W VA d/o Wm L. & R.A. Dudley O: farming; by W.H. Ayers.

182. 10 Nov 1897 E.L. WIRTH 22 yrs single b. Bland Co VA to MARY A. THOMPSON 16 yrs single d/o Larkin & Jennie Thompson O: laborer; by John H. Honaker.

183. 10 Nov 1897 HENRY BANISTER 30 yrs single b. Pittsylvania Co VA s/o James to ROSY WILLIAMS 21 yrs single b. Tazewell Co VA d/o Charles & Sarah O: merchant; by J.D. Leftwich; REMARKS: col'd.

184. 8 Nov 1897 F.J. BROWN 36 yrs single b. Giles Co VA s/o Lewis & Malinda to LULA HIGHT 36 yrs wid. b. Wythe Co VA d/o Elbert & Emma Lyons O: Justice of the Peace; by J.A. Burrow.

185. 10 Nov 1897 S.G. MOYER 29 yrs single b. Wythe Co Va to SARAH RUNNELS 28 yrs wid. O: shoemaker; by A.H. Lambert.

186. 15 Nov 1897 CHAS V. THOMPSON 22 yrs single b. Mercer Co W VA s/o Allen & Minerva Thompson to D.V.E. HOLDREN 21 yrs single b Mercer Co W VA s/o Saml & D.W. Holdren O: farming; by W.L Gantier.

187. 18 Nov 1897 JAMES G. BOWDEN 35 yrs wid. b. Pulaski Co VA s/o James G. & Lucinda to MARY ALOFF 36 yrs div. b. Mercer Co W VA d/o Elisha & Zerine Jones O: farmer; by W.L Gantier.

188. 18 Nov 1897 RUFUS H. PENNINGTON 23 yrs single b. Mercer Co VA s/o B.P & R.H. Pennington to NANCY J. FLETCHER 28 yrs wid. b. Floyd Co VA d/o Robt & M.A. Hill O: farmer; by L. Goodwyn.

189. 17 Nov 1897 LEWIS C. ROBISON 21 yrs single b. Mercer Co W VA s/o Henry & E. Robison to SARAH F. SKEENS 19 yrs single b. Mercer Co W VA d/o Henry & Mary Skeens O: farmer; by R.A. Miller.

190. 21 Nov 1897 LEE McNUTT 25 yrs single b. Pulaski Co VA s/o ? & Margaret to DELAY SMITH 24 yrs single b. Russell Co VA d/o Susan Smith O: farmer; by J.S. Leftwich; REMARKS: col'd.

Page 91

191. 25 Nov 1897 LEROY F. BAILEY 35 yrs wid. b. Mercer Co W VA s/o Floyd & Ziltha to L.C. WALKER 24 yrs single b. Mercer Co W VA d/o Counsil R. & Emma O: farmer; by J.M. Meadows.

192. 25 Nov 1897 E.K. BOURNE 30 yrs div. b. Grayson Co VA s/o H. & Julia to H.V. JONAS 30 yrs single b. Bland Co VA d/o Peter & Julia O: laborer; by A.H. Lambert.

193. 30 Nov 1897 J.M. BAUGNESS 36 yrs single b. Wilkes Co NC s/o Reuben & Mary to JULIA E. YOUNG 17 yrs single b. Monroe Co W VA d/o S.H. & ? O: stone mason; by John H. Honaker.

194. 30 Nov 1897 OSKER CROCKETT 20 yrs single b. Tazewell Co Va s/o James A. & Rachel to ARNES SWADER 19 yrs single b. Mercer Co W VA d/o Henry & Katie O: farmer; by A.M. Craft.

195. 5 Nov 1897 EWARD(sic) STONE 21 yrs single b. Pittsylvania Co VA s/o Wm & Dasha to MARY WALKER 21 yrs single b. Campbell Co VA d/o Sam & Juda O: miner; by J.W. Johnson; REMARKS: col'd.

196. 30 Nov 1897 LEDFORD HILL 28 yrs single b. Covington VA s/o John & Mary to LAURA CALOWAY 24 yrs wid. b. Bedford Co VA O: RR; by Geo t. Wright; REMARKS: col'd.

197. 2 Dec 1897 ALFRED E. GOODWYN 23 yrs single b. Richmond VA s/o Geo T. Rhodes & Magie Goodwin to LITTIE F. WARREN 22 yrs single b. Tazewell Co VA d/o Wade & Elmira O: barber; by Geo R. Wright; REMARKS: col'd.

198. 5 Dec 1897 GEORGE W. LYLE 23 yrs single b. Washington Co VA s/o Jackson & Rose to ELIZABETH MILLS 20 yrs single O: miner; by E. Olivier.

199. 7 Dec 1897 JAMES WOOD 29 yrs wid. b. Wythe Co VA to FRANCES MILES 27 yrs wid. b. Pulaski Co VA O: L engineer; by J.S. French.

200. 9 Dec 1897 B.L. HEDRICK 24 yrs single b. Wayne Co W VA s/o Harvey & Nancy J. to MARY J. TABOR 24 yrs single b. Tazewell Co VA d/o Russel & Martha O: laborer; by A.B. Hunter.

201. 9 Dec 1897 C.L. DEATON 45 yrs wid. b. Alleghany Co VA now living in McDowell Co VA s/o John & G. to EFFIE E. VERNON 32 yrs single b. Kanawha Co WA d/o Wm H. & Jennie O: miner; by D.A. Daugherty.

202. 9 Dec 1897 H.S. POFF 48 yrs wid. b. Floyd Co VA s/o Peter & Catharine Poff to JUDA MEADOWS 35 yrs single b. Mercer Co W VA d/o ? & Malinda Meadows O: farmer; by Allen M. McKinney.

203. 15 Dec 1897 YANCY J. FOLDEN 28 yrs single b. VA s/o Geo F. & ? to SARAH SUSAN HEONE 25 yrs single b. Raleigh Co W VA d/o Wm & Jane O: farmer; by G.C. Anderson.

204. 16 Dec 1897 CHARLES E. CAUSBY 19 yrs single b. Giles Co VA s/o A.T. Causby & ? to CORA Z. BELCHER 24 yrs single b. Tazewell Co VA s/o W.C. & H.H. O: miner; by A.M. Craft.

205. 16 Dec 1897 R.L. SHELTON 22 yrs single b. Franklin Co VA now living in McDowell Co VA s/o Ann Elizabeth Williams to SARAH R. BELCHER 27 yrs single b. Tazewell Co VA d/o W.C. & H.H. O: miner; by A.M. Craft.

206. 22 Dec 1897 HERBERT L. MORRIO 21 yrs to JULIA LUSK 22 yrs d/o William Lusk; by John H. Honaker. *NOTE: No other information given.*

207. 16 Dec 1897 WM D. CLINE 21 yrs single b. Wyoming Co W VA now living same s/o Gordon & Elizabeth Cline to LILLY B. MORGAN 18 yrs single b. Mercer Co W VA d/o Thos P. & Martha Morgan O: farmer; by E.W. Tiller.

208. 16 Dec 1897 FLOYD H. FARMER 19 yrs single b. Mercer Co W VA s/o R.C. & H.M. Farmer to E.J. BECKELHIMER 19 yrs single b. Floyd Co VA d/o A.& M. Beckelhimer O: farmer; b J.H. McClaugherty; REMARKS: parent of both present.

209. 22 Dec 1897 FELIX L. BOURNE 26 yrs single b. Tazewell Co VA s/o Chas A. & Angelina to MAUD E. WOHLFORD 18 yrs single b. Bland Co VA d/o Thos E. & E.O. Wohlford O: railroader; by J.W. West.

210. 22 Dec 1897 GUY M. ROCKEY 25 yrs single b. Lancaster OH now living in Phila PA s/o H.T. & Cordelia E. to EVYLIN GRACE HIGHT 20 yrs single b. Lynchbury VA d/o Alex & Lula O: private clerk; by J.T. Frazier.

211. 21 Dec 1897 ANDERSON BLANKENSHIP 21 yrs single b. Giles Co VA now living same s/o Wm H. & margaret to ADA G. HOLDREN 18 yrs single b. Mrcer Co W VA d/o Jas H. & Mary R. O: farming; by R.A. Miller; REMARKS: father present.

212. 22 Dec 1897 W.P. WINFREY 23 yrs wid. b. Mercer Co W VA s/o H.W. & O.H. Winfrey to BERTHA M. TAYLOR 23 yrs single b. Craig Co VA d/o ? & Polly A. Taylor O: farming; by S.E. Houk; REMARKS: C.W. Taylor.

213. 22 Dec 1897 RUFUS A. STAFFORD 25 yrs single b. Mercer Co W VA s/o Wm & Louisa Stafford to CARRIE V. FARLEY 16 yrs single b. Giles Co VA d/o A.F. & N.E. Farley O: farming; by G.H. Johnston; REMARKS: N.F. Farley.

214. 22 Dec 1897 JOHN E. BOOTH 24 yrs single b. Tazewell Co Va now living same s/o ? & L.J. Booth to HATTIE HICKMAN 16 yrs single b. Tazewell Co VA d/o John & ? Hickman O: farming; by J.W. West.

215. 23 Dec 1897 C.W. ONEY 28 yrs single b. Mercer Co W VA s/o E.M. & V.F. Oney to MARY C. CARBAUGH 24 yrs single b. Mercer Co W VA d/o W.T. & ? Carbaugh O: farming; by S.E. Houk.

216. 23 Dec 1897 WM B. LILLY 22 yrs single b. Washington Co TN s/o J.J. & Martha Lilly to SARAH J. BLANKENSHIP 19 yrs single b. Mercer Co W VA d/o W.H. & Louisa Blankenship O: miner; by J.O. Cassaday.

217. 25 Dec 1897 ALBERT WORLDS 24 yrs single b. VA s/o Jessie & Elizabeth to NANNY WIRTZ 17 yrs single b. Mercer Co W VA s/o Dick & Lizzie O: farmer; by R.H. Ashworth.

218. 29 Dec 1897 ELBERT F. PETERS 20 yrs single b. Summers Co W VA s/o Jos & M.A. Peters to ROSA E. SHREWSBURY 21 yrs single b. Mercer Co W VA d/o L.C. & nancy Shrewsbury O: teachng; by James W. Lilly.

219. 28 Dec 1897 THOS E. PEERY 23 yrs single b. Andriau Co MO s/o J.E. & C.D. Peery to SHRILDIA BROWN 24 yrs single b. Tazewell Co VA d/o Frank & Julia Brown O: dry goods clk; by W.A. Pearson; REMARKS: T.E. Peery sworn.

220. 22 Dec 1897 ROY L. EPLINE 22 yrs single b. Giles Co VA s/o L.A. & Ellen Epling to MARY A. POOL 18 yrs single b. Bland Co VA d/o Milam & M.L. Pool O: farmer; by W.I. Gantier.

221. 31 Dec 1897 W.C. BELCHER 24 yrs single b. Mercer co W VA s/o T.I. & A.H. Belcher to EVA BAILEY 18 yrs single b. Mercer Co W VA d/o G.P. & ? Bailey O: merchant; by John H. Honaker.

222. 29 Dec 1897 R.M. ASHWORTH 46 yrs wid. b. Pulaski Co VA s/o A.A. & Nancy Ashworth to LINA BIRD 29 yrs single b. Mercer Co W VA d/o B.W. & Letha A. Bird O: mnister; by D.H. Thornton.

223. 29 Dec 1897 M.L. CARTER 27 yrs sngle b. Wythe Co VA s/o J.C. & R.S. Carter to SARAH J. MULLEN 27 yrs single b. Tazewell Co VA d/o Austn & C.E. Mullan O: farming; by W.H. Ayera.

224. 29 Dec 1897 CHARLES E. POWELL 20 yrs sngle b. Rockingham Co VA s/o H.F. & R.J. to IDA E. THOMPSON 17 yrs single b. Mercer Co W VA d/o J.D. & Emma O: farming; by A.J. Thompson.

225. 29 Dec 1897 JOHN BARBERIE, JR. 32 yrs sngle b. England s/o John & Julia to MATILDA J. DAVIDSON 22 yrs sngle b. Mercer Co W VA d/o Henry & R.H. O: railroading; by S.E. Houk.

226. 29 Dec 1897 JOHN H. THMPSON 27 yrs wid. b. Montgomery Co VA s/o J.W. & Mary to OLLIE G. CAVES 17 yrs sngle b. Pulaski Co Va d/o J.W. & Eliza O: railroading; by A.M. Lambert.

227. 29 Dec 1897 C.F. BAND 23 yrs single b. Coburn VA now livng same s/o G.W. & E.R. to LIZZIE KIRK 21 yrs single d/o John S. & R.A. O: merchant; by Authur S. Thorn.

1. 5 Jan 1898 V.W. COOPER 49 yrs wid. b. Wyoming Co W VA now living in Summers Co W VA s/o Josiah & Narciss to CORA J. KING 26 yrs single b. Franklin Co VA d/o J.H. & M.I. King O: farmer; by James W. Lilly.

2. 12 Jan 1898 SAML L. MAXEY 32 yrs single b. Franklin Co VA now living in Pocahontas VA s/o Jas B. & Alice Maxey to ALICE ELIZABETH WALL 23 yrs single b. Mercer Co W VA d/o Jas C. & Martha F. Wall O: constable; by R.A. Kelly.

3. 12 Jan 1898 WADE BAILEY 24 yrs single b. McDowell Co W VA s/o Elijah & Mary A. to LURA F. STEWART 18 yrs single b. Montgomery Co VA d/o J.W. Stewart & ? O: farming; by H.C. Reed; REMARKS: witness sworn.

4. 13 Jan 1898 HENRY C. CARTER 23 yrs single b. Tazewell Co VA s/o Dan & ? to MOLLIE BELCHER 19 yrs single b. Mercer Co W VA d/o ? Belcher O: farming; by W.H. Ayres.

5. 15 Jan 1898 ISAAC LOGAN 26 yrs single b. Pitsylvania Co VA s/o Isaac & Anna Logan to ANNA COOK 23 yrs wid. d/o Jacob & ? Tober O: miner; by J.W. Johnson; REMARKS: colored.

6. 17 Jan 1898 CHAS AKERS 27 yrs single b. Kanawha Co W VA s/o Creed & Martha F. to RUCIA DYE 30 yrs wid. b. Tazewell Co VA s/o Pryer & Sarah O: farming; by J.A. Burrow.

7. 25 Jan 1898 ELBERT W. FORD 19 yrs single b. Monroe Co W VA s/o ? & A.B. Ford to VIRGINIA B. BURDETT 22 yrs div. b. Monroe Co W VA d/o R.B. & D.S. Crawford O: farming; by J.O. Cassaday.

8. 26 Jan 1898 ALBERT J. BASHAM 23 yrs single b. Mercer Co W VA s/o Jas A. & Polly A. to CASIE V. BAILEY 16 yrs single b. Mercer Co W VA d/o Wm C. & Mary E. Bailey O: farming; by G.C. Anderson.

9. 26 Jan 1898 CHAS C. BRAKE 24 yrs single b. Franklin Co PA now living in Roanoke Co VA s/o Israel & Louisa Brake to HARRIET E. KIRK 24 yrs single b. Giles Co VA d/o Absolom & H.M. Kirk O: loco. fireman; by G.M. Johnston; REMARKS: Chas C. Brake sworn.

10. 26 Jan 1898 Brammel W VA WM L. PEAK 24 yrs single b. s/o Joseph & Nancy J. to EMMA SMITH 22 yrs single b. Monroe Co W VA d/o Henry A. & H.M. Smith O: miner; by R.A. Kelly.

11. 26 Jan 1898 CHAS A. MATHANA 24 yrs single b. Tazewell Co VA s/o Geo & Emily Mathana to LEDA M. MUNSEY 17 yrs single b. Mercer Co W VA d/o J.A. & Katie F. Munsey O: farming; by J.O. Cassaday.

12. 28 Jan 1898 WM R. GODFREY 20 yrs single b. Wyoming Co W VA now living same s/o L.B. & N.R. Godfrey to LAANZA A. LESTER 17 yrs single b. Mercer Co W VA d/o L.J. & Rebecca Lester O: teaching; by G.C. Anderson.

13. 2 Feb 1898 Simmons WARREN S. COPE 29 yrs single b. Chester Co PA now living in McDowell Co W VA s/o Geo H. & Lydia J. Cope to MABEL J. SHEPHERD 24 yrs single b. England d/o Peter & ? Shepherd O: mining engineer; by Norman E. Marshall; REMARKS: W.S. Cope sworn.

14. 31 Jan 1898 G.H. CHASE 33 yrs single b. Shepherdstown W VA s/o Geo W. & Elizabeth A. to SALLIE B. FUNK 31 yrs wid. b. Knoxville TN d/o Maggie A. Jones O: railroading; by S.E. Houk.

15. * * * HOWE RIDER 42 yrs single b. Bland Co VA s/o Hiram & S.W. Rider to OCTAVIA C. LUCHORUE 36 yrs wid. b. Floyd Co VA d/o ? & Martha Argabright O: railroader. (*Note: no date given.)

16. 6 Feb 1898 GEORGE P. COLE 23 yrs single b. Raleigh Co W VA now living same s/o Bartley D. & Adeline to SALLIE A. ALLEN 21 yrs single b. Mercer Co W VA d/o John & Susie O: farmer; by G.A. Hatcher; REMARKS: D.C. Hedric sworn.

17. 9 Feb 1898 L.C. DELP 19 yrs single b. Mercer Co W VA s/o Ballard P. & S.E. to IDA B. BAILEY 22 yrs single b. Mercer Co W VA d/o Jas F. & Martha O: farmer; by G.C. Anderson; REMARKS: Allen C. Bailey sworn.

18. 17 Feb 1898 PRESTON VANCE 25 yrs wid. b. Mercer Co W VA to FLORA E. LESTER 22 yrs single b. Montgomery Co VA d/o Wilson & Rachel Lester O: miller; by R.A. Miller; REMARKS: Wilson Lester.

19. 13 Feb 1898 RILEY T. BOOTHE 21 yrs single b. Mercer Co W VA s/o W.G. & Nancy to MARTHA SHEPHERD 17 yrs single b. Montgomery Co VA d/o Wm & Eve J. O: farmer; by W.H. Ayres; REMARKS: witness B.P. McGuire sworn.

20. 12 Feb 1898 CHAS M. KING 22 yrs single b. Bland Co VA s/o James & Jane King to ADDIE WIMMER 22 yrs single b. Mercer Co W VA d/o Isaac & R.J. Wimmer O: farmer; by S.E. Houk; REMARKS: C.M. King & Addie Wimmer sworn.

21. 23 Feb 1898 HENRY A. NEAL 23 yrs single b. Mercer Co W VA s/o Wm & Martha to VIRGINIA A. WRIGHT 20 yrs single b. Bland Co VA d/o James D. & Sarah E. O: farmer; by G.C. Anderson; REMARKS: witness J.B. Neal sworn.

22. 20 Feb 1898 G.H. LEE 28 yrs div. b. Chattanooga TN s/o Liza Lee to LOUISA EGGLESTON 24 yrs div. b. Pitsylvania Co VA d/o George & Jane O: RR; by G.T. Wright.

23. 23 Feb 1898 BALLARD PRESTON SHUMATE 22 yrs single b. Mercer Co W VA s/o R.A. & Elizabeth to JOANNA B. BURTON 19 yrs single b. Mercer Co W VA d/o Elijah & Martha O: farmer; by J.O. Cassaday; REMARKS: B.P. Shumate sworn.

24. 22 Feb 1898 CHAS E. REED 21 yrs single b. Mercer Co W VA s/o H.A. & Susan Reed to S. MAUD BURGESS 16 yrs single b. Raleigh Co W VA d/o J.C. & Nancy Burgess O: farmer; by James W. Lilly; REMARKS: C.E. Reed sworn.

25. 1 Mar 1898 BARTLEY B. POE 24 yrs wid. b. Mercer Co W VA s/o H. & H.J. to INDIA C. BELCHER 24 yrs single b. Tazewell Co VA d/o James E. & Amanda O: farmer; by W.H. Ayres; REMARKS: H. Poe sworn.

26. 3 Mar 1898 NEWTON PATTERSON 23 yrs single b. Tazewell Co VA s/o John & Mary to SHANUA COLE 17 yrs single b. Mercer Co W VA d/o A.J. & Mary O: miner; by John H. Honaker; REMARKS: A.J. Cole present.

27. 2 Mar 1898 CHARLEY T. SHAFER 23 yrs single b. Christiansburg VA s/o Charley & Missey to SUSAN R. BARNETT 26 yrs single b. Christiansburg VA d/o Henry & Mary O: RR; by S.M. Gaines; REMARKS: col'd.

28. 8 Mar 1898 DOCK FUDGE 29 yrs div. b. Tazewell Co VA s/o Milton & ? Fudge to NANNIE A. WARREN 23 yrs single b. Tazewell Co VA d/o John & Lizzie Warren O: railroader; by S.M. Gaines; REMARKS: col'd.

29. 9 Mar 1898 R.J. PHIPPS 23 yrs wid. b. Ash Co NC s/o Harvey & Sallie Phipps to NANNIE A. BIRD 21 yrs single b. Mercer Co W VA d/o Bluford & Letha A. Bird O: brick layer; by R.M. Ashworth; REMARKS: Wm Holdren sworn.

30. 10 Mar 1898 PEARL KIRK 25 yrs single b. Giles Co VA s/o A.& H.M. Kirk to LIZZIE BRAGG 21 yrs single b. Summers Co W VA d/o A.J. & Malinda Bragg O: farming; by G.H. Johnston.

31. 9 Mar 1898 F.F. REPASS 60 yrs wid. b. Giles Co Va now living in Bland Co VA s/o Saml & Rhoda Repass to REBECCA M. WHEELER 35 yrs single b. Bland Co VA d/o Henry P. & B. Wheeler O: minister; by J.E. Bruce.

32. 10 Mar 1898 ALBERT L. GILBERT 25 yrs single b. Patrick Co VA s/o Wm P. & Larinda Gilbert to MARY E. MEADOWS 17 yrs single b. Giles Co Va d/o J.J. & M.E. Meadows O: railroader; by A.B. Hunter.

33. 15 Mar 1898 NELSON ROBINSON 28 yrs single b. Nelson Co VA s/o Ryle & Mahala Robinson to MOLLIE COOPER 23 yrs wid. b. Franklin Co VA O: coal miner; by J.W. Johnson; REMARKS: colored.

34. 16 Mar 1898 LAWSON W. SYERS* 24 yrs single v. Mercer Co W VA s/o David & Zylphia Syres* to ROSA B. BAILEY 19 yrs single b. Mercer Co W VA d/o G.M. & Ella E. Bailey O: farmer; by John H. Honaker; REMARKS: W.W. Bailey sworn. (*Note: name spelled both ways.)

35. 20 Mar 1898 WM H. LILLY 66 yrs wid. s/o Elijah & Sally Lilly to R.J. BOWLING 58 yrs wid. d/o Jos & M.W. Reed O: farming; by James W. Lilly.

36. 17 Mar 1898 JOHN L. MEADOWS 32 yrs single b. Mercer Co W VA s/o Woodson & A. Meadows to CATHARINE C. HOONEY 36 yrs wid. b. Mercer Co W VA d/o Nathaniel & Acres O: farming; by Drury Farley.

37. 12 Mar 1898 G.R. WILLIAMS 22 yrs single b. Giles Co VA s/o Jas H. & Oney to L.B. SMITH 21 yrs single b. Mercer Co W VA d/o J.H. & Louisa O: farming; by R.A. Miller; REMARKS: G.R. Williams sworn.

38. 23 Mar 1898 A.V. McCOMAS 23 yrs single b. Mercer Co W VA s/o J.C. & Etty to FANNIE K. CALDWELL 20 yrs single b. Mercer Co W VA d/o Glen & Sarah O: farming; by J.W. Bailey; REMARKS: J.O. Mangus & Robt Caldwell sworn.

39. 24 Mar 1898 H. MADISON ELHORE 27 yrs single b. Giles Co VA now living in Giles Co VA to DELLA M. MEADOWS 26 yrs single b. Mercer Co W VA d/o Henry & Laurena Meadows O: laborer; by R.A. Miller.

40. 26 Mar 1898 R.A. HALL 18 yrs single b. Bland Co VA s/o J.P. & Victoria Hall to VIRGINIA A. WHITE 21 yrs single b. Mercer Co W VA d/o Wm R. & Polly J. White O: farming; by D.H. Thornton.

41. 27 Mar 1898 WM BERRYMAN 32 yrs single b. Montgomery Co VA s/o Wm & Juda Berryman to MARY J. ROBERTS 27 yrs single b. Wythe Co VA d/o Jno & Mary Roberts O: railroader; by J.D. Leftwich; REMARKS: col'd.

42. 30 Mar 1898 LEONARD M. WALKER 20 yrs single b. Mercer Co W VA s/o John M. & Millie to LAURA D. BELCHER 20 yrs single b. Tazewell Co VA d/o R.H. & Realy O: farmer; by J.W. Bailey.

43. 31 Mar 1898 DANIEL B. THOMAS 18 yrs single b. Mercer Co W VA s/o M.F. & Sarah Thomas to PEGGY THOMAS 20 yrs single b. Mercer Co W VA d/o J.H. & Caroline Thomas O: farmer; by R.A. Miller; REMARKS: M.F. & J.H. Thomas.

44. 6 Apr 1898 C.J. SLOAN 21 yrs single b. Mercer Co W VA s/o David A. & Emily L. to MINNIE MARTIN 20 yrs single b. Mercer Co W VA d/o Wm H. & Martha O: farmer; by W.L Gantier.

45. 6 Apr 1898 M.E. KING 28 yrs single b. Floyd Co VA s/o Jas M. & H.J. to DAISEY P. BAILEY 18 yrs single b. Mercer Co W VA d/o M.E. & ? O: blacksmith; by Horace Strong.

46. 6 Apr 1898 R.G. BOLIN 23 yrs single b. Mercer Co W VA s/o Alen H. & Elizabeth to JULIA V. STEVENS 21 yrs single b. Knox Co KY d/o ? & Virginia Campbell O: farmer; by Frank Jackson; REMARKS: R.G. Bolin sworn.

47. 6 Apr 1898 W.J. HUTTON 25 yrs single b. Washington Co VA now living in Tazewell Co VA s/o John A.P. & S.H. to A.L. KELLY 25 yrs wid. b. Giles Co VA d/o Jacob L. & Sarah Peters O: RR; BY Eugene Blake.

48. 9 Apr 1898 BRYANT ROSE 50 yrs wid. b. NC s/o Isah & Mary to ELIZA FARMER 27 yrs single b. Mercer Co W VA d/o Wm & ? O: farmer; by J.B. Simpson.

Page 93

49. 10 Apr 1898 JOHNSON HAWKINS 35 yrs wid. b. Pulaski Co VA s/o J. & eliza to ELLA SLAUGHTER 22 yrs single b. Pulaski Co VA O: miner; by G.W. Alexander; REMARKS: col'd.

50. 12 Apr 1898 J.H. HOVMAN 27 yrs single b. Buckingham Co VA now living in McDowell Co W VA s/o J.T. & M. to IDA H. HARMAN 19 yrs single b. Tazewell Co VA d/o W.B. & P.J. O: RR; by J.E. Bruce.

51. 13 Apr 1898 C.H. KING 42 yrs single b. Laporte IN now living in Bluefield W VA s/o J.J. & Ellen to HENRIETTA TARR 33 yrs single b. IN O: blacksmith; by S.E. Houk; REMARKS: sworn.

52. 13 Apr 1898 R.C. ROWLAND 29 yrs single b. Mercer Co W VA s/o J.J. & Sally Rowland to KATE L. SHELTON 24 yrs single b. Mercer Co W VA d/o Robt & N.J Shelton O: laborer; by S.E. Houk.

53. 20 Apr 1898 J.J. ANDERSON 36 yrs single b. Montgomery Co VA now living same s/o Cary & Malinda to ADDIE L. THOMAS 33 yrs single b. Montgomery Co VA d/o Geo W. & Josie V. O: farmer; by A.B. Hunter.

54. 20 Apr 1898 JAS W. THOMPSON 28 yrs single b. Mercer Co W VA s/o Eli & ? Thompson to ADA G. HUGHES 18 yrs single b. Mercer Co W VA d/o Sarah Hughes O: farmer; by W.L Gantier.

55. 20 Apr 1898 VAL H. NEAL 21 yrs single b. Mercer Co W VA s/o J.H. & Cynthia Neal to MARY A. HONAKER 19 yrs single b. Raleigh Co W VA d/o Jno H. & S.A. Honaker O: farmer; by G.C. Anderson.

56. 19 Apr 1898 ANDREW J. BOYD, JR. 27 yrs single b. Smyth Co VA s/o A.J. & Margaret Boyd to LOU HOLBROOK 27 yrs wid. b. Smyth Co VA d/o Jack Lyle O: laborer; by A.B. Hunter.

57. 19 Apr 1898 M.A. ELLIS 24 yrs single b. Summers Co W VA s/o O.J. & Jane Ellis to JENNIE HICKMAN 23 yrs single b. Tazewell Co VA d/o John Hickman O: laborer; by A.B. Hunter; REMARKS: M.A. Ellison & A.J. Boyd sworn.

58. 7 May 1898 JAMES C. MASON 34 yrs wid. b. Dinwidda VA s/o James Mason & Lucy to SINA J. RATLIFF 23 yrs single b. Wilkes Co NC d/o Richard & Sarah O: miner; by G.W. Alexander.

59. * * * J.H. WINFREY 47 yrs wid. b. Scott Cand s/o John & Francis to MARY E. LUCADE 32 yrs single b. Giles Co VA d/o George & Ann O: RR. (*Note: no date given.)

60. 27 Apr 1898 W.L. FLESHMAN 28 yrs single b. Appomatax(sic) VA s/o J.P.L. & H.J. to ROZALIA GROVE 21 yrs single b. Lanesa(sic) VA d/o F.S. & ? O: miner; by S.E. Houk.

61. 20 Apr 1898 C.D. SCOTT 37 yrs wid. b. Charlotte Co VA s/o L. & Eliza to LITTIE SANDERS 31 yrs wid. b. TN d/o H. & Bettie O: miner; by S.E. Houk.

62. 27 Apr 1898 C. CUNNINGHAM 26 yrs single b. KY s/o W.H. & Louiza to ANNA LOUISA COLE 19 yrs single b. Mercer Co W VA d/o A.F. & Denisha O: machinist; by J.W. West.

63. 27 Apr 1898 CHARLES P. CALDWELL 35 yrs single b. VA now living in Craig Co VA s/o Jacob & Sarah J. to MARY S. JOHNSTON 32 yrs single b. Mercer Co W VA d/o Wm & Sarah E. O: farming; by S.E. Houk.

64. 1 May 1898 WILLIAM TUNE 26 yrs single b. VA s/o Alexander & Emily to MARY HOURAN 25 yrs single b. Lynchburg VA O: teamster; by G.W. Alexander.

65. 5 May 1898 G.M. PERDUE 20 yrs single b. Giles Co VA s/o Wm A. & Louisa to R.M. THOMAS 16 yrs single b. Mercer Co W VA d/o M.F. & Sarah O: farmer; by R.A. Miller.

66. 4 May 1898 FRANCIS TRESISE 19 yrs single b. Arbrzonia PA now living in Tazewell Co VA s/o Wm & H.J. to MYRTIE M. HOUK 17 yrs single b. Grayson Co VA d/o S.E. & N.C; by S.D. Long.

67. 8 May 1898 C.S. PATTON 27 yrs single b. Washington Co TN s/o W.J. & C.E. to IDA H. WAVELRING 24 yrs single b. Centre Co PA d/o G.W. & R.E. O: RR; by J.A. Burrow.

68. 15 May 1898 W.C. GORDEN 23 yrs single b. Giles Co VA s/o G.W. & Elizabeth to CARRIE E. TRACY 16 yrs single b. Giles Co VA d/o G.P. & ? O: farmer; by R.A. Miller.

69. 18 May 1898 SAHL K. REID 22 yrs single b. Giles Co VA s/o Jas B. & H.J. Reid to ONIE M. EPLING 19 yrs single b. Giles Co VA d/o L.A. & E.J. Epling O: farmer; by James W. Lilly; REMARKS: S.K. Reid sworn.

70. 17 May 1898 J.H. MEADOWS 24 yrs single b. Mercer Co W VA s/o Jacob & Julia to MANDA BROYLES 21 yrs single b. Mercer Co W VA d/o Joshua G. & Ollie O: farmer; by L. Goodwyne.

71. 18 May 1898 RUFUS B. BELCHER 23 yrs single b. Mercer Co W VA s/o ? & Jane Belcher to ETTA WORRELL 17 yrs single b. Mercer Co W VA O: laborer; by S.E. Houk.

72. 18 May 1898 RICHARD CHARLEY MITCHEL 20 yrs single b. McDowell Co W VA now living same s/o J.W. & C to GEORGIA ELLEN FERGUSON 17 yrs single b. McDowell Co W VA d/o G.W. & Mary O: laborer; by C.A. Chrisman.

73. 25 May 1898 ALFRED H. HOCK 26 yrs single b. Shamakin PA s/o Wm H. & Kate Hock to SALLY J. BRADLEY 22 yrs single b. Bedford Co VA d/o Chas F. & H.J. Bradley O: loco engineer; by A.B Hunter.

74. 25 May 1898 CHARLES L. CLARK 30 yrs single b. Summers Co W VA now living same s/o A.J. & Isabell H to STELLA A. FRENCH 16 yrs single b. Giles Co VA d/o Wm L. & Lanesa O: farming; by J.E. Bruce.

75. 25 May 1898 J.L. MARKHAM 30 yrs single b. VA s/o Fleming & E.J. to DORA ANNIE SMITH 20 yrs single b. VA d/o Henry C. & Mary E. O: miner; by R.A. Kelly.

76. 25 May 1898 G.F. JOHNSON 24 yrs single b. VA s/o Wm & Mary to P.M. BAUGUESS 17 yrs single b. NC d/o John & ? O: miner; by D.A. Ramey.

77. 30 May 1898 JOHN T. HARTWELL 24 yrs single b. VA to ELLA BRANCH 22 yrs single; by G.W. Alexander; REMARKS: col'd.

78. 29 May 1898 THOMAS WOODY 26 yrs single b. VA s/o Abraham & Eliza to SALLIE GAMMON 21 yrs single b. VA d/o W.T. & Dollie; by R.H. McCoy; REMARKS: col'd.

79. 28 May 1898 J.D. KIRBY 23 yrs single b. VA s/o Robert R. & Mary to WILLIE R. HURST 16 yrs single b. VA d/o W.J. & ? O: miner; by John H. Honaker.

80. 28 May 1898 A.W. HOWARD 24 yrs single b. IL now living in Hingo Co W VA s/o Chas A. & Elizabeth to B.R. SAHUELS 19 yrs single b. Spotsylvania VA d/o A.J. & M.E. O: RR; by Wm Wistar Hamilton.

81. 1 June 1898 D.B. LAMBERT 20 yrs single b. Mercer Co W VA s/o S.P & M.J. to T.O. GODFREY 19 yrs single b. Mercer Co W VA d/o A.B. & S.M. O: farmer; by G.W. Bailey.

82. 2 June 1898 C.L. BAILEY 33 yrs single b. Mercer Co W VA s/o Addison C. & Octavia to SARAH J.E. TALIAFERRO 16 yrs single b. Mercer Co W VA d/o P.N. & Frances O: farmer; by G.W. Bailey.

83. 31 May 1898 W.A. EPLING 24 yrs single b. Giles Co VA s/o A.E. & M.F. to H.E. BOGLE 25 yrs single b. Bland Co VA O: RR; by S.E. Houk.

84. 1 June 1898 RUFUS W. LAXTON 23 yrs single b. Wyoming Co W VA s/o Henkich & Jane to LAURA BELL ZORA COOK 17 yrs single b. Mercer Co W VA d/o John N. & Margaret A. O: farmer; by G.W. Bailey.

85. 1 June 1898 W.J. CARPER 22 yrs engle b. Mercer Co W VA s/o Flern & Martha to FANNIE J. WINFREY 19 yrs single b. Mercer Co W VA d/o Lum & Lidilia O: farmer; by S.e. Houk.

86. 9 June 1898 ALBERT WINGFIELD 51 yrs single b. VA s/o Albert & Martha to LUCINDA POE 36 yrs single b. Mercer Co W VA d/o Jenny & ? O: farmer; by D.C. Sanders.

87. 8 June 1898 WILLIAM SMITH 18 yrs single b. Mercer Co W VA s/o William H. & Victoria to ALLIE WIMMER 18 yrs single b. Mercer Co W VA d/o Samuel D. & Rhoda J. O: farmer; by R.A. Miller.

88. 15 June 1898 ARTHUR T. SHUMATE 18 yrs single b. Mercer Co W VA s/o r.A. & Elizabeth to MELVINA B. THORNTON 18 yrs single b. Mercer Co W VA d/o F.M. & A.J. Thornton O: farmer; by J.O. Cassaday; REMARKS: A.T. Shumate sworn.

89. 16 June 1898 JAS C. HAZLEWOOD 23 yrs single b. Mercer Co W VA s/o W.J. & A.e. Hazlewood to MAHALA E. SOUTHERN 16 yrs single b. Mercer Co W VA d/o J. Southern O: farmer; by W.L. Gantier; REMARKS: Jas C. Hazlewood sworn.

90. 22 June 1898 ROBT L. SNIDER 32 yrs single b. Mercer Co W VA s/o W.R. & D. Snider to BIR K. KEATLEY 28 yrs single b. Mercer Co W VA d/o John & Susan Keatley O: farmer; by S.E. Houk.

91. 24 June 1898 GENERAL LEE PENNINGTON 29 yrs wid. b. Lincoln Co W VA s/o LG. & R.E. to ALICE PENDLETON 25 yrs single b. Mercer Co W VA O: farmer; by James G. Tabor.

92. 26 June 1898 GEO W. JARRELL 33 yrs single b. Mercer Co W VA s/o Wash & Lizzie Jarrell to LULA BARKER 21 yrs single b. TN d/o D.S. & ? Barker O: railroader; by Wm Wistar Hamilton.

93. 28 June 1898 DOUGLASS SHIELDS 27 yrs single b. Pitts Co W VA now living in McDowell Co s/o J.H. & Elizabeth to ELLA HANSHEED 19 yrs single b. Mercer Co W VA d/o Charles & ? O: conductor; by D.A. Ramey.

94. 29 June 1898 WILLIAM BAKER 27 yrs b. Henry Co VA s/o Mat & L. Baker to LUTICIA CALLAWAY 20 yrs b. Franklin Co VA d/o A. & P. Miller O: coal miner; by J.W. Johnson.

95. 29 June 1898 LEWIS WARD 37 yrs wid. b. Campbell Co VA s/o Fany to KITTY WHITE 39 yrs wid. b. Bedford Co VA O: laborer; by Rev. A.J. Brown.

96. 29 June 1898 EDWARD WARD 25 yrs single b. Campbell Co VA s/o Dave & P. to SALLIE SPENCER 19 yrs single b. VA d/o C.H. & Rhoda O: mining; by Rev. A.J. Brown.

Page 94

97. 6 July 1898 C.A. PECK 33 yrs b. Monroe Co W VA s/o ? & Amanda M. to JUELLA HASTIN 33 yrs d/o E.W. Peck & Martha O: Express Agt; by A.B. Hunter.

98. 29 June 1898 FLOYD A. FRANCISCO 29 yrs b. Cable(sic) Co W VA s/o E.E. & Nannie to CHRISTINA V. PETERS 20 yrs b. Giles Co VA d/o Jacob L. & Mary S. O: RR; by Eugene Blake.

99. 3 July 1898 WINGO HARMAN 19 yrs single b. Mercer Co W VA s/o P. & S.J. Harman to TERRESA P. ROSS 19 yrs single b. Mercer Co W VA d/o J.B. & S. Ross O: farmer; by J.E. Bruce; REMARKS: Wingo Harman sworn.

100. 6 July 1898 ELMAS BAILEY 21 yrs single b. Mercer Co W VA s/o D.P. & M.J. Bailey to AMY MAY SHREWSBURY 16 yrs single b. Mercer Co W VA d/o E.B. & Tela Shrewsbury O: farmer; by I.W. Bailey; REMARKS: Elmas Bailey.

101. 20 July 1898 SIMON ERBY 24 yrs single b. Halifax Co VA s/o Jarrett & Julia Erby to CORHA JONES 21 yrs single d/o Jennie Jones O: coal miner; by J.W. Johnson.

102. 9 July 1898 ROBERT W. LILLY 26 yrs wid. b. Mercer Co W VA s/o Daniel Lilly to PEARL E. FARLEY 19 yrs single b. Summers Co W VA d/o O.J. Farley & Nannie Y. O: farmer; by Drury Bailey; REMARKS: father present.

103. 9 July 1898 J.H. JENKINS 23 yrs single b. Pulaski Co VA s/o Hugh & Catherine to SARAH SLADE 21 yrs single b. Pulaski Co VA d/o Oscar & Kittie O: hotel porter; by G.T. Wright; REMARKS: J.H. Jenkins sworn.

104. 8 July 1898 J.W. WINSTON 44 yrs div. b. VA s/o Lewis & Moriah to MARY DIXON 33 yrs wid. b. VA d/o William & Mariah Hill O: clerk; by F.T. Wright.

105. 12 July 1898 WILLIAM H. RAINES 30 yrs single b. Roanoke VA now living in McDowell to ROSA M.B. PENCE 24 yrs single b. Mercer Co W VA d/o P.G. Pence & J.K. O: miner; by J.B. Ward.

106. 13 July 1898 CHARLES EMORY CHAMBERS 24 yrs single b. Monroe Co W Va s/o J.A. & Elizabeth S. to RETTA LEDY 22 yrs single b. KY d/o J.C. & ? O: RR; by Wm Winstar Hamilton; REMARKS: Chambers sworn.

107. 14 July 1898 A.W. WHITLOW 23 yrs single b. Floyd Co VA s/o F.H. & Rebecca Whitlow to HARRIET C. HILL 21 yrs single b. Floyd Co VA d/o Robt & M.A. Hill O: farmer; by L. Goodwyne; REMARKS: J.H. Henry sworn.

108. 22 July 1898 GEO W. PALMER 21 yrs single b. Floyd Co VA s/o Ben & Mary to ROSA IRVIN 20 yrs single b. Bland Co VA d/o Isaac & Lucinda O: RR; by D.N. Saunders; REMARKS: Palmer sworn.

109. 27 July 1898 JAS H. GADD 23 yrs single b. Mercer Co W Va s/o W.H. & L.E. Gadd to MINNIE D. PETERS 17 yrs single b. Mercer Co W VA d/o Jas & M.A. Peters O: teacher; by James W. Lilly; REMARKS: C.C. Peters sworn.

110. 27 July 1898 W.C. PENN 25 yrs single b. Henry Co VA s/o ? & Lucy Penn to PEARL CISCO 17 yrs single b. Smith Co VA d/o ? & Stella Cisco O: railroader; by A.J. Brown; REMARKS: colored.

111. 27 July 1898 JAS L. McCLAUGHERTY 21 yrs single b. Mercer Co W VA s/o Jos H. & E.E. McClaugherty to LAURA MARTIN 21 yrs single b. Mercer Co W VA d/o Geo B. & Mary Martin O: farming; by J.H. McClaugherty.

112. 3 Aug 1898 JAS H. GRAHAM 19 yrs single b. Mercer Co W VA s/o Lynch & Mary Graham to ANNA J. WOOD 18 yrs single b. Mercer Co W VA d/o A.N. & E. Wood O: farming; by James W. Lilly; REMARKS: J.H. Graham sworn.

113. 20 Aug 1898 GRANT FULTON 27 yrs single b. Pitts Co VA s/o Charles & Juda to MANERVA ROBINSON 22 yrs single b. Pitts Co VA d/o Bob & Sarah O: miner; by J.W. Johnson; REMARKS: Powaten Wilson sworn.

114. 4 Aug 1898 WM H. WORTH 23 yrs single b. Rockbridge Co VA s/o ? & Mary Worth to MINNIE HOLSTON 25 yrs single b. Mercer Co W VA d/o A.J. & E. Holston O: butcher; by D.N. Saunders; REMARKS: both parties sworn.

115. 11 Aug 1898 ALLEN H. COX 21 yrs single b. Summers Co W VA s/o Matthew & Mary Cox to ARTHELIA C. SHREWSBURY 22 yrs single b. Mercer Co W VA d/o ? & Melissa Shrewsbury O: farmer; by Jas W. Lilly; REMARKS: A.H. Cox & J.F.M. Lilly.

116. 11 Aug 1898 CHAS W. MARTIN 24 yrs single b. Mercer Co W VA s/o Levi & Lula Martin to CORA A. FLETCHER 19 yrs single b. Mercer Co W VA d/o LG. & Ella Fletcher O: farmer; by J.W. Bennett; REMARKS: C.W. Martin sworn.

117. 14 Aug 1898 JOHN W. DUDLEY 22 yrs single b. Mercer Co W VA s/o Wm L. & Rebeca to VIOLA MEREDITH 21 yrs single b. Montgomery Co VA d/o John & Lucinna O: farmer; by W.H. Ayers; REMARKS: John Meredith sworn.

118. 17 Aug 1898 JOHN M. MEADOWS 33 yrs single b. Monroe Co W VA now living in Summers Co s/o G.C. & Isibel to MARY A. TILLER 21 yrs single b. Mercer Co W VA d/o J.F. & A.C. O: farmer; by M.C. Reed; REMARKS: father present.

119. 18 Aug 1898 A.J. MOORE 23 yrs single b. Roanoke Co VA s/o N.D. & M.M. Moore to ZELLA MICHALL 20 yrs single b. Mercer Co W VA d/o J.W. & Katie O: farmer; by H. Strong; REMARKS: P.H. Stanley sworn.

120. 18 Aug 1898 J.C. STEVENS 46 yrs to MOLLIE BISHOP 38 yrs; by J.S. French; REMARKS: Ed Cooper.

121. 24 Aug 1898 J.M. SHREWSBURY 21 yrs single b. Mercer Co W VA s/o E.B. & T.F. to L.C. HURST 21 yrs single b.

Mercer Co W VA d/o Jas H. & Sarah O: farmer; by L.H. Bailey; REMARKS: J.M. Shrewsbury sworn.

122. 24 Aug 1898 E.L. DAVIDSON 23 yrs single b. Mercer Co W VA s/o H.P. & Lucinda to L.B. TILLER 18 yrs single b. Mercer Co W VA d/o C.L & E. O: farmer; by J.W. Rader; REMARKS: father present.

123. 24 Aug 1898 GEO W. TAYLOR 20 yrs single b. Mercer Co W VA s/o John & H.F. Taylor to ARDELIA FARMER 18 yrs single b. Mercer Co W VA d/o S.W. & r. Farmer O: farmer; by G.C. Anderson; REMARKS: John Taylor sworn.

124. 24 Aug 1898 ISAAC H. MEADOR 46 yrs wid. b. Raleigh Co W VA s/o Sylvester & Mary to MARY F. COX 31 yrs single b. Summers Co W VA d/o Mathew & Mary O: farmer; by Jas W. Lilly; REMARKS: M.A. Cox sworn.

125. 31 Aug 1898 LEE CONNER 22 yrs single b. Pulaski Co W VA s/o Henry & Maranda to LAURA GALLAWAY 17 yrs single b. Wythe Co VA d/o George & Sarah O: miner; by G.W. Alexander; REMARKS: col'd, W.J. Rumburg.

126. 4 Sept 1898 BENJAMIN F. PORTER 22 yrs single b. Caroll Co VA s/o Steven D. & Victory to IDA M. CONNER 17 yrs single b. Halifax Co VA d/o Tanvill T. & Bell O: miner; by D.A. Ramsey; REMARKS: W.J. Rumburg.

127. 31 Aug 1898 W.C. MAYS 27 yrs single b. Amherst Co VA s/o L.M. & H.J. to NETTIE N. DOUTHAT 17 yrs single b. Giles Co VA d/o Wm H. & S.Va. O: RR; by A.B. Hunter.

128. 1 Sept 1898 CHARLEY CHRYSTON 22 yrs single s/o Cumfrey to JULIA B. BURTON 17 yrs single b. Mercer Co W VA d/o Wm H. & Elvira O: farmer; by John H. Honaker; REMARKS: J.E. Belcher sworn.

129. 4 Sept 1898 C.H. ROSENFILD 22 yrs single b. Richmond VA s/o John & Margaret to M.C. JOHNSON 19 yrs single b. Mercer Co W VA d/o J.C. & Martha J. O: farmer; by J.W. Bennett; REMARKS: father present.

130. 6 Sept 1898 W.R. BAILEY 27 yrs single b. Mercer Co W VA s/o Daniel P. & Mary J. to IDA L. KINZER 21 yrs single b. Mercer Co W VA d/o Tom & L.S. Kinzer O: merchant; by J.E. Bruce; REMARKS: sworn.

131. 6 Sept 1898 C.C. TABOR 27 yrs single b. Tazewell Co VA s/o G.W. & ? Tabor to MARY A. RODGERS 34 yrs wid. b. Mercer Co W VA d/o Jas & Matilda Dillon O: farmer; by W.H. Ayers.

132. 7 Sept 1898 ALFRED F. SLIGH 25 yrs sigle b. Bedford Co VA s/o Isaac & Julia to RACHEL BALES 26 yrs single b. Tazewell Co VA d/o Wm & Rebeca O: RR; by S.E. Houk; REMARKS: Sligh sworn.

133. 15 Sept 1898 JOS W. SMITH 29 yrs single b. Tazewell Co VA s/o J.L. & M.A. Smith to MAGGIE J. ALBERT 23 yrs single b. TN d/o J.R. & ? Albert O: miner; by R.A. Kelly.

134. 22 Sept 1898 GUS BAILEY 21 yrs single b. Htn City TN s/o John & ? Bailey to CORA A. SMITH 18 yrs single b. VA d/o Wm & Ada Smith O: miner; by G.W. Alexander; REMARKS: colored.

135. 21 Sept 1898 W.L COX 19 yrs single b. Summers Co now living same s/o J.M. & S.C. to FANNIE D. ELLISON 16 yrs single b. Mercer Co W VA d/o R.F. & H.J. O: farmer; by Drewry Farley; REMARKS: father present.

136. 19 Sept 1898 R.S. WILLIAMS 27 yrs single b. Tazewell Co VA now living in Buffalo NY s/o W.C. & O.E. Williams to LEONA MURRELL 25 yrs single b. MO d/o James & ? Murrell O: civil engineer; by P.C. Clark.

137. 28 Sept 1898 JNO W. THOMPSON 23 yrs single b. Campbell Co VA s/o Peter & A. Thompson to MARY B. SCOTT 23 yrs single b. Franklin Co VA d/o Saml & Nancy Scott O: laborer; by A.J. Brown; REMARKS: col'd.

138. 28 Sept 1898 GEO W. JOHNSON 23 yrs single b. Charlotte Co VA s/o Wm & Nancy Johnson to ENDORA CLAYTON 22 yrs wid. b. Campbell Co VA d/o Peter & Adaline Rose O: laborer; by A.J. Brown; REMARKS: col'd.

139. 29 Sept 1898 J.O. CLENDENEN 24 yrs single b. Mercer Co W VA s/o R.G. & M.E. to MAGGIE V. LONG 21 yrs single b. PA d/o P.J. & ? O: RR; by E. Olivier; REMARKS: sworn.

140. 4 Oct 1898 W.G. COOPER 24 yrs single b. IN now living in Summers s/o V.W. & L.G. to H.E. RICHMOND 16 yrs single b. W VA d/o Park & Elizabeth O: farmer; by Drewry Farley; REMARKS: J.E. Cooper sworn.

141. 5 Oct 1898 C.R. BROWN 27 yrs single b. VA s/o J.K. & E.J. to ALICE JONES 17 yrs single b. VA d/o Jacob & F.A. O: RR; by A.B. Hunter; REMARKS: father present.

142. 8 Oct 1898 BENNETT C. BRYAN 22 yrs single b. Floyd Co VA now living in McDowell s/o James K. & Susan to NANNIE M. YOUNG 25 yrs single b. Franklin Co VA d/o S.H. & Ann O: miner; by John H. Honaker; REMARKS: sworn.

143. 5 Oct 1898 JOS K. FAULKNER 24 yrs single b. Mercer Co W VA s/o Gordan & A.E. Faulkner to M.E. POE 19 yrs single b. Mercer Co W VA d/o T.E. & M.E. Poe O: railroad fireman; by W.H. Ayres.

144. 6 Oct 1898 CLAY NOSLER 21 yrs single b. Giles Co VA s/o W.A. & Hattie to NANNIE ALIFF 18 yrs single b. Montgomery Co VA d/o Thos & Nannie O: RR; by A.B. Hunter; REMARKS: Nosler sworn.

Page 95

145. 12 Oct 1898 ROBERT M. KING 24 yrs single b. VA s/o J.H. & Jane to MALINDA FRANCES PENNINGTON 29 yrs single b. W VA d/o Riley & ? O: farmer; by Jos W. Lilly; REMARKS: J.H. King sworn.

146. 11 Oct 1898 R.H. THOMAS 24 yrs single b. Monroe Co VA s/o J.w. & Sarah to D.W. THOMAS 28 yrs single b. Mercer Co W VA d/o Wm G. & Annie O: farmer; by R.A. Miller; REMARKS: affidavit.

147. 19 Oct 1898 ROBERT M. WAYODS 24 yrs single b. Tazewell Co VA s/o Isaac & Rachel to BILLIE WOODSON 34 yrs single b. VA d/o Rose O: miner; by G.W. Alexander.

148. 11 Oct 1898 GEO A. SMITH 24 yrs single b. VA s/o Bill & Mary to MYRTLE JENNINGS 21 yrs single b. Mercer Co W VA d/o W.H. Jennings O: RR; by John F. Stone.

149. 12 Oct 1898 H.P. BAILEY 20 yrs single b. McDowell Co W VA s/o Mastin & Nancy Bailey to ELLEN PRICHARD 17 yrs single b. Mercer Co W VA d/o Thos & Sally Prichard O: farming; by J.W. Bennett.

150. 14 Oct 1898 CHARLES MACK 23 yrs single b. VA to MALINDA COLIVER 16 yrs single b. VA d/o J.C. & Martha O: miner; by R.H. McKoy.

151. 13 Oct 1898 W.H. WHITWORTH 25 yrs single b. Montgomery Co VA s/o G.R. & S.H. to MAGGIE F. RATCLIFFE 18 yrs single b. Tazewell Co VA d/o Nannie J. O: RR; by J.E. Bruce.

152. 13 Oct 1898 C.M. BELCHER 18 yrs single b. Mercer Co W VA s/o A.G. & Martha A. to JOSEPHINE BAILEY 19 yrs single b. Mercer Co W VA d/o John H. & Julia O: farmer; by Jno H. Honaker; REMARKS: father present.

153. 16 Oct 1898 JOHN T. TAYLOR 21 yrs single b. Mercer Co W VA s/o John & Mary I. to EDEN VIRGRELEE TAYLOR 20 yrs single b. Mercer Co W VA d/o ? & Matilda O: miner; by G.W. Bailey.

154. 18 Oct 1898 JOHN F. MATHESON single b. SC s/o John F. & Mary E. to KATE F. JENNINGS 19 yrs single b. VA d/o A.M. & Bessie O: minister; by R.G. Matheson.

155. 19 Oct 1898 LEWIS N. FARRAN 27 yrs single b. Appomattox Co VA s/o S.D. & A.M. Farran to ELLA L. CLIFFORD 17 yrs single b. Alleghany Co Va d/o H.M. & R.A. Clifford O: RR engineer; by E.Olivier.

156. 19 Oct 1898 F.P. FRENCH 23 yrs single b. Mercer Co W VA s/o H.R. & Hollie A. to ANNIE L. HEDRECK 16 yrs single b. Mercer Co W Va d/o H.M. & N.L. O: RR; by Wm W. Hamilton; REMARKS: French sworn.

157. 19 Oct 1898 HERBERT E. APPLE 30 yrs single b. Augusta Co VA s/o Wm H. & E.A. to MARGARET FRENCH 24 yrs single b. Mercer Co W VA d/o David & Mary O: merchant; by Frank Jackson.

158. 20 Oct 1898 GEORGE MORRIS 22 yrs single b. Albemarle Co Va s/o Allen & Julia Morris to REBECCA A. HALL 17 yrs single b. Mercer Co W VA d/o Harvey & E. Hall O: farming; by J.O. Cassaday.

159. 2 Nov 1898 MILLARD F. McCOMAS 19 yrs single b. Mercer Co W VA s/o R.B. & O.A. McComas to LAUVERNIA LILLY 18 yrs single b. Mercer Co W VA d/o A.J. & S.E. Lilly O: farming; by James W. Lilly.

160. 26 Oct 1898 KURNEY A. HOUCHINS 21 yrs single b. Mercer Co W VA s/o Ballard & ? Houchins to DAISY B. AKERS 18 yrs single d/o H.H. & Elizabeth Akers O: farming; by James W. Lilly.

161. 26 Oct 1898 BENJAMINE ENGLISH 21 yrs single b. Franklin Co VA s/o S.D. & M. to MYRTLE POWELL 16 yrs single b. Ada W VA d/o Mc H. & H.J. O: miner; by R.A. Kelly; REMARKS: Thos Dowdy sworn.

162. 26 Oct 1898 THOMAS DOWDY 29 yrs single b. Franklin Co VA s/o John & Betie to HATTIE MAY DICKERSON 24 yrs single b. Bedford Co VA d/o D. & Martha O: miner; by R.A. Kelly; REMARKS: Thos Dowdy sworn.

163. 28 Oct 1898 R.W. HOSLEY 48 yrs div. b. NC s/o H.D. & Martha to ALICE WESTLAND 38 yrs single b. NC d/o James & ? O: miner; by C.A. Chrisman; REMARKS: r.W. Hosley.

164. 26 Oct 1898 JAMES E. BUCKLEY 26 yrs single b. Smith Co VA s/o J.R. & Margaret to MARTHA ERECIA BICKER 22 yrs single b. Franklin Co VA s/o T.H & Florence L. O: RR; by C.A. Chrisman; REMARKS: father present.

165. 26 Oct 1898 W.H. CORNETT 24 yrs single b. Grayson Co VA now living same s/o F.R. & E.H. to EDNA F. McCLAUGHERTY 22 yrs single b. Giles Co VA d/o R.C. & S.W. O: farmer; by S.D. Long.

166. 27 Oct 1898 H.B. MILLER 25 yrs single b. Mercer Co W VA s/o ? & Margaret Miller to MARY M. MARTIN 20 yrs single b. Mercer Co W VA d/o W.R. & C.J. Martin O: laborer; by G.W. Terry; REMARKS: H.B. Miller sworn.

167. 2 Nov 1898 J.K. CARBAUGH 23 yrs single b. Mrcr Co W VA s/o Jno H. & s. Carbaugh to BETTIE A. SAUNDERS 23 yrs single b. Mercer Co W VA d/o D.N. & N. Saunders O: farming; by S.E. Houk.

168. 15 Nov 1898 ED P. NEELY 19 yrs single b. Summers Co W VA now living same s/o J.H. & H.A. Neely to WILLIE M. WYRICK 19 yrs single b. Mercer Co W VA d/o J.H. & ? Wyrick O: farming; by G.M. Johnston; REMARKS: Absolom Kirk sworn.

169. 20 Nov 1898 THOS J. BELCHER 44 yrs wid. b. Mercer Co W VA s/o Chris & Polly Belcher to MARY C. SHEPPARD 24 yrs wid. b. NC d/o ? & Julia Shepard O: merchant; by Jno H. Honaker.

170. 16 Nov 1898 HARRISON SHRADER 26 yrs single b. Mercer Co W VA s/o A.J. & Elvira Shrader to NORA H. STAMP 25 yrs single b. Floyd Co VA d/o J.B. & Sally Stamp O: farming; by G.W. Bailey.

171. 16 Nov 1898 CLARANCE F. RAHLE 22 yrs single b. Mercer Co W VA s/o Jno B. & Maggie Kahle to LOU E. HARMAN 18 yrs single b. Mercer Co W VA d/o Chas & M.J. Harman O: farming; by Eugene Blake; REMARKS: Clarence F. Kahle sworn.

172. 16 Nov 1898 C.D. HAMBRICK 23 yrs single b. Mercer Co W V s/o Geo & Amy to INDIA PEARL FARLEY 18 yrs single b. Giles Co VA d/o H.F. & Nannie E. O: farming; by G.M. Johnston; REMARKS: father present.

173. 17 Nov 1898 JERRY HAYWOOD 23 yrs single b. Mercer Co W Va s/o Vicy to ELIZA FINLEY 18 yrs single b. Mercer Co W VA O: farming; by W.H. Parkins; REMARKS: guardian present.

174. 20 Nov 1898 ISAIAH HILL 20 yrs single b. Mercer Co W VA to ALICE BRIGGS 18 yrs single b. NC d/o D.H. & M.E. Briggs O: farming; by G.C. Anderson; REMARKS: L Hill sworn.

175. 19 Nov 1898 JAS H. HALL 24 yrs single b. Montgomery Co VA s/o Jas & Lucinda Hall to MARIAH L. CARTER 17 yrs single b. McDowell Co W VA d/o Wm & Mary Carter O: farming; by S.E. Houk.

176. 23 Nov 1898 JAS O. ARCHER 21 yrs single b. Mercer Co W VA s/o James & ? Archer to LOUISA L MAXEY 20 yrs single b. Mercer Co W VA d/o Josiah & L.A. Maxey O: farming; by James W. Lilly; REMARKS: G.W. Maxey sworn.

177. 23 Nov 1898 WADE H. BAILEY 30 yrs single b. Tazewell Co VA s/o Estill & Agnes C. to EFFIE E. TUGGLE 21 yrs single b. Mercer Co W VA d/o Henry & Easter J. O: farming; by Jas H. Johnston.

178. 23 Nov 1898 TILDEN H. HOLT 26 yrs single b. Mercer Co W VA s/o ? & Gracie Holt to ORA STINSON 20 yrs single b. Mercer Co W VA d/o J.W. & ? Stinson O: merchant; by S.E. Houk.

179. 27 Nov 1898 L.H. QUESENBERRY 24 yrs single b. Carroll C VA s/o Thos & Louisa to EMILY CARTER 20 yrs single b. Floyd Co VA d/o J.H. & Mary O: farmer; by R.A. Miller; REMARKS: father present.

180. 28 Nov 1898 SAMUEL CRUSE 24 yrs single b. Halifax Co VA s/o James & Sarah to MARY HILLER 24 yrs wid. b. Montgomery Co VA d/o Nelson & ? O: miner; by J.D. Leftwich; REMARKS: col'd.

181. 30 Nov 1898 HOE THOMAS 25 yrs single s/o John & Lucy to MARY CAMPBELL 27 yrs single d/o Pleasant & Martha O: miner; by R.H. McKoy; REMARKS: col'd.

182. 30 Nov 1898 GREEN W. MEADOWS 23 yrs single b. Summers Co W VA s/o Chas & Oma Meadows to VIRGINIA DOVE 32 yrs single b. Mrcer Co W VA d/o Jas & ? Lilly O: farming; by German P. Hatcher.

183. 30 Nov 1898 GEO W. LITTLE 23 yrs single b. Grayson Co VA s/o Johnathan & Mary to EMMA DENT 20 yrs single b. Carroll Co VA d/o Thos & Charlott A. O: miner; by R.A. Kelly; REMARKS: father present.

184. 8 Dec 1898 WALLER McHARTIN 22 yrs single b. Mercer Co W VA s/o Wm K. & Syntha to ANGELINE BOLEN 17 yrs single b. Mercer Co W VA d/o G.W. & H.E. O: farmer; by W.I. Gantier.

185. 7 Dec 1898 E.H. NEAL 28 yrs single b. Mercer Co W VA s/o James H. & Syntha R. to MARY EFFIE BELCHER 22 yrs single b. Mercer Co W VA O: conductor; by J.W. Rader.

186. 14 Dec 1898 THOS J. RADER 24 yrs single b. Tazewell Co VA now living same s/o Wm E. & Jennie Rader to ELSIE LEE WALRUP 18 yrs single b. Mercer Co W VA d/o H.W. & Elizabeth Walrup O: mechanic; by R.H. Ashworth.

187. 18 Dec 1898 T.T. WATTS 23 yrs div. to D.D. DUNCAN 19 yrs single b. Mercer Co W VA d/o A.H. & Rebeca O: sawmilling; by J.F. Matheson; REMARKS: father present.

188. * * * L. LEWELLYN BREEDLOVE 23 yrs single s/o J. & C.H. to LUCY LEE PERDUE 21 yrs single b. Mercer Co W VA d/o J.H. & Sarah F. O: electrician; REMARKS: witness sworn. (*Note: no date given.)

189. 22 Dec 1898 WILLIAM F. JENNINGS 22 yrs single b. Carroll Co VA s/o Robert & Evaline to MARY E. MOORE 17 yrs single b. Pulaski Co VA d/o John A. & Amanda J. O: miner; by A.M. Craft; REMARKS: Jennings sworn.

190. 21 Dec 1898 CORNELIUS ROBINSON 26 yrs single b. Franklin Co Va s/o James A. & B. to M.J. BROYLES 27 yrs single b. Mercer Co W VA d/o Erastus & Josephine O: carpenter; by Wm W. Hamilton.

Page 96

191. 21 Dec 1898 E.C. BAILEY 21 yrs single b. Mercer Co W VA s/o R.H. & L.J. Bailey to EDNA A. DARE 17 yrs single b. mercer Co W Va d/o Jos H. & S.N. Dare O: farmer; by J.A. Ellison.

192. 21 Dec 1898 A.E. BIVIUS 22 yrs single b. Monroe Co W VA now living same s/o R.H. & E.A. Bivius to STELLA M. CALFEE 21 yrs single b. Mercer Co W VA d/o W.D. & M.F. Calfee O: drummer; by Jno W. West.

193. 22 Dec 1898 LEVY RADCLIFF 25 yrs wid. b. Washington Co VA s/o Jessie to ALICE THOMPSON 22 yrs single b. Washington Co VA d/o John & Caroline O: miner; by G.W. Alexander.

194. 22 Dec 1898 T.H. PATTERSON 40 yrs single b. VA to M.E. PENNINGTON 18 yrs single b. Mercer Co W V d/o J.A. & M.E. O: farmer; by W.L Gautier; REMARKS: father present.

195. 22 Dec 1898 THOMAS FITZBURGH 18 yrs single to FLORA BELCHER 37 yrs wid. b. Mercer Co W VA d/o Henry & Sarah; by D.N. Saunders; REMARKS: guardian present.

196. 22 Dec 1898 GEORGE BROWN 19 yrs single b. Mercer Co W VA s/o W.S. Brown & Harriet to FANNIE HAZLEWOOD 18 yrs single b. Mercer Co W VA d/o Starling & Octave O: farmer; by S.E. Houk; REMARKS: father present.

197. 23 Dec 1898 J.A. KARNES, JR. 21 yrs single b. Mercer Co W VA s/o J.A. & E.A. to KATE BALLARD 19 yrs single b. Monroe Co W VA d/o G.G. & L.A. O: farmer; by Thos B. Cook; REMARKS: certificate witnessed.

198. 24 Dec 1898 CHARLIE STAHL 19 yrs single b. PA now living in Fayette Co W VA s/o Elias & Susan Stahl to FANNIE BLESSING 18 yrs single b. Mercer Co W VA d/o ? & Caroline Blessing O: miner; by G.W. Bailey; REMARKS: Chas Stahl sworn.

199. 23 Dec 1898 L.C. WOOLWINE 21 yrs single b. Montgomery Co VA s/o R.P. & S.P. Woolwine to FLOSSIE E. WALTERS 22 yrs single b. Montgomery Co VA d/o Mollie D. O: railroader; by Wm W. Hamilton; REMARKS: guardian present & sworn.

200. 24 Dec 1898 JAMES A. PENINGTON 20 yrs single b. Mercer Co W VA s/o J.A. & M.E. to E.J. MEADOWS 19 yrs single b. Mercer Co W Va d/o Jas C. & Mary O: farmer; by W.B. Booth; REMARKS: witness sworn.

201. 27 Dec 1898 WM A. WILLIAMS 23 yrs single b. Mercer Co W VA s/o J.A. & Rebeca to ALBERTA ROSE NICEWANDER 18 yrs single b. Bland d/o W.H.H. & N. O: farmer; by R.A. Kelly.

202. 2* Dec 1898 W.P. HARMAN 21 yrs single b. Mercer Co W VA s/o Patrick & Sarah J. to MARY E. BROWN 17 yrs single b. Mercer d/o Wm S. & Harriet A. O: farmer; by G.W. Terry; REMARKS: father present. (*Note: unable to clearly read date.)

203. 2* Dec 1898 JAMES JONES 26 yrs single b. Charlott VA s/o Emeline to MARY CARTER 22 yrs single b. Amherst VA d/o Walter & ? O: RR; by A.J. Brown. (*Note: unable to clearly read date.)

204. 27 Dec 1898 C.J. SARVER 20 yrs single b. Mercer s/o W.A. & Mary A. to LULA HARE 18 yrs single b. Bland Co d/o James O: farmer; by L. Goodwyn; REMARKS: witness sworn.

205. 28 Dec 1898 N.A. MILLS 26 yrs single b. Pittsylvania Co VA s/o W.C. & Bettie to LAUDONA HAMBRICK 23 yrs single b. Mercer Co W VA d/o Joseph & Ellen O: sawmilling; by G.W. Bailey; REMARKS: witness sworn.

206. 29 Dec 1898 A.E. GADD 19 yrs single b. Mercer s/o W.H. & L.E. to NONA A. LILLY 16 yrs single b. Raleigh d/o Joseph & J.A. O: farmer; by Jas W. Lilly; REMARKS: witness sworn.

207. 28 Dec 1898 JOHN FORD 25 yrs single b. Monroe s/o George & ? to MARTHA VIA 23 yrs single b. Patrick d/o S.& Mary O: farmer; by W.B. Booth; REMARKS: witness sworn.

208. 29 Dec 1898 WM VIA 21 yrs single b. Patrick s/o G.W. & Moriah to XANTIPPER SHRADER 16 yrs single b. Mercer d/o Conrad & Virginia O: cabinet maker; by W.B. Booth; REMARKS: witness sworn.

209. 29 Dec 1898 JOHN W. DOSS 22 yrs single b. Pittsylvania VA s/o F. & S.J. to LILLY B. BOWLING 17 yrs single b. Tazewell Co VA d/o G.W. & Martha O: miner; by D.A. Ramsey.

210. 26 Dec 1898 SAMUEL B. MILLS 22 yrs single b. Mercer Co W VA s/o James & Mary to NICATIE F. NICHOLS 22 yrs single b. Giles Co VA O: farmer; by J.O. Cassaday.

211. 29 Dec 1898 C.J. LYONS 35 yrs wid. b. TN s/o T.C. & Emeline to LUCY A. JONES 22 yrs single b. Mercer Co W VA d/o Kenna & Anna O: miner; by J.W. Johnson; REMARKS: witness sworn.

212. 27 Dec 1898 O.B. CAMPBELL 25 yrs single b. Monroe Co W VA now living same s/o Lewis P. & Isabelle Campbell to NANNIE CRAWFORD 21 yrs single b. Mercer Co W VA d/o S.M. & Emily L. Crawford O: school teacher; by Will L. Hall.

213. 29 Dec 1898 ANDREW ANDERSON 33 yrs single b. VA s/o Lewis & Nancy to ELLA WILSON 30 yrs wid. b. VA d/o J. & Nancy O: waiter hotel; by S.M. Gaines; REMARKS: sworn, col'd.

214. 28 Dec 1898 JAMES DICKERSON 30 yrs single b. KY s/o Robt & Caroline to SOPHIA CLARK 25 yrs single b. VA d/o John & ? O: RR; by S.M. Gaines.

215. 28 Dec 1898 C.E. WINDSON 28 yrs single b. Fayett Co W VA s/o Anderson & Martha to FANNIE E. SPICER 18 yrs single b. Mercer Co W VA d/o Wm & ? O: miner; by D.a Ramsey; REMARKS: sworn.

216. 29 Dec 1898 ANDREW G. HIGGENBOTHAM 35 yrs single b. Mercer Co W VA s/o ? & Sarah E. to DOSHA L. HAZLEWOOD 18 yrs single b. Mercer Co W VA d/o E.E. & E.N. O: farmer; by W.L Gautier; REMARKS: sworn.

217. 30 Dec 1898 W.R. DAVIS 24 yrs single b. Mercer s/o Wm & Nancy to ADA M.E. HARVEY 17 yrs single b. Mercer Co W VA d/o Floyd & Emeline O: sawmilling; by r.M. Ashworth.

218. 31 Dec 1898 W.R. PHIPPS 31 yrs single b. Raleigh Co s/o J.R. & Mary to FLORENE MAY BELCHER 19 yrs single b. Mercer Co W VA d/o Allen & Sallie E. O: merchant; by Wm W. Hamilton.

Page 97

1. 8 Jan 1899 GEORGE GILLS 22 yrs single b. Bland VA s/o Benj & Mary to LOLY BELCHER 17 yrs single b. Mercer Co W VA d/o A.R. & ? O: RR & farmer; by G.W. Bailey; REMARKS: sworn witness Crockett Scott & W.M. Gills.

2. 9 Jan 1899 SIDNEY SIMPSON 37 yrs wid. b. Wythe Co VA s/o Bob & Charlotte Simpson to MILLY LEE 39 yrs wid. b. Wythe Co VA d/o Humphrey & ? Austin O: blacksmith; by S.M. Gaines; REMARKS: S.M.G, col'd.

3. 19 Jan 1899 JOHN SMITH 27 yrs single b. NC s/o Jos & Lillie Smith to ELIZA WATSON 26 yrs single b. Russell Co VA d/o Killy & Julia Watson O: farmer; by W.H. Ayers.

4. 12 Jan 1899 W.A. TACKET 53 yrs wid. b. NC s/o Alex & Caroline to JANE HOLCOMB 48 yrs wid. b. Franklin Co VA d/o Preston & Mary Hall O: farmer; by D.A. Ramey.

5. 18 Feb 1899 ROBERT T. MILLER 20 yrs single b. Mercer s/o Maggie to BETTIE PETTRY 20 yrs single b. Mrcer d/o A.T. & N.J. O: farmer; by J.T. Tabor.

6. 18 Jan 1899 JOHN A. THORNTON 39 yrs single b. Mercer Co W VA s/o Jas A. & Louisa to DARINDA BONHAM 23 yrs wid. b. Mercer d/o W.H. & Victoria O: farmer; by L. Goodwyn.

7. 19 Jan 1899 F.D. MORING 40 yrs wid. b. Richmond VA now living in Tazewell Co VA s/o W.W. & M.J. to ALICE M. WILSON 26 yrs wid. b. Mercer Co W VA d/o John W. & M.D. Johnston O: merchant; by T.F. Suthers.

8. 19 Jan 1899 W.A. COOPER 23 yrs single b. Franklin Co VA s/o Jos & Mandy to DELIA MELVIN 25 yrs single b. Mercer Co W VA d/o P.H. & Ann O: farmer; by J.O. Cassaday; REMARKS: sworn.

9. 25 Jan 1899 CHARLES L. SMITH 21 yrs single b. McDowell Co VA s/o G.F. & Martha L. to MINNIE E. KADE 18 yrs single b. Mercer Co W VA d/o G.W. & Mary M. O: farmer; by Eugene Blake; REMARKS: sworn.

10. 26 Jan 1899 ELBERT COMBS 22 yrs single b. Carol Co VA to ALICE McKINNEY 21 yrs single b. Mercer Co W VA d/o L.F. & Margaret O: farmer; by W.B. Booth; REMARKS: sworn.

11. 26 Jan 1899 L.P. HARRISON 29 yrs single b. Floyd Co VA s/o E.F. & Sarah to KATIE STITES 20 yrs single b. Russel Co VA d/o R.F. & Emily O: RR; by John F. Stone.

12. 25 Jan 1899 WM MARTIN 33 yrs single b. Bedford Co VA s/o Booker & Mildred to CHARLOTT ELLIOTT 31 yrs wid. b. Montgomery VA d/o Adaline Palmer O: RR; by A.J. Brown.

13. 2 Feb 1899 CHARLEY N. COLLINS 21 yrs single b. NC s/o G.W. & Elizabeth to WILLIE SMITH 27 yrs single b. VA d/o James & Ann O: miner; by D.A. Ramey.

14. 25 Jan 1899 JOHN S. CLARK 64 yrs wid. b. AL s/o Jack Bruce & Nicy Clark to EMILINE EAVES 64 yrs wid. b. VA O: farmer; by Eugene Blake.

15. 1 Feb 1899 SAMUEL P. WHITE 24 yrs single b. Mercer Co W VA s/o J.K. & J.H. to OLIVIA M. STEELE 21 yrs single b. Mercer Co W VA d/o W.F. & Rhoda O: farmer; by W.B. Booth.

16. 1 Feb 1899 FLOYD HYPES 26 yrs single b. Mercer Co W VA s/o J.L. & Jane to IDA F. BROYLES 21 yrs single b. Mercer Co W VA d/o Leroy & Lizzie O: farmer; by Eugene Blake.

17. 1 Feb 1899 M.H. HILL 53 yrs wid. b. Montgomery s/o J.L. & F.W. to CHARLOTT F. BAILEY 25 yrs single b. Mercer Co W VA d/o W.L. & ? O: farmer; by G.W. Bailey.

18. 2 Feb 1899 J.W.S. BURNETT 23 yrs single b. Floyd Co VA s/o J.B. & F. to ANNIE KATE PERDUE 17 yrs single b. Franklin Co VA d/o J.A. & N.A. O: miner; by D.A. Daugherty.

19. 1 Feb 1899 G.W. HELMS 20 yrs single b. Franklin Co VA d/o Thomas O. & M. to VIRGIE A. CLARK 16 yrs single b. Mercer Co W VA d/o Elijah & Judith A. O: farmer; by German P. Hatcher.

20. 2 Feb 1899 O.O. KARNES 29 yrs single b. Mercer Co W VA s/o R.F. & Elizabeth to IDA K. THOMPSON 24 yrs single b. Bland VA d/o David & Catharine O: merchant; by J.H. McClaugherty.

21. 5 Feb 1899 RUSH ODELL 20 yrs single b. Mercer s/o Abraham & Martha to LOUISA REED 18 yrs single b. Raleigh c/o G.W. & R.C. O: farmer; by L.H. Bailey; REMARKS: father present.

22. 9 Feb 1899 JAMES H. FRAZIER 21 yrs single b. Giles Co VA s/o C.J. & S.A. to BERTIE CRAWFORD 16 yrs single b. Summers Co W VA d/o R.B. & D.S. O: RR; by A.B. Hunter; REMARKS: witness sworn.

23. 15 Feb 1899 GEO S. DANNER 37 yrs wid. b. Roanoke Co VA s/o J.E. & J.E. Danner to LUCY CADWALANDER 26 yrs single b. Bedford Co VA d/o Jas & Frances O: carr inspector; by A.B. Hunter.

24. 16 Feb 1899 JAS MARVIN CECIL 19 yrs single b. Pulaski Co Va now living same s/o W.B. & Mollie Cecil to JOSIE BLANCH CECIL 19 yrs single b. Pulaski Co VA d/o Jno G. & M.J. Cecil O: farmer; by S.E. Houk.

25. 23 Feb 1899 JAMES SANDERS 24 yrs single b. NC s/o Riley & ? to VICTORY HARMAN 18 yrs single b. Mercer Co W VA d/o A.J. & L. O: farmer; by G.W. Bailey.

26. 22 Feb 1899 C.L. MEADOR 22 yrs single b. Summer Co VA s/o James & Bettie to ZIZA M. ALIFF 18 yrs single b. Mercer Co W VA d/o F.A. & Mary O: farmer; by John H. Honaker.

27. 22 Feb 1899 GILES C. SUBLETT 22 yrs single b. Montgomery Co VA s/o Wm & R.F. Sublett to THEORA J. DUNN 18 yrs single b. Mercer Co W VA d/o J.W. & Mary C. Dunn O: farmer; by W.I. Gantier; REMARKS: father, J.W. Dunn, pres.

28. 1 Mar 1899 R.H. BAILEY 23 yrs single b. Mercer Co W VA s/o Henderson & Sarah to HARRIET A. BROYLES 18 yrs single b. Mercer Co W VA d/o Leroy & Lizzie O: farmer; by S.E. Houk; REMARKS: R.H. Bailey sworn.

29. 3 Mar 1899 ALEXANDER HEATH 36 yrs wid. b. Russell Co VA s/o Milton & Elizabeth to LIDDIE WARD 21 yrs single b. Tazewell Co VA d/o Reese & Jane O: miner; by J.W. Johnston.

30. 4 Mar 1899 O. CECIL HEDRICK 22 yrs single b. Mercer Co W VA s/o C.S. & S.E. to ELIZA F. LILLY 19 yrs single b. Raleigh Co W VA d/o John & ? O: farmer; by James P. Thompson.

31. 8 Mar 1899 S.P. MARTIN 27 yrs single b. Henry Co VA s/o Wm & Matilda to LIZZIE M. HOUCHINS 27 yrs wid. b. Mercer Co W VA O: RR; by John F. Stone.

32. 9 Mar 1899 ALEXANDER ROLES 68 yrs wid. to ESTALINE HEDRICK 37 yrs single b. Greenbrier Co W VA d/o D.W. & M.J. O: farmer; by J.H. Meadows.

33. 13 Mar 1899 CHARLEY MINOR 22 yrs single b. McDowell Co s/o Peter & Nancy to MAGGIE BELL FAROLER 17 yrs single b. Pulaski Co VA d/o Martin & Nancy O: miner; by G.W. Bailey.

34. 9 Mar 1899 CHARLES RYAN 23 yrs single b. Mercer Co W VA s/o ? & Rebecca Ryan to CLEMENTINE WEBB 17 yrs single b. Washington Co VA d/o F.N. & Oakley Webb O: farmer; by S.E. Houk; REMARKS: F.N. Webb present.

35. 9 Mar 1899 ASA PERDUE 26 yrs single b. Mercer County W VA s/o Tobe & Peggy Perdue to ALLIE B. THOMAS 26 yrs single b. Mercer Co W VA d/o Jas H. & C. Thomas O: farmer; by R.A. Miller.

36. * * * J.A. SYNAN 27 yrs single b. KY now living in McDowell s/o Jas & Bettie C. to JENNIE MOSIER 24 yrs single b. PA d/o D. & ? O: gardner(sic); REMARKS: Not Returned. (*Note: no date given.)

37. 11 Mar 1899 JAMES LINEBERRY 22 yrs single b. Caroll Co VA s/o Alex & Polly to GRACIE A. HOUCHINS 17 yrs single b. Mercer d/o G.H. & Mary O: farmer; by W.W. West; REMARKS: Lineberry sworn.

38. 12 Mar 1899 WM JOHNSON 30 yrs single b. NC s/o Alph & Sarah to TILDA CRAIG 25 yrs single b. Tazewell Co VA d/o Sam & Eliza O: RR; by J.D. Leftwich.

39. 16 Mar 1899 N.T. LILLY 25 yrs single b. Summers Co W VA s/o Wm H. & Lucinda to MARTHA A. OAKS 21 yrs single d/o W.S. & Catherine Oaks O: farming; by Drewery Farley; REMARKS: N.T. Lilly sworn.

40. 15 Mar 1899 CHARLES GILMORE 22 yrs single b. Montgomery Co VA to LELIA H. NOELL 16 yrs single b. Roanoke Co VA d/o Jas R. & M.E. Noell; by D.A. Ramey.

41. 14 Mar 1899 MAURICE CRAGHEAD 23 yrs single b. VA s/o Wm & J. Craghead to BERTHA PETTRY 18 yrs single b. Mercer Co W VA d/o Nelie & Shaffia Pettry O: farming; by W.I. Gantier.

42. 15 Mar 1899 ALBERT G. NISWANDER 32 yrs single b. Bland Co VA s/o Alex & Mary to LULA HAVEN 16 yrs single b. Bland Co VA d/o Alex & E. Haven O: miner; by A.M. Craft.

43. 20 Mar 1899 EDGAR PAYNE 22 yrs single b. Giles Co Va s/o Wm & Annie to MARY FANNING 25 yrs div. b. Wyoming Co W VA d/o Berry & Martha McComas O: carpenter; by John H. Honaker; REMARKS: Payne sworn.

44. 23 Mar 1899 M.W. EDWARDS 21 yrs single b. Floyd Co VA s/o John & Sarah Edwards to ELIZA LESTER 21 yrs single b. Montgomery Co VA d/o Lloyd & ? Lester O: farming; by R.A. Miller.

45. 29 Mar 1899 BURNETT LAXTON 19 yrs single b. Wyoming Co W VA s/o Hesikiah & Martha J. to NANCY ORA DILL COOK 16 yrs single b. Mercer Co W VA d/o John N. & Margaret O: farming; by L.H. Bailey; REMARKS: Laxton sworn.

46. 28 Mar 1899 IREAL HAWKINS 38 yrs wid. b. Roanoke VA s/o Daniel & Hester to HATTIE WASHINGTON 20 yrs single b. Roanoke VA; by G.W. Alexander; REMARKS: A.L. Godfrey.

NOTE #47 was omitted due to the numbering of entries being off by one.

Page 98

48. 29 Mar 1899 JAS C. FARLEY 28 yrs single b. Summers Co W VA s/o Jackson & Mary A. to HOLLIE BOLIN 18 yrs sngle b. Mercer Co W VA d/o J.J. & Isabella O: saw milling; by G.H. Johnston.

49. 29 Mar 1899 ALBERT S. MORGAN 24 yrs single b. Mercer Co W VA s/o Thos P. & Martha to ORSA F. FRENCH 21 yrs single b. Mercer Co W Va d/o Jas E. & Emma O: farmer; by A.B. Hunter; REMARKS: sworn.

50. 29 Mar 1899 J.H. GEARHEART 22 yrs single b. Floyd VA s/o Lawson & ? to N.J. COLE 23 yrs sngle b. Mercer Co W VA d/o A.J. & Mary O: miner; by G.W. Bailey.

51. 11 Apr 1899 J.H. LOGAN 42 yrs wid. now living in Raleigh to H.H. BOWLING 37 yrs wid. b. Mercer Co W VA d/o Hiram & Susan Reed O: farmer; by R.A. Bryant.

52. 29 Mar 1899 JOHN A. PENN 32 yrs wid. b. Henry Co Va s/o Albert & Charlotte to HENRY ANN FERGUSON 22 yrs single b. Franklin Co VA O: laborer; by Eugene Blake; REMARKS: col'd, Penn sworn.

53. 4 Apr 1899 W.O. ALLEY 25 yrs single b. Tazewell s/o J.H. & T.L. to NANNIE B. ANDERSON 22 yrs single b. Tazewell O: RR; by A.B. Hunter; REMARKS: sworn.

54. 7 May 1899 JAMES O. WILEY 23 yrs single b. Mercer s/o ? & Sarah Wiley to NANNIE COMER 19 yrs single b. Mercer d/o A. Comer & Martha O: farmer; by W.B. Boothe; REMARKS: S.G. Via sworn.

55. 6 Apr 1899 B.D. AYERS 21 yrs single b. Roanoke VA s/o B.A. & Julia A. to FANNIE WILLIAMS 23 yrs single b. Giles d/o F.G. & ? O: RR; by P.C. Clark; REMARKS: Ayers sworn.

56. 7 Apr 1899 W.E. ANSBONNE 27 yrs single b. Buckingham VA s/o Wm E. & Nannie G. to BESSIE B. PENNINGTON 20 yrs single b. Mercer d/o Green & Ann O: clerk; by S.E. Houk; REMARKS: father present.

57. 13 Apr 1899 DENNIS C. McCOHAS 19 yrs single b. Mercer s/o J.I. & Mary A. to LUTHERA L. THOMPSON 17 yrs single b. Mercer d/o James A. & Virginia O: farmer; by T.B. Cook; REMARKS: father present.

58. 12 Apr 1899 C.N. MILLER 21 yrs single b. Monroe now living same s/o S.A. & Mary F. to LIZZIE LOU HOUCHINS 26 yrs single b. Monroe d/o Wm & Lou O: farmer; by D.H. Thornton; REMARKS: sworn.

59. 13 Apr 1899 W.R. PARKER 29 yrs wid. b. Floyd s/o Saml & Mary Jane to LIZZIE ADAMS 30 yrs single b. Pulaski d/o Ples & Manerva O: farmer; by Author S. Thorn.

60. 19 Apr 1899 A.G. RICHMOND 24 yrs single b. Raleigh Co W VA s/o ? Richmond to D.C. COX 23 yrs single b. Summers Co W VA d/o Matthew & Mary Cox O: farmer; by James W. Lilly; REMARKS: L.H. Meadows sworn.

61. 19 Apr 1899 J.C. BENNETT 21 yrs sngle b. Mercer Co W VA s/o J.W. & C.A. Bennett to KATE B. FRENCH 22 yrs single b. Mercer Co W VA d/o Henry & M. French O: farmer; by S.E. Houk; REMARKS: W.A. Bennett sworn.

62. 20 Apr 1899 JEHU C. HONAKER 24 yrs sngle b. Raleigh Co W VA s/o J.H. & S.A. Honaker to ALMEDA D. NEAL 26 yrs single b. Mercer Co W VA d/o J.H. & Cynthia Neal O: farmer; by J.E. Bruce.

63. 27 Apr 1899 JAS R. LILLY 56 yrs wid. b. Mercer Co W VA now living in Summers Co W VA s/o Jonathan & Margaret Lilly to SUSAN E. OAKS 19 yrs single b. Floyd Co VA d/o W.S. & Catharing Oaks O: farmer; by Drewry Farley; REMARKS: W.S. Oaks present.

64. 30 Apr 1899 P.L. WOODY 28 yrs single b. Franklin Co VA now living in Tazewell VA s/o Pete & Eliza to MARY F. CRAGHEAD 25 yrs wid. b. Franklin Co VA d/o Miles & Lucy Jane O: miner; by J.W. Johnston.

65. 26 Apr 1899 JAMES A. PENNINGTON 21 yrs single b. Mercer s/o J.W. & Ellen to BERTIE GOODE 20 yrs single b. Giles Co VA d/o G.W. & Permelia O: farmer; by Giles M. Johnston; REMARKS: G.W. Goode, Jr. sworn.

66. 27 Apr 1899 JOHN McLOUD 22 yrs single b. Russell Co VA s/o Henry & Elizabeth to LETIE BELL GREEN 17 yrs single b. Wyoming Co W VA d/o Shadrick & Louise O: railroader; by Chas J. Jones; REMARKS: Joseph Norris sworn.

67. 26 Apr 1899 ISAAC FLOYD BALDWIN 20 yrs single b. Buchanan Co VA s/o S.A.D. & Hannah to FLORA ALICE BOWER 16 yrs single b. Floyd Co VA d/o R.H. & Sarah E. O: laborer; by R.A. Kelly; REMARKS: father of wife present and written consent of mother of husband.

68. 3 May 1899 WILLIAM A. NEELY 20 yrs single b. Mercer s/o I.G. & V.E. to ROXANNE SNEED 17 yrs single b. Raleigh Co d/o B.J. & R.E. O: farmer; by James W. Lilly; REMARKS: E.R. Ferguson sworn.

69. 3 May 1899 WM O. NELSON 23 yrs single b. Mercer Co W VA s/o Jas R. & E. Nelson to ADA J. MEADOWS 24 yrs single b. Mercer Co W VA d/o Henderson & B. Meadows O: farmer; by W.L. Gantier; REMARKS: Jas R. Nelson.

70. 10 May 1899 RUFUS BIRD 23 yrs single b. Mercer Co W VA s/o Steven J. & Susan to LANEHA TABOR 17 yrs single b. Mercer Co W VA d/o Henderson & Rebecca O: miner; by R.A. Kelly; REMARKS: Bird sworn.

71. 17 May 1899 LUSTER R. EPLING 21 yrs single b. Giles Co s/o Lewis A. & Ellen J. to L.E. HAXEY 16 yrs single b. Mercer d/o Joseph & J.V. O: merchant; by James W. Lilly; REMARKS: R.L. Epling sworn.

72. 15 May 1899 F.C. HALEY 39 yrs wid. b. Pittsylvania VA s/o E.W. & S.C. to FANNIE SIMPSON 28 yrs single b. Roanoke VA d/o R. & F.L. O: RR; by W.W. Hamilton.

73. 17 May 1899 GEORGE W. MEADOWS 19 yrs single b. Wyoming Co s/o Wm T. & Martha E. to VIRGIE L. CUNNINGHAM 16 yrs single b. Mercer Co W VA d/o James & S.J. O: farmer; by H.L Cook; REMARKS: Henry L Cook sworn.

74. 17 May 1899 JNO L. MOTLEY 20 yrs single b. Mercer Co W VA s/o W.B. & P. Motley to ESTHER G. STEELE 17 yrs single b. Mercer Co W VA d/o W.F. & Rhoda Steele O: farmer; by W.L. Gantier; REMARKS: J.N. Pennington sworn.

75. 23 May 1899 R.E. FREEMAN 23 yrs single b. Clifton Forge VA s/o John & Isabella to LIZZIE GILMORE 18 yrs single b. Brownstown W VA d/o Hilton & Alice O: operator; by R.A. Kelly.

76. 21 May 1899 W.M. DUNFORD 44 yrs wid. b. Giles Co VA s/o Albert & Eliza to MARTHA RASH 23 yrs single b. Pulaski O: farmer; by G.W. Bailey.

77. 24 May 1899 ALEXANDER WOOD 50 yrs wid. b. German to LAURA R. CRAY 30 yrs single b. Giles s/o Isaac & Sarah F. O: farmer; by J.M. Meadows.

78. 26 May 1899 H.G. HUDSON 40 yrs single b. Dunwidy Co VA s/o W.D. & M.H. to CORDELIA PEDIGO 20 yrs single b. Franklin Co VA d/o S.E. & Susan O: engineer; by S.E. Houk; REMARKS: H.G. Hudson sworn.

79. 31 May 1899 L.E. WHITE 21 yrs single b. Mercer s/o B.P. & M.J. to V.E. PENDLETON 21 yrs single b. Mercer d/o L.M. & Ann O: farmer; by L. Goodwyn; REMARKS: fathers present.

80. 7 June 1899 HERBERT B. HAWES 26 yrs single b. Farmville VA s/o H.H. & Harriet Hawes to BESSIE A. PRINCE 23 yrs single b. Hinton W VA d/o Burke & B.J. Prince O: atty; by H.H. Hawes.

81. 6 June 1899 ROBT LUTHER BROWN 23 yrs single b. Mercer s/o Evan H. & M.E. to CARRIE C. THOMPSON 19 yrs single b. Mercer d/o W.S. & Emma O: farmer; by W.B. Boothe; REMARKS: father present.

82. 7 June 1899 GEORGE PEARSON 34 yrs single b. NC s/o P. & J. to ANNIE WHITE 24 yrs single b. VA O: stable boss; by A.J. Brown.

83. 14 June 1899 JNO N. SWEENEY 22 yrs single b. Raleigh now living same s/o Wm J. & E.F. to LOTTIE D. LILLY 19 yrs single b. Mercer d/o R.F. & S. O: farmer; by James W. Lilly; REMARKS: Jno N. Sweeney sworn.

84. 15 June 1899 P.J. KELLEY 32 yrs single b. PA s/o John & Ellen to L.V. BALDWIN 24 yrs single b. Tazewell d/o D.V. & Sallie O: taylor; by E. Olivia.

85. 16 June 1899 JOHN L. MITCHUM 28 yrs single b. Raleigh Co now living same s/o Gus & L.P. to PHELENA FOLEY 17 yrs single b. Mercer d/o C.A. & Mary J. O: farmer; by Horace Strong; REMARKS: father present.

86. 15 June 1899 EVERETT W. LESTER 23 yrs single b. Mercer s/o A.B. Lester & Martha J. to LIZZIE WOOD 17 yrs single b. Giles s/o L.W.A. & ? O: farmer; by D.N. Saunders; REMARKS: A.L. Lester sworn.

87. 16 June 1899 W.H. HERNDON 27 yrs single b. Mercer s/o W.H.H. & M.E. Herndon to MARY TAYLOR 20 yrs single b. Northumberland Co PA d/o Jas & Mary Taylor O: clerk; by R.A. Kelly.

88. 21 June 1899 W.N. BALLARD 24 yrs single b. Mercer to CYNTHA SURFACE 25 yrs single b. Mercer d/o Robt & Jane O: sawmilling; by G.W. Terry.

89. 22 June 1899 MILTON GILHORE 52 yrs wid. b. VA to ANNIE E. EARLY 19 yrs single b. Carroll Co VA d/o R.J. & H.C. Early O: miner; by R.A. Kelly.

90. 21 June 1899 GILES O. HAMBRICK 27 yrs single b. Mercer s/o C.O. & A.P. to NANNIE K. HYPES 22 yrs single b. Mercer d/o G.A. & S.E. O: farmer; by J.E. Bruce.

91. 24 June 1899 THOS T. BARKER 24 yrs single b. Washington Co VA s/o Jos & L.S. Barker to DAISY FOY 19 yrs single b. PA d/o J.W. & H.A. Foy O: Loco. engineer; by A.B. Hunter.

92. 28 June 1899 WILLARD GRAVLEY* 22 yrs single b. Pittsylvania Co VA s/o ? & Anna Gravly* to EMMA ARTHER 23 yrs single b. Pittsylvania Co VA d/o Benj & Ann Arther O: miner; by J.W. Johnson; REMARKS: col'd.

93. 22 June 1899 C.E. HYPES 25 yrs single b. Mercer s/o G.A. & S.E. to ANNIE MAY FRANCISCO 23 yrs single b. Tazewell d/o Elisha & ? O: fireman; by J.E. Bruce.

94. 28 June 1899 THOS L. LITTLE 20 yrs single b. Mercer Co W VA s/o H. & H.A. Little to NELLY L. LEHAN 20 yrs single b. Franklin Co VA d/o G.H. & N.C. Leman O: miner; by A.M. Craft; REMARKS: G.H. Leman.

95. 26 June 1899 ROBT MONTGOMERY 25 yrs single b. VA s/o J.R. & H.C. to ANNIE F. CRAMAR 18 yrs single b. VA d/o Jno F. & ? O: miner; by A.M. Craft.

96. 29 June 1899 W.H. NICEWANDER 60 yrs wid. b. VA to BELL GRAVELEY 27 yrs wid. b. VA O: miner; by Jno B. Perry.

Page 99

97. 2 July 1899 SAMUEL WALKER 28 yrs single b. Campbell Co VA s/o Sam & July Walker to CARRY GRAVES 22 yrs single b. Pittsylvania Co VA d/o Raymond & Rhoda Graves; by J.W. Johnston; REMARKS: col'd.

98. 28 June 1899 CHAS T. DANIEL 25 yrs single b. VA s/o J.D. & Sally Daniel to LAURA A. MORGAN 20 yrs single b. Mercer Co W VA d/o Douglass & Sarah Morgan O: clerk; by G.M. Johnston.

99. 28 June 1899 HENRY ALLEN 28 yrs single b. VA s/o Geo & Martha Allen to ARDELIA ALLEN 38 yrs wid. b. Mercer Co W VA d/o A. & ? Tiller O: miner; by L. Goodwyn.

100. 2 July 1899 LUTHER T. FALLS 23 yrs single b. Mercer Co W VA s/o Lewis & ? Falls to CORA M. MEADOWS 18 yrs single b. Mercer Co W VA d/o H.D. & v. Meadows O: lumberman; by J.W. Bennett.

101. 4 July 1899 WM MASSEY 25 yrs single b. Floyd Co VA s/o Jas & Bettie Massey to MARY JOHNSON 21 yrs single b. TN d/o J. & Martha Johnson O: miner; by Emmet F. Mason.

102. 9 July 1899 J.W.F. BAILEY 32 yrs single b. Mercer Co s/o A.C. & Octavia to NANNIE M. HELHANDOLOR 16 yrs single d/o T.H. & J.N. O: farmer; by Peter Grim; REMARKS: Bailey sworn.

103. 11 July 1899 CHARLES CLARK 24 yrs single b. Franklin Co VA s/o Nathaniel & Susan to LIZZIE CONNER 16 yrs single b. Halifax d/o Tasvill & Bell O: miner; by A.M. Craft.

104. 11 July 1899 GEORGE MARTIN 22 yrs single b. Pittsylvania Co s/o Daniel & Emily to CAROLINE STEVENS 21 yrs single b. Lynchburg d/o Harvy & Caroline; by J.W. Johnston.

105. 11 July 1899 JOSEPH BECK 24 yrs single b. Montgomery s/o Henry & Henrietta to CARRY ERBY 23 yrs single b. Montgomery d/o ? & Amanda; by J.W. Johnston.

106. 10 July 1899 ALBERT HODGE 21 yrs single b. Mercer s/o G. Wash & Elizabeth to SARAH CARVER 21 yrs single b. Tazewell d/o John & Mary O: miner; by John H. Honaker.

107. 12 July 1899 DAVID L. POE 23 yrs single b. Mercer s/o Jerry Poe & Cynthia to MINNIE WIMMER 34 yrs div. b. Bland d/o Havery & ? O: farmer; by D.N. Saunders.

108. 12 July 1899 GEO W. HALDREN 18 yrs single b. Mercer s/o B.M. & H.E. to H.E. HALDREN 20 yrs single b. Giles d/o Charley & D.A. O: farmer; by W.I. Gantier; REMARKS: father & Guardian pres.

109. 19 July 1899 JOHN C. BAILEY 21 yrs single b. Mercer s/o Letwich(sic) & Sarah to AMERICA BELCHER 17 yrs single b. Mercer d/o Bal & Cleo O: farmer; by D.N. Saunders; REMARKS: A.J. White sworn.

110. 23 July 1899 JOHN YOUNG 24 yrs single b. VA to FLORA PERKS 17 yrs single b. Giles VA d/o Henderson & Rachel O: miner; by R.H. McKoy; REMARKS: J.F. Smith sworn.

111. 22 July 1899 WILEY W. NEAL 18 yrs sngle b. Mercer Co W VA s/o D.N. & S.A. Neal to LOLLIE G. ARGABRIGHT 17 yrs single b. Montgomery Co VA d/o r.L. & O.A. Argabright O: farmer; by Eugene Blake; REMARKS: D.N. Saunders.

112. 27 July 1899 HOWARD M. WHITE 28 yrs single b. Mercer Co W VA to DORA A. SHREWSBURY 25 yrs single b. Mercer d/o Thornton & Iowa O: farmer; by W.I. Gantier; REMARKS: David P. Shrewsbury sworn.

113. 23 July 1899 WILLIAM R. RAYMOND 38 yrs div. b. Main(sic) to LOTTIE E. SHREWSBURY 23 yrs single b. Mercer d/o Thornton & Iowa O: stone mason; by W.L Gantier; REMARKS: David P. Shrewsbury sworn.

114. 27 July 1899 MARIAN JONAS 30 yrs single b. Wythe Co VA s/o Peter & Julia Jonas to JULIA NEAL 35 yrs single b. Bland Co VA d/o ? & Sally Neal O: carpenter; by A.B. Hunter.

115. 19 Sept 1899 GEORGE CALLOWAY 23 yrs single b. Montgomery s/o Wm & Bettie to ADDIE JONES 22 yrs single b. Montgomery c/o Winston & Ester O: miner; by J.W. Johnston.

123

116. * * * LEE CHARLTON 25 yrs wid. b. Mercer s/o Sam & Katie to LELIA FORD 22 yrs single b. NC d/o ? & Elizabeth O: miner.(*Note: no date given.)

117. 3 Aug 1899 ISAAC JANEY 23 yrs single b. Franklin Co VA s/o John & Malinda to DORA M. HALL 18 yrs single b. Franklin d/o J.H. & Elizabeth O: RR; by W.H. Ayers; REMARKS: father present.

118. 3 Aug 1899 O.C. HARVEY 24 yrs single b. Summers Co W VA now living same s/o John W. & Eliza to NOTIE J. LILLY 23 yrs single b. Mercer d/o James & ? O: farmer; by German F. Hatcher.

119. 10 Aug 1899 R.L. TAYLOR 25 yrs single b. Mercer s/o Tompson & Martha to EMMAZELLA KING 22 yrs single b. Mercer d/o W.R. King & ? O: farmer; by Henry L. Cook; REMARKS: R.S. Taylor.

120. 16 Aug 1899 WM WALACE 29 yrs single b. Charlott NC s/o Jack & Ann to MORIAH BATEMAN 45 yrs wid. b. NC d/o Carter & Hannah Johnson O: miner; by G.W. Alexander.

121. 9 Aug 1899 HARVEY FLETCHER 18 yrs single b. Mercer s/o Anderson & Alice to LOU FISHER 21 yrs single b. Mercer d/o ? & Molinda O: farmer; by G.W. Terry.

122. 12 Aug 1899 J. WES LOVELL 23 yrs single b. Carroll Co VA to HAHALA J. WYATT 17 yrs single b. Wyomng Co W VA d/o Jno & H.J. Wyatt O: farmer; by Peter Grim.

123. 11 Aug 1899 HUDSON L. BRUGH 29 yrs wid. b. Botetourt Co VA s/o Jacob & Luvna Brugh to LOULA E. PAYNE 17 yrs single b. Bristol TN d/o S.E. & A.E. Payne O: miner; by R.A. Kelly.

124. 11 Aug 1899 SAMUEL BRAZEIL 24 yrs single b. VA to MARY L. PAYNE 23 yrs single b. Bristol TN d/o S.E. & A.E. Payne O: miner; by R.A. Kelly.

125. 16 Aug 1899 WM SHREWSBURY 27 yrs single b. Mercer to ARABELL LINKENS 17 yrs single b. Bland d/o J.L. & Mary M. O: farmer; by D.N. Saunders; REMARKS: father present.

126. 19 Aug 1899 SAWYER TAYLOR 24 yrs single b. Mercer s/o John & M.F. Taylor to POLLY HEARN 25 yrs wid. b. Mercer Co W VA d/o Sampson & Martha Taylor O: farmer; by G.W. Bailey.

127. 23 Aug 1899 JOHN W. MORE 21 yrs single b. VA s/o Peter & Sue to MARY DAVIS 21 yrs single b. NC d/o Mershall & Jane O: miner; by G.W. Alexander; REMARKS: sworn to before Rumburg.

128. 23 Aug 1899 SAM H. BECK 25 yrs single b. VA s/o Henry & Henrietta to LILLIE B. MILLS 21 yrs single b. VA d/o L. & M. O: miner; by G.W. Alexander.

129. 23 Aug 1899 CHARLES A. VAUGHT 29 yrs wid. b. OH s/o Ransom & Sarah H. to DORAH E. ALVIS 21 yrs single b. W VA d/o John & Josephine O: farmer; by James H. Johnston.

130. 29 Aug 1899 E.L. WRIGHT 33 yrs single b. W VA s/o C.G. & Betty to M.G. CROTTY 17 yrs single b. W VA d/o ? & M.A. White O: farmer; by L. Goodwyn.

131. 30 Aug 1899 F.T. HARVEY 25 yrs single b. Mercer s/o Floyd & Emeline to BERTHA E. LESTER 21 yrs single b. Montgomery VA d/o Wilson & Rachel O: farmer; by R.A. Miller; REMARKS: father present.

132. 30 Aug 1899 G.W. FINZER 25 yrs single b. VA to MAUD WILLIAMS 17 yrs single b. VA d/o W.P. & C.A. O: RR; by Wm Wiston Hamilton.

133. 2 Sept 1899 FOUNTAIN T. THOMPSON 28 yrs single b. Mercer s/o Allen & Manerva to LENNIE WHITE 18 yrs single b. Mercer d/o Thomas & Rebeca O: farmer; by W.I. Gantier; REMARKS: guardian present.

134. 2 Sept 1899 WILBURN GUNTER 19 yrs single b. Carroll VA s/o Wm & F.I. to NANCY LUETTA TILLEY 17 yrs single b. Wyoming W VA d/o John C. & Sarah O: farmer; by W.I Gantier; REMARKS: guardian present.

135. 6 Sept 1899 N.E. HELTON 32 yrs single b. Washington Co VA s/o B.A. & Nancy B. to LILLIE L. WILSON 20 yrs sngle b. Mercer Co W VA d/o James H. & Marinda O: farmer; by Wm Wiston Hamilton; REMARKS: father present.

136. 2 Sept 1899 JOS M. HOLDREN 58 yrs wid. b. mercer Co s/o Polly Holdren to ZORA E. BLANKENSHIP 36 yrs single b. Mercer Co W VA d/o Rebecca Blankenship O: farmer; by W.I. Gantier.

137. 4 Sept 1899 ALLEN THOMAS 22 yrs single b. Campbell Co VA s/o Charles & Sallie to PINKEY MADISON 19 yrs wid. d/o ? & Caroline Calloway O: laborer; by J.F. Prigmore.

138. 6 Sept 1899 JOHN NELL FICH 28 yrs wid b. Campbell Co VA s/o Jordan & Caroline Fich to SALENA LEFLICK 23 yrs single b. Campbell Co VA d/o John & Martha Leflich O: night watchman; by R.H. McKoy.

139. 6 Sept 1899 L.H. PETTYJOHN 31 yrs single b. Amherst Co Va s/o John W. & Mariah E. to MAUD V. BURTON 21 yrs single b. Bedford Co Va d/o Geo H. & ? O: RR; by A.B. Hunter; REMARKS: Pettyjohn sworn.

140. 5 Sept 1899 L.G. PRUETT 30 yrs single b. NC s/o T.H. & Polly to CASBY MAY BROOKS 22 yrs single b. VA d/o Jas & Margaretta O: miner; by Wm Wiston Hamilton; REMARKS: Pruett sworn.

141. 7 Sept 1899 GASTON WILEY 22 yrs single b. Mercer s/o Manerva Wiley to FANNIE HUFFMAN 29 yrs single b. Mercer O: sawmill; by R.H. Ashworth; REMARKS: Henry W. Wiley sworn.

142. 7 Sept 1899 R.C. LILLY, JR. 27 yrs wid. b. Summers Co now living in Raleigh s/o R.C. & Virginia to H.O. REED 21 yrs single b. Mercer d/o V.C. & Eliza J.E. O: Co Supr; by Jas W. Lilly.

Page 100

143. 9 Sept 1899 ROBT L. HARLESS 26 yrs b. Monroe Co W VA s/o Miles & E. Harless to ANGIE P. SMITH 21 yrs b. Monroe Co W VA d/o S. Perry & L. Smith O: farmer; by T.H. Shannon.

144. 16 Sept 1899 S.W. MILLS 19 yrs single b. Monroe Co W VA s/o Samuel G. & Mary to MAUD L. WALKER 16 yrs single b. Mercer d/o G.P. & Bettie O: farmer; by Jas W. Lilly; REMARKS: S.W. Mills sworn, Mills' father.

145. 11 Sept 1899 ISHAM D. BELCHER 58 yrs wid. to MARY ELIZA MELVIN 44 yrs wid. d/o Jas & Mildred Thomhill; by Wm Wiston Hamilton.

146. 13 Sept 1899 J.L. KEPFINGER 22 yrs single b. NY s/o Mile & Anna Kepfinger to GRACE LEFLER 21 yrs single b. Giles VA d/o Jas A. & Fannie Lefler O: lumberman; by D.N. Saunders; REMARKS: J.L. Kepfinger & W.H. Lefler sworn.

147. 15 Sept 1899 G.L. FERFUSON 18 yrs single b. Mercer s/o G.N. & Octavia to E.M. WALKER 17 yrs single b. Mercer d/o G.P. & Harriett O: farmer; by Jas W. Lilly; REMARKS: G.N. Ferguson sworn.

148. 17 Sept 1899 FAYETTA IRVIN 22 yrs div. b. Giles Co VA s/o Isaac & Lucinda to DELFIE THOMPSON 21 yrs single d/o Mary & ? O: laborer; by W.H. Ayers.

149. 13 Sept 1899 J.A. ROTHWELL 41 yrs wid. b. Upshin Co W VA s/o Thos B. & Mary F. to MAUD L. HOPKINS 22 yrs single b. Mercer d/o Joel & Louisa O: laborer; byu S.E. Houk.

150. 17 Sept 1899 CHARLIE PENNINGTON 22 yrs single b. Mercer Co W VA s/o Wm H. & Mary Pennington to SUSAN D. SNYDER 20 yrs single b. Giles Co VA d/o Z.H. & R.A. Snyder O: farmer; by Wm L. Ball; REMARKS: J.H. Snyder.

151. 16 Sept 1899 W.F. FRITH 22 yrs single b. Franklin Co VA s/o Silas & Julianna Frith to H.M. McALEXANDER 26 yrs wid. b. Mercer Co W VA d/o Jos & ? Doss O: farmer; by Jas F. Lilly; REMARKS: W. Frith sworn.

152. 20 Sept 1899 L.M. BAILEY 20 yrs single b. Wyomng now living same to s/o S.& R. to BERTHA A. COOK 19 yrs single b. Mercer Co W VA d/o T.B. & Louisa O: farmer; by Horace Strong; REMARKS: guardian present Bailey sworn.

153. 20 Sept 1899 C.C. FARLEY 26 yrs wid. b. Mercer Co W VA s/o Wm & Ann Farley to ELIZA J. GADD 28 yrs single b. Mercer Co W VA d/o Andrew & D. Gadd O: farmer; by Jas W. Lilly; REMARKS: Alex. Wallace.

154. 17 Sept 1899 E.T. CHAPMAN 39 yrs wid. b. Tazewell Co Va now living in Tazewell Co VA s/o Geo & H. Chapman to NANCY C. NEAL 30 yrs single b. Mercer Co W VA d/o Aug & Agnes Neal O: farmer; by W.H. Perkins; REMARKS: Aug. Neal, col'd.

155. 20 Sept 1899 JOSEPH BUTTRY 22 yrs single b. Russell Co VA s/o Nat & Mary Buttry to DOROTHY KILHER 18 yrs single b. Montgomery Co VA d/o G.W. & Mary Kilmer O: teamster; by J.H. McClaugherty; REMARKS: G.W. Kilmer.

156. 21 Sept 1899 WOOD L. MOORE 22 yrs single b. VA s/o D.N. & Martha to NINA WISSIE MICHAEL 20 yrs single b. W VA d/o J.W. & Kate O: farmer; by S.E. Houk; REMARKS: W.L. Moore sworn.

157. 21 Sept 1899 HENRY UNDERWOOD 18 yrs angle b. Mercer Co W VA s/o Asa & H.J. Underwood to MINNIE SHREWSBURY 18 yrs single b. Mercer Co W VA d/o Geo & Ellen Shrewsbury O: farmer; by Henry I Cook; REMARKS: Asa Underwood & J.L. Jennings.

158. 21 Sept 1899 J.D. COBURN 52 yrs wid. b. Mercer Co W VA s/o David & E. Coburn to BELL HALL 27 yrs wid. b. Carroll Co VA d/o Jordan & C. Hall O: farmer; by Peter Grim.

159. 21 Sept 1899 JNO C. EVANS 34 yrs single b. Roanoke Co Va s/o G.C. & Susie Evans to MARY E. DANNER 25 yrs single b. Roanoke Co VA d/o J.E. & Jane Danner O: plasterer; by A.B. Hunter.

160. 25 Sept 1899 DOUGLASS McELRATH 27 yrs wid. b. NC s/o Henry & Louisa to NANNIE S. FRANKLIN 21 yrs single b. Franklin Co VA d/o Sam & Harriett O: miner; by G.W. Alexander.

161. 27 Sept 1899 B.M. GUNTER 24 yrs single b. VA s/o Wm Gunter & P.J. to AVIS PRINCE 23 yrs single b. Mercer d/o Mary O: farmer; by Eugene Blake.

162. 27 Sept 1899 JOHN KING 24 yrs single b. VA s/o George & Mary to SALLIE COLEMAN 21 yrs single b. OH d/o Tucker & Ada O: RR; by J.F. Prigmore.

163. 28 Nov 1899 CHARLES GRIFFIN 24 yrs single b. VA s/o John & Lidda to ALICE SANDERS 17 yrs single b. VA d/o Felix & Fanny O: miner; by J.W. Johnston.

164. 28 Nov 1899 HAYES SANDERS 23 yrs single b. VA s/o ? & Emily to SALLIE SANDERS 18 yrs single b. VA d/o ? & Hariet O: miner; by J.W. Johnston.

165. 27 Sept 1899 W.H. WHITE 26 yrs wid. b. Wythe s/o Robt & Margaret to DORAH HERNDON 19 yrs single b. Mercer d/o Chas & Mariah O: miner; by S.E. Houk.

166. 1 Oct 1899 BARTHELUMEW HALDREN 23 yrs single b. Mercer s/o James H. & Rhoda to MARTHA C. DEWEESE 27 yrs div. b. Mercer d/o J.L. & Minerva O: farmer; by R.A. Miller.

167. 30 Sept 1899 JOSEPH REED 21 yrs single b. Mercer s/o H.A. & Susan to FRANCES DALTON 22 yrs single b. Carroll VA O: farmer; by Eugene Blake; REMARKS: R. Floyd Karnes sworn.

168. 2 Oct 1899 L.C. DAMEWOOD 26 yrs single b. Bland s/o S.M. & ? to BLANCHE M. JOHNSON 24 yrs single b. VA d/o G.S. & Nannie O: clerk; by W.L. Ball.

169. 4 Oct 1899 HENRY TRIGG 22 yrs single b. Kanawha W VA s/o Wm B. & Martha to FRANCIS BROOKS 22 yrs single d/o Nathan & Amanda O: miner; by D.A. Daugherty.

170. 4 Oct 1899 F.A. GUNTER 22 yrs single b. VA s/o A. Gus & R.E. to MOLLIE E. HOPKINS 18 yrs single b. Mercer d/o Joel E. & Louisa L. O: farmer; by J.W. Bennett; REMARKS: F.A. Gunter sworn.

171. 4 Oct 1899 J.D. SHUFFLEBARGER 37 yrs single b. Mercer s/o Louis & A.J. to LOLA E. DAVIDSON 20 yrs single b. Mercer d/o H.P. & Lucinda O: farmer; by S.E. Houk; REMARKS: J.H. Davidson sworn.

172. 4 Oct 1899 PETER T. McGUE 22 yrs single b. OH s/o Peter & Ellen to SADIE L. HUTCHINSON 18 yrs angle b. W VA d/o J.L. & S.P. O: machinist; by E. Oliver; REMARKS: father present.

173. 5 Oct 1899 L. ANVILL 24 yrs angle now living in McDowell s/o S.H. & Nancy to IDA ASHWORTH 24 yrs single b. VA d/o R.M. & S.E.; by S.W. Bourne.

174. 10 Oct 1899 A.J. REED 30 yrs wid. b. Monroe s/o J.M. & S.C. to HATTIE J. HELVIN 24 yrs angle b. Mercer d/o N. & Ann O: laborer; by A.B. Hunter; REMARKS: A.J. Reed sworn.

175. 7 Oct 1899 J.W. MILLER 27 yrs wid. b. Mercer s/o R.A. & A. to DORA M. MULLINS 17 yrs single b. Mercer d/o J.R. & M.J. O: laborer; by J.O. Cassaday; REMARKS: father present.

176. * * * JOHN HOBBS 37 yrs wid. b. VA s/o Madison & Nancy to A.Z. THOMPSON 27 yrs wid. b. Bland d/o Elias & Rhoda Henderson O: laborer. (*Note: no date given.)

177. 12 Oct 1899 DANL S. ADKINS 23 yrs single b. Mercer Co W VA s/o Preston & E. Adkins to LEAH A. MEADOWS 26 yrs wid. b. Summers Co d/o Mathew & Mary Hock O: farmer; by James W. Lilly.

178. 11 Oct 1899 W.M. HOBBS 21 yrs single b. Giles Co VA now living same s/o E.W. & R.B. Hobbs to LENNA CAMPER 18 yrs angle b. VA d/o C.H. & L. Camper O: carpenter; by Wm W. Hamilton.

179. 16 Oct 1899 ARTHER RICHMOND 42 yrs wid. b. Raleigh Co W VA s/o Arthur & H.J. Richmond to SARAH JANE SPICER 22 yrs single O: farmer; by Granville Houchins.

180. 18 Oct 1899 ALAWAY HAUR 21 yrs single b. Patrick Co VA s/o Jordan & C. Haur to BELL COBURN 22 yrs single b. Wyoming Co W VA d/o Jno & ? Coburn O: farmer; by Peter Grim; REMARKS: Alaway Haur.

181. 19 Oct 1899 WM A. GAUTIER 19 yrs single b. Mercer Co W VA s/o R.A. & H.A. Gautier to MARY C. NOBLE 16 yrs angle b. Mercer Co W Va d/o H.P. & Nannie Noble O: farmer; by G.M. Johnston; REMARKS: R.A. Gautier.

182. 19 Oct 1899 G.W. GRIFFITH 23 yrs single b. KY s/o S.B. & ? to TELITHA L. HAMBRICK 22 yrs single b. Mercer Co W VA d/o L.T. & R.J. O: miner; by G.W. Terry; REMARKS: father present.

183. 19 Oct 1899 ROBERT MILLS 19 yrs single b. Raleigh Co W Va now living same s/o Jno B. & Minerva Mills to JESTEU BAILEY 18 yrs single b. Mercer Co W VA d/o A.J. & Ann Bailey O: farmer; by Wm A. Bailey; REMARKS: F.R. Bailey.

184. 25 Oct 1899 JAMES ROLES 31 yrs wid. b. Summers s/o Jas & H.J. to MARGARETT ATKINS 31 yrs single b. Smythe VA O: RR; by Wm W. Hamilton.

185. 25 Oct 1899 HENRY J. HARRIS 22 yrs single b. VA s/o G.W. & H.E. to ELLA H. FOLDEN 17 yrs angle b. VA d/o E.W. & M.J. O: miner; by G.W. Bailey; REMARKS: father present.

186. 25 Oct 1899 G.C. ARTHUR 22 yrs single b. VA s/o J.H. & F.J. to JARUSHA A. PHILLIPS 17 yrs angle b. VA d/o Noah J. & Sarah Va O: miner; by Chas J. Jones; REMARKS: witness sworn.

187. 23 Nov 1899 RANDAL CANNADAY 29 yrs wid. b. VA now living in McDowell s/o Lewis & Rhoda to FLORENCE MACK 21 yrs single b. Monroe Co W VA d/o Calvin & M. O: miner; by J.W. Johnston.

188. 29 Oct 1899 S.C. VIA 27 yrs single b. Floyd Co VA now living in Summers Co to GEORGIANA PENNINGTON 25 yrs single b. Monroe Co W VA d/o Wm & Nancy Pennington O: dry goods clerk; by W.B. Booth; REMARKS: H.D. Pennington.

189. 26 Oct 1899 R.O. LUSK 19 yrs single b. Mercer s/o Eli C. & Lizzie to O.T. WALKER 16 yrs single b. Mercer d/o C.W.J. & Ardelia O: miner; by G.C. Anderson; REMARKS: J.P. Walker sworn.

190. 25 Oct 1899 GEO W. STEELE 24 yrs sngle b. Tazewell Co VA s/o John & Julia Steele to WILLIE BISHOP 16 yrs single b. Montgomery Co VA d/o Asa & martha Bishop O: teamster; by A.N. Jackson; REMARKS: G.W. Steele & A. Bishop.

Page 101

191. 29 Oct 1899 JNO HENRY COBBS 27 yrs to FLORA FRANKLIN 22 yrs d/o Thos & Charlotte Franklin; by A.B. Hunter; REMARKS: colored.

192. 1 Nov 1899 JNO W. REED 32 yrs single b. Mercer Co W VA s/o Hiram & Susan Reed to VICTORIA STILLWELL 16 yrs single b. Caroll Co VA d/o ? & Olive Stillwell O: merchant; by J.W. Lilly; REMARKS: Jno W. Reed.

193. 9 Oct 1899 GEORGE W. SMITH 28 yrs single b. TN to BERTHA HENDERSON 22 yrs sngle b. VA d/o Walter & Lucinda; by A.J. Brown.

194. 1 Nov 1899 WM JNO MAYS 28 yrs single b. Smythe Co VA s/o S.H. & E.B. Mays to MINNIE E. MARCUS 18 yrs single b. Bland Co VA d/o R.N. & F.A. Marcus O: farmer; by A.N. Jackson.

195. 2 Nov 1899 GEO W. SHOCKEY 59 yrs wid. b. Morgan Co W VA now living in Winchester Va s/o Jno & Nancy Shockey to OCTAVIA LUCHORNE 38 yrs wid. b. Floyd Co VA d/o ? & M.J. Argabright O: salesman; by A.N. Jackson.

196. 7 Nov 1899 S.H. YOUNG 28 yrs single now living in McDowell s/o S.H. & ? to JERUSHA B. SHRADER 32 yrs wid. b. Mercer d/o Henderson & Marcena Dillon O: miner; by G.C. Anderson.

197. 8 Nov 1899 JAS A. GILLESPIE 42 yrs wid. b. Tazewell Co VA s/o H. & M. Gillespie to MINTIE FUQUA 34 yrs wid. b. Pulaski Co VA O: cnboner; by J.F. Prigmore; REMARKS: col'd.

198. 9 Nov 1899 GARFIELD LIGHT 19 yrs single b. Floyd Co VA s/o Mat & Ganzettie to SARAH ALICE HEARN 24 yrs single b. Mercer d/o Andrew & Max O: laborer; by J.W. Bennett; REMARKS: guardian present.

199. 12 Nov 1899 Z.B. ABSHER 21 yrs single b. Tazewell Co VA s/o Jacob & ? Absher to EMMA D. BALES 23 yrs sngle b. Tazewell Co VA d/o ? & Rebecca Bales O: farmer; by Wm W. Hamilton.

200. 15 Nov 1899 ELI W. WALTER 20 yrs single b Mercer Co VA s/o E.H. & N. Walter to LOUEMMA J. SIRE 18 yrs single b. Mercer Co W VA d/o David & Z. Sire O: farmer; by Peter Grim; REMARKS: D. Sire & A.A. Parker.

201. 15 Nov 1899 DAVID E. FRENCH 28 yrs single b. Giles Co VA now living in McDowell Co W VA s/o H.C. & H.T. French to MINNIE REID 23 yrs single b. Summers Co W VA d/o Wm & Louisa Reid O: atty at law; by W.L. Ball; REMARKS: David E. French.

202. 16 Nov 1899 WILEY LUSK 20 yrs sngle b. Wyoming Co W VA now living same s/o T. & M.L. Lusk to LOUISA J. SHREWSBURY 18 yrs sngle b. Mercer Co W VA d/o W.R. & C.O. Shrewsbury O: farmer; by Granvill Houchins; REMARKS: J.R. Blankenship.

203. 19 Nov 1899 JOHN KESSELL 37 yrs wid. b. Richmond VA s/o Thos & Sarah Kessell to MARY L. CORNER 31 yrs single d/o r.W. & H.A. Corner O: machinist; by Chas J. Jones; REMARKS: H.D.c. Beaufort.

204. 21 Nov 1899 JNO L. WILLIAMS 22 yrs single b. Wyoming Co W VA s/o R.G. & R.J. Williams to MARIETTA A. FARMER 20 yrs sngle b. Mercer Co W VA d/o Wm H. & Sarah Farmer O: farming; by H.J. Wynor; REMARKS: J.L. Williams sworn.

205. 22 Nov 1899 ALLEN N. PHILLIPS 24 yrs single b. Mercer Co W VA s/o P.B. & C.P. Phillips to MARY M. PHILLIPS 16 yrs sngle b. Mercer Co W VA d/o Floyd & M.I. Phillips O: farming; by W.L Gautier; REMARKS: Allen N. Phillips sworn.

206. 3 Dec 1899 BOYD CECIL 20 yrs sngle b. Wyoming Co W VA now living in McDowell Co W VA s/o J.W. & Jane Cecil to LOTTIE BAILEY 17 yrs single b. Tazewell Co VA d/o Z.H. & L. Bailey O: miner; by H.C. Smith; REMARKS: H.A. Cecil sworn.

207. 29 Nov 1899 P.T. BELCHER 22 yrs single b. Mercer Co W VA s/o A.C. & H.A. Belcher to SARAH HERDISTER 26 yrs wid. b. Grayson Co VA O: miner; by A.B. Hunter; REMARKS: P.T. Belcher sworn.

208. 28 Nov 1899 THOMAS ATKINS 26 yrs wid. b. Franklin Co Va s/o Danl & M. Atkins to ANNIE REYNOLDS 19 yrs single b. Montgomery Co VA d/o Thos & Mary Reynolds O: laborer; by S.W. Patterson; REMARKS: Geo E. Webster sworn, col'd.

209. 29 Nov 1899 JNO H. SMITH 24 yrs single b. Hawkins Co TN s/o Thos & Rachel Smith to CORA MOTLEY 23 yrs single b. Summers Co W VA d/o W.B. & R.J. Motley O: railroader; by John F. Stone; REMARKS: Jno Smith & W.B. Motley.

210. 29 Nov 1899 JNO W. WALL 29 yrs single b. Guilford Co NC s/o Pink & Victoria Wall to LOUELLA MOTLEY 22 yrs single b. Summers Co W VA d/o W.B. & R.J. Motley O: RR conductor; by John F. Stone; REMARKS: Jno. W. Wall & W.B. Motley.

211. 29 Nov 1899 A.B. WATTS 22 yrs single b. Campbell Co VA s/o Jas & Roxie Watts to ROSA PATTERSON 19 yrs single b. Campbell Co VA d/o Nelson & M.A. Patterson O: miner; by G.W. Bailey; REMARKS: col'd, Jas Fitch & A.B. Watts.

212. 29 Nov 1899 GEORGE CHEATHAM 27 yrs single b. VA s/o Wash & Maria Cheatham to FANNIE CARDWELL 24 yrs single b. Campbell Co VA d/o Thos & ? Cardwell O: miner; by S.W. Patterson; REMARKS: Geo. Cheatham, col'd.

213. 30 Nov 1899 SAML J. HENRY 26 yrs wid. b. Roanoke Co VA s/o Thos & Virginia Henry to MARTHA M. EARLY 17 yrs single b. Carroll Co VA d/o robt J. & M.C. Early O: miner; by D.A. Ramey; REMARKS: certificate from Rumburg.

214. 29 Nov 1899 LEMHEL J. BELCHER 23 yrs single b. Mercer Co W VA s/o Obediah & M. Belcher to ARAMINTA S. CARBAUGH 22 yrs single b. Mercer Co W VA d/o Wm & Ester Carbaugh O: farming; by D.A. Carr; REMARKS: L.J. Belcher sworn.

215. 5 Dec 1899 EDWIN MANN 33 yrs single b. Greenbrier W VA s/o Mathew & Elizabeth to MARY L HANSBOROUGH 19 yrs single b. VA d/o ? & Blanch R. Shirey O: banker; by Norman F. Marshall; REMARKS: guardian in writing.

216. 6 Dec 1899 A.B. HELTON 37 yrs single b. Washington Co VA now living same s/o B.A. & Nancy to MITYLENA WILSON 28 yrs single b. Mercer Co W VA d/o J.H. & Marinda O: farmer; by I.D. Looney.

217. 6 Dec 1899 W.H. STRALEY 22 yrs single b. TN s/o ? & M.E. to ROSA B. BAILEY 18 yrs single b. Mercer d/o Elijah & ? O: farmer; by W.L Jenkins.

218. 13 Dec 1899 JOHN W. FERGUSON 24 yrs single b. Mercer Co W VA s/o G.N. & Octavia Ferguson to FLORA A. GRAHAM 21 yrs single b. Mercer d/o Lynch & Nancy Graham O: teacher; by James W. Lilly.

219. 19 Dec 1899 ALBERT PENNINGTON 20 yrs single b. Mercer Co W VA s/o G.W. & Wilmoth to ELLA PETTREY 18 yrs single b. Mercer d/o A.L. & Camelia O: fireman; by John F. Stone; REMARKS: J.W. Pennington sworn.

220. 14 Dec 1899 FERD. SMITH 50 yrs wid. b. VA to MARY EVANS 26 yrs wid. b. VA d/o Harve & ? Lambert O: carpenter; by W.H. Ayers.

221. 13 Dec 1899 ROBT C. OXLEY 31 yrs single b. Mercer s/o Sandford & D. to MARY C. BARBARIE 21 yrs single b. Mercer d/o John & Julia O: farmer; by Norman F. Marshall; REMARKS: A.H. Suthers sworn.

222. 13 Dec 1899 WM H. MILES 23 yrs single b. Tazewell Co VA s/o Ballard & Ollie Miles to LAVINA GILLESPIE 16 yrs single b. Franklin Co VA d/o Isac & Jemima Gillespie O: laborer; by John F. Stone; REMARKS: Melvin Blizzard.

223. 20 Dec 1899 THOMAS BAKER 48 yrs wid. b. Mercer Co W VA to KEMMIE SMITH 42 yrs wid. b. Carroll Co VA d/o Riley & Becca Jennings O: farmer; by Jas W. Lilly; REMARKS: J.H. Hoye.

224. 29 Dec 1899 CHARLES VADEN 22 yrs single b. VA s/o Alex & Susan to RUTHA HASTON 21 yrs single b. VA d/o riley & Nicey O: miner; by R.H. McKoy; REMARKS: col'd, sworn to beford Rumburg.

225. 20 Dec 1899 CHARLES F. CARPER 20 yrs angle b. Mercer s/o Flen & Martha to MARY L. WALL 17 yrs single b. Mercer d/o Robert & Margaret O: teamster; by J.O. Cassaday; REMARKS: witnesses sworn.

226. 25 Dec 1899 GEORGE LESLIE 21 yrs single b. Mercer Co W VA s/o J.P. & Melvina Leslie to LAURA A. SMITH 18 yrs single b. Mercer Co W VA d/o D.H. & Alice Smith O: miller; by L. Goodwyn; REMARKS: J.P. Smith.

227. 22 Dec 1899 WH PLATER 34 yrs div. b. Patrick VA s/o T.J. & Mary to ALMEDA DUDLEY 33 yrs single b. Giles Co VA O: farmer; by A.B. Hunter.

228. 22 Dec 1899 BEN RIGGS 22 yrs single b. Kanawha W VA s/o Robt & Harriett to HESTER BLANKENSHIP 18 yrs single b. Bland Co VA d/o Ed & Julia O: farmer; REMARKS: J.H. & Ben Riggs sworn.

229. 25 Dec 1899 JAMES C. THOMPSON 22 yrs angle b. Mercer s/o Henderson & Jane to DORA D. KIDWELL 17 yrs single b. Mercer d/o Green & Sarah O: farmer; by W.I. Gautier; REMARKS: Greely Haldren sworn.

230. 25 Dec 1899 H.C. KNIGHT 21 yrs single b. Grayson Co VA s/o ? & Hilda Bird to ELLA MARTIN 24 yrs single b. Mercer Co W VA d/o French & Nancy Martin O: farmer; by J.W. Bennett; REMARKS: Geo W. Birch & H.C. Knight.

231. 26 Dec 1899 JAS E. CLARK 27 yrs single b. Bland Co VA s/o R.W. & N.L. Clark to HATIE PERDUE 22 yrs angle b. Mercer Co W VA d/o G.W. & Fannie Perdue O: RR conductor; by A.B. Hunter; REMARKS: Jas E. Clark.

232. 29 Dec 1899 JAMES R. AYERS 24 yrs single b. VA to ALICE LUSK 18 yrs single b. Mercer Co W VA d/o W.B. & H.J. O: farmer; by G.W. Bailey; REMARKS: O.S. Hurst sworn.

233. 29 Dec 1899 T.S. COMPTON 19 yrs single b. Tazewell now living same s/o W.S. & H.L. to MAHIE M. OLLIS 17 yrs single b. VA d/o G.L. & E.A. O: miner; by Wm W. Hamilton; REMARKS: W.H. Shelton sworn.

234. 26 Dec 1899 JAMES E. LEFEW 39 yrs div. b. Montgomery VA s/o Isaac & Sarah to ELVIAR BELCHER 42 yrs div. b. Tazewell VA d/o Obidiah & Vicey O: farmer; by W.H. Ayers; REMARKS: witness sworn.

235. 24 Dec 1899 J.B. EADES 24 yrs single b. Surry Co NC s/o Robt & S.A. to LAURA L. LILLY 16 yrs single b. Mercer d/o J.K. & A. O: farmer; by W.L Gautier.

236. 29 Dec 1899 E.H. HARSTON 50 yrs wid. b. Franklin Co VA now living in McDowell s/o Mary to HANNAH SIMPSON 30 yrs single b. miner; by J.B. Ward.

237. 23 Dec 1899 J.E. GODFREY 24 yrs single b. Mercer s/o R.H. & Arzula to VIRGIE HARTWELL 16 yrs single b. Mercer d/o John & Isabell O: farmer; by G.W. Terry; REMARKS: father present.

238. 25 Dec 1899 WH LAWSON 26 yrs single b. Tazewell Co VA s/o Silas & Jane Lawson to ELLEN GRAHAM 28 yrs single b. Mercer d/o Jas & Jane Graham O: miner; by A.B. Hunter; REMARKS: J.D. Hare.

239. 26 Dec 1899 JAS H. EAVES 24 yrs single b. VA s/o Lewis & Dora to BESSIE PURSELL 22 yrs single b. VA d/o Jas & Laura O: breakman(sic); by J.F. Prigmore; REMARKS: see H.M. Smith.

240. 26 Dec 1899 LEW MEAD 23 yrs single b. VA to LULA MUSE 22 yrs single b. VA d/o John & Lucy; by J.F. Prigmore; REMARKS: see H.M. Smith.

241. 28 Dec 1899 BRUCE LESTER 19 yrs single b. Floyd VA s/o Loyd & Angeline to IDA HAZLEWOOD 17 yrs angle b. Mercer d/o H.D. Hazlewood & Sarah O: farmer; by R.A. Miller; REMARKS: certificate sworn to.

242. 27 Dec 1899 A.A. LUSK 21 yrs single b. Mercer Co W VA s/o W.B. & H.J. Lusk to JOSIE MORRIS 18 yrs single b. Montgomery Co VA d/o Jno R. & S.A. Morris O: farmer; by G.W. Bailey; REMARKS: Herbert Morris.

243. 31 Dec 1899 JOHN RAYLONDS 24 yrs single b. VA s/o Mathew & Mariah to FANNIE JOYCE 23 yrs angle b. VA d/o Lewis & ? O: waiter; by J.F. Prigmore.

244. 29 Dec 1899 DAVID FUQUA 21 yrs single b. VA s/o Tom & ? to DORA L. BUDD 16 yrs single b. VA d/o Thomas & Ann O: RR; by J.G. Prigmore; REMARKS: guardian.

245. 28 Dec 1899 JOHN W. SUTTON 27 yrs single b. Lee Co VA s/o Phillip & Victory to LILLIAN A. KARNES 23 yrs single b. Mercer d/o G.L. & Easter O: printer; by H.J. Wysor.

246. 31 Dec 1899 W.R. STEWART 21 yrs angle b. Montgomery VA now living same s/o Giles A. & Julia A. to IRENIA C. CONNER 18 yrs angle b. Montgomery VA d/o ? & Mary J. O: farmer; by John F. Stone; REMARKS: W.R. Stewart sworn.

247. 3 Jan 1900 R.S. BIRD 25 yrs single b. Mercer Co W VA s/o Wm & Cintha to LUCINDA HIGGINBOTHAM 16 yrs single b. Mercer Co W VA d/o Lewis Higginbotham O: farmer; by W.I. Gautier; REMARKS: Lewis Higginbotham sworn.

248. 3 Jan 1900 JOHN MULLINS 21 yrs angle b. Mercer Co W VA s/o ? & Jane to ELIZA WELLS 18 yrs single b. Mercer Co W VA d/o Daniel & Dorcus; by J.O. Cassaday; REMARKS: sworn.

*Written at bottom of page: "Beginnng(sic) the 1900 Mr Bailey Clink."

1. 10 Jan 1900 JAMES H. MOYERS 34 yrs single b. Wytheville VA s/o T.J. & Mary to VICTORIA FARIS 18 yrs single b. Monroe Co W VA d/o A.W. & Henrietta O: bar keeper; by E.A. Shugart.

2. 3 Jan 1900 BENJ DUSTHIMER 69 yrs wid. b. OH now living same s/o Jno & Elizabeth to SARAH JANE GUTRIDGE 59 yrs wid. b. OH O: farming; by J.H. McClaugherty.

3. 6 Jan 1900 W.T. PUCKETT 39 yrs single to MOLLIE WILLIAMS 38 yrs wid; by W.W. Hamilton. (NOTE: No other info given.)

4. 7 Jan 1900 EDWARD SADLER 26 yrs single b. Mercer Co W VA s/o Henry & Minta Sadler to AMANDA CECIL 17 yrs single b. Mercer Co W VA d/o Wm & N.E. Cecil O: miner; by A.M. Craft; REMARKS: Edward Sadler sworn.

5. 10 Jan 1900 H.E. COOK 22 yrs single b. Mercer Co W VA s/o J.N. & Margaret to ELLA M. BLANKENSHIP 21 yrs single b. Mercer Co W VA d/o R.M. & Syntha O: farmer; by H.L Cook; REMARKS: Cook sworn.

6. 10 Jan 1900 T.W. CRESSEL 22 yrs single b. Pulaski VA s/o J.A. & M.E. to LULA M. BALES 19 yrs single b. Russell VA d/o Wm & R.B. O: farmer; by Wm W. Hamilton; REMARKS: Cressel sworn.

7. 14 Jan 1900 W. JOSEPH VAUGHN 30 yrs single b. NC s/o B.F. & M.J. to MARGARET PERDUE 30 yrs wid. b. W VA d/o James & ? O: miner; by A.M. Craft.

8. 17 Jan 1900 THOMAS SHEFFEY JOHNSON 27 yrs single b. Rusell Co VA s/o C.W. & A. to ALICE ANN VIRGINIA THORNTON 25 yrs single b. Mercer Co W VA d/o Wm H. & Eliza J. O: minister; by T.C. Shuler.

9. 7 Feb 1900 FLOYD J. BROWN 38 yrs wid. b. Giles Co VA s/o Lewis & Lucinda to ANNIE G. BROUSE 28 yrs single d/o Henry H. & ? Brouse O: justice; by Norman F. Marshall.

10. 24 Jan 1900 WEBSTER MOORE 24 yrs single b. VA s/o John & Chess to LENNIA OWENS 25 yrs single b. VA d/o Osker & Bettie O: miner; by J.H. Gardener.

11. 20 Jan 1900 WM J. FARLEY 35 yrs wid. b. Mercer Co W VA s/o Wm & Lucy A. Farley to ELIZA C. FERGUSON 25 yrs single b. Mercer Co W VA d/o E.R. & Elizabeth Ferguson O: farmer; by German P. Hatcher; REMARKS: Wm J. Farley.

12. 31 Jan 1900 C.H. CARRELL 32 yrs single b. Montgomery VA s/o John B. & Ann to MINNIE J. WILSON 21 yrs single b. Montgomery VA O: RR; by John F. Stone.

13. 31 Jan 1900 GEORGE GRAY 21 yrs single b. NC s/o Bill & Elizabeth to EASTER J. MEANS 21 yrs wid. b. W VA d/o Green Hager & Nancy O: farmer; by D.N. Saunders; REMARKS: George Gray sworn.

14. 2 Feb 1900 JNO BENJ STAMP 19 yrs single b. Franklin Co VA s/o Geo W. & Martha A. to TEXAS COOPER 19 yrs single b. Giles Co VA d/o Joseph & S.M. O: farmer; by J.O. Cassaday; REMARKS: Stamp sworn.

15. 14 Feb 1900 ELI T. BAILEY 23 yrs single b. Mercer Co s/o W.L. & E.A. to ROSIE MOORE 23 yrs single b. Franklin VA d/o John & Mary O: miner; by G.W. Bailey; REMARKS: Eli T. Bailey sworn.

16. 7 Feb 1900 FLETCHER FLOYD 22 yrs single b. SC s/o H.F. & ? to BESSIE GEORGE 22 yrs single b. Mercer d/o Sam & Elvira O: barber; by J.F. Prigmore; REMARKS: col'd.

17. 14 Feb 1900 J.H. WRIGHT 26 yrs single b. Campbell Co VA s/o J.W. & A.M. to DAISY D. KINGSBURY 20 yrs single b. Grayson VA d/o L.D. & M.A. O: clerk; by P.C. Clark; REMARKS: Wright sworn.

18. 14 Feb 1900 C.H. GOODWYN 26 yrs single b. Lunenburg Co VA to CORA L. PENDLETON 19 yrs single b. Mercer d/o W.A. & M.J. O: clerk; by L. Goodwyn; REMARKS: father present.

19. 16 Feb 1900 WILEY W. SETTLE 23 yrs single b. Russell Co VA s/o Jno & M.A. Settle to MARY E. SLUSS 17 yrs single b. Tazewell Co VA d/o M.A. & H.F. Sluss O: miner; by D.A. Ramey; REMARKS: W.W. Settle sworn.

20. 28 Feb 1900 FRANCES M. TILLEY 35 yrs wid. b. NC s/o Jno C. & Sarah to ENDORA F. FERGUSON 23 yrs div. b. Mercer d/o John & Elizabeth O: farmer; by W.F. Jenkins.

21. 27 Feb 1900 C.H. McKINNEY 20 yrs single b. Mercer s/o L.F. & M.A. to LAURA TANNER 18 yrs single b. Mercer d/o A.& M. O: farmer; by W.B. Booth; REMARKS: father present.

22. 28 Feb 1900 BOSTON BOOKER 28 yrs to CARRIE HENDRICKS 25 yrs d/o Margaret; by J.F. Prigmore.

23. 3 Mar 1900 C.P. HANKS 69 yrs wid. b. VA to IDA WILLIS 34 yrs single b. Mercer O: farmer; by W.L. Gautier.

24. 1 Mar 1900 WILLIAM ADAMS 23 yrs single b. Smyth Co VA s/o Nick & Fannie to ELLA ROBERTSON 21 yrs single b. Roanoke VA d/o Bob & Sallie O: RR; by J.F. Prigmore; REMARKS: sworn Adams.

25. 3 Mar 1900 EDWARD DUNFORD 23 yrs single b. Franklin Co VA s/o Wm & Polina to MARY BELL BILEY 17 yrs single b. Bland Co VA d/o Alexander & Nancy O: farming; by G.W. Bailey; REMARKS: Dunford sworn.

26. 7 Mar 1900 L.C. CARTER 41 yrs wid. b. Washington Co VA now living in Tazewell VA s/o Lewis & M. to JENNIE L. GLASCO 31 yrs wid. b. Tazewell Co VA d/o Jas & Marg O: miner; by J.F. Prigmore.

27. 7 Mar 1900 W.F. ROYAL 31 yrs single b. Ashe Co NC s/o John & ? to ROSIE YOUNG 17 yrs single b. VA d/o S.H. & L.J. O: sawmill man; by G.W. Bailey; REMARKS: Roby Dunn sworn.

28. 7 Mar 1900 JAS I.C. SANDERS 21 yrs single b. Scott Co VA s/o Wm & Clara Sanders to IDA L. HAGER 21 yrs single b.

Mercer Co W VA d/o Saml & Rebecca Hager O: farming; by C.A. Brown; REMARKS: Saml J. Hager & J.L.C. Sanders sworn.

29. 14 Mar 1900 JANDER R. MARTIN 26 yrs single b. Smith Co VA s/o Robt & Nettie Martin to ELIZA E. KILLIP 19 yrs single b. England d/o Geo & R. Killip O: railroader; by John F. Stone; REMARKS: Geo Killip.

30. 14 Mar 1900 JAS T. PERDUE 21 yrs single b. Herer Co W VA s/o Jas H. & Sarah E. Perdue to ROSA E. TABOR 17 yrs single b. Tazewell Co VA d/o Geo & Martha Tabor O: farming; by W.H. Ayers; REMARKS: Geo Perdue.

31. 14 Mar 1900 TINY N. GIBSON 22 yrs single b. Montgomery Co VA s/o Thos & Emma Gibson to MARY SUE BROWN 19 yrs single b. Montgomery Co VA d/o W.H. & M.J. Brown O: farming; by A.B. Hunter; REMARKS: T.N. Gibson & K.A. Brown.

32. 15 Mar 1900 LEWIS JOHNSON 39 yrs wid. b. Monroe Co W VA to L. NORA WESLEY 22 yrs wid. b. Tazewell Co VA d/o Jo & A. Williams O: farming; by O.T. Harris; REMARKS: col'd.

33. 27 Mar 1900 EDGAR N. ALBERT 21 yrs single b. Pulaski Co VA to FRANCES BUSKILL 21 yrs wid; by John F. Stone.

34. 28 Mar 1900 R.B.H. McKINZIE 22 yrs single b. Mercer s/o J.A. & L.E. to EUGENIA J. EATON 20 yrs single b. Mercer d/o L.M. & E.S. O: farmer; by Will L. Ball; REMARKS: McKinzie sworn.

35. 29 Mar 1900 LEVI DUNN 21 yrs single b. NC s/o J. & Millie to AMY CADLE 18 yrs single b. Raleigh Co VA d/o John A. & A.E. O: farmer; by G.C. Anderson; REMARKS: Levi Dunn sworn.

36. 28 Mar 1900 HENRY W. STOWERS 28 yrs single b. Bland Co VA now living in McDowell Co W VA s/o Grayson & Lucinda to LAURA G. WILLIAMS 19 yrs single b. Giles Co VA d/o J.H. & Ona E. O: farmer; by H.J. Wysor; REMARKS: J.H. Williams.

37. 29 Mar 1900 JNO M. KING 28 yrs single b. Knox Co TN s/o Russell & Fannie to ELIZA A. LAMPERD 28 yrs wid. b. Pulaski Co VA d/o Sol & Sarah King O: laborer; by H.J. Wysor.

38. 4 Apr 1900 RUSH BLACKWELL 23 yrs single b. Tazewell s/o ? & Amanda to JANE MOWLES 23 yrs single b. Tazewell d/o Tomey & Allie O: laborer; by A.B. Hunter; REMARKS: R.A. Tackett.

39. 6 Apr 1900 WILLIAM CLEAVER 22 yrs single b. Mercer s/o Abshir to LAURA HELVIN 21 yrs single b. Pole & Ann O: laborer; by J.O. Cassaday.

40. 8 Apr 1900 THOMAS J. MULLINS 52 yrs div. b. Franklin Co VA d/o Ade & Polly to EMMA FARMER 27 yrs single b. Mercer d/o John & ? O: laborer; by G.W. Terry.

41. 12 Apr 1900 E.J. HONAKER 21 yrs single b. Giles s/o J.W. & E. Susan to LULA ATKINS 16 yrs single b. Bland d/o H.B. & ? O: laborer; by J.H. Franklin; REMARKS: E.J. Honaker sworn.

42. 18 Apr 1900 GEORGE P.B. WHITE 34 yrs single b. Mercer s/o H.G. & S.E. to MARIE E. LONG 20 yrs single b PA d/o P.J. & P.J. O: conductor; by E. Oliver; REMARKS: G.P.B. White.

43. 17 Apr 1900 C.H. COMPTON 29 yrs single b. Tazewell Co VA to ROSA WREN WOHLFORD 24 yrs single b. Bland Co VA d/o Thomas & Edna O. O: conductor; by A.B. Hunter.

44. * * * JAMES SCOTT 31 yrs single b. Rockbridge VA s/o Wm & Mariah to SARAH C. PERKINS 23 yrs wid. b. Franklin VA d/o Edd & Margaret Turner O: miner. (*Note: no date given.)

45. 20 Apr 1900 WM T. DOUGLASS 25 yrs single b. Pittsylvania VA s/o Green & P.A. to HENRETTA JASPER 21 yrs single b. Montgomery VA d/o ? & Polly O: brakeman; by A.B. Hunter.

Page 104

46. 28 Apr 1900 A.C. LEFFEW 28 yrs div. b. Franklin Co Va s/o W.K. & Elizabeth to HINA DANIEL 20 yrs wid. b. Lee Co VA d/o ? & ? Tanner O: miner; by E.A. Shugart.

47. 25 Apr 1900 WATSON TERRY 27 yrs single b. Pittsylvania VA s/o Watson & V. to HELEN LYBROOK 21 yrs single b. Giles VA d/o John & ? O: RR; by J.F. Prigmore.

48. 23 Apr 1900 CHARLEY PAXTON 22 yrs single b. Tazewell Co VA s/o Richard & Malinda to POLLY McDONALD 21 yrs single b. Tazewell VA d/o George & Harinda O: RR; by J.F. Prigmore; REMARKS: Dave Harris sworn.

49. 25 Apr 1900 A.H. HAWLEY 51 yrs wid. b. Pulaski Co VA s/o Anderson & ? Hawley to MOLLIE E. NEWKIRK 26 yrs single b. Mercer Co W VA d/o Jno R. & M.E. Newkirk O: merchant; by J.F. Stone.

50. 2 May 1900 W.R. THOMPSON 22 yrs single b. Wyoming Co W VA s/o G.W. & Cora L. to ALLA DORA MORGAN 20 yrs single b. Mercer Co W VA d/o A.B. & M.D. O: farmer; by J.B. Simpson.

51. 2 May 1900 WM C. WILLIAMS 22 yrs single b. Smythe Co VA s/o W.P. & C.A. Williams to BESSIE G. GLOVER 17 yrs single d/o C.W. & L.E. Glover O: RR fireman; by R.M. Ashworth.

52. 9 May 1900 E.S. SMITH 28 yrs single b. Franklin VA now living in McDowell W VA s/o Joshua & Susan to EVIE COUSINS 31 yrs single b. Campbell VA d/o A.G. & Martha O: miner; by W.J. Carter.

53. 4 May 1900 JOHN MEADOWS 26 yrs single b. Giles VA s/o Floyd & ? to VIRGIE HALEY 24 yrs single d/o Harden & Virginia O: laborer; by J.F. Prigmore.

54. 2 May 1900 J.E. KADE 23 yrs single b. Mercer Co W VA s/o G.W. & Mary C. to CLARA BELCHER 25 yrs single b. Summers Co W VA d/o M.F. & Mary O: railroader; by Jno F. Stone.

55. 6 May 1900 HIRAM DAVIS 60 yrs wid. b. Mercer Co W VA s/o Joshua & ? Davis to MARY MEADOWS 32 yrs single b. Mercer Co W VA d/o Jerry & Virginia O: farmer; by R.A. Miller.

56. 6 May 1900 URE ISAACS 24 yrs single b. Wayne Co W VA s/o John & Mary A. to L.M. WHEELING 16 yrs single b. Mercer Co W VA d/o ? & H.V. Wheeling O: farmer; by T.S. Johnson; REMARKS: Aaran Kirk sworn.

57. 10 May 1900 L.P. SPANGLER 56 yrs wid. b. Monroe Co W Va now living in Giles Co VA s/o Floyd & ? Spangler to S.M. SHUMATE 55 yrs wid. b. Giles Co VA d/o Parkerson & R. Shumate O: farmer; by J.E. Thorn.

58. 16 May 1900 E.H. BROWN 28 yrs single b. Petersburg VA to ADA C. MEADOWS 2 yrs single b. Mercer Co d/o James & M.E. O: merchant; by A.B. Hunter.

59. 22 May 1900 H.G. JOHNSON 22 yrs single to MARY M. JAMISON 17 yrs single b. Tazewell Co VA d/o ? & Annie G. Jamison; by J.F. Stone.

60. 23 May 1900 C.W. PENNINGTON 24 yrs single b. Mercer Co W VA s/o Green & H.A. to LULA HOPKINS 23 yrs single b. Mercer Co W VA d/o ? & Louisa O: farmer; by J.O. Cassaday; REMARKS: Pennington.

61. 30 May 1900 WM T. GRAHAM 24 yrs single b. Tazewell Co VA now living in Wise Co VA s/o James & Sphrana to AMY Z. SHREWSBURY 18 yrs single b. Mercer Co W VA d/o P.T. & Iowa O: miner; by W.L Gautier.

62. 30 May 1900 CHAS C. BAILEY 30 yrs single b. Mercer Co W VA s/o Jno M. & S.A. to ADA MAY HALL 23 yrs single b. Tazewell Co VA d/o T.K. & ? Hall O: L. Engineer; by A.B. Hunter.

63. 30 May 1900 J. PRICE STUART 25 yrs single b. Greenbrier Co W VA now living n Scott Co VA s/o W.R. & S.K. to NANNIE E. BURTON 27 yrs single b. Amherst Co VA d/o Geo H. & Ves O: carpenter; by A.B. Hunter.

64. 6 June 1900 LUTHER JOHNSON 26 yrs single b. Campbell Co VA s/o Jefferson & Elvira to RHODA BELCHER 22 yrs single b. Roanoke Co VA d/o Joseph & Ellen O: fireman; by Wm Green; REMARKS: col'd.

65. 31 May 1900 SAMUEL G. NICKERSON 33 yrs single b. Pulaski Co VA s/o Pearis & Millie to FRANCES BEASLEY 22 yrs single b. Mercer Co W VA d/o Daniel & H.A. O: laborer; by C.A. Brown; REMARKS: col'd.

66. 1 June 1900 LEE CURRY 22 yrs single b. Wilks(sic) Co NC s/o Fate & Hannah to SUSAN SMITH 24 yrs wid. b. Campbell Co VA O: miner; by G.W. Bailey; REMARKS: col'd.

67. 15 June 1900 WM T. DUDLEY 31 yrs single b. Tazewell Co VA s/o J.C. & M.L. to ALMEDA CARVER 25 yrs div. b. Mercer Co W VA d/o Wm K. & C. Pennington O: farmer; by A.N. Jackson.

68. 6 June 1900 ROBT E. CHUMBLEY 26 yrs single b. Pulaski Co VA now living same s/o Geo H. & Nannie H. to VIRGINIA L. BROWN 22 yrs single b. Montgomery Co VA d/o W.H.H. & Mary J. O: physician; by P.C. Clark.

69. 5 June 1900 JNO L. BRAMMER 48 yrs wid. b. Mercer Co W VA s/o Jonathan & Mariah to LESSIE BOWLING 41 yrs wid. b. Mercer Co w VA d/o Woodson & ? O: farmer; by G.H. Johnston.

70. 7 June 1900 J.E. FARLEY 19 yrs single b. Mercer s/o Riley & Ellen to LOUIZA A. FARLEY 20 yrs single b. Mercer d/o B.D. & Mary A. O: farmer; by James W. Lilly; REMARKS: father present.

71. 6 June 1900 W.A. NELSON 25 yrs single b. Monroe Co w VA s/o Wm & Caroline to FANNIE E. JOHNSTON 23 yrs single b. Mercer d/o Erastus & Ella O: merchant; by W.J. Wysor.

72. 3 July 1900 W.L. BALLARD 29 yrs single b. Boon(sic) Co W VA now living in Charleston W VA s/o John & Emma to NETTIE GARRETT 22 yrs single b. Logan Co W VA d/o John & ? O: bartender; by Jno T. Stone.

73. 14 June 1900 SMITH SELLARS 42 yrs single b. TN s/o Hadison & Ann to JANE SELLARS 32 yrs wid. b. NC O: miner; by J.C. Carper; REMARKS: C.W. Lilly.

74. 14 June 1900 G.F. AKERS 53 yrs div. b. Montgomery Co VA s/o Jordan & Julina to SARAH J. KIDWELL 46 yrs wid. b. Giles Co VA d/o Jos & Nancy Skeens O: farmer; by r.A. Miller.

75. 18 June 1900 JOHN ROBINSON 23 yrs single s/o Wm & Julia to EFFIE BRIGGS 22 yrs single d/o Geo & L.C. Briggs O: miner; by S.W. Patterson; REMARKS: colored.

76. 20 June 1900 JAMES H. MARTIN 27 yrs single b. Mercer Co W Va s/o Wm H. & Martha A. to MARY BURCH 20 yrs single b. Mercer Co W VA d/o Jos & Catharine O: postal clerk; by M.J. Wysor.

77. 20 June 1900 F.L. RODMAN 34 yrs single now living in IL s/o EMILY GEILINGER 27 yrs single d/o ? & S.E. Geilinger; by P.C. Clark.

78. 21 June 1900 L.G. THORNTON 22 yrs single b. Mercer Co W VA s/o Sidney & Jane to MILLIE G. MEADOWS 19 yrs single b. Mercer Co W VA d/o Jno W. & Ardelia O: merchant; by R.A. Miller.

79. 20 June 1900 CARL B. BURKS 21 yrs single b. Summers Co W VA now living same s/o B.B. & F.M. Burks to SALLIE J. DOVE 22 yrs single b. Mercer Co W VA d/o P.W. & R. Dove O: saw milling; by G.H. Johnston; REMARKS: Carl B. Burks sworn.

80. 27 June 1900 JOHN P. ROLES 32 yrs wid. to LUCINDA A. JENNINGS 27 yrs wid. d/o ? & ? Whig O: farmer; by R.A. Bryant.

81. 20 June 1900 DAVID HOLTZCLAW 25 yrs single b. Lincoln Co KY now living same s/o W.R. & Mary A. to LOU E. BAILEY 27 yrs single b. mMcDowell Co W VA d/o Hastin & Nancy O: minister of the gospel; by M.H. Wyson.

82. 27 June 1900 S.E. CLENDENIN 29 yrs single b. Alamance Co NC s/o Geo A. & Mary to M.F. WHITWORTH 18 yrs single b. Montgomery Co VA d/o G.R. & S.M. O: RR conductor; by J.F. Stone.

83. 28 June 1900 CHAS W. LILLY 28 yrs wid. b Washington Co TN s/o Jno & mrtha Lilly to LULA JONES 22 yrs angle b. Mercer Co W VA d/o A.P. & Zerna Jones O: miner; by R.A. Miller; REMARKS: W.B. Jones sworn.

84. 3 July 1900 R.I. TULLY 21 yrs single s/o B.& E. to ROSA M. LIGON 18 yrs single d/o L.P. & ?; by E.Oliver; REMARKS: affidavit.

85. 26 June 1900 ANDREW JACKSON 32 yrs wid. b. Campbell Co VA s/o Mat & Ann Jackson to EMMA WILLIAMSON 22 yrs wid. b. Greenbrier Co W VA d/o ? & Octavia Dolan O: miner; by C.A. Pearson; REMARKS: colored.

86. 27 June 1900 J.R. CALLOWAY 32 yrs single b. Franklin Co VA to NELIE ARMSTRONG 24 yrs single d/o Ed & ?; by Wm Green.

87. 27 June 1900 MACK D. LEWIS 27 yrs wid. b. Appomatox Co VA s/o thos & Martha to LULAR STEWART 17 yrs single b. Campbell VA d/o Frank & Ann O: fireman; by L.C. Carter.

88. 27 June 1900 THOMAS CRAWFORD 41 yrs agle b. Mrcer s/o R. & Margaret to MATTIE J. UNDERWOOD 29 yrs angle b. Mercr d/o James & Mary O: farmer; by J.O. Cassaday.

89. 27 June 1900 E.R. PEDERHAN 22 yrs single b. Montgomery VA s/o H.S. & Anne to JANE E. KILLIP 20 yrs single b. England d/o George & Rozella O: RR; by John F. Stone; REMARKS: father present.

90. 27 June 1900 W.E. BENNETT 21 yrs single b. Franklin VA s/o G.D. & M.L. to ANNIE B. ALBERT 19 yrs single b. Montgomery VA d/o H.W. & Amanda O: miner; by R.A. Kelly; REMARKS: guardian present.

91. 4 July 1900 GRANVILLE L. LILLY 20 yrs single b. Summers Co W VA s/o J.S. & V.E. Lilly to ZORA J. EPLING 16 yrs single b. Mercer Co W VA d/o L.A. & Ellen Epling O: farmer; by James W. Lilly; REMARKS: G.L. Lilly sworn.

92. 30 June 1900 J.A. TROUTMAN 33 yrs single b. Cabrarous Co NC now living in McDowell Co s/o John & Elizabeth to NINA GRAVLY* 22 yrs single b. VA d/o John & ? Gravely* O: L. engineer; by A.N. Jackson. (*Note: name spelled both ways.)

93. 5 July 1900 JOHN J. HELMS 19 yrs single b. Franklin Co Va s/o Thos O. & Mary to CORA ROSE 17 yrs single b. Mercer Co W VA d/o Wm & D.A. O: farmer; by Ja W. Lilly; REMARKS: Jno J. Helms sworn.

Page 105

94. 4 July 1900 W.T. CORUM 26 yrs wid. b. TN s/o P.M. & Elizabeth to NORA B. FOWLER 19 yrs single b. Mercer Co W VA d/o Martin & N.A. O: miner; by A.M. Craft; REMARKS: Henry Ball.

95. 4 July 1900 WM B. ELMORE 23 yrs single b. Mercer s/o F.W. & P.F. to THEODOCIA PALMER 21 yrs single b. Mercer Co W VA d/o S.L. & Texas O: farmer; by J.O. Cassaday; REMARKS: father present.

96. 11 July 1900 CHARLES HEDRICK 19 yrs single b. Mercer s/o ? & Beckey to D.E. UNDERWOOD 21 yrs angle b. Mercer Co W VA d/o Asa & M.J. Underwood O: teamster; by Peter Grim; REMARKS: Asa Underwood sworn.

97. 18 July 1900 JOSEPH L. HAZLEWOOD 24 yrs single b. mercer s/o W.J. & Nannie to PEARL S. KIDWELL 19 yrs agle b. Giles Co Va d/o Benj & Martha O: farmer; by W.L Gautier; REMARKS: J.L. Hazlewood sworn.

98. 18 July 1900 GEO W. HAZLEWOOD 22 yrs single b. Mercer s/o W.J. & Nannie to NANNIE B. KIDWELL 16 yrs angle b. Giles Co VA d/o Benj & Martha O: farmer; by W.L Gautier; REMARKS: Geo W. Hazlewood sworn.

99. 16 July 1900 JOHN SANDERS 21 yrs single s/o Wm & Therrissa to JENNIE SANDERS 16 yrs single d/o ? & Fannie O: miner; by R.A. Kelly; REMARKS: certificate of J.P.

100. 26 July 1900 SAMUEL SISK 38 yrs angle b. Wytheville Va s/o Logan Scott & Eliza to MARIAH CALLOWAY 26 yrs wid. b. Christiansburg d/o Sinola Curtis O: RR; by J.F. Prigmore.

101. 25 July 1900 ADDIE C. JOHNSTON 28 yrs single b. Mercer s/o Jas E. & Ella C. to NELLIE L. EATON 25 yrs single b. Giles d/o L.H. & F.S. O: school teacher; by D.H. Carr.

102. 2 July 1900 WM F. LARRISON 35 yrs single b. OH s/o Samuel & Allice to ROSA M. MONROE 27 yrs single b. Mercer d/o John & Amanda O: mining; by W.B. Boothe.

103. 28 July 1900 W.I. WATSON 29 yrs wid. b. Grayson Co VA s/o Eli H. & M.E. to ELIZABETH GRIM 24 yrs angle b. W VA d/o James & Elizabeth O: mason; by G.W. Bailey.

104. 30 July 1900 ED LOGAN 22 yrs single b. VA s/o Monk & Emma to MARY PORTER 19 yrs single b. VA d/o John & Annie O: miner.

105. 30 July 1900 JAMES H. DUNCAN 21 yrs sigle b. Mercer Co W VA s/o A.M. & R.S. to RHODA J. MULLINS 19 yrs single b. Mercer Co W VA d/o T.J. & M.J. O: farmer; by M.J. Wyson; REMARKS: J.H. Duncan & K.W. McClaugherty sworn.

106. 21 July 1900 J.H. HOLLOWAY 20 yrs angle b. Franklin Co Va now living in McDowell Co s/o C.E. & E.A. to NITA BAILEY 18 yrs angle b. Mercer Co W VA d/o G.H. & F.A. O: miner; by G.C. Anderson.

107. 1 Aug 1900 JNO R. CALDWELL 25 yrs single b. Mercer Co W VA s/o Glen & Sarah to EALLA LESTER 21 yrs angle b. Mercer Co W VA d/o A.B. & M.L. O: railroader; by A.N. Jackson.

108. 1 Aug 1900 J.W. O'DONNEL 23 yrs single b. Mercer Co W VA s/o W.R. & Elizabeth to LUCY SADLER 18 yrs single b. Mercer Co W VA d/o Eli & Nancy O: railroader; by G.W. Bailey.

109. 2 Aug 1900 RIBBLE W. SUBLETT 19 yrs single b. Mercer Co W VA s/o Wm & R.F. to LILLIE M. PETTRY 20 yrs angle b. Mercer Co W VA d/o A.B. & Eliza O: farmer; by W.L Gautier; REMARKS: R.W. Ribble sworn.

110. 9 Aug 1900 S.I. VIA 21 yrs single b. VA s/o G.W. & ? to E.A. PENNINGTON 17 yrs angle b. W VA d/o J.H. & H. O: farmer; by W.B. Boothe; REMARKS: father present.

111. 9 Aug 1900 RUSELL ROBINSON 21 yrs agle b. VA s/o Wm & Julia to MINNIE GILLS 20 yrs single b. VA d/o Sam & Halinda O: mner; by Benj F. Newson.

112. 10 Aug 1900 HENRY G. THOMPSON 23 yrs single b. Summers Co W VA now living same s/o Jos & L.E. Thompson to WINNIE A. LILLY 19 yrs angle b. Mercer Co W VA d/o E.H. & C.E. Lilly O: farmer; by G.H. Johnson; REMARKS: E.H. Lilly present.

113. 12 Aug 1900 JOSEPH W. COOPER 35 yrs single b. Grayson Co Va s/o Jas M. & Phaney to MOLLIE REYNOLDS 35 yrs single b. Mercer Co W VA d/o S.T. & Araminta O: farmer; by T.S. Johnson.

114. 15 Aug 1900 A.B. HYLTON 28 yrs wid. b. Floyd co VA s/o Hiram & Louisa to HEDA SWADER 20 yrs single b. Mercer Co W VA d/o Jackson & Elvira O: farmer; by G.W. Terry; REMARKS: father present.

115. 19 Aug 1900 EDWARD SYOVENYI 29 yrs single b. Hungary s/o August & Elizabeth to MARY STUPALSKI 35 yrs single b. Hungary O: grocery clerk; by E. Olivier.

116. 29 Aug 1900 JNO L. PERDUE 23 yrs single b. Franklin Co VA s/o Jno A. & N.A. Perdue to MOLLIE BELL 17 yrs single b. Mercer Co d/o Henry & J.A. Bell O: miner; by D.H. Thornton.

117. 4 Sept 1900 JAMES T. THRONTON 24 yrs single b. Mercer s/o Wm M. & Eliza to BERTHA WRIGHT 21 yrs single b. Carroll VA d/o Isac & ? O: merchant; by D.H. Thornton.

118. 29 Aug 1900 GEO L. LETCHER DODD 26 yrs single b. Summers Co W VA s/o F.W. & C.E. Dodd to JOSIE R. LAWSON 17 yrs single b. Giles Co Va d/o W.J. & Amanda A. O: laborer; by J.H. Franklin.

119. 29 Aug 1900 O.B. TABOR 20 yrs single b. Tazewell VA s/o Geo W. & Martha A. to JULIA B. BELCHER 16 yrs single b. Mercer d/o Ballard & Cloe O: laborer; by W.H. Ayers.

120. 28 Aug 1900 CALVIN GODFREY 22 yrs single b. Mercer s/o Robt & Julia to ELIZABETH UNDERWOOD 19 yrs single b. Mercer d/o Acy & M.J. O: laborer; by J.B. Simpson; REMARKS: father present.

121. 29 Aug 1900 W.B. BELCHER 21 yrs single b. Mercer s/o I.B. & Nancy to SUSAN E. HOLSTON 19 yrs single b. Mercer d/o L.C. & S.L. O: laborer; by M.J. Wysor.

122. 30 Aug 1900 HENRY GULLION 22 yrs single b. Mercer s/o Reuben & E.H. to ROSA ANN TABOR 16 yrs single b. Mercer d/o John & Amanda O: laborer; by T.B Cook.

123. 5 Sept 1900 A.J. MABRY 39 yrs wid. b. VA to JULIA YEATTS 26 yrs wid; by D.A. Ramey.

124. 31 Aug 1900 WILLIAM PRUETT 27 yrs single b. Smythe Co Va s/o John & Jane Pruett to AMANDA BLACKWELL 36 yrs single b. Tazewell Co VA d/o David & Sarah Cordell O: teamster; by P.C. Clark.

125. 5 Sept 1900 ARTY BLESSNG 23 yrs single b. KY s/o John & Caroline to MARY DENT 23 yrs single b. Wythe VA d/o Thomas & Charlott O: miner; by G.W. Bailey; REMARKS: Blessing sworn.

126. 6 Sept 1900 JOHN SNEED 44 yrs b. Mercer to MATILDA SNEED 29 yrs b. Mercer O: farmer; by Pleasant H. Lilly.

127. 12 Sept 1900 ROBT LEE WHITE 34 yrs wid. b. Monroe Co W VA s/o Robt & Martha to ELLA B. PARKER 26 yrs wid. b. Monroe Co W VA d/o Saml & ? Parker O: laborer; by J.O. Cassaday; REMARKS: colored.

128. 17 Sept 1900 CLEM LANE 27 yrs wid. b. Chatham Co NC s/o Wm P. & H. Lane to MATIE G. BARROW 22 yrs single b. Pulaski Co VA d/o Wm & Bettie F. O: telegrapher; by A.N. Jackson.

129. 17 Sept 1900 A.G. BELCHER 55 yrs wid. b. Mercer Co s/o Jno N. & Nancy to CELIA SOUTH 48 yrs wid. O: farmer; by John H. Honaker.

130. 18 Sept 1900 W.H. HARRY 23 yrs angle b. Mercer Co s/o Calvin & Mary to ANN NETTIE HINCHU 19 yrs angle b. Giles d/o C.H. & Mahaly O: clerk; by J.F. Stone; REMARKS: father present.

131. 19 Sept 1900 C.L. HATCHER 18 yrs single b. Mercer Co s/o Jno P. & Julia A. to D.A. COX 20 yrs single b. Summers Co W VA d/o Jas F. & Mary O: farmer; by German P. Hatcher; REMARKS: C.L. Hatcher sworn.

132. 19 Sept 1900 ALBERT MORGAN 23 yrs angle b. Wyoming W VA now living same s/o Amos & Mary to ORA ELSIE McCOY 17 yrs single b. Mercer d/o Wm H. & ? O: farmer; b J.H. Franklin; REMARKS: W.H. Caldwell.

133. 19 Sept 1900 GEO W. BERKHART 24 yrs single b. Lee Co VA s/o N.C. & Marena to TEMPA McFADDEN 22 yrs single b. Russell Co VA d/o Richard & Mary O: agent; by P.C. Clark.

134. 26 Sept 1900 J.H. SHUFFLEBARGER 26 yrs single b. Pulaski Co VA now living Tazewell Co W VA s/o M. & Susan to MOLLIE C. HARRIS 21 yrs single b. Amherst Co VA d/o G.S. & ? Harris O: baggage man; by R.A. Kelly.

135. 26 Sept 1900 JOSEPH HYLTON 27 yrs single b. Floyd VA s/o Hiram & Louisa to LUCY M. MARTIN 20 yrs single b. Mercer d/o Wm & Martha O: farmer; by J.B. Simpson.

136. 26 Sept 1900 THOMAS SHRADER 25 yrs single b. Mercer s/o Greenvill & Rebecca to MOLLIE SMITH 17 yrs single b. Montgomery d/o W.J. & Ann M. O: farmer; by J.B. Simpson.

137. 27 Sept 1900 JAMES F. HARVEY 29 yrs single b. VA to BETTIS JOHNSON 24 yrs wid. O: miner; by J.T. Gibbins.

138. 1 Oct 1900 F.D. TRAIL 34 yrs wid. b. Franklin Co VA s/o Flem & Latitia to MAGGIE N. HARVEY 21 yrs single b. Montgomery Co VA d/o Wm T. & Lydia O: painter; by P.A. Anthony; REMARKS: C.E. Harvey sworn.

139. 3 Oct 1900 W.C. CRINER 20 yrs single b. VA now living in Tazewell s/o E.E. & Emma to MOLLIE PERDUE 19 yrs single b. W VA d/o J.H. & Sarah E. O: laborer; by E.T. Mason; REMARKS: G.H. Perdue sworn.

140. 2 Oct 1900 OWEN HEDRICK 21 yrs single b. W VA s/o Granvill & Rebecca to BULEY ESTHER SCOTT 19 yrs single b. W VA d/o J.O. & ? O: laborer.

141. * * * G.S. HEDRICK to P.F. BISHOP; by P.C. Clark. (*Note: no date given.) NOTE: No other information given.

Page 106

NOTE: Numbered as original is numbered.
141. 11 Oct 1900 THOS L. NOURLIN single b. Franklin Co VA s/o W.F. & Sarah H. to NANNIE CLARK single b. Franklin Co VA d/o James & Susan; by T.B. Cook.

142. 4 Oct 1900 R.H. HENDERSON 22 yrs single b. TX now living in McDowell Co s/o W.A. & M.B. Henderson to DELIA B. HUGHES 21 yrs single b. Mercer Co W VA d/o J.C. & E.D.; by A.S. Thorn; REMARKS: father present.

143. 6 Oct 1900 S.L. HURST 19 yrs single b. Mercer Co W VA s/o J.H. & Sarah to NITA WOOD 16 yrs angle b. Mercer Co W VA d/o ? & Sallie E. O: merchant; by Peter Grim; REMARKS: J. Jordan sworn.

144. 10 Oct 1900 JAS B. STOVALL 23 yrs single b. Mercer Co W VA s/o Levi & Ann to LAVERNIA SIMPSON 20 yrs wid. b. Mercer Co W VA d/o P.A. & Lucy A. Hubbard O: farmer; by James W. Lilly.

145. 10 Oct 1900 WILLIAM H. GADD 45 yrs wid. b. Mercer Co W VA s/o Andrew & Delilah to CATHERINE MEADOR 38 yrs wid. b. Mercer Co W VA s/o Nat & Sally Aders O: farmer; by James W. Lilly.

146. 10 Oct 1900 J.J. RUFFIN 29 yrs single b. Tazewell to BARBARIE L. CECIL 21 yrs single b. Tazewell d/o Charlott; by P.R.a. Smith; REMARKS: F.J. Brown.

147. 11 Oct 1900 J.F. PERDUE 35 yrs single b. NC now living in McDowell to ROSA E. BALLARD 29 yrs wid. b. Mercer d/o Hawks O: laborer; by W.I. Gautier.

148. 13 Oct 1900 FLOYD BROWN 30 yrs single b. Pulaski Co VA s/o Geo & Letha A. to CALLIE HOWARD 18 yrs single b. Pulaski Co VA d/o ? & Rhoda Adams O: farming; by C.A. Brown; REMARKS: colored, guardn present.

149. 17 Oct 1900 CHARLES CLARK 20 yrs single b. Mercer s/o John & Nancy M. to ZOLLA GADD 19 yrs single b. Mercer d/o J.B. & Z.T. O: farming; by R.A. Bryant; REMARKS: J.B. Gadd present & sworn.

150. 17 Oct 1900 MARCUS SNYDER 25 yrs single b. Fayett now living same to LIZZIE BUTLER 21 yrs single b. Mercer d/o Z.R. & Linn O: breakman(sic); by G.M. Johnson; REMARKS: E.E. ANDERSON SWORN.

151. 21 Oct 1900 B.J. BRUSTER 22 yrs single b. Tazewell Co VA s/o R.B. & Sarah to LAURE ARGABRIGHT 22 yrs single b. Montgomery Co VA d/o R. & O.A. O: railroading; by G.W. Hutchinson; REMARKS: B.J. Bruster sworn.

152. * * * S.W. CORNWELL 32 yrs wid. b. SC s/o Jno D. & Hannah to ANGIE PERRY 39 yrs angle b. Tazewell Co VA O: electrician. (*Note: no date given.)

153. 24 Oct 1900 O.E. CHAPMAN 26 yrs single b. Salem VA s/o O.B. & H.B. to LUCY C. MUNDY 23 yrs single b.

Charlottsville VA d/o J.D. & ? Mundy O: boiler maker; by P.C. Clark.

154. 24 Oct 1900 J.W. RAGLAND 23 yrs single b. Newsferry VA s/o C.J. & L.J. to ANNIE B. MUNDY 20 yrs single b. Charlottsville VA d/o J.D. & ? Mundy O: merchant; by P.C. Clark.

155. 24 Oct 1900 GEORGE SHORT 21 yrs single b. Bland Co VA s/o Henry & Nannie to REBECCA M. BRUSTER 18 yrs single b. Tazewell Co VA d/o R.B. & Sarah O: miner; by D.N. Saunders; REMARKS: G.W. Bruster & Geo Short sworn.

156. 29 Oct 1900 JOHN H. GAENS 30 yrs single b. Campbell Co VA s/o Jas E. & Sophia to NANCY TRENT 19 yrs single b. Giles Co VA d/o a.M. & Mary Trent O: miner; by P.A. Anthony; REMARKS: father present.

157. 31 Oct 1900 GREEN MEADOWS 25 yrs wid. b. Mercer Co W VA to MARGARET COX 18 yrs single b. Mercer Co W VA d/o Wellington & Lizzie O: farmer; by Pleasant H. Lilly; REMARKS: Irvin Meadows sworn.

158. 31 Oct 1900 H.S. WALKER 24 yrs single b. Gila Co VA s/o G.H. & S.B. Walker to ADA B. CLENDENEN 22 yrs single b. Mercer Co W VA d/o R.G. & mary E. O: engineer; by J.T. Frazier.

159. 31 Oct 1900 J.B. NEWMAN 27 yrs single b. Franklin Co VA s/o Asa & Lyddia to MATTIE E. BENNETT 17 yrs single b. Franklin Co VA d/o G.D. & M.L. O: mining; by R.A. Kelly; REMARKS: father present.

160. 31 Oct 1900 GEO C. KITTS 24 yrs single b. Bland Co VA s/o Peter & Mary Kitts to ADALINE R. LANDRUM 21 yrs single b. Pulaski Co VA d/o Thos & Latiria O: Loco fireman; by R.A. Owens; REMARKS: Leroy Landrum sworn.

161. 31 Oct 1900 JOHN CODWELL 23 yrs single b. Lynchburg VA s/o Fayette & Sallie to ELIZA ALEH 28 yrs single O: miner; by R.H. McRay; REMARKS: colored.

162. 31 Oct 1900 B.S. ADKINS 20 yrs angle b. Bland Co Va s/o H.G. & Victoria to NANCY C. GOLD 17 yrs single b. Smythe Co Va d/o A.L. & Arena O: farmer; by W.H. Ayers; REMARKS: A.L. Gold sworn.

163. 2 Nov 1900 JAMES H. BROOKS 25 yrs angle b. Russell Co VA s/o Nathan & Amanda to LAURA G. HOLLINS 19 yrs single b. Gloyd Co Va d/o W.H. & F.E. O: miner; by R.A. Kelly; REMARKS: father present.

164. 4 Nov 1900 J.I. CECIL 21 yrs sgle b. Mercer Co W VA s/o Wm P. & Emma to C.E. HENNINGS 16 yrs single b. Surry Co NC d/o M.R. & Amanda O: miner; by G.C. Anderson; REMARKS: G.H. Harman sworn.

165. 1 Nov 1900 DEXTER COLLINS 23 yrs single b. Ash Co NC s/o Henry & Bell to AMERICA RUDICIL 28 yrs wid. b. Mercer Co W VA d/o J.F. & A.E. Ratliff O: miner; by G.W. Terry; REMARKS: J.F. Ratliff.

166. * * * D.J. HYLTON 40 yrs wid. b. Patrick VA s/o M. & H. to MARY HAYES 25 yrs single b. NC d/o H. & A. O: mason. (*Note: no date given.)

167. 7 Nov 1900 FRANK STEWART 30 yrs single to DEALY RIPPY 23 yrs single O: miner; by B.F. Newsom.

168. 14 Nov 1900 GEO W. VIA 47 yrs wid. b. Patrick Co Va now living in Giles Co VA s/o Spirel & Mary J. to NANCY J. VIA 44 yrs wid. b. Franklin Co VA d/o Dave & Betsy Gunley O: farmer; by W.L Gautier.

169. 7 Nov 1900 ODEN C. MUNSEY 22 yrs single b. Giles CoVA s/o Winton & Sarah to EUNICE A. CALDWELL 19 yrs single b. Mercer Co W VA d/o Glen & S.A. O: farmer; by J.T. Frazier; REMARKS: J.R. Caldwell sworn.

170. 14 Nov 1900 CHAS P. HOWARD 30 yrs now living in Bedford VA s/o Jno A. & Cleopatra to ELIZABETH V. STUDIVANT 31 yrs d/o Pleasant M. & Nancy S. O: farmer; by R.A. Kelly.

171. 9 Nov 1900 JESSE W.B. JENKINS 22 yrs angle b. Smythe Co VA s/o S.P. & Cynthia A. to JOSIE CECIL 19 yrs single d/o W.F. & ? Cecil O: farmer; by G.C. Anderson; REMARKS: S.P. Jenkins sworn.

172. 8 Nov 1900 A.T. CAULEY 45 yrs single b. Tazewell Co VA s/o G.C. & Eliza J. to CORDELIA EWING 25 yrs single b. Lee Co VA d/o James & Catharine O: miner; by R.A. Kelly.

173. 11 Nov 1900 GEO C. COLES 34 yrs wid. b. Charlotte Co VA s/o Catharine Coles to LIZZIE SANDERS 22 yrs single d/o Milton & Frances O: miner; by R.A. Kelly.

174. * * * JOHN DAYS 26 yrs angle b. Montgomery Co VA s/o John & Lucy Days to LIDA HARDEN 24 yrs angle b. Lexington KY d/o John & Mary Harden O: miner. (*Note: no date given.)

175. 13 Nov 1900 JOSEPH PARKER 23 yrs single b. Floyd Co VA s/o Jas A. & M.J. to VIRGINIA ADAMS 16 yrs single b. Mercer Co W VA d/o ? & Lizzie Parker O: farmer; by C.A Brown; REMARKS: Joseph Parker sworn, col'd.

176. 13 Nov 1900 JAS C. BROWN 21 yrs single b. VA to ADDIE R. VAUGHN 21 yrs single b. VA d/o H.C. & Mollie; by P.R.A. Smith.

177. 21 Nov 1900 JAMES W. THOMASON 51 yrs wid. b. VA now living in Tazewell Co VA s/o Daniel & Elizabeth to COLUMBIA J. DAWSON 50 yrs single b. VA d/o Hiram & Sarah O: farmer; by G.W. Terry.

178. 21 Nov 1900 JAMES L. HAWTHORN 22 yrs single b. Petersburg VA s/o Jas F. & M.B. to KATHRYN JAMES 24 yrs single b. Pittsylvania Co VA d/o B.A. & S.R. O: liveryman; by P.C. Clark; REMARKS: James L. Hawthorn.

179. 21 Nov 1900 HARVEY D. BROWN 42 yrs wid. b. Tazewell Co VA now living same s/o Jno & Rinda to NELLIE COE 22 yrs single b. Smythe Co VA d/o J.J. & Martha Coe O: farmer; by T.B. Cook.

180. 22 Nov 1900 G.W. CREGER 28 yrs single b. Tazewell CoVA s/o Wash & Amanda to MAUD HARVEY 24 yrs single b. Montgomery Co VA d/o Wm & Eliza O: laborer; b P.A. Anthony; REMARKS: Creger sworn.

181. 22 Nov 1900 G.W. DAVIDSON 42 yrs wid. b. Mercer now living in Summers s/o Hiram & Nancy to MALINDA J. GORE 23 yrs single b. Mercer d/o Jacob & Jane O: farmer; by R.D. Haynes; REMARKS: C.C. Gore sworn.

182. 24 Nov 1900 WM R. KENT 22 yrs single b. Mercer s/o Morris & Alice to EMMA SEABOLT 19 yrs angle b. Tazewell Co VA d/o James & Conby O: L. fireman; by James W. Lilly; REMARKS: W.R. Kent.

183. 25 Nov 1900 E.F. SHRADER 20 yrs angle b. Mercer s/o Rusell & Sarah A. to G.H. HOLLAND 17 yrs angle b. Russell Co VA O: farmer; by J.B. Simpson; REMARKS: guardian & father present.

184. 28 Nov 1900 L.W. GORE 34 yrs angle b. Mercer s/o H.F. & ? to BURTIE KEATLEY 21 yrs single b. Mercer d/o G.W. & Mary O: farmer; by J.W. Bennett; REMARKS: H.F. Gore.

185. 28 Nov 1900 CHAS L. SNEED 21 yrs single b. Mercer now living in Bland Co VA s/o Chas & Kate to MINNIE E. BOWLING 24 yrs single b. Mercer d/o P.A. & C.J. O: printer; by D.H. Thornton.

186. * * * GARRET COX 21 yrs single b. Glade Springs VA s/o Jas & Eliza Cox to FRANCES HACK 21 yrs wid. b. NC O: miner; REMARKS: Garret Cox, col'd, No Return.(*Note: no date given.)

187. 29 Nov 1900 H.A. MELVIN 21 yrs angle b. Mercer Co s/o Maggie Melvin to ALBERTA TAYLOR 16 yrs single d/o Geo W. & Etta O: farmer; by D.N. Saunders.

(188.) * * * GEORGE HELVIN 18 yrs single b. Mercer s/o Margaret to DASIE HELVIN 21 yrs single b. Mercer d/o Poll & Ann O: farmer; by D.N. Saunders; REMARKS: Margaret sworn. (*Note: date torn off original.)

(189.) * * * C.A. DILLON s/o ?.F. & S.A. to NANNIE L. HALE d/o B. & M.A. O: RR; by W.H. Ayers. (*Note: date torn off original.) NOTE:this entry difficult to read.

Page 107

190. 5 Dec 1900 ROBERT JACKSON 30 yrs single to KATE M. TAYLOR 21 yrs single d/o Jane & Jackson; by P.R.A. Smith; REMARKS: F.J. Brown.

191. 15 Dec 1900 W.H.H. BELCHER 55 yrs wid. b. Tazewell VA s/o L.& R. to LIDIA C. HOBBS 39 yrs single O: laborer; by P.A. Anthony.

192. 12 Dec 1900 L.L. NICHOLS 21 yrs single b. Summers s/o Z. & S.E. to V.A. MARTIN 26 yrs single b. Mercer d/o W.F. & M.E. O: sawmilling; by W.L. Ball; REMARKS: L.L. Nichols sworn.

193. 20 Dec 1900 WALTER LEE WOOD 20 yrs single b. Wyoming Co W VA now living same s/o Jas A. & S.A. Wood to MARY C. McBRIDE 19 yrs single b. Mercer d/o T. & Mary McBride O: farming; by Jacob Hylton; REMARKS: Walter Lee Wood sworn.

194. 26 Dec 1900 HOBART H. ELLISON 20 yrs single b Mercer Co W VA s/o R.F. & M.J. Ellison to SADIE CLARK 16 yrs single b. Mercer d/o Henry & V.Clark O: teacher; by J.W. Lilly; REMARKS: Henry Clark.

195. 19 Dec 1900 JAMES HOLLAND 22 yrs single b. Franklin Co VA s/o James & C. to LAURA SINKFORD 21 yrs single b. Tazewell Co VA d/o Adam & H.; by D.A. Ramey; REMARKS: Rumburg.

196. 19 Dec 1900 S.J. PETERS 23 yrs single b. VA s/o W.J. & Tulia to ALPH O. HOLSTON 21 yrs single b. Mercer d/o L.C. & S.L. O: carpenter; by R.A. Owens; REMARKS: sworn Peter & J.M. Holston.

197. 23 Dec 1900 JAMES DOSS 24 yrs single b. Tazewll s/o Sam & N. Lambert to MARY RADLIFF 20 yrs single b Montgomery d/o Bin & Jennie O: RR; by P.C. Clark; REMARKS: James Doss sworn.

198. 22 Dec 1900 ISAIAH E. BEE 33 yrs single b. Mercer Co W VA s/o Isaiah & Mary L. Bee to KATHLEEN P. NELMS 25 yrs single b. Hamlin Co TN d/o John H. & Letitia V. Nelms O: physician; by R.A. Owens; REMARKS: I.E. Bee.

199. 26 Dec 1900 DAVID H. KING 23 yrs single b. Franklin Co VA s/o Jas M. & M.J. King to JOSIE M. SHREWSBURY 17 yrs single b. Mercer Co W VA d/o John & Victoria Shrewsbury O: farmer; by G.C. Anderson; REMARKS: James M. King sworn.

200. 25 Dec 1900 J.G. GOFF 24 yrs single b. Bedford Co VA s/o Joseph & Ellen to LETTIE MAY FISHER 18 yrs single b. Montgomery Co VA d/o J.A. & E.J. O: fireman; by J.F. Stone; REMARKS: father present.

201. 26 Dec 1900 O.D. MEADOWS 22 yrs single b. Mercer s/o James & Sarah to ALHA F. CREWS 18 yrs single b. Mercer d/o Ann & Delinh O: farmer; by Pleasant H. Lilly; REMARKS: M.S. Poff sworn.

202. 24 Dec 1900 WM GREGGS 24 yrs single b. Franklin Co Va now living in McDowell to PEARLY SWADER 17 yrs single b. Mercer d/o H. & Catherine O: miner; by a.M. Craft; REMARKS: Henry Swader present.

203. 24 Dec 1900 JOSEPH HOWLES 19 yrs single b Mrcer s/o D.C. & N.J. to JANE IRVIN 19 yrs single d/o ? & Lucinda O: farmer; by J.F. Stone; REMARKS: W.H. Croy & H.R. Ballard sworn.

204. 30 Dec 1900 JAMES DENNIS 24 yrs single b. Bedford VA s/o Gilford & Nancy to NANNIE KATE CURRY 28 yrs wid. b. Franklin Co VA; by J.W. Johnson; REMARKS: Rumburg.

205. 24 Dec 1900 P.C. COX 22 yrs single b. Tazewell VA s/o John & Barbary to SALLIE ABSHER 20 yrs single b Mercer Co W VA d/o Wm & Martha O: farmer; by D.N. Sanders; REMARKS: father present.

206. 27 Dec 1900 WM R. COMER 29 yrs single b. Mercer s/o Jacob & Elizabeth to ADA M. SKEENES 18 yrs single b. VA d/o L.H. & Elvira O: farmer; by R.M. Ashworth; REMARKS: R.J. Hill sworn.

207. 2 Feb (1901) L.W. ALBERT 38 yrs single b. Montgomery VA s/o Henry & Jane to VICIE E. DAWSON 36 yrs single b. Tazewell VA d/o A.D. & Martha O: carpenter; by A.S. Thorn; REMARKS: J.P. Heptinstill.

208. 28 Dec 1900 W.W. WHITE 37 yrs single b. Mercer s/o Wm & margaret to BEE WHITE 25 yrs wid. b. Mercer d/o B.P. & ? O: farmer; by L. Goodwyn.

209. 30 Dec 1900 J.M.B. ROLAND 19 yrs single b. Tazewell Co VA s/o M.B. & M.E. Roland to MARTHA DORA SHIELDS 18 yrs single b. Tazewell Co VA d/o A.M. & M.A. Shields O: black smith; by D.N. Saunders; REMARKS: J.H.B. Roland sworn.

210. 1 Jan 1901 S.W. AKERS 21 yrs single b. Summers Co W VA s/o Jno E. & ? to L.J. LILLY 17 yrs single b. Raleigh Co W VA d/o Jos & J.A. Lilly O: farming; by James L. Lilly; REMARKS: L.F. Meador sworn.

211. 3 Jan 1901 MONROE HELTON 22 yrs single s/o ? & Sina Helton to ROZETTA JONES 19 yrs single b. Mercer Co W VA d/o Rufus F. & Sallie Jones O: railroading; by J.O. Cassaday; REMARKS: W.B. Jones.

212. 2 Jan 1901 DAVID WIMMER 23 yrs single b Mercer Co W VA s/o S.D. & R.J. Wimmer to MARY L BOWDEN 18 yrs single b. Mercer Co W VA d/o Jas G. & ? Bowden O: farming; by L. Goodwyn; REMARKS: David Wimmer.

Page 108

1. 1 Jan 1901 New Hope ROBT W. GOTT 28 yrs single b. Mercer Co W VA s/o A. & L.J. Gott to ALLIE R. CARR 24 yrs single b. Mrcer Co W VA d/o J.T. & N.A. Carr O: farmer; by R.A. Owen.

2. 2 Jan 1901 Bluefield H.L. LAUGHTER 23 yrs single b. Buncum Co NC s/o H.P. & M. Laughter to JENNIE HAMBRICK 22 yrs single b. Tazewell Co VA d/o Dudley & Laura O: L. Engineer; by P.A. Anthony; REMARKS: H.L. Laughter.

3. 2 Jan 1901 Princeton JAS E. GOTH 30 yrs wid. b. Mercer Co W VA s/o A.& L.J. Goth to HATTIE O. OLIVER 20 yrs single b. Mercer Co W VA d/o J.T. & J.D. Oliver O: farmer; by R.A. Owen; REMARKS: J.T. Oliver.

4. 2 Jan 1901 Oakvale ARTHUR THOMAS 18 yrs single b. Mercer Co W VA s/o Wilson & Jane to DORA B. SMITH 17 yrs single b. Mercer Co W VA d/o D.H. & A.J. Smith O: farmer; by L. Goodwin; REMARKS: Arthur Thomas sworn.

5. 4 Jan 1901 G.W. TAYLOR 19 yrs single to H.C. VAUGHAN 23 yrs single d/o ? & Mollie Vaughan; by P.R.A. Smith; REMARKS: F.J. Brown certified.

6. 5 Jan 1901 FRAZIER FARMER 23 yrs single b. Mercer Co W VA s/o J.P. & S.E. Farmer to LAURA B. FLETCHER 20 yrs single b. Mercer Co w VA d/o J.H. & ? Fletcher O: farmer; by J.B. Simpson; REMARKS: Frazier Farmer sworn.

7. 10 Jan 1901 C.C. TAYLOR 24 yrs single b. Mercer Co w VA s/o W.M. & Mary to MARY ROSABELL AKERS 17 yrs single b. Mercer Co W VA d/o Lewis J. & Manerva O: farmer; by E. Hawiston; REMARKS: C.C. Taylor sworn.

8. 10 Jan 1901 JOHN L. JOHNSTON 20 yrs single b. Mercer Co W VA s/o G.A. & Louisa to SARAH MITCHUM 17 yrs single b. Mercer Co W VA d/o James & Harriett O: farmer; by J.O. Cassaday; REMARKS: J.L. Johnston sworn.

9. 15 Jan 1901 ROBERT FLOWERS 22 yrs single b. Bedford Co VA s/o James & Bettie Flowers to EMMA TABOR 18 yrs single b. Tazewell Co VA d/o C.L. & M.A. Tabor O: laborer at B.I.W.; by D.N. Sanders; REMARKS: father present.

10. 17 Jan 1901 F.M. DUNCAN 31 yrs single b. Craig Co VA s/o Jos & N.A. Duncan to MARTHA E. PENDLETON 19 yrs single b. Patrick Co VA d/o Reed & Tilda A. O: farming; by L. Goodwin; REMARKS: father present.

11. 24 Jan 1901 F.C. THOMPSON 21 yrs single b. Alleghany Co VA s/o J.W. & F.C. Thompson to NORA G. ELLIS 21 yrs single b. Mercer Co W VA d/o Griffith & A.J. Ellis O: railroader; by A.S. Thorn; REMARKS: F.C. Thompson & N.G. Ellis sworn.

12. 31 Jan 1901 ARTHUR D. BASHAM 23 yrs single b. Monroe Co W VA s/o J.A. & P.A. Basham to MATIE L. WHITE 20 yrs single b. Mercer Co W VA d/o J.S. & josie White O: farmer; by Peter Grim; REMARKS: R.H. Basham.

13. 31 Jan 1901 RUFUS H. BASHAM 39 yrs div. b. Monroe Co W VA s/o J.A. & P.A. Basham to RUSHA RICHIE 23 yrs div. b. Mercer Co W VA d/o Wm C. & H.E. Bailey O: farmer; by Peter Grim; REMARKS: R.H. Basham.

14. 27 Jan 1901 JAMES IRA PENNINGTON 24 yrs single b. Monroe Co W VA s/o Green & M.A. to CORA MAY CONNER 19 yrs single b. Montgomery VA d/o J.H. & Louisa T. O: farmer; by A.L. Cathers; REMARKS: Pennington sworn.

15. 30 Jan 1901 ROBT MARSHALL BUTLER 26 yrs single b. Giles Co VA s/o Richard & Matilda to ELLEN PERKINS 28 yrs wid. b. Bland Co VA d/o J. & Annie Perkins O: laborer; by P.A. Anthony.

16. 31 Jan 1901 THOMAS SMITH 21 yrs single b. England s/o Eli & Emma Smith to L.N.G. PEUCE 21 yrs single b. Monroe Co W VA d/o P.J. & J.K. Peuce O: miner; by W.C. Carden; REMARKS: Thos Smith & A.K. Haynes.

17. 6 Feb 1901 W.B. WILLIAMS 27 yrs single b. Mercer s/o A.M. & H.J. to LOU J. WYRICK 23 yrs single b. Summers Co d/o J.C. & S.E. O: farmer; by J.W. Bennett; REMARKS: Williams sworn.

18. 9 Feb 1901 ROBT E. COX 28 yrs single b. Scott Co VA s/o Jno L. & Mary Cox to DARA FIELDS 21 yrs single b. Dickerson Co VA d/o Jno & Mattie Fields O: railroader; by J.T. Frazier.

19. 10 Feb 1901 JAS M. GRAVLEY 24 yrs single b. Carroll Co VA to MISSOURI L JENNINGS 17 yrs single b. Carroll Co VA d/o G.H. & Sarah Jennings O: farming; by J.W. Bennett; REMARKS: Jno M. Jennings sworn.

20. 20 Feb 1901 J.R.S. KENNEDY 22 yrs single b. Roanoke Co VA s/o J.E. & S.J. to LILLY E. HURST 21 yrs single b. Mercer Co W VA d/o O.S. & L. Hurst O: miner; by G.W. Bailey; REMARKS: C.H. Lester sworn.

21. 18 Feb 1901 JAMES R. CHRISTIAN 30 yrs single b. Giles Co VA now living in Summers Co s/o A.J. & H.J. to A.A. LILLY 25 yrs single b. Mercer Co W VA O: farmer; by A.L. Cole; REMARKS: D.C. Dobbins sworn.

22. 20 Feb 1901 HENRY F. FERGUSON 23 yrs single b. Mercer s/o E.R. & Elizabeth to JOCIE M. SNEED 17 yrs single b. Raleigh Co W VA d/o C.W. & M.A. O: farmer; by James W. Lilly; REMARKS: father present.

23. 21 Feb 1901 ISHAM B. BELCHER 59 yrs wid. b. Mercer to LUE KIDD 45 yrs single O: farmer; by R.A. Owen.

24. 25 Feb 1901 J.W. THOMPSON 30 yrs wid. b. Giles to AVAZOR HALL 16 yrs single b. Tazewell Co VA O: laborer; by A.S. Thorn.

25. 24 Feb 1901 J.H. VEST 28 yrs single b. Floyd Co VA s/o S.A. & D.A. to LENA V. BELCHER 23 yrs single b. Mercer Co W VA d/o M.H. & Valentine O: saw milling; by J.B. Simpson; REMARKS: J.H. Vest sworn.

26. 28 Feb 1901 M.F. ELLISON 50 yrs div. b. Mercer to HAHALA G. HICKS 43 yrs div. O: farmer; by James W. Lilly.

27. 27 Feb 1901 WESLEY WASHINGTON 21 yrs single b. Ellison VA s/o Geo & Susan Washington to ROSA THOMAS 21 yrs single b. Mercer Co W VA d/o Ed & Rosa Thomas O: miner; by B.J. Newsom; REMARKS: col'd, Wesley Washington sworn.

28. 11 Mar 1901 WALTER R. HICKEY 28 yrs single b. VA s/o Micael & Athea to MARGARET MILLER 24 yrs single b. VA d/o Mitchell & Kate R. O: machinist; by F.C. Clark.

29. 1 Mar 1901 MACK PEARSY 24 yrs single b. VA now living in W VA s/o J.W. & Lucy to ROSA HOWLES 26 yrs div. b. VA d/o ? & Mary O: laborer; by J.T. Frazier; REMARKS: J.W. Pearsy sworn.

30. 5 Mar 1901 H.H. CLAY 35 yrs single b. AL s/o H. & Ellen to REBECA DAVIS 22 yrs single b. VA d/o ? & America O: miner; by Anderson Davis; REMARKS: certificate A.J. Godfrey.

31. 7 Mar 1901 H.P. SHUMATE 27 yrs wid b. Mercer Co W VA s/o H.H. & Allie to MAGGIE B. PHIPPS 23 yrs single b. Mercer Co W VA d/o B. & ? O: farmer; by D.H. Thornton.

32. 14 Mar 1901 M.P. CAIN 40 yrs wid. b. Roanoke Co VA s/o Chas & Mariah Cain to ROSETTA BRICE 24 yrs single b. Marion Co VA d/o Ned & Rebecca Brice O: L. engineer; by Anderson Davis.

33. 21 Mar 1901 GEO F. DAVIS 35 yrs wid b. Mercer Co W VA s/o Hiram & J.A. Davis to MELISSA M.E. HARVEY 25 yrs single b. Mercer Co W VA d/o floyd & Emaline Harvey O: farmer; by R.A. Miller.

34. 20 Mar 1901 E.L. TILLEY 27 yrs single b. Mercer Co W VA s/o J.C. & ? to A.L. SHREWSBURY 25 yrs single b. Mercer Co W VA d/o George & L. O: laborer; by Peter Grim; REMARKS: J.E. Blankenship sworn.

35. 20 Mar 1901 C.H. McQUENE 29 yrs single b. AL to MELLIE JANE LAWSON 16 yrs single b. VA d/o W.J. & Amanda A. O: clerk; by P.A. Anthony.

36. 14 Mar 1901 MARTIN HARRA 35 yrs single b. NY s/o John & Julia to KATE RICHARDSON 28 yrs single b. VA d/o John & ? O: RR; by P.C. Clark.

37. 26 Mar 1901 W.L. DONALLY 34 yrs single b. VA s/o A. & S.A. to ANNIE L. FLETCHER 16 yrs single b. W VA d/o J.H. & ? O: farmer; by G.W. Terry.

38. 28 Mar 1901 J.G. DENNIS 27 yrs single b. Monroe Co W VA s/o S.T. & H.E. to CLARKIE MAY ELLIS 18 yrs single b. Mercer d/o Shan & Amanda J. O: breakman; by A.M. Craft; REMARKS: J.G. Dennis.

39. 27 Mar 1901 MARTIN LUTHER BURTON 22 yrs single b Mercer s/o John W. & Martha J. to SARAH LUVENIA TABOR 20 yrs single b. Wyoming d/o Chas T. & Cynthia H. O: farmer; by A.S. Thorn; REMARKS: M.L. Burton sworn.

40. 27 Mar 1901 JUSTIN SACKETT 33 yrs wid. b. OH s/o Chester & Roena to SALLIE HETHERINGTON 29 yrs single b. Mercer Co W VA d/o J.T. & Juliet H. O: saw milling; by R.A. Owen; REMARKS: Caldwell sworn.

41. 27 Mar 1901 W.B. CALDWELL 29 yrs single b. Mercer s/o Madison A. & Ann to NANNIE A. MARTIN 18 yrs single b. Mercer Co W VA d/o L.V. & Lula O: farmer; by D.H. Carr.

42. 28 Mar 1901 WM HAROLD 35 yrs wid. b. Tazewell Co VA s/o Wm & Margaret to DELLA MEADOWS 22 yrs single b. Summers Co O: farmer; by R.a. Owen; REMARKS: Wm Harold sworn.

43. 30 Mar 1901 GEO W. GRAHAM 24 yrs single b. Montgomery VA s/o ingle & Mary to MARY ARNOLD 22 yrs single b. NC d/o Andrew & Mary O: miner; by A.M. Craft.

44. 2 Apr 1901 JOSEPH W. MAXEY 27 yrs wid b. Mercer s/o Edgar & Anne to IDA E. LILLY 19 yrs single b. Raleigh d/o W.A. & Ellen O: farmer; by James W. Lilly.

45. 3 Apr 1901 DAVID A. WILEY 21 yrs single b. Mercer s/o Gas & Emily to MATIE MONROE 21 yrs single b. Mercer d/o John & Amanda O: farmer; by W.L. Gautier; REMARKS: Harve Pennington sworn.

46. 3 Apr 1901 R.L. SMITH 36 yrs wid. b. Tazewell s/o Geo P. & Martha J. to FANNIE J. BELCHER 25 yrs single b. Mercer d/o J.C. & Mary E. O: farmer; by R.A. Owen.

47. 10 Apr 1901 CHARLEY THOMAS 23 yrs single b. VA s/o Henry & Sarah to LULA ELDRIDGE 21 yrs single b. VA d/o Wm & Rachel O: miner; by B.F. Newson; REMARKS: A.L. Godfrey.

MERCER COUNTY, WEST VIRGINIA
Marriages 1854 - 1901

48. 8 Apr 1901 ED BECK 22 yrs single b. VA s/o Henry & Henriety to ELLA GAINES 21 yrs single b. VA d/o ? & Julia O: miner; by Anderson Davis; REMARKS: A.L. Godfrey.

Page 109

49. 10 Apr 1901 WM A. PANKEY 23 yrs single b. Appomatix Co VA s/o John R. & Bell to JESSIE KATHARINE KAHLE 17 yrs single b. Mercer Co W VA d/o John B. & M.C. O: electrician; by E.F. Kahle; REMARKS: Ernest Kitts sworn.

50. 14 Apr 1901 E.W. CROMER 32 yrs single b. Montgomery VA now living in Roanoke VA s/o C.D. & Sarah C. to ANNIE W. ATKINSON 25 yrs single b. Montgomery VA d/o J.W. & ? O: carpenter; by G.W. Bailey.

51. 10 Apr 1901 JAMES A. WIMMER 30 yrs wid. b. W VA s/o S.D. & Rhoda J. to CORA MAYBERRY 19 yrs single b. W VA d/o James & Lucinda O: farmer; by R.A. Miller.

52. 8 Apr 1901 WM D. YOUNG 23 yrs single b. KY s/o Gas & Bell Young to LUCY SPENCER 21 yrs single b. Charlotte Co VA d/o Abe & Delsie Spencer O: railroader; by R.A. Owen; REMARKS: col'd, Lucy Spencer sworn.

53. 18 Apr 1901 LEWIS SKEENES 40 yrs wid. b. VA s/o Joseph & Nancy to LEE CLEMENS 35 yrs single b. W VA d/o John & Mary O: farmer; by W.L Gautier.

54. 20 Apr 1901 JOSEF GEDER 25 yrs single b. Hungary s/o Josef & Terez to SORVEC TEREZ 25 yrs single b. Hungary d/o Steve I & Sherwitz O: miner; by E. Olivier; REMARKS: E. Freeman.

55. 17 Apr 1901 ELI O. LILLY 19 yrs single b. Mercer s/o Josiah & Mary to CORA J. CLARK 19 yrs angle b. Mercer d/o ? & J.A. O: farmer; by James W. Lilly; REMARKS: Eli O. Lilly & Giles Lilly sworn.

56. 17 Apr 1901 C.D. HOYE 20 yrs single b. Mercer s/o E.W. & S.E. to C.E. LILLY 20 yrs single b. Mercer d/o Danl & ? O: farmer; by James W. Lilly; REMARKS: father present.

57. 17 Apr 1901 JAMES R. WALTERS 21 yrs single b. Montgomery s/o Robt & Virginia to EFFIE D. BUCHANAN 17 yrs single b. Tazewell VA d/o A.& C.J. O: carpenter; by W.C. Corden; REMARKS: A. Buchan(sic) present sworn.

58. 20 Apr 1901 CHAS E. BROWN 31 yrs single b. Mason Co W VA s/o James & E.A. to LILLY B. HAMBRICK 21 yrs single b. Mercer d/o Geo & A.P. O: farmer; by J.B. Simpson; REMARKS: Jas McCluskey.

59. 19 Apr 1901 JOHN H. REED 34 yrs div. b. Grayson Co VA s/o John & Louisa to JENNIE WELSH 23 yrs single b. Patrick Co VA O: laborer; by L. Goodwin.

60. 23 Apr 1901 JAMES BAILEY 22 yrs single b. W VA s/o John H. & Sarah to SARAH J. COOPER 21 yrs single b. W VA d/o Lewis & M.A. O: farmer; by R.A. Miller; REMARKS: father present & J.W. Skeenes sworn.

61. 23 Apr 1901 JOHNSON B. ROSS 54 yrs wid. b. VA s/o Grifith & Harriett to ANN KIDD 44 yrs div. b. Bland Co VA d/o Wm & Polly O: farmer; by J.O. Cassaday.

62. 30 Apr 1901 L.L. McINTIRE 26 yrs single b. NC to M.D. WALKER 22 yrs angle b. VA d/o ? & Sarah O: RR man; by J.T. Frazier.

63. 30 Apr 1901 R.T. BOWEN 30 yrs single b. Tazewell VA s/o Thos & ? to LINA A. WALKER 26 yrs single b. VA d/o Sarah O: conductor; by Peter C. Clark.

64. 25 Apr 1901 JINK TINES 24 yrs single b. Bland Co VA s/o Jack & Julia to WILLIE M. THOMPSON 18 yrs single b. Mercer Co W VA d/o Charlie & Harriet O: railroading; by R.W. Hill; REMARKS: Tines sworn.

65. 28 Apr 1901 PRESTON EARLEY 26 yrs angle b. Wythe Co VA s/o Milton & Celia to POLINA BROWN 23 yrs single b.

Montgomery VA d/o Berney & Cynthia; by S.E. Williams; REMARKS: F.J. Brown.

66. 30 Apr 1901 ROBT L. HENCH 28 yrs single b. PA s/o S.T. & Annie E. to MARY E. CLIFFORD 21 yrs single b. W VA d/o M.H. & R.A. O: engineer; by E. Olivier; REMARKS: Hench sworn.

67. 1 May 1901 P.A. SMITH 29 yrs single b. Wyoming Co W VA s/o G.P. & M.I. Smith to MINNIE E. POE 17 yrs single b. Montgomery Co VA d/o J.I & M.J. Poe O: teacher; by D.N. Saunders; REMARKS: J.L. Poe.

68. 30 Apr 1901 H.A. SHORTER 21 yrs single b. Mercer s/o ? & Southern to WILLIA A. WILEY 21 yrs single b. Mercer d/o ? & Jocie Wiley; by W.I. Gautier.

69. 1 May 1901 EDWARD E. BAILEY 23 yrs single b. Mercer s/o Henderson & Sarah to JOSIE BROOKMAN 19 yrs single b. Giles Co VA d/o Gus & R.G. O: railroading; by G.W. Terry; REMARKS: Ed E. Bailey sworn.

70. 1 May 1901 JNO L. BASHAM 55 yrs div. b. Monroe Co W VA s/o John & Catharine to ELLA A. GLENDY 30 yrs single b. Pulaski Co VA d/o R.A. & Nancy M. O: Dept Clk Co Ct; by P.C. Clark.

71. 5 May 1901 P.H. BAILEY 21 yrs single b. McDowell s/o E.B. & Mary A. to LOTTIE SNODGRASS 16 yrs single b. VA d/o Geo & Mary E. O: farmer; by A.L. Cothers; REMARKS: P.H. Bailey.

72. 12 May 1901 ALBERT HARRIS 33 yrs single to HATTIE LIPSCOMB 22 yrs single d/o Squire & Harriett O: miner; by R.H. McKay.

73. 15 May 1901 EDWARD A. SPENCER 25 yrs single b. Lynchburg Va now living same s/o Warwick & Mary to ANN B. SCULES 21 yrs single b. Winston NC d/o ? & Sarah O: merchant; by N.F. Marshall; REMARKS: A.L Godfrey.

74. 13 May 1901 GEORGE R. BRECKENRIDGE 30 yrs wid. b. Mercer s/o Carrie & Hatilda to DESSIE GORE 18 yrs angle b. Mercer d/o Jacob & Sarah O: blacksmith; by R.W. Hill.

75. 13 May 1901 CHARLES W. HOWARD 21 yrs single b. Mercer s/o Charles & Elmira to ROXIE L. GORE 24 yrs single b. Mercer d/o Jacob & Sarah O: teamster; by R.W. Hill.

76. 16 May 1901 W.L. BAILEY 21 yrs single b. Mercer s/o Wm A. & Virginia to MOLLIE G. FOLEY 18 yrs single b. Mercer d/o Richard F. & Mag O: farmer; by J.T. Tabor; REMARKS: L. Foley.

77. 27 May 1901 NELSON JONES 29 yrs single b. Appomattix Co VA s/o Nathan & Lucy to MATTIE WELCH 22 yrs single b. Montgomery Co VA d/o Fountain & Mary O: miner; by R.A. Kelly; REMARKS: A.L. Godfrey.

78. 15 May 1901 ROBERT McCLION 24 yrs single b. NC s/o J. & M. to MALINDA LUKE 18 yrs single b. NC d/o Henry & Jane O: miner; by S.H. Gaines.

79. 19 May 1901 GEORGE CLEMENS 22 yrs single b. Webster now living Knawha Co s/o ? & Elizabeth to V.E. HALDREN 16 yrs single b. Mercer d/o P.T. & R.A. O: miner; by W.L Gautier; REMARKS: P.T. Haldren present.

80. 20 May 1901 ELIJAH P. MEADOWS 50 yrs wid. b. Giles Co Va now living in Raleigh Co W VA s/o Richard & Mary Meadows to MARTHA J. SNEED 50 yrs wid. b. Raleigh Co W VA d/o Hiram & Mary Farley O: farmer; by J.T. Tabor.

81. 23 May 1901 IKE SHREWSBURY 22 yrs single b. Mercer s/o Jas W. & Julia to HINNIE SHUTT 22 yrs single b. Montgomery VA d/o H.F. & Ellen O: farmer; by I.H. Bailey; REMARKS: LK Shrewsbury & J.W. Shutt sworn.

82. 22 May 1901 FRED W. YOST 26 yrs single b. IL to WILLIE A. SMITH 19 yrs single b. Mercer d/o J.M. & L.A. O: blacksmith; by R.A. Miller; REMARKS: father present.

83. 22 May 1901 GEORGE S. BURTON 20 yrs angle b. Mercer s/o John & Martha to JULIA B. BURTON 20 yrs single b. Mercer d/o W.H. & Elvira O: farmer; by I.H. Bailey.

135

84. 23 May 1901 WM BALLARD JONES 31 yrs wid. b. Mercer s/o E.P. & JeRus to MARY SNODGRASS 28 yrs wid. b. Mercer d/o Jas P. & A.A. O: farmer; by J.O. Cassaday.

85. 25 May 1901 ANDREW NAGY 23 yrs single b. Hungary to MARY SIKIER 26 yrs single b. Hungary O: miner; by E. Olivier.

86. 29 May 1901 J.W. JONES 20 yrs single b. VA s/o Wm & G.A. to ADA G. WHITE 19 yrs single b. Mercer d/o T.H. & Z.D. O: teamster; by A.S. Thorn; REMARKS: J.W. Jones.

87. 1 June 1901 STEVE DANESECZ 24 yrs single b. Hungary to TEREZO POZVEK 22 yrs single b. Hungary O: miner; by E. Olivier.

88. 30 May 1901 JOHN L. JOHNSON 70 yrs wid. b. Giles co VA s/o ? & S. Johnson to VIRGINAI HAMLIN 54 yrs single b. Giles Co VA d/o Stephen & Sarah Hamlin O: farming; by R.A. Miller.

89. 29 May 1901 SONNIE SPINNER 30 yrs b. Bedford Co Va s/o ? & Fannie Spinner to NANNIE K. PARKER 16 yrs single b. Mrcer Co W VA d/o S.H. & M.J. Parker O: farming; by J.O. Cassaday; REMARKS: col'd, father present.

90. 29 May 1901 ED W. BAILEY 33 yrs angle b. Mercer Co W VA s/o Wm C. & Mollie E. Bailey to MOLLIE SHUTT 26 yrs single b. Mercer Co W VA d/o ? & ? Hazlewood O: surveyor; by G.W. Bailey.

91. 29 May 1901 WM T. BRADBURY 21 yrs single b. Pulaski Co Va s/o Eldridge & Elizabeth to LENA BROOKMAN 18 yrs single b. Giles Co VA d/o R.L. & & Brookman O: railroader; by G.W. Terry; REMARKS: Wm T. Bradbury sworn.

92. 4 June 1901 C.B. STRICKLER 22 yrs single b. Roanoke Co Va now living same s/o D.S. & Nannie E. to LIZZIE O. PECK 22 yrs single b. Marshall Co RA d/o J.P. & Annie G. O: clerk; by P.A. Anthony; REMARKS: C.B. Strickler sworn.

93. 5 June 1901 A.F. PENNINGTON 23 yrs single b. Mercer s/o H.W. & C.A to WILLIE

JERNSHA JANE BIRD 23 yrs single b. Mercer d/o Wm A. & C.J. O: laborer; by W.L Gautier.

94. 5 June 1901 FRANK POINDEXTER 31 yrs single b. Campbell Co VA s/o Patrick & Dicey to AERENA TAYLOR 21 yrs single b. Roanoke Co Va d/o Creed & Emily O: miner; REMARKS: col'd, F. Poindexter sworn.

95. 5 June 1901 JOHN SHUTT 24 yrs wid. b. Mercer Co W VA s/o French & Ellen Shutt to RUFINA BELCHER 23 yrs single b. Mercer Co w VA d/o ? & Martha Belcher O: farmer; by H.L. Cook; REMARKS: Wm Carr sworn.

96. 5 June 1901 SAMUEL CARR 23 yrs single b. Bland Co VA s/o Jas & Fanny Carr to LILLIE MAY BASHAM 17 yrs angle b. Mercer co W VA d/o Lewis A. & Mary F. Basham O: laborer; by H.L Cook; REMARKS: Wm Carr sworn.

Page 110

97. 12 June 1901 C.C. PETERS 22 yrs single b. Mercer Co W VA s/o Jas & Mary A. Peters to EMMA L. SHREWSBURY 23 yrs single b. Mercer Co W VA d/o L.C. & Nancy Shrewsbury O: farming; by James W. Lilly; REMARKS: C.C. Peters sworn.

98. 12 June 1901 C.M. WINFREY 33 yrs wid. b. Mercer Co W VA s/o C. & J. to HAY J. BROYLES 20 yrs angle b. Mercer Co W VA d/o J.G. & M.C. O: farming; by R.M. Ashworth.

99. * * * BYRD FERRELL 36 yrs wid. b. VA s/o ? & Mary to ISADORE FROE 24 yrs single b. VA d/o D. & Mary O: miner; REMARKS: Not Returned.

100. 12 June 1901 GEO McGHEE 36 yrs div. b. VA s/o Henry & Nancy to MAGGIE MILLER 26 yrs single b. VA d/o James & Nancy O: miner; by Anderson Davis.

101. 14 June 1901 RICHARD JONES 42 yrs to NANCY WARF 36 yrs; by S.E. Williams; REMARKS: colored.

102. 17 June 1901 GILES THOS EPLING 28 yrs single b. Giles Co VA now living in McDowell Co W VA to NANNIE A. WHITE 20 yrs single b. Mercer Co W VA d/o B.P. & Laura A. White O: dentist; by J.W. Browning; REMARKS: B.P. White present.

103. 19 June 1901 SAML E. PRINCE 29 yrs wid. b. Mercer Co W VA s/o Henderson & Mary Prince to ALICE JANE LILLY 25 yrs wid. b. Summers Co w VA d/o Rufus & ? Lilly O: farming; by H.L Cook.

104. 18 June 1901 OSCAR ROLES 41 yrs single b. Mercer Co W VA s/o James & Mary J. Roles to CORA L. WOHLFORD 32 yrs single b. Bland Co VA d/o thos & Edna Wohlford O: RR conductor; by P.C. Clark.

105. 19 June 1901 LUTHER C. BIVINS 20 yrs single b. Monroe co W VA now living same s/o R.H. & E.A. Bivins to DELLA L. BLANKENSHIP 18 yrs single b. Giles Co VA d/o Henry & Margaret O: lawyer; by R.A. Miller; REMARKS: G.G. Thomas sworn.

106. 27 June 1901 CHAS H. SPENCER 60 yrs wid. b. Charlotte Co VA to AGNES GAINES 35 yrs div. b. Nelson Co VA d/o Edmond & Lucy Shipman O: laborer; by S.E. Williams; REMARKS: colored.

107. 20 June 1901 MACK ORTON 26 yrs single b. NC to MARY ELLEN HAMBLIN 21 yrs single b. Montgomery Co VA d/o T.H. & Catharne O: laborer; by G.W. Terry; REMARKS: A.J. Yopp sworn.

108. 25 June 1901 S.E. WILLIAMS 33 yrs single b. Franklin Co VA s/o S.E. & Harriet Williams to ROSA LEE MERRIMAN 22 yrs single b. Bedford Co VA d/o Geo & Ada Merriman O: minister; by R.D. Washington.

109. 25 June 1901 J.L. WATKINS 25 yrs angle b. charlott VA s/o W.T. & Carrie S. to LILA J. ZINK 22 yrs single b. Montgomery VA d/o Wm H. & Dorath O: machinist; by P.A. Anthony; REMARKS: J.L. Watkins sworn.

110. 26 June 1901 JOHN CARR HANES 26 yrs angle b. NC s/o Jacob W. & Amanda to ARDELIA BOWEN 20 yrs single b. Tazewell Co VA d/o Geo & Amanda O: barber; by S.E. Williams.

111. 26 June 1901 WM E. BAILEY 19 yrs single b. Mercer Co W VA to MARY E. BAILEY 23 yrs single b. Mercer Co W VA d/o Saml & Virginia O: railroader; by P.A. Anthony.

112. 29 June 1901 SHANON P. BAILEY 20 yrs single b. Mercer Co W VA s/o D.P. & M.J. Bailey to EDNA C. BAILEY 17 yrs single b. Mercer Co W VA d/o C.W. & S.A. Bailey O: farmer; by G.C. Anderson; REMARKS: Shanon P. Bailey sworn.

113. 27 June 1901 W.C. BRYANT 25 yrs single b. Grayson Co VA s/o Frank & Bettie to WILLIE J. MACK 24 yrs div. d/o J.C. & Martha O: miner; by S.E. Williams.

114. 30 June 1901 JAMES H. FLETCHER 49 yrs wid. b. Mercer Co W VA s/o Anderson & Rhoda Fletcher to ELIZA J. PENNINGTON 17 yrs single b. Mercer Co W VA d/o A.W. & M.F. Pennington O: farmer; by G.W. Terry; REMARKS: father, A.W. Pennington present.

115. 3 July 1901 WM E. LAWSON 23 yrs wid. b. Tazewell Co VA s/o Clabe & Mary Ann to MARY L. MARTIN 18 yrs single d/o Jno A. & Mary V. Martin O: miner; by A.H. Craft; REMARKS: W.E. Lawson sworn.

116. 4 July 1901 ALLION DUDLEY 19 yrs single b. Mercer s/o Wm L. Dudley & Rebeca to NORA HARMAN 17 yrs single b. Tazewell VA d/o T.C. & Rebeca O: timberman; by D.a. Ramey; REMARKS: father present.

117. 4 July 1901 BERRELL McCORMICK 21 yrs single b. Floyd Co VA s/o Richard & Jane to LOUVENIA THOMAS 16 yrs single b. Mercer Co W VA d/o Waine & Sarah O: farmer; by J.O. Cassaday; REMARKS: McCormick sworn.

118. 3 July 1901 VICTOR CORDER 23 yrs sigle b. Mercer s/o Sam & Ettie to MARY STAR 19 yrs single b. Tazewell VA d/o James & Hattie O: teamster; by Peter C. Clark; REMARKS: Victor Corder sworn.

119. 10 July 1901 D.H. MILLER 20 yrs single b. Mercer s/o G.C. & Margaret to LIZZIE BROYLES 24 yrs single b. Mercer d/o Wm J. & M.J. O: farming; by L. Goodwyn; REMARKS: D.H. Miller sworn.

120. 13 July 1901 HARKEV ULINOH 36 yrs single b. Russia s/o Ulenan & Palagia to MARY DEMKO 22 yrs single b. Hungary d/o John & Anna O: miner; by E. Olivier; REMARKS: E.W. Freeman.

121. 9 July 1901 J.F. CHURCH 25 yrs single b. NC s/o S.E. & S.A. Church to AMANDA HARMAN 18 yrs single b. Mercer Co W VA d/o A.J. & Lydia Harman O: carpenter; by G.c. Anderson; REMARKS: A.J. Harman present.

122. 10 July 1901 HUGH C. HOLSTON 33 yrs single b. Mercer Co W VA s/o Lewis & Sarah to AMELIA WILLIAMS 32 yrs single b. Carroll Co VA d/o Martin & Polly O: farming; by R.A. Owen; REMARKS: J.H. Holston.

123. 11 July 1901 W.R. HOLLIDAY 25 yrs single b. Wyth Co VA s/o John H. & Francis to BELL PRATT 22 yrs wid. b. Wyth Co VA d/o Thomas & Lizzie Smith O: fireman; by R.A. Owen; REMARKS: W.r. Holliday sworn.

124. 18 July 1901 JAS R. RICHARDSON 28 yrs div. b. Summers Co W VA s/o Jno R. & Jane Richardson to MARY FRANCES MILLS 19 yrs single b. Mercer Co W VA d/o H.G. & Elizabeth H. O: farmer; by J.H. Meadows; REMARKS: father present.

125. 18 July 1901 J.E. WHITE 49 yrs wid. b. SC s/o Joe & Nannie to KATIE CUNNINGHAM 44 yrs wid. b. Montgomery Co VA d/o Thomas & Mary Jane O: laborer; by D.a. Ramey; REMARKS: A.L Godfrey.

126. 17 July 1901 T.J. AUTON 30 yrs wid. b. NC s/o John & Annie to MAY ELLEN SAUNDERS 26 yrs single b. Mercer Co d/o Wm & Clara O: laborerl by J.B. Simpson.

127. 19 July 1901 ALI W. LILLY 20 yrs single b. Summers Co now living same s/o J.T. & Margaret M. to TENARIE C. MANN 20 yrs single b. Mercer Co d/o Andy &

N.C. O: laborer; by James W. Lilly; REMARKS: father present & sworn.

128. 17 July 1901 IRA W. KINZER 19 yrs single b. Mercer s/o Wm & Margaret E. to MARY E. SCOTT 16 yrs single b. Mercer d/o Geo P. & Amanda O: laborer; by G.C. Anderson; REMARKS: Gideon Birchet sworn.

129. 17 July 1901 S.G. JOHNSTON 28 yrs single b. Grayson Co VA s/o Jessie & Malinda to HENRY ETTIE CROTTY 38 yrs single b. Monroe Co W VA d/o D.L. & Angeline O: carpenter; by J.T. Frazier.

130. 21 July 1901 WM A. WEEKS 26 yrs single b. Floyd Co VA now living in McDowell Co s/o John & ? Weeks to ORA MAY NEELY 18 yrs single b. Mercer Co W VA d/o John & Rachel Neely O: saw milling; by J.M. Ashworth; REMARKS: John Neely present.

131. 21 July 1901 WM B. LILLY 25 yrs wid. b. TN s/o J.J. & Martha Lilly to EMMA BLANKENSHIP 24 yrs single b. Giles Co VA d/o A.J. & Sallie Blankenship O: miner; by J.O. Cassaday.

132. 21 July 1901 H.J. SMITH 33 yrs single b. Montgomery Co VA s/o Lewis & Annie Smith to MARY CLARK 39 yrs single b. Russell Co VA d/o ? & Matilda Garrett; by S.E. Williams.

133. 31 July 1901 LONZY KEFFER 23 yrs single b. W VA now living in Summers s/o G.A. & Margaret to KATIE ROBERTSON 18 yrs single b. VA d/o C.D. & Mary E. O: farming; by G.A. Comer.

134. 26 July 1901 JOHN HALMANDOLLAR 30 yrs now living in Tazewell Co VA to SALLIE WHIT 30 yrs d/o ? & Polly; by Peter C. Clark.

135. 31 July 1901 J.E. WRIGHT 23 yrs single b. Mercer Co W VA s/o J.H. & Nannie to MINNIE M. DAVIS 18 yrs angle b. OH d/o M.W. & M.S. O: farmer; by J.B. Simpson; REMARKS: father present.

136. 31 July 1901 H.C. HULL 21 yrs angle b. Mercer Co W VA to NORA CALFEE 17 yrs single b. Mercer d/o A.B. & Virginia O: farmer; by G.C. Anderson; REMARKS: H.C. Hill sworn.

137. 31 July 1901 WALTER EDWARD PEARSON 26 yrs single b. Richmond VA s/o W.A. & M.C. to GEORGIA VIRGINIA JOHNSTON 27 yrs single b. Mercer Co W VA d/o D.E. & S.E. Johnston O: clerk; by P.A. Anthony.

138. 31 July 1901 LUTHER GIBSON 22 yrs single b. Bland Co VA s/o Sam & Emma to HARTHA HEDRICK 22 yrs single b. Mercer Co W VA d/o Harvey & N.J. O: RR; by W.W. Williamson; REMARKS: L.H. Bailey sworn.

139. 4 Aug 1901 CHAS H. HUNT 30 yrs single b. Tazewell Co VA s/o H.F. & Louisa to MOLLIE SHUFFLEBARGER 26 yrs single b. Mercer Co W VA d/o Lewis & Jane O: railroader; by W.W. Williamson.

140. 6 Aug 1901 LAWRENCE DWYER 32 yrs single b. New Orleans LA now living in New Port News VA to LILLY F. SHORTER 22 yrs single b. Mercer Co W VA d/o W.T. & Mary Shorter O: ship filler; by G.H. Johnston; REMARKS: father present.

141. 8 Aug 1901 OSCAR BYRD* 20 yrs single b. Mercer s/o Stephen & Susan to ROSA LEE CAVIS 16 yrs single b. Pulaski VA d/o J.W. & Eliza O: miner; by A.H. Craft; REMARKS: Oscar Bird* sworn. (*Note: name spelled both ways.)

142. 7 Aug 1901 JOHN LAMBERT 26 yrs to MATTIE HOULES 17 yrs d/o ? & Ollie; by J.T. Frazier.

143. * * * ADAM SMITH 39 yrs to LOU WHITE 23 yrs. (*Note: no date given.) NOTE: No other information given.

144. 8 Aug 1901 S.R. SHREWSBURY 22 yrs single b. Mercer s/o Bill & J. to ANNIE L. WYATT 17 yrs single b. Wyoming d/o John & M.J. O: farmer; by Peter Grim; REMARKS: E.L. Tilley.

Page 111

145. 8 Aug 1901 JAS S. WHITTAKER 20 yrs single b. Yadkin Co NC s/o John & Nancy to BARBARA C. HELSEL 16 yrs single b. Mercer Co W VA d/o Jacob A. &

Susan O: farmer; by J.O. Cassaday; REMARKS: Jas H. Champ & Davis Thorn sworn.

146. 11 Aug 1901 PRIDEMORE CLINE 25 yrs single to DICY A. REED 17 yrs single b. Mercer Co W VA d/o C.W. & Harnda O: miner; by C.W. Bailey; REMARKS: Floyd Odle sworn.

147. 12 Aug 1901 ERNEST L. BURTON 22 yrs single b. Giles VA s/o Peavis & Mary to BELLE McELRATH 21 yrs single b. Giles VA d/o Robert & Emma O: farmer; by Peter C. Clark; REMARKS: Ernest L. Burton sworn.

148. 13 Aug 1901 JAMES JONES 24 yrs single b. VA s/o H. & Adaline to SALLIE THRIFF 25 yrs single b. VA O: miner; by Anderson Davis; REMARKS: colored.

149. 14 Aug 1901 ROY T. WRIGHT 19 yrs single b. Mercer Co W VA s/o E.C. & Sue Wright to HATTIE McCLAUGHERTY 22 yrs single b. Mercer Co W VA d/o Jos H. & Evaline O: farmer; by G.C. Anderson; REMARKS: Roy T. Wright sworn.

150. 20 Aug 1901 JAMES R. WIMMER 19 yrs single b. Mercer Co W VA to CLOA D. SHREWSBURY 17 yrs single b. Mercer Co W VA d/o W.R. & Olive Shrewsbury O: farmer; by W.I. Bailey; REMARKS: W.R. Wimmer sworn.

151. 22 Aug 1901 JOHN W. ALIFF 22 yrs single b. Franklin Co Va s/o J.S. & S.C. Aliff to HINNETTIE DOWDY 16 yrs single b. Giles Co VA d/o Chas & Mandy Dowdy O: teamster; by Peter C. Clark; REMARKS: Jas W. Aliff sworn.

152. 28 Aug 1901 LEWIS R. STATON 22 yrs single b. Buchan VA s/o W.H. & O.r. to SALLIE H. WALL 25 yrs single b. Mercer Co W VA d/o James C. & Fannie O: Express messenger; by W.C. Carden; REMARKS: J.W. Johnston & L.R. Staton sworn.

153. 28 Aug 1901 WILLIS D. FOLEY 21 yrs single b. Mercer Co s/o R.F. & Mat to SARAH B. REED 16 yrs single b. Wyoming d/o Samuel W. & C.C. O: farmer; by J.T. Tabor; REMARKS: A.L. Foley.

154. 28 Aug 1901 ROBERT L. BISHOP 23 yrs single b. Montgomery VA s/o Acy & Martha to BERTHA ALLEY 22 yrs single b. Grayson VA d/o Enoch & ? O: railroading; by W.W. Williamson.

155. 29 Aug 1901 JAMES WELLS 26 yrs single to ELLA THOMPSON 21 yrs single; by S.e. Williams.

156. 29 Aug 1901 WILLIAM OSCAR SNOW 23 yrs single b. Mercer s/o Anthony & Lucinda to IDA JOSEPHINE CAMPBELL 19 yrs single b. Mercer d/o ? & Rosana O: farmer; by J.O. Cassaday.

157. 4 Sept 1901 JAMES CARVER 25 yrs single b. KY s/o Pearce & Elizabeth to MARY McCLOUD 18 yrs single b. VA d/o Henry & Betty O: railroading; by Rufus E. Halden; REMARKS: James Carver sworn.

158. 2 Sept 1901 WM H. DAVIS 20 yrs single s/o H.W. & M.S. to SALLIE E. WRIGHT 19 yrs single b. Mercer d/o J.H. & Nannie O: farmer; by J.B. Simpson; REMARKS: J.W. Wright sworn.

159. 4 Sept 1901 F.E. THOMASON 24 yrs single b. Wyoming now living same s/o George & C.L. to LILLIE M. MORGAN 19 yrs single b. Mercer d/o A.B. & R. O: farmer; by J.B. Simpson; REMARKS: W.K. Thomasson sworn.

160. 3 Sept 1901 J.R. MILLS 21 yrs single b. Mercer s/o W.F. & Electra to VIRGIE FAULKNER 16 yrs single b. Mercer d/o Gorden & Rhoda O: miner; by J.B. Simpson; REMARKS: guardian present.

161. 5 Sept 1901 J.J. TICE 30 yrs single b. VA to EVA E. RATLIFFE 21 yrs single b. VA O: RR; by J.T. Frazier; REMARKS: D.G. Lilly.

162. 4 Sept 1901 W.H. DEQUASIE 40 yrs single b. Fayett Co W VA s/o L.& Rebeca to MARGIE PAYNE 27 yrs single b. VA; by Robt A. Owen; REMARKS: Preston Clark sworn.

163. 3 Sept 1901 PRESTON CLARK 56 yrs wid. b. Monroe Co W VA now living same s/o Thomas & Eliza to JULIA A. BALLARD 36 yrs single b. Monroe Co W VA d/o John

& Julia O: farmer; by A.L. Cathers; REMARKS: Preston Clark sworn.

164. 5 Sept 1901 MONTGOMERY LONGHORN 24 yrs single to NANNIE CHRISTIAN 27 yrs single O: laborer; by R.D. Washington; REMARKS: E.T. Oliver J.P.

165. 4 Sept 1901 GARFIELD ROBRTSON 21 yrs single b. Mercer s/o W.H. & Margaret to VIRGINIA F. BUTTERWORTH 17 yrs single b. TN d/o J.H.T. & Mary J. O: farmer; by D.H. Carr; REMARKS: father present.

166. 4 Sept 1901 LAWSON STEWART 21 yrs single b. VA to FRANCIS LUMPKIN 23 yrs sngle b. VA O: RR; by R.D. Washington; REMARKS: E.T. Oliver.

167. 5 Sept 1901 BENJAMIN W. PENDLETON 35 yrs sngle b. Mercer s/o D.B. & N.V. to CARRIE HALE 29 yrs single b. Monroe d/o J.W. & C.e. O: Atty; by Arthur S. Thorn.

168. 5 Sept 1901 OSCAR H. CARDEN 32 yrs single b. Monroe s/o A.A. & Virginia to GEORGIA HALE 22 yrs single b. Monroe d/o L.M. & M.J. O: hotel prop; by J.O. Cassaday.

169. 11 Sept 1901 J.R. SHANKLIN 26 yrs single b. Monroe now living in OH s/o John & Ellen to MARY CARPER 23 yrs single b. W VA d/o John & Mariah; by J.T. Frazier.

170. 10 Sept 1901 PAUL H. HARRIS 24 yrs single now living in McDowell to OCIE LEE CORE 23 yrs single b. Mercer d/o A.W. & S.E.; by W.L. Ball.

171. 18 Sept 1901 J.M. WRIGHT 22 yrs single b. Bland Co VA s/o J.D. & S.E. to FLORENCE M. SHUTT 16 yrs single b. Mercer d/o J.D. & M.C. O: farmer; by J.B. Simpson; REMARKS: T.B. Browning sworn.

172. 25 Sept 1901 WILLET PENNINGTON 20 yrs single b. Mercer s/o A.W. P. & Scinda to LILLIE MARTIN 26 yrs single b. Mercer d/o French & Nannie O: farmer; by W.I. Gautier; REMARKS: Willet Pennington.

173. 18 Sept 1901 A.C. CROUCH 20 yrs single b. Glen Co VA s/o Wm & S.K. to VIRGINIA R. MILLS 19 yrs single b. Mercer d/o S.D. & Mary O: farmer; by H.I. Cook; REMARKS: S.D. Mills sworn.

174. 18 Sept 1901 H.C. CREWS 24 yrs single b. KY s/o O.W. & Mollie to EVA AMOS 20 yrs wid. b. Montgomery d/o R.P. & S.J. Wolwine O: carpenter; by W.W. Williamson.

175. 19 Sept 1901 J.H. McCORMACK 21 yrs single b. Floyd Co VA s/o Dick & Jane to MOLLIE FITZWATER 21 yrs single b. Mercer d/o I.N. & Rhoda O: farmer; by L. Goodwyn; REMARKS: father present.

176. 15 Sept 1901 JAMES RILEY PERDUE 20 yrs single b. Mercer Co W VA s/o Harrison & Margaret to MASURA JANE THOMAS 20 yrs single b. Mercer d/o James D. & Sarah C. O: railroader; by R.A. Miller; REMARKS: A.C. Perdue sworn.

177. 25 Sept 1901 HENRY H. BLANCHARD 27 yrs single s/o Martin V. & Fred to HARRIETT, W. MOORE 22 yrs single b. NJ d/o Bethuel & Emma O: bookeeper; by Norman F. Marshall; REMARKS: J.E.T. Suitz.

178. 18 Sept 1901 HENRY H. SHRADER 28 yrs single b. Bland VA now living same s/o I.N. & A.H. to LILLIE F. BAILEY 23 yrs single b. McDowell d/o P.F. & Mary A. O: farmer; by A.L. Cathers; REMARKS: P.W. Bailey.

179. 29 Sept 1901 GRANT WILSON BALLARD 34 yrs single b. Monroe Co W VA now living same s/o Harrison & ? Ballard to ELIZA EDMONIA BONHAM 24 yrs single b. Monroe Co W VA d/o Pendleton & ? Bonham O: farmer; by J.W. Bennett.

180. 26 Sept 1901 J.B. UNDERWOOD 23 yrs single b. Mercer s/o Asa & M.J. to LARENY M. LYN 17 yrs single b. Mercer d/o David & Z O: farmer; by Peter Grim; REMARKS: J.B. Underwood sworn.

181. 25 Sept 1901 PEARLY F. MILLER 27 yrs single b. Giles Co VA s/o T.K. & E.V. to DASIS BUCHANAN 22 yrs single b. Giles

Co VA d/o W.H. & Eliza O: salesman; by J.T. Frazier; REMARKS: P.S. Buchanan sworn.

182. 2 Oct 1901 SAMUEL GRAY 29 yrs wid. b. Franklin Co VA s/o Henry & Octavia to MATILDA THOMPSON 21 yrs single b. Mercer d/o Charley & Harriet O: RR; by S.E. Williams; REMARKS: J.H. Owens.

183. 2 Oct 1901 J.M. OWENS 30 yrs single b. Roanoke Co VA now living same s/o Franklin & Mary to SERRENA PRICE 26 yrs single b. Montgomery Co VA O: RR; by P.A. Anthony.

184. 6 Oct 1901 KENT McKEE 24 yrs single b. VA s/o Peter & P. to MARY FIRESLINE 20 yrs single b. VA d/o D.H. & Angeline O: miner; by A.M. Craft; REMARKS: Kent McKee.

185. 6 Oct 1901 JOSEPH JOHN R. HARMAN 18 yrs single b. Mercer s/o W.A. Harman & M.E. to MARGARET E. BELCHER 17 yrs single b. Mercer d/o Henry E. & Amy O: farmer; by J.B. Simpson; REMARKS: W.A. Harman made oath that the said J.J.R. Harman was over the age of 18 yrs not with standing the record only. * * 17 witness. H.G. Woods. (*Note: unable to read.)

186. 5 Oct 1901 KENNISON BARRETT 30 yrs single b. Grayson s/o Reuben & Margaret to DELIA BANDY 30 yrs wid. b. Tazewell O: farmer; by R.A. Owen.

187. 8 Oct 1901 AMOS ADKINS 22 yrs single b. Mercer s/o Preston & Elizabeth to ISABELLA COX 17 yrs single d/o Wellington & ? O: farmer; by Jas W. Lilly; REMARKS: Amos Adkins sworn.

188. 7 Oct 1901 A.F. WRIGHT 21 yrs single b. Mercer s/o J.M. & Nancy to EFFIE HALL 17 yrs single b. Mercer d/o John & Jane O: farmer; by J.B. Simpson.

189. 9 Oct 1901 J.P. BROOKMAN 23 yrs single b. Mercer s/o Augustus & Rachel to MARY A. BRYANT 23 yrs single b. Patrick VA d/o Wm F. & S.R. O: farmer; by Isaac Wright.

190. 8 Oct 1901 J.T. McCRAW 21 yrs single b. VA s/o Samuel H. & H.J. to LUELLA MYERS 23 yrs single b. VA O: fireman; by P.A. Anthony.

191. 9 Oct 1901 J.R. WINTER 29 yrs single b. KY s/o F.& S.J. to MARY E. FORELINE 21 yrs single b. VA d/o Joe & ? O: engineer; by D.A. Ramey; REMARKS: J.R. Winter.

192. 10 Oct 1901 J.W. FORD 28 yrs single b. Monroe s/o J.L. & Amanda B. to RHODA CLEMINTINE FRENCH 21 yrs single b. Mercer d/o H.B. & M.A. O: miner; by Eugene Douglass; REMARKS: Charley French sworn.

Page 112

193. 9 Oct 1901 JOHN HENRY THOMAS LYNCH 28 yrs single b. VA s/o John & A.R. to SALLIE SHRADER 17 yrs single b. Mercer d/o R.H. & J.V. O: railroading; by A.H. Craft; REMARKS: father present.

194. 16 Oct 1901 LUM JERVIS 27 yrs single b. NC s/o John & Mary to LILLIE N. BURNETT 20 yrs single b. W VA d/o J.A. & M.N. O: farmer; by G.C. Anderson; REMARKS: Lum Jervis sworn.

195. 23 Oct 1901 NOAH D. CLARK 18 yrs single b. Mercer s/o Elijah Clark & E.E. to KATE ELLEN ELLISON 16 yrs single b. Mercer d/o L.I. & Elizabeth O: farmer; by J.T. Tabor; REMARKS: father present.

196. 17 Oct 1901 ERNEST B. HALL 22 yrs single b. Mercer Co W VA s/o James & Lucinda Hall to INDIA CARTER 17 yrs single b. Mercer d/o Wm & Mary Carter O: well contractor; by G.W. Bailey; REMARKS: L.E. Carter sworn.

197. 18 Oct 1901 E.E. WALKER 20 yrs single b. Mercer Co W VA s/o J.B. & R.C. to FANNIE ALLEN 22 yrs single b. Mercer d/o John & ? O: farmer; by W.W. West; REMARKS: father present.

198. 17 Oct 1901 CHARLES W. BAILEY 40 yrs wid. b. Mercer Co W VA to MARY E. BURTON 20 yrs single b. Mercer d/o John & Martha J. O: farmer; by G.W. Bailey; REMARKS: Geo Burton.

199. 17 Oct 1901 S.P. BAILEY 21 yrs single b. Wyoming now living same s/o A.P. & Polly to LILLY WITT 21 yrs single b. Montgomery d/o ? & Nannie O: farmer; by D.N. Saunders.

200. 23 Oct 1901 V.T. LILLY 18 yrs single b. Mercer s/o Daniel & Holly to STELLA SWEENEY 17 yrs single b. Mercer d/o Wm G. & A.D. O: farmer; by James W. Lilly; REMARKS: V.T. Lilly sworn.

201. 23 Oct 1901 THOMAS CRAWFORD 25 yrs single b. Mercer s/o Reuben & Rebecca to ELIZA JANE CAMPBELL 30 yrs wid. b. Giles Co VA O: farmer; by T.S. Johnson.

202. 23 Oct 1901 C.N. THOMISON 20 yrs single b. Mercer s/o F.L. & Ellen to FLORRENCE C. HAGER 20 yrs single b. Mercer d/o H.B. & Clarinda O: farmer; by D.N. Saunders; REMARKS: A.C. Hager & W.L. Hager sworn.

203. 23 Oct 1901 C.B. MEADOR 27 yrs single b. Bedford Co VA now living in KS s/o C.J. & Sallie J. to O.P. & M.J. O: farming; by P.A. Anthony; REMARKS: C.B. Meador.

204. 27 Oct 1901 GEORGE ROBERSON 23 yrs single b. Mercer s/o Frank & ? to LIZZIE STUARD 22 yrs single b. Pulaski d/o ? & Francis O: laborer; by R.D. Washington; REMARKS: F.J. Brown.

205. 23 Oct 1901 W.H. SHREWSBURY 21 yrs single b. Summers now living in Raleigh Co s/o Johnathan & Malina to ROXIE B. DOVE 21 yrs single b. Mercer d/o Bill & Elizabeth O: miner; by James W. Lilly; REMARKS: W.H. Shrewsbury sworn.

206. 23 Oct 1901 LUTHER MARTIN 23 yrs single b. Mercer s/o G.B. & Mary to ETHEL H. McCLAUGHERTY 18 yrs single b. Mercer d/o J.H. & Evaline O: farmer; by R.A. Owen; REMARKS: guardian present.

207. 23 Oct 1901 WM WHITE 39 yrs wid. b. VA s/o Charles & Minnie to LELIA SMITH 22 yrs single b. NC d/o Monk & Lelia O: laborer; by S.E. Williams.

208. 24 Oct 1901 SKYE V. STRALEY 29 yrs single b. Mercer s/o H.W. & D.A to SALLIE A. McNUTT 22 yrs single b. Monroe d/o J.P. & Jennie O: N.F.; by W.L. Ball.

209. 30 Oct 1901 WM H. MUSE 28 yrs single b. Franklin Co VA now living in McDowell s/o Wm A. & Rozella to ALLIE E. CALANDER 27 yrs single b. Mercer d/o Wm & Ann O: miner; by R.D. Washington.

210. 30 Oct 1901 A.B. PHIPPS BELCHER 22 yrs single b. Mercer s/o Wm M.H. & Julia to ALICE CALFEE 22 yrs div. b. Mercer d/o Bal & Chloe O: farmer; by W.H. Ayres.

211. 27 Oct 1901 RUBIN FARREL 28 yrs single b. NC s/o R. & O. to SENIA FITZGERALD 25 yrs single b. VA d/o ? & C; by S.E. Williams.

212. 30 Oct 1901 JAMES C. DAVIDSON 32 yrs single b. Mercer s/o Henry & C. to BESSIE BARBARIE 24 yrs single b. Mercer d/o John & Julia O: farmer; by R.A. Owen.

213. 30 Oct 1901 O.L. HUFFMAN 27 yrs single b. Summers now living same s/o John & ? to BERTIE M. WILLIAMS 20 yrs single b. Mercer d/o A.M. & Mary J. O: RR; by G.H. Johnston.

214. 30 Oct 1901 T.E. ARMSTRONG 25 yrs single b. Nova Scotia s/o George & Jessie to JANIE M. FRENCH 22 yrs single b. Mercer d/o David & Mary O: physician; by W.L. Ball.

215. 6 Nov 1901 H.O. WHITWORTH 26 yrs single b. VA s/o G.R. & S.M. to CORA BURTON 19 yrs single b. VA d/o H.P. & Mary A. O: guard state; by P.A. Anthony; REMARKS: B.F. Kennett sworn.

216. 6 Nov 1901 J.W. SHREWSBURY 26 yrs single b. Mercer s/o Sam & Elizabeth to FANNIE BELCHER 20 yrs single b. Tazewell Co VA d/o R.H. & A. O: farmer; by R.A. Owen; REMARKS: H.E. Belcher sworn.

217. 6 Nov 1901 W.T. DOUTHAT 33 yrs single b. Pulaski Co VA s/o J.H. & M.E. Douthat to N.M. WOODRING 25 yrs single b. Canter Co PA d/o G.W. & E.E. Woodring O: L. engineer; by J.T. Frazier; REMARKS: Geo. G. Belcher sworn.

218. 6 Nov 1901 GEO G. BELCHER 22 yrs single b. W VA s/o J.F. & H.J. to EVA RATCLIFF 18 yrs single b. W VA d/o B.B. & Eliza O: stone mason; by G.W. Terry.

219. 13 Nov 1901 ROBT H. THORNHILL 44 yrs wid. now living in Giles Co VA s/o James & Milly Thornhill to FRANCES COMER 26 yrs single b. Mercer Co W VA d/o Wm & Martha Comer O: farmer; by R.A. Miller; REMARKS: A.H. Thornton.

220. 7 Nov 1901 ROBT LEE TAYLOR 24 yrs single b. Mason Co W VA s/o C.B. & Victoria Taylor to LECTRA DACRE BAILEY 23 yrs single b. Mercer Co W VA d/o M.E. & N.B. Bailey O: carpenter; by Peter C. Clark.

221. 13 Nov 1901 D.W. HEARN 26 yrs single b. Mercer Co W VA s/o ? & Nancy Hearn to ANNIE R. SHUTT 26 yrs single b. Montgomery Co VA d/o H.F. & Ellen Shutt O: farmer; by G.W. Bailey; REMARKS: S.P. Wheeler.

222. 10 Nov 1901 JAMES L. YOUNCE 25 yrs single b. NC s/o Elijah & Harriett to JULIA BELCHER 20 yrs single b. Mercer d/o J.F. & H.J; by J.T. Frazier; REMARKS: F.J. Brown.

223. 13 Nov 1901 HARRY COLIS 23 yrs single b. VA s/o A. & Lillie to LIZZIE PARKER 21 yrs single b. Franklin d/o James & ? O: miner; by Anderson Davis.

224. 12 Nov 1901 HAL BELL 26 yrs wid. b. Prince Edward VA s/o Charles & Judy to EMMA WASHINGTON 30 yrs wid. b. Blacksburg VA d/o James & Catherine O: laborer; by R.A. Miller.

225. 13 Nov 1901 M.W. TILLER 21 yrs single b. Mercr s/o J.F. & A.C. to IDA BOWLING 16 yrs single b. Mercer d/o A.I. & Alla O: laborer; by R.A. Owen; REMARKS: P.M. Matheney sworn.

226. 16 Nov 1901 O.H. BAILEY 22 yrs single b. Wyoming Co now living same s/o Harrison & L.J. to FANNIE E. SHREWSBURY 19 yrs single b. Mercer d/o John & Elizabeth O: farmer; by H.C. Cook; REMARKS: guardian present.

227. 28 Nov 1901 J.N. CROZIER 40 yrs wid. b. Monroe Co now living in McDowell to LAURA SPANGLER 30 yrs wid. b. Monroe; by D.A. Ramey.

228. 27 Nov 1901 DANIEL J. WOODWARD 23 yrs single b. Washington Co VA s/o J.S. & L.J. to SRAH J. DOOLEY 16 yrs single b. Kanawha d/o I.C. & M.A; by J.E. Wolfe.

229. 18 Nov 1901 LUTHER SMITH 18 yrs single b. Pulaski VA s/o Chas P. & Jennie JENNIE MELVIN 16 yrs single b. Giles VA d/o ? & Mary; by P.A. Anthony; REMARKS: Luther Smith sworn.

230. 21 Nov 1901 S.L. WYATT 26 yrs wid. b. NC s/o Robert & Julia to ELIZABETH WEST 30 yrs wid. b. Mercer d/o George & ? O: farmer; by R.H. Ashworth; REMARKS: S.L. Wyatt sworn.

231. 20 Nov 1901 DAVIS McBRIDE THORN 19 yrs single b. Tazewell now living in Giles Co VA s/o R.T. & Laura to MARY BESSIE BLANKENSHIP 19 yrs single b. Mercer d/o Thompson & L. O: farmer; by R.A. Owen; REMARKS: D.B. Thorn sworn.

232. 24 Nov 1901 CHARLES HILL 21 yrs single b. Giles Co VA s/o Robert & Martha A. to ADA LISTER 19 yrs single d/o Loyd & ? O: farmer; by R.A. Miller; REMARKS: J.H. Harvey sworn.

233. 27 Nov 1901 C.N. HICKS 21 yrs single b. Mercer s/o E.G. & Mary to MARY A. BROYLES 21 yrs single b. Mercer d/o Leroy & Lizzie O: farmer; by G.A. Conner; REMARKS: E.G. Hicks present.

234. 27 Nov 1901 ARTHUR L. WHITE 19 yrs single b. Mercer s/o W.R. & P.J. to MARY L. AKERS 17 yrs single b. Floyd d/o W.S. & E.S. O: farmer; by W.B. Booth; REMARKS: Authur L. White sworn.

235. 27 Nov 1901 W.C. PATTERSON 52 yrs wid. b. Wythe Co VA s/o A.H. & e.E. Patterson to RHODA E. GAYHART 38 yrs wid. b. Montgomery Co VA O: miner; by G.W. Bailey.

236. 27 Nov 1901 PLEASANT H. LILLY 57 yrs wid. to DELILAH R. CREWS 45 yrs wid. b. Montgomery Co VA O: farmer; by Drewry Farley.

237. 27 Nov 1901 ALBERT CARTER 35 yrs single b. Wythe Co VA s/o Craig & Kittie Carter to NORA W. MARTIN 24 yrs single b. Montgomery Co VA d/o A.J. & Nannie O: RR conductor; by W.W. Williamson.

238. 27 Nov 1901 CHARLES PILLERS 22 yrs single b. Carroll Co VA s/o Ella Pillers to LOTTIE PILLERS 18 yrs single b. Mercer Co W VA d/o Thos G. & M.C. O: farming; by W.C. Carden; REMARKS: Robt Pillers sworn.

239. 27 Nov 1901 T.H. HAMBLIN 50 yrs wid. b. Montgomery Co VA to MARY THOMPSON 47 yrs wid. O: laborer; by W.W. Williamson.

240. 28 Nov 1901 JACKSON HEDRICK 22 yrs single b. Mercer s/o Robt & B. to SALLIE O. SHRADER 20 yrs single b. Mercer d/o Robt & S.J. O: farming; by G.A. Conner; REMARKS: father present.

Page 113

241. 27 Nov 1901 HENRY C. RUBLE 20 yrs single b. Tazewell s/o Calvin & State Ira to NANCY ELIZABETH BAILEY 25 yrs single b. Mercer d/o G.F. & E.A. O: farmer; by J.T. Frazier; REMARKS: R.N. Ruble sworn.

242. 3 Dec 1901 T.F. COX 22 yrs single b. Summers Co s/o Mathew & Mary to L.C. HATCHER 17 yrs single b. Mrcer d/o J.P. & J.A. O: farmer; by James W. Lilly; REMARKS: T.F. Cox sworn.

243. 3 Dec 1901 F.E. GODSEY 24 yrs sngle b. Bristol TN s/o J.P. & M.E. to MINNIE L. BAILEY 24 yrs single b. Mercer d/o Nancy O: clerk; by D.N. Saunders.

244. 11 Dec 1901 ROBERT L. SKEENES 24 yrs single b. Mercer s/o John T. & Amanda to LIEN A. NELSON 17 yrs single b. Mercer d/o James R. & Elizabeth O: farmer; by R.H. Ashworth; REMARKS: Dave Burch sworn.

245. 11 Dec 1901 CHARLIE W. SKEENES 22 yrs single b. Mercer s/o John T. & Amanda to DORA D. NELSON 23 yrs single b. Mercer d/o James R. & Elizabeth O: farmer; by R.H. Ashworth; REMARKS: Dave Burch sworn.

246. 18 Dec 1901 J. REESE HUTCHINSON 27 yrs single b. Franklin Co VA s/o B.R. & P.F. Hutchinson to LALA F. DUDLEY 26 yrs single b. Franklin Co VA d/o P.S. & ? Dudley O: merchant; by J.T. Frazier; REMARKS: R.E. Lazenby.

247. 8 Dec 1901 HENRY PRICE 68 yrs wid. b. Montgomery to MARGARET COOK 54 yrs wid. b. Wyoming O: farmer; by W.A. Bailey.

250. 11 Dec 1901 DONALD S. BELCHER 23 yrs single b. Mercer Co W VA s/o C.C. & Nannie C. Belcher to CLIDA MITCHELL 19 yrs single b. Kanawha Co W VA d/o J.H. & Gertrude O: carpenter; by J.E. Wolfe; REMARKS: J.H. Mitchell.

251. 11 Dec 1901 STEWART MAXEY 23 yrs single b. Summers Co W VA s/o Daniel & Martha to EFFIE MAY BENNETT 18 yrs single b. Bedford Co VA d/o Wm C. & Laura O: miner; by D.A. Ramey.

252. 11 Dec 1901 FRANK SMITH 18 yrs single b. Fayette co W VA s/o Jas R. & Ann to CHARLOTTE ELLIOTT 18 yrs single b. Fayette Co W VA d/o Robert & Esther O: miner; by D.A. Ramey.

253. 22 Dec 1901 FRANK CHAFFIN 22 yrs single b. NC s/o Frank Chaffin to MARY BOWEN 16 yrs single b. Tazewell VA d/o Mary Bowen O: waiter; by S.E. Williams; REMARKS: S.E. Williams.

254. 18 Dec 1901 WM CABELL 27 yrs single b. Roanoke Co VA s/o Fountain & Maria to JOSIE JOHNSON 22 yrs single b. Augusta Co VA d/o Anderson & Alice O: cook; by S.E. Williams; REMARKS: S.E. Williams.

255. 25 Dec 1901 JAMES R. CARTER 19 yrs single b. Tazewell Co VA now living same s/o S.N. & Susana to DELIA A. HYPES 19 yrs single b. Mercer Co W VA d/o J.L. & Frances J. O: saw milling; by W.L. Ball; REMARKS: J.L. Hypes present.

256. 18 Dec 1901 GEORGE W. FLETCHER 18 yrs single b. Mercer Co W VA s/o Jas H. & Mary Ann to SADIE E. COOK 16 yrs single b. Mercer Co w VA d/o A.C. & Virgnia O: farming; by G.M. Johnston; REMARKS: A.C. Cook present.

257. 18 Dec 1901 J.G. MILLER 52 yrs wid. b. Monroe Co W VA now living same s/o Samuel & Susan to HARRIET R. HARRY 51 yrs single b. Mercer co W VA d/o Romulus & G. O: farming; by J.M. Ashworth.

258. 18 Dec 1901 JOHNSON D. BAILEY 22 yrs single b. Mercer Co W VA s/o Liftwich & ? Bailey to LILLY M. THOMASON 17 yrs single b. Mercer Co w VA d/o F.L. & E.A. Thomason O: farming; by D.N. Saunders; REMARKS: F.L. Thomason present.

259. 22 Dec 1901 ELLIOTT A. SWEENY 18 yrs single b. Montgomery Co VA s/o J.T. & Martha A. to TEXAS VIPPERMAN 28 yrs single b. Pulaski Co VA O: farming; by J.E. Wolfe; REMARKS: J.T. Sweeny sworn.

260. 24 Dec 1901 AARAN* UNDERWOOD 24 yrs single b. Franklin Co VA s/o Martin & Elizabeth to ALMA B. KING 16 yrs single d/o W.H. & Hollie King O: laborer; by J.E. Wolfe; REMARKS: Aaron* Underwood sworn. (*Note: name spelled both ways.)

261. 25 Dec 1901 WM E. JACKSON 22 yrs single b. Montgomery s/o J.L. & S.J. to HATTIE J. KIRBY 23 yrs single b. Montgomery d/o James & C.A. O: brakeman; by J.T. Frazier; REMARKS: W.E. Jackson sworn.

262. 23 Dec 1901 POWELL JONES 22 yrs single b. Mercer s/o Kenna & Sarah A. to ADA COLEMAN 22 yrs sngle b. Mercer d/o Wilson & Clara O: miner; by R.A. Owen.

272. 25 Dec 1901 E.W. CARBAUGH 29 yrs single b. Mercer Co v VA s/o J.H & Allie to VIVA G. WALKER 16 yrs single b. Mercer Co W VA d/o Ira W. & ? Walker O: farming; by R.A. Owen; REMARKS: E.W. Carbaugh.

273. 25 Dec 1901 LACY L. WOODS 19 yrs single b. Giles Co VA now living same s/o John H. & R.J. to HANNIE F. KIRK 22 yrs single Co VA d/o A. & H.H. O: tanner; by G.H. Johnston; REMARKS: Lacy L. Woods sworn.

274. 26 Dec 1901 THOMAS BUDD 22 yrs single b. TN s/o Jerry & Annie to HATTIE GREEN 21 yrs single b. Bland d/o Clabern & Viney; by S.E. Williams; REMARKS: sworn to before F.J. Brown.

275. 29 Dec 1901 WILLIAM MORRIS 35 yrs single b. VA s/o Joe & Matilda to MAGGIE HOWARD 25 yrs single b. VA d/o Thomas & Fannie; by R.P. Washington; REMARKS: F.J. Brown.

276. 8 Feb 1902 LEWIS ELLIS 28 yrs single b. VA s/o James & S. to BELL LUSTHSCUH 24 yrs single b. VA d/o Sam & Rosa O: miner; by R.W. Harris.

277. 2 Jan 1902 LEWIS H. FARLEY 29 yrs single b. Mercer now living in Summers s/o A.P. & Emline to MARTHA J. COOK 26 yrs single b. Mercer d/o Danl & Mahala O: sawmilling; by G.H. Johnston.

278. 2 Jan 1902 WALTER B. COOK 24 yrs single b. Mercer now living in Summers s/o Daniel & Mahala to OFFIE J. BRAHHER 21 yrs single b. Mercer d/o John & Sarah O: farmer; by G.H. Johnston.

279. 31 Dec 1901 H.G. BRYANT 24 yrs single b. VA s/o A. & L. to C.P. HICKS 23 yrs single b. Mercer d/o Rus & Hannah O: miner; by J.E. Wolfe; REMARKS: J.G. Bryant.

280. 31 Dec 1901 ALBERT BYRD 26 yrs single b. Franklin s/o D.H. & Sallie to CLARA COLE 17 yrs single b. Mercer d/o A.J. & Mary O: miner; by G.W. Bailey; REMARKS: D.B. Cole.

281. 1 Jan 1902 ALVIS TABOR 20 yrs single b. Mercer s/o F.J. & Sarah to SALLIE HALL 16 yrs single b. Mercer d/o John & Jane O: father; by G.H. Comer; REMARKS: A.F. Wright sworn.

263. 24 Dec 1901 WILLIAM L. HAM 23 yrs single b. Mercer s/o W.W. & L.V. to ANNIE HAY HELHANDOLLAR 19 yrs single b. Mercer d/o T.H. & Annie O: railroading; by J.E. Wolfe.

264. 24 Dec 1901 L.B. BAILEY 22 yrs single b. Mercer s/o W.W. & L.V. to EMMA H. HAM 16 yrs single b. Mercer d/o J.W. & I.N. O: railroading; by C.C. Anderson; REMARKS: Wm L. Ham sworn.

265. 25 Dec 1901 WM CRAFT 28 yrs single b. Pittsylvania VA s/o Rollin & Lizzie to FLORENCE MOORE 22 yrs single b. Henry Va d/o John & Lucy O: railroading; by S. E. Williams; REMARKS: Saml E. Williams sworn.

266. * * * CHARLIE PATTERSON 35 yrs single b. VA s/o F. & R. to BETTIE WOODS 33 yrs single b. VA d/o Sam & Jennie O: miner; REMARKS: Not returned. (*Note: no date given.)

267. * * * FRANK D. BRADY 26 yrs single to VIRGINIA HAZLEWOOD 29 yrs single b. Mercer d/o W.I. & Amanda; REMARKS: J.C. Hazlewood sworn. (*Note: no date given.)

268. 25 Dec 1901 AXEL ALEXANDER 31 yrs single b. Sweeden(sic) now living in Washington s/o M. & Annie to ALLIE GORE 27 yrs single O: farming; by G.H. Johnston; REMARKS: Axel Alexander sworn.

269. 25 Dec 1901 ERNEST HARRIS 25 yrs single b. NC s/o Henry & Kansas to NANCY JONES 28 yrs wid. b. Mercer d/o Wm & Manerva Gore O: RR; by O.T. Harris.

270. 25 Dec 1901 J.H. ROBERTS 42 yrs single b. Washington Co VA s/o Wm & Susan to BELL ELLIS 35 yrs single b. Mercer d/o O.J. & ? O: RR; by J.T. Frazier.

271. 25 Dec 1901 CHAS HALL 19 yrs single b. Tazewll Co s/o W.R. & Mattie to BERTIE WOOLWINE 16 yrs single b. Montgomery d/o R.P. & S.J. O: smith; by W.W. Williamson; REMARKS: R.P. Woolwine sworn.

ERRATA

Pg 4 #30 Corbelius = Cornelius
#39 Boling/Bowling are both in original as this shows.

Pg 6 #36 Rugh = Ruth

Pg 8 #47 Whittabke = Whittaker
#19 Soprter = Shorter

Pg 9 $47 Leory = Leroy

Pg 10 #26 Judity = Judith

Pg 14 #9 Sophis = Sophia

Pg 16 #15 Waught = Vaught
#24 Kpmatjam C. Jarvel = Jonathan C. Harvey

Pg 17 #25 Cylistina = this is how it is written, however cf. pg 112 1860 Mercer Co. WV Census the name is written Celestine Holstine d/o Joseph and Elizabeth Holstine

#37 & #38 B. T. & Vina Bird on #37 and B. T. and Neva Bird on #38 may or maynot be the same as the two children were born in different counties.

Pg 22 #10 Comas = Comer

Pg 23 #1 Poly = Polly

Pg 21 #33 [no groom] = Andrew J. Payne

Pg 25 #47 Cathering = Catherine
#48 Skeong = Skeen

Pg 27 #45 Decor = Devot

Pg 28 #10 Farler = Farley

Pg 29 #43 ...lewood = Inglewood

Pg 30 #2 Lanbert = Lambert

Pg 31 #25 Bride = Sarah J. S. R. Meader age 14

single b. Mercer Co. d/o G. W. & Elizabeth Meader
#47 Saray = Sarah

Pg 32 #26 Blark = Clark

Pg 33 #2 John = Julia

Pg 34 #33 Smal = Sam'l

Pg 35 #31 Fieding = Fielding

Pg 39 #48 Octabia = Octavia
#3 Wilim = William

Pg 44 #30 Eliza Reed = Elisa Reed
#34 Ronulus = Romulus

Pg 45 #24 Jula = Julia

Pg 46 #29 Pricsilla = Priscilla

Pg 49 #30 Andsr = And'sn
#41 Daul = Dan'l

Page 53 #28 Hsrewsbury = Shrewsbury

Pg 56 #9 Abdrew = Andrew

Pg 57 #24 Andrw = Andrew

Pg 59 #2 martn = Martin

Pg 64 #13 Daviw = Davis
#23 Jeo. = Geo.

Pg 65 #47 Liaaie = Lizzie
#20 Cathering = Catherine

Pg 67 #31 Niswandes = Niswander
#1 Susah = Sarah

Pg 69 #47 Issac = Isaac
#3 Cambell = Campbell
#14 Pery = Perry

Pg 70 #36 Chaterine = Catherine
#43 Austn = Austin
#45 Sanl = Sam'l

Pg 71 #5 Austn = Austin

Pg 75 #35 Givson = Gibson

Pg 76 #15 Julin = Julia

Pg 77 #20 Thomson = Thomsen

Pg 78 #41 Isac = Isaac

Pg 79 #21 Yater = Yates

Pg 80 #10 Feo. = Geo.

Pg 81 #6 Cadlwell = Caldwell

Pg 83 #10 Harison = Harrison

Pg 84 #2 Lucnda = Lucinda
#4 Sweney = Sweeney

Pg 85 #29 Stededcide/Stindell = Heindrick

Pg 86 #42 Phetthlace = Phettyplace
#21 & 22 Ferguson = Ferguson

Pg 88 #30 M. McC Duckwall = J. McC. Duckwall

Pg 89 #10 Lucnda = Lucinda

Pg 91 #33 S. V. Vaught = S. B. Vaught

Pg 92 #41 M. R. Griffith = M. H. Griffith
#48 Hallano = Hallans
Robacca = Robeeca [sic]
#11 Js. T. Wimmer = Jas. T. Wimmer

Pag 93 #2 Olilia Munsy = Otilia Munsy

Pg 96 #3 Andrson = Anderson

Pg 100 #22 Chaterine = Catherine

Pg 102 #44 Gillaspia = Gillaspie

Pg 106 #21 Austn = Austin

Pg 107 #8 Brides parents are David & Mary Pauley

#28 Tnie = Tinie Melvin

Pg 108 #10 Kester = Kesler

Pg 109 #47 King Wirght = King Wright

Pg 112 #154 Garrett = Garrett

Pg 114 #220 Epline = Epling
#223 Austn = Austin
#226 Thmpson = Thompson

Pg 116 #57 Hichman = Hickman

Pg 122 #63 Catharing = Catharine

Pg 123 #107 Havery = Harvey

Pg 126 #222 Isac = Isaac

Pg 127 #234 Elviar = Elvina Belcher

Pg 129 #61 Sphrana = Sphrona

Pg 130 #83 Mrtha = Martha

Pg 131 #117 Thronton = Thornton
Isac = Isaac

Pg 134 #25 Smpson = Simpson

Pg 136 #88 Virgina = Virginia

Pg 139 #203 Bride is DOLLIE A. MEADER 22 single b. Bedford Co. VA

Pg 140 #228 Srah = Sarah

—	ELIZABETH J., 12	PRESTON, 125, 138	MARTHA A., 101	ISABELL, 87	MIRIAM, 75	116, 118, 119, 125,	ANGLE
	G.A., 12	REBECCA JANE, 98	MARTHA E., 110	J.S., 99, 137	ROSEBEL, 75	126, 128, 130,	ARON, 52, 20-B
—LEWOOD	ACORD	SARAH E., 111	MARTHA F., 114	J.T., 87	ALVIS	132(2), 133, 136,	CALEB, 14
WILLIAM J., 29	ELIZABETH, 53	SHERARD, 11	MARY, 5	JAS W., 137	ARTEMISIA, 1	137(4), 139, 141	CLOEY A., 69
	FLOYD, 53	VICTORIA, 132	MARY D., 23	JOHN W., 137	DAVID, 10	GAR C., 84	DANL., 20-D
-A-	JULIA A., 53	WM, 69	MARY J., 67	JOS S., 101	DORAH E., 124	GAR. C., 83, 84	DAVID, 14
	ACRES	WM R., 69	MARY L., 140	JOSIAH, 99	GEO W., 92	GARLAND C., 62	DON, 20-B
ABBOT	AMANDA L., 20-D	ADKINSON	MARY ROSABELL, 133	JULIA A., 38	GEORGE A., 108	GEO, 100	DUDLEY, 69
CHARLES, 7	NATHANIEL, 20-D	NANCY, 12	N.B., 50, 20-D	MARTHA A., 99	J.D., 77	GEO W., 86	E., 14
ABBOTT	SARAH, 20-D	POLLY, 12	NANCY, 5, 19	MARY, 99, 121	JAMES D., 64	H., 112	ELIZ, 20-B
CHAS., 39	ADAIR	SHEDRICK, 12	NATHANIEL, 23	NANNIE, 101, 118(2)	JANE, 74	J.A., 20-D	ELIZABETH, 20-D
ELLEN W., 7	SARAH, 31	WILLIAM, 11	NATHANIEL B., 40	PERRY, 38	JAS D., 64	J.J., 116	HENRY BOSWELL, 56
IDA, 27, 39	WILLIAM, JR., 31	AGEE	NATHL B., 63	RHODA FLORENCE, 101	JHN H., 110	JABEZ, 10, 20-D	
JOSEPH, 21, 20-F	WM, 31	ABSOM, 74	POLLY A., 101		JNO H., 92	JACK, 47	JOHN, 20-D
MINERVA, 21, 20-F	ADAMS	DANL H., 3	RACHEL, 39, 79	S.C., 87, 137	JOCIE, 112	JAMES, 112	MATTIE S., 56
SALLIE, 7	A.A., 37	ELVIRA, 74	ROSA BELL, 108	SARAH C., 99, 101	JOHN, 64, 112, 124	JAMES D., 12	PAULINA, 56
SARAH A., 39	CHARLES, 70	LEVI, 3	S.J., 20-D	THOMAS, 101	JOHN H., 77, 108	JAS H., 61	SARAH, 52
ST. CLAIR, 7, 21, 20-F	DANIEL E., 56	SARAH, 3	S.W., 133	THOS, 118	JOSEPHINE, 64, 92,	JNO T., 62(2)	SILAS, 69
ABHER	ELIZABETH, 56	WM T., 74	SARAH, 23, 63	THOS E., 86	110, 124	JOHN, 12	VICTORIA, 52
JAMES, 31	ESTER, 70	AIKINSON	SARAH J., 40, 50, 68	ZIZA M., 121	JOSEPHINE M., 77	JOHN T., 10	ANSBONNE
JOHN, 31	FANNIE, 128	FLORA L., 81	SUSAN, 79	ALLEN	MARGARET J., 10, 108	JUDY, 12	NANNIE G., 122
NANCY ANN, 31	GEORGE, 70	L.F., 81	W.S., 140	ALICE, 104		JULIA, 10	W.E., 122
ABINGDON	HUMPHREY, 68	MARY P., 81	WILLIAM T., 39	ANN M., 4, 12	MARTHA, 14	JULIA A., 75	WM E., 122
LUCINDA, 107	J.H., 81(2), 83, 85,	AKER	WM B., 67	ANNIE L., 104	MARY, 2, 10	LEWIS, 120	ANTHONY
NANNIE B., 107	87, 91, 94	W.S., 94	WM S., 106	ARDELIA, 123	MINNIE J., 77	LIZZIE, 109	EMILY, 73
PETER, 107	JAMES, 37	AKERS	AKERSON	CATHERINE G., 65	NANNIE, 112	LOUISE M., 12	P.., 139
ABINGTON	LIZZIE, 122	BETTIE, 58	GEO, 75	ELIJAH, 104	NORA A., 110	MALINDA, 116	P.A., 131, 132(2),
BARBARA, 84	LOLLIE, 48	C.W., 68	ROSE, 75	ELLEN M., 12	WM, 32, 74	MANERVA, 86	133(2), 134(2),
LUCNDA, 84	M.C., 84	CHAS, 114	SARAH, 75	FANNIE, 139	AMERINGTIN	MANERVA J., 10	136(3), 137, 138,
PETER, 84	MANERVA, 122	CLARA C., 63	ALBERT	GEO, 123	ALBERT, 92	MARCUS P., 20-D	139(2), 140
ABOS	MARGARET A., 27	CORA L., 109	ALBERT, 118	GEO G., 86	ISAAC G., 92	MARTHA W., 62(2)	WM, 73
LIZZIE W., 108	MELISSA, 84	CREED, 114	AMANDA, 130	GEORGE, 65	NANCY, 92	MARY, 47	ANTON
S.P., 108	MINERVA, 48, 79, 108	CROCKETT, 45, 48, 67,	ANNIE B., 130	GEORGE G., 49	AMOS	MINNIE J., 86	ANNIE, 100
WM H., 108	NICK, 128	101, 110	EDGAR N., 128	HENRY, 123	ELVIRA F., 108	NANCY, 19, 120	JOHN, 100
ABSHER	PEASANT, 79	DAISY B., 119	H.W., 130	J.B., 94	EVA, 138	NANNIE B., 122	THOS J., 100
CHRISTIAN, 38	PLEASANT, 48, 68, 108	DAVID, 39	HENRY, 133	JANE S., 49, 65, 86	JAMES W., 108	NANNIE S., 85	ANVILL
JACOB, 126	PLES, 122	DAVID H., 20-D	I.W., 133	JAS, 94	JOHN W., 108	OLIVA, 101	L., 125
JAS, 26	RHODA, 68, 79, 131	DRUCILLA, 50	J.R., 118	JNO J.T., 49	PATRICA, 112	OLIVIA C., 89	NANCY, 125
JAS A., 93(2)	S.A., 37	E.S., 140	JANE, 133	JOHN, 114, 139	ANAHEIM	P.W., 82	S.H., 125
JNO B., 3	SUSAN, 56	ELIZABETH, 45, 106,	MAGGIE J., 118	MARIA, 94	ADRIAN, 93	PAYNE, 10	APPLE
JOHN, 38	SUSAN A., 97	119	ALEM	MARTHA, 123	EDWARD, 93	PEARL MOORE, 101	E.A., 119
LUCINDIA, 93	VIRGINIA, 132	FLOYD L., 50	ELIZA, 132	MARY E.C., 4	EDWD, 93		HERBERT E., 119
MARTHA, 133	WILLIAM, 108, 128	G.F., 98, 129	ALEXANDER	R.M., 4	SARAH, 93	RALEIGH M., 62	WM H., 119
NANCY, 26, 34	WM C., 84	GEO W., 100	ANNIE, 141	RICHARD M., 12	ANDERSON	REUBEN, 61	APSHER
NANCY E., 26	ADDISON	H.H., 106, 109, 119	AXEL, 141(2)	SALLIE A., 114	ANDREW, 120	ROBT A., 101	C., 110
SALLIE, 133	DICEY, 41, 76	HENRY, 19	FRANKLIN, 112	SUSIE, 114	ANTHONY, 47	S., 112	CELINA, 110
SARAH, 3	ELVIRA, 41	HENRY H., 100	G.H., 92	U.S., 86	BERRY, 46	SALLY, 46	J.E., 110
SARAH JANE, 93	LEWIS, 41, 76	HUDSON, 5, 19	G.N., 109, 110	ULYSSUS S., 86	C.T., 89(2)	SUSAN, 10	ARCHER
WILLIAM, 34	M.T., 62	IDA J., 58	G.W., 84(2), 90, 92,	ALLEY	CARY, 116	THOS. C., 46	EMMA F., 53
WM, 133	MARY J., 62	J.W., 68	93, 107, 108(3), 110,	BERTHA, 138	CORINNE, 89	ANDREWS	J.S., 75(2)
Z.B., 126	WILLIAM, 62	JAMES P., 40	111, 115, 116(3),	ENOCH, 138	E.E., 131	A.J., 34, 53	JAMES, 53, 67, 119
ABSHERE	ADERS	JAS T., 61	118(3), 120, 122,	J.M., 122	E.T., 101	CAROLINE, 90	JAS O., 119
ALEX, 54	NAT, 131	JNO E., 133	124(3), 125	T.L., 122	ELIZABETH, 18	F.D., 53	JAS S., 92(2)
ALEXR., 54	SALLY, 131	JORDAN, 98, 129	M., 141	W.O., 122	F.J., 92	JACKSON, 20-C	JOHN W., 19
JAS A., 54	ADKINS	JOSIE F., 67	MARY, 112	ALLISON	FRANCES, 61	JOHN, 90	JULINA, 53, 75, 92
JOHN, 54	AMOS, 138(2)	JULINA, 98, 129	W.F., 112	JAMES, 77	G.C., 76, 77, 78,	JOHN W., 34	L.S., 67
NANCY, 54	B.S., 132	LEWIS J., 48, 133	ALIFF	JAS, 60	79(2), 80, 83, 85,	JULIA, 20-C	LYDIA J., 12
ABSHIRE	CAROLINE, 69	LIZIE, 109	A.J., 86	L.E., 60, 77	88, 89, 91, 92,	LIZZIE, 109	M.G., 92
CHRISTIAN, 16	DANL S., 125	LOUIS, 67	ALEXANDER, 38	MARY, 60, 77	93(2), 95(3), 96(2),	NANCY, 53	S., 19
CLARESSA C., 16	E., 125	LUKE, 79	BUDD, 101(2)	ALOFF	97(2), 99(4), 101(2),	NANCY M., 34	SAMPSON, 12
J., 16	ELIZABETH, 138	MANERVA, 133	ELISHA, 99	MARY, 113	104, 105(2), 106(2),	RUSSELL, 20-C	SAMSON, 8
ABIESHIN	H.G., 132	MARTHA, 45, 48, 67,	F.A., 121	ALTIZER	109, 111, 112(3),	WM, 90	SARAH, 8, 12, 19
	MARY, 11	110	FLUVANNA, 86	J.E., 75	113, 114(2), 115(2),		SARAH A., 8

SARAH E., 75
ARBS
  HY, 95
ARGABRIGHT
  A.B., 58
  BITTIE A., 42
  CALLIE R., 54
  CATHERINE, 54
  ELIZABETH, 58
  ELIZABETH A., 43, 47
  EBNERZETER E., 43
  G.W., 58
  GEO W., 42, 43
  GEORGE W., 47
  J.H., 84
  JACOB, 55
  JOS B., 55
  JOSEPH R., 47
  LAURE, 131
  LOLLIE G., 123
  LUCY J., 84
  M.J., 126
  MARTHA, 114
  O.A., 123, 131
  R., 131
  R.L., 123
  SARAH A., 84
  SENE, 55
  WM E., 42
ARMENTROUT
  B., 3
  ELIZTH E., 3
  JNO, 3
ARMONTROUT
  B., 15, 17
  BAR., 20
  GEORGE, 36
  J., 15, 17
  JAS., 20
  JOANNA, 36
  JOHN W., 15
  MARY A., 20
  MARY ANN, 36
  SARAH, 17
  WILLIAM M., 20
ARMSTEAD
  ANNA, 87
  HENRY, 84
  JACOB, 84
  MALINDA, 65
  POLLY, 84
  REUBEN, 87
  ROSE, 77
  WM J., 87
ARMSTRONG
  ED, 130
  ELIZABETH, 49
  GEORGE, 139
  JESSIE, 139
  JOHN, 82, 98
  MARY M., 82
  NELIE, 130
  OBADIAH, 49
  POCA, 98
  SAML, 49
  SUSAN, 82, 98
  T.E., 139
ARNOLD
  ANDREW, 134
  C.M., 76
  G.W., 111
  JAS S., 76
  MARY, 111, 134(2)
  SARAH, 76
  THOMAS, 111
ARTHER
  ANN, 123
  BENJ, 123
  EMMA, 123
ARTHUR
  A., 14
  F.J., 125
  G.C., 125
  J.H., 125
  JOHN, 111
  SARAH, 111
  STEPHEN, 14
  T., 14
  WM, 111
ASHWORTH
  A.A., 14, 28, 29, 35, 81, 114
  B.M., 110
  ELIZA A., 87
  F.A., 93
  IDA, 125
  J.M., 137, 140
  J.S., 87
  J.W., 93
  JOEL, 16
  JOHN, 16
  NANCY, 16, 114
  R.M., 43, 44, 45(2), 69(2), 82, 84, 92, 93, 97, 98, 99, 100, 101, 105(2), 107, 108, 110, 112(2), 114(2), 115, 119, 120, 124, 125, 129, 133, 136, 140(3)
  ROBT M., 42
  S.E., 125
  SUSAN, 93
  T.J.P., 87
ATKINS
  DANIEL, 108
  DANL, 126
  ELIZTH, 16
  F.M., 107
  H.B., 128
  JACKSON, 107
  LULA, 128
  M., 126
  MARGARETT, 125
  MATTHEW, 16
  MATTHEW B., 16
  NANNIE, 71
  PATSEY, 108
  SUSAN, 107
  THOMAS, 108, 126
ATKINSON
  ANNIE W., 135
  BRADE, 112
  E.W., 109
  J.W., 135
  L.F., 109
AUER
  IGNATY, 91
  JOSEPH, 91
  MARY, 91
AUSTIN
  A., 84
  A.J., 76, 84, 85
  ALBERT, 90
  ALBERT G., 74
  ALICE B., 104
  ANTHONY, 108
  ATHALINDA, 76, 85
  BLEDSO, 4
  D.M., 104
  E.A., 26
  E.J., 26, 37
  EDWD, 57
  ELIZTH J., 10
  ELLA P., 80
  ELLEN, 108
  EMMA F., 76
  G.A., 13, 22, 23, 26, 27, 29, 37(2), 40, 43
  G.W., 81, 89
  GARLAND A., 8, 10(3), 11(2), 13, 15(3), 17, 18, 37
  GEO, 10
  H., 88
  H.R., 90
  HUMPHREY, 120
  I.E., 89, 106
  ISAAC E., 32, 37
  ISAC E., 48
  ISAIAH, 4
  JAMES E., 37
  JAS, 88
  JNO J., 84
  L.E., 104
  LUCY, 4
  M.L., 104
  MACY, 106
  MAGGIE, 81
  MALINDA, 32, 57, 89
  MALINDA L., 37
  MALVINA, 48
  MARGARET, 84
  MARTHA W., 10
  MARY A., 85
  MARY S., 26
  MARY W., 32
  MATILDA, 90
  MATILDA B., 74
  MILES, 106
  MILLIE, 88
  QUEEN V., 48
  ROBERT W., 108
  ROBT LEE, 57
  THEODOCIA E., 84
  THOS, 76
  UMPHERY, 84
  V.V., 74
  VICTORIA J., 37
AUSTN
  I.E., 106
  ISAAC B., 106
  MALINDA, 106
AUTON
  ANNIE, 137
  JOHN, 137
  T.J., 137
AVINGTON
  LOUCINDA A., 103
  PETER, 103(2)
AYERS
  B.A., 122
  B.D., 122
  BISHOP A., 108
  CORDELIA, 98
  FLORA, 112
  JAMES R., 127
  JENNE, 108
  JULIA A., 122
  L.L., 112
  N.H., 110
  THOMAS, 108
  W.H., 99, 101, 113(2), 114, 117, 118, 120, 124(2), 126, 127, 128, 131, 132, 133
  WM H., 112
AYMES
  AGNESS, 20-D
AYRES
  GRANVILLE, 45
  SUSAN, 45
  W.H., 99, 107(4), 111, 114, 115(2), 118, 139
  WM H., 45

-B-

BABER
  P.B., 60
BACHELOR
  ANN, 33
  FERDINAND, 33
  REUBEN, 33
BAGLEY
  BETTIE, 87
  SAM, 87
  TINA, 87
BAILEY
  A.C., 28, 97, 123
  A.I., 111
  A.J., 69, 125
  A.L., 97
  A.P., 139
  ADDISON, 38, 43, 84
  ADDISON C., 1, 116
  AGNES, 58, 59
  AGNES C., 76, 119
  ALBANY V., 51
  ALBERT EDWIN, 58
  ALEX J., 43, 45
  ALEX W., 49
  ALEXANDER, 2, 6
  ALICE E., 75
  ALICE L., 20-B
  ALLEN C., 115
  ALMEDA, 22
  AMOS, 16
  AMOS W., 5
  ANDERSON M., 29
  ANDREW, 47
  ANDREW J., 10
  ANN, 65, 96, 125
  ANNA, 9
  ANNIE, 111
  ARAMINTA, 56
  ARCH, 6, 9, 23
  ARCHD, 2
  AUGUSTUS I., 65, 96
  AUGUSTUS J., 27
  B.B., 19, 69
  BALLARD P., 9, 46(2), 54, 96
  BALLARD R., 45
  BETIE E., 103
  BETTY F., 84
  BLUFORD B., 47
  BURON, 50
  BURREL, 25
  BURREL B., 59
  BURRELL, 22
  BURRELL B., 30
  BURWELL, 83
  C.A., 87
  C.J., 97
  C.L., 116
  C.N., 69
  C.W., 69, 77(2), 110, 136
  CALLIE D., 54
  CASIE V., 114
  CATHARINE, 4
  CATHERINE T., 9
  CHAR., 20-B
  CHARLES W., 2, 139, 20-E
  CHARLOTT F., 121
  CHARLOTTE, 10, 20, 22, 32, 47
  CHARLOTTE S., 65
  CHAS B., 84
  CHAS C., 129
  CHAS W., 45
  CHAS. W., 42
  CHLOE, 18
  CHRISTINA, 38
  CLAY, 2, 3
  CLEMANTINE C., 20-B
  CLIAS, 22
  CLIAS W., 23
  CORNELIUS W., 22, 81
  COUSBY T., 109
  CYNTHIA, 20
  CYNTHIA M., 24
  CYRUS M., 57, 65
  D.P., 77, 117, 136
  DAISEY P., 115
  DANIEL P., 46, 118
  DANIEL R., 46
  DAVID K., 72
  DAVID P., 20
  DRURY, 117
  E., 15, 109, 20-C
  E.A., 128, 140
  E.B., 135
  E.C., 120
  E.P., 103, 104, 109
  ED E., 135
  ED W., 136
  EDNA C., 136
  ELECTRA ANN, 39
  ELECTRA P., 32
  ELI, 10, 20, 22(2), 25, 32, 41, 47, 49, 20-B
  ELI T., 128(2)
  ELIAS, 99
  ELIJAH, 21, 79, 90, 114, 126, 20-F
  ELIJAH L., 58
  ELIZ, 23
  ELIZA, 87
  ELIZA J., 64(2)
  ELIZABETH, 3, 16, 25, 42, 45, 48, 53, 56(2), 67, 73, 81, 86, 93, 97, 98, 101
  ELIZTH, 2, 3(2), 4, 6, 8, 9(2), 21, 32, 57, 20-F
  ELIZTH A., 57
  ELLA A., 50
  ELLA E., 115
  ELLOTTA, 25
  ELMAS, 117(2)
  ELZ, 28, 30
  EMMA, 85, 93
  EMMA J., 55
  ENOS, 42
  ESTER A., 35
  ESTILL, 9, 58, 59, 76, 119
  EUGENIA, 81
  EUGENIA A., 54
  EUNICE E., 72
  EVA, 114
  F., 19
  F.A., 130
  F.R., 125
  FAMIE E., 39
  FANNIE, 68
  FANNIE W., 57
  FLORA H., 68
  FLOYD, 27, 32, 37, 40, 46, 83, 113
  FRANCES, 3, 9, 30
  FRANCIS, 6, 27
  FRANKIE, 90
  FRENCH, 20-D
  G.C., 78, 86
  G.D., 93
  G.F., 28, 140
  G.M., 115, 130
  G.P., 114
  G.T., 84(2)
  G.W., 102(2), 107(2), 112, 116(3), 118, 119, 120(3), 121(3), 122(2), 124, 125, 126, 127(2), 128(3), 129, 130(2), 131, 134, 135, 136, 137, 139(3), 140, 141
  GASTON C., 20-A
  GENNETTIE, 111
  GEO, 3, 6, 30
  GEO C., 19
  GEO P., 37, 56, 98
  GEORGE, 9
  GEORGE D., 6, 38
  GEORGE M., 34, 73
  GREENVILLE C., 72
  GUS, 118
  H.E., 72, 74, 75, 76(2), 77, 80(4)
  H.F., 47(2)
  H.P., 118
  HANNAH L., 43, 45
  HARRISON, 140
  HARRY, 48, 66
  HARVEY G., 84
  HARVY R., 20-D
  HENDERSON, 121
  HENDERSON F., 46, 52, 62
  HENRY, 21, 24, 27, 30, 32, 53, 20-A, 20-F
  HENRY B., 39
  HESTER A.C., 43
  HY, 20-D
  I.H., 103(2), 108, 118, 121, 122, 135(2)
  I.W., 117
  IDA A., 97
  IDA B., 104, 115
  IDA I., 96
  IDA K., 78
  INDICA F., 64
  IRVAN H., 9
  IRVIN, 39, 65
  IRVIN E., 54
  IRVIN H., 60, 65, 67, 99
  J., 4, 15, 95
  J.F., 92
  J.H., 75(2)
  J.J., 20-C
  J.K.P., 103, 110
  J.M., 33, 20-E
  J.S., 73, 84
  J.W., 115(2)
  J.W.P., 123
  JABA P., 33
  JAHU, 91
  JAMES, 46, 68, 72, 135
  JAMES B., 43
  JAMES F., 25
  JAMES L., 9, 10, 20-B
  JAMESON, 8, 9, 20, 46, 20-B
  JAMISON, 23, 25, 28, 34, 35, 54
  JAMISON, JR., 21, 20-F
  JANE, 22, 72, 78, 20-D
  JAS, 9
  JAS F., 52, 94, 115
  JAS K.P., 61
  JAS L., 90
  JAS M., 30, 56, 20-A, 20-C
  JAS McH., 56
  JAS O., 40
  JAS. ESTEL, 46
  JAS. L., 21, 20-F
  JAS. M., 18
  JENNIE J., 61
  JESTEU, 125
  JNO M., 54, 129
  JNO S., 24
  JOHN, 12, 29, 50, 67, 79, 85, 97, 118
  JOHN A., 11, 49
  JOHN C., 9, 123
  JOHN H., 9, 22, 118, 135
  JOHN HARRISON, 30
  JOHN M., 38, 56, 68(2), 90
  JOHN P., 35
  JOHN S., 30
  JOHN W., 7, 20(3),

20-A(2)
JOHNATHAN, 25
JOHNATHAN S., 25, 20-B

JOHNSON D., 140
JONATHAN, 30, 45, 50
JONATHAN S., 29, 34
JONTH, 3
JONTHAN S., 65
JOSEPHINE, 118, 20-B
JOSEPHINE C., 39
JUANITA B., 90
JULA, 45
JULIA, 29, 118
JULIA A., 67
JULIA ANN, 85, 97, 99
JULIA T., 20-A
JUTST, 49
L, 126
L.B., 72, 141
L.J., 120, 140
L.K.P., 104
L.M., 124, 137
L.V., 141
LAURA B., 78
LAURA L., 64
LEANDER H., 40
LECTRA DACRE, 139

LEE, 91
LEFTWICH, 9, 35, 52, 58, 77, 78, 91
LELAND, 43, 49, 51, 56
LEROY F., 40, 113
LETWICH (SIC), 123
LIFTWICH, 140
LILLIE, 92
LILLIE F., 138
LIZZIE, 75, 105
LOTTIE, 41, 49, 126
LOU E., 129
LOU J., 104
LOUELLA, 41
LOUIE, 79
LOUISA, 11
LOUISA C., 3
LOUISA J., 11
LUCINDA, 3
LURISA C., 50
LUVENIA C., 38
M., 3, 16, 20-B, 20-E
M.C., 47
M.E., 115, 134, 139
M.J., 117, 136
MACIJAH, 3
MADISON, 31
MAGGIE, 82
MAIIALA, 2
MALISA A., 91
MARGARET, 16
MARINDA, 15
MARTELIA V., 90
MARTHA, 9(2), 10, 21,

39, 50, 77, 104, 115, 20-F
MARTHA A., 41
MARTHA J., 40, 62, 97
MARY, 2, 7, 12, 45, 52, 57, 68, 77, 101, 20-D(2)
MARY A., 109, 114, 135, 138
MARY A.P., 25
MARY E., 5, 25, 27, 28, 38, 46, 47, 114, 136
MARY J., 25, 46, 77, 118, 20-C
MARY JANE, 59
MARY I., 57
MARY N., 53
MARY P., 84
MARY S., 53
MARYELINE M., 8

MAS. W., 29
MASHU, 49
MASTIN, 35, 72, 118, 129
MATHEW E., 35
MATILDA, 35, 39, 41, 76
MATILDA J., 3
MELDORA D., 110
MELISSA C., 56
MELVINA M., 49
MERTIE R., 77
MICAJAH, 2(2), 16
MINNIE L., 140
MOLLIE E., 136
MOLLY C., 52
N.B., 139
N.K., 106
NANCY, 19, 22, 25, 30, 35(2), 47, 57(2), 59, 83, 94, 105, 118, 129, 140
NANCY ELIZABETH, 140
NANCY J., 9, 84
NANNIE, 94
NANNIE C., 72
NANNIE J., 68
NATHAN, 48
NICHOLAS B., 12
NITA, 130
O.H., 140
OCTAVA, 43, 84
OCTAVIA, 38, 116, 123
ONIE, 2
P.F., 67
P.H., 93, 135(2)
P.P., 138
P.W., 138
PAULINA, 110
PERLINA, 61

PHILIP, 106
PHILIP J., 42
PHILIP P., 27
PHILLIP P., 11
POLLIE E., 65
POLLY, 3, 9, 19, 20, 21, 24, 25, 27, 34, 35, 42, 47, 54, 83, 90, 139, 20-A, 20-B, 20-F
POLLY W., 20-B
POLY, 23, 20-E
R., 124
R.H., 79, 93, 120, 121(2)
RACHEL, 11
RACHEL E., 73
REBECCA, 3, 21, 43, 49, 50, 51, 56, 98, 20-F
REBECCA A., 46
REBECCA J., 21, 31, 48, 60, 20-F
REUBEN, 20-D
REUBIN R., 22
RHODA, 5
RHODA G., 10
RHODA J., 45
ROBERT, 57, 85
ROBT H., 55
ROSA B., 115, 126
ROSABEL, 67
ROSINA, 48, 66
ROXIE L., 86
ROZENIA, 53
S., 124, 20-C
S.A., 81, 129, 136
S.E. JANE, 86
S.P., 139
S.W., 68
SALLIE A., 90
SALLIE J., 50
SALLY, 30, 31
SAML., 2, 3, 42, 136
SAML., 19, 20-D
SAMPSON TAYLOR, 47

SAMUEL, 7, 20-B
SAMUEL A., 34
SARAH, 18, 33, 35, 46(2), 47(3), 52(2), 54, 56, 58, 62, 75, 77, 90, 91, 92, 96, 121, 123, 135
SARAH A., 9, 38
SARAH E., 46, 54
SARAH E.J., 72
SARAH F., 19, 79
SARAH H., 55
SARAH J., 38, 46, 61, 68, 87, 20-C
SARAH JANE, 47
SARAH M., 78, 91

SHANON P., 136(2)
SIDNEY J., 66
SPARRIL, 83
SUE A., 69
SUSAN, 81, 110
SYLVIA, 83
TELIA, 39, 65, 67
TELIA C., 60
THOMPSON, 57, 68
THOMPSON P., 19, 25, 41, 53, 56
THOS W., 109
TILICE, 25
TIMANDRY M., 84
U., 20-B
U.A., 90
URIAH A., 20-B
URSULA, 24, 34, 50, 65
URZULA, 73
VIOLA JANE, 96
VIRGINIA, 41, 76, 135, 136
VIRGINIA E., 46
W.A., 105, 111, 140
W.I., 137
W.L., 121, 128, 135
W.R., 118
W.W., 115, 141
WADE, 114
WADE H., 119
WALTER, 94
WALTER T., 76
WESLEY H., 86
WILEY W., 29
WILLIAM, 39, 76
WILLIAM A., 32
WILLIAM C., 20-A
WILLIAM M., 2
WILSON L., 93, 97
WILSON LEE, 59, 83, 105
WINTON E., 43
WM A., 125, 135
WM C., 114, 134, 136
WM D., 67
WM E., 136
WM M., 35, 41
Z., 67
Z.H., 48, 81, 101, 109, 126
ZACH, 11
ZACHARIAH, 73
ZACHARIAH H., 86

ZELPHA, 27
ZILPHA, 46
ZILPHIA, 32, 37, 40
ZILPHIA A., 27
ZILTHA, 113
ZULA, 61
BAILY
ARCH., 14
CHARLOTTE, 13

CHRISTIAN F., 13
ELI, 13
ELIZTH, 14
FLOYD, 14
G.W., 106
GREENVILLE C., 13

JAS. K.P., 14
JAS. L., 13
JOHN, 13
M., 13
N., 13
NANCY, 13
RUSSEL B., 13
SARAH, 13
SARAH A.J., 14
WILSON L., 13
ZELPHA, 14
BAKER
ELIJA J., 10
I., 117
JNO., 13
JOHN, 7, 20, 42
LIZZIE, 93
MARY, 13
MAT, 117
NANCY, 87
POLLY, 7, 10, 20, 42
RHODA A., 20
SARAH E., 13
SARAH J., 93
SUSANNAH, 7
THOMAS, 127
WILLIAM, 117
WM, 93
WM T., 42
BALDWIN
D.O., 110
D.V., 123
DENISON O., 110
DON B., 74
HANNAH, 122
ISAAC FLOYD, 122
J.S., 67
JOHN M., 67
L.V., 123
S.A.D., 122
SALLIE, 123
SALLIE C., 74
SALLIE W., 74
SUSAN J., 109
TABITHA, 67
BALES
EMMA D., 126
LULA M., 127
MARY A., 87
R.B., 127
RACHEL, 118
REBECA, 118
REBECCA, 126
WM, 118, 127
BALEY
J.C., 112

J.H., 112
MARY, 112
BALKE
EUGENE, 81
BALL
ALFORD, 90
ALFRED, 52, 57
ANNA, 57
ANNIE, 52
AUGUSTUS, 3
C.M., 111
CAROLINE, 52, 90
CATH, 107
CATHERINE, 104
CHARLES A., 104
ELIZA S., 3
ELIZABETH, 47
HENRY, 130
JAMES, 57, 104
JAMES W., 20-D
JOS H., 47
MARY M., 111
NOAH, 107
PETER H., 111
R., 3
W.L., 125, 126, 133, 138, 139(2), 140
WM, 47
WM L., 124
BALLARD
A.M., 87
EMILY, 101
EMMA, 129
G.G., 120
GRANT WILSON, 138

H.R., 133
HARRISON, 24, 138
HAWKS, 131
JOHN, 129, 138
JULIA, 138
JULIA A., 138
KATE, 120
L.A., 120
MARY ANN, 6
MARY E., 24
R.F., 87
RILEY, 101
ROSA E., 131
SARAH, 6
W.H., 87(2)
W.L., 129
W.N., 123
W.R., 101
WILSON, 6
BALLENGER
ISAAC, 16
LORENZA, 16
POLLY, 16
BALPHAM
MARY, 16
MEADOR, 16

BAND
C.F., 114
E.R., 114
G.W., 114
BANDY
DELIA, 138
BANE
JOSEPH H., 28
NANCY, 28
WM R., 28
BANGLES
MARY, 47
R.T., 47
REUBEN, 47
BANISTER
HENRY, 113
JAMES, 113
BANKS
ADALINE, 109
ANDREW J., 3
ANNA, 3
BESSIE L., 109
GEO, 109
SAML, 3
BANNER
A., 95
JAMES, 95
M., 95
BARBARIE
BESSIE, 139
JOHN, 126, 139
JULIA, 126, 139
MARY C., 126
BARBER
ALEX, 11
ELIZTH, 11
HERBERT B., 49
HUBERT B., 11
MARY H., 49
TAMMIE C., 49
BARBERIE
JOHN, 114
JOHN, JR., 114
JULIA, 114
BARBERIES
EUPHERNIA, 36
JOHN, 36
MARIA ANN, 36
BARBOR
ALEX H., 82
FANNIE, 72
FANNIE C., 82
H.B., 72, 82
IRENE H., 72
BARBORA
BERTHA, 67
JNO, 67
JULIA, 67
BARBRIE
JOHN, 102
JULIA, 102
MARGRIET, 102
BARGER

BESSIE, 101
DANIEL, 101
DAVID A., 36
DIANNA, 36
GEO M., 101
GEO W., 43
JACOB, 36, 43, 81
LUCY, 81
MARY J., 78
TINA, 81
W.G., 78
W.H., 78
BARILEY
ALICE G., 52
HARRY, 52
ROSENA, 52
BARKER
D.S., 117
JOHN W., 23
JOS, 123
JULIA A., 13, 23
L.S., 123
LULA, 117
M.C., 13, 23
M.E., 103
MARY, 46
MARY E., 13
SAML. L., 46
SARAH J., 46
THOS T., 123
WM C., 103(2)
BARKSDALE
BENJAMIN, 86, 93
CHANEY, 74
CLEM, 103
DANIEL, 86, 93
LILLIE, 103
SALLIE, 86, 93
WM, 103
BARLEY
ALBERT, 78
MARY, 78
PETER, 78
BARNES
E.B., 46
LUCY (SIC), 106
LULA, 93
MARY, 46
SARAH, 106
W.H., 36
WILLIAM H., 36
WM, 46, 106
WM H., 36(2), 39, 40(3), 41(2)
WM K., 41
BARNETT
ELLA O., 92
HENRY, 115
MAGGIE, 92
MARY, 115
SUSAN R., 115
WILLIAM, 92
BARR

EDWIN V., 59
BARRETT
JAMES, 99
JAS, 99
KENNISON, 138
MARGARET, 60, 138

NANCY, 99
REUBEN, 60, 138
SAML, 99
WM, 60
BARROW
BETTIE F., 131
MATIE G., 131
WM, 131
BARTLEY
II., 108
HENRY A., 108
MINOR B., 108
BARTON
ELIZABETH, 23
POLY, 23
BARTRUM
MALISSA, 54
WM, 54(3)
BASHALDER
ANN S., 7
BASHAM
ALBERT J., 114
ANDERSON, 41
ARAMINTA, 63
ARTHUR D., 134
CATHARINE, 135
D.A., 109
ELIZA E., 80
ELIZABETH, 42
ELLA JANE, 45
EMMA A., 62
ERASTUS L., 60
HENRY J., 43
HENRY W., 42
J.A., 134(2)
JNO L., 135
JOHN, 5, 41, 42(2), 60, 63, 80, 135
JOS, 92
JOS A., 45, 114
JOSEPH, 45, 76
JOSEPH A., 51, 62
JULINA, 43
LEWIS A., 136
LIDA, 109
LILLIE MAY, 136
MANERVA, 109
MARTHA, 42(2)
MARTHA A., 41, 60, 63
MARTHA ANN, 80

MARY F., 136
MATTIE, 76
MEADOR, 5
P.A., 134(2)
PATTY, 5

POLLY, 45, 62
POLLY A., 45, 51, 92, 114
R.H., 134(2)
REBECCA, 45
RUFUS H., 51, 134
W.T., 92
WILLIAM, 43
BASSHAM
ALEXANDER, 9
DAV, 19
ELIZA, 10
JOHN, 9, 45
JOS A., 45
LEWIS A., 45
M., 18(2)
MARTHA, 45
MARY, 9(2), 10, 19
MARY J., 16
MEADOR, 9(2), 10
POLLY A., 45
R., 19
RHODA, 4
SARAH E., 45
WILLIAM, 4
BATCHELOR
ARINE, 23
EMILINE V., 23
REUBEN, 23
BATEMAN
ALBERT, 103
AMANDA, 50
JOSEPH, 50
MARY, 103
MORIAH, 124
OPIE, 103
THOS H., 50
BATTLES
E.M., 86
G.E., 86
LOUISA M., 86
BAUGHNESS
J.M., 113
MARY, 113
RUEBEN, 113
BAUGUESS
JOHN, 116
P.M., 113
BAUMER
CHLOE, 55
DICK, 55
RICHARD, 55
BAXLER
GEO, 24
GEORGE, 24
SARAH, 24
BAXTER
ANN, 102, 108
CHAS H., 102
GEORGE, 39(2), 102, 108
GEORGE EDWARD, 108

JAS S., 42
M.H., 51
MARTHA, 42
SARAH, 39
W.D., 51
WILLIAM, 42
WM M., 51
BAYS
C., 83
CHAS, 83
LOUISA, 83
WM, 83
BEACKENRIDGE

BELLE, 46
CARY, 46
MATILDA, 46
BEAMER
B.F., 73
JANE, 73
MICHAEL, 73
BEARD
CHAS H., 79
GEO W., 79
M.A., 79
BEASLEY
AMY, 33
DANIEL, 33, 129
FRANCES, 129
H.W., 90
HANNAH, 48
JAS. HERBERT, 48
JEMIMA, 90
JERRY, 48
M.A., 129
THOS, 33
BEAU
MARTHA L., 41
SALLIE A., 41
SAML LEE, 41
BEAUFORT
H.D.C., 126
BECHELHYMER

ABRAHAM, 48
LAURA ANN E., 48
MARY, 48
BECK
ED, 135
HENRIETTA, 123, 124
HENRIETY, 135
HENRY, 123, 124, 135
JOSEPH, 123
SAM H., 124
BECKELHIMER

A., 113
E.J., 113
M., 113
BECKER
JESSE, 94

MARY, 94
U.S., 94
BECKET
JAMES J., 34
SARAH, 34
SOLOMON, 34
BECKETT
MARGARET, 60, 74
MARGT., 20-D
R.D., 74(2)
WILBER F., 20-D
WILLIAM, 74
WILLIE H., 60
WM, 60
WM C., 20-D
BECKLEHEIMER

ABRAM, 68
G E N E R A L
WASHINGTON, 68
MARY A., 68
BECKLEHYMER

M.J., 51
BECKLEY
N.C., 21(5), 20-D, 20-E, 20-F(5)
BECKNER
JOSEPH S., 39
MOAB, 39
SARAH A., 39
BEE
I.E., 93(2), 133
ISAIAH, 93
ISAIAH E., 133(2)
MARY L., 133
MARY V., 93
BELCHER
A., 139
A.A., 26, 20-B
A.B. PHIPPS, 139
A.D., 96
A.G., 96, 118, 126, 131
A.H., 114
A.R., 97, 120
ALEXANDER, 24
ALLEN, 120
ALLEN D., 8, 47
AMANDA, 91, 115
AMANDA BEL., 53

AMANDA E., 101
AMDERSON, 29
AMERICA, 123
AMERICA L., 32
AMY, 138
AND. A., 48
ANDERSON, 31, 39, 43, 46, 84
ANDERSON A., 7, 41
ANN, 24, 29, 112
ANNA, 5, 15, 19, 47

ANNIE, 42
ARROLIE, 72
ASA, 4, 5, 8, 11, 15, 16, 21, 25, 20-E, 20-F
AUGUSTUS B., 46
B.H., 92
B.P., 100
BAL, 123
BALLARD, 131
BARTLEY, 28, 32, 66
BEN, 79
BESSIE, 113
BOYD S., 41
C., 15, 17, 100
C.C., 140
C.L., 72
C.M., 118
CASVILLE C., 34
CH., 20-E
CHAS M., 59
CHAS W., 98
CHRIS, 14, 27, 119, 20-B
CHRISTEN, 82
CHRISTIAN, 7, 22, 32, 34, 64, 66
CLARA, 4, 5, 8, 15, 16, 21, 129, 20-F
CLARA A., 100
CLARE, 20-E
CLARINDA, 11, 25, 48
CLARISSA, 31
CLARY C., 23
CLEMENTINE, 107
CLEMINTINE, 58
CLEO, 123
CLOE, 131
COLBY, 106
CORA Z., 113
D.P., 88
DANIEL, 67
DANIEL W., 20-B
DANL W., 74
DAVID, 96
DELIA A., 48
DONALD S., 140
ED J., 51
EDWARD J., 93
ELBERT A., 1
ELISA J., 5
ELIZA L., 7
ELIZABETH, 1
ELIZTH H., 26
ELLEN, 46, 129
ELLEN R., 48
ELVIAR, 127
EMALINE, 42
EZEKIEL B., 86
FANNIE, 139
FANNIE A., 56
FANNIE J., 134
FLORA, 120
FLORENCE MAY, 120

FLOYD, 98
G.B., 76
GEO G., 139(2)
GEO W., 27
GREEN, 82
H.D., 5, 15
H.M., 113(2)
HARRIET P., 58
HENRY, 7, 24, 42, 47, 120
HENRY D., 19, 29, 47
HENRY E., 138
HIRAM P., 68
HUGH H., 17, 89
I.D., 66, 131
INDIA C., 115
ISAAC, 10
ISABELLA, 46
ISAM, 25(2)
ISHAM, 4, 23, 51, 93, 97
ISHAM B., 134
ISHAM D., 29, 124
ISOM, 14, 21, 64, 111, 20-B, 20-F
ISOM D., 15
ISOM G., 59
J. FLOYD, 56
J.C., 134
J.E., 96, 101, 118
J.F., 87, 89, 139(2)
JAMES, 12, 18, 84
JAMES A., 10
JAMES E., 115
JANE, 32, 39, 43, 84, 116
JAS E., 53, 89
JAS. C., 20-A
JNO N., 131
JOHN, 1
JOHN N., 32
JOHN W., 19
JONATHAN H., 5
JOSEPH, 129
JOSEPHUS, 25
JULIA, 2, 67, 139(2)
JULIA A., 56, 70, 112
JULIA ANN, 29
JULIA B., 131
JULIANA V., 28
L., 133
L.A., 74
L.J., 126
L.O., 74
LAURA D., 115
LAVENIA, 42
LEAH, 107
LEMMEL J., 126
LENA V., 134
LETTA A., 20-B
LETTIE, 41
LEWIS, 2, 10, 16, 18,

46
LILLY F., 37
LOLY, 120
LOUISE L., 59
LUCETTA, 84
LUCINDA, 111
LUCINDA C., 20-B
M., 4(2), 18, 126, 20-C, 20-E
M. MN, 17
M.A., 126
M.E., 139
M.F., 75, 91, 129
M.H., 134
M.J., 75, 87, 139(2)
M.M., 58
MADISON F., 4
MAHALA, 12, 20-A
MALINDA, 14, 66
MANDA C., 89
MARCY C., 89
MARGARET, 46
MARGARET C., 16

MARGARET E., 138

MARGARET J., 46
MARGT W., 86
MARINDA C., 87
MARTHA, 18, 27, 56, 64, 82, 97, 98, 136
MARTHA A., 96, 118
MARTHA J., 11, 32
MARY, 4, 14, 15, 27, 28, 91, 129
MARY E., 15, 59, 134
MARY EFFIE, 119
MARY J., 48
MARY JANE, 53
MARY M., 32, 20-B
MARY R., 97
MATILDA, 1, 84, 97
MAY, 22
MAZARINO, 32
MELVINA, 21, 20-F
MICAJAH, 14, 20-C
MIDDLETON H., 20-A

MILLA, 7
MILTON, 107
MILTON M., 16
MISAJAH, 1
MOLLIE, 114
MOLLIE E., 92
MOLLIE M., 70
MOLLIE V., 88
MOSES E., 72
NANCY, 4, 25, 32, 51, 64, 93, 111, 131(2)
NANCY R., 53
NANNIE, 67
NANNIE C., 140
NANNIE JANE, 106

OBADIAH, 26
OBEDIAH, 27, 53, 64, 86, 113(2), 126, 20-B
OBEDIAH D., 113
OBIDIAH, 127
OCTABIA L., 39
OCTAVIA J., 47
ORINIE J., 64
P.T., 126(2)
PHOEBE A., 82
POLLY, 7, 119
R., 4, 16, 18, 133
R.H., 72, 115, 139
RACHEL H., 59
RHALY, 115
REBECCA, 2, 10(2), 21, 43, 46, 20-B, 20-F
REBECCA J., 74, 96, 20-B
REELY, 72
RELIE, 68
RHODA, 129
ROBERT, 68, 92
ROIT C., 59
ROIT H., 72
RUFINA, 136
RUFUS B., 116
RUFUS R., 21, 20-F
RUSSELL, 37
S. STOWERS, 106
SALLIE, 10, 23, 28
SALLIE E., 47, 98, 120
SAMUEL W., 27
SARAH, 32, 37, 66, 74, 120
SARAH A., 56, 20-B
SARAH L., 101
SARAH R., 113
SARAH V., 31
T.J., 114
THOS J., 22, 119
THOS., 26
VALENTINE, 134
VICEY, 127
VIOLA, 89
VISA, 113(2)
W. McH., 70
W.B., 113
W.C., 112, 113(2), 114
W.M.H., 133
W.O., 66
WADDY C., 82
WILLIAM, 46
WILLIAM H., 12
WILLIAM M.H., 18
WINFIELD, 75
WM A., 48
WM M.H., 139
WM W., 56, 82
ZEPHANIAH, 97
BELL
ADILAH A., 38
CANDIS, 92

CAUSHY, 32
CHARLES, 59, 139
DAVID E., 38
DORA JANE, 106
EDWARD, 83
ELIZA, 70
ELIZABETH, 38
EMILY, 40
GEO, 72
GEO W., 106
GEO. W., 26
H., 70
HAL, 139
HAVNER, 105
HENRY, 29, 70, 79(2), 92, 99, 130
J.A., 26, 130
JAMES, 29, 32, 38, 40, 42, 59
JAS, 83
JAS., 26
JUDY, 139
JULIA, 40, 42, 59, 72, 79, 99
JULIA A., 29, 92
JULIA ANN, 38, 79, 83
MAGGIE, 105
MARTHA A., 38
MARTHA J., 99
MARY A., 38
MOLLIE, 105, 130
SARAH, 42, 72
SARAH E., 79, 106
THOMAS, 38
VIRGINIA, 79
BENNET
CATHARINE, 2
ISAAC, 2
J.W., 78
ROBERT, 2
BENNETT
AMANDA, 105
ANDREW, 24
ANN W., 23
C.A., 122
DELILAH, 50
EFFIE MAY, 140
ELCINDA, 13
G.D., 130, 132
G.W., 24
GABE, 106
GEO D., 89
GREEN, 65
J.C., 122
J.W., 20, 29(2), 31(2), 32, 33(3), 34(2), 35(3), 36(3), 37(2), 38, 40, 41, 42(2), 43(2), 44, 45, 46(6), 47(5), 48(6), 49(4), 50(2), 51, 52, 53(5), 54, 55(2), 56(2), 57, 59(3),

60(5), 62, 65, 66(2), 67(2), 68, 70, 71(4), 72(2), 74, 75, 76(2), 77, 78(2), 79(3), 81, 84, 87(2), 88(2), 90(2), 91(2), 92, 93, 94, 95(2), 97, 98, 99(3), 100(2), 101(3), 102(3), 104(3), 106(2), 108, 110, 111, 117, 118(2), 122, 123, 125, 126, 127, 132, 134(2), 138, 20-B(3), 20-C(2)
JACKSON, 105
JAS. W., 23
JEFF., 13
JEFFERSON, 24
JNO M., 106
LARKIN J., 65
LAURA, 140
M.L., 130, 132
MARTHA J., 13
MARTHA L., 89
MARY, 24
MARY E., 65
MARY H., 89
MATH. F., 13
MATTIE E., 132
NANCY, 13, 106
ROBT, 13
T.J., 50(2)
T.W., 20-E
THOS., 23
W.A., 122
W.E., 130
W.F.M., 105
WM C., 140
BENTLEY
JANE W., 6
MARTHA M., 6
SAML, 6
BERKHART
GEO W., 131
MARENA, 131
N.C., 131
BERKS
SARAH, 75
BERNES
MARTIN, 86
MAY, 86
NAOMI, 86
BERRYMAN
JUDA, 115
WM, 115(2)
BETHEL
JOSEPH, 73
LUCY, 73
MAT, 73
BETTIS
E.S., 92, 97, 98, 100, 101(2), 102, 103,

104(4), 105(2), 106(2), 107(3), 108, 109, 112
BIBB
MARTIN, 15
BIBY
JOHN, 109(2)
NANCY, 109(2)
NICHOLAS, 109(2)
BICKER
FLORENCE L., 119
MARTHA ERECIA, 119

T.H., 119
BICKNELL
A.L., 56
A.R., 56
LARKIN, 62
M., 56
MARTHA E., 62
MYRINDA, 62
BIGGS
AUGUSTUS C., 70
JOHN L., 70
LYDIA, 70
BILBIE
CAROLINE, 67
ISABELLA, 67
JOSEPH, 67
BILEY
ALEXANDER, 128

EDWARD E., 135
HENDERSON, 135

LEFTWICH, 77
MARY BELL, 128
NANCY, 128
SARAH, 135
BILLINGS
ELIZA, 82
LUCY B., 81
M.J., 81
W.M., 81
BILLINGSLY
ELIZABETH, 42
SAMUEL T., 42
BILLIPS
ADELINE, 49
ALICE A., 34
E.L., 85
ELIZA, 85
FRANCIS, 34, 52
GEORGE, 34
GIDIEON, 85
JOHN, 34
KIAH, 49
NANCY, 34
NANNIE, 52
RHEW, 49
WESLEY, 34
BINGHAM
CHRIS T., 63

EMALINE, 63
HORACE L., 63
BIRCH
GEO W., 12, 127
MARTHA, 12
BIRCHET
GIDEON, 137
BIRCHFIELD
A., 14
ABR. R., 14
THOS., 14
BIRD
A., 15
AGINETH, 16
ANDREW A., 78
ANN, 72
B.F., 21
D.T., 13(12), 14(2), 19(2), 23, 24, 25, 27(4), 28, 29(2), 31(2), 32, 33, 37(2), 20-C(4), 20-D(5), 20-E, 20-F
B.W., 114
BENJ F., 34
BENJ T., 27(2), 38
BENJ. F., 21
BENJ. T., 12, 14(2), 19, 22, 34, 37, 20-D, 20-F
BENJAMIN T., 15(3), 16(3), 17(3), 18, 19(4), 20(3), 24, 25, 27, 34, 37, 38(2), 20-A(3), 20-B(3), 20-D
BLUFORD, 115
BLUFORD W., 19
C.J., 136
CATH., 20-B
CINTHIA, 127
CYNTHIA, 48, 78, 95
CYNTHIA J., 29, 60, 61
E.J., 20-C
ELIZABETH, 82, 88, 97
EMILY J., 20
F., 111
F.A., 26
HANNAH J., 48
HARMON W., 25
HILDA, 127
IDA A.H., 60
IRENA, 19
IRENE, 34
IRENE M., 107
J., 94
J.B., 82(2)
J.S.H., 107
JAMES, 72
JAMES O., 44
JAS W., 97
JNO S.H., 88, 97
JOHN, 15, 16, 27

JOHN S.H., 19
JOHN W., 20-C
JOSEPH H., 27
JULIA F., 15
JULIANA H., 14
L. VICTORIA, 110
LETHA A., 114, 115
LINA, 114
LIZZIE, 107
M.A.E., 26
MALINDA, 25, 44
MARTHA, 72
MARY, 110
MARY J., 82
MARY JANE, 101
MINERVA E., 34
NANCY, 111
NANCY J., 16
NANNIE A., 115
NENA, 19
NOMMIE LEE, 88
OSCAR, 137
PRICE K.M., 20-B
R.S., 127
RAISON A., 28
RHODA A., 19, 95
RICHARD, 82
RUFUS, 122
SALLY, 94
SARAH, 27
SARAH E., 61
SILAS J., 20
STEP G.J., 26
STEPHEN, 44, 101
STEPHEN J., 82
STEPHEN W., 25
STEVEN J., 122
SUSAN, 101, 122
SUSAN J., 82
SUSAN JANE, 111
TAYLOR, 110
THOS A., 20-C
THOS. A., 20
VINA, 14, 19
WILLIE JERNSHA JANE, 136
WM, 127
WM A., 48, 60, 61, 78, 95, 136
WM M., 20-B
BIRKY
DOMINEK, 112
BISHOP
A., 99, 126
ACY, 138
ASA, 126
BENJ. W., 11
BENJ. W.S., 12(3)
DORA, 99
MARTHA, 99, 126, 138
MOLLIE, 117
P.E., 131

ROBERT L., 138
WILLIE, 126
BIVINS
E.A., 136
LUTHER C., 136
R.H., 136
BIVIUS
A.E., 120
E.A., 120
R.H., 120
BLACKBURN
ELIZA, 89
JAS A., 89
JORDAN, 89
BLACKWELL
AMANDA, 128, 131
RUSH, 128
BLAKE
EUGENE, 77, 78(2), 80(2), 82(3), 92, 93, 95, 97, 115, 117, 119, 121(3), 122, 123, 125(2)
MARY V.E., 82
VIR BELLE, 82
W.E., 82
BLAKEY
CHARLOTTE, 77
HENRY, 77
JOHN, 77(2)
BLANCHARD
FRED, 138
HENRY H., 138
MARTIN V., 138
BLANKENSHIP
A.J., 64, 85, 137
A.M., 15, 16
ALBERT W., 90, 111
ALICE, 62
ALICE J., 87
ANDERSON, 114
ARDELIA, 85
BALLARD, 14, 62
BARRY, 10
C., 15
CATH., 16
CATHARINE, 2
CYNTHIA J., 71
CYNTHIA, 59, 105
DANIEL, 61
DARCUS, 19
DELILAH, 22
DELLA I., 136
E., 3, 14, 17, 26
E.G., 30
ED, 127
ED., 26
EDITH, 10
EDMOND, 16
EDWARD, 70
ELI H., 16, 60
ELI S., 52
ELIZA, 52

ELIZABETH, 16, 60, 79, 87, 20-B
ELLA M., 127
ELLEN, 54, 69
EMMA, 137
FRANCES E., 17
FRANCES J., 2
GASTON, 20-B
H., 16
H.W., 82
HANNAH, 33
HARRISON, 68, 79, 90, 111
HENRY, 136
HENRY C., 33
HENRY P., 70
HESTER, 127
J.E., 134
J.M., 105
J.N., 105
J.R., 126
JAMES, 79
JAMES M., 30
JAS A., 60
JAS M., 82
JASPER, 93
JENNIE, 52
JESSE, 16, 33
JOHN W., 54
JULIA, 51, 127
JULIA A., 18
JULIA ANN, 93
L., 4, 17, 19, 140, 20-C, 20-D
LARKIN, 61
LEANTHA, 18, 20-B, 20-E
LEWIS, 27, 32, 41
LOUISA, 79, 90, 111, 114
LOUISA J., 83
LUCINDA, 58, 60, 68
LUISA, 68
M., 4, 17, 19, 20-D
MARGARET, 114, 136

MARTHA, 22, 62, 83
MARTHA M., 20-B
MARY, 27, 32, 41, 61, 64
MARY E., 64
MARY OLA, 79
MINNIE B., 59
N., 3(2)
NANCY, 20
NOAH, 20, 79
NOAH G., 3
OLIE B., 60
OSCAR, 69, 87
OSCAR E., 17
P., 20-C

PASCHAL B., 53
PATRICK, 42
PHIL K., 105
R.A., 60, 82
R.G., 41
R.L., 87
R.M., 127
R.M.B., 105
RACHEL A., 105
REBECCA, 42, 124
REBECCA S., 20-C
REUBEN G., 32
RHODA H., 27
ROBERT M., 20-D
ROBT, 59
ROBT M., 71
S., 3, 17
S.M., 2
SARAH, 30, 87, 93(2)
SARAH E., 58
SARAH J., 82, 114
SHAD, 10
SILVESTER, 33
SLALIE, 137
STEPH., 14
STEPHEN, 16, 69
SUS., 26
SYNTHA, 127
THOMPSON, 3, 33, 87, 140
W.H., 114
WILEY B.W., 4
WILLIAM M., 15
WM H., 114
WM H.H., 83
WM K., 71
ZENA B., 105
ZORA E., 124
BLANTON
BARTLEY, 66
M.D., 71
NANNIE, 71
S.M., 71
S.N., 66
SARAH, 66
BLEDIUS
ALEY, 98
DAVID A., 98
NATHAN A., 98
BLESSING
ARTY, 131
CAROLINE, 99, 107, 120, 131
FANNIE, 120
JOHN, 131
LUCY E., 99
BLEVENS
DANIEL, 64
LAURA, 64
ROBT F., 64
BLIZZARD
MELVIN, 126
BOAG

JAMES, 10
TASHA S., 10
WILLIAM R., 10
BOARD
  EMMA, 105
  JAS A., 88
  NANCY, 88
  WM, 88
BOBER
  P.B., 11
BOBON
  P.B., 88
BOEHM
  CATHERINE, 112
  J.S., 90
  J.T., 90
  JOHN S., 112
  S.L., 112
  W.W., 90
BOGGESS
  JNO L., 35
  KINROD, 35
  M.A., 87
  MARGARET, 35, 73
  N.A.H., 87
  NIMROD, 73, 87
  PORTER W., 38
  RACHEL, 112
  SAML, 112
  W.P., 73
BOGGLESS
  D.E., 80
  POLLY, 80
  REUBEN, 80
BOGLE
  M.E., 116
BOLEN
  ANGELINE, 119
  G.W., 119
  ISAAC, 111
  JOHN C., 14
  M.E., 119
  MARVEL, 14
  MARY E., 111
  SARAH, 14
  T.J., 111
BOLES
  ALICE, 113
  JAMES, 113
  LITTLETON, 113
BOLIN
  ALEN H., 115
  ALLEN H., 64
  ANNIE J., 76
  BETTIE, 76
  E.M., 78
  ELIZA T.T., 37
  ELIZABETH, 37(3), 43, 115
  ELIZTH, 64
  ELMIRA C., 78
  FLOYD A., 37
  G.S., 76, 78, 111

GEORGE W., 43
HOLLIE, 122
ISABELL, 108
ISABELLA, 45, 111, 122
J.J., 45, 108, 111, 122
J.L., 95
JAMES W., 45
JANE, 91, 111
JAS W., 60
JESSE, 91
JESSIE, 111
MARY E., 37
MARY JANE, 64
MOLLIE B., 111
N.L., 108
R.G., 115(2)
SARAH E., 91
WILLIAM, 37, 43
WM, 37(2), 38(2)
BOLING
  ANDERSON, 40
  BARBER B., 40
  CHARLES A., 5
  DEMENTH, 40
  ELIZTH, 6, 8, 26
  HENRY, 63
  ISABEL, 90
  J.J., 90
  JACKSON, 63, 110
  JAMES, 8
  JAMES J., 8
  JOHN, 5
  LUCINDA E., 8
  LULA, 90
  MARY C., 20-C
  MINERVA A., 26
  RUTH, 8
  SARAH, 5
  SUSAN V., 110
  URIAH A., 6
  WILLIAM A., 4
  WM, 6, 8, 26
BOLTON
  ELIZABETH, 8
  EMMA E., 52
  FANNIE L., 42
  JACOB, 8
  JOSIE M., 73
  MARY, 42, 73
  MARY F., 52, 90
  MATTHEW, 42, 90
  MATTHEW W., 52
  MATTHEW, 73
  MATTHEW W., 8
  WIRT, 90
BOND
  BETTIE A., 72
  J.E., 72
  WM P., 72
BONDS
  MARY, 79
  THOS, 79

WM, 79
BONHAM
  A.J., 109
  A.P., 109
  ALBERT P., 79
  AMANDA, 70, 85, 107
  AMANDA S., 72
  ANDREW R., 72
  DARINDA, 120
  E.W., 109
  ELIZA EDMONIA, 138

  JNO, 107
  JNO F., 85
  JOHN F., 72
  JOS F., 85
  LAURA M., 107
  NEHEMIAH, 79
  PENDLETON, 138
  REGINA, 79
  SARAH M., 70
  VICTORIA, 120
  W.H., 120
BONSLANG
  MINTERY R., 28
BOOK
  HENRY L., 60
  WM HENRY, 60
BOOKER
  BOSTON, 128
  C.H., 104
  CALVIN, 95
  EMMA, 95
  MARY, 95
  SYLVIA, 75
BOONE
  MAGDALINE, 4
BOOSE
  ARAMINTA, 63
  LEW, 109
  N.A., 109
  NANCY A., 63
  W.G., 109
  WM G., 63
BOOTH
  CHARLES, 51
  ELLEN, 67, 86
  JAS R., 67
  JOHN E., 114
  JOHN W., 86
  L.J., 114
  THOMAS, 67
  THOS, 86
  W.B., 120(3), 121(2), 125, 128, 140
  WILLIAM C., 10, 11(2), 14
  WM, 59
BOOTHE
  ELISHA, 101
  JOS W., 101

MARY J., 101
NANCY, 115
RILEY T., 115
W.B., 122, 123, 130(2)
W.G., 115
BOOZE
  EASTER JANE, 73
  NANCY, 73
  WM, 73
BORSDICKS
  ANN, 102
  SUSIE, 102
  WILBURN, 102
BOSTWICK
  ALICE, 102
  IRA H., 102
  PELERIAM, 102
BOURNE
  ANGELINA, 113
  CHAS A., 113
  E.K., 113
  EMMET K., 77
  FELIX L., 113
  H., 113
  H.A., 77
  JULIA, 113
  JULIA F., 77
  S.W., 125
BOWDEN
  ELIZABETH, 22
  J.C., 54
  JAMES G., 41(2), 113(2)
  JAS G., 133
  JOHN, 22
  JOHN L., 54
  LUCINDA, 41, 113
  MARY L., 133
  MARY JANE, 54
  SARAH, 11
BOWEN
  AMANDA, 136
  ARDELIA, 136
  GEO, 136
  JONATHAN, 58
  MARY, 140(2)
  PHOEBE W., 58
  R.T., 135
  THOS, 135
BOWER
  DAVID, 46
  FLORA ALICE, 122
  JAS T., 46
  JENNIE D., 111
  NANCY, 46
  R.H., 111, 122
  S.E., 111
  SARAH E., 122
BOWERS
  ELIZABETH, 7
  JAMES, 7
  LUCY W., 7
BOWES

JOSEPH, 75
L.A., 75
MARY E., 75
BOWINE
  ELLIS M., 105
  HOUSTIN, 105
  JULIA, 105
BOWLES
  AMANDA A., 96
  COLUMBUS, 81
  DANIEL, 81
  LUCINDA, 81
  MARY, 96
  MARY A., 78
  MARY LOUISA, 78

  MELVINA, 110
  RICHD, 110
  SALLY A., 110
  THOS T., 78
  WM, 96
BOWLING
  A.J., 84(2), 139
  A.K., 91
  A.L., 95
  A.W., 44, 51(2), 64, 82, 94, 99(2)
  ALBERT C., 39
  ALLA, 139
  ALLEN H., 20-A
  ALLIE, 84
  ALMANSIE, 103
  ANDREW, 101
  ANDREW J., 103
  ARDELIA, 43
  ARMINDA R., 51
  ARTHELLA E., 41
  C.J., 132
  CHAS A., 70
  CHAS. A., 39
  DEMARIES, 44
  DEMARRIS, 80
  DEWARIUS, 47
  ELISHA, 16
  ELIZABETH, 12(2), 40
  ELIZTH, 20-A
  EMMA L., 79
  FLOURNOY, 99
  G.W., 109, 120
  GEO S., 13
  GEO W., 51
  HELEN, 100
  IDA, 139
  IDA M., 109
  IOWA M., 64
  ISABELLA, 71
  ISSAC A., 69
  J.J., 71
  J.L., 71
  JACKSON, 17
  JAMES, 42
  JAMES W., 40
  JANE, 13(2), 33, 82

JAS H., 80
JAS., 20
JENNIE F., 95
JESSE, 13, 33
JESSE I., 18, 82
JNO, 13
JNO W., 44
JOHN, 4, 18, 26, 44, 100, 20-B
JOSEPHINE V., 70
JOSHUA, 16, 17
KEZIAH C., 20
L.B., 94
LELIA C., 54
LESSIE, 129
LILLY B., 120
LUCINDA, 44, 51(2), 82, 94, 99, 101
LUCINDA A., 103
LUCY, 70
LUCY M., 39
LURINDA A., 82
M.A., 44, 48, 54, 69
M.H., 122
M.J., 109
MALINDA A., 48
MARTHA, 120
MARY E., 84
MINNIE E., 132
NANCY, 16, 17, 26
ORPHA, 82
P.A., 132
PURVIS A., 29
R.J., 48, 54, 115
REBECCA J., 41, 69, 91
ROBT I., 100
RUTH M., 20, 42
RUTHA M., 33
S., 18
S.G.C., 42
SALLIE, 26, 20-B
SALLY, 4
SAML A., 101
SARAH, 13
SARAH J., 20-B
T.J., 95
THOS J., 79
THOS. J., 13
U.A., 91
URIAH A., 41
WATSON C., 47
WM, 12, 40, 20-A
WM A., 47, 80
WOODSON, 129
BOWLLING
  ELIZA E., 28
BOWLS
  DANL, 80
  LOUCINDA, 80
  NELSON, 80
BOWMAN
  FRANCIS H., 112
  H.W., 112

MATTIE, 109
PETER, 109
ROSALIE, 112
W.T., 109
BOYD
  A.J., 80, 89, 116(2)
  ANDREW J., JR, 116
  CHLOE, 15
  FANNIE, 80
  FANNY, 77
  HENRY, 62
  JOHN R., 57
  MANERVA, 17
  MARGARET, 80, 89, 116

  MARINDA, 57, 73
  MARY M., 73
  S.E., 89, 90
  THOS., 17
  W.W., 89(2)
  WILLIAM H., 17
  WM H., 73
  WM S., 57
BRACKENBRIDGE

  CAREY, 78
  ELLA, 78
  MATILDA, 78
BRADBURY
  ELDRIDGE, 136
  ELIZABETH, 136
  WM T., 136(2)
BRADLEY
  ANN, 67
  C.F., 110
  C.H., 110
  CHAS F., 116
  DAVID, 67
  HENRY W., 67
  M.J., 110, 116
  SALLY J., 116
BRADY
  ESTHER, 82
  FRANK D., 141
  ISAIAH W., 104
  JOHN, 82
  SAML, 104
BRAFF
  JOHN, 2
BRAG
  J.W., 112
  JOHN, 20-D
  THOMAS S., 12
BRAGG
  A.J., 97, 115
  ABRAHAM, 12
  ELIZABETH, 7
  JOHN, 1(3), 2(3), 4(7), 9(2), 10, 21, 23, 24, 26, 45, 20-D, 20-F
  LIZZIE, 115
  LUTHER R., 97

MALINDA, 97, 115
MICHAEL, 7
RACHEL, 12
SYLVESTER, 7
DRAKE
  CHAS C., 114(2)
  ISRAEL, 114
  LOUISA, 114
BRAMMER
  A. CHARLOTTE, 46

  AD. R., 21, 20-F
  ANDERSON, 10
  ANNA, 2(2), 3, 5
  CHAS C., 78
  EFFIE, 111
  EMALINE, 20-A
  EVA, 77
  GREEN C., 19
  J., 20-C
  J.H., 19
  JAMES, 17, 46, 77
  JAMES A., 57
  JAS, 3, 5
  JAS A., 3, 78
  JESSE, 21, 20-F
  JESSE H., 42
  JNO, 2
  JNO L., 129
  JOHN, 17, 141
  JOHN H., 42
  JOHN L., 34, 111
  JON, 20-A
  JONATHAN, 10, 34, 129
  LOU, 77
  LOUISA, 57, 78
  LUCY M., 5
  M., 20-C
  MADALINE, 20-C
  MARIA, 10, 34, 20-A
  MARIAH, 129
  MARY, 19
  NANCY, 24
  OFFIE J., 141
  SARAH, 17, 21, 141, 20-F
  SARAH E., 111
  SARAH L., 42
  THOS F., 57
BRANCH
  ADAM, 108(2)
  ELLA, 116
  FANNIE, 96
  JANE, 108
BRANDART
  T.J., 79
BRANDON
  T.A., 94
  T.J., 65, 66(2), 92(2), 93, 94(4), 95(2), 96, 101(2), 102
BRANDORS

T.J., 92
BRANHAM
BEVERLY, 17
JAMES N., 17
RACHEL, 17
BRATTEN
MELISSA V., 29
BRATTON
ALLEN I., 107
B.P., 69
ELIZABETH, 78
ELIZTH, 83
JOHN R., 78
L.R., 77
LEWIS D., 47
MARY, 3
MARY E., 47(3), 69, 77
MARY ELIZTH, 107

MARY V., 47
SARAH E., 47
THOMAS, 3, 47, 78
THOS, 3, 47(2), 69, 77, 83, 107
WM J., 83
BRAY
C.D., 83
FANNIE, 68
LELIA M., 70
M.H., 68(2), 70, 79
NANNIE J., 79
VERONE P., 68
VINNIE R., 60
BRAZEIL
SAMUEL, 124
BREAZEALE
CHAS, 84
SALLIE, 84
THOS E., 84
BRECKENRIDGE

CARRIE, 135
CARY, 49
GEORGE R., 135
MATILDA, 49, 135
SELENIA, 49
BREEDLOVE
C.M., 119
J., 119
L LEWELLYN, 119
BREWER
HOPKINS, 71
SALLIE J., 71
SUSAN A., 71
BRIANS
ALBERT P., 14
CHLOE, 14
J.M., 14
BRICE
NED, 134
REBECCA, 134
ROSETTA, 134
BRICKEY

CHRISTINA, 70
E.G., 70
L.D., 70
BRID
B.W., 92
BENJAMIN T., 20-B
JENNIE H., 92
L.A., 92
BRIDGES
MARY, 1
MARY C., 57
N.T., 70
NED T., 53(2), 57
ROBT E., 70
SALLIE P., 70
TUPPS, 57
WILLIAM, 1
WILLIAM L., 1
WM M., 74
BRIGGS
ALICE, 119
D.M., 119
EFFIE, 129
GEO, 129
L.C., 129
M.E., 119
BRILLHART
JACOB, 16(6)
BRINDLE
AMANDA R., 62
CHAS A., 62
IRVIN DANL, 62
MARGARET, 112
BRINKEY
J.H., 111
RACHEL, 111
THEODOSIA, 111
BRINKLEY
GREEN, 32
HEN, 108
HENRY C., 108
ISHAM, 1
JAS H., 32, 76
NANCY, 32
NELLY, 1
RACHEL, 108
RACHEL A., 76
SARAH E., 76
BRITTON
EDIE, 72
R.C., 72
SCOT, 72
BROADNAX
ADAM, 64
LEE, 64
LOUISA, 64
BROCE
B.P., 98
MARY, 98
SUNDY M., 98
BROOKMAN
AUGUSTUS, 55, 89, 106, 138

DECATUR, 106
ETTABELL, 54
G., 54
GUS, 135
J.P., 138
JOSIE, 135
LEE, 89
LENA, 136
MARY M., 54, 55
MOLLIE, 89
NANNIE B., 55
R.G., 135
R.L., 136
RACHEL, 106, 138
BROOKS
A.J., 43, 44
A.T., 42(2), 45(3), 47, 50
AARON, 84
AMANDA, 125, 132
BETIE J., 77
CASBY MAY, 124
CHAS F., 102
CLOUGH M., 102
ELIZABETH, 104
EMARILO, 104
EMALINE, 102
FANNIE, 77
FRANCIS, 125
JAMES H., 132
JAS, 124
JENNIE, 84
JOHN, 7, 84
JOHN W., 7
LIZZIE, 93
MARGARETTA, 124

MARY, 93
MARY A., 98
NANCY, 7
NATHAN, 125, 132
PAULINA, 105
POLLY, 84
ROBT L., 98
ROSIE E., 98
SALLY, 84
WILLIAM, 104
WM, 93, 105
BROTHERTON

ELIZABETH, 12
ROBERT H., 12
THOMAS, 12
BROUSE
ANNIE G., 127
HENRY H., 127
BROWN
A.E., 86
A.J., 117, 118(2), 120, 121, 123, 126
A.J., REV., 117(2)
ADOLPHUS E., 51
ALEX, 44

ALICE, 34
ALLEN, 4, 28, 62
ALLEN W., 52
ANDERSON, 7
ANDREW, 108
ANDREW B., 5
ARCHIE, 82
BIRNEY, 135
BOYD M., 99
C.A., 128, 129, 131, 132
C.R., 57, 75(3), 78, 118
C.S.W., 110
C.W., 109
CARRIE, 75
CATHARINE, 44
CHAS, 86
CHAS E., 135
CHAS I., 64
COLUMBIA, 6
CYNTHIA, 135
CYRIS M., 44
E.A., 135
E.G., 44
E.H., 21, 23, 29, 129, 20-F
E.J., 118
EDNA, 108
ELIZA ANN, 82
ELIZABETH, 7, 54, 66, 95, 99, 102
ELIZABETH B., 96
ELIZTH, 6, 36
ELLA, 108
ELLEN, 109
EVAN H., 3, 4(3), 5(2), 6(3), 7(3), 9, 13(2), 18(3), 19(2), 20(3), 21, 22, 24, 26(2), 27(2), 28(2), 29, 30(3), 32, 35(4), 36, 37, 38, 39, 40, 41, 42, 43(3), 44(2), 45(3), 47(5), 48, 49(3), 50, 51(5), 52(2), 53(2), 55(3), 57(2), 59(4), 61(3), 64, 123, 20-A, 20-B(2), 20-C, 20-F
EVANS H., 3(2)
F.J., 113, 131, 133(2), 135, 139(2), 141(2)
FANNIE, 108
FLOYD, 131
FLOYD J., 127
FRANK, 109, 114
GEO, 131
GEO P., 6, 14, 20
GEO W., 5
GEORGE, 120
GEORGE P., 20-C

GEORGIA, 110
HANNAH, 54
HANSON, 95
HARRIET, 120
HARRIET A., 120
HARVEY D., 132
HENRY, 3, 61
ISABELL H., 18
J., 20-C
J.F., 102
J.H., 70, 95, 110
J.K., 118
JACOB H., 95
JAMES, 22, 135
JAMES L., 36
JANE, 61
JAS C., 132
JENNIE, 64
JIM, 109
JNO, 132
JOHN, 6, 7, 76, 108
JOHN A., 14
JOHN W., 7, 11, 46, 52, 54, 55
JOSIE, 62, 86
JULIA, 114
K.A., 124
KATE, 90
L., 18
LETHA A., 131
LEVINA, 8
LEWIS, 113, 127
LILLIE E., 55
LOUISA J., 28
LUCINDA, 4, 5, 11, 127
LUCY, 76
M., 72
M.E., 123
M.J., 128
MALINDA, 113
MARCHALL B., 36
MARGARET, 3, 6, 8
MARGARET B., 6
MARGARET J., 20-D

MARGT, 10
MARIA A., 48
MARSHAL, 96, 99
MARSHALL, 102
MARTHA, 64, 72
MARTHA E., 43, 47, 55
MARTHA J., 15, 52, 20-D
MARY, 28, 109
MARY A., 64
MARY ANN, 96
MARY E., 17, 62, 64, 120
MARY J., 129
MARY SUE, 128
MARY V.M., 28
McDONALD, 84
MEDA G., 72

MIRAM, 5
MOLLIE L., 89
NANA, 76
NANNIE E., 109
NANNIE M., 47
NED, 22
NELLY, 22
NOKE, 82
PARIS, 64
PATTEN R., 48
PATTON R., 10
POLINA, 135
PRISCILLA, 7
R., 20-C
R.J., 102
RANDALL, 76
REBECCA, 44
REBECCA J., 6
RHODA M., 46, 54, 55
RICHARD, 44
RINDA, 132
ROBT LUTHER, 123

ROLEN, 90
ROSA, 86
ROSS, 54
RUSH H., 64
S.P., 84
S.W., 88
SALLIE A., 36
SALLIE P., 6
SARAH, 20
SARAH P., 14
SARAH W., 48
SHRILDIA, 114
SMAL, 34
SUSAN, 88
THOMAS, 6, 8
THOS, 3, 10, 66
THOS R., 66
THOS W., 55
TISHY, 90
VIRGINIA D., 43
VIRGINIA F., 20
VIRGINIA L., 129
W.H., 128
W.H.H., 129
W.R., 88
W.S., 120
WILLIAM S., 36
WILLIE, 108
WILLIE B., 76
WM, 4, 5, 11, 18, 61
WM A., 46
WM J., 84
WM S., 120
BROWNING
L.H., 66
J.W., 72, 136
JOHN V., 66
L.D., 88
LUCINDA, 66
MARY J., 88

T.B., 138
THOS B., 88
BROYLES
A.W., 49, 61
AMANDA, 46, 49, 55, 61, 83
ANDREW W., 46, 55
ELIZA J., 64
ELIZABETH, 107
ERASMUS, 20-B
ERASTUS, 119
H.S., 107
HARRIET A., 121
IDA E., 121
J.G., 93, 136
JOHN S., 90
JOSEPHINE, 119
JOSHUA G., 63, 116
JOSIE B., 63
KATHERINE, 85
L.M., 109, 110(6), 111, 112
LAURA V., 83
LEROY, 25, 80, 90, 107, 121(2), 140
LIZZIE, 121(2), 137, 140
LUCINDA, 25, 31, 32
LUCINDA JANE, 31

LUCINDA O., 61
M., 20-B
M.A., 4
M.C., 136
M.J., 119, 137
M.O., 93
MAHALA M.A., 93
MANDA, 116
MARY A., 20, 140
MARY E., 49
MARY J., 4
MAY J., 136
OLIVIA, 63
OLIVIA K., 46
OLLIE, 116
R.B., 80
REBECCA A., 55
S.E., 80
S.M., 111
SALLIE A., 28
SARAH E., 90
SOLOMON D., 25
THOMPSON, 25, 31, 32
W.A., 83
W.C., 85
W.H., 85
WASH, 20
WASHG, 4
WASHINGTON, 25, 20-B

WM J., 137
WM R., 32
BRUCE

AGNES, 71
CATHARINE J., 48
CATHERINE, 7
CHARLES, 48
CORA L., 87
ELIZABETH, 88
ESTELL B., 48
GARLAND, 71
HERALD FULTON, 88

J.B., 115, 116(2), 117, 118(2), 122, 123(2)
JACK, 121
JAMES, 88
JOANNA, 101
JOHN, 7
JOSIAH G., 22
MARTHA, 73, 101, 112
MARTHA C., 22
MARTHA H., 48, 87
MARY, 22
POLLY, 48
SARAH J., 73
W.W., 87, 101
WILLIAM W., 7
WILLIE, 112
WILLIS, 71
WM, 112
WM A., 48
WM W., 73
BRUGH
HUDSON L., 124
JACOB, 124
LUVNA, 124
BRUMFIELD
JANE, 87
T.W., 87
WM R., 87
BRUNTY
JAMES, 11(2)
LUMMA L., 25
MATILDA J., 11
SARAH, 11
TABITHA, 11(2)
BRUSE
CORA L., 103
JOS N., 103
M.J., 103
BRUSTER
B.J., 131(2)
G.W., 132
R.B., 90, 131, 132
REBECCA M., 132
RHODA J., 90
SARAH, 90, 131, 132
BRYAN
BENNETT C., 118
JAMES K., 118
SUSAN, 118
BRYANS
ARAMINTA E., 34
CHLOE, 34

JNO, 34
BRYANT
A., 141
BETTIE, 136
FRANK, 136
GABRIEL, 82
H.G., 141
J.G., 141
J.M., 62
JAS E., 62
L., 141
MARY A., 138
MATTIE A., 88
R.A., 122, 129, 131
S.R., 138
SARAH J., 62
W.C., 136
WM F., 138
BUCHANAN
A., 135
ANDREW, 83
C.J., 135
CAROLINE, 87
CYRUS, 83
DASIS, 138
EDWARD, 87
EFFIE D., 135
ELIZA, 138
GEO, 87, 99
HENRY, 71
KIZIAH, 71
MARY, 83
P.S., 71, 138
S.E., 93
W.H., 99, 138
BUCHANON
ANNIE, 88
GEORGE, 88
MARY L., 88
BUCKLAND
HUGH, 58
JOHN, 5, 21, 20-F
JOSEPH J., 21, 20-F
KAIBURN, 20-E
LORENZO D., 5
MALINDA, 20-E
MARTHA, 58
MARY, 5
NANCY, 21, 20-F
STEPHEN, 20-E
BUCKLEY
J.K., 119
JAMES E., 119
MARGARET, 119
BUCKNER
A.J., 68
R.J., 63, 64, 65(3), 67(5), 69(3)
BUDD
ANN, 127
ANNIE, 141
DORA L., 127
JERRY, 141

THOMAS, 127, 141
BUEL
BETTIE, 105
DOUGLASS, 105
SAMUEL, 105
BUFFALOW
SUSAN, 49
WILLIAM, 49
WILLIE, 49
BUGGER
WM, 75(2)
BUICE
CHARLES, 25
DANL H., 28
HENLEY, 39
JAMES, 39
MARY E., 25
SARAH, 25
BULLARD
CHESTER, 1
BUMGARDNER
ANN, 65
GEORGE, 65, 67
LORIE, 65
MARY, 67
O.E., 98
OVID, 67
BUNYON
NANCY, 11
RICHARD, 11
STEPHAN, 11
BURCH
B.Z., 76
CATHARINE, 129
DAVE, 140(2)
DAVID A., 112
GEO W., 71, 76, 102, 112
GEORGE W., 65
JOS, 94(2), 129
KATHERINE, 94
MARY, 129
MOLLIE L., 71
NANNIE, 102
S.J., 102
SAREPTA, 71
SORRAPTRA, 112
WILLIE, 65
BURCHETT
ELIZABETH, 42, 88
GIDEON, 29
GILFORD, 42, 106
JAMES, 84
L., 105
LAWSON, 42, 88
LAWSON G., 88
BURDETT
ADELADE, 24
ANNA W., 52
CA., 20-C
CHAS H., 52, 91
CYNTHIA J., 24

IRENE, 91
JOS C., 52
JOSEPH, 24, 91, 20-C
MARY E., 20-C
NANCY H., 20-C
SY., 20-C
VIRGINIA B., 114
BURDISS
FANNIE M., 82
JAMES, 82
MARTHA, 82
BURDITT
A., 17
DICY, 16
J.C., 17, 24
JOSEPH, 16
JOSEPH C., 16
L., 24
MARTHA L., 24
WILLIAM J., 17
BURDITTE
ARRENA W., 67
EMMA C., 67
JOS C., 67
BURGE
JNO, 26
LUCINDA, 26
N., 26
BURGERS
ADA C., 105
JAS C., 105
BURGESS
ALMEDA H., 28
AMANDA, 106
DANIEL C., 25
DANL E., 106
FLORENCE L., 106
GEO W., 43, 79
HIRAM, 25, 43
J.C., 115
NANCY, 25, 43, 115
S. MAUD, 115
WM, 86
BURK
JAMES, 80
SELAH, 80
WALLACE, 80
BURKET
ABRAHAM, 100
ANN, 49
B.S., 49
GEORGE, 49
SOFIA H., 100
T.J., 100
BURKHARDT
W.H., 74, 78
WM H., 77
BURKHART
W. HULLIHAN, 86
BURKS
ADAMS, 105
ANN, 81
ARTHELIA, 80

B.B., 129
CARL B., 129(2)
F.M., 129
JOSEPH, 81
M.E., 77
R.S., 77
SCOTT, 105
SUTTON, 50
U.L., 77
VICTORIA, 105
WM, 81
BURNETT
ADELINE, 38
AINCETTA A., 38
B.C., 38
BENJ., 56
CYNTHIA C., 58
ELIZA, 66
F., 121
J.A., 139
J.B., 57, 58, 121
J.W.S., 121
JAMES A., 30
JAS A., 82
JEMIMA, 50
JOHN, 82
JOSIAH, 50
LILLIE N., 139
LORENZO D., 50
LOUVENIA J., 57
M.N., 139
MARY, 56
OLIBIA (SIC) T., R2
S.D., 57, 58
BURNETTE
JEREMIAH, 69
LAYNE, 69
SARAH, 69
BURNEY
JAMES, 56
ROBT, 56
SARAH, 56
BURNS
ELIZA O., 85
JAMES, 65
MICHAEL, 65
NORAH, 65
SARAH O., 85
BURROUGHS
L.R., 81
TAZEWELL W., 81
WM T., 81
BURROW
J.A., 113, 114, 116
BURTON
A.D., 70
ALFRED E., 70
ARDELL, 70
BEN H., 45
COBE, 110
CORA, 139
DAISY LILLIAN, 100
EASTER, 63

ELIAS, 30, 32, 47(2), 63
ELISH, 115
ELISHA, 43, 110
ELVIRA, 118, 135
ELVIRA A., 96
ELVIRA E., 86
ERNEST L., 137(2)
GEO, 139
GEO H., 100, 124, 129
GEORGE S., 135
H.B., 80
H.P., 84, 100, 139
JAS C., 110
JOANNA B., 115
JOHN, 75, 135, 139
JOHN W., 32, 110, 134
JULIA ANN, 30
JULIA B., 118, 135
JULIA E., 80
LUCINDA, 110
M.A., 84
M.L., 134
MARTHA, 43, 115, 135
MARTHA J., 110, 134, 139
MARTIN LUTHER, 134

MARY, 137
MARY A., 80, 100, 139
MARY E., 139
MARY H., 103
MAUD V., 124
NANCY R., 96
NANNIE E., 129
NANNIE J., 103
NORA ANN, 100
PEAVIS, 137
RHODA C., 43
S.J., 84
SALLY, 30
SAML F., 45
SARAH, 32, 47
SARAH C., 86
SARAH L., 47
SARAH R., 45
SUE, 75
TRAVIS, 103
VES, 129
VESTINA J., 100
W.H., 135
WM E., 63
WM H., 86, 96, 118
BUSKILL
FRANCES, 128
BUTLER
CAROLINE, 95
CHARLES W., 32
D., 15(2)
DAVIEN, 32
GEO, 103
IDA D., 95
JAMES H., 15

JAS H., 93, 98
JOEL A., 19, 62, 66
L.E., 98
LINA, 131
LIZZIE, 131
LOCHIE, 66
LOUISA, 19
LUCY N., 62
LUTHER L., 93
M.E., 93, 98
MARINDA, 20
MARTHA A., 15
MARY, 103
MATILDA, 134
NANCY J., 20-C
NANNIE, 103
P., 15(2), 19
PASCAL, 28
POWELL, 20, 32, 20-C
REBECCA J., 20-C
RICHARD, 110
ROBT MARSHALL, 134

S.E., 66
SARAH E., 62
VEROCA, 20
Z.R., 89, 131
ZACHARIAH R., 95

ZONA M., 89
BUTT
ABRAM, 97
CHAS W., 102
GEORGE A., 48
GILES M., 42
HARRISON, 42(2), 48
LUCRETIA, 42(2)
PEGGY, 97
R., 102
RANSOM, 102
VIRGINIA C., 102
WM E., 42
WM HARRISON, 97

BUTTERWORTH

CHARLES E., 111
J.H.T., 138
JULIE A., 111
MARY J., 138
SARAH E., 111
VIRGINIA F., 138
BUTTREY
J.F., 52
J.T., 52
BUTTRY
JOSEPH, 125
MARY, 42, 125
NAT, 125
NATHANIEL, 42
SUSAN A., 42
BYRD
ALBERT, 141

ARCH A., 108
CYNTHIA, 37
D.M., 141
EMMA S., 108
FRANCIS, 108
JOHN S., 50
JOS B., 50
MARY E., 37
OSCAR, 137
SALLIE, 141
SARAH C., 50
STEPHEN, 137
SUSAN, 137
WM, 37
BYRONSIDE
DELILAH S., 1
ISAAC, 1
MARY, 1

-C-

CABELL
FOUNTAIN, 140
MARIA, 140
WM, 140
CADE
ELIZABETH, 32
GEORGE W., 32
CADLE
A.E., 128
AMY, 128
DANIEL, 21, 20-F
ELIZABETH, 21, 23, 20-F
FRANCES J., 5
JAMES, 5
JOHN A., 128
JOHN H., 12
JULIA, 12
LUCINDA M., 12
MARTIN, 21, 23, 20-F
REBECCA, 23
SARAH, 5
CADWALANDER
FRANCES, 121
JAS, 121
LUCY, 121
CAHILL
ELIZ., 50
ELIZABETH A., 73
ELIZTH A., 58
NANNIE J., 58
PERRY G., 50, 73
PERRY J., 50, 58, 73
CAIN
CHAS, 134
CHS, 74
M.P., 134
MADISON, 74
MARIAH, 74, 134
CALAHAN
ABNER C., 20-D

P., 20-D
STEPHEN E., 20-D
CALANDER
ALLIE E., 139
ANN, 109, 139
SUSAN, 109
WM, 109, 139
CALAWAY
ANNIE, 86
GRANVILLE, 2
MARY, 2
PARTHENIA, 86
SIMEON, 86
SUSAN, 2
CALBIRD
JOHN T., 51
CALDWELL
ALBERT F., 101
ANN, 36, 51, 67, 134
ARAMINTA, 20-B
CHARLES P., 116
D.A., 39
E.A., 66, 101
ED, 25
EDNA, 113
EDWARD, 39, 44, 50
ELIZA, 8, 15, 22, 24, 38, 98
ELIZABETH, 43
ELIZABETH A., 41, 56
ELVIRA V., 36
EMENIRA, 41
EMMA, 38
EUNICE A., 132
F., 20-A
F.M., 37
FANNIE K., 115
FRANCES, 81
FRANCIS, 21, 20-F
FRANCIS M., 37
G.W., 66, 73
GEO E., 50
GEO W., 43, 56, 98, 101
GEO W.E., 41
GEORGE W., 41
GLEN, 96, 115, 130, 132
HARPER W., 44
HARRIET O.O., 81
HUGH, 21, 37, 81, 20-A, 20-F
J.H., 57, 79
J.R., 132
JACOB, 116
JAMES, 41, 113
JAMES M., 25
JAS H., 56
JENNIE, 79
JENNIE L., 106
JNO, 24, 38, 98
JNO R., 130
JOHN, 8, 15, 22, 38

JOHN D., 43
JOSEPH, 44
JULIA, 79
LOUISA, 106, 107
M.F., 41
MAD, 67
MADISON A., 36, 51, 134
MANELIUS, 15
MANELIUS C., 22, 23
MARGARET, 25, 39, 44, 50
MARGARET A., 51

MARY, 44
MARY A., 8
O.E., 44
OLIVA A., 23
POLLY, 113
PRISCILLA, 38
ROBT, 115
RUTHA J., 38
S.A., 132
SAML. G.W., 21, 20-F
SARAH, 115, 130
SARAH A., 96
SARAH E., 24
SARAH J., 67, 116
SARAH L., 20-A
SARAH V., 11
SARAH W., 57
SOFA, 27
SOPHIA, 11
SOPHS, 14
SQUIRE, 63
SUE E., 38
W.B., 134
W.H., 131
WILLIAM, 11, 38(2)
WM, 14, 27, 106, 107
WM H., 66
WM J., 96
CALENDER
ELIZA, 44
GEORGE, 44
M.C., 26
SUSAN, 26
CALES
EPHRAIM, 56
JAMES, 32
JOHN, 56
MARY, 56
SARAH, 32
WM H., 32
CALFEE
A.B., 95, 137
A.J., 79, 84, 95
AGNES C., 9
AGNES J., 54
ALICE, 139
AUGUSTUS B., 45
BAL, 139

BELLE, 95
CATHARINE F., 29
CHAS W., 35
CHAS. W., 25
CHLOE, 139
EASTER ANN, 50
ELIZABETH, 23, 44, 49, 71, 95
ELZTH, 33
ESTHER A., 8
ESTHER F., 32
ESTHER JANE, 23
EVALINE, 20-A
FANNIE J., 58
H.S., 68
HANNAH, 20-D
HENRY, 9, 97, 100
HENRY S., 11, 58
JACKSON, 20-D
JAMES, 1(10), 2(4), 3, 4(4), 5(4), 6(3), 7(2), 8(2), 9(7), 10(3), 11(6), 12(2), 14, 15(3), 16(2), 17(2), 19, 20(2), 21, 23, 25(4), 26, 27, 28, 29(2), 30, 31, 32, 33(3), 34(3), 35(6), 37, 38(2), 39(2), 40, 41(2), 42(2), 43, 44(2), 46, 47, 48(2), 49(2), 50, 51, 52, 53, 20-A(5), 20-B(2), 20-C, 20-D, 20-F
JANE, 9, 11, 32, 35, 54, 58, 59
JANE C., 8
JANE P., 45, 51
JAS, 43, 53, 71, 95
JAS L., 59
JAS., 14, 29, 42, 45, 46, 52, 53(2)
JOHN, 21, 54, 20-F
JOHN A., 20-A
JOSEPH M., 79
L.J., 58, 68
LAURA F., 49
LOUCINDA N., 53
LOULA N., 84
M.F., 120
MAGGIE, 79, 84
MARGARET, 95
MARY A., 44
MARY ELLEN, 58
MARY F., 76
MARY MARGT., 21, 20-F

MATILDA, 27
MATILDA D., 25
MATILDA E., 35
NANCY D., 25, 35
NANNIE C., 76

NORA, 137
PATSY, 39
REBECCA, 8, 9
RUSSEL K., 51
RUTLEDGE, 8
RUTLEGE, 50
S.L., 100
S.T., 27
SAML, 9
SAML L., 100
SAML T., 8, 9, 25
SAML., 8
SAMUEL T., 11
SARAH, 71, 97, 100
SARAH F., 25, 35
STELLA M., 120
THOS J., 95
V.B., 27
VIRGINIA, 21, 137, 20-F
VIRGINIA L., 25
W.D., 120
WALKER, 97
WILLIAM, 33
WILLIE E., 68
WILSON D., 32, 45, 51, 58, 59
WM, 20-A
WM D., 76
WM G., 50
CALIVER
AMANDA, 81
JOS, 81
JOSEPH, 81
CALLAHAN
BEN, 103
ESTELLA, 103
J.W., 20-E
MARTHA, 103
CALLANDER
JULIA, 22
SARAH, 37
SUSAN, 22, 37
CALLAWAY
ELIZTH, 13
GRANVILLE, 13
J.F., 69
J.R., 69
LUTICIA, 117
MARY, 69
CALLENDER
MATILDA N., 20-B
SUSAN, 20-B
CALLIS
SARAH, 61
CALLOWAY
ANDREW L., 22
ANTHONY, 101
BETTIE, 123
CAROLINE, 124
CATHARINE, 71
CHLOE, 81
CHORA ALICE, 20-E

G., 20-C
GEORGE, 123
GRANVILLE, 12, 22
J.R., 130
JAS, 81
JAS., 15
JNO R., 101
JOHN, 60
JOHN R., 101
LOUISA, 71, 101
MARGARET T., 12
MARGT., 15
MARIAH, 130
MATTIE, 81
S., 20-C
SARAH J., 15
SUSAN, 12
SUSAN G., 22
WM, 123
CALOWAY
GRANVILLE, 20-E
LAURA, 113
MATHEW, 20-B
SARAH J., 20-C
SUSAN, 20-E
CALSAW
ELIZA, 85
HATTIE, 85
NATHAN, 85
CAMBELL
JOHN, 69
CAMPBELL
A., 85
AMI, 104
ANDREW, 85
B.J., 41
CAROLINE, 20-A
CHARLOTTE, 104
CYRUS, 57
DELAWAR, 104
ELIZA, 73
ELIZA JANE, 139
ELIZA T., 32
FANNIE, 76
FRANCIS M., 20-A
I.A., 91
ISAAC H., 91
ISABELLE, 120
J.H., 73
J.O., 88
J.P., 55, 57(3), 59(2), 61, 62(2), 64(2), 65, 70, 71, 72, 76, 78, 88, 90, 91, 95, 96, 102, 103(2), 104, 110
JAMES P., 111
JM H., 22
JOHN, 73
JOSEPHINE, 138
L.A., 82
LELIA G., 76

LEWIS P., 120
LUCINDA, 49
MARY, 32, 41, 119
MATILDA, 57
NANCY A., 91
O.B., 120
ROSANA, 138
ROSIE E., 73
SUSAN, 57
SUSANAH B., 49
THOMAS K., 41
THOS K., 22, 32, 49
THOS M., 49
VIRGINIA, 115
WM E., 49
CAMPER
C.M., 125
L., 125
LENNA, 125
CANADAY
CLARA, 95
CANADY
CLARA, 111
FLERN S., 111
CANDIFF
MARGARET C., 53

NANCY, 53
CANDLER
EDGAR, 61
JOHN W., 61
SALLIE, 61
CANNADAY
CLARA, 36
FLEMMING, 36
LEWIS, 125
RANDAL, 125
RHODA, 125
RHODA J., 36
CANNADY
CLARA, 36
FLEMMING, 36
LIZZIE F., 36
CANTERBURY

D.D., 23
ELLET. H., 23
JOHN W., 38
LUCINDA, 23
CANTRELL
ELIZABETH, 51
JAMES M., 55
CAPERTON
A.J., 85
A.W.J., 19
ADAM, 12, 13
ADAM H., 61, 108
ALBERTEANY, 60

ALBERTENA, 96
ALBERTINA, 5, 61
ALBERTINY, 98
ALICE V., 38

ALLAN, 60
ALLEN T., 60
AUGS, 5
AUGUSTUS W.J., 1
ELIZTH G., 36
JNO G., 12, 13, 61
JOHN, 40
JOHN G., 60, 96, 98
JOHN S., 30, 46
JOHN W., 46
JULIA F., 41
LAURA, 36, 38, 60, 65
LORA, 46
MANERVA, 30, 98
MARGARET A., 30

MARTHA H., 104, 108
MARY A., 17, 96
MARY J., 40
MINERVA, 40
MINERVA A., 46
NANCY G., 35
O.H., 104(2), 108
R., 19
RACHEL, 5
ROBERT G., 65
SEREPHA, 1
T.H., 17, 65
THEODOSIA E., 46
THOMPSON, 36, 38, 41
THOMPSON H., 60
THOMPSON K., 46
THOMPSON N., 35
CAR
CHAS, 97
CARBAUGH
A., 119
ALLIE, 141
ALMEDA, 78
ARAMINTA S., 126
B.W., 141(2)
ELIZTH, 2
ESTER, 126
ESTHER, 67
GEO, 2
J.H., 141
J.K., 119
JNO H., 119
JOHN, 78
MARY, 2
MARY C., 114
NANNIE E., 78
SALLIE E., 67
W.T., 67, 114
WM, 126
CARBOUGH
ELIZABETH, 35, 20-E
GEO, 20-E
GEORGE, 35
JOHN, 20-E
JOHN H., 35
CARDEN
A.A., 138

ISAAC, 47
ISAAC G., 47
M.M., 102
OSCAR H., 138
REBECCA, 47
VIRGINIA, 138
W.C., 134, 137, 140
CARDWELL
FANNIE, 126
L., 68
THOS, 126
VIOLA, 74
WATSON, 68
WM, 68
CARINGTON
ELIZA, 80
CARLIN
LEWIS E., 89
MAY, 89
WM, 89
CARMACK
N., 20-C
R., 20-C
SARAH JANE, 20-C
CARNEFIX
BENJ F., 46
ELIZABETH A., 46
GEO E., 46
CARNER
DAVID, 3
ELIZABETH, 3
JUBAL, 3
CARNES
CATHERINE, 111
WM, 111(2)
CARPENTER
M., 20
MARY J., 20
NANCY, 16
SAML, 20
SAMUEL, 16(2)
CARPER
B.P., 100, 109
CHARLES F., 127
CHARLES L., 94
E.C., 3
B.J., 100
F.D., 86
FLEMING, 86
FLEN, 127
FLERN, 116
GEO D., 49
J.C., 4
JEREMH, 59
JOHN, 138
M.F., 3
M.L., 109
MARIAH, 138
MARTHA, 100, 109, 116, 127
MARY, 49, 50, 82, 138
MARY H., 50
MARY J., 94

MOLLIE, 59
REBECCA, 59
ROBERT O., 29
ROBT, 82(2)
SALLY, 86
SARAH E., 3
W.I., 116
WESLEY, 82
CARPET
HENRY, 96
MARTHA A., 96
REBECCA E., 96
CARR
ALLEN H., 47
ALLIE R., 133
ARAMINTA J., 47
ARDELIA, 71
CHARLES, 97
D.A., 126
D.H., 44, 47(3), 48, 49, 51(2), 130, 134, 138
DINAH, 20-D
DOCIE, 18
FANNIE, 69, 102
FANNY, 116
FRANCIS M., 20-D
HARRY, 25
HAYWOOD, 97
J., 18
J.E., 98
J.T., 133
J.V., 70
JAMES, 69, 20-B
JANE K., 6
JAS, 102, 136
JNO, 3
JNO T., 78
JOHN, 20, 26, 27
JOHN S., 47
JOHN T., 51, 71
JULIETTE H., 20
K.H., 43
LIZZIE, 73
LUCINDA, 98
M.A.J., 27
MARGARET C., 3
MARTHA M., 28
MARY, 10, 44
MARY A., 19
MARY J., 20-B
MAY M., 71
N.A., 133
NANCY, 20-B
NANCY A., 51, 78
NANNIE E., 47, 78
NORA, 44
RACHEL, 19
ROBERT, 28, 73
ROBT, 3, 6
RUFUS J., 51
S., 20 H(2)
SALLIE, 6, 27, 20-B

SAMUEL, 136
SARAH, 3(2), 20, 26, 28, 47, 73
SARAH A., 3
SARAH E., 25
SUSAN E., 26
THOMAS, 20-D
THOS, 98
THOS., 19
WILLIAM, 10, 44, 102
WM, 69, 136(2), 20-B(3)
WM R., 29
CARRELL
ANN, 128
C.H., 128
JOHN B., 128
CARROLL
ELISHUA, 96
HENRY, 96
SARAH C., 96
CARTER
A.J., 68
AARON, 75
ABRAM L., 35
ALBERT, 140
BELL, 81
C.A., 75, 110
CATHERINE, 39
CHARLES, 55
CLOYD AUSTIN, 75

CRAIG, 140
DAB, 112
DAN, 114
ELIZA, 112
ELIZABETH, 57
ELIZABETH J., 59
ELLA, 91
EMILY, 119
GORDAN, 35
GORDON, 39
H.J., 87
HENRY C., 114
INDIA, 139
ISAAC, 55
J.C., 114
J.H., 87, 119
JAMES R., 140
JOHN H., 29
KATE, 35
KITTIE, 140
L.C., 128, 130
L.E., 139
LEWIS, 128
LUCY, 102
M., 128
M.L., 114
MARGT L., 57
MARIAH L., 119
MARTIN L., 39
MARY, 8, 96, 106, 119(2), 120, 139

MARY E., 37
NANCY, 75
POLLY, 59
R.S., 114
RACHEL, 91
S.N., 140
SALLIE, 102
SARAH, 55, 99
SIDNEY, 112
SUSANA, 140
THOS, 57
VICIR J.E., 96
W.J., 66, 67, 72, 80, 81(2), 83, 87, 90, 102, 129
WALTER, 120
WM, 96, 106, 119, 139
CARTERBURY

EMALINE, 79
FOUNTAIN, 79
GEORGE, 79
CARVER
ALMEDA, 129
ELIZABETH, 138
H., 57
HENRY, 81
HENRY L., 57
JAMES, 57, 138(2)
JANE, 87
JAS, 90
JNO W., 90
JOHN, 123
MARTHA, 81
MARY, 57, 81, 87, 90, 123
PEARCE, 138
SARAH, 123
CASEY
GEO., 69
HENRY, 75
HENRY D., 38
JOHN, 69
MATTHIAS J., 38
MILLIE, 75
SARAH, 38
SUSAN, 69
THOMAS M., 75
CASLEY
BERRY, 1
GERMNAH, 1
RODA, 1
CASON
ELZTH D., 33
JAS B., 33
P.A., 33
CASPER
E., 14
HARDIN H., 17
ISAAC, 9
JANE, 17
JOSEPH, 17
M., 14

MARTHA C., 14
REBECCA, 9
SARAH E., 9
CASSADAY
H., 14(2)
HIRAM, 5
J.O., 24(4), 25(4), 26(4), 27(6), 28(4), 29(2), 30, 31(4), 32(2), 33(5), 34(5), 35(4), 36(4), 37(5), 38, 39(7), 40(3), 41(6), 42(5), 43(4), 44(4), 45, 46(6), 47(4), 48(3), 49(3), 50(6), 51(3), 52, 54, 55, 57(3), 58(2), 59(2), 60, 61(2), 63, 64, 67, 68(3), 69, 70(2), 71(3), 72, 74(2), 75(3), 76(5), 77, 78(5), 79(4), 82(4), 83(4), 84, 85(2), 86(3), 87(3), 88(2), 89(2), 90(2), 91, 92(2), 94(4), 95(2), 96(2), 98, 99(2), 100, 102, 103, 107(2), 109, 111(2), 114(3), 115, 117, 119, 120, 121, 125, 127(2), 128(2), 129, 130(2), 131, 133(2), 135, 136(3), 137(2), 138(2), 20-B, 20-D, 20-E
JAMES O., 14, 20(2), 22, 20-A(3), 20-C
JAS O., 54, 58, 64, 66(2), 73, 78
JAS. O., 29, 48, 51, 52
LOUISA, 20-A
M., 14(2)
MARTHA, 5
ROBERT P., 5
CASSADY
J.O., 20-B
JAMES O., 26
CASTLE
ABRAM, 96
MARY D., 96
OTIS T., 96
CATHERS
A.L., 134, 138(2)
CATO
DAVID, 59
RACHEL, 59
THOS L., 59
CATRAN
J.W., 112
NANCY, 112
WM W., 112

CAULEY
A.T., 132
BENJN, 5
BERRY, 11, 16
DAVID, 16
ELIZA J., 132
ELIZTH, 16
G.C., 132
JAMES, 16
JOHN, 11
PHOEBA, 5
RHODA, 11
CAUSBY
A.T., 113
CHARLES E., 113
CAVES
ELIZA, 114
J.W., 114
OLLIE G., 114
CAVILL
ELLEN, 73
FRANK, 73
MOLLIE, 73
CAVIS
ELIZA, 137
J.W., 137
ROSA LEE, 137
CAWLEY
ADA P., 107
L.A., 107
PEARL, 107
CECIL
AMANDA, 127
BARBARIE L., 131
BOYD, 126
CHARLOTT, 131
EMMA, 132
H.A., 126
HENRY, 71
J.J., 132
J.W., 126
JAMES, 71
JAMES W., 51
JANE, 43, 51, 71, 126
JAS, 43
JAS MARVIN, 121
JNO G., 121
JOSIE, 132
JOSIE BLANCH, 121

M.J., 121
MARY J., 7
MOLLIE, 121
N.E., 127
SARAH, 51, 88
SARAH E., 7
SERRILDIA, 43
SHELBY, 7
W.B., 121
W.F., 132
WM, 127
WM P., 132
CEPHAS

BOB, 87
HENRY, 87
CHAFFIN
FRANK, 140(2)
CHAMBERS
A.F., 72
CHARLES EMORY, 117

ELIZABETH S., 117
J.A., 117
J.B., 102
JAS S., 72
JOEL W., 1
MARY J., 72
CHAMP
ELKAHAH, 36
JAS H., 137
LAFAYETTE, 36
NANCY, 36
CHAMPE
ELKANAH, 37
NANCY, 37
WM H., 37
CHANDLER
SARAH M., 104
WM, 104
CHANESS
COSBY C., 68
JAS H., 68
VIRGINIA B., 68
CHANNING
E.A., 66
J.H., 66
W.J., 66
CHAPELL
JOHN, 97
NETTIE, 97
SUSAN, 97
CHAPMAN
AARON D., 74
ALLEN, 82
CLARISSA, 56
E.T., 125
GEO, 125
GEORGE, 82
H., 125
H.H., 131
HULDA, 82
J., 56
J.A., 74
JAS A., 74
MARY, 56
O.B., 131
O.E., 131
SARAH, 90
SARAH J., 74
THEODORE, 90
WM, 90
CHARLES
N.J., 83
CHARLTON
GODFREY, 46
HULDAH, 44

KATIE, 124
KIS., 46
KISY J., 37
KIZIMA, 44
KIZZIAH, 47, 87
KIZZIE M.J., 80
LEE, 124
LEE A., 80
NOAH, 37(2)
SAM, 87, 124
SAML, 44, 46, 80
SARAH, 87
CHASE
ELIZABETH A., 114
G.M., 114
GEO W., 114
CHATTING
ELIZABETH, 30
GEORGE W., 108
GRIZELLE W., 20-D
JOHN A., 55
JOS, 30
JULIA, 108
LUCINDA, 55
MARTHA A., 44
MARY, 11, 30, 43, 44, 20-D
OZELLO R., 55
SARAH J., 11
W.W., 43, 108
WILLIAM, 11, 44
WM, 20-D
WM T., 43
WM W., 30
WM R., 107
CHAUEP (?)
CAUSBY, 49
JAMES H., 49
SUSAN J., 49
CHEATHAM
CHARITY, 86
ELIZA, 67
GEO, 126
GEORGE, 126
LILLY, 67
MARIA, 126
ROBERT, 86
SPENCER, 86
WASH, 67, 126
CHILDERS
JAMES, 100
M.H., 100
OLLIE, 100
CHILDRESS
EDW, 97
JAS, 97(2)
MARY E., 97
CHOCKLET
CYNTHIA, 108
MARY, 108
WM, 108
CHRISMAN
C.A., 116, 119(2)
CHRISTIAN

A.J., 134
ARTHUR, 107
CARRIE T., 107
CATH., 9
ELI W., 11, 72
ELIZABETH, 10, 110
ESTER, 2
FANNY, 107
GIDEON, 77
JAMES R., 134
JANE, 63, 77, 80, 83
JNO H., 33
JOHN, 2
JOHN H., 10, 11, 20-C
L., 72
LOTTIE T., 110
LUTICIA A., 77
M.J., 134
MANELIUS A., 9
MARTHA, 33
NANNIE, 138
NELLIE J., 63
NELLY, 2
PERMILIA, 11
PRISCILLA, 20-C
R.B., 110
R.T., 107
ROBT G., 63, 80
ROBT L., 80
S.B., 72
SARAH E., 33
SEREPTA P., 20-C
THOMAS M., 9
W.W., 107
WM R., 107
CHRISTIE
C., 16
CYNTHIA P., 39, 55, 67
DEMARIUS K., 16
JAMES M., 16, 39, 67
JAS M., 55
M.W., 55
R.C., 57
RICHARDSON C., 39

SAML M., 67
SARAH G., 111
T.M., 111
T.W., 111
CHRISTIN
ELI, 97
LUTICIA, 97
VIRGINIA G., 97
CHRISTY
CATH., 28
THOS, 28
TILLUSON, 28
CHRYSTON
CHARLEY, 118
CUMFREY, 118
CHUMBLEY
GEO H., 129
NANNIE H., 129

ROBT E., 129
CHURCH
J.F., 137
S.A., 137
S.E., 137
CISCO
PEARL, 117
STELLA, 117
CLARE
CLARINDA, 59
J.H., 59
THOMAS, 59
CLARK
A.F., 95
A.J., 79, 116
A.V., 112
ALFRED, 98
ALLEN T., 18
ALLEY, 11
ANKAR, 32
ANNIE, 91
BROOK, 84
C., 51, 53(3), 56, 60
C.A., 112
CARROLL, 32, 36(2), 38(3), 40(2), 41(2), 44, 45, 50, 54(2), 57(3), 58, 62(3)
CATHERINE, 65
CELIA, 32
CHARLES, 123, 131
CHARLES L., 116
CL, 54
CORA J., 135
DERINDA, 9
DIONY, 2
E., 94
E.E., 94, 139
E.J., 78
E.L., 78
EDGAR, 91
ELI, 3
ELIJAH, 19, 75, 121, 139
ELIJAH C., 41
ELIZA, 75, 83, 103, 138
ELLEN, 84
EMMA, 63
GEO, 59, 64
H.H., 58
HARRIET, 64
HENRY, 2, 6, 9(2), 11, 17, 19, 98, 133(2), 20-B(2)
ISABELL H., 116
J.A., 101, 135
JAMES, 9, 17, 41, 75, 131
JAMES G., 20
JAS E., 127(2)
JINN V., 91
JNO, 3

JOHN, 8, 29, 63, 84, 91, 120, 131
JOHN S., 121
JOSEPH, 75
JUDATH, 41
JUDITH A., 121
KATHARINE, 78
LEWIS, 64
LOW, 63
M.E., 94
MARIA, 112
MARTHA, 95
MARY, 3, 18, 19, 20, 64, 137
MARY E., 97
MARY P., 8
MERRITT, 64
MICHAEL, 65
MIRAINE, 8
N.L., 127
NANCY M., 131
NANNIE, 131
NANNIE L., 97
NATHANIEL, 123
NICY, 29, 121
NIZY, 29
NOAH D., 139
P.C., 118, 122, 128, 129(2), 131(3), 132(3), 133, 134(2), 135, 136
PATRICK, 65
PETER C., 135, 136, 137(3), 139
POLLY, 9
PRESTON, 138(3)
R., 18
R.W., 127
REBECCA, 9
RUFUS, 9, 19, 20
RUFUS W., 97
RUTH, 2, 6, 9(2), 11, 17, 19, 20-B
SADIE, 133
SALLIE, 75
SALLIE A., 75
SAML, 64
SAMUEL, 32
SARAH E., 19
SOPHIA, 120
SUSAN, 123, 131
SUSAN E., 58
THOMAS, 29, 138
THOS M., 58
V., 133
VICTORIA A., 52
VIRGIE A., 121
VIRGINIA, 98
W.J., 76
WILLIAM, 103
WILLIE, 83, 95
WM, 27(2), 83
WM J., 77(3)

CLAXTON
WM A., 39, 44, 47(2)
CLAY
BURG, 70
ELLEN, 134
H., 134
H.C., 70
H.H., 134
SARAH, 70
CLAYTON
ALICE, 66
ENDORA, 118
MARY, 74
CLAYTOR
BETTIE, 76
ELIZABETH, 106
EMMA G., 84
FLETCHER, 84
HARRIET, 84
JENTRY, 75
LAURA, 77
LELIA, 75
NED, 76
PETER, 84
PLEASANT, 106
R.G., 106
RACHEL, 76
CLEAVER
ABSIIR, 128
DAVID, 26
ELLEN, 79
JOHN, 26
M.J., 79
POLLY, 26
WILLIAM, 128
WM, 79
CLEGHON
ELIZ. J., 50
J.A., 49
J.B., 49, 50
JEROME B., 64
MARY, 49, 50, 64
STEPHEN F., 64
CLEGHORN
FANNIE C., 50
J.B., 50
CLEMENS
ELIZABETH, 135
GEORGE, 135
JOHN, 135
LEE, 135
MARY, 135
CLEMENT
J.W., 83
SARAH, 83
STEPHEN, 83
CLEMENTS
JOHN, 25
JULIA A., 25
MARY, 25
CLEMMONS
ARRISTER, 60
BETSY, 60

JAMES H., 60
JOHN R., 44
MARY, 44
MOLLIE S., 30
RUTH E., 44
CLEMONS
EMMA F., 30
JNO R., 80
JNO W., 80
JOHN R., 22, 36
MARTHA J., 22
MARY, 22, 80
MARY S., 36
SERVILLA J., 36
CLENDENEN
ADA B., 132
EMMA J., 97
J.O., 118
JULIET Y., 29
M.E., 118
MARY E., 76, 132
N.J., 97
R.G., 76, 118, 132
S.J., 76
CLENDENIN
GEO A., 130
LINNIE B., 92
MAC, 92
MARY, 130
N.J., 92
S.E., 130
CLENDENON
A. Mc., 60
AGORA N., 26
ALMEDA, 26
ANGLEN, 34
ARGLEN, 26
ELECTRA JANE, 34

GEO G., 94
M., 26
MARGERY, 34
MARY, 26
MARY E., 60
Mc, 94
MILTON L., 14(2), 15(2), 16(3)
NANCY J., 60, 94
ROBERT C., 26
CLENDERSON
JOHN, 14
MARY, 14
ROBERT G., 14
CLENDONEN
MARY, 107
REVOANVY, 1
ROBT G., 107
SHADY, 1
VIOLA M., 107
CLICK
HENRY, 68
JASPER, 68
MARY F., 68

CLIFFORD
ELLA L., 118
K.A., 118, 135
M.M., 118, 135
MARY E., 135
CLINE
ELIZABETH, 113
ELIZTH, 16
GORDON, 113
JAMES, 16
JOHN H., 16
PRIDEMORE, 137
WM D., 113
CLOVER
J.T., 52
CLOWER
E.R., 93
J.T., 93
JAS, 93
LEONAH B., 93
M.E., 93
CLOWERS
JOHN D., 65
MARY J., 72
MARY JANE, 65(2)
CLTER (SIC)
JANE, 110
JOHN, 110
WM, 110
CLYBURN
ANGELINE, 43
E.B., 95
ELIZA, 95
J.W., 111
JAMES, 43
JONAS, 43, 95
JOSHUA L., 55
MARIA, 55
MARIAH, 111
WM B., 55, 111
COBBS
CAROLINE, 72
JACOB, 72
JNO HENRY, 126
SILAS, 72
COBERN
JOHN D., 75
SARAH, 75(2)
COBURN
A.B., 107
BELL, 125
CATHARINE, 62
CATHERINE, 57
CYNTHIA, 33
DANL S., 88
DAVID, 1(2), 32, 33, 57, 62, 79, 125
E., 125
J.D., 125
J.H., 66
JAMES, 32
JEREMIAH, 62
JNO, 125

JNO D., 88
JOHN, 66
MARY, 57
SARAH, 66
SARAH A., 88
SARAH E., 79, 107
URSULA, 32, 33
WM T., 107
COCHRAN
ANDREW, 69
BRICK, 14
DANL, 69
ISOM, 20-C
MARY, 14
NANCY, 69
S., 20-C
W., 14
CODWELL
FAYETTE, 132
JOHN, 132
SALLIE, 132
CODWILL
ROBT, 84
SALLIE, 84
WILLIE, 84
COB
J.J., 132
MARTHA, 132
NELLIE, 132
COFER
SARAH ANN, 31
SARAH J., 31
COFFEY
ALICE, 95
J.G., 95
LOIS, 95
COGER
A., 109
CHARLES R., 109
S., 109
COHEN
H., 94
J., 94
MARRIE, 94
COLE
A.F., 116
A.J., 60, 76, 93, 115(2), 122, 141
A.L., 134
A.W., 112
ADELINE, 114
ALB., 23
ALLEN, 103
ALLEN G., 23
ALLEN T., 39, 75
ANDREW, 12
ANDREW J., 53, 75
ANNA LOUISA, 116

AUG., 18
AUGUSTUS D., 12
AUGUSTUS W., 39
BARTLEY D., 89, 114

BEDFORD, 112
CATHERINE, 112
CLARA, 141
COY R., 103
D.B., 93(2), 141
DELLIE M., 53
DENISHA, 116
DORA G., 60
E.A., 89
GEORGE P., 114
HANAH, 12
JAMES W., 89
JANE, 81
JENNIE, 75
JNO W., 62
JOHN, 112(3)
JOHN H., 18
JOSEPH K., 51
M., 23
M.M., 76
MAGDALENA C., 76

MARGARET, 39
MARGT, 18
MARGT JANE, 62
MARTHA, 112(2)
MARTHA J., 62
MARY, 53, 60, 75, 93, 115, 122, 141
MINNIE L., 75
N.J., 122
PEARLY MAY, 75

SHANUA, 115
VIRGINIA, 103
COLEMAN
ADA, 125, 140
CLARA, 140
ELIZA, 36
ELIZABETH, 36
JNO, 95
JNO., 36
KELSON, 34
NAPOLION, 20-D
SALLIE, 125
THOS, 78
TUCKER, 125
WILSON, 34, 140
COLES
CATHARINE, 132
ED, 66
EDWARD, 83
GEO C., 132
JANE, 66, 83(2)
LOUISA, 83
WYATT, 83
COLIS
A., 139
HARRY, 139
LILLIE, 139
COLIVER
J.C., 118
MALINDA, 118

MARTHA, 118
COLLINS
BELL, 132
CHARLEY N., 121
DAVID, 18, 65
DEXTER, 132
EDW, 73
ELIZABETH, 73, 121
ELIZTH, 106
G.W., 121
HENRY, 132
J.R., 81
J.S., 102
JAMES, 106
JAS H., 65
JEM, 18
JOHN T., 73
LULA B., 106
LUVINA, 65
MARTHA, 81
SALLIE, 81
SOL, 18
COLRIN
LUZENA A., 41
MARION, 41
COLVARD
ROBT L., 104
SALLIE, 104
WM M., 104
COMAS
JANE, 22
JOHN, 22
COMBS
ELBERT, 121
COMER
A., 122
AMANDA L., 95
AUGUSTUS, 22, 104, 106

BETSY, 62
ELIZA ANN, 60
ELIZA J., 37
ELIZABETH, 37, 51(2), 133
ELIZTH S., 32
ELZTH, 32
EMMA, 51
FRANCES, 139
G.A., 137
G.H., 141
HESTER J., 106
IDA, 94
JACOB, 32, 37, 51(2), 62, 133
JAMES, 94
JANE, 18, 107
JOHN, 18, 107
JOS H., 51
LEVI G., 51
LEWIS A., 112
MARTHA, 94, 95, 104, 106, 112, 122, 139
MARTHA J., 18

MARY J., 32
MARY S., 62
NANNIE, 122
SARAH, 32, 60
SARAH A., 85
SARAH C., 85
SEVILLA, 104
W.J., 32, 107
WALLACE J., 60, 85
WM, 112, 139
WM R., 133
WM S., 95
COMMACK
EMILY, 20-C
NANCY, 20-D
ROBERT, 20-D
COMPTON
ALICE O., 85
BALLARD P., 61
BATHELDA, 85(2)
BATHILDA, 89
BERTHILDA, 107
C.H., 128
CALLEAR (?), 8
CAR, 4
CHAS E., 61
CORRIE, 89
DELILAH, 61
DOCN, 85(2)
E.G., 96
F.P., 89
FEILDEN T., 107
FIELDING, 30
FLEMING, 101
GRANGA B., 96
KANSAS S., 107
LOU, 86
LUCRETIA, 4
M.L., 127
MAGGIE E., 86
MALINDA, 55
MARGAT, 1
MARY, 90
MARY E., 1
MICAJAH, 8(2)
NAOMA, 8(2)
NAOMA J., 8
PEYTON, 90
R.J., 4
STARLING, 86, 90, 101
STELLA C., 85
T.S., 127
TEMPERANCE, 101

VIRGIE E., 96
W.S., 127
COMSTOCK
NANCY E., 92
CONDEXTER
JOHN, 74
CONIMACK
M. SUE, 110
CONLEY

ALMEDIA, 63
GUY P., 63
RUSSEL P., 63
CONNER
BELL, 118, 123
CORA MAY, 134
DANL R., 60
ELIJAH, 7(2)
O.A., 140(2)
HADEN, 60
HENRY, 118
IDA M., 118
IRENIA C., 127
J.H., 134
JAS H., 86
L.F., 86
LAURA A., 83
LEE, 118
LIDDIE, 60
LIZZIE, 123
LOUISA T., 134
MARANDA, 118
MARY I., 127
McCRACKEN, 110

PRISCILLA, 110
R.J., 83
TASVILL, 123
TASVILL T., 118
W.N., 83
ZORA M., 86
CONNOR
DANL R., 62
HENRY, 67
LYDIA, 62
MARTHA, 67
MIRANDA, 67
SAML J., 62
CONWELL
HARRIET, 86
JAMES, 86
SAM, 86
COOK
A.C., 140(2)
ALICE BELLE, 98
ANN, 29, 59, 20-C
ANNA, 5, 9, 11, 27,
114, 20-A
ANNIE, 31, 20-B
BERTHA A., 124
C., 20-B
C.W., 52
CALVIN, 21, 20-F
CALVIN J., 95
CATHERINE, 20-C
COR., 20-A
CORNELIUS, 5, 9, 11,
29, 31, 59
CORNELIUS W., 20-C

CORNS, 20-C
DANIEL, 141
DANIEL P., 29

DANL, 141
DANL O., 89
DAVID, 9, 19
DAVID H., 20-B
DAVID P., 29
E., 15
E.A., 95
ELIZA F., 11
EMILY L., 31
FLOYD, 79
GEO W., 98
H.C., 141
H.E., 127
H.I., 127, 136(3), 138
H.L., 122
HARRIET, 20-B
HATTIE, 77
HENRY I., 124, 125
HENRY L., 122
ISAAC, 19
J.C., 69, 70(4)
J.N., 127
JAMES, 20-D
JAS, 20-B
JAS W., 69
JENNIE, 15
JNO C., 78(2), 82
JOHN N., 85, 116, 122
JULIAS, 69
LAURA BELL ZORA,
116
LEORA EFFA, 99
LEVI J., 97
LOUENNA J., 52
LOUISA, 99, 124
LUVERNIE V., 59
MAHALA, 73, 141(2)
MAHALA Y., 20-A
MANDEVILLE, 15

MARGARET, 85, 116,

122, 127, 140
MARGARET A., 98

MARTHA J., 9, 141,
20-D
MARTHA L., 60
MARY A., 79
MARY E., 104
MARY M., 69
MAT F., 97
MONTGOMERY, 77

NANCY, 9, 19, 27,
20-B, 20-D
NANCY ORA DILL, 122

NANCY P., 60
OLLIE V., 77
R.J., 95
REBECCA, 21, 35, 20-F
RHODA, 52, 89, 95, 104

RHODA A., 60
ROBERT S., 85
SADIE B., 140
SARAH, 97
SARAH ANN, 5
SUSAN, 9
SUSAN B., 79
T.B., 111, 122, 124,
131(2), 132
THOMAS, 27
THOMAS B., 35
THOMAS M., 35, 60,
20-C
THOS, 20-F
THOS B., 99, 104, 120
THOS., 21
VIRGINIA, 140
W.M., 95
WALTER B., 141
WARD, 89, 95, 104
WM, 20-C
WM B., 109
COOLEY
BETIE, 76
ISAIAH, 76
L.C., 76
COOPER
ALEX, 32
ALEXANDER, 20-B

ALICE, 94
AMANDA J., 20-E
ANDREW L., 20-C
ANN, 20-E
ANN E., 21, 20-F
ANNIE E., 58
AUSTIN, 19
AX, 20-E
BALLARD P., 25
C.W., 45
DOSHA H., 24
E.A., 110
E.F., 95
E.W., 81, 85(2)
E.W., REV., 89
ED, 117
ELIZABETH C., 11
EMMA L., 106
ERASTUS W., 54
F., 20-E
HARRIET, 45
ISAAC, 25
J., 15
J.E., 118
J.M., 112(2)
JANE, 19, 112
JAS M., 94, 130
JNO, 106
JOHN, 19, 27, 58, 73,
77, 78, 83, 20-C
JOHN S., 54
JONAH, 21, 20-F
JOS, 121

JOSEPH, 75, 77, 128
JOSEPH W., 130
JOSIAH, 24, 114
KATIE B., 96
L.G., 118
LEWIS, 27, 112, 135
LEWIS M., 32
LILLY A., 75
LULA JANE, 96
M.A., 112, 135
MALVINA, 95
MANDY, 121
MARGARET, 2
MARIA, 58, 78, 106
MARY, 32
MARY E., 112
MARY J., 15
MELVINA, 34, 65
MILLISON, 83
MOLLIE, 115
N., 20-E
NANCY, 11, 13, 15(2),
20-C
NANCY A., 15
NANNIE M., 65
NARCISSA, 114
NARCISSUS, 21, 20-F
NORIUM, 24
PHAMY, 94
PHANEY, 130
POLLY A., 27
RACHEL S., 73
REBECCA, 25
RHODA A.E., 20-E
ROBERT M., 45
S.M., 128
SALLIE IRENE, 78
SARAH A., 77
SARAH J., 135
SARAH M., 75
TEXAS, 128
V.W., 114, 118
VALEIUS W., 20-E
W.A., 121
W.G., 118
WILLIAM, 2
WILLIAM A., 95
WILLIAM C., 34
WILLIAM L., 83
WM A., 34, 53, 65, 73,
96(2)
WM C., 65
COPE
GEO H., 114
LYDIA J., 114
W.S., 114
WARREN S., 114
COPERTON
CYNTHIA, 12
COPING
L.A., 81
M.F., 81
CORAN

JOHN P., 1
CORDELL
DAVID, 131
SARAH, 131
CORDEN
W.C., 135
CORDER
BENJ., 35
ETTIE, 136
JULIA, 35
SAM, 136
SAMUEL S., 35
VICTOR, 136(2)
CORE
ALLEN T., 36
ELIZABETH, 36
ROBERT, 36
CORNER
CATHERINE, 98
H.A., 126
JAMES A., 98
MARY L., 126
R.W., 126
WILLIAM, 98
CORNETT
E.M., 119
F.R., 119
JAMES, 54
W.M., 119
CORNWELL
HANNAH, 131
JNO D., 131
S.W., 131
CORUM
ELIZABETH, 92, 130
JANCKNEY, 92
P.M., 130
W.T., 92, 130
COSE
MOLLIE C., 20-A
SARAH, 20-A
SCISUL, 20-A
COSNER
JANE, 22
JOHN, 22
WM S., 22
COTHERS
A.L., 135
COTTLE
GEORGE, 11
JOHN J., 11
MARIA, 11
COUCHINS
BEN, 20-B
JAMES M., 13
N., 20-B
COULEY
ALICE J., 66
J.F., 66
MARY, 66
COUSINS
A.G., 129
CARTER, 60

DAISY, 60
EVIE, 129
GEORGE, 65
JAS, 65
LOU, 65
MARTHA, 129
SARAH H., 60
COWAN
HORTON, 103
MAGGIE, 103
SAML W., 103
COWGILL
J.A., 17
COWLING
IDA M., 31
L.M., 110
MARY, 31, 110
MARY E., 49
SOPHONIA, 27
VIRGINIA E., 49
W.J., 110
WILLIS J., 31, 49
COX
A.H., 117
ABSOLUM, 107
ALLEN H., 117
ANDERSON, 74
ANNIE, 74
ANSELIN, 67
ASLUM, 69
BARBARY, 133
BONINA, 2
C.H., 37
CYNTHIA, 17
D.A., 131
D.C., 122
DANL R., 20-B
DOCIA, 62, 64
EDWARD, 69
ELIZA, 132
ERSKIN R., 2
ERSKINE, 20-B
F. MANAR, 52
FRANCIS, 2
GARRET, 132(2)
IDA E., 103
ISABELLA, 138
J.C., 37
J.M., 118
JAMES, 1, 62, 64, 107
JAS, 132
JAS F., 131
JNO L., 134
JOHN, 26, 133
JOS H., 62
JOSEPH, 1, 21, 22, 52,
20-F
JUDA, 74
JUDIA, 69, 107
JULY, 67
LIZZIE, 132
M.A., 118
MARGARET, 132

MARTHA ISABELL, 37

MARY, 52, 117, 118,
122, 131, 134, 140
MARY F., 118
MARY J., 21, 20-F
MATHEW, 118, 140
MATTHEW, 117, 122
MOSES, 17
NANCY, 1, 22
P.C., 133
ROBT E., 134
S.A., 20-B
S.C., 118
SARAH, 22
SARAH A., 17
SIDNEY, 21, 20-F
T.F., 140(2)
W., 67
W.I., 118
WELLINGTON, 64, 103,

132, 138
WESLEY, 67
COY
MAGGIE M., 97
CRACKEN
D.M., 81
CRADDOCK
EZEKIAH, 36
EZEKIAL, 46
LUCY R., 36, 46
RUFUS, 46
W.R., 36
CRAFT
A.M., 65, 66, 73, 77,
78, 79(3), 81(2), 82,
83, 86(4), 87, 88,
89, 90, 92, 93(2),
95(2), 96(5), 97,
99(5), 100, 101(2),
102(2), 105(3),
106(2), 107, 111,
112(2), 113(3), 119,
121, 123(3), 127(2),
130, 133, 134(2),
136, 137, 138, 139
ARMSTEAD, 65
CLARA, 65
DISSIE, 65
GEO W., 44
IDA E., 99
JNO W., 44
LIZZIE, 141
MARY E., 44
ROLLIN, 141
SALLY, 99
WM, 141
CRAGHEAD
J., 121
LUCY JANE, 122
MARY F., 122
MAURICE, 121

MILES, 122
WM, 121
CRAIG
ELIZA, 121
POLLY, 53
SAM, 121
TILDA, 121
CRAMAR
ANNIE F., 123
JNO P., 123
CRAWFORD
ALEC J., 36
ALEXR D., 61
ANNIE, 24
ARAMINTA C., 56
BERTIE, 121
C., 33(2)
CAROLINE W., 56
CHAS, 68
CYNTHIA M., 100
D.S., 114, 121
ELIZA E., 104
ELIZABETH, 36, 56, 61,
68
ELIZTH, 26
EMILY, 104
EMILY L., 120
ISAAC, 24, 31, 53
JANE, 5(2), 6, 10
JENNIE F., 69
JOHN, 51
JOHN B., 5
LAURA J., 57
LILLIE, 101
MARGARET, 57, 100,

101, 130
MARGARET B., 69

MARGARET H., 5
MARGT B., 56
MARINDA A., 50, 51
MARY, 71
NANCY, 31, 53
NANNIE, 120
R., 130
R.A., 26
R.B., 114, 121
REBECCA, 139
REBECCA J., 61
REUBEN, 6, 56, 57, 69,
100, 101, 139
REUBEN A., 61
ROBT B., 71
S.M., 120
SALLIE, 10
SAML M., 104
SAMUEL M., 31
SUSAN, 51
THOMAS, 130, 139
THOS, 26, 56, 61
THOS B., 56, 68
THOS P., 53

154

W.M., 31
WM, 71
WM M., 29, 30(2), 31(2)
ZACH, 10
ZACHARIAH, 5, 6
ZACHIRAH, 5
CRAY
ISAAC, 122
LAURA R., 122
SARAH F., 122
CREGER
AMANDA, 132
G.W., 132
WASH, 132
CRENSHAW
FLORA, 64
FRED, 64
JOHN, 64
CRESSEL
J.A., 127
M.E., 127
T.W., 127
CREWS
A.G.W., 96
ACY, 54, 65
AEG, 53
ALMA F., 133
ANNIE L., 65
ASA, 37, 44, 56, 133
ASA V., 22
D.R., 96
DAVID, 1, 50
DELIAH, 133
DELILAH R., 140
H.C., 138
J.D., 96
JAMES, 89
JAMES M., 22
JAS W., 63
JEFFERSON D., 44
JNO D., 53
JOHN W., 1, 41, 42, 63
LOUISIANA, 1
LOUISIANA D., 42
LUCINDA, 37
MARTHA, 56
MOLLIE, 138
NANCY, 37, 44, 53, 54, 65
NANNIE, 89
O.W., 138
ROBT L., 54
SARAH A., 41
SARAH F., 56
SUSAN, 42, 63
V.L., 69
WILLIAM T., 65
WM H., 65
CRICKENBURGEN
J.J., 23
CRIDER

CATHERINE, 108
J.W., 108
JENNIE, 108
CRIMP
AMANDA, 69
ARMINTA, 69
THOS, 69
CRINER
E.E., 131
EMMA, 131
W.C., 131
CROCKETT
ADDISON, 79
CAROLINE, 67
ELIZABETH, 52
J., 67
JAMES A., 52, 113
JANE, 79
JAS A., 50, 78, 97
MAGGIE, 78
N.C., 67
OSKER, 113
RACHEL, 52, 78, 97, 113
RACHEL E., 50
REBECCA, 97
WM B., 50
CROFT
A.M., 71
D.M., 109
M.C., 109
T.C., 109
CROMER
C.D., 135
CHAS F., 60
E.W., 135
J.C., 60
JOHN C., 93
MARY, 60, 93
SAMUEL D., 93
SARAH C., 135
WILLIE H., 81
CROOK
G.W., 23, 20-E
GEO W., 23, 24
GEORGE W., 20-E(2)
JNO W., 22
CROTTY
ANGELINE, 137
C.L., 57
D.L., 137
DANIEL L., 69
GEO W., 47, 80
HARRIET E., 91
HENRY ETTIE, 137
INDIA M., 47, 80
JOHN M., 84
JOSEPH O., 39
JULIA, 39, 62(2), 84, 101
LUTHER, 47
M.G., 124

MARGARET A., 62, 69

MARY, 57, 91
MARY ANN, 21, 20-F

MICHAEL, 21, 57, 20-F
ROSA A., 80
S.R., 91
SAML P., 101
SAMUEL R., 21, 20-F
SARAH E., 62
WM, 39, 101
WM A., 62(2), 84
CROUCH
A.G., 138
L.W., 2(3), 3(2)
S.K., 138
WM, 138
CROW
FAYETTE, 88
KATE, 88
WILLIAM, 88
CROWDER
AMAS, 94
AUGUSTA, 77
FRED L., 77
LUCY, 94
MUNFORD, 94
SARAH C., 86
WM, 77
CROY
ELLEN M., 95
G.E., 83(2)
ISAAC, 83(2)
SAML E., 83
SARAH F., 83(2)
W.H., 133
WM D., 95
WM H., 95(2)
CROZIER
J.N., 140
CRUM
A., 14
ABR, 20
ALMEDA, 93
ARAMINTA, 93
ARMINTA, 84
HIRAM, 93
J.A., 14
JULIA, 20
JULIA A., 84
MARY E., 14
SAMUEL T., 20
THOS, 84
CRUMB
ARAMINTA, 45
POLLY, 45
SAMPSON, 45
CRUMBE
ARAMINTA, 80
NANNIE C., 80
THOMAS, 80
CRUSE

JAMES, 119
SAMUEL, 119
SARAH, 119
CRUSENBURY

JAMES A., 18
CUESADAY
HIRAM, 5
MARTHA, 5
MARY E., 5
CULLISS
HEZEKIAH, 57
NELLIE, 57
SARAH ANN, 57
CUMBY
AARON T., 96
ANNIE, 96
ARMINTA, 85
C., 85(2)
L. EASLEY, 96
THOS, 85
CUMFORD
JAS D., 83
MARGT, 83
WM H., 83
CUMINS
A.J., 24
CUNDIFF
ELI, 54
REBECCA, 54
WM, 54
CUNINGHAM
HENRY, 70
LUCY, 70
MILES, 70
CUNNINGHAM

C., 116
ELIZABETH, 6, 25
GEO, 64
JAMES, 25, 122
JAS C., 89
JAS H., 58, 89
JAS. H., 25
JOCKEY, 108
KATIE, 80, 137
LOUIZA, 116
LUCY, 108
MARY JANE, 137
MILES, 108
S.J., 122
SARAH, 89
SARAH E., 58
SARAH J., 58
THOMAS, 137
VIRGIE L., 122
W.M., 116
CURRY
FATE, 129
HANNAH, 129
JOHN, 92
LEE, 129
MARIA, 92

MESHACK, 92
NANNIE KATE, 133
CURTIS
CLAIBOURNE, 17
SINOLA, 130
CUSTARD
CATHERINE, 12
FANNIE D., 12
JOHN D., 12
CUX
ELIZABETH S., 109
MARY, 109
MATHEW, 109
CYPERS
J.S., 69
MOLLIE, 69
OLLIE M., 69

-D-

DABNEY
BETTIE, 105
ELIZA V., 105
D'AGOSTIN
ANGELO, 82(2)
MARIE, 82
DAHRING
C.H., 58
DALTON
FRANCES, 125
JAS L., 98
MAHALA, 98
DAMERON
CATHERINE, 48
MICHAEL, 48
THOS G., 48
DAMEWOOD
CYNTHIA, 54
GEO P., 91
I.C., 125
S.M., 54, 125
SAML M., 91
DANCE
HENRY, 71
MOSES, 71
SOPHIA, 71
DANESECZ
STEVE, 136
DANGERFIELD

ELIZABETH, 7
JAS F., 62
JAS T., 62
LEONARD H., 7, 26
LUCINDA, 12
MATILDA, 62
NANCY, 7, 12, 26
OWEN, 62
RIGHT E., 26
SAMUEL H., 12
DANIEL
CHAS T., 123

J.D., 123
JAMES H., 21, 20-F
JANE, 21, 20-F
MARY, 75
MINA, 129
SALLY, 123
DANIELEY
ANN, 57
DERUSHA, 55, 57
JANE, 58
JERISHA, 58
NEHEMIAH, 55, 57, 58
RENIE, 55
DANIELLEY
JERNSHA, 34
JOHN H., 34
NEHEMIAH, 34
DANIELS
A.A., 94
DANILY
ELEN, 85
THOMAS, 85
WILLMOUIE, 85
DANNELBY
GERUSHA, 49
HUGH A., 49
NEHEMIAH, 49
DANNER
GEO S., 121
J.E., 121(2), 125
JANE, 125
MARY E., 125
DARBIN
MARY, 64
NANNIE, 64
DARE
CHAS, 31
CHAS, 20-A
EDNA A., 120
ELIZABETH, 31
ELIZTH., 20-A
H.J., 89
J.H., 64
JAMES H., 31
JENNIE, 89
JOS H., 120
LOUISA J., 20-A
MARY E., 3
MOLLIE, 89
S.N., 120
DARY
RICHARD PHASIN, 93

DAUGHERTY
D.A., 103, 106, 113, 121, 125
H.T., 101
HENRY FRANK, 101

LANDONIA, 101
DAULTON
JNO A., 107
POLLY, 107

DAUMER
JANE, 62
JOHN E., 62
LUCY J., 62
DAVENPORT
ANNA, 69
BETTIE, 65
ELIZA, 69
JENNIE, 65
THOMAS, 69
TOM, 65
DAVID
EVAN, 89(3)
JOSHUA, 2
KATHERINE, 89
SALLY, 2
DAVIDSON
A., 16
A.C., 65, 72, 77
AILSA, 98
ANDREW, 92
ARAMINTA, 16, 20
BETSY, 12
C., 139
CASS, 79
CASSANDER, 72
CHARLES, 43, 98
CHRISTINA, 42
DAVID, 16
E.L., 118
EDWARD G., 87
ELIZA J., 2
ELVIRA, 49
EVALANOR C., 92
G.W., 132
GEO T., 59
H.P., 118, 125
HANNAH M., 30
HEIRAM, 43
HENRY V., 62
HENRY, 12, 72, 114, 139
HENRY P., 62, 65, 98
HIRAM, 42, 132
HOWARD W., 2
HUGH, 98
J.H., 125
JAMES, 53, 87, 92
JAMES C., 4, 83, 139
JANE, 30, 59, 20-A
JAS, 92(2)
JOS, 4, 20-A
JOSEPH, 30, 59
JOSEPHINE, 49
JULIA, 83
JULIA A., 20-A
LOLA E., 125
LUCINDA, 62, 98, 118, 125
LUCINDA A., 65
LUCY B., 65
M., 4
MARGARET, 53, 92

MARGARET A., 92

MARGRET, 92
MARY S., 98
MATILDA J., 114
NANCY, 42, 43, 132
R.H., 114
RUFUS M., 53
SAML, 49
SM G., 2
WILLIAM G., 12
WILLMATH D., 92
WM B., 83
DAVIS
A.K., 89
ALBERT, 66
ALICE, 66
ALICE J., 63
ALICE V., 71
ALWILDAY, 25
AMELIA, 65
AMERICA, 134
ANDERSON, 134(2), 135, 136, 137, 139
ANDW. J., 13
ANNIE L., 94
ARDELIA, 20-E
ASA B., 100
BELL, 79
BETTY, 66, 86
C.C., 89, 94
C.S., 79
CATHERINE, 7
CATHERINE, 25
CHRISTINA, 31, 68(2)
CHRISTINE, 35, 63, 100
D.J., 75
DAVID D., 112
DELLIE B., 68
DOCTOR, 20
EASTHA S., 31
EDMUND, 101
ELBERT, 111
ELIJAH, 22
ELIZ. C., 37
ELIZA JANE, 35
ELIZABETH, 15, 22, 36, 112
ELIZABETH J., 52
ELIZABETH L., 25
GEO, 52
GEO F., 134
GEO T., 55
GEORGE R., 36
GREEN, 1, 25, 37, 61
H.G., 89, 94
HANNIE A., 33
HARRIET, 2
HENRY W., 24, 61
HIRAM, 8, 55, 129, 134
HIRAM G., 20-B
IRA W., 24

ISAAC J., 65
ISABELLA, 68
ISSAC J., 85
J., 20-E
J.A., 134
J.L., 75(2)
J.W., 20-A
JAMES B., 35
JAMES O., 111
JANE, 20, 24, 124
JAS W., 56
JENNIE, 8
JESSE, 35, 20-B
JNO, 101
JNO W., 13, 25
JOEL, 22
JOHN, 22, 25, 33, 61,
  94, 101
JOHN W., 5, 20, 77
JOSHUA, 1, 3, 8, 112,
  129, 20-C
JOSHUA A., 74
JULIA A., 8
JULIA ANN, 55
KIZZIAH, 79
LANDON, 3, 30
LANDON E., 53
LAUPEE, 20-A
LEE, 31, 35, 63,
  68(2), 94, 100, 112,
  20-C
LEN, 56, 71
LINDSAY, 8
LINDSEY, 24(2)
LINSEY, 20-B
LONEMA, 24
LOUISA, 5
LUCINDA T., 36
M., 85
M.S., 137, 138
M.W., 137, 138
MARGARET, 35
MARGT, 20-B
MARIA, 11
MARIA J., 52
MARIAE R.E., 54
MARTHA, 101
MARTHA M.J., 30
MARY, 22, 30, 77, 94,
  124
MARY C., 28
MARY E., 112
MARY F., 52
MARY N., 24
MERSHALL, 124
MINNIE M., 137
MOLLIE, 86
NANCY, 52, 75, 110,
  120
NANCY C., 61
P., 20-C
PAULINE A., 58
PERFINA, 77

POLLY, 71
POLLY ANN, 56
PURRIS L., 20
R., 68(2)
REBECA, 134
RHODA, 58, 63
ROBT, 68
RUTH J., 11
SALLIE P., 65
SALLY, 1
SAML, 61, 75
SANDY, 77
SARAH, 3, 8, 25(2),
  37, 61
SARAH E., 24
SARAH F., 22
SOL, 86
SUSAN, 61, 75
TEMPA, 20
TEMPE, 33
TEMPERANCE, 5, 13, 24,
  25
TERRIPY, 61
THOMAS, 112
TINY, 61
V.A., 75
W.R., 120
WALTER S., 110
WILLIAM, 54
WILLIAM L., 30
WILMOTII C., 63
WM, 20, 68, 74, 110,
  120
WM G., 52
WM L., 58
WM M., 138
DAVIS
  CHRISTINA, 64
  LEE, 64
  WM R., 64
DAWSON
  A.D., 133
  A.R., 70
  ALBERT S., 31
  ALICE, 80
  COLUMBIA J., 132
  ELIZA B., 79
  HIRAM, 70, 132
  HIRAM A., 31, 52
  MARTHA, 133
  MARY L., 52
  MOSES, 47, 56
  NANCY, 47, 56
  R.D., 79
  SALLIE, 52
  SARAH, 31, 70, 132
  VICIE E., 133
  WILLIS, 47, 56
DAY
  AMANDA, 44
  C.C., 97
  CHAS, 87

D.R., 79
DAVID, 80
DAVIS, 87
E., 18
ELL, 89
ELECTRA V., 29
ELIZ. ANN, 39
ELIZABETH, 45, 66
ELIZTH A., 59
ELLA L., 66
GILES, 66
JAMES I., 3
JAMES S., 44
JOSEPHINE, 80, 87
JOSHUA, 18, 79, 89
L.G., 39, 43(2), 44
LEWIS, 3, 18
LEWIS G., 36, 37, 38,
  39(2), 40(2), 44, 45,
  59
LOUISA C., 44, 20-D
LYDIA, 22
MAGGIE M., 59
MARINDA ANN, 39
MARY, 97
MARY E., 45
MARY W., 30
OCTAVIA A.M., 1
PATIENCE, 3
SARAH E., 79, 89
THOMAS, 80
WALTER, 97
DAYS
  JOHN, 132(2)
  LUCY, 132
DEAN
  FANNY, 66
  GEO W., 66
  LEE, 66
DEARMON
  ANTHONY, 92
  CAROLINE, 92
  DANL, 92
DEATIN
  CHARLES A., 30
DEATON
  C.L., 113
  CHARLES L., 31
  CHAS A., 49
  G., 113
  JOHN, 31, 113
  NATHAN, 35, 49
  SARAH, 49
  SARAH F., 35
DECOR
  COSBULL, 27
  JOHN, 27
DEEDS
  C.B., 22
  ELIZTH M., 4
  HANNAH, 4, 17
  JOHN, 20-E

JOHN F., 17
JOHN M., 20-E
JOS, 4
JOSEPH, 17
MARY, 13
PATSEY, 20-E
S.G., 22
WILSONIA JOSEPHINE,
  22
DEEK
  J.E., 90
DEEP
  PHRAIM, 53
  EPHRAIM G., 53
  LUCY, 53
DEER
  ELIZTH R.L., 76
  J.E., 76
  WM H., 76
DEETON
  JOHN, 112
  MARY, 111
  PARCILLA, 112
DEEWEES
  ANDREW, 20-D
  B., 20-D
DEHART
  HULA, 93
  MARTHA, 93
  THOMAS, 93
DeHAVEN
  JNO P., 87
  SARAH, 87
DELLION
  MASTIN, 26
DELP
  BALLARD P., 36, 115
  E., 110
  ELPHRAIM, 36
  L.C., 115
  LUCY, 110
  LUCY A., 36, 110
  S.E., 115
  SARAH, 51
DELPH
  EPHRAIM, 65
  JAMES W., 65
  LUCY, 65
DEMKO
  ANNA, 137
  JOHN, 137
  MARY, 137
DENNIS
  BENJ., 53
  GILFORD, 133
  J.G., 134(2)
  JAMES, 133
  M.E., 134
  NANCY, 133
  S.T., 134
DENNSON
  ISABELLA, 51
DENT

CHARLOTT, 131
CHARLOTT A., 119
CHARLOTTE, 87
EMMA, 119
LINDA J., 87
MARY, 131
THOMAS, 131
THOS, 87, 119
DENTON
  S.T., 66
DEOV (SIC)
  CHARLES, 12
  SALLIE, 12
DEQUASH
  L., 138
  REBECA, 138
  W.H., 138
DESPER
  JOHN, 54
  LUCY, 54
  PATIENCE, 54
DESWIM
  AMANDA, 74
  CALVIN, 74
  M.F., 74
DEVANEY
  JAS W., 62
  MARTHA, 62
  THOMAS, 62
DEVOR
  GEO. W., 27
DEWEES
  VIRGINIA P., 20-D
DEWEESE
  A., 14
  ANDREW, 11
  ESTHER, 11
  J.L., 125
  MANERVA, 125
  MARTHA C., 125
  MATILDA J., 14
  R., 14
  ROSINE, 11
DEWESE
  A., 17
  ANDR., 24
  ANDREW, 12, 30, 55
  ANDREW J., 28
  JANE, 77
  JAS W., 55
  JULIA ANN, 30
  LORIA E., 24
  MARY M., 12
  MATILDA J., 17
  ROSANAH, 28
  ROSENA, 12, 17
  ROZENA, 55
  SARAH G., 28
  T., 30
  W.S., 77
  WM LEE, 77
  WM P., 77
DEWEY

A.G., 14
EMILY N., 14
ROSA, 14
DEYERLE
  JOHN, 10
  MARY H., 14
DICKENSON
  HENRY, 78
  JAS H., 78
  JENNIE, 74
  NANCY, 78
  RADFORD, 74
  SAML, 74
DICKERSON
  CAROLINE, 120
  D., 119
  HATTIE MAY, 119
  HENRY, 70, 71
  JAMES, 120
  JANE, 71
  JENETTE, 104
  JENNETT, 70
  JNO H., 104(2)
  JOHN, 71
  MARTHA, 119
  MARY, 71
  MATIE, 71
  ROBT, 120
  SAM, 104
  SAML, 70
  SUE, 71
DICKINSON
  ANSEL, 20-E
  HATTIE, 93
  HENRY, 37, 44
  J.B., 85
  J.V., 76, 77(3), 84,
    85, 91
  LUCINDA, 20-E
  NANCY, 37
  NANCY ANN, 44
  PHEBE, 20-E
  THOMPSON W., 37
  W.A., 48
  WM N., 44
DICKISON
  JOHN, 81
  LEWIS, 75
  LUCY, 75
  PAYTON, 75
  PHOEBE ELLEN, 81
  SALLIE, 81
DICKSON
  GINNET, 80
  JOHN, 63
  SALLIE, 63
  SUSAN, 63
  WM, 80
DIE
  ELLIE, 77
  JOHN, 77

SARAH, 77
DIERLE (DEYIRLE)
  JOHN, 11
DIGGS
  L., 67
DILLARD
  ADDIE, 101
  EMILY, 84(2)
  JAS, 72
  JNO, 72
  JOHN, 84
  LUCY, 72
  MARSH, 101
DILLION
  ANGIE LEE, 95
  BALLARD P., 7
  CYNTH., 20-B
  CYNTHIA, 7, 11, 20, 27
  CYNTHIA E., 6
  CYNTHIA J., 28
  ELIZA L, 14
  EMARILLA, 14
  FREEBLIN H., 76
  GERUSHA B., 59
  H.F., 59
  H.G., 66
  H.J., 5
  HARRIET A., 45
  HENDERSON, 76
  HENDERSON F., 20
  JAMES, 51
  JAMES H., 11, 45
  JAMES F., 6, 11
  JAS. HARVEY, 47
  JAS. P., 14
  JESSE, 7, 11, 20, 27,
    20-B
  JOHN H., 107
  JULIA, 6, 81
  JULIET, 11, 14
  M.E., 51
  M.F., 76
  MARGARET A., 36, 20-B
  MARGARET W., 20-D(2)
  MARTHA, 36, 51
  MARY, 80(2), 106, 107
  MARY A., 47
  MASTIN, 26, 36,
    20-D(2)
  MATILDA, 45, 47, 51
  MATILDA J., 58
  MERCINA, 59
  OSBORN T., 5
  PEGGY, 36
  POLLY, 2, 4
  POLLY A., 4
  POLLY D., 11
  R., 26

RACHEL, 26
REBECCA J., 20-D
RHODA G., 2
S., 13
SAML, 2, 4
SARAH E., 36
SQUIRE, 13
T.T., 27
VIRGINIA F., 58
W.H., 81
WILLIAM, 80
WILLIAM H., 81
WM, 36, 51, 106(2),
  107
DILLON
  AMOS E., 101
  C.A., 133
  EMMA L., 99
  F., 133
  HENDERSON, 126
  HENDERSON F., 65
  JAS, 90, 118
  LULY, 65
  M.F., 95
  MARCENA, 126
  MATILDA, 118
  MATILDA J., 90
  MERCENA, 65
  PATRIA F., 90
  S.A., 133
  SALLIE, 101
  SALLY, 99
  T.F., 86(2), 101
  WM, 86
  Z.T., 99
  ZACH, 101
DILLS
  CYNTHIA, 83
  MILLARD C., 40
  NANCY J., 40
  PETER H., 40
  ROSA, 83
DINGER
  AUG, 59
  CHAS A., 59
  KATE, 59
DINGMAN
  BERT F., 68
DISHMEL
  HILA ANN, 55
  LEANDER, 55
  WM, 55
DIXIE
  LOUISA, 76
  W.P., 76
DIXON
  CHAS, 65
  MARY, 117
  NINIE, 65
  WALTER E., 65
DOBBINS

D.C., 134
W.C., 52, 56, 88
WM C., 22, 23(3), 27
DOBINS
WILLIAM C., 21(3), 20-F(3)
WM C., 22
DODD
A.A., 76
ANDERSON, 32, 43, 94
ANDERSON A., 33
C.E., 131
E.C., 76, 94
ELIZABETH, 43
ELZTH, 32, 33
F.W., 131
GEO L. LETCHER, 131

HARRETT (SIC) M., 94

MARY J., 33
MINERVA E., 43
SARAH A., 3
SARAH A.E., 32
W.W., 76
DOLAN
OCTAVIA, 130
DONAHOE
AGNES D., 20-E
JANE, 20-E
THOS. H., 20-E
DONAHOO
JUNE, 21, 20-F
MARY B., 21, 20-F
THOS H., 21, 20-F
DONALLEY
ANDRSON, 96
ELISHA K., 96
SARAH, 96
DONALLY
A., 134
ANDERSON, 90
JULIA A., 90
S.A., 134
SALLIE A., 90
W.L., 134
DONATHAN
AARON, 98
H.L., 98
MARTHA, 98
DONEHOE
JANE, 23
JULIA, 23
THOS, 23
DONITHAN
ROBT LEE, 65
DOOLEY
M.A., 140
SARAH J., 140
T.C., 140
DORMAN
MARY, 39
DORSEY

S.C., 72(3), 73, 74, 75, 76
DOSS
ELZINE, 104
F., 120
FLOYD, 51
FLOYD W., 104
JAMES, 133(2)
JNO, 3
JNO R., 104
JOHN W., 120
JOS, 124
S.J., 120
SARAH, 3
DOUDY
JNO, 90
MARY L., 90
DOUGLASS
ELEANOR, 10
EUGENE, 139
GREEN, 128
J.M., 69(5), 70, 71(4), 72
JNO M., 60(2), 63
JOHN A., 10(2)
JOHN M., 60, 63, 64(4), 65(2), 66(2)
P.A., 128
WM T., 128
DOUTHAT
C.F., 72
EMMA, 72
J.H., 139
M.E., 139
MARY F., 72
NETTIE N., 118
S. VA., 118
W.T., 139
WM H., 118
DOVE
B., 129
BERTIE O., 88
BILL, 139
ELIZABETH, 76, 139
FERDIMAN, 22
FOOTE, 88
FOOTE W., 105
ISABELLA, 70, 88, 105
JUDA A., 76
LAURA, 105
P.W., 129
POWHATTAN, 33

R.L., 70
ROXIE B., 139
S.B., 33
SALLIE, 33
SALLIE J., 129
SALLY, 22
SHERWOOD, 22
TOOT. W., 70
VIRGINIA, 119
WM, 76

DOWDY
BENJN, 60
BEBE, 119
CHAS, 137
JAMES C., 60
JOHN, 119
MANDY, 137
MINNETTIE, 137
SUSAN, 60
THOMAS, 119
THOS, 119(2)
DOWNS
ELISHA, 87
EMMA, 87
MARY JANE, 87
DOYERLE
JOHN, 4
DOYLE
CHAS THOS, 86
ENRIVA J., 44
JAMES A., 44, 46
JOHN J., 46
MARTHA, 46, 86, 88
MARTHA A., 42, 44, 57
MARTHA E., 57
MARTHA O., 110
MARY A., 42
MATTIE, 100
ROSA A., 88
S.E., 110
SARIAH, 100
WM M., 110
DOYLES
JAMES A., 35
MARTHA A., 35
WILLIAM M., 35
DREBERT
J.F., 82
JOHN, 82
MARY, 82
DRIGGINS
MARY C., 20-D
NANCY, 20-D
THOMAS, 20-D
DRISCOLL
DENNIS, 106
VIRGINIA E., 106
W.R., 106(2)
DRUGAN
JANE, 84
JOHN, 84
JOSEPH, 84
DUCKWALL
J. McC., 75, 77, 81, 83(3), 84(2), 86, 89(2), 90(3), 91, 93, 96(2), 99(2), 100
J.M.C., 71, 79
M. McC., 88
DUDLEY
A.E., 66
A.J., 66

ALLION, 136
ALMEDA, 127
ANDREW J., 52
CENA, 36
ELIZ A., 37
ELIZABETH, 52
H.D., 111
HARVEY W., 48
HUGH D., 42
J.C., 129
JANE, 42, 48, 111
JNO S., 37
JOHN, 36
JOHN W., 117
LALA F., 140
LUCY, 36, 37
LUCY J., 113
M.L., 129
MARY E., 66
MAURICE R., 52
P.S., 140
R.A., 113
REBECA, 136
REBECCA, 117
TOBIAS, 48
W.E., 111
WILLIAM L., 29
WM E., 42
WM L., 113, 117, 136
WM T., 129
DUGGER
MARY, 58
W.C., 58
WM, 58
DUHRING
CHARLOTTE, 94
ELIZA, 94
GEO, 94
DUNAGAN
L., 20-B
LEWIS, 44(2), 20-B
N., 20-B
NANCY, 44
DUNBAR
CINTHIA, 1
CYNTHIA A., 1
SUSAN, 1
WILLIAM, 1(2)
DUNCAN
A.M., 119, 130
BRADY B., 67
CHAS R., 64
D.D., 119
E.G., 14
ELISHA G., 2, 8, 10, 15, 16(3)
ELLA M., 94
F.M., 133
G.W., 100, 102
GEORGIA A.F., 100
J.H., 130
JAMES H., 130
JANE, 102

JAS W., 94
JOS, 133
JOSEPHUS, 39
LANDON, 1, 8
LUCINDA, 48
LUCINDA E., 67, 20-B
LUCNDA, 89
MALINDA J., 39
MARTHA A., 102
MARTHA S., 39
MARY A., 64
MINNIE A., 89
N.A., 133
R.S., 130
REBECA, 119
SARAH, 100, 102
SARAH A., 94
THOS, 102
WM, 48, 89, 102
WM H., 67
WM M., 48
DUNEVANT
BECKY, 66
JAMES, 66
JASPER, 66
DUNFORD
ALBERT, 48, 122
C., 100
CANEY, 100
EDWARD, 128
ELIZA, 48, 122
ELIZA A., 89
J.W., 52, 56
JAS R., 56
JENNIE, 112
JESSE G J., 48
JULIA A., 52
LINA, 89
P.E., 56
PAULINA, 100
PHOEBE E., 52
POLINA, 128
W.M., 122
WM, 89, 100, 128
DUNIGAN
LEWIS, 55
NANCY JANE, 55
ROSA BELLE, 55
DUNKIN
A.T., 104
HARVEY, 104
REBECCA, 104
DUNLAP
PATTIE, 109
DUNN
AMANDA, 51
BALLARD P., 51
C.V., 100
ELIZABETH A., 28
FELDON, 66
IDA B., 105
ISAIAH W., 27
J., 128

J.W., 106, 121(2)
JAS SANDERS, 100
JNO W., 105(2)
JOHN W., 28, 60, 106
JUNIUS, 66(2)
LEVI, 128(2)
M.W., 27
MARY, 105
MARY C., 105, 106, 121
MILLEY, 66
MILLIE, 128
MILLIE J., 27
MILLY, 66
NANNIE E., 106
ROBEY, 66
ROBY, 128
T.E., 100
THEORA J., 121
THOS A., 51
ZORA J., 105
DUNSON
ELISHA G., 11
KATE U., 104
M.B., 104
EAST
ELIZABETH, 12
GALEN, 98
MARY ANN, 98
NANCY, 98
SAMUEL A., 12
THOMAS, 12
DWIGGINS
LOUISA CATH, 20-D

MARY, 20-D
SARAH F., 24
THOMAS, 20-D
THOMAS C., 11, 24
WILLIAM G., 11
DWYER
LAWRENCE, 137
DYALE
CROCHETO, 7
MARY, 7
REBECA C., 7
DYE
FANNIE, 92
FLORENCE, 90
PRIOR, 90, 92
FRYER, 114
RUCIA, 114
SARAH, 92, 114
SARAHAN, 90
DYERLE
JOHN, 8
DYERLY
HELEN, 93
DYLA
CALLIE, 110
ELLEN, 110
JEFF, 110

-E-

EADES
J.B., 127
ROBT, 127
S.A., 127
EAKLE
JACOB, 69
JANE, 69
WM B., 69
EANS
EMMA, 75
EARLEY
CELIA, 135
PRESTON, 135
EARLY
ANNIE E., 123
M.C., 123, 126
MARTHA M., 126
R.J., 123
ROBT J., 126
EASLEY
JOHN W., 104
EAST
ELIZABETH, 12
GALEN, 98
MARY ANN, 98
NANCY, 98
SAMUEL A., 12
THOMAS, 12
EASTBURN
DAVID, 56
SARAH, 56
WALTER D., 56
EASTER
BETTIE E., 79
CHAS M., 84
E.W., 79
L.W., 79(2)
MAHALA, 22
MARTHA J., 18, 112
MARY S., 112
R.S., 112
ROBT S., 30
SUSAN, 18, 22, 30
SUSAN A., 84
W.W., 30
WM, 22
WM W., 18, 84
EATON
DANIEL H., 8
E.S., 128, 130
ELIZABETH, 8
EUGENIA J., 128
JOHN, 8
L.M., 128, 130
NELLIE L., 130
EAVES
DORA, 127
ELIZABETH, 104
EMILINE, 121
EMMA, 104

JACOB, 104
JAS M., 127
LEWIS, 127
NELSON, 54
ECHOLS
ROBT N., 89
EDMUNDS
CAVNESS, 77
DILSEY, 77
MAC, 77
EDWARDS
BETTIE R., 89, 90
BIA R., 73
CHARITY, 61
DOLLIE, 73
FANNIE, 91
JACOB, 106(2)
JANE, 91, 96
JOHN, 122
LEWIS F., 61
M.H., 91, 96
M.W., 122
MARTHA J., 106
MARY C., 82
NANNIE P., 90
NEWEL M., 61
SALLY J., 110
SARAH, 122
SUSIE, 96
THOMAS, 106
W.H., 73, 89, 90
W.N., 89
WM, 109
WM H., 90
EGGLERTON
BEVERLY, 83
H.W., 83
MARY, 83
EGGLESTON
GEORGE, 115
JANE, 115
LOUISA, 115
ELDRIDGE
CHAS, 102
LULA, 134
MARGARET, 72
RACHEL, 72, 102, 134
WM, 102, 134
ELISON
BURLEY, 2
F.T., 20-D
M., 20-C
U., 20-D
ELKINS
EMILY C., 22
ELLIOTT
CHARLOTT, 121
CHARLOTTE, 140
ESTHER, 84, 140
J.C., 81
ROBERT, 140
ROBT F., 81
SARAH A., 81

ELLIS
A.J., 134
AMANDA J., 59, 134
BELL, 141
CLARKIE MAY, 134

ELIZTH F., 56
ELLA, 82
GRIFFITH, 39, 134
HARRIET E., 46
JAMES, 141
JANE, 39, 42, 56, 76, 116
LEWIS, 141
M.A., 116
MARTHA E., 39
MARY S., 42
MINNIE J., 76
N.G., 134
NORA G., 134
O.J., 56, 76, 116, 141
OBEDIA, 39
OVERTON, 42
PRICSILLA, 46
S., 141
SALLY, 82
SHAN, 134
WILLIAM H., 16
WM, 46
ELLISON
ANDREW, 2
ASA, 2, 12
BENJ, 73
E., 19
EASTER, 42
ELIZA, 21, 20-F
ELIZABETH, 31, 39, 43, 46, 139
ELIZABETH J., 19
ELIZTH, 9
FANNIE D., 118
GIRTRUDE, 74
HENDERSON F., 17

HOBART H., 133
I.J., 46, 139
ISAAC, 5(2), 31
ISAAC J., 9, 21, 39, 43, 46, 20-F
J.A., 120
J.M., 41
JAMES, 20-D
JAS, 20-B
JAS., 17, 33
JOHN R., 5
JOS., 13
JOSEPHINE, 20-D
JULIAN A., 9
KATE ELLEN, 139
L.B., 73
LARKIN, 42
LUCY ANN, 96
M., 3, 42

M.A., 116
M.F., 74, 134
M.J., 74, 118, 133
MARINDA, 13
MARY, 2, 12, 13, 17, 20-B, 20-D
MARY A., 31
MARY A.V., 40
MARY ANN, 5
MARY S., 20-B
MATTHEW, 20-A
MATTIE L., 39
MILLARD F., 21, 20-F
MILLY, 2
N.V., 96
NANCY T., 5(2)
P.A., 96
POLLY, 33
R.F., 118, 133
ROBERT P., 39
S.J., 19
SAML, 39
SAMUEL, 40
SAMUEL G., 41
SARAH, 20-D
SARAH E., 43
SUSAN, 39, 40, 41
WILLIAM, 2, 42
WM OR., 33
WM T., 12
ELMORE
A.P., 81
CLEMENTINE, 81
ELLEN, 66
F.W., 130
H. MADISON, 115
J.E., 81
JAMES, 66
P.F., 130
WM B., 66, 130
EMMONS
B., 4
MARY E.C., 57
MORTON, 4
MORTON R., 57
OSCAR J., 4, 57
EMSWELLER
BIRDIE, 34
IRA, 34
ENGLAND
AUG J.S., 61
JAS MAD., 61
MARY E., 61
ENGLISH
BENJAMINE, 119
M., 119
S.D., 119
ENOCHS
HENRY, 22
JOSEPH, 22
LOLLIE, 22
RHODA, 22
ENSLEY

JOHN, 69
MARY, 69
MOLLIE, 69
EPLING
A.E., 116
D.L., 72
E.J., 116
ELLEN, 72, 81, 114, 130
ELLEN J., 122
GILES THOS, 136
L.A., 72, 81, 114, 116, 130
LEWIS A., 122
LUSTER R., 122
M.F., 116
MOLLIE E., 81
ONIE M., 116
R.L., 122
ROY L., 114
W.A., 116
ZORA J., 130
ERBY
AMANDA, 123
ANNA, 69
C.M., 77
CARRY, 123
ISAAC, 77
JARRETT, 117
JOHN, 69
JULIA, 117
LUCINDA, 77
LUCY, 69
SIMON, 117
ERWIN
ANDREW, 64
FANNIE, 64
HANNAH, 64
ESKEY
AVIS, 35
JOSEPH L., 35
WILLIAM, 35
ESKRIDGE
T.J., 103, 104(2), 105
THOS J., 102
ETTER
ELLEN J., 111
MINNIE B., 111
EUBANKS
CAROLINE, 48
DAWNIE, 48
NAPOLEON, 48
EVANS
AB., 15
ABRAHAM, 101
ANGELINE, 111
ANNIE V., 110
CAROLINE, 38
CHAS H., 104
D.S., 104
ED, 53
EDWIN, 40
ELIZABETH C., 101

EVAN, 51
F.D., 71
FANNIE A., 77
G.C., 125
G.E., 111
GEORGE, 25, 38
J.W.R., 55
JNO B., 107
JNO C., 125
JOHN J., 71
JOSEPH, 110
K.L., 63
LEE, 85
LEWIS, 15, 55, 77, 101
LOUISA, 77
MARTHA, 77
MARY, 126
MARY ANN, 40
OSBORNE, 53
REBECCA, 53
ROHT, 111
RUTH A., 71
S.A., 110
SAML J., 107
SARAH, 85, 101
SARAH A., 15, 85, 107
SARAH E., 104
STEPHEN, 38
SUSAN, 55, 77
SUSIE, 125
THOMAS, 40
THORNTON, 77
WILLIAM H., 25
WM, 63, 112
EVATT
BARBARA J., 6
JOSEPH, 6
PHOEBE, 6
EVERLY
AMANDA E., 20-E
IRA, 20-E
MARTHA, 20-E
EWING
CATHARINE, 132
CORDELIA, 132
JAMES, 132

-F-

FALEY
A.B., 25
J.H., 112
MANERVA, 25
P., 25
SUSAN, 112
TOLIVER, 112
FALKE
C.C., 92
ELIZA, 92
H.M., 92
FALLS
LEWIS, 123
LUTHER T., 123

FANING
BENJN, 2, 3
NANCY, 2, 3
FANNING
ANDREW J., 2
ANNIE J., 76
BENJ, 20-D
BENJ., 18, 22
BENJ. F., 12
BENJAMIN, 27
BENJN, 2
CYRUS B., 20-C
ELIZABETH, 9
G.B., 20-C
GARLAND, 40
GARLAND B., 5, 7, 9
GARLIN, 2
GEORGE W., 30
HUGH J., 5
ISABELLA, 22
J.J., 76
JANE, 30
JAS R., 76
JOSEPH, 30
MARTHA, 7
MARY, 121
MARY D., 7
MATILDA, 40
MILLA, 9
MILLIE, 5
MILLY, 2
NANCY, 2, 18, 22, 27, 40, 20-C, 20-D
NANCY E., 18
NANCY J., 2
S.J., 12
SARAH E., 3
SUSAN S., 2
T.T., 27
FANTROY
NANCY, 59
FARIS
A.W., 127
HENRIETTA, 127
VICTORIA, 127
FARLEY
A.F., 114
A.P., 141
ADALINE, 29
ADAM, 21, 20-F
ALBERT G.P., 21, 20-F
ALEXANDER, 24
ALICE, 88
ALICE M., 22
ALLIE H., 83
ALMIRA F., 28
AND, 27
ANDERSON, 7
ANDREW, 7, 11, 20, 21, 22, 28, 35, 41, 20-F
ANDREW P., 20-A
ANN, 125
ANNA, 7(2), 11(2), 15,

20, 27
ARCH, 10, 11, 17, 20-A(2)
ARCH'D, 21, 20-F
AUDSN. P., 49
B.D., 129
BAITLEY D., 34
BARBARA A., 48
C.C., 125
CARRIE V., 114
CLARISON A., 52
D., 69, 71
DINAH, 1, 2, 11, 12, 20
DREWERY, 52, 121
DREWRY, 55, 62, 63, 73, 94, 98, 101, 102, 103(2), 108, 118(2), 122, 140
DRURY, 24, 64, 87, 88(2), 90, 91, 115
ELIZA J., 20-D
ELIZABETH, 21(2), 39, 40, 44, 54, 20-F(2)
ELIZABETH A., 54
ELIZABETH J., 41
ELIZTH, 20
ELLEN, 129, 20-D
EMALINE, 49
EMILINE, 141
FRANCIS, 11
FRANCIS K., 39
GIDEON, 1, 2, 11, 12(2), 20
H.F., 119
HENDERSON F., 10

HENDLEY, 38, 40
HENLEY, 29
HENRY, 44, 97
HENRY L., 57
HEUDLEY C., 20-A
HIRAM, 21, 135, 20-D, 20-F
IDA, 7
INDIA PEARL, 119
ISAAC, 20, 21(2), 20-F(2)
ISAAC E., 20-E
J., 20-A
J.E., 129
J.R., 83
JACKSON, 122
JAMES, 7, 20-A
JAMES A., 29
JAMES H., 57
JAMES R., 20-A
JANE, 2
JAS, 20-A
JAS C., 122
JAS H., 52, 78
JAS N., 62
JEM., 20-A

JEMIMA, 10, 11, 17, 21, 20-F
JOHN, 20, 24, 34, 91, 20-D
JOHN R., 91
JOHN W., 39, 40, 44
JUDAH, 21, 20-F
JUDITH, 22, 35
LEVI, 88
LEWIS M., 141
LOUISA, 11
LOUIZA A., 129
LUCINDA, 40, 52
LUCINDA E., 49
LUCY, 34, 20-D
LUCY A., 29, 34, 128
LUCY ANN, 44, 62, 97
LUVERNA, 21, 20-F
M., 20-A
M.J., 83
MAHALA, 17
MALINDA, 49
MARG, 21, 20-F
MARGARET, 62
MARTHA, 10, 88, 20-A
MARY, 15, 21, 52, 57, 78, 135, 20-F
MARY A., 34, 122, 129, 20-D
MARY J., 91
MINERVA A., 21, 20-F
N.E., 114
N.F., 114
N.H., 26
NANNIE E., 119
NANNIE Y., 117
NELSON, 1, 49
O.J., 117
OSCAR J., 35
PEARL E., 117
PLEASANT H., 38
R.L., 85
RACHEL, 12, 20
RACHEL J., 20-A
RHODA, 44
RILEY, 129
ROBERT W., 40
RUFUS W., 52
S.E., 26
S.R., 26
SALINA, 24
SARAH, 21, 28, 29, 38, 40, 48, 20-F
SARAH E., 24
SARAH J., 24
SUSAN, 21, 20-F
THOS C., 49
VICTORIA, 89
VIRGINIA ALICE, 78

VIRGINIA R., 89
W.T., 13
WILLIAM, 29, 44

WILLIAM J., 12
WILLIAM R., 20-E
WILSON, 20, 52
WM, 34, 54, 62, 85, 89, 97, 125, 128
WM C., 21, 20-F
WM J., 62, 128(2)
FARLIN
ADA A., 94
OCTVA, 94
W.C., 94
FARLY
DINAH, 12, 13
GIDEON, 13
FARMER
ALEXANDER, 41
ARDELIA, 118
AUGUSTA L., 61
AUGUSTUS, 41
BOYD, 111
DAVID, 16, 32
ELIJAH, 9, 10, 11
ELIZA, 115
ELIZA J., 61
EMMA, 128
FANNIE C., 112
FLOYD H., 113
FRANK M., 71
FRAZIER, 133(2)
GEO W., 70
J.L., 18
J.P., 133
J.R., 89
J.T., 93
JAMES, 70, 111
JAMES H., 112
JANE, 112
JAS T., 61, 75, 93
JNO, 13
JOHN, 14, 61, 128
JOHN D., 10
JOHN H., 24, 61, 112
JOHN L., 11, 24
JOHN M., 41
JOHN N., 81
LENA G., 71
LIZZIE, 102
M.M., 113
MARGARET E., 18

MARGARET J., 57
MARIETTA A., 126
MARTHA A., 89
MARY, 9, 11, 14
MARY E., 10
MARY ELLEN, 75
MARY M., 34, 50, 61, 68, 92
MARY MIRTIE, 112

N., 18
NANCY, 11, 13, 24, 81
NANCY A.A., 50

NANCY D., 11
NANCY E., 52
OLENA M., 34
POLLY, 70
R., 118
R.C., 92, 113
REUBEN, 34, 68
REUBEN C., 11, 50, 61, 81
RHODA, 32
RHODA E., 68
ROXANA, 112
S.E., 133
S.W., 118
SALLIE, 70
SARAH, 52, 57, 126
SARAH A., 61
SARAH E., 75, 93, 102, 111
SARAH M., 9
STEPHEN, 32
SUSAN A., 61
VICTORIA, 71
VIRGINIA, 52
VIRGINIA E., 92
VIRGINIA V., 89
W.K., 93
WILLIAM, 102
WILLIAM HENRY, 109

WM, 13, 14, 115
WM H., 52, 57, 126
FAROLER
MAGGIE BELL, 121

MARTIN, 121
NANCY, 121
FARRAN
A.M., 118
LEWIS N., 118
S.D., 118
FARRELL
O., 139
R., 139
RUBIN, 139
FARROR
JAS, 97
JULIA, 97
FARTHING
A.P., 66
JAMES, 66
PARTHENIA, 66
FAULKNER
A.E., 118
ANN E., 49, 101
ANNA E., 47
ANNE, 43
ANNIE E., 70
BELL, 91
ELLEN P., 17
EMMA, 8
FIELDING E., 47
GORDAN, 118

GORDEN, 138
GORDON, 43, 44, 47, 49, 61, 70
GORDON P., 101
H.M., 17, 91(2), 110
HANNAH L., 21, 20-F
HARDY, 22
HARRIET L., 28
HUGH M., 6, 8, 21, 28, 44, 47, 20-F
JNO T., 101
JORDAN, 6
JOS K., 118
LAURA, 47
M.D., 110
MARGARET L., 49
MARY, 22, 47
MEDORA A., 51
MOLLIE, 91
RHODA, 138
S., 17
SARAH E., 43, 61
SUSAN, 44, 51
SUSANNAH, 6, 8, 21, 28, 20-F
THEE L., 61
VINT C., 70
VIRGIE, 138
VIRGILLA G., 110
VIRGINIA S., 22
FEAZEL
JNO M., 20
M., 14
MARSHALL, 14
MARSHALL M., 20

MARTHA M., 14
MARY E., 20
FERFUSON
EDNA E., 86
M.W., 86(2)
MARTHA W., 86
THOS S., 86(2)
FERGUSON
AMELIA, 13
ANDREW, 105
ANNETTA J., 29
AURELIA, 20
BETTIE, 56
C.L., 71
CHAS A., 100
CHAS V., 100
D.M., 36
D.W., 79(3)
DANIEL W., 21, 20-F
E.R., 66, 94, 122, 128, 134
EFFE, 105
ELEANA, 21, 20-F
ELIJAH, 20
ELIZA C., 128
ELIZABETH, 32, 66, 80, 94, 128(2), 134

ELIZTH, 22
EMMADORA S., 80

ENDORA F., 128
FEO W., 80
FLOYD P., 94
G.L., 124
G.N., 84, 124(2), 126
G.W., 116
GEORGIA ELLEN, 116

GREEN W., 26
HENRY ANN, 122
HENRY F., 134
J.A., 66
J.B., 55
JERE., 15
JEREMIAH, 4
JESSE G.L., 23
JNO, 30
JOHN, 23, 26, 30, 128
JOHN W., 126
JOS., 22
JOSIAH, 30
LIRONIA, 21, 20-F
LIVONIA, 36
MAGGIE, 65
MARY, 65, 80, 116
MARY J., 15
MARY JANE, 22
MARY LOUISA, 100

MILLA, 30
N., 4
NANCY, 15
NANCY E., 20
NANCY P., 55
NORA D., 71
OCTAVA, 84
OCTAVIA, 124, 126
RHODA J., 30
RODK. B., 105
S.M., 71
SARAH C., 4, 55
SUE F., 13
SUSANA, 30
SUSANNAH, 23
SWAUNA S., 26
V.E., 36
VIRGINIA F., 84
W.E., 13
FERRELL
BYRD, 136
DAVID, 4
E., 4
J., 4
MARY, 136
FICH
CAROLIN, 124
JOHN NELL, 124
JORDAN, 124
FIELDER
C.F., 50

CHAS. T., 43
CYNTHIA, 57
DENNIS, 30, 50, 55, 59
DEWEESE, 43
ELIZTH C., 59
FRANK C., 55
GRANVILLE M., 30

JOSEPH, 57
MARY, 43, 50, 59
MARY M., 55
POLLY, 30
R.J., 68
S.E., 68
VIOLA T., 57
WM S., 68
FIELDS
AMANDA, 74
CARRIE, 74
DARA, 134
J.W., 93
JNO, 134
LISIA, 101
MATTIE, 134
ROBERT, 101
ROBT, 74
FIERCE
SAML, 72
FILLY
E.A., 58
FINCH
LIZZIE, 105
SADIE F., 105
THOMAS R., 105
FINK
ANDREW E., 39
ANDREW L., 39
CHARLES H., 39
RACHAEL S., 39
RACHEL, 20-B
RUTH, 39
TURPIN M., 20-B
WM A., 39, 20-B
FINLEY
ELIZA, 92, 119
ROSA, 92
RUFUS, 92
FINNEY
C.A., 94(2)
J.W., 85
JAS W., 85
LILBURN, 78
LULA K., 78
MARINDA, 94
MELISSA, 78
RINDA, 85
SILAS, 94
FINZER
G.W., 124
FIRESLINE
ANGELINE, 138
D.M., 138
MARY, 138

FISHER
E.J., 133
HENRY, 40
I.B., 109
J.A., 133
JAMES, 109
LETTIE MAY, 133
LOU, 124
MALINDA J., 40
MOLINDA, 124
NANCY, 40, 20-C
FITCH
CAROLINE, 72
DAISY B., 67
GEORGE B., 67
HATTIE A., 67
JAS, 126
JORDON, 72
NEEL, 72
FITSWATER
JOHN, 20-D
MARTHA, 20-D
SARAH, 20-D
FITZBURGH
THOMAS, 120
FITZGERALD
C., 139
CHRIS, 103
DAVID, 103
R.W., 62, 63(2), 68(2), 69
RACHEL, 103
SENIA, 139
FITZWATER
B.N., 94
I.N., 138
ISAAC N., 20-B
ISAIAH, 94
J.C., 111
JNO, 33, 98, 20-B
JNO C., 98
JOHN C., 33
LAURA A., 111
M.E., 111
MOLLIE, 138
OCTAVIA, 94
RHODA, 138
SARAH, 33, 98, 20-B
FIZER
CHARLES, 44
REBECCA, 44
SUSAN, 44
FIZIER
CHAS F., 71
MINNIE N., 71
SUE K., 71
FLAMMER
ELIZABETH, 55
JAS H., 55
JEHIAL M., 55
FLEMING
CAROLINE, 54
ELIZA LIN, 54

JERRY, 54
FLESHMAN
J.P.L., 116
JANE, 41
MJ., 116
SARAH E., 41
W.L., 116
FLETCHER
ALICE, 46, 50, 124
ANDERSON, 124, 136

ANDREW J., 73
ANNIE L., 134
ARAMINTA, 43
ARDELIA E., 57
CALVIN, 31, 48, 103
COLUMBIA, 37
COLUMBIA J., 32
COLUMBIA JANE, 73

CORA A., 117
DAVISON, 46
E., 18
ELIZTH, 14
ELLA, 117
ELLA A., 32
ELLEN, 32, 36
EMMA C., 31
GEORGE W., 140
H.A., 50
HARRISON, 40
HARVEY, 124
HIRAM A., 40, 43, 45, 20-D
HIRAM H., 37
I., 18
I.G., 117
ISAAC, 14, 32, 36, 48, 59, 107
ISAAC G., 36, 57
J.H., 133, 134
J.W. HENDERSON, 48

JAMES H., 40, 136, 20-D
JANE, 24, 32, 40(2), 20-D
JAS H., 32, 37, 73, 103, 107, 140
JAS., 14
JAS. H., 24
JOHN D., 37
JOHN W., 57
JOSIE L., 60
JULIA A., 24
JULIA E., 54
LAURA B., 133
LILLY D., 107
LOUISA, 40(2)
LOUISA F., 45
LOUISA J., 59
LUCY ANN, 40
LUEMMA VICTORIA,

107
MARTHA, 46, 60
MARTHA J., 67
MARY, 20-D
MARY ANN, 107, 140

MARY J., 54
MINERVA J., 48
NANCY, 37
NANCY J., 113
POLLY ANN, 40
R.H., 67
RHODA, 31, 37, 40, 43, 45, 48, 103, 136, 20-D
ROBERT, 20-D
SARAH, 48
SARAH E., 40, 107
WILLIAM, 40
WILLIAM H., 18
WM H., 60, 67
FLICK
ANN, 106
ANN M., 27
ECL, 27
EDWARD, 106
JN. M.N., 27
JNO, 106
FLORANCE
CYNTHIA M., 29
FLOWERS
BETTIE, 133
JAMES, 12, 133
JOHN H., 12
ROBERT, 133
SARAH, 12
FLOYD
BILLIE L., 94
FLETCHER, 128
H.D., 94
H.F., 128
MARY L., 97
N.S., 97
W.H., 97
FLUMMER
C.E., 62
CATHERINE, 44
JAS H., 44, 62
VIRGINIA, 62
WM J.E., 44
FOLDEN
E.W., 125
ELLA M., 125
GEO F., 113
M.J., 125
YANCY J., 113
FOLEY
A.L., 93, 137
ALF., 20-B
BERNARD F., 33
C.A., 123
CHAS A., 92

CORNELIUS H., 45
ELIZABETH E., 2
J.A., 68
JAMES, 2, 6, 10, 15
JAMES T., 10
JUDA, 2, 6
JUDITH, 15
JUDITY, 10
L., 135
L.A., 92
LOUISA, 6
MAG, 135
MANEY A., 20-B
MARY, 74
MARY D., 44, 68
MARY J., 92, 123
MAT, 137
MOLLIE G., 135
P., 19, 32, 33
PARSHANDATHA, 50

PARSHAUDALHA, 45

PHELENA, 123
R.B., 19
R.F., 68, 137
REED M., 15
RICHARD, 44, 20-B
RICHARD B., 33, 45
RICHARD F., 135
RICHD, 32
ROSABELLA, 19
SUSAN, 45
TEXAS, 51
TOLIVER, 45
VICTORIA A., 44
VILEY JANE, 45
VIRGINIA E., 32
WILLIS D., 137
FOLKNER
BETTIE, 91
FONTY
MICHEAL (SIC), 72
REBECCA, 72
WM S., 72
FORD
A.B., 114
AMANDA B., 139
BENJAMIN, 6
ELBERT W., 114
ELIZABETH, 124
GEO A., 56
GEORGE, 94, 120
J.L., 139
J.W., 139
JOHN, 120
JOHN J., 6
LELIA, 124
LEWIS, 56
LIZZIE, 94
LOUCINDA, 84
LUTITIA, 19
MARY, 56, 94

159

MAY G., 84
PEGGY, 6
SAML, 84
FORDE
 LEWIS, 19
FORELINE
 JOE, 139
 MARY E., 139
FORTNER
 HARVEY, 81
 JNO, 56
 MINERVA, 56
 NOW (SIC), 81
 WM W., 56
FORTUNE
 ELIZABETH, 58
FOSTER
 BURGRESS, 3
 GEORGE, 2
 JAMES, 2
 JAMES R., 50
 JOHN W., 108
 KATIE, 108
 LUCY, 53
 MARY, 2, 83
 MARY B., 3
 MATISON, 108
 MILTON, 50
 NANCY, 97
 RICHARD, 24
 RICHD, 64
 SQUIRE, 97
 W.M., 97
 W.R., 83
 WM, 53, 83
 WM K., 3
 WM M., 24, 64
 ZALPHA, 24
 ZILTHA, 64
FOUND
 ALISON, 98
 ELEANOR, 98
FOWLER
 CORA A., 103
 D.W., 98
 ELIZABETH, 79
 JOHN L., 79
 MARSHAL, 79
 MARTIN, 130
 N.A., 130
 NORA B., 130
 S.E., 103
 S.M., 98, 103
FOX
 ANN C., 99
 MARIA V., 99
 MATHIAS, 99
 R.C., 101(2), 102, 105(2), 106(2), 108(5), 109(2), 110
FOY
 DAISY, 123
 GEO, 77

J.F., 77, 82(2)
J.W., 123
KATHARINE, 77
M.A., 123
FRANCISCO
 ANNIE MAY, 123
 E.E., 117
 ELISHA, 123
 FLOYD A., 117
 JOHN L., 99
 L.M., 99
 NANNIE, 117
 S.E., 99
FRANKLIN
 ABBIE, 32
 ANDERSON, 109
 C.W., 99
 CHARLOTTE, 126
 DOLLIE M., 90
 FLORA, 126
 HARIET, 83
 HARRIETT, 125
 J.A., 71
 J.H., 128, 131(2)
 JAMES P., 32
 JEANIE, 109
 JOHN, 106
 M.W., 39
 MARY, 39
 MARY E., 99
 MARY J., 71
 NANNIE B., 99
 NANNIE S., 125
 SAM, 125
 T.J.J., 90(2)
 THOMAS, 32
 THOS, 109, 126
 THOS G., 90
 VICTORIA, 106
 WILLIAM, 39
 WM, 71
 WM J., 106
FRANSCOW
 CHARLOTTE, 45
FRAZIER
 A.J., 40
 C.J., 121
 CHRISTOPHER A., 34

 GILLIE E., 90
 J.T., 19, 86, 97, 113, 132(2), 134(2), 135, 137(2), 138(3), 139(2), 140(3), 141
 JAMES H., 121
 LOUISA, 33
 ROBT, 34
 S.A., 121
 SARAH O., 33
 WILLIAM, 33
FREEMAN
 BELL, 71
 E., 135

E.W., 84, 137
EDWARD, 87
ISABELLA, 122
JOHN, 59, 66, 71, 122
KATE, 66, 71
MARY, 87
MARY A., 59
R.E., 122
WM, 87(2)
FRENCH
 A., 20-E
 A.G., 22
 A.L., 22(2), 23(3), 25, 28(3), 29(2)
 A.L.P., 32
 A.P.L., 29(2), 30(6), 31(3), 32(3), 33(2), 34
 A.R.L., 29(4)
 AND, 20-B
 ANDREW, 20-B
 ANDREW J., 27, 20-A
 ANDREW L., 21(3), 23(4), 25(4), 20-D(4), 20-E(4), 20-F(3)
 ANDREW P.L., 34
 ANDRW C.F., 57
 AUSTIN, 20
 BELINDA, 104
 C.C., 20-B
 CHARLES, 12
 CHARLES C., 7
 CHARLEY, 139
 CLARA A., 23
 D.E., MRS., 90
 DAVID, 44, 119, 139
 DAVID E., 126(2)
 DAVID W., 20-B
 EDWARD K., 36
 ELEANOR F., 12
 ELIZABETH, 20-C
 EMMA, 122
 EVALINE, 104
 F.P., 119
 G.T., 57
 GEO B., 91
 GEO THOS, 57
 H.B., 91, 119, 139
 H.C., 126
 H.T., 126
 HARRIET A., 31
 HARVEY, 104
 HENRIETTA, 87
 HENRY, 122
 HUGH C., 1
 ISAAC E., 20
 J.D., 87
 J.S., 87, 113, 117
 J.T., 93
 JAMES, 34
 JAMES M., 44
 JAMES P., 55

JANE, 10, 31
JANE B., 36
JANIE M., 139
JAS, 90
JAS D., 57
JAS E., 122
JAS M., 93
JNO W., 57
JOHN, 39
JOHN E., 55
JOSEPH E., 23
K., 20-B
KATE B., 122
LANESA, 116
LAURA B., 102
LEE, 20
LIMMONA, 1
LIZZIE, 90
LOUISA, 102
M., 122
M. BLAIR, 20-D
M.A., 139
MAHALA, 23
MALINDA, 55
MARGARET, 119
MARIA, 20-D
MARTHA, 57
MARTHA A., 21, 37, 48, 20-F
MARTHA J., 21, 90, 20-F
MARY, 44, 91, 119, 139
MARY A., 88
MARY E., 10
MARY J., 39
MILLARD F., 48
MILLON H., 7
MINNIE B., 44
MOLLIE A., 119
N.B., 10, 31
NANCY A., 37
NANCY J., 20-B
NAPOLEON B., 36
NETTA L., 106
ORSA F., 122
OSHIE, 93
R., 20-H(2), 20-H
R.D., 23
R.G., 24(4), 26, 28(3), 30, 31(2), 32(3), 33(2), 34, 37, 48, 20-C(2), 20-D, 20-E
REBECCA, 7, 12, 30
REDDIE E., 57
RHODA, 44
RHODA CLEMINTINE, 139
RHODA L., 93
RHONDA, 20-A
ROBERT U., 44
RUSSEL G., 19, 21, 44, 20-A, 20-B(2), 20-F

RUSSELL G., 8, 9(6), 11(3), 12, 14, 15(2), 20, 29(2)
S.N., 20-D
SALLIE, 57
SARAH B., 20-B
STELLA A., 116
SUSAN, 34
U. VICTORIA, 44
VICTORIA W., 30
W.L.G., 57
WILLIAM, 20-E
WM K., 57
WM L., 102(2), 116
WM M., 23, 20-A
FRITH
 JULIANNA, 124
 SILAS, 124
 W., 124
 W.F., 124
FROE
 D., 136
 ISADORE, 136
 MARY, 136
FRY
 JULIA A., 22
 REBECCA J., 22
FUDGE
 DOCK, 77, 115
 ELYN, 77
 MILTON, 77, 115
FUGATE
 JOSEPH P., 7
 PHERMBA, 7
 ZACHARIAH, 7
FULLEN
 BETTIE, 68
 JOHN, 68
FULLER
 CHAINIE, 75
 CHANEY, 73
 HENRY, 75
 JOHN, 58
 MARY, 49, 58
 SALLY ANN, 73
FULTON
 CHARLES, 117
 GRANT, 117
 JUDA, 117
FUNK
 SALLIE B., 114
FUNNELS
 SARAH, 1
FUQUA
 DAVID, 127
 MINTIE, 126
 TOM, 127
FURGUSON
 ELIZABETH, 61
 ENDORA F., 61
 GREEN N., 74(2)
 J.J., 76
 JNO, 61

MARY E., 76
NANCY V., 74
OCTOVA F., 74
S.C., 76
SARAH, 20-E

-G-

GADD
 A.E., 120
 A.P., 27, 79
 ANDREW, 24, 125, 131
 ANDREW P., 28, 39, 40(2)
 D., 125
 DELILA, 24, 27
 DELILA E., 27, 28
 DELILAH, 40(2), 79, 131
 DELILAH E., 39
 ELECTRA, 24
 ELIZA A., 91
 ELIZA J., 125
 ELIZABETH R., 39
 J.B., 131(2)
 JAS H., 117
 JOSEPH B., 40
 L.E., 91, 117, 120
 MARY ANN, 40
 R.W., 27
 SARAH M., 27
 VICTORY MELISSA, 79

 W.H., 117, 120
 WILLIAM H., 28, 131
 WM H., 91
 Z.T., 131
 ZOLA, 131
GAENS
 JAS E., 132
 JOHN H., 132
 SOPHIA, 132
GAILRES
 S.M., 112
GAINES
 AGNES, 136
 CHARLOTTE, 19
 ELLA, 135
 JULIA, 111, 135
 MARGARET A., 19

 NANNIE, 111
 S.M., 82(2), 83(2), 84(3), 87, 91, 93(3), 94, 96(2), 97, 98, 110, 111, 112, 115(2), 120(3), 135
GAINS
 ANDERSON, 82
 HARRIET, 82
 WM H., 82
GAINTER

W.L., 120
GALDIN
 FLORENCE L., 68
 LOUISA, 68
 WILLIAM, 68
GALE
 ANNA, 40
 GEORGE B., 40
 LEVIN, 40
GALLAWAY
 GEORGE, 118
 LAURA, 118
 SARAH, 118
GALLIER
 ELLA, 68
 JOHN, 68
 MARY A., 68
GALLIHER
 JACK, 47, 75
 JULIANN, 47
 POLLY, 47, 75
GAMMON
 DOLLIE, 116
 SALLIE, 116
 W.T., 116
GAND
 ALEXANDER, 8
 SARAH, 8
 WM, 8
GANDY
 CORNELIUS, 82
 LAWRENCE S., 82
 MARY J., 82
GANOE
 DICIA, 20-B
GANT
 ANNA L., 112
 ELIZABETH, 112
 THOS, 112
GANTHER
 ALICE, 105
 J.R., 105
 JAMES, 22
 JOS, 22
 JOSEPH, 92
 LUCY, 92
 MARY F., 22
 RUFUS A., 105
 W.I., 92, 103, 104, 105, 106, 110, 111, 112(2), 113(3), 114, 115, 116, 117, 119, 120, 121(2), 122(2), 123(3), 124(3)
GARDENER
 J.H., 128
GARDNER
 ADA, 108
 ANNIE, 108
 HARDIN, 34
 J.H., 93

LINA, 108(2)
MOLLIE, 70
ROSANAH, 34
RUSH, 34, 108(2)
RUTH, 70
T.H., 81
VINEY, 70
GARETSON
 AHAM, 29
GARETT
 ELLEN, 112
 WM, 112
GARHART
 MARY, 83
 W.L., 83
 WASHINGTON, 83
GARLICK
 CHAS T., 58
 F.T., 61
 JAS F., 58
 MINNIE A., 61
 SARAH J., 61
 SARENA, 58
GARNER
 ARCHIE, 95
 CHARLOTTE, 48
 JAS., 48
 JOSEPH, 53
 LEWIS, 20, 48
 MARY, 95
GARNETT
 ED B., 110
 ELLEN T., 110
 S.W., 110
GARRETSON
 A., 17
 ABM, 3
 ABRAHAM, 1(2), 2(4), 3, 4(2), 5(3), 6(2), 7(3), 8(4), 9(3), 10(2)
 ABRAHAM L., 61
 ABRAM, 3
 ABSALOM, 1
 ANN, 1, 53
 ARDELIA, 40, 42
 B., 17
 C.A., 68
 COLUMBIA A., 33
 CORA C., 77
 DELIA, 40, 41
 ELIZABETH S., 38
 EMMA J., 80
 FRANCIS P., 21, 20-F
 H. INGRAM, 53
 H.F., 80
 H.L., 45
 HIRAM G., 38
 HIRAM J., 38
 HIRAM L., 1
 IDA, 8
 INGRAHAM, 82

JOHN, 8, 21, 40(2),
  41, 42, 20-D,
  20-E(3), 20-F
JOS. H., 45
JULIA, 41
JULIA A., 42
M.B., 53
MARIA E., 33
MARY, 77
MARY A., 38, 45
MARY ANN, 21, 20-F

MARY J., 61, 80
MARY M., 40
NANCY, 6
NANCY E., 40
POLLY, 82
RUAH, 32
THARISA, 17
THOMAS, 77
THOMAS J., 32
WILLIAM, 1, 6
WM, 33
WM P., 61
GARRETT
  B.S., 110
  CARRIE D., 110
  HENRY C., 108
  JIM, 108
  JOHN, 129
  MATILDA, 137
  NETTIE, 129
  RACHEL, 108
  WM, 112
GARRISON
  ALBERT, 75
  C.A., 75
  WILLIAM, 75
GARY
  AILSIE, 72
GASH
  ANNIE E., 107
  ERNEST M., 107
  J.R., 107
GATTON
  REBECCA, 20-C
GAUTIER
  ALISA, 110
  GEORGIA, 95
  JAMES, 95
  JANE, 32
  JOSEPH, 10(2), 32, 44
  LILLY B.P., 110
  LUCY, 44
  M.A., 125
  MARY, 10
  MARY E., 32
  PAULINA, 95
  R.A., 125(2)
  RUFUS A., 110
  W.I., 108(3), 109,
    110(2), 126, 127(3),
    128, 129, 130(3),

    131, 132, 134,
    135(3), 136, 138
  WILSON E., 44
  WM A., 125
GAYHART
  RHODA E., 140
GEARHART
  ANNIE A., 84
  EVALINE, 86
  HENRY J., 84
  MINERVA, 86
  ROSA, 88
  W.L., 86
GEARHEART
  A.J., 80
  ANDREW, 62
  ELIZABETH, 62
  H.I., 109
  H.L., 70
  J.M., 122
  JENRY, 80
  LAWSON, 122
  M. DELLA, 109
  MARY, 70
  MICHAEL J., 62
  MOLLIE, 80
  SARAH, 109
  WASHINGTON, 70

GEDER
  JOSEF, 135(2)
  TEREZ, 135
GEILINGER
  EMILY, 129
  S.E., 129
GENT
  J.H., 86
  MAGARET (SIC), 86

  MARGARET, 92
  PETER, 92
  WM, 86, 92
  WM, JR., 90
GEORGE
  ANNIE, 107
  BESSIE, 128
  E.H., 4
  EDITH, 69
  ELEANOR, 1
  ELLISON, 64
  ELVIRA, 64, 82, 88,
    128
  F.M., 107
  FRANCIS M., 24
  G.C., 69
  HENRIETTA, 26
  HIRAM, 69
  HUGH, 96
  JOHN, 39
  JULIA A., 64
  LARRISSA M., 1
  MARGARET, 96
  MARY, 82

MATILDA P., 4
MOLLIE, 39
NANNIE B., 77
POLLY, 96
SAM, 82, 128
SAMUEL P., 26
THOS, 4
THOS J., 1
W.T., 107
WM W., 39
GHERRANT
  LIDIA, 81
  MARTHA, 81
GIBBINS
  J.T., 131
GIBBS
  LOUISA, 26
GIBERTSON
  ISAAC, 105
  JAMES, 105
GIBSON
  —, 35
  ALICE, 84
  ALICE J., 27
  CHARLES, 74
  CHAS, 74
  ELIZTH, 8
  EMMA, 128, 137
  EVILINE, 111
  J.P., 5
  JAS M., 27
  L.M., 27
  LENESOR G., 8
  LUTHER, 137
  NANCY, 74
  SAM, 137
  SAML., 8
  T.N., 128
  THOMPSON, 75
  THOS, 128
  TINY N., 128
  W.D., 102
  WM T., 75
GIFFITH
  M.H., 92
GILBERT
  ALBERT L., 115
  LARINDA, 115
  WM P., 115
GILES
  NAT, 74
  SALLY, 74
  VAIDEN, 74
GILLASPIA
  ISAAC, 102
  JENNIE, 102
  TERESSA C.P., 102
GILLESPIE
  CHAS G., 63
  H., 126
  ISAC, 126
  JANE, 63, 67
  JAS A., 126

JEMIMA, 126
JULIA A., 67
KATE E., 42
LAVINA, 126
M., 126
MAGGIE L., 42
ROBT, 42
W.E., 67
WM E., 63
GILLISPIE
  MARTHA, 84
  ROBT, 84
  SOLOMON, 84(2)
GILLOM
  L.A., 93
GILLS
  BENJ, 120
  BENJ F., 63, 65
  BENJN, 103
  BINGMAN, 56
  GEORGE, 120
  MALINDA, 130
  MARY, 63, 65, 103, 120
  MARY M., 56
  MINNIE, 130
  ROBERT, 63
  SAM, 130
  SAML H., 65
  SARAH E., 56
  W.M., 120
  WM M., 103
GILLUM
  J.W., 93
  M.A., 93
GILMORE
  ALICE, 64, 94, 122
  BLANCH, 67
  CHARLES, 121
  FANNIE, 67
  HETTIE, 64
  LILLIE, 94
  LIZZIE, 122
  MILTON, 64, 93, 94(2),
    122, 123
  WM, 67
GILPEN
  ELIZABETH, 84
  JAS T., 84
  WM, 84
GINTHER
  CLAIRSY M., 106
  G.Z., 106
  J.S., 106
GIRST
  BLANCH, 111
  LUKE, 111
GIVENS
  EMMA, 57
  FRANCIS, 14
  HARRIET, 57
  ISAIAH, 57
  JAS. H., 14
  MARY, 14

GLASCO
  JAS, 128
  JENNIE L., 128
  MARG, 128
GLASCOW
  ALFRED, 45
  EMELINE, 45
  OSCAR, 45
GLASS
  JESSE M., 73
  MARTHA, 73
  OLIVER M., 73
GLENDY
  ELLA A., 135
  NANCY M., 135
  R.A., 135
GLETCHER
  ISAAC, 109
  MARY E., 109
  SARAH E., 109
GLOVER
  ANNIE, 67
  BESSIE G., 129
  BETTIE, 70
  BETTY, 67
  C.W., 84, 129
  HATTIE, 70
  J.T., 51
  JOHN, 67, 70
  L.E., 129
  MARY J., 84
GODFREY
  A.B., 108, 116
  A.C., 76, 102
  A.F., 74
  A.I., 97, 122, 134(2),
    135(2), 137
  A.L., 135
  ALICE A., 30
  AMAJIAH I., 70
  ARZULA, 127
  AUGUSTUS B., 28
  AUGUSTUS C., 18
  CALVIN, 131
  CLOIA, 76
  GEO D., 60
  J.E., 127
  JAMES, 23(2), 20-D
  JAMES B., 10
  JAS A., 44
  JAS B., 5
  JAS T., 76
  JNO D., 62(2)
  JNO. D., 25
  JOHN D., 28, 38, 44,
    60, 65, 70
  JOHN E., 65
  JOSIE E., 62
  JULIA, 131
  L.B., 114
  LINA N., 30
  MARGT., 18
  MARTHA, 25, 28, 38,

    44, 60, 62(2), 65
  MARTHA B., 70
  MARY A., 10
  MARY J., 5, 102
  MATILDA J., 29
  N., 20-D
  N.R., 114
  NANCY, 5, 10
  NANCY M., 23(2)
  R.M., 127
  R.V., 26
  REBECCA, 38
  ROBT, 99, 131
  ROBT M., 23
  ROBT. M., 23
  S.M., 108, 116
  SINAI, 99
  T.O., 116
  THOMAS B., 108
  THOS., 18
  TIMEANDRE M., 25

  VICTORIA, 20-D
  VIRGINIA B., 91
  VIRGINIA J., 62
  WM R., 114
GODFRY
  E.A., 28
GODREY
  GEO D., 76
  JOHN D., 76
  MARTHA, 76
GODRREY
  A.I., 102
GODSEY
  CHARLOTTE, 106
  F.P., 140
  J.P., 140
  JNO C., 106
  M.E., 140
  T.C., 106
GOFF
  BELLE, 66
  E.M., 68
  ELLEN, 133
  FRANK, 59
  J.G., 133
  JEPH L., 68
  JOHN, 59
  JOSEPH, 133
  MAGGIE, 59
  SARAH E., 68
GOFORTH
  HANNAH, 96
  JAS H., 96
  JAS T., 96
GOIN
  S., 17
  WM, 17
GOINS
  CHESTINE, 54
  ELIZA, 54
  GEORGE, 54

GOLD
  A.L., 132(2)
  ARENA, 132
  NANCY C., 132
GOLDSMITH
  J.M., 98
  JOS S., 98
  MARY I., 98
GOLLIER
  ELIZABETH, 11
  JOHN, 11(2)
GOOCH
  ALONZO, 4, 10, 76
  B.J., 4, 110
  ELIZA J., 4
  JANE E., 10, 76
  NANCY J., 65, 110
  SUE M., 65
  T.C., 110
  THOMAS C., 10
  THOS C., 65, 76
GOODALL
  ELIZTH, 9
  JOS, 9
  LULA M., 106
GOODE
  BERTIE, 122
  EMMA L., 67
  G.W., 66, 90, 122
  G.W., JR., 90, 122
  GEO. W., 47
  GEORGE W., 56
  IDELLA S., 66
  J.P., 71
  JOSEPH R., 47
  LEWIS H., 45
  LUCY J., 87
  MALINDA, 67, 87
  MARY F., 56
  PAMELIA, 47
  PARINDIA, 67
  PARMELIA, 45
  PERMELA, 90
  PERMELIA, 66, 67, 71,
    122
GOODMAN
  CALLIE B., 95
GOODSON
  CARRIE T., 108
  FLOYD, 105, 108
  MARY, 105
  SALLIE, 108
  SARAH, 105
GOODWIN
  L., 28, 34, 36, 59
GOODWYN
  ALFRED E., 113
  C.M., 128
  F., 107(4)
  L., 36, 41, 43(2),
    41(3), 45(3), 46(4),

    47, 48, 49(4), 50(2),
    51, 52, 53, 54(4),
    55(4), 56(6), 57, 58,
    59, 60(3), 61(2),
    62(3), 63(2), 64, 66,
    67, 69, 70(3), 71(2),
    72(3), 73(3), 74(2),
    75(5), 76(4), 77,
    79(3), 80(3), 81(3),
    82, 83(3), 84(3),
    85(4), 86, 87, 89,
    90, 91(2), 93(3), 94,
    96(2), 97(2), 98(3),
    99, 100, 101(3),
    103(2), 108, 110,
    111(4), 112(2),
    113(2), 116, 117,
    120(2), 123(2), 124,
    127, 128, 133(4),
    135, 137, 138
  LEONIDAS, 36, 37(3),
    38, 39, 41(2)
  LONIDAS, 35
  LOUIDAS, 35
  MAGIE, 113
  T., 107
GORDEN
  ELIZABETH, 68, 116
  G.W., 116
  GEO W., 68
  W.C., 116
  W.J., 68
GORDON
  ALICE, 81
  COLUMBUS, 81
  ELIZABETH, 100
  G.W., 100
  GEORGE W., 72
  GRANVILLE, 58
  LAURA E., 58
  MARY, 58
  SALLIE, 72
  SALLIE M., 100
  SOPHIA, 81
  ZEALIE E., 72
GORE
  A.W., 30(2), 138
  ALABAMA, 13
  ALLIE, 141
  AMOS, 57, 75
  ANGELINE, 43
  C.C., 132
  C.W., 40
  CAROLINE, 29, 85
  CATHARINE, 35
  DESSIE, 135
  ELIZ. M., 45
  ELIZA, 50
  ELIZABETH, 40, 75
  GEORGE, 43
  GRANGER H., 46
  GREEN, 42
  H.F., 46, 61, 96, 110,

132(2)
H.L., 96
HENDERSON F., 1, 35

HENRY, 1, 42
IDA, 1, 8, 13, 14
ISAAC, 1(2), 8, 13, 14, 31
J.F., 71
JACOB, 37, 132, 135(2)
JAKE, 104
JANE, 132
JOHN A., 35
JOHN C., 37
L.W., 132
LEVI, 36
LOUISA, 50
LUCY V., 85
M.D.L., 14
MALINDA J., 132
MANERVA, 141
MANIRVA A., 8
MARY, 20, 35, 43
MARY B., 45
MARY J., 57
MATILDA, 20, 29, 37
MINERVA, 72
MINERVA JANE, 37

MINNIE S., 61
NANCY R., 72
OCIE LEE, 138
RACHEL C., 110
ROBERT, 31, 40, 45
ROXIE L., 135
S.E., 138
S.K., 71
S.R., 35, 71, 96, 110
SARA J., 104
SARAH, 35, 36(2), 37, 42, 135(2)
SARAH E., 104
SARAH JANE, 37
SAREPTA R., 46, 61
SEREPTA, 30
VIRGINIA, 1
WILLIAM, 85
WILLIS, 35
WM, 72, 75, 141
WM A., 36
WM C., 37
GOSER
CATHERINE, 8
HENRY, 8
JOSEPH, 8
GOTH
A., 133
JAS E., 133
L.J., 133
GOTT
A., 133
ALICE, 22
ANDREW, 22(2), 27, 48,

53, 77, 107
FRANCIS, 27
JAMES E., 77
JNO D., 48
JOHN R., 27
L.F., 53
L.G., 77
L.J., 133
LOUCINDA, 53
LOUEMONA J., 107

MARY J., 107
ROBT W., 133
GOUCH
ED. JOHNSTON, 82
MARY JANE, 82
THOMAS C., 82
GOWINGS
ALICE, 71
ANDREW, 71
HARIET, 71
GRAD
ANDREW J., 106
CALLEY, 106
MAGGIE, 106
GRAHAM
ANDREW, 104
CHAS. W., 47
DAVID E., 47
ELIZABETH, 90
ELLEN, 127
FANNIE, 70
FLORA A., 126
GEO W., 134
INGLE, 134
J.H., 117
J.W., 102
JAMES, 31, 129
JANE, 127
JAS, 50, 127
JAS H., 117
JAS. W., 50
LOUISA, 102
LUCILLA S., 96
LYNCH, 31, 97, 117, 126
M.M., 90
MARTHA J., 97
MARY, 97, 117, 134
MARY A., 88
MARY W., 104
NANCY, 126
REBECCA, 47
SARAH, 31, 50
SPHRANA, 129
SUE, 70
TINSEY, 104
W.E., 96
WM A., 102
WM T., 129
GRALEY
ISAAC N., 3
JAS, 3

SARAH, 3
GRAVELBY
BELL, 123
GRAVELLY
JOHN, 26
PETER H., 26
WINNEY, 26
GRAVELY
JOHN, 130
GRAVES
CARRY, 123
DOCTOR, 82
GEO, 67, 69
GIRTIE, 103
JESSE, 103
JOHN, 67
LUCY, 82
MARY A., 103
MILLIE, 67
MILLIE, 69
NANCY, 69
OLLIE, 84
RADER, 92
RAYMOND, 123
RHODA, 123
GRAVLEY
JAS M., 134
STEVE, 68
VICTORIA, 68(2)
WILLARD, 123
GRAVLY
ANNA, 123
NINA, 130
GRAY
BILL, 128
ELIZABETH, 128
G.T., 17
GEORGE, 128(2)
GEORGE T., 18(2)
HENRY, 89, 138
JAMES, 94
MARY, 94
OCTAVIA, 89, 138
SAMUEL, 89, 138
THOS, 94
GRAYBILL
ANN E., 3
ISABELLA, 8
JNO, 3
JOHN, 8
SUSAN, 3, 8
GREAR
JOHN C., 42
REBECCA E., 42
GREAVER
J.B., 68
GREBAR
J.C., 66
JOASIA, 66
R.E., 66
GREELY
MARY, 31
GREEN

ALBERT, 74
CLABERN, 141
EMMA J., 66
FRANK, 66
G.W.K., 37, 38(2), 39, 20-E
GEANNA, 22
HATTIE, 141
JANE, 66
JAS D., 74
LETH BELL, 122
LOUISA, 85
LOUISE, 122
NANCY, 85
SHADRICK, 122
VINEY, 141
W., 76
WINNIE, 74
WM, 77, 78, 129, 130
GREENAWALT

DORCAS, 94
JOHN R., 94
PHILIP, 94
GREENER
S.H., 109
W.A., 109
GREENS
ADA B., 80
AMANDA H., 80
JOHN L., 80
GREENSPAN
A., 94
I., 94
SAUL, 94
GREER
E.A., 107
ELIZABETH, 87(2)
J.L., 87(2), 107
JAS T., 87
JOHN C., 40
RENA O., 107
SARAH J., 40
WALTER S., 87
GREEVER
J.R., 56
GREGGS
WM, 133
GREWER
J.B., 66
GRIFFIN
ALEX, 66
BELL, 59
CHARLES, 125
ELLIOTT, 59
HENRIETTA, 66
JOHN, 125
LIDDA, 125
MAGGIE, 59
GRIFFITH
BEVERLY, 55, 70
CATHARINE, 58, 63
CATHERINE, 51, 55, 56,

60
CHATHERINE, 70
FLORIDA, 83
FRANCIS, 101
G.W., 125
ISAAC, 92, 20-C
ISAAC F., 60
J., 20-C
JANE, 55
JAS S., 101
JOHN, 21, 35, 83, 20-A, 20-C, 20-F
JOHN T., 20-A
JOSEPHINE, 58
JUDA, 21, 35, 20-A, 20-F
LOUISA, 51
M.C., 58
MAKALA C., 63
MARY, 83
MARY J., 51
MARY L., 57
NANCY, 70
OWEN P., 92
R.C., 57
ROSA B., 56
S.B., 51, 56, 57, 58(2), 63, 125
SARAH E., 58
SHADRACK B., 51
SHADRECK B., 60
SHEDRACH, 58
STAUNTON, 21, 35, 20-F

THOS, 80
W.A., 101
GRIGGSBY
EDMOND, 108
GEORGIANA, 59
MARGARET, 108
MARY, 59
ROBERT, 108
GRIGSBY
FANNIE E.C., 11
HARRIET, 41
JAS S., 11
JUDITH E., 11
GRIM
C.W., 69
CAHINE, 21
CAHINE (SIC), 20-F
CATH, 20-A
CATHERINE, 31
CATHERINE A., 47
DELLER C., 109
ELIZABETH, 130(2)
ELLEN, 11
HARRIET A., 99
JAMES, 68, 130, 20-A
JENNETTA A., 47
JOHN, 31
LUTICIA V., 68
LUVINA, 66

M.A., 66
MARTHA, 69
MARTHA A., 47(2), 99, 109, 111
NEVADA MAY, 111

PETER, 47(2), 66, 69, 99, 109, 111(3), 123, 124, 125(2), 126, 130, 131, 134(3), 137, 138
REBECCA, 11
SARAH A., 21, 20-F
WM, 11, 21, 31, 20-A, 20-F
GRIMES
A.M., 96
P.M., 96
S.M., 109
WM P., 96
GRIMM
CATH., 13
DRUCILLA P., 13
JAMES, 74
JANE, 74
JOHN, 39
LAURA A., 74
LUCY A., 39
WM, 13
GROSS
FRANK, 78
GROVE
F.S., 116
ROZALIA, 116
GULLION
CARRIE, 111
DOCK, 111
E.M., 89, 131
ELIZABETH, 97
ELIZTH M., 85
HENRY, 131
R.E., 85
REUBEN, 85, 89, 97, 131
REUBEN A., 89
ROBT E., 85
THOS J., 97
TILDA, 111
GUNOE
DISA, 9
HULDAH A.H., 9
ISAAC, 2
JNO, 2
MARY, 2
WM, 9
GUNTER
A. GUS, 125
B.M., 125
F.A., 125(2)

F.J., 124
FRANCIS E., 100
JNO R., 94(2)
P.J., 125
PHEBA, 100
PHEBY JANE, 94
R.E., 125
WILBURN, 124
WILLIAM, 100
WM, 94, 124, 125
GUSLBY
BETSY, 132
DAVE, 132
GUTRIDGE
CLARENCE, 103
SARAH JANE, 127

-H-

HACKER
NANNIE, 69
PERY, 69
R., 69
HAGAN
ELIZTH, 2
JOHN, 2
WILLIAM J., 2
HAGAR
A. GREEN, 47
A.G., 57
AND. G., 62
BALLARD J., 47
EASTER J., 57
MARY E.A., 62
NANCY, 47, 57, 62
HAGEN
J.R., 84
MARY, 84
NANNIE N., 84
HAGER
A. BAILEY, 110
A. GREENVILLE, 40

A.C., 139
A.G., 34, 90
A.J., 110
ALEXANDER, 33
CLARINDA, 139
CYNTHIA, 106
DAVID B., 110
ELIZTH, 34
FLORRENCE C., 139

FLOYD, 106
GREEN, 128
H.B., 139
HENDERSON B., 40

IDA I., 128
LOUDERMA, 98
LUCINDA, 98
N.E., 98
NANCY, 34, 40, 90, 128

PETER, 106
PHOEBY, 110
R.A., 71, 104
R.M.L., 71
REBECCA, 128
RUSSEL, 28
RUSSELL, 33
S.H., 104
SAML, 128
SAML J., 128
SAMUEL H., 34
SARAH, 20, 28, 33
SQUIRE, 34
SYNTHA F., 110
VICTORIA, 110
W.I., 139
W.W., 71
WILLIAM H., 34
WILLIAM W., 28
WILLIS I., 104
WM R., 90
HAGERMAN
CELIA, 47
WM, 47
HAIDY
GEORGE, 67
HENRY, 67
MARTHA, 67
HAIN
EMMA, 88
HANNAH M., 88
P.J., 88
HAINES
HARRIET, 74
JOHN, 74
WILLIE, 74
HAIRMAN
ELVIRA C., 92
PAULINA J., 92
WM B., 92
HAIRSTON
BETTIE, 90
MARTHA, 90
HAIRTZ
NANCY, 23
REUBEN, 23
HALDEN
RUFUS E., 138
HALDREN
AND L., 105
B.M., 123
BARTHELUMEW, 125

BENJAMIN, 31
C.W., 113
CHARLES, 7
CHARLEY, 123
D.A., 123
DARCUS W., 113
DORCAS W., 105
GEO W., 123
GREELY, 127
HENRY, 8, 30

JAMES H., 125
JULIA ANN, 27
LONSAN, 27
M.E., 123(2)
MAHALA, 8, 30
NANCY, 30
P.T., 135(2)
R.A., 135
RHODA, 125
SAML, 105, 113
SAML HARASS, 31

SAML., 27
SARAH, 7, 8
V.E., 135
HALDRON
  BALLARD R., 11
  CHARLES LEWIS, 38

  GEORGE W., 10
  HENRY, 10, 11
  MAHALA, 10, 11
  NANCY, 38
  SMITHEN, 38
  TYRESSA J., 51
HALDSON
  NANCY, 1
  SAMUEL, 1
HALE
  AMA, 103
  ANN, 27
  BAILEY, 89
  C.A., 107
  C.B., 74
  C.E., 138
  CARRIE, 138
  CHAS R., 66
  DANIEL P., 38
  DANL F., 57
  DANL P., 33, 36, 57
  E.A., 82
  ED, 20-A
  EDWARD, 110
  ELIAS, 25, 61, 20-A
  ELIAS JAS., 56
  ELIZA, 66
  ELIZA F., 44, 61
  ELLEN, MRS., 69
  F.W., 48
  G.W., 95, 108
  GEORGIA, 138
  GEORGIE, 103
  HARRIET N., 26
  J., 95
  J.A., 110
  J.B., 110
  J.W., 138
  JAMES E., 89
  JANE, 27, 95
  JAS E., 82
  JAS W., 74
  JNO C., 26
  JNO D., 27

JNO E., 56
JOHN, 95, 100, 103
JULIA, 20-D
JULIDE, 107
L.M., 138
LEWIS M., 38
LUDERNA, 100
LULA I., 74
M.J., 138
MARINDA A., 20-D
MARTHA, 33, 57, 89, 20-A
MARTHA A., 36, 38
MARTHA H., 48
MARY K., 56
MATTIE B., 107
MIRIAM E., 36
NANCY, 25, 33
NANNIE L., 133
R., 100
RHODA J., 61
ROBERT, 100
RUFUS A., 25
SPARREL, 82
SPARRELL, 66
W.G., 111
WM W., 48
HALEY
  E.W., 122
  F.C., 122
  HARDEN, 129
  S.C., 122
  VIRGIE, 129
  VIRGINIA, 129
HALL
  A., 71
  A.B., 105(2)
  ABSALOM B., 105
  ADA MAY, 129
  ADALINE, 91
  ALLIE, 107
  ALZORA J., 81
  AMANDA, 70, 92, 112
  AMANDA E., 54, 67, 87
  ANDREW J., 45
  ASA, 102
  ASA R., 93
  AVAZOR, 134
  BASCOM, 105
  BECKY ANN, 29
  BELL, 125
  BETTIE, 74, 95
  BOOKER, 91
  C., 125
  C.D., 91
  CHAS, 95, 141
  CHAS H.F., 58
  CHAS L., 54
  CHAS W., 66
  DANIEL, 40, 42
  DANL W., 92
  DAVID, 9, 16
  DORA M., 124

E., 119
EFFIE, 138
ELIZA, 45
ELIZABETH, 71, 105, 124
ELVIRA M., 40
ERNEST B., 139
F.M., 83
FLORENCE D., 86
GEO N., 26
GEO THOS, 96
HARVEY, 106, 119
HARVEY R., 102
HENDERSON H., 54

HENRIETTA, 53, 54
HENRIETTA D., 46
HENRY, 107
IDA F., 87
IRA D., 81
J. MARSH, 57
J. MARSHALL, 57
J.D., 70
J.H., 124
J.N.J., 66
J.P., 115
J.R., 87, 112
J.T., 86, 107
J.W., 71
JACOB, 95
JAMES, 9, 139
JAMES M., 9
JANE, 138, 141
JANE H., 27
JAS, 86, 119
JAS H., 119
JAS K., 96
JAS S., 106
JNO M., 54
JNO R., 92
JOHN, 27, 72, 138, 141
JOHN H., 45
JOHN M., 46, 53
JOHN R., 54, 67
JOHN S., 112
JOHNSTON, 27
JORDAN, 125
JULIA, 72
JULIA F., 83
JULITIA, 42
L.S., 70
LAURA B., 91
LILIAN I., 83
LIZZIE, 106
LUCINDA, 119, 139
LUCY, 93, 102
MALINDA, 103
MARGARET G., 66

MARY, 9, 27, 42, 72, 85, 91, 120
MARY E., 9, 16, 67, 81
MARY J., 57, 58, 87

MARY M., 40
MARY S., 105
MATTIE, 141
MELISSA, 86
MOLLIE S., 96
NANNIE K., 93
P.B., 87
PRESTON, 85, 91, 120
PRESTON B., 27, 57, 58
R.A., 115
REBECCA A., 119
RHODA, 27
SALLIE, 141
SAML A., 83(2)
SAML H., 105
SARAH E., 9, 86
SUSAN, 45
T.K., 129
THOS J., 87
VICIE J.F., 106
VICTORIA, 115
W.R., 141
WALTER, 86
WM J., 45
WM T., 53
XANTIPPI E., 46
HALLANO
  EVALINE, 92
  F.A., 92
  WILLIAM, 92
HALMANDOLLAR

  JOHN, 137
HALO
  DOC, 58
  LANDAN, 58
  LOUISA, 58
HALSTEAD
  ADAM, 2, 20-A
  ELIZTH, 20-A
  GRANVILLE S., 2
  JOHN, 20-A
  SARAH, 2
HAM
  EMMA M., 141
  I.N., 141
  J.W., 141
  L.V., 141
  W.W., 141
  WILLIAM L., 141
  WM L., 141
HAMBLIN
  CATHARINE, 136
  MARY ELLEN, 136

  T.H., 136, 140
HAMBRIC
  LEONARD T., 21, 20-F
  MARG, 21, 20-F
  RILEY, 21, 20-F
HAMBRICK
  A.P., 123, 135
  ALLEN H., 65

AMY, 96, 119
AMY P., 45, 53
C.D., 119
CHARLES A., 20
DUDLEY, 133
E.P., 113
ELLEN, 65, 72, 120
ELVIRA J., 58
EMMA P., 45
G.O., 45, 123
GEO, 96, 119, 135
GEO O., 45, 53
GEORGE O., 8
GILES O., 123
HARRIET V., 41
J.H., 113
JAMES L., 45
JANE, 41
JENNIE, 133
JOHN, 41
JOHN A., 4, 44(2)
JOS H., 65
JOSEPH, 72, 120
JOSEPH H., 17
L.T., 87(2), 99, 125
LAUDONA, 120
LAURA, 133
LIRUVENIA, 72
LILLY B., 135
LIONA R., 17
LOVIE, 96
M., 4, 17(2)
MARGARET, 8, 58
MARGT, 20
MARTHA E., 87
MARY A., 20
MARY JANE, 44
MAY I., 113
R., 4, 17(2), 20
R.J., 99, 125
R.S., 99
REBECCA J., 87
RIGHLY, 8
RILEY, 58(2)
SUSAN M., 45
TELITHA L., 125
WM R., 53
HAMILTON
  CARRIE, 63
  D.H., 62
  FANNIE, 61
  JOHN, 61
  ROXIE, 62
  W.W., 62, 122, 127
  WM J., 61
  WM W., 119(2), 120(2), 125(2), 126, 127(2)
  WM WINSTAR, 117

  WM WISTAR, 116, 117

  WM WISTON, 124(4)

HAMLIN
  CASSIE, 100
  JANE, 30
  LUCINDA, 21, 20-F
  NANCY L., 100
  S.W., 21, 20-F
  SARAH, 136
  STEPHEN, 136(2)
  T.H., 100
  THOS J., 20-F
  THOS. J., 21
  VIRGINIA, 136
HAMMERSLEY

  JAS, 98
  M.L., 98
  MIRA L., 98
  MOSES, 98
HAMMOCK
  NANNIE F., 57
HAMMON
  CATHARINE, 2
  JACOB M., 2
  JNO., 2
HAMPTON
  ISAAC, 91
  JANE, 91
  JAS ED., 91
  KATIE, 77
  LAWSON, 77, 86
  LOUISA, 77
  SARAH, 86
HANCE
  GEO W., 105
  LENA, 105
HANCOCK
  ELLA, 65
  FLORENCE, 70
  GEORGE, 54
  JULIA, 54, 65
  M., 15
  M.W., 54
  MARCUS W., 54
  N., 15
  WILLIAM, 15
  WM H., 65
HANES
  AMANDA, 136
  JACOB W., 136
  JOHN CARR, 136
HANGER
  A.H., 85
  FANNY, 85
  SARAH, 85
HANK
  W.F., 76
HANKS
  C.P., 84, 88, 128
  ELENA B., 88
  MOLLIE D.C., 84
  NAOMI, 54
  ONEY E., 84, 88
  SUSAN, 54
  V.P., 88

WM, 54
HANSBOROUGH

  MARY I., 126
  NANCY I., 100
HANSHED
  CHARLES, 117
  ELLA, 117
HANUAU
  ISAAC S., 42
HARDEN
  JOHN, 132
  LIDA, 132
  MARY, 132
HARDNEY
  FERD H., 78
  J. VNEY, 78
HARDY
  JOHN, 44
  JOHN L., 66
  SARAH, 44
  SARAH C., 66
  WM M., 66
HARE
  ARAMINTA, 56, 59, 74
  CATHARINE A., 56
  EDNA E., 59
  EMMA V., 108
  ISAAC, 1, 56, 59, 74
  J.D., 127
  JAMES, 120
  JAS F., 69
  JOHN, 74
  JOSEPH, 57
  JULIA, 57
  JULIA A., 57
  LULA, 120
  MINNIE J., 69
  SARAH, 1
  WILLIAM, 1
HARGO
  REBECCA, 20
  WILLIAM, 20
HARGRAVES
  B.J., 61(2)
HARISON
  GUS, 83
HARLESS
  ALEXANDER, 8
  BETTIE A., 66
  CASPER L., 8
  E., 124
  ELIZABETH, 8, 31
  ELIZTH, 20
  EMILY, 66
  EMMA S., 60
  JOHN, 20
  LORA, 80
  MARTHA E., 31
  MARY, 93
  MARY F., 14
  MILES, 124
  MOLLIE, 93

N.F., 60, 66
NAPOLEON F., 20
PHIL, 14
PHILIP, 31
PHILEGAR, 93
ROBT I., 124
SUSAN, 14
WM S., 60
HARLEY
  EMILINA, 29
HARMAN
  A.H., 102
  A.J., 79(2), 97, 109, 121, 137(2)
  AMANDA, 137
  ANDREW, 22, 56, 78
  ANDY, 78
  ANN, 98
  ARLEVA B., 39
  ARTHA C., 52
  B.P., 26
  BAL, 93
  BALLARD, 71
  BETTIE, 22
  C.W., 67
  CAUSBY, 29
  CELIA, 38
  CHARLES, 93
  CHAS, 83, 91, 119
  DANL C., 37
  DICIE S., 79
  ELIZABETH T., 15
  ELIZTH N.B., 59
  ELIZTH, 30
  FANNIE, 71
  G.M., 132
  G.W., 78
  GEO, 22, 30
  GEORGE, 18, 38
  IDA M., 116
  ISAAC, 54
  ISAAC S., 55(2)
  J.A., 52
  J.J.R., 138
  JAMES, 39
  JAMES C., 20-C
  JAMES P., 15
  JANE, 39
  JAS W., 51
  JAS. P., 20-C
  JOHN M., 98
  JOHN W., 98
  JOS, 51
  JOSEPH, 39, 40, 67
  JOSEPH JOHN R., 138

  KATE, 53
  L., 109, 121
  L.B., 109
  LAURA, 71
  LIZZIE, 79
  LOU E., 119
  LYDIA, 56, 78, 97, 137

163

M., 20-C
M.E., 138
M.J., 119
MAGGIE, 86
MARGARET, 37
MARTHA, 93
MARY, 53, 67
MARY J., 83, 91
MOLLIE L., 80
NANCY, 39, 40, 51
NANCY J., 56
NORA, 136
NORA BELL, 109
P., 117
P.J., 80, 116
PATRICK, 52(2), 59, 92, 102, 120
PAULINA, 86
PETE, 18
PHOEBE K., 39
POLLY, 18
REBECA, 136
REESE A., 37
RICHARD, 53
RINDA, 15
ROBERT, 20-B
S.J., 117
SALLIE, 26, 20-B
SALLIE M., 83
SARAH J., 52(2), 59, 92, 102, 120
SUSAN, 30
T.C., 136
VICTORIA C., 92
VICTORY, 121
W.A., 138(2)
W.B., 116
W.E., 97
W.P., 120
WINGO, 117(2)
WM A., 40
WM B., 80
WM B.C., 86
WM R., 91
HARMON
  ISAAC S., 49
HARNDON
  REBECCA M., 2
HAROLD
  EDIE, 102
  FLORA A., 102
  M.C., 102
  MARGARET, 134
  WM, 134(3)
HARPER
  FLETCHER J., 110
HARRELL
  CATHERINE, 105
  MARY, 65
  ROBT, 105
  SALLIE B., 105
HARRIS
  AB, 55

ALBERT, 135
ANDERSON, 58
CHARLOTTE, 105
CORNELIUS, 20-A
DAVE, 129
DAVID, 109
E.I., 106
ELIZABETH, 2, 21, 20-F
ELLEN, 109
ERNEST, 141
G.A., 105(2)
G.S., 131
G.W., 125
GEO E., 94
HENRY, 58, 141
HENRY J., 125
IDA, 67
JANE, 55
JAS, 20-A
JOHN, 109
JOHN S., 2
KANSAS, 141
LOUISA, 104
LULA B., 105
M.E., 125
MARY, 55
MARY A., 111
MARY M., 67
MOLLIE C., 44
NANCY, 20-A
NORA L., 94
O.T., 104, 108(2), 128, 141
PAUL H., 138
R., 72
R.W., 141
ROBERT, 2
ROBERTA, 98
ROBT, 21, 20-F
S.S., 94
SUSAN, 58
VIRGINIA, 94
W.G., 112
W.H., 82(2), 83, 86, 88, 94
WINSTON, 104
WM, 98
WM A., 21, 67, 20-F
HARRISON
  CAROLINE, 110
  E.F., 121
  JANE, 50
  L.P., 121
  MARTHA H., 50
  SARAH, 121
  VINIA, 110
HARRUP
  JAS., 18
  MARY, 18
  SAMUEL, 18
HARRY
  CALVIN, 27, 39, 44, 51, 78, 90, 107, 131

CAPHAS D., 46
CHARLES W., 107
G., 140
GEO A., 78
HARRIET R., 140
HATTA A., 51
JULIA V., 39
LILLY ALICE, 51
MARY, 27, 39, 44, 131
MARY A., 20-A
MARY E., 51, 90, 107
MOLLIE, 44
NANCY C., 27
R., 72, 92, 93, 96, 20-A
ROBT R., 64
ROMULUS, 37, 44(2), 46, 49, 51(5), 52, 53, 54(2), 58, 64(2), 76, 92(2), 140
RONULUS, 44
RUTH, 20-A
RUTHA, 64
RUTHA J., 46, 51
RUTHY JANE, 44
SARAH E.V., 44
W.E., 90
W.H., 131
HARSTON
  E.H., 127
  MARY, 127
HART
  W.E., 78
HARTWELL
  ALONZO G., 43
  ANDREW, 8
  ANDREW D., 6
  ANDREW J., 43
  CYNTHIA, 43, 46, 99
  CYNTHIA E., 43
  EVY, 83
  FANNEY L., 59
  GOOCH, 83
  ISABELL, 127
  JANE, 6, 8, 83
  JNO L., 43
  JOHN, 42, 43, 46, 99, 127
  JOHN B., 46
  JOHN L., 6
  JOHN T., 116
  JULIET M., 42
  MARK, 99
  MARY, 44
  MARY ANN, 59, 101
  MARY F., 8
  R.R., 44
  SARAH E., 101
  SYNTHIA E., 42
  VIRGIE, 121
  Z.T., 59, 101(2)
HARVES
  ALICE, 89

H.H., 89
HARVEY
  A.H., 100
  A.M., 100
  ADA M.E., 120
  ADAM, 24
  ADAM M., 55, 84
  ALBERT, 45
  ALLHY, 44
  ALLIE, 45
  AMANDA, 44
  AMANDA G., 8
  AUSTIN B., 5, 42
  C.E., 131
  CATH, 11
  CATHARINE, 40
  CATHERINE, 24
  CELIA A., 16
  CHAS L., 54
  D.C., 40
  E., 19
  ELECTRA A., 55, 84
  ELIZA, 124, 132, 20-C
  ELIZA. E., 19
  ELIZABETH, 20-C
  ELIZTH, 31
  EMALINE, 5, 134
  EMELINE, 61, 120, 124
  F.T., 124
  FLOYD, 61, 120, 124, 134
  FREDERICK, 11, 44, 45
  HENRY A., 20-C
  ISAAC G., 16
  ISAAC N., 19, 31, 20-C
  J.H., 101, 140
  JACOB, 33
  JACOB A., 35
  JACOB H., 16
  JACOB W., 11, 24, 35, 40
  JAMES F., 131
  JAMES G., 8, 9
  JAMES L., 20-C
  JAS H., 84
  JASPER M., 29
  JOHN, 97
  JOHN H., 61
  JOHN W., 16(2), 124
  JONATHAN C., 16
  JOSHUA, 80
  KATHARINE, 35
  LEAH M., 20-C
  LEWIS WHIZH., 100

  LORENZO D., 80
  LYDIA, 131
  M.W., 18
  MAGGIE N., 131
  MARTHA K., 33
  MARY E., 16
  MARY J., 18
  MATILDA, 5

MATTIE, 102
MAUD, 132
MELISSA M.E., 134
MICHAEL, 5(3)
MICHAEL W., 16
MURAIN Y., 42
N., 16
N.N., 18
NANCY, 5, 8, 9
NANCY K., 33
O.C., 124
SAML M., 60
SAMUEL C., 31
SARAH, 16(2)
SARAH C., 16
SARAH J., 100
SUSAN, 60, 80
SUSAN E., 60
VANDALIN B., 9
VIRGINIA EMMA TEXAS, 55
W., 5(2)
WILSON, 16
WM, 132
WM GORDON, 97

WM L., 29
WM T., 131
WYETT, 102
HARVY
  ADALINE, 20-C
  C., 20-C
  CALVIN, 89
  E., 20-C
  J.N., 20-C
  JACOB W., 20-C
  JAMES H., 20-C
  MARY, 89
HARWELL
  J.H., 61, 62
HARWOOD
  J.G., 87
  SARAH, 87
  WM, 87
HASKIN
  ELEN, 20-E
  HENRY, 20-B
  JOHN, 76
  JULIA, 76
  LACEY, 76
HASKINS
  DAVID, 32
  DOCK, 32
  JOHN, 76
  JULIA, 75
  LACY, 75
  LOUISA, 32
  ROBT, 75
HASTON
  NICEY, 127
  RILEY, 127
  RUTHA, 127

HATCHER
  AGNES PERMELIA, 30
  AMMON T., 19
  ANADIA, 20
  C.I., 131(2)
  C.W., 66
  DORTHA J., 111
  EDMOND, 3, 99
  EDMOND H., 16, 63
  ELIJAH, 16, 30, 35, 45, 108
  ELIZ J., 4
  ELIZA A., 88
  ELIZABETH, 3
  G.A., 114
  GERMAN P., 98, 119, 121, 124, 128, 131
  J.A., 140
  J.G., 102
  J.P., 140
  JEMIMA, 35, 108
  JENNIE, 16
  JESSEE G., 35
  JESSIE C., 108
  JNO P., 131
  JNO R., 98
  JNO W., 32
  JOHN, 111
  JOHN R., 20, 66
  JULIA A., 131
  L.C., 140
  LETHA A., 19
  LUCETTIA, 99
  LUCETTIE P., 109
  MARTHA J., 45
  MINNEY, 45
  N.E., 109
  NANCY, 3, 30, 63, 99, 102
  NANCY E., 66, 98, 111
  NORA ESTALINE, 102

  PERMELIA, 32
  SARAH, 87
  SARAH J., 63
  SILAS, 20, 32
  SIMMON, 5
  TEMPA, 5
HATHERINGTON

  J.H., 71
  J.T., 71
  MARY E., 71
HAUHKS
  AMELIA, 51
  POLLY, 51
  WM, 51
HAULDRON
  MARGARET A., 51

HAUR
  ALAWAY, 125(2)
  C., 125

JORDAN, 125
HAVELY
  CHARLES, 57
  ELIZA, 57
  W.D., 57
HAVEN
  ALEX, 121
  E., 121
  LULA, 121
HAVENS
  JOHN, 93
  LIZZIE, 93
  SALLIE, 93
HAVIS
  CAMPLINE, 105
  JAMES, 105
  LILLIE R., 105
HAWISTON
  E., 133
HAWKINS
  ABRAM, 60
  DANIEL, 60
  ELIZA, 115
  ELIZA JANE, 60
  HESTER, 122
  IREAL, 122
  J., 115
  JAMES, 60
  JOHN A., 68
  JOHNSON, 60, 115
  JOHNSTON, 75
  MAJOR, 60
  MELVINA, 70
  POLLY, 70
  SARAH B., 60
HAWKS
  A., 30
  ABRAHAM, 45
  ARMITTA, 111
  BEULA, 45
  BULIA, 30
  ELI, 80, 101
  ELIZABETH, 80
  FRANK, 59
  H.H., 98(2)
  HATTIE B., 98
  HENDERSON C., 79

  HERBERT H., 98
  MARY ANN, 79
  MARY V., 98
  MITCHELL, 30, 97
  NANCY, 80
  NANCY J., 101

POLLEY A., 87
POLLY, 59, 99
POLLY ANN, 65
RHODA C., 95
ROSA E., 87
ROSETTA, 99
SUSAN, 97
THIRSEY, 111
W.J., 65
W.R., 111
WILBUR J., 65
WM, 101
WM R., 45, 59, 65, 79, 87, 95, 99
HAWLEY
  A.U., 129
  ADDISON M., 70
  ANDERSON, 129
  CHARLOTTE, 20, 49, 50

  CHAS D., 50
  J.W., 28
  JOHN, 20
  JOHN A., 49
  JOHN H., 50
  MARY E., 70
  W.S., 49
  WINFIELD S., 20
  WM P., 70
HAWS
  HERBERT H., 89
HAWTHORN
  JAMES L., 132(2)
  JAS F., 132
  M.D., 132
HAYES
  A., 132
  H., 132
  MARY, 132
HAYMAKER
  ELIZA W., 8
  MARY, 8
  MICHAEL, 8
HAYNES
  A.K., 134
  ANN, 69
  ISAAC N., 69
  LIZZIE L., 69
  R.D., 132
HAYS
  WM H., 87
HAYWOOD
  ELLEN, 5
  JERRY, 119
  JULIA, 106
  PATSY, 5(2)
  RHODA, 35, 58
  SAML, 5(2)
  SARAH, 35, 40
  VICY, 119
  WILLIAM, 5
  WILLIAM E., 40
  WM, 35, 40

HAZELWOOD

ASA, 37, 38
CHARITY, 27, 30
ELISHA E., 38
JOHN, 39, 20-D
JOSEPH, 30
JOSHUA, 27(2), 30
LAZARUS, 37
NANCY, 39
RACHAEL, 38
RACHEL, 37
STARLING, 39
HAZLEWOOD

A.E., 117
A.N., 53, 80
AASY (SIC), 80
ALICE B., 49
AMANDA, 141
ARDELIA, 102
ASA, 40, 53
CHARITY, 20-D
DOSIA L., 120
E.E., 120
E.N., 120
FANNIE, 120
GEO W., 70, 130(2)
H.D., 127
HIRAM, 40
IDA, 127
J.C., 141
J.L., 130
J.W., 111
JAS C., 117(2)
JOHN, 30, 49, 53, 56, 93, 102
JOSEPH L., 130
JOSHUA, 30, 20-D
LILLY, 53
MARY, 93, 102
MARY J., 49
NANCY, 53, 56, 87
NANCY J., 70
NANNIE, 93, 130(2)
OCTAVE, 120
RACHAEL, 40
RACHEL, 53, 80
SARAH, 127
STARLING, 120
SUSANNA, 70
THOS P., 56
VIRGINIA, 141
W.J., 117, 130(2), 141
W.S., 87
HEAD
ALEXD, 66
ELSIE, 68
J.A., 66
NANCY, 66
SUSAN, 68
ZEB, 68
HEARE

SARAH, 14
WM, 14
HEARN
A., 20-C
A.G., 103
AMY, 22
AND J., 45
ANDREW, 22, 102, 126
ANNA, 11
ARORA, 10
D.W., 139
E.C., 61
EASTER, 45
EASTER C., 103
EDWD S., 100
ESTHER C., 55
GEO W., 52
IDA, 52
J., 112
JAMES, 11, 45, 100, 103
JAS, 55, 61, 84
JNO B., 55
L.G., 20-C
L.L., 70
LEVI, 22, 28
LEVI G., 10, 11, 36, 46, 55
LEVI L., 20-C
MARTHA A., 36
MARY J., 102
MARY JANE, 28
MATTIE, 102
MAX, 126
METTIE J., 70
NANCY, 139
ORA, 36, 46, 55
PAULINA, 28
POLLY, 124
QUINDORA, 61
RHODA L., 70
RHOLLETA MAY, 112

SARAH ALICE, 126
SARAH C., 46
VICTORIA J., 55
WILLIAM, 10, 52
WM, 112
HEATH
ALEXANDER, 121

ELIZABETH, 80, 121
JAS R., 80
JEFFERSON, 48
MILTON, 80, 121
NANNIE, 48
PERLINIA, 48
HEDRECK
ANNIE L., 119
H.M., 119
N.L., 119
HEDRIC
D.C., 114

HEDRICK
ANN, 33
ASKEN, 107
B., 140
B.L., 113
BECKEY, 130
BIDDY, 107
C.S., 121
CATHRINE, 107
CHARLES, 130
CLONNEY S., 31
CORRIE L., 99
D.W., 121
DIANAH, 13
DIANNA, 32
ESTALINE, 121
G.H., 49
G.S., 131
GEO J., 107
GEORGE W., 20-B
GRANVILL, 131
GRANVILLE, 33, 56
GRANVILLE H., 32, 34, 63
H., 32
H.M., 99
HARVEY, 113, 137
HARVEY M., 104
HARVY M., 13
JACKSON, 140
JEANNETTIE N., 40
JOS A., 104
JOS., 13
JOSEPH, 32
M., 32
M.J., 121
MARTHA, 137
MARY, 56, 107
MARY JANE, 40
MARY L., 34
MARY O., 34
N.J., 137
NAN., 20-B
NANCY, 99
NANCY J., 113
NANNIE J., 104
O. CERCIL, 121
OWEN, 131
PERRY, 40
PETER, 31
PHIL, 20-B
POLLY, 63
REBECCA, 131
ROBERT, 32
ROBT, 140
RUFUS, 107
S.E., 121
SARAH J., 33
THOS J., 63
VIRGINIA B., 49
WM P., 56
HEINDRICK
CHARLES, 142

JACK, 142
LYTHA, 142
HELM
ADAM, 20-A
ANN, 20-A
RACHEL, 20-A
HELMANDOLLAR

ANGA G., 91
ANGIE G., 91
ANNIE, 141
ANNIE MAY, 141
LINDA, 2
MARY J., 91
MATILDA, 2
T.H., 141
THOMAS, 91(2)
WM, 2
WM G., 91
HELMANDOLOR

J.N., 123
NANNIE M., 123
T.H., 123
HELMS
G.W., 121
JNO J., 130
JOHN H., 130
M., 121
MARY, 130
THOMAS O., 121
THOS O., 130
HELSEL
BARBARA, 49
BARBARA C., 137
JACOB, 49
JACOB A., 137
JOSEPH, 49
SUSAN, 137
HELTON
A.B., 126
B.A., 124, 126
ELIJAH, 52
EMILY, 52
JENNIE, 104
MARY, 104
MONROE, 133
N.E., 124
NANCY, 44, 126
NANCY B., 124
NEWMAN, 44
SINA, 133
WM A., 44
WM G., 52
HENCH
ANNIE E., 135
ROBT L., 135
S.T., 135
HENDERSON
ANNIE, 100
BENJ., 58
BERTHA, 126
CHRISTIAN, 103

CHRISTIANNA, 26
CHRISTINA, 32, 44, 56, 58
ELIAS, 125
GILLIE A., 49
HANNAH, 48
HIRAM, 56
LUCINDA, 126
M.B., 131
MALINDA, 26
MARY, 14
MAY B., 100
PARTHENIA, 82
PEER, 56, 58
PERRY, 26, 44, 103
PIER, 32
POLLY, 44
R., 14
R.H., 131
REBECCA, 32
REBECCA J., 100
RHODA, 125
SAMUEL G., 16
VICTORIA, 48
W.A., 131
WALTER, 126
WM, 100
WM A., 100
HENDRICKS
CARRIE, 128
MARIA, 69
WM, 69(2)
HENING
FRANK, 100
MINA, 100
ORAB A., 100
HENNINGS
AMANDA, 132
C.E., 132
M.R., 132
HENRITZE
T.L., 58
HENRY
J.H., 117
JANE, 81
MILTON, 81(2)
SAML J., 84, 126
THOS, 126
THOS H., 84
VIRGINIA, 84, 126
HEONE
JANE, 113
SARAH SUSAN, 113

WM, 113
HEPTINSTILL
J.P., 133
HERDISTER
SARAH, 126
HERNDEN
CHARLES, 29
HERNDON
A., 15, 20-A

A.B., 91
A.G., 88
ALICE V., 74
ARCHER, 1, 2
ARTHUR, 27, 28, 31, 74, 20-A
ARTHUR M., 86
AUTHUR, 21, 20-F
CHAS, 105, 125
DONNIE, 28
DORAH, 125
ELIZA, 1, 31
ELIZABETH B., 1
HATTIE, 105
IDA M., 97
J.L., 88
J.W., 88(2)
JNO W., 34
LELIA S., 31
LOUISA, 37
LOUISIA, 34
M.E., 123
MADISON, 37
MARIA, 47
MARIAH, 105, 125
MARTHA, 34
MARTHA E., 21, 20-F
MARY E., 66, 86, 97
N.L., 74, 91
NANCEY, 37
S.E.B., 15, 21, 27, 28, 20-A, 20-F
SALLIE A., 27
SARAH E.B., 2
W.H., 86, 123
W.H.H., 123
WM H., 97
WM H.H., 15
HERON
JOHN, 73
MARY, 73
WILLIAM, 73
HESLIP
JOSEPH, 20-D
REBECCA, 20-D
TIMOTHY N., 20-D
HESS
CATHARINE, 2
JOHN, 2
MARY A., 2
HETHERINGTON

GEORGE T., 30
J.S., 106
J.T., 106, 134
JOHN, 20-B
JOS J., 20
JOSEPH T., 20
JULIET H., 134
JULIETT H., 106
MARY C., 20-B
R., 20-B
RHODA, 20

SALLIE, 134
HETTERMAN
MARY, 64
PATRICK, 64
WM, 64
HEUDUCK
AGNES, 45
HEYLTON
A., 15
GEORGE W., 15
MARTHA, 15
HEYPES
WM W., 52
HIBBS
MARY E., 49
THOMAS W., 49
WILLIAM, 49
HICKEY
ATHEA, 134
MICAEL, 134
WALTER R., 134
HICKMAN
HATTIE, 114
JENNIE, 116
JOHN, 91, 114, 116
PHILLIS, 91
SARAH M., 91
HICKS
ANNIE, 105
C.N., 141
C.P., 141
E.G., 140(2)
EDWARD G., 40
H.L., 96
HANNAH, 65, 141
J.T., 20-A
JANE, 107
JESSE, 102
LEWIS G., 37
LORENZIE, 40
LORENZO D., 21, 20-F

LUCINDA, 21, 40, 20-F
MAHALA G., 134
MARY, 140
MINNIE, 96
MOLLIE, 65
NANCY, 107
PULINA, 102
REBECCA, 20-A
RUS, 141
RUSSEL S., 20-A
W.W., 105
WESLEY, 105
WILLIAM R., 21, 20-F
WM, 102
WM R., 65, 96
HICKSON
SARAH, 28
HIGGENBOTHAM

ANDREW G., 120
FANNIE, 111

GEORGE, 111
JANE B., 111
SARAH E., 120
HIGGINBOTHAM

B.S., 81
ELIZTH, 64
ELMIRA, 26
G.L., 64
H., 26
J.C., 89
J.H., 29, 89
JNO B., 84, 87
JNO C., 87
JOHN B., 81
LEWIS, 127(2)
LUCINDA, 127
M.C.H., 89
M.E., 81, 84
MARIA ELZTH, 31

MARTHA E., 64
MARY, 26, 87
ROBT H., 60
S.J., 23
SARAH, 60
SARAH E., 23
SUSAN, 26
T.J., 84
HIGGINS
C.E., 49
HIGHT
ALEX, 113
EVYLIN GRACE, 113

J.H., 101
JULIUS C., 101
LULA, 113(2)
REBECCA, 101
HILL
A.B., 101
AARAS, 32
ALA, 32, 35, 99
ALEXR., 19
ALIE, 43
ANDREW J., 61
CATHARINE, 35
CHARLES, 140
CHAS C., 92
CHAS M., 86
CORA L., 83
DAVEY, 53
DAVID, 71
DELIA, 38
EDWARD, 79
ELIZABETH, 38
ELLEN, 86
F.S., 83
F.W., 121
GEORGE H., 86
H.C., 137(2)
HARDEN, 47
HARDIN H., 35

HARDON, 78
HARIUM, 47
HARRIET C., 117
HARRIET E., 92
I., 119
ISAIAH, 119
J.F., 79
J.L., 121
J.R., 99
JAMES F., 47
JAMES R., 38
JANE, 35, 47, 78
JANEY, 47
JAS F., 78
JAS R., 93
JENNETTA U., 43
JOHN, 1, 113
JUDEL, 87
JULINE, 100
LEDFORD, 113
LOUISA, 53, 71
LULA ALBERTA, 99

M.A., 93, 113, 117
M.C., 100
M.H., 121
MARGARET, 87
MARIAH, 117
MARTHA, 61, 63, 71, 73, 79, 99, 107
MARTHA A., 61, 101, 140
MARY, 19, 47, 113
MOLLIE, 77
NANCY JANE, 73, 100

NANNIE S., 83
PEGGY ANN, 53
PETER ALEXD, 63
PHILIP W., 92
POLLY, 1
R.J., 133
R.K., 99
R.W., 135(3)
REUBEN, 79
ROBERT, 61(2), 63, 101, 140
ROBT, 113, 117
ROBT J.L., 63
ROSENA, 19
S.S., 93
SARAH E., 104
SOPHIA, 87
SUSAN E., 61
WILEY G., 35
WILLIAM, 117
WILLIAM S., 1
HILLON
DAVIS, 57
MARY J., 57
HILTON
DAVID, 63
ELIZA, 48

HENRY S., 48
JACOB E., 63
LOUISA, 101
MARY A., 63
MARY S., 101
WM A., 48
HINCHU
ANN NETTIE, 131
C.H., 131
MAHALY, 131
HINES
ADELINE, 72
BEN, 72
CALLIE L., 72
HINTON
ANS., 23
J., 13
JNO, 23
WM, 23
HITE
JAMES H., 20-C
MARY, 20-C
SAMUEL, 20-C
HIX
JANE, 58
MINERVA E., 58
WILLIAM J., 28
HOBBS
ALABAMA, 15
CALVIN, 15
D.C., 108
E.W., 125
JACOB, 57
JAMES A., 15
JOHN, 125
JULIA, 54
JULINA, 16
LEWIS, 54
LIDIA C., 133
MADISON, 125
MAGIE M., 108
NANCY, 125
R.H., 125
THOS, 54
THOS., 16
W.M., 125
W.S., 108
WILLIAM S., 16
HOCK
ALFRED H., 116
KATE, 116
MARY, 125
MATHEW, 125
WM H., 116
HODGE
ALBERT, 123
ANDERSON, 19
ARAMINTA, 59
E., 19
ELIZABETH, 52, 123
ELLA B., 59
G. WASH, 123
GEORGE W., 52

JAMES, 59
JAMES M., 19
WELTHY C., 52
HOGAN
AMANDA E., 17
ELIZABETH E., 20-D
GRANVILLE H., 17
MARY A., 17
NANCY, 17(3), 21, 20-D, 20-F
PETER, 17(3), 21, 20-D, 20-F
VIRGINIA A., 21, 20-F
HOGE
ELLEN, 49
JAMES, 49
JAS H., 49
HOGGE
DALE, 31
DELLAH, 31
FOUNTAIN J., 31
HOGINS
CHLOE, 53
DENNIS, 53
PATRICK, 53
HOLBROOK
GEORGIA, 65
JOHN C., 36
LOU, 116
MARY H., 36
POLLY, 40
RANDAL, 40
RANDALL, 36
W.D., 40
HOLCOMB
GEO L., 85
JANE, 120
NANCY, 85
WM, 85
HOLDERN
ADA G., 114
ANDREW J., 20-A
D.V.E., 113
D.W., 113
DORCAS W., 100
ELIZABETH, 24
ELLA, 90
GEO, 24
HENRY, 20-A, 20-D
J.A., 97
JAMES, 20-D
JAMES M., 17
JAS H., 91, 114
JOHN A., 30
JOS M., 124
LIDA H., 97
M., 20-A
M.S., 97
MAHALA, 20-D
MARY R., 114

MATHEW, 91
POLLY, 17, 124
RHODA, 91
SAMI, 100, 113
SAMUEL, 19
SARAH, 19
WALTER S., 100
WM, 115
HOLDRON
BENJAMIN M., 38
DORCAS, 100
H.G., 100
HARRY, 44
HENRY, 41, 97
JAS H., 97
JULIA A., 74
MAC C., 41
MAHAIA, 41
MAHALA, 44, 97
PHILIP T., 44
SALLY, 14
SAML, 74, 100
SAMUEL, 38
WM, 14
HOLLAND
A.J., 79(2)
BETTIE, 92
C., 133
CORNELIUS, 79, 95
CREASY, 106
FANNIE, 106
G.M., 132
GEO, 106
GRISELDA, 79
GRUZELA, 95
JAMES, 133(2)
JENNIE, 109
JOHN, 92
MINNIE, 95
NANNIE, 92
HOLLAWAY
C.E., 110
E.A., 110
JAMES, 110
HOLLIDAY
FRANCIS, 137
JOHN M., 137
W.R., 137(2)
HOLLIN
MINNIE, 65
HOLLINS
F.E., 132
J.M., 81
LAURA G., 132
MARY E., 81
W.M., 132
HOLLOWAY
C.E., 130
CHAS E., 75, 77, 78, 93
E.A., 130
ELIZA, 75
ELIZA A., 93

ELIZA ANN, 77, 78
J.H., 130
JAS C., 78
MINNIE LEE, 77
MOLLIE, 93
NANNIE, 75
HOLLY
AMERICA J., 42
CHARLES, 42
GEORGE, 55
HENDERSON, 55
MAURINDA, 42
HOLROYD
J.F., 71
NANNIE T., 40
S.R., 76
SALLIE E., 75
SARAH, 40, 49, 75
W., 23(2), 25
WILLIAM, 2, 4, 5(3), 6(2), 7(3), 8(2), 10(3), 11, 14, 16, 17(2), 18(3), 20, 26, 27(3), 32(2), 33(3), 34(2), 36(3), 37, 40, 49, 20-A(5), 20-B, 20-C(3), 20-D
WM, 11(4), 12(2), 28(2), 34(2), 35, 36, 37, 41, 42(3), 45, 46, 47, 48(4), 60(2), 61, 62, 63, 70(2), 71(2), 75, 78, 79, 81, 82, 83, 85, 91, 20-C, 20-D, 20-E
WM H., 49
HOLSON
RHODA, 60
HOLSTIN
JOHN M., 28
HOLSTINE
ADELINE M., 16
ANDREW J., 24
ANN S., 16
CYLISTINA E., 17
CYNTHIA J., 4
E., 15, 17
ELIZ, 20-E
ELIZABETH, 7, 24
ELIZABETH E., 15
ELIZTH, 16(2)
ELIZTH, 20-A
HARRIET J., 7
HENRY, 4
HUGH, 1, 17
J., 15
J.C., 17
JAS W., 4
JAS. C., 16
JES. C., 20-A
JOS, 20-E
JOS. C., 24
JOSEPH C., 7, 16

LEWIS C., 97, 20-A
M., 4(2)
MARY E., 4
NICHOLAS E., 1
O.W., 97
SARAH, 1, 17
SARAH L., 97
HOLSTON
A.J., 117
ALPH O., 133
E., 117
HUGH C., 137
J.M., 133, 137
L.C., 131, 133
LEWIS, 137
MINNIE, 117
PETER, 133
S.L., 131, 133
SARAH, 137
SUSAN E., 131
HOLT
DENNIS, 58
ELEANOR, 50
ELENDER, 35
ELJENDER, 67
GRACEY, 42
GRACIE, 119
GRACY A., 69
JACOB J., 67
JAMES, 58
JOSEPH T., 50
JOSEPHINE J., 42
JULIA, 58
PAMALATEA E., 35

R.EL., 69
RICHARD, 35, 50, 67
TILDEN H., 119
HOLTZCLAW
DAVID, 129
MARY A., 129
W.R., 129
HONAKER
A.J., 68, 76, 90
ABRAM, 20
ANDREW, 69, 73
ARAMINTA, 105
BELL, 69
CHAS W., 81, 90
CHAS WM, 87
E. SUSAN, 128
E.J., 128(2)
ELIZABETH, 38, 47
ELLEN, 38
F.P., 87
G.W.L., 73
GEORGE P., 87
HENRY, 20, 38, 47
J., 19
J.H., 25, 27(2)
J.R., 81
J.W., 22, 128
JAMES D., 69

JAS B., 20-C
JAS C., 69
JAS J., 68
JAS R., 69
JAS., 20-E
JOHN H., 89
JNO D., 22(2)
JNO H., 28, 81, 92(6), 93, 95, 96(2), 97(3), 98, 99, 100(2), 116, 118, 119
JNO. W., 22
JOHN A., 88
JOHN H., 21(2), 23(4), 24(4), 25(2), 26(5), 27, 28(7), 84, 85, 86(2), 87(2), 88(3), 89, 90(2), 105(2), 109(4), 112(2), 113(3), 114, 115(2), 116, 118(2), 121(2), 123, 131, 20-E(4), 20-F(2)
JOHN M., 47
LUCY, 73, 76, 90
LUCY A., 68
M., 19
M.A., 20-C
MANERVA, 20-E
MARGARET N., 65

MARY, 76
MARY A., 42, 116
MARY J., 81
MARY JANE, 65
MOLLIE J., 87
O.A., 20-E
PETER C., 42
PETTER, 20-C
S., 20-E
S.A., 109, 116
SARAH, 20
SARAH C., 19
W.C., 105(2), 109
W.S., 109
WM B., 42
WM C., 65(2), 20-E
HONCHINS
EDME J., 33
GEO H., 55
MALINDA E., 33
MINNIE M., 55
SARAH A., 55
SHOM, 33
HONKER
J.H., 122
JEHU C., 122
S.A., 122
HOOGE
ELIZ. J., 49
GEO D., 49
REBECCA, 49
HOON

CELIA, 19
JOHN, 19
WILLIAM A., 19
HOPKINS
ELIZABETH, 34
GEO W., 37, 42
J., 4(2)
J.T., 17
JAMES F., 28
JAMES T., 17
JAS. T., 34
JEMIMA, 8
JEMIMAH, 12
JOEL, 97, 124
JOEL E., 28, 125
JOHNATHAN, 20-D

JONATHAN, 8, 12
JOSEPH H., 77
L.E., 97
LOUISA, 124, 129
LOUISA J., 66
LOUISA L., 125
LULA, 129
LULA H., 97
M., 17
MARN P., 28
MARY P., 34
MAUD L., 124
MOLLIE E., 125
NANCY, 37, 42
RACHEL, 77
REUBEN, 37, 42
SAML, 77
SAMUEL, 12
SIMEON D., 4, 8
TEMPERANCE, 20-D

HOPSON
CATHARINE, 74
HENRIETTA, 74
WILLIS, 74
HORNE
D.C., 64, 65(2), 66, 67(6), 68(4), 69
HORNESBY
C., 20-C
JOHNATHAN, 20-C

NANCY JANE, 20-C

HORTON
A.J., 65
ANA, 65
BENJ C., 83
CHAS, 78
ESTHER, 78, 88
HENRY, 54
JACOB, 54
JNO C., 83
JOHN L., 78
L.H., 88
LEAN, 88

166

LEWIS, 78
LUCINDA, 78
NANCY J., 83
SINE, 54
WILLIE, 78
HORUE
D.C., 64
HOSTIN
DICY, 81
HOSTON
ABRAHAM, 73
H., 73
HARVEY, 73
JENNETTE, 73
HOUCHER
S.A., 20
SARAH L, 20
WM C., 20
HOUCHINGS
GRANVILLE, 125
HOUCHINS
BALLARD, 18, 119
C., 18(2)
CALLIE, 86
CATHARINE, 13
CELIA, 20-E
CHAS., 13
CLARA P., 97
CORA N., 66
ELIZABETH, 69
EMILY, 19
G., 95
G.H., 66, 121
GEO, 86
GEO H., 60, 84
GRACIE A., 121
GRAN, 83
GRAN., 81
GRANVILL, 86, 126
GRANVILLE, 86(2), 94, 108, 20-E
GRAVILL, 103
H.A., 69
IRVIN, 34
J.B., 86(2), 97
JAMES, 13, 20-D
JAS, 4
JAS., 19, 20-A
JULIA, 20-A
KURNEY A., 119
LIZZIE LOU, 122
LIZZIE M., 121
LOU, 122
LOUISA J., 13
MAGGIE, 86
MARY, 86, 121
MARY J., 4
MOLLIE, 105
MOLLIE L., 84
PATRIA, 86
ROSA LEE, 60
S., 4, 13, 20-D
SARAH, 19, 60, 20-A

SARAH A., 84
SAREPTA, 20-D
VIRGINIA, 34
VIRGINIA P., 18
W., 18
W.R., 69
WILMON, 20-E
WM, 18, 122, 20-E
WM R., 13
HOUELIUS
CAROLINE, 15
WILMOUTH, 15
WM, 15
HOUK
MYRTLE M., 116
N.C., 116
S.E., 101, 102(4), 103, 104, 105(3), 106(2), 107(2), 108(2), 112(3), 114(4), 115, 116(9), 117, 118, 119(3), 120, 121(3), 122(3), 124, 125(3)
HOWARD
A.W., 116
AUGUSTUS, 83
BETSEY, 41
CALLIE, 131
CHARLES, 41, 135
CHARLES W., 135
CHAS A., 116
CHAS P., 132
CLEOPATRA, 132
DELPHIA, 103
ELIZA M., 83
ELIZABETH, 116
ELMIRA, 76, 135
FANNIE, 141
GRANDVILLE, 41
J.H., 77
JAMES, 77
JNO A., 132
JULIA, 110
KITTY, 103
MAGGIE, 141
MALINDA, 65
MARY, 77
MINIE, 65
SARAH, 65
THOMAS, 141
WM, 83
HOWEL
JAMES, 80
THOMAS, 80
VIRGINIA, 80
HOWELL
EMMA Z., 40
JENNIE, 84, 85
JNO, 13
JOHN, 84
JOHN D., 31
JOHN P., 40

LETHA, 40
MARK W., 99
NANCY, 80
NANCY M., 31
ROSA E., 85
SETHA., 13
SETHE, 31
THOMAS, 85
THOS, 80, 84, 99
VINICE S., 13
VIRGINIA, 80, 99
HOWERTON
E., 42, 45, 52, 65
JOHN, 20-C
HOWERY
IRENE, 88
JNO A., 88
HOWNEN
CHAS, 107
CORDELIA, 107
ELIZA, 107
HOY
L.L., 110
J.L.L., 110
S.M., 110
HOYE
CALVIN C., 88
MARY E., 88
MILES C., 88
HUBBARD
A.A., 96
ANNA, 20-A, 20-E
BELL, 68
CHAS G., 79
E., 20-E
ELIZABETH, 7(2)
ELIZTH, 9(2), 24
ELLEN, 85, 103
EMALINE, 20-A
GEO W., 77
GREEN, 78, 89
H.E., 98
J.C., 21(2), 24, 26, 20-A, 20-C(2), 20-D(2), 20-E, 20-F(2)
J.L., 49
JAMES B., 109
JANE, 54
JNO C., 13(2)
JOHN C., 1(6), 2(4), 3(6), 4(5), 5(6), 6(2), 7, 15(2), 18(5), 19(5), 20(2), 23, 20-A(3), 20-B(2)
JONATHAN, 53, 54, 68, 75, 92
JONATHAN A., 9
JOSEPH, 20-E
L.A., 77, 109
L.C., 85
LOUISA A., 7
LOURINDA, 53

LUCINDA A., 78
LUCY A., 79, 86, 131
LUCY ANN, 98, 107
LUVERNIE, 107
M.F., 96
MAHALA A., 9
MANERVIA, 78
MARTHA, 92
MARTHA A., 96
MARY E., 24
MATTIE F., 103
MINERVA J., 38
MORUS, 89
P.A., 77, 79, 107, 131
PATERO A., 7
PAYTON A., 109
PEYTON A., 86, 98
ROSIA F., 89
RUTH, 16
S., 20-E
SAML, 9(2), 85, 103
SAML., 26
SAMUEL, 7(2), 24
SAMUEL G., 20-E
T.C., 77
THOS C., 86
V.E., 68, 75
VIRGINIA, 53, 92
WM S., 75
HUDGENS
LEE, 53
HUDNALL
JOS ALEX, 95
MARY E., 95
RICHD A., 95
HUDSON
ELIZTH, 17, 54
H.G., 122(2)
HARRIET, 6
JAMES, 6
JATHINA A., 73
JOHN S., 6
JOSEPH P., 6
KATE, 86
M.H., 122
MARTHA E., 73
R., 17
R.R., 73
ROBERT, 86
ROBERT R., 17
ROSA, 3
ROSANA, 6
VINCENT, 3, 6, 17
VINCENT P., 17
W.D., 122
WM, 17, 54
WM ROBT., 54
HUDUSON
WILLIAM, 3
HUFF
EDWARD, 58
HARVEY, 61
JAS V., 58

MARTHA, 61
MELINDA, 86
MIMA, 61
PRUDENCE, 86
WATT, 86
HUFFMAN
A.J., 63, 85
ANDREW J., 38, 43, 52
BETTIE E., 85
CHAS J.W., 109
CHAS L., 84
DICIE E., 85
ELLEN, 38, 63
ELVIRA, 109
FANNIE, 124
J.H., 63
JAMES, 84
JAS H., 63
JNO, 17
JOHN, 109, 139
JOHN L., 17
MARGT., 17
MARTHA Z., 43
MARY C., 27, 84
O.L., 139
SOLAMAN, 38
WM, 52
HUGG
EDWARD, 59
HUGHES
A.A., 110
ADA G., 116
ARAMINTA, 92
ARAMINTA D., 10
ARMINTA, 83
CLUFF, 55, 66, 94
DELIA B., 131
DELILA, 14
E.D., 131
ELLEN, 86
GABE, 86
GEORGE, 14, 54
GORDAN J., 110
H.J., 110
HOLLEY, 66
HOLLIE, 55, 94
HOWARD, 61
HUGH J., 19, 84
J.C., 131
JAS C., 55, 71
JOHN, 14
JOHN C., 66
LOUISA, 14
MAHALA, 54
MARGARET D., 41

R.H., 52
ROBT, 61
RUHAMER, 83
SARAH, 116
SARAH V., 55
SUSAN, 54
THOMS R., 94

THOS, 90
WASHN, 83
WM, 10, 19
WM A., 84
HUGHS
GEO W., 27(2)
LOUISA, 14
MARY E., 14
NANCY J., 27
REUBEN G., 27
SUSAN, 27(2)
WM, 14
HULL
ANDREW J., 7
ELIZABETH, 76
EMALY, 7
HENRY, 7
LEWIS, 76
WM P., 76
HULLER
H.L., 111
J.J., 111
HUMPHREYS
JAMES M., 25
JOHN, 50
MALINDA, 50
NELIA J., 50
HUNT
ANNA J., 47
CHAS H., 137
CYNTHIA, 10
ELI, 10
H.F., 105, 137
H.W., 37
HANNAH, 47
HANNAH C., 37, 47
HARVEY, 47
HARVEY W., 47
JAMES, 20-C
JOHN, 75
LOUISA, 105, 137
M.A., 20-C
MARY A., 37
MARY E., 105
MEDDLETON, 20-C

NANNIE L., 47
S.P., 18
SALLIE, 75
SAML., 18
SAMUEL, 18
WEBB, 75

HUNTER
A.B., 79, 83(2), 85(3), 86, 87(2), 88, 112(3), 113, 115, 116(4), 117, 118(3), 121(2), 122(2), 123(2), 124, 125(2), 126(2), 127(3), 128(4), 129(3)
ALFRED B., 84
CHAPMAN, 100

EVELINE, 73
GEO W., 73
JOSIE E., 73
L.D., 74
HURLEY
DAVID, 46(2)
LAURA A., 63
MARY, 46
HURST
AMANDA B., 59
ARMSTEAD, 65
ARMSTED A., 19
C.W., 74
FLOYD, 22
J.H., 95, 131
JAMES H., 19, 74
JAMES W., 65
JAS H., 59, 72, 79, 95, 118
JEMIMA, 28
JOSIE M., 95
L., 134
LC., 117
LILLY E., 134
LURA M., 72
MARTHA, 29
MARY J., 23
MATILDA, 29
MILLE, 28
N.A.E., 79
O.S., 127, 134
OWEN S., 38
PHEBE, 9, 19
POLLIE, 80
ROSA E., 80
S.L., 131
SARAH, 59, 95, 118, 131
SARAH E., 65
SARAH F., 74, 79
SARAH P., 72
SUSAN, 19, 38, 43
THOMAS J., 43
THOS, 28
VIRGINIA E., 9
W.J., 116
WILLIAM, 28
WILLIE R., 116
WM, 9, 19(2), 23, 38, 43, 80
HURT
DELIE, 77
DELPHA, 77
EPP, 77
JOHN, 87
LOUISA, 104
MAC, 87
MANDY, 87
MARTHA J., 72, 76, 82
NANCY, 83
ROBT McNUTT, 76
SARAH F., 72

VANIE, 104
W.B., 82
W.E., 79
W.S., 72, 82
WM SAML, 76
HUTCHINSON
ALEX, 38, 71
ALEXANDER S., 15
ANN, 13
B.R., 140
CYNTHIA J., 38
ELIZ., 13
G.W., 131
H., 13
J. REESE, 140
J.L., 125
LIZZIE, 71
LYDIA, 71
LYDIA ANN, 38
P.F., 140
S.P., 125
SADIE L., 125
HUTTON
JAMES T., 88
JOHN A.P., 115
MARTHA E., 88
S.A., 88
S.H., 115
W.J., 115
HYE
HENRY, 76
SILVIA, 76
WM, 76
HYLE
SUSANAH, 27
HYLTON
A.B., 130
ABSOLOM, 90
CHAS P., 102
D.J., 132
ELLEN T., 110
H., 132
HARVEY, 75
HENRY, 1
HIRAM, 75, 84, 104, 130, 131
ISAAC L., 84
J., 68
JACOB, 62, 133
JEREMIAH, 1
JNO A., 90
JOSEPH, 131
LEWIS, 102
LEWIS PRESTON, 103

LOUISA, 84, 104, 130, 131
LYDIA A., 104
M., 132
MARY J., 90
MILLIE, 102
NANNIE, 112

RUTHA E., 103	ISAAC, 100	LOUVENIA, 54	W.I., 126	R.A., 80	J.C., 118	W.H., 89	JAMES D., 2, 55, 71
SARAH, 1, 75	ISAAC N., 44	MARY M., 129	JENKS	ELIZABETH, 55	J.H., 107	WESLEY, 62	JAMES E., 24
WM A., 103	LUCINDA, 44, 57, 100	NANNIE, 54	IANNA R., 74	ELIZTH ANN, 64, 77	J.T., 91	WM, 116, 118, 121	JAMES H., 33, 40(2),
HYPES	MARY F., 44	SIDNEY, 54	WM J., 74	H.C., 59	J.W., 103(3), 104(5),	JOHNSTON	46(2), 54, 111, 112,
C.E., 123	ISAACS	STEPTOE, 54	WM S., 74	HAMILTON, 64	105(3), 106, 107(2),	A., 20-C	124, 20-B
DELIA A., 140	JOHN, 129	STEPTOR, 54	JENNING	J.G., 58, 84(2), 95	108, 113, 115,	ADAM, 8, 10, 24, 33,	JAS A., 89
FLOYD, 121	MARY A., 129	JANEY	C.M., 63	JANH, 59	117(3), 120, 123, 133	68, 20-B	JAS B., 95
FRANCES J., 140	URE, 129	ISAAC, 124	JENNINGS	JNO S., 95	JACOB S., 95	ADDIE C., 130	JAS D., 42
FRANCES JANE, 96		JOHN, 124	A.M., 118	JOHN, 6, 13, 19	JAMES, 105	ADISON, 14	JAS E., 130
	-J-	MALINDA, 124	BECCA, 127	M.E., 77	JAMES H., 85, 86	ALEX, 26	JAS H., 36, 51, 55(3),
FRANCIS J., 49, 85		JANNEY	BESSIE, 118	M.M., 58	JAS D., 59	ALEXANDER, 7, 34, 61	56(2), 57, 58, 59,
G.A., 70, 123(2)	JACK	ADELINE Y., 17	C.M., 80(2)	MARTHA BELL, 64	JAS H., 78		80, 92, 95(3), 119
GEO A., 45	ALEX, 87	ELIZTH, 17	CHURCHWELL M., 53,		JAS W., 97	ALICE, 106(2)	JAS N., 44
J.L., 85, 96, 121,	J.C., 87	JOHN, 17	59	MARY E., 55	JEFFERSON, 129	ALICE M., 66	JAS W., 58
140(2)	S.E., 87	JARMER	CROCKETT, 96	MARY M., 84, 95	JESSIE E., 89	ANNIE LAURA, 87	JAS. D., 31
JACOB L., 49	JACKSON	CORA, 86	EVALINE, 119	NANNIE C., 84	JOHN, 62		JAS. H., 36, 55
JANE, 121	A.N., 126(3), 129,	JNO J., 86	FREDERICK, 53	S.D., 80	JOHN L., 136	ARCHD, 3	JENNIE, 70
JOHN M., 96	130(2), 131	LUCY, 86	G.H., 134	SOLOMAN, 59	JOHN W., 51	BETTIE B., 49	JESSIE, 137
JOS M., 49	ABEL, 11, 85	JARRELL	GARLAND, 102	W.A., 69	JOS C., 67, 87, 99	C.F., 36	JNO H., 99
MAGGIE L., 70	ANDREW, 44, 130	ELIZABETH T., 55	GARLAND H., 100	W.H., 80	JOSEPH W., 8	C.T.J., 30	JNO L., 36, 37
MARTHA ANN, 45	ANN, 130	GEO, 79	GEO H., 102	WM A., 58	JOSIE, 140	CHARLOTTE, 58	JNO W., 24, 27, 34, 35
	BETTIE, 110	GEO W., 69, 117	J.L., 125	WM H., 55, 77	LEWIS, 87, 128	D.B., 106	JOHN, 34, 97, 106
NANNIE K., 123	BOSE, 74	GEO. W., 20-A	JNO M., 100, 134	JOHNSO	LILLIE S., 59	D.E., 137	JOHN A., 33
S.E., 70, 123(2)	CHARLES, 74	GEORGE W., 15	JONATHAN K., 59	J.C., 99	LOTTA, 65	DAVID E., 68	JOHN D., 36
SALLIE E., 45	CLARK, 65	JAMES, 55	KATE F., 118	JOHNSON	LUCY, 48	ELIAS, 17	JOHN L., 27, 43, 45,
SARAH V., 85	ELIZTH, 11	JERE., 15	LEWIS, 96	A., 127	LUTHER, 129	ELIZ., 14	48, 55, 133
	EMILY, 85	LAURA A., 79	LUCINDA A., 129	ABE, 48, 55	M.A., 109	ELIZA F., 50	JOHN R., 26
-I-	FRANK, 72, 73, 74,	LIZZIE, 117	MARY, 53, 59, 80	ADIUS, 98	M.C., 118	ELIZABETH, 61, 68	JOHN S., 45
	75(2), 76, 81, 84,	LIZZIE T., 69	MARY E., 69	ALICE, 140	M.D., 51	ELIZTH, 34	JOHN W., 26, 33, 35,
IDDINGS	115, 119	MATTIE, 79	MISSOURI I., 134	ALPH, 121	M.S., 72	ELLA, 129	66, 121
OLLIE, 111	G.M., 85(2)	MOLLIE M., 20-A	MYRTLE, 118	ANDERSON, 140	MARIETTA, 92	ELLA C., 130	JOSEPH C., 70
RALEIGH, 111	GARNET, 110	REB., 20-A	POLLY, 96	ANNIE R., 51	MARTHA, 87, 123	ELLA C., MRS., 76	JOSHUA L., 37, 45
IMFREWILLER (?)	GEO W., 75	SALLIE B., 69	REBECCA, 69	ANTHONY, 92	MARTHA J., 118	ELLA L., 97	L.P., 88
	HARRIET, 74	SARAH, 15	RILEY, 69, 127	AURORA, 109	MARTHA L., 99	ELVIRA, 20-B	LANDONIA P., 33
NANCY, 64	J.L., 140	WASH, 117	ROBERT, 119	BELLE, 56	MARY, 73, 105, 116,	EMMA H., 61	LAURA E., 35
PERLINA D., 64	LIZZIE, 102	JASPER	SARAH, 100, 102, 134	BETTIS, 131	123	ERASTUS, 129	LEEOTA D., 87
SAML, 64	MAT, 130	HENRETTA, 128	W.H., 118	BLANCHE M., 125	MARY E., 72, 92	ERASTUS N., 32	LIZZIE J., 68
IRBY	MINNEY, 44	POLLY, 128	WILLIAM F., 119	C.W., 127	MARY ELIZA, 112	FANNIE, 34	LLOYD E., 88
ISAAC, 71	ROBERT, 133	JEFFERSON	JENNINS	CARTER, 124	MARY H., 97, 99, 112	FANNIE E., 129	LOUISA, 95, 133
JENNIE, 71, 74	S.J., 140	ANDREW, 71	ALX, 107	CATHERINE, 67	MARY V., 59	G.A., 133	LUCY, 58
LONDON, 74	SAMUEL W., 11	HARRIET, 71	REBECCA, 107	CHAS, 62	MINNIE B., 99	G.F., 72	LULA A., 68
PEYTON, 71, 74	STEPHEN, 110	ROBT, 71	RILEY, 107	CHAS G., 89	MOSES, 56	G.M., 62, 68, 72, 73,	M.D., 121
IRSKINS	W.E., 140	JEFFRES	JERVIS	CORDELIA E., 95	NANCY, 118	89(2), 95(2), 97, 98,	M.N., 27
EARSLEY, 26	WINTON, 102	JOHN J., 32	JOHN, 139	CREED, 73	NANNIE, 72(2), 125	110, 111, 114(2),	M.S., 49, 87
GEO., 26	WM E., 140	SARAH A., 32	LUM, 139(2)	EDMON D., 105	NATHAN, 98	115, 119(2), 122,	MADISON W., 20-B
IRVAN	WRITON, 44	JEMISON	MARY, 139	EDMOND, 62	PATRICK, 8	123, 125, 129(2),	MALINDA, 137
ANDREW, 53	JAMES	MARY, 61	JESSIE	ELIZABETH, 8	PHOEBE, 62	137, 139, 140, 141(4)	MANL S., 61
FRANK, 53	ANDERSON, 49	STEP, 61	B.A., 51	ELVIRA, 62	R.L., 99	GEORGIA VIRGINIA,	MARG., 24
SARAH, 53	B.A., 132	SYDNEY, 61	MARY J., 51	EMELINE, 62	R.O., 82	137	MARGARET, 27, 34, 35,
IRVIN	JASPER, 49	JENKINS	SARAH, 51	EMILINE, 102	REBECCA, 92	GILES M., 53, 54, 66,	
FAYETTA, 124	JOSEPH, 26	CATHERINE, 117	JESSUT	ESTHER, 62	RICHARD, 67, 102	80, 83, 99, 122	66
HANNAH, 53	KATHRYN, 132	CHAS, 100	ALFRED, 96	G.F., 73(2), 74(5),	S., 136	GREEN A., 27, 45, 95	MARGARET A., 55
ISAAC, 117, 124	MARTHA, 26	CYNTHIA A., 132	JENNIE, 96	75(3), 76, 116	SALLIE, 74	H.E., 68	
ISAAC N., 51	NELSON, 107	HUGH, 117	RUTH, 96	G.M., 77, 130, 131	SALLIE B., 72	HUGH, 2, 31	MARGARET D., 35
JANE, 133	S.R., 132	J.H., 117(2)	JEWEL	G.S., 125	SALLY, 95	ISAAC R., 20-C	
LUCINDA, 51, 117, 124,	SARAH, 107	JESSE W.B., 132	CATHERINE, 57	G.W., 88, 92	SARAH, 55, 121	J.H., 44, 58, 65,	
133	THOMAS, 107	LAURA, 100	FLOURNOY C., 57	GEO, 102	T.J., 109	68(4), 69(2)	MARTHA C., 55
ROSA, 117	JAMEY	MARIA, 100	THOS, 57	GEO S., 72(2)	T.S., 129, 130, 139	J.L., 133	MARTHA E., 39
WM R., 51	ELIZTH, 15	O.H., 109	JEWELL	GEO W., 118	THOMAS SHEFFEY, 127	J.R., 39	MARTHA J., 61, 70
IRVINE	JOHN W., 15	PATRA H., 109	ASA H., 19	H.G., 129		J.W., 112, 114, 121,	MARY, 50, 68, 71
CHRIS C., 57	MALINDA, 15	S.P., 132(2)	C., 19	HANNAH, 124	THOMAS W., 92	122, 123(4), 125(3),	MARY A., 71
F.S., 100(2)	JAMISON	TABITHA, 109	CHRISTIAN, 13	ISABELL, 48	W.C., 91, 97(2), 99,	137	MARY A.E., 7, 8
I.N., 57	ANNIE G., 129	W.F., 128	CHRISTIANA, 6(2)	J., 123	112	JAMES, 50	MARY B., 55
							MARY C., 55

168

MARY F., 51
MARY J., 26, 48
MARY L., 97
MARY M., 27
MARY P., 88
MARY S., 116
MINERVA, 36, 45
MINERVA A., 37, 45
MINNIE T., 55
N., 20-C
NANCY, 7, 42
NANCY D., 26, 61
NANCY J., 10
NELLIE V., 106
PAT, 14
R.W., 42
REBECCA, 75
REUBEN, 3
RICHARD, 58, 61, 68
ROSA W., 106
RUTHA, 3
S., 20-B
S.E., 87, 137
S.G., 137
SALLIE A., 61, 87
SAML, 26, 61
SAML., 51
SARAH, 2, 31, 32, 49,
  58
SARAH ANN, 20-E
SARAH E., 68, 99, 104,
  116
SUSAN, 33
SUSAN C., 43
SUSANAH, 8, 24
SUSANNAH, 10
VIRGINIA W., 24
WATSON, 55
WILLIAM, 50, 104, 20-B
WILLIAM M., 35
WM, 17, 32, 58, 87,
  99, 116
WM E.B., 104
WM J., 39
WM L., 51
JONAS
  H.V., 113
  JULIA, 113, 123
  MARIAN, 123
  PETER, 113, 123
JONES
  A.P., 130
  ADALINE, 137
  ADDIE, 123
  ALEX, 59, 103
  ALICE, 65, 118
  ALICE J., 20-A
  ANN, 5, 60, 88, 98
  ANNA, 3, 4, 120
  BALLARD P., 68
  CALLIE, 98
  CAROLINE, 36, 72
  CATHARINE, 4

CHANCY, 63
CHARLES, 87
CHARLOTTE, 77, 82
CHAS J., 122, 125, 126
CORUA, 117
DELILA, 3
DORA, 62
E.P., 75(2), 78, 136
EDWD., 55
ELI, 51
ELISHA, 32, 46, 94,
  113
ELISHA P., 38, 55, 61
ELISHA R., 34
ELIZA, 94
ELIZABETH, 45, 54(2)
ELIZE, 87
ELLA, 74
ELMIRA, 73
EMELINE, 120
ESTER, 123
F.A., 118
FANNY, 55
FRANCES, 42, 46, 68
FRANCIS, 46, 74
FRANCIS J., 40
FREDERICK, 63
G.A., 136
GEO W., 103
GORDON, 88
GRIFFITH, 97
H., 137
H.G., 54
HARRY, 74
HARVEY, 45
HELEN, 14, 20-B
HENRY, 21, 51, 54, 62,
  91, 93, 20-F
HIRAM, 88
ISAAC, 17
ISRAEL, 4
J.C., MRS., 85
J.E., 103
J.W., 136(2)
JACOB, 118
JAMES, 55, 87, 94,
  120, 137
JAMES A., 9
JAMES E., 59
JAMES H., 45, 20-B
JAMES P.D., 72
JANE, 4
JAS W., 55
JENNIE, 117
JEREMIAH, 14
JERUHA, 55
JERUS, 136
JERUSHA, 94
JESSE, 4
JOANNA, 52, 98
JOHN, 9, 12, 18, 34,
  68
JOSEPH, 77

JUDAH, 9
JULIA A., 20-A
KENNA, 120, 140
KINNEY, 60
KINNEN, 98
LAURA, 103
LEWIS, 94
LINDSEY, 63
LIZZIE, 73
LUCINDA, 93
LUCY, 36, 135
LUCY A., 120
LULA, 130
M., 4
M. EMMA, 103
MAGGIE A., 114
MARGRET ANN, 74

MARIA, 112
MARINDA E., 17
MARTHA, 17
MARTHA J., 62, 103
MARY, 38, 51, 54, 74,
  82
MARY A., 54, 112
MARY E., 4, 46
MOLLIE, 60
MOLLIE R., 93
NANCY, 97, 141
NATHAN, 135
NELSON, 135
OLLIE, 65
PAYTON, 112
PERCILLA M., 52
PICKNEY, 98
PINKNEY, 52
POWEL, 36
POWELL, 140
PRISCILLA, 46, 77
R.F., 75
RACHAEL, 32
RACHEL, 21, 20-F
REBA, 68
REBECCA, 9, 12, 34
REBECCA S., 18
REBECCE, 18
RHODA, 75
RHUEY, 46
RICHARD, 136
RNAH, 34
ROBERT, 42
ROBT, 72, 73
ROZETTA, 133
RUFUS F., 34, 68, 133
RUTHA J., 46
SALLIE, 72(2), 133
SARAH, 2, 32, 54
SARAH A., 140
SARAH C., 40
SARAH M., 34

SHIELDS BALLARD, 98

SILAS B., 9, 54

THOMAS, 21, 20-F
THOS J., 45
TINA, 45
VALARY, 94
VIRGINIA, 61
W.B., 130, 133
WILEY, 4
WILLIAM, 5
WILSON, 2, 40, 46(2),
  68, 74
WILSON R., 2
WINSTON, 123
WM, 3, 4, 5, 54, 136
WM B., 75
WM BALLARD, 136

WM J., 65
WM M., 45
Z., 78
ZERHUA, 61
ZERINE, 113
ZERNA, 130
ZERNAH, 38
ZERUAH, 75(2)
JORDAN
  ---, 27
  CATLETT, 108
  DOLLY, 108
  ELIJAH, 73
  J., 131
  JAMES, 73
  MARTHA, 73
  ROBERT W., 108
JOSEPH
  BENJ, 94
  DAVID S., 94
  MARY J., 94
JOYCE
  FANNIE, 127
  JAKE, 60
  LEWIS, 127
  MOLLIE, 60
  RICHARD, 60
JUIKONS
  ELLEN, 102
  THOMAS, 102
  VICTORIA, 102
JUSTICE
  CATHARINE, 1, 10
  HEN., 10
  HENDERSON, 1
  HENRY, 24
  HUGH M., 1
  J.H., 20-A
  JOHN H., 10
  MARGRET A., 24
  MARGT., 20-A
  MARTHA J., 20-A
  POLLY A., 24

-K-

KADE

G.W., 121, 129
J.E., 129
MARY C., 129
MARY M., 121
MINNIE E., 121
KAHLE
  ARAMINTA A., 42
  CATHERINE K., 38
  CATHERINE T., 44
  CHAS. S., 44
  CLARANCE F., 119
  CLARENCE F., 119
  E.F., 36, 53(2),
    54(4), 55(4), 56,
    57(3), 58, 65, 67(2),
    135
  JESSIE KATHARINE, 135

  JNO B., 83, 119
  JOHN B., 135
  KATHARINE, 42
  KATHERINE, 83
  M.C., 135
  MAGGIE, 119
  MARY H., 43
  SAML, 42, 83
  SAMUEL, 43, 44
  SAMUEL K., 38
  SAVELETT D., 29
  WILLIAM T., 38
KARNES
  ADALINE, 110
  ADDIE E., 48
  ADELINE, 86
  ALMEDA, 20-B
  AMANDA H., 59
  AMY R., 40
  ANGELINE, 20-B
  CATHERINE, 51
  E.A., 73, 120
  EASTER, 127
  ELIZABETH, 26, 53, 70,
    121, 20-C
  ELIZABETH A., 70
  ELIZABETH C., 59
  ELIZABETH M., 48
  G.L., 127
  GAD, 100
  GEORGE L., 32
  H.A., 109
  HATTIE L., 70
  HENRY, 18, 26, 59,
    20-B, 20-C
  ISAAC, 37, 40
  J.A., 73, 110, 120
  J.A., JR., 120
  JACOB, 48
  JAMES A., 70(2)
  JANE, 18
  JAS A., 53, 57, 86
  JAS. A., 48
  JAS.R., 48
  JULIA A., 10

LILLIAN A., 127
LOUISA, 20-A
LUCINDA, 37
LUCRETIA, 40
M., 20-A
M.E., 109
MAD., 10, 20-B
MADISON, 32, 41, 20-B
MARY J., 26
MAY, 37
MOLLIE L., 48
NANCY, 10, 32, 41,
  20-A, 20-B, 20-E(2)
NANCY A., 51
NANNIE E., 86
O.O., 121
R., 18, 109, 20-B
R. FLOYD, 125
R.F., 121
ROBECCA, 100
ROBERT A., 70
ROBERT D., 41
RUSSELL F., 20-C
SALLIE, 73
SAMUEL S., 100
SENORA BELL, 57
W.W., 110
WINTON, 53
WM, 51
KARR
  ROBERT, 20-C
  S., 20-C
  SARAH ANN, 20-C
KEARNS
  MADISON, 13
  N., 13
  VIRGINIA, 13
KEATEN
  JOSEPH, 50
  MARY, 50
  WM, 50
KEATLEY
  ALBERT, 61
  BIR K., 117
  BURTIE, 132
  G.W., 132
  GEO W., 34
  JOHN, 34, 61, 117
  MARY, 29, 132
  SUSAN, 34, 61, 117
KEATON
  ELIZA J., 26
  HANNON, 9, 24
  HARMON, 20-D
  JANE, 9, 24, 46, 20-D
  JUDSON, 49
  LEROY, 1(3), 2(2), 3,
    5(2), 6(4), 7(3),
    8(2), 9(5), 10(5),
    11(6), 12(6), 16, 18,
    19, 26
  MARIETTA, 38
  MARTHA J., 49, 20-E
  R.A., 69, 82

MARY A., 38
MARY ANN, 35
N.A., 111
NELSON, 46
S.R., 111
SARAH V., 89
SAREPTA, 89
W.B., 46
W.C., 60
W.F., 111
WARD C., 24, 49, 50,
  52, 20-D
WILLIAM J., 9
WM F., 26
WM J., 49
WM R., 89
KEELEY
  CHAS W., 81
KEENES
  JOS M.S., 72
  JOSEPH, 72
KEESEE
  J.D., 85
KEFFER
  G.A., 137
  LONZY, 137
  MARGARET, 137
KEGLEY
  DANIEL, 18, 19
  DANL, 33
  LOUISA E., 19
  M., 18, 19
  MARGARET, 33
  SARAH E., 18
  WILLIAM R., 33
KEISER
  JOS, 82
  WM, 82
KEISLER
  CECELIA, 84
  H.J., 84
  U.M., 84
KEISTER
  JAMES B., 108
  JAMES H., 108
  NANNIE, 108
KELLER
  JOHN, 86
  LULA, 86
KELLEY
  C.W., 72(2), 73(5),
    74(5), 75, 77(3),
    78(2), 80(2)
  CHAS W., 77, 80(4),
    81, 82(5), 83(2)
  CHS W., 82
  ELLEN, 123
  JAMES O., 81
  JOHN, 123
  KIZZIAH, 81
  MOSES G., 81
  P.J., 123
  R.A., 69, 82

KELLY
  A.J., 115
  C.W., 73, 79
  JOHN E., 77
  MARGARET, 101
  R.A., 61, 65(4), 66,
    67, 68(2), 71, 108,
    109, 111(3), 112,
    114(2), 116, 118,
    119(3), 120, 122(3),
    123(2), 124(2),
    130(2), 131, 132(5),
    135
  RACHEL, 77
  ROBT S., 101
  W.C., 77
KENDALL
  ELIAS, 7(2)
KENNEDY
  HENRY, 109
  J.E., 134
  J.H., 58, 59, 61(2),
    62, 63, 64(1), 67,
    68, 69(2), 70(3), 71,
    73, 74
  J.L., 109
  J.R.S., 134
  JAMES, 107
  JAS L., 58
  JOHN H., 65, 72, 73
  JOSEPH E., 67
  MARTHA J., 58
  MARY, 58, 109
  MARY O., 67
  S.J., 134
  SUSAH J., 67
KENNEIT
  B.F., 139
KENSLEY
  AARON, 46
  AVALINE, 46
  ROBT, 46
KENT
  ALICE, 132
  HENRY, 33
  LUCY, 13, 33
  MORRIS, 132
  MORRIS H., 33
  W.R., 132
  WM R., 132
KENTLEY
  ELIZABETH, 57
  JOHN, 57
  SUSAN, 57
KENZER
  SARAH, 29
KEPFINGER
  ANNA, 124
  J.L., 124(2)
  MILE, 124
KERNS
  CLAUDE, 109
  H., 109

S., 109
KERR
ABNER, 4, 11
ELIZA J., 11
MARY F., 4
SARAH, 4, 11
KESINGER
CHAS W., 82
JAS M., 82
MARTHA, 82
KESLER
ELIZABETH, 42
JENNIE B., 108
JOHN M., 42
MARTHA S., 42
KESSEE
GALLISA, 85
JESSE D., 85
JOHN, 85
KESSELL
JOHN, 126
SARAH, 126
THOS, 126
KESSINGER
ANNA JANE, 47
ANNIE J., 52, 55
AS N., 55
CHARLOTTE, 73
CHARLOTTE ANN, 64

J.J., 73
L.S., 64
LUTHER S., 64
M.A., 77
MANERVA, 77
MARY O., 47
ONIE E., 48
RO. N., 52
SILAS, 47, 48
SILAS M., 52, 55, 64, 73
TOLLEY, 48
WM, 77
KESTER
ARMANDA, 77
ELIZABETH, 42, 77
ELIZABETH F., 53
J.C., 111
J.L., 111
JAMES, 108
JANNIE, 108
JNO M., 53
JOHN, 42, 53, 77
MARY L., 42
NANCY, 111
KEYS
JAMES, 90(2)
MARTHA, 90
KEYTON
MARY, 46
MARY A., 46
KIDD
ANN, 135

ELVIRA E.A., 42
GEORGE A., 51
J.K., 71
JENK, 73
LUE, 134
MARY J., 42
MARY T., 71
MAY, 39
MAY E., 39
POLLY, 135
W.M., 71
WILLIAM, 39, 42
WM, 135
KIDWELL
A., 33
AMANDA E., 53
BENJ, 130(2)
BENJAMIN F., 34
DORA D., 127
FROG, 98
GREEN, 79, 127, 20-B
JOSEPHINE, 20-B
LATISHA, 34
LITTA, 20-B
MARTHA, 98, 130(2)
MARY ANN, 33
MARY E., 53
MICH., 20-B
MICHAEL B., 33, 34
MINNIE, 79
NANCY, 98
NANCY J., 20-B
NANNIE B., 130
PEARL S., 130
SARAH, 79, 127, 20-B
SARAH J., 129
KIESTER
HASSIE J., 100
J.H., 100
S.M., 100
KILLIP
ELIZA E., 128
GEO, 128(2)
GEORGE, 130
JANE E., 130
R., 128
ROZELLA, 130
KILMER
AUDREY, 89
BIRDY, 110
DOROTHY, 125
G.W., 89, 125(2)
MARY, 125
MARY J., 89
MOLLIE, 110
KIMBLE
JNO A., 100
JOHN A., 100
MAHALA, 100
KIMKAID
----, 30
KINCADE
J.H., 58

KINCAID
ELIZA J., 71
HARVEY, 71
KING
ALMA B., 140
C.H., 116
C.M., 115
CHAS M., 115
CORA J., 114
DAVID H., 133
DORA LEE, 44
E., 86
E.W., 95
EDMON, 95
ELIAS, 86
ELIZABETH, 113
ELLA E., 73
ELLEN, 116
EMILY ANN, 22
EMMAZELLA, 124

EULAS, 69
EURAH E., 71
F.H.J., 21, 20-F
F.H.K., 20-E
FANNIE, 128
FLEMING, 72
FRANCIS A.J., 11
GEORGE, 125
H.A., 108
HANNAH, 39
HENRY A., 71
I.H., 108
ISABELLA, 67
ISAIN, 69
ISHAM, 67
J.E., 71
J.J., 116
J.M., 114, 118(2)
JACOB O., 73
JAMES, 115
JAMES M., 133
JANE, 102, 115, 118
JAS, 102
JAS M., 58, 95, 115, 133
JNO H., 59
JNO M., 128
JNO T., 49
JOHN, 125
JOHN T., 59
JOHN W., 58
LAURA A., 78
LILLIE, 95
LUCINDA J., 66
M.E., 115
M.H., 133
M.J., 114, 115
MARGARET, 66
MARY, 11, 67, 69, 72, 113, 125
MATILDA, 86
MILDRED, 95

MILDREGE J., 58
MOLLIE, 140
NALE, 59
REBECCA C., 72, 73
RILEY, 39
ROBERT, 102
ROBERT M., 118
CHAS M., 115
ROBERTIE H., 108
RUSSELL, 128
SALLY, 22
SAMUEL, 11
SARA O.S., 95
SARAH, 49, 128
SARAH ANN, 39
SARAH V., 95
SERELDA F., 59
SOL, 128
T.H. JENNIE, 12
THOMAS, 49
W.H., 140
W.R., 124
WALTER, 86
WM, 113
WM R., 66
ZANCY, 95
KINGBURY
LAWRENCE D., 68

MARIAM A., 68
SD. VIOLA, 68
KINGRY
FLEMING, 94
I.J., 94
ISAAC J., 94
MARTHA, 94
KINGSBURY
DAISY D., 128
L.D., 128
M.A., 128
KINZER
ANN, 4
CATH., 10
CATHARINE, 1, 2
ELIZABETH, 10, 18
IDA L., 18
IRA W., 137
J.P., 111
JOHN, 1, 2, 10
L.S., 118
LIORIA C., 48
LUCRETIA, 39, 48, 53
M.F., 95
MARGARET, 61, 95
MARGARET E., 99, 137

MARTHA J., 53
MARY, 18
MICHAEL, 4
NANCY E., 61
NANCY J., 46
PHILIP, 2, 46
REBECCA, 1
REBECCA J., 18

RICHD. H., 30
S.S., 111
SALLIE B., 46
SALLY, 46
SAMUEL, 99
SARAH, 14
SARAH E., 39
SUCRETIA A., 46
THOMAS, 48
THOMAS B., 4
THOS B., 39, 46, 53, 111
TOM, 118
WILLIAM R., 18
WM, 137
WM R., 61, 95, 99
KIOUS
ISABELLA, 58
JAS H., 58
MATTIE E., 58
KIPPINGER
ADAM, 102
CATHERINE, 102
MICHAEL, 102
KIRBY
C.A., 140
C.H., 97
CALLEY A., 99
CHAS, 99
E.E., 82
ELIZABETH, 82
HATTIE J., 140
J.D., 116
JAMES, 140
JAS, 99
JAS W., 82
MARY, 116
MARY A., 97
R.R., 97
ROBERT R., 116
KIRK
A., 115, 141
AARAN, 129
ABSOLOM, 114, 119
ANN, 66
ANNA, 68
ANNIE, 55
E.V., 64
H.M., 114, 115, 141
HARRIET E., 114
J.F., 68
J.G., 66
JAMES, 64
JENNIE B., 68
JNO S., 68
JOHN F., 55
JOHN S., 114
JOS, 68
LIZZIE, 114
MANNIE F., 141
MARIA B., 66
PEARL, 115
R.A., 114

SARAH, 55, 64, 68
KIRKPATRICK
LAURA, 82
KIRTNER
ANGELINE C., 18
C.I., 101
C.T., 63
CROCKET C., 40
CROCKETT, 40, 20-D
CROCKETT J., 38, 42
E., 18
EDGAR P., 38, 42
EDWARD B., 101
ELLEN, 40
ELLEN E., 18, 38, 42, 101, 20-D
LOUISE F., 20-D
KISSINGER
ANNA JANE, 48
DOLLY, 48
SILAS, 48

WM, 95
LAMBERT
A.M., 110, 113(2), 114
AMANDA, 53
ANDREW M., 52
ANNA, 16
BENJ F., 57
C., 30
CHARLOTTE, 24, 30, 52, 53
CYNTHIA M., 100
D.B., 116
D.L.G., 53
E., 14
E.B., 84
EDWARD, 57
ELEANOR, 6(2), 9
ELEANOR P., 14
ELIZH, 17
HANNAH L., 6
HARVE, 126
J. BALLARD, 100
J.K., 33
JAS H., 53
JAS. W., 29
JERE., 6
JEREMIAH, 6, 14
JNO, 17
JOHN, 16, 137
KENLY, 30, 20-E
LOTTIE, 43
M.J., 116
MARY, 53, 57
MARY E., 84
N., 133
PHILLIP B., 43
S.P., 116
SAM, 133
SARAH, 6, 20-E
SHAR., 20-E
SUDOMA JANE, 30

E.M., 78
J.H., 67

-L-

LACY
B.T., 25
HENRY, 25
MARY, 25
MARY C., 25
LADD
E., 15
MARGARET, 15
THOS., 15
LALEY
ALFOID, 94
RICHARD D., 94
LAMB
A., 95
MARTHA LOUISA, 95

T.K., 30(3), 31, 34(2), 35(4), 37, 38(2), 39, 40(3), 42(2), 43(4), 44, 45, 47(3), 49(2), 51, 52(5), 53(2), 56, 59, 60(2), 65, 67(2), 72, 86, 88(2), 90, 94, 100, 105
THOMAS, 16
THOMAS K., 24, 31, 37
THOS K., 24(2), 53, 100
WILLIAM, 84
LAMPERD
ELIZA A., 128
LANBERT
SAML P., 30
LANDRUM
ADALINE R., 132
LATTHA, 132
LEROY, 132
THOS, 132
LANE
C., 4
CINTHA, 2
CLEM, 131
CYNTHA, 3
CYNTHIA, 10, 11
GEORGIA, 106
H.N., 106
JOHN, 2
M., 131
M.C., 106
MARIETTA, 11
MARTHA, 3
MATILDA J., 10
MOSES, 2, 3, 4, 10, 11
WM P., 131
LANES
SARAH, 4
LANIER
ALFRED, 65
BETTY, 65
WILLIAM, 65
LAREW
BIDDY, 32
FORTNER, 61
JOHN, 32
LIZZIE, 61
LIZZIE M., 61
MARY, 32
LARRISON
ALLICE, 130
SAMUEL, 130
WM F., 130
LARRUE
BATHILDA, 30
LAUGHTER
H.E., 133(2)
H.P., 133
M., 133

LAUVE
  CLINTON G., 34
  JOHN, 34
  MARY, 34
LAVENDER
  JANE, 5
  JOHN, 5
LAW
  ALLEN, 23(2)
  EMMA, 93
  JANE, 17
  MARY A., 17
  WM, 17
LAWLESS
  G.W., 86
  R.M., 86
  ROBT L., 86
LAWRENCE
  CYNTHIA, 85
  J., 85
  JAMES, 85
  JOHN, 6, 85
  SARAH, 6
  WILLIAM, 6
LAWSON
  ALBERT, 71, 72
  AMANDA A., 131, 134
  ARCHIE S., 106
  BARBARA J., 98
  CLARE, 136
  EMMA, 71
  EVELINE, 104
  GEO S., 104
  HENRY, 54
  JANE, 127
  JOANNAH, 68
  JOHN, 72
  JOHN J., 68
  JOSEPH, 54
  JOSIE R., 131
  LUCY, 106
  LUE, 104
  LUIE, 104
  MARY, 72
  MARY ANN, 136
  MARY J., 96
  MELLIE JANE, 134
  RACHEL, 71
  ROSS, 109
  SARAH E., 98, 109
  SILAS, 127
  VINA, 54
  W.E., 136
  W.J., 131, 134
  WM, 106, 127
  WM E., 136
  WM W., 104(2)
  Z.P., 96
LAXTON
  BURNETT, 122
  HESIKIAH, 122
  HESKICK, 116
  JANE, 116

MARTHA J., 122
RUFUS W., 116
LAYNE
  CHAS A., 82
  ELIZABETH, 89
  MINERVA, 82
  W.C., 89
  W.P., 89
  WM, 82
LAZENBY
  R.E., 140
LEDY
  J.C., 117
  REITA, 117
LEE
  ANN, 75
  ANNA BERTA, 75
  C.B., 95
  EDWARD, 71
  ELIZABETH, 76
  G.H., 115
  HENRY, 65
  J.R., 68
  JNO L., 68
  JOHN B., 8
  LIZA, 115
  MANERVA, 71
  MARTHA J., 68
  MARY, 7
  MILLY, 120
  NANNIE S., 95
  ROBERT CRAIG, 7

  SULLIS, 75
  W.P.F., 95
  WM, 71, 76
LeFEW
  C.B., 82
LEFEW
  ISAAC, 127
  JAMES E., 127
  SARAH, 127
LEFFEW
  A.C., 103, 129
  ELIZABETH, 103, 129
  W.K., 103, 129
LEFLER
  AARON, 66
  C.W., 66, 73
  E.M., 98
  ELLIE, 102
  FANNIE, 102(2), 124
  GRACE, 124
  JAMES, 98
  JAS A., 102(2), 124
  JOHN, 64
  M.A., 66
  M.B., 73
  M.C., 66
  M.O., 64
  NORA J.E., 64
  OSCAR, 102
  SARAH A., 66

W.M., 124
LEFLICK
  JOHN, 124
  MARTHA, 124
  SALENA, 124
LEFTRIDGE
  FANNIE, 96
  JERRY, 96
  WILLIE, 40
LEFTWICH
  C.D., 113
  GLENNA, 88
  J.D., 108, 109(2),
    110, 113, 115, 119,
    121
  J.S., 113
  SALLIE, 88
  WM R., 88
LEMAN
  G.H., 123(2)
  N.C., 123
  NELLY L., 123
LEOVEL
  ALEXANDER, 46
  B.G., 46
  MARY, 46
LESLIE
  ELVINA, 38
  GEORGE, 127
  J.P., 61, 127
  JAMES W., 38
  JNO P., 38
  JOHN C., 50
  JOHN P., 38, 54
  MALINDA, 61
  MARTHA JANE, 38

  MELVINA, 38, 50, 54,
    61, 127
  R.L., 59
  ROZENA, 54
  S. SUE, 50
LESLY
  B.P., 67
  PEARIS, 67
LESTER
  A.B., 62, 83, 105,
    123, 130
  ANGELINE, 127
  ARCHIBALD B., 18
  BERTHA E., 124
  BRUCE, 127
  BURD, 9
  C.M., 134
  CHLOE L., 105
  DICIE, 18
  EALLA, 130
  ELIZA, 122
  EVERETT W., 123
  FLORA E., 115
  ISAAC, 38
  J.L., 18
  JOHN H., 106

JOSEPH M., 9
L.J., 114
LAANZA A., 114
LAURA A., 83
LEWIS J., 38
LLOYD, 122
LOYD, 127
M.L., 130
MAHILDA, 18
MARTHA, 83, 105
MARTHA J., 123
MARTHA L., 62
MARY, 38
MARY A., 106
MATILDA, 9
RACHEL, 115, 124
REBECCA, 114
SARAH E., 62
W.F., 106
WILSON, 115(2), 124
LEVALLEY
  CHARLES, 79
  JOSEPHINE, 79
  LIZZIE, 79
LEVERAGE
  ANNA, 102
  DANIEL, 102
LEVIDEER
  JAMES W., 54
  LOUIS, 54
  PHOEBE E., 54
LEWEY
  CATHERINE, 110
LEWIS
  AGNES, 106
  ANN, 102
  G.N., 90
  GAY, 94
  HARRIET, 102
  HARRY, 106
  JAMES L., 93
  JANE, 94
  JAS, 80
  JOHN, 94
  LACEY, 88
  LEWIS, 110
  M.J., 93
  MACK D., 130
  MARGARET, 57
  MARTHA, 88, 130
  MARY, 80
  MARY O., 34
  ROBT, 57, 80
  ROSA, 34
  SANDERS, 102
  THOMAS, 57
  THOS, 130
  W.J., 93
  WM, 88, 106
  WM E., 110
LIGHT
  GANZETTIE, 91, 126
  GARFIELD, 126

MAT, 91, 126
ORESTES, 91
LIGHTHOURN
  JNO S., 91
LIGON
  L.P., 130
  ROSA M., 130
LIKENS
  ELIZA JANE, 50
  GEO, 51
  MARTHA J., 50, 51
  WM, 50, 51
LILLEY
  A., 20-E
  A.L., 21, 20-F
  ANDREW, 20-C
  DAVID, 20-C, 20-E
  ELIJAH, 21, 20-F
  ELIZABETH, 35
  FRANCIS, 20-D
  ISAAC J., 29
  J.W., 32
  JAMES F.M., 29
  JAMES W., 29(2), 30,
    31, 32(2), 33(2), 35
  JANE, 20-D
  JAS H., 45
  JAS P., 20-C
  JAS. W., 29, 35
  JOHN, 20-D, 20-E
  JOHN A., 21, 20-F
  JOHN F., 20-E
  JOHN T., 20-D
  JONATHAN, 29
  JONATHAN, 34
  JOS., 45
  JOSEPH, 35, 45
  JOSEPH A., 21, 20-F
  JOSEPHINE, 34
  JOSHUA, 34
  JOSIAH, 20-D(2)
  JULIA A., 21, 20-F
  LOUISA, 35
  M.A., 20-E
  M.J., 56
  MARINDA, 20-C
  MARY, 21, 56, 20-C,
    20-E, 20-F
  MARY V., 29, 20-C
  NANCY, 20-D
  ROBERT, 20-C, 20-D
  RUFUS, 56
  RUHAMA, 29
  SAMUEL D., 20-C
  SARAH, 21, 20-F
  SARAH A., 21, 20-F
  SARAH E., 20-E
  T., 20-E
  TABITHA, 20-D
  TURNER, 20-E
  TURNER T., 20-E
  URTO (SIC), 20-E
  VALLERIA, 20-C

WASH., 21, 20-F
WILLIAM, 20-D
WILSON, 20-D, 20-E
WILSON A., 20-D
WM P., 56
LILLY
  A., 127
  A.A., 134
  A.E., 109
  A.H., 100
  A.J., 119
  A.L., 16, 19
  A.M., 100
  ADALINE, 109
  ADAM L., 101
  ALA. B., 48
  ALABAMA, 53, 60, 92,
    103, 104
  ALABAMMA, 103

  ALEXANDER H., 31

  ALI W., 137
  ALICE JANE, 136
  ALLABAMMA, 106

  ALLEN G., 38
  ALLIE, 50
  ALLIE R., 97
  ALLYFARE V., 40
  ALMIRA, 90
  ALMIRA V., 106
  AMANDA L., 104
  ANDREW J., 39
  ANDREW L., 15, 43
  ANDW L., 82
  ANN, 18
  ANNA L., 44
  ARAMINTA, 101
  ARMINTA, 5
  ARTIE, 45, 58
  ARTY, 5
  B.F., 97(2)
  BAL W., 98
  BALLARD P., 24
  BELLE J., 50
  BENJ B., 88
  BENJ J., 101
  BETSEY, 73
  C.C., 90
  C.D., 80
  C.E., 130, 135
  C.W., 129
  CELIA, 12
  CELIA A., 5
  CELIA J., 88
  CEPHAS, 40
  CHARLES W., 85
  CHAS W., 130
  CLARIE E., 106
  D.G., 138
  DANIEL, 31(2), 60(2),
    117, 139

DANIEL T., 28
DANL, 88, 135
DANL T., 64, 88, 90
DAVID, 21, 20-F
DAVID G., 43
DAVID H., 4
DAVID T., 19
DELILA, 17
DOSIA, 1
DRUCILLA, 91
E., 18(2), 19, 20-C
E.H., 130(2)
E.P., 96
ED., 113
ELECTRA A., 100
ELI O., 135(2)
ELIJAH, 5, 115
ELISHA D., 104
ELIZA F., 121
ELIZA J., 5
ELIZABETH, 6, 11(2),
  13, 18, 19, 33, 38,
  40, 53, 101, 113
ELIZABETH C., 73
ELIZABETH E., 17
ELIZBTH C., 82
ELIZBTH E., 82
ELIZTH, 2, 5, 20-B
ELLEN, 4, 13, 134
ELMIRA, 64
EMILY, 17
ENON E., 50
ERASTUS B., 37
EST., 106
ESTALINE, 57
FRANCES, 6, 39
FRANCIS, 23, 40
G.L., 130
GEO W., 20-C
GILES, 135
GRANVILLE L., 130
HARMON, 24
HIRAM, 20-C
HOLLY, 139
HUFF J., 31
IDA B., 92
IDA E., 134
ISAAC H., 60
J., 4
J.A., 90, 110, 120,
  133
J.E., 66
J.F.M., 117
J.H., 101
J.J., 85, 114, 137
J.K., 53, 92, 103(2),
  104, 106, 127
J.L., 18(2)
J.S., 130
J.T., 137
J.W., 21, 68(2),
  69(2), 72, 84, 86,
  89, 91(5), 100, 102,

126, 133, 20-F
JAMES, 5, 7, 13, 17,
  24, 53, 57, 124
JAMES A., 82
JAMES H., 24
JAMES L., 133
JAMES M., 5
JAMES R., 20
JAMES W., 22, 23(2),
  24(3), 27, 28(2), 34,
  36, 38, 41, 42,
  47(2), 48(3), 49, 50,
  51, 53, 54, 57,
  58(3), 60, 63(2), 77,
  83, 85, 87, 89,
  100(2), 108, 109(4),
  114(2), 115(2), 116,
  117(2), 119(3),
  122(3), 123, 125,
  126, 129, 130,
  131(2), 132, 134(3),
  135(2), 136, 137,
  139(2), 140
JANE, 5, 36, 38, 41,
  44, 48, 65, 81, 88
JAS, 4, 97, 119
JAS A., 60
JAS F., 124
JAS R., 122
JAS W., 22, 44(2), 45,
  48, 49, 51, 52, 53,
  54(2), 56, 62(2),
  63(3), 64, 65, 73(2),
  74, 75(2), 76(2), 77,
  78(2), 79(3), 80(2),
  81(2), 82, 83(2),
  84(2), 88, 91(2),
  94(3), 95, 96(2), 97,
  98(4), 99(2), 100,
  101, 103, 113, 117,
  118, 120, 124(3),
  125, 127, 130, 138
JAS., 13
JAS. W., 13, 36
JEFFERSON D., 73
JNO, 4, 13, 130
JNO E., 57
JNO W., 81
JOHN, 1, 2, 5(2), 12,
  13, 17, 53, 121
JOHN A., 19
JOHN A.L., 46
JOHN E., 5, 46, 88
JOHN S., 16, 24, 82,
  108
JOHN W., 13, 20-B
JOHNATHAN, 24(3)

JOHNSTON K., 50, 60
JON, 20
JONATHAN, 5, 14, 37,
  38, 122
JONATHAN K., 13

JONATHAN W., 66
JONTII, 20
JOS, 4, 133, 20-B
JOS W., 118
JOS., 13
JOSEPH, 5, 20, 23, 37, 38(3), 39(3), 40(3), 41(6), 42(2), 43(2), 45, 46, 73, 82, 91, 96, 120, 20-C
JOSEPH R., 20-A
JOSEPHUS, 88
JOSHUA, 51
JOSIAH, 24, 54, 135
JOSIE, 73
JUDATH A., 41
JULIA, 80
JULINA, 4, 5, 46, 57, 66, 88
KELLEY J., 106
L., 15
L.J., 133
L.W.D., 43
LAURA B., 80
LAURA L., 127
LAUVERNIA, 119
LAVINA, 31
LEAH, 24
LEANDER J., 58, 109
LEERIE, 41
LEVI, 20-C
LEWIS, 23, 33, 39, 40, 83
LEWIS G., 88
LINA, 97
LONNIE L., 110
LOTTIE D., 123
LOUISA E., 88
LOUISA J., 14
LUCINDA, 39, 121
LUCINDA A., 20-C
LUCINDA V., 38
LULA A., 103
LULA MAUD, 101
M., 4, 14, 19
M.J., 108
MAHALA J., 31
MALISSA A., 54
MARG. M., 13
MARGARET, 4, 5(2), 13, 19, 24(2), 88, 122
MARGARET M., 137
MARGT, 20(2)
MARTHA, 12, 92, 114, 130, 137
MARY, 1, 4, 5, 12, 13(2), 14, 19(2), 24, 26, 28, 39, 41, 52, 76, 98, 101, 104, 135
MARY A., 19, 91
MARY ANN, 100

MARY D., 96
MARY E., 53, 64
MARY J., 21, 45, 20-F
MARY JANE, 5
MARY L.F., 21, 20-F
MARY M., 50, 91
MARY V., 21, 20-F
MILLY, 23
MINERVA J., 39
MIT., 110
N.T., 121(2)
NAAMAN W., 101
NANCY, 1, 2, 5, 12, 13, 17
NANCY C., 3, 20-B
NANCY E., 51
NANCY M.J., 88
NARCISSA, 54
NELLY, 7, 13, 17, 24
NONA A., 120
NOTIE J., 124
P.J., 108
P.R., 20-C
PLEASANT, 23
PLEASANT C., 20-C
PLEASANT H., 19, 131, 132, 133, 140
POLLY, 4(2), 82, 87
PROFOANA (?), 13
R.C., 124
R.C., JR., 78, 124
R.F., 123
RACHEL, 39, 45, 73, 83, 91
RACHEL E.B., 57
REBECA, 21, 20-F
REBECCA, 37, 38
RHODA, 5
RHODA C., 104
RHODA J., 60, 82
ROBERT, 1, 2, 6, 11, 17, 104
ROBERT C., 1
ROBERT W., 117
ROBT, 5, 13, 26
ROBT C., 43, 78
ROBT., 14, 19(2)
ROMANZIE B., 57
ROSANA, 34
ROXIE B., 91
RUFUS, 98, 101, 136
RUFUS B., 4, 52, 104
RUFUS E., 83
RUSSEL F., 38
RUTHA, 20-B
S., 123
S.E., 119
S.P., 97, 108
SALLIE, 5
SALLY, 115
SAML. G., 14
SAMUEL G., 20
SARAH, 16, 19

SARAH A., 4, 19, 88
SARAH E., 36, 43, 52, 97, 108, 113
SERVINA, 60
SIMON B., 24
SUSAN, 13
T.A., 19
TABATHA A., 13
TABITHA, 14
THEORA R., 103
THOMAS, 17, 21, 26, 34, 38, 20-F
THOMAS B., 24
THOMAS E., 5
THOS E., 88
THOS., 13(2)
THOS. T., 45
TURNER, 5, 45, 58, 20-B
TURNER A., 3
V.E., 130
V.T., 139(2)
VALERIA, 92
VINA, 85
VIRGINIA, 43, 78, 108, 124
VIRGINIA A., 38
VIRGINIA J., 62
W., 4, 15, 19(2)
W.A., 134
W.M., 13
W.P., 13
WASH., 12
WASH., 13, 19
WASHG, 76
WASHINGTON, 5, 24, 28, 39, 87
WILBERT J., 82
WILLIAM H., 5
WILLIAM J., 7
WILLIAM N., 91
WILLIAM P., 39, 41, 42(3)
WILSON, 13, 14
WILTON W., 82
WINNIE A., 130
WM, 13, 23, 24, 101
WM B., 114, 137
WM H., 36, 38, 39, 41, 44, 48, 62, 81, 115, 121
WM J., 104
WM MOODY, 62
WM P., 40, 41, 46, 47, 48, 50, 52, 55(2), 57(2), 60(2), 61, 62, 63, 66, 92
LINCONS
ELLEN, 91
NANNIE H., 91
THOMAS, 91

LINDSAY
ALLEN, 19
J.L.C., 109
J.W., 109
JOSHUA, 19
MARGARET A., 33
NANCY, 19, 109
W.C., 100
WM C., 102
LINDSEY
W.C., 100, 103
LINEBERRY
ALEX, 121
JAMES, 121
POLLY, 121
LINHONS
ELLEN, 105
ROBT, 105
THOMAS, 105
LINIS
RUSH H., 28
LINKENS
ARABELL, 124
J.L., 124
MARY M., 124
LINROWE
MARTHA, 104
W.C., 104
LINSEY
ALFORD, 105
JESSE H., 105
MARTHA, 105
LINSLEY
W., 23
LIPFORD
FANNIE, 52
R.A., 52
RICHARD A., 52
LIPSCOMB
HARRIETT, 135
HATTIE, 135
SQUIRE, 135
LIST
JNO, 88
JNO S., 88
KATHERINE, 88
LISTER
ADA, 140
LOYD, 140
LITCHFORD
CATHERINE, 69
CHAS E., 69
EDWARD L., 69
LITTLE
EDNA, 73
ELEANOR, 7
ELLEN, 19, 44
GEO W., 119
H., 123
HIRAM, 36
JOHNATHAN, 119
L.D., 55, 20-E

LARISSA E., 53
LORENZA, 62
LORENZO D., 38
LOTTIE, 62
M.A., 123
MARY, 119
MARY D., 53, 55
PERCILLA, 38
RHODA, 19
RHUA, 55
RUCY, 62
RUE, 20-E
THOMAS, 7, 19, 44
THOMAS G., 44
THOS L., 123
U.S., 20-E
URLEY W., 53
WILLIAM H., 7
WM H., 53
ZERNAH, 38
LIUKONS
ELLEN, 54
MONTGOMERY, 54

THOS, 54
LIVELY
FRANCIS, 88
JOS, 88
LOCK
ELIZA, 58
JOHN, 58
JOSEPH, 58
LOFFLIN
ADITH, 54
BENJ, 54
ELMIRA, 54
LOGAN
ANNA, 114
ED, 130
EMMA, 130
ISAAC, 114(2)
J.M., 122
MONK, 130
LONG
MAGGIE V., 118
MARIE E., 128
P.J., 118, 128(2)
S.D., 116, 119
LONGHORN
MONTGOMERY, 138

LONGWORTH

SARAH, 52
WM, 52
WM F., 52
LOONEY
I.D., 126
LORBETT
JOSIAH, 8, 9
LORD
ADELLA CO, 81
F.C., 81

W.F., 81
LOUERN
CATHERINE, 83
J.K., 83
MARY M., 83
LOUTHEN
ISAAC P., 84
SARAH, 84
LOVE
CALLIE D., 103
JAMES, 103
M.F., 103
LOVELL
J. WES, 124
M.A., 67
M.E., 67
MARGT A., 64
SARAH M., 64
WM, 67
WM C., 64
LOVERN
CATHERINE, 98
J.C., 98
JOHN C., 98
JOHN K., 98
LOVILL
H.L., 91
J.W., 111
M.A., 91, 111
WM, 91
WM C., 111
LOVINGS
ADALINE, 53
LURENDA, 53
THOS, 53
LOWDER
GEO W., 85
LURANIE B., 85
RAY B., 85
LOWRY
FANNIE A., 104
LUCY, 104
MARIA, 103
S.M., 104
LOYD
J.F., 86
LUCADE
ANN, 116
GEORGE, 116
MARY E., 116
LUCAS
HARRY, 105
JAMES, 9
JAS, 105
JAS M., 30
JNO M., 63
JOHN B., 40
MARIA E., 40
MARTHA, 105
MARY, 40
MARY ANN, 63
MATTIE L., 63
SARAH, 9

WM, 9
LUCHORNE
OCTAVIA, 126
LUCHORUE
OCTAVIA C., 114
LUCUS
JAMES M., 31
LUDLOW
MAY, 40
THOMAS, 40
LUKAC
ANDREW, 103
JOHN, 103
MARY, 103
LUKE
HENRY, 135
JANE, 135
MALINDA, 135
LUMPKIN
FRANCIS, 138
LUMPKINS
BETTIE, 94
HENRY, 94
MARIA, 94
LUSK
A.A., 127
ABSALOM, 1
ABSOLAM, 3
ABSOLOM, 5, 7
ABSOLOM, JR., 1
ALFRED E., 35, 46, 51, 53
ALICE, 127
AMANDA, 43, 66
ANN S., 25
CHICO, 1
CLOE, 1
D.M., 109
DAVID, 1
DAVID K., 7
DELIAH, 1
DELILA, 3
DILLA, 7
DILLY, 5
E.C., 109
ELI, 6
ELI C., 35, 125
ELIZA, 3
ELIZABETH, 6
HENRIETTA, 35, 53
HENRIETTA W., 46
ISAAC, 7
J.H., 127
JAMES A., 35
JANES F., 1
JAS M., 37
LEWIS A., 7
LIZZIE, 125
LUCINDA, 23(2)
M.C., 51
M.J., 127
M.L., 126
MALINDA, 67

MARY, 25
MARY A.E., 23
MATTHEW E., 6
NANCY P., 20-C
NANNIE E., 46
R.O., 125
R.T., 23(2)
REBECCA, 26, 31, 35, 37
REECE T., 5
REESE, 31, 37
REESE T., 1, 35
ROBERT, 25
ROSA BELL, 53
RUFUS A., 109
SARAH M., 31
T., 126
THOMAS B., 43
THOS B., 66
W.B., 127(2)
WILBY, 126
WILLIAM, 43, 66, 113
WM, 67
WM B., 23
WM I., 67
LUSTER
BIRD, 1
MALINDA, 1
MARY L., 1
LUSTISCUM
BELL, 141
ROSA, 141
SAM, 141
LYBROOK
EDNA R., 112
HARRY, 22
HELEN, 129
JOHN, 112, 129
MAIMA, 22
VIRGINIA, 22
LYLE
GEORGE W., 113
JACK, 116
JACKSON, 113
ROSE, 113
LYN
DAVID, 138
LARENY M., 138
Z., 138
LYNCH
A.R., 139
ANN, 45, 51
ANN C., 25
ELIZABETH A., 31
EMALINE, 25
EMILIA, 31
JOHN, 51, 139
JOHN C., 31, 45
JOHN HENRY THOMAS, 139
THOS N., 45
THOS W., 51
LYON

DANIEL, 7
ELIJAH, 73
JAMES J., 41
JANE, 64
JAS, 64
JNO D., 39
JOHN D., 7, 41, 56
LUCY, 7, 73
MARY, 35
MARY A., 41, 56
MARY ANN, 39
NANCY ELLEN, 53

SARAH E., 39
SQUIRE T., 35
THOS A., 64
WM J., 56
LYONS
C.J., 120
ELBERT, 113
EMELINE, 120
EMMA, 113
S.F., 73
T.C., 120

-M-

MABE
C., 75
ELIZA, 42
JAMES F., 42
JOSEPH, 75
LOUISA, 40
SOPHIA, 75
WM, 40
WM B., 40
MABRY
A.J., 131
McALEANDER
BIRD E., 94
HORRUS H., 94
LESTER, 94
McALEXANDER
H.M., 124
McBRIDE
BIRD, 84
BIRD E.F., 84
CATHARINE, 13
CHARLES, 16, 21, 20-F
CHAS, 9, 49
CHAS., 13
ELIJAH W., 55
ELIZA J.E., 63
ELIZABETH, 21, 20-F
FLOWRETTA, 84
JESSE, 9
JNO, 82
JNO B., 63, 99
JOHN, 62, 65
JOHN B., 13
LUCETTA, 55

MARTHA ALICE, 94

MARY, 133
MARY C., 133
NANCY, 16
S.F., 67
SALLIE, 99
SARAH, 9, 13, 16, 21,
  49, 63, 20-F
SOPHIA A.M., 99
T., 133
THOMAS, 67
THOS., 13(2), 55
WM G., 67
McCAHN
MILLA, 12
STEPHEN, 12
SUSAN, 12
McCANN
ALEX, 47
McCLAGHERTY

JOHN, 5
MARTHA E., 5
PHOEBE, 5
McCLANAHAN

A., 20-B
DAVID, 20-B
WM, 20-B
McCLAUGHERTY

E.E., 117
EDNA E., 119
EMALINE, 68
EMMA M., 68
ETHEL H., 139
EVALINE, 137, 139
EVELINE, 101
HATTIE, 137
J., 18
J.H., 107, 113, 117,
  121, 125, 127, 139
JAS L., 117
JNO, 20-A
JOHN, 7
JOHN M., 7
JOS H., 68, 117, 137
JOS W., 101
JOSEPH H., 18
K.W., 130
NELSON H., 20-A
P., 20-A
PHEBE, 7
R.C., 119
S.W., 119
SARAH E., 30
T.H., 109
W.W., 101
McCLAUGHETY

EVALINE, 64
JOS H., 64

NANNIE V., 64
McCLINTOCK
SOPHIA A., 56
McCLION
J., 135
M., 135
ROBERT, 135
McCLOSKEY
BYRNARD, 60
CATHARINE, 60
JAMES, 60
McCLOUD
BETTY, 138
HENRY, 111, 138
MARY, 138
RACHEL, 111
SARAH, 111
McCLUSKEY
JAS, 135
McCOMAS
A., 37, 38, 43(2),
  45(2), 51(2), 54(2)
A.V., 115
ALLEN B., 103
ARCH, 20-B
ARCH., 52
ARCHABALD, 103

ARCHD, 46, 58, 59, 60,
  61, 62
ARCHD., 42(2), 43, 45,
  57, 59, 61, 62(2)
ARCHIBALD, 37(3), 38,

  39(2), 40(3), 41(4),
  45, 46(2), 48(2),
  50(3), 53
BERRY, 121
DENNIS, 122
E., 30
ELI, 19, 22, 23
ELIZTH, 13
ELSIE A., 105
ELZ A., 30
ETTY, 115
J., 30
J.A., 19
J.C., 115
J.I., 122
JAMES, 1, 6, 25
JAMES A., 37
JAS., 26, 20-C
JOS., 13
JULIA ANN, 22
JULIA F., 53
JULIE, 23
L.F., 20-E
LEWILLA, 53
LOUISA E., 45
LUCINDA ELIZTH, 22

MARTHA, 25, 121
MARTHA J., 30

MARY A., 122
MARY M., 76
MILLARD F., 119
NANCY P., 6
O.A., 119
OA'EOC, 85
OLIVA A., 105
OLIVIA A., 62, 76
POLLY E., 40
R.B., 76, 85, 105, 119
REBECCA, 1(2), 6, 13,
  25, 26
REBECCA J., 28
RUFUS A., 23
RUFUS B., 62, 20-E
SAVILLA, 37, 103
SERVILLA T., 62
SERVILLA F., 40, 41
SURVILLA, 45
VICTORIA, 19
VIR E., 85
WM R., 41
McCORKLE
JAMES T., 6
JOHN, 6
JULIA, 36
MASTIN C., 36
SAMUEL, 36
SARAH, 6
McCORMACK
DICK, 138
J.M., 138
JANE, 138
McCORMICK
BERRELL, 136
JANE, 136
RICHARD, 136
McCOY
CHARLES F., 41
D., 86
LUCINDA, 41
ORA HESIE, 131
R.H., 106, 116
R.S., 86
WM H., 41, 131
McCRACKEN
D., 66, 67(2), 76
DAVID, 66
McCRACKIN
D., 75
DAVID, 62
McCRAY
FANNIE, 64
FANNY, 64
G.S., 64
JOHN LOHR, 64
MARGT L., 64
WM L., 64
McCREERY
DAURARIUS, 25
JOHN W., 25
WM, 25
McCRURY

DEMARUS, 31
WM, 31
WM H., 31
McCUE
A.G., 67
E.J., 73
H. WINTERS, 73
HANNAH, 4
JAMES, 73
JAMES M., 4
JAS, 67
JOHN, 4
JOSEPHINE, 67
McCULLOCH
D.J., 75
BENJ, 75
ELIZABETH, 75
McDANIEL
ANNIE C., 94
DAVID, 73, 74
E.F., 99
IDA, 74
JOHN W., 94
LELIA M., 99
LIZZIE, 99
MARY L., 94
PAULINA, 74
ROSE, 73
McDONALD
CROCKETT, 16
FRANCIS, 50
GEORGE, 129
JOHN, 50
MALISSA O., 50
MARINDA, 129
POLLY, 129
S., 16
STEPHEN, 16
McDOWELL
AUGUSTUS, 20
McELRATH
BELL P., 137
DOUGLAS, 111
DOUGLASS, 125
EMMA, 137
HENRY, 125
JAMES, 111
LOUISA, 111, 125
ROBERT, 137
T.J., 79
McEWEN
ALEX C., 79
MARY A., 79
SARAH WILLIS, 79
McFADDEN
MARY, 131
RICHARD, 131
TEMPA, 131
McFADEN
F.T., 89
McGEE
BETSIE, 62
JOHN, 62

REUBEN, 62
McGEO
AILSEY, 24
ANN, 24
CHAS., 24
McGHEE
GEO, 136
HENRY, 136
NANCY, 136
THOMAS, 79
McGINNIS
JAMES H., 75
MARY, 75
WM H., 75
McGLOCKLIN
WM L., 77
McGRAW
J.T., 139
JAS A., 99
JOHN, 99
M.J., 139
MITCHELL, 99
SAMUEL H., 139
SARAH, 99
McGUE
ELLEN, 125
PETER, 125
PETER T., 125
McGUIRE
A.C., 90(2)
B.P., 115
BALLARD P., 73
FRANKLIN, 88
GRANVILLE, 88
JNO, 90
LUE, 73
M.E., 90
MATILDA, 88
SARAH E., 73
McGURK
J.J., 94
McGUYER
A., 101
M.F., 101
W.R., 101
McINDOR
CATHERINE, 64
JAMES, 64(2)
McINNES
CATHARINE, 50
JOHN, 50
WM, 50
McINTIRE
L.L., 135
McINTOSH
JACOB, 106
MARY, 106
MARY J., 106
MACK
CALVIN, 125
CAROLINE, 108
CHARLES, 104, 118
ELIJAH, 108

FLORENCE, 125
FRANCES, 132
J.C., 136
JOHN, 108
JOSEPH, 104
M., 125
MARGERET, 105
MARTHA, 136
NANCY, 104
WILLIAM, 105
WILLIE J., 136
McKAY
R.H., 110, 135
McKEE
KENT, 138(2)
LUCY, 99
P., 138
PETER, 138
WM, 99
WM H., 99
McKENZIE
ALEXR., 3
JAMB H., 3
JNO, 43
JNO A., 60
JOHN, 40
JOHN A., 50
KATE, 60
LUCINDA, 40, 50
LUCINDA E., 43, 60
MALINDA, 3
NECTHE (SIC) V., 40
OZELLA R., 43
W.S.O., 50
McKINEY
GEO R., 101
JANE, 101
JNO W., 101
McKINNEY
ALICE, 121
ALLEN M., 80, 104(2),
  113
C.H., 128
D.A., 20
ELIAH, 24
ELIZABETH, 100, 107
ELIZTH S., 83
GEO W., 48
GEORGE R., 50
I.F., 121, 128
ISAAC F., 17
ISAAC R., 30
J.W., 107
JOHN F., 38
JOHN W., 26
JOS., 26
JULIA A., 37
LUCY A., 59
M., 59
M.A., 128
MARGARET, 121
MATILDA, 24
NAN, 26

NANCY E., 25
NANNIE E., 100
P., 17, 18
P.B., 30(2), 34(2),
  107
PAUHANAN, 30
POLLY, 18
POWHATAN, 59
POWHATAN B., 18

POWHATTAN, 37

POWHATTAN H., 38

POWHATTON B., 25

POWSTAN, 83
PRISCILLA B., 20
R.B., 30
RHODA, 20
S., 17, 18
S.H., 83
S.M., 67, 101, 102,
  103
SAML M., 78
SAML W., 86
SARAH M., 18
SUSAN, 30, 37
SUSAN E., 25, 38
VICTORIA E., 37
WILSON, 24
McKINZIE
ALEX., 8
ARDELIA C., 29
DEHENZHEH, 23
J.A., 128
JNO, 23
JNO A., 27, 84
JNO A., JR., 84
JOHN A., 8
JOHN O., 7
L.H., 128
LOUCINDA, 84
MALINDA, 8
MARTHA, 23
PRISCILLA, 7
R.B.H., 128
VICTORIA, 7
McKOY
R.H., 118, 119, 123,
  124, 127
McLANE
GILLIAM, 1
HANNAH, 1
SARAH A., 1
McLAUGHLIN
CLARINDA, 72
HARVEY, 72
SERILDA A., 72
McLOUD
ELIZABETH, 122
HENRY, 122
JOHN, 122

173

McMANAWAY

A.D., 49
CHAS D., 47
JAMES, 47
JOHN W., 49
MARY E., 49
SARAH A., 47
McMARTIN
SYNTHA, 119
WALLER, 119
WM K., 119
McNABB
PETER, 67
McNEIL
DANL D., 67
R., 67
McNUTT
ALLEN, 22, 69, 109
CHARLES R., 46
ELIZABETH E., 46
ELLEN, 26
ELLEN E., 97
EMMA, 109
EMMA L., 69
J.P., 139
JENNIE, 139
LEE, 113
LEWIS, 109
MARGARET, 113
MARY, 69
MARY G., 26
NITA, 97
R.D., 46
ROBT B., 26, 97
SALLIE A., 139
McPEEK
CELIA A., 54
CHAS W., 54
CLAYBURN, 54
McPHERSON
ALLIE R., 75
ANDREW, 12
CYNTHIA, 41
E., 20-C
ELIZABETH, 64, 20-D
ELLA, 41
G., 20-C
GEORGE, 41, 20-D
H.H., 64
J.L., 98
J.R., 75
JACOB, 64, 20-D
JACOB R., 75
JULIA, 64(2)
LIZZIE, 75
LIZZIE E., 75
M.L., 64
M.S., 98
MARY A., 20-C
PHEBA J., 3
PHOEBE L., 75
POLLY, 3, 12

S.E., 98
McPHILLIPS
LETCHER, 88
M.F., 88
R.S., 88
McQUEEN
C.M., 134
McRAY
R.H., 132
McVEY
JAMES, 37
PHOEBE, 37
SILAS J., 37
McWALL
E.R., 41
HENRY D., 41
JANE, 41
MADISON
ELIZA, 42
GORDAN C., 42(2)
PINKEY, 124
MAFEY
ELLEN A., 26
JAMES B., 26
JULIA A., 26
MAHAN
C.W., 93(2)
MAHOOD
ALEXR, 3
BETTIE O., 79
MARTHA, 3
WM A., 3, 79
WM M., 79
MALONE
JONATHAN, 39
MARY, 39
WM P., 39
MANAWAY
JAMES, 68
REBECCA M., 68
SARAH, 68
MANESS
J.C., 57, 58(7),
59(4), 60(2), 61(2),
63(3), 64(3), 65(2),
66, 68
MANGUS
J.O., 115
JOSEPH, 37
JULINA, 37
MARY A., 37
MANN
ANDREW, 68, 108
ANDREW W., 20-A

ANDY, 137
BALLARD A., 22
EDWIN, 126
ELI, 88
ELIZA J.B., 49
ELIZABETH, 9, 126
ELIZTH, 3, 6, 20-A
EZEKIAH, 6

HEZ, 20-A
HEZEKIAH, 3
ISAAC H., 9
JACOB, 22
JAS W., 88
LOUISA, 6
LUCINDA E., 68
M.E., 108
MARGARET, 3
MARY, 49, 80
MARY L., 48
MATHEW, 126
N.C., 108, 137
NANCY, 88
NANCY C., 68
ROSA, 80
SARAH E., 22
SIMON L., 56
TENABIE C., 137
THOS, 55
WILIAM, 39
WILLIAM, 95
WM, 49, 80
MANNESS
J.C., 63
MANNING
ANDREW, 56, 70
HESTER ANN, 42
JAMES, 42
MARGARET, 42
MARGARET E., 41

MARGARET J., 50
MARY C., 70
NANCY J., 41, 56, 70
SALLIE, 50
WM R., 56
MANNS
LEWIS, 109
LULA, 109
MARTHA, 109
MANUAL
JENNIE, 59
JORDAN, 59
MANUEL
E., 13, 26
KATY, 75
MARCUS
F.A., 126
MINNIE E., 126
R.N., 126
MARKHAM
E.J., 116
FLEMING, 116
J.L., 116
MARRA
JOHN, 134
JULIA, 134
MARTIN, 134
MARROW
JUDIA, 64
SAML., 64
WM., 64
MARSHALL

CHAS A., 72
ELIZABETH, 72
GEO C., 86
M., 86
MILTON, 86
MINERVA, 86
N.F., 94(2), 98, 135
NORMA F., 106
NORMAN E., 114
NORMAN F., 101(2),
126(2), 127, 138
WM, 72
MARTIN
A., 76, 20-A
A.J., 140
A.W.U., 110
ACHILLES, 46, 47
ACLES, 26, 29, 30, 101
ADAM, 20, 27, 64, 20-C
ADAM H., 63
AILS A., 101
AILSBY, 46, 47
ALCY, 30
AMY LEE, 111
ANDREW J., 4
ANN, 8, 18, 25, 27,
31, 49
ANNA, 16
ARCH, 13
BOOKER, 4, 7, 121
C., 4(2)
C.J., 119
C.W., 71, 117
CHAS, 57
CHAS W., 110, 117
CORNELIUS, 73
CYNTHIA J., 10, 59
D., 18
DANIEL, 123
DANL, 32
DAVID, 2, 4, 7, 13,
23, 34, 35, 41, 48,
77, 20-D
DONSIL W., 11
E., 13, 26
E.A., 4
E.M., 27
ELIZA, 24, 31,
20-A(2), 20-E
ELIZA A., 92
ELIZABETH, 56, 57
ELIZABETH E., 20
ELIZABETH S., 4, 20-A
ELIZTH, 3, 10
ELIZTH O., 3
ELLA, 127
ELZ. ISABELLA, 30
EMILY, 123
EMILY E., 57
ESTHER, 18, 23, 34, 35
ESTHER A., 32(2)
FANNY, 112
FRANCH, 127

FRENCH, 138
G.B., 139
GEO B., 117
GEO W., 48, 49, 54,
56, 91, 20-C
GEORGE, 123
GEORGE B., 29
GEORGE W., 15, 18(3),
19(2), 20, 20-A
H., 20-A
H.H., 92
HARDIN K., 18
HENDERSON F., 18

HENRY L., 101
HESTER, 41, 48, 20-D
HESTER A., 2, 16
HUDSON, 13, 20-E
IDA, 71
ISAAC D., 20-D
ISAAC P., 83
J.B., 70
JAMES A., 20-E
JAMES M., 129
JANE, 77
JAS, 112
JAS B., 48
JAS H., 50
JAS J., 59
JAUDER R., 128
JNO A., 136
JOHN, 2, 7, 10, 14,
50, 74
JOHN D., 8
JOHN E., 24
JOHN F., 20-C
JOSEPH H., 11
JUDSON, 24
JULIA V., 104
L.D., 30, 48(2), 70
L.P., 6
L.V., 134
LAURA, 117
LEM L., 104
LEVI, 117
LEVI N., 20-D
LEWIS, 41
LEWIS A., 41
LEWIS D., 48
LILLIE, 138
LORENZO D., 10
LOUISA, 35
LUCY M., 131
LULA, 117, 134
LUTHER, 139
M.E., 133
MAHALA, 13
MARGARET, 49
MARTHA, 71, 73, 115,
131
MARTHA A., 129
MARY, 117, 139
MARY J., 34, 71, 20-A

MARY L., 136
MARY M., 119
MARY V., 136
MAT. J., 76
MATILDA, 121
MILDRED, 121
MINNIE, 115
NANCY, 7, 49, 56, 127,
20-C
NANCY F., 2
NANNIE, 138, 140
NANNIE A., 134
NETTIE, 128
NORA W., 140
PEGGY, 74
POLLY, 7
POLLY J., 20-C
R., 4, 20-C
REBECCA, 7, 20, 41,
54, 63, 64
RHODA, 112
RHODA A., 91
ROBT, 128
ROBT A., 81(2)
S., 14
S.P., 121
SALLIE, 11
SALLY, 20-D
SAMUEL, 4
SAMUEL W., 20-D
SANFORD, 49
SARAH, 2, 10, 48(2),
50, 64, 70
SARAH C., 77
SARAH J., 27
SARAH L.N., 30
SARAH M.P., 49
SARAH V., 14
SUSAN, 2, 30
THOS, 73
THOS A., 47
V.A., 133
VICTORIA, 92, 110
VIRGINIA, 81, 110
W.A., 110
W.C., 13, 21, 22, 24,
20-C(2), 20-F
W.E., 26, 110
W.F., 133
W.H., 88
W.J., 71
W.R., 119
WASH, 69
WILLIAM A., 25, 20-C
WILLIAM C, 10
WILLIAM C., 1(2),
2(2), 4, 5, 6(3),
7(2), 8(4), 9, 10(3),
12(2), 14, 15(2), 17,
18(2), 19(2), 20(3),
21, 22, 25(2), 28,
36, 20-A, 20-B(6),
20-C(2), 20-D(4),

20-E, 20-F
WILLIAM F., 23
WILLIAM K., 10
WM, 71, 121(2), 131
WM A., 81
WM C., 1, 2(5), 8, 12,
13, 14, 16, 18, 22,
26, 27, 29, 30(3),
31(4), 34, 36, 37,
39, 20-E(2)
WM E., 46, 92, 104
WM H., 63, 115, 129
WM K., 59
WM L., 3
WM R., 13
MASON
CALVIN, 105
E.T., 131
EMMET F., 123
HENRY, 77
JAMES, 116
JAMES C., 116
LUCY, 116
MASSEY
BETTIE, 123
CATHERINE C., 90
CELIA R., 62
CHARLES, 47
CLARINDA E., 47
CYNTHIA E., 48
ELIZABETH, 47, 20-D
ELIZTH, 10
EMILY, 44
EMMA A., 33
ETHAL ELIZTH, 28
INSEL, 10
JACKSON, 43, 62, 90
JAMES J. 1, 27, 44
JAS, 123
JAS J., 63
JEMSHA H., 23
JOHN, 1(2), 24, 43
LOUISA, 23, 35, 20-D
MARTHA, 27
MARY, 10, 32, 48
MARY A., 29
MARY J., 20-D
MATILDA, 35
MINERVA B., 35
NANCY, 1, 24
PATSEY, 90
PATSY, 44, 62, 63
RICHARD S., 32, 48
THEODORE, 35
THOMAS B., 1, 35
THOMAS J., 20-D
THOMAS K., 32
THOS., 23
WM, 123
WM J., 63
MASSIE
F.B., 62

J.A., 79
JAS J., 36
JAVA, 79
JOHN, 17
JOHN F., 40
JULIA E., 36
LOUISA, 40, 62
LOUISA M., 62
MARY A., 79
NANCY, 17(2)
PATSEY, 36
THOMAS B., 40
MASTEN
V.I., 96
MASTIN
AMANDA M., 44
C.M., 62
ELIZABETH, 62
ENDORA, 70
JUELLA, 117
LEE D., 44
MARY H., 49
WILLIAM C., 3
WILLIAM E., 44
WM E., 49, 62, 70
MASTON
ELIZABETH, 37
JOHN, 37
JOSEPHINE, 43
W.E., 37
WILLIAM E., 43
MATEEN
ELIZABETH, 60
FRANK E., 60
HENRY, 60
MATHANA
CHAS A., 114
EMILY, 114
GEO, 114
MATHENA
C.W., 64
FLOYD, 83
GEO W., 101
HARRIET, 101
HARRIETT, 64
HENRY, 83
HULDA, 83
JEO W., 64
MAGGIE C., 101
PARIS M., 64
MATHENEY
P.M., 139
MATHEREY
FLOYD W., 70
HULDA J., 70
NANNIE B., 70
MATHERLY
JAS A., 97, 98
MATHESON
J.F., 119
JOHN F., 118(2)
MARY E., 118
R.G., 118

MATHEWS
ALICE, 56
C.R., 107
F.M., 107
G.W., 94, 98
GEO W., 96
H.L., 96
H.L.E., 98
HARRIET L., 94
HULDAH J., 107
L.L., 96
LEWIS L., 96
MARIA L., 98
MILLEY, 56
MILLIE, 80
PEARLS M., 94
MATHIS
J.J.W., 63, 64(3), 65, 66(2), 67
MATHLEY
BETTIE A., 86
EDNA J., 86
WM, 86
MATSIN
MARY, 74
NEHEMIAH, 74
WM, 74
MAULY
EMMA J., 32
MAURY
CUDIE, 63
EJ., 63
STIRLING, 63
MAXBY
ALA, 31, 34
ALICE, 114
ANNE, 134
ANNIE, 91
AUGUSTUS C., 29
BURRELL, 34
CELIA, 34(2), 102
CELIA A., 26, 42
CORA A., 102
DANIEL, 140
EDGAR, 18, 91, 134
ELIZTH MARY, 30

G.W., 119
J.E., 122
IOWA, 26
J., 18
J.V., 122
JAMES B., 31
JAS B., 114
JOSEPH, 34, 122
JOSEPH W., 134
JOSIAH, 5, 27, 29, 30, 40, 80, 119
JULIA A., 42
L.A., 119
LOUISA A., 40
LOUISA H., 91
LOUISA L., 119

MADISON P., 31
MARGELINA, 5
MARTHA, 140
MARTHA F., 27
MARY, 27, 29, 40
NANCY B., 34
PRESTON, 26, 34(2), 42, 102
SALLIE, 5
SAML L., 114
SARAH, 18, 30, 80
SARAH A., 74
SARAH E., 34
STEWART, 140
MAXIE
ANNIE, 58, 93, 103
EDGAR, 58, 93, 103
ETTIE, 93
J.W., 103
JOHN, 91
JOSEPH W., 91
NANCY E., 91
SARAH E., 58
MAXWELL
CELESTIA A., 72
E.V., 73
ELBERT W., 78
GRAYSON, 95
MELVINA, 71, 73, 95
MELVINA P., 78
SARAH A., 71
WM, 71, 72, 73, 78, 95
MAY
ALLEN H., 61
AMANIAS, 61
ANNIE, 74
DUT., 74
EMMA, 61
IDA, 74
MARY, 50
SARAH J., 50
WILLIAM, 50
MAYBERRY
CORA, 135
JAMES, 135
LUCINDA, 135
MAYES
FRANCIS, 106
HERBERT, 106
PETER, 106
MAYFIELD
LUCY, 84
MAYNARD
COSBY, 101
FLORENCE, 101
MAYS
E.B., 126
L.M., 118
M.J., 118
P.C., 52, 53(2), 54(2), 55
S.H., 126
W.C., 118

WM JNO, 126
MEAD
BETTIE, 70
JOS, 70
LEW, 127
OVERTON, 70
MEADER
BEDDY, 50
D.C., 102
DOLLIE A., 142
ELIZABETH, 31
G. W., 31
ISAAC, 102
J.G.W., 50
JOSIAH, 47
MARY JANE, 102
SARAH J. S. R., 31
SUSAN, 50
SUSANNA, 47
WM H.H., 47
MEADOR
A., 20-E
A.J., 41, 103
ABE, 17
ABRAM, 17
ADALINE, 20-E
ADAM, 24
ALICE S., 90
ALLEN H., 1
ALLEYFAIR V., 52
AMANDA M., 3
ANDREW, 20-C
ANN, 1, 17, 32, 20-B
ANNA, 3(2), 4(2), 13
AVIS A., 60
BENJAMIN L., 32
BETTIE, 121
C., 4, 15
C.B., 139(2)
C.J., 139
C.L., 121
CATHARINE, 60
CATHERINE, 73, 131
CELIA, 1, 4, 7, 22
CELIA A., 4
CELIA E., 17, 64
CLARISSA, 20-A
CLINANTINA, 24
DASHA, 1
DAVID, 8
DAVID C., 73
E., 14, 18, 20-C(2)
ELIZA A., 46
ELIZABETH, 24(2), 29, 52, 64
ELIZABETH A., 20-B
ELIZABETH C., 24
ELIZABETH N., 71
ELIZABETH, 29
ELIZTH, 16
EMELINE, 41
EMILA, 2
EMILY, 13, 14, 20-B(2)

EMILY C., 20-B
ERASTUS B., 7
FLOYD G., 16
FOLON, 46
FOUNTAIN S., 21, 20-F
G.W., 71, 20-B(2)
GEO, 103
GEO W., 87
GEORGE W., 5, 41
GREEN, 3, 64
GREEN F., 22
GREEN W., 2, 13, 14
HENRY, 22
HUGH J., 4
ISAAC, 5, 41, 73, 90
ISAAC H., 118
J., 4, 18, 19, 20-A
J.C., 91
J.J., 35, 90, 91, 101, 108, 110
J.N., 71
JACOB, 24
JAMES, 16, 121
JERE, 20-A
JNO, 3(2), 4(2)
JNO W., 30
JOHN, 1, 13, 17, 32, 20-B
JOHN A., 29
JOHN J., 4, 37, 38, 39, 71
JOHN L., 91
JOHN W., 24, 40, 20-B
JORDAN, 13, 20-C
JOS., 13
JOSEPH, 23, 52, 20-C
JOSEPHUS, 73
JOSIAH, 1, 3, 4, 5, 7, 19, 24(2), 30, 60
JUDA, 5
JUDAH, 30
JUDITH, 1, 7, 19
JUDITH E., 15
JUDITY, 3
JUDITY F., 2
JUDY, 40
JULIA, 13, 23
L.F., 133
LALUDA, 24
LORENZO, 23
LUCINDA, 24
LYCURGUS, 35
LYCURGUS, 60
LYDA, 5
LYENSGUS, 4
MALINDA, 19, 32, 41, 46, 69, 91
MANORA A., 60
MARY, 8, 118
MARY A., 7
MARY E., 38, 87
MARY J, 41
MARY JANE, 73

MARY M., 23
MARY V., 4
MATTHEW, 19
NANCY, 35
NANCY C., 20-C
NANCY J., 18
NANCY M., 35
O.E., 98
ONEY, 87
P.E., 90
R.B., 71
RACHEL, 13
RACHEL A., 29
REBECCA, 23
RHODA, 41, 103
RUFUS G., 29
RUTH, 17
S., 20-C
SALLIE J., 139
SAMP. G., 13
SARAH, 24, 20-E
SARAH A., 17
SARAH ANN, 24
SARAH E., 41
SARAH F., 20-C
SELIA, 21, 20-F
SOLAR, 41
SOLERI, 69
SOLON, 32, 91
SUSAN, 13, 60
SUSANA, 1
SUSANNAH, 38
SYLVESTER, 118
T., 19
THOMAS, 5
VIRGINIA, 20-B
VIRGINIA A., 73
W.H., 23
W.M., 13
WILLIAM M., 7
WM, 13, 15
WM M., 1, 4(2), 21, 22, 20-F
WOODSON B., 3, 22
MEADORS
ELLEN, 54
HARVEY D., 12
JANE, 12
JEREMIAH, 12
MARTHA, 9
MEADOW
AMANDA, 55
ISAAC, 108
LYCURGUS, 49
MARY C., 49
MARY J., 108
ROMANSA C., 49
WM G., 55
WOODSON, 55
MEADOWS
A., 115
A.H., 81
A.J., 49

A.P., 81
ABRAHAM, 2, 6
ABRAM, 69
ADA C., 129
ADA J., 122
ADAM, 3, 37
ALAHAMA, 21, 20-F
ANDELIA, 69
ANTHONY, 9
ARDELIA, 129
ARDELIA A., 54
B., 122
B.P., 36
CAROLINE, 69, 87
CARRIE A., 55
CATHERINE, 112
CHAS, 119
CLARA, 5
CORA M., 123
DELLA, 134
DELLA M., 115
E.J., 120
ELIJAH P., 22
ELIZA, 31
ELIZA J., 100
ELLEN, 14, 49
ERASTUS, 102
FLORA JANE, 107
FLOYD, 54, 129
FLOYD, REV., 87
G.C., 117
GEO W., 47
GEORGE W., 122
GREEN W., 119
H.D., 75, 123
HARVEY, 44, 66, 70
HARVEY D., 54
HENDERSON, 122
HENRY, 24, 33, 110, 115
HULDAH, 45, 78, 94
HUNT, 109
I.H., 122
IRVIN, 132
ISAAC H., 18
ISHEL, 117
J., 14, 18, 20-C
J.F., 85(2), 112
J.H., 116
J.J., 115
J.M., 113, 121, 122, 137
J.W., 69
JACOB, 37, 116
JAMES, 129, 133
JAMES J., 31
JAMES T., 78
JANE, 5, 25
JANE C., 25
JAS A., 44
JAS C., 120
JAS D., 69

JEFFERSON, 2
JERE, 5
JEREMIAH, 6, 24, 25(2)
JERRY, 22, 129
JNO L., 92
JNO W., 129
JOAB, 21, 20-F
JOHN, 129
JOHN C., 52
JOHN L., 65, 86, 111, 115
JOHN M., 117
JOHNATHAN P., 25
JORDAN, 8, 14
JOS B., 54
JOS R.A., 45
JOSEPH, 3, 102
JOSHUA S., 85
JOSIAH, 3
JUDA, 113
JUDITH, 3
JULIA, 116
KATHERINE, 85
LAURENA, 115
LEAH A., 125
LIDA, 21, 20-F
LILLIE, 70
LURESY, 14
LUTHER, 66
M.E., 115, 129
M.L., 109
MALINDA, 113
MARDINA, 111
MARGARET, 2
MARINDA, 65, 86
MARTHA E., 122
MARY, 3, 9, 21, 33, 37, 47, 54, 120, 129, 20-F
MARY E., 107, 115
MARY J., 2, 92
MELINA, 92
MILLIE G., 129
MINERVA, 98
MINTIE E., 108
MOLLIE, 75
N., 18, 20-C
NANCY, 22, 55
NANCY A., 100
NANCY ANN, 86
NELSON, 65
NINNIE M., 110
O.D., 133
OMA, 119
PHILIP, 87
R.E., 111
RHODA, 8
RICHARD, 37
ROBERT D., 37
ROSA, 69
RUFUS, 20-C
RUGH, 6
RUSSELL, 100

RUTH, 2
S., 14
S.A., 36
S.G., 33, 69
SALLIE, 69
SAMPSON, 54, 87
SARAH, 3, 37, 110, 133
SARAH E., 33
SARAH J., 69, 102
ST. CLAIR, 31
SU, 14
SUSANN, 8
SYLVESTER, 21, 47, 20-F
THELBERT, 75
THOMAS, 2
THOMAS J., 36
URIAH, 55
V., 123
VICTORIA, 54, 66, 70, 75
VINNY, 81
VIRGINIA, 129
WARD, 9, 45, 78, 94
WARD B., 94
WILLIAM H., 25
WM A., 21, 20-F
WM D., 112
WM T., 122
WOODSON, 115
MEADR.
F.A., 49
MEANS
CHARLES, 38
EASTER J., 128
ELIZABETH, 38
SARAH C., 38
MEAROR
ADAM, 20-C
SARAH, 20-C
MEASE
BINDIE, 76
BOOKER, 76
FRANCES, 76
MEDLEY
AMANDA M., 76
ARAMINTA, 35
FIELDING, 35
GEORGIE A., 55
ISAAC, 76
J.J.D., 76
MARY L., 52
MISTIE, 80
WILLIAM, 35
MEDLIN
ARAMINTA, 20-B
MARTHA, 29
MEDLIN, 20-B
WILLIAM, 20-B
MEDLY
ABERT J., 85
MINNIE, 85
MEDOR

J.O.W., 77
JOSIAH, 77
SUSAN, 77
MEDOW
ISAAC, 49
JANE, 49
MATILDA, 49
MEDOWS
ELIJAH P., 135
GREEN, 132
MARY, 135
RICHARD, 135
MEEKS
C., 17
SUSAN, 17
THOMAS C., 17
MELVIN
ANDREW, 26
ANN, 107, 121, 125, 128, 132
B., 107
BECKEY, 63
DASIE, 132
DELIA, 121
E., 20-B
EDWD L., 63
ELIZ., 20-C
ELIZA, 124
ELIZABETH, 37
ELIZTH, 26
GEORGE, 132
H.A., 132
HEZ, 20-C
HEZ., 20-B
HEZEKIAH, 26, 37
J. WEAVER, 20-C
JENNIE, 140
JNO W., 37
JOHN W., 63, 97
LAURA, 128
MACK, 106
MAGGIE, 132
MARGARET, 132
MARIA S., 44
MARY, 140
MATTIE J., 125
N., 125
N.B., 107
P.U., 121
POLE, 128
POLL, 132
REBECCA, 44, 97
RUFUS, 20-B
SARAH, 106
TNIE, 107
W.B., 97
WEAVER, 44
MEMX
DOTSEY, 27
MAUR, 27
WM G., 27
MERCER
ANDREW, 62

MARY A., 62
NANCY C., 62
WILLIAM C., 4(2)
MERCHANT
CHAS, 56
LOUISA, 56
MEREDITH
ANGELINE, 109
JOHN, 117(2)
LUCINNA, 117
VIOLA, 117
MEREIDTH (SIC)
RUSSELL, 71
MERRETT
DRURY T., 44
ELLEN, 44
MANNIE E., 44
MERRICK
BARNEY, 20-C
DODSON, 20-C
MARY, 20-C
MERRIMAN
ADA, 136
GEO, 136
ROSA LEE, 136
MICHAEL
J.W., 125
KATE, 125
NINA WISSIE, 125
MICHIALL
J.W., 117
KATIE, 117
ZELLA, 117
MIDCAFF
JAMES M., 39
JANE, 39
MATHEW, 39
MIDTIFF
I., 95
NANCY, 95
MILES
BALLARD, 126
FRANCES, 113
MILLY OLEY (SIC), 58

MOSES, 58
OLLIE, 126
RACHAEL, 63
THOMAS, 58
THOS, 58
THOS M., 63
WM, 63
WM H., 126
MILKE
HENRY S., 34
JOHN W., 34
MARY J., 34
MILLER
A., 117, 125
ALBERT, 80
ALICE T., 41
ARMSTEAD, 67
BEN, 80

C.N., 122
CLARA, 34
D.H., 137(2)
E., 17
E.J., 112
E.V., 138
EDIE E., 41
ELIZ., 20-D
ELIZABETH, 44, 56, 67
ELLEN C., 74
ELPHICY, 20-A
F., 20-A
FANNIE L., 91
FLOYD, 12, 21, 36, 20-F
G.C., 137
GEO A., 29
GEO C., 83
GEO. C., 46
GEORGE, 74
GEORGE C., 17, 43
GEORGE D., 24
GEORGE P., 9
GRIEF, 1
H.B., 119(2)
HARRIETT, 57
J., 17
J.G., 140
J.R., 75, 112
J.W., 81, 125
JAMES, 10, 34, 36, 39, 136
JOHN, 57
JOHN H., 43
JOHN L., 36
JOS, 80
JULIA, 21, 20-F
KATE R., 134
L.A., 135
LUCRETIA, 36
M.A., 91(2)
MAGGIE, 120, 136
MARCUS M., 1
MARGARET, 119, 134, 137

MARK M., 41
MARTHA M., 22
MARY, 9, 27, 56, 80(2), 93, 119
MARY A., 12, 13
MARY E., 44
MARY F., 122
MARY J., 81
MARY JANE, 36
MEDIA A., 44
MILVINA, 74
MITCHELL, 134
MOSES, 24
NANCY, 1, 35, 80, 83, 136
NANCY M., 20-A
NELSON, 119

P., 117
PEARLY P., 138
PERLINA, 45
PETER, 27(2), 93
POLLY, 12, 60
R.A., 26, 29, 30(5), 31(4), 32(5), 39, 75, 76, 81, 110, 112(2), 113, 114, 115(4), 116(2), 117, 118, 119, 121, 122, 124, 125(2), 127, 129(3), 130, 134, 135(2), 136(2), 138, 139(2), 140
R.E., 96
RACHEL, 34, 36
REBECCA, 76
REBECCA J., 54, 75
RHODA, 26
RHODA A., 54
RICHARD, 54
RICHARD A., 10, 27(2), 28(2), 33(2), 45
RICHD. A., 28, 32
ROBERT T., 120
RUCY, 21, 20-F
S.A., 122
SALLIE, 39
SAML, 70
SAMUEL, 140
SANL S., 70
SARAH, 10
SARAH E., 96
SARAH M.E., 76
SUSAN, 24, 140
SUSAN C., 34
T.K., 138
THOMAS, 56, 93
VIRGINIA B., 110
W., 82
W.H., 91
WADE, 112
WILLIAM, 12, 67, 20-D
WILLOUGHBY, 35, 44(2), 96

WM, 9, 27, 57, 60
WM A., 83
MILLISON
D.V., 76
MILLS
ADA E., 94
AMANDA E., 70
ANDERSON, 102
ANNA, 71
ANNIE, 106
BENJ, 26
BENJ., 16
BETTIE, 120
C. KATHARINE, 89
C.C., 96
C.M., 70

C.W., 107
CATHARINE, 63
CATHERINE, 63
CH. W., 26
CHARLES A., 102
D., 15
D.B., 96
D.T., 70, 90(2)
DAVID, 13
DOLLIVER B., 96
E.A., 107
E.E., 69
E.G., 100
ELEANOR P., 9
ELECTRA, 138
ELIZABETH, 68, 82, 83, 113, 137
ELIZATH, 69
ELIZTH M., 70
EMILY, 106
EMMARILLA, 20, 20-A

FANNIE M., 107
FANNY, 90
GREEN, 63
H.G., 70, 96, 137
HARRIET, 103
HENRY G., 27
HUGH, 99
HUGH G., 63
HUGHEY G., 99
HUGHIE G., 49
HY G., 89
IDA B., 90
J.A., 82, 83
J.R., 138
JACOB, 71
JAMES, 120
JAMES R., 15
JANE, 66
JAS H., 52, 82, 94
JEREMIAH J., 63
JNO A., 69
JNO B., 25
JOHN, 13, 66(2)
JOHN A., 68
JOHN B., 25
JOSEPH, 38
JULIA F., 83
L., 124
LECTORY J., 52
LERNAH, 7
LIDDY, 25
LILLIE B., 124
LYDIA, 34, 62
M., 71, 124
MAGGIE, 82
MAGGIE A., 100
MARGT E., 99
MARILIA, 38
MARY, 52, 71, 120, 124, 138
MARY A., 82, 94

MARY FRANCES, 137

MARY FRANCIS, 82

MARY M., 16
MARY O., 26
MINERVA, 125
N.A., 120
NANCY, 10, 13, 15, 16
NATHANIEL R., 10
PRISCILLA, 7, 10
R.W., 89
RACHEL, 20-B
REBECCA, 49
RHODA, 71
RHODA J., 20-A
ROBERT, 25, 27, 62, 125
ROBT, 34, 49
ROBT BENJ, 63
S.D., 138(2)
S.W., 124(2)
SALLIE, 70
SALLIE A., 68
SAML, 10(2), 20-B
SAMUEL, 7, 16, 20-B
SAMUEL B., 120
SAMUEL O., 124
SAMUEL ZERUAH, 9

SARAH E., 16
TEPLA, 27
THOMPSON, 100
VIRGINIA R., 138
W.C., 120
W.F., 138
WAL E., 62
WALKER, 71
WILLIAM, 38
WILLIAM F., 20, 34
WM, 20, 20-A
ZERNAH, 10
MIMICK
RABECCA, 95
MINCY
D., 18
P.P., 18
SARAH M., 18
MINER
ELIZTH E., 54
SALLIE J., 54
T.P., 54
MINK
EELIZABETH, 62
GEORGIE ANN, 62

SILAS, 62
MINOR
AMANDA, 30
CHARLEY, 121
E., 26, 20-E
ELIZ, 88
ELIZ., 30

ELIZABETH, 19
ELIZETH, 31
NANCY, 85, 105, 121
NEHEMIAH, 105
PETER, 85, 105, 121, 20-E
S.A., 85
SAML A., 85
SAMUEL, 26
THOMPSON, 30, 31, 88, 20-E
THOS, 26
WILLIAM P., 31
MIREAL
M.S., 81
MARY A., 81
ZORAH M., 81
MIRICK
JOHN, 22
LUCINDA, 22
WILLIAM, 22
MITCHEL
C., 116
ELVIRA, 108
J.W., 116
JACK, 108
JOHN, 108
RICHARD CHARLEY, 116
MITCHELL
AGNES, 73
AMANDA, 94
C., 23
CAUSBY, 63
CLIDA, 140
ELIJAH, 40
F.W., 56
FERDINAND, 23
GERTRUDE, 140
HENRY, 94
J.H., 140(2)
JAMES, 40
JEFF, 73(2)
JOEL, 23
JOHN, 70
JOHN W., 45, 63
LELIA E., 94
LUCINDA, 70
MARTHA J., 45
MATILDA, 40
PHOEBE A., 63
STEWART C., 45
W.E., 103
MITCHEM
JANE, 85
MITCHUM
ELIJAH D., 58
GUS, 123
HANNAH, 58
HARRIETT, 133
JAMES, 133
JOHN L., 123
JORDAN, 58

L.P., 123
SARAH, 133
MIZE
BERRY, 6
ELIZABETH, 6
SAMSON, 6
MOGE
ELIJAH, 9
JOHN W., 9
MARY, 9
MOMOARN (SIC)
D., 95
E., 95
LULA, 95
MONK
FRANCES, 89
JAMES A., 63
JESSE A., 89
MINNIE E., 89
SARAH J., 94
SILAS, 63, 94
MONROE
AMANDA, 130, 134
ANNIE, 93
BERTIE, 91
CALVIN, 93
JAMES, 93
JAMES R., 7
JOHN, 59, 130, 134
LOU, 91
MATIE, 134
PARMELIA, 59
RHODA, 7
ROSA M., 130
SUSAN A., 7
THOS J., 59
MONSEY
ANNA, 70
TERESSA, 70
W.J., 70
MONTGOMERY
D., 84
DEL, 85
E.F., 80
E.M., 85
ESTELLA, 84
J.R., 76, 81, 123
JAMES M., 74
JOHN, 74
M.C., 123
MARY, 81
MARY C., 76
ROBT, 123
S.M., 80, 84
SYDNEY M., 85
T.C., 73
W.H., 76
W.K., 81(2)
MOONEY
AERES, 115
ALBERT, 105

ALEXR H., 8
AMELIA, 7
CATHARINE C., 115
ELIZA, 57
JNO L., 3
JOHN, 6
JOHN L., 8
LAURA, 50
MARTIN D., 7
NATHANIEL, 115
ROBT L., 63
ROSA M.J., 3
RUTH S., 6
S.L., 63
STONIX L., 105
STYNAIS L., 7
STYNAX L., 50, 57
SUSANA, 3
SUSANAH, 50
SUSANNA, 8
SUSANNAH, 6, 57, 63, 105
MOONY
AMELIA H., 77
S.L., 77
SUSANNAH, 77
MOORE
A.J., 117
ADELINE, 106
AMANDA J., 119
ANNA, 1
B., 68, 69, 73, 74(2), 75(2), 76, 78, 79, 85
BELL A., 59
BETHUEL, 138
CHESS, 128
D.N., 125
ELLEN, 37
EMMA, 138
FLORENCE, 141
FRANCES, 37
GEO, 108
GORDON J., 61
H.G., 106
HARRIETT W., 138
HY LEWIS, 106
JESSE, 108
JOHN, 128(2), 141
JOHN A., 119
LEWIS, 37
LIZZIE, 95
LUCY, 141
M.H., 14
M.M., 71, 101, 117
MAPOLEON A., 59

MARTHA, 59, 125
MARTHA M., 61
MARY, 128
MARY ANN, 53
MARY E., 119
MARY J., 71
MINTY, 108

N.D., 61, 71, 101, 117
NANCY, 37
PAULINE, 93
PETER, 96, 107
PULINA F., 107
REESE, 37
RICHARD, 37
ROBERT, 53
ROSIE, 128
S.W., 96
SALLY, 50
SAM, 93
SAMUEL, 1
SUE, 96, 107
THOMAS, 1
THOS, 50
W.L., 125
WALTER, 96
WEBSTER, 128
WILLIAM S., 14
WILLIAM T., 50
WM, 53
WM. S., 14
WOOD L., 125
MORAN
JAMES M., 38
JAS M., 26
JOHN C., 38
LEE C., 26
SARAH, 26, 38
MORE
JOHN W., 124
PETER, 124
SUE, 124
MOREHEAD
DAN F., 64
DAN P., 64
MORELAND
ELIZABETH, 64
MORGAN
A., 18
A.B., 129, 138
ALBERT, 131
ALBERT S., 122
ALLA DORA, 129
AMOS, 131
ANTHONY, 37, 41
ARCHIBALD B., 37
BASWELL, 21(2), 20-F(2)
C.A., 102
CHAS A., 53
CHLOE, 18, 37, 41
D.A., 95
DOUGLASS, 31, 91, 123
FRANCIS A., 53, 91, 102
FRANCISA., 48
GILBERT, 21, 20-F
JOHN, 21, 20-F
L.J., 95
LAURA A., 123
LAURA P., 48

LILLIE M., 138
LILLY B., 113
M.D., 129
M.H., 95
MARTHA, 96, 113, 122
MARTHA L., 18
MARY, 131
MINNIE E., 96
R., 138
ROBT H., 71
SARAH, 123
SARAH E., 71
SAVILLA J., 41
SWAN H., 48, 53, 91, 102
THOS P., 29, 96, 113, 122
URWEAN, 21(2), 20-F(2)

W.E., 71
MORING
F.D., 121
M.J., 121
W.W., 121
MORRIO
HERBERT L., 113
MORRIS
ALLEN, 119
ANN, 106
E.B., 80
GEORGE, 119
HERBERT, 127
J.R., 68(2), 70(2), 71
JENNIE, 80
JNO R., 127
JOE, 141
JOHN, 106
JOSIE, 127
JULIA, 119
KITTY, 64
LOUISA, 106
MATILDA, 141
RACHEL, 80
S.A., 127
SAML H., 80
THOS R., 56, 57, 59(2), 61, 62, 64
WILLIAM, 141
MORRISON
EMELINE, 102
EPHRAIM, 102
JOHN, 102
P.A., 81
MORTIN
EMELINE, 64
MARTHA, 64
MOSIER
D., 121
JENNIE, 121
MOSLEY
H.D., 119
MARTHA, 119
NANCY J., 20 B

R.W., 119(2)
MOSS
JAMES, 103
LYDIA, 8
TILDA, 103
WM, 103
MOTLEY
CATHARINE, 2
CORA, 126
E., 15
ELIZTH, 2, 9, 16
GRIGGELLE P., 15
JNO L., 122
JOEL F., 9
JOHN, 9
LOUELLA, 126
MARY E., 112
P., 122
PARTHENA P., 112
R.J., 126(2)
RUFINA, 16
SARAH, 2
THOMAS D., 2
W.B., 122, 126(4)
WM, 2(2), 15, 16, 112
MOULES
MATTIE, 137
OLLIE, 137
MOUNTZ
GREEN, 52
MOURAN
MARY, 116
MOVMAN
J.H., 116
J.T., 116
M., 116
MOWLES
ALLIE, 128
D.C., 95, 133
ELIZTH, 9
JANE, 128
JOSEPH, 133
JUDIA, 95
LOUISA, 9
MARY, 134
N.J., 133
NANCY G., 95
ROSA, 134
THOS, 9
TOMEY, 128
MOWLS
D.C., 101
DAVID C., 64
HENSLEY, 64
MATTIE, 101
NANCY, 64
NANCY G., 101
MOYA
JONATHAN H., 52
MARTHA J., 52
WM, 52
MOYE
ADA MARIA, 98

ANNA L., 68
C.D., 135
CAROLINE, 17
E.W., 81, 98(2), 135
ELIJAH, 17(2)
EVERMONT W., 36

J.H., 46, 127
JNO D., 91
JNO W., 68
JOHN D., 27
JOHN W., 36, 48
JULIA A., 48, 68
JULIA ANN, 36
LILLY MAY, 98
LUCINDA, 49
M.J., 20-C
MAR., 17
MARTHA, 53
MARTHA F., 91
MARTHA J., 27, 46
MARY, 17
MARY J., 53
MARY JANE, 91
NEWTON F., 48
ROBERT C., 20-C
ROBT E., 49
S.E., 98(2), 135
VICTORIA L., 49
WILLIAM, 53
WILLIAM W., 46
WM, 27, 20-C
MOYER
S.G., 113
MOYERS
JAMES H., 127
MARY, 127
T.J., 127
MULLEN
AUSTIN, 114
C.E., 114
JOSEPH, 53
SARAH J., 114
MULLIN
CALVIN, 46
ELIZABETH, 46
JAMES, 64
JANE, 101
JOHN, 101
JOHN E., 46
LOUISA L., 64
SALLY, 64
SALLY M., 101
MULLINS
ABAGAIL, 44, 51
ABAGIE ANN, 38
ABE, 32
ADE, 128
ADELINE, 98
AUSTIN, 39
CHAS M., 112
DORA M., 125
ELIZ C., 51

J.B., 125
JAMES B., 38
JANE, 112, 127
JEFFERSON D., 44
JOHN, 127
JOHN J., 39
JOHN S., 41, 20-C
JOS, 105, 112
M.J., 125, 130
MOLLIE, 105
NANCY, 41
P.H., 98
POLLY, 32, 105, 128
R., 98
RHODA J., 130
RICHARD, 98
SAML, 41
SARAH J., 39
T.J., 130
THOMAS J., 32, 128
WM P., 38, 44, 51
MUNCEY
MARTHA, 44
MARY J., 44
WILEY W., 44
MUNCY
ANNIE R., 102
MARTHA, 102
W.W., 102
MUNDA
JOHN, 52
MUNDY
ANNIE B., 132
J.D., 132(2)
LUCY C., 131
MUNSBY
ANNIE J., 101
J.A., 114
J.L., 109
JAS A., 94
JOSEPHINE S., 33
JULIA, 33
KATIE E., 114
LEDA M., 114
M.P., 101
McC., 94
N.A., 94
ODEN C., 132
SARAH, 109, 132
SKIDMORE, 33
W.M., 109
WINTON, 132
MUNSY
HANNAH, 93
OLILIA, 93
W.J., 93
MURFY
JANE, 39
JOSEPH, 39
Z.A., 39
MURKEY
SIDNEY, 76
MURPHY

ANNORA, 94
GEO R., 75
GEO., 75
JANE, 52
JAS E., 94
JOHN, 52, 94
JOSEPH, 52
LOUCINDA, 85
LUCINDA, 75
SALLIE, 85
MURRAY
JAMES A., 26
JOHN, 52
JULIA A., 26
MARY, 52
MARY A., 104
SKIDMON, 26
STERLING, 104
THOMAS, 52
MURRELL
DRURY T., 11, 53
ELIZABETH E., 19
ELLEN, 53
HESEKEAH, 41
JAMES, 11, 19, 118
JAMES A., 41
JAS A., 31
LAURA E., 53
LEONA, 118
MARY, 11
REBECCA J., 31
S., 19
SARAH A., 41
SARAY, 31
MURRY
CURDY, 96
LEWIS, 96
OLLIE, 108
STERLING, 96
MUSE
ABE, 48, 60(2)
ABRAM, 75
AUSTN, 71
CARR, 48
FANNY, 60
JACK, 89
JNO P., 71
JOHN, 89, 127
LUCINDA, 89
LUCY, 127
LULA, 127
MATILDA, 75
MILLE, 48
MILLIE, 60(2)
MILLY, 75
ROSAZELLA, 71
ROZELLA, 139
VICTORIA, 60
WM A., 139
WM H., 139
MUSGROVE
ADELINE, 95
JNO, 95

MARSHALL, 95
MUSSELFIELD (?)

MARSHALL, 112
OLLIE, 112
MUSTARD
PARKINSON, 88
RHODA, 88
SARAH M., 88
MYERS
A.J., 95
C.W., 68
CHRISTENA, 95
HARDEN, 68
JANE, 68
LUELLA, 139
ROSANA, 18
SALLY, 95

-N-

NADDLE
GEORGE B., 36
JNO A., 36
POLLY, 36
NAFF
JNO E., 84, 96(2), 97
NAGY
ANDREW, 136
NANCE
CASSIE, 88
E.L., 88
GEO, 88
NAPIER
MARY ANN, 75
NASH
ABNER, 20-A
ALBERT B., 20-A
BETTIE D., 40
JOHN F., 54
REBECCA, 20-A
NEAL
A.P., 100
A.S., 100
AGNES, 125
ALMEDA D., 122
ANDW JACKN, 59
ANN E., 33
ARMINUS L., 25
AUG, 125(2)
AUGUSTUS, 49
BETTIE C., 47
CHRISTENA ELIZ., 55
CLEMENTINE A., 83
CYNTHIA, 116, 122
D.N., 46, 86, 123(2)
DANIEL, 8(2)
DANIEL N., 8
DANL N., 43
DAVID, 10

E.H., 119
ELIZA J., 86
ELIZABETH F., 43
ELLEN, 99
ELLEN V., 85
EMMA T., 58
ERASTUR G., 111
GEO E.L., 68
GUS, 55
H.M., 20
H.P., 99
HANNAH, 8(2)
HARRIET D.B., 40
HATTIE, 105
HENRY A., 115
HENRY M., 22, 25, 32(3), 33, 47, 58, 104
HENRY P., 59
I.V., 111
J.B., 115
J.H., 116, 122
JAMES H., 20, 119
JOHN B., 97
JOHN H., 46
JULIA, 123
LELIA H., 85
LEONIDAS JASPER, 100

MARTHA, 40, 59, 115
MARTHA A., 85
MARTHA J., 68, 83, 97
MATTHEW, 40
MOLLIE, 70
NANCY, 92
NANCY C., 125
NANNIE B., 70
PHIL, 85
RANDALL, 92
REBECCA V., 85
RHODA J., 105
ROBT M., 59, 85
S.A., 123
SALLIE, 33, 58, 92
SALLY, 123
SARAH, 10, 25, 47
SARAH A., 20, 22, 43, 46, 86, 104
SARAH G., 8
SOPHRONIA J., 111
STONEWALL J., 104
SUSAN A., 22
SYNTHIA R., 119
TERRY, 49
VAL H., 116
W.C., 105(2)
W.W., 6, 9, 10
WILEY W., 123
WILLIAM R., 10
WM, 115
WM E., 26, 36
WM R., 68, 83, 97
NEALE

AGNUS, 14
THOS., 14
NEALEY
J.G., 99
NEALL
ELLEN V., 16
NEEL
ANNA LAURA, 111

D.E., 99
E.V., 97(2)
H.P., 99
HENRY M., 97
JAS M., 106
LYDIA, 99
M.A., 111
MARTHA, 111
MARTHA A., 106
MARY, 99
R.M., 99, 111(2)
ROBERT, 111
ROBT M., 106
SARAH A., 97
SARAH E. (SIC), 106
THOS J., 106
NEELEY
CATHARINE, 36, 49
DELILAH, 33, 35, 47
FANNIE G., 35
JESSE G., 36
JOHN, 33
KATHERINE, 35
N.M., 36
NANCY ELIZABETH, 35

NATHANIEL M., 35
WILLIAM G., 35
WM, 47
WM F., 47, 86
WM G., 33
NEELY
ALLEN L., 21, 20-F
AMANDA M., 54
CLARA, 17, 21, 20-D, 20-F
DELILA, 10, 14, 17
DELILAH, 22, 54, 81
DELILY, 83
ED F., 119
EVAN, 20-D
I.G., 122
J.H., 119
JOHN, 10, 83, 137(2)
M.A., 119
MARTHA, 14
MARY A., 17
NELSON, 20-D
NELSON H., 17, 21, 20-F
ORA MAY, 137
RACHEL, 137
S.L., 83
SUSAN, 10

SUSAN C., 17
V.E., 122
VICTORIA, 86
VIRGIN M., 86
W.F., 86
WILLIAM A., 122
WM, 14, 17, 81
WM F., 22
WM G., 22, 54
NELLY
LEVI, 20-E
MARY E., 20-B
REBECA, 20-B
NELMS
JOHN H., 133
KATHLEEN P., 133
LETTIA V., 133
NELSON
CAROLINE, 129
CHARDY, 24
DORA D., 140
E., 122
EDGAR G., 41
ELISHA, 24
ELIZA, 37
ELIZABETH, 140(2)
EMMILINE, 83
HENRY, 103
JAMES, 6
JAMES R., 140(2)
JARVIS, 24
JAS R., 122(2)
JOHN R., 41
JOHN W., 6
JORDAN, 65
JULIA A., 94
LIEN A., 140
LYDIA, 6
MARY, 94, 103
MONDACAI, 28
MORGAN, 94(2)
SALLIE, 41
SARAH, 65
TEMPERANCE, 65

W.A., 129
WARD, 103
WM, 129
WM O., 122
NESBIT
BELLE, 94
FRANK, 81
ISAAC, 81, 94
NANCY, 81
NANNIE, 94
NEWBILL
ANDERSON, 93
HARRIET, 93
POMPEY, 93(2)
NEWBURY
A.J., 15
E., 15
SAMUEL H., 15

SARAH, 5
THOMAS, 5(2)
NEWKIRK
JNO R., 129
JOHN R., 23
M.E., 129
MARY A., 23
MOLLIE E., 129
PRATHER, 52
RUTHY, 52
STEPHEN, 23
NEWLEE
AMANDA, 23
ELIZTH, 8
GEO. B., 23
JOHN G., 8
MARY C., 23
SARAH E., 8
NEWLON
HARRIET, 23
NEWMAN
ASA, 132
J.B., 132
LYDDIA, 132
NEWSOM
B.F., 132
B.J., 134
HENRY, 103
JAMES, 6
EMELINE, 62
NEWSON
B.F., 134
BENJ F., 130
NICEWANDER

ALBERTA ROSE, 120

ANN, 91(2)
ARDELIA J., 99
CHRISTINA, 98
DELIA R., 91
H.P., 125
FRANK, 91
JOSIE L., 99
JULIA, 91
JULIA A., 91
N., 120
NANNIE, 99
R.F., 91(2)
ROMA V., 91
RUFUS, 98
SAML M., 99
VERNIE, 98
W.H., 123
W.H.H., 120
WILLIE A., 91
WM H., 91(2)
NICHISON
MILLE, 29
NICHOLAS
ROXY, 47
NICHOLS
CALVIN, 64
EVALINE, 73
JAS S., 61
JOHN, 73

KATE, 61
L.L., 133(2)
NICATIE F., 120
ROSY, 73
S.E., 133
SUSAN, 64
W.A., 78
WM, 64
WM G., 61
Z., 133
NICKERSON
MILLIE, 129
PEARIS, 129
SAMUEL G., 129
NICKISON
MANA, 29
NICKLES
THOMAS, 35
WILLIAM A., 35
NORMAN
ELIZABETH, 111
J.M., 58
MARY, 58
NORRIS
DEANEY, 107
E.F., 85, 92
EMILY, 105, 107
H.L., 85
HARVEY, 92, 105
JOHN, 107
JOS M., 85
JOSEPH, 122
SHILOH, 92
WM, 105(2)
NORTHCUTT
THOS, 49
NOSLER
CLAY, 118
MATTIE, 118
W.A., 118
NOURLIN
SARAH H., 131
THOS L., 131
W.F., 131
NUNLEY
JAMES, 106
MARY J., 106
WM, 106

-O-

PERMELIA, 37
SARAH F., 20-B
WILLIAM, 7
WM, 20-B
WM A., 37
NOEL
JAMES S., 88
MARTHA, 88
T.C., 88
NOELL
CALEB, 4
JAS R., 121
LELIA H., 121

M., 4
M.E., 121
SARAH L., 4
NOFF
JNO E., 85(4), 86, 87(2), 93(3), 94(2), 95
JOHN E., 89, 90
NOLL
DAVID, 23
NONE
JAMES, 37
NANCY, 37
THOMAS, 37
NORE
ABRAHAM, 104, 121
FLOYD, 104
O'DELL
J.J., 80
JACOB, 80
MANERVA, 80
ODELL
MARTHA, 104, 121
RUSH, 121
ODLE
A., 93
ABRAM, 65, 93
FLOYD, 137
MARTHA, 65
MARY, 93
SARAH, 65
O'DONALD
ALICE L., 94
ODONALD
ELIZABETH, 88
O'DONALD
LIZZIE, 94
ODONALD
NANCEY J., 88
WILLIAM, 88
O'DONALD
WM, 94
O'DONELL
ELIZABETH, 93
ROSA, 93
WILLIAM, 93
ODONNEL
ELIZABETH, 130
J.W., 130
W.R., 130
OGDEN
MARTHA, 77
OILER
PATSY, 20-D
OKES
ELLA M., 63
JESSE A., 63
POLLY, 63
OLESER
WM J., 22
OLEY
ALICE, 58
EDWARD, 58
LUCINDA, 58

POLLY, 104
SUSAN E., 122
W.S., 121, 122(2)
O'BRYANT
FRANCIS, 76
JULIANNE, 76
WM LEE, 76
O'DANIEL
ISAAC, 32
JESSE G., 64
LIZZIE, 64
REBECCA, 32(2)
WM, 64
ODELL
ABRAHAM, 104, 121
FLOYD, 104
O'DELL
J.J., 80
JACOB, 80
MANERVA, 80
ODELL
MARTHA, 104, 121
RUSH, 121

OLIVER
ANNY, 21, 20-F
CATHE, 3
CLARA, 27
E., 27, 125, 128, 130
E.T., 138(2)
ELIZA, 27, 34
ELZA, 29
FREEMAN, 3
HATTIE O., 133
J.D., 133
J.T., 133(2)
JAS, 11
JOHN, 3
JOSEPH T., 39
LIZZIE, 21, 20-F
LYNN, 11
MARY, 11
NANCY, 39, 48
WILLIAM J., 21, 20-F
WM, 39, 48
WM C., 48
OLIVIA
E., 123
OLIVIER
E., 103, 113, 118(2), 130, 135(2), 136(2), 137
OLLIS
E.A., 127
G.I., 127
MAMIE M., 127
O'NEAL
DANIEL, 62
ELLEN, 62
TAYLOR, 62
ONEY
ALICE V., 76
C.W., 114
E.J., 78
E.M., 76(2), 78, 114
EDWARD M., 20
M.G., 76
NANCY, 20
V.F., 76(2), 78, 114
WM, 20
ORNEFER
ANNIE, 103
JOHN, 103
MARY, 103
ORR
MARGARET, 110
MARTHA, 110
SAM, 110
ORTON
MACK, 136
OSBORN
H.C., 95
J.R., 95
JOHN, 20-E
NANCY, 20-E
SARAH, 20-E
SARILDA, 95

OSBORNE
ELIZTH, 20-A
LEO, 20-A
OSBURN
AARON, 76
ELIZABETH, 76
JOHN, 22
SARAH, 22
THOS, 76
OVERSTREET
ABNEW H., 56
SOPHIA, 56
WM W., 56
OWEN
R.A., 133(2), 134(4), 135, 137(2), 138, 139(4), 140(2), 141
ROBT A., 138
OWENS
BETTIE, 128
FRANKLIN, 138
J.M., 138(2)
LENNIA, 128
MARY, 138
OSKER, 128
R.A., 132, 133(2)
OWENSBY
C., 19
M., 19
SARAH J., 19
OWNBY
CHARLOTTA, 68
CHARLOTTE J., 29
H.F.P., 68
MONROE, 68
OWNES
GEO L., 94
J.B., 94
JULIA M., 94
OWNEY
LIVE, 79
OXLEY
AMANDA A., 45
BUFORD H., 33
CYNTHIA J., 41
D., 126
DANIEL L., 33
DELILA A., 41, 45
DELILAH, 78
DELILAH A., 23
ELZ. R., 29
GEORGE S., 78
MARY E., 23
RHODA J., 33
ROBT G., 126
SANDFORD, 126
SANFORD, 23
SANFORD H., 41, 45, 78
OXLY
BENJN. H., 22
DELILAH, 22
SANFORD, 22
OYLER

A.A., 71
ARBELIA, 10
EMANUEL, 71
MALLIE R., 71
MARTHA, 10

-P-

PACK
AMANDA, 20-B
ANDERSON, 1, 7, 20-B

CELIA, 20-B
CLARA B., 7
E.B., 20-B
ELIZ., 20-B
ELIZA, 16, 18
ELIZABETH, 20-B
ELIZABETH J., 1
ELIZTH, 9(2)
ELIZTH B., 9, 10
FLEMING, 18
FRANCES, 16
ISABELLA, 5
J.A., 20-B
JAMES A., 20-B
JAS W., 61
JNO A., 33
JOHN, 9(3), 10, 16, 20-E(2)
JOHN CONRAD, 61

JOHN R., 10
M., 20-E
MARY, 20-B
MARY A., 61
MARY J., 9
MARY R., 33
MATILDA A., 21, 20-F
MATTHEW, 16
NANCY, 1, 9
PRESTON, 20-E
RACHEL, 9
REBECCA, 1, 7, 23
RHODA, 1, 5, 23
ROBERT, 1, 5
ROBT, 23
RUFUS, 5(4), 6, 7(4), 9(2), 13, 14(2), 16(2), 17(3), 19(3), 21(3), 22(2), 23(2), 24, 20-B(3), 20-C, 20-D(2), 20-E(6), 20-F(3)
SALLIE M., 33
SAMUEL, 20-B(2)
TANDY, 21, 20-F
THOMAS, 20-B
VGA, 21, 20-F
VIRGINIA V., 20-E
WILLIAM A., 20-E
PAFFORD
MARY E., 88

WM, 88
PAGE
ALFRED, 62
AMANDA, 62
DELAWARE, 107
DELAWARE L., 108

DORA, 83
FLOYD, 62
HAROLD, 108
HEROD, 104
HEROD A., 104
LOUISA, 104, 108
PAINE
ISAAC, 38
JAMES, 38
JOHN M., 27
JULY, 27
MARY, 38
WM, 27
PAINTER
C.E., 87, 88, 89, 95
ELVIRA, 95
JOHN A., 95
PALMER
ADALINE, 121
AGNES, 88
BEN, 117
EDEN, 107
ELIZABETH A., 36
GEO W., 117
JAS, 102
JERRY, 102
JULIA, 15
MARY, 117
NANCY, 107
NANCY ALICE, 107

PRISCILLA, 102
ROBT T., 36
S.L., 130
SAMUEL L., 36
TEXAS, 130
THEODOCIA, 130
W.W., 88
WALTER W., 88
WM, 15
PANE
BARTLEY, 20-E
JULIET, 20-E
WM, 20-E
PANKEY
BELL, 135
JOHN R., 135
WM A., 135
PANLEY
H.C., 112
HATTIE I., 112
S.M., 112
PANNILL
M.A., 65, 66(2), 70, 71, 73(2), 75(3), 77(2), 78, 80, 82,

85, 86, 89
MOSES A., 60(2), 62
PARK
AMA, 20-B
ELIZTH B., 16
JOHN, 16
RHODA, 20-B
ROB, 20-B
PARKER
A., 20-A
A.A., 59, 74, 126
ALLEN A., 59
ANDERSON, 20-B
ANN E., 20-B
BENJAMIN, 34
BETSY, 64
ELIZA F., 20-A
ELIZABETH S., 61
ELIA B., 108, 131
ISAAC, 64
JAMES, 42, 61, 139
JANE, 79
JAS A., 132
JAS., 34, 59
JOHN B., 75
JOSEPH, 132(2)
LAURA A., 64
LIZZIE, 132, 139
M., 20-B
M.J., 132, 136
MARY, 34, 42, 61, 74, 20-A
MARY J., 59, 108
MARY JANE, 122
NANNIE H., 74
NANNIE K., 136
OLLIE, 42
S.H., 136
SAML, 122, 131
SAML H., 108
W.R., 79, 122
PARKINS
ELIZTH, 16
JOHN A., 16
SAML, 16
W.H., 119
PARMER
JULIA, 17
MARTHA E., 17
WM, 17
PARRETT
LUCY, 91
MARGARET, 91
REUBEN, 91
PARRIS
THOS, 67, 73
PARRY
AGNES, 89
ELIZA, 87, 89
MAGGIE, 87
WILLIAM, 87
WM, 89
PARSON

W.A., 87
PASSEL
MARY E., 55
PATRICK
FLORENCE E., 94
GEORGE E., 80
JAMES, 86
JAS, 80
JOHN W., 86
L.D., 51
NANNIE, 80
NANNIE A., 86
ROBERT, 16
RUTH, 16
WILSON, 16
PATSEY
JACKSON, 43
PATTERSON
A.H., 140
A.W., 112
CHARLIE, 141
E.E., 140
ELIZABETH S., 25
F., 141
GILEN, 25
GILFORD, 63
H.B., 105
J.W., 55
JACKSON, 105
JAS., 25
JOHN, 63, 73, 115
JULIA, 87
M.A., 126
MARY, 115
MATTIE, 87
NANCY, 63
NELSON, 126
NEWTON, 115
R., 141
ROSA, 126
S.N., 110
S.W., 112, 126(2), 129
SALLY ANN, 73
SURRY, 87
T.H., 120
THOS, 83
W.C., 85, 140
PATTON
C.E., 116
C.S., 116
W.J., 116
PAULEY
ALBERT G., 15
B., 15
B.A., 20-D
BARBARA, 11
BERTHILDA, 107
ELIZABETH, 68
ELLEN, 43
FEILDEN T., 107
GEORGE, 68
GEORGE W., 20-A
H., 15

HARRY, 20-D
HARVEY, 11
JOHN, 43
JOS, 18
LEVINA, 18
LUCINDA B., 107
MINNIE B., 68
NANCY, 12, 15, 20-A
REBECCA J., 15
ROSELLA E., 43
SU, 18
SUDOMY C., 11
PAULY
MARY B., 20-D
NANCY, 13
PAXTON
CHARLEY, 129
MALINDA, 129
RICHARD, 129
PAYNE
A.E., 124(2)
ALICE C., 72
ANDREW, 65, 81, 98, 105
ANN E., 6
ANNIE, 121
AUGUSTA, 89, 110
BARTLEY, 103
BARTLY, 72
C.H., 95
CAROLINE, 72
DAVID R., 22
EDGAR, 121
ELIJAH C., 105
ELIZA, 65, 98
ELIZABETH, 81
ELIZTH, 105
GILES F., 110
I.M., 89
ISAAC, 95
J.W., 87
JAMES, 22, 95
JAS., 24
JUDY, 1
JULIA A., 19(3)
LIZZIE, 103
LOUISA, 19
LOUIA E., 124
MAHALA, 6
MARGIE, 138
MARY, 22, 24, 95
MARY E., 98
MARY L., 124
MATILDA B., 1
NANCY, 19
NOAH, 89, 110
REBECCA, 19
S.E., 124(2)
SARAE, 65
WILLIAM, 1
WM, 19(3), 81, 121
PAYTON
ELLA, 97

PEAK
JOSEPH, 114
NANCY J., 114
WM L., 114
PEAKS
AMANDA, 110
CLAYBORNE, 110

THOMAS, 110
PEARIES
GEORGE W., 49
PHOEBE C., 49
SAMUEL P., 49
PEARIS
AGNES, 42
JOHN, 42
P.C., 42
PEARISH
FOUNTAIN, 104
MARTHA, 104
S., 104
STEPHEN, 104
PEARSON
C.A., 130
GEORGE, 123
J., 123
M.C., 137
P., 123
W.A., 85, 86, 87(2), 88(2), 90(2), 91, 92, 97(3), 98(2), 99(5), 100, 101(4), 102(2), 104(3), 105, 106, 107(2), 108(3), 109(3), 110, 111(2), 112, 113, 114, 137
WALTER EDWARD, 137

PEARSY
J.W., 134(2)
LUCY, 134
MACK, 134
PECK
ALBERTA C., 60
AMANDA M., 117
ANNIE G., 101, 136
BEN W., 100
BENJAMIN, 1
C.A., 117
C.M., 100
E.W., 117
ERASTUS, 54
ERASTUS H., 100
FLEMING, 45
FLORA B., 101
J. AUSTIN, 102
J.P., 136
JACOB A., 1, 54, 60, 64
LARISSA, 54, 64, 102
LIZZIE O., 136
MALISSA, 60
MARTHA, 117

MATILDA, 76
MATILDA G., 64
NANNIE, 45
POLLY, 1
ROSA, 45
SARAH, 54
SUE, 54
WALTER V., 54
WM A., 102
PEDERMAN
ANNE, 130
E.R., 130
H.S., 130
PEDIGO
CHAS J., 107
CORDELIA, 122
LEWIS, 112
MOLLIE, 46
NANCY, 112
S.E., 122
SAML E., 46, 107, 112
SUSAN, 107, 122
SUSAN M., 46
WM A., 51
PEERY
ALICE M., 86
C.D., 114
J.E., 114
T.E., 114
THOS E., 114
PEFRAM
JOHN W., 28
PEGRAM
GEORGE, 3
GEORGE W., 3
MARY, 3
PENCE
J.K., 117
JENNIE K., 90
P.G., 90, 117
ROSA M.B., 117
WM MOSES, 90
PENDLETON
ALICE, 117
ANN, 123
BENJAMIN B., 35
BENJAMIN W., 138
CORA L., 128
D.B., 79, 107, 138
DAVID B., 14
ELZTH, 31
L.M., 123
LEONIDAS M., 31
M., 14
M.J., 128
MARTHA E., 133
MARY J., 56
N.V., 138
NANCY VA, 107
R.E., 74
RACHAEL, 35, 70
RACHEL A., 29
REED, 134

ROBT E., 70
S.A., 56
SAMUEL, 31
SUSAN, 14, 79
SUSAN E., 79
TILDA A., 133
V.E., 123
W.A., 128
WILLIAM A., 29
WM D., 107
WYATT, 70
WYATT W., 29, 35
PENDRY
  JONATHAN L., 23
  MORGAN, 23
PENINGTON
  ALONZO W., 44
  GORDON E., 44, 68
  J.A., 120
  JAMES A., 120
  JULIA, 44
  JULIA P., 68
  KATHERINE, 85
  M.E., 120
  M.G., 68
  ROSANE, 85
  W.J., 71
  WM K., 85
PENLEY
  G.W., 15
PENLY
  G.W., 15
PENN
  ALBERT, 122
  AMANDA, 101
  CHARLES, 81
  CHARLOTTE, 122
  FANNY, 66
  GEO W., 101
  GEORGE H., 81
  GERMAN, 56
  JAMES, 66
  JOHN A., 122
  JOHN H., 101
  LUCY, 117
  R.A., 66
  W.C., 117
PENNINGTON
  A.F., 136
  A.W., 111, 136(2)
  A.W.P., 138
  ALBERT, 126
  ALBERT G., 97
  ALMEDA, 57
  ALMEDIA V.M.J., 51
  AMANDA E., 43
  ANN, 122
  ARAMINTA K., 36
  AVENA, 36
  B.A., 48
  B.H., 113
  B.P., 74, 93, 97(3), 113

BALLARD P., 28
BENJ P., 57
BESSIE B., 122
C., 129
C.A., 136
C.W., 129
CATHERINE, 41, 44, 56, 57, 107
CHARLIE, 124
DANIEL F., 94
E.A., 130
ELIZ., 32
ELIZA J., 136
ELIZA JANE, 108
ELIZABETH, 29, 36, 43, 48, 54
ELLA J., 112
ELLEN, 25, 26, 28, 32, 35, 57, 122
ELZTH, 31
ERASTUS W., 31
EVA, 78
FANNIE J., 81
FORDON E., 59
G.K., 90
G.W., 74, 94(2), 126
GASTON K., 90
GENERAL LEE, 117

GEORGIANA, 125
GORDAN, 43
GORDAN E., 36(2)
GORDON, 2, 51
GORDON E., 50
GREEN, 26, 36, 122, 129, 134
H., 130
H.D., 109, 125
H.W., 136
HARRIET A., 36
HARVE, 134
HENDERSON M., 107

HENNY A.W., 33
I.G., 117
IRENE, 78
ISAC G., 78
J.A., 120
J.H., 130
J.N., 122
J.W., 106, 122, 126
JAMES, 2, 7
JAMES A., 122
JAMES IRA, 134
JANE, 43
JAS A., 54
JAS W., 74
JNO, 26
JNO A., 36
JOHN A., 25, 28, 32, 33, 35, 57
JOHN F., 34, 108
JOHN W., 32

JOSEPH N., 35
JULIA A., 36
JULIA ANN, 50, 51
JULIET, 36, 43, 59
KATE K., 90
LEE, 78
LEVI, 28, 32, 36, 43, 48, 54, 107, 112
LEWIS H., 48
LUCINDA, 111
M. JANE, 74
M.A., 129, 134
M.E., 20, 33, 120(2)
M.F., 136
MALINDA E., 32
MALINDA FRANCES, 118
MARGARET, 43, 54
MARTHA, 7
MARTHA J., 25
MARY, 41, 109(2), 124
MARY E., 43, 111
MILTON G., 50
NANCY, 48, 97, 109, 125, 20-A
NELSON, 54
NICHOLAS, 36
P.F., 33
PARKINSON F., 34
R.E., 117
RILEY, 1, 29, 31, 43, 54, 118
ROSANIA, 56
ROZENA, 109
ROZENIA, 109
RUAH, 74
RUFUS H., 113
S.A., 107, 112
SARA A., 78
SARAH, 1, 5, 33
SARAH A., 7
SARAH J., 29
SARAY A., 20-A
SCINDA, 138
SUSAN, 34
SUSAN C., 108
THOS J., 59
W.D., 107
W.M., 109
WAYNE H., 44
WHEELER, 71
WILLET, 138(2)
WILLIAM, 5, 33, 41, 44, 48, 97
WILMOTH, 94, 126
WILMOUTH, 71, 74
WM, 1, 5, 125
WM H., 71
WM K., 56, 57, 90, 107, 129
WM M., 124
PENTUREE
  CATHERINE, 95

GERTRUDE, 91
MARY C., 91
RICHARD C., 95
W.J., 91, 95
PERDIEW
  HARRISON, 97
  PEGGY, 97
  ROSA, 97
PERDIN
  J.H., 61
  JNO OTE, 61
  SARAH E., 61
PERDUE
  A.C., 138
  ALICE, 60, 63
  ALLIE L., 98
  ANNIE KATE, 121
  ASA, 121
  ASA C., 38
  AUSCAI, 49
  BALLARD L., 67
  BOOKER T., 45
  C., 14, 111
  CHRISTINA, 66
  CHRISTINA, 10
  DEMARIES W., 43
  DICY A., 51
  ELIZTH, 8
  FANNIE, 98, 99, 127
  FERGUS, 25
  FIERG., 26
  FORGUS, 34, 49, 51
  FRANCES, 37
  G.H., 131
  G.M., 116
  G.W., 98, 127
  GEO, 128
  GEO W., 98, 99
  GEORGE W., 20-C
  HARISON, 63
  HARRISON, 25, 138
  HATIE, 127
  ISAAC, 105
  J.A., 89, 121
  J.F., 131
  J.H., 66, 119, 131
  JAMES, 59, 127
  JAMES A., 14
  JAMES H., 10, 47, 67
  JAMES O., 25
  JAMES RILEY, 138
  JAS H., 59, 96, 128
  JAS T., 128
  JAS., 14
  JNO A., 130
  JNO L., 130
  JOHN, 8, 111, 20-A
  JOSEPHINE V., 45
  JOSIE, 108
  JULIA E., 23
  LAURA, 71
  LAURESY, 20-C
  LOUISA, 116

LUCY H., 45
LUCY LEE, 119
MAC, 60
MACK, 71, 91
MANDA I., 91
MARGARET, 105, 127, 138
MARGARETT, 63
MARTHA A., 35
MARTHA E., 34
MARTHA JANE, 31
MARTHA P., 59
MARY, 8
MARY ANN, 111
McCLELLAN, 99
McHENRY, 67
MINNIE M., 89
MOLLIE, 131
N.A., 89, 121, 130
NANCY, 25(2), 26, 34, 35(3), 51, 60, 67
NANCY B., 35
NANCY C., 96
NANCY F., 37, 67, 71, 91
NANCY J., 10, 23, 45
NANCY JANE, 45(2), 20-C
NANNIE, 49
PATRIA A., 35
PEGGY, 121
POLLY, 20-A
RHODA J., 38
RIAS, 20-A
ROSA M., 105
SAMUEL T.C., 8
SARAH, 43
SARAH E., 10, 47, 59(2), 66, 96, 128, 131
SARAH JANE, 59
SARAH L., 38
SARAH P., 119
SILAS, 10, 23, 25, 35(3), 45(3), 67, 20-C
SILAS W., 47
SUSAN J., 26
THOMAS, 37
TINAH, 31
TOBE, 121
WILLIAM, 43
WM, 10, 31
WM A., 116
ZACH, 8
PERKINS
  ANGELINE, 101
  ANNIE, 134
  E., 20-D
  ELIZA, 61

ELLEN, 134
HENRY, 61
ISOM, 8
J., 134
J.W., 86
JAMES, 20-D
JNO A., 86
JOHN, 101
MARTHA A., 8
MARY, 61, 86, 101
NANCY P., 20-D
POLLY, 8
SARAH C., 128
TERUPA, 90
W.H., 125
PERKS
  FLORA, 123
  HENDERSON, 123

RACHEL, 123
PERMINGTON
  ELLEN, 60
  JNO A., 60
  JOS N., 60
PERRY
  ANGIE, 131
  DAVID P., 41
  E.J., 90
  JAS H., 90
  JNO B., 123
  MAGGIE E., 90
PERRYMAN
  J.J., 94
  R.B., 94
  S.E., 94
PETERS
  A., 12
  ALBINA R.J., 60
  ALICE, 101
  AMCILLE, 12
  ARTHUR L., 76
  C.C., 117, 136(2)
  CHRIS, 3, 9, 18
  CHRISTIAN, 6, 12(2), 51
  CHRISTIAN B., 12
  CHRISTIAN S., 7
  CHRISTINA V., 117
  E.C., 103
  ELBERT F., 114
  ELIJAH C., 53, 60
  ELIZABETH, 16, 31
  FIDELLA, 3
  G.P., 102
  GEO P., 91
  GEORGE W., 7
  HARVEY, 25, 96
  HENRY L., 51
  ISABELLE F., 18
  J.D., 76
  JACOB L., 115, 117
  JAMES, 95
  JAMES C., 9, 44

JAS, 117, 136
JOHN, 18
JOHN C., 7
JOS, 101, 114
JOSEPH, 31, 101
JULIANN, 13
JULINA, 51
LORETTA B., 53
M.A., 114, 117
MARGARET B., 7
MARIA, 91, 102
MARTHA, 83, 96
MARY, 3, 6, 7, 18
MARY A., 136
MARY ANN, 6
MARY E., 9
MARY S., 117
MARY T., 12
MINNIE D., 117
MOLLIE, 76
NANCY, 25
NANCY E., 83
NANCY L., 91
POLLIE, 95
POLLY, 12
POLLY ANN, 96
R.V., 103
REBECCA J., 7
S.J., 133
SARAH, 18, 115
SARAH E., 44
STEPHEN, 31
TAINER, 53
TAMOR, 60, 103
THOMPSON, 18, 25
TULIA, 133
W.J., 102, 133
WILLIE G., 101
WM H., 83
WM K, 95
PETIT
  GEO L., 72
  MATILDA, 72
  WM W., 72
PETRIE
  ELIZABETH, 21, 20-F
  JACOB, 21(2), 20-F(2)
  JAMES WM, 21, 20-F
  JAS, 62
  MARTIN, 62
  MELIE, 62
  NANCY, 21, 20-F
PETRY
  ALBERTINE, 19
  AMOS L., 30
  ANDREW B., 31
  ANN, 8
  ARDELIA, 19
  BALLARD P., 19
  DANIEL C., 36
  ELIZABETH, 37
  ELIZTH, 20-B
  ELZ., 30

ELZTH, 31
HENDERSON, 5
I.B., 22
J., 20-B
JACOB, 30, 31, 37
JACOB L., 30
JAMES, 8, 18
JOHN, 20-B
L.S., 37
LOUISA, 20-B
MARTHA, 20-B
MARTIN, 8
MARY A., 5
NANCY, 18, 20-B
NANCY B., 20-D
PERMELIA, 30
POLLIE, 18
POLLY, 2, 5, 19, 22, 20-D
SARINA, 20-B
SYLVESTER, 20-B
TERRY, 36
THOMSY (SIC), 5
WILLIAM, 2, 22
WM, 2, 5, 19, 20-D
PETTET
  HARRIET M., 85
  JAS H., 85
  W.W., 85
PETTIFORD
  REUBEN, 36
PETTIS
  GEO H., 94
PETTIT
  MARTHA, 39
  MARTHA V., 39
  ROBERT, 39
PETTITT
  ELIZABETH, 66
  GEORGE, 66
  WM L., 66
PETTREY
  A.L., 126
  AMOS L., 74, 106
  B.F., 68
  CAMELIA, 126
  CORNELIA, 74, 106
  ELIZABETH, 68
  ELLA, 126
  ISABELL, 103
  J.L., 103
  JACOB, 68
  JAS W., 89
  JULIA, 89
  LIZZIE, 89
  LOUISA M., 74
  S.E., 106
  SUSAN S., 103
PETTRY
  A.B., 130
  A.T., 120
  ALBERTENA, 47
  ALFRED, 55

ARTHELIA, 93
BERTHA, 121
BETTIE, 120
DRUCILLA, 87
ELIZA, 130
ELIZABETH, 53
JACOB, 53
JAS, 93
JULIA, 93
LILLIE M., 130
LOUISA, 55
N.J., 120
NELIE, 121
POLLY, 53
SARAH A., 47
SHAFFIA, 121
PETTYJOHN
JOHN W., 124
L.M., 124
MARIAH E., 124
PEUCE
J.K., 68, 134
L.N.G., 134
LAURA E., 68
P.J., 134
PENDLETON G., 68

PEYTON
CHARLES A., 87
JOHN C., 87
JULINA, 87
PHETHLACE
DANL H., 86
ELIZABETH, 86
L.H., 86
PHETTYPLACE
DAN'L H., 142
ELIZABETH, 142
L. H., 142
PHILIP
CATHARINE S., 107(2)

MELANCHON
PEERMAN, 107
WM H., 107(2)
PHILIPS
AMANDA P., 42
BALLARD P., 22
CLARA, 42
CLARY, 22
JAMES, 42
JAS., 22
W.J., 27
PHILIPS
ALICE, 92
ALLEN N., 126(2)
ANDREW, 92
C.P., 126
CATHERINE, 72
CLARA, 8, 11, 38
CLARA A., 33
CLARE, 20-C
CLARK, 72

ELIZABETH, 11
FLOYD, 126
HENRY, 92
JAMES, 11, 13(2), 33, 38, 20-C
JARUSHA A., 125
JAS, 8
JNO A., 88
JOHN A., 20-C
M.B., 72
M.I., 126
MARY E., 88
MARY M., 126
NOAH J., 125
P.B., 126
SARAH, 13
SARAH J., 8
SARAH VA, 125
SEREPTA J., 88
TEXAS A., 38
W.O., 28
PHILPS
BALLARD P., 70
C.P., 70
MARY M., 70
W.J., 28
PHIPPS
A.B., 34, 77(3)
A.J., 96
AARON, 32
AARON B., 36, 49
B., 134
BENJ, 75
CHARLOTTE, 32
EMMA, 36
FLOYD, 96
HARVEY, 96, 115
J.R., 120
JNO R., 77
JOHN R., 49
MAGGIE B., 134
MARGARET, 49
MARGARET A., 34

MARGT A., 77
MARY, 120
MARY JANE, 34
NANCY, 96
NANNIE P., 32
NOAH, 96
R.J., 115
REBECCA, 75
ROBIE, 75
SALLIE, 115
SALLY, 96
W.K., 120
PHRITCHARD (SIC)

JOHN H., 88
SARAH J., 88
THOS, 88
PICKERING
D.Y., 66

DAVID, 57
IDA B., 57
MINNIE D., 66
SARAH, 57, 66
PICKETT
R.A., 76
SUSANNAH M., 76
W.W., 76
PIGGOTT
J.R., 67
MINERVA, 67
PERSON, 67
PILLARS
M.C., 88, 92, 112
RICE, 88(2), 112
THOMAS, 92
THOS G., 88, 112
WM W., 92
PILLERS
CHARLES, 140
ELLA, 140
LOTTIE, 140
M.C., 140
ROBT, 140
THOS G., 140
PINE
ALEX, 48, 51, 53
ALEXANDER, 37, 57

ALEXD, 31
ALEXDR, 47
ELIZABETH, 37
EMILY F., 31
JOSIE, 53
LEWIS A., 57
MARTHA M., 47
MARY C., 51
R., 48
REBECA, 53
REBECCA, 31, 37, 47, 51, 57
SARAH L., 48
PINKARD
ELLEN, 61
FANNIE, 81
G.W., 76(3), 77(4), 80
GARLAND, 61
JOHN, 81
TERRIS, 61
THOMAS, 81
PITMAN
CYNTHIA, 58, 82
D., 82
DOUGLAS, 82
JOHN, 1, 58
MALINDA, 58
MICHICAL, 1
NANCY, 1
PETER, 82
PITTMAN
JOSEPH, 44
MICHAEL, 44
REBECCA M., 44

PITZER
BARBARA, 8
CARY A., 8
GEO W., 30
JAS P., 30
JOHN H., 8
MARTHA, 30
WM B., 43
PLASTER
MARY, 127
TJ., 127
WM, 127
PLUNTER
HARRIETT, 70
MARTHA, 70
POE
ANGELINE, 71
B.A., 96
BARTLEY B., 115
CURVIN L., 59
CYNTHIA, 71
CYNTHIA, 58, 61, 109, 123
DAVID L., 123
EMMA J., 61
FANNIE, 86
H., 96(2), 115(2)
H.J., 115
H.P., 90
HENRIETTA, 59
HENRIETTA J., 96
HENRY, 80
HENRY D., 58
HENRY P., 90
HEZEKIAH, 59
J.I., 135(2)
JAMES, 80, 86
JAMES A., 61
JAMES EVEN, 61
JANE, 80
JAS E., 58
JENNY, 116
JEREMIAH, 58, 61
JERERY, 71
JERRY, 109, 123
L.R., 80
LUCINDA, 116
M.E., 70, 118(2)
M.J., 135
MARTHA, 61
MINNIE E., 135
N.E., 80
NANCY E., 58, 90
SARAH M.J., 70
T.E., 80, 118
THOMAS E., 58
THOS E., 70, 80, 90
POFF
CATHARINE, 113
M.S., 113, 133
PETER, 113
POINDEXTER
DICEY, 136

F., 136
FRANK, 136
JOHN D., 7
LOUISA, 7
PATRICK, 136
SARAH J., 7
POLLIE
ALLEN, 84
LILLIE M., 84
POOL
CHAS R., 45
JAS H., 51
M.I., 114
MARY A., 114
MATILDA, 45
MILAM, 114
MOSES, 45
PORTER
ANNIE, 130
BENJAMIN F., 118
JOHN, 130
MARY, 130
STEVEN D., 118
VICTORY, 118
PORTERFIELD
I.F., 60
POSTLETHWAITE
AGNES, 99

G.W., 90
MARION B., 90
OLIVE, 90
POWEL
FRANCES, 20-C
JULIA, 20-C
WM A., 20-C
POWELL
ALICE L., 72
C.C., 111
CATHERINE, 101
CHARLES E., 114
E.L., 111
H.J., 119
HADEN M., 66
JANE, 55
JNO W., 55
JOHN W., 55
JULIA, 23, 66
L.A., 111
M.F., 85, 114
MARY E., 101
Mc H., 119
MOLLIE, 72
MYRTLE, 119
R.J., 114
REBECCA, 85
W.A., 72, 101
W.H., 85
WM, 66
WM A., 23(2), 101
POWERS
BESSIE, 82
C.M., 80
GERTRUDE, 82

MARY, 80
MARY S., 82(2)
W.J., 80
POZVEK
TEREZO, 136
PRANT
ALBERT, 72
CHARLES, 72
PRATER
J.C., 72
J.L., 70(2), 72(2), 76, 79, 86, 87(2), 88(2), 90(2), 91, 92, 93, 95, 96(2)
P.L., 95
W.J., 70
PRATT
ASH, 111
BELL, 137
NELLIE S., 111
OVERTON, 111
PRAUS
CHARLOTTE, 22
PREECH
W.J., 73
WM J., 62
PRESTON
CAROLINE, 45
CHARLES, 110
GEORGE, 45
REECE, 45
PRICE
ALEX, 102
ALLEN J., 85
AMANDA M., 63
AMY, 60
ANNIE, 108
CAMPBELL, 47
CATHERINE, 50
CHARLES, 47
EDITH M., 108
FRANK W., 63
GEO J., 60
GEO W., 60
HENRY, 50, 140
HENRY D., 76
J.W., 72
JACOB L., 63
JNO C., 50
KATHARINE, 76
LEON K., 85
MARY, 47, 72
MELIA C., 76
MORRIS, 72
OCTAVIA, 75
R.H., 75
REBECCA, 102
SERRENA, 138
THOS F., 108
PRICHARD
ELLEN, 118
SALLY, 118

THOS, 118
FRIER
MARY, 90
MORRIS, 90
UNDERWOOD, 90
PRIGMORE
J.F., 124, 125, 126, 127(3), 128(4), 129(3), 130
J.G., 127
PRIM
MARTHA A., 89
MARTHA E., 89
PETER, 89
PRINCE
A.C., 82
ANDREW C., 17
AVIS, 125
B.J., 123
BESSIE A., 123
BURKE, 123
ELENDER, 34
ELLEN, 34
FRANCES, 87
H.E., 99
HENDERSON, 136

HENDERSON F., 24

HIRAM, 37(2)
HIRAM A., 46, 58
HUGH G., 62
JAMES, 17
JAS, 34, 82
JAS A., 3
JOS., 24
JOSEPH, 99
JUDITH, 3
JULIA, 82
JULIET, 17
LOUISA A., 63
LUCY, 5
MARGALINA, 62
MARGALINE, 45, 46, 58

MARGELINE, 63
MARTHA M., 62
MARY, 125, 136
MATILDA C., 33
NARCISSA, 3
O.F., 45
O.T., 62
OSCAR F., 46, 58, 63
OSCAR T., 5
SAML E., 136
SAML H., 62
SARAH J., 45
SUSAN, 24, 99
WM, 5
PRITCHARD
CATHARINE, 95
MAGGIE A., 93

MARY, 15
SALLIE, 93
THOMAS, 15, 95
THOS, 93
THOS., 15
PRIVETT
AMANDA M., 20-A

ISAAC, 89, 20-A
MARY, 12
SARAH, 12, 89, 20-A
WILLIAM, 12
PRIVOTT
ELIZABETH F., 11
PROCTOR
MARY A., 6
PROFIT
BETSY, 50
HIRAM, 50
JOHN G., 50
PROPHET
ANDERSON, 90
JESSIE, 90
REBECCA, 90
PRUITT
HENRY M., 45
I.F., 83(2)
ISABELLA, 45
JANE, 131
JAS M., 45
JOHN, 131
L.G., 124
LUCINDA F., 83
MELISSA E., 83
POLLY, 124
T.M., 124
WILLIAM, 131
PRUNTY
E.J., 28
ELLA, 75
JOHN, 75
JOSEPH, 75
PUCKETT
THOMAS, 29
W.T., 127
PUGH
ADELIA, 87
EMILINE, 97
FLEM, 97
FLERN, 87
MARY E., 87
ROBT S., 97
PULLERMAN
JOHN, 108
NANNIE, 108
PULLIAM
J.C., 39
JOHN C., 16
M.B., 16
T.C., 40, 62, 63, 64, 73, 103
THOMAS C., 16, 38(5)
THOS C., 38

PULMAN
CHAS, 103
PULUM
T.C., 87(2)
PURDUE
COUNCIL, 56
JNO WM, 56
MARY, 56
PURSELL
BESSIE, 127
JAS, 127
LAURA, 127

-Q-

QUESENBERRY

L.M., 119
LOUISA, 119
THOS, 119
QUINN
MICHAEL, 10
PATRICK, 10
WINNIE M., 10

-R-

RADCLIFF
JESSIE, 120
LEVY, 120
RADER
J.S., 100
J.W., 90, 92, 97,
98(2), 118, 119
JENNIE, 119
THOS J., 119
WM E., 119
RADFORD
ANNIE, 92
CHATERINE, 100
JACOB, 100
LOUISE, 58
MARY D., 100
MOSE, 58
RADLIFF
BIN, 133
JENNIE, 133
MARY, 133
RAGLAND
CJ., 132
J.W., 132
L.J., 132
RAINES
WILLIAM H., 117
RAINS
JONATHAN, 29
RAMBURG
NANCY J., 100
RACHEL E., 100
WM J., 100
RAMEY
D.A., 89(2), 90(2),
91, 99, 102(2), 103,

109(4), 111(2), 116,
117, 120, 121(2),
126, 128, 131, 133,
136, 137, 139, 140(3)
EMMA, 103
M.M., 103
OWN (SIC), 103
RAMSEY
D.A., 99, 118, 120(2)
RANDOLPH
DARRIE, 68
RANEY
D.A., 86
RANSOM
CAROLINE, 51
HENRY T., 51
ISADOR O., 89
JOHN, 89
WM H., 51
RANSON
JAMES T., 50
LUCINDA, 50
LUVENA, 50
RASH
MARTHA, 122
RATCLIFF
AMERICA, 59
B.B., 139
ELIZA, 139
ELIZABETH, 59
EVA, 139
JAMES, 59
RATCLIFFE
D.S., 100
DAVID S., 104
DELLA M., 100
ELIZABETH D., 101
JAS S., 101
JNO B., 104
M.V., 100
MAGGIE F., 118
MARY V., 104
NANNIE J., 118
SARAH C., 101
RATLIFEE
ELIZ A., 41
MARY, 41
MILTON, 41
RATLIFF
A.E., 132
AGNES, 9, 11
AMERICAS S., 11
BELLE, 49
ELIZABETH, 87
J.F., 132(2)
JANE, 49, 57
JAS, 87
JAS F., 86
JOHN, 9, 11
M.E., 86
MILTON, 9
RICHARD, 116
SARAH, 87, 116

SINA J., 116
SUSAN, 86
VIRGINIA A., 28
RATLIFFE
AMANDA E., 55
ELIZABETH, 52
EVA E., 138
GEO T., 52
JAMES, 52, 55
MARY L.G., 81
MISSOURI C., 81
REBECCA J., 55
WM D., 81
RAUNEY
D.A., 86
RAUSLY
D.A., 88
RAYLONDS
JOHN, 127
MARIA, 127
MATHEW, 127
RAYMOND
WILLIAM R., 123
READ
A.D., 110
ALFRED, 110
EMMA, 110
REASE
JESSE, 11
NANCY C., 11
ROSANNA, 11
RECK
GEORGE H., 26
JAMES B., 26
SARAH, 26
REDDIX
CAROLINE, 79
HENRY, 79
SARAH, 79
REDIX
HENRY, 96
IDA, 96
VIRGINIA, 96
REDMAN
EDMOND, 36
JOSEPH, 36
SARAH, 36
REED
A.J., 125(2)
ABRAHAM, 64
ADELINE, 64
ALICE, 61
AMANDA M., 111
ANDERSON, 78
BETTIE, 105
C.C., 137
C.E., 115
CALVIN, 38, 105
CATHERINE, 103
CHAS E., 115
CLARKSTON C., 30
DICA, 16
DICY, 16

DICY A., 137
DICY J., 22(2)
DISA, 15, 22
DISA J., 22
E.E., 79
ELIAS, 27(2), 31, 32,
33(2), 34, 35(2), 38,
39, 40(3), 44, 103(2)
ELIJAH, 15, 16(2),
22(3)
ELIUS, 16
ELIZA, 78
ELIZA J.E., 124
ELLEN, 78
FLERN, 72
G.W., 97, 121, 137
GEO W., 104
GEORGE, 89
H.A., 115, 125
H.O., 124
HARRIET, 78
HIRAM, 47, 102, 122,
126
HIRAM A., 6, 48
IDA, 41
J.M., 125
JAMES, 72
JAMES M., 86
JAS, 97
JAS. A., 48
JN C., 109
JNO W., 126(2)
JOHN, 135
JOHN C., 26
JOHN H., 135
JOS, 115
JOSEPH, 1, 6(2), 22,
125
JULIET JANE, 44
KEZIAH, 113
L.C., 102
LEWIS C., 97
LOUISA, 121, 135
M.C., 110, 114, 117
M.W., 115
MALINDA, 1, 6(2), 22
MARINDA C., 104
MARNDA, 137
MARY, 78
MARY J., 103
MARY LANN, 1
MIRAM, 15
MOLLIE J., 47
NANCY, 38
NANCY E., 22
NANNIE J., 69
OSCAR, 78
PAULINA L., 104
PEMBROOK F., 26
R.C., 121
RACHEL, 16
REBECCA A., 49, 86, 97
REBECCA J., 6

RHODA, 69, 86, 97
RHODA ANN, 22
ROBERT F., 35
S.C., 125
SAMUEL W., 137
SAPHRONA, 61, 79
SAPHRONIA, 44
SARAH, 72
SARAH B., 137
SARAH J., 26
SEPHRONA, 41
SOFRANA, 89
SUFFRONIA, 35
SUSAN, 47, 48, 102,
115, 122, 125, 126
T.L., 97
THOMAS, 35, 41, 44,
61, 79
THOMAS, SR., 113
THOS, 89
TRIFANIE, 38
V.C., 78, 124
WASHINGTON, 69

WILLIE E., 78
WM, 64(2)
WM H., 105
REEDE
JOS, 69
MALINDA, 69
WM G., 69
REID
BERTHA J., 106
GEORG L., 81
JAMES, 81
JAS B., 116
JENNIE, 81
LOUISA, 90, 126
M.J., 116
MARY E., 106
MAUD, 90
MINNIE, 126
SAML K., 116
V.E., 82
VIRA E., 82
WM, 126
WM A., 90
WM F., 106
RENFRO
L.M., 33
RENN
IRVIN S., 82
J.S., 82
KATHERINE, 82
REPASS
E.J., 15
F.F., 115
J.I., 15
MARY A., 15
RHODA, 115
SAML, 115
REYNOLDS
ADAM, 93

ANNIE, 126
ARAMINTA, 45, 130
CHARLES, 39
CHAS, 69
DANL, 82
ELIZA, 27
ELIZABETH, 20-E
FRANCIS, 93
JAMES L., 20-E
JOHN, 16
JOHN H., 4
KIZZIAH, 82
M., 4
M.E., 45
MANERVA A., 39
MANNIE, 62
MARY, 126
MILLA, 16
MOLLIE, 130
RICHD, 4
RICHD., 16
S.T., 130
SILAS T., 45, 62
THOS, 126
WASH, 69
WM E., 27(2), 20-E
RHOADS
BETTIE, 93
CHARLES H., 93
G.W., 93
RHODES
E.W., 91
GEO T., 113
HULDAH, 91
ISAAC, 91
RIBBLE
R.W., 130
RICE
A.D., 83
ADDIE S., 33
AMANDA, 100
CHARLES, 100
CHAS H., 98
DAVID, 26, 33, 55, 58,
83(2)
DOCTOR, 100
GEO, 98
ISABELLE A., 83
LULA, 59
MALINDA, 59
MALINDA J., 98
MARY E., 26
NANCY, 33, 55
NANCY A., 26, 58, 83
S.M., 55
WM J., 58
RICH
E.H., 111
RICHARDS
B.W., 107
RHODA, 107
SAML, 115
BRUCE W., 64
RIGGIN
HENRY, 67
JAS H., 64

JENNIE, 67
JNO L., 62
JNO P., 61
MARTHA A., 107
ROBT E., 61
S., 67
S.M., 107
SARAH J., 61
SOPHIA M., 64
RICHARDSON
JANE, 137
JAS R., 137
JNO R., 137
JOHN, 134
KATE, 134
MARY, 58
W.L., 44
RICHIE
RUSHA, 134
RICHMAN
HARRY L., 23
JAMES, 23
LUCINDA, 23
RICHMOND
A.G., 122
ARTHER, 125
ARTHUR, 125
ASTER, 80
B.D., 103
C.L., 103
ELIZABETH, 36, 62,
103(2), 118
HARRISON A., 36
JNO P., 103
JOHN P., 62
M.E., 118
M.J., 125
MALINDA J., 80
MOSEA, 36
MOSES C., 80
PARK, 118, 122
PARKERSON, 103
PARKISON, 62
RIDDLE
JULIA ANN, 33
SOPHIA, 33, 44
SUSAN M., 44
TOBIA, 33
TOBIAS, 44
RIDER
CALLIE J., 91
ELLA, 91
HIRAM, 114
HOWE, 114
S.W., 114
W.H., 91
RIFFE
CINDERILLA, 9
JOEL, 9
SUSAN, 9
RIGGIN
JOSHUA R., 111
RIGGIN, 111

RIGGS
BEN, 127(2)
HARRIETT, 127
J.H., 127
ROBT, 127
RIGHT
ELIZABETH A., 17
RILEY
CATHARINE, 94
EDWARD, 94
ELIZABETH A., 94
FRANCIS, 63
JOHN S., 63(2)
RINEHART
EMILY F., 26
ERASTUS G., 40
JNO, 26
JOHN, 40
JULIET, 26, 40
RIPPEY
JOHN, 63
OLLIE, 63
SANDERS, 108
SARAH, 63, 108
RIPPY
DEALY, 132
JOHN, 75(2)
SARAH, 75
SAUNDERS, 75
RISK
JOSEPH, 10
REBECCA H., 10
SICILY, 10
RISKY
ANNA, 58
JOSEPH, 58
WILLIAM, 58
WM, 58
ROACH
JAS L., 71
M., 13, 14
MARGARETT, 13

MARY, 71
REUB., 13
REUBEN, 13
RUBEN, 14
SARAH E., 13, 14
W.H., 13
WM, 71
ROBBINS
JOHN, 96
NANCY, 91
NANCY P., 96
WALLACE, 91, 96
ROBERSON
CHARLOTT, 108
FRANK, 139
GEORGE, 139
JOHN, 108
JOHN H., 107
JULIA, 107
MARGIE, 108

RESSIE, 107
ROBERTS
FRANK, 111
H.H., 108
J.H., 67, 141
JNO, 115
L.J., 108
MARION T., 108
MARY, 115
MARY J., 115
PEGGY, 111
RANDALL, 74
RISSIE, 74
ROBT, 111
SUSAN, 141
WM, 141
ROBERTSON
A. JULIA, 74
AMANDA, 27
BIAH, 74
BOB, 128
C.D., 137
CATHARINE, 46
CATHERINE, 44
CHAS, 81
CHAS P., 46
CHAS., 44
ELLA, 128
ELMIRA H., 27
GARFIELD, 138
HENRY, 32
JANE, 81
JENNIE, 81
JNO L., 27
KATIE, 137
MARGARET, 138
MARGARET A., 32

MARY A., 104
MARY E., 137
MOLLIE B., 104
PATSIE, 65
REED, 65
RHODA C., 46
RICHD W., 28
ROBERT, 81
RUTHA, 81
SALLIE, 128
W.H., 104, 138
WILLIE, 65
WM C., 44
ROBINET
NANCY J., 55
ROBINETT
CHRISTERINA, 20
DICA, 20
HIRAM, 20
J.P., 73
JOHN, 73
MARY, 73
ROBINS
HENRIETTA, 63
LUCINDA R.R., 63

WM H., 63
ROBINSON
ARDELIA, 10
B., 119
BERRY, 77
BOB, 117
CHARLES D., 37
CHARLES H., 38
CHAS, 105
CHAS., 37
CORNELIUS, 119
ELLEN, 12
FRANK, 56
G.L., 93(2)
G.W., 80
H., 26(2), 20-D
HAR., 10
HARISON, 20-F
HARRET, 25
HARRIET, 21, 33, 50,
51, 20-F
HARRIETT, 7
HARRISON, 7, 20,
21(2), 25, 29(3),
33(2), 34(2), 50, 51,
20-C, 20-E, 20-F
HART., 10
HENRY, 38, 73, 100,
108
HENRY, JR., 100
JACOB P., 33
JAMES A., 119
JOHN, 12, 108, 129
JOHN H., 25
JOHN T., 35
JOSEPHUS, 7
JULIA, 129, 130
KATHARINE, 37
KYLE, 115
L.W., 51
LEANNA, 94
LETTA, 100
LOUISA, 33, 35
M.E., 16
MAHALA, 115
MANERVA, 117
MARGARET, 93
MARY E., 21, 20-F
NARCISSUS, 105
NELSON, 115
OCTAVIA H., 50
PHOEBE, 38, 73
R.G., 94
RACHEL, 108
RHODA C., 33
ROBT, 30
RUSELL, 130
SARAH, 117
SIBERT, 77
SILY, 77
THOMAS, 35, 73
THOS, 33
VIRGINIA, 94

W.H., 93
WILLIAM H., 12
WM, 129, 130
ROBISON
E., 113
HENRY, 113
LEWIS C., 113
ROCKEY
CORDELIA, 113
GUY M., 113
H.T., 113
RODE
ARTHUR W., 65
BRIDGET, 65
JOHN C., 65
RODGERS
MARY A., 118
Z.T., 71
RODMAN
F.L., 129
ROGERS
ISAAC E., 33
JEFFERSON, 47
JOHN, 33
LOT, 23
MARY ANN, 47
PHEBA, 23
SARAH, 33
WM P., 23
Z.T., 75
ZACH TAYLOR, 47

ROGGERS
AMANDA, 112
ROGUS
JAS LAFAYETEE, 62

WM P., 62
ROLAND
FANNIE E., 67
J.M.B., 133(2)
JAS R., 103
M.B., 67, 133
M.E., 67, 133
MARY, 72
MARY E., 103
MILES B., 72, 103
NANCY C., 72
ROLES
ALEX., 32
ALEXANDER, 121

ANDREW, 48
ELIZABETH, 48
ELZTH, 32
HENRY W., 48
JAMES, 125, 136
JAS, 125
JOHN, 18
JOHN P., 129
M., 18
M.J., 125
MARY J., 136

MINNIE, 93
MORDICA, 20
NANCY, 20
OSCAR, 136
SUSAN, 18, 20
WILLIAM C., 32
ROLLINS
JONATHAN, 35
JONATHAN A., 35
NANCY, 35
ROLLISON
ELIZTH, 13
JOS., 13
PETER, 13
ROLLYSON
BETTIE, 21, 20-F
E., 14, 16
ELIZABETH, 2, 16
ELIZTH, 16, 20-B
GABELLA, 21, 20-F
J., 14
JOS, 20-B
JOS., 21, 20-F
JOSEPH, 2, 16(2)
MARY, 2
NANCY A., 20-B
RACHEL, 14
ROLYSON
SUSAN, 16
ROMAN
BETSY, 91
CHRIS COL, 91
JAMES, 91
ROMANO
JOHN M., 58
ROMANS
J.M., 63, 64, 65(2),
90
JOHN M., 61, 64
ROPPY
OLLIE, 107
RORER
DERENZIE, 48
LUCINDA R., 81
MARY, 48
MARY A., 81
MARY J., 78
WM R., 48, 81
RORRER
B.L., 86
D.C., 103
EDDIE B., 111
GENORA A., 94
MARY A., 103
NANCY, 111
NANCY J., 94
P.T., 94
PETER, 111
W.R., 103
ROSE
ADALINE, 118
ALICE, 85
ALICE BEE, 82

AMANUEL, 79
BARLIN, 103
BARTON, 82
BASTON, 28
BRYAN, 74
BRYAN F., 68
BRYANT, 26, 115
COLUMBUS, 58
CORA, 130
D.A., 130
ELI B., 62
H.B., 1(2), 3(6), 4,
5(3), 6
H.R., 5
HENRY B., 4, 6
ISAH, 115
JAMES M., 74
KIZZIE R., 79
LAWSON, 75
LEVI, 68
LILLY D., 103
MARY, 75, 115
NANCY, 26
PETER, 118
RANZY, 26
REBECCA J., 82, 103
ROSAMAND, 68, 74

SAML, 79
WESLEY, 75
WM, 130
ROSENFILD
C.H., 118
JOHN, 118
MARGARET, 118
ROSER
MARY C., 24
ROSS
AMANDA J., 25
ANNA, 110
BURLEY, 57
C.D., 52
CORA A., 43
DAVIDSON C., 18, 43
ELIZABETH, 102
EMELINE, 43
G., 18
GRIFFITH, 25(2)
GRIFITH, 135
HARRIET, 25(2)
HARRIET E., 18
HARRIETT, 135
J.B., 102(2), 117
JOANAH, 20
JOHN B., 52
JOHNSON B., 135
JOHNSTON B., 30
LEE A., 52
NANCY, 57
NANNIE B., 110
S. ROSS, 117
SARAH, 83
SARAH E., 25

THERRESA P., 117
WM, 110
WM F., 57
ROTHWELL
J.A., 124
MARY F., 124
THOS B., 124
ROUR
ISOM H., 20
JANE, 20
NANCY J., 20
ROUSLY
D.A., 88
ROWDEN
DANL, 96
FLOYD, 96
WINNIE, 96
ROWEN
ARRAMAH E., 59
NANCY J., 59
P.F., 59
ROWLAND
CHARLES, 75
E., 4
ELIZABETH, 1
ELIZTH, 17
ELZ. F., 29
GEO R., 50
J.J., 50, 116
JACKSON, 29, 42
JAMES, 1, 4
JAMES A., 42
JAS., 17
JONATHAN J., 49
JULIA A., 49
K.C., 116
KINZIE, 75, 79
LOUISA J., 1
MARY E., 4
NANCY, 75, 79
ROBT L., 79
SALLY, 116
SARAH, 29, 42, 49, 50
SUSAN, 14
ROY
JOHN, 112
MARTHA, 112
WM, 112
ROYAL
JOHN, 128
JOHN, 12
W.F., 128
ROYESTER
MARY, 82
SPOTTS, 82
THOS, 82
ROYSTER
CHARLES, 84
MARINDA, 84
RUBLE
CALVIN, 140
HENRY C., 140
R.N., 140
STATE IRA, 140

RUCKER
AMBROS, 72
MARTHA, 72
W.H., 72
RUDD
ARELIUS, 74
CAROLINE, 74
JOHN W., 74
RUDICIL
AMERICA, 132
RUDISILL
ALVERTY, 101
JAMES, 59
LOUZENA, 101
RUFFIN
J.J., 131
RUHLE
CATHERINE, 8
SAMUEL, 8
SARAH E., 8
RULOFF
ANNIE, 58
FRANCIS H., 58
HERMAN, 58
RUMBURG
CHAS C., 93, 113
E.N., 57
EMMA, 48
EMMA I., 75
MARIA J., 103
NANCY, 48
NANCY J., 57, 75, 77,
93, 103, 113
W.J., 113, 118(2)
WM H., 77
WM J., 48, 57, 75, 77,
93(2), 103
RUNION
ANNA E., 51
ELIZABETH, 51
RUNNELS
ANNA, 1
JOHN, 1
SARAH, 113
RUNYON
ALLA, 53
BETSY, 53
ELIZABETH, 44(2)
JAMES, 53
JAS F., 44
JOHN, 12
MARBARY E., 44
MARY JANE, 44
NANCY, 12
STEPHEN, 12
RUSSBURG
WILLIAM J., 20
RUSSEL
B.O., 49
BENJ O., 49
HARRIET O., 40
JANE, 40, 49
NOAH R., 49

RUSSELL
BENJ., 17, 22
BENJAMIN, 15
DAVID, 10
HENRY, 33
HESTER M., 17
MARY, 10, 15
PRISCILLA, 16
ROBERT, 15
ROBT, 10
SARAH, 17
SARAH A., 22
SUSAN, 33
VICTORIA CYNTHIA, 22

WILLIAM H., 33
RUTLEDGE
ADELINE, 45
SAML, 45
TAZEWELL C., 45
RUTTER
JOHN A., 49
REBECCA J., 49
RYAN
CHARLES, 121
DAVID M., 68
JOHN F., 68, 74
JOSEPH, 48
MATTIE L., 74
N.J., 48
REBECCA, 68, 121
REBECCA S., 74
W.G., 48
RYE
HIRAM, 101
SARAH, 101

-S-

SACKETT
CHESTER, 134
JUSTIN, 134
ROENA, 134
SADDLER
CHLOE, 39
FANNY E., 26
GEORGE D., 39
HENRY, 26, 30, 32, 39,
43
JACOB, 32
JAMES, 43
MARY, 32
VICTORIA, 30
SADLER
ALEXANDER, 88
ANN, 53
ARAMINTA, 24, 53, 68,
92
EDWARD, 127(2)
ELI, 130
HENRY, 24, 53, 68, 88,
92(2), 127
LUCY, 130

MARY E., 24
MINTA, 127
MINTIE, 88
NANCY, 130
WILEY W., 68
SAFERTY
FRANCES, 46
SAGE
WM J., 63
ST. CLAIR
ALICE, 96, 99
BETSEY, 33
CORNELIUS B., 38
D.P., 99
DAVID P., 96, 20-A
EDWARD, 38
ELIZ., 20-D
ISAAC, 8, 20-A
JANE, 8, 20-A
JAS K.P., 33
JNO D., 99
JOHN B., 8
MARY J., 20-D
MINNIE, 96
WILLIAM, 20-D
WM, 33
SALE
ESLIE, 72
SARAH, 72
WM H., 72
SALES
ANN, 71
ANNIE, 71
HARRY, 71
SALYER
TYRE T., 20-A
SAMMONS
ALFRED, 80
J.A., 80
ZAIDA, 80
SAMPLES
EMELINE, 67
HARVEY, 67
SAML W., 67
SAMUELS
A.J., 116
B.R., 116
M.E., 116
SANDERS
ABSOLUM, 84
ADELINE, 84
ALICE, 125
AMY, 108
BETTIE, 116
CALVIN, 108
CLARA, 128
D.C., 116
D.N., 133(2)
EMILY, 125
FANNIE, 130
FANNY, 125
FELIX, 125
FRANCES, 132

GUSTAVUS, 108
H., 116
HARRIET, 125
HAYES, 125
J.I.C., 128
JAMES, 108, 121
JAS I.C., 128
JEMIMA, 108
JENNIE, 130
JOHN, 130
LITTIE, 116
LIZZIE, 132
MARGARET, 108
MILTON, 132
RILEY, 96, 121
SALLIE, 125
SARAH, 96
THERRISSA, 130
THOS J., 96
W.B., 84(2)
WM, 128, 130
SANDRIDGE
AUSTN, 70
E.A., 70
SARAH J., 70
SANFARD
GEORGE, 60
LIZZIE, 60
SALLIE, 60
SANFORD
VAN, 6
W.D., 66
SARVER
BALLARD P., 12
C.J., 120
ELIZABETH, 1
ELIZTH, 16
EMILY, 16
FRANCIS, 12, 81
H., 69
JAMES, 1, 16, 38
JAMES M., 57, 72
JERRY, 81
JOHN, 12, 81
MALINDA, 11
MARY A., 1, 38, 69, 85, 120
MATILDA, 57
MATILDA A., 72
NOGIE, 85
SARAH E., 72
SUSAN E., 82
W.A., 57, 120
WM A., 38, 69
SATTERFIELD
CAROLINE, 88
GEO, 88(2)
SAUDERS
DAVID U., 23
JULIUS, 23
LYDIA, 23
SAUL
JAMES, 110

SAUNDERS
A.J., 90
ANN, 90
ANN M., 1
BETTIE A., 119
CALVIN, 81
CHARITY, 74
CHARLES, 103
CHAS, 103
CHRIS, 109
CLARA, 137
D.N., 44, 45, 50, 52(2), 53, 54(2), 55, 56(3), 57(2), 58(5), 59(3), 61(3), 65(3), 66(4), 67, 69(2), 70(3), 71(2), 72(3), 73, 74, 75(2), 76, 79, 80, 81, 83, 85(3), 87, 88, 89, 90(2), 92, 94, 95, 97(2), 100, 101, 103, 106, 107, 109(2), 110, 117(2), 119, 120, 123(3), 124(2), 128, 132(3), 133, 135, 139(2), 140(2)
D.P., 60
DAVID, 1
DAVID N., 44, 45, 47, 50, 78
DRUCILLA, 105
EMILY, 78
EMMA, 109
GEORGE, 50
GORDON, 105
GORDON L., 47
HARRIET L., 58
HENRY, 50, 85, 91
J.E., 105
JACOB R., 50
JANE, 58
JANIE, 67
JEMIMA, 81
JENNIE, 105
JOSEPH, 91
JULIAS, 13
JULIUS, 6, 23, 31(2), 47
LEROY, 74
LIDIA, 23
LILLIE, 31(2)
LIONA, 50
LIZZIE, 89
LUCY, 91
LYDIA, 6, 13, 47
LYDIA A., 31
M.B., 60
M.H., 90
MARIA, 103
MARTHA, 85
MARY, 89
MAY ELLEN, 137

MICAJAH, 105
MICAJAH B., 13
MORA, 85
N., 119
NANCY, 105
NANCY J., 78
NOAH, 103
RHODA, 78
ROBERT, 6
ROBERT W., 1
S., 67
SAMUEL, 81
SARAH C., 60
STEPHEN, 31
THEODOSIA, 78
THOS., 50
VIOLET, 74
WILLIAM, 109
WM, 89, 137
WM J., 23
SAWER
SAML G., 53
SAYERS
ELIZABETH, 111
JAS A., 111
ROBT LEE, 111
SAYLOR
JOHN H., 80
KATHERINE E., 80
W.A., 80
SCALES
A.P., 60
ANN, 59
GEO, 56
JAS, 4
JNO, 59
JOHN, 59, 60
NATHAN, 60
SARAH, 4
SCARBORO
ED, 83
SCHWANN
CORA M., 83
JOS, 83
MATILDA, 83
SCON
ELIZABETH, 40
MARTHA C., 40
WILLIAM, 40
SCOTT
ALBERT, 34
ALFRED, 112
AMANDA, 88, 106, 137
AMANDA A., 70
AMELIA, 87
ANDREW, 87
ANN, 112
BELINDA, 7
BROWN, 41, 60, 67
BULEY ESTHER, 131

C.D., 116
CHINA, 3, 7(2)

CLARINDA B., 7
CROCKIET, 55
CROCKETT, 47, 84, 120
E.N., 41
ELIZ., 21, 20-F
ELIZA, 116
ELIZABETH, 39, 63, 70
ELIZABETH M., 18
ELIZTH, 2
EMALINE V., 6
FRANCIS, 2
GEO P., 30, 137
GEO W., 60, 67
J.O., 131
JACOB, 87
JAMES, 128
JAMES O., 39
JAMES W., 25
JANE, 21, 20-F
JANE E., 55
JAS WM., 52
JNO, 3
JOHN, 7(2), 105
JOHN D., 33, 66
JOHN S., 47
JOSEPH, 52
L., 116
LETTIE, 72
LOUISA, 105
MARGARET A., 25, 28

MARIAH, 128
MARTHA M., 2
MARY, 112
MARY B., 118
MARY E., 30, 66, 85, 137
MOLLIE P., 89
N., 18
NANCY, 2, 6, 18, 52, 89, 105, 118, 20-C
NANCY C., 20-C
P.E., 85
PEARIS, 106
PICKNEY, 89
PRESTON, 106
RHODA JANE, 28
ROBT, 56, 72
ROBT C., 3
SAML, 2, 6, 13(2), 56, 118
SAML., 14(2), 18, 25
SAMUEL, 1(2), 2, 3, 5, 8(5), 10, 12(2), 14(3), 15(2), 17(5), 18(3), 20, 24, 26, 28, 72, 20-B, 20-C
SARAH, 34, 47
SARAH A., 55
SARAH E., 63
SUSAN, 41, 60, 67
SUSAN S., 20-D
W.R., 30

WILLIAM, 34
WILLIAM B., 2
WM, 33, 39, 85, 89, 128
WM R., 63, 66, 70, 84
SCULES
ANN B., 135
SARAH, 135
SEABOLT
COSBY, 132
EMMA, 132
JAMES, 132
SEAL
CATHERINE, 56
JAMES W., 56
LOUISA, 78
SAML E., 56
SEALS
CHARLES, 112
HENRY, 112
LILLY, 112
VIRGINIA C., 18
SEANLAND
EUGENE B., 109
NATHAN, 109
SALLIE, 109
SELLARS
ANN, 129
JANE, 129
MADISON, 129
SMITH, 129
SELLERS
ELIZA J., 33
GEORGE WILLIAM, 33

WM, 33
SENTY
J.E.T., 82
SERGE
SAM, 80
SERUTH
ELIZ., 45
GEORGE, 45
KITTIE, 45
SETTLE
F.A., 76
J.B., 76
JNO, 128
M.A., 128
M.F., 76
W.W., 128
WILEY W., 128
SEUCE
J.E.T., 58
SALLIE F., 51
SAML H., 51
SARAH F., 51
SEVELL
PRISCILLA, 78
SHACK
MARY M., 20-A
SHADE
RHODA, 50
SAML A., 50

SHAFER
CHARLEY, 115
CHARLEY T., 115
JULIA, 94
MARY, 93
MISSEY, 115
PETER, 93
ZORA, 93
SHAFFER
FRANK, 86
KATE, 86
SIDNEY, 86
SHANKLIN
ELLEN, 138
J.R., 138
JOHN, 138
NANCY, 20-B
POLLY, 20-B
SHANNEN
JOHN, 18
M., 18
SHANNON
AMANDA, 25
CHAS W., 55
CHRIS, 11
JAMES M., 11
JNO, 2
JOHN, 7(2), 19
JOHN L., 7
JOHN R., 7
LAURA N., 81
M., 19
MARGARET, 2, 7
MARGARET J., 62
MARGARET T., 2
MARY, 14
MARY A., 79
MARY ANN, 62
MARY E., 20
RACHEL W., 30
REBECCA, 7
ROBERT S., 19
SAM, 81
SAML, 62, 79, 81
SAML., 55
SAMUEL, 20
SARAH, 20(2), 25, 30
SARAH A., 32, 55
SARAH E., 32
SUSAN, 11
T.H., 124
W.A., 79
WILLIAM, 14
WM, 14, 20(2), 25, 30, 32
SHARP
B.F., 99
CATHARINE, 66
EMILY, 93
JUS, 99
REBECCA, 66
SARAH, 99

STEPHEN, 66
W.E., 93
WM ED, 93
SHAWVER
ALICE, 110
EDWARD J., 110
J.M., 110
SHEANARD
LUTIE, 97
SARAH, 97
SHEARER
NAOMIA, MRS., 88
SHEELER
T.C., 89
SHEFFEY
J.E., 110
JANE, 110
THOMAS, 110
SHEGGS
JESSE, 56
MARY, 56
OLIVER J., 56
SHELDON
ALVIRA, 82
E.D., 82
E.T., 82
JEFFERSON, 56
THOS S., 82
SHELTIN
SYNCH P., 28
SHELTON
A.H., 105
AGNES L., 59
ALANZO P., 61
ALONZO P., 96
C.J., 84(2)
CREED, 98
CREED F., 98
EASTER, 55
ELIZA, 105
ELIZABETH, 98
ESTHER, 31, 33, 20-A
EUNICE, 61
F.H., 105
FRED, 84, 20-A
FREDERICK, 31, 33, 55
FREDERICK H., 31
G.H., 105
H., 20-B
JOHN H., 28
KATE L., 116
LILLILAM, 105
LONDON, 59
M.E., 109
MARY, 85
MARY E., 33
MARY J., 96
MATILDA E., 55
N.J., 116
P.T., 85
R.L., 113
REBECCA, 84, 85
ROBERT L., 20-B

ROBT, 116
ROSE M., 109
S.V., 105
SARAH V., 97
W.M., 127
WILLIAM A., 20-A
WM, 61, 96
SHELVY
LEWIS, 104
LUCY, 104
MARTHA, 104
SHENALL
CALVIN, 105
ORRIE JANE, 105
WM H., 105(2)
SHEPARD
CAROLINE, 64
GEORGE, 64
JAMES, 105
JULINA, 105
MATTIE, 105
W., 64
WM., 64
SHEPHARD
MARIA L-V., 28
SHEPHERD
EVIE J., 115
MABLE J., 114
MARTHA, 115
MARY, 82
PETER, 82, 114
SALLIE, 82
WM, 115
SHEPHERDSON
JAMES F., 92
SADIE E., 92
WILLIE, 92
SHEPPARD
JULIA, 119
MARY C., 119
SHERMAN
ADDIE, 66
MARTHA, 66
SHERWOOD
ELIZE, 55
GEORGE, 55(2)
JNO W., 95
M.A., 95
SHIELDS
A.M., 109, 133
ALICE V., 109
DOUGLASS, 117
ELIZABETH, 117
HAMILTON, 44
J.H., 117
JOHN A., 44
M.A., 133
MARTHA DORA, 133

MARY A., 109
PRISCILLA, 10
SHILLING

CYNTHIA, 89
SHINALL
WM H., 98
SHIP
GAINES, 80
LEE J., 80
MARGARET, 80
SHIPMAN
EDMOND, 97, 136
LUCY, 136
MARTHA, 97
SHIRBY
BLANCH R., 126
FRANK M., 98
KATHERINA A., 95
L.M., 95
LUCY M., 98
ROBERT M., 89
W.H., 95
WM H., 98
SHOAS
CATHERINE, 7
SHOCKEY
GEO W., 126
JNO, 126
NANCY, 126
SHORT
ELIZA C., 57
ELIZABETH, 57
G.W., 110
GEO, 132
GEORGE, 132
HENRY, 132
JAMES, 57
NANNIE, 110, 132
WM L., 110
SHORTER
AVARILLA, 111
BEATRICE A., 33
BETTIE, 85
CELESTIA G., 40
CLEOPATRIA, 22
ELIZ., 36
ELIZABETH, 52, 60, 111
FABIAS N., 36
GEO, 33
GEO W., 15
GEORGE W., 8
ILA., 135
J.O., 102
JNO, 37
JOHN W., 52
LEONIDAS A., 46
LILLY F., 137
LOUISA V., 78
M.C., 20-E
MABEL CLARE, 102

MARTHA A., 22
MARTHA A.C., 46
MARTHA C., 36, 40, 43
MARY, 78, 137

MARY A., 97
MARY E., 36
MAUD, 60
NANCY, 8, 11, 97
P., 15
PERMELIA, 15
REBECCA A., 102
SARAH A., 37
SARAH J., 33
SOUTHERN, 135
T.C., 100
VICTORIA E., 37
W.A., 36, 20-E
W.T., 78(2), 137
WINFIDA T., 29
WM A., 20-E
WM T., 97
WOODSON, 85(2)
WOODSON A., 11, 22, 36, 40, 46, 52, 60, 111
SHOTH
D.W., 110
L.B., 110
MILDRED R., 110
SHOWALTER
JENNIE, 63
SHOWARLER
ANNIE, 63
JENNIE, 63
SHELTON, 63
SHOWVEN
ALEX, 11
WILLIAM A., 11
SHRADER
A.H., 138
A.J., 119
ALEX, 103
AMY, 47
CHLOE, 31, 34, 39, 44, 54
CLOE, 28
GLORIA, 70
CONRAD, 28, 82, 120
CYNTHIA D., 81
CYNTHIA J., 49, 54, 81, 89
CYNTHIA JANE, 35

DAVID, 28, 31, 34, 36(2), 39, 44, 54, 70
E.F., 132
ELECTRA, 31
ELLEN, 74
ELVIRA, 80, 119
GRANVILLE, 67
GREENVILL, 131
H.F., 49
H.H., 89(2)
HARRISON, 119
HENRY, 35, 47, 52
HENRY H., 138
I.N., 138

J. ROBT, 103
J.V., 139
JACKSON, 80
JANE, 74
JERUSHA B., 126
JOHN, 28, 31, 47, 50, 61
JULIA A., 52
KATHERINE, 103
LOUISA, 67
LUCINDA, 50
LYDIA, 39
MACK H., 70
MARGARET M., 61

MARTHA, 54
MARY ANN, 34
MARY E., 82
MILLE F., 44
NANCY, 28, 31, 47, 50, 61
R.H., 139
RACHEL, 80
RALPH, 28
REBECCA, 67, 131
REBECCA J., 31
RHODA, 36
ROBERT, 49, 74, 81
ROBT, 35, 54, 89, 140
ROBT T., 54
RUSSEL, 132
S.J., 140
SALLIE, 139
SALLIE O., 140
SARAH, 47, 52
SARAH A., 47, 132
THOMAS, 131
VIRGINIA, 82, 120
XANTIPPER, 120
SHREWBURY
H., 20-D
J., 20-D
JOHN S., 20-D
RED, 20-C
SHREWSBURY
A.J., 93
A.L., 134
ALLEN P., 16
ALLIE, 105
ALMEDA F., 54
AMY MAY, 117
AMY Z., 129
ARAMINTA E., 56
ARMINTA E., 99
ARTHELIA C., 117
B.W., 53
BILL, 137
C.O., 126
CHAR, 10
CHARLOTTE, 1, 5, 10, 26, 45
CHAS A., 46

CLARA C., 27
CLOA D., 137
CYNTHIA, 99
DANIEL, 5
DAVID P., 123(2)
DORA A., 123
E.B., 117(2)
ELECTRA V., 54
ELI, 25
ELI B., 108
ELIZABETH, 1, 32, 39, 46, 53, 62, 99, 105, 139, 140
ELIZABETH E., 20-D
ELIZABETH R., 40, 56
ELIZTH, 3, 6, 8, 9, 10, 14, 16, 26, 27
ELLEN, 103, 125
EMMA L., 136
F.J., 51
F.K.J., 34
FANNIE E., 140
GEO, 125
GEO W., 58
GEO WM, 103
GEO., 33
GEORGE, 134
GEORGE W., 30
H.G.C., 62
HENRY, 11, 23(2), 24, 38, 51, 66, 20-D
HUGH J., 45
I.K., 135
IKE, 135
IOWA, 93, 123(2), 129
IRVIN H., 39
IVIN H., 29
J., 137
J.B., 99
J.M., 117, 118
J.W., 85, 139
JAMES, 27, 54, 81
JAMES B., 29
JAMES W., 78
JANE, 11, 23(2), 24, 49, 66, 20-D
JANETTE A.D., 108
JAS, 26, 38
JAS H., 58
JAS P., 59
JAS W., 85, 89, 135
JAS., 14
JERE, 6, 9
JERE., 16
JNO, 3, 25
JNO S., 84
JNO., 25
JNO. H., 49
JOHN, 8, 10, 32, 39, 41, 46, 87, 133, 140, 20-E
JOHN A., 45
JOHN B., 105

JOHN S., 102
JOHN W., 34
JOHNATHAN, 139
JOSIE M., 133
JULIA, 85, 89, 135
JULIA A., 34, 78
JULIN A., 76
L., 134
L.C., 114, 136
L.E., 20-E
LEWIS C., 26
LOTTIE E., 123
LOUISA, 54
LOUISA J., 126
LUCY A., 10
LUEWINA, 81
LUKOUS H., 81
M., 108
M.J., 50, 81, 20-E
MALINA, 139
MALINDA, 58
MARCUS L., 6
MARGALINE, 46
MARGARET, 110
MARGERY, 37
MARGHI., 51, 59
MARGHI A., 65
MARGY, 35
MARTHA, 25
MARTHA M., 25(2), 34

MARTIN V., 9
MARY, 23
MARY E., 78
MARY J., 65
MARY M., 11
MARY M.S.E.E., 35
MASSIE M., 105
MATILDA, 108
MELISSA, 117
MILLEY, 24
MINNIE, 125
NANCY, 5, 114, 136
OLIVE, 137
OSCAR J., 10
P.T., 26, 93, 129
PHIL, 10, 23
PHIL M., 62
PHILIP, 1, 37, 45, 59, 65
PHILLIP, 5, 10(2), 26, 110
RACHAEL, 38
REBECCA, 45
REESE B., 32
RHODA, 45, 66
RIERDELL, 37
RILEY, 49
ROBT A., 40
ROSA A., 110
ROSA E., 114
S.A., 103
S.K., 137

S.R.J., 81
SAM, 139
SAML, 3, 53, 56, 62
SAMUEL, 40
SARAH, 23, 38, 50
SARAH A., 62
SARAH A J., 54
SARAH F., 20, 34
SUSAN, 20-B
T.F., 117
TELA, 117
THOMAS, 35
THOMAS M., 8
THORNTON, 123(2)
THOS, 46
THOS S., 84
URSULA M., 23(2)
V.R., 89
VANTY ANN, 41
VASHTI, 20
VASTIE, 45
VASTY, 37(2)
VICTORIA, 84, 102, 133
VICTORIA E., 46
VIRGINIA, 39(2), 20-B
W.A., 76
W.H., 139(2)
W.R., 126, 137
W.W., 102
WILLIAM, 54
WILLIAM A., 105
WILLIAM G., 105
WILLIAM H., 99
WILLIAM R., 28
WM, 20, 37, 41, 45, 50, 62, 81, 124
WM A., 76
WM BASTY, 33
WM R., 99
SHUCK
ANDREW, 69
MALINDA, 40
MARGARET, 40
MARY J., 69
WM, 69
SHUB
AWANDA, 39
JOSEPH B., 39
SARAH, 39
SHUFFELBARGER

MATILDA, 2
SHUFFLEBARGER

A.J., 125
DAVID, 27
ELIZABETH, 27
J.D., 125
J.H., 131
JANE, 137
JOHN, 2
LEWIS, 137
LOUIS, 125

M., 131
MARIS, 2
MOLLIE, 137
SUSAN, 131
WM E., 27
SHUFFLEBURGER

LEWIS, 12
SHUGART
B.A., 127
SHULER
T.C., 98(4), 101, 102, 103(2), 104(2), 106, 107, 127
THOS C., 93, 94(2), 95(2), 96(4), 105
SHULL
EADY, 110
SHUMATE
A., 15
A.T., 117
ALLIE, 99, 134
ANDERSON, 9, 55, 62, 88
ARTHUR T., 117
B.P., 115
BALLARD, 15
BALLARD PRESTON, 115
ELIZABETH, 115, 117
ELIZATH, 68
H.M., 134
H.N., 99
H.P., 134
HENRY H., 43
J.T., 88
JOHN T., 29, 55
L.A., 103
MARGARET, 35
MARY, 37
MARY ANN, 99
MARY V., 68
MATTHEW, 99
MINNIE A., 99
PARKERSON, 129
PARKESON, 9
PARKINSON, 3(2)
R., 3, 129
R.A., 68, 115, 117
RHODA, 3, 9
RUFUS, 54
RUFUS A., 9, 43
RUFUS E., 62
S., 15
S.M., 129
SALLIE, 55
SARAH, 9, 88
SARAH E., 9, 43, 54
SUSAN A., 54
WM H., 3
SHUPE
ELIZABETH, 57
JOHN, 57

THOS R., 57
SHUTT
ANNIE B., 139
BETSY, 42
DAVID, 42, 70, 20-A
ELIZABETH, 70
ELIZTH, 20-A
ELLEN, 45, 88, 92, 135, 136, 139
FLORENCE M., 138

FRENCH, 136
H.F., 88, 92, 135, 139
HENDERSON F., 45

J.D., 138
J.W., 92, 135
JEFFERSON D., 52
JOHN, 136
LELA JANE, 88
M.C., 138
MARY E.M.B., 20-A
MARY F., 45
MINNIE, 135
MOLLIE, 136
SALLIE E., 70
SAMUEL, 28
VIRGINIA, 42
SIAS
FRANCES, 4
JAS, 4
JESSE, 4
SIER
DAVID, 27
SARAH, 27
SOLOMAN, 27
SIKIER
MARY, 136
SIMMONS
AMANDA J., 23
EPHRAIM, 23
M.S., 110, 111, 112
SARAH J., 23
WM L., 78
SIMMS
KIZZIE, 68
MILLE, 68
SIMPKINS
ELIAS, 33, 83
ELIZABETH, 33
ELIZABTH, 83
MARGARET S., 33
T.W.H., 83
SIMPSON
ALONZO B., 107
BOB, 120
CHARLOTTE, 120
ELIZA, 107
ENZER, 104
F.L., 122
F.T., 104
FANNIE, 122
FRANIE J., 81

GEO, 92
GEO W., 103
GEORGE, 92
HANNAH, 127
J.B., 58, 63, 68(2), 100, 101, 115, 129, 131(3), 132, 133, 134, 135, 137(2), 138(6)
JACOB C., 64
JAMES, 32, 107
JOHN W., 81
LAVERNIA, 131
LUCY, 64
MARTHA, 88
MARY A., 103
SHACK, 64
SIDNEY, 120
SUSAN, 92
T.T., 88
V.R., 104, 122
VINCENT R., 81
W.A., 103
SIMS
ALMEDA, 100
SINCLAIR
BETTY, 100
BLUFORD, 100
E.G.F., 97
GEO A., 97
GEO B., 97
MARY E., 100
SINCOCK
EDWIN, 93
JOHN, 93
MARY, 93
SINGLETON
ADAM, 20
JACOB T., 20
WINNIE, 20
SINK
DANIEL, 41, 43
EMILY, 41
EMILY A., 43
HARRIETT L., 57
JULIA A., 43
MORRIS, 57
NANNIE J., 41
SUSAN, 57
THOMAS D., 28
SINKFORD
ADAM, 133
H., 133
LAURA, 133
SIPHERS
ANDREW, 51
ELIZABETH, 51
WM, 51
SIRE
D., 126
DAVID, 126
LOUEMMA J., 126
Z., 126

SISCLE
JAMES, 78
MARGRET E., 78
PRUCILIA, 78
SISK
ELIZA, 88, 130
GIDEON, 88, 99
JAMES A., 88
LOGAN SCOTT, 130

SAMUEL, 130
SIZEMORE
COSBY, 111
JANE, 13(2)
JNO, 13
SKAGGS
ANDREW A., 100
FRANK E., 100
MARTHA, 100
SKEENES
ADA M., 133
AMANDA, 140(2)
CHARLIE W., 140
ELVIRA, 133
J.W., 135
JOHN T., 140(2)
JOSEPH, 135
L.H., 133
LEWIS, 135
NANCY, 135
ROBERT L., 140
SKEENS
AMANDA, 112
AMANDA H., 63
EMMA S., 112
FANNIE, 17
FLORA B., 60
H., 17
H.A., 73
HENRY, 113
HENRY A., 97
JNO T., 112
JOHN F., 63
JOHN T., 25
JOS, 129
JOSEPH, 25, 60
JOSIAH, 60
LOCKEY ISABEL, 97

M.E., 73
MARY, 113
MARY E., 73, 97
NANCY, 60(2), 129
NANCY A., 25
NANNIE L., 60
SARAH F., 113
TINEY E., 63
SKELTON
ELIZABETH, 46
JOHN M., 46
MILTON, 46
SKEONG
FRANCIS, 25

MARGARET J., 25
THOS., 25
SLADE
KITTIE, 117
OSCAR, 117
SARAH, 117
SLAUGHTER
EDWARD, 64
ELLA, 115
JAS M., 92
JENNIE, 64
MARTHA, 92
NANCY R., 64
WM, 92
SLIGH
ALFRED F., 118
ISAAC, 118
JULIA, 118
SLOAN
ANNIE, 111
C.J., 115
DAVID, 22
DAVID A., 115
DEBORAH, 22
EMILY L., 115
JACK, 22
JOEL, 111
K., 111
SLOANE
DAVID, 31
JOEL, 31
SLONE
DAVID A., 62
MALONA, 62
MARTHA M., 62
SLUSHER
A.M., 86
LAFAYETTE, 86
LOUISA, 86
SLUSS
CLARINDA, 44
JAMES, 44
M.A., 128
M.F., 128
MARCUS A., 44
MARY E., 128
SMELCHER
MARY, 61
MOLLIE, 61
SMITH
A., 18
A.J., 133
ABS., 18
ADA, 73, 78, 118
ADAM, 137
AGNES, 5, 16
AGNESS, 50
ALBERT B., 24
ALICE, 83, 93, 127
ANGIE P., 124
ANN, 121, 140
ANN M., 131
ANNA, 78

ANNIE, 70(2), 137
ANNIE B., 64
ARREDELLA, 82
ASBURY, 65
AUSTIN, 50
BALLARD P., 64
BECKEY, 28
BECKY A., 28
BENJ, 10
BENJ., 8
BENJAMIN, 8, 11
BILL, 118
C.P., 106
C.W., 67, 91
CAROLINE, 60, 106
CATH J., 64
CATHERINE, 52, 64
CHARLES L., 121
CHAS, 73
CHAS P., 140
CLARKIE H., 77
CLOUY, 65
CORA A., 118
CORA L., 81
COSBY L., 96
D.H., 93, 127, 133
D.L., 88
DAN, 111
DANIEL, 92
DANIEL L., 55, 87(2)
DANIEL M., 111
DANL L., 64
DARCAS, 15
DAVID, 55
DAVID H., 30
DELAY, 113
DERINZIE B., 72
DINAH, 91
DORA ANNIE, 116
DORA B., 133
E.S., 129
E.V., 109
EDMONIA C., 55
ELI, 66, 134
ELIZ. S., 8
ELIZA, 29
ELIZA A., 55
ELIZA J., 67
ELIZABETH, 8, 11
ELIZTH, 10, 15
ELIZTH J., 24
ELLA, 70
ELLEN B., 87
EMMA, 52, 68, 70, 74, 114, 134
ERI, 68, 77
ESTHER, 74
EU, 74
F.A., 65
FANNIE, 92
FANNIE B., 55, 87(2), 88
FERD, 126

FLORA, 78
FRANK, 91, 140
G.H., 87, 109
G.L., 79
G.P., 96, 121, 135
GEO A., 118
GEO P., 86, 97, 134
GEORGE, 27(2), 75, 91
GEORGE W., 126
GUSTUS, 66
H.A., 109
H.B., 71, 79
H.C., 82, 100, 126
H.J., 137
H.M., 127(2)
H.W., 63
HAMPTON, 66
HARRIET, 66
HENRY, 78
HENRY A., 114
HENRY C., 116
HENRY M., 60
HIRAM M., 60
HUSSIE, 106
IDA J., 11
ISAAC A., 11, 73, 83
J.B., 92
J.F., 123
J.J., 80
J.L., 118
J.M., 115, 135
J.P., 127
J.W., 88
JAMES, 70, 121
JAMES A., 4
JANE, 27
JAS R., 140
JEFF, 65
JENNIE, 106(2), 140
JNO, 126
JNO J., 91
JNO M., 126
JNO N., 25
JNO W., 10
JOHN, 79, 106, 120
JOHN B., 8, 55
JOHN D., 15
JOHN E., 104
JOHN H., 53, 70
JOHN J., 71
JOHN M., 25, 37, 87
JOHN T., 77
JOHN W., 9, 10, 65, 73
JOS, 120
JOS L., 84
JOS W., 118
JOSHUA, 129
JULIA, 74
JULIA ANN, 65
K.H., 109
KEMMIE, 127
L., 124
L.A., 1, 135

L.B., 115
LAURA A., 127
LAURA E., 87
LELIA, 139(2)
LEONARD H., 87
LEWIS, 137
LILLIE, 120
LIZZIE, 137
LOUISA, 115
LOUISA A., 87
LUCY A., 106
LUTHER, 140(2)
M.A., 118
M.B., 27
M.I., 135
M.M., 109, 114
MABRIDA, 89
MALINDA, 111
MARGARET A., 91

MARIA, 66
MARTHA, 68, 84
MARTHA I., 86, 96, 97, 121, 134
MARTHA J., 10
MARTHA W., 87
MARY, 80, 81, 118
MARY A., 88
MARY E., 9, 82, 116
MARY F., 8
MARY J., 53
MARY W., 5
MOLLIE, 92
MOLLIE E., 87
MONK, 139
MOSES, 50
OLIVIA J., 65
P.A., 135
P.R.A., 131, 132, 133(2)
PAT J., 97
PAUL, 104
PAUL C., 92
R.A., 80
R.L., 134
RACHEL, 71, 126
REBECCA, 9, 10(2)
RHODA J., 18, 89
RICH, 64
RICHARD, 74(2)
RICHD L., 64
ROBERT, 81, 84
ROBT B., 65
ROBT L., 86
ROMA A., 109
S. PERRY, 124
S.T., 88
SALLIE, 27
SALLIE B., 16
SAML B., 16
SAML P., 5, 53
SARAH, 4, 37, 73, 80, 83, 92

SARAH A., 88
SARAH C., 25
SARAH E., 64
SARAH G., 55
SARAH L., 70
SARAH W., 10
SHIRLE K., 93
SUSAN, 113, 129(2)
SYLVIA, 74
T.T., 4
THEODORE, 22(5), 24, 25(2), 26(2), 67, 20-D, 20-E
THOMAS, 134, 137
THOS, 70, 126, 134
THOS., 27
VEARIS, 15
VERONIA, 104
VICTORIA, 63, 75, 82(2), 117
VICTORIE, 72
VIRGINIA J., 63
W.B., 89
W.J., 131
W.W., 100
WASH, 78
WILEY, 75
WILLIAM, 117
WILLIAM H., 117
WILLIE, 121
WILLIE A., 135
WILSON W., 37
WM, 15, 73, 78, 80, 106(2), 118
WM A., 64
WM B., 15
WM FLETCHER, 112

WM H., 72
WM L., 92
WM M., 83
SMITHICANN
ELIZA. A., 51
JNO K., 51
ROBERT M., 51
SMOOT
A.B., 72
AMANDA, 72
WASH. COWAN, 72

SMYTH
PETER, 81
SARAH, 81
SYLVIA, 81
SNAPP
CATHARINE, 3
CATHERINE, 8
DANIEL M., 41
JNO, 3
JNO W., 41
JNO W.O., 3
JOHN, 8
MATILDA J., 41

SAMUEL M., 8
SNEAD
A.J., 106
ALICE, 93
BARNETT J., 39
E., 4
EMMAZELLA, 20
ENEMARELLA, 43
ESTHER, 15
JAMES, 4
JAMES M., 11
JOHN, 39
JOHN B., 11
JOHN G., 15
JOHN T., 9
JUDITH E., 9
LULA, 106
MARTHA, 93
MARY, 47
MARY A., 47
MARY C., 106
NANCY JANE, 43
SAML, 4
SAMUEL, 15
SARAH, 9
SARAH B., 11
WILEY, 93
SNEED
ANN, 92
D.J., 122
CHAS, 132
CHAS L., 132
CHAS W., 40
E.A., 85
J.H., 109
JAMES, 41, 109
JAS, 63
JEREMIAH B., 49
JNO, 27
JNO T., 27
JOHN, 49, 85(2), 92, 131
JOHN T., 12, 40
KATE, 132
MARTHA J., 135
MARY, 41
MARY J., 49
MARY L., 85
MARY V., 63, 109
MATILDA, 131
R.E., 122
ROXANNE, 122
S.J., 92
SALLY, 27
SAMUEL J., 12
SARAH, 12, 40
THOS G., 63
WILLIAM, 41
SNEEDS
C.W., 134
JOCIE M., 134

M.A., 134
SNIDER
ALMETA, 85
BEN. ISAAC, 99
D., 110, 117
D.A., 110
DIMORTHA, 46
DIMOTHA, 70
DIMOTHEUS, 82
DIMOTHY, 99
EASOM, 10
ELI W., 70
ESOM, 60, 85, 90, 99, 109
FOUNTAIN, 60
G.W., 82
GEO WAS, 82
H.P., 90
JOHN, 7, 10, 12(2)
JOHN O., 7
L.A., 108
LETHA A., 109
NANCY J., 99
O.M., 108
RHODA, 85, 90, 99
RHODA A., 60
RHODA ANN, 109

ROBT L., 117
SARAH, 12
SUSAN, 7, 10
W.R., 110, 117
WM H., 46
WM R., 82, 99
WM RILEY, 46, 70
SNIDOW
HARVEY, 78
JNO MILTON, 52
JOHN, 9(2)
M.V., 78
MAHALA, 9
MARY, 9
MINNIE, 78
NANCY B., 52
SUSAN, 9(2)
SUSAN E., 28
WM B., 52
SNODGRASS
A.A., 136
ANNIE, 27
ARAMINTA, 90
E., 27
E.N., 20-B
ESTILL, 31, 34, 42, 97
GEO, 135
JAS P., 136
JESSE F., 56
JOHN, 90
JOHN H., 20-B
KATHARINE, 34
LOTTIE, 135
MARY, 136
MARY E., 135

OLLIE, 90
S.A., 20-B
SARAH, 27, 34
SARAH M., 42
SARAH V., 31
SNOW
ANTHONY, 138
HENRY, 47
LUCINDA, 138
WILLIAM OSCAR, 138

SNYDER
BALLARD, 20-E
DIMOTHA, 56
ESOM, 56
J., 20-E
J.H., 124
MALINDA J., 56
MARCUS, 131
R.A., 124
RHODA A., 56
S., 20-E
SUSAN D., 124
WM R., 56
WM RILEY, 56
Z.H., 124
SOLESBURY
ELIZTH, 14, 26
JNO, 26
NANCY, 23
PHIL., 14
R.B., 26
RHODA E., 23
WM, 14
SOLSBERY
LOUISA, 2
PHEBE, 2
SONGER
A.J., 41
CHARLOTTE, 41
CHRISTIAN, 6
EVA A., 6
JNO, 3
MARTHA, 3
MARY ANN, 6
NANCY M., 3
V.H., 41
SONSENIE
JOHN, 82
ROSA, 82
VISSENSO, 82
SOUTH
CELIA, 131
SOUTHERN
ASA, 63
BETTY, 101
ELIZA JANE, 96
EMMA G., 63
FANNIE M., 47
HENRY A., 106
JOHN ANDREW, 104

MAHALA E., 117

MINTA, 96
NANCY J., 72
RACHAEL, 72
RACHEL, 47, 104, 106, 111
ROSIE, 101
SARAH, 63
WM, 47, 72, 104, 106
SOWERS
C.B., 54
DOCIA A.M., 54
MAJOR, 54
SPADE
ELIZTH F., 36
REBECCA J., 52
RHODA, 36, 52, 95
SAML, 95
SAML A., 36, 52
SPANGLER
ALICE A., 76
CONRAD, 54
D.W., 76, 78
DANL W., 54, 56
ELI, 97
ELMEITIE L., 97
FLOYD, 129
G.W., 63
JANE, 11
JNO L., 78
JOHN, 11
JOHN O., 11
L.P., 129
LAURA, 140
LOUISA C., 56
MYRTLE, 99
RHODA, 97
ROBT L., 78
S.C., 76, 78
SARAH C., 54, 56
SUSAN E., 63
VALARIA I., 78
WILLIE, 99
SPARKS
ANNIE, 104
GEO, 104
JNO, 104
SPENCER
ABE, 135
C.H., 72, 90(2), 117
CHAS H., 136
DELSIE, 135
EDWARD A., 135
FRANCIS, 90
J.M., 53, 54(2), 56, 58
J.S., 55
JULIAN, 72
LUCY, 135(2)
MARY, 135
RHODA, 72, 117
RHODY, 90
SALLIE, 117
WARWICK, 135

SPENSE
MARY, 18
S., 18
SPICER
FANNIE E., 120
FLORA E., 77
HARVEY, 56
JOSEPHINE, 69
MARTHA, 104
MARTHA M., 57, 67, 77
MARY ANN, 67
NANCY, 56, 69, 112
NANCY L., 57
SALLIE, 104
SARAH JANE, 125
URA, 56
WILLIAM, 57, 104
WM, 67, 77, 120
SPINNER
FANNIE, 136
SONNIE, 136
SPRADLIN
CARDWELL M.D., 20-D

JNO, 13
JOHN, 20-D
L., 20-D
LOUISA, 8, 13
N.E., 13
SPRINKLE
JAS, 57
SPURLOCK
BURWELL, 16
STACK
ELIZABETH, 12
FIELDING, 12
WM, 12
STAFFMAN
JOHN L., 52
MINIAM S., 52
STAFFORD
DAVID, 55
EDWARD, 36
HENRIETTA, 55
JOSEPH A., 36
JULIA F., 82
L.P.G., 36
LOUISA, 94, 114
LOUISA A., 33, 104
LOUISA H., 36, 82
LUCILLA, 36
MARY, 94
RUFUS A., 114
SARAH E., 33
VIRGIE R.V.S., 104
WM, 114
WM H., 55
WM M., 33, 36, 82, 94, 104
STAHL
ALFRED, 93(3)
CAHRLIE, 120
CHAS, 120

ELIAS, 93(2), 106, 120
HATTIE, 106
LIDDIE ANN, 93
SUSAN, 106, 120
SUSANNAH, 93(2)
STAMBRICK
A.L., 64
ANDREW L., 64
REBECCA, 64
STAMP
GEO W., 128
J.B., 119
JNO BENJ, 128
MARTHA A., 128
NORA H., 119
SALLY, 119
STAMPER
CATHERINE, 75
J.D., 75
M.D., 75
STANLEY
BETTIE, 72
STANLY
ELIZABETH, 13
JNO, 13
MARTHA D., 13
STAR
HATTIE, 136
JAMES, 136
MARY, 136
STARKWELL
F.T., 56
MARY ANN, 56
NANCY M., 56
STARMAN
JOSEPH, 61
JOSEPH E., 61
MACK, 61
NANCY, 61
PATRICK, 61
PRISCILLA, 61
REBECCA, 61
SARAH J., 61
WM, 61
STATON
L.R., 137
LEWIS R., 137
O.R., 137
W.M., 137
STAUFFER
C.E., 68
CHAS S., 68
MARY E., 68
STEARN
A.L.J., 57
AURY, 47
PASTER S., 47
I.L., 57
HEVIG., 47
RHODA, 57
STEDEDCIDE
CHARLES, 85

STEEL
RHODA, 67
SARAH, 8
TERRY, 20
W.S., 67
WILLIAM F., 8
WM R., 67
STEELE
AUGUSTUS L., 48
ESTHER G., 122
FRANCIS MARION, 81

G.W., 126
GEO W., 126
JAMES, 70
JOHN, 126
JULIA, 126
LAURA F., 63
M.L., 112
MARY, 70
OLIVIA M., 121
REBECCA M.F., 55
RHODA, 48, 55, 63, 81, 112, 121, 122
SEXTON, 70
W.F., 112, 121, 122
WM F., 48, 55, 63, 81
STEELS
FLORA M., 105
RHODA, 105
W.F., 105
WM F., 105
STEPHENS
ALICE BELLE, 107
I.M., 107
MARIA, 49
NANCY J., 104
S.B., 107
SOL D., 104
WM, 104
STEPHENSON
CALVIN E., 13
N., 13
STESSEL
PETER, 100
STEVENS
ANNA, 89
CAROLINE, 123(2)
CHAS C., 59
HARVY, 123
J.C., 117
JOHN, 59, 64, 89
JULIA V., 115
MATILDA, 64
SARAH, 89
SARAH A., 59, 64
STEWARD
CYNTHIA, 65
GRANVILLE, 65
LEWIS, 65
STEWART
A.M., 110
ANN, 130

CATHERINE, 20-D
FRANK, 130, 132
GEO, 2
GEO., 26
GEORGE, 9, 10(3)
GILES A., 127
HARRY H., 100
J.W., 114
JAMES, 100
JAS M., 65
JNO H., 83
JULIA A., 127
LAWSON, 138
LAWSON E.P., 83
LULAR, 130
LURA F., 114
MARTHA, 83
SARAH, 100
SYLVESTER, 20-D
W.R., 127(2)
WM, 20-D
STILLS
LETTIE, 56
STILLWELL
OLIVE, 126
VICTORIA, 126
STINDELL
JACK, 85
LYTHIA, 85
STINSON
C., 18
CELESTINE, 69
CHARLES, 25, 38, 45
CHAS, 33, 52(2), 69
E., 18
ELIZABETH, 25, 38, 45, 52, 112
ELZTH, 33
EUGENIA L., 83
J.W., 119
JACOB, 52
JAS. W., 33
JOSEPHINE, 38
L., 83
L.I., 112
LARKIN L., 25
LORAINE, 18
MARY B., 112
MARY S., 52
ORA, 119
PAMELA, 52
RHODA, 83
VIRGINIA, 45
STINSTON
CHAS, 27
ELIZABETH, 27
MINVERVA J., 27
STOBBS
JACOB, 57
MADISON, 57
NANCY, 57
STOCK
ELEM, 46

HESTER, 46
SALLY, 46
STOCKTON
JOHN, 73
PATSY, 73
STOKE
JOSIAH, 53
MARGARET, 53
R.J., 53
STOKES
DEXTER, 74
PARTHENA, 74
SCOTLAND, 74
STONE
CLEMENTINE, 96
DASHA, 113
EWARD (SIC), 113
FLEMING E., 96
O.L., 79(2)
J.F., 129(2), 130,
    131, 133(2)
JNO F., 129
JNO T., 129
JOHN F., 118, 121(2),
    126(4), 127, 128(3),
    130
JULIA, 97
MALINDA, 79
OLIVER, 97
STEPHEN, 96
WM, 113
STOPLES
G.W., 65
J.W., 65
STOVALL
A.G., 51, 71, 20-B
ALBERT, 22
ALBERT G., 29
ANN, 79, 81, 91, 103,
    131
ARCHAD F., 31
C.W., 91
EFFIE A., 79
J.T., 50
JAS B., 131
L.V., 79, 81
LEVI, 91, 131
LEVI V., 103, 20-B
LUCINDA A., 31
MARY, 31
N.K., 20-B
NANCY, 29
NANCY K., 51, 71
NANNIE R., 103
NORAH E., 81
PED., 99
R.L., 71
ROBT, 98
S.M.K., 22
SARAH, 99
SARAH E.A., 22
SILAS, 99
SUSAN B., 29

WM A., 51
STOWERS
A., 19
DISA, 20
ELIZTH, 19
GRAYSON, 128
HENRY W., 128
HIEK, 17
JAMES M., 17
JNO L., 20
JOHN W., 19
LUCINDA, 128
MOLLIE, 17
ROWLAND F., 20
SARAH, 17
STOWERTON
GEO W., 52
MARTHA ANN, 52

REUBEN, 52
STRABY
ARAMINTA, 21, 20-F
ELIZTH, 21, 20-F
JOHN, 21, 20-F
STRADER
BETTIE, 76
J.D., 92
RACHEL, 76
SIDNEY, 76
STRALEY
D.A., 79, 139
D.C., 76, 78
DORIAS C., 20-D
ELIZ., 20-D
ELIZABETH, 1
ELIZTH, 2, 11
H.W., 79, 139
HARRIETT A., 2
HARRISON W., 1
J.L., 78
JOHN, 1, 2, 11, 20-D
KATIE A., 79
M.E., 126
S.A.E., 76, 78
SKYE V., 139
VALERA J., 11
VIRGINIA, 94
W.A., 76
W.H., 126
STRANGER
ELIZABETH, 69
JESSIE, 69
THOS, 69
STREET
HOUSTON, 62
JAS P., 62, 68
MARY E., 62, 68
SARAH, 68
STREWBUCHER

FRED H., 57
HENRIETTA, 57
STARMOND, 57

STRICKLER
C.B., 136(2)
D.S., 136
NANNIE E., 136
STRING
DANIEL, 40
RHODA, 40
SARAH C., 40
STROCK
JNO F., 96
S.A., 96
SAMI. A., 96
SARAH, 96
STRONG
ABBIE C., 37
ABBY C., 5
BAILEY, 88
D., 69(2), 71
DANIEL, 37, 88
DAVID, 5
ELIZTH, 37
H., 117
HORACE, 115, 123, 124
HORAN, 5
MARY E., 88
STROUD
NANCY M., 6
THOS, 6
WILLIAM D., 6
STROUSE
JOHN, 82
JOSEPH, 82
MARY, 82
STRUM
C.H., 79
STUARD
FRANCIS, 139
LIZZIE, 139
STUART
GEO., 26
GEORGE, 31(2)
J. PRICE, 129
PETTER S., 2
R.H., 46, 48
S.K., 129
W.R., 129
STUAT
CHARLES H., 101
KITT, 101
VILET, 101
STUDIVANT
ELIZABETH V., 132
NANCY S., 132
PLEASANT M., 132
STUMP
CLORIE E., 109
GEORGE W., 4
J.B., 109
JOHN, 76
MARTHA J., 76
MARY, 20
POLLY, 4
ROBT L., 76

S.M., 109
WM, 4, 20
STUPALSKI
MARY, 130
STURGIS
WILLIAM, 16
STUTES
EMILY, 121
KATIE, 121
R.F., 121
STWART (SIC)
MARY, 89
MELVINA, 89
SPAREL, 89
SUBLETT
A.W., 85(2)
ANNIE L., 79
DOCK, 79
E.J., 46
FRANCIS, 85
GILES C., 121
JAMES W., 98
MATHEW, 85
R.F., 121, 130
REBECCA, 79, 98
REBECCA F., 46
RIBBLE W., 130
W.R., 46, 98
WM, 121, 130
SUGART
E.A., 129
SUITER
FRANKLIN T., 103
MARGARET, 103
PETER, 103
SARAH J., 110
THOS W., 110
WM, 110
SUITZ
BELLE, 64
J.E.T., 138
S.H., 64
S.T., 64
SULLENDER
AGNES, 20
CHRISTENIA, 20(2)
SULLIVAN
ROBERT, 109
SUMMERS
G.W., 89
SUMMONS
WM L., 94
SURFACE
A., 14
AMARILIAH, 54
AMARILLA, 69
AUGUSTUS, 59, 81
CATHERINE A., 17
CYNTHA, 123
EMIRILLA, 83
G.W., 54, 83
GEO W., 15, 17(2), 69
GEORGE W., 14

JAMES H., 64
JANE, 123
JANE A., 59
JAS D., 59
JAS F., 83(2)
JOHN H., 64
JULIA, 64
LEE, 81
LEE A.S., 15
LEE, 52
LEFERIDGE, 47
LEEFWICH A., 43
LEUDIENA J., 17
M.H., 69
MARTN, 59
MARY A., 14
MARY E., 59
ROBT, 102
S.D., 75
SALLIE, 54
SARAH, 15, 17(2), 43,
    47, 52
SUSAN, 47
TOBITHA, 59
VICTORIA, 52
ZORAH E., 75
SUTER
JAND, 75
JOSHUA, 75
LISHA C., 75
SUTHERLAND
R.K., 97, 100(2)
SUTHERS
A.M., 126
T.F., 103, 106(2),
    111, 121
T.T., 105
SUTPHIN
BAZEWELL., 20-A
CHRIS, 20-A
CHRISTOPHER, 18

M., 20-A
WM, 18
SUTTON
ALX M., 102
JOHN W., 127
KATIE A., 82
LOUISE, 102
MARY, 102
MARY S., 67
P.S., 34, 42(2), 43,
    44(3), 45(3), 46,
    49(2), 50(6), 51(2),
    68(3), 69, 70(3),
    71(2), 72, 75, 85(3),
    91, 102
PHIL A., 34
PHIL E., 35
PHIL S., 34(3), 42(2),
    44, 46(3), 47, 48,
    49(2), 50, 52(2), 53,
    55, 56, 58, 59,

61(2), 62(2), 64(2),
    65, 66(2), 67, 73(2),
    74(2), 75, 76, 77(3),
    78(2), 79(2), 80,
    81(2), 82(4), 83(2),
    84(3), 85, 86(2),
    87(3), 88(3), 89, 90,
    92(2), 93, 94(2),
    95(2), 97, 98, 99,
    100
PHILIP S., 67
PHILIP, 127
PHILIP S., 39
S.I., 102
VICTORIA, 67, 82, 102
VICTORY, 127
SWADER
ALEX, 106
ALEXANDER, 17, 49, 96

ALICE, 106
ARNES, 113
CASSIE, 106
CATHERINE, 49, 96, 133

CHLOE, 20-B
CLARINDA, 40
CLORA, 63
COSBY, 56
CYNTHA, 42
CYNTHA J., 42
DAVID, 7, 63, 20-B
DELILA, 63
ELVIRA, 130
GREENVILLE, 17
H., 133
HENRY, 40, 59, 113,
    133
HUGH, 22
JACKSON, 130
JAMES, 42
JNO, 22
JOHN, 17, 56, 59
JULIA, 17, 20-B
JULIET, 42
KATIE, 113
MALINDA, 65
MEDA, 130
MILLEY, 4
NANCY, 17, 22, 37, 56
PEARLY, 133
RASTUS B., 96
RHODA, 7, 20-B
ROBERT, 4, 42
ROMULUS, 20-B
RUSSELL, 28
SARAH, 40, 59
VIRGINIA, 49
WM, 17, 42, 20-B
SWANGGIN
ARMINTA, 69
JAMES, 69
JULET, 69

SWEENEY
A.D., 139
E.F., 123
FRANK, 101
J., 43(2)
JAMES, 41, 42, 44,
    73(2), 81, 84(2), 89
JAS, 43, 57, 68, 70,
    71(2), 79, 83(2), 89,
    93
JAS E.V., 101
JAS., 38, 43, 71
JNO N., 121(2)
JOHN D., 90
MARTIN, 3, 6
MARTIN W., 3
N., 18
NANCY, 3, 6
NANCY E., 6
STELLA, 139
WILLIAM J., 18
WM, 18
WM G., 139
WM J., 123
SWEENY
ELLIOTT A., 140
J.T., 140(2)
MARTHA A., 140
SWIM
AMANDA J., 92
M.F., 78, 99
MANDY, 78
MANDY J., 99
MELVIN, 99
ROBECCA, 92
RUTH J., 78
SWIMMEY
MARTIN, 1
NANCEY, 1
PATSEY, 1
SWIMNEY
ANN E., 27
SWINDLER
HATTIE, 54
JOHN, 54
SWINNEY
ARCH, 17
J.T., 62
LUCINDA, 17
MALINDA, 17
SYERS
LAWSON W., 115
SYNAN
BETTIE C., 121
J.A., 121
JAS, 121
SYOVENYI
AUGUST, 130
EDWARD, 130
ELIZABETH, 130
SYRES
DAVID, 115
ZYLPHIA, 115

-T-

TABB
L.C., 77
TABOR
A.M., 96(2)
ABRAHAM, 30
ABRAM, 37
ALBERT, 59(2), 70
ALVIS, 141
AMANDA, 131
AMANDA L., 56
ANDREW, 43
ANDREW J., 42
ARCH, 100
BARKLEY, 43
C.C., 118
C.E., 67
C.L., 133
CHAS L., 42
CHAS T., 134
CYNTHA H., 134
CYRUS, 30
DELLA J., 89
DORA L., 50
ELGIN C., 112
ELIZA, 11, 17
ELLEN, 37
EMMA, 133
EZRA, 60
F.J., 70, 141
G.W., 118
GEO, 94, 128
GEO O., 48, 72
GEO R., 48
GEO W., 131
GEO. C., 34
GEO. O., 48
GEORGE, 56
GEORGE O., 11
GEORGE W., 35
H.H., 111
HENDERSON, 122

HENRY H., 50, 67
HENRYH., 96
J.H., 20-B
J.T., 120, 135(2),
    137, 139
JAMES, 24
JAMES G., 117
JAMES T., 48, 108,
    109, 110, 111(2)
JAS, 93(2)
JAS. H., 34
JEFFERSON, 35
JENNIE, 105
JESSE, 11
JOHN, 131
JOHN C., 38
JULINA, 42, 43
L., 85

LANEMA, 122
LEVI, 85
LONIE C., 72
LOUCINDA, 85
LUCINDA, 93
LUCINDA O., 38
LUCY, 77
M.A., 133
M.M., 111
MARTHA, 113, 128
MARTHA A., 131
MARY, 89
MARY A., 110
MARY J., 113
MARY M., 50, 67, 96
MATILDA, 59, 70
MILLIE, 39, 95
MOSES, 70, 91
NANCY, 24, 30, 34, 37
NANNIE, 85
NELL, 20-B
O.B., 131
OLIVA, 56
OLIVE, 48(2), 94
OLLIE, 72
PERMILLIA, 70
REBECCA, 122
RICHARD, 39, 70, 95
ROB, 107
ROSA ANN, 131
ROSA E., 128
RUSSEL, 113
S.G., 85, 108
S.H., 85, 111
SAM A., 94
SAML, 105
SAMUEL G., 24
SARAH, 35, 60, 77, 112, 141
SARAH LUVENIA, 134

STELLAR S., 108
STEPHEN, 93
STEPHEN H., 38
THOMAS G., 20-B
VIRGINIA, 85, 108
WILLIAM J., 77
WM, 112
WM J., 39, 60, 95
TABOT
SARAH, 43
VIOLA T., 43
WILLIAM J., 43
TACKET
ALEX, 120
CAROLINE, 120
ELLEN J., 65
NANCY V., 65
W.A., 120
W.W., 65
WM A., 65
TACKETT
ELLEN, 102

ELLEN G., 98
MARY MATILDA, 98

R.A., 102, 128
W.A., 98, 102
TAGUE
ANDREW, 93
J.A., 93
MOLLIE, 93
TALBERT
G.W., 106
LYDIA C., 106(2)
MARY M., 106
TALIAFERRO
FRANCES, 116
P.N., 116
SARAH J.E., 116
TALLICHET
CHARLOTTE, 63
FRANCOIS, 63
LOUIS N., 63
TALO
GEO, 65
HENRY, 65
MARY, 65
TAMPLIN
ELIZABETH, 63
LUCY K., 63
WM, 63
TANNER
A., 128
A.L., 69
B.E., 74
CHARLOTTE A., 35

FREDERICK, 31, 35
G.H., 69
JAS, 107
JOHN M., 69
LAURA, 128
M., 128
M.A., 69
MANERVA E., 31
MARTHA C., 69
MARY J., 74
MARY JANE, 29
MIUONSI (SIC), 35
NATHAN, 69
ZULA, 31
TARPLER
BEN, 112
HARRIET, 112
LEWIS, 112
TARR
HENRIETTA, 116
TATE
C., 110
VIRA, 110
WM C., 110
TATURN
COLEMAN, 110
HANNAH, 110
JOHN, 110

TAYLER
BLLA, 92
IDA J., 66
JAS W., 53
JOHN, 53
MARY L., 53
W.T., 66
TAYLOR
A.J., 105
AERENA, 136
ALBERTA, 132
ALEY, 31
ALICE, 48
ALMIRA, 66
AND J., 63
ANN, 84
ARAMINTA, 20
ARAMINTA JANE, 77

ARDELIA, 41
B., 93
BERTHA M., 114
BETTIE, 105
C.B., 139
C.C., 90, 92, 133(2)
C.W., 94, 114
CORA, 67
CREED, 136
CYNTHIA, 27
CYNTHIA A., 105
EDEN VIRGRELEE, 118

EDNA A., 63
ELEANOR, 14
ELIAS, 54
ELLA C., 94
ELMIRA, 87, 94
EMILY, 136
EMMA, 69
ETTA, 132
G.W., 100, 109, 133
GEO A., 87, 94
GEO W., 118, 132
GEORGE, 14
GEORGE A., 66
GEORGE W., 31
HARRIETT, 109
HENRY, 69
IDA F., 90
JABA, 20-D
JACKSON, 133
JACOB, 90
JAMES, 14, 76, 93, 109
JAMES C., 24
JANE, 133
JAS, 123
JESSE, 31
JNO, 13, 80, 112
JNO N., 56
JOHN, 8(2), 15, 18, 31, 48, 50, 95, 105, 112, 118(3), 124
JOHN R., 56

JOHN T., 118
JOS., 54
JOSEPH A., 24
JULIA, 76
KATE M., 133
LAURA, 73
LELIA A., 50
LEVI, 77
LIDA, 76
LUCINDA, 97
M., 93
M.E., 118, 124
MARINDA, 95
MARTHA, 13, 27, 47, 90, 94, 100(2), 124(2)
MARTHA E., 50
MARTHA J., 56
MARY, 8, 13, 15(2), 18, 20, 22, 30, 31, 43, 49, 52, 54, 90, 92, 97, 105, 112, 123(2), 133
MARY A., 15
MARY ANNIE, 73
MARY B., 24
MARY F., 48, 50, 118
MARY J., 29, 49
MATILDA, 67, 77, 118
MAZIE B., 100
MIMA, 69
NANCY, 30, 99
NANCY E., 50
NANNIE, 76, 100
POLLY, 43, 100
POLLY A., 87, 114
R.L., 124
R.S., 124
REBECCA, 32
REBECCA A., 100
ROBT LEE, 139
ROSA, 47, 52
S., 30
SAM, 20
SAMP., 13
SAMPSON, 15, 22, 27, 31, 32, 41, 43(3), 77, 100(2), 124
SARAH, 92, 100
SARAH M., 66
SAWYER, 124
SERENA, 20-D
SYNTHIA M., 90
THEO, 22
THOMAS, 105
THOMPSON, 124
TRACY, 32
VICEY, 52
VICTORIA, 63, 139
W., 94
W.M., 133
W.T., 94
WADE H., 100

WALTER, 80
WEALTHY, 13, 18
WEST, 73
WILLIAM, 15, 47, 52(2)
WILLOUGHBY, 43, 80

WM, 49, 90, 92(2), 95, 97, 100
WM F., 50
WM NELSON, 84
WM P., 52
TEMPLETON
J.R., 61
TEREZ
SHERWITZ, 135
SORVEC, 135
STEVE I., 135
TERRY
A.J., 55, 98
CORA L., 98
ELIZA JANE, 62
G.W., 75, 119, 120, 123, 124, 125, 127, 128, 130, 132(2), 134, 135, 136(3), 139
GEO W., 42
JAMES B., 54
JNO W., 55
JOSEPH, 42
LUCINDA, 54, 62
MARTHA J., 55, 98
MARY ANN, 42
MAY B., 99
MEGGIE, 99
SAML, 99
SAML B., 54
SAML. B., 62
V., 129
WATSON, 129(2)
TESTER
DANL, 91
LINA, 91
TELIA, 91
TESTERMAN
STEPHEN, 109
STEPHEN F., 109
SUSAN, 109
THAXTON
CHAS W., 70
JO., 92
SALLIE, 70
SAML, 70
THOMAS
ADDIE L., 116
ALLEN, 124
ALLIE B., 121
ALMEDA, 96
ANDREW, 99
ANN, 2
ANNIE, 35, 38, 118
ARENA W., 16
ARTHUR, 133(2)
H P., 74

BERTHA A., 15
BOSTON, 59
C., 121
C.A., 75
CAROLINE, 8, 13, 40, 60, 67, 68, 83, 115
CHARLES, 124
CHARLEY, 134
D.H., 106
D.W., 118
DANIEL B., 115
DAVID W., 62
ED, 14, 134
EDWARD, 8, 15, 42
ELLEN, 49, 62, 75
EMMA, 65
EMMA V., 76
F. JANE, 74
G.B., 105
G.G., 136
G.W., 112
GEO G., 68
GEO W., 116
GEOR W., 76
GILES B., 105
H., 15
HANLEY, 2
HARLY, 69
HARVEY E., 60
HENDERSON F., 5

HENLEY, 8, 16
HENRIETTA, 48
HENRY, 134
HOE, 119
J.H., 115(2)
J.W., 74(2), 118
JAMES, 96
JAMES A., 11, 48, 20-B
JAMES D., 40, 138
JAMES H., 8, 33, 40, 60
JANE, 133
JAS H., 67, 68, 83, 121
JEFF, 75
JEFF W., 42
JEFFREY, 14
JEMIMA, 1, 11, 13
JEMISON, 20-B
JENNELLIE A., 67
JEREMIAH, 20-C
JESSE, 2, 5, 16, 27, 59, 20-B
JESSEE, 20-D, 20-E(2)
JESSEE, JR., 20-E
JNO W., 26
JOHN, 2, 8, 15, 16, 27, 119
JOSEPH, 42
JOSEPHINE, 112
JOSH, 76, 83
JOSIE V., 116

JULETT, 8
JULIET, 5(2)
L.F., 42
L.M., 75
LAMPKIN, 62
LAMPKIN M.K., 1
LAURA E., 112
LOUVENIA, 136
LUCINDA F., 99
LUCY, 119
M., 15
M.F., 115(2), 116
M.M., 99
MALVINA, 26
MARGARET, 2, 8, 42, 58, 124
MARGT, 16
MARTHA A., 5
MARY, 48, 65
MARY FRANCIS, 109

MARY J., 96
MASURA JANE, 138

MAY, 14
MICHEY, 16
MILLARD F., 38
MINTA JANE, 105
MONTIE, 102
NANCY, 69
OLLIE A., 109
PEGGY, 69, 115
PHEBA, 27
PHEBE, 2, 8, 15, 16
R., 20-E
R.H., 118
R.M., 116
RACHAEL, 20-D
RACHEL, 2, 5, 59, 20-B, 20-E
RHODA, 36, 20-B
ROBERT M., 20-D
ROBT M., 102
ROSA, 134(2)
ROSA L., 105
SALLIE, 33, 124
SAMPKIN, 49
SAMUEL, 5(2), 8, 16
SARAH, 1, 5, 115, 116, 118, 134, 136
SARAH C., 138
SARAH M., 102
TEMPY, 20-B
VICTORIA, 35
W.G., 35
W.H., 106
WAIN, 20-E
WAINE, 136
WILLIAM G., 2, 38
WILSON, 33, 133
WM G., 118
WM H., 58(2), 109
THOMASON

C.L., 138
DANIEL, 132
E.A., 140
ELIZABETH, 132
ELLEN, 104
EUGENIA, 104
F.E., 138
F.L., 140(2)
GEORGE, 138
JAMES W., 132
LILLY C., 140
T.L., 104
W.K., 138
THORNHILL
JAS, 124
MILDRED, 124
THOMILY
EMALINE V., 18
THOMISON
C.N., 139
ELLEN, 139
F.L., 139
THOMPSON
---, 38
A., 18, 118, 20-C
A.G., 14
A.J., 14, 22(3), 23, 24(3), 25(3), 26(2), 28, 29, 30(6), 31, 32(3), 33(2), 35, 36, 37(3), 38(2), 39, 40(3), 41, 43(2), 46(2), 47(2), 48(3), 49(2), 50(2), 51(3), 53(4), 54(2), 55(3), 56(2), 57(2), 59, 60(7), 61(3), 63(4), 61(2), 69(2), 70, 72(3), 73, 74(3), 79, 80(2), 82(2), 85, 89, 91(2), 93, 95, 96, 97, 98, 100, 103, 104, 105(3), 106(2), 107, 114, 20-D(3)
A.J.E., 20-D
A.L., 102
A.N., 14, 96
A.Z., 125
ABBE, 40
ADALINE, 88
ADELINE, 15
AIDON, 1
ALBERT, 80
ALICE, 120
ALLEN, 8, 53, 103, 113, 124
ALLIE M., 45
ALMEDA L., 32
AMOS D., 28
AND. J., 41
ANDREW, 1
ANDREW J., 7, 9, 17(3), 18(5), 19(4),

20, 22, 27(2),
20-A(4), 20-B(2)
ANG., 14
ANGELINE, 28, 31, 45,
68, 20-D
ANNA B., 79
ARCH, 15, 20-D
ARCHIBALD, 24
ARTHELIA N., 53
BELLE, 101
BERTHA M., 103
CAROLINE, 120
CARRIE C., 123
CATHARINE, 121
CATHERINE, 80
CATHERING, 66
CHARLEY, 138
CHARLIE, 135
CHAS, 41
CHAS C., 79
CHAS R., 66
CHAS S., 60
CHAS V., 113
CHAS. E., 41
CLABURN, 27
CORA L., 129
D., 18, 20-C
DANL, 100
DAVID, 14, 28, 31, 45,
68, 88, 121, 20-D
DELFIE, 124
DOCIA, 20
EDITHA, 7
EDWARD, 98
ELI, 33, 69, 116
ELIHU, 77
ELIZA R., 32
ELIZABETH, 7(2), 20-D

ELIZABETH R., 37
ELIZTH, 9, 14, 15, 24
ELLA, 138
EMMA, 103, 114, 123
F.C., 134(3)
FANNIE C., 88
FANNIE M., 102
FANSBY, 52
FOUNTAIN T., 124
FRANCES, 2
FRANCIS, 77
G.W., 129
GEO T., 79
GEORGE, 98
GORDAN, 35
GORDON, 20, 32, 41
H.C., 24, 70, 102
H.E., 68
HARRIET, 135, 138
HAYWOOD, 77
HEN B., 104
HENDERSON, 127

HENRY, 52

HENRY G., 130
HIRAM, 27, 65, 112
IDA E., 114
IDA K., 121
ISA H., 78
ISAAC, 103
J.D., 106, 114
J.H., 74, 96
J.N., 68
J.W., 114, 134(2)
JACKSON, 52
JAMES, 8, 40, 48, 99
JAMES A., 41, 122
JAMES C., 127
JAMES D., 93
JAMES P., 121
JANE, 1, 37, 58, 65,
112, 127
JAS, 6
JAS E., 81
JAS W., 116
JENNIE, 100, 113
JEREMIAH S., 42
JNO A., 80
JNO D., 14
JNO H., 77(2)
JNO W., 84, 118
JOHLE, 84
JOHN, 7, 120
JOHN D., 93, 106
JOHN H., 114
JOHN McH., 2
JOS, 130
JOS H., 78
JOS W., 106
JOSHUA B., 14
JULIA E., 20-C
K., 91
KATHARINE, 77
KATHERINE, 79
L., 32, 74
L.E., 96, 130
L.H., 84
LARKIN, 113
LEROY, 20-D
LEVI, 79
LEVI E., 66
LEVY, 80(2)
LOUISA, 20, 35
LOUISA E., 35
LOUISA F., 29
LOUISA J., 41
LUCY, 6, 48, 99
LUCY A., 8
LUTHERA L., 122
LYONS, 2(2)
MALTILDA, 41
MANERVA, 38, 124
MARGARET, 14, 74
MARGARET E., 43

MARGT, 31
MARGT F., 84

MARGT. F., 78
MARIA A., 18
MARIAH J., 80
MARINDA, 37, 70
MARY, 24, 55, 58, 79,
91(2), 114, 124, 140
MARY A., 98, 113
MARY B., 56
MARY E., 44, 69
MARY I., 65
MARY J., 6, 20, 29, 43
MARY M., 80
MATILDA, 138
MINERVA, 53, 100, 103,
113
N., 15
NANCY, 2(2), 6
NANCY E., 93, 106
NANCY H., 15
NANCY J., 55, 100
NANNIE E., 41
NANNIE R., 110
OMBY, 27
PEIIER, 118
PHILIP, 31, 43, 55
PHILLIP, 29
POLLY A., 9
PRESTON B., 58
R.J., 29, 32(2)
REBECA JANE, 1
REBECCA, 56
REBECCA J., 60, 61
ROBERT, 91
S., 15
SALLIE, 101
SALLY, 1
SARAH, 33, 41, 42, 69,
71, 104
SARAH B., 40
SARAH E., 31, 37
SARAH J., 48
SYMS, 6
VICIE, 92
VICTORIA A., 33
VIRGINIA, 122
W.A., 71
W.H., 101
W.K., 129
W.S., 103, 123
WATSON, 112
WILLIAM, 38, 70
WILLIAM H., 6, 7
WILLIE M., 70, 135
WINFIELD, 31
WINTON, 32
WM, 37
WM A., 61
WM H., 41, 42, 56, 60,
61, 71, 104
WM R., 37
THOMSEN
ANNA K., 77
THEODOR, 77

WM, 77
THOMSON
MARY ANN, 66
W.C., 66
THORN
A.S., 91, 93, 94, 131,
133, 134(3), 136
ARTHUR S., 74, 106(2),
108(2), 138
AUTHOR S., 122
AUTHUR S., 114
D.B., 140
DAVIS, 52, 137
DAVIS McBRIDE, 140

J.D., 83, 91
J.E., 129
JAMES P., 48, 52, 74,
95
JANE R., 48
LAURA, 140
MAGGIE E., 91
MAHALA T., 48
MAHAVALA, 74, 95

MAHAVALA T., 52

MARY, 95
NANCY, 83, 91
NANNIE E., 83
R.T., 140
THORNHILL
JAMES, 139
MILLY, 139
ROBT H., 139
THORNILY
JAMES, 6
MARY, 6
THOMAS H., 6
THORNTON
A.J., 69, 79, 117
A.M., 59, 108, 139
ALICE ANN VIRGINIA,

127
AMANDA, 70, 89
ANDREW, 14, 17, 32
C.W., 107
CHARLOTTE, 32
D.H., 114, 115, 122,
130, 131, 132, 134
ELIZA J., 107, 127
F.B., 103
F.M., 117
FILLMORE M., 36
G.J., 86(3)
G.W., 70
GEORGE W., 43
H.C., 70
HARRIET J., 50
HARRIET L., 50
HENRY, 108
HENRY C., 20-A

JAMES A., 50, 80
JAMES H., 79
JANE, 129
JAS, 84
JAS A., 59, 120
JOHN A., 120
JULIA L., 38
L., 14
L.G., 129
LILLIE G., 84
LOU P., 108
LOUISA, 9, 24(2), 59,
80, 120, 20-A
LOUISA W., 36, 80
LOUISE, 4, 17
M., 14, 17, 20-A
M.J., 79
MARGT E., 86
MARY, 43
MARY E., 103
MARY H., 24
MARY S., 103
MELVINA B., 117
MER., 19
MEREDITH, 9, 36
MEREDITY, 4
MERIDETH, 24(2)
NANCY, 27
NANCY V., 14, 38
O.E., 69
PETER, 43
ROBT, 32
S.E., 26(2)
SIDNEY, 129
SIDNEY A., 24
SUSAN E., 19
THOMAS P., 9, 42
THOS P., 38
THOS. H., 42
WILLIAM M., 4
WM M., 107, 127
WM R., 26
THORP
NELLIE, 48
THRASHER
G.W., 71, 72, 73,
74(2), 75(2)
THREET
HENRY, 76
THRIFF
SALLIE, 137
THRONTON
ELIZA, 131
JAMES T., 131
WM M., 131
TICE
J.J., 138
TICKEL
D.P., 90
MARY, 90
TICKLE
DANIEL C., 35
F.C., 35

FRANCIS C., 65
S., 35
SOLOMAN D., 65
STEPHEN M., 65
TILLER
A., 15, 20, 123
A.C., 117, 139
ANDERSON, 8
ANDR, 2
ANNIE J., 61
C.I., 89(2), 118
CHAS G., 55
CHAS. J., 26
CLEMENTINE, 61
D., 15
DORA, 64
E., 118
E.W., 91(2), 94, 98,
100, 102(2), 103(3),
101, 105(3), 106(2),
109, 110(2), 113
EDW H., 107
ELIZABETH, 89
ELLEN P., 1
ETTA M., 107
EVERMONT W., 38

GEO L., 90
HALLIE A., 67
HARVEY G., 20
HIRAM, 19, 38
HIRAM D., 15
J., 20-C
J.F., 61, 117, 139
JAS. F., 25
JNO, 107
JOHN, 38
JOHN M., 60
JOHN P., 8
JOHN W.N., 19
JUDA, 10
JUDIE, 81
JUDITH, 17
K., 20-C
KINZER, 17
KINZIE, 10, 81
L.B., 118
LAURA, 46
LOUISA, 38(2), 46, 55,
64
LOUISA ELLISE, 89
M.W., 139
MANERVA H., 17
MARY A., 117
MARY E., 45
MARY L., 60
MINERVA A., 78
MOSES D., 16
POLLY, 19
PRISCILLA, 2, 8, 20
R., 25
REBECCA, 38
REBECCA J., 10

RHODA, 26, 28, 45, 66,
67, 90
RHODA J., 66
RHODA L., 20-C
RHODA M., 7
SAMUEL, 12
SARAH M., 28
SUSAN E., 60
WILEY J., 78
WILLIAM, 12, 38, 45,
55
WILLIAM A., 2
WILLIAM D., 28
WM D., 26, 66, 67, 90
WM McH., 28
WM McH., 78
TILLEY
E.L., 134, 137
E.W., 103
FRANCES M., 128
J.C., 111, 134
JNO C., 128
JOHN C., 124
LEE, 92
NANCY LUETTA, 124

SARAH, 111, 124, 128
TILLY
EDMUND, 57
EDMUND A., 55
EDMUND F., 57
JAMES W., 106(2),
107(2)
JOHN C., 99
MARY, 99
TIMER
JOHN, 65
VICTORIA, 65
TINCHER
E.A., 58
FRANK W., 58
W.C., 58
TINES
JACK, 135
JINK, 135
JULIA, 135
TINLEY
DIER., 71
JINNIE, 71
MARY, 71
TINNER
N., 24
TINSLEY
BENJAMIN M., 20-D

ELIZ., 20-D
H.C., 20-D
N., 24
W., 21, 20-E, 20-F
WILLIS, 6, 19, 20-D

TOBER
JACOB, 114
TOBOR
CHARLES, 92
CYNTHIA, 92
J.F., 92
TOLBERT
G.W., 79
M.B., 79
MARY M., 79
TOLER
GEORGE, 111
HENRY, 111
MARY, 111
TOLIVER
CREED, 88
FRANKIE, 88
HENRY, 77
MARY, 88
TONEY
ELIZTH, 2
GEORGE W., 2
JONATHAN, 2
TORBETT
CATHERINE, 9
JOHN, 9
JOSIAH, 9
TOTTON
ELIZTH, 26
S.E., 26
WM, 26
TOWN
J.E., 85
TOY
MARY, 67
S.A., 75
SAML, 67
SAML A., 67
TRACEY
FRANKIE, 42
LAURA V., 42
ROWLAND J., 42
TRACY
CARRIE E., 116
DICEY, 4
E., 18
G.P., 116
HARVEY S., 17
JOHN, 18
SARAH A., 4
WINTON B., 18
WM, 4, 17
TRAIL
E.R., 98
ELIJAH, 5
F.D., 131
FLEM, 131
JACOB, 18, 98
JANE, 5
JOHN W., 63
LATITIA, 131
LEWIS, 5
LOCKA, 18

LOCKIE, 98
MARY E., 14
SAML M., 63
SAMUEL M., 18
SARAH M., 63
TRAILE
DELIA W., 36
JACOB, 36
LOCKEY, 36
TRAYNHAM
ANNIE, 77
SALLY, 77
TRENT
A.M., 132
MARY, 132
NANCY, 132
TRESISE
FRANCIS, 116
M.J., 116
WM, 116
TRETWELL
NANIE M., 97
S.H., 97
TRIGG
DEBORAH, 102
ELIJAH, 102
HENRY, 125
JOHN, 37
MARTHA, 125
SIMON L., 102
WM B., 125
TROTTER
SALLY, 91, 95
TROUTMAN
ELIZABETH, 130
J.A., 130
JOHN, 130
TUCKER
F.B., 79
JULIA A., 63, 112
L.W., 112
LITTLETON W., 63
MARY E., 112
REBECCA E., 63
S.L., 100
SALLIE, 109
WM, 79
TUCKETT
JAMES, 59
MARY, 59
TUGGLE
EASTER J., 119
EFFIE E., 119
EMILY, 23, 39
GEORGE W., 39
HENRY, 23, 119
JOHN, 3, 23, 25, 39, 43
LARKIN, 3
LUCINDA, 43
MALINDA, 3
MALINDA C., 43
MARY J., 25

TULLY
B., 130
B.I., 130
E., 130
TUNE
ALEXANDER, 116

EMILY, 116
WILLIAM, 116
TURNER
AARON, 84
ANDY, 66
CHARLES G., 35
CHARLES L., 46
CHARLES S., 7
CORA, 98
EDD, 128
ELIZA, 66
GEO, 65
JAXEINA, 84
JOS H., 100
JULIA A., 58
LAFAYETT F., 109
LAFAYETTE, 92
LAURA ALICE, 100

LIA AIE, 65
LUEMMA A., 35
LUNDA V., 79
MAGGIE, 84
MARGARET, 128
MARY J., 79, 98
MARY M., 100
MATTIE, 65
MEADOR, 113
P., 109
PEYTON, 92
ROBERT B., 24
ROBT B., 79
ROBT D., 98
SARAH, 24, 46
SARAH C., 7
SUSAN, 92, 109
VICTORIA, 27, 35, 46
WILLIAM, 113
WILSON, 7, 24
TURNES
FANNIE, 103
LOUIS, 103
PLEASANT, 103
TURPIN
CORNELIUS, 59
EMILY, 59
HENRY, 20(2)
JUDITH, 20
MARTHA, 20
NANCY, 20
REBECCA, 20
TUTOR
HENRY, 15
RICHARD, 15
SUSAN, 15
TWEDDLE

ISABELLA, 73
MARY, 73
ROBERT, 73
TWIGGS
ELIZA, 93
TIMOTHY, 93
WM, 93
TYLER
CHARLES, 108
S.P., 108
SARAH, 108
TYREE
FANNIE B., 92
MARY, 92
TYRUS
JACK, 22
PEYTON, 22

-U-

ULINOH
MARKEV, 137
PALAGIA, 137
ULENAN, 137
UMBERGER
R.S., 73
UNDERWOOD

A.L., 98
AARAN, 140
AARON, 140
ACY, 131
ADAM, 5
ARAMINTA, 49
ASA, 125(2), 130(2), 138
ASA L., 73
C.R., 101(2)
CLA A., 101
D.E., 130
DOSIE, 100
ELEANOR, 5
ELIZABETH, 47, 100, 131, 140
ELIZTH, 5, 34(2), 20-A(2)
ESTER, 49
GABRIEL, 47
HENRY, 125
HESTER M., 20-A
ISHAM, 34
J.A., 92
J.B., 138(2)
J.L., 71
JAMES, 130
JAMES A., 20-A
JANE, 1
JAS A., 83(2)
JESSE, 5(2), 43
JOSHUA, 39
LITHA, 39
M.J., 73, 125, 130, 131, 138

MALINDA F., 43
MARSHALL H., 43
MARTHA, 34, 71
MARTIN, 47, 100, 140
MARY, 130
MARY ANN, 83, 92
MARY C., 92
MARY J., 59, 98
MATTIE J., 130
MISHEL, 5
MOSES, 59
MURRELL, 71
R.E., 83
RACHEL, 1
SARAH F., 98, 101
SERENA, 59
SINA A., 73
VICTORIA, 39
WILLIAM, 34
WM, 1, 34, 20-A(2)
UPTON
AGNES, 19
CAROLINE, 7
CLIFFORD, 20-D
ELIZABETH, 2
GEORGE, 14
L., 4(2)
LEITIA, 13, 14
LEWIS, 4
LOUISA, 20-D
M., 19
MANERVA, 13
MARTHA, 19, 23
MARY, 4, 12
MARY L., 61
MEREDITH, 2, 7, 12
NANCY, 23
SALLIE, 12
SARAH, 2
SYLVESTER, 4(2), 13, 14, 23

-V-

VADEN
ALEX, 127
CHARLES, 127
SUSAN, 127
VAIDEN
ALEX, 76
SANDY, 76(2)
SUSAN, 76
VAILEY
JAMES F., 78
JOSEPHINE V., 78
MARGARET, 78
VANCE
J.J., 109
MARGARET, 75, 109

MARVEL, 75
PRESTON, 75, 115
WM, 109

VANDERWOOD

PAUL, 7, 8(3)
VANDIKE
JOHN F., 101
LOUISA, 101
VANVAETER
CHARITY, 16
JOSEPH W., 16
SOL., 16
VASS
A.C., 98
ANGELINE, 6
BENJN, 6
ELIZABETH J., 3
H.D., 98
JULIA, 6
M.E., 98
MARY, 3
ROBT, 3
VAUGHAN
EASTER J., 63
EMMA, 98
ESTHER J., 98
JAS E., 63
THOS J., 63, 98
VAUGHN
ADDIE R., 132
B.F., 127
JOSEPH, 127
M.C., 132, 133
M.J., 127
MOLLIE, 132, 133
VAUGHT
AMERICA J., 64
C.A., 90
C.C., 76, 82
C.L., 46, 76, 82(2)
CHARLES A., 124
CHAS A., 65
CLARA, 46
CLARA C., 72, 82
E.H., 88, 104
ELIZABETH, 82
ELIZABETH H., 79
EMMA J., 78
FLORA C., 88
J. CHANCY, 104
JAS W., 72
LEVI H., 99
LEWIS C., 72
LIZZIE C., 79
LUCINDA, 99
LUCRECIA, 95
LUCY W., 46
MARTHA A., 82
MARY J., 46
MINERVA, 46
PEGGY, 16
R.F., 88
RANSOM, 46, 64, 65, 78, 95, 99, 124
RUFUS, 104

RUFUS F., 79
S.B., 91(2), 95, 98, 106, 110
S.V., 91
SALINA M., 76
SARAH M., 64, 65, 78, 95, 124
WILLIAM, 16
VAWTER
EDWARD, 91
ELIZTH D., 102
JNO WM, 102
W.A., 102
WM A., 102
WM R., 91
VEAL
CHAS, 2
ELIZTH, 2
JACKSON, 2
VERMILLION
E., 19(2)
ELIZABETH, 22
ELIZABETH S., 19
ELIZTH, 25
HESTER F., 25
J.A., 19
J.B., 55
J.R., 19
JAS A., 22
JAS. R., 25
JNO C., 55
NANCY M., 22
RHODA, 103
S.T., 103
STEPHEN T., 19
THALESTROUS, 103

VERNON
EFFIE E., 113
JENNIE, 113
WM H., 113
VEST
A., 18, 20-C
AUD., 22
B.H., 47
CHARLES J., 18
CHAS M., 62
D.A., 134
DELPHIA, 20-B
E.A., 93
FLEMING, 20-C
J.M., 134(2)
JANE, 45, 20-C
JOHN, 18, 20-B
JOHN J., 20-C
JOHN M., 20-C
LUCY A., 22
M., 18
MALINDA F., 53
MARTHA JANE, 45

MARY E., 12
MARY J., 47

MARY JANE, 20-B
MINNESOTA, 93
NICY A., 20-C
RHODA, 18, 22
S.A., 134
SALINA M., 76
S.J., 47, 93
SALLIE, 44
SARAH, 18, 20-C
SARAH J., 15
SUSAN A.B., 47
WILLIAM, 47
WM, 45, 62
VIA
ABAGAIL, 49
ANDERSON, 52
ANN, 55
G.W., 120, 130
GEO W., 132
GEORGE, 55
J.J., 82
JAS J., 52
JOHN T., 51, 73
MALINDIA, 80
MARTHA, 120
MARY, 120
MARY J., 70(2), 80, 82, 132
MORIAH, 120
NANCY, 52
NANCY J., 132
RACHEL, 49, 51
S., 70, 120
S.G., 122, 125
S.J., 130
SPIREL, 82, 132
THOS H., 55
WM, 120
VICARS
J.G., 54
VIDWELL
AMANDA, 29
VIERNOW
ALBERT, 74
ALVENA, 74
HENRY, 74
VINES
ALEX C., 113
ELIZA, 25
ELIZA F., 39(2), 40
ELIZA S., 39
JAMES W., 25, 40
JANE E., 39
JNO W., 39
SILAS, 25, 39(2)
SILAS S., 39, 40
SUSAN, 113
W.F., 113
VIPERMAN
E.J., 69
MARTHA, 69
RACHEL, 69
VIPPERMAN
DANL, 107

E. JACKSON, 107
TEXAS, 140
VIPPERMON
EMANL J., 58
FLORENCE A.L., 58
RACHEL, 58
VIRMILLION
IREAN E., 95
RODA, 95
S.T., 95
VORG
LOUISA, 106
W.L., 106
VORGE
HARRIET, 36(2)

-W-

WADDLE
ALEXANDER, 7
ALEXR, 3
GEORGE B., 26
JAMES, 16
JANE B., 49
JOHN A., 26
JOSEPH, 7
LOU, 66
MARY, 3, 7, 60
POLLY, 26
SARAH, 49
SARAH E., 60
SARAH G., 16
SUSAN, 16
WILLIAM, 3, 49
WM, 60, 66
WADE
ABIGAIL, 61
BALLARD, 61
BETTIE, 96
CATHERINE, 59
FLORENCE, 96
G.H., 94
GEO, 67
H.D., 94
HARRIETT, 67
JACKSON, 59
JACOB, 6
JAKE, 65
JAMES, 65
JANE, 95
JOSHUA, 35
M.E., 94
MARGARET, 35, 59
MARGARET M., 35

MARTIN V., 6
MOSES, 61
NED, 96
SARAH, 67
SUSAN, 6
WINNIE, 65
WAGGONER
ADAM, 9

191

HANNAH, 9
MARY A., 8
WAGNER
ADAIR E., 45
D., 20-B
DANIEL J., 45
JULINA E., 45
M., 20-B
MARGARET J., 20-B

WAGONER
ADAM C., 35
ADAM E., 42
DAVID D., 40
GEO O., 60
HULDAH, 84
JNO W., 84
JULINA E., 35
MAGGIE S., 60
MARY A., 32
MARY E., 32
NANCY, 40
PARIS W., 35
SARAH, 84
WILLIAM, 40
WAIMER
EMMA, 51
ISAAC, 51
REBECCA, 51
WAKEFIELD
ISABELLA D., 86
PRISCILLA, 86
THEODORE, 86
WALACE
ANN, 124
JACK, 124
WM, 124
WALDRON
ANDREW, 57
MARTHA, 57
T.D., 57
WALDSON
CATHERINE F., 12
JAMES, 12
MARGARET, 12
WALKER
ADALINE, 23
ALBERT K., 60
AMANDA J., 23
ANDERSON, 30
ARDELIA, 125
ARLENIA E., 106
AUGUSTUS, 70
B.U., 61
BETTIE, 124
BIRREL W., 19
BURREL, 67
C., 19, 20(2), 40(2)
C.A., 18
C.W.J., 125
CAROLINE, 72
CHARLES, 13, 15(3),
16(5), 17(5), 18(3),

21(2), 25, 26, 32,
36, 39(3), 40, 49(2),
50, 51, 55, 74, 76,
78, 89, 91, 20-C,
20-F(2)
CHAS, 63, 65, 66, 67,
70(2), 82, 83, 94
CHAS C., 50
CHAS G.C., 52
CHAS W.J., 41
CHAS., 13(5), 14,
26(2), 30(3)
CHRISPIANOS, 6, 41, 50
CHRISTIAN, 24
COUCIL, 48
COUNCIL, 12, 23,
41(2), 50
COUNSEL K., 88
COUNSIL K., 113
DRURY LACY, 63

E.E., 139
E.M., 124
E.S., 6
ELEANOR, 6
EMILY, 88
EMMA, 113
EMOZELLA, 12
F., 18
FERD, 70
FIELDEN, 80
FLORA E., 103
FLOYD, 105
FRANCES, 41
FRANCIS, 50
FRANKIE J.C., 23
G.H., 132
G.P., 88, 124(2)
G.W., 72(2)
GEORGE W.N., 21, 20-F

GILBERT L., 105
H.S., 132
HANNAH, 29
HARRIET, 88
HARRIETT, 124
HARRISON C., 103
HENRY, 6
IRA W., 48, 141
J.D., 139
J.P., 125
JACOB A., 24
JAMES C., 30
JAMES M., 20-C
JANE D., 52
JANE K., 50
JANE N., 51
JAS B., 105
JNO M., 60
JOHN, 19
JOHN L., 6, 50, 51
JOHN M., 103, 115
JOHN T., 6

JOHN W.C., 30, 103
JOHNATHAN K., 88

JORDAN, 29
JUDA, 113
JULIA, 105
JULY, 123
L.C., 113
LEONARD M., 115
LEWIS, 52
LINA A., 135
LOLA D., 88
LOUICIE E., 35
LOUISA, 30, 35, 70
LOYD P., 57
LUCY A., 52
M.D., 135
M.M., 28
MAHALA, 24
MARTHA A., 52
MARTHA E., 52
MARY, 113
MARY A., 63
MARY B., 6
MARY J., 60
MAUD I., 124
MEREAUIA F., 20
MILLIE, 103, 115
NANCY, 12, 19, 23, 103
NANCY D., 19, 20(2),
41, 48
NELLIE C., 61
NUMA, 52
O.T., 125
R., 20-C
R.C., 139
RACHEL, 21, 20-F
REBECCA C., 105
ROBT HY, 63
S.B., 132
SALLIE, 57
SALLIE B., 51, 105
SAM, 113, 123
SAMI., 57
SAMUEL, 123
SARAH, 135(2)
THOS H., 57
UNDERWOOD, 35

VICTORIA, 61, 67
VIVA G., 141
WALTER C., 52
ZANIE, 111
WALKINS
CYNTHIA A., 53
FANNIE J.E., 53
WILSON, 53
WALKUP
JOSEPH, 36
LIZZIE F., 95
MARSHAL W., 36
SUSAN J., 36
WALL

ALICE ELIZABETH, 114

CHAS McF., 51
CORA E., 97
ELIZABETH, 21, 43, 51,
76, 20-F
ELIZTH, 24
ELLA C.E., 24
FANNIE, 137
G. MILTON, 83
HARVEY, 102
HELEN, 102
HENRY, 70, 83
HENRY D., 48
JAMES C., 21, 137,
20-F
JANE, 24, 70, 83
JAS C., 97, 114
JNO W., 126(2)
JOHN, 43
MARGARET, 127
MARTHA F., 114
MARY J., 48
MARY L., 127
PINK, 126
ROBERT, 127
RUFUS K.G., 48
SALLIE H., 137
SIDNEY M., 70
VICTORIA, 126
WILLIAM, 43
WM, 21, 24, 51, 76,
20-F
WALLACE
ALEX, 90
ALEX., 125
MARY, 102, 107
NANCY E., 102
SARAH J., 107
THOS, 102
WALLER
GABE, 66
J.W., 66
MINNIE, 66
WALRUP
ELIZABETH, 119
ELSIE LEE, 119
M.W., 119
WALTER
DRURY, 2
E.H., 126
ELI W., 126
H.B., 112
HENRY, 112
N., 126
RUTHA, 112
WALTERS
ELI H., 34
FLOSSIE E., 120
JAMES R., 135
MARY JANE, 34
MOLLIE D., 120
MOSES, 30, 34(2)

ROBT, 135
S., 30
SERENIA, 34(2)
VIRGINIA, 135
W.R., 30
WALTHALT
MARY B., 51
ROBT B., 51
WILLIE N., 51
WALTON
DAVIS, 103
JAMES H., 103
JOHN L., 89
MARY, 103
WANHOP
ELIZA J., 57
ELIZABETH, 57
ELIZTH, 42
JOHN K., 42, 57
NANCY J., 42
WARD
ANDERSON, 86, 87
CHARLES, 46
DAVE, 117
DAVID, 72
EDWARD, 117
ELIZA, 92, 107
FANNIE, 68, 107
FANY, 117
GEO, 92, 107
HENRY, 61
HENRY F., 61
J.B., 107, 112, 117,
127
JANE, 121
JNO H., 87
KATE, 72
LEWIS, 68, 117
LIDDIE, 121
MALINDA, 87
MARY, 46
P., 117
REASE, 121
SARAH A., 72
SARAH P., 65
WARE
NANCY, 136
WARNER
BELLE, 104
FRANCES M., 104
GEO, 104
WARREN
CHARLIE, 101
ELMIRA, 113
JOHN, 115
LITTIE F., 113
LIZZIE, 115
MARY J., 101
NANNIE A., 115
RICHARD, 101
WADE, 113
WARWICK
ANNA, 110

EMANUEL S., 110
RICHD, 110
WASHINGTON
ALICE, 112
CATHERINE, 139
ED, 110
EMMA, 139
FANNIE, 62
GEO, 29, 34, 134
GEORGE, 52, 62
HARRIET, 29, 34, 52
HATTIE, 122
JAMES, 139
PHIL, 52
PHILIP, 29
R.D., 136, 138(2),
139(2)
R.P., 141
SAM, 112
SAMUEL, 34
SARAH, 110
SUSAN, 134
SUSAN ANN, 112
WESLEY, 134(2)
WATKINS
ANNIE H., 112
C.S., 112
CARRIE S., 136
CHAVESS, 55(2)
J.L., 136(2)
SARAH, 55
W.J., 112
W.T., 136
WATSON
ELI H., 130
ELIZA, 120
JULIA, 120
KILLY, 120
M.E., 130
NEHEMIAH, 50
W.J., 130
WATTS
A.B., 126(2)
ELIJAH, 103
JANE, 89
JAS, 126
JESSE, 89
LAURINDA, 103
LEE, 89
ROXIE, 126
T.T., 119
THOS, 103
WAUGH
BARBARA, 6
HENRY P., 6(2)
JOHN, 6
RUTH, 6
WAUGHT
CHRISTIAN L., 16
WAUHOP
E., 20-A
JOHN, 20-C
JOHN K., 20-A

MARY M., 20-C
SARAH M., 20-A
WAVELRING
G.W., 116
IDA H., 116
R.E., 116
WAYODS
ISAAC, 118
RACHEL, 118
ROBERT M., 118
WEATHERFORD

ADELINE M., 23, 37
JAMES T., 37
JNO. M., 23
JOHN M., 37
NANCY E., 23
WEAVER
ELIZA, 55, 66
IMOGENE, 112
JAMES, 55, 66, 68
LIZIE, 68
LIZZIE H., 112
MALINDA, 55
MARGARET E., 66

MARY L., 94
MATILDA, 42
ROBT L., 106, 112
VICTORIA, 68
WEBB
CLEMENTINE, 121
ELIZE J., 75
F.N., 89, 121(2)
J.O., 89
J.R., 89
MARTHA, 75
OAKLEY, 121
W., 67
WARNER, 75
WEBSTER
GEO E., 126
WEEKS
ADDIE L., 112
ARBELA, 112
E.J., 85, 112
HASEY, 112
J.W., 112
JNO W., 85
JOHN, 137
JOSEPH, 112
MARY R.J., 85
WM A., 137
WEIMER
CYNTHIA, 28
ELLEN MANDINE, 111

MASSEY, 25
SAM., 25
SARAH J., 25
WEINER
ELIZTH, 26
ESTHER A., 26

JAS., 26
WEISER
CHAS G., 83
WELCH
E.W., 78
ELIZABETH, 78
ELLEN, 15
FOUNTAIN, 135
MARY, 135
MATTIE, 135
NANNIE, 78
SILA, 78
WILLIAM J., 15
WM, 15
WELKS
JOHN, 12
TEMPA J., 12
WELL
DANL, 27
ELIZABETH, 27
WELLER
E.B., 45, 56
HENI J., 56
M.B., 45
MARGARET, 56
MARY H., 45
WELLS
ALEXANDER, 53
D., 94
DANIEL, 35, 99, 127
DANL, 94
DANL, 20-A
DAVID, 34
DORCAS, 99
DORCUS, 127
ELIZA, 127
ELIZABETH, 34
ELIZTH, 20-A
EMMA, 99
JAMES, 138
LETTIE, 94
LOUISA, 27
MARTHA, 34
MARY C., 53
MARY J., 20-A
NANCY, 35
TURNER D., 53
WELSH
JENNIE, 135
WERT
CHAS, 75
LUCY, 75
WESLEY
NORA, 128
WEST
DELILA, 65
ELIZABETH, 56, 140
GEORGE, 140
GEORGE W., 20-B
J.W., 113, 114, 116
JAS, 4
JESSE J., 56
JNO W., 120

192

JOHN, 14(2), 16(2), 17, 20(2), 24, 25(2), 31, 32, 42, 45, 46, 54, 62, 64, 20-B(3), 20-C(5)
LEEANNA, 69
MALINDA, 4(2)
MARINDA, 20-B
PETER, 69
RHODA A., 19
RUSSEL, 65
W.W., 121, 139
WASH, 69
ZACH, 56
WESTLAND
ALICE, 119
JAMES, 119
WESTMORELAND

ELLEN, 99
WETHERFOOT

JAMES, 65
WHALES
JAMES, 108
LUCY, 108
WILLIE, 108
WHEELER
ANDREW M., 43
B., 115
BATHSHEBA, 53
EMMA, 95
FRANCES, 73
HENRY, 95
HENRY P., 53, 115
JACOB, 73
MARY, 73
MOLLIE, 88
NANCY, 43
REBECCA M., 115
ROBERT N., 43
RUFUS M., 88
S.P., 53, 139
SAML R., 55
T.B., 88
ZOLLIE M., 88
WHEELING
L.M., 129
M.V., 129
WHIRLEY
JAS W., 62
WHIT
POLLY, 137
SALLIE, 137
WHITE
A., 92
A.J., 123
ABRAHAM, 46
ADA G., 136
ALBERT J., 42, 49, 20-E
ALICE JANE, 36
ALLEN, 47, 102, 105

ALZODO M., 81
AMANDA, 41
AND, 26
ANDREW, 2, 48, 20-C
ANDREW J., 47
ANGELA, 80
ANN, 94
ANNIE, 123
ARDENIA, 104
ARTHUR L., 140
AUTHUR L., 140
B.P., 68, 123, 133, 136(2)
B.V., 105
BALLARD P., 23, 63, 68
BEE, 133
BENJ, 39
BENJ., 45
BENJK, 20-E
BENTON, 2
BETTIE M., 85
C.M., 33
CAROLINA, 15
CHARLES, 139
CHAS A., 63
CHAS H., 71
CHRISTIE, 113
CORNELIUS, 4(3), 8, 24, 94
CYNTHIA M., 53, 59, 78
D.H., 107
DELILA, 16
DEMERIUS, 4
DESSIE, 81
EDATHA, 2(2)
EDWARD E., 40
ELI, 31
ELIJAH, 15
ELIZ, 20-E
ELIZA, 31, 47
ELIZABETH, 39, 45, 48
ELIZABETH P., 39
ELIZTH, 26
ELIZZIE, 71
ELLEN, 3
ELLY C., 42
EVERMONT W., 40

FLORA, 48
FLOYD, 15
FRANCIS, 81
FRED, 70
G.P.B., 128
G.W.P., 63
GEO P., 37
GEO W.P., 86
GEORGE, 41, 61, 82, 20-E
GEORGE P.B., 128
GEORGE W., 18
GREELY, 102
H., 80
H.G., 88(2), 128

HARMAN, 29, 33, 53, 59, 78, 80
HARMAN A., 49
HARRISON, 78
HARVEY G., 8, 42
HENRY, 41
HESTER PEARLY, 108

HOWARD M., 123
IDA, 93
IDA E., 65
IRA L., 107
J.A., 48, 74, 88
J.E., 137
J.G., 71
J.H., 121
J.K., 60, 121
J.S., 78, 90, 134
JACOB H., 27
JAMES, 15, 40, 80
JAMES K., 27
JAMES R., 19
JANE, 80
JAS, 3
JAS A., 74, 93, 107
JAS ANDERSON, 23

JAS K., 74
JAS R., 23, 63, 71
JAS. R., 23
JAS. W., 48
JENNIE A., 42
JENNIE F., 106
JOE, 137
JOHN, 36, 20-C
JOHN A., 62, 108
JOHN ALLEN, 113
JOHN H., 78
JOHN M., 81
JOHN W., 4, 80
JOSEPH S., 33
JOSIE, 134
JUDA V., 26
JULIA, 23, 63
JULIET, 23, 40
KATE, 70(2)
KITTY, 117
L.E., 123
LAURA A., 136
LAURA F., 66
LENNIE, 124
LILLIE V., 86
LOUISA V., 20-E
LOUSA, 1
LUCIEN, 85
M., 4(2)
M.A., 124
M.J., 105, 123
M.S.J., 90
MAHALA, 15
MARGARET, 125, 133

MARIETTA, 53

MARINDA J., 5
MARTHA, 37, 38, 48, 50, 63, 97, 131
MARTHA A., 96
MARY, 5, 18, 19, 47, 78, 80, 88, 102, 20-C
MARY A., 61
MARY E., 48(2)
MARY ELLA, 87
MARY J., 62, 71, 105, 108, 113
MARY JANE, 68
MARY P., 63
MARY S., 106
MATIE L., 134
MELVINA, 36
MICHAE, 3
MILLY F., 46
MINERVA A., 28
MINNIE, 139
MINNIE B., 90
N.A., 37
N.F., 81
NANCY A., 47
NANCY E., 38
NANNIE, 137
NANNIE A., 136
NELSON, 104
OPIE O., 80
OVERTON C., 4
P., 4
P.J., 140
PATTON, 27(2), 31, 40, 60, 74
POLLY, 2, 8, 10, 24
POLLY J., 115
R., 60
R.C., 96
R.J., 61
REBECA, 124
REBECCA L., 53
REBECCA S., 63, 86
REUBEN, 5, 18, 19, 37, 38, 48, 63, 96, 97
RHODA, 15, 27(2), 31, 37, 40, 74
RICHD JNO, 61
ROBERT C., 37
ROBT, 50, 125, 131
ROBT L., 50
ROBT LEE, 131
ROSA L., 62
S., 20-E
S.E., 128
SALLIE, 80
SAML, 94
SAML M., 85
SAML O., 88
SAMPSON, 47
SAMUEL, 94
SAMUEL P., 121
SARAH A., 42, 49
SARAH E., 42, 88

SARAH J., 71
SARAH L., 45
SNOWIE J., 97
SUSAN, 82, 20-C
SUSANNAH, 10
SYNTHA J., 20-D
T.H., 65, 81, 107, 136
TAYLOR, 106
THOMAS, 10, 74, 124, 20-C
THOS, 2
THOS H., 82
U.S., 46
VIRGINIA, 24
VIRGINIA E., 30
VIRGINA A., 115
W.E., 107
W.H., 125
W.R., 140
W.S., 104
W.T., 104
W.W., 133
WALTER L., 78
WILLIAM, 1
WILLIAM H., 2
WILLIAM R., 20-C
WILLIS C., 59
WM, 2(2), 133, 139
WM E., 107
WM L., 68
WM R., 74, 115
Z.D., 107, 136
ZURIAH, 65
WHITED
FRANKLIN, 32
RHODA, 32
WHITEHEAD
ANNIE F., 69
F.C., 57
FRANKLIN C., 54
KADE, 69
MARY A., 54
RHODA, 57
ROSA E., 69
WM R., 54
WHITEKER
ANDREW, 57
VIRGINIA, 57
WM C., 57
WHITTENBURGER

MARY, 79
WHITLOCK
ANNA, 11
ANNIE, 21, 20-F
CALVIN, 21, 20-F
CHARLES E., 11, 41
ELIZABETH M., 41
JOSEPH R., 11, 21, 20-F
P.H., 41
WHITLOW
A.W., 117

E.H., 95
E.R., 95
F.H., 117
JOS W., 83
LILLIE M., 97
P.H., 83, 97, 98
REBECCA, 83, 97, 98, 117
SALLIE C., 95
W.S., 98
WHITT
BURGESS, 51
CHARTER M., 60
JAS H., 51
JOS B., 56
MARGARET M., 41

MARTHA S., 60
MARY, 51, 56
MARY E., 60
WHITTAKER
AARON, 8
MARGARET, 8
WHITTAKER
A., 17
A. SUE, 101
AARON, 44, 62
ALLICE J., 30
ANDREW J., 17
CATH, 3
CORLIE V., 52
E., 18
ELIZA, 44
ELIZABETH C., 15
ELIZTH, 20-A
ELLA A., 92
ELLEN, 15
F., 14, 15
FRANKLIN, 3, 9
GEORGE, 52
GEORGE C., 40
HARVEY, 42
HULDA, 22, 30
J.B., 43
JAMES H., 24
JAS, 3
JAS S., 137
JAS., 22, 30
JOHN, 137
JOHN T., 18
JULIA, 9, 14
KATIE, 40
LAURA C.C., 42
M., 17
MARGARET, 44, 62
MARTHA, 26
MARY A.P., 41
MARY J., 103
MATILDA E., 20-A
N., 18
NANCY, 137
NANCY V., 9

OLIVE M., 30
PALINA V., 22
PENELOPE, 8
R.M., 111
RHODA E., 103
RUTH, 26, 44
RUTHA, 24, 43
S.J., 20-A
SARAH, 42
T.C., 92
WILLIAM, 41, 43, 44, 92, 103
WM, 24, 26, 28, 44, 62, 101
WHITTEN
C., 4
CHARLOTTE, 1, 4, 7, 13(2)
ELIZA, 1
HENRY, 98
JOHN, 19
L., 13
LEWIS, 1, 4, 7, 13, 19
MARGARET L., 7
MARTHA, 13
WHITWORTH
G.R., 118, 130, 139
H.O., 139
M.F., 130
MOLLIE, 90
ONEY, 90
RUTH, 67
S.M., 118, 130, 139
THOS, 90
THOS L., 67
W.H., 118
WHORLEY
G.W., 20-C
MARTHA J., 20-C
P., 20-C
WIBIRT
IDA B., 76
WICE
JOHN, 41
J.B., 43
NANCY, 41
R.J., 41
WIDNER
LYDIA, 90
SALLIE, 90
STEVEN, 90
WIGGINTON
J.S., 102
WILBURN
GORDON L., 20-A
LEWIS, 20-A
M.B., 20-A
NANCY, 12
PRISCILLA J., 12
STEPHEN, 12
WILCOX
ELIZABETH, 85
J.B., 85
THOS O., 85

WILEY
A.P., 92
ABS., 20-A
ABSALOM, 20-C
ABSOLOM, 11, 35
ALBERT, 4, 71, 108, 20-B
ALBTA., 13
ALLEN, 110(2)
ALLEN C., 76
ALLEN L., 79
ALLIE D., 72
AMERICA, 46
ANNIE, 82
ARDELIA L., 109
ARMINE, 108
BALLARD P., 46
C.H., 100(2)
CATHERINE, 46
CHAS W., 46
CLARA F., 34
CYNTHIA, 29
CYNTHIA, 10, 13(2), 25, 41, 43, 73, 79, 95
DAVID A., 134
E., 20-C
EDWARD, 10
ELIZABETH, 11, 27
ELIZTH, 33, 20-A
ELLEN, 92, 20-A
EMILY, 97, 134
ERASTUS, 108
F., 71
FOUNTAIN, 71
G., 4
G.N., 97
GAS, 134
GASTON, 124
GASTON M., 30
GEORDON, 63
GINEY, 60
GOR., 20-B
GORDAN, 22
GORDON, 60, 61, 103
HENRY W., 124
J.R., 100
JAMES, 12, 27, 33, 35
JAMES A., 11
JAMES L., 46
JAMES N., 20-A
JAMES O., 122
JAO., 13
JAS, 82
JAS H., 95
JAS. W., 23
JNO, 92
JNO A., 72, 101
JOCIE, 135
JOHN, 25, 20-A
JOHN A., 76(2), 108
JOHN L., 43
JULINA, 12

LEWIS A., 25
LEWIS H., 103
LIONA, 97
LOCHIE J., 108
LOUISA, 71, 108, 110(2)
LOUISA C., 10
LOUISA J., 100
LOUVENY, 83
LURA J., 76
MACK H., 63
MAHALA, 29(2), 72, 76(2)
MAHALA J., 108
MAHALA Y., 101
MANERVA, 124
MARTHA F., 41
MARY, 25, 29
MARY E., 51
NANCY, 12, 27
OLIVE, 110
PARTHELA J., 61
RACHEL, 33
RAVENA E., 101
RHODA A., 10, 20-C
SARAH, 60, 122
SARAH A., 110
SAREFITA, 22
SINA, 51, 61
SINAI, 103
SOPHIA A., 34
SQUIRE, 20-A
SUICY, 63
SUSAN E., 60
T., 4
TOMSEY, 22
TOMSY, 20-B
VINCENT, 10, 13, 25, 29, 41, 43, 73, 79, 82, 95
VIRGINIA, 25
WILLIA A., 135
WILKES
  ARCHIBALD, 15
  JOHN T., 64
  MARY D., 20-B
  R.F., 64
  SARAH C., 64
  TERROPY, 15
WILKIE
  H.J.M., 90
  HOSEA J., 90
  L.E., 90
WILKINSON
  CAUSBY ANN, 87
  LETITIA H., 87
WILKMAN
  AECE., 28
WILKS
  LIZZIE, 76
  SUSAN, 76
  VICTORIA, 12
WILLIAMS

A., 15(2), 128
A.M., 104, 134, 139
ABSOLUM, 85(2)
ALEX, 62
ALICE H., 81
AMELIA, 137
ANA, 20-B
AND., 20-B
ANDREW, 12, 14, 17, 23
ANDREW J., 15
ANDREW P., 38
ANDW., 21, 20-F
ANN, 12
ANN ELIZABETH, 113

ANNA, 2
ANNIE, 30
B.P., 68, 81, 109
BERTIE M., 139
C.A., 78, 124, 129
CATHARINE, 27
CATHERING, 65
CHARLES, 113
CHAS, 96
CHAS A., 20-F
CHAS B., 100
CHAS. A., 21
CHRISTINA, 62
CONNADY, 85
D.W., 89
E.T., 75
EDWARD P., 33
ELIZA, 15
ELIZA JANE, 85
ELIZABETH, 89
ELIZABETH L., 46
ELMORA, 104
ELZ. EJ., 30
F.E., 109
F.G., 122
FANNIE, 102, 122
FIELDING, 13
FLOYD G., 73
FRANCES E., 68, 81
FRANCES M., 100
FRANCIS, 35
G., 96
G.G., 84, 102
G.J., 75
G.P., 75
G.R., 115(2)
G.W., 95
GEO, 23
GEO E., 67
GEO P., 27, 65(2)
GEORGE, 96
GILES M., 64
HARRIET, 51, 63, 136
HARVEY, 73
HENRIETTA, 35
J., 20-E
J.A., 120
J.B., 78

J.H., 89, 128(2)
J.L., 15, 126
J.M., 95
J.S., 15
JACOB L., 14
JAMES, 15
JAMES A., 67
JAMES H., 81
JAMES P., 20-B
JAS A., 91
JAS H., 84, 115
JNO A., 56
JNO L., 30, 126, 20-B
JNO M., 27, 81
JO, 128
JOB, 20-B
JOHN, 2, 68
JOHN A., 15
JOHN C., 73
JOHN L, 33
JOHN M., 65
JOS, 95(2)
JULIA, 46
KATHERINE, 95
LANDON, 17
LARKIN, 5
LAURA G., 128
LEO J., 75
LONDON, 46
LORI, 68
LOUISA, 20-B
M., 95
M.A., 33
M.J., 134
M.M., 62
MALINDA, 68
MAMIE, 101
MANIVA, 101
MARGARET, 2
MARTHA A., 78
MARTIN, 137
MARY, 73
MARY A., 13, 33, 20-B
MARY H., 70
MARY E., 20-B
MARY J., 84, 104, 139
MATTHEW, 89
MAUD, 124
MINNIE L., 102
MOLLIE, 127
MOLLIE B., 87
N., 13
NANNIE C., 70
O.E., 118
ONA E., 128
ONEY, 115
ORA, 14
ORE LUCY, 21, 20-F
OSHIE, 72
PERMELIA A., 56
POLLY, 137
PRESTON, 35
R., 17

R. LEE, 91
R.E., 67
R.G., 126
R.J., 126
R.S., 118
RACHEL, 15
REBECA, 120
RHODA, 5
ROBERT G., 28
ROBT H., 109
ROSY, 113
S., 95
S.E., 135, 136(6), 137, 138(2), 139(2), 140(4), 141(2)
SAML, 89
SAML E., 141
SAML L., 33
SAMUEL L., 5
SARAH, 81, 96, 113
SUE ANNIE, 75
SUSANNA, 89
T.L., 87
THOS P., 87
VIOLIA, 73
W.B., 134
W.C., 118
W.J., 78(2)
W.P., 124, 129
WILLIAM, 37
WILLIAM H., 12
WILLIAM L., 33
WM, 63
WM A., 120
WM B., 68
WM C., 129
WM E., 100
WILLIAMSON
  EMMA, 130
  W.W., 137(2), 138(2), 140(2), 141
WILLIE
  CORA LEE, 88
  D.R., 88
WILLIS
  A. JACKSON, 53
  ANNA MAUD, 55

  D.R., 53, 78
  IDA, 128
  J., 95
  J.T., 108
  JEFF, 79
  JEFFERSON, 95
  JOSEPH W., 108
  LIDA W., 78
  LOUISA, 55
  MAHALA, 79, 95
  MARGT., 62
  MATTIE, 79
  N.J., 108
  NANNIE A., 81
  STANA, 53

WHITNEY E., 62
WM M., 55
WM V., 62
WILLS
  E.G., 24
  ELIZA, 85
  JOHN, 85
  LELAND, 1
  LULA, 85
  LYDIA, 1
  MARIAH L., 24
  MEREDITH, 1
WILLSON
  B.C., 88
  J.B., 88
  M.E., 85
  MARY, 88
WILLY
  ALBERTINA, 12
WILSON
  A.A., 100
  ALEAN, 96
  ALICE, 80
  ALICE M., 121
  ANDREW, 11
  BALLARD P., 43
  BELLE, 54
  CATHERINE, 45
  CELESTE V., 96
  E., 15
  E.J., 68
  EDWARD, 9, 43
  ELIZTH J., 57
  ELLA, 120
  EMILY, 66
  ERASTUS, 20-A
  EVA C., 110
  F.L.A., 68
  ISAAC E., 9
  J., 120
  J.H., 82, 126
  J.W., 82
  JAMES H., 15, 124
  JANE A., 20-A
  JOHN A., 66
  JOS R., 66
  KATHARINE, 36
  LILLIE L., 124
  M.A., 52, 53, 55, 57(2), 59(2), 60, 61(2), 62, 64, 66, 67, 68(5), 69(3), 70(2), 71(3), 73, 74, 75(2), 76(3), 77, 79, 81, 84(3)
  M.E., 110
  MARINDA, 82, 124, 126
  MARTHA, 57
  MINNIE J., 128
  MITYLENA, 126
  NANCY, 120
  NANCY JANE, 23
  NANCY M., 11

NORA B., 100
POWATN, 117
R., 15
R.G., 100
RALEIGH G., 96
REBECCA, 9, 43
RHODA, 80
RICHARD, 45
RUFINA C., 11
S., 20-A
VINCENT W., 57
VIRGINIA E., 57
W.T., 110
WALKER, 80
WM, 57
WIMER
  ELIZTH, 25
  JAS, 25
  MARTHA, 25
WIMMER
  ADDIE, 115(2)
  ALLIE, 117
  CATHARINE, 1
  DAVID, 133(2)
  ELIZABETH, 42, 54
  ELLEN, 61
  HARVEY, 79
  HAVERY, 123
  ISAAC, 72, 115
  ISAAC C., 92
  J.M., 85
  JAMES, 42, 54(2)
  JAMES A., 135
  JAMES K., 137
  JAMES T., 72
  JAS M., 61
  JS T., 92
  MARY A., 42
  MARY E., 66
  MASSIE, 79, 20-A
  MINNIE, 123
  R.J., 80, 115, 133
  REBECCA, 92
  REBECCA J., 72
  RHODA J., 66, 117, 135
  S.D., 80, 133, 135
  SAML, 79
  SAML C., 92
  SAML D., 66
  SAML, 20-A
  SAMUEL, 1, 20-A
  SAMUEL D., 117
  SARAH, 80
  W.R., 137
WINBUSH
  CATHERINE, 76
  LAURA, 61
  RALEIGH, 61
  SARAH, 61
  SMITH, 76
  WILSON, 76
WINDSON
  ANDERSON, 120

C.E., 120
MARTHA, 120
WINESETT
  CARTHULA, 92
  NOAH, 92
  W.J., 92
WINFREY
  AMERICUS, 103
  BIRREL, 14
  BRUWELL, 78
  BURRELL, 28, 30, 31(2), 34, 35(2), 67
  C., 136
  C.M., 136
  CHARLES, 53, 69, 98
  CHAS, 83
  CHAS M., 83
  COLUMBUS, 95, 103
  DORCAS E., 35
  ELLA M., 69
  EURY ELLAN, 31
  FANNIE J., 116
  FRANCIS, 116
  G.A., 98
  GEO A., 53
  J., 136
  J.B., 78
  J.H., 116
  JOHN, 116
  JULINA, 53, 69, 83, 98
  LAURA B., 95
  LIDDIA, 116
  LUM, 116
  LYDIA, 95, 103
  M.W., 101, 114
  MARGARET J., 30
  MIFFLIN W., 28
  NANCY, 14
  O.M., 114
  OINA, 31
  ONINA, 31
  ORINA, 28, 30, 34, 35, 67, 78
  ORINA J., 35
  PUNNARD C., 31
  REBECCA, 34
  RENEY, 14
  SARAH E., 35
  V.M., 101
  W.P., 101, 114
  WM, 67
WINFRY
  BURRELL, 13
  CHAS, 13
  ORINA, 13
WINGERISH
  ANNIE, 74
  PETER, 74
  TUCK S., 74
WINGFIELD
  ALBERT, 116(2)
  J.H., 79
  M.L., 79

MARTHA, 116
S.E.V., 79
WINSON
  ANDERSON, 71
  MARTHA, 71
  W.J., 71
WINSTON
  EDWARD P., 86
  J.W., 117
  LEWIS, 117
  MARY, 39, 86
  MORIAH, 117
  REESE, 39
  ROBERT, 39
  ROBT, 86
WINTER
  F., 139
  J.R., 139(2)
  S.J., 139
WIRTH
  E.L., 113
WIRTZ
  DICK, 114
  LIZZIE, 114
  NANNY, 114
WISDOM
  HUMPHREY, 101
  JULIA, 101
WISE
  BETTIE G., 79
  CHAS R., 79
  W.G., 79
WISEMAN
  CHAS A., 62
  JNO L., 62
  MARGT A., 62
WISEMOUR
  JOHN S., 16
WITEN
  LAURA J., 78
  WM H., 78
WITT
  ABRAHAM, 73
  EMALINE, 73
  J.F., 72(3)
  J.T., 72
  JAMES, 73
  JESSE, 23
  LILLY, 139
  NANNIE, 139
  NANNIE A., 90
  SEPHROUS T., 23
  THOMAS H., 23
WITTEN
  BELLE D., 50
  CORA, 72
  EDMOND, 21, 20-F
  EMALINE, 21, 20-F
  GEORGE, 21, 20-F
  HATTIE H., 83
  JACOB, 21, 20-F
  JAMES R., 44
  JNO L., 99

JULIA A., 55
LEVICIE, 71
MANNIE, 44
MARY, 28, 36(2), 50, 70, 71, 83
MATILDA J., 44
MAXEY G., 55
NANCIE, 72
NINA, 21, 20-F
PATIENCE, 21, 20-F
RACHEL C., 28
SOPHIA, 70
WILLIAM, 50, 83
WM H., 28, 36, 70, 71, 72
ZACHARIAH S., 55
WOHLFORD
CORA L., 136
E.O., 113
EDNA, 128, 136
MAUD E., 113
ROSA WREN, 128
THOMAS, 128
THOS, 136
THOS E., 113
WOLF
ANNA, 71
LUCINDA W., 32
MARY, 71
NANCY R., 32
PETER, 71
RICHARD A., 32
WOLFE
GEO., 110
J.E., 140(4), 141(2)
LUCINDA, 17
REBECCA, 17
WOLFORD
C., 72
JOHN A., 72
WOLLEN
ALVIN, 53
HENRY, 53
LUCINDA E., 53
WOLWINE
R.P., 138
S.J., 138
WOMACK
GEORGE, 82
SALLIE, 82
SAMUEL, 82
WONK
SILAS, 45
WILLIS, 45
WOOD
A.N., 67, 117
ALEX, 14
ALEX., 12
ALEXANDER, 122, 20-C
ALEXANDER M., 20-D
ALEXANDER N., 50

ALEXR, 3, 8
ALEXR., 13
ANNA J., 117
BATHENA, 8
BETHANY, 12
BETHENA, 14
BETHINA, 13
CAROLINE, 31, 39
CATHERINE E., 11
CORNELIUS, 51
CRAWFORD H., 13

DAVID, 77
DEBIE, 99
E., 117
ELIZ., 50
ELIZA ANN, 58
ELIZABETH, 32, 67
EMMA C., 67
FANNIE, 77
FRANCES, 6, 9, 10, 11
FRANKIE, 23
G.W., 15
GABRIEL, 31
GERMAN, 24, 26, 41, 57, 122, 20-D
GUMARD, 24
H.A., 112
H.B., 3
H.M., 110
J.B., 71
J.W., 77
JAMES, 113
JAMES A., 32
JAMES N., 6
JAS A., 133
JAS B., 110
JAS W., 57
JNO W., 12
JOHN, 31
JOHN H., 10, 111
JOSEPH F., 9
K.E., 3
KATHARINE, 39
L.W.A., 123
LIZZIE, 123
LOUISA, 8
LUANDA, 32
LUCINDA, 15
LUCINDA E., 28
LUETTA, 31
LYDIA A., 23
MARTHA, 97, 112
MARTHA J., 41
MARY E., 111
MARY J., 14
NANCY, 6, 24, 26, 31, 57, 20-D
NANCY A., 24
NANCY M.J., 31
NITA, 131
OCTAVIA, 26

PETER, 6, 112
PHILENA A., 50
R., 20 C(2)
R.H., 71
RACHEL, 24
RANSOM, 51, 99
RBT., 23
RICHARD, 24
RICHARD A., 32
ROBERT, 6, 11
ROBT, 9, 10
ROBT A., 99
S., 97
S.A., 133
S.F., 15
SALLIE E., 131
SARAH E., 6
SIDNEY, 97(2)
SUSAN, 71
VIRGIE, 111
W.T., 110
WALTER LEE, 133(2)

WOODALL
FRANCES J., 20-A
J., 14
JACOB, 14, 15, 58
JOHN A.J., 15
LUSANE, 60
MAHALA A., 31
MARTHA, 58
MARTHA B., 15
MAT S., 58
MATTHEW S., 1
R., 14
S., 20-A
SALLY, 31
SAMPSON, 31
SARAH, 20-A
SUSANA, 1
WOODEY
BETTY, 85
CHARLES, 85
JOSEPH, 85
WOODIN
AMBROSE, 74
BETTY, 74
GEORGE, 74
WOODING
GEO, 77(3)
JAMES, 77
KITTY, 77
WOODRING
G.W., 139
N.M., 139
R.E., 139
WOODS
ARCHER, 71
BALLARD P., 61
BETTIE, 141
GEO, 71
H.G., 87, 138
HENRY, 105

J.P., 71
JAMES, 71
JANE, 61, (7)
JENNIE, 141
JOHN, 59
JOHN H., 141
LACY L., 141(2)
LOUDENIA, 105
LUDEMIA, 59
MARY, 71
NANCY E., 71
O.J., 44
R.J., 141
SAM, 141
SAML, 61
THOS, 69
WM T., 69
WOODSON
AGNES PRESTON, 49

BILLIE, 118
CHAS W., 49
ROSE, 118
WESLEY, 99
WOODWARD

DANIEL J., 140
J.S., 140
L.J., 140
WOODY
ABRAHAM, 116
BRYANT, 88
ELIZA, 116, 122
J.B., 88
NANCY, 88
P.L., 122
PETE, 122
THOMAS, 116
WOODYARD
LON, 46
NANCY J., 46
WM S., 46
WOOLFORD
S., 20
WOOLWIN
L.C., 120
R.P., 120
S.P., 120
WOOLWINE
ANNA B., 76
BERTIE, 141
EVIE M., 108
JANE, 76
JNO L., 27, 36
JOHN L., 36
JOSEPH W., 36
JUS. L., 23
LEWIS, 27
MARY JANE, 23
NANCY, 23, 27, 36(2)
R.P., 76, 141(2)
REBECCA A., 36
RUBEN P., 108

S.J., 141
SALLIE J., 108
WORKMAN
ANDELIA, 68
ANDREW, 22, 20-C
BOBT (SIC), 68
DOLLY, 17
DORA, 95
ELIZABETH, 95
JAMES, 80
JANE, 59, 68, 96
LEVI, 95
MALINDA, 59
MARGARET J., 28
MARY, 96
POLLY, 80
ROBERT, 17(2), 96
ROBT, 59, 111
RUFUS, 111
SALLIE, 111
W.W., 79, 80(2), 81
WORKMON
ANDREW, 11
WORLDS
ALBERT, 114
ELIZABETH, 114
JESSIE, 114
WORLEY
EMILIA A., 20-D
G., 20-E
GEORGE, 12, 20-D
LOUISA M., 20-E
M., 20-E
MARY, 20-D
POLLY, 12
TAZEWELL, 12
WORRELL
AMERICA A., 46
ELEANDER, 33
ELI, 46, 69
ELI B., 10
ELIZA, 69
ELIZA J., 30
ELIZA JANE, 46
ELIZABETH, 92
ETTA, 116
F.A., 69, 78
GRANVILLE, 7
JAMES, 10, 11
JAMES B., 7(2)
JAS B., 6, 42
JESSE, 92
JOHN A., 32
LUCY A., 7
LUKE, 32, 33, 42(2)
MAGGIE, 92
MILLE, 32, 33
MILLIE, 42
OLIVE, 7(2)
OLIVIA, 10, 11(2)
RHODA, 6
SUSAN, 6
WILBURN, 42

WORREN
RACHEL ANN, 87
WORTH
MARY, 117
WM H., 117
WRIGHT
A.F., 138, 141
A.M., 128
A.W., 60
AD., 93
AGNUS, 16
ALICE, 93
BERTHA, 131
BETSY, 49
BETTIE, 94
BETTY, 124
C., 4
C.G., 50, 94, 124
C.O., 73
CAMDEN G., 24, 43, 50
CATHARINE A., 50
CLARA A., 24
D.E., 89
DANL E., 56
DAUL., 49
DAVID O., 81
E., 18, 20-E
E.C., 137
E.L., 124
ELBERT C., 42
ELIZ., 24
ELIZABETH, 50(2), 89
EMALINE E., 18
EMILY, 82
F.T., 117
FANNIE, 63
FANNY, 77
FLORILLA B., 55
G.T., 102, 105, 110, 111, 112, 115, 117
GEO R., 113
GEO T., 96, 113
GEORGE, 16
H.G., 50
HENRIETTA M., 43
HENRY, 77
ISAAC, 138
ISAC, 131
J.D., 138
J.E., 137
J.H., 128
J.J., 4
J.M., 137, 138(4)
J.W., 128
JAMES, 63, 77
JAMES D., 115
JANE, 105
JAS D., 88
JAS., 18
JAS. M., 35
JOHN D., 82
JOHN H., 89
JOHN J., 4, 73

JOS DAVID, 60
JOSEPH, 1, 2(2), 3(5), 4(4), 5(2), 6(3), 7(4), 8(3), 9, 10(2), 11, 13(5), 14(5), 15(4), 17(5), 18(3), 19(6), 20(3), 20-B(2)
KING, 109
LAURA A., 50
LUCY A., 55, 60, 76
LUCY M., 16
M.J., 81
M.R., 73
MAGGIE J., 43
MARY C., 50
MATILDA, 69
MAY S., 28
MOSES, 63
NANCY, 138
NANNIE, 137, 138
NORA E., 88
PETER, 93
RANSON, 50
ROBT A., 82
ROY T., 137(2)
S.B., 105
S.E., 138
SALLIE E., 138
SARAH E., 88, 115
SARAH J., 42
SARAH JANE, 35
SARAH M., 50
SUE, 137
TEINEY, 56
THOMAS, 42
THOS, 35
VIRGINIA A., 115
W., 20-E
W.G., 76
W.H.B., 57
W.W., 81
WATSON, 105
WM, 56, 94
WM J., 57
WRISTON
WM, 31
WURRELL
ELIZABETH, 99
ROSA, 99
WYANT
ISABELLA A., 62
P.B., 62
WM G., 62
WYATT
ANNIE L., 137
BOSTON, 111
JNO, 124
JOHN, 111, 137
JULIA, 140
M.J., 124, 137
MAHALA J., 124
MARY JANE, 111
MARY L., 111

ROBERT, 140
S.I., 140(2)
WYGAL
J.G.W., 109
J.L., 109
M.W., 109
WYNN
WM A., 112
WYNNE
W.A., 100, 101
WYRICK
ASA, 70
DANIEL, 43
HENRY, 111
J.C., 134
J.H., 119
JAMES H., 111
JAMES S., 70
JOHN H., 43
LEANNA, 43
LOU J., 134
MARINDA, 70
S.E., 134
WILLIE M., 119
WYSON
M.H., 129
M.J., 129, 130
WYSONG
HENRY, 80
MILLIE, 80
WYSOR
M.J., 126, 127, 128(2), 131
W.J., 129

-Y-

YATER
NANNIE, 79
WASH, 79
YATES
GEO W., 75
GILLIE, 75
JOHN, 110
MARY EULA, 79
NANNIE A., 75
YEATS
GEO W., 72
JAMES, 72
NANNIE, 72
YEATTS
JULIA, 131
YOPP
A.J., 136
YORK
FRED B., 104
LOU F., 104
R.W., 104
YOST
FRED W., 135
YOUNCE
ELIJAH, 139
HARRIETT, 139

JAMES L., 139
YOUNG
  A.J., 45, 46, 47(3),
    48, 51, 52(4), 53,
    56, 57, 58(7), 59(4),
    60(3), 61(2), 62(2),
    63(2), 64(2), 76
  ANDREW J., 47, 51
  ANDW J., 80, 81, 84
  ANN, 118
  AUGUSTUS A., 20-E

  BELL, 135
  CAUSBY, 33
  CHARLES R., 20-D
  DAN'L, 82
  ELLA, 75
  FANNIE, 87, 111
  GAS, 135
  HENRY, 87(2), 111
  HENRY R., 111
  ISAAC, 86
  ISAAC S., 20
  J.S., 76, 80, 82
  JAMES W., 33
  JNO S., 22
  JOHN, 22, 43, 123,
    20-D, 20-E
  JOS, 77, 80
  JOSIAH, 23
  JULIA E., 113
  L.J., 128
  LEWIS, 23, 33
  LOCHIE A., 106
  M.A., 20-E
  M.A.W., 43
  MARGARET L., 107

  MARGT A., 107
  MARY, 23, 82, 20-D
  MARY A., 43
  MARY ANN, 22
  MARY E., 20
  MILLIE, 112
  NANCY, 33
  NANNIE, 106
  NANNIE M., 118
  R.W., 107
  ROBT W., 107
  ROSIE, 128
  S.H., 106, 113, 118,
    126(2), 128
  SARAH, 20, 82, 86
  W.M., 86
  WM D., 135

        -Z-

ZINK
  DORATH, 136
  LILA J., 136
  WM H., 136
ZOLL

CHARLES LEWIS, 79

JACOB, 79
MARY, 79

www.ingramcontent.com/pod-product-compliance
Lightning Source LLC
Chambersburg PA
CBHW080421270326
41929CB00018B/3115